Library of Congress Cataloging-in-Publication Data

Parkin, Michael, 1939–
    Economics/Michael Parkin.—4th ed.
       p.   cm.
    Includes bibliographical references and index.
    ISBN 0-201-52668-9 (hardcover)
    1. Economics.   I. Title.
  HB171.5.P313   1997
  330—dc21
                    97–13594
                          CIP

Printed in the United States of America.

3 4 5 6 7 8 9 – RNT – 01009998

Senior Editor:	Denise J. Clinton
Project Editor:	Lena Buonanno
Editorial Assistant:	Jennifer Vito
Senior Development Manager:	Sylvia Mallory
Supplements Editor:	Joan Twining
Development Assistant:	Rebecca Ferris
Managing Editor:	James Rigney
Senior Production Supervisor:	Nancy H. Fenton
Art and Design Director:	Karen Rappaport
Senior Design Supervisor:	Barbara T. Atkinson
Technical Illustrator:	Richard Parkin, RWP Graphics
Photo Researchers:	Billie Porter and Sandy Schneider
Prepress Buying Manager:	Sarah McCracken
Electronic Production Administrator:	Sally Simpson
Copyeditor:	Barbara Willette
Production Services:	Sarah Hallet Corey
Permissions Editor:	Mary Dyer
Indexer:	Alexandra Nickerson
Senior Manufacturing Manager:	Roy Logan
Manufacturing Supervisor:	Hugh Crawford
Executive Marketing Manager:	Beth Toland
Marketing Manager:	Quinn Perkson
Marketing Coordinator:	Lois Carter
Printer:	World Color

Reprinted with corrections, July 1998

ECONOMICS

FOURTH EDITION

MICHAEL PARKIN

UNIVERSITY OF WESTERN ONTARIO

 ADDISON-WESLEY

AN IMPRINT OF ADDISON WESLEY

READING, MASSACHUSETTS • MENLO PARK, CALIFORNIA
DON MILLS, ONTARIO • SYDNEY • MEXICO CITY

About **Michael Parkin**

Michael Parkin received his training as an economist at the Universities of Leicester and Essex in England. Currently in the Department of Economics at the University of Western Ontario, Canada, Professor Parkin has held faculty appointments at Brown University, the University of Manchester, the University of Essex, and Bond University. He has served on the editorial boards of the *American Economic Review* and the *Journal of Monetary Economics* and as managing editor of the *Canadian Journal of Economics*. Professor Parkin's research on macroeconomics, monetary economics, and international economics has resulted in over 160 publications in journals and edited volumes, including the *American Economic Review*, the *Journal of Political Economy*, the *Review of Economic Studies*, the *Journal of Monetary Economics*, and the *Journal of Money, Credit and Banking*. It became most visible to the public with his work on inflation that discredited the use of wage and price controls. Michael Parkin also spearheaded the movement toward European monetary union. Professor Parkin is an experienced and dedicated teacher of introductory economics.

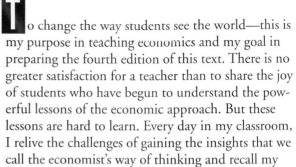

Preface

To change the way students see the world—this is my purpose in teaching economics and my goal in preparing the fourth edition of this text. There is no greater satisfaction for a teacher than to share the joy of students who have begun to understand the powerful lessons of the economic approach. But these lessons are hard to learn. Every day in my classroom, I relive the challenges of gaining the insights that we call the economist's way of thinking and recall my own early struggles with this discipline. In preparing this edition, I have been privileged to draw on the experiences not only of my own students but also of the many teachers and students who have used the previous editions.

The principles of economics course is constantly evolving, and the past few years have seen some major shifts of emphasis, especially in macroeconomics. Today's principles course springs from today's concerns about productivity growth, the information revolution, the emerging market economies of Central Europe and Asia, and the expansion of global trade and investment. Increasingly, we recognize the value of teaching long-run fundamentals as a basis for understanding these issues and as a springboard to understanding short-run economic fluctuations. With a tradition established in my third edition, this book allows you to place an early emphasis on long-run fundamentals and to teach the theory of long-run economic growth using nothing more than the tools of supply and demand.

The Fourth Edition Approach

THIS BOOK HAS BEEN CRAFTED TO ACHIEVE FIVE overriding goals:

- Focus on the core ideas.
- Explain the issues and problems of our time.
- Create a flexible teaching and learning tool.
- Make modern economics accessible.
- Make efficient use of new information technologies.

Focus on Core Ideas

A flood of new concepts and a new way of thinking can overwhelm students. Our goal as teachers is to help students cut through to the core concepts that a student needs to think like an economist, both during and beyond the principles course. Consistent with this goal, I focus on a few central ideas: choice, tradeoff, opportunity cost, choosing at the margin, incentives, the gains from voluntary exchange, the power of markets, and the role of government. For the economy as a whole, the value of production equals total expenditure and total income. Living standards improve when production per person increases. Prices rise when the quantity of money increases faster than production. Unemployment can result from market failure but can be productive.

The core tool of demand and supply is thoroughly explained and repeatedly used throughout both the micro and macro chapters.

Explain the Issues and Problems of Our Time

The core ideas and tools are *used* repeatedly to help students understand the issues that confront them in today's world. These issues include the environment, immigration, widening income gaps, the productivity growth slowdown, budget deficits, restraining inflation, watching for the next recession, avoiding protectionism, and the long-term growth of output and incomes.

Create a Flexible Teaching and Learning Tool

We teachers of economics hold strong views about what to teach and how to teach, yet we do not all hold the *same* view. This diversity of opinion poses a special challenge to textbook authors, especially in macro. This book is carefully organized to be useful in a wide range of situations and to appeal to a diversity of teachers. The book's flexibility is demonstrated in the "Flexibility Chart" that appears on p. XIV–XV. This book can be used to teach all the traditional macro sequences, which place the main emphasis on short-term fluctuations in output, prices, and unemployment. It can support a course with a Keynesian emphasis or one with a monetarist emphasis. This

book can also be used to teach a course that places an early emphasis on the long-term growth of output and incomes.

Make Modern Economics Accessible

This book presents economics as a serious, lively, and evolving science that tries to explain the economic world around us. It presents new ideas, such as dynamic comparative advantage, game theory and its applications, the modern theory of the firm, information, public choice, new growth theory, and real business cycle theory. But it presents these new topics by using the familiar core ideas and tools.

In some areas, economics is relatively settled. In other areas, controversy persists. Where matters are settled, I present what is known; where controversy persists, I present the alternative viewpoints. This positive approach to economics is vital for students who will enter a world in which simple ideologies have become irrelevant and the economic landscape is changing at a rapid pace.

Always recalling my own early struggles with economics, I place the student at center stage and write for the student. I am conscious that many students find economics hard. Consequently, my goal has been to make the material as accessible as possible. I use language that makes for an easy read and that doesn't intimidate.

Each chapter opens with a clear statement of learning objectives, a real-world, student-friendly vignette that grabs attention, and a brief chapter preview. Once in the chapter, I do not reduce economics to a set of recipes to be memorized. Instead, I encourage the student to try to understand each concept. To accomplish this goal, I illustrate every principle with examples that have been selected both to hold the student's interest and to bring the subject to life. And to foster an enthusiasm and confidence in the student, when I present a new principle, I put it to work right away and use it to illuminate a current real-world problem or issue.

Make Efficient Use of New Information Technologies

The supplements that accompany this text, and the text itself, make carefully thought out and efficient use of the new information age technologies. We have worked hard to avoid the hype that often surrounds software and Web-based supplements and create true value for students and teachers. Our *Economics in Action* tutorial and quizzing software has been thoroughly redesigned and revised in the light of the lessons we've learned from its earlier versions. And new to this edition, we have created a World Wide Web site that provides features and content that is timely and constantly updated. The text has extensive links both to *Economics in Action* and the Internet.

Key Revisions in the Fourth Edition

ECONOMICS, FOURTH EDITION, HAS BEEN CAREfully revised on the basis of extensive reviews to:

- Place stronger emphasis on core economic principles
- Reflect the most modern and recent economic developments
- Shorten and make the material even more accessible, and
- Strengthen the pedagogical features.

To achieve these goals, I have added new chapters and topics, reorganized and streamlined existing chapters, and created three new pedagogical features.

New Chapters

Chapter 1, "What is Economics?" uses a photo essay approach to lay out the key questions and big ideas of economics. The photos were carefully selected to motivate students and show them that economics is truly a part of their lives.

Chapter 6, "Efficiency," and a new early introduction of efficiency in Chapter 3, gives a new unity to the micro chapters and provides a stronger framework and preparation for Chapter 7, "Markets in Action."

New Coverage

Chapter 7, "Markets in Action," now includes a discussion of the inefficiency of rent ceilings, minimum wages, and taxes. Chapter 15, "Demand and Supply in Resource Markets," includes a new section on exhaustible natural resources. Chapter 16, "Labor Markets," includes a new section on immigration. Chapter 23, "Measuring GDP, Inflation, and Economic Growth," presents the chain-weighted measure

of real output. Chapter 29, "Fiscal Policy," includes a new section on the supply-side effects of fiscal policy.

New Macro Organization

"Aggregate Supply and Aggregate Demand" now appears as Chapter 24 and is used as the overview model for both long-run and short-run macro issues. A flexible modular structure is maintained that allows the teacher to cover the *AS-AD* setup and then move to either Part VIII, "Aggregate Supply and Economic Growth," or Part IX, "Aggregate Demand and Inflation," depending on preferences.

More Accessible Macro

Chapter 26, "Capital, Investment, and Saving," has been extensively revised. Consumption coverage has been removed from this chapter, and the chapter focus has been placed on investment and saving. This chapter now covers long-run aspects of fiscal policy.

Chapter 28, "Expenditure Multipliers," includes a clearer and more accessible discussion of the multiplier. Chapter 29, "Fiscal Policy," includes a revised, simplified, presentation of fiscal policy multipliers.

Chapter 36, "The Balance of Payments and the Dollar," is extensively revised to make the theory of the exchange rate a more standard application of demand and supply.

Streamlined

Using new technology to deliver information, I have removed selected material from the text and made it available in electronic form over the Internet. You can access at the Parkin Web site material on producing at least cost, formerly an appendix to the cost curves chapter, old Chapter 16 on capital and natural resource markets, and old Chapter 37 on emerging economies.

Updated

The text, graphics, and examples have been updated to reflect the most current available data.

Three New Pedagogical Features

The three new pedagogical features are:

- Reading Between the Lines with Policy Watch
- Web and Critical Thinking Exercises
- Part Openers

Policy Watch   I have added an element to many of the *Reading Between the Lines* features that asks the student to think about the policy issues raised by a news article and to participate in the public policy debate through "You're the Voter" questions. All the old Reading Between the Lines features have been replaced by new articles from *The Wall Street Journal, The Economist, The New York Times,* and from many regional newspapers.

Web and Critical Thinking Exercises   The pedagogy of the fourth edition has been carefully developed to encourage students to learn more about economics and to use technology as a means of researching and analyzing current events.

New to the fourth edition are end-of-chapter Internet-based exercises that ask students to access real-world data from Web sites such as those of the Bureau of Labor Statistics, the Federal Reserve Board, and the Penn World Table. An icon ⊕ in the margin identifies these questions.

Also new to this edition are a set of Critical Thinking exercises that further test and build students' analytical skills.

Selected end-of-chapter questions are linked to *Economics in Action* Version 3.0 and coverage will expand with subsequent releases of the software.

Part Openers   Economic Legends Past & Present is a new part opener that traces the evolution of economic thought and connects the ideas of economics with the events that shaped those ideas. This new feature unites the past and the present with interviews with key economists of today including Nobel Prize winners Gary Becker and Robert E. Lucas, Jr., and Claudia Goldin, a leading labor economist.

Features that Enhance the Learning Process

THIS FOURTH EDITION, LIKE ITS PREDECESSORS, is packed with special features designed to enhance the learning process.

The Art Program: Showing the Economic Action

Earlier editions of this book set new standards with their highly successful and innovative art programs. My goal has always been to show "where the economic action is." The figures and diagrams in this book continue to generate an enormously positive response, confirming my view that graphical analysis is the most important tool for teaching and learning economics. But it is a tool that gives many students much difficulty. Because many students find graphs hard to work with, the art has been designed to communicate economic principles unambiguously and clearly. The data-based art clearly reveals the data and trends. In addition, diagrams that illustrate economic processes consistently distinguish among key economic players (firms, households, governments, and markets).

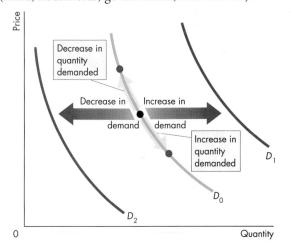

A consistent protocol in style, notation, and use of color, includes:

- Highlighting shifted curves, points of equilibrium, and the most important features in red
- Using arrows in conjunction with color to lend directional movement to what are usually static presentations
- Pairing graphs with data tables from which the curves have been plotted
- Using color consistently to underscore the content and referring to such use of color in the text and captions
- Labeling key pieces of information in graphs with boxed notes

The entire art program has been developed with the study and review needs of the student in mind. It has the following features:

- Marking the most important figures and tables with a red icon and listing them at the end of the chapter under the head "Key Figures and Tables"
- Using complete, informative captions that encapsulate major points in the graph so that students can preview or review the chapter by skimming through the art

Learning Aids: Pedagogy that Leads to Active Learning

The careful pedagogical plan has been refined to ensure that this book complements and reinforces classroom learning. Each chapter contains the following pedagogical elements:

Objectives   A list of learning objectives that enable students to see exactly where the chapter is going and to set their goals before they begin the chapter. The goals are linked directly to the chapter's major heads.

Chapter Openers   Intriguing puzzles, paradoxes, or metaphors frame questions that are unraveled and resolved as the chapter progresses.

Highlighted In-Text Reviews   Frequent, succinct summaries in list format are included for review.

Key Terms   Highlighted terms within the text form the first part of a three-tiered review of vocabulary. These terms are repeated with page references in the chapter summary and in the end-of-book glossary.

Key Figures and Tables   The most important figures and tables are identified with the ◆ and are listed in the summary at the end of each chapter.

End-of-Chapter Study Material   Chapters close with a summary that includes lists of key terms, figures and tables (with page references); and questions, problems, and critical thinking exercises. New to this edition, the end-of-chapter summaries are in a concise list form.

End-of-chapter problems have been revised to include many new problems and many that use diagrams. Problems identified by an icon 🖳 are linked to my *Economics in Action* software package or the Parkin Web site. New to this edition, each chapter has a set of *critical thinking* questions based on *Reading Between the Lines* and on current policy topics. In many problems and critical thinking

questions, identified by an icon ⊕, I send the student to *Internet sites* such as the Bureau of Labor Statistics, the Department of Commerce, and the Fed and the Parkin Web site. My hope is to encourage the student to stay up to date and gain confidence using the Internet to access information.

The Learning and Teaching Package

ADDISON-WESLEY'S EDITORS, THE SUPPLEMENTS authors, and I have worked closely together to ensure that our integrated text and supplements package provides students and teachers with a seamless learning and teaching experience.* The authors of the supplements are outstanding economists and teachers who have brought their own human capital (and that of their students) to the job of ensuring that the supplements are of the highest quality and value. The package contains three broad components:

- Tools to enhance learning
- Tools to enhance teaching
- Tools for the electronic classroom

Tools to Enhance Learning

Study Guide   Available in microeconomics and macroeconomics split versions, the fourth edition Study Guide was prepared by Mark Rush of the University of Florida. Carefully coordinated with the main text and the Test Bank, each chapter of the Study Guide contains:

- Key concepts
- Helpful hints
- True/false/uncertain questions that ask students to explain their answers
- Multiple-choice questions
- Short-answer questions
- You're the Teacher, which lets the student explain common questions or misconceptions
- New to this edition, end-of-chapter quizzes and practice final exams

*Some supplement items might not be available to adopters outside the United States.

Several elements of the Study Guide are geared to building critical thinking skills: True/false/uncertain questions; multiple-choice answers that include explanations of why the answer is correct; *You're the Teacher* sections; and *Reading Between the Lines* exercises. Other elements are geared to make studying economics a bit easier. The key concepts are a study aid. The helpful hints focus on ways to better understand the principles or to avoid common pitfalls. The multiple-choice questions are plentiful and their answers contain detailed explanations; the part overview midterm examination allows the student to simulate an exam.

The study guide includes an essay, "Should the Study of Economics Be Part of Your Future?," written by Robert Whaples of Wake Forest University. This essay describes the value of studying economics for both majors and non-majors. It includes information on career options for those with an economics degree, what the study of economics entails, what graduate school is like, and references for further reading.

Economics in Action Interactive Software

Students across the nation and around the world have used the path-breaking *Economics in Action*, a widely acclaimed computer learning tool, to increase their success in the principles course.

With *Economics in Action* Release 3.0, which accompanies the fourth edition, students will have fun working the tutorials, answering questions that give instant explanations, and testing themselves ahead of their mid-term exams. One of my students told me that using *EIA* is like having a private professor in your dorm room! The new release of the software has the following features:

- Step-by-step, graph-based tutorials
- A graph-making tool with data for the United States, Canada, twelve European countries, Japan, and Australia
- A quiz tool that generates drag-and-drop, true/false, multiple-choice, and numeric questions
- A self-testing tool that simulates tests and gathers results
- A problem-solving tool that allows students to solve homework problems from the text
- A figure gallery that builds text figures and captions.

The Parkin Web Site

The Parkin Web site provides a rich array of learning tools that are carefully integrated with the text and other components of the package. A weekly electronic *Reading Between the Lines* provides an effective way of motivating students and keeping them up to date on economics in the news. A periodic electronic *Point-Counterpoint* feature encourages students to participate in the contemporary policy debate. A weekly quiz that uses completely new questions (not found in the study guide, test banks, or *Economics in Action*) provides students with frequent review and testing material. On-line office hours enable students to consult me directly with their learning problems. And carefully selected links provide students with a guide to economic resources on the Internet.

The Parkin Web site will become a must-visit site for all teachers and students of the principles of economics. Whether you are a teacher or a student, you can reach all my Internet services at http://hepg.awl.com/parkin/econ100.

Tools to Enhance Teaching

Test Bank

Revised test items in **Volume I** were prepared by Robert Whaples of Wake Forest University and Carol Dole of the University of North Carolina to thoroughly reflect the content and terminology of the fourth edition. The file includes 5,000 multiple-choice questions, of which about one third are new to this edition. Each chapter includes a section of questions that parallel questions in the study guide.

New to the fourth edition, **Volume II** Test Bank contains 5,000 new questions comprising multiple-choice, true/false, and short answers. These test items were prepared by Carol Dole of the University of North Carolina and James Giordano and Peter Zaleski of Villanova University.

Computerized Test Bank

Testing software is available for DOS, Windows, and Macintosh. It includes all questions in the printed test banks. This software gives instructors the ability to view graphs on the screen, add questions, edit questions, scramble question order and answer options, and more. An on-line quiz component is also provided with the Computerized Test Bank.

Instructor's Manual

A revised instructor's manual has been prepared by Mark Rush of the University of Florida. The instructor's manual is designed to integrate the teaching and learning package, serving as a guide to all supplements. Each chapter includes a chapter outline, changes in the fourth edition, teaching suggestions, the big picture (how the chapter relates to what has come before and what comes later), cross-references to the acetates, software units, additional discussion questions, answers to the review questions, and answers to the problems.

An introductory section written by Byron Brown of Michigan State University and Dennis Hoffman of Arizona State University presents technology ideas for professors who are just getting started with electronic teaching tools. This section talks about teaching in a multimedia classroom, how to use electronic tools in the lecture, and how to integrate *Economics in Action* into the course.

Acetates and Overlays   Key figures from the text are rendered in full color on the acetates. Several figures include overlays that make it easy to walk through the figure as you lecture. The acetates are enlarged and simplified to be more legible in large classrooms. They are available to qualified adopters of the textbook (contact your Addison-Wesley sales representative).

Tools for the Electronic Classroom

PowerPoint Electronic Lectures   A complete lecture framework in Microsoft PowerPoint is available for Macintosh and Windows. Prepared by Jeffrey Caldwell of Rose State College, this presentation support system breaks chapters down into lecture-size bites and includes key figures from the text, animated graphs, and speaking notes.

Economics in Action Software   Instructors can use *Economics in Action* interactive software in the classroom. Its full-screen display option makes it possible to use its many analytical graphs as "electronic transparencies" and to do live graph manipulation and curve-shifting in lectures. Its figure gallery of animated slides from the text provides high quality graphics for the classroom. Its real-world data sets and graphing utility enable time-series graphs and scatter diagrams to be made and displayed in the classroom. Additionally, *Economics in Action* is a helpful review tool for instructors to use with their students or assign to their students to help reinforce economic principles before tests or exams.

Parkin on the World Wide Web   Instructors can use the Parkin Web site in a suitably equipped classroom. The weekly electronic *Reading Between the Lines* provides an effective way of motivating and organizing a lecture. And the electronic *Point-Counterpoint* feature provides a handy way of organizing a classroom debate. The weekly quiz can also be used for in-class review.

The Parkin Internet Exchange   This medium of on-line support includes mailing list discussion groups, access to information through ftp, and a World Wide Web home page. You can share teaching tips and ideas for using the book and supplements and discuss current economic events. To subscribe to the Parkin mailing list, send an e-mail to majordomo@aw.com and write Subscribe ParkinPr in the body of the message. An Internet discussion group is also available for students. They can talk with other students about the course, the book, and economics. To subscribe to the Parkin student mailing list, send a e-mail to majordomo@aw.com and write Subscribe ParkinSt in the body of the message.

Acknowledgments

WHILE THE EXTENT OF MY DEBTS CANNOT BE fully acknowledged, it is a joy to record my gratitude to the many people who have helped me to produce this book, some without realizing just how helpful they were.

I thank those of my current and former colleagues at the University of Western Ontario who have taught me a great deal that can be found in these pages: Jim Davies, Jeremy Greenwood, Ig Horstmann, Peter Howitt, Greg Huffman, David Laidler, Phil Reny, Chris Robinson, John Whalley, and Ron Wonnacott. I also thank Doug McTaggart of Bond University and Christopher Findlay of the University of Adelaide, co-authors of the Australian edition. Their suggestions arising from their adaptation of earlier editions have been extremely helpful in preparing this edition.

It is a special pleasure to acknowledge my debt and express my thanks to the several thousand students whom I have been privileged to teach. The instant response that comes from the look of puzzlement or enlightenment has taught me, more than anything else, how to teach economics.

My sponsoring editor, Denise Clinton, has been a constant source of inspiration and encouragement. I want to place on record her crucial role in developing our new approach to macroeconomics. I could not have undertaken the transformation of macro without her clear-headed vision and tough empirical approach. I am enormously impressed by and grateful to her.

It has been a pleasure to work day by day with Lena Buonanno, my development editor. Lena even went so far as to enroll in a principles of economics course (using a competing text!) in order to be well prepared for her task. She organized conference calls, focus groups, and reviewers. She also took care of the interviews and helped the interviewees and me to make our conversations accessible to our student readers. Lena has brought a personal and professional commitment to this project that is rare and impressive. I am deeply grateful to her.

Joan Twining, Supplements Editor, has planned, organized, and managed the task of creating a large and high-quality supplements package. All of the supplements authors and I thank Joan for her extraodinary editorial and personal skills and for the energy and commitment she has given us.

Our Senior Development Manager, Sylvia Mallory, has been a steady source of support and it is she who proposed that we revise Chapter 1 as a photo essay. I am excited about the way this suggestion evolved, and I thank Sylvia for her inspiring idea. I thank Marjorie Singer Anderson for her development support on the macro chapters. Billie Porter and Sandy Schneider did the photo research. Nancy Fenton has been my level-headed, no-nonsense, I-can-do-anything, senior production editor for two editions and I renew my thanks to her for directing the design and production effort. Barbara Willette has again been copyeditor and I thank her for continuing to coax yet better English from my keyboard. I also thank Ed Moura, Vice President and General Manager of Addison-Wesley's Higher Education Publishing Group, for his support of this project and for ensuring that it is directed by the most talented editors in the business.

I thank the supplements authors: Mark Rush, Jeffrey Caldwell, Carol Dole, Robert Whaples, James Giordano, Peter Zaleski, Byron Brown, and Dennis

Hoffman. Mark has played a crucial role in the creation of this edition and has been a constant source of good advice and good humor. Robert Whaples is another extraordinary helper who went well beyond the call of duty or the scope of the checkbook in his manuscript, accuracy, and study guide reviews; his participation in conference calls; and his writing of an essay for the study guide. I am deeply grateful to him. I also thank Carol Dole and Robert Whaples for their accuracy reviews of page proof. Byron Brown and Dennis Hoffman have written excellent essays for the instructor's manual. Others who helped shape my ideas for the new macro sequence are Robert Gillette, Dennis Hoffman, Manfred Keil, Robert Rossana, Scott Simkins, and Larry Wimmer.

I thank my research assistants. Jeannie Gillmore helped me to find good news articles and wrote useful outlines and first drafts of each *Reading Between the Lines* feature. She also provided other general research assistance, along with Christine Bies, Jane McAndrew, and Tom Adam.

I thank Richard Parkin, who created the electronic art manuscript and final art files and has contributed many ideas that have improved the figures in this book.

As with the previous editions, this one owes an enormous debt to Robin Bade. I dedicate this book to her and again thank her for her work. She has read every word that I have written, commented in detail on every draft, created many of the end-of-chapter review questions and problems, inspired me when I have been flagging, and managed the entire project from its initial conception through its three editions and through seven editions published in other countries. I could not have written this book without the unselfish help she has given me. My thanks to her are unbounded.

The empirical test of this book's value continues to be made in the classroom. I would appreciate hearing from instructors and students about how I can continue to improve it in future editions.

Michael Parkin
Department of Economics
University of Western Ontario
London, Ontario, N6A 5C2
Parkin@sscl.uwo.ca

Reviewers

Tajudeen Adenekan, Bronx Community College; Milton Alderfer, Miami-Dade Community College; William Aldridge, Shelton State Community College; Stuart Allen, University of North Carolina—Greensboro; Sam Allgood, University of Nebraska—Lincoln; Neil Alper, Northeastern University; Alan Anderson, Fordham University; Jeff Ankrom, Wittenberg University; Fatma Antar, Manchester Community Technical College; Kofi Apraku, University of North Carolina—Asheville; Moshen Bahmani-Oskooee, University of Wisconsin—Milwaukee; Donald Balch, University of South Carolina; Mehmet Balcilar, Wayne State University; A. Paul Ballantyne, University of Colorado; Sue Bartlett, University of South Florida; Valerie R. Bencivenga, University of Texas—Austin; Ben Bernanke, Princeton University; Margot Biery, Tarrant County Community College South; John Bittorowitz, Ball State University; Sunne Brandmeyer, University of South Florida; Baird Brock, Central Missouri State University; Byron Brown, Michigan State University ; Jeffrey Buser, Columbus State Community College; Alison Butler, Florida International University; Tania Carbiener, Southern Methodist University; Kevin Carey, University of Miami; Kathleen A. Carroll, University of Maryland—Baltimore County; Michael Carter, University of Massachusetts—Lowell; Adhip Chaudhuri, Georgetown University; Gopal Chengalath, Texas Tech University; Daniel Christiansen, Albion College; John J. Clark, Community College of Allegheny County—Allegheny Campus; Meredith Clement, Dartmouth College; Michael B. Cohn, U.S. Merchant Marine Academy; Robert Collinge, University of Texas—San Antonio; Doug Conway, Mesa Community College; Larry Cook, University of Toledo; Bobby Corcoran, Middle Tennesee State University; Kevin Cotter, Wayne State University; James Peery Cover, University of Alabama—Tuscaloosa; Eleanor D. Craig, University of Delaware; Jim Craven, Clark College; Stephen Cullenberg, University of California—Riverside; David Culp, Slippery Rock University; Norman V. Cure, Macomb Community College; Dan Dabney, University of Texas—Austin; Andrew Dane, Angelo State University; Joseph Daniels, Marquette University; David Denslow, University of Florida; Mark Dickie, University of Georgia; James Dietz, California State University—Fullerton; Carol Dole, University of North Carolina—Charlotte; Ronald Dorf, Inver Hills Community College; John Dorsey, University of Maryland—College Park; Amrik Singh Dua, Mt. San Antonio College; Thomas Duchesneau, University of Maine—Orono; Lucia Dunn, Ohio State University; Donald Dutkowsky, Syracuse University; John Edgren, Eastern Michigan University; David J. Eger, Alpena Community College; Ibrahim Elsaify, State University of New York—Albany; Kenneth G. Elzinga, University of Virginia; M. Fazeli, Hofstra University; Philip Fincher, Louisiana Tech University; F. Firoozi, University of Texas—San Antonio; David Franck, University of North Carolina—Charlotte; Alwyn Fraser, Atlantic Union College; Eugene Gentzel, Pensacola Junior College; Andrew Gill, California State University—Fullerton; Robert Giller, Virginia Polytechnic Institute and Sate University; Robert Gillette, University of Kentucky; James N. Giordano, Villanova University; Maria Giuili, Diablo College; Richard Gosselin, Houston Community College; John Graham, Rutgers University; John Griffen, Worcester Polytechnic Institute; Robert Guell, Indiana State University; Jamie Haag, University of Oregon; Daniel Hagen, Western Washington University; David R. Hakes, University of Northern Iowa; Craig Hakkio, Federal Reserve Bank, Kansas City; Ann Hansen, Westminster College; Jonathan Haughton, Northeastern University; Randall Haydon, Wichita State University; Jolien A. Helsel, Kent State University; John Herrmann, Rutgers University; John M. Hill, Delgado Community College; Lewis Hill, Texas Tech University; Tom Hoerger, Vanderbilt University; Calvin Hoerneman, Delta College; Dennis L. Hoffman, Arizona Sate University; Paul Hohenberg, Rensselaer Polytechnic Institute; Jim H. Holcomb, University of Texas—El Paso; Harry Holzer, Michigan State University; Djehane Hosni, University of Central Florida; Harold Hotelling, Jr., Lawrence Technical University; Calvin Hoy, County College of Morris; Julie Hunsaker, Wayne State University; Beth Ingram, University of Iowa; Michael Jacobs, Lehman College; Dennis Jansen, Texas A & M University; Frederick Jungman, Northwestern Oklahoma Sate University; Paul Junk, University of Minnesota—Duluth; Leo Kahane, California State University—Hayward; E. Kang, St. Cloud State University; Arthur Kartman, San Diego State University; Manfred W. Keil, Claremont McKenna College; Rose Kilburn, Modesto Junior College; Robert Kirk, Indiana University—Purdue University—Indianapolis; Norman Kleinberg,

City University of New York, Baruch College; **Robert Kleinhenz**, California Sate University—Fullerton; **Joseph Kreitzer**, University of St. Thomas; **David Lages**, Southwest Missouri State University; **Leonard Lardaro**, University of Rhode Island; **Kathryn Larson**, Elon College; **Luther D. Lawson**, University of North Carolina—Wilmington; **Elroy M. Leach**, Chicago State University; **Jay Levin**, Wayne State University; **Tony Lima**, California State University—Hayward; **William Lord**, University of Maryland—Baltimore County; **K.T. Magnusson**, Salt Lake City Community College; **Mark Maier**, Glendale Community College; **Beth Maloan**, University of Tennessee—Martin; **Jean Mangan**, California State University—Sacramento; **Michael Marlow**, California Polytechnic State University; **Akbar Marvasti**, University of Houston; **Wolfgang Mayer**, University of Cincinnati; **John McArthur**, Wofford College; **Amy McCormick**, College of William and Mary; **Russel McCullough**, Iowa State University; **Gerald McDougall**, Wichita State University; **Stephen McGary**, Ricks College; **Richard D. McGrath**, College of William and Mary; **Richard McIntyre**, University of Rhode Island; **John McLeod**, Georgia Institute of Technology; **Charles Meyer**, Iowa State University; **Peter Mieszkowski**, Rice University; **John Mijares**, University of North Carolina—Asheville; **Judith W. Mills**, Southern Connecticut State University; **Glen Mitchell**, Nassau Community College; **Jeannette C. Mitchell**, Rochester Institute of Technology; **Khan Mohabbat**, Northern Illinois University; **W. Douglas Morgan**, University of California—Santa Barbara; **William Morgan**, University of Wyoming; **Joanne Moss**, San Francisco State University; **Edward Murphy**, Southwest Texas State University; **Kathryn Nantz**, Fairfield University; **William S. Neilson**, Texas A & M University; **Bart C. Nemmers**, University of Nebraska—Lincoln; **Anthony O'Brien**, Lehigh University; **Mary Olson**, Washington University; **Jim B. O'Niell**, University of Delaware; **Farley Ordovensky**, University of the Pacific; **Z. Edward O'Relley**, North Dakota State University; **Jan Palmer**, Ohio University; **Michael Palumbo**, University of Houston; **G. Hossein Parandvash**, Western Oregon State College; **Randall Parker**, East Carolina University; **Robert Parks**, Washington University; **David Pate**, St. John Fisher College; **Donald Pearson**, Eastern Michigan University; **Mary Anne Pettit**, Southern Illinois University—Edwardsville; **Kathy Phares**, University of Missouri—St. Louis; **William A. Phillips**, University of Southern Maine; **Dennis Placone**, Clemson University; **Charles Plot**, California Institute of Technology—Pasadena; **Mannie Poen**, Houston Community College; **Kathleen Possai**, Wayne State University; **Ulrika Praski-Stahlgren**, University College in Gavle-Sandviken, Sweden; **K.A. Quartey**, Talladega College; **Herman Quirmbach**, Iowa State University; **Peter Rangazas**, Indiana University—Purdue; **Vaman Rao**, Western Illinois University; **Laura Razzolini**, University of Mississippi; **J. David Reed**, Bowling Green State University; **Robert H. Renshaw**, Northern Illinois University; **W. Gregory Rhodus**, Bentley College; **John Robertson**, Paducah Community College; **Malcolm Robinson**, University of North Carolina—Greensboro; **Richard Roehl**, University of Michigan—Dearborn; **Thomas Romans**, State University of New York—Buffalo; **David R. Ross,** Bryn Mawr College; **Thomas Ross**, St. Louis University; **Robert J. Rossana**, Wayne State University; **Rochelle Ruffer**, Ithaca College; **Mark Rush**, University of Florida; **Gary Santoni**, Ball State University; **John Saussy**, Harrisburg Area Community College; **David Schlow**, Pennsylvania State University; **Paul Schmitt**, St. Clair County Community College; **Martin Sefton**, Indianapolis University; **Rod Shadbegian**, University of Massachusetts—Dartmouth; **Gerald Shilling**, Eastfield College; **Dorothy R. Siden**, Salem State College; **Scott Simkins**, North Carolina Agricultural and Technical State University; **Chuck Skoro**, Boise State University; **Phil Smith**, DeKalb College; **William Doyle Smith**, University of Texas—El Paso; **Frank Steindl**, Oklahoma Sate University; **Jeffrey Stewart**, New York University; **Allan Stone**, Southwest Missouri State University; **Courtenay Stone**, Ball State University; **Mark Strazicich**, Ohio State University—Newark; **Robert Stuart**, Rutgers University; **Gilbert Suzawa**, University of Rhode Island; **David Swaine**, Andrews University; **Kay Unger**, University of Montana; **Anthony Uremovic**, Joliet Junior College; **David Vaughn**, City University, Washington; **Francis Wambalaba**, Portland State University; **Rob Wassmer**, Wayne State University; **Paul A. Weinstein**, University of Maryland—College Park; **Lee Weissert**, St. Vincent College; **Robert Whaples**, Wake Forest University; **Larry Wimmer**, Brigham Young University; **Mark Witte**, Northwestern University; **Willard E. Witte**, Indiana University; **Cheonsik Woo**, Clemson University; **Douglas Wooley**, Radford University; **Ann Al Yasiri**, University of Wisconsin—Platteville; **John T. Young**, Riverside Community College; **Michael Youngblood**, Rock Valley College.

Flexibility Chart

Core	Policy	Optional
1. What is Economics?		**2.** Making and Using Graphs
		Good chapter for students with fear of graphs.
3. The Economic Problem		
4. Demand and Supply		
5. Elasticity		
6. Efficiency	**7.** Markets in Action	
A new chapter that unifies the entire coverage of micro	A unique chapter that gives extensive applications of demand and supply.	
8. Utility and Demand		**9.** Possibilities, Preferences, and Choices
Some teachers like to cover this material before Chapter 4. Some like to skip it. Both are possible		Easy to teach coverage of indifference curves. Strictly optional.
10. Organizing Production		
This chapter may be skipped.		
11. Output and Cost		
12. Competition		
13. Monopoly		
14. Monopolistic Competition and Oligopoly		
15. Demand and Supply in Resource Markets		**16.** Labor Markets
This chapter gives an overview of all resource markets–labor, capital, and natural resources.		
	17. Income Distribution	
	18. Market Failure and Public Choice	
	A general introduction to the role of government in the economy and the positive theory of government.	
	19. Competition Policy	

Core	Policy	Optional
	20. Externalities, the Environment, and Knowledge	**21.** Uncertainty and Information

22. A First Look at Macroeconomics

23. Measuring GDP, Inflation and Economic Growth

> Chapter 25, Employment, Wages, and Unemployment may be studied immediately following Chapter 23.

24. Aggregate Supply and Aggregate Demand

> Chapter 24 may be delayed and studied after Chapter 28

25. Employment, Wages, and Unemployment

> If you wish to emphasize short-term fluctuations, you may delay coverage of this block of chapters on aggregate supply and long-term growth.

26. Investment, Capital, and Interest

> Includes a section on long-run aspects on fiscal policy

27. Economic Growth

> The section on growth theory is optional

Core	Policy	Optional
28. Expenditure Multipliers	**29.** Fiscal Policy	If you wish to emphasize short-term fluctuations, you may cover this block of chapters before those on aggregate supply and long-term growth.
30. Money	**31.** Monetary Policy	

32. Inflation

33. The Business Cycle

34. Macroeconomic Policy Challenges

35. Trading with the World

36. The Balance of Payments and the Dollar

Brief Contents

Contents

Summary (Key Points, Key Figures and Tables, and Key Terms), Questions, Problems, and Critical Thinking Exercises appear at the end of each chapter.

part 3 A Closer Look at Demand and Supply

Chapter 8

Utility and Demand 155

Chapter 9

Possibilities, Preferences, and Choices 173

part 4 Competition Versus Monopoly

Chapter 13

Monopoly 263

Chapter 14

Monopolistic Competition and Oligopoly 285

part 5   Resource Markets

Chapter 15

Demand and Supply in Resource Markets 317

Chapter 16

Labor Markets 341

part 6 Market Failure and Government

part **8** Aggregate Supply and Economic Growth

Chapter 25

Employment and Unemployment 543

Chapter 26

Capital, Investment, and Saving 565

part 9   Aggregate Demand and Inflation

Chapter 29

Fiscal Policy **641**

Chapter 30

Money **665**

part 10 Stabilization Problems and Policies

part 11 | The Global Economy

It's a Small World 793

Your Economics Course

You are living at a time that future historians will call the *Information Revolution*. We reserve the word "Revolution" for big events that influence all future generations. ◆ During the *Agricultural Revolution*, which occurred 10,000 years ago, people learned to domesticate animals and plant crops. They stopped roaming in search of food and settled in villages and eventually towns and cities, where they developed markets in which to exchange their products. ◆ During the *Industrial Revolution*, which began 240 years ago, people used science to create new technologies. This revolution brought extraordinary wealth for most, but created conditions in which some were left behind. It brought social and political tensions that we still face today. ◆ During today's *Information Revolution*, people who have the ability and opportunity to embrace the new technologies are prospering on an unimagined scale. But the incomes and living standards of the less educated are falling behind, and social and political tensions are increasing. Today's revolution has a global dimension. Some of the winners live in previously poor countries in Asia, and some of the losers live in the United States. ◆ So you are studying economics at an interesting time. Whatever *your* motivation is for studying economics, *my* objective is to help you do well in your course, to enjoy it, and to develop a deeper understanding of the economic world around you. ◆ There are three reasons why I hope that we both succeed. First, a decent understanding of economics will help you become a full participant in the Information Revolution. Second, an understanding of economics will help you play a more effective role as a citizen and voter and enable you to add your voice to those who are looking for solutions to our social and political problems. Third, you will enjoy the sheer fun of *understanding* the forces at play and how they are shaping our world. ◆ If you do find economics interesting, think seriously about majoring in the subject. A degree in economics gives the best training available in problem solving, offers lots of opportunities to develop conceptual skills, and opens doors to a wide range of graduate courses, including the MBA, and to a wide range of jobs. You can read more about the benefits of an economics degree in Robert Whaples's essay in your *Study Guide*. ◆ Economics was born during the Industrial Revolution. We'll look at its birth and meet its founder, Adam Smith. Then we'll talk with one of today's creative economic thinkers, Professor Mancur Olson of the University of Maryland. ◆ In the next three chapters, we'll begin to study the science that Adam Smith began. You will encounter the questions, methods, and ideas of economics in Chapter 1. And in Chapter 3, you will learn about Adam Smith's key insight: specialization and exchange bring economic wealth. In optional Chapter 2, you have an opportunity to learn about the graph tools that we use in economics. But first, let's meet Adam Smith.

Understanding the Sources of Economic Wealth

The Father of Economics: Adam Smith

Adam Smith was a giant of a scholar who contributed to ethics and jurisprudence as well as economics. Born in 1723 in Kirkcaldy, a small fishing town near Edinburgh, Scotland, Smith was the only child of the town's customs officer (who died before Adam was born).

His first academic appointment, at age 28, was as Professor of Logic at the University of Glasgow. He subsequently became tutor to a wealthy Scottish duke, whom he accompanied on a two-year grand European tour, following which he received a pension of £300 a year—ten times the average income at that time.

With the financial security of his pension, Smith devoted ten years to writing *An Inquiry into the Nature and Causes of the Wealth of Nations*, which was published in 1776. Many people had written on economic issues before Adam Smith, but he made economics a science. Smith's account was so broad and authoritative that no subsequent writer on economics could advance ideas without tracing their connections to those of Adam Smith.

> *"It is not from the benevolence of the butcher, the brewer, or the baker that we expect our dinner, but from their regard to their own interest."*
>
> ADAM SMITH
>
> THE WEALTH OF NATIONS

The Issues and Ideas

Why are some nations wealthy while others are poor? This question lies at the heart of economics. And it leads directly to a second question: What can poor nations do to become wealthy?

Adam Smith, who is regarded by many scholars as the founder of economics, attempted to answer these questions in his book *The Wealth of Nations*, published in 1776. Smith was pondering these questions at the height of the Industrial Revolution. During these years, new technologies were invented and applied to the manufacture of cotton and wool cloth, iron, transportation, and agriculture.

Smith wanted to understand the sources of economic wealth, and he brought his acute powers of observation and abstraction to bear on the question. His answer:

- The division of labor
- Free markets

The division of labor—breaking tasks down into simple tasks and becoming skilled in those tasks—is the source of "the greatest improvement in the productive powers of labor," said Smith. The division of labor became even more productive when it was applied to creating new technologies. Scientists and engineers, trained in extremely narrow fields, became specialists at inventing. Their powerful skills accelerated the advance of technology, so by the 1820s, machines could make consumer goods faster and more accurately than any craftsman could. And by the 1850s, machines could make other machines that labor alone could never have made.

But, said Smith, the fruits of the division of labor are limited by the extent of the market. To make the market as large as possible, there must be no impediments to free trade both within a country and among countries. Smith argued that when each person makes the best possible economic choice, that choice leads as if by "an invisible hand" to the best outcome for society as a whole. The butcher, the brewer, and the baker each pursue their own interests but, in doing so, also serve the interests of everyone else.

THEN...

Adam Smith speculated that one person, working hard, using the hand tools available in the 1770s, might possibly make 20 pins a day. Yet, he observed, by using those same hand tools but breaking the process into a number of individually small operations in which people specialize—by the division of labor—ten people could make a staggering 48,000 pins a day. One draws out the wire, another straightens it, a third cuts it, a fourth points it, a fifth grinds

it. Three specialists make the head, and a fourth attaches it. Finally, the pin is polished and packaged. But a large market is needed to support the division of labor: One factory employing ten workers would need to sell more than 15 million pins a year to stay in business.

...AND NOW

If Adam Smith were here today, he would be fascinated by the computer chip. He would see it as an extraordinary example of the productivity of the division of labor and of the use of machines to make machines that make other machines. From a design of a chip's intricate circuits, cameras transfer an image to glass plates that work like stencils. Workers prepare silicon wafers on which the circuits are printed. Some slice the wafers, others polish them, others bake them, and yet others coat them with a light-sensitive chemical. Machines transfer a copy of the circuit onto

the wafer. Chemicals then etch the design onto the wafer. Further processes deposit atom-sized transistors and aluminum connectors. Finally, a laser separates the hundreds of chips on the wafer. Every stage in the process of creating a computer chip uses other computer chips. And like the pin of the 1770s, the computer chip of the 1990s benefits from a large market—a global market—to buy chips in the huge quantities in which they are produced efficiently.

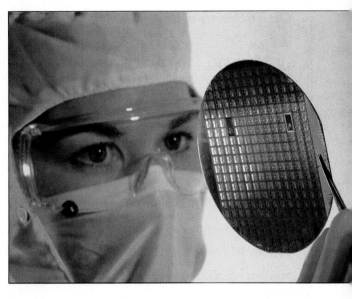

Many economists have worked on the big themes that Adam Smith began. One of these economists is Mancur Olson, of the University of Maryland, whom you can meet on the following pages.

Mancur Olson, Jr., is Distinguished University Professor of Economics at the University of Maryland, a position he has held since 1978. Professor Olson was born in Grand Forks, North Dakota, in 1932. He was an undergraduate at North Dakota State University, a Rhodes Scholar at Oxford University (M.A. 1960), and a graduate student at Harvard University (Ph.D. 1963).

Professor Olson's research covers a wide area, and his major work is on the problems that lead to and are caused by collective choices by groups such as businesses, labor unions, or governments. He has studied the effects of collective choices on economic growth and on the transition from Communism to a market economy.

Michael Parkin talked with Professor Olson about his work, how it connects with the origins of economics and the work of Adam Smith, and the insights it offers us in facing today's problems.

What attracted you to economics?

I became enchanted with the first economics book that I read, *Defense Without Inflation* by Albert Gaylord Hart. I had never before come upon anything that used logical deduction from basic assumptions to derive general principles about how the world worked. The fun and relevance of economics captivated me and made me want to be an economist. When economics writing and teaching are really good, they make clear what a wonderful and fascinating subject economics is.

Can you describe the connection between this set of ideas and your own and the earlier ideas of Adam Smith?

I'm enormously indebted to Adam Smith and to the other great economists who have written over the last two and a quarter centuries. Long ago the great physicist Isaac Newton said that if he was able to see farther, it was because he stood on the shoulders of giants. Not only do economists of today have the legacy of Adam Smith, but also other giants such as Ricardo, Malthus, Mill, and Marshall. Thus the economist today stands on the shoulders of giants standing on shoulders of giants—on a great pyramid of genius.

Adam Smith thought that he understood the major reason for differences in the wealth of nations, and he attributed this mainly to the extent to which people exploited the advantages of the division of labor and specialization on the one hand and then coordinated their individual activities by allowing self-interest to rule in the marketplace. Was Smith right?

Adam Smith put forth one of the most important truths ever told, but it's still not the whole truth. What he neglected to point out is that, to achieve prosperity, societies need what I call "market-augmenting government." Many suppose that governments only repress or interfere with markets, but the richest societies have governments that, on balance, increase the number of markets. In an anarchy, people are fighting instead of trading. The government that replaces the anarchy is already augmenting markets because a peaceful order increases the incentive to produce and to trade.

Many people think that once there is peace, all the needed markets arise spontaneously, but this is true of only one of the two types of markets. One kind of market does arise simply because the gains from trade are often very large and the parties can reap these gains without any outside help. When people trade goods and cash on the spot, these trades are self-enforcing. When trades are self-enforcing, markets spring up by themselves, and if governments make them illegal, they may even exist as black markets.

The other kind of market exists only when there is third-party enforcement of contracts. Consider long-term loans. A lender has to give up the money at the outset, so the lender is a fool to lend unless he or she can be reasonably confident that the money will be paid back with interest. Thus lenders lend and borrowers can borrow only if an impartial third party, such as the government's legal system, will enforce the loan contract, often by seizing the assets purchased with the loan in the interest of the lender. The gains from trade in capital markets, insurance markets, and many other markets can be realized only if there is a contract-enforcing and thus market-augmenting government. The richest (or First World) countries have such governments and thus have not only self-enforcing markets but also a huge range of markets that depend upon third-party enforcement. By contrast, the countries of the Third World and those that are in transition from Communism (the Second World) do not have mar-ket-augmenting governments, and they usually have little more than self-enforcing markets.

You place a great deal of emphasis on collective action. Why?

While most goods and services are provided most efficiently through the market, there are some goods and services that the market cannot provide. Firms can make money producing the kinds of goods that we find in the stores because they can keep us from getting the goods unless we pay the going price. But there are other kinds of goods that are collective or public goods—goods that, if available to anyone, are automatically available to everyone in some category or country, whether or not a person contributed anything toward the cost of providing the good. A population cannot obtain such goods through voluntary or market behavior. Virtually everyone prefers clean air to polluted air, but that does not mean that the people in a metropolitan area will voluntarily spend a few hundred extra dollars to have their cars equipped with pollution abatement technology. If there were, say, a million individuals in a metropolitan area, a typical individual would get only about one millionth of the benefit from the increment in clean air that resulted because that individual paid for pollution abatement technology. But that individual would pay the whole cost of any pollution abatement technology that the individual purchased. A person would also obtain the benefit of any pollution abatement by others, whether or not that person had done anything to reduce pollution or not.

This means that, even if absolutely everyone agreed that clean air was worth more than it cost and everyone would vote in favor of making the pollution abatement technology compulsory, no one individual would gain from voluntarily contributing to or "buying" this good. Voluntary or market mechanisms therefore cannot provide any substantial population with pollution abatement or any other collective good. This is the paradoxical logic of collective action: Rational individual behavior leads to a collectively irrational outcome. It is because of the logic of collective action that certain goods and services, such as law and order and national defense, have to be funded through compulsory taxation. It is because of this logic that we need government.

This logic also helps to explain the behavior of some types of non-governmental organizations. Consider, for example, the benefits that a lobby provides to an industry. If a lobby gets a tariff for an

A key idea is that the incentive structures of societies overwhelmingly determine how well their economies perform.

industry, the price rises for all of the producers in that industry. Every producer in the industry gets the benefit of the tariff, whether that producer paid any of the costs of the lobbying or not. Therefore lobbying organizations provide a benefit that is a collective good to their constituents. Similarly, by restricting output and raising prices, cartels also provide a collective good to those who sell the product that benefits from the monopoly price.

A key idea is that the incentive structures of societies overwhelmingly determine how well their economies perform. One important determinant of this is the power of the special interest organizations that I mentioned in response to your last question. As time goes on in stable democracies, more organizations representing the firms or workers in an industry or occupation develop the selective incentives that enable them to overcome the difficulties of collective action. Each individual industry is small in relation to the economy as a whole. Suppose, for the sake of easy arithmetic, that the firms or workers in a special interest organization earn exactly 1 percent of the nation's income. Then they gain from using their lobbying or cartel power to change the distribution of income in their favor. They seek such things as tariff protection, tax loopholes, and higher prices or wages. This makes the economy less productive. The members of the special interest organization will, when they earn 1 percent of income, bear on the average only about 1 percent of the total loss arising from the redistribution to themselves, but they receive everything that is redistributed to them. Thus they gain from their lobbying or cartel power until the nation's income falls by a hundred times as much as they obtain! So an economy with a dense network of special interest organizations is like a china shop filled with wrestlers battling over its contents—and breaking much more than they carry away.

Another important determinant of the structure of incentives is the quality of the legal system's enforcement of contracts and com-

pany law and its protection of property rights. This mainly determines whether a society can mobilize the capital—and the modern technologies that are normally embodied in capital goods—needed for either capital-intensive or large scale production. Most of the countries in the First World have the rule of law with respect to property and contract as to other things. Most countries in the Second and Third Worlds do not have the rule of law and thus also lack good property and contract rights. This is, I believe, the single most important reason why the First World

> *Economic development requires ... governments so strong that they're expected to last indefinitely but so inhibited that they never abridge individual rights.*

countries are rich and the countries of the Second and the Third Worlds are mostly still poor.

The structure of incentives that a society needs to prosper does not spring up spontaneously but is a result of social accumulation and governmental design. There is no private property, for example, without government; there may be possessions, in the sense that a dog possesses a bone, but no socially sanctioned property right. Just as governments are indispensable for private property, so they are often the greatest threat to private property. Governments have the power to seize whatever property they want. In much of the world, private property is insecure because governments often expropriate it or because governments are so unstable or weak that individuals cannot be sure the government will be able to protect private property indefinitely. Economic development requires something that's rather rare: governments so strong that they're expected to last indefinitely but so inhibited that they never abridge individual rights.

Economics, far more than any other social science, has a body of powerful ideas that illuminate the problems that individuals and societies face. Economics ideas will be indispensable in the next century as in the present one. The problem is to make their value apparent to the student. Some economics instruction sets out the logic of models without relating them frequently to observation. It's said, "The glory of opera is that it is words and music," and the glory of economics is that it is both logic and observation. Only when the two go together—only when the teacher of economics makes it clear how the logic of economic theory illuminates what we observe around us—does the great practical value of economics become apparent.

What is Economics?

From the moment you wake up each morning to the moment you fall asleep again each night, your life is filled with *choices*. Your first choice is when to get up. Will you start running the moment the alarm goes off, or will you linger for a few minutes and listen to the radio? What will you wear today? You check the weather forecast and make that decision. Then, what will you have for breakfast? Will you drive to school or take the bus? Which classes will you attend? Which assignments will you complete? What will you do for lunch? Will you play tennis, swim, run, or skate today? How will you spend your evening? Will you study, relax at home with a video, or go to the movies? ◆ You face decisions like these every day. But on some days, you face choices that can change the entire direction of your life. What will you study? Will you major in economics, business, law, or film? ◆

A Day in Your Life

While you are making your own decisions, other people are making theirs. And some of the decisions that other people make will have an impact on your own subsequent decisions. Your school decides its course offerings for next year. Stephen Spielberg decides what his next movie will be. General Motors decides what new models to introduce and how many of this year's models to produce. A team of eye doctors decides on a new experiment that will lead them to a cure for nearsightedness. The U.S. Congress decides to cut defense spending and to lower taxes. The Federal Reserve Board decides to raise interest rates. ◆ All these choices and the decisions made by you and everyone else are examples of economics in your life. ◆ This chapter takes a first look at the subject you are about to study. It defines economics. Then it expands on that definition with five big questions that economists try to answer and eight big ideas that define the economic way of thinking. These questions and ideas are the foundation on which your course is built. The chapter concludes with a description of how economists go about their work, the scientific method they use, and the pitfalls they try to avoid. When you have completed your study of this chapter, you will have a good sense of what economics is about and you'll be ready to start learning economics and using it to gain a new view of the world.

After studying this chapter, you will be able to:

■ Define economics

■ Explain the five big questions that economists seek to answer

■ Explain eight ideas that define the economic way of thinking

■ Describe how economists go about their work

Big Economic Questions

A Definition of Economics

All economic questions and problems arise from **scarcity**—they arise because our wants exceed the resources available to satisfy them.

We want good health and long life, material comfort, security, physical and mental recreation, and knowledge. None of these wants is completely satisfied for everyone, and everyone has some unsatisfied wants. While many people have all the material comfort they want, many others do not. And no one feels entirely satisfied with her or his state of health and expected length of life. No one feels entirely secure, even in the post-Cold War era, and no one has enough time for sport, travel, vacations, movies, theater, reading, and other leisure pursuits.

The poor and the rich alike face scarcity. A child wants a 75¢ can of soft drink and a 50¢ pack of gum but has only $1.00 in her pocket. She experiences scarcity. A student wants to go to a party on Saturday night but also wants to spend that same night catching up on late assignments. He experiences scarcity. A millionaire wants to spend the weekend playing golf *and* attending a business strategy meeting and cannot do both. She experiences scarcity. Even parrots face scarcity—there just aren't enough crackers to go around!

Not only do I want a cracker—we all want a cracker!

Drawing by Modell; ©1985 The New Yorker Magazine, Inc.

Faced with scarcity, we must *choose* among the available alternatives.

Economics is the *science of choice*—the science that explains the choices we make and how those choices change as we cope with scarcity.

All economic choices can be summarized in five big questions about the goods and services we produce. These questions are: What? How? When? Where? Who?

1 **What** goods and services are produced and in **what** quantities?

Goods and services are all the things that we value and are willing to pay for. We produce a dazzling array of goods and services that range from necessities such as houses to leisure items such as camping vehicles and equipment. We build more than a million new homes every year. And these homes are more spacious and better equipped than they were 20 years ago. We make several mil-

lion new leisure vehicles, tents, portable microwaves, refrigerators, telephones, television sets, and VCRs, all of which make outdoor living and vacations more attractive and more comfortable.

What determines whether we build more homes or make more camping gear and develop more campsites? How do these choices change over time? And how are they affected by the ongoing changes in technology that make an ever-widening array of goods and services available to us?

2 How are goods and services produced?

In a vineyard in France, basket-carrying workers pick the annual grape crop by hand. In a vineyard in California, a huge machine and a few workers do the same job that a hundred French grape harvesters do. Look around you and you will see many examples of this phenomenon—the same job being done in different ways. In some supermarkets, checkout clerks key

in prices. In others, they use a laser scanner. One farmer keeps track of livestock feeding schedules and inventories by using paper and pencil records, while another uses a personal computer. GM hires workers to weld auto bodies in some of its plants and uses robots to do the job in others.

Why do we use machines in some cases and people in others? Do mechanization and technological change destroy more jobs than they create? Do they make us better off or worse off?

3 When are goods and services produced?

On a building site, there is a surge of production activity and people must work overtime to keep production flowing fast enough. An auto factory closes for the summer, temporarily laying off its workers, and its production dries up.

Sometimes, economy-wide production slackens off and even shrinks in what is called a *recession*. At other times, economy-wide production expands rapidly. We call these ebbs and flows of production the *business cycle*. When production falls, jobs are lost and unemployment climbs. Once, during the Great Depression of the 1930s, production fell so much that one quarter of the work force was jobless.

During the past few years, production has decreased in Russia and its Central and Eastern Europe neighbors as these countries try to change the way they organize their economies.

What makes production rise and fall? When will production fall again in the United States? Can the government prevent production from falling?

4 Where are goods and services produced?

The Kellogg Company, of Battle Creek, Michigan, makes breakfast cereals in 20 countries and sells them in 160 countries. Kellogg's business in Japan is so huge that it has a Web site in Japanese to promote its products! Honda, the Japanese auto producer, makes cars and motorcycles on most continents.

"Globalization through localization" is its slogan. But it produces some cars in one country and ships them for sale in another. We in the United States even import some cars from Japan.

In today's global economy, people who are separated by thousands of miles cooperate to produce many goods and services. Software engineers in Silicon Valley work via the Internet with programmers in India. American Express card charge slips are processed in Barbados. But there is a lot of local concentration of production as well. Most American carpets are made in Dalton, Georgia. And most of our movies are made in Los Angeles.

What determines where goods and services are produced? And how are changing patterns of production location changing the jobs we do and the wages we earn?

5 Who consumes the goods and services that are produced?

Who consumes the goods and services produced depends on the incomes that people earn. Doctors earn much higher incomes than nurses and medical assistants. So doctors get more of the goods and services produced than nurses and medical assistants do.

You probably know about many other persistent differences in incomes. Men, on the average, earn more than women. Whites, on the average, earn more than minorities. College graduates, on the average, earn more than high school graduates. Americans, on the average, earn more than Europeans, who in turn earn more, on the average, than Asians and Africans. But there are some significant exceptions. The people of Japan and Hong Kong now earn an amount similar to that of Americans. And there is a lot of income inequality throughout the world.

What determines the incomes we earn? Why do doctors earn larger incomes than nurses? Why do women and minorities earn less than white males?

These five big economic questions give you a sense of what economics is *about*. They tell you about the *scope of economics*. But they don't tell you what economics *is*. They don't tell you how economists *think* about these questions and seek answers to them. Let's find out how economists approach economic questions by looking at some big ideas that define the *economic way of thinking*.

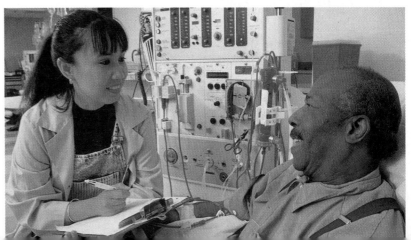

Big Ideas of Economics

1 **A choice is a trade-off— we give up something to get something else—and the highest-valued alternative we give up is the opportunity cost of the activity chosen.**

Whatever we choose to do, we could have done something else instead. We trade off one thing for another. "There ain't no such thing as a free lunch" is not just a clever throwaway line. It expresses the central idea of economics— that every choice involves a cost.

We use the term **opportunity cost** to emphasize that when we make a choice in the face of scarcity, we give up an opportunity to do something else. The opportunity cost of any action is the highest-valued alternative forgone. The action that you choose not to do—the highest-valued alternative forgone—is the cost of the action that you choose to do.

You can quit school right now, or you can remain in school. If you quit and take a job at McDonald's, you might earn enough to buy some CDs, go to the movies, and spend lots of free time with your friends. If you remain in school, you can't afford these things. You will be able to buy these things later, and that is one of the payoffs from being in school. But for now, when you've bought your books, you have nothing left for CDs and movies. And doing assignments means that you've got less time for

hanging around with your friends. The opportunity cost of being in school is the alternative things that you would have done if you had quit school.

Opportunity cost is the highest-valued alternative forgone. It is not *all* the possible alternatives forgone. For example, your economics lecture is at 8:30 on a Monday morning. You contemplate two alternatives to attending the lecture: staying in bed for an hour or jogging for an hour. You can't stay

in bed and jog for that same hour. The opportunity cost of attending the lecture is not the cost of an hour in bed and the cost of jogging for an hour. If these are the only alternatives you contemplate, then you have to decide which one you would do if you did not go to the lecture. The opportunity cost of attending a lecture for a jogger is a forgone hour of exercise; the opportunity cost of attending a lecture for a late sleeper is a forgone hour in bed.

2 We make choices in small steps, or at the **margin**, and choices are influenced by **incentives**.

Everything that we do involves a decision to do a little bit more or a little bit less of an activity. You can allocate the next hour between studying and e-mailing your friends. But the choice is not "all-or-nothing." You must decide how many minutes to allocate to each activity. To make this decision, you compare the benefit of a little bit more study time with its cost.

The mother of a young child must decide how to allocate her time between being with her child and working for an income. Like your decision about study time, this decision too involves comparing the benefit of a little bit more income with the cost of a little bit less time with her child.

The benefit that arises from an increase in an activity is called **marginal benefit.** For example, suppose that a mother is working 2 days a week and is thinking about increasing her work to 3 days. Her marginal benefit is the benefit she will get from the additional day of work. It is *not* the benefit she gets from all 3 days. The reason is that she already has the benefit from 2 days work, so she doesn't count this benefit as resulting from the decision she is now making.

The cost of an increase in an activity is called **marginal cost.** For the mother of the young child, the marginal cost of increasing her work to 3 days a week is the cost of the additional day not

spent with her child. It does not include the cost of the two days she is already working.

To make her decision, the mother compares the marginal benefit from an extra day of work with its marginal cost. If the marginal benefit exceeds the marginal cost, she works the extra day. If the marginal cost exceeds the marginal benefit, she does not work the extra day.

By evaluating marginal benefits and marginal costs and choosing only those actions that bring greater benefit than cost, we use our scarce resources in the way that makes us as well off as possible.

Our choices respond to incentives. An **incentive** is an inducement to take a particular action. The inducement can be a benefit—a carrot—or a cost—a stick. A change in opportunity cost—in marginal cost—and a change in marginal benefit changes the incentives that we face and leads to changes in our actions.

For example, suppose the daily wage rate rises and nothing else changes. With a higher daily wage

rate, the marginal benefit of working increases. For the young mother, the opportunity cost of spending a day with her child has increased. She now has a bigger incentive to work an extra day a week. Whether or not she does so depends on how she evaluates the marginal benefit of the additional income and marginal cost of spending less time with her child.

Similarly, suppose the cost of day care rises and nothing else changes. The higher cost of day care increases the marginal cost of working. For the young mother, the opportunity cost of spending a day with her child has decreased. She now has a smaller incentive to work an extra day a week. Again, whether or not she changes her actions in response to a change in incentives depends on how she evaluates the marginal benefit and marginal cost.

The central idea of economics is that by looking for changes in marginal cost and marginal benefit, we can predict the way choices will change in response to changes in incentives.

3 Voluntary exchange makes *both* buyers and sellers better off, and **markets** are an **efficient** way to organize exchange.

When you shop for food, you give up some money in exchange for a basket of vegetables. But the food is worth the price you have to pay. You are better off having exchanged some of your money for the vegetables. The food store receives a payment that makes its operator happy too. Both you and the food store operator gain from your purchase.

Similarly, when you work at a summer job, you receive a wage that you've decided is sufficient to compensate you for the leisure time you must give up. But the value of your work to the firm that hires you is at least as great as the wage it pays you. So again, both you and your employer gain from a **voluntary exchange.**

You are better off when you buy your food. And you are better off when you sell your labor during the summer vacation. Whether you are a buyer or a seller, you gain from voluntary exchange with others.

What is true for you is true for everyone else. Everyone gains from voluntary exchange.

In our organized economy, exchanges take place in **markets** and for money. We sell our labor in exchange for an income in the labor market. And we buy the goods and services we've chosen to consume in a wide variety of markets—markets for vegetables, cof-

fee, movies, videos, muffins, haircuts, and so on. At the other side of these transactions, firms buy our labor and sell us the hundreds of different consumer goods and services we buy.

Markets are **efficient** in the sense that they send resources to the place where they are valued most highly. For example, a frost kills Florida's orange crop and sends the price of orange juice through the roof. This increase in price, with all other prices remaining unchanged, increases the opportunity cost of drinking orange juice. The people who place the highest value on orange

juice are the ones who keep drinking it. People who place a lower value on orange juice now have an incentive to substitute other fruit juices.

Markets are not the only way to organize the economy. An alternative is called a command system. In a **command system,** some people give orders (commands) and other people obey those orders. A command system is used in the military and in many firms. And it was used in the former Soviet Union to organize the entire economy. But the market is a superior method of organizing an entire economy.

4 The market does not always work efficiently and sometimes, government action is necessary to overcome **market failure** and lead to a more efficient use of resources.

Market failure is a state in which the market does not use resources efficiently.

If you pay attention to the news media, you might get the impression that the market almost never does a good job. It makes credit card interest rates too high. It makes the wages of fast food workers too low. It causes the price of coffee to go through the ceiling every time Brazil has a serious frost. It increases the world price of oil when political instability threatens the Middle East. These examples are not cases of market failure. They are examples of the market doing its job of helping us to allocate our scarce resources and ensure that they are used in the activities in which they are most highly valued.

Buyers never like it when prices rise. But sellers love it. And sellers never like it when prices fall. But buyers are happy. Rising and falling prices make news because they bring changes in fortunes. Some people win and some lose. Everyone gains from voluntary exchange, as you've just seen, but other things remaining the same, the higher the price, the more the seller gains and the less the buyer gains.

Because a high price brings a bigger gain to the seller, there is

an incentive for sellers to try to control a market. When a single producer controls an entire market, the producer can restrict production and raise the price. This action brings market failure. The quantity of the good available is too small. Some people believe that Intel restricts the quantity of computer chips when it introduces a new design in order to get a high price for it. Eventually, the price falls, but at first, Intel sells its new design for a high price and makes a bigger profit.

Market failure can also arise when producers don't take into account the costs they impose on other people. For example, electricity utilities create pollution such as acid rain that destroys plants and forests and lowers farm production. If these costs were taken into account, we would produce less electricity.

Market failure can also arise because some goods, such as the air traffic control system, must be consumed by everyone equally. None of us has an incentive voluntarily to pay our share of the cost of such a service. Instead, we try to free ride on everyone else. But if everyone tries to free ride, no one gets a ride!

To overcome market failure, governments regulate markets with antitrust laws and environmental protection laws. And the government discourages the production and consumption of some goods and services (tobacco and alcohol for example) by taxing them and encourages the production and consumption of some other items (health care and schooling for example) by subsidizing them.

5 For the economy as a whole, **expenditure** *equals* **income** *equals* the **value of production.**

When you buy a coffee milkshake, you spend $2. But what happens to that money? The server gets some of it in wages, the owner of the building gets some of it as rent, and the owner of the milk bar gets some of it as profit. The suppliers of the milk, ice cream, and coffee also get some of your $2. But these suppliers spend part of what they receive on wages and rent. And they keep part of it as profit. Your $2 of expenditure creates exactly $2 of incomes for all the people who have contributed to making the milkshake, going all the way back to the farmer in Brazil who grew the coffee beans.

Your expenditure generates incomes of an equal amount. The same is true for everyone else's expenditure. So for the economy as a whole, total expenditure on goods and services equals total income.

One way to value the things you buy is to use the prices you pay for them. So the value of all the goods and services bought equals total expenditure. Another way to value the items you buy is to use the cost of production. This cost is the total amount paid to the people who produced the items—the total income generated by your expenditure. But we've just seen that total expenditure and total income are equal, so they also equal the value of production.

6 Living standards improve when **productivity** increases.

By automating a car production line, one worker can produce a greater output. But if one worker can produce more cars, then more people can enjoy owning a car. The same is true for all goods and services. By increasing output per person, we enjoy a higher standard of living and buy more goods and services.

The dollar value of production can increase for any of three reasons: because prices rise, because production per person—**productivity**—increases or because the population increases.

But only an increase in productivity brings an improvement in living standards. A rise in prices brings higher incomes, but only in dollars. The extra income is just enough to pay the higher prices, not enough to buy more goods and services. An increase in population brings an increase in *total* production but not an increase in production per person.

7 Inflation occurs when the quantity of money increases faster than production.

Prices rise in a process called **inflation** when the quantity of money in circulation increases faster than production. This leads to a situation of "too much money chasing too few goods." As people bring more money to market, sellers see that they can raise their prices. But when these sellers go to buy their supplies, they find that the prices they face increase. With too much money around, money starts to lose value.

In some countries, inflation has been rapid. One such country is Poland. Since 1990, prices in Poland have risen more than sevenfold. In the United States, we have moderate inflation of about 3 percent a year.

Some people say that by increasing the quantity of money, we can create jobs. The idea is that if more money is put into the economy, when it is spent, businesses sell more and so hire more labor to produce more goods.

Initially, an increase in money might increase production and create jobs. But eventually, it only increases prices and leaves production and jobs unchanged.

8 Unemployment can result from market failure but some unemployment is productive.

Unemployment is ever present. Sometimes its rate is low and sometimes it is high. Also, unemployment fluctuates over the business cycle.

Some unemployment is normal and efficient. We choose to take our time finding a suitable job rather than rushing to accept the first one that comes along. Similarly, businesses take their time in filling vacancies. The unemployment that results from these careful searches for jobs and workers improves productivity because it helps to assign people to their most productive jobs.

Some unemployment results from fluctuations in expenditure and can be wasteful.

These eight ideas lie at the heart of economics, and you will repeatedly return to them at every point in your study of the subject. To complete your introduction to economics, we next describe how economists go about their work. We're going to describe what economists do.

What Economists Do

Economists work on the wide array of problems that arise from the five big questions that you reviewed at the start of this chapter. And they use the big ideas that you've just studied to search for answers. How do they go about their work? What special problems and pitfalls do they encounter? Let's look at these questions.

Microeconomics and Macroeconomics

You can take either a micro or a macro view of the spectacular display of national flags in a Korean sports stadium. The micro view is of a single participant and the actions he or she is taking. The macro view is the patterns formed by the joint actions of all the individuals participating in the entire display.

You can look at the economy with either a micro or a macro view. These two views define the two major branches of the subject: microeconomics and macroeconomics.

Microeconomics is the study of the decisions of individual people and businesses and the interaction of those decisions in markets. It seeks to explain the prices and quantities of individual goods and services. Microeconomics also studies the effects of government regulation and taxes on the prices and quantities of individual goods and services. For example, microeconomics studies the forces that determine the prices of cars and the quantities of cars produced and sold. It also studies the effects of regulations and taxes on the prices and quantities of cars.

Macroeconomics is the study of the national economy and the global economy as a whole. It seeks to explain *average* prices and the *total* employment, income, and production. Macroeconomics also studies the effects of taxes, government spending, and the government budget deficit on total jobs and incomes. It also studies the effects of money and interest rates.

Economic Science

Economics is a social science (along with political science, psychology, and sociology). A major task of economists is to discover how the economic world works. In pursuit of this goal, economists (like all scientists) distinguish between two types of statements:

- What *is*
- What *ought* to be

Statements about what *is* are called *positive* statements. They say what is currently believed about the way the world operates. A positive statement might be right or wrong. And a positive statement can be tested by checking it against the facts. When a chemist does an

experiment in her laboratory, she is attempting to check a positive statement against the facts.

Statements about what *ought* to be are called *normative* statements. These statements depend on values and cannot be tested. When Congress debates a motion, it is ultimately trying to decide what ought to be. It is making a normative statement.

To see the distinction between positive and normative statements, consider the controversy over global warming. Some scientists believe that centuries of the burning of coal and oil are increasing the carbon dioxide content of the earth's atmosphere and leading to higher temperatures that eventually will have devastating consequences for life on this planet. "Our planet is warming because of an increased carbon dioxide buildup in the atmosphere" is a positive statement. It can (in principle and with sufficient data) be tested. "We ought to cut back on our use of carbon-based fuels such as coal and oil" is

a normative statement. You may agree with or disagree with this statement, but you can't test it. It is based on values. Health-care reform provides an economic example of the distinction. "Universal health care will cut the amount of work time lost to illness" is a positive statement. "Every American should have equal access to health care" is a normative statement.

The task of economic science is to discover and catalog positive statements that are consistent with what we observe in the world and that enable us to understand how the economic world works. This task is a large one that can be broken into three steps:

■ Observation and measurement

■ Model building

■ Testing models

Observation and Measurement

First, economists keep track of the amounts and locations of natural and human resources, of wages and

work hours, of the prices and quantities of the different goods and services produced, of taxes and government spending, and of the quantities of goods and services bought from and sold to other countries. This list gives a flavor of the array of things that economists can observe and measure.

Model Building

The second step toward understanding how the economic world works is to build a model. An **economic model** is a description of some aspect of the economic world that includes only those features of the world that are needed for the purpose at hand. A model is simpler than the reality it describes. What a model includes and what it leaves out result from *assumptions* about what is essential and what are inessential details.

You can see how ignoring details is useful—even essential— to our understanding by thinking about a model that you see every day: the TV weather map. The weather map is a model that helps

to predict the temperature, wind speed and direction, and precipitation over a future period.

The weather map shows lines called isobars—lines of equal barometric pressure. It doesn't show the interstate highways. The reason is that our theory of the weather tells us that the pattern of air pressure, not the location of the highways, determines the weather.

An economic model is similar to a weather map. It tells us how a number of variables are determined by a number of other variables. For example, an economic model of the 1994 Los Angeles earthquake might tell us the effects of the earthquake and the government's relief efforts on the number of houses and apartments, rents and prices, jobs, and commuting times.

Testing

The third step is testing the model. A model's predictions may correspond to or be in conflict with the facts. By comparing the model's predictions with the facts, we are able to test a model and develop an economic theory. An **economic theory** is a generalization that summarizes what we think

we understand about the economic choices that people make and the performance of industries and entire economies. It is a bridge between an economic model and the real economy.

A theory is created by a process of building and testing models. For example, meteorologists have a theory that if the isobars form a particular pattern at a particular time of the year (a model), then it will snow (reality). They have developed this theory by repeated observation and by carefully recording the weather that follows specific pressure patterns.

Economics is a young science. It was born in 1776 with the publication of Adam Smith's *The Wealth of Nations* (see pp. 2-3). Over the past 220 years, economics has discovered many useful theories. But in many areas, economists are still looking for answers. The gradual accumulation of economic knowledge gives most economists some faith that their methods will, eventually, provide usable answers to the big economic questions.

But progress in economics comes slowly. Let's look at some

of the obstacles to progress in economics.

Obstacles and Pitfalls in Economics

We cannot easily do economic experiments. And most economic behavior has many simultaneous causes. For these two reasons, it is difficult in economics to unscramble cause and effect.

Unscrambling Cause and Effect

By changing one factor at a time and holding all the other relevant factors constant, we isolate the factor of interest and are able to investigate its effects in the clearest possible way. This logical device, that all scientists use to identify cause and effect, is called *ceteris paribus*. **Ceteris paribus** is a Latin term that means "other things being equal" or "if all other relevant things remain the same." Ensuring that other things are equal is crucial in many activities, including athletic events, and all successful attempts to make scientific progress use this device.

Economic models (like the models in all other sciences) enable the influence of one factor at a time to be isolated in the imaginary world of the model. When we use a model, we are able to imagine what would happen if only one factor changed. But *ceteris paribus* can be a problem in economics when we try to test a model.

Laboratory scientists, such as chemists and physicists, perform experiments by actually holding all the relevant factors constant except

for the one under investigation. In the nonexperimental sciences, such as economics (and astronomy), we usually observe the outcomes of the *simultaneous* operation of many factors. Consequently, it is hard to sort out the effects of each individual factor and to compare the effects with what a model predicts. To cope with this problem, economists take three complementary approaches.

First, they look for pairs of events in which other things were equal (or similar). An example might be to study the effects of unemployment insurance on the unemployment rate by comparing the United States with Canada on the presumption that the people in the two economies are sufficiently similar. Second, economists use statistical tools—called *econometrics.* And third, when they can, they perform experiments. This relatively new approach puts real subjects (usually students) in a decision-making situation and varies their incentives in some way to discover how they respond to one factor at a time.

Economists try to avoid *fallacies*—errors of reasoning that lead

to a wrong conclusion. But two fallacies are common, and you need to be on your guard to avoid them. They are the:

- Fallacy of composition
- *Post hoc* fallacy

Fallacy of Composition

The fallacy of composition is the (false) statement that what is true of the parts is true of the whole or that what is true of the whole is true of the parts. Think of the true statement "Speed kills" and its implication that going more slowly saves lives. If an entire freeway moves at a lower speed, everyone on the highway has a safer ride.

But suppose that only one driver slows down and all the other drivers try to maintain their original speed. In this situation, there will probably be more accidents because more cars will change lanes to overtake the slower vehicle. In this example, what is true for the whole is not true for a part.

The fallacy of composition arises mainly in macroeconomics, and it stems from the fact that the parts interact with each other to produce an outcome for the

whole that might differ from the intent of the parts. For example, a firm lays off some workers to cut costs and improve its profits. If all firms take similar actions, incomes fall and so does spending. The firm sells less, and its profits don't improve.

Post Hoc Fallacy

Another Latin phrase—*post hoc ergo propter hoc*—means "after this, therefore because of this." The *post hoc* fallacy is the error of reasoning that a first event *causes* a second event because the first occurred before the second. Suppose you are a visitor from a far-off world. You observe lots of people shopping in early December, and then you see them opening gifts and partying on

Christmas day. Does the shopping cause Christmas, you wonder. After a deeper study, you discover that Christmas causes the shopping. A later event causes an earlier event.

Unraveling cause and effect is difficult in economics. And just looking at the timing of events often doesn't help. For example, the stock market booms, and some months later the economy expands—jobs and incomes grow. Did the stock market boom cause the economy to expand? Possibly, but perhaps businesses started to plan the expansion of production because a new technology that lowered costs had become available. As knowledge of the plans spread, the stock market reacted to *anticipate* the economic expansion. To disentangle cause and effect, economists use economic models and data and, to the extent that they can, perform experiments.

Economics is a challenging science. Does the difficulty of getting answers in economics mean that anything goes and that economists disagree on most questions? Perhaps you've heard the joke: "If you laid all the economists in the world end to end, they still wouldn't reach agreement." Does the joke make a valid point?

Agreement and Disagreement

Economists agree on a remarkably wide range of questions. And surprisingly, the agreed view of economists often disagrees with the popular and sometimes politically correct view. When Fed Chairman Alan Greenspan testifies before the Senate Banking Committee, his words are rarely controversial among economists, even when they generate endless debate in the press and Congress.

Here are 12 propositions[1] with which at least 7 out of every 10 economists broadly agree:

- Tariffs and import restrictions make most people worse off.

- A large federal budget deficit has an adverse effect on the economy.

- Cash payments to welfare recipients make them better off than do transfers-in-kind of equal cash value.

- A minimum wage increases unemployment among young workers and low-skilled workers.

- A tax cut can help to lower unemployment when the unemployment rate is high.

- The distribution of income in the United States should be more equal.

- Inflation is primarily caused by a rapid rate of money creation.

- The government should restructure welfare along the lines of a "negative income tax."

- Rent ceilings cut the availability of housing.

- Pollution taxes are more effective than pollution limits.

- The redistribution of income is a legitimate role for the U.S. government.

- The federal budget should be balanced on the average over the business cycle, but not every year.

Which are positive and which are normative? Notice that economists are willing to offer their opinions on normative issues as well as their professional views on positive questions. Be on the lookout for normative propositions dressed up as positive propositions.

You are now ready to start *doing* economics. As you get into the subject, you will see that we rely heavily on graphs. You must be comfortable with this method of reasoning. If you need some help with it, take your time in working carefully through Chapter 2. If you are already comfortable with graphs, then you are ready to jump right into Chapter 3.

---

[1] These are propositions generally supported or supported with provisos by more than 7 out of 10 economists according to a survey by Richard M. Alston, J.R. Kearl, and Michael B. Vaughan, "Is There a Consensus Among Economists," *American Economic Review*, 82 (May 1992), pp. 203-209. I have simplified the language in some cases and you should check the original for the exact propositions and percentages agreeing.

SUMMARY

Key Points

A Definition of Economics (p. 8)

- Economics is the *science of choice*—the science that explains the choices that we make to cope with scarcity.

Big Economic Questions (pp. 8–11)

- Economists try to answer five big questions about goods and services:
  1. What?
  2. How?
  3. When?
  4. Where?
  5. Who?
  What are the goods and services produced, *how*, *when*, and *where* are they produced, and *who* consumes them?

- These questions interact to determine the standards of living and the distribution of well-being in the United States and around the world.

Big Ideas of Economics (pp. 12-17)

- A choice is a tradeoff, and the highest-value alternative forgone is the opportunity cost of what is chosen.

- Choices are made at the margin and are influenced by incentives.

- Markets enable both buyers and sellers to gain from voluntary exchange.

- Sometimes government actions are needed to overcome market failure.

- For the economy as a whole, expenditure equals income and equals the value of production.

- Living standards rise when production per person increases.

- Prices rise when the quantity of money increases faster than production.

- Unemployment can result from market failure but can also be productive.

What Economists Do (pp. 18-22)

- Microeconomics is the study of individual decisions, and macroeconomics is the study of the economy as a whole.

- Positive statements are about what *is* and normative statements are about what *ought* to be.

- To explain the economic world, economists build and test economic models.

- Economists use the *ceteris paribus* assumption to try to disentangle cause and effect, and they are careful to avoid the fallacy of composition and the *post hoc* fallacy.

- Economists agree on a wide range of questions about how the economy works.

Key Terms

Ceteris paribus, 20	Marginal benefit, 13
Command system, 14	Marginal cost, 13
Economic model, 19	Market, 14
Economic theory, 20	Market failure, 15
Economics, 8	Microeconomics, 18
Efficient, 14	Opportunity cost, 12
Expenditure, 16	Productivity, 16
Goods and services, 8	Scarcity, 8
Incentive, 13	Tradeoff, 12
Income, 16	Unemployment, 17
Inflation, 17	Value of production, 16
Macroeconomics, 18	Voluntary exchange, 14
Margin, 13	

QUESTIONS

1. Give a definition of economics.
2. What is scarcity? Give some examples of rich people and poor people facing scarcity.
3. Why does scarcity force us to make choices?
4. Give some examples, different from those in the chapter, of each of the five big economic questions.
5. Why do you care about *what* goods and services are produced? Give some examples of goods that you value highly and goods on which you place a low value.
6. Why do you care about *how* goods and services are produced? [Hint: Think about cost.]
7. Why do you care about *when* or *where* goods and services are produced?

8. Why do you care about *who* gets the goods and services that are produced?

9. What do we mean by the related ideas of *tradeoff* and *opportunity cost?* Give some examples of tradeoffs that you have made today and of opportunity costs that you have incurred.

10. What is *marginal* cost and *marginal* benefit and why are they relevant for making a decision? Give some examples.

11. What is a market and why does it enable both buyers and sellers to gain from exchange?

12. Give some examples for market failure.

13. Explain why for the economy as a whole, expenditure equals income and the value of production.

14. What makes living standards rise?

15. What makes prices rise?

16. Why does unemployment occur? Is all unemployment a problem?

P R O B L E M S

1. You plan to go to school this summer. If you do, you won't be able to take your usual job that pays $6,000 for the summer and you won't be able to live at home for free. The cost of your tuition will be $2,000, textbooks $200, and living expenses $1,400. What is the opportunity cost of going to summer school?

2. On Valentine's Day, Bernie and Catherine exchanged gifts: Bernie sent Catherine red roses and Catherine bought Bernie a box of chocolates. Each spent $15. They also spent $50 on dinner and split the cost evenly. Did either Bernie or Catherine incur any opportunity costs? If so, what were they? Explain your answer.

3. The local mall has free parking, but the mall is always very busy and it usually takes 30 minutes to find a parking space. Today when you found a vacant spot, Harry also wanted it. Is parking really free at this mall? If not, what did it cost you to park today? When you parked your car today, did you impose any costs on Harry? Explain your answers.

C R I T I C A L   T H I N K I N G

1. This man is homeless and you can see all his possessions in the photograph.

Use the five big questions and the eight big ideas of economics to organize a short essay about the economic life of the man in the photograph. Does he face scarcity? Does he make choices? Can you interpret his choices as being in his own best interest? Can either his own choices or the choices of others make this man better off? If so, how?

Chapter 2

Making and Using Graphs

British Prime Minister Benjamin Disraeli is reputed to have said that "There are three kinds of lies: lies, damned lies, and statistics." One of the most powerful ways of conveying statistical information is in the form of a graph. And like statistics, graphs can lie. But the right graph does not lie. It reveals a relationship that would otherwise be obscure. ◆ Graphs are a modern invention. They first appeared in the late eighteenth century, long after the discovery of logarithms and calculus. But today, in the age of the personal computer and video display, graphs have become as important as words and numbers. How do economists use graphs? What types of graphs do they use? What do graphs reveal and what can they hide? ◆ The big questions that economics tries to answer—questions that you studied in

Three Kinds of Lies

Chapter 1—are difficult ones. They involve relationships among a large number of variables. Almost nothing in economics has a single cause. Instead, a large number of variables interact with each other. It is often said that in economics, everything depends on everything else. Changes in the quantity of ice cream consumed are caused by changes in the price of ice cream, the temperature, and many other factors. How can we make and interpret graphs of relationships among several variables? ◆ In this chapter, you are going to look at the kinds of graphs that economists use. You are going to learn how to make them and read them. You are also going to learn how to determine the magnitude of the influence of one variable on another by calculating the slope of a line and of a curve. ◆ There are no graphs or techniques used in this book that are more complicated than those explained and described in this chapter. If you are already familiar with graphs, you may want to skip (or skim) this chapter. Whether you study this chapter thoroughly or give it a quick pass, you can use it as a handy reference, returning to it whenever you need extra help in understanding the graphs that you encounter in your study of economics.

After studying this chapter, you will be able to:

■ Make and interpret a time-series graph, a scatter diagram, and a cross-section graph

■ Distinguish between linear and nonlinear relationships and between relationships that have a maximum and a minimum

■ Define and calculate the slope of a line

■ Graph relationships among more than two variables

Graphing Data

GRAPHS REPRESENT A QUANTITY AS A DISTANCE ON a line. Figure 2.1 gives two examples. A distance on the horizontal line represents temperature, measured in degrees Fahrenheit. A movement from left to right shows an increase in temperature. A movement from right to left shows a decrease in temperature. The point marked 0 represents zero degrees Fahrenheit. To the right of 0, the temperatures are positive. To the left of 0, the temperatures are negative (as indicated by the minus sign in front of the numbers).

A distance on the vertical line represents altitude or height, measured in thousands of feet above sea level. The point marked 0 represents sea level. Points above 0 represent feet above sea level. Points below 0 (indicated by a minus sign) represent feet below sea level.

There are no rigid rules about the scale for a graph. The scale is determined by the range of the variables being graphed.

The main point of a graph is to enable us to visualize the relationship between two variables. And to accomplish this, we set two scales perpendicular to each other, like those in Fig. 2.1.

The two scale lines are called *axes*. The vertical line is called the *y*-axis, and the horizontal line is called the *x*-axis. The letters *x* and *y* appear on the axes of Fig. 2.1. Each axis has a zero point, which is shared by the two axes. This zero point, common to both axes, is called the *origin*.

To show something in a two-variable graph, we need two pieces of information. We need the value of the variable *x* and the value of the variable *y*. For example, off the coast of Alaska on a winter's day, the temperature is 32 degrees, which we will call the value of *x*. A fishing boat is located at 0 feet above sea level, which we'll call the value of *y*. These two bits of information appear as point *a* in Fig. 2.1. A climber at the top of Mount McKinley on a very cold day is 20,320 feet above sea level and the temperature is 0 degrees. These two pieces of information appear as point *b*. The position of the climber on a warmer day might be at the point marked *c*. This point represents the peak of Mt. McKinley when the temperature is 32 degrees.

Two lines, called coordinates, can be drawn from point *c* in the graph. One of these lines runs from *c* to the horizontal axis. This line is called the *y*-coordinate. Its length is the same as the value marked off on

FIGURE 2.1
Making a Graph

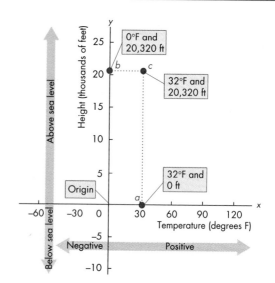

All graphs have axes that measure quantities as distances. Here, the horizontal axis (*x*-axis) measures temperature. A rightward movement shows an increase in temperature. The vertical axis (*y*-axis) measures height. An upward movement shows an increase in height. Point *a* represents a fishing boat at sea level (0 on the *y*-axis) on a day when the temperature is 32° (32° on the *x*-axis). Point *b* represents a climber at the top of Mt. McKinley (20,320 feet above sea level on the *y*-axis) on a day when the temperature on Mt. McKinley is 0° (0° on the *x*-axis). Point *c* represents a climber at the top of Mt. McKinley, 20,320 feet above sea level (on the *y*-axis) on a day when the temperature on Mt. McKinley is 32° (on the *x*-axis).

the *y*-axis. The other of these lines runs from *c* to the vertical axis. This line is called the *x*-coordinate. Its length is the same as the value marked off on the *x*-axis. To describe a point in a graph, we simply use the values of its *x*- and *y*-coordinates.

Graphs like that in Fig. 2.1 can be used to show any type of quantitative data about two variables. Economists use graphs similar to the one in Fig. 2.1 to reveal and describe the relationships among economic variables. To do so, they use three main types of graphs, which we'll now study. They are:

■ Scatter diagrams

■ Time-series graphs

■ Cross-section graphs

Scatter Diagrams

A **scatter diagram** plots the value of one economic variable against the value of another variable. Such a graph is used to reveal whether a relationship exists between two economic variables. It is also used to describe a relationship.

Consumption and Income   Figure 2.2(a) shows a scatter diagram of the relationship between consumption and income. The *x*-axis measures average income, and the *y*-axis measures average consumption. Each point shows consumption per person (on the average) and income per person in the United States in a given year from 1986 to 1995. The points for the ten years are "scattered" within the graph. Each point is labeled with a two-digit number that shows us its year. For example, the point marked 92 shows us that in 1992, income per person was $18,000 and consumption per person was $16,500.

The dots in this graph form a pattern, which reveals a positive relationship between these two variables. That is, when income increases, consumption also increases.

Phone Calls and Price   Figure 2.2(b) shows a scatter diagram of the relationship between the number of international phone calls made from the United States and the average price per minute.

The dots in this graph reveal that as the price per minute falls, the number of calls increases.

Unemployment and Inflation   Figure 2.2(c) shows a scatter diagram of inflation and unemployment in the United States. The dots in this graph form a pattern that shows us there is no clear relationship between these two variables. By its lack of a distinct pattern, the graph shows us that there is no simple relationship between inflation and unemployment in the United States.

Correlation and Causation   A scatter diagram that shows a clear relationship between two variables, such as Fig. 2.2(a) or Fig. 2.2(b), tells us that the two variables have a high correlation. When a high correlation is present, we can predict the value of one variable from the value of the other variable. But correlation does not imply causation. Sometimes a high correlation is just a coincidence, but sometimes it does

---

FIGURE 2.2

Scatter Diagrams

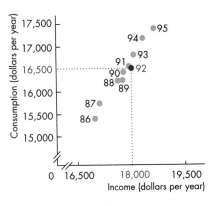

(a) Consumption and income

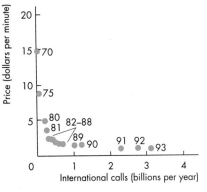

(b) International phone calls and prices

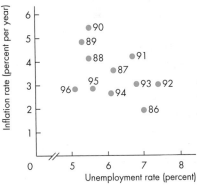

(c) Unemployment and inflation

A scatter diagram reveals the relationship between two variables. Part (a) shows the relationship between consumption and income between 1986 and 1995. Each point shows the values of the two variables in a specific year. For example, in 1992, average income was $18,000 and average consumption was $16,500. The pattern formed by the points shows that as income increases, so does consumption. Part (b) shows the relationship between the price of an international phone call and the number of phone calls made per year between 1970 and 1993. This graph shows that as the price of a phone call has fallen, the number of calls made has increased. Part (c) shows the inflation rate and unemployment rate in the United States between 1986 and 1996. This graph shows that inflation and unemployment are not closely related.

arise from a causal relationship. It is likely, for example, that increasing income causes increasing consumption (Fig. 2.2a) and that falling phone call prices cause more calls to be made (Fig. 2.2b).

Breaks in the Axes   Two of the graphs you've just looked at, Fig. 2.2(a) and Fig. 2.2(c), have breaks in their axes, as shown by the small gaps. The breaks indicate that there are jumps from the origin, 0, to the first values recorded.

In Fig. 2.2(a), the breaks are used because the lowest value of consumption exceeds $15,000 and the lowest value of income exceeds $16,500. With no breaks in the axes of this graph, there would be a lot of empty space, all the points would be crowded into the top right corner, and we would not be able to see whether a relationship exists between these two variables. By breaking the axes, we are able to bring the relationship into view.

Putting a break in the axes is like using a zoom lens to bring the relationship into the center of the graph and magnify it so that it fills the graph.

Misleading Graphs   Breaks can be used to highlight a relationship. But they can also be used to mislead and create a wrong impression—to make a graph that lies. The most common way of making a graph lie is to use axis breaks and to also either stretch or compress a scale. The most effective way to see the power of this kind of lie is to make some graphs that use this technique. For example, redraw Fig. 2.2(a) but make the y-axis that measures consumption run from zero to $45,000 and keep the x-axis the same as the one shown. The graph will now create the impression that despite huge income growth, consumption has barely changed.

To avoid being misled, it is a good idea to get into the habit of always looking closely at the values and the labels on the axes of a graph before you start to interpret it.

Time-Series Graphs

A **time-series graph** measures time (for example, months or years) on the x-axis and the variable or variables in which we are interested on the y-axis. Figure 2.3 shows an example of a time-series graph. In this graph, time (on the x-axis) is measured in years, which run from 1966 to 1996. The variable that we are interested in is the price of coffee, and it is measured on the y-axis.

A time-series graph conveys an enormous amount of information quickly and easily, as this example illustrates. It shows:

- The *level* of the price of coffee—when it is *high* and *low*. When the line is a long way from the x-axis, the price is high. When the line is close to the x-axis, the price is low.

- How the price *changes*—whether it *rises* or *falls*. When the line slopes upward, as in 1976, the price is rising. When the line slopes downward, as in 1978, the price is falling.

- The *speed* with which the price changes—whether it rises or falls *quickly* or *slowly*. If the line is very steep, then the price rises or falls quickly. If the line is not steep, the price rises or falls slowly. For example, the price rose very quickly in 1976 and 1977. The price went up again in 1993 but slowly. Similarly, when the price was falling in 1978, it

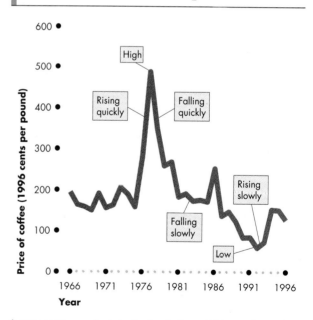

FIGURE 2.3

A Time-Series Graph

A time-series graph plots the level of a variable on the y-axis against time (day, week, month, or year) on the x-axis. This graph shows the price of coffee (in 1996 cents per pound) each year from 1966 to 1996. It shows us when the price of coffee was *high* and when it was *low*, when the price *increased* and when it *decreased*, and when it changed *quickly* and when it changed *slowly*.

fell quickly, but during the early 1980s, it fell more slowly.

A time-series graph also reveals whether there is a trend. A **trend** is a general tendency for a variable to rise or fall. You can see that the price of coffee had a general tendency to fall from the mid-1970s to the early 1990s. That is, although there were ups and downs in the price, there was a general tendency for it to fall.

A time-series graph also lets us compare different periods quickly. Figure 2.3 shows that the 1980s were different from the 1970s. The price of coffee fluctuated more violently in the 1970s than it did in the 1980s. This graph conveys a wealth of information, and it does so in much less space than we have used to describe only some of its features.

Comparing Two Time-Series   Sometimes we want to use a time-series graph to compare two different variables. For example, suppose you want to know whether the balance of the government's budget fluctuates with the unemployment rate. You can examine the government's budget balance and the unemployment rate by drawing a graph of each of them on the same time scale. But we can measure the government's budget balance either as a surplus or as a deficit. Figure 2.4(a) plots the budget surplus. The scale of the unemployment rate is on the left side of the figure, and the scale of the government's budget surplus is on the right. The orange line shows unemployment, and the blue line shows the budget surplus. This figure shows that the unemployment rate and the government's budget surplus move in opposite directions.

Figure 2.4(b) uses a scale for the government's budget balance measured as a deficit. That is, we flip the right-side scale over. This figure shows that the unemployment rate and the government's budget deficit move in the same direction.

Scatter Diagram for Comparing Two Time Series
We can compare two time series in a graph like Fig. 2.4 or in a scatter diagram like Fig. 2.2. Which is better? There is no right answer to this question. If the purpose of the graph is to show *both* the way two variables have changed over time and how they are related to each other, then the time-series graph does the better job. But if the purpose of the graph is to check the strength of the relationship between two variables, then a scatter diagram does a better job. A relationship that looks strong in a time-series graph often looks weak in a scatter diagram.

FIGURE 2.4

Time-Series Relationships

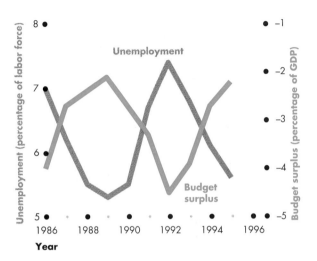

(a) Unemployment and budget surplus

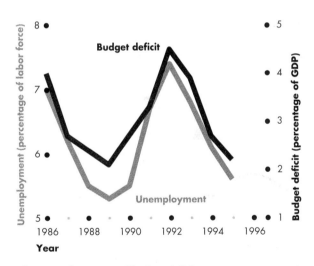

(b) Unemployment and budget deficit

These two graphs show the unemployment rate and the balance of the government's budget. The unemployment line is identical in the two parts. Part (a) shows the budget surplus—*taxes minus spending*—on the right scale. It is hard to see a relationship between the budget surplus and unemployment. Part (b) shows the budget as a deficit—*spending minus taxes*. It inverts the scale of part (a). With the scale for the budget balance inverted, the graph reveals a tendency for unemployment and the budget deficit to move together.

Cross-Section Graphs

A **cross-section graph** shows the values of an economic variable for different groups in a population at a point in time. Figure 2.5 is an example of a cross-section graph. It shows average income per person in the ten largest metropolitan areas in the United States in 1995. This graph uses bars rather than dots and lines, and the length of each bar indicates average income per person. Figure 2.5 enables you to compare the average incomes per person in these ten cities. And you can do so much more quickly and clearly than by looking at a list of numbers.

The cross-section graph in Fig. 2.5 is also an example of a *bar chart*. We often use bars rather than lines in cross-section graphs, but there are no fixed rules about whether to use lines, dots, or bars. It is a matter of taste.

You've now seen how we can use graphs in economics to show economic data and to reveal relationships between variables. Next, we're going to learn how to use graphs in a more abstract way. We'll learn how economists use graphs to construct and display economic models.

FIGURE 2.5

A Cross-Section Graph

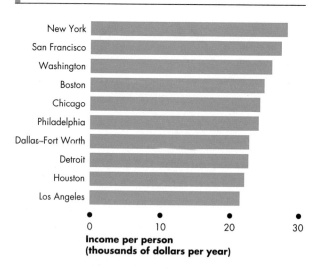

A cross-section graph shows the level of a variable across the members of a population. This graph shows the average income per person in each of the ten largest metropolitan areas in the United States in 1995.

Graphs Used in Economic Models

THE GRAPHS USED IN ECONOMICS ARE NOT always designed to show real-world data. Often they are used to show general relationships among the variables in an economic model.

An **economic model** is a stripped down, simplified description of an economy or of a component of an economy such as a business or a household. It consists of statements about economic behavior that can be expressed as equations or as curves in a graph. Economists use models to explore the effects of different policies or other influences on the economy in ways that are similar to the use of model airplanes in wind tunnels and models of the climate.

You will encounter many different kinds of graphs in economic models, but there are some repeating patterns. Once you've learned to recognize these patterns, you will instantly understand the meaning of a graph. Here, we'll look at the different types of curves that are used in economic models, and we'll see some everyday examples of each type of curve. The patterns to look for in graphs are the four cases in which:

- Variables move in the same direction
- Variables move in opposite directions
- Variables have a maximum or a minimum
- Variables are unrelated

Let's look at these four cases.

Variables That Move in the Same Direction

Figure 2.6 shows graphs of the relationships between two variables that move up and down together. A relationship between two variables that move in the same direction is called a **positive relationship** or a **direct relationship**. Such a relationship is shown by a line that slopes upward.

Figure 2.6 shows three types of relationships, one that has a straight line and two that have curved lines. But all the lines in these three graphs are called curves. Any line on a graph—no matter whether it is straight or curved—is called a *curve*.

A relationship shown by a straight line is called a **linear relationship.** Figure 2.6(a) shows a linear

FIGURE 2.6

Positive (Direct) Relationships

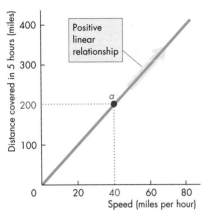

(a) Positive linear relationship

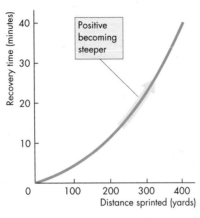

(b) Positive becoming steeper

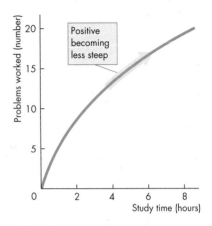

(c) Positive becoming less steep

Each part of this figure shows a positive (direct) relationship between two variables. That is, as the value of the variable measured on the *x*-axis increases, so does the value of the variable measured on the *y*-axis. Part (a) shows a linear relationship—as the two variables increase together, we move along a straight line. Part (b) shows a positive relationship such that as the two variables increase together, we move along a curve that becomes steeper. Part (c) shows a positive relationship such that as the two variables increase together, we move along a curve that becomes flatter.

relationship between the number of miles traveled in 5 hours and speed. For example, point *a* shows us that we will travel 200 miles in 5 hours if our speed is 40 miles an hour. If we double our speed to 80 miles an hour, we will travel 400 miles in 5 hours.

Part (b) shows the relationship between distance sprinted and recovery time (the time it takes the heart rate to return to its normal resting rate). This relationship is an upward-sloping one shown by a curved line that starts out fairly flat but then becomes steeper as we move along the curve away from the origin. The reason this curve slopes upward and becomes steeper is because the additional recovery time needed from sprinting an additional 100 yards increases. It takes less than 5 minutes to recover from 100 yards but more than 10 minutes to recover from the third 100 yards.

Part (c) shows the relationship between the number of problems worked by a student and the amount of study time. This relationship is shown by an upward-sloping curved line that starts out fairly steep and becomes flatter as we move away from the origin. Study time becomes less productive as you study for more hours and become more tired.

Variables That Move in Opposite Directions

Figure 2.7 shows relationships between things that move in opposite directions. A relationship between variables that move in opposite directions is called a **negative relationship** or an **inverse relationship**.

Part (a) shows the relationship between the number of hours available for playing squash and the number of hours for playing tennis. One extra hour spent playing tennis means one hour less playing squash and vice versa. This relationship is negative and linear.

Part (b) shows the relationship between the cost per mile traveled and the length of a journey. The longer the journey, the lower is the cost per mile. But as the journey length increases, the cost per mile decreases, and the fall in the cost is smaller, the longer the journey. This feature of the relationship is shown by the fact that the curve slopes downward, starting out steep at a short journey length and then becoming flatter as the journey length increases. This relationship arises because some of the costs are fixed,

---

FIGURE 2.7

Negative (Inverse) Relationships

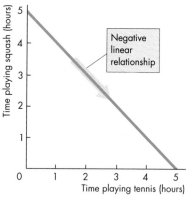

(a) Negative linear relationship

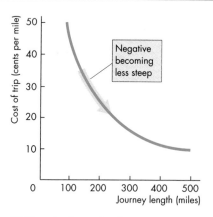

(b) Negative becoming less steep

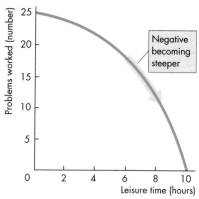

(c) Negative becoming steeper

Each part of this figure shows a negative (inverse) relationship between two variables. Part (a) shows a linear relationship—as one variable increases and the other variable decreases, we move along a straight line. Part (b) shows a negative relationship such that as the journey length increases, the curve becomes less steep. Part (c) shows a negative relationship such that as leisure time increases, the curve becomes steeper.

---

such as auto insurance, and the fixed costs are spread over a longer journey.

Part (c) shows the relationship between the amount of leisure time and the number of problems worked by a student. Increasing leisure time produces an increasingly large reduction in the number of problems worked. This relationship is a negative one that starts out with a gentle slope at a small number of leisure hours and becomes steeper as the number of leisure hours increases. This relationship is a different view of the idea shown in Fig. 2.6(c).

Variables That Have a Maximum or a Minimum

Many relationships in economic models have a maximum or a minimum. For example, firms try to make the maximum possible profit and to produce at the lowest possible cost. Figure 2.8 shows relationships that have a maximum or a minimum.

Part (a) shows the relationship between rainfall and wheat yield. When there is no rainfall, wheat will not grow, so the yield is zero. As the rainfall increases up to 10 days a month, the wheat yield also increases. With 10 rainy days each month, the wheat yield reaches its maximum at 40 bushels an acre (point *a*). Rain in excess of 10 days a month starts to lower the yield of wheat. If every day is rainy, the wheat suffers from a lack of sunshine and the yield falls back to zero. This relationship is one that starts out sloping upward, reaches a maximum, and then slopes downward.

Part (b) shows the reverse case—a relationship that begins sloping downward, falls to a minimum, and then slopes upward. An example of such a relationship is the gasoline cost per mile as the speed of travel increases. At low speeds, the car is creeping along in a traffic snarl-up. The number of miles per gallon is low, so the gasoline cost per mile is high. At very high speeds, the car is traveling faster than its most efficient speed, and again the number of miles per gallon is low and the gasoline cost per mile is high. At a speed of 55 miles an hour, the gasoline cost per mile traveled is at its minimum (point *b*). This relationship is one that starts out sloping downward, reaches a minimum, and then slopes upward.

FIGURE 2.8

Maximum and Minimum Points

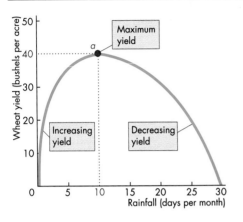

(a) Relationship with a maximum

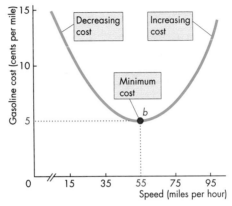

(b) Relationship with a minimum

Part (a) shows a relationship that has a maximum point, *a*. The curve slopes upward as it rises to its maximum point, is flat at its maximum, and then slopes downward. Part (b) shows a relationship with a minimum point, *b*. The curve slopes downward as it falls to its minimum, is flat at its minimum, and then slopes upward.

Variables That Are Unrelated

There are many situations in which no matter what happens to the value of one variable, the other variable remains constant. Sometimes we want to show the independence between two variables in a graph, and Fig. 2.9 shows two ways of achieving this.

In describing the graphs in Fig. 2.6 through 2.9, we have talked about the slopes of curves. Let's look more closely at the concept of slope.

FIGURE 2.9

Variables That Are Unrelated

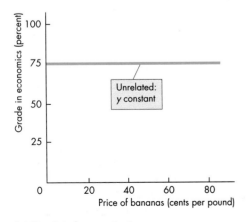

(a) Unrelated: *y* constant

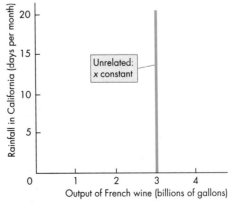

(b) Unrelated: *x* constant

This figure shows how we can graph two variables that are unrelated to each other. In part (a), a student's grade in economics is plotted at 75 percent regardless of the price of bananas on the *x*-axis. The curve is horizontal. In part (b), the output of the vineyards of France does not vary with the rainfall in California. The curve is vertical.

The Slope of a Relationship

WE CAN MEASURE THE INFLUENCE OF ONE variable on another by the slope of the relationship. The **slope** of a relationship is the change in the value of the variable measured on the *y*-axis divided by the change in the value of the variable measured on the *x*-axis. We use the Greek letter Δ (*delta*) to represent "change in." Thus Δ*y* means the change in the value of the variable measured on the *y*-axis, and Δ*x* means the change in the value of the variable measured on the *x*-axis. Therefore the slope of the relationship is

$$\Delta y \, / \, \Delta x.$$

If a large change in the variable measured on the *y*-axis (Δ*y*) is associated with a small change in the variable measured on the *x*-axis (Δ*x*), the slope is large and the curve is steep. If a small change in the variable measured on the *y*-axis (Δ*y*) is associated with a large change in the variable measured on the *x*-axis (Δ*x*), the slope is small and the curve is flat.

We can make the idea of slope sharper by doing some calculations.

The Slope of a Straight Line

The slope of a straight line is the same regardless of where on the line you calculate it. Thus the slope of a straight line is constant. Let's calculate the slopes of the lines in Fig. 2.10. In part (a), when *x* increases from 2 to 6, *y* increases from 3 to 6. The change in *x* is +4—that is, Δ*x* is 4. The change in *y* is +3—that

---

FIGURE 2.10

The Slope of a Straight Line

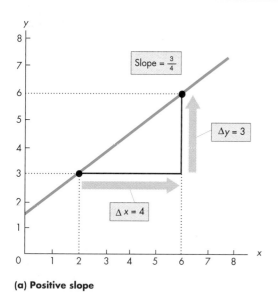

(a) Positive slope

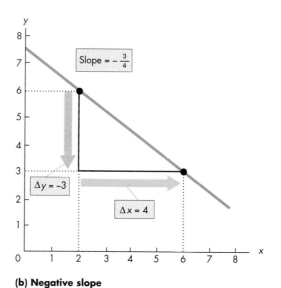

(b) Negative slope

To calculate the slope of a straight line, we divide the change in the value of the variable measured on the *y*-axis (Δ*y*) by the change in the value of the variable measured on the *x*-axis (Δ*x*) as we move along the curve. Part (a) shows the calculation of a positive slope. When *x* increases from 2 to 6, Δ*x* equals 4.

That change in *x* brings about an increase in *y* from 3 to 6, so Δ*y* equals 3. The slope (Δ*y*/Δ*x*) equals ³⁄₄. Part (b) shows the calculation of a negative slope. When *x* increases from 2 to 6, Δ*x* equals 4. That increase in *x* brings about a decrease in *y* from 6 to 3, so Δ*y* equals –3. The slope (Δ*y*/Δ*x*) equals –³⁄₄.

is, Δy is 3. The slope of that line is

$$\frac{\Delta y}{\Delta x} = \frac{3}{4}.$$

In part (b), when x increases from 2 to 6, y decreases from 6 to 3. The change in y is *minus* 3—that is, Δy is –3. The change in x is *plus* 4—that is, Δx is 4. The slope of the curve is

$$\frac{\Delta y}{\Delta x} = \frac{-3}{4}.$$

Notice that the two slopes have the same magnitude (3/4), but the slope of the line in part (a) is positive (+3/+4 = 3/4), while that in part (b) is negative (–3/+4 = –3/4). The slope of a positive relationship is positive; the slope of a negative relationship is negative.

The Slope of a Curved Line

The slope of a curved line is trickier. The slope of a curved line is not constant. Its slope depends on where on the line we calculate it. There are two ways to calculate the slope of a curved line: You can calculate the slope at a point, or you can calculate the slope across an arc of the line. Let's look at the two alternatives.

Slope at a Point To calculate the slope at a point on a curve, you need to construct a straight line that has the same slope as the curve at the point in question. Figure 2.11 shows how this is done. Suppose you want to calculate the slope of the curve at point a. Place a ruler on the graph so that it touches point a and no other point on the curve, then draw a straight line along the edge of the ruler. The straight red line is this line, and it is the tangent to the curve at point a. If the ruler touches the curve only at point a, then the slope of the curve at point a must be the same as the slope of the edge of the ruler. If the curve and the ruler do not have the same slope, the line along the edge of the ruler will cut the curve instead of just touching it.

Now that you have found a straight line with the same slope as the curve at point a, you can calculate the slope of the curve at point a by calculating the slope of the straight line. Along the straight line, as x increases from 0 to 4 ($\Delta x = 4$), y increases from 2 to 5

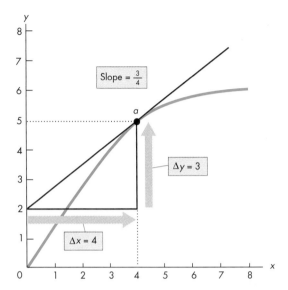

FIGURE 2.11

Slope at a Point

To calculate the slope of the curve at point a, draw the red line that just touches the curve at a—the tangent. The slope of this straight line is calculated by dividing the change in y by the change in x along the line. When x increases from 0 to 4, Δx equals 4. That change in x is associated with an increase in y from 2 to 5, so Δy equals 3. The slope of the red line is 3/4. So the slope of the curve at point a is 3/4.

($\Delta y = 3$). Therefore the slope of the line is

$$\frac{\Delta y}{\Delta x} = \frac{3}{4}.$$

Thus the slope of the curve at point a is 3/4.

Slope Across an Arc An arc of a curve is a piece of a curve. In Fig. 2.12, you are looking at the same curve as in Fig. 2.11. But instead of calculating the slope at point a, we are going to calculate the slope across the arc from b to c. You can see that the slope at b is greater than the slope at c. When we calculate the slope across an arc, we are calculating the average slope between two points. As we move along the arc from b to c, x increases from 3 to 5 and y increases from 4 to 5.5. The change in x is 2 ($\Delta x = 2$), and the

FIGURE 2.12

Slope Across an Arc

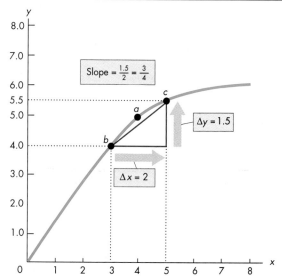

Slope $= \dfrac{1.5}{2} = \dfrac{3}{4}$

$\Delta y = 1.5$

$\Delta x = 2$

To calculate the average slope of the curve along the arc *bc*, draw a straight line from *b* to *c*. The slope of the line *bc* is calculated by dividing the change in *y* by the change in *x*. In moving from *b* to *c*, Δx equals 2 and Δy equals 1.5. The slope of the line *bc* is 1.5 divided by 2, or $^3/_4$. So the slope of the curve across the arc *bc* is $^3/_4$.

change in *y* is 1.5 ($\Delta y = 1.5$). Therefore the slope of the line is

$$\frac{\Delta y}{\Delta x} = \frac{15}{2} = \frac{3}{4}.$$

Thus the slope of the curve across the arc *bc* is 3/4.

This calculation gives us the slope of the curve between points *b* and *c*. The actual slope calculated is the slope of the straight line from *b* to *c*. This slope approximates the average slope of the curve along the arc *bc*. In this particular example, the slope across the arc *bc* is identical to the slope of the curve at point *a*. But the calculation of the slope of a curve does not always work out so neatly. You might have some fun constructing counterexamples.

You now know how to make and interpret a graph. But so far, we've limited our attention to graphs of two variables. We're now going to learn how to graph more than two variables.

Graphing Relationships Among More Than Two Variables

WE HAVE SEEN THAT WE CAN GRAPH THE relationship between two variables as a point formed by the *x*- and *y*-coordinates in a two-dimensional graph. You may be thinking that although a two-dimensional graph is informative, most of the things in which you are likely to be interested involve relationships among many variables, not just two. For example, the amount of ice cream consumed depends on the price of ice cream and the temperature. If ice cream is expensive and the temperature is low, people eat much less ice cream than when ice cream is inexpensive and the temperature is high. For any given price of ice cream, the quantity consumed varies with the temperature, and for any given temperature, the quantity of ice cream consumed varies with its price.

Figure 2.13 shows a relationship among three variables. The table shows the number of gallons of ice cream consumed each day at various temperatures and ice cream prices. How can we graph these numbers?

To graph a relationship that involves more than two variables, we use the *ceteris paribus* assumption.

Ceteris Paribus   The Latin phrase **ceteris paribus**, means "other things remaining the same." Every laboratory experiment is an attempt to create *ceteris paribus* and isolate the relationship of interest. We use the same method to make a graph.

Figure 2.13(a) shows an example. There, you can see what happens to the quantity of ice cream consumed when the price of ice cream varies while the temperature is held constant. The line labeled 70°F shows the relationship between ice cream consumption and the price of ice cream if the temperature is 70°F. The numbers used to plot that line are those in the third column of the table in Fig. 2.13. For example, if the temperature is 70°F, 10 gallons are consumed when the price is 60¢ a scoop, and 18 gallons are consumed when the price is 30¢ a scoop. The curve labeled 90°F shows consumption as the price varies if the temperature is 90°F.

We can also show the relationship between ice cream consumption and temperature while the price of ice cream remains constant, as shown in Fig. 2.13(b). The curve labeled 60¢ shows how the consumption

FIGURE 2.13

Graphing a Relationship Among Three Variables

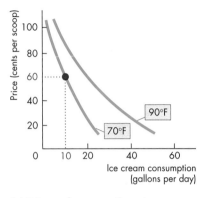

(a) Price and consumption at a given temperature

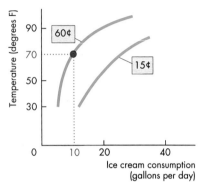

(b) Temperature and consumption at a given price

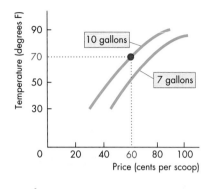

(c) Temperature and price at a given consumption

Price	Ice cream consumption			
(cents per scoop)	(gallons per day)			
	30°F	50°F	70°F	90°F
15	12	18	25	50
30	10	12	18	37
45	7	10	13	27
60	5	7	10	20
75	3	5	7	14
90	2	3	5	10
105	1	2	3	6

The quantity of ice cream consumed depends on its price and the temperature. The table gives some hypothetical numbers that tell us how many gallons of ice cream are consumed each day at different prices and different temperatures. For example, if the price is 60¢ a scoop and the temperature is 70°F, 10 gallons of ice cream are consumed. This set of values is highlighted in the table and each part of the figure. To graph a relationship among three variables, the value of one variable is held constant. Part (a) shows the relationship between price and consumption when temperature is held constant. One curve holds temperature at 90°F and the other at 70°F. Part (b) shows the relationship between temperature and consumption when the price is held constant. One curve holds the price at 60¢ a scoop and the other at 15¢ a scoop. Part (c) shows the relationship between temperature and price when consumption is held constant. One curve holds consumption at 10 gallons and the other at 7 gallons.

of ice cream varies with the temperature when ice cream costs 60¢ a scoop, and a second curve shows the relationship when ice cream costs 15¢ a scoop. For example, at 60¢ a scoop, 10 gallons are consumed when the temperature is 70°F and 20 gallons when the temperature is 90°F.

Figure 2.13(c) shows the combinations of temperature and price that result in a constant consumption of ice cream. One curve shows the combination that results in 10 gallons a day being consumed, and the other shows the combination that results

in 7 gallons a day being consumed. A high price and a high temperature lead to the same consumption as a lower price and a lower temperature. For example, 10 gallons of ice cream are consumed at 90°F and 90¢ a scoop, at 70°F and 60¢ a scoop, and at 50°F and 45¢ a scoop.

◆ With what you have learned about graphs, you can move forward with your study of economics. There are no graphs in this book that are more complicated than those that have been explained here.

SUMMARY

Key Points

Graphing Data (pp. 26–30)

▨ Time-series graphs show trends, cycles, and other fluctuations in economic data.

▨ Scatter diagrams show the relationship between two variables. They show whether two variables are positively related, negatively related, or unrelated.

▨ Cross-section graphs show how variables change across the members of a population.

Graphs Used in Economic Models (pp. 30–33)

▨ Graphs are used to show relationships among variables in economic models.

▨ Relationships can be positive (an upward-sloping curve), negative (a downward-sloping curve), positive and then negative (have a maximum point), negative and then positive (have a minimum point), or unrelated (a horizontal or vertical curve).

The Slope of a Relationship (pp. 34–36)

▨ The slope of a relationship is calculated as the change in the value of the variable measured on the y-axis divided by the change in the value of the variable measured on the x-axis—that is, $\Delta y/\Delta x$.

▨ A straight line has a constant slope.

▨ A curved line has a varying slope. To calculate the slope of a curved line, we calculate the slope at a point or across an arc.

Graphing Relationships Among More Than Two Variables (pp. 36–37)

▨ To graph a relationship among more than two variables, we hold constant the values of all the variables except two.

▨ We then plot the value of one of the variables against the value of another.

Key Figures

Key Terms

QUESTIONS

1. What are the three types of graphs used to show economic data?

2. Give an example of a time-series graph.

3. List three things that a time-series graph shows quickly and easily.

4. Give three examples, different from those in the chapter, of scatter diagrams that show a positive relationship, a negative relationship, and no relationship.

5. Draw some graphs to show the relationships between two variables:
   a.   That move in the same direction.
   b.   That move in opposite directions.
   c.   That have a maximum.
   d.   That have a minimum.

6. Which of the relationships in question 5 is a positive relationship and which a negative relationship?

7. What are the two ways of calculating the slope of a curved line?

8. How do we graph a relationship among more than two variables?

PROBLEMS

🖥 1. The official inflation rate in the United States and the interest rate on U.S. Treasury bills between 1976 and 1996 were as follows:

Year	Inflation rate (percent per year)	Interest rate
1976	5.8	5.0
1977	6.5	5.3
1978	7.6	7.2
1979	11.3	10.0
1980	13.5	11.5
1981	10.3	14.0
1982	6.2	10.7
1983	3.2	8.6
1984	4.3	9.6
1985	3.6	7.5
1986	1.9	6.0
1987	3.6	5.8
1988	4.1	6.7
1989	4.8	8.1
1990	5.4	7.5
1991	4.2	5.4
1992	3.0	3.4
1993	3.0	3.0
1994	2.6	4.3
1995	2.5	5.5
1996	3.3	5.0

a. Draw a time-series graph of the inflation rate and use your graph to determine (i) the year in which inflation was highest, (ii) the year in which it was lowest, (iii) the years in which it increased, (iv) the years in which it decreased, (v) the year in which it increased most, and (vi) the year in which it decreased most.

b. What have been the main trends in U.S. inflation?

🖥 2. Use the data in problem 1.

a. Draw a time-series graph of the interest rate and use your graph to determine (i) the year in which the interest rate was highest, (ii) the year in which it was lowest, (iii) the years in which it increased, (iv) the years in which it decreased, (v) the year in which it increased most, and (vi) the year in which it decreased most.

b. What have been the main trends in the interest rate?

🖥 3. Use the data in problem 1.

a. Draw a scatter diagram to show the relationship between the inflation rate and the interest rate.

b. Describe the relationship, if one exists, between the inflation rate and the interest rate.

🖥 4. Use the information in the following table to draw a graph that shows the relationship between two variables x and y.

x	y
0	0
1	1
2	4
3	9
4	16
5	25
6	36
7	49
8	64

a. Is the relationship between x and y positive or negative?

b. Does the slope of the relationship increase or decrease as the value of x increases?

c. Try to think of some possible economic relationships that might be similar to this one.

🖥 5. Use the information in the following table to draw a graph that shows the relationship between two variables x and y.

x	y
0	50
1	48
2	44
3	32
4	16
5	0

a. Is the relationship between x and y positive or negative?

b. Does the slope of the relationship increase or decrease as the value of x increases?

c. Try to think of some possible economic relationships that might be similar to this one.

🖥 6. Use the data in problem 5 to:
   a. Calculate the slope of the relationship between x and y when x equals 4.
   b. Calculate the slope of the arc when x increases from 3 to 4.
   c. Calculate the slope of the arc when x increases from 4 to 5.
   d. Calculate the slope of the arc when x increases from 3 to 5.
   e. What do you notice that is interesting about your answers to (b), (c), and (d) compared with your answer to (a)?

7. Use the information in the following figure to calculate the slope of the relationship shown at point a.

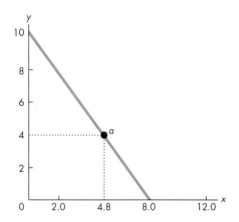

8. Use the information in the following figure to calculate:
   a. The slope of the relationship shown at point a.
   b. The slope of the relationship shown at point b.
   c. The slope of the relationship across the arc ab.
   d. Can you find a point between a and b that has the same slope of the arc ab? Approximately, what are the values of x and y for this point?

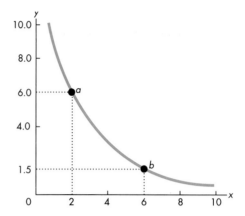

9. The following table gives data on the price of a balloon ride, the temperature, and the number of rides taken per day.

Price (dollars per ride)	Balloon rides (number per day)		
	50°C	70°C	90°C
5.00	32	40	50
10.00	27	32	40
15.00	18	27	32
20.00	10	18	27

Draw graphs that show the relationship among:
   a. The price and the number of rides taken, holding the temperature constant.
   b. The number of rides taken and temperature, holding the price constant.
   c. The temperature and price, holding the number of rides taken constant.

🌐10. Visit the Parkin Home Page on the World Wide Web (at http://hepg.awl.com/parkin/econ100).
   a. Use the link provided to find data for the latest twelve months on the Consumer Price Index (CPI).
   b. Make some graphs to show whether the CPI is rising or falling and whether its rate of rise or fall is increasing or decreasing.
   c. Write a brief description of the data and draw some conclusions about what your findings mean for you and your family.

3

The Economic Problem

We live in a style that surprises our grandparents and would have astonished our great-grandparents. Most of us live in more spacious homes than they did. We eat more, grow taller, and are even born larger than they were. Video games, cellular phones, gene splices, and personal computers did not exist even 20 years ago. But today it is hard to imagine life without these things. Economic growth has made us richer than our grandparents. And we are not alone in experiencing an expansion in the goods and services that we consume. Many nations around the world are not only sharing our experience: They are setting the pace. Hong Kong, Taiwan, Singapore, Korea, and China are expanding at unheard of rates. But economic growth does not liberate us from scarcity. Why not? Why, despite our immense wealth, must we still make choices and face costs? Why are there no "free lunches"? ◆ We see an incredible amount of specialization and trade in the world. Each one of us specializes in a particular job—as a lawyer, a car maker, a home maker. We have become so specialized that one farm worker can feed 100 people. Less than one sixth of the U.S. work force is employed in manufacturing. More than half of the work force is employed in wholesale and retail trade, banking and finance, government, and other services. Why do we specialize? How do we benefit from specialization and trade? ◆ Over many centuries, institutions and social arrangements have evolved that we take for granted. One of them is property rights and the political and legal system that protects them. Another is markets. Why have these social arrangements evolved? How do they increase production? ◆ These are the questions that we study in this chapter. We begin with the core economic problem: scarcity and choice and the concept of the production possibility frontier. We then learn about the central idea of economics—efficiency. We also discover how we can expand production by accumulating capital and by specializing and trading. ◆ What you will learn in this chapter is the foundation on which all economics is built. You will receive big dividends from a careful study of this material.

Making the Most of It

After studying this chapter, you will be able to:

- Explain the fundamental economic problem

- Define the production possibility frontier

- Define and calculate opportunity cost

- Explain the conditions in which resources are used efficiently

- Explain how economic growth expands production possibilities

- Explain how specialization and trade expand production possibilities

Resources and Wants

TWO FACTS DOMINATE OUR LIVES:

- We have limited resources.
- We have unlimited wants.

These two facts define **scarcity**, a condition in which the resources available are insufficient to satisfy people's wants.

Scarcity is a universal fact of life. It confronts each one of us individually, and it confronts our families, local communities, and nations.

The fundamental economic problem is to use our limited resources to produce the items that we value most highly. **Economics** is the study of the *choices* people make to cope with *scarcity*. It is the study of how we each individually try to get the most out of our own limited resources and of how in that endeavor, we interact with each other. Let's look a bit more closely at our limited resources and unlimited wants.

Limited Resources

The resources that can be used to produce goods and services are grouped into four categories:

- Labor
- Land
- Capital
- Entrepreneurship

Labor is the time and effort that we devote to producing goods and services. It includes the physical and mental work of people who make cars and cola, gum and glue, wallpaper and watering cans.

Land is the gifts of nature that we use to produce goods and services. It includes the air, the water, and the land surface as well as the minerals that lie beneath the surface of the earth.

Capital is the goods that we have produced and that we can now use to produce other goods and services. It includes interstate highways, buildings, dams and power projects, airports and jumbo jets, car production lines, shirt factories, and cookie shops.

Capital also includes **human capital**, which is the knowledge and skill that people obtain from education and on-the-job training. You are building human capital right now as you work on your economics course and other subjects. And your human capital will continue to grow when you get a full-time job and become better at it. Human capital improves the *quality* of labor.

Entrepreneurship is the resource that organizes labor, land, and capital. Entrepreneurs come up with new ideas about what, how, when, and where to produce, make business decisions, and bear the risks that arise from these decisions.

Our limited resources are converted into goods and services by using the technologies available. These technologies are limited by our knowledge—our human capital—and by our other resources.

Unlimited Wants

Our wants are limited only by our imaginations and are effectively unlimited. We want food and drink, clothing, housing, education, and health care. We want some of these things so badly that we call them *necessities*. But we also want many other things. We want cars and airplanes, movie theaters and videos, popcorn and soda, Walkmans and tapes, books and magazines, restaurant meals, vacations at the beach and in the mountains, music and poetry, and instant telecommunication across the globe.

Some of these wants are less pressing than others, but they are all wants. We even want things that are technologically impossible today but about which we fantasize. We want to live longer and healthier lives. Some of us want to hitchhike the galaxy and be beamed around the universe.

Because our wants exceed our resources, we must make choices. We must rank our wants and decide which wants to satisfy and which to leave unsatisfied. We try to get the most out of our resources.

R E V I E W

- Economics is the study of the choices that people make to cope with scarcity.
- Our limited resources are labor, land, capital, and entrepreneurship.
- Our unlimited wants must be ranked, and we must choose which wants to satisfy.
- In making choices, we try to get the most out of our resources.

We'll begin our study of the choices people make by looking at the limits to production and at a fundamental implication of choice—opportunity cost.

Resources, Production Possibilities, and Opportunity Cost

EVERY WORKING DAY, IN MINES, FACTORIES, shops, and offices and on farms and construction sites across the United States, 125 million people produce a vast variety of goods and services valued at around $27 billion. The quantities of goods and services that can be produced are limited by our available resources and by technology. That limit is described by the production possibility frontier.

The **production possibility frontier** (*PPF*) is the boundary between those combinations of goods and services that can be produced and those that cannot.

To illustrate the production possibility frontier in a graph, we focus our attention on two goods at a time. In focusing on two goods, we hold the quantities produced of all the other goods and services constant—a device called the *ceteris paribus* assumption. That is, we look at a *model* of the economy in which everything remains the same except for the production of the two goods we are currently considering.

Let's look at the production possibility frontier for two goods that most students buy: bottles of soda and blank audio tapes.

Production Possibility Frontier

The *production possibility frontier* for soda and tapes shows the limits to the production of these two goods, given the total resources available to produce them. Figure 3.1 shows this production possibility frontier. The table lists some combinations of the quantities of tapes and soda that can be produced given the resources available, and the figure graphs these combinations. The quantity of tapes produced is shown on the *x*-axis, and the quantity of soda produced is shown on the *y*-axis. (The numbers are hypothetical.)

Because the *PPF* shows the *limits* to production, we cannot attain the points outside the frontier. They are points that describe wants that cannot be satisfied. We can produce at all the points *inside* the *PPF* and *on* the *PPF*. They are attainable points.

Suppose that in a typical month, 4 million tapes and 5 million bottles of soda are produced. Figure 3.1 shows this combination as point *e* and as possibility *e* in the table. Figure 3.1 also shows other production possibilities. For example, we might stop

FIGURE 3.1

Production Possibility Frontier

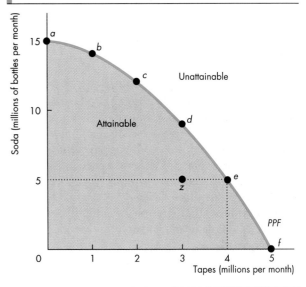

Possibility	Tapes (millions per month)		Soda (millions of bottles per month)
a	0	and	15
b	1	and	14
c	2	and	12
d	3	and	9
e	4	and	5
f	5	and	0

The table lists six points on the production possibility frontier for tapes and soda. Row *a* tells us that if we produce no tapes, the maximum quantity of soda we can produce is 15 million bottles a month. The rows of the table are graphed as points *a, b, c, d, e,* and *f* in the figure. The line passing through these points is the production possibility frontier (*PPF*). It separates the attainable from the unattainable. We can produce at any point inside the orange area or on the frontier. Points outside the frontier are unattainable. Points inside the frontier such as point *z* are inefficient because it is possible to use the available resources to produce more of either or both goods.

producing tapes and move all the people who produce them into bottling soda. This case is shown as point *a* in the figure and possibility *a* in the table.

The quantity of soda produced increases to 15 million bottles a month, and tape production dries up. Alternatively, we might close down the bottling plants and switch all the resources into producing tapes. In this situation, we produce 5 million tapes a month. This case is shown as point *f* in the figure and possibility *f* in the table.

Production Efficiency

We achieve **production efficiency** if we cannot produce more of one good without producing less of some other good. When production is efficient, we are at a point *on* the *PPF*. If we are at a point *inside* the *PPF*, such as point *z*, production is *inefficient* because we have some *unused* resources or we have some *misallocated* resources or both.

Resources are unused when they are idle but could be working. For example, we might leave some of the bottling plants idle or some workers might be unemployed.

Resources are *misallocated* when they are assigned to tasks for which they are not the best match. For example, we might assign skilled bottling machine operators to work in a tape factory and skilled tape makers to work in a bottling plant. We could get more tapes *and* more bottles of soda from these same workers if we reassigned them to the tasks that more closely match their skills.

If we produce at a point inside the *PPF* such as *z*, we can use our resources more efficiently to produce more tapes, more soda, or more of *both* tapes and soda. But if we produce at a point *on* the *PPF*, we are using our resources efficiently and we can produce more of one good only if we produce less of the other. We face a *tradeoff*.

Tradeoff

On the production possibility frontier, every choice involves a **tradeoff**—we must give up something to get something else. On the *PPF* in Fig. 3.1, we must give up some soda to get more tapes (or give up some tapes to get more soda).

Tradeoffs arise in every imaginable real-world situation. At any given point in time, we have a fixed amount of labor, land, capital, and entrepreneurship. By using our available technologies, we can employ these resources to produce goods and services. But we are limited in what we can produce. This limit defines a boundary between what we can attain and what we

cannot attain. This boundary is the real-world's production possibility frontier, and it defines the tradeoffs that we must make. On our real-world *PPF*, we can produce more of any one good or service only if we produce less of some other goods or services.

When doctors say we must spend more on AIDS and cancer research, they are suggesting a tradeoff: more medical research for less of some other things. When Bill Clinton says he wants to spend more on education and health care, he is suggesting a tradeoff: more education and health care for less national defense or less private spending (because of higher taxes). When your parents say that you should study more, they are suggesting a tradeoff: more study time for less leisure or less sleep. When an environmental group argues for less logging, it is suggesting a tradeoff: greater conservation of endangered wildlife for less paper.

All tradeoffs involve a cost—an opportunity cost.

Opportunity Cost

The **opportunity cost** of an action is the highest-valued alternative forgone. We can make the concept of opportunity cost more precise by using the production possibility frontier. Along the frontier, there are only two goods, so there is only one alternative forgone—some quantity of the other good. Given our current resources and technology, we can produce more tapes only if we produce fewer bottles of soda. The opportunity cost of producing an additional tape is the number of bottles of soda we must forgo. Similarly, the opportunity cost of producing an additional bottle of soda is the quantity of tapes we must forgo.

For example, at point *c* in Fig. 3.1, we produce fewer tapes and more bottles of soda than we do at point *d*. If we choose point *d* over point *c*, the additional 1 million tapes *cost* 3 million bottles of soda. One tape costs 3 bottles of soda.

We can also work out the opportunity cost of choosing point *c* over point *d* in Fig. 3.1. If we move from point *d* to point *c*, the quantity of soda produced increases by 3 million bottles and the quantity of tapes produced decreases by 1 million. So if we choose point *c* over point *d*, the additional 3 million bottles of soda *cost* 1 million tapes. One bottle of soda costs 1/3 of a tape.

Opportunity Cost Is a Ratio Opportunity cost is a ratio. It is the decrease in the quantity produced of one good divided by the increase in the quantity produced of another good as we move along the production possibility frontier.

Because opportunity cost is a ratio, the opportunity cost of producing soda is equal to the *inverse* of the opportunity cost of producing tapes. Check this proposition by returning to the calculations we've just worked through. When we move along the *PPF* from *c* to *d*, the opportunity cost of a tape is 3 bottles of soda. The inverse of 3 is 1/3, so if we decrease the production of tapes and increase the production of soda by moving from *d* to *c*, the opportunity cost of a bottle of soda must be 1/3 of a tape. You can check that this number is correct. If we move from *d* to *c*, we produce 3 million more bottles of soda and 1 million fewer tapes. Because 3 million bottles cost 1 million tapes, the opportunity cost of 1 bottle of soda is 1/3 of a tape.

Increasing Opportunity Cost The opportunity cost of a tape increases as the quantity of tapes produced increases. Also, the opportunity cost of soda increases as the quantity of soda produced increases. This phenomenon of increasing opportunity cost is reflected in the *shape* of the *PPF*—it is bowed outward.

When a large quantity of soda and a small quantity of tapes are produced—between points *a* and *b* in Fig. 3.1—the frontier has a gentle slope. A given increase in the quantity of tapes *costs* a small decrease in the quantity of soda, so the opportunity cost of a tape is a small amount of soda.

When a large quantity of tapes and a small quantity of soda are produced—between points *e* and *f* in Fig. 3.1—the frontier is steep. A given increase in the quantity of tapes *costs* a large decrease in the quantity of soda, so the opportunity cost of a tape is a large amount of soda.

The production possibility frontier is bowed outward because resources are not all equally productive in all activities. Production workers with many years of experience working for PepsiCo are very good at producing soda but not very good at making tapes. So if we move these people from PepsiCo to 3M, we get a small increase in the quantity of tapes but a large decrease in the quantity of soda.

Similarly, plastics engineers and production workers who have spent many years working for 3M are good at producing tapes but not so good at bottling soda. So if we move these people from 3M to PepsiCo, we get a small increase in the quantity of soda but a large decrease in the quantity of tapes.

The more we try to produce of either good, the less productive are the additional resources we use to produce that good and the larger is the opportunity cost of a unit of that good.

Increasing Opportunity Costs Are Everywhere
Just about every activity that you can think of is one with an *increasing* opportunity cost. Two examples are the production of food and the production of health-care services. We allocate the most skillful farmers and the most fertile land to the production of food. And we allocate the best doctors and least fertile land to the production of health-care services. If we shift fertile land and tractors away from farming to hospitals and ambulances and ask farmers to become hospital porters, the production of food drops drastically and the increase in the production of health-care services is small. The opportunity cost of a unit of health-care services rises. Similarly, if we shift our resources away from health care toward farming, we must use more doctors and nurses as farmers and more hospitals as hydroponic tomato factories. The decrease in the production of health-care services is large, but the increase in food production is small. The opportunity cost of a unit of food rises.

This example is extreme and unlikely, but these same considerations apply to any pair of goods that you can imagine: housing and diamonds, wheelchairs and golf carts, pet food and breakfast cereals.

R E V I E W

- The production possibility frontier (*PPF*) is the boundary between production levels we can attain and cannot attain.
- When we produce at a point on the *PPF*, production is efficient.
- In choosing among points on the *PPF*, we face a tradeoff of one good for another.
- Every tradeoff involves an opportunity cost—the highest-valued alternative forgone.
- As we move along the *PPF* and produce more of one good, the opportunity cost of a unit of that good increases.

We've seen that production possibilities are limited by the production possibility frontier. And we've seen that production on the *PPF* is efficient. But there are many possible quantities we can produce on the *PPF*. How do we choose among them? How do we know which point on the frontier is the best one?

Using Resources Efficiently

HOW DO WE DECIDE WHETHER TO SPEND MORE on AIDS and cancer research? Whether to vote for an education and health-care package or a tax cut? Whether to join an environmental group and press for a greater conservation of endangered wildlife?

These are big questions that have enormous consequences. But the essence of the answer can be seen by thinking about the simpler question: How do we decide how many tapes and how many bottles of soda to produce?

We decide by calculating and comparing two numbers:

- Marginal cost
- Marginal benefit

Marginal Cost

Marginal cost is the opportunity cost of producing *one more unit* of a good or service. You've seen how we can calculate opportunity cost as we move along the production possibility frontier. The marginal cost of a tape is the opportunity cost of *one* tape—the quantity of soda that must be given up to get one more tape—as we move along the *PPF*.

Figure 3.2 illustrates the marginal cost of a tape. If all the available resources are used to produce soda, 15 million bottles of soda and no tapes are produced. If we now decide to produce 1 million tapes, how much soda do we have to give up? You can see the answer in Fig. 3.2(a). To produce 1 million more tapes, we move from *a* to *b* and the quantity of soda decreases by 1 million bottles to 14 million a month. So the opportunity cost of the first 1 million tapes is 1 million bottles of soda.

If we decide to increase the production of tapes to 2 million, how much soda must we give up? This time, we move from *b* to *c* and the quantity of soda decreases by 2 million bottles. So the second million tapes costs 2 million bottles of soda.

You can repeat this calculation for an increase in the quantity of tapes produced from 2 million to 3 million, then to 4 million, and finally to 5 million. Figure 3.2(a) shows these opportunity costs as a series of steps. Each additional million tapes costs more bottles of soda than the preceding million did.

We've just calculated the opportunity cost of tapes in blocks of 1 million at a time and generated

FIGURE 3.2

FIGURE 3.2

Opportunity Cost and Marginal Cost

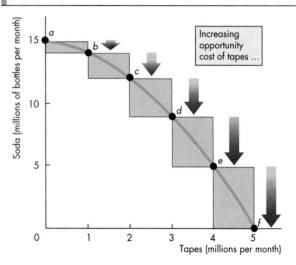

(a) PPF and opportunity cost

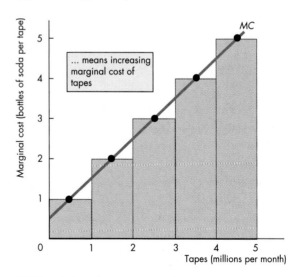

(b) Marginal cost

Opportunity cost is measured along the *PPF* in part (a). If the production of tapes increases from zero to 1 million, the opportunity cost of the first 1 million tapes is 1 million bottles of soda. If the production of tapes increases from 1 million to 2 million, the opportunity cost of the second 1 million tapes is 2 million bottles of soda. The opportunity cost of tapes increases as the production of tapes increases. Marginal cost is the opportunity cost of producing one more unit. Part (b) shows the marginal cost of a tape as the *MC* curve.

the steps in Fig. 3.2(a). If we now calculate the opportunity cost of tapes one at a time, we obtain the *marginal cost* of a tape. In Fig. 3.2(b), the line labeled *MC* shows the marginal cost of a tape. The marginal cost of each additional tape in terms of forgone soda increases, so the marginal cost curve slopes upward.

To use our resources efficiently, we must compare the marginal cost of a tape with its marginal benefit. Let's now look at marginal benefit.

Marginal Benefit

The **marginal benefit** is the benefit that a person receives from consuming one more unit of a good or service. The marginal benefit from a good or service is measured as the maximum amount that a person is willing to pay for one more unit of it. It is a general principle that the more we have of any good or service, the smaller is our marginal benefit from it—the principle of *decreasing marginal benefit.*

To understand the principle of decreasing marginal benefit, think about your own marginal benefit from tapes. If tapes are very hard to come by and you can buy only one or two a year, you might be willing to pay a high price to get one more tape. But if tapes are readily available and you have as many as you can use, you are willing to pay almost nothing for yet one more tape.

In everyday life, we think of prices as money— as dollars per tape. But you have just been thinking about cost as opportunity cost, which is not a dollar cost but a cost in terms of a forgone alternative. You can also think about prices in the same terms. The price you pay for something is not the number of dollars you give up, but the goods and services that you would have bought with those dollars.

To see this idea more clearly, let's continue with the example we used to study the *PPF* and opportunity cost: tapes and soda. The marginal benefit from a tape can be expressed as the number of bottles of soda that a person is willing to forgo to get a tape. This amount decreases as the quantity of tapes available increases. Figure 3.3 illustrates the marginal benefit from tapes. (Again, the numbers are hypothetical.)

In row *a*, 0.5 million tapes a month are available and at that quantity, people are willing to pay 5 bottles of soda for a tape. As the quantity of tapes available increases, the amount that people are willing to pay for a tape falls. When 4.5 million tapes a month are available, people are willing to pay only 1 bottle of soda for a tape.

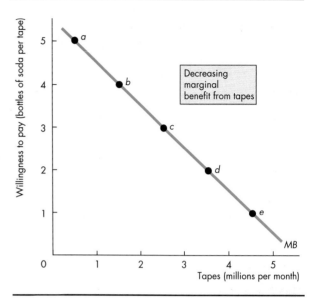

FIGURE 3.3
Marginal Benefit

Possibility	Tapes (millions per month)	Willingness to pay (bottles per tape)
a	0.5	5
b	1.5	4
c	2.5	3
d	3.5	2
e	4.5	1

The fewer the number of tapes available, the more soda people are willing to give up to get an additional tape. If only 0.5 million tapes a month are available, people are willing to pay 5 bottles of soda for a tape. But if 4.5 million tapes a month are available, people will pay only 1 bottle of soda for a tape. Decreasing marginal benefit is a universal feature of people's preferences.

The marginal benefit from a tape and the opportunity cost of a tape are both measured in bottles of soda. But they are not the same concept. The *opportunity cost* of a tape is the amount of soda that people *must forgo* to get another tape. The *marginal benefit* from a tape is the amount of soda that people *are willing to forgo* to get another tape.

You now know how to calculate marginal cost and marginal benefit. Let's use these concepts to discover the efficient quantity of tapes to produce.

Efficient Use of Resources

Resource use is **efficient** when we produce the goods and services that we value most highly. That is, when we are using our resources efficiently, we cannot produce more of any good without giving up something that we value even more highly.

We always choose *at the margin*. We compare marginal cost and marginal benefit. If the marginal benefit from a good exceeds the marginal cost of the good, we increase production of that good. If marginal cost exceeds marginal benefit, we decrease production of the good. And if marginal benefit equals marginal cost, we stick with the current production.

This principle is just like the decisions you make when you go shopping. You have $10 to spend and are thinking about buying a CD or a box of floppy disks. You figure that you will get more value from the CD than from the floppy disks, so you spend your $10 on the CD. You have allocated scarce resources to their highest-value use. The marginal benefit from a CD is greater than (or equal to) its marginal cost, the box of floppy disks. The marginal benefit from a box of floppy disks is less than its marginal cost. No matter what the good or service, if you can afford it and you think it is worth the price, you buy it. If you think it not worth its price, you pass it up.

We can illustrate an efficient use of resources by continuing to use the example of soda and tapes. Figure 3.4 shows the marginal cost and marginal benefit of tapes. Suppose we produce 1.5 million tapes a month. The marginal cost of a tape is 2 bottles of soda. But the marginal benefit from a tape is 4 bottles of soda. Because someone values an additional tape more highly than it costs to produce, we can get more value from our resources by moving some of them out of soda production and into tape production.

Now suppose we produce 3.5 million tapes a month. The marginal cost of a tape is now 4 bottles of soda. But the marginal benefit from a tape is only 2 bottles of soda. Because an additional tape costs more to produce than anyone thinks it is worth, we can get more value from our resources by moving some of them away from tape production and into soda production.

But suppose we produce 2.5 million tapes a month. Marginal cost and marginal benefit are now equal at 3 bottles of soda. This allocation of resources between tapes and soda is efficient. If more tapes are produced, the forgone soda is worth more than the additional tapes. If fewer tapes are produced, the forgone tapes are worth more than the additional soda.

FIGURE 3.4

Efficient Use of Resources

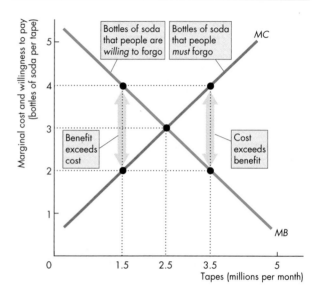

The greater the quantity of tapes produced, the smaller is the marginal benefit (*MB*) from a tape—the fewer bottles of soda people are willing to give up to get an additional tape. But the greater the quantity of tapes produced, the greater is the marginal cost (*MC*) of a tape—the more bottles of soda people must give up to get an additional tape. When marginal benefit equals marginal cost, resources are being used efficiently.

R E V I E W

■ The marginal cost of a good or service is the opportunity cost of increasing its production by one unit.

■ The marginal benefit from a good or service is the maximum amount that someone is willing to pay for an additional unit.

■ Resources are used efficiently when they cannot be reallocated to increase the value of production.

■ When marginal benefit equals marginal cost, resources are used efficiently.

You now understand the limits to production and the conditions under which resources are used efficiently. Your next task is to study the expansion of production possibilities.

Economic Growth

DURING THE PAST 30 YEARS, PRODUCTION IN THE United States has expanded by 80 percent. Such an expansion of production is called **economic growth**. Can economic growth enable us to overcome scarcity and avoid opportunity cost? You are going to see that economic growth does not overcome scarcity and avoid opportunity cost. You are also going to see that the faster we make production grow, the greater is the opportunity cost of economic growth.

The Cost of Economic Growth

Two key factors influence economic growth: technological change and capital accumulation. **Technological change** is the development of new goods and of better ways of producing goods and services. **Capital accumulation** is the growth of capital resources.

As a consequence of technological change and capital accumulation, we have an enormous quantity of cars that enable us to produce more transportation than when we had only horses and carriages; we have satellites that make global communications possible on a scale that is much larger than that produced by the earlier cable technology. But new technologies and new capital have an opportunity cost. In order to use resources in research and development and to produce new capital, we must decrease our production of consumption goods and services. Let's look at this opportunity cost.

Instead of studying the *PPF* of tapes and soda, we'll hold the quantity of soda produced constant and examine the *PPF* for tapes and tape-making machines. Figure 3.5 shows this *PPF* as the blue curve *abc*. If we devote no resources to producing tape-making machines, we produce at point *a*. If we produce 3 million tapes a month, we can produce 6 tape-making machines at point *b*. If we produce no tapes, we can produce 10 tape-making machines a month at point *c*.

The amount by which our production possibilities expand depends on the resources we devote to technological change and capital accumulation. If we devote no resources to this activity (point *a*), the frontier remains at *abc*—the blue curve in Fig. 3.5. If we cut the current production of tapes and produce 6 machines a month (point *b*), then in the future, we'll have more capital and our *PPF* rotates outward to the

FIGURE 3.5
Economic Growth

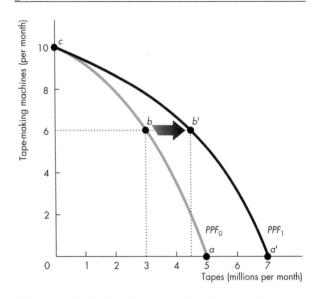

PPF_0 shows the limits to the production of tapes and tape-making equipment, with the production of all other goods and services remaining constant. If we devote no resources to producing tape-making machines and produce 5 million tapes a month, we remain stuck at point *a*. But if we decrease tape production to 3 million a month and produce 6 tape-making machines a month, at point *b*, our production possibilities will expand. After a year, the production possibility frontier shifts outward to PPF_1 and we can produce at point *b'*, a point outside the original *PPF*. We can shift the *PPF* outward, but we cannot avoid opportunity cost. The opportunity cost of producing more tapes in the future is fewer tapes today.

position shown by the red curve. The fewer resources we devote to producing tapes and the more resources we devote to producing machines, the greater is the expansion of our production possibilities.

Economic growth is not free. To make it happen, we devote resources to producing new machines and less to producing tapes. In Fig. 3.5, we move from *a* to *b*. There is no free lunch. The opportunity cost of more tapes in the future is fewer tapes today. Also, economic growth is no magic formula for abolishing scarcity. On the new production possibility frontier, we continue to face opportunity costs.

The ideas about economic growth that we have explored in the setting of the audio tape industry also apply to nations. Let's look at two examples.

Economic Growth in the United States and Hong Kong

If as a nation we devote all our resources to producing consumer goods and none to research and capital accumulation, our production possibilities in the future will be the same as they are today. To expand our production possibilities in the future, we must devote fewer resources to producing consumption goods and some resources to accumulating capital and developing technologies so we can produce more consumption goods in the future. The decrease in today's consumption is the opportunity cost of an increase in future consumption.

The experiences of the United States and Hong Kong make a striking example of the effects of our choices on the rate of economic growth. In 1960, the production possibilities per person in the United States were more than four times those in Hong Kong (see Fig. 3.6). The United States devoted one fifth of its resources to accumulating capital and the other four fifths to consumption. In 1960, the United States was at point *a* on its *PPF*. Hong Kong devoted one third of its resources to accumulating capital and two thirds to consumption. In 1960, Hong Kong was at point *a* on its *PPF*.

Since 1960, both countries have experienced economic growth, but growth in Hong Kong has been more rapid than growth in the United States. Because Hong Kong devoted a bigger fraction of its resources to accumulating capital, its production possibilities expanded more quickly.

In 1997, the *PPF* per person in the United States and Hong Kong were similar. If Hong Kong continues to devote a similar proportion of its resources to accumulating capital (at point *b* on the 1997 *PPF*), it will continue to grow more rapidly than the United States and its frontier will move out beyond our own. But if Hong Kong increases its consumption and decreases its capital accumulation (moving to point *c* on its 1997 production possibility frontier), then its rate of economic growth will slow.

The United States is typical of the rich industrial countries, which include Western Europe, Japan, and Canada. Hong Kong is typical of the fast-growing Asian economies, which include Taiwan, Thailand, South Korea, and China. These countries have grown at between 5 percent a year and almost 10 percent a year, which is much faster than the growth rate of the United States. If the current differences in growth rates persist, these other countries will eventually close the gap on the United States as Hong Kong has done.

FIGURE 3.6

Economic Growth in the United States and Hong Kong

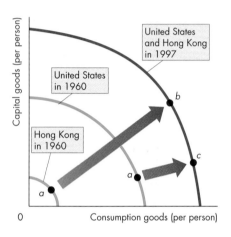

In 1960, the production possibilities per person in the United States were much larger than those in Hong Kong. But Hong Kong devoted more of its resources to accumulating capital than did the United States, so its production possibility frontier has shifted out more quickly than has that of the United States. In 1997, the two production possibilities per person were similar.

R E V I E W

■ Economic growth results from technological change and capital accumulation.

■ The opportunity cost of economic growth is a decrease in current consumption.

■ By decreasing current consumption, we can devote more resources to developing new technologies and accumulating capital and can speed up the rate of economic growth.

Next, we're going to study another way we expand our production possibilities—the amazing fact that buyers and sellers gain from specialization and trade.

Gains from Trade

PEOPLE CAN PRODUCE FOR THEMSELVES ALL THE goods that they consume, or they can concentrate on producing one good (or perhaps a few goods) and then trade with others—exchange some of their own goods for those of others. Concentrating on the production of only one good or a few goods is called *specialization*. We are going to discover how people gain by specializing in the production of the good in which they have a *comparative advantage* and trading with each other.

Comparative Advantage

A person has a **comparative advantage** in an activity if that person can perform the activity at a lower opportunity cost than anyone else. Differences in opportunity costs arise from differences in individual abilities and from differences in the characteristics of other resources.

No one excels at everything. One person is an outstanding pitcher but a poor catcher; another person is a brilliant lawyer but a poor teacher. In almost all human endeavors, what one person does easily, someone else finds difficult. The same applies to land and capital. One plot of land is fertile but has no mineral deposits; another plot of land has outstanding views but is infertile. One machine has great precision but is difficult to operate; another machine is fast but often breaks down.

Although no one excels at everything, some people excel and can outperform others in many activities. But such a person does not have a *comparative* advantage in every activity. For example, John Grisham is a better lawyer than most people. But he is an even better writer of fast-paced thrillers. His *comparative advantage* is in writing.

Because people's abilities and the quality of their resources differ, they have different opportunity costs of producing various goods. Such differences give rise to comparative advantage. Let's explore the idea of comparative advantage by looking at two audio cassette factories, one operated by Tom and the other operated by Nancy.

Tom's Factory   To simplify the story quite a lot, suppose that audio cassettes have just two components: a length of tape and a plastic case. Tom has two production lines, one for tape and one for cases.

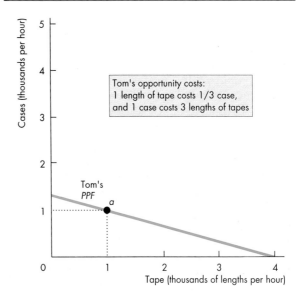

FIGURE 3.7

Production Possibilities in Tom's Factory

Tom's opportunity costs:
1 length of tape costs 1/3 case,
and 1 case costs 3 lengths of tapes

Tom can produce tape and cassette cases along the production possibility frontier *PPF*. For Tom, the opportunity cost of 1 length of tape is 1/3 of a case and the opportunity cost of 1 case is 3 lengths of tape. If Tom produces at point *a*, he can produce 1,000 cassette cases and 1,000 lengths of tape an hour.

Figure 3.7 shows Tom's production possibility frontier for tape and cases. It tells us that if Tom uses all his resources to make tape, he can produce 4,000 lengths of tape an hour. The *PPF* in Fig. 3.7 also tells us that if Tom uses all his resources to make cases, he can produce 1,333 cases an hour. But to produce cases, Tom must decrease his production of tape. For each 1 case produced, he must decrease his production of tape by 3 lengths.

Tom's opportunity cost of producing 1 case is 3 lengths of tape.

Similarly, if Tom wants to increase his production of tape, he must decrease his production of cases. For each 1,000 lengths of tape produced, he must decrease his production of cases by 333. So

Tom's opportunity cost of producing 1 length of tape is 0.333 case.

Nancy's Factory   The other factory, operated by Nancy, can also produce cases and tape. But Nancy's factory has machines that are custom made for case production, so they are more suitable for producing cases than tape. Also, Nancy's work force is more skilled in making cases.

This difference between the two factories means that Nancy's production possibility frontier—shown along with Tom's *PPF* in Fig. 3.8—is different from Tom's. If Nancy uses all her resources to make tape, she can produce 1,333 lengths an hour. If she uses all her resources to make cases, she can produce 4,000 an hour. To produce tape, Nancy must decrease her production of cases. For each 1,000 additional lengths of tape produced, she must decrease her production of cases by 3,000.

Nancy's opportunity cost of producing 1 length of tape is 3 cases.

Similarly, if Nancy wants to increase her production of cases, she must decrease her production of tape. For each 1,000 additional cases produced, she must decrease her production of tape by 333 lengths. So

Nancy's opportunity cost of producing 1 case is 0.333 length of tape.

Suppose that Tom and Nancy produce both tapes and cases and that each produces 1,000 lengths of tape and 1,000 cases—1,000 cassettes—an hour. That is, each produces at point *a* on their production possibility frontiers. Total production is 2,000 cassettes an hour.

In which of the two goods does Nancy have a comparative advantage? Recall that comparative advantage is a situation in which one person's opportunity cost of producing a good is lower than another person's opportunity cost of producing that same good. Nancy has a comparative advantage in producing cases. Nancy's opportunity cost of a case is 0.333 length of tape, whereas Tom's is 3 lengths of tape.

You can see her comparative advantage by looking at the production possibility frontiers for Nancy and Tom in Fig. 3.8. Nancy's production possibility frontier is steeper than Tom's. To produce one more case, Nancy gives up less tape than Tom. Hence Nancy's opportunity cost of a case is less than Tom's. This means that Nancy has a comparative advantage in producing cases.

FIGURE 3.8

The Gains from Trade

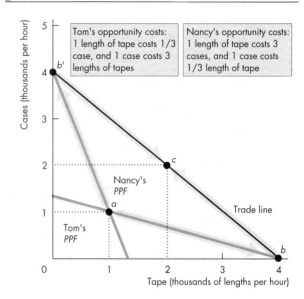

Tom and Nancy each produce at point *a* on their respective *PPF*s. Nancy has a comparative advantage in cases, and Tom has a comparative advantage in tape. If Nancy specializes in cases, she produces at point *b'* on her *PPF*. If Tom specializes in tape, he produces at point *b* on his *PPF*. They then exchange cases for tape along the red "Trade line." Nancy buys tape from Tom for less than her opportunity cost of producing it, and Tom buys cases from Nancy for less than his opportunity cost of producing them. Each goes to point *c*—a point outside his or her *PPF*—where each has 2,000 cassettes an hour. Tom and Nancy double their rate of production with no change in resources.

Tom's comparative advantage is in producing tape. His production possibility frontier is less steep than Nancy's. This means that Tom gives up fewer cases to produce one more length of tape than Nancy does. Tom's opportunity cost of producing a length of tape is 0.333 case, which is less than Nancy's 3 cases. So Tom has a comparative advantage in producing tape.

Because Nancy has a comparative advantage in cases and Tom in tape, they can both gain from specialization and exchange.

Achieving the Gains from Trade

If Tom, who has a comparative advantage in tape production, puts all his resources into that activity, he can produce 4,000 lengths of tape an hour—point *b* on his *PPF*. If Nancy, who has a comparative advantage in producing cases, puts all her resources into that activity, she can produce 4,000 cases an hour—point *b* on her *PPF*. By specializing, Tom and Nancy together can produce 4,000 cases and 4,000 lengths of tape an hour, double their total production without specialization. By specialization and exchange, Tom and Nancy can get *outside* their production possibility frontiers.

To achieve the gains from specialization, Tom and Nancy must trade with each other. Suppose they agree to the following deal: Each hour, Nancy produces 4,000 cases, Tom produces 4,000 lengths of tape, and Nancy supplies Tom with 2,000 cases in exchange for 2,000 lengths of tape. With this deal in place, Tom and Nancy move along the red "Trade line" to point *c*. At this point, each produces 2,000 cassettes an hour—double their previous production rate. These are the gains from specialization and trade.

Both parties to the trade share the gains. Nancy, who can produce tape at an opportunity cost of 3 cases per length of tape, can buy tape from Tom for a price of 1 case per length. Tom, who can produce cases at an opportunity cost of 3 lengths of tape per case, can buy cases from Nancy at a price of 1 length per case. Nancy gets her tape more cheaply, and Tom gets his cases more cheaply.

Absolute Advantage

Suppose that Nancy invents and patents a production process that makes her *four* times as productive as she was before in the production of both cases and tape. With her new technology, Nancy can produce 16,000 cases an hour (4 times the original 4,000) if she puts all her resources into that activity. Alternatively, she can produce 5,332 lengths of tape (4 times the original 1,333) if she puts all her resources into that activity. Nancy now has an **absolute advantage** in producing *both* goods—using the same quantity of resources as Tom, she can produce more of both goods than Tom can produce.

But Nancy does not have a *comparative* advantage in both goods. She can produce four times as much of *both* goods as before, but her *opportunity cost* of 1

length of tape is still 3 cases. And this opportunity cost is higher than Tom's. So Nancy can still get tape at a lower cost by exchanging cases for tape with Tom.

A key point to recognize is that it is *not* possible for *anyone* to have a comparative advantage in everything. So gains from specialization and trade are always available when opportunity costs diverge.

Dynamic Comparative Advantage

At any given point in time, the available resources and technologies determine the comparative advantages that individuals and nations have. But just by repeatedly producing a particular good or service, people become more productive in that activity, a phenomenon called **learning-by-doing**. Learning-by-doing is the basis of *dynamic* comparative advantage. **Dynamic comparative advantage** is a comparative advantage that a person (or country) possesses as a result of having specialized in a particular activity and, as a result of learning-by-doing, having become the producer with the lowest opportunity cost.

Hong Kong, South Korea, and Taiwan are examples of countries that have pursued dynamic comparative advantage vigorously. They have developed industries in which initially they did not have a comparative advantage but, through learning-by-doing, became low opportunity cost producers in those industries. An example is the decision to develop a genetic engineering industry in Singapore. Singapore probably did not have a comparative advantage in genetic engineering initially. But it might develop one as its scientists and production workers become more skilled in this activity.

R E V I E W

- A person has a comparative advantage in producing a good if that person's opportunity cost of producing the good is lower than everyone else's.
- Production increases if people specialize in the activity in which they have a comparative advantage.
- By specializing in the activities in which they have a comparative advantage and trading, everyone can gain.
- Dynamic comparative advantage can result from learning-by-doing.

The Market Economy

INDIVIDUALS AND COUNTRIES GAIN BY SPECIALIZ-
ing in the production of those goods and services in
which they have a comparative advantage and trading
with each other. This source of economic wealth was
identified by Adam Smith in his *Wealth of Nations,*
published in 1776—see pp. 2–3.

But for billions of people who specialize in producing millions of different goods and services to be
able to reap these gains, trade must be organized. But
trade need not be *planned* or *managed* by a central
authority. In fact, when such an arrangement has
been tried, as it was for 60 years in Russia, the result
has been less than dazzling.

Trade is organized by using social institutions.
The two key ones are:

■ Property rights
■ Markets

Property Rights

Property rights are social arrangements that govern the ownership, use, and disposal of resources,
goods, and services. *Real property* includes land and
buildings—the things we call property in ordinary
speech—and durable goods such as plant and equipment. *Financial property* includes stocks and bonds
and money in the bank. *Intellectual property* is the
intangible product of creative effort. This type of
property includes books, music, computer programs,
and inventions of all kinds and is protected by copyrights and patents.

If property rights are not enforced, the incentive
to specialize and produce the goods in which each
person has a comparative advantage is weakened, and
some of the potential gains from specialization and
trade are lost. If people can easily steal the production
of others, then time, energy, and resources are devoted
not to production, but to protecting possessions.

Establishing property rights is one of the greatest
challenges facing Russia and other Eastern European
nations as they seek to develop market economies.
Even in countries where property rights are well
established, such as the United States, protecting
intellectual property is proving to be a challenge in
the face of modern technologies that make it relatively easy to copy audio and video material, computer programs, and books.

Markets

In ordinary speech, the word *market* means a place
where people buy and sell goods such as fish, meat,
fruits, and vegetables. In economics, a *market* has a
more general meaning. A **market** is any arrangement that enables buyers and sellers to get information and to do business with each other. An example
is the market in which oil is bought and sold—the
world oil market. The world oil market is not a place.
It is the network of oil producers, oil users, whole-
salers, and brokers who buy and sell. In the world oil
market, decision makers do not meet physically. They
make deals throughout the world by telephone, fax,
and direct computer link.

In the example we've just studied, Nancy and
Tom get together and do a deal. They agree to
exchange cassette cases for lengths of tape. But in a
market economy, Nancy sells cassette cases to a dealer
in plastic products and buys lengths of tape from a
dealer in electronic recording media. Similarly, Tom
buys cassette cases and sells lengths of tape in these
same two markets. Tom can use Nancy's cases and
Nancy can use Tom's lengths of tape and yet be
unaware of each other's existence.

Circular Flows in the Market Economy

Figure 3.9 identifies two types of markets: goods
markets and resource markets. *Goods markets* are
those in which goods and services are bought and
sold. *Resource markets* are those in which productive
resources are bought and sold.

Households decide how much of their labor,
land, capital, and entrepreneurship to sell or rent in
resource markets. They receive incomes in the form
of wages, rent, interest, and profit. Households also
decide how to spend their incomes on goods and services produced by firms. Firms decide the quantities
of resources to hire, how to use them to produce
goods and services, what goods and services to
produce, and in what quantities.

Figure 3.9 shows the flows that result from these
decisions by households and firms. The red flows
are the resources that go from households through
resource markets to firms and the goods and services
that go from firms through goods markets to households. The green flows in the opposite direction are
the payments made in exchange for these items.

How do markets coordinate all these decisions?

FIGURE 3.9

Circular Flows in the Market Economy

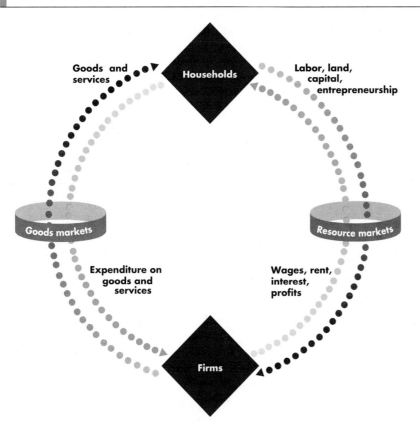

Households and firms make economic choices. Households choose the quantities of labor, land, capital, and entrepreneurship to sell or rent to firms in exchange for wages, rent, interest, and profits. Households also choose how to spend their incomes on the various types of goods and services available. Firms choose the quantities of resources to hire and the quantities of the various goods and services to produce. Goods markets and resource markets coordinate these choices of households and firms. Resources and goods flow clockwise (red), and money payments flow counterclockwise (green).

Coordinating Decisions

Markets coordinate individual decisions through price adjustments. To see how, think about your local market for hamburgers. Suppose that some people who want to buy hamburgers are not able to do so. To make the choices of buyers and sellers compatible, buyers must scale down their appetites or more hamburgers must be offered for sale (or both must happen). A rise in the price of hamburgers produces this outcome. A higher price encourages producers to offer more hamburgers for sale. It also curbs the appetite for hamburgers and changes some lunch plans. Fewer people buy hamburgers, and more buy hot dogs. More hamburgers (and more hot dogs) are offered for sale.

Alternatively suppose that more hamburgers are available than people want to buy. In this case, to make the choices of buyers and sellers compatible, more hamburgers must be bought or fewer hamburgers must be offered for sale (or both). A fall in the price of ham-

burgers achieves this outcome. A lower price encourages firms to produce a smaller quantity of hamburgers. It also encourages people to buy more hamburgers.

◆ You have now begun to see how economists approach economic questions. Scarcity, choice, and divergent opportunity costs explain why we specialize and trade and why property rights and markets have developed. You can see the lessons you've learned in this chapter all around you. *Reading Between the Lines* on pp. 56–57 gives an example. It explores the *PPF* that you face as you make your decisions about whether to remain in school or quit school and take a job.

In Chapter 4, you are going to learn how markets work and see why prices adjust to coordinate buying plans and selling plans. And in Chapter 6, you are going to discover that markets are an effective way of achieving an efficient use of resources. Markets generally move resources into those activities in which they are valued most highly.

Policy
WATCH

Opportunity Cost: The Cost and Benefit of a College Degree

PORTLAND PRESS HERALD, MAY 2, 1996

High Cost Blocks Education

Robin McAlister of South Portland has fallen into a disheartening routine: Sit down at the kitchen table, scan the classifieds, apply for a job, get turned down.

"I need computer experience," said McAlister, a 39-year-old single mother, who lost her clerical job at a physician's office in January. "Because of the lack of computer training, I don't qualify for general office positions." ...

Like thousands of other Mainers, McAlister has learned a fundamental truth: People who don't have the skills needed in today's high-tech, highly competitive environment rarely find good jobs. ...

A five-month investigation by The Portland Newspapers found that education increasingly separates successful workers who earn good pay from those who are struggling to find a job that pays a livable wage. Yet the cost of getting the skills needed for a decent job is spiraling out of reach for many Mainers. ...

Jobs that pay a livable wage increasingly demand computer-literate, college-educated workers. A college degree doesn't guarantee a good-paying job, but it gives workers a better chance at getting one. An estimated 78 percent of the jobs in Maine that pay $15 an hour or more generally require a college degree. ...

Although a college degree doesn't guarantee a job, the economy is creating work for highly educated people. A computer analysis by The Portland Newspapers found the number of jobs in Maine for people with advanced degrees and technical training is rapidly increasing.

Since 1989, the number of jobs for people with a master's degree has jumped an estimated 21 percent; jobs demanding associate degrees from technical colleges have grown by 16 percent; work for people with a doctorate increased about 11 percent; and jobs that generally require a bachelor's degree have increased about 5 percent.

By comparison, jobs that generally don't require a college education have declined an estimated 1 percent.

There's a huge gap in pay between the two groups. In Maine, the average hourly wage for jobs that generally require a college degree is twice that for occupations that don't, about $18 an hour vs. $9 an hour, according to an analysis by The Portland Newspapers of state and federal databases. ...

Mainers must strive to increase their skills and continue their education after high school to succeed in today's intensely competitive global market. ...

Essence of THE STORY

■ People who lack high-tech skills rarely find good jobs in today's competitive environment.

■ Education is a factor in wage determination. The average hourly wage for jobs requiring a college degree is twice as much as that for jobs requiring less than a completed college education.

■ Although a college degree does not guarantee a job, the economy is creating more jobs for college graduates than for non–college graduates.

Economic

A N A L Y S I S

■ The opportunity cost of a college degree is forgone consumption. The payoff is an increase in lifetime production possibilities.

■ Figure 1 shows the choices facing a high school graduate. This person can consume education goods and services such as tuition, books and other supplies, and study time, measured on the y-axis, or other goods and services, measured on the x-axis.

■ The person can consume at any point along the blue PPF. By going to college, the student chooses point a. She increases her use of educational goods and services to A and decreases her consumption of other goods and services.

■ With a college degree, consumption possibilities expand to the red PPF in Fig. 1.

■ A college graduate can choose to spend even more on education to get a professional degree.

■ Figure 2 shows the choices facing a college graduate. To get a professional degree, a college graduate selects point c on the blue PPF, forgoes consumption and increases

the use of educational goods and services to B.

■ The red PPF in Fig. 2 shows the expanded possibilities with a professional degree. It is now possible for this person to consume at point d or at another point along the red PPF.

■ The greater the resources devoted to education, the greater are the future consumption possibilities. For people who have the required ability, the future benefits from education exceed the costs by a significant amount.

■ The news article says that a college graduate earns twice the income of a non–college graduate. Other data suggest that the difference is about 60 percent. Either way, the difference is large.

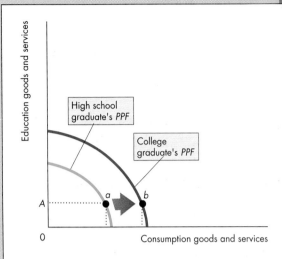

Figure 1 High school graduate's choices

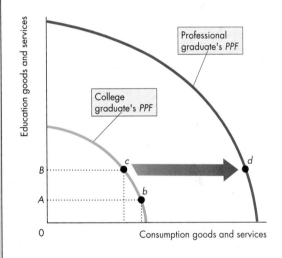

Figure 2 College graduate's choices

You're

T H E   V O T E R

■ In his 1997 State of the Union address, President Clinton said that he wants every American to have a college education.

■ Why do you think the President needs to worry about college education?

■ With such huge returns from education, why don't more people remain in school for longer?

■ What is the opportunity cost of President Clinton's plan?

■ Would you vote for or against a tax increase to enable everyone to attend college? Why or why not?

SUMMARY

Key Points

Resources and Wants (p. 42)

- Economic activity arises from scarcity—resources are insufficient to satisfy people's wants.
- Resources are labor, land, capital (including human capital), and entrepreneurship.
- We choose how to use our resources and try to get the most out of them.

Resources, Production Possibilities, and Opportunity Cost (pp. 43–45)

- The production possibility frontier, *PPF*, is the boundary between production levels that are attainable and those that are not attainable when all the available resources are used to their limit.
- Production efficiency occurs at points on the *PPF*.
- Along the *PPF*, the opportunity cost of producing more of one good is the amount of the other good that must be given up.
- The opportunity cost of a good increases as the production of the good increases.

Using Resources Efficiently (pp. 46–48)

- The marginal cost of a good is the opportunity cost of producing one more unit.
- The marginal benefit from a good is the maximum amount of another good that a person is willing to forgo to obtain more of the first good.
- The marginal benefit of a good decreases as the amount available increases.
- Resources are used efficiently when the marginal cost of each good is equal to its marginal benefit.

Economic Growth (pp. 49–50)

- Economic growth, which is the expansion of production possibilities, results from capital accumulation and technological change.
- The opportunity cost of economic growth is forgone current consumption.

Gains from Trade (pp. 51–53)

- A person has a comparative advantage in producing a good if that person can produce the good at a lower opportunity cost than everyone else can.
- People gain by specializing in the activity in which they have a comparative advantage and trading with others.
- Dynamic comparative advantage arises from learning-by-doing.

The Market Economy (pp. 54–55)

- Property rights and markets enable people to gain from specialization and trade.
- Markets coordinate decisions and help to allocate resources to *higher* value uses.

Key Figures

Key Terms

| QUESTIONS | PROBLEMS |

QUESTIONS

1. What is the fundamental economic problem?
2. What are the resources used to produce goods and services?
3. How does the production possibility frontier illustrate scarcity?
4. How does the production possibility frontier illustrate the fact that every choice involves a tradeoff?
5. How does the production possibility frontier illustrate production efficiency?
6. How does the production possibility frontier illustrate opportunity cost?
7. Why is opportunity cost a ratio?
8. Why does the production possibility frontier for most goods bow outward?
9. Why does opportunity cost generally increase as the quantity produced of a good increases?
10. What is marginal cost and how is it measured?
11. How do we measure the marginal benefit from a good?
12. How does the marginal benefit from a good change as the quantity of that good increases?
13. What is production efficiency and how does it relate to the production possibility frontier?
14. Under what conditions are resources used efficiently?
15. What shifts the production possibility frontier outward?
16. How do choices influence the pace of economic growth?
17. What is the opportunity cost of economic growth?
18. Why do people specialize and trade?
19. How do people gain from specialization and trade?
20. Is production still efficient when people specialize? Explain why or why not.
21. What are the gains from specialization and trade?
22. Distinguish between comparative advantage and absolute advantage.
23. What is dynamic comparative advantage and how does it arise?
24. Why are social arrangements such as markets and property rights necessary?
25. What are the main functions of markets?

PROBLEMS

1. Wendell enjoys playing tennis, but the more time he spends on tennis, the lower is his grade in economics. The figure shows the tradeoff he faces.

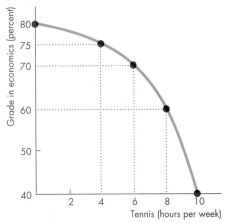

Calculate Wendell's opportunity cost of two hours of tennis if he increases the time he plays tennis from:
   a. 4 to 6 hours a week.
   b. 6 to 8 hours a week.

2. In problem 1, describe the relationship between the time Wendell spends playing tennis and the opportunity cost of an hour of tennis.

3. If Wendell's opportunity cost of increasing his grade were constant regardless of how much time he spent playing tennis, what would be the shape of his *PPF*? Which shape seems more likely, the one in the figure above or the one that answers this question?

4. Suppose that Leisureland produces only two goods: food and sunscreen. The table gives its production possibilities.

Food (pounds per month)		Sunscreen (gallons per month)
300	and	0
200	and	50
100	and	100
0	and	150

   a. Draw a graph of Leisureland's production possibility frontier.
   b. What are the opportunity costs of producing food and sunscreen in Leisureland? List them at each output given in the table.

c. Why are these opportunity costs the same at each output level?

5. Suppose that the people in Leisureland are willing to give up 5 pounds of food per gallon of sunscreen if they have 25 gallons of sunscreen, 2 pounds of food per gallon of sunscreen if they have 75 gallons of sunscreen, and 1 pound of food per gallon of sunscreen if they have 125 gallons of sunscreen.
   a. Draw a graph of Leisureland's marginal benefit from sunscreen.
   b. On the same graph, plot the opportunity cost of producing sunscreen.
   c. What is Leisureland's efficient use of sunscreen?
   d. What is the efficient production of food?

6. Busyland produces only food and sunscreen, and its production possibilities are as follows:

Food (pounds per month)		Sunscreen (gallons per month)
150	and	0
100	and	100
50	and	200
0	and	300

   a. Draw a graph of Busyland's production possibility frontier.
   b. What are the opportunity costs of producing food and sunscreen in Busyland? List them at each output given in the table.

7. Suppose that in problems 4 and 6, Leisureland and Busyland do not specialize and trade with each other. Leisureland produces and consumes 50 pounds of food and 125 gallons of sunscreen per month. Busyland produces and consumes 150 pounds of food per month and no sunscreen. Now the countries begin to trade with each other.
   a. What good does Leisureland sell to Busyland and what good does it buy from Busyland?
   b. What are the maximum quantities of food and sunscreen that the two countries can produce if each country specializes in the activity at which it has a comparative advantage?

8. Wendell in problem 1 has the marginal benefit curve shown in the figure.

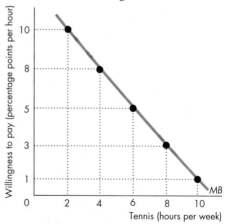

   a. If Wendell uses his time efficiently, what grade will he get?
   b. Why would Wendell be worse off getting a higher grade?

CRITICAL THINKING

1. After you have studied *Reading Between the Lines* on pp. 56–57, answer the following questions:
   a. Draw a graph that shows the opportunity cost of education. Does the opportunity cost of education increase as the quantity of education increases?
   b. If all colleges and universities were private institutions that charged full-cost tuition, would the opportunity cost of a college education increase, decrease, or remain unchanged? Explain your answer.
   c. Most colleges and universities operate a school year of around 30 weeks. So for 22 weeks each year, classrooms are empty and professors do no teaching. Is this arrangement inefficient or efficient? Explain your answer.
   d. What do you think are the main benefits from education? Do all the benefits accrue to the people who receive education? Do other people benefit as well?

Part 2

How Markets Work

The Amazing Market

The market is an amazing instrument. It enables people who have never met and who know nothing about each other to interact and do business. It also enables us to allocate our scarce resources to the uses that we value most highly. Markets can be very simple or highly organized. ◆ A simple market is one that the American historian Daniel J. Boorstin describes in *The Discoverers* (p. 161). In the late fourteenth century,

> The Muslim caravans that went southward from Morocco across the Atlas Mountains arrived after twenty days at the shores of the Senegal River. There the Moroccan traders laid out separate piles of salt, of beads from Ceutan coral, and cheap manufactured goods. Then they retreated out of sight. The local tribesmen, who lived in the strip mines where they dug their gold, came to the shore and put a heap of gold beside each pile of Moroccan goods. Then they, in turn, went out of view, leaving the Moroccan traders either to take the gold offered for a particular pile or to reduce the pile of their merchandise to suit the offered price in gold. Once again the Moroccan traders withdrew, and the process went on. By this system of commercial etiquette, the Moroccans collected their gold.

An organized market is the New York Stock Exchange that trades many millions of stocks each day. Another is an auction at which the U.S. government sells rights to broadcasters and cellular telephone companies for the use of the air waves. ◆ All of these markets determine the prices at which exchanges take place and enable both buyers and sellers to benefit. ◆ Everything and anything that can be exchanged is traded in markets. There are markets for goods and services; for resources such as labor, capital, and raw materials; for dollars, pounds, and yen; for goods to be delivered now; and for goods to be delivered in the future. Only the imagination places limits on what can be traded in markets. ◆ The next four chapters explain how markets work. We begin, in Chapter 4, by learning about the laws of demand and supply. We'll discover the forces that make prices adjust to coordinate buying plans and selling plans. In Chapter 5, we study the concept of elasticity—a tool for measuring the responsiveness of quantities bought and sold to prices. In Chapter 6, we study efficiency. We'll discover the conditions under which a market sends resources to uses in which they are valued most highly and we'll discover that markets do a good job of achieving this outcome. Finally, in Chapter 7, we study markets in action. We'll see how markets cope with change. We'll also see how markets operate when governments intervene to fix prices or prohibit trading in some types of goods. ◆ But first, we'll spend a few minutes with the economists who discovered the laws of demand and supply and we'll also talk with Paul Milgrom of Stanford University, who is one of today's most influential economists who studies and even helps to create auction markets.

Discovering the Laws of Demand and Supply

The Economist: Alfred Marshall

Alfred Marshall (1842–1924) grew up in an England that was being transformed by the railroad and by the expansion of manufacturing. Mary Paley Marshall was one of Marshall's students at Cambridge, and when Alfred and Mary married, in 1877, celibacy rules barred Marshall from continuing to teach at Cambridge. By 1884, with more liberal rules, the Marshalls returned to Cambridge, where Alfred became Professor of Political Economy.

Many others had a hand in refining the theory of demand and supply, but the first thorough and complete statement of the theory as we know it today was set out by Alfred Marshall, with the acknowledged help of Mary. Published in 1890, the monumental treatise *Principles of Economics*, became the textbook on economics on both sides of the Atlantic for almost half a century. Marshall was an outstanding mathematician, but he kept mathematics and even diagrams in the background. His supply and demand diagram appears only in a footnote.

> *"The forces to be dealt with are ... so numerous, that it is best to take a few at a time. ... Thus we begin by isolating the primary relations of supply, demand, and price."*
>
> ALFRED MARSHALL
>
> *THE PRINCIPLES OF ECONOMICS*

The Issues and Ideas

The laws of demand and supply that you will study in the following chapter were discovered during the 1830s by Antoine-Augustin Cournot (1801–1877), a professor of mathematics at the University of Lyon, France. Although Cournot was the first to use demand and supply, it was the development and expansion of the railroads during the 1850s that gave the newly emerging theory its first practical applications. Railroads then were at the cutting edge of technology just as airlines are today. And as in the airline industry today, competition among the railroads was fierce.

Dionysius Lardner (1793–1859), an Irish professor of philosophy at the University of London, used demand and supply to show railroad companies how they could increase their profits by cutting rates on long-distance business on which competition was fiercest and by raising rates on short-haul business on which they had less to fear from other transportation suppliers. Today, economists use the principles that Lardner worked out during the 1850s to calculate the freight rates and passenger fares that will give airlines the largest possible profit. And the rates calculated have a lot in common with the railroad rates of the nineteenth century. On local routes on which there is little competition, fares per mile are highest, and on long-distance routes on which the airlines compete fiercely, fares per mile are lowest.

Known satirically among scientists of the day as "Dionysius Diddler," Lardner worked on an amazing range of problems from astronomy to railway engineering to economics. A colorful character, he would have been a regular guest of David Letterman if late-night talk shows had been around in the 1850s. Lardner visited the École des Ponts et Chaussées (School of Bridges and Roads) in Paris and must have learned a great deal from Jules Dupuit.

In France, Jules Dupuit (1804–1866), a French engineer/economist, used demand to calculate the benefits from building a bridge and, once the bridge was built, for calculating the toll to charge for its use. His work was the forerunner of what is today called *cost-benefit analysis.* Working with the principles invented by Dupuit, economists today calculate the costs and benefits of highways and airports, dams, and power stations.

THEN...

Dupuit used the law of demand to determine whether a bridge or canal would be valued enough by its users to justify the cost of building it. Lardner first worked out the relationship between the cost of production and supply and used demand and supply theory to explain the costs, prices, and profits of railroad operations. He also used the theory to discover ways of increasing revenue by raising rates on short-haul business and lowering them on long-distance freight.

...AND NOW

Today, using the same principles devised by Dupuit, economists calculate whether the benefits of expanding airports and air-traffic control facilities are sufficient to cover their costs, and airline companies use the principles developed by Lardner to set their prices and to decide when to offer "seat sales." Like the railroads before them, the airlines charge a high price per mile on short flights, for which they face little competition, and a low price per mile on long flights, for which competition is fierce.

Markets do an amazing job. And the laws of demand and supply help us to understand how markets work. But in some situations, a market must be designed and institutions must be created to enable the market to operate. In recent years, economists have begun to use their tools to design and create markets. And one of the chief architects of new style markets is Paul Milgrom of Stanford University, whom you can meet on the following pages.

Paul R. Milgrom is Professor of Economics at Stanford University and an Associate Editor of the *American Economic Review*, the leading journal that publishes economic research. He is founder and president of Market Design, Inc., a young company that designs new auction and market rules for businesses and governments. Born in Detroit, Michigan, in 1948, Professor Milgrom was an undergraduate at the University of Michigan and a graduate student at Stanford University (Ph.D. 1979). He taught at Northwestern University and Yale University before returning to Stanford in 1987.

Professor Milgrom is an economic theorist, which means that he uses mathematical techniques to study economic behavior. His work on auctions has been especially influential and has found practical applications in auctioning items ranging from radio spectrum (used in paging and cellular telephones) to mining rights.

Michael Parkin talked with Professor Milgrom about his work, how it connects with the theory of demand and supply developed by Cournot and Marshall.

Professor Milgrom, how did you become an economist?

I came into the house of economics through an unmarked side door, not knowing where I was until I was well inside. The main entrance is through a graduate degree in economics, but I have no university degree in economics at any level. My undergraduate studies were in mathematics and statistics, and my graduate studies were in business. It was in graduate school that I stumbled across a brilliant study of auction theory by William Vickrey—work for which he was awarded the Nobel Prize 21 years later, in 1996. Vickrey's work surprised me and convinced me that mathematical analysis could help me to understand auctions and could even point the way to new, improved types of auctions.

Auctions, like all market arrangements, bring buyers and sellers together. Doesn't the supply and demand model explain how auctions work?

The supply and demand model is the economist's workhorse for day-to-day market analysis. It provides a wonderful way to summarize some of the main factors affecting prices and quantities and to explain how prices guide important choices.

But the model is silent about how the rules that govern trade are set or how they affect economic outcomes. Also, it is not very helpful for thinking about technology decisions that can have a huge impact on economic outcomes. For example, the way standards are set for cellular telephone systems determines whether the same phone will work on different systems in different parts of the nation and the world. In Europe, a single standard allows a consumer to go from country to country and still have a working telephone. In the United States, where no single standard exists, a consumer may find that her telephone fails to operate even with the system in the next town.

Obviously, that failure depresses the sales of cellular phone service, although it has nothing to do with the consumer preferences for communications or with the cost or availability of the cellular telephone technology.

So institutions influence prices and quantities and the kinds of plans that people make. And sometimes, institutions such as standards-setting bodies can solve problems that a market guided only by prices can't deal with effectively.

Let's return to auctions. What is auction theory? How does it relate to supply and demand?
Auctions are institutions that determine the prices and other terms at which buyers and sellers will trade. Auction theory explains how the rules of an auction affect its outcome.

Sellers want auctions that generate the highest price. Buyers want auctions that generate the lowest price. Auction houses want auctions that balance the interests of buyers and sellers and ensure a continuing flow of customers for future auctions.

In the U.S. auctions of radio spectrum, the government's main objective was to assign spectrum efficiently.

The supply and demand model does not include a place for auction rules. It supposes that buyers and sellers know all the relevant prices when they make their decisions. In reality, that is not always true.

Often in an auction, bidders must make a choice without knowing all the relevant prices.

What are the main types of auctions and why are there so many different types? Why isn't one type best?
An auction may be either sealed or open. In a sealed auction, the bids are written and the best bids win. In open auctions, there is usually a sequence of bids with each bidder getting an opportunity to respond to the bids of others. Within these two auction types, there is great variety.

The sealed bid has two advantages over the open auction. First, the bidders don't have to be gathered together physically at one time to conduct the auction. In bidding at a used car warehouse, for example, the bidders (usually used car dealers) examine the cars at times that are convenient for themselves and leave behind a sealed envelope with their bids. There is a deadline for bids. When the deadline passes, the bids are opened and the bidders are notified of the results.

Second, it is harder for bidders to collude and depress the price received by the seller. With sealed bids, a member of a ring of buyers who agree to keep prices low might be tempted to submit a slightly higher bid and take advantage of the low bids by other ring members. The temptation to cheat in an open auction is much less, because the other ring members can punish the cheater by driving up the price when the member violates the agreement.

Open auctions have advantages, too. When a single item is being sold and price is the key factor, an open auction eliminates the guesswork of sealed bids. The bidder with the highest value can outbid the competitors. Also, when a large number of items are to be sold and the bidders are present for an open auction, the items can be sold quickly in sequence.

What advances have we made in auction theory?
Since Vickrey initiated auction theory some 35 years ago, we have improved our ability to predict how different types of auctions perform. And we've learned how to design auctions with particular objectives in mind. We even have developed mathematical descriptions of "optimal auctions," which are theoretically the best auction designs for achieving particular objectives.

We still haven't implemented an optimal auction in a real situation, but a small group of economists have used auction theory to design significant new auctions. Recently, I was among a group that proposed a brand-new auction design called a "simultaneous ascending auction." This type of auction is an open auction of many different items, all of which can be bid for simultaneously.

The U.S. Federal Communications Commission used such an auction to sell licenses to use radio spectrum for telecommunications services. The auction was the largest in history and generated gross revenues of $24 billion.

More important to me, the new auction design performed as predicted and led to much more efficient license assignments than other kinds of auctions could have achieved.

The radio spectrum auctions have shaped competition in wireless communications and have determined which firms will operate businesses in which parts of the country.

Why did selling the frequency spectrum need a simultaneous ascending bid auction? And how does such an auction work?

Bidders want to acquire licenses to provide a wireless communications service covering certain geographic areas. A bidder might want to use one of two available bands of spectrum to provide services in, say, Los Angeles County. If either spectrum band will do and the bidder needs just one, then the licenses to use these bands are economic substitutes.

But a bidder might also be willing to pay more to acquire a license covering southern California if he or she could also acquire a license covering northern California. These licenses are complements. One reason why licenses might be complements is that the two areas can share some facilities and lower costs. Another reason is that an owner of both licenses might be able to provide a more valuable service to consumers and so charge a higher price for it.

The simultaneous ascending bid auction handles both situations well. In such an auction, the bidding for the northern and southern California licenses, and in fact *all* the licenses, goes on at the same time, and bidding remains open on all the individual licenses until bidding for all licenses is complete. In an auction like this, a bidder who is interested in the California licenses can bid for both and can cease bidding when the combination price gets too high. This is a far from perfect solution, but it is much better

than any of the traditional alternatives and seems to have performed well in the sale of spectrum licenses in the United States.

What differences are today's information technologies making to the problems of auction design?

Without modern information technology, the simultaneous ascending auction of radio spectrum licenses couldn't have been conducted. In a large version of the auction, both the auctioneer and the bidders need to keep track of bids on hundreds or even thou-

sands of licenses simultaneously. Software programs have been created to facilitate submitting bids and tracking the auction results.

How do you advise today's undergraduate to prepare for a career in economics? What besides economics should he or she study?

The best economists are technically able, curious about the world, concerned about human welfare, flexible in their perspectives, and dedicated to clear, analytical thinking. Courses can help with some of these things. Students can certainly learn mathematical and statistical concepts as undergraduates.

To enjoy a career as an economist, you have to go beyond the academic abstractions and incorporate elements that excite you. Many students study economics because of their specific social concerns, for example, wanting to understand the sources of poverty in their home countries and to discern the paths out of poverty. For those students, I recommend reading widely and studying other social sciences to learn about the culture and politics of poverty and the kinds of barriers they create to good economic policies. There are so many ways to incorporate one's pleasures in an economics career! I have friends and colleagues who've studied the economics of sports, of wine prices, of the performing arts, and of the Internet. By weaving their personal and professional interests together, they eliminate the sharp divide between their career and their leisure. These are the folks I hold up as role models.

> *The best economists are technically able, curious about the world, concerned about human welfare, flexible in their perspectives, and dedicated to clear, analytical thinking.*

4

Demand and Supply

Slide, rocket, and roller coaster—
Disneyland rides? No. Commonly used
descriptions of prices changes. ◆ CD
players have taken a price slide from around
$1,100 (in today's money) in 1983 to less than
$100 today. And during these years, the quantity of
CD players bought has increased steadily. What caused
this price slide? Why didn't brisk buying keep the
price high? ◆ The price of health care has rocketed. Yet
despite rocketing prices, people buy more health services every
year. Why did people buy ever larger amounts of health care during
the 1980s and early 1990s when its price rocketed? ◆ The prices of
bananas, coffee, and other agricultural commodities follow a roller
coaster. Why does the price of bananas roller-coaster even when people's tastes for bananas barely change? ◆ The prices of many things we

Slide, Rocket, and Roller Coaster

buy are remarkably steady. For example, the
price of an audio cassette tape has not changed
much. But despite its steady price, the number
of tapes people buy increases each year. Why
do people buy more tapes even though their
price is no lower than it was a decade ago? And
why do firms sell more tapes even though they
can't get higher prices for them? ◆ Economics
is about the choices people make to cope with
scarcity. These choices are guided by costs and benefits and are coordinated through markets. ◆ The tool that explains how markets
work is demand and supply. It is central to the whole of economics. It
is used to study issues as diverse as wages and jobs, rents and housing,
pollution, crime, consumer protection, education, welfare, health care,
the value of money, and interest rates. ◆ Your careful study of this
topic will bring big rewards both in your further study of economics
and in your everyday life. Once you understand demand and supply,
you will view the world through new eyes. When you have completed
your study of demand and supply, you will be able to explain how
prices are determined and make predictions about price slides, rockets,
and roller coasters. But first, we're going to take a closer look at the idea
of price. Just what is a price?

After studying this chapter, you will be able to:

- Distinguish between a money price and a relative price

- Explain the main influences on demand

- Explain the main influences on supply

- Explain how prices and quantities bought and sold are determined by demand and supply

- Explain why some prices fall, some rise, and some fluctuate

- Use demand and supply to make predictions about price changes

Price and Opportunity Cost

ECONOMIC ACTIONS ARISE FROM SCARCITY—wants exceed the resources available to satisfy them. Faced with *scarcity,* people must make choices. And to make choices, they compare *costs* and *benefits*. Choices are influenced by opportunity costs. If the opportunity cost of a good or service increases, consumers look for less costly substitutes and decrease their purchases of the more costly item.

We are going to build on this fundamental idea and study both the way people respond to *prices* and the forces that determine prices. But to pursue these tasks, we need to understand the relationship between price and opportunity cost.

In everyday life, the *price* of an object is the number of dollars that must be given up in exchange for it. Economists refer to this price as the *money price*.

The *opportunity cost* of an action is the highest-valued alternative forgone. If, when you buy a cup of coffee, the highest-valued thing you forgo is some gum, then the opportunity cost of buying a coffee is the *quantity* of gum forgone. We can calculate this quantity from the money prices of coffee and gum.

If the money price of coffee is $1 a cup and the money price of gum is 50¢ a pack, then the opportunity cost of one cup of coffee is two packs of gum. To calculate this opportunity cost, we divide the price of a cup of coffee by the price of a pack of gum and find the *ratio* of one price to the other. The ratio of one price to another is called a **relative price**, and a *relative price is an opportunity* cost. It is the price of good *X* divided by the price of good *Y*, and it tells us how many units of good *Y* must be given up to get one more unit of good *X*.

There are many relative prices—coffee to gum, coffee to Coke, coffee to everything else, gum to Coke, gum to everything else, Coke to everything else—and we need a convenient way of expressing relative prices.

The normal way of expressing a relative price is in terms of what a "basket" of all goods and services cost in a particular year. To calculate this relative price, we divide the money price of a good by the money price of a "basket" of all goods (called a *price index*). The resulting relative price tells us the opportunity cost of an item in terms of how much of the "basket" of all goods must be given up to buy it.

Figure 4.1 illustrates the distinction between a money price and a relative price. The green curve shows the money price of wheat and tells us that the

FIGURE 4.1
The Price of Wheat

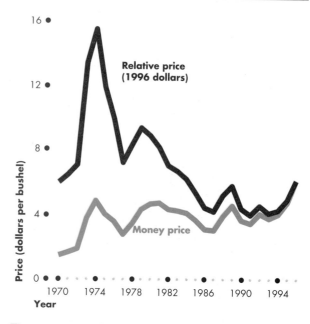

The money price of wheat—the number of dollars that must be given up for a bushel of wheat—has fluctuated between $1.50 and $6.20. But the *relative* price or *opportunity* cost of wheat, expressed in 1996 dollars, has fluctuated between $4.00 and $15.60 and has tended to fall. The fall in the relative price of wheat is obscured by the behavior of the money price.

Sources: Price of wheat, *International Financial Statistics*, International Monetary Fund, Washington, D.C., 1997; Consumer Price Index, *Economic Report of the President*, U.S. Government Printing Office, Washington, D.C., 1997.

money price has fluctuated but has tended to rise. The red curve shows the relative price of wheat—the price relative to that of a basket of goods and services in 1996. This curve tells us about the opportunity cost of wheat. It shows what the price would have been each year if the price of the basket had been the same as it was in 1996. The relative price of wheat peaked in 1974 and has tended to fall since that year.

The theory of demand and supply that we are about to study determines *relative prices,* and the word "price" means *relative* price. When we predict that a price will fall, we do not mean that its *money* price will fall—although it might. We mean that its *relative* price will fall. That is, its price will fall *relative* to the average price of other goods and services.

Let's now begin our study of demand and supply, starting with demand.

Demand

I̲F̲ ̲Y̲O̲U̲ ̲D̲E̲M̲A̲N̲D̲ ̲S̲O̲M̲E̲T̲H̲I̲N̲G̲,̲ ̲T̲H̲E̲N̲ ̲Y̲O̲U̲

- Want it,
- Can afford it, and
- Have made a definite plan to buy it.

Wants are the unlimited desires or wishes that people have for goods and services. How many times have you thought that you would like something "if only you could afford it" or "if it weren't so expensive"? Scarcity guarantees that many—perhaps most—of our wants will never be satisfied. Demand reflects a decision about which wants to satisfy.

The **quantity demanded** of a good or service is the amount that consumers plan to buy during a given time period at a particular price. The quantity demanded is not necessarily the same amount as the quantity actually bought. Sometimes the quantity demanded is greater than the amount of goods available, so the quantity bought is less than the quantity demanded.

The quantity demanded is measured as an amount per unit of t̲i̲m̲e̲.̲ For example, suppose that you consume one cup of coffee a day. The quantity of coffee that you demand can be expressed as 1 cup a day or 7 cups a week or 365 cups a year. Without a time dimension, we cannot tell whether a particular quantity demanded is large or small.

What Determines Buying Plans?

The amount of any particular good or service that consumers plan to buy depends on many factors. The main ones are:

- The price of the good
- The prices of related goods
- Income
- Population
- Preferences
- Expected future prices

We first look at the relationship between the quantity demanded and the price of a good. To study this relationship, we hold constant all other influences on consumers' planned purchases and ask: How does the quantity demanded of the good vary as its price varies, other things remaining the same?

The Law of Demand

The law of demand states:

Other things remaining the same, the higher the price of a good, the smaller is the quantity demanded.

Why does a higher price reduce the quantity demanded? For two reasons:

1. Substitution effect
2. Income effect

Substitution Effect   When the price of a good rises, other things remaining the same, its *relative* price—its opportunity cost—rises. Although each good is unique, it has *substitutes*—other goods that can be used in its place. As the opportunity cost of a good rises, people buy less of that good and more of its substitutes.

Income Effect   When a price changes and all other influences on buying plans remain unchanged, the price rises *relative* to people's incomes. So faced with a higher price and an unchanged income, people cannot afford to buy all the things they previously bought. The quantities demanded of at least some goods and services must be decreased. Normally, the good whose price has increased is one of those bought in a smaller quantity.

To see the substitution effect and the income effect at work, think about the effects of changes in the price of blank audio cassette tapes. Many different goods provide a service similar to that provided by a tape. For example, a compact disc, a prerecorded tape, a radio or television broadcast, and a live concert all provide similar services to a tape. Suppose that tapes initially sell for $3 each and then the price doubles to $6. People now substitute compact discs and prerecorded tapes for blank tapes—the substitution effect. And faced with a tighter budget, they buy fewer tapes as well as less of other goods and services—the income effect. The quantity of tapes demanded decreases for these two reasons.

Now suppose the price of a tape falls to $1. People now substitute blank tapes for compact discs and prerecorded tapes—the substitution effect. And with a budget that now has some slack from the lower price of tapes, people buy more tapes as well as more of other goods and services—the income effect. The quantity of tapes demanded increases for these two reasons.

Demand Curve and Demand Schedule

You are now about to study one of the two most used curves in economics, the demand curve. And you are going to encounter one of the most critical distinctions: the distinction between *demand* and *quantity demanded*.

The term **demand** refers to the entire relationship between the quantity demanded and the price of a good, and it is illustrated by the demand curve and the demand schedule. The term *quantity demanded* refers to a point on a demand curve—the quantity demanded at a particular price.

Figure 4.2 shows the demand curve for tapes. A **demand curve** shows the relationship between the quantity demanded of a good and its price when all other influences on consumers' planned purchases remain the same.

The table in Fig. 4.2 is the demand schedule for tapes. A *demand schedule* lists the quantities demanded at each different price when all the other influences on consumers' planned purchases—such as income, population, preferences, and future prices—remain the same. For example, if the price of a tape is $1, the quantity demanded is 9 million tapes a week. If the price of a tape is $5, the quantity demanded is 2 million tapes a week. The other rows of the table show the quantities demanded at prices of $2, $3, and $4.

We graph the demand schedule as a demand curve with the quantity demanded on the horizontal axis and the price on the vertical axis. The points on the demand curve labeled *a* through *e* represent the rows of the demand schedule. For example, point *a* on the graph represents a quantity demanded of 9 million tapes a week at a price of $1 a tape.

Willingness and Ability to Pay   Another way of looking at the demand curve is as a willingness-and-ability-to-pay curve. And the willingness-and-ability-to-pay is a measure of *marginal benefit.*

If a small quantity is available, the highest price that someone is willing and able to pay for one more unit is high. But as the quantity available increases, the marginal benefit of each additional unit falls and the highest price that someone is willing and able to pay for it also falls along the demand curve.

In Fig. 4.2, if 2 million tapes are available each week, the highest price that someone is willing to pay for the 2 millionth tape is $5. But if 9 million tapes are available each week, someone is willing to pay only $1 for the last tape bought.

FIGURE 4.2
The Demand Curve

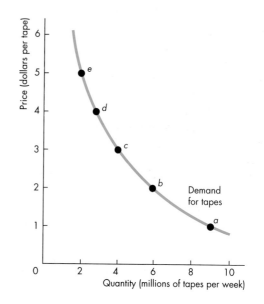

	Price (dollars per tape)	Quantity (millions of tapes per week)
a	1	9
b	2	6
c	3	4
d	4	3
e	5	2

The table shows a demand schedule listing the quantity of tapes demanded at each price if all other influences on buyers' plans remain the same. At a price of $1 a tape, 9 million tapes a week are demanded; at a price of $3 a tape, 4 million tapes a week are demanded. The demand curve shows the relationship between quantity demanded and price, everything else remaining the same.

The demand curve slopes downward: As price decreases, the quantity demanded increases. The demand curve can be read in two ways. For a given price, it tells us the quantity that people plan to buy. For example, at a price of $3 a tape, the quantity demanded is 4 million tapes a week. For a given quantity, the demand curve tells us the maximum price that consumers are willing and able to pay for the last tape available. For example, the maximum price that consumers will pay for the 6 millionth tape is $2.

A Change in Demand

When any factor that influences buying plans other than the price of the good changes, there is a **change in demand**. Figure 4.3 illustrates an increase in demand. When demand increases, the demand curve shifts rightward and the quantity demanded is greater at each and every price. For example, at a price of $5, on the original (blue) demand curve, the quantity demanded is 2 million tapes a week. On the new (red) demand curve, the quantity demanded is 6 million tapes a week. Look closely at the numbers in the table in Fig. 4.3 and check that the quantity demanded is higher at each price.

Let's look at the factors that bring a change in demand. There are five key factors to consider.

1. Prices of Related Goods   The quantity of tapes that consumers plan to buy depends in part on the prices of substitutes for tapes. A **substitute** is a good that can be used in place of another good. For example, a bus ride is a substitute for a train ride; a hamburger is a substitute for a hot dog, and a compact disc is a substitute for a tape. If the price of a substitute for a tape increases, people buy less of the substitute and more tapes. For example, if the price of a CD rises, people buy fewer CDs and more tapes. The demand for tapes increases.

The quantity of tapes that people plan to buy also depends on the prices of complements of tapes. A **complement** is a good that is used in conjunction with another good. Hamburgers and fries are complements. So are spaghetti and meat sauce, and so are tapes and Walkmans. If the price of a Walkman falls, people buy more Walkmans *and more tapes*. It is a fall in the price of a Walkman that increases the demand for tapes in Fig. 4.3.

2. Income   Another influence on demand is consumer income. When income increases, consumers buy more of most goods, and when income decreases, they buy less of most goods. Although an increase in income leads to an increase in the demand for *most* goods, it does not lead to an increase in the demand for *all* goods. A **normal good** is one for which demand increases as income increases. An **inferior good** is one for which demand decreases as income increases. Long-distance transportation has examples of both normal goods and inferior goods. As incomes increase, the demand for air travel (a normal good) increases and the demand for long-distance bus trips (an inferior good) decreases.

FIGURE 4.3

An Increase in Demand

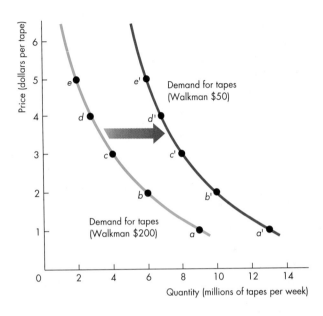

| Original demand schedule | | | New demand schedule | | |
Walkman $200			Walkman $50		
	Price (dollars per tape)	Quantity (millions of tapes per week)		Price (dollars per tape)	Quantity (millions of tapes per week)
a	1	9	a'	1	13
b	2	6	b'	2	10
c	3	4	c'	3	8
d	4	3	d'	4	7
e	5	2	e'	5	6

A change in any influence on buyers' plans other than the price of the good itself results in a new demand schedule and a shift of the demand curve. A change in the price of a Walkman changes the demand for tapes. At a price of $3 a tape (row c of the table), 4 million tapes a week are demanded when the Walkman costs $200 and 8 million tapes a week are demanded when the Walkman costs only $50. A *fall* in the price of a Walkman *increases* the demand for tapes because the Walkman is a complement of tapes. When demand *increases*, the demand curve shifts *rightward*, as shown by the shift arrow and the resulting red curve.

3. Population   Demand also depends on the size and the age structure of the population. The larger the population, the greater is the demand for all goods and services. And the smaller the population, the smaller is the demand for all goods and services.

For example, the demand for car parking spaces or movies or tapes or just about anything you can imagine is much greater in New York City (population 7.5 million) than it is in Boise City, Idaho (population 150,000).

Also, the larger the proportion of the population in a given age group, the greater is the demand for the types of goods and services used by that age group.

For example, in 1995, there were about 3.3 million 19-year-olds in the United States compared with almost 4 million in 1990. As a result, the demand for college places decreased during the 1990s. During these same years, the number of people living in the United States aged 85 years and over increased from 3 million in 1990 to 3.7 million. As a result, the demand for nursing home services increased.

4. Preferences   Demand depends on preferences. *Preferences* are an individual's attitudes toward goods and services. For example, a rock music fanatic has a much greater taste for tapes than does a tone-deaf workaholic. As a consequence, even if they have the same incomes, their demands for tapes will be very different.

5. Expected Future Prices   If the price of a good is expected to rise in the future and if the good can be stored, the opportunity cost of obtaining the good for future use is lower now than it will be when the price has increased. So people retime their purchase—they substitute over time. They buy more of the good now before its price is expected to rise (and less after), so the current demand for the good increases.

For example, suppose that Florida is hit by a severe frost that damages the season's orange crop. You expect the price of orange juice to soar. So, anticipating the higher price, you fill your freezer with enough frozen juice to get you through the next six months. Your current demand for frozen orange juice has increased (and your future demand has decreased).

Similarly, if the price of a good is expected to fall in the future, the opportunity cost of buying the good in the present is high relative to what it is expected to be in the future. So again, people retime their purchases. They buy less of the good now before its price is expected to fall (and more after), so the current demand for the good decreases.

TABLE 4.1
The Demand for Tapes

THE LAW OF DEMAND

The quantity of tapes demanded

Decreases if:	*Increases if:*
■ The price of a tape rises	■ The price of a tape falls

CHANGES IN DEMAND

The demand for tapes

Decreases if:	*Increases if:*
■ The price of a substitute falls	■ The price of a substitute rises
■ The price of a complement rises	■ The price of a complement falls
■ Income falls*	■ Income rises*
■ The population decreases	■ The population increases
■ The price of a tape is expected to fall in the future	■ The price of a tape is expected to rise in the future

*A tape is a normal good.

Computer prices are constantly falling, and this fact poses a dilemma. Will you buy a new computer now, in time for the start of the school year, or will you wait until the price has fallen some more? Because people expect computer prices to keep falling, the current demand for computers is less (the future demand is greater) than it otherwise would be.

Table 4.1 summarizes the influences on demand and the direction of those influences.

A Change in the Quantity Demanded Versus a Change in Demand

Changes in the factors that influence buyers' plans cause either a change in the quantity demanded or a change in demand. Equivalently, they cause either a movement along the demand curve or a shift of the demand curve.

The distinction between a change in the quantity demanded and a change in demand is the same as that between a movement along the demand curve and a shift of the demand curve.

change in quantity demanded = change in price
change in demand = change of other factors

A point on the demand curve shows the quantity demanded at a given price. So a movement along the demand curve shows a **change in the quantity demanded**. The entire demand curve shows demand. So a shift of the demand curve shows a **change in demand**. Figure 4.4 illustrates and summarizes these distinctions.

Movement Along the Demand Curve   If the price of a good changes but everything else remains the same, there is a movement along the demand curve. The negative slope of the demand curve reveals that a decrease in the price of a good or service increases the quantity demanded—the law of demand.

In Fig. 4.4, if the price of a good falls when everything else remains the same, the quantity demanded of that good increases and there is a movement down the demand curve D_0. If the price rises when everything else remains the same, the quantity demanded decreases and there is a movement up the demand curve D_0.

A Shift of the Demand Curve   If the price of a good remains constant but some other influence on buyers' plans changes, there is a change in demand for that good. We illustrate a change in demand as a shift of the demand curve. For example, a fall in the price of the Walkman—a complement of tapes—increases the demand for tapes. We illustrate this increase in the demand for tapes with a new demand schedule and a new demand curve. If the price of the Walkman falls, consumers buy more tapes regardless of whether the price of a tape is high or low. That is what a rightward shift of the demand curve shows—that more tapes are bought at each and every price.

In Fig. 4.4, when any influence on buyers' planned purchases changes, other than the price of the good, the demand curve shifts and there is a *change* (an increase or a decrease) *in demand*. A rise in income (for a normal good), in population, in the price of a substitute, or in the expected future price of the good or a fall in the price of a complement shifts the demand curve rightward (to the red demand curve D_1). This represents an *increase in demand*. A fall in income (for a normal good), in population, in the price of a substitute, or in the expected future price of the good or a rise in the price of a complement shifts the demand curve leftward (to the red demand curve D_2). This represents a *decrease in demand*. (For an inferior good, the effects of changes in income are in the direction opposite to those described above.)

FIGURE 4.4

A Change in the Quantity Demanded Versus a Change in Demand

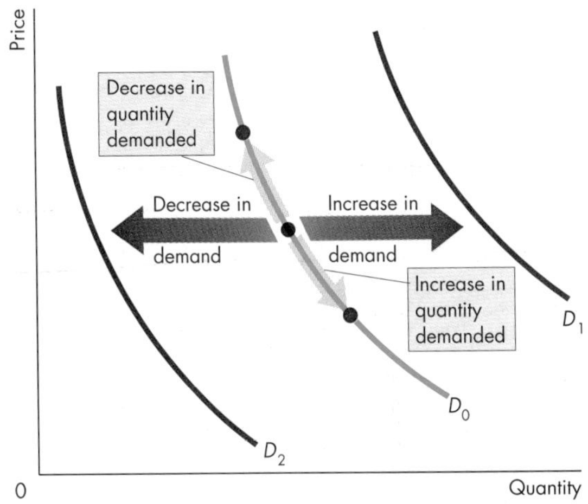

When the price of the good changes, there is a movement along the demand curve and a *change in the quantity demanded*, shown by the blue arrows on demand curve D_0. When any other influence on buying plans changes, there is a shift of the demand curve and a *change in demand*. An increase in demand shifts the demand curve rightward (from D_0 to D_1). A decrease in demand shifts the demand curve leftward (from D_0 to D_2).

R E V I E W

- The quantity demanded is the amount of a good that consumers plan to buy during a given period of time at a particular price. Other things remaining the same, the quantity demanded increases as price decreases.
- Demand is the relationship between quantity demanded and price, other things remaining the same.
- When the price of the good changes and all other influences on buying plans remain the same, there is a change in the quantity demanded and a movement along the demand curve.
- When any influence on buying plans other than the price of the good changes, there is a change in demand and a shift of the demand curve.

Supply

IF A FIRM SUPPLIES A GOOD OR SERVICE, THE FIRM

- Has the resources and technology to produce it,
- Can profit from producing it, and
- Has made a definite plan to produce it and sell it.

A supply is more that just having the *resources* and the *technology* to produce something. *Resources and technology* are the constraints that limit what is possible.

Many useful things can be produced, but they are not produced unless it is profitable to do so. Supply reflects a decision about which technologically feasible items to produce.

The **quantity supplied** of a good or service is the amount that producers plan to sell during a given time period at a particular price. The quantity supplied is not necessarily the same amount as the quantity actually sold. Sometimes the quantity supplied is greater than the quantity demanded, so the quantity bought is less than the quantity supplied.

Like the quantity demanded, the quantity supplied is measured as an amount per unit of time. For example, suppose that GM produces 1,000 cars a day. The quantity of cars supplied by GM can be expressed as 1,000 a day or 7,000 a week or 365,000 a year. Without the time dimension, we cannot tell whether a particular number is large or small.

What Determines Selling Plans?

The amount of any particular good or service that producers plan to sell depends on many factors. The main ones are:

- The price of the good
- The prices of resources used to produce the good
- Technology
- The number of suppliers
- The prices of related goods produced
- Expected future prices

Let's first look at the relationship between the price of a good and the quantity supplied. To study this relationship, we hold constant all the other influences on the quantity supplied. We ask: How does the quantity supplied of a good vary as its price varies?

The Law of Supply

The law of supply states:

Other things remaining the same, the higher the price of a good, the greater is the quantity supplied.

Why does a higher price increase the quantity supplied? It is because of *increasing marginal cost*. As the quantity produced of any good increases, the marginal cost of producing the good increases. (You can refresh your memory of increasing marginal cost in Chapter 3, p. 46.)

It is never worth producing a good if the price received for it does not at least cover marginal cost. So when the price of a good rises, other things remaining the same, producers are willing to incur the higher marginal cost and increase production. The higher price brings forth an increase in the quantity supplied.

Let's now illustrate the law of supply with a supply curve and a supply schedule.

Supply Curve and Supply Schedule

You are now going to study the second of the two most used curves in economics, the supply curve. And you're going to learn about the critical distinction between *supply* and *quantity supplied*.

The term **supply** refers to the entire relationship between the quantity supplied and the price of a good, and it is illustrated by the supply curve and the supply schedule. The term *quantity supplied* refers to a point on a supply curve—the quantity supplied at a particular price.

Figure 4.5 shows the supply curve of tapes. A **supply curve** shows the relationship between the quantity supplied of a good and its price when all other influences on producers' planned sales remain the same. It is a graph of a supply schedule.

The table in Fig. 4.5 sets out the supply schedule for tapes. A *supply schedule* lists the quantities supplied at each different price when all the other influences on producers' planned sales remain the same. For example, if the price of a tape is $1, the quantity supplied is zero—on row *a* of the table. If the price of a tape is $2, the quantity supplied is 3 million tapes a week—on row *b*. The other rows of the table show the quantities supplied at prices of $3, $4, and $5.

Why is it that when people are buying less, producers supply more??

FIGURE 4.5
The Supply Curve

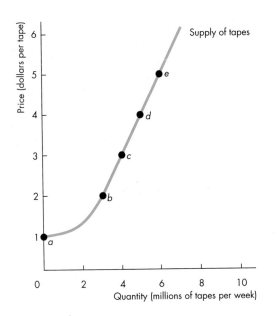

The table shows the supply schedule of tapes. For example, at $2 a tape, 3 million tapes a week are supplied; at $5 a tape, 6 million tapes a week are supplied. The supply curve shows the relationship between the quantity supplied and price, everything else remaining the same. The supply curve usually slopes upward: As the price of a good increases, so does the quantity supplied.

A supply curve can be read in two ways. For a given price, its tells us the quantity that producers plan to sell. And for a given quantity, it tells us the minimum price that producers are willing to accept for that quantity.

	Price (dollars per tape)	Quantity (millions of tapes per week)
a	1	0
b	2	3
c	3	4
d	4	5
e	5	6

To make a supply curve, we graph the quantity supplied on the horizontal axis and the price on the vertical axis, just as in the case of the demand curve. The points on the supply curve labeled *a* through *e* represent the rows of the supply schedule. For example, point *a* on the graph represents a quantity supplied of zero at a price of $1 a tape.

Minimum Supply Price Just as the demand curve has two interpretations, so too does the supply curve. The demand curve can be interpreted as a willingness-and-ability-to-pay curve. The supply curve can be interpreted as a minimum-supply-price curve. It tells us the lowest price at which someone can profitably sell another unit.

If a small quantity is produced, the lowest price at which someone can profitably sell one more unit is low. But if a large quantity is produced, the lowest price at which someone can profitably sell one more unit is high. *How about McDonalds vs. Trotters?*

In Fig. 4.5, if 6 million tapes are produced each week, the lowest price that a producer is willing to accept for the 6 millionth tape is $5. But if only 4 million tapes are produced each week, the lowest price that a producer is willing to accept for the 4 millionth tape is $3.

A Change in Supply

When any factor that influences selling plans other than the price of the good changes, there is a **change in supply**. Let's look at the five key factors that change supply.

1. Prices of Productive Resources The prices of productive resources influence supply. The easiest way to see this influence is to think about the supply curve as a minimum-supply-price curve. If the prices of productive resources rise, the lowest price a producer is willing to accept rises so supply decreases. For example, during 1996, the price of jet fuel increased and the supply of air transportation decreased. Similarly, a rise in the minimum wage decreased the supply of hamburgers. If the wages of tape producers rise, the supply of tapes decreases. *But doesn't price affect supply??*

2. Technology Advances in technology are the single biggest influence on supply. New technologies create new products and lower the costs of producing existing products. As a result, they change supply. For example, the development of a new technology for tape production by Sony and Minnesota Mining and Manufacturing (3M) has lowered the cost of producing tapes and increased the supply of tapes.

3. The Number of Suppliers   Supply also depends on the number of suppliers. The larger the number of firms that produce a good, the greater is the supply of the good. As firms enter an industry, the supply in that industry increases. As firms leave an industry, the supply in that industry decreases. For example, over the past two years, there has been a huge increase in the number of firms that produce and manage World Wide Web sites. As a result, the supply of Internet and World Wide Web services has increased enormously.

4. Prices of Related Goods Produced   The prices of related goods and services that firms produce influence supply. For example, if the price of prerecorded tapes rises, the supply of blank tapes decreases. Blank tapes and prerecorded tapes are *substitutes in production*—goods that can be produced by using the same resources. If the price of beef rises, the supply of cowhide increases. Beef and cowhide are *complements in production*—goods that must be produced together.

5. Expected Future Prices   If the price of a good is expected to rise, the return from selling the good in the future is higher than it is in the present. So the current supply decreases.

Figure 4.6 illustrates an increase in supply. When supply increases, the supply curve shifts rightward and the quantity supplied is larger at each and every price. For example, at a price of $2, on the original (blue) supply curve, the quantity supplied is 3 million tapes a week. On the new (red) supply curve, the quantity supplied is 6 million tapes a week. Look closely at the numbers in the table in Fig. 4.6 and check that the quantity supplied is larger at each price.

Table 4.2 summarizes the influences on supply and the directions of those influences.

A Change in the Quantity Supplied Versus a Change in Supply

Changes in the factors that influence producers' planned sales cause either a change in the quantity supplied or a change in supply. Equivalently, they cause either a movement along the supply curve or a shift of the supply curve.

A point on the supply curve shows the quantity supplied at a given price. So a movement along the

FIGURE 4.6

An Increase in Supply

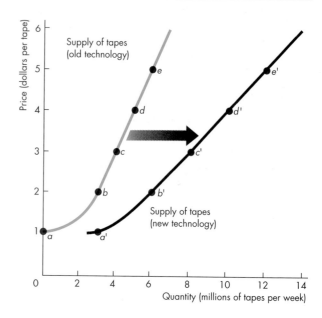

Original supply schedule Old technology			New supply schedule New technology		
	Price (dollars per tape)	Quantity (millions of tapes per week)		Price (dollars per tape)	Quantity (millions of tapes per week)
a	1	0	a'	1	3
b	2	3	b'	2	6
c	3	4	c'	3	8
d	4	5	d'	4	10
e	5	6	e'	5	12

A change in any influence on sellers' plans other than the price of the good itself results in a new supply schedule and a shift of the supply curve. For example, if Sony and 3M invent a new, cost-saving technology for producing tapes, the supply of tapes changes.

At a price of $3 a tape, 4 million tapes a week are supplied when producers use the old technology (row c of the table) and 8 million tapes a week are supplied when producers use the new technology. An advance in technology *increases* the supply of tapes and shifts the supply curve *rightward*, as shown by the shift arrow and the resulting red curve.

supply curve shows a **change in the quantity supplied**. The entire supply curve shows supply. So a shift of the supply curve shows a **change in supply**.

Figure 4.7 illustrates and summarizes these distinctions. If the price of a good falls and everything else remains the same, the quantity supplied of that good decreases and there is a movement down the supply curve S_0. If the price of a good rises and everything else remains the same, the quantity supplied increases and there is a movement up the supply curve S_0. When any other influence on selling plans changes, the supply curve shifts and there is a change in supply. If the supply curve is S_0 and if production costs fall supply increases and the supply curve shifts to the red supply curve S_1. If production costs rise, supply decreases and the supply curve shifts to the red supply curve S_2.

FIGURE 4.7

A Change in the Quantity Supplied Versus a Change in Supply

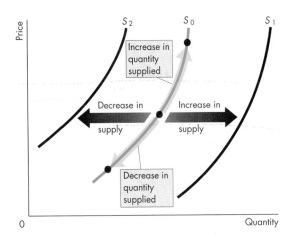

When the price of the good changes, there is a movement along the supply curve and a *change in the quantity supplied*, shown by the blue arrows on supply curve S_0. When any other influence on selling plans changes, there is a shift of the supply curve and a *change in supply*. An increase in supply shifts the supply curve rightward (from S_0 to S_1). A decrease in supply shifts the supply curve shifts leftward (from S_0 to S_2).

TABLE 4.2

The Supply of Tapes

THE LAW OF SUPPLY

The quantity of tapes supplied

Decreases if:	*Increases if:*
■ The price of a tape falls	■ The price of a tape rises

CHANGES IN SUPPLY

The supply of tapes

Decreases if:	*Increases if:*
■ The price of a resource used to produce tapes rises	■ The price of a resource used to produce tapes falls
	■ More efficient technologies for producing tapes are discovered
■ The number of tape producers decreases	■ The number of tape producers increases
■ The price of a substitute in production rises	■ The price of a substitute in production falls
■ The price of a complement in production falls	■ The price of a complement in production rises
■ The price of a tape is expected to rise in the future	■ The price of a tape is expected to fall in the future

R E V I E W

■ The quantity supplied is the amount of a good that producers plan to sell during a given period at a given price. Other things remaining the same, the quantity supplied increases as price increases.

■ Supply is the relationship between quantity supplied and price, other things remaining the same.

■ When the price of the good changes, other things remaining the same, there is a change in the quantity supplied and a movement along the supply curve.

■ Changes in other influences on selling plans change supply and shift the supply curve.

Let's now bring demand and supply together and see how prices and quantities are determined.

Market Equilibrium

WE HAVE SEEN THAT WHEN THE PRICE OF A good rises, the quantity demanded *decreases* and the quantity supplied *increases*. We are now going to see how prices coordinate the plans of buyers and sellers and achieve an equilibrium.

An *equilibrium* is a situation in which opposing forces balance each other. Equilibrium in a market occurs when the price balances the plans of buyers and sellers. The **equilibrium price** is the price at which the quantity demanded equals the quantity supplied. The **equilibrium quantity** is the quantity bought and sold at the equilibrium price. A market moves toward its equilibrium because:

■ Price regulates buying and selling plans
■ Price adjusts when plans don't match

Price as a Regulator

The price of a good regulates the quantities demanded and supplied. If the price is too high, the quantity supplied exceeds the quantity demanded. If the price is too low, the quantity demanded exceeds the quantity supplied. There is one price at which the quantity demanded equals the quantity supplied. Let's work out what that price is.

Figure 4.8 shows the market for tapes. The table shows the demand schedule (from Fig. 4.2) and the supply schedule (from Fig. 4.5). If the price of a tape is $1, the quantity demanded is 9 million tapes a week, but no tapes are supplied. The quantity demanded exceeds the quantity supplied by 9 million tapes a week. In other words, at a price of $1 a tape, there is a shortage of 9 million tapes a week. This shortage is shown in the final column of the table. At a price of $2 a tape, there is still a shortage, but only of 3 million tapes a week. If the price of a tape is $5, the quantity supplied exceeds the quantity demanded. The quantity supplied is 6 million tapes a week, but the quantity demanded is only 2 million. There is a surplus of 4 million tapes a week. The one price at which there is neither a shortage nor a surplus is $3 a tape. At that price, the quantity demanded is equal to the quantity supplied: 4 million tapes a week. The equilibrium price is $3 a tape, and the equilibrium quantity is 4 million tapes a week.

Figure 4.8 shows that the demand curve and supply curve intersect at the equilibrium price of $3 a

FIGURE 4.8
Equilibrium

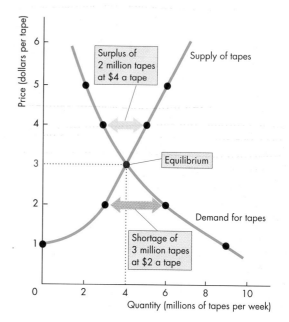

Price (dollars per tape)	Quantity demanded	Quantity supplied	Shortage (–) or surplus (+)
	(millions of tapes per week)		
1	9	0	–9
2	6	3	–3
3	4	4	0
4	3	5	+2
5	2	6	+4

The table lists the quantities demanded and quantities supplied as well as the shortage or surplus of tapes at each price. If the price is $2 a tape, 6 million tapes a week are demanded and 3 million are supplied. There is a shortage of 3 million tapes a week, and the price rises. If the price is $4 a tape, 3 million tapes a week are demanded and 5 million are supplied. There is a surplus of 2 million tapes a week, and the price falls. If the price is $3 a tape, 4 million tapes a week are demanded and 4 million are supplied. There is neither a shortage nor a surplus. Neither buyers nor sellers have any incentive to change the price. The price at which the quantity demanded equals the quantity supplied is the equilibrium price.

tape. At each price *above* $3 a tape, there is a surplus of tapes. For example, at $4 a tape, the surplus is 2 million tapes a week, as shown by the blue arrow. At each price *below* $3 a tape, there is a shortage of tapes. For example, at $2 a tape, the shortage is 3 million tapes a week, as shown by the red arrow.

Price Adjustments

You've seen that if the price is below equilibrium there is shortage and if the price is above equilibrium there is a surplus. But can we count on the price to change and eliminate a shortage or surplus? We can, because such price changes are mutually beneficial to both buyers and sellers. Let's see why the price changes when there is a shortage or a surplus.

A Shortage Forces the Price Up   Suppose the price of a tape is $2. Consumers plan to buy 6 million tapes a week, and producers plan to sell 3 million tapes a week. Consumers can't force producers to sell more than they plan, so the quantity actually offered for sale is 3 million tapes a week. In this situation, powerful forces operate to increase the price and move it toward the equilibrium price. Some producers, noticing lines of unsatisfied consumers, move their prices up. Some producers increase their output. As producers push their prices up, the price rises toward its equilibrium. The rising price reduces the shortage because it decreases the quantity demanded and increases the quantity supplied. When the price has increased to the point at which there is no longer a shortage, the forces moving the price stop operating and the price comes to rest at its equilibrium.

A Surplus Forces the Price Down   Suppose the price of a tape is $4. Producers plan to sell 5 million tapes a week, and consumers plan to buy 3 million tapes a week. Producers cannot force consumers to buy more than they plan, so the quantity that is actually bought is 3 million tapes a week. In this situation, powerful forces operate to lower the price and move it toward the equilibrium price. Some producers, unable to sell the quantities of tapes they planned to sell, cut their prices. In addition, some producers scale back production. As producers cut prices, the price falls toward its equilibrium. The falling price decreases the surplus because it increases the quantity demanded and decreases the quantity supplied. When the price has fallen to the point at which there is no longer a surplus, the forces moving the price

stop operating, and the price comes to rest at its equilibrium.

The Best Deal Available for Buyers and Sellers
When the price is below equilibrium, it is forced upward toward the equilibrium. Why don't buyers resist the increase and refuse to buy at the higher price? Because they value the good more highly than the current price and they cannot satisfy all their demands at the current price. In some markets—an example is the market for rental accommodation in Atlanta during the 1996 Olympic Games—the buyers might even be the ones who force the price upward by offering higher prices to divert the limited quantities away from other buyers.

When the price is above equilibrium, it is bid downward toward the equilibrium. Why don't sellers resist this decrease and refuse to sell at the lower price? Because their minimum supply price is below the current price and they cannot sell all they would like to at the current price. Normally, it is the sellers who force the price downward by offering lower prices to gain market share from their competitors.

At the price at which the quantity demanded and the quantity supplied are equal, neither buyers nor sellers can do business at a better price. Buyers pay the highest price they are willing to pay for the last unit bought, and sellers receive the lowest price at which they are willing to supply the last unit sold.

When people freely make offers to buy and sell, and when demanders try to buy at the lowest possible price and suppliers try to sell at the highest possible price, the price at which trade takes place is the equilibrium price—the price at which the quantity demanded equals the quantity supplied. The price coordinates the plans of buyers and sellers.

R E V I E W

■ The equilibrium price is the price at which buyers' and sellers' plans match each other—the price at which the quantity demanded equals the quantity supplied.

■ At prices below the equilibrium price, there is a shortage and the price rises.

■ At prices above the equilibrium price, there is a surplus and the price falls.

■ Only at the equilibrium price are there no forces acting on the price to make it change.

change in demand ⟹ change in quantity supplied

Predicting Changes in Price and Quantity

THE DEMAND AND SUPPLY THEORY WE HAVE JUST studied provides us with a powerful way of analyzing influences on prices and the quantities bought and sold. According to the theory, a change in price stems from either a change in demand or a change in supply or a change in both. Let's look first at the effects of a change in demand.

A Change in Demand

What happens to the price and quantity of tapes if the demand for tapes increases? We can answer this question with a specific example. Suppose the price of a Walkman falls from $200 to $50. Because the Walkman and tapes are complements, the demand for tapes increases, as is shown in the table in Fig. 4.9. The original demand schedule and the new one are set out in the first three columns of the table. The table also shows the supply schedule for tapes.

The original equilibrium price is $3 a tape. At that price, 4 million tapes a week are demanded and supplied. When demand increases, the price that makes the quantity demanded equal the quantity supplied is $5 a tape. At this price, 6 million tapes are bought and sold each week. When demand increases, both the price and the quantity increase.

Figure 4.9 shows these changes. The figure shows the original demand for and supply of tapes. The original equilibrium price is $3 a tape, and the quantity is 4 million tapes a week. When demand increases, the demand curve shifts rightward. The equilibrium price rises to $5 a tape, and the quantity supplied increases to 6 million tapes a week, as highlighted in the figure. There is an *increase in the quantity supplied* but *no change in supply*—a movement along, but no shift of, the supply curve.

We can reverse the exercise that we've just conducted. We can work out what happens if we start at a price of $5 a tape with 6 million tapes a week being bought and sold and then demand decreases to its original level. Such a decrease in demand might arise from a fall in the price of CDs or CD players (both substitutes for tapes). The decrease in demand shifts the demand curve leftward. The equilibrium price falls to $3 a tape, and the equilibrium quantity decreases to 4 million tapes a week.

FIGURE 4.9

The Effects of a Change in Demand

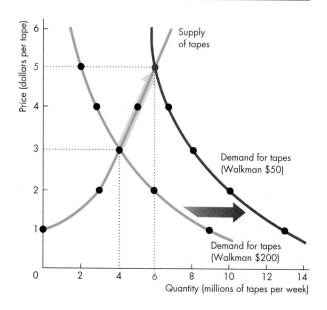

Price (dollars per tape)	Quantity demanded (millions of tapes per week)		Quantity supplied (millions of tapes per week)
	Walkman $200	Walkman $50	
1	9	13	0
2	6	10	3
3	4	8	4
4	3	7	5
5	2	6	6

With the price of a Walkman at $200, the demand for tapes is the blue curve. The equilibrium price is $3 a tape, and the equilibrium quantity is 4 million tapes a week. When the price of a Walkman falls from $200 to $50, the demand for tapes increases and the demand curve shifts rightward to become the red curve.

At $3 a tape, there is now a shortage of 4 million tapes a week. The price of a tape rises to a new equilibrium of $5 a tape. As the price rises to $5, the quantity supplied increases—shown by the blue arrow on the supply curve—to the new equilibrium quantity of 6 million tapes a week. Following an increase in demand, the quantity supplied increases but supply does not change—the supply curve does not shift.

← and vice versa

We can now make our first two predictions:

- When demand increases, both the price and the quantity increase.

- When demand decreases, both the price and the quantity decrease.

A Change in Supply

Suppose that Sony and 3M introduce a new cost-saving technology in their tape production plants. The new technology increases the supply of tapes. The new supply schedule (the same one that was shown in Fig. 4.6) is presented in the table in Fig. 4.10. What are the new equilibrium price and quantity? The answer is highlighted in the table: The price falls to $2 a tape, and the quantity increases to 6 million a week. You can see why by looking at the quantities demanded and supplied at the old price of $3 a tape. The quantity supplied at that price is 8 million tapes a week, and there is a surplus of tapes. The price falls. Only when the price is $2 a tape does the quantity supplied equal the quantity demanded.

Figure 4.10 illustrates the effect of an increase in supply. It shows the demand curve for tapes and the original and new supply curves. The initial equilibrium price is $3 a tape and the quantity is 4 million tapes a week. When the supply increases, the supply curve shifts rightward. The equilibrium price falls to $2 a tape, and the quantity demanded increases to 6 million tapes a week, highlighted in the figure. There is an *increase in the quantity demanded* but *no change in demand*—a movement along, but no shift of, the demand curve.

The exercise that we've just conducted can be reversed. If we start out at a price of $2 a tape with 6 million tapes a week being bought and sold, we can work out what happens if supply decreases to its original level. Such a decrease in supply might arise from an increase in the cost of labor or raw materials. The decrease in supply shifts the supply curve leftward. The equilibrium price rises to $3 a tape, and the equilibrium quantity decreases to 4 million tapes a week.

We can now make two more predictions:

- When supply increases, the quantity increases and the price falls.

- When supply decreases, the quantity decreases and the price rises.

FIGURE **4.10**

The Effects of a Change in Supply

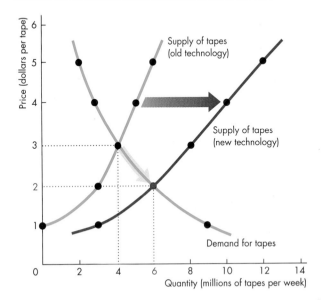

Price		Quantity supplied (millions of tapes per week)	
(dollars per tape)	Quantity demanded (millions of tapes per week)	old technology	new technology
1	9	0	3
2	6	3	6
3	4	4	8
4	3	5	10
5	2	6	12

With the old technology, the supply of tapes is shown by the blue supply curve. The equilibrium price is $3 a tape, and the equilibrium quantity is 4 million tapes a week. When the new technology is adopted, the supply of tapes increases and the supply curve shifts rightward to become the red curve.

At $3 a tape, there is now a surplus of 4 million tapes a week. The price of a tape falls to a new equilibrium of $2 a tape. As the price falls to $2, the quantity demanded increases—shown by the blue arrow on the demand curve—to the new equilibrium quantity of 6 million tapes a week. Following an increase in supply, the quantity demanded increases but demand does not change—the demand curve does not shift.

A Change in Both Demand and Supply

You can now predict the effects of a change in either demand or supply on the price and the quantity. But what happens if *both* demand and supply change together? To answer this question, we look first at the case in which demand and supply move in the same direction—either both increase or both decrease. Then we look at the case in which they move in opposite directions—demand decreases and supply increases or demand increases and supply decreases.

Demand and Supply Change in the Same Direction   We've seen that an increase in the demand for tapes increases the price of tapes and increases the quantity bought and sold. And we've seen that an increase in the supply of tapes lowers the price of tapes and increases the quantity bought and sold. Let's now examine what happens when both of these changes occur together.

The table in Fig. 4.11 brings together the numbers that describe the original quantities demanded and supplied and the new quantities demanded and supplied after the fall in the price of the Walkman and the improved tape production technology. These same numbers are illustrated in the graph. The original (blue) demand and supply curves intersect at a price of $3 a tape and a quantity of 4 million tapes a week. The new (red) supply and demand curves also intersect at a price of $3 a tape but at a quantity of 8 million tapes a week.

An increase in either demand or supply increases the quantity. So when both demand and supply increase, so does quantity.

An increase in demand raises the price, and an increase in supply lowers the price, so we can't say whether the price will rise or fall when demand and supply increase together. In this example, the price does not change. But notice that if demand increases by slightly more than the amount shown in the figure, the price will rise. And if supply increases by slightly more than the amount shown in the figure, the price will fall.

We can now make two more predictions:

■ When *both* demand and supply increase, the quantity increases and the price increases, decreases, or remains constant.

■ When *both* demand and supply decrease, the quantity decreases and the price increases, decreases, or remains constant.

FIGURE 4.11

The Effects of an Increase in Both Demand and Supply

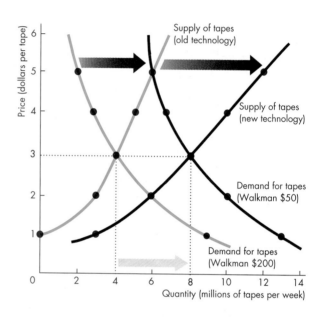

	Original quantities (millions of tapes per week)		New quantities (millions of tapes per week)	
Price (dollars per tape)	**Quantity demanded** Walkman $200	**Quantity supplied** old technology	**Quantity demanded** Walkman $50	**Quantity supplied** new technology
1	9	0	13	3
2	6	3	10	6
3	**4**	**4**	**8**	**8**
4	3	5	7	10
5	2	6	6	12

When a Walkman costs $200 and the old technology is used to produce tapes, the price of a tape is $3 and the quantity is 4 million tapes a week. A fall in the price of a Walkman increases the demand for tapes, and improved technology increases the supply of tapes. The new supply curve intersects the new demand curve at $3 a tape, the same price as before, but the quantity increases to 8 million tapes a week. These increases in demand and supply increase the quantity but leave the price unchanged.

Demand and Supply Change in Opposite Directions

Let's now see what happens when demand and supply change together but move in *opposite* directions. An improved production technology increases the supply of tapes as before. But now the price of CD players falls. A CD player is a *substitute* for tapes. With less costly CD players, more people buy them and switch from buying tapes to buying discs, and the demand for tapes decreases.

The table in Fig. 4.12 describes the original and new demand and supply schedules. These schedules are shown as the original (blue) and new (red) demand and supply curves in the graph. The original demand and supply curves intersect at a price of $5 a tape and a quantity of 6 million tapes a week. The new supply and demand curves intersect at a price of $2 a tape and at the original quantity of 6 million tapes a week.

A decrease in demand or an increase in supply lowers the price. So when a decrease in demand and an increase in supply occur together, the price falls.

A decrease in demand decreases the quantity, and an increase in supply increases the quantity, so we can't say for sure which way the quantity will change when demand decreases and supply increases at the same time. In this example, the decrease in demand and the increase in supply are such that the increase in quantity brought about by an increase in supply is offset by the decrease in quantity brought about by a decrease in demand—so the quantity does not change. But notice that if demand had decreased slightly more than shown in the figure, the quantity would have decreased. And if supply had increased by slightly more than shown in the figure, the quantity would have increased.

We can now make two more predictions:

■ When demand decreases and supply increases, the price falls and the quantity increases, decreases, or remains constant.

■ When demand increases and supply decreases, the price rises and the quantity increases, decreases, or remains constant.

Make Your Own Summary Figure

You've now seen the eight combinations of changes in demand and supply, each on its own and both together. Problem 6 on p. 90 invites you to review the predictions for each case. Don't skip this problem. And make your own summary figure for each case. There is no good substitute for drawing your own figures and becoming thoroughly familiar with these eight predictions.

FIGURE 4.12

The Effects of a Decrease in Demand and an Increase in Supply

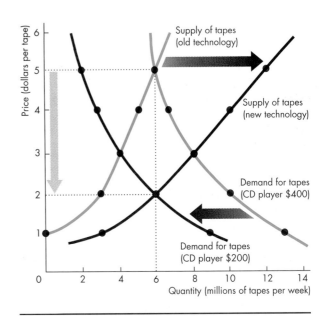

	Original quantities (millions of tapes per week)		**New quantities** (millions of tapes per week)	
Price (dollars per tape)	**Quantity demanded** CD player $400	**Quantity supplied** old technology	**Quantity demanded** CD player $200	**Quantity supplied** new technology
1	13	0	9	3
2	10	3	6	6
3	8	4	4	8
4	7	5	3	10
5	6	6	2	12

When a CD player costs $400 and the old technology is used to produce tapes, the price of a tape is $5 and the quantity is 6 million tapes a week. A fall in the price of a CD player decreases the demand for tapes, and improved technology increases the supply of tapes. The new supply curve intersects the new demand curve at $2 a tape, a lower price, but in this case the quantity remains constant at 6 million tapes a week. The decrease in demand and increase in supply lower the price but leave the quantity unchanged.

CD Players, Health Care, and Bananas

Earlier in this chapter, we looked at some facts about prices and quantities of CD players, health care, and bananas. Let's use the theory of demand and supply that we have just studied to explain the movements in the prices and quantities of those goods.

A Price Slide: CD Players   Figure 4.13(a) shows the market for CD players. In 1983, when CD players were first manufactured, very few producers made them and the supply was small. The supply curve was S_0. In 1983, there weren't many titles on CDs and the demand for CD players was small. The demand curve was D_0. The quantities supplied and demanded in 1983 were equal at Q_0, and the price was $1,100 (1994 dollars). As the technology for making CD players improved and as more and more factories began to produce CD players, the supply increased by a large amount and the supply curve shifted rightward from S_0 to S_1. At the same time, increases in incomes, a decrease in the price of CDs, and an increase in the number of titles on CDs increased the demand for CD players. But the increase in demand was much smaller than the increase in supply. The demand curve shifted rightward from D_0 to D_1. With the new demand curve D_1 and the new supply curve S_1, the equilibrium price fell to $170 in 1994 and the quantity increased to Q_1. The large increase in supply combined with a smaller increase in demand resulted in an increase in the quantity of CD players and a dramatic fall in the price. Figure 4.13(a) shows the CD player price slide.

A Price Rocket: Health Care   Figure 4.13(b) shows the market for health-care services. In 1980, the supply curve for health-care services was S_0. Advances in medical technology have greatly increased the range and complexity of conditions that can be treated and have increased the supply of health-care services. But large increases in doctors' compensation and costs have escalated the cost of providing health care and have decreased supply. The net change in supply resulting from these two opposing forces has been an increase. The supply curve has shifted rightward from S_0 to S_1. At the same time that supply increased by a relatively modest amount, the demand for health care increased enormously. Some of the increase resulted from higher incomes, some from an aging population, and some from a demand for newly available treatments. The combination of these

influences on demand resulted in the demand curve shifting from D_0 to D_1. The combined effect of a large increase in demand and a small increase in supply was an increase in the quantity from Q_0 to Q_1 and an increase in price from 100 (an index number) in 1980 to 160 in 1995. Figure 4.13(b) shows the health-care price rocket.

A Price Roller Coaster: Bananas   Figure 4.13(c) shows the market for bananas. The demand for bananas—curve D—does not change much over the years. But the supply of bananas, which depends mainly on the weather, fluctuates between S_0 and S_1. With good growing conditions, the supply curve is S_1. With bad growing conditions, supply decreases and the supply curve is S_0. As a consequence of fluctuations in supply, the quantity fluctuates between Q_0 and Q_1. The price of bananas fluctuates between 33 cents per pound (1995 cents), the maximum price, and 20 cents per pound, the minimum price. Figure 4.13(c) shows the banana price roller coaster.

The Invisible Hand   Adam Smith said that each buyer and seller in a market "is led by an invisible hand to promote an end which was no part of his intention." What did he mean? He meant that when each one of us makes decisions to buy or sell to achieve the best outcome for ourselves and when our decisions are coordinated in free markets, we end up achieving the best outcome for everyone.

Although markets are amazing instruments, it turns out that they do not always work quite as perfectly as Adam Smith imagined. If you go on to study *micro*economics, you will discover the conditions under which markets are efficient and why they sometimes fail to achieve the best possible outcome for everyone. If you go on to study *macro*economics, you will discover the reasons why the market economy produces fluctuations in output and employment and sometimes creates persistent unemployment.

◆ You now know the basic theory of demand and supply. By using this theory, you can explain past fluctuations in prices and quantities and also make predictions about future fluctuations. *Reading Between the Lines* on pp. 86-87 shows you the theory in action in the world price of wheat and in the U.S. price of bread in 1996. You will see lots of news articles about this type of issue. Watch for stories on frosts in Brazil and the price of coffee or frost in Florida and the price of orange juice.

FIGURE 4.13

Price Slide, Rocket, and Roller Coaster

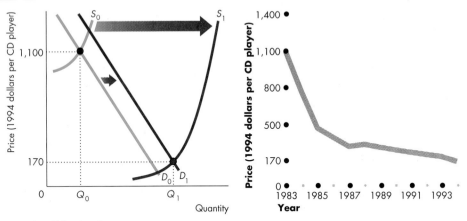

(a) Price slide: CD players

A large increase in the supply of CD players, from S_0 to S_1 combined with a small increase in demand, from D_0 to D_1, resulted in an increase in the quantity of CD players bought and sold from Q_0 to Q_1. The average price of CD players fell from $1,100 in 1983 to $170 in 1994—a price slide.

Source: U.S. Bureau of the Census, Statistical Abstract of the United States: 1994 (114th edition.) Washington, D.C., 1994.

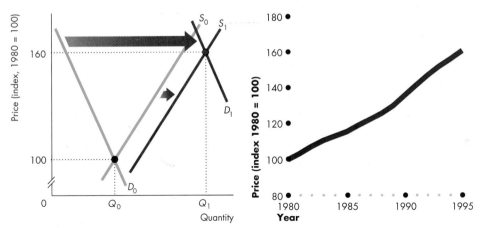

(b) Price rocket: health care

A large increase in demand for health care, from D_0 to D_1, combined with a small increase in the supply, from S_0 to S_1, has resulted in an increase in the quantity of health care, from Q_0 to Q_1 and a rise in the price of health care from 100 in 1980 to 160 in 1995—a price rocket.

Source: Economic Report of the President, 1996.

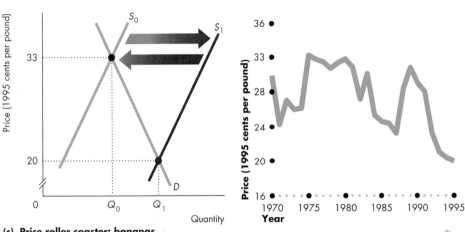

(c) Price roller coaster: bananas

The demand for bananas remains constant at D. But supply fluctuates between S_0 and S_1. As a result, the price of bananas has fluctuated between 20 cents per pound and 33 cents per pound—a price roller coaster.

Source: International Financial Statistics Yearbook, International Monetary Fund, Washington, D.C., 1996.

Demand and Supply: The Price of Bread

RALEIGH NEWS OBSERVER, JUNE 28, 1996

It Takes a Lot of Bread to Buy a Loaf

BY DUDLEY PRICE

... Record wheat prices this spring are finding their way to grocery stores, where shoppers are paying more for bread than almost anyone can remember. ...

Bob Dirkes, senior vice president for marketing for Interstate Brands Corp. of Kansas City, Mo., says it's the biggest increase in 15 years. "The increase in the cost of flour is primarily what's causing that."

Bakers and grocery chains say they tried to keep prices down despite rising wheat and flour costs during the past two years. But now, they are passing along those costs to the consumers.

Nationally, bread prices in May were 8 percent higher than they were a year ago, Dirkes said. ...

A loaf of Sunbeam bread, for example, now costs $1.63, up 42 percent from $1.19 a year ago, said David Colling, a company route salesman in Raleigh. ... Bakery owners and agriculture experts say further declines predicted for this year's wheat harvest probably will lead to even higher prices. ...

Bob Murphy, chief statistician for the state Department of Agriculture, said farmers in the nation's largest wheat-producing states—Kansas, Texas and Oklahoma—weren't spared by droughts that cut the nation's other grain crops. ...

Wheat farmers have seen production decline every year since 1994, when 1.66 billion bushels were harvested, Murphy said.

This year's harvest is expected to be 1.37 billion bushels, a 17 percent decline in just two years.

As a result, wheat and flour prices have increased. A bushel of wheat that Wednesday sold for $5.93 on the Kansas City exchange cost $5.06 just a year ago.

Although the higher cost of wheat is the primary reason bread prices have risen, Dirkes said, high prices at the gas pumps also play a role in higher food costs. ... "Thirty-five percent of the cost of a loaf of bread is the cost of getting it from the bakery to the grocery store."

Reprinted with permission.

Essence of THE STORY

■ Between mid-1995 and mid-1996, the price of bread increased from $1.19 to $1.63 a loaf and the price of wheat increased from $5.06 to $5.93 a bushel.

■ Droughts decreased U.S. wheat production from 1.66 billion bushels in 1994 to an estimated 1.37 billion bushels in 1996.

■ The rise in the price of wheat was the primary cause of the rise in the price of bread.

■ But a rise in gasoline prices also contributed to the rise in the price of bread.

Economic

A N A L Y S I S

■ U.S. wheat production is about 12 percent of the world total, and U.S. wheat consumption is about 6 percent of the world total (see the table).

■ Because wheat is easy to transport, its price is determined by supply and demand in a *world* market, which is shown in Fig. 1.

■ In 1995, demand was D_{95} and supply was S_{95}. The price was $5 a bushel, and the quantity consumed was 20.6 billion bushels.

■ In 1996, the price of wheat increased to $6 a bushel but the quantity of wheat consumed remained constant at 20.6 billion bushels.

■ This outcome occurred because supply decreased to S_{96} and demand increased to D_{96}. With a decrease in supply and an increase in demand, the price increased. But the decrease in supply and increase in demand left the quantity unchanged.

■ The news article says that supply decreased in 1996 because of a drought in the United States. The U.S. drought contributed to the decrease in world supply.

■ But another factor that decreased world supply was the expected *future* price of wheat. The table shows that traders held on to more inventories. Traders hold wheat to sell later when they expect a higher price in the future.

■ The news article identifies the rise in the price of wheat as a main cause of the rise in the price of bread.

■ Figure 2 shows the market for Sunbeam bread. The demand is D. In 1995, supply was S_{95} and the price was $1.19 a loaf.

■ The rise in the price of wheat increased the cost of producing bread and decreased the supply of bread. The supply curve shifted leftward from S_{95} to S'. Other factors, such as higher fuel costs, also decreased supply and the supply curve shifted farther leftward to S_{96}.

■ The price increased to $1.63 a loaf.

■ The rise in the price of bread brought a decrease in the quantity of bread demanded, which is shown by a movement along the demand curve for bread.

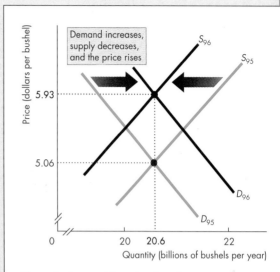

Figure 1 The world market for wheat

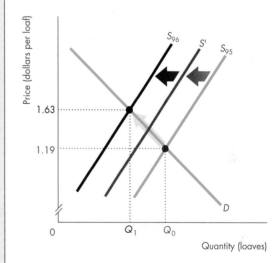

Figure 2 The market for Sunbeam bread

World Wheat Consumption (billions of bushels)	1994–95	1995–96
United States	1.3	1.2
Rest of world	19.3	19.4
World	20.6	20.6
World Wheat Production	**1994–95**	**1995–96**
United States	2.4	2.2
Rest of world	17.3	18.2
World	19.7	20.4
Change in wheat inventory	–1.0	–0.2

SUMMARY

Key Points

Price and Opportunity Cost (p. 68)

- Opportunity cost is a relative price. We measure relative price by dividing the price of one good by the price (index) of a basket of all goods.
- Demand and supply determines relative prices.

Demand (pp. 69–73)

- Demand is the relationship between the quantity demanded of a good and its price when all other influences on buying plans remain the same.
- The higher the price of a good, other things remaining the same, the smaller is the quantity demanded.
- Demand depends on the price of the good, the prices of substitutes and complements, income, population, preferences, and expected future prices.

Supply (pp. 74–77)

- Supply is the relationship between the quantity supplied of a good and its price when all other influences on selling plans remain the same.
- The higher the price of a good, other things remaining the same, the greater is the quantity supplied.
- Supply depends on the price of the good, the prices of resources used to produce it, technology, the number of producers, the prices of related goods produced, and expected future prices.

Market Equilibrium (pp. 78–79)

- At the equilibrium price, the quantity demanded equals the quantity supplied.
- At prices above equilibrium, there is a surplus and the price falls.
- At prices below equilibrium, there is a shortage and the price rises.

Predicting Changes in Price and Quantity (pp. 80–85)

- An increase in demand brings a rise in price and an increase in the quantity supplied. (A decrease in demand brings a fall in price and a decrease in the quantity supplied.)
- An increase in supply brings a fall in price and an increase in the quantity demanded. (A decrease in supply brings a rise in price and a decrease in the quantity demanded.)
- An increase in demand and an increase in supply bring an increased quantity but an ambiguous price change. An increase in demand and a decrease in supply raise the price and bring an ambiguous quantity change.
- Fill in the table in problem 6 (p. 90) for a complete summary of the predictions.

Key Figures

Key Terms

QUESTIONS

1. Distinguish between a money price and a relative price. Which is an opportunity cost and why?
2. Define the quantity demanded of a good or service.
3. Define the quantity supplied of a good or service.
4. List the main factors that influence the amount that consumers plan to buy and say whether an increase in each factor increases or decreases consumers' planned purchases.
5. List the main factors that influence the quantity that producers plan to sell and say whether an increase in each factor increases or decreases firms' planned sales.
6. State the law of demand and the law of supply.
7. If a fixed amount of a good is available, what does the demand curve tell us about the price that consumers are willing to pay for that fixed quantity?
8. If consumers are willing to buy only a certain fixed quantity, what does the supply curve tell us about the price at which firms will supply that quantity?
9. Distinguish between:
   a. A change in demand and a change in the quantity demanded.
   b. A change in supply and a change in the quantity supplied.
10. Why is the price at which the quantity demanded equals the quantity supplied the equilibrium price?
11. What are the forces that operate in a market if:
    a. The price is below the equilibrium price?
    b. The price is above the equilibrium price?
12. What is the effect on the price of a tape and the quantity of tapes sold if:
    a. The price of a CD increases?
    b. The price of a Walkman increases?
    c. The supply of CD players increases?
    d. Consumers' incomes increase and firms that produce tapes switch to new cost-saving technology?
    e. The prices of the resources used to make tapes increase?
13. What is the effect on the price of a tape and the quantity of tapes sold in question 12 if:
    a. Events (a) and (e) occur simultaneously?
    b. Events (b) and (e) occur simultaneously?

PROBLEMS

1. Suppose that one of the following events occurs:
   a. The price of gasoline rises.
   b. The price of gasoline falls.
   c. All speed limits on highways are abolished.
   d. An engine that runs on cheap alcohol is invented.
   e. Robot production plants lower the cost of producing cars.
   f. The rates for auto insurance double.
   g. A massive and high-grade oil supply is discovered in Mexico.
   h. The price of cars rises.
   i. The price of cars falls.
   j. The summer temperature is 10 degrees lower than normal.

   State which of the above events produces the following effects. (Each event might have more than one effect.)
   (i) An increase in the demand for gasoline
   (ii) A decrease in the demand for gasoline
   (iii) An increase in the supply of gasoline
   (iv) A decrease in the supply of gasoline
   (v) An increase in the quantity of gasoline demanded
   (vi) An increase in the quantity of gasoline supplied
   (vii) A decrease in the quantity of gasoline demanded
   (viii) A decrease in the quantity of gasoline supplied

2. The demand and supply curves for pizza are as follows:

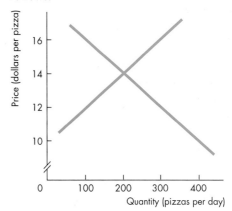

   a. What is the equilibrium price of pizza?
   b. What is the equilibrium quantity of pizza?

⊡ 3. The demand and supply schedules for gum are as follows:

Price (cents per pack)	Quantity demanded (millions of packs a week)	Quantity supplied (millions of packs a week)
20	180	30
30	160	60
40	140	90
50	120	120
60	100	140
70	80	160
80	60	180

a. What is the equilibrium price of gum?
b. What is the equilibrium quantity of gum?

Suppose that a huge fire destroys one half of the gum-producing factories. The supply of gum decreases to one half of the amount shown in the above supply schedule.

c. What is the new equilibrium price of gum?
d. What is the new equilibrium quantity of gum?
e. Has there been a shift in or a movement along the supply curve of gum?
f. Has there been a shift in or a movement along the demand curve for gum?
g. As the gum factories destroyed by fire are rebuilt and gradually resume gum production, what will happen to:
   (i) The price of gum?
   (ii) The quantity of gum bought?
   (iii) The demand for gum?
   (iv) The supply curve of gum?

⊡ 4. Suppose the demand and supply schedules for gum are those in problem 3. An increase in the teenage population increases the demand for gum by 40 million packs per week.
a. Write out the new demand schedule for gum.
b. What is the new equilibrium quantity of gum?
c. What is the new equilibrium price of gum?
d. Has there been a shift in or a movement along the demand curve for gum?
e. Has there been a shift in or a movement along the supply curve of gum?

⊡ 5. Suppose the demand and supply schedules for gum are those in problem 3. An increase in the teenage population increases the demand for gum by 40 million packs per week, and

simultaneously the fire described in problem 2 occurs, wiping out one half of the gum-producing factories.
a. Draw a graph of the original and new demand and supply curves.
b. What is the new equilibrium quantity of gum?
c. What is the new equilibrium price of gum?

6. Complete the table by inserting in each column an up arrow (↑) for increase, a down arrow (↓) for decrease and a question mark (?) for indeterminate (can increase or decrease depending on the size of the change in demand and supply). To fill in this table, draw a separate demand and supply diagram for each of the eight cases.

	Increase in demand	No change in demand	Decrease in demand
Increase in supply	*P* *Q*	*P* *Q*	*P* *Q*
No change in supply	*P* *Q*	*P* — *Q* —	*P* *Q*
Decrease in supply	*P* *Q*	*P* *Q*	*P* *Q*

CRITICAL THINKING

1. Study the story about the price of bread and the price of wheat in *Reading Between the Lines,* pp. 86–87 and then:
a. Describe the changes in the price of wheat in the United States and the rest of the world.
b. Explain what happened to the quantity of wheat demanded by consumers in the United States and show the change in the quantity demanded in the figure.
c. Explain why the price of wheat is determined in a world market but the price of bread is determined in local markets.

⊕ 2. Visit the World Wide Web site of the FAO (the Food and Agricultural Organization of the United Nations) in Rome. (You will find a link to it at the Parkin home page.) Gather data on world and U.S. production and consumption of wheat for the most recent period available and update the table on p. 87. Then draw a new version of Fig. 1 on p. 87 to explain what has happened to the world economy since 1996.

5

Elasticity

You've just been hired as Intel's marketing manager, and you face your first challenge. Intel is about to launch a new memory chip that outperforms its predecessors. But Intel has a dilemma that you must resolve. You must decide the price at which to sell the new chip. Will you recommend a high price or a low price? You know that the quantity of chips sold depends on the price and that the higher the price, the smaller is the quantity sold. What price will bring Intel the most revenue? Will a high price depress sales and lower revenue? Or will a low price fail to stimulate sales by enough and bring in a lower revenue? Many firms share Intel's dilemma. A bumper grape crop is good news for wine consumers. It lowers the price of wine. But is it good news for

Intel's Dilemma

grape growers? Do they get more revenue? Or does the lower price more than wipe out their gains from larger quantities sold? ◆ The government faces a similar dilemma. Looking for greater tax revenue to balance its budget, it decides to increase the tax rates on tobacco and gasoline. Do the higher tax rates bring in more tax revenue? Or do people switch to substitutes for tobacco and gasoline on such a large scale that the higher tax rates bring in less tax revenue? ◆ Back at Intel, as marketing manager, you have a lot more questions about the demand for chips. How will growth in the world economy translate into an increase in demand for computers and memory chips? What are the substitutes for Intel chips and how will their prices evolve? Will Motorola, Sun Microsystems, and Asian companies produce inexpensive alternatives to Intel chips? ◆ In this chapter, you will learn how to tackle questions such as the ones just posed. You will learn how we can measure in a precise way the responsiveness of the quantities bought and sold to changes in prices and other influences on buyers and sellers.

After studying this chapter, you will be able to:

- Define and calculate the price elasticity of demand
- Explain what determines the price elasticity of demand
- Use the price elasticity to determine whether a price change will increase or decrease total revenue
- Define and calculate other elasticities of demand
- Define and calculate the elasticity of supply

Elasticity of Demand

L AS INTEL'S MARKETING MANAGER, YOU ARE TRYING to decide whether to advise that a new chip be sold for a high price or a low price. To select Intel's pricing strategy, you need to know how the quantity of chips demanded and the revenue from chip sales will respond to a change in price. You also need some way to measure that response.

You are going to discover that the concept of the price elasticity of demand can help you to calculate the influence of a price change on the quantity demanded and sales revenue. The **price elasticity of demand** is a measure of the responsiveness of the quantity demanded of a good to a change in its price with all other influences on buyers' plans remaining the same. The price elasticity of demand is a measure that compresses a large amount of information into a single number. Before you learn how to calculate this number, let's look a bit more closely at your task as Intel's marketing manager.

The Responsiveness of the Quantity Demanded to Price

You can appreciate the importance of the responsiveness of the quantity demanded to price by comparing the two scenarios shown in Fig. 5.1. Initially, the price of a chip is $400 and the quantity of chips sold is 40 million a year.

The **total revenue** from the sale of a good equals the price of the good multiplied by the quantity sold. The total revenue from chip sales is $400 multiplied by 40 million chips a year, which equals $16,000 million ($16 billion) a year.

You are trying to decide whether to launch a new Intel chip at a price of $400 or whether to go for a lower price of $200. You know that Intel can sell more chips at $200 than at $400. But how many more? And will the quantity increase by enough to bring in more total revenue than at $400 a chip? The answer depends on whether the demand curve is D_a in Fig. 5.1(a) or D_b in Fig. 5.1(b).

A fall in price has two opposing effects on total revenue. It increases the quantity sold, which increases total revenue (blue areas in Fig. 5.1), but it lowers the revenue on each unit sold (red areas in Fig. 5.1). Either of these two opposing effects could be larger. In case (a), the first effect is larger (blue area exceeds

FIGURE 5.1
Demand and Total Revenue

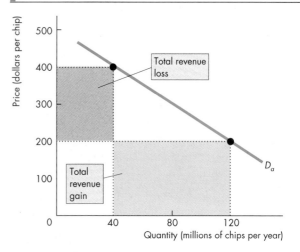

(a) More total revenue

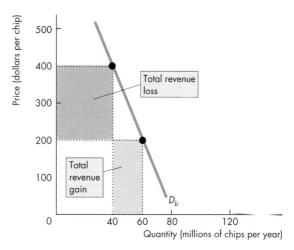

(b) Less total revenue

Initially, the price of a computer chip is $400 and the quantity of chips sold is 40 million a year. The total revenue from chip sales—the price multiplied by the quantity—is $16 billion. In part (a), if the price is cut to $200 a chip, the quantity of chips demanded increases to 120 million a year and total revenue *increases* to $24 billion. The increase in total revenue from greater sales (blue area) exceeds the decrease in total revenue from a lower price (red area). In part (b), if the price is cut to $200 a chip, the quantity of chips demanded increases to 60 million a year and total revenue *decreases* to $12 billion. The increase in total revenue from greater sales (blue area) is less than the decrease in total revenue from a lower price (red area).

red area), so total revenue increases. In case (b), the second effect is larger (red area exceeds blue area), so total revenue decreases. So if demand is D_a, you recommend a price of $200, and if demand is D_b, you recommend a price of $400.

Slope Depends on Units of Measurement

What is different in these two cases is the responsiveness of the quantity demanded to a change in price. Demand curve D_b is steeper than demand curve D_a. In this example, we can compare the slopes of the demand curves. But we can't always do so. Slope depends on the units in which we measure the price and quantity. And we often need to compare the demand curves for different goods and services that are measured in unrelated units. For example, the government, anxious to increase its tax revenues, wants to know whether to increase the tax on tobacco or the tax on gasoline. Which item can the government tax at a higher rate without decreasing the tax revenue? The answer can't be found by comparing the slope of the demand curve for tobacco with the slope of the demand curve for gasoline. This comparison has no meaning. We measure tobacco in pounds, and we measure gasoline in gallons—completely unrelated units.

To overcome this problem, we need a measure of responsiveness that is independent of the units of measurement of prices and quantities. Elasticity is such a measure.

Elasticity: A Units-Free Measure

The *price elasticity of demand* is a units-free measure of the responsiveness of the quantity demanded of a good to a change in its price. It is calculated by using the formula

$$\text{Price elasticity of demand} = \frac{\text{Percentage change in quantity demanded}}{\text{Percentage change in price}}.$$

Elasticity is a units-free measure because the percentage change in a variable is independent of the units in which the variable is measured. For example, if we measure a price in dollars, an increase from $1.00 to $1.50 is a $0.50 increase. If we measure a price in cents, an increase from 100¢ to 150¢ is a 50¢ increase. The first increase is 0.5 of a unit (dollars) and the second increase is 50 units (cents), but they are both 50 percent increases.

Minus Sign and Elasticity   When the price of a good *increases* along a demand curve, the quantity demanded *decreases*. Because a *positive* price change results in a *negative* change in the quantity demanded, the price elasticity of demand is a negative number. But it is the magnitude, or *absolute value*, of the price elasticity of demand that tells us how responsive—how elastic—demand is. To compare elasticities, we use the magnitude of the price elasticity of demand and ignore the minus sign.

Calculating Elasticity

To calculate the price elasticity of demand, we need to know the quantities demanded at different prices, all the other influences on buyers' plans remaining the same. Let's assume that we have the relevant data on prices and quantities demanded of memory chips and calculate the elasticity of demand for chips.

Figure 5.2 zooms in on the demand curve for chips and shows how the quantity demanded responds to a small change in price. Initially, the price of a chip is $410 and 36 million chips a year are sold—the original point in the figure. The price then falls to $390 a chip, and the quantity demanded increases to 44 million chips a year—the new point in the figure. When the price falls by $20 a chip, the quantity demanded increases by 8 million chips a year.

To calculate the price elasticity of demand, we express the changes in price and quantity demanded as percentages of the *average price* and the *average quantity*. By using the average price and average quantity, we calculate the elasticity at a point on the demand curve midway between the original point and the new point. The original price is $410 and the new price is $390, so the average price is $400. The $20 price decrease is 5 percent of the average price. That is,

$$\Delta P/P_{ave} = (\$20/\$400) \times 100 = 5\%.$$

The original quantity demanded is 36 million chips and the new quantity demanded is 44 million chips, so the average quantity demanded is 40 million chips. The 8 million chip increase in the quantity demanded is 20 percent of the average quantity. That is,

$$\Delta Q/Q_{ave} = (8/40) \times 100 = 20\%.$$

FIGURE 5.2

Calculating the Elasticity of Demand

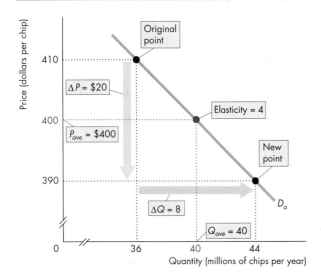

The elasticity of demand is calculated by using the formula*

$$\text{Price elasticity of demand} = \frac{\text{Percentage change in quantity demanded}}{\text{Percentage change in price}}$$

$$= \frac{\%\Delta Q}{\%\Delta P}$$

$$= \frac{\Delta Q / Q_{ave}}{\Delta P / P_{ave}}$$

$$= \frac{8 / 40}{20 / 400}$$

$$= 4.$$

This calculation measures the elasticity at an average price of $400 a chip and an average quantity of 40 million chips a year.

*In the formula, the Greek letter delta (Δ) stands for "change in" and %Δ stands for "percentage change in."

So the price elasticity of demand, which is the percentage change in the quantity demanded (20 percent) divided by the percentage change in price (5 percent) is 4. That is,

$$\text{Price elasticity of demand} = \frac{\%\Delta Q}{\%\Delta P}$$

$$= \frac{20\%}{5\%} = 4.$$

Average Price and Quantity   We use the *average* price and *average* quantity to avoid having two values for the elasticity of demand, depending on whether the price increases or decreases. A $20 price decrease from $410 to $390 is 4.9 percent of $410, the original price, 5.1 percent of $390, the new price, and 5 percent of $400, the average price. An 8 million chip quantity increase from 36 million to 44 million is 22.2 percent of 36 million, the original quantity, 18.2 percent of 44 million, the new quantity, and 20 percent of 40 million, the average quantity. If we use percentages of the original price and quantity, we get 22.2 divided by 4.9, which equals 4.5. If we use percentages of the new price and quantity, we get 18.2 divided by 5.1, which equals 3.6. If we use percentages of the average price and average quantity, we get 20 divided by 5, which equals 4. Using percentages of the average price and quantity gives the same value for the elasticity regardless of whether the price rises or falls.

Percentages and Proportions   Elasticity is the ratio of the *percentage* change in the quantity demanded to the *percentage* change in the price. It is also, equivalently, the proportionate change in the quantity demanded divided by the proportionate change in the price. The proportionate change in price is $\Delta P/P_{ave}$, and the proportionate change in quantity demanded is $\Delta Q/Q_{ave}$. The percentage changes are the proportionate changes multiplied by 100. So when we divide one percentage change by another, the 100s cancel and the result is the same as we get by using the proportionate changes.

Inelastic and Elastic Demand

Figure 5.3 shows three demand curves that cover the entire range of possible elasticities of demand. In Fig. 5.3(a), the quantity demanded is constant regardless of the price. If the quantity demanded remains constant when the price changes, then the price elasticity of demand is zero and demand is said to be **perfectly inelastic.** One good that has a very low price elasticity of demand (perhaps zero over some price range) is insulin. Insulin is so important to some diabetics that if the price rises or falls, they do not change the quantity they buy.

If the percentage change in the quantity demanded equals the percentage change in price, then the price elasticity equals 1 and demand is said to be **unit elastic**. The demand in Fig. 5.3(b) is an example of unit elastic demand.

FIGURE 5.3

Inelastic and Elastic Demand

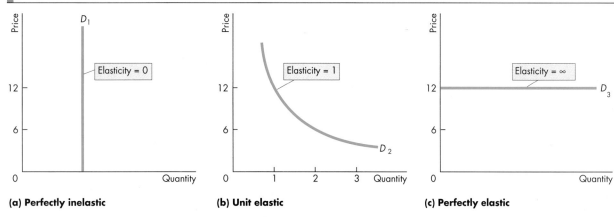

(a) Perfectly inelastic **(b) Unit elastic** **(c) Perfectly elastic**

Each demand illustrated here has a constant elasticity. The demand curve in part (a) illustrates the demand for a good that has a zero elasticity of demand. The demand curve in part

(b) illustrates the demand for a good with a unit elasticity of demand. And the demand curve in part (c) illustrates the demand for a good with an infinite elasticity of demand.

Between the cases shown in parts (a) and (b) of Fig. 5.3 is the general case in which the percentage change in the quantity demanded is less than the percentage change in price. In this case, the price elasticity of demand is between zero and 1 and demand is said to be **inelastic.** The demand for food and the demand for housing are inelastic.

If the quantity demanded changes by an infinitely large percentage in response to a tiny price change, then the price elasticity of demand is infinity, and demand is said to be **perfectly elastic.** The demand curve in Fig. 5.3(c) is an example of perfectly elastic demand. An example of a good that has a very high elasticity of demand (almost infinite) is marker pens from the campus bookstore and from the convenience store next door to the bookstore. If the two stores offer pens for the same price, some people buy from one and some from the other. But if the bookstore increases the price of a pen, even by a small amount, while the convenience shop maintains the lower price, people will buy their pens from the convenience store and the bookstore will have zero sales of pens. Marker pens from the two stores are perfect substitutes.

Between the cases in parts (b) and (c) of Fig. 5.3 is the general case in which the percentage change in the quantity demanded exceeds the percentage change in price. In this case, the price elasticity is greater than 1 and demand is said to be **elastic**. The demand for automobiles and the demand for furniture are elastic.

Elasticity Along a Straight-Line Demand Curve

Elasticity is not the same as slope, but the two are related. To understand how they are related, let's look at elasticity along a straight-line demand curve—a demand curve that has a constant slope.

Figure 5.4 illustrates the calculation of elasticity along a straight-line demand curve. We've already calculated the elasticity at an average price of $400 a chip and an average quantity of 40 million chips a year. Check that calculation by imagining that the price falls from $500 a chip to $300 a chip. The average price (P_{ave}) is $400 (average of $300 and $500), which means that the proportionate change in price is

$$\frac{\Delta P}{P_{ave}} = \frac{200}{400}.$$

At a price of $500 a chip, the quantity demanded is zero, and at a price of $300 a chip, the quantity demanded is 80 million chips a year. So the change in the quantity demanded (ΔQ) is 80 million chips a year, and the average quantity (Q_{ave}) is 40 million chips a year (the average of 80 million and zero), so the proportionate change in the quantity demanded is

$$\frac{\Delta Q}{Q_{ave}} = \frac{80}{40}.$$

FIGURE **5.4**

Elasticity Along a Straight-Line Demand Curve

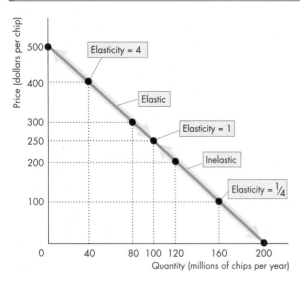

On a straight-line demand curve, elasticity decreases as the price falls and the quantity demanded increases. Demand is unit elastic at the midpoint of the demand curve (elasticity of demand is 1). Above the midpoint, demand is elastic; below the midpoint, demand is inelastic.

Dividing the proportionate change in the quantity demanded by the proportionate change in the price gives

$$\frac{\Delta Q / Q_{ave}}{\Delta P / P_{ave}} = \frac{80 / 40}{200 / 400} = 4.$$

By using this same method, we can calculate the elasticity of demand at any price and quantity along the demand curve. Because the demand curve is a straight line, a $200 price change brings an 80 million quantity change at every average price. So in the elasticity formula, $\Delta Q = 80$ and $\Delta P = 200$ regardless of average quantity and average price. But the lower the average price, the greater is the average quantity demanded. So the lower the average price, the less elastic is demand.

Check this proposition by calculating the elasticity of demand at the midpoint of the demand curve, where the price is $250 a chip and the quantity

demanded is 100 million chips a year. The proportionate change in price is 200/250 = 0.8, and the proportionate change in the quantity demanded is 80/100 = 0.8, so the elasticity of demand is 1. On *all* straight-line demand curves, the price elasticity is 1 at the midpoint. Above the midpoint, demand is elastic, and below the midpoint, demand is inelastic. Demand is perfectly elastic (elasticity is infinity) where the quantity demanded is zero and perfectly inelastic (elasticity is zero) where the price is zero.

The Factors That Influence the Elasticity of Demand

Table 5.1 gives some actual elasticities for the United States. You can see that these real-world elasticities of demand range from 1.52 for metals, the good with the most elastic demand in the table, to 0.12 for food, the good with the most inelastic demand in the table. What makes the demand for some goods elastic and the demand for others inelastic? Elasticity depends on three main factors:

- The closeness of substitutes
- The proportion of income spent on the good
- The time elapsed since a price change

Closeness of Substitutes   The closer the substitutes for a good or service, the more elastic is the demand for it. For example, oil has substitutes but none that are very close (imagine a steam-driven, coal-fueled car or a nuclear-powered jetliner). As a result, the demand for oil is inelastic. In contrast, metals have good substitutes such as plastics, so the demand for metals is elastic.

In everyday language we call some goods, such as food and housing, *necessities* and other goods, such as exotic vacations, *luxuries*. A necessity is a good that has poor substitutes and that is crucial for our well-being. So generally, a necessity has an inelastic demand. A luxury is a good that usually has many substitutes, one of which is doing without the good. So a luxury generally has an elastic demand.

The degree of substitutability between two goods also depends on how narrowly (or broadly) we define them. For example, computer chips do not have close substitutes, but different types of chips are substitutes for each other. So if the price of one type of chip falls and the prices of all other chips remain the same, the quantity demanded of that chip increases by a larger

TABLE 5.1
Some Real-World Price Elasticities of Demand

Good or Service	Elasticity
Elastic Demand	
Metals	1.52
Electrical engineering products	1.39
Mechanical engineering products	1.30
Furniture	1.26
Motor vehicles	1.14
Instrument engineering products	1.10
Professional services	1.09
Transportation services	1.03
Inelastic Demand	
Gas, electricity, and water	0.92
Oil	0.91
Chemicals	0.89
Beverages (all types)	0.78
Clothing	0.64
Tobacco	0.61
Banking and insurance services	0.56
Housing services	0.55
Agricultural and fish products	0.42
Books, magazines, and newspapers	0.34
Food	0.12

Sources: Ahsan Mansur and John Whalley, "Numerical Specification of Applied General Equilibrium Models: Estimation, Calibration, and Data," in *Applied General Equilibrium Analysis*, eds. Herbert E. Scarf and John B. Shoven (New York: Cambridge University Press, 1984), 109, and Henri Theil, Ching-Fan Chung, and James L. Seale, Jr., *Advances in Econometrics, Supplement 1, 1989, International Evidence on Consumption Patterns* (Greenwich, Conn: JAI Press Inc., 1989). Reprinted with permission.

amount than it would if the prices of all chips fell. The demand for a single type of chip is more elastic than the demand for chips in general.

This example, which distinguishes between chips in general and different types of chips, applies to many other goods and services. The elasticity of demand for meat in general is low, but the elasticity of demand for beef, lamb, or chicken is high. The

elasticity of demand for personal computers is low, but the elasticity of demand for a Compaq, Dell, or IBM is high.

Proportion of Income Spent on the Good
Other things remaining the same, the greater the proportion of income spent on a good, the more elastic is the demand for it. If only a small proportion of income is spent on a good, then a change in its price has little impact on the consumer's overall budget. In contrast, even a small percentage rise in the price of a good that commands a large proportion of a consumer's budget induces the consumer to make a radical reappraisal of expenditures.

To appreciate the importance of the proportion of income spent on a good, consider your own elasticity of demand for textbooks and chewing gum. If the price of textbooks doubles (increases 100 percent), there will be a big decrease in the quantity of textbooks bought. There will be an increase in sharing and in illegal photocopying. If the price of chewing gum doubles, also a 100 percent increase, there will be almost no change in the quantity of gum demanded. Why the difference? Textbooks take a large proportion of your budget, while gum takes only a tiny proportion. You don't like either price increase, but you hardly notice the effects of the increased price of gum, while the increased price of textbooks puts your budget under severe strain.

Figure 5.5 shows the proportion of income spent on food and the price elasticity of demand for food in 20 countries. This figure confirms the general tendency we have just described. The larger the proportion of income spent on food, the larger is the price elasticity of demand for food. For example, in Tanzania, a poor African nation where average incomes are 3.3 percent of incomes in the United States and where 62 percent of income is spent on food, the price elasticity of demand for food is 0.77. In contrast, in the United States, where 12 percent of income is spent on food, the elasticity of demand for food is 0.12.

Time Elapsed Since Price Change   The longer the time that has elapsed since a price change, the more elastic is demand. When a price changes, consumers often continue to buy similar quantities of a good for a while. But given enough time, they find acceptable and less costly substitutes. As this process of substitution occurs, the quantity purchased of a good or service that has become more expensive gradually decreases.

FIGURE 5.5

Price Elasticities in 20 Countries

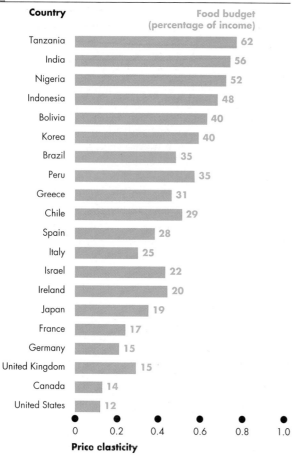

As income increases and the proportion of income spent on food decreases, the demand for food becomes less elastic.

Source: Henri Theil, Ching-Fan Chung, and James L. Seale, Jr., *Advances in Econometrics, Supplement 1, 1989, International Evidence on Consumption Patterns* (Greenwich, Conn: JAI Press Inc., 1989).

To describe the effect of time on demand we distinguish between two time frames:

1. Short-run demand
2. Long-run demand

Short-run demand describes the response of buyers to a change in the price of a good *before* sufficient time has elapsed for buyers to have made all the possible substitutions. Long-run demand describes the response of buyers to a change in price *after* sufficient

time has elapsed for all the possible substitutions to be made.

An example of a long-lasting price change is the fall in the price of computers. A few years ago, a multimedia PC with a fast chip, a CD-ROM drive, a huge amount of memory, and a modem to connect to the Internet cost around $5,000. Today, the price is not much more than $1,000. Because the price has fallen, the quantity demanded has increased. But most people still do not have a computer. And many people who can afford one and who will eventually buy one have not yet got around to doing so. Some of these people are waiting for even lower prices. But many would be willing to buy at today's prices if they could see a benefit from owning a computer. They are waiting for a more compelling reason to buy. But as more and more applications become available and as services such as the World Wide Web become more useful, the quantity of computers demanded increases.

A given fall in the price of computers brings a larger increase in the quantity demanded in the long run than it does in the short run. The long-run demand for computers is more elastic than the short-run demand.

Elasticity, Total Revenue, and Expenditure

This chapter began with a dilemma. Can a producer of computer chips (or anything else) increase total revenue by cutting its price? We can now answer this question.

The change in a producer's total revenue depends on the extent to which the quantity sold changes as the price changes—the elasticity of demand.

- If demand is elastic, a 1 percent price cut increases the quantity sold by more than 1 percent and total revenue increases.

- If demand is unit elastic, a 1 percent price cut increases the quantity sold by 1 percent and so total revenue does not change.

- If demand is inelastic, a 1 percent price cut increases the quantity sold by less than 1 percent and total revenue decreases.

Total Revenue Test   We can use this relationship between elasticity and total revenue to estimate elasticity using a total revenue test. The **total revenue test** is a method of estimating the price elasticity of

FIGURE 5.6

Elasticity and Total Revenue

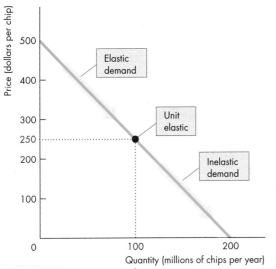

(a) Demand

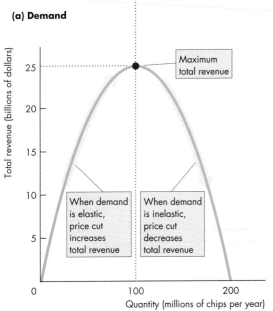

(b) Total revenue

When demand is elastic, in the price range from $500 to $250, a decrease in price (part a) brings an increase in total revenue (part b). When demand is inelastic, in the price range from $250 to zero, a decrease in price (part a) brings a decrease in total revenue (part b). When demand is unit elastic, at a price of $250 (part a), total revenue is at a maximum (part b).

demand by observing the change in total revenue that results from a price change (all other influences on the quantity sold remaining unchanged).

- If a price cut increases total revenue, demand is elastic.
- If a price cut decreases total revenue, demand is inelastic.
- If a price cut leaves total revenue unchanged, demand is unit elastic.

Figure 5.6 shows the connection between the elasticity of demand and total revenue. In part (a), over the price range from $500 to $250, demand is elastic. Over the price range from $250 to zero, demand is inelastic. At a price of $250, demand is unit elastic.

Figure 5.6(b) shows total revenue. At a price of $500, the quantity sold is zero, so total revenue is also zero. At a price of zero, the quantity demanded is 200 million chips a year but total revenue is again zero. A price cut in the elastic range brings an increase in total revenue—the percentage increase in the quantity demanded is greater than the percentage decrease in price. A price cut in the inelastic range brings a decrease in total revenue—the percentage increase in the quantity demanded is less than the percentage decrease in price. At unit elasticity, total revenue is at a maximum. A small price change on either side of $250 keeps total revenue constant. The loss in total revenue from a lower price is offset by a gain in total revenue from a greater quantity sold.

REVIEW

- The price elasticity of demand measures the responsiveness of the quantity demanded of a good or service to a change in its price, all other influences on buyers' plans remaining the same.
- The price elasticity of demand is the percentage change in the quantity demanded of a good divided by the percentage change in its price.
- The price elasticity of demand for a good is determined by the closeness of substitutes for it, the proportion of income spent on it, and the time elapsed since its price changed.

So far, we've studied the most widely used elasticity: the *price* elasticity of demand. But there are some other useful elasticity of demand concepts. Let's look at them.

More Elasticities of Demand

BACK AT INTEL, YOU ARE TRYING TO FIGURE OUT how your competitors' prices are going to affect the demand for Intel chips. You have heard a rumor that a Taiwan source is about to enter the market with a lower priced chip that claims to be as good as Intel's. What is going to be the effect on the demand for your chips?

But all is not bleak. The world economy is expanding, and income growth is bringing an increase in demand for all types of computers and related items. So you are feeling confident about future demand growth. But just how much demand growth can you expect?

To answer these questions, you need to calculate two other types of an elasticity of demand. Let's examine these other elasticities.

Cross Elasticity of Demand

We measure the influences of changes in the prices of substitutes and complements by using the concept of the cross elasticity of demand. The **cross elasticity of demand** is a measure of the responsiveness of the demand for a good to a change in the price of a substitute or complement, other things remaining the same. It is calculated by using the formula

$$\text{Cross elasticity of demand} = \frac{\text{Percentage change in quantity demanded}}{\text{Percentage change in price of a substitute or complement}}.$$

The cross elasticity of demand can be positive or negative. It is positive for a substitute and negative for a complement.

Figure 5.7 illustrates the cross elasticity of demand. The Walkman and the CD player are substitutes. Because they are substitutes, when the price of a CD player rises, the demand for Walkmans increases. The demand curve for Walkmans shifts rightward from D_0 to D_1. Because a *rise* in the price of a CD player brings an *increase* in the demand for Walkmans, the cross elasticity of demand for Walkmans with respect to the price of a CD player is *positive*.

The Walkman and tapes are complements. Because they are complements, when the price of a tape rises, the demand for Walkmans decreases. The

FIGURE 5.7
Cross Elasticity of Demand

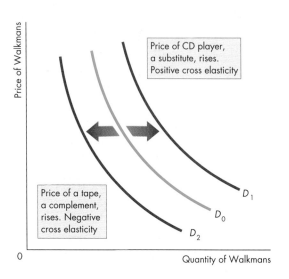

When the price of a CD player, a *substitute* for a Walkman, rises, the demand for Walkmans increases and the demand curve for Walkmans shifts rightward from D_0 to D_1. The cross elasticity of demand for Walkmans with respect to the price of a CD player is *positive*. When the price of a tape, a *complement* of a Walkman, rises, the demand for Walkmans decreases and the demand curve for Walkmans shifts leftward from D_0 to D_2. The cross elasticity of demand for Walkmans with respect to the price of a tape is *negative*.

demand curve for Walkmans shifts leftward from D_0 to D_2. Because a *rise* in the price of a tape brings a *decrease* in the demand for Walkmans, the cross elasticity of demand for Walkmans with respect to the price of a tape is *negative*.

Income Elasticity of Demand

As income grows, how does the demand for a particular good change? The answer depends on the income elasticity of demand for the good. The **income elasticity of demand** is a measure of the responsiveness of the demand for a good or service to a change in income, other things remaining the same.

It is calculated by using the formula

$$\text{Income elasticity of demand} = \frac{\text{Percentage change in quantity demanded}}{\text{Percentage change in income}}.$$

Income elasticities of demand can be positive or negative and fall into three interesting ranges:

1. Greater than 1 (*normal* good, income elastic)
2. Between zero and 1 (*normal* good, income inelastic)
3. Less than zero (*inferior* good)

Figure 5.8(a) shows an income elasticity of demand that is greater than 1. As income increases, the quantity demanded increases, but the quantity demanded increases faster than income. Examples of goods in this category are ocean cruises, custom clothing, international travel, jewelry, and works of arts.

Figure 5.8(b) shows an income elasticity of demand that is between zero and 1. In this case, the quantity demanded increases as income increases, but income increases faster than the quantity demanded. Examples of goods in this category are food, clothing, furniture, newspapers, and magazines.

Part (c) shows an income elasticity of demand that eventually becomes negative. In this case, the quantity demanded increases as income increases until it reaches a maximum at income *m*. Beyond that point, as income continues to increase, the quantity demanded declines. The elasticity of demand is positive but less than 1 up to income *m*. Beyond income *m*, the income elasticity of demand is negative. Examples of goods in this category are small motorcycles, potatoes, and rice. Low-income consumers buy most of these goods. At low incomes, the demand for such goods increases as income increases. But as income increases above point *m,* consumers replace these goods with superior alternatives. For example, a small car replaces the motorcycle; fruit, vegetables, and meat begin to appear in a diet that was heavy in rice or potatoes.

Real-World Income Elasticities of Demand

Table 5.2 shows estimates of some income elasticities of demand in the United States. Necessities such as food and clothing are income inelastic,

---

FIGURE **5.8**
Income Elasticity of Demand

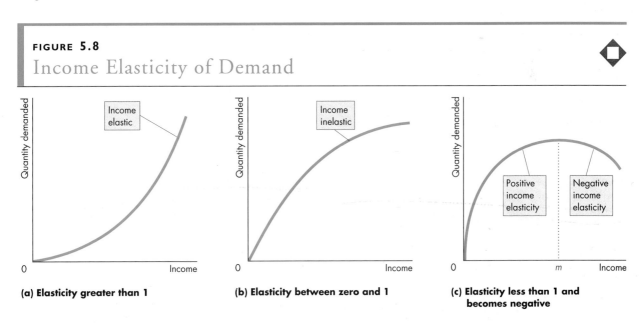

(a) Elasticity greater than 1

(b) Elasticity between zero and 1

(c) Elasticity less than 1 and becomes negative

Income elasticity of demand has three ranges of values. In part (a), income elasticity of demand is greater than 1. As income increases along the x-axis, the quantity demanded increases but by a bigger percentage than the increase in income. In part (b), income elasticity of demand is between zero and 1. As income increases, the quantity demanded increases but by a smaller percentage than the increase in income. In part (c), the income elasticity of demand is positive at low incomes but becomes negative at incomes above level *m*. Maximum consumption of this good occurs at the income *m*.

TABLE 5.2

Some Real-World Income Elasticities of Demand

Elastic Demand

Airline travel	5.82
Movies	3.41
Foreign travel	3.08
Electricity	1.94
Restaurant meals	1.61
Local buses and trains	1.38
Haircutting	1.36
Cars	1.07

Inelastic Demand

Tobacco	0.86
Alcoholic beverages	0.62
Furniture	0.53
Clothing	0.51
Newspapers and magazines	0.38
Telephone	0.32
Food	0.14

Sources: H.S. Houthakker and Lester D. Taylor, *Consumer Demand in the United States* (Cambridge, Mass.: Harvard University Press, 1970), and Henri Theil, Ching-Fan Chung, and James L. Seale, Jr., *Advances in Econometrics, Supplement 1, 1989, International Evidence on Consumption Patterns* (Greenwich, Conn: JAI Press Inc., 1989). Reprinted with permission.

while luxuries such as airline and foreign travel are income elastic.

What is a necessity and what is a luxury depend on the level of income. For people with a low income, food and clothing can be luxuries. So the *level* of income has a big effect on income elasticities of demand. Figure 5.9 shows this effect on the income elasticity of demand for food in 15 countries. In countries with low incomes, such as Tanzania and India, the income elasticity of demand for food is high. In countries with high incomes, such as the United States, it is low. A 1 percent increase in income leads to an increase in the demand for food of 0.75 percent in India and only 0.14 percent in the United States. These numbers confirm that necessities have a lower income elasticity of demand than do luxuries.

FIGURE 5.9

Income Elasticities in 15 Countries

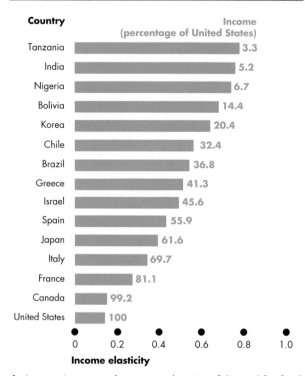

As income increases, the income elasticity of demand for food decreases. For low-income consumers, a larger percentage of any increase in income is spent on food than for high-income consumers.

Source: Henri Theil, Ching-Fan Chung, and James L. Seale, Jr., *Advances in Econometrics, Supplement 1, 1989, International Evidence on Consumption Patterns* (Greenwich, Conn: JAI Press Inc., 1989).

R E V I E W

- The cross elasticity of demand measures the responsiveness of the quantity demanded of a good or service to a change in the price of a substitute (a positive number) or a complement (a negative number).

- The income elasticity of demand measures the responsiveness of the quantity demanded of a good or service to a change in income. Income elasticity is positive for a normal good and negative for an inferior good.

Elasticity of Supply

DURING THE 1996 SUMMER OLYMPICS, THE demand for accommodation in Atlanta surged. There was a *change in the demand* for hotel rooms and apartments for short-term lease. Hotel operators and apartment owners were very interested in the likely changes in the prices that this increase in demand would bring. Would the rise be large or moderate? A change in demand shifts the demand curve and leads to an *increase in the quantity supplied*, which is shown by a *movement along the supply curve*. To predict the changes in price and quantity, we need to know how responsive the quantity supplied is to the price of a good. That is, we need to know the elasticity of supply.

The **elasticity of supply** measures the responsiveness of the quantity supplied of a good to a change in its price. It is calculated by using the formula

$$\text{Elasticity of supply} = \frac{\text{Percentage change in quantity supplied}}{\text{Percentage change in price}}.$$

There are two extreme cases of the elasticity of supply. If the quantity supplied is fixed regardless of the price, the supply curve is vertical and the elasticity of supply is zero. Supply is perfectly inelastic. If there is a price at which sellers are willing to supply any quantity demanded, the supply curve is horizontal and the elasticity of supply is infinite. Supply is perfectly elastic.

The magnitude of the elasticity of supply depends on:

■ Resource substitution possibilities
■ Time frame for the supply decision

Resource Substitution Possibilities

Some goods and services can be produced only by using unique or rare productive resources. These items have a low, and perhaps a zero, elasticity of supply. Other goods and services can be produced by using commonly available resources that could be allocated to a wide variety of alternative tasks. Such items have a high elasticity of supply.

A Van Gogh painting has been produced by a unique type of labor—Van Gogh's. No other productive resource can be substituted for this labor. And there is just one of each painting, so its supply curve is vertical and its elasticity of supply is zero. At the other extreme, wheat can be grown on land that is almost equally good for growing corn. So it is just as easy to grow wheat as corn, and the opportunity cost of wheat in terms of forgone corn is almost constant. As a result, the supply curve of wheat is almost horizontal and its elasticity of supply is very large. Similarly, when a good is produced in many different countries (for example, sugar and beef), the supply of the good is highly elastic.

The supply of most goods and services lies between the two extremes. The quantity produced can be increased but only by incurring a higher cost. If a higher price is offered, the quantity supplied increases. Such goods and services have an elasticity of supply between zero and infinity.

Elasticity of Supply and the Time Frame for Supply Decisions

To study the influence of the length of time elapsed since a price change, we distinguish three time frames of supply:

■ Momentary supply
■ Long-run supply
■ Short-run supply

Momentary Supply   When the price of a good rises or falls, the *momentary supply curve* shows the response of the quantity supplied immediately following a price change.

Some goods, such as fruits and vegetables, have a perfectly inelastic momentary supply—a vertical supply curve. The quantities supplied depend on crop-planting decisions made earlier. In the case of oranges, for example, planting decisions have to be made many years in advance of the crop being available.

Other goods, such as long-distance phone calls, have an elastic momentary supply. When many people simultaneously make calls, there is a big surge in the demand for telephone cable, computer switching, and satellite time, and the quantity supplied increases (up to the physical limits of the telephone system) but the price remains constant. Long-distance carriers monitor fluctuations in demand and reroute calls to ensure that the quantity supplied equals the quantity demanded without raising the price.

Long-Run Supply The *long-run supply curve* shows the response of the quantity supplied to a change in price after all the technologically possible ways of adjusting supply have been exploited. In the case of oranges, the long run is the time it takes new plantings to grow to full maturity—about 15 years. In some cases, the long-run adjustment occurs only after a completely new production plant has been built and workers have been trained to operate it—typically a process that might take several years.

Short-Run Supply The *short-run supply curve* shows how the quantity supplied responds to a price change when only *some* of the technologically possible adjustments to production have been made. The first adjustment that is usually made is in the amount of labor employed. To increase output in the short run, firms work their labor force overtime and perhaps hire additional workers. To decrease their output in the short run, firms lay off workers or reduce their hours of work. With the passage of time, firms can make additional adjustments, perhaps training additional workers or buying additional tools and other equipment. The short-run response to a price change, unlike the momentary and long-run responses, is not a unique response but a sequence of adjustments.

Three Supply Curves Figure 5.10 shows three supply curves that correspond to the three time frames. They are the supply curves in the world market for oranges in a given week in which the price is $2 a pound and the quantity of oranges grown is 3 million pounds. Each supply curve passes through that point. Momentary supply is perfectly inelastic, as shown by the blue curve *MS*. As time passes, the quantity supplied becomes more responsive to price as the short-run supply curve, *SS*, shows. As yet more time passes, the supply curve becomes the red long-run curve *LS*, the most elastic of the three supplies.

The momentary supply curve is vertical because, on a given day, no matter what the price of oranges, producers cannot change their output. They have picked, packed, and shipped their crop to market, and the quantity available for that day is fixed. The short-run supply curve slopes upward because producers can take actions quite quickly to change the quantity supplied in response to a price change. They can, for example, stop picking and leave oranges to rot on the tree if the price falls by a large amount. Or they can use more fertilizers and improved irrigation

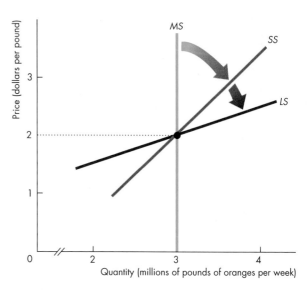

FIGURE 5.10

Supply: Momentary,
Short-Run, and Long-Run

The momentary supply curve, *MS*, shows how the quantity supplied responds to a price change the moment that it occurs. The blue momentary supply curve shown here is perfectly inelastic. The purple short-run supply curve, *SS*, shows how the quantity supplied responds to a price change after some adjustments to production have been made. The red long-run supply curve, *LS*, shows how the quantity supplied responds to a price change when all the technologically possible adjustments to the production process have been made.

and increase the yields of their existing trees if the price rises. In the long run, they can plant more trees and increase the quantity supplied even more in response to a given price rise.

◆ You have now studied the theory of demand and supply, and you have learned how to measure the elasticities of demand and supply. All the elasticities that you've met in this chapter are summarized in Table 5.3. In the next chapter, we are going to study the efficiency of competitive markets. But before doing that, take a look at *Reading Between the Lines,* on pp. 106-107 to see the price elasticity of demand and the cross elasticity of demand in action.

TABLE 5.3

A Compact Glossary of Elasticities

PRICE ELASTICITIES OF DEMAND

A relationship is described as	When its magnitude is	Which means that
Perfectly elastic or infinitely elastic	Infinity	The smallest possible increase in price causes an infinitely large decrease in the quantity demanded*
Elastic	Less than infinity but greater than 1	The percentage decrease in the quantity demanded exceeds the percentage increase in price
Unit elastic	1	The percentage decrease in the quantity demanded equals the percentage increase in price
Inelastic	Greater than zero but less than 1	The percentage decrease in the quantity demanded is less than the percentage increase in price
Perfectly inelastic or completely inelastic	Zero	The quantity demanded is the same at all prices

CROSS ELASTICITIES OF DEMAND

A relationship is described as	When its value is	Which means that
Perfect substitutes	Infinity	The smallest possible increase in the price of one good causes an infinitely large increase in the quantity demanded of the other good
Substitutes	Positive, less than infinity	If the price of one good increases, the quantity demanded of the other good also increases
Independent	Zero	The quantity demanded of one good remains constant, regardless of the price of the other good
Complements	Less than zero	The quantity demanded of one good decreases when the price of the other good increases

INCOME ELASTICITIES OF DEMAND

A relationship is described as	When its value is	Which means that
Income elastic (normal good)	Greater than 1	The percentage increase in the quantity demanded is greater than the percentage increase in income
Income inelastic (normal good)	Less than 1 but greater than zero	The percentage increase in the quantity demanded is less than the percentage increase in income
Negative income elastic (inferior good)	Less than zero	When income increases, quantity demanded decreases

ELASTICITIES OF SUPPLY

A relationship is described as	When its magnitude is	Which means that
Perfectly elastic	Infinity	The smallest possible increase in price causes an infinitely large increase in the quantity supplied
Elastic	Less than infinity but greater than 1	The percentage increase in the quantity supplied exceeds the percentage increase in the price
Inelastic	Greater than zero but less than 1	The percentage increase in the quantity supplied is less than the percentage increase in the price
Perfectly inelastic	Zero	The quantity supplied is the same at all prices

*In each description, the directions of change may be reversed. For example, in this case: The smallest possible *decrease* in price causes an infinitely large *increase* in the quantity demanded.

Elasticity in Action: The Demand for Gas

Essence of **THE STORY**

WINSTON-SALEM JOURNAL, MAY 28, 1996

Gas Prices Changing Venezuelans' Driving Habits

BY BART JONES
THE ASSOCIATED PRESS

Standing in his lot, Oswaldo Ochoa, a used-car dealer, recalls how easily he used to sell Ford LTDs, Conquistadors and other models with full-size bodies and thirsty engines.

Cheap gas was considered a birthright in this oil-rich South American nation. ... [At] 7 cents a gallon, gasoline cost less than bottled water or a can of soda.

Not any more. Last month, the government increased gas prices more than sixfold—hitting 44 cents a gallon—and such car dealers as Ochoa are stuck with lots full of the gas guzzlers that once ruled Venezuela's roads.

"People don't want them, even if you gave them one," Ochoa said glumly, his eyes taking in a dozen old cars parked near a line of palm trees. "Sales are paralyzed."...

People in the United States—or Europe, or elsewhere in South America—who pay far more for gasoline may wonder what Venezuelans are fretting over.

The key difference is that salaries here are a fraction of what they are in more developed countries. Most workers make about $112 dollars a month, which is the national minimum wage.

Few drivers have turned in their clunkers yet because money is tight and even the smallest new cars are prohibitively expensive at $8,000. But driving habits already are starting to change.

Carlos Rodriguez used to think nothing of driving his 1972 Buick LeSabre to visit his family in the southern plains, a five-hour ride from Caracas. When he could fill his 24-gallon tank for under $2, he'd make the 470-mile round trip as frequently as several times a month.

Now, at $11 a tank, "It's going to have to be once a year," Rodriguez, a 31-year-old subway-security supervisor, said. ...

Reprinted with permission.

- In 1996, the price of gasoline in Venezuela increased from 7 cents a gallon to 44 cents a gallon.
- Demand for large gas-guzzling cars decreased.
- Venezuelans could not afford to replace their automobiles with smaller, fuel-efficient models.
- Instead, they decreased their automobile use.
- At 7 cents a gallon, Carlos Rodriguez would journey to the southern plains from Caracas to visit his family several times a month. With gasoline at 44 cents a gallon, he makes the trip only once a year.

Economic

A N A L Y S I S

■ The figure shows Carlos's demand curve for gasoline for trips to the southern plains.

■ The y-axis measures the price of gasoline in cents per gallon. The x-axis measures the quantity of gasoline that Carlos uses, not in gallons but in trips to the southern plains.

■ At a price of 7 cents a gallon, Carlos makes 30 trips a year—point a.

■ At a price of 44 cents a gallon, Carlos makes only 1 trip a year—point b.

■ We can use these facts to calculate Carlos's price elasticity of demand for gasoline midway between points a and b. The table summarizes the calculation.

■ The price rises from 7 cents to 44 cents, a rise of 37 cents. The average price is 25.5 cents, the average of 7 cents and 44 cents. The percentage change in price, which is the change in price divided by the average price and multiplied by 100 is 145.1 percent.

■ The quantity decreases from 30 trips to 1 trip, a decrease of 29 trips. The average number of trips is

15.5, the average of 30 and 1. The percentage change in quantity, which is the change in quantity divided by the average quantity and multiplied by 100, is –187.1 percent.

■ The price elasticity of demand is the absolute value percentage change in quantity divided by the percentage change in price, which is 187.1 divided by 145.1. This elasticity is 1.3.

■ Carlos's demand for gasoline to visit the southern plains is elastic.

■ It seems likely that Carlos would cut his expenditure on gasoline for long trips because he is faced with a much higher cost of getting around Caracas. He almost certainly has an inelastic demand for gasoline for local travel and so must spend more on that.

■ The news article says that auto dealers are having a hard time in Venezuela.

■ The reason is that the automobile and gasoline are complements. When the price of gasoline rises, the demand for gas-guzzling automobiles decreases.

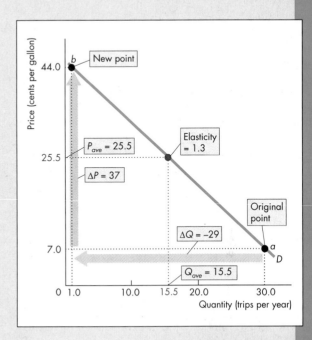

■ The increase in the price of gasoline results in a decrease in the quantity demanded of automobiles at each price—the demand curve for autos shifts leftward.

■ The cross elasticity of demand for automobiles with respect to the price of gasoline is negative.

Carlos's trips

Original price	7	cents per gallon
New price	44	cents per gallon
Change in price	37	cents per gallon
Average price	25.5	cents per gallon
Percentage change in price	145.1	percent
Original quantity	30	trips per year
New quantity	1	trips per year
Change in quantity	–29	trips per year
Average quantity	15.5	trips per year
Percentage change in quantity	–187.1	percent
Elasticity	**187.1/145.10 = 1.3**	

SUMMARY

Key Points

Elasticity of Demand (pp. 92–99)

▪ Price elasticity of demand is a measure of the responsiveness of the quantity demanded of a good to a change in its price.

▪ Price elasticity of demand equals the percentage change in the quantity demanded divided by the percentage change in price.

▪ The larger the magnitude of the price elasticity of demand, the greater is the responsiveness of the quantity demanded to a given change in price.

▪ Price elasticity of demand depends on how easily one good serves as a substitute for another, the proportion of income spent on the good, and the length of time elapsed since the price change.

▪ If demand is elastic, a decrease in price leads to an increase in total revenue. If demand is unit elastic, a decrease in price leaves total revenue unchanged. And if demand is inelastic, a decrease in price leads to a decrease in total revenue.

More Elasticities of Demand (pp. 100–102)

▪ Cross elasticity of demand measures the responsiveness of demand for one good to a change in the price of a substitute or a complement.

▪ The cross elasticity of demand with respect to the price of a substitute is positive. The cross elasticity of demand with respect to the price of a complement is negative.

▪ Income elasticity of demand measures the responsiveness of demand to a change in income. For a *normal good*, the income elasticity of demand is positive. For an *inferior good*, the income elasticity of demand is negative.

▪ When the income elasticity is greater than 1, as income increases, the percentage of income spent on the good also increases.

▪ When the income elasticity is less than 1 but greater than zero, as income increases, the percentage of income spent on the good decreases.

Elasticity of Supply (pp. 103–105)

▪ Elasticity of supply measures the responsiveness of the quantity supplied of a good to a change in its price.

▪ Elasticities of supply are usually positive and range between zero (vertical supply curve) and infinity (horizontal supply curve).

▪ Supply decisions have three time frames: momentary, long-run, and short-run.

▪ Momentary supply refers to the response of sellers to a price change at the instant that the price changes.

▪ Long-run supply refers to the response of sellers to a price change when all the technologically feasible adjustments in production have been made.

▪ Short-run supply refers to the response of sellers to a price change after some adjustments in production have been made.

Key Figures and Table

Key Terms

1. What is the price elasticity of demand and why is it a more useful measure of responsiveness than is the slope of the demand curve?

2. Draw a graph or describe the shape of a demand curve, which represents a good or service that has an elasticity of demand equal to:
   a. Infinity.
   b. Zero.
   c. Unity.

3. Which item in each of the following pairs has the larger price elasticity of demand:
   a. *People* magazine or magazines
   b. Vacations or vacations in Florida
   c. Broccoli or vegetables

4. What three factors determine the size of the elasticity of demand?

5. What do we mean by short-run demand and long-run demand?

6. Explain why the short-run demand for a good is usually less elastic than the long-run demand.

7. What is the connection between elasticity and total revenue? If the elasticity of demand for dental work is 1, by how much does a 10 percent increase in the price of dental work change total revenue?

8. Define the cross elasticity of demand. Is the cross elasticity of demand positive or negative?

9. Define the income elasticity of demand.

10. Give an example of a good or service whose income elasticity of demand is:
    a. Greater than 1.
    b. Positive but less than 1.
    c. Less than zero.

11. State the sign (positive or negative) of the following elasticities:
    a. The cross elasticity of demand for ice cream with respect to the price of frozen yogurt.
    b. The cross elasticity of demand for corn ready to be popped with respect to the price of popcorn machines.
    c. The income elasticity of demand for Caribbean cruises.
    d. The income elasticity of demand for toothpaste.

12. Define the elasticity of supply. Is the elasticity of supply positive or negative?

13. Give an example of a good or service whose elasticity of supply is:
    a. Zero.
    b. Greater than zero but less than infinity.
    c. Infinity.

14. What do we mean by momentary, short-run, and long-run supply?

15. Why is momentary supply perfectly inelastic for many goods?

16. Why is long-run supply more elastic than short-run supply?

1. The figure shows the demand for videotape rentals.

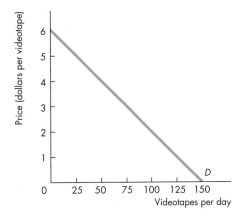

   a. At what prices is the elasticity of demand equal to 1, infinity, and zero?
   b. At what price is total revenue maximized?
   c. Calculate the elasticity of demand for a rise in the rental price from $4 to $5.

2. Assume that the demand for videotape rentals in problem 1 increases by 10 percent at each price.
   a. Draw the old and new demand curves.
   b. Calculate the elasticity of demand for a rise in the rental price from $4 to $5. Compare your answer with that of problem 1(c).

3. You have been hired as an economic consultant by Intel and given the following world demand schedule for Intel chips:

Price (dollars per chip)	Quantity demanded (millions of chips per year)
100	60
200	50
300	40
400	30
500	20

Your advice is needed on the following questions:

a. What will happen to Intel's total revenue if the price of a chip falls from $400 to $300?
b. What will happen to Intel's total revenue if the price of a chip falls from $300 to $200?
c. What is the price at which Intel's total revenue is maximized?
d. What quantity of chips will be bought at the price that answers problem 3(c)?
e. At an average price of $350, is the demand for chips elastic or inelastic? Use the total revenue test and your answer to problem 3(a) to answer this question.
f. At an average price of $250, is the demand for chips elastic or inelastic? Use the total revenue test and your answer to problem 3(b) to answer this question.
g. What is the elasticity of demand for chips at the price that maximizes Intel's total revenue?

4. The following table gives some data on the demand for long-distance telephone calls:

Price (cents per minute)	Quantity demanded (millions of minutes per day)	
	Short-Run	Long-Run
10	700	1,000
20	500	500
30	300	0

At a price of 20¢ a minute:
a. Calculate the elasticity of short-run demand.
b. Calculate the elasticity of long-run demand.
c. Is the demand for calls more elastic in the short run or the long run?

5. In problem 4, does total expenditure on calls increase or decrease as the price of a call decreases from 20¢ a minute to 10¢ a minute?
a. In the short run
b. In the long run

6. The following table gives some data on the supply of long-distance phone calls:

Price (cents per minute)	Quantity supplied (millions of minutes per day)	
	Short-Run	Long-Run
10	300	0
20	500	500
30	700	1,000

At 20¢ a minute, calculate the elasticity of:
a. Short-run supply.
b. Long-run supply.

CRITICAL THINKING

1. Study *Reading Between the Lines* on pp. 106–107 on the markets for gasoline and automobiles in Venezuela and then answer the following questions:
a. What are the main consequences of the rise in the price of gasoline from 7 cents a gallon to 44 cents a gallon that are reported in the news article?
b. What other consequences can you think of that are *not* reported in the news article?
c. Does the news article tell us or give us any clues as to whether the *relative* price of gasoline increased?
d. The news article does not tell us that prices on the average increased by 100 percent (doubled) during 1996 in Venezuela. What does this fact tell you about the change in the relative price of gasoline?
e. Use the price elasticity of demand and the cross elasticity of demand to explain the events described in this news article and take into account the fact in part (d).
f. Why do you think Carlos doesn't sell his gas-guzzler and replace it with a similar aged-smaller car that is more fuel-efficient?
g. What do you expect happened to the demand for bus and train travel in Caracas as a result of the gas price increase? Do you think the demand for these modes of transportation is price elastic or inelastic? Explain your answer.
h. What do you expect happened to the incomes of the owners of gas stations?
i. What do you expect happened to the incomes of workers at gas stations?

6

Efficiency

People constantly strive to get more for less. As consumers, we love to get a bargain. We enjoy telling our friends about the great deal we got on CDs or some other item we bought at a surprisingly low price. Every time we buy something, or decide to *not* buy something, we express our view about how scarce resources should be used. We try to spend our incomes in ways that get the most out of our scarce resources. For example, we balance the pleasure we get from our expenditure on leisure and entertainment against that we derive from our textbooks and other educational materials. ◆ Is the allocation of our resources between leisure and education, pizza and submarine sandwiches, roller-blades and squash balls, and all the other things we buy the right one? Could we get more out of our resources if we spent

More for Less

more on some goods and services and less on others? ◆ Scientists and engineers devote enormous efforts to finding more productive ways of using our scarce land, labor, and capital resources to produce goods and services. Workers in factories and on assembly lines make suggestions that increase productivity. Is

our economy an efficient mechanism for producing goods and services? Do we get the most out of our scarce resources in our factories, offices, and shops? ◆ Some firms make huge profits year after year. Microsoft, for example, has generated enough profit over the past ten years to rocket Bill Gates, one of its founders, into the position of being one of the richest people in the world. Is that kind of business success a sign of efficiency? ◆ These are the kinds of questions that you will explore in this chapter. You will first learn some concepts that enable you to think about efficiency more broadly than the everyday use of that word. You will discover that competitive markets can be efficient. But you will also discover some sources of inefficiency that can be addressed with government action. You will also discover that firms that make huge profits, while efficient in one sense, might be inefficient in a broader sense.

After studying this chapter, you will be able to:

■ Distinguish between value and price

■ Define consumer surplus

■ Distinguish between cost and price

■ Define producer surplus

■ Explain why consumer surplus and producer surplus are the gains from trade

■ Explain why competitive markets move resources to their highest-valued uses

■ Explain the sources of inefficiency in our economy

Efficiency: A Refresher

IT IS HARD TO TALK ABOUT EFFICIENCY IN ordinary conversation without generating both disagreement and misunderstanding. Many people see efficiency as a clearly desirable goal. To an engineer, an entrepreneur, a politician, a working mother, or an economist, getting more for less seems like an obviously sensible thing to aim for. But some people think that the pursuit of efficiency conflicts with other goals. And they believe the other goals are more worthy of pursuit. Environmental protection groups worry about contamination from "efficient" nuclear power plants. And car producers worry about competition from "efficient" foreign producers.

Economists use the idea of efficiency in a way that avoids these conflicts. Resource use is **efficient** when we produce the goods and services that people value most highly (see Chapter 3, pp. 46-48). Equivalently, resource use is efficient when we cannot produce more of a good or service without giving up some other good or service that we value more highly.

If people value a nuclear-free environment more highly than they value cheap electric power, it is efficient to use higher-cost, non-nuclear technologies to produce electricity. Efficiency is not a cold, mechanical concept. It is a concept based on value, and value is based on people's feelings.

Think about the efficient quantity of pizza. To produce more pizza, we must give up some other goods and services. For example, we might give up some submarine sandwiches. To get more pizzas, we forgo submarines. If we produce fewer pizzas we can produce more submarines. What is the efficient quantity of pizza to produce? The answer depends on marginal benefit and marginal cost.

Marginal Benefit

If we consume one more pizza, we receive a marginal benefit. **Marginal benefit** is the benefit that a person receives from consuming one more unit of a good or service. The marginal benefit from a good or service is measured as the maximum amount that a person is willing to pay for one more unit of it. So the marginal benefit from a pizza is the maximum amount of other goods and services that people are willing to give up to get one more pizza. The marginal benefit from pizza decreases as the quantity of pizza consumed increases— the principle of *decreasing marginal benefit*.

We can express the marginal benefit from a pizza as the number of submarine sandwiches that people are willing to forgo to get one more pizza. But we can also express marginal benefit as the dollar value of other goods and services that people are willing to forgo. Figure 6.1 shows the marginal benefit from pizza expressed in this way. As the quantity of pizza increases, the value of other items that people are willing to forgo to get yet one more pizza decreases.

Marginal Cost

If we produce one more pizza, we incur a marginal cost. **Marginal cost** is the opportunity cost of producing *one more unit* of a good or service. The marginal cost of a good or service is measured as the

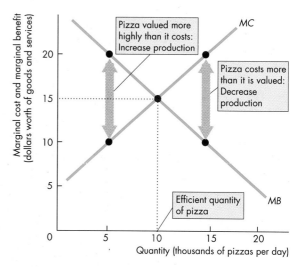

FIGURE 6.1

The Efficient Quantity of Pizza

The marginal benefit curve (*MB*) shows what people *are willing to* forgo to get one more pizza. The marginal cost curve (*MC*) shows what people *must* forgo to get one more pizza. If fewer than 10,000 pizzas a day are produced, marginal benefit exceeds marginal cost. Greater value can be obtained by producing more pizzas. If more than 10,000 pizzas a day are produced, marginal cost exceeds marginal benefit. Greater value can be obtained by producing fewer pizzas. If 10,000 pizzas a day are produced, marginal benefit equals marginal cost and the efficient quantity of pizza is available.

value of the best alternative forgone. So the marginal cost of a pizza is the value of the best alternative forgone to get one more pizza. The marginal cost of a pizza increases as the quantity of pizza produced increases—the principle of *increasing marginal cost*.

We can express marginal cost as the number of submarine sandwiches we must forgo to get one more pizza. But we can also express marginal cost as the dollar value of other goods and services we must forgo. Figure 6.1 shows the marginal cost of pizza expressed in this way. As the quantity of pizza produced increases, the value of other items we must forgo to get yet one more pizza increases.

Efficiency and Inefficiency

To determine the efficient quantity of pizza, we compare the marginal cost of a pizza with the marginal benefit from a pizza. There are three possible cases:

- Marginal benefit exceeds marginal cost.
- Marginal cost exceeds marginal benefit.
- Marginal benefit equals marginal cost.

Marginal Benefit Exceeds Marginal Cost

Suppose the quantity of pizza produced is 5,000 a day. Figure 6.1 shows that at this quantity, the marginal benefit of a pizza is $20. That is, when the quantity of pizza available is 5,000 a day, people are willing to pay $20 for the 5,000th pizza.

Figure 6.1 also shows that the marginal cost of the 5,000th pizza is $10. That is, to produce one more pizza, the value of other goods and services that we must forgo is $10. If pizza production increases from 4,999 to 5,000, the value of the additional pizza is $20 and its marginal cost is $10. By producing this pizza, the value of the pizza produced exceeds the value of the goods and services forgone by $10. Resources are used more efficiently—they create more value—if we produce an extra pizza and fewer other goods and services. This same reasoning applies all the way up to the 9,999th pizza. Only when we get to the 10,000th pizza does marginal benefit not exceed marginal cost.

Marginal Cost Exceeds Marginal Benefit

Suppose the quantity of pizza produced is 15,000 a day. Figure 6.1 shows that at this quantity, the marginal benefit of a pizza is $10. That is, when the quantity of pizza available is 15,000 a day, people are willing to pay $10 for the 15,000th pizza.

Figure 6.1 also shows that the marginal cost of the 15,000th pizza is $20. That is, to produce one more pizza, the value of the other goods and services that we must forgo is $20.

If pizza production decreases from 15,000 to 14,999, the value of the one pizza forgone is $10 and its marginal cost is $20. So by not producing this pizza, the value of the other goods and services produced exceeds the value of the pizza forgone by $10. Resources are used more efficiently—they create more value—if we produce one fewer pizza and more other goods and services. This same reasoning applies all the way down to the 10,001st pizza. Only when we get to the 10,000th pizza does marginal cost not exceed marginal benefit.

Marginal Benefit Equals Marginal Cost

Suppose the quantity of pizza produced is 10,000 a day. Figure 6.1 shows that at this quantity, the marginal benefit of a pizza is $15. That is, when the quantity of pizza available is 10,000 a day, people are willing to pay $15 for the 10,000th pizza.

Figure 6.1 also shows that the marginal cost of the 10,000th pizza is $15. That is, to produce one more pizza, the value of other goods and services that we must forgo is $15.

In this situation, we cannot increase the value of the goods and services produced by either increasing or decreasing the quantity of pizza. If we increase the quantity of pizza, the 10,001st pizza costs more to produce than it is worth. If we decrease the quantity of pizza produced, the 9,999th pizza is worth more than it costs to produce. So when marginal benefit equals marginal cost, resource use is efficient.

R E V I E W

- If marginal benefit exceeds marginal cost, we can use resources more efficiently by increasing the production of pizza and decreasing the production of other goods. The value of the extra pizza exceeds the value of other goods forgone.
- If marginal cost exceeds marginal benefit, we can use our resources more efficiently by decreasing the production of pizza and increasing the production of other goods. The value of the other goods exceeds the value of the pizza forgone.
- If marginal benefit equals its marginal cost, we are producing the efficient quantity of pizza.

Does a competitive pizza market produce the efficient quantity of pizza? Let's answer this question.

Value, Price, and Consumer Surplus

TO INVESTIGATE WHETHER A COMPETITIVE market is efficient, we need to learn about the connection between demand and marginal benefit and supply and marginal cost.

Value, Willingness to Pay, and Demand

In everyday life, we talk about "getting value for money." When we use this expression we are distinguishing between *value* and *price*. Value is what we get, and price is what we pay.

The **value** of one more unit of a good or service is its *marginal benefit*. Marginal benefit can be expressed as the maximum price that people are willing to pay for another unit of the good or service. The willingness to pay for a good or service determines the demand for it.

In Fig. 6.2(a), the demand curve shows the quantity demanded at each price. For example, when the price of a pizza is $15, the quantity demanded is 10,000 pizzas a day. In Fig. 6.2(b), the demand curve shows the maximum price that people are willing to pay when there is a given quantity. For example, when 10,000 pizzas a day are available, the most that people are willing to pay for a pizza is $15. This interpretation means that the marginal benefit from the 10,000th pizza is $15.

When we draw a demand curve, we use a *relative price*, not a *money price*. A relative price is expressed in dollar units, but it measures the number of dollars worth of other goods and services forgone to obtain one more unit of the good in question (see Chapter 4, p. 68). So a demand curve tells us the quantity of other goods and services that people are willing to forgo to get an additional unit of a good. But this is what a marginal benefit curve tells us, too. So:

A demand curve is a marginal benefit curve.

We don't always have to pay the maximum price that we are willing to pay. When we buy something, we often get a bargain. Let's see how.

FIGURE 6.2

Demand, Willingness to Pay, and Marginal Benefit

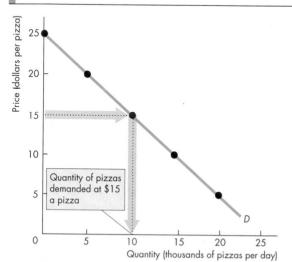

Quantity of pizzas demanded at $15 a pizza

(a) Price determines quantity demanded

The demand curve for pizza, *D*, shows the quantity of pizza demanded at each price, other things remaining the same. It also shows the maximum price that consumers are willing to pay if a given quantity of pizza is available. At a price of $15,

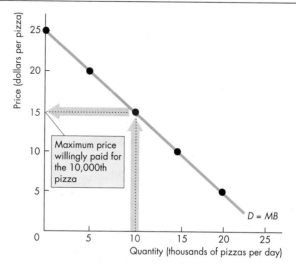

Maximum price willingly paid for the 10,000th pizza

(b) Quantity determines willingness to pay

the quantity demanded is 10,000 pizzas a day (part a). If 10,000 pizzas a day are available, the maximum price that consumers are willing to pay for the 10,000th pizza is $15 (part b).

Consumer Surplus

When people buy something for less than it is worth to them, they receive a consumer surplus. A **consumer surplus** is the value of a good minus the price paid for it.

To understand consumer surplus, let's look at Lisa's demand for pizza, which is shown in Fig. 6.3. Lisa likes pizza, but the marginal benefit she gets from it decreases quickly as her consumption increases.

To keep things simple, suppose Lisa can buy pizza by the slice and that there are 10 slices in a pizza. If a pizza costs $2.50 a slice (or $25 a pizza), Lisa spends her fast food budget on items that she values more highly than pizza. At $2 a slice (or $20 a pizza), she buys 10 slices (one pizza) a week. At $1.50 a slice, she buys 20 slices a week; at $1 a slice, she buys 30 slices a week; and at 50 cents a slice ($5 a pizza), she eats nothing but pizza and buys 40 slices a week.

Lisa's demand curve for pizza in Fig. 6.3 is also her *willingness-to-pay* or marginal benefit curve. It tells us that if Lisa can have only 10 slices a week, she is willing to pay $2 slice. Her marginal benefit from the 10th slice is $2. If she can have 20 slices a week, she is willing to pay $1.50 for the 20th slice. Her marginal benefit from the 20th slice is $1.50.

Figure 6.3 also shows Lisa's consumer surplus from pizza when the price of pizza is $1.50 a slice. At this price, she buys 20 slices a week. A price of $1.50 a slice is the most she is willing to pay for the 20th slice, so its marginal benefit is exactly the price she pays for it.

But Lisa is willing to pay almost $2.50 for the first slice. So the marginal benefit from this slice is close to $1 more than she pays for it. She receives a *consumer surplus* of almost $1 from her first slice of pizza. At a quantity of 10 slices of pizza a week, Lisa's marginal benefit is $2 a slice. So on this slice, she receives a consumer surplus of 50 cents. To calculate Lisa's consumer surplus, we must find the consumer surplus on each slice and add these surpluses together. This sum is the area of the green triangle in Fig. 6.3. This area is equal to the base of the triangle (20 slices of pizza per week) multiplied by the height of the triangle ($1) divided by 2, or $10 a week.

The blue rectangle in Fig. 6.3 is the amount that Lisa pays for pizza, which is $30 a week—20 slices at $1.50 a slice.

All goods and services are like the pizza example you've just studied. Because of decreasing marginal benefit, people receive more benefit from their consumption than the amount they pay.

FIGURE 6.3
A Consumer's Demand and Consumer Surplus

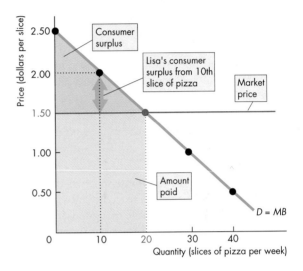

Lisa's demand curve for pizza tells us that at $2.50 a slice, she does not buy pizza. At $2 a slice, she buys 10 slices a week; at $1.50 a slice, she buys 20 slices a week. Lisa's demand curve also tells us that she is willing to pay $2 for the 10th slice and $1.50 for the 20th. She actually pays $1.50 a slice—the market price—and buys 20 slices a week. Her consumer surplus from pizza is $10—the area of the green triangle.

REVIEW

- The value or marginal benefit from a good or service is the maximum amount that someone is willing to pay for it.
- The demand curve shows marginal benefit.
- Consumer surplus is the marginal benefit minus the price of each item consumed.

You've seen how we distinguish between value—marginal benefit—and price. And you've seen that consumers receive a surplus because marginal benefit exceeds price. Next, we're going to study, the connection between supply and marginal cost and learn about producer surplus.

Cost, Price, and Producer Surplus

WHAT YOU ARE NOW GOING TO LEARN ABOUT cost, price, and producer surplus parallels the related ideas about value, price, and consumer surplus that you've just studied.

Firms are in business to make a profit. To do so, they must sell their output for a price that exceeds the cost of production. Let's look at the relationship between cost and price.

Cost, Minimum Supply-Price, and Supply

Firms undertake the most elaborate schemes to earn profits. Earning a profit means receiving more (or at least receiving no less) for the sale of a good or service than the cost of producing it. Just as consumers distinguish between *value* and *price*, so producers distin-

guish between *cost* and *price*. Cost is what a producer gives up, and price is what a producer receives.

The cost of producing one more unit of a good or service is its *marginal cost*. Marginal cost is the minimum price that producers must receive to induce them to produce another unit of the good or service. This minimum acceptable price determines supply.

In Fig. 6.4(a), the supply curve shows the quantity supplied at each price. For example, when the price of a pizza is $15, the quantity supplied is 10,000 pizzas a day. In Fig. 6.4(b), the supply curve shows the minimum price that producers must be offered to produce a given quantity of pizza. For example, if 10,000 pizzas a day are to be produced, the minimum price that producers must be offered is $15 a pizza. This second view of the supply curve means that the marginal cost of the 10,000th pizza is $15.

Because the price is a relative price, a supply curve tells us the quantity of other goods and services that *sellers must forgo* to produce one more unit of the good. But a marginal cost curve also tells us the quantity of other goods and services that we must

---

FIGURE 6.4

Supply, Minimum Supply-Price, and Marginal Cost

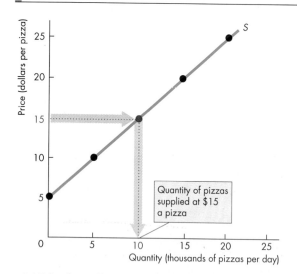

(a) Price determines quantity supplied

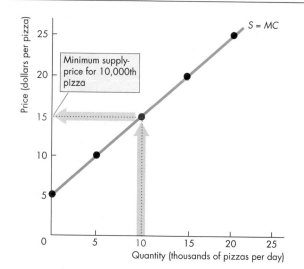

(b) Quantity determines minimum supply-price

The supply curve of pizza, S, shows the quantity of pizza supplied at each price, other things remaining the same. It also shows the minimum price that producers must be offered if a given quantity of pizza is to be produced. At a price of $15,

the quantity supplied is 10,000 pizzas a day (part a). If 10,000 pizzas a day are produced, the minimum price that producers must be offered for the 10,000th pizza is $15 (part b).

forgo to get one more unit of the good. So:

A supply curve is a marginal cost curve.

Producers don't always wind up receiving their minimum supply-price. If the price they receive exceeds the cost they incur, they earn a surplus. This surplus earned by producers is analogous to consumer surplus. Let's look at producer surplus.

Producer Surplus

When a firm sells something for more than it costs to produce, the firm obtains a producer surplus. A **producer surplus** is the price of a good minus the opportunity cost of producing it. To understand producer surplus, let's look at Max's supply of pizza in Fig. 6.5.

Max can produce pizza or bake bread that people like a lot. The more pizza he bakes, the less bread he can bake. His opportunity cost of pizza is the value of the bread he must forgo. This opportunity cost increases as Max increases his production of pizza. If a pizza sells for only $5, Max produces no pizza. He uses his kitchen to bake bread. Pizza just isn't worth producing. But at $10 a pizza, Max produces 50 pizzas a day, and at $15 a pizza, he produces 100 a day.

Max's supply curve is also his *minimum supply-price* curve. It tells us that if Max can sell only one pizza a day, the minimum that he must be paid for it is $5. If he can sell 50 pizzas a day, the minimum that he must be paid for the 50th pizza is $10, and so on.

Figure 6.5 also shows Max's producer surplus. If the price of pizza is $15, Max plans to sell 100 pizzas a day. The minimum that he must be paid for the 100th pizza is $15. So its opportunity cost is exactly the price he receives for it. But his opportunity cost of the first pizza is only $5. So this first pizza costs $10 less to produce than he receives for it. Max receives a *producer surplus* from his first pizza of $10. He receives a slightly smaller producer surplus on the second pizza, less on the third, and so on until he receives no producer surplus on the 100th pizza.

Figure 6.5 shows Max's producer surplus as the blue triangle formed by the area above the supply curve and beneath the price line. This area is equal to the base of the triangle ($10 a slice) multiplied by the height (100 pizzas a week) divided by 2, or $500 a week. Figure 6.5 also shows Max's opportunity costs of production as the red area beneath the supply curve.

FIGURE 6.5

A Producer's Supply and Producer Surplus

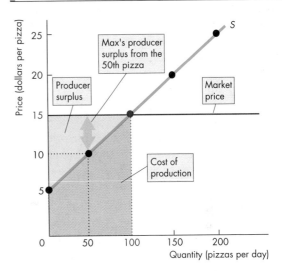

Max's supply curve of pizza tells us that at a price of $5, Max plans to sell no pizza. At a price of $10, he plans to sell 50 pizzas a day; and at a price of $15, he plans to sell 100 pizzas a day. Max's supply curve also tells us that the minimum he must be offered is $10 for the 50th pizza a day and $15 for the 100th pizza a day. If the market price is $15 a pizza, he sells 100 pizzas a day and receives $1,500. The red area shows Max's cost of producing pizza, which is $1,000 a day, and the blue area shows his producer surplus, which is $500 a day.

R E V I E W

- The marginal cost or opportunity cost of producing a good or service is the minimum supply price—the minimum price that producers must be offered. *"Breaking even"*
- Marginal cost is shown by the supply curve.
- Producer surplus is the price received from the sale of a good minus the opportunity cost of producing it.

Consumer surplus and producer surplus can be used to measure the efficiency of a market. Let's see how we can use these concepts to study the efficiency of a competitive market.

Is the Market Efficient?

FIGURE 6.6 SHOWS THE MARKET FOR PIZZA. THE demand for pizza is shown by the demand curve, *D*. The supply of pizza is shown by the supply curve *S*. The equilibrium price is $15 a pizza, and the equilibrium quantity is 10,000 pizzas a day.

The market forces that you studied in Chapter 4 (pp. 78-79) will pull the pizza market to this equilibrium. If the price is greater than $15, a surplus will force the price down. If the price is less than $15, a shortage will force the price up. Only if the price is $15 is there neither a surplus nor a shortage and no forces operating to change the price.

So the market price and quantity are pulled toward their competitive equilibrium values. But is a competitive market efficient? Does it produce the efficient quantity of pizza?

Efficiency of a Competitive Market

The equilibrium in Fig. 6.6 is efficient. Resources are being used to produce the quantity of pizza that people value most highly. It is not possible to produce more pizza without giving up some other good or service that is valued more highly. And if a smaller quantity of pizza is produced, resources are used to produce some other good that is not valued as highly as the pizza forgone.

To see why the equilibrium in Fig. 6.6 is efficient, think about the interpretation of the demand curve as a marginal benefit curve and the supply curve as a marginal cost curve. The demand curve tells us the marginal benefit from pizza. The supply curve tells us the marginal cost of pizza. So where the demand curve and the supply curve intersect, marginal benefit equals marginal cost.

But this condition—marginal benefit equals marginal cost—is the condition that delivers an efficient use of resources. It puts resources to work in the activities that create the greatest possible value. So a competitive market is efficient.

If production is less than 10,000 pizzas a day, the marginal pizza is valued more highly that its opportunity cost. If production exceeds 10,000 pizzas a day, the marginal pizza costs more to produce than the value that consumers place on it. Only when 10,000

FIGURE **6.6**

An Efficient Market for Pizza

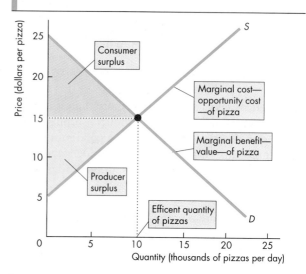

Resources are used efficiently when the sum of consumer surplus and producer surplus is maximized. Consumer surplus is the area below the demand curve and above the market price line—the green triangle. Producer surplus is the area below the price line and above the supply curve—the blue triangle. Here consumer surplus is $50,000, and producer surplus is also $50,000. The total surplus is $100,000. This surplus is maximized when the willingness to pay equals the opportunity cost. The efficient quantity of pizza is 10,000 pizzas per day.

pizzas a day are produced is the marginal pizza worth exactly what it costs. The competitive market pushes the quantity of pizza produced to its efficient level of 10,000 a day. If production is less than 10,000 a day, a shortage raises the price, which stimulates an increase in production. If production exceeds 10,000 a day, a surplus lowers the price, which decreases production.

When the market is using resources efficiently at a competitive equilibrium, the sum of consumer surplus and producer surplus is maximized. At this equilibrium, resources are used in the activities in which they are valued most highly.

Buyers and sellers each attempt to do the best they can for themselves and no one plans for an efficient outcome for society as a whole. Buyers seek the lowest possible price and sellers seek the highest possible price. And the market comes to an equilibrium in which the gains from trade are as large as possible.

The Invisible Hand

Writing in his *Wealth of Nations* in 1776, Adam Smith was the first to suggest that competitive markets send resources to the uses in which they have the highest value—see pp. 2–3. Smith believed that each participant in a competitive market is "led by an invisible hand to promote an end [the efficient use of resources] which was no part of his intention."

You can see the invisible hand at work in the cartoon. The cold drinks vendor has both cold drinks and shade. He has an opportunity cost of each and a minimum supply-price of each. The park-bench reader has a marginal benefit from a cold drink and from shade. You can see that the marginal benefit from shade exceeds the marginal cost, but the marginal cost of a cold drink exceeds its marginal benefit. The transaction that occurs creates gains from trade. The vendor obtains a producer surplus from selling the shade for more than its opportunity cost, and the reader obtains a consumer surplus from buying the shade for less than its marginal benefit. In the third frame of the cartoon, both the consumer and the producer are better off than they were in the first frame. The umbrella has moved to its highest-valued use.

The Invisible Hand at Work Today

The market economy relentlessly performs the activity illustrated in the cartoon and in Fig. 6.6 to achieve an efficient use of resources. And rarely has the market been working as hard as it is today. Think about a few of the changes taking place in our economy that the market is guiding toward an efficient use of resources.

New technologies have cut the cost of producing computers. As these advances have occurred, supply has increased and the price has fallen. Lower prices have encouraged an increase in the quantity demanded of this now less costly tool. The marginal benefit from computers is brought to equality with their marginal cost.

A Florida frost cuts the supply of oranges. With fewer oranges available, the marginal benefit from an orange increases. A shortage of oranges raises their price to allocate the smaller quantity available to the people who value them most highly.

Market forces persistently bring marginal cost and marginal benefit to equality and maximize value.

Drawing by M. Twohy; © 1985 The New Yorker Magazine, Inc.

Sources of Inefficiency

Although markets generally do a good job at sending resources to where they are most highly valued, they do not always get the correct answer. Sometimes markets overproduce a good or service, and sometimes they underproduce. The most significant obstacles to achieving an efficient allocation of resources in the market economy are

- Price ceilings and floors
- Taxes, subsidies, and quotas
- Monopoly
- Public goods
- External costs and external benefits

Price Ceilings and Floors A price ceiling is a regulation that makes it illegal to charge a higher price than a specified level. An example is a ceiling on apartment rents, which some cities impose. A price floor is a regulation that makes it illegal to pay a lower price than a specified level. An example is the minimum wage. (We study both of these restrictions on buyers and sellers in Chapter 7.)

The presence of a price ceiling or a price floor blocks the forces of demand and supply, resulting in a level of production that might exceed or fall short of the quantity determined in an unregulated market.

Taxes, Subsidies, and Quotas Taxes increase the prices paid by buyers and lower the prices received by sellers. Taxes decrease the quantity produced (for reasons that are explained in Chapter 7, on pp. 135–139). All kinds of goods and services are taxed, but the highest taxes are on gasoline, alcohol, and tobacco.

Subsidies, which are payments by the government to producers, decrease the prices paid by buyers and increase the prices received by sellers. Subsidies increase the quantity produced.

Quotas, which are limits to the quantity that a firm is permitted to produce, restrict output below the level that a competitive market produces. Farms are sometimes subject to quotas.

Monopoly A **monopoly** is a firm that has sole control of a market. For example, Microsoft has a near monopoly on operating systems for personal computers. Although monopolies earn large profits, they prevent markets from achieving an efficient use of resources. The goal of a monopoly is to maximize profit; to achieve this goal, it restricts production and raises price. (We study monopoly in Chapter 13.)

Public Goods A **public good** is a good or service that is consumed simultaneously by everyone, even if they don't pay for it. Examples are national defense and the enforcement of law and order. Competitive markets would produce too small a quantity of public goods because of a *free-rider problem*: It is not in each person's interest to buy her or his share of a public good. So a competitive market produces less than the efficient quantity. (We study public goods in Chapter 18.)

External Costs and External Benefits An **external cost** is a cost not borne by the producer but borne by other people. The cost of pollution is an example of an external cost. When an electric power utility burns coal to generate electricity, it puts sulfur dioxide into the atmosphere. This pollutant falls as acid rain and damages vegetation and crops. The utility does not consider the cost of pollution when it decides the quantity of electric power to supply. Its supply is based on its own costs, not on the costs that it inflicts on others. As a result, the utility produces more power than the efficient quantity.

An **external benefit** is a benefit that accrues to people other than the buyer of a good. An example is when someone in a neighborhood paints her home or landscapes her yard. The homeowner does not consider her neighbor's marginal benefit when she decides whether to do this type of work. So the demand curve for house painting and yard improvement does not include all the benefits that accrue. In this case, the quantity falls short of the efficient quantity. (We study externalities in Chapter 20.)

The impediments to efficiency that we've just reviewed and that you will study in greater detail in later chapters result in two possible outcomes:

- Underproduction
- Overproduction

Underproduction

Suppose that one firm owned all the pizza outlets in a city and that it restricted the quantity of pizzas produced to 5,000 a day. Figure 6.7(a) shows that at this quantity, consumers are willing to pay $20 for the marginal pizza—marginal benefit is $20. The marginal cost of a pizza is only $10. So there is a gap between what people are willing to pay and what producers must be offered—between marginal benefit and marginal cost.

The sum of consumer surplus and producer surplus is decreased by the amount of the gray triangle in Fig. 6.7(a). This triangle is called deadweight loss. **Deadweight loss** is the decrease in consumer surplus and producer surplus that results from an inefficient level of production.

The 5,000th pizza brings a benefit of $20 and costs only $10 to produce. If we don't produce this pizza, we are wasting almost $10. Similar reasoning applies all the way up to the 9,999th pizza. By producing more pizza and less of other goods and services, we get more value from our resources.

The deadweight loss is borne by the entire society. It is not a loss for the consumers and a gain for the producer. It is a *social* loss.

FIGURE 6.7

Underproduction and
Overproduction

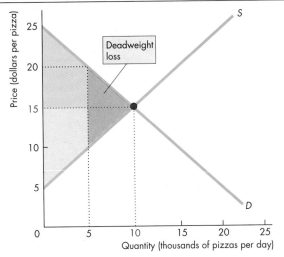

(a) Underproduction

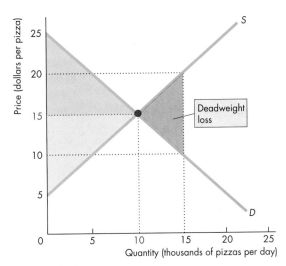

(b) Overproduction

If production is restricted to 5,000 a day, a deadweight loss (the gray triangle) arises. Consumer surplus and producer surplus are reduced to the green and blue areas. At 5,000 pizzas, the benefit of one more pizza exceeds its cost. The same is true for all levels of production up to 10,000 pizzas a day. If production increases to 15,000, a deadweight loss arises. At 15,000 pizzas a day, the cost of the 15,000th pizza exceeds its benefit. The cost of each pizza above 10,000 exceeds its benefit. Consumer surplus plus producer surplus equals the green and blue area minus the deadweight loss.

Overproduction

Suppose the pizza lobby gets the government to pay the pizza producers a fat subsidy and that production increases to 15,000 a day. Figure 6.7(b) shows that at this quantity, consumers are willing to pay only $10 for that marginal pizza but the opportunity cost of that pizza is $20. It now costs more to produce the marginal pizza than consumers are willing to pay for it. The gap gets smaller as production approaches 10,000 pizzas a day, but it is present at all quantities greater than 10,000 a day.

Again, deadweight loss is shown by the gray triangle. This loss must be subtracted from the producer and consumer surplus to calculate the gains from trade. The 15,000th pizza brings a benefit of only $10 but costs $20 to produce. If we produce this pizza, we are wasting almost $10. Similar reasoning applies all the way down to the 10,001st pizza. By producing less pizza and more of other goods and services, we get more value from our resources.

R E V I E W

■ Competitive markets make marginal benefit equal marginal cost and use resources efficiently.

■ Price ceilings and floors; taxes, subsidies, and quotas; monopoly; public goods; and externalities all result in markets producing an inefficient quantity.

■ If production is less than or greater than the efficient level, a deadweight loss occurs and resources are not used in their most valuable ways.

■ Only if production is at the competitive equilibrium level is deadweight loss zero and resource use efficient.

◆ You now know the conditions under which resources are used efficiently. You've seen how a competitive market can be efficient, and you've seen some impediments to efficiency. Some of these arise from government intervention in markets; others require government intervention to overcome them. In the next chapter, we study some sources of inefficiency. And at many points throughout this book, you will return to and use the ideas about efficiency that you've learned in this chapter. *Reading Between the Lines* on pp. 122-123 looks at an example of inefficiency our economy today.

Inefficiency in Software

AUSTIN AMERICAN-STATESMAN, JANUARY 18, 1997

Microsoft Cautious After Its Earnings Beat Expectations

BY LAWRENCE M. FISHER

On Friday, Microsoft Corp. reported second quarter earnings that far exceeded Wall Street analysts' expectations. But the software giant also said that its growth could slow in fiscal 1998. ...

For the quarter ended Dec. 31, the Redmond, Wash., company reported earnings of $741 million, or 57 cents a share, up 29 percent from $575 million, or 45 cents a share, in the comparable period a year earlier. Revenue totaled $2.68 billion, a 22 percent increase over the $2.20 billion reported a year earlier.

Analysts had expected the company to earn 51 cents a share, ...

Maffei said the company had strong performances across all of its businesses, with particularly robust sales of its Windows 95 operating systems for desktop computers and Back Office applications for large enterprises. He said the company intentionally tapered off sales of its Office 95 suite of applications in anticipation of the launch of Office 97 this week.

"We are pleased with the current financial results and growth prospects for the next two quarters, particularly with the outlook for sales of Office 97," Mike Brown, Microsoft's chief financial officer, said in a statement. "However, I do anticipate lower revenue increases in our maturing businesses and margin pressure from continuing aggressive spending on research and development and new business ventures," he said. ...

Reprinted with permission.

Essence of THE STORY

■ In January 1997, Microsoft reported earnings for the quarter ended December 31, 1996, that exceeded Wall Street analysts' expectations.

■ Sales of the Windows 95 operating systems for desktop computers were particularly strong.

■ Microsoft intentionally cut sales of its Office 95 suite of applications in anticipation of the launch of Office 97 during January 1997.

Economic

A N A L Y S I S

■ Figure 1 shows the demand curve for Windows 95, labeled D. The demand curve is also the marginal benefit curve, so it is also labeled MB. It tells us the value to users of one more copy of Windows 95.

■ Figure 1 also shows Microsoft's marginal cost curve, MC, for producing Windows 95. The curve has a gentle slope, which reflects the assumption that the marginal cost of software does not increase by much as the quantity produced increases.

■ If Windows 95 was produced in a competitive market, the marginal cost curve would also be a supply curve. In this case, equilibrium would occur at point a, where the demand curve and the supply curve intersect.

■ At point a, production is efficient—marginal benefit equals marginal cost.

■ The consumer surplus arising from Windows 95 is shown by the green area. The producer surplus arising from Windows 95 is shown as the blue area.

■ But Microsoft does not produce at point a. Instead, it produces at point b in Fig. 2.

■ Microsoft knows that it can make a bigger profit by reducing its output and charging a higher price.

■ By reducing output to Q_b, Microsoft can raise the price of Windows 95 to $90 per unit.

■ Point b is good for Microsoft, but it is inefficient. Marginal benefit exceeds marginal cost, and a deadweight loss arises, as shown by the gray area.

■ With the higher price and smaller quantity at point b, Microsoft's producer surplus is greater than at point a. But consumer surplus is smaller. And the decrease in consumer surplus is larger than the increase in producer surplus by the size of the deadweight loss.

■ The reason why Microsoft's earnings were greater than expected is that the demand for Windows 95 was greater than Wall Street analysts expected. The demand curve was farther to the right than expected. The increase in demand occurred because the marginal benefit of Windows 95 increased.

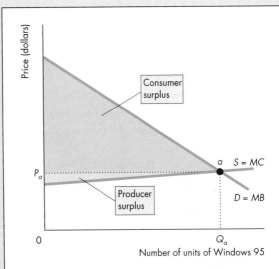

Figure 1 Efficient quantity

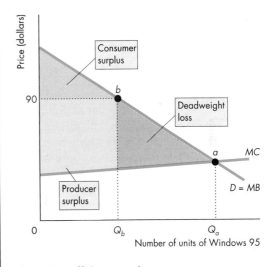

Figure 2 Inefficient quantity

■ The increase in marginal benefit most likely arose from the lower cost of computers and the availability of more highly valued applications such as Office 97.

123

SUMMARY

Key Points

Efficiency: A Refresher (pp. 112–113)

- The marginal benefit received from a good or service—the benefit of consuming one additional unit—is the *value* of the good or service to its consumers.
- The marginal cost of a good or service—the cost of producing one additional unit—is the *opportunity cost* of one more unit to its producers.
- Resources are used efficiently when marginal benefit equals marginal cost.
- If marginal benefit exceeds marginal cost, an increase in production increases the value of production.
- If marginal cost exceeds marginal benefit, a decrease in production increases the value of production.

Value, Price, and Consumer Surplus (pp. 114–115)

- Marginal benefit is measured by the maximum price that consumers are willing to pay for a good or service.
- Marginal benefit determines demand, and a demand curve is a marginal benefit curve.
- Value is what people are *willing to* pay; price is what people *must* pay.
- Consumer surplus equals value minus price, summed over the quantity consumed.

Cost, Price, and Producer Surplus (pp. 116–117)

- Marginal cost is measured by the minimum price producers must be offered to increase production by one unit.
- Marginal cost determines supply, and a supply curve is a marginal cost curve.
- Opportunity cost is what producers pay; price is what producers receive.

- Producer surplus equals price minus opportunity cost, summed over the quantity produced.

Is the Market Efficient? (pp. 118–121)

- In a competitive equilibrium, marginal benefit equals marginal cost and resource use is efficient.
- If production is less than the competitive quantity, marginal benefit exceeds marginal cost. If production exceeds the competitive quantity, marginal cost exceeds marginal benefit. In either case, resource use is inefficient and a deadweight loss arises.
- Monopoly restricts production and creates deadweight loss.
- A competitive market provides too small a quantity of public goods because of the free-rider problem.
- A competitive market provides too large a quantity of goods and services that have external costs and too small a quantity of goods and services that have external benefits.

Key Figures

Key Terms

QUESTIONS

1. What is the distinction between *price* and *value*? How do economists define the value of a good or service?

2. Explain the connection between the demand curve and the concept of the willingness to pay for a good or service.

3. How does the willingness to pay for a good or service change as the quantity available of that good or service changes? Why does willingness to pay change in the way you describe?

4. What is consumer surplus? How do we measure consumer surplus?

5. What is the distinction between *price* and *cost*? How do economists define cost?

6. Explain the connection between the supply curve and the concept of the minimum supply-price of a good or service.

7. How does the minimum supply-price of a good or service change as the quantity bought of that good or service changes? Why does the minimum supply-price change in the way you describe?

8. What is producer surplus? How do we measure producer surplus?

9. What conditions must be satisfied if resources are used efficiently?

10. When does a competitive market achieve an efficient use of resources?

11. What is a deadweight loss?

12. Does a deadweight loss occur only if production is less than the efficient level?

13. List the main impediments to achieving an efficient use of resources?

14. Give an example of each of the impediments to achieving an efficient use of resources?

15. How does monopoly prevent a market from achieving an efficient use of resources?

16. How do public goods prevent a market from achieving an efficient use of resources?

17. How do external costs prevent a market from achieving an efficient use of resources?

18. How do external benefits prevent a market from achieving an efficient use of resources?

PROBLEMS

1. The figure shows the demand for and supply of floppy disks.

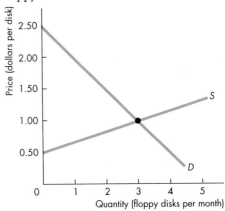

a. What are the equilibrium price and equilibrium quantity of floppy disks?
b. What is the consumer surplus?
c. What is the producer surplus?
d. What is the total surplus?

2. The demand for and supply of submarine sandwiches is as follows:

Price (dollars per sub)	Quantity demanded	Quantity supplied
	(thousands of submarine sandwiches per day)	
0	400	0
1	350	50
2	300	100
3	250	150
4	200	200
5	150	250
6	100	300
7	50	350
8	0	400

a. What is the maximum price that consumers are willing to pay for the 250th submarine sandwich?
b. What is the minimum price that producers must be offered to produce the 250th submarine sandwich?
c. Are 250 submarine sandwiches a day less than or greater than the efficient quantity?
d. What is the consumer surplus if the efficient quantity of submarine sandwiches is produced?

e.   What is the producer surplus if the efficient quantity of submarines is produced?

f.   What is the deadweight loss if 250 submarines are produced?

🖳 3. The following table contains demand schedules for train travel for Ben, Beth, and Bo:

Price (cents per passenger mile)	Quantity demanded (passenger miles)		
	Ben	**Beth**	**Bo**
10	500	300	60
20	450	250	50
30	400	200	40
40	350	150	30
50	300	100	20
60	250	50	10
70	200	0	0

a.   If the price of train travel is 40 cents a passenger mile, what is the quantity demanded by each consumer?

b.   What is the consumer surplus of each consumer?

c.   Which consumer has the largest consumer surplus? Explain why.

b.   If the price of train travel rises to 50 cents a passenger mile, what happens to the consumer surplus of each consumer?

🖳 4. The table gives the demand and supply schedules for chocolate brownies.

Price (cents per brownie)	Quantity demanded	Quantity supplied
	(millions per day)	
50	5	3
60	4	4
70	3	5
80	2	6
90	1	7

a.   What is the price of a brownie and how many are produced and consumed?

b.   What is the total benefit from brownies?

c.   What is the total amount spent on brownies?

d.   What is the consumer surplus on brownies?

e.   What is the producer surplus on brownies?

CRITICAL   THINKING

1. Study *Reading Between the Lines* on pp. 122–123 on Microsoft and then answer the following questions:

a.   Is the quantity of Microsoft software greater than, less than, or equal to the efficient quantity? Explain your answer by using the concepts of marginal benefit, marginal cost, price, consumer surplus, and producer surplus.

b.   What, if anything, do you think could be done to increase the quantity of software and decrease its price?

c.   Microsoft sells copies of its programs in campus software stores at a huge educational discount. Does this practice increase or decrease consumer surplus? Does it increase or decrease Microsoft's producer surplus? Does it bring the quantity of software closer to the efficient quantity? Explain your answer by using the concepts of marginal benefit, marginal cost, price, consumer surplus, and producer surplus.

d.   Chinese software producers have been accused of making illegal copies of Microsoft products and selling them at much lower prices than Microsoft's own price. Does this practice increase or decrease consumer surplus? Does it increase or decrease Microsoft's producer surplus? Does it bring the quantity of software closer to the efficient quantity? Explain your answer by using the concepts of marginal benefit, marginal cost, price, consumer surplus, and producer surplus.

2. How would you set about calculating your own consumer surplus on some item that you buy regularly?

3. How would you set about determining whether the allocation of your time between studying different subjects is efficient? In what units would you measure marginal benefit and marginal cost? Explain your answer by using the concepts of marginal benefit, marginal cost, price, consumer surplus, and producer surplus.

7

Markets in Action

In 1906, San Francisco suffered a devastating earthquake that destroyed more than half the city's homes but killed few people. How did San Francisco's housing market cope with this enormous shock? What happened to rents? Did they have to be controlled to keep housing affordable? Were scarce housing resources allocated to their highest-value uses? ◆ Almost every day, a new machine is invented that saves labor and increases productivity. How do labor markets cope with labor-saving technological change? Does decreasing demand for low-skilled labor drive wages lower and lower? Do we need minimum wage laws to prevent wages from falling? Do minimum wages enable us to use labor efficiently? ◆ Almost everything we buy is taxed. How do taxes affect prices? Do they increase by the full amount of the tax so that we, the buyers, pay all the tax? Or does the seller pay part of the tax? Do taxes help or hinder the market in its attempt to move resources to where they are valued most highly? ◆ Trade in items such as drugs, automatic firearms, and enriched uranium is prohibited. How does the prohibition of trade affect the actual amounts of prohibited goods consumed? And how does it affect the prices paid by those who trade illegally? ◆ In 1991, ideal conditions brought high grain yields. But in 1996, crops were devastated by drought and grain yields were low. How do farm prices and revenues react to such output fluctuations? And how do the actions of speculators and government agencies influence farm revenues? ◆ In this chapter, we study a variety of markets. We use the theory of demand and supply (Chapter 4) and the concepts of elasticity (Chapter 5) and efficiency (Chapter 6) to answer the questions just posed. We'll begin by studying two markets that have the biggest impacts on our lives: the housing market and the labor market. Because these markets are so vital to the economic welfare of everyone, governments often intervene in them to try to control prices. They impose rent ceilings and minimum wages. To set the scene for each, we're going to see how a market responds to turbulent events. We'll begin by seeing how a housing market copes with an extremely severe supply shock.

Turbulent Times

After studying this chapter, you will be able to:

- Explain how price ceilings create shortages and inefficiency

- Explain how price floors create surpluses and inefficiency

- Explain the effects of the sales tax

- Explain how markets for illegal goods work

- Explain why farm prices and revenues fluctuate

- Explain how speculation limits price fluctuations

Housing Markets and Rent Ceilings

To SEE HOW A MARKET COPES WITH A SUPPLY shock, let's transport ourselves to San Francisco in April 1906, as the city is suffering from a massive earthquake and fire. You can sense the enormity of San Francisco's problems by reading a headline from the *New York Times* on one of the first days of the crisis, April 19, 1906:

Over 500 Dead, $200,000,000 Lost in San Francisco Earthquake

Nearly Half the City Is in Ruins and 50,000 Are Homeless

The commander of federal troops in charge of the emergency described the magnitude of the problem:

> Not a hotel of note or importance was left standing. The great apartment houses had vanished . . . two hundred-and-twenty-five thousand people were . . . homeless.[1]

Almost overnight, more than half the people in a city of 400,000 had lost their homes. Temporary shelters and camps alleviated some of the problem, but it was also necessary to utilize the apartment buildings and houses left standing. As a consequence, they had to accommodate 40 percent more people than they had before the earthquake.

The *San Francisco Chronicle* was not published for more than a month after the earthquake. When the newspaper reappeared on May 24, 1906, the city's housing shortage—what would seem to be a major news item that would still be of grave importance—was not mentioned. Milton Friedman and George Stigler describe the situation:

> *There is not a single mention of a housing shortage*! The classified advertisements listed sixty-four offers of flats and houses for rent, and nineteen of houses for sale, against five advertisements of flats or houses wanted. Then and thereafter a considerable number of all types of accommodation except hotel rooms were offered for rent.[2]

How did San Francisco cope with such a devastating reduction in the supply of housing?

[1.] Reported in Milton Friedman and George J. Stigler, "Roofs or Ceilings? The Current Housing Problem," in *Popular Essays on Current Problems*, vol. 1, no. 2 (New York: Foundation for Economic Education, 1946), 3–159.

[2.] *Ibid.*, 3.

The Market Response to a Decrease in Supply

Figure 7.1 shows the market for housing in San Francisco. The demand curve for housing is *D*. There is a short-run supply curve, labeled *SS*, and a long-run supply curve, labeled *LS*.

The short-run supply curve shows the change in the quantity of housing supplied as the price (rent) changes while the number of houses and apartment buildings remains constant. The short-run supply response arises from changes in the intensity with which existing buildings are used. The quantity of housing supplied increases if families rent out rooms that they previously used themselves, and it decreases if families use rooms that they previously rented out to others.

The long-run supply curve shows how the quantity of housing supplied responds to a change in price after enough time has elapsed for new apartment buildings and houses to be erected or for existing ones to be destroyed. In Fig. 7.1, the long-run supply curve is *perfectly elastic*. We do not actually know that the long-run supply curve is perfectly elastic, but it is a reasonable assumption. It implies that the cost of building an apartment is pretty much the same regardless of whether there are 50,000 or 150,000 apartments in existence. *No→ real estate value changes based on that!*

The equilibrium price (rent) and quantity are determined at the point of intersection of the *short-run* supply curve and the demand curve. Before the earthquake, the equilibrium rent is $16 a month and the quantity is 100,000 units of housing.

Figure 7.1(a) shows the situation immediately after the earthquake. The destruction of buildings decreases the supply of housing and shifts the short-run supply curve *SS* leftward to *SS*$_A$. If the rent remains at $16 a month, only 44,000 units of housing are available. But with only 44,000 units of housing available, the maximum rent that someone is willing to pay for the last available apartment is $24 a month. So rents rise. In Fig. 7.1(a), the rent rises to $20 a month. As the rent rises, the quantity of housing demanded decreases and the quantity supplied increases to 72,000 units. These changes occur because people economize on their use of space and make spare rooms, attics, and basements available to others. The higher rent allocates the scarce housing to those people who value it most highly and are willing to pay most for it.

But the higher rent has other, long-run effects. Let's look at these long-run effects.

→ No, just to the richest!

FIGURE 7.1

The San Francisco Housing Market in 1906

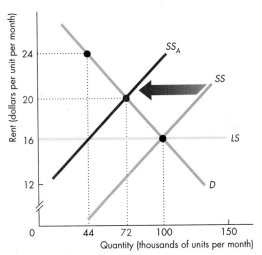

(a) After earthquake

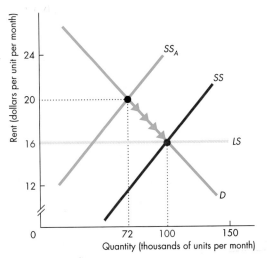

(b) Long-run adjustment

Part (a) shows that before the earthquake, 100,000 housing units were rented at $16 a month. After the earthquake, the short-run supply curve shifts from SS to SS$_A$. The rent rises to $20 a month, and the quantity of housing decreases to 72,000 units.

With rent at $20 a month, there is profit in building new apartments and houses. As the building program proceeds, the short-run supply curve shifts rightward (part b). The rent gradually falls to $16 a month, and the quantity of housing increases to 100,000 units—as the arrowed line shows.

Long-Run Adjustments

With sufficient time for new apartments and houses to be constructed, supply increases. The long-run supply curve in Fig. 7.1(a) tells us that in the long run, housing is supplied at a rent of $16 a month. Because the rent of $20 a month exceeds the long-run supply price, there is a building boom. More apartments and houses are built, and the short-run supply curve shifts gradually rightward.

Figure 7.1(b) shows the long-run adjustment. As more housing is built, the short-run supply curve shifts rightward and intersects the demand curve at lower rents and larger quantities. The market equilibrium follows the arrows down the demand curve. When the process ends, there is no further profit in building. The rent is back at $16 a month, and 100,000 units of housing are available.

A Regulated Housing Market

We've just seen how a housing market responds to a decrease in supply. And we've seen that a key part of the adjustment process is a rise in the rent.

Suppose the government passes a law to stop the rent from rising. Such a law is called a price ceiling. A **price ceiling** is a regulation that makes it illegal to charge a price higher than a specified level. When a price ceiling is applied to housing markets, it is called a **rent ceiling**. How does a rent ceiling affect the housing market?

The effect of a price (rent) ceiling depends on whether it is imposed at a level that is above or below the equilibrium price (rent). A price ceiling set above the equilibrium price has no effect. The reason is that the price ceiling does not constrain the market forces. The force of the law and the market forces are not in conflict. But a price ceiling set below the equilibrium price has powerful effects on a market. The reason is that it attempts to prevent the price from regulating the quantities demanded and supplied. The force of the law and the market forces are in conflict, and one (or both) of these forces must yield to some degree. Let's study the effects of a price ceiling set below the equilibrium price by returning to San Francisco. What would have happened in San Francisco if a rent ceiling of $16 a month—the rent before the earthquake—had been imposed?

This question and some answers are illustrated in Fig. 7.2. At a rent of $16 a month, the quantity of housing supplied is 44,000 units and the quantity

FIGURE 7.2
A Rent Ceiling

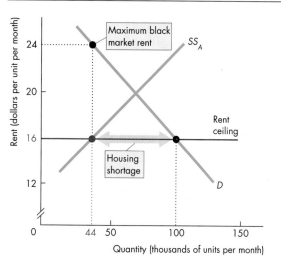

If there had been a rent ceiling of $16 a month, then the quantity of housing supplied after the earthquake would have been stuck at 44,000 units. People would willingly have paid $24 a month for the 44,000th unit. Because the last unit of housing available is worth more than the rent ceiling, frustrated renters will spend time searching for housing and frustrated renters and landlords will make deals in a black market.

demanded is 100,000 units. So there is a shortage of 56,000 units of housing.

But the story does not end here. Somehow, the 44,000 units of available housing must be allocated among people who demand 100,000 units. How is this allocation achieved? When a rent ceiling creates a housing shortage, two developments occur. They are:

■ Search activity
■ Black markets

Search Activity

The time spent looking for someone with whom to do business is called **search activity**. We spend some time in search activity almost every time we buy something. You want the latest hot CD, and you know 4 stores that stock it. But which store has the best deal? You need to spend a few minutes on the telephone finding out. In some markets, we spend

a lot of time searching. An example is the used car market. People spend a lot of time checking out alternative dealers and cars.

But when a price is regulated and there is a shortage, search activity increases. In rent-controlled housing markets, frustrated would-be renters scan the newspapers, not only for housing ads but also for death notices! Any information about newly available housing is useful. And they race to be first on the scene when news of a possible supplier breaks.

The *opportunity cost* of a good includes not only its price but also the value of the search time spent finding the good. So the opportunity cost of housing is equal to the rent (a regulated price) plus the time and other resources spent searching for the restricted quantity available. Search activity is costly. It uses time and other resources, such as telephones, cars, and gasoline, that could have been used in other productive ways. A rent ceiling controls the rent portion of the cost of housing, but it does not control the opportunity cost, which might even be *higher* than the rent would be if the market were unregulated.

Black Markets

A **black market** is an illegal market in which the price exceeds the legally imposed price ceiling. Black markets occur in rent-controlled housing, and scalpers run black markets in tickets for big games and rock concerts.

When rent ceilings are in force, frustrated renters and landlords constantly seek ways to increase rents. One common way is for a new tenant to pay a high price for worthless fittings such as $2,000 for threadbare drapes. Another is for the tenant to pay an exorbitant price for new locks and keys—called "key money."

The level of a black market rent depends on how tightly the rent ceiling is enforced. With loose enforcement, the black market rent is close to the unregulated rent. But with strict enforcement, the black market rent is equal to the maximum price that renters are willing to pay.

With strict enforcement of the rent ceiling in the San Francisco example shown in Fig. 7.2, the quantity of housing available remains at 44,000 units. A small number of people offer housing for rent at $24 a month—the highest rent that someone is willing to pay—and the government detects and punishes some of these black market traders.

Inefficiency of Rent Ceilings

In an unregulated market, the market determines the rent at which the quantity demanded equals the quantity supplied. In this situation, scarce housing resources are allocated efficiently. The sum of *consumer surplus* and *producer surplus*—the gains from trade—is maximized (see Chapter 6, pp. 114–115).

Figure 7.3 shows the inefficiency of a rent ceiling. If the rent is fixed at $16 per unit per month, 44,000 units are supplied. The producer surplus is shown by the blue triangle above the supply curve and below the rent line. Because the quantity of housing is less than the competitive quantity, there is a deadweight loss shown by the gray triangle. This loss is borne by the consumers who can't find housing and the producers who can't supply housing at the new lower price. Consumers who do find housing at the controlled rent gain. If no one incurs search cost, consumer surplus is shown by the sum of the green triangle and the pink rectangle. But search costs might eat up part of the consumer surplus, possibly as much as the entire amount that consumers are willing to pay for the available housing, which is shown by the pink rectangle.

So rent ceilings prevent scarce resources from flowing to their highest-valued use. But don't they ensure that scarce housing goes to the people whose need is greatest? The idea of need is complex. Who is to determine whether one person's "need" is greater than another person's? The unregulated market respects everyone's assessment of "need" by permitting each person's willingness to pay to allocate scarce resources.

When the law prevents rents from adjusting to bring the quantity demanded into equality with the quantity supplied, factors other than rent allocate the scarce housing. One of these factors is discrimination on the basis of race, ethnicity, or sex.

There are many modern examples of rent ceilings, but the best is New York City. One consequence of New York's rent ceilings is that families that have lived in the city for a long time—including some rich and famous ones—enjoy low rents, while newcomers pay high rents for hard-to-find apartments. At the same time, landlords in rent-controlled Harlem abandon entire city blocks to rats and drug dealers.

The effects of rent ceilings have led Assar Lindbeck, chairman of the economic science Nobel Prize committee, to suggest that rent ceilings are the most effective means yet for destroying cities, even more effective than the hydrogen bomb.

FIGURE 7.3
The Inefficiency of a Rent Ceiling

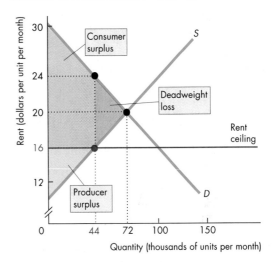

A rent ceiling of $16 a month decreases the quantity of housing supplied to 44,000 units. People are willing to pay $24 a month for the 44,000th unit, so there is a large consumer surplus. Producer surplus shrinks to the blue triangle. A deadweight loss (the gray triangle) arises. If people use no resources in search activity, consumer surplus is shown by the green triangle plus the pink rectangle. But people might use resources in search activity equal to the amount they are willing to pay for the available housing, the pink rectangle.

R E V I E W

- A decrease in the supply of housing increases the equilibrium rent.
- The higher rent decreases the quantity of housing demanded and allocates the scarce housing to its highest-value use.
- In the long run, the higher rent stimulates building, which increases supply and lowers the rent.
- Rent ceilings limit the ability of the housing market to respond to change and can result in a permanent housing shortage. They create inefficiency.

We next study the labor market. We see how an unregulated market adjusts to new technologies and how the minimum wage slows the adjustment.

The Labor Market and the Minimum Wage

FOR EACH ONE OF US, THE LABOR MARKET IS THE most important market in which we participate. It is the market that influences the jobs we get and the wages we earn. Firms decide how much labor to demand, and the lower the wage rate, the greater is the quantity of labor demanded. Households decide how much labor to supply, and the higher the wage rate, the greater is the quantity of labor supplied. The wage rate adjusts to make the quantity of labor demanded equal to the quantity supplied.

But the labor market is constantly hit by shocks, and wages and employment prospects constantly change. The most pervasive source of these shocks is the advance of technology.

New labor-saving technologies become available every year. As a result, the demand for some types of labor, usually the least skilled types, decreases. During the 1980s and 1990s, for example, the demand for telephone operators and television repair persons has decreased. Throughout the past 200 years, the demand for low-skilled farm laborers has steadily decreased.

How does the labor market cope with this continuous decrease in the demand for low-skilled labor? Doesn't it mean that the wages of low-skilled workers are constantly falling?

To answer these questions, we must study the market for low-skilled labor. And just as we did when we studied the housing market, we must look at both the short run and the long run.

In the short run, there is a given number of people who have a given skill, training, and experience. The short-run supply of labor describes how the number of hours of labor supplied by this given number of workers changes as the wage rate changes. To get workers to work more hours, they must be offered a higher wage rate.

In the long run, people can acquire new skills and find new types of jobs. The number of people in the low-skilled labor market depends on the wage rate in this market compared with other opportunities. If the wage rate of low-skilled labor is high enough, people will enter this market. If the wage rate is too low, people will leave it. Some will seek training to enter higher-skilled labor markets, and others will stop working and stay at home or retire.

The long-run supply of labor is the relationship between the quantity of labor supplied and the wage rate after enough time has passed for people to enter or leave the low-skilled labor market. If people can freely enter and leave the low-skilled labor market, the long-run supply of labor is *perfectly elastic*.

Figure 7.4 shows the market for low-skilled labor. Other things remaining the same, the lower the wage rate, the greater is the quantity of labor demanded by firms. The demand curve for labor, D in part (a), shows this relationship between the wage rate and the quantity of labor demanded. Other things remaining the same, the higher the wage rate, the greater is the quantity of labor supplied by households. But the longer the period of adjustment, the greater is the *elasticity of supply* of labor. The short-run supply curve is SS, and the long-run supply curve is LS. In the figure, long-run supply is assumed to be perfectly elastic (the LS curve is horizontal). This market is in equilibrium at a wage rate of $5 an hour and with 22 million hours of labor employed.

What happens if a labor-saving invention decreases the demand for low-skilled labor? Figure 7.4(a) shows the short-run effects of such a change. The demand curve before the new technology is introduced is the curve labeled D. After the introduction of the new technology, the demand curve shifts leftward to D_A. The wage rate falls to $4 an hour, and the quantity of labor employed decreases to 21 million hours. This short-run effect on the wage rate and employment is not the end of the story.

People who are now earning only $4 an hour look around for other opportunities. They see many other jobs (in markets for other types of skills) that pay more than $4 an hour. One by one, workers decide to go back to school or take jobs that pay less but offer on-the-job training. As a result, the short-run supply curve begins to shift leftward.

Figure 7.4(b) shows the long-run adjustment. As the short-run supply curve shifts leftward, it intersects the demand curve D_A at higher wage rates and lower levels of employment. The process ends when workers have no incentive to leave the market for low-skilled labor and the short-run supply curve has shifted all the way to SS_A. At this point, the wage rate has returned to $5 an hour and employment has decreased to 20 million hours a year.

Sometimes, the adjustment process that we've just described is rapid. At other times, it is slow and wages remain low for a long period. To boost the incomes of the lowest-paid workers, the government intervenes in the labor market and sets the minimum wage that employers are required to pay. Let's look at the effects of the minimum wage.

FIGURE 7.4

A Market for Low-Skilled Labor

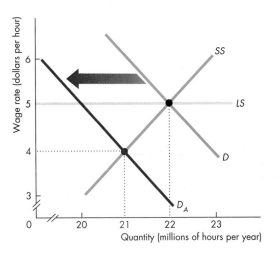

(a) After invention

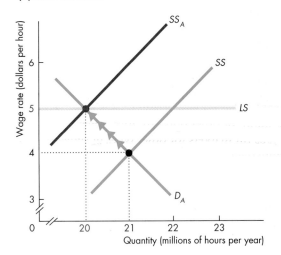

(b) Long-run adjustment

Part (a) shows the immediate effect of a labor-saving invention on the market for low-skilled labor. Initially, the wage rate is $5 an hour and 22 million hours of labor a year are employed. A labor-saving invention shifts the demand curve from D to D_A. The wage rate falls to $4 an hour, and employment decreases to 21 million hours a year. With the lower wage rate, some workers leave this market, and the short-run supply curve starts to shift gradually to SS_A (part b). The wage rate gradually increases, and the employment level decreases. In the long run, the wage rate returns to $5 an hour, and employment falls to 20 million hours a year.

The Minimum Wage

A **minimum wage law** is a regulation that makes the hiring of labor below a specified wage illegal. If the minimum wage is set *below* the equilibrium wage, the minimum wage has no effect. The minimum wage law and market forces are not in conflict. But if a minimum wage is set *above* the equilibrium wage, the minimum wage is in conflict with the market forces and does have some effects on the labor market. Let's study these effects by returning to the market for low-skilled labor.

Suppose that with an equilibrium wage of $4 an hour (Fig. 7.4a), the government imposes a minimum wage of $5 an hour. What are the effects of this law? Figure 7.5 answers this question. It shows the minimum wage as the horizontal red line labeled "Minimum wage." At this minimum wage, 20 million hours of labor are demanded (point *a*) and 22 million hours of labor are supplied (point *b*), so 2 million hours of available labor go unemployed.

The Minimum Wage in Practice

The minimum wage in the United States is set by the federal government's Fair Labor Standards Act. Some state governments have passed state minimum wage laws that exceed the federal minimum. In 1997, the minimum wage is $5.15 an hour. The minimum has been increased from time to time and has fluctuated between 35 percent and more than 50 percent of the average wage of production workers.

Figure 7.5 shows that the minimum wage brings unemployment. But how much unemployment does it bring? Economists do not agree on the answer to this question. Until recently, most economists believed that the minimum wage was a big contributor to high unemployment among low-skilled young workers. But recently this view has been challenged, and the challenge has been rebutted.

David Card and Alan Krueger, two economists at Princeton University, say that increases in the minimum wage have not decreased employment and created unemployment. They say that in California, New Jersey, and Texas, the employment rate of low-income workers increased following an increase in the minimum wage. They suggest three reasons why higher wages might increase employment. First, workers become more conscientious and productive. Second, workers are less likely to quit, so labor

FIGURE 7.5

Minimum Wage and Unemployment

The demand curve for labor is D_A, and the supply curve is SS. In an unregulated market, the wage rate is $4 an hour and 21 million hours of labor a year are employed. If a minimum wage of $5 an hour is imposed, only 20 million hours are hired but 22 million hours are available. Unemployment—*ab*—of 2 million hours a year is created. With only 20 million hours demanded, some workers are willing to supply that 20 millionth hour for $3. Frustrated unemployed workers will spend time and other resources looking for a job.

in the minimum wage, are responsible for the patterns that Card and Krueger found.

One effect of the minimum wage, according to Fig. 7.5, is an increase in the quantity of labor supplied. If this effect occurs, it might show up as an increase in the number of people who quit school before completing high school. Some economists say that this response does occur.

Inefficiency of the Minimum Wage

An unregulated labor market allocates scarce labor resources to the jobs in which they are valued most highly. The minimum wage frustrates the market mechanism and results in unemployment—wasted labor resources—and an inefficient amount of job search.

In Fig. 7.5, with firms employing only 20 million hours of labor at the minimum wage, many people who are willing to supply labor are unable to get hired. You can see that the 20 millionth hour of labor is available for $3. That is, the lowest wage at which someone is willing to supply the 20 millionth hour—read off from the supply curve—is $3. Someone who manages to find a job earns $5 an hour—$2 an hour more than the lowest wage rate at which someone is willing to work. So it pays unemployed people to spend time and effort looking for work. Even though only 20 million hours of labor actually get employed, each person spends time and effort searching for one of the scarce jobs.

turnover, which is costly, is reduced. Third, managers make a firm's operations more efficient.

Most economists remain skeptical about Card and Krueger's suggestions. If higher wages make workers more productive and reduce labor turnover, why don't firms freely pay the wage rates that encourage the correct work habits? And if managers can get greater productivity out of their workers, why don't they do so at any wage rate?

Daniel Hamermesh, of the University of Texas at Austin, believes that firms cut employment *before* the minimum wage is increased in anticipation of the increase. If he is correct, looking for the effects of an increase *after* it has occurred will miss its main effects. Finis Welch of Texas A&M University and Kevin Murphy of the University of Chicago believe that regional differences in economic growth, not changes

R E V I E W

◼ A decrease in the demand for low-skilled labor lowers the equilibrium wage rate.

◼ The lower wage rate encourages some people to leave the labor force and others to train and obtain more skill. In the long run, the supply of low-skilled labor decreases and the wage rate rises.

◼ A minimum wage above the equilibrium wage blocks the adjustment and creates unemployment.

Next we're going to study a more widespread government intervention in markets, taxes, such as the state sales tax. We'll see how taxes change prices and quantities. We'll discover that the sales tax is not paid entirely by the consumer. And we'll see that usually, taxes create a deadweight loss.

Taxes

ALMOST EVERYTHING YOU BUY IS TAXED. But who really pays the tax? Because the sales tax is added to the price of a good or service when it is sold, isn't it obvious that *you*, the buyer, pays the tax? Isn't the price higher than it otherwise would be by an amount equal to the tax? It can be, but usually it isn't. And it is even possible that you actually pay none of the tax! Let's see how we can make sense of these apparently absurd statements.

Who Pays the Sales Tax?

Suppose the government puts a $10 sales tax on CD players. What are the effects of the sales tax on the price and quantity of CD players? To answer this question, we need to work out what happens to demand and supply in the market for CD players.

Figure 7.6 shows this market. The demand curve is *D*, and the supply curve is *S*. With no sales tax, the equilibrium price is $100 per CD player and 5,000 players are bought and sold each week.

When a good is taxed, it has two prices: a price that excludes the tax and a price that includes the tax. Buyers respond only to the price that includes the tax, because that is the price they pay. Sellers respond only to the price that excludes the tax, because that is the price they receive. The tax is like a wedge between these two prices.

Think of the price on the vertical axis of Fig. 7.6 as the price paid by buyers—the price that *includes* the tax. When a tax is imposed and the price changes, there is a change in the quantity demanded but no change in demand. That is, there is a movement along the demand curve and no shift of the demand curve.

But the supply changes and the supply curve shifts. The sales tax is like an increase in cost, so supply decreases and the supply curve shifts leftward to *S + tax*. To determine the position of this new supply curve, we add the tax to the minimum price that sellers are willing to accept for each quantity sold. For example, with no tax, sellers are willing to offer 5,000 players a week for $100 a player. So with a $10 tax, they will supply 5,000 players a week for $110—a price that includes the tax. The curve *S + tax* describes the terms on which sellers are willing to offer players for sale now that there is a $10 tax.

Equilibrium occurs where the new supply curve intersects the demand curve—at a price of $105 and

FIGURE 7.6

The Sales Tax

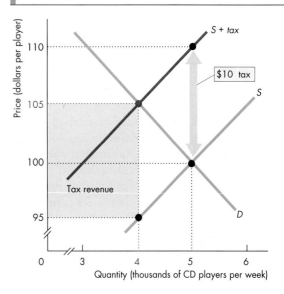

With no sales tax, 5,000 players a week are bought and sold at $100 each. A sales tax of $10 a player is imposed, and the supply curve shifts leftward to *S + tax*. In the new equilibrium, the price rises to $105 a player and the quantity decreases to 4,000 CD players a week. The sales tax raises the price by less than the tax, lowers the price received by the seller, and decreases the quantity. The sales tax brings in revenue to the government equal to the blue rectangle.

a quantity of 4,000 CD players a week. The $10 sales tax increases the price paid by the buyer by $5 a player. And it decreases the price received by the seller by $5 a player. So the buyer and the seller pay the $10 tax equally. *"Happy Medium"*

The tax brings in tax revenue to the government equal to the tax per item multiplied by the number of items sold. The blue area in Fig. 7.6 illustrates the tax revenue. The $10 tax on CD players brings in a tax revenue of $40,000 a week.

In this example, the buyer and the seller split the tax equally: The buyer pays $5 a player, and so does the seller. This equal sharing of the tax is a special case and does not usually occur. But some split of the tax between the buyer and seller is usual. Also, there are other special cases in which either the buyer or the seller pays the entire tax. The division of the tax between the buyer and the seller depends on the elasticities of demand and supply.

Tax Division and Elasticity of Demand

The division of the tax between the buyer and the seller depends, in part, on the elasticity of demand. There are two extreme cases:

- Perfectly inelastic demand—buyer pays.
- Perfectly elastic demand—seller pays.

Perfectly Inelastic Demand   Figure 7.7(a) shows the market for insulin, a vital daily medication of diabetics. Demand is perfectly inelastic at 100,000 doses a day, regardless of the price as shown by the vertical curve *D*. That is, a diabetic would sacrifice all other goods and services rather than not consume the insulin dose that provides good health. The supply curve of insulin is *S*. With no tax, the price is $2 a dose and the quantity is 100,000 doses a day.

   If insulin is taxed at 20¢ a dose, we must add the tax to the minimum price at which drug companies are willing to sell insulin. The result is a new supply curve *S* + *tax*. The price rises to $2.20 a dose, but the quantity does not change. The buyer pays the entire sales tax of 20¢ a dose.

Perfectly Elastic Demand   Figure 7.7(b) shows the market for pink marker pens. Demand is perfectly elastic at $1 a pen as shown by the horizontal curve *D*. If pink pens are less expensive than the others, everyone uses pink. If pink pens are more expensive than the others, no one uses them. The supply curve is *S*. With no tax, the price of a pink marker is $1, and the quantity is 4,000 pens a week.

   If a sales tax of 10¢ a pen is imposed on pink marker pens, we add the tax to the minimum price at which sellers are willing to offer them for sale and the new supply curve is *S* + *tax*. The price remains at $1 a pen, and the quantity decreases to 1,000 a week. The 10¢ sales tax leaves the price paid by the buyer unchanged but lowers the amount received by the seller by the full amount of the sales tax. As a result, sellers decrease the quantity offered for sale.

   We've seen that when demand is perfectly inelastic, the buyer pays the entire tax, and when demand is perfectly elastic, the seller pays it. In the usual case, demand is neither perfectly inelastic nor perfectly elastic, and the tax is split between the buyer and the seller. But the division depends on the elasticity of demand. The more inelastic the demand, the larger is the amount of the tax paid by the buyer.

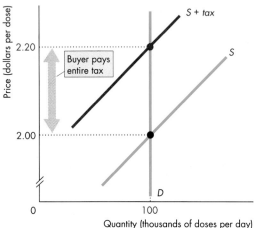

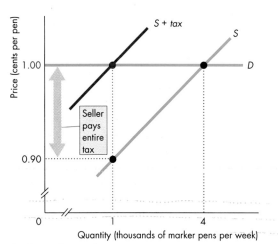

FIGURE 7.7

Sales Tax and the Elasticity of Demand

(a) Inelastic demand

(b) Elastic demand

Part (a) shows the market for insulin. The demand for insulin is perfectly inelastic. With no tax, the price is $2 a dose and the quantity is 100,000 doses a day. A sales tax of 20¢ a dose shifts the supply curve to *S* + *tax*. The price rises to $2.20 a dose, but the quantity bought does not change. Buyers pay the entire tax. Part (b) shows the market for pink marker pens. The demand for pink pens is perfectly elastic. With no tax, the price is $1 a pen and the quantity is 4,000 pens a week. A sales tax of 10¢ a pink pen shifts the supply curve to *S* + *tax*. The price remains at $1 a pen, and the quantity of pink markers sold decreases to 1,000 a week. Sellers pay the entire tax.

Tax Division and Elasticity of Supply

The division of the tax between the buyer and the seller also depends, in part, on the elasticity of supply. Again, there are two extreme cases:

■ Perfectly inelastic supply—seller pays.
■ Perfectly elastic supply—buyer pays.

Perfectly Inelastic Supply   Figure 7.8(a) shows the market for water from a mineral spring that flows at a constant rate that can't be controlled. Supply is perfectly inelastic at 100,000 bottles a week as shown by the supply curve S. The demand curve for the water from this spring is D. With no tax, the price is 50¢ a bottle and the 100,000 bottles that flow from the spring are bought.

Suppose this spring water is taxed at 5¢ a bottle. The supply curve does not change because the spring owners still produce 100,000 bottles a week even though the price they receive falls. But buyers are willing to buy the 100,000 bottles only if the price is 50¢ a bottle. So the price remains at 50¢ a bottle, and the seller pays the entire tax. The sales tax reduces the price received by sellers to 45¢ a bottle.

Perfectly Elastic Supply   Figure 7.8(b) shows the market for sand from which computer-chip makers extract silicon. Supply of this sand is perfectly elastic at a price of 10¢ a pound as shown by the supply curve S. The demand curve for sand is D. With no tax, the price is 10¢ a pound and 5,000 pounds a week are bought.

If this sand is taxed at 1¢ a pound, we must add the tax to the minimum supply-price. Sellers are now willing to offer any quantity at 11¢ a pound along the curve S + tax. A new equilibrium is determined where the new supply curve intersects the demand curve—at a price of 11¢ a pound and a quantity of 3,000 pounds a week. The sales tax has increased the price paid by the buyer by the full amount of the tax—1¢ a pound—and has decreased the quantity sold.

We've seen that when supply is perfectly inelastic, the seller pays the entire tax, and when supply is perfectly elastic, the buyer pays it. In the usual case, supply is neither perfectly inelastic nor perfectly elastic, and the tax is split between the buyer and the seller. But the division between the buyer and the seller depends on the elasticity of supply. The more elastic the supply, the larger is the amount of the tax paid by the buyer.

FIGURE 7.8

Sales Tax and the Elasticity of Supply

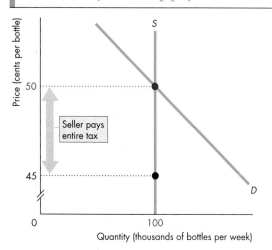

(a) Inelastic supply

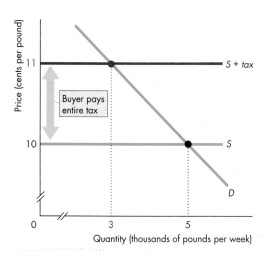

(b) Elastic supply

Part (a) shows the market for water from a mineral spring. Supply is perfectly inelastic. With no tax, the price is 50¢ a bottle. With a sales tax of 5¢ a bottle, the price remains at 50¢ a bottle. The number of bottles bought remains the same, but the price received by the seller decreases to 45¢ a bottle. The seller pays the entire tax. Part (b) shows the market for sand. Supply is perfectly elastic. With no tax, the price is 10¢ a pound and 5,000 pounds a week are bought. The sales tax of 1¢ a pound increases the minimum supply-price to 11¢ a pound. The supply curve shifts to S + tax. The price increases to 11¢ a pound. The buyer pays the entire tax.

Sales Taxes in Practice

Heavily taxed items such as alcohol, tobacco, and gasoline have a low elasticity of demand. So the buyer pays most of the tax. Also, because demand is inelastic, the quantity bought does not decrease much and the government collects a large tax revenue.

But sometimes, the government makes a mistake. In 1991, the Federal government was scraping around for every dollar it could find to cut its deficit. It came up with a plan to put a 10 percent "luxury tax" on pleasure boats, private airplanes, high-priced cars, furs, and jewelry, which it estimated would bring in $300 million a year. But the government did not reckon on the high elasticity of demand for these items. The quantities of pleasure boats and other luxury items bought decreased by up to 90 percent, and the tax revenue collected was only one tenth the amount expected. The luxury tax was quickly abandoned.

This short-lived experiment with a luxury tax explains why the items that are taxed are those that have inelastic demands and why, in practice, buyers pay most of the taxes.

Taxes and Efficiency

You've seen that a sales tax places a wedge between the price paid by buyers and the price received by sellers. The price paid by buyers is also the buyers' willingness to pay, which measures marginal benefit. And the price received by sellers is the sellers' minimum supply-price, which equals marginal cost.

So, because a tax places a wedge between the buyers' price and the sellers' price, it also puts a wedge between marginal benefit and marginal cost and creates inefficiency. With a higher buying price and a lower selling price, the tax decreases the quantity produced and consumed and a deadweight loss arises. Figure 7.9 shows the inefficiency of taxes. Both the consumer surplus and producer surplus shrink. Part of each of these surpluses goes to the government in tax revenue—the purple area in the figure. And part of the surpluses becomes a deadweight loss—the gray area.

In the extreme cases of perfectly inelastic demand and perfectly inelastic supply, the quantity does not change and there is no deadweight loss. The more inelastic is either demand or supply, the smaller is the decrease in quantity and the smaller is the deadweight loss. When demand or supply is perfectly inelastic, the quantity remains constant and there is no deadweight loss.

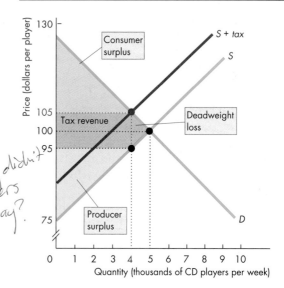

FIGURE 7.9
Taxes and Efficiency

With no sales tax, 5,000 players a week are bought and sold at $100 each. With a sales tax of $10 a player, the buyers' price rises to $105 a player, the sellers' price falls to $95, and the quantity decreases to 4,000 CD players a week. Consumer surplus shrinks to the green area, and producer surplus shrinks to the blue area. Part of the loss of consumer surplus and producer surplus goes to the government as tax revenue, which is shown as the purple area. A deadweight loss also arises, which is shown by the gray area.

R E V I E W

■ The less elastic the demand, the larger is the price increase, the smaller is the quantity decrease, and the larger is the portion of the tax paid by the buyer.

■ The more elastic the supply, the larger is the price increase, the larger is the quantity decrease, and the larger is the portion of the tax paid by the buyer.

■ Taxes are normally placed on goods with inelastic demands.

■ Taxes create inefficiency and deadweight loss.

Governments prohibit the trading of some types of goods such as drugs. Let's see how the market works when trade in a prohibited good takes place.

Markets for Prohibited Goods

THE MARKETS FOR MANY GOODS AND SERVICES
are regulated, and the buying and selling of some
goods are prohibited—the goods and services are
illegal. The best-known examples of such goods
are drugs, such as marijuana, cocaine, and heroin.

Despite the fact that these drugs are illegal, trade
in them is a multibillion-dollar business. This trade
can be understood by using the same economic
model and principles that explain trade in legal
goods. To study the market for prohibited goods,
we're first going to examine the prices and quantities
that would prevail if these goods were not prohibited.
Next, we'll see how prohibition works. Then we'll see
how a tax might limit consumption of these goods.

A Free Market for Drugs

Figure 7.10 shows the market for drugs. The demand
curve, *D,* shows that, other things remaining the same,
the lower the price of drugs, the larger is the quantity
of drugs demanded. The supply curve, *S,* shows that,
other things remaining the same, the lower the price of
drugs, the smaller is the quantity supplied. If drugs
were not prohibited, the quantity bought and sold
would be Q_c and the price would be P_c.

Prohibition on Drugs

When a good is prohibited, the cost of trading in the
good increases. By how much the cost increases and
on whom the cost falls depend on the penalties for
violating the law and the effectiveness with which the
law is enforced. The larger the penalties and the more
effective the policing, the higher are the costs. Penalties might be imposed on sellers, buyers, or both.

Penalties on Sellers   Drug dealers in the United
States face large penalties if their activities are
detected. For example, a marijuana dealer could pay
a $200,000 fine and serve a 15-year prison term. A
heroin dealer could pay a $500,000 fine and serve a
20-year prison term. These penalties are part of the
cost of supplying illegal drugs, and they bring a
decrease in supply—a leftward shift in the supply
curve. To determine the new supply curve, we add
the cost of breaking the law to the minimum price
that drug dealers are willing to accept. In Fig. 7.10,

A Market for a Prohibited Good

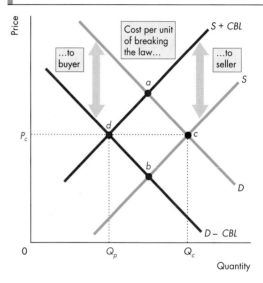

The demand curve for drugs is *D*, and the supply curve is *S*.
With no prohibition on drugs, the quantity bought and sold is
Q_c at a price of P_c—point *c*. If selling drugs is illegal, the cost of
breaking the law by selling drugs (*CBL*) is added to the minimum supply-price and supply decreases to *S* + *CBL*. The price
rises, and the quantity bought decreases—point *a*. If buying
drugs is illegal, the cost of breaking the law is subtracted from
the maximum price that buyers are willing to pay, and demand
decreases to *D* – *CBL*. The price falls, and the quantity bought
decreases—point *b*. If both buying and selling are illegal, both
the supply and demand curves shift, the quantity bought
decreases even more, but (in this example) the price remains
at its unregulated level—point *d*.

the cost of breaking the law by selling drugs (*CBL*) is
added to the minimum price that dealers will accept,
and the supply curve shifts leftward to *S* + *CBL*. If
penalties are imposed only on sellers, the market
moves from point *c* to point *a*. The price increases,
and the quantity bought decreases.

Penalties on Buyers   In the United States, it is
illegal to *possess* drugs such as marijuana, cocaine,
and heroin. For example, possession of marijuana
can bring a prison term of 1 year and possession of
heroin can bring a prison term of 2 years. Penalties
fall on buyers, and the cost of breaking the law must
be subtracted from the value of the good to determine

the maximum price buyers are willing to pay for the drugs. Demand decreases, and the demand curve shifts leftward. In Fig. 7.10, the demand curve shifts to $D - CBL$. With penalties imposed only on buyers, the market moves from point c to point b. The price and the quantity bought decrease.

Penalties on Both Sellers and Buyers If penalties are imposed on sellers *and* buyers, both supply and demand decrease, and both the supply curve and the demand curve shift leftward. In Fig. 7.10 the costs of breaking the law are the same for both buyers and sellers, so both curves shift leftward by the same amount. The market moves to point d. The price remains at P_c, but the quantity bought decreases to Q_p.

The larger the penalties and the greater the degree of law enforcement, the larger is the decrease in demand and/or supply and the greater is the shift of the demand and/or supply curve. If the penalties are heavier on sellers, the supply curve shifts farther than the demand curve and the price rises above P_c. If the penalties are heavier on buyers, the demand curve shifts farther than the supply curve and the price falls below P_c. In the United States, the penalties on sellers are larger than those on buyers, so the quantity of drugs traded decreases and the price increases compared with an unregulated market.

With high enough penalties and effective law enforcement, it is possible to decrease demand and/or supply to the point at which the quantity bought is zero. But in reality, such an outcome is unusual. It does not happen in the case of illegal drugs. The key reason is the high cost of law enforcement and insufficient resources for the police to achieve effective enforcement. Because of this situation, some people suggest that drugs (and other illegal goods) should be legalized and sold openly but also be taxed at a high rate in the same way that legal drugs such as alcohol are taxed. How would such an arrangement work?

Legalizing and Taxing Drugs

From your study of the effects of taxes, it is easy to see that the quantity of drugs bought could be decreased if drugs were legalized and taxed. A sufficiently high tax could be imposed to decrease supply, raise the price, and achieve the same decrease in the quantity bought as with a prohibition on drugs. The government would collect a large tax revenue.

Illegal Trading to Evade the Tax It is likely that an extremely high tax rate would be needed to cut the quantity of drugs bought to the level prevailing with a prohibition. It is also likely that many drug dealers and consumers would try to cover up their activities to evade the tax. If they did act in this way, they would face the cost of breaking the law—the tax law. If the penalty for tax law violation is as severe and as effectively policed as drug-dealing laws, the analysis we've already conducted applies also to this case. The quantity of drugs bought would depend on the penalties for law breaking and on the way in which the penalties are assigned to buyers and sellers.

Some Pros and Cons of Taxes Versus Prohibition
So which works more effectively, prohibition or taxing? The two methods can be made equivalent if the taxes and penalties are set at the appropriate levels. But there are some other differences.

In favor of taxes and against prohibition is the fact that the tax revenue can be used to make law enforcement more effective. It can also be used to run a more effective education campaign against drugs. In favor of prohibition and against taxes is the fact that a prohibition sends a signal that might influence preferences, decreasing the demand for drugs. Also, some people intensely dislike the idea of the government profiting from trade in harmful substances.

R E V I E W

- Penalizing sellers of an illegal good decreases supply and penalizing buyers decreases demand.
- Penalizing either buyers or sellers of an illegal good decreases the quantity bought.
- Taxing a good at a sufficiently high rate can achieve the same consumption level as prohibition.

You've seen how government intervention in markets in the form of price ceilings, price floors, and taxes limits the quantity and creates inefficient resource use. You've also seen how in a market for an illegal good, the quantity can be decreased by imposing penalties on either buyers or sellers or by legalizing and taxing the good. In the next and final section of this chapter, we look at agricultural markets and see how governments try to stabilize farm revenues.

Stabilizing Farm Revenues

WHEN FLOODS COVERED VAST TRACTS OF THE MID-west in the summer of 1993, many farmers saw their crops wiped out. Farm output fluctuates a great deal because of fluctuations in the weather. How do changes in farm output affect farm prices and farm revenues? And how might farm revenues be stabilized? Let's begin to answer these questions by looking at an agricultural market.

An Agricultural Market

Figure 7.11 shows the market for wheat. In both parts, the demand curve for wheat is *D*. Once farmers have harvested their crop, they have no control over the quantity supplied, and supply is inelastic along a *momentary supply curve*. In normal climate conditions, the momentary supply curve is MS_0 (in both parts of the figure).

The price is determined at the point of intersection of the momentary supply curve and the demand curve. In normal conditions, the price is $4 a bushel. The quantity of wheat produced is 20 billion bushels, and farm revenue is $80 billion. Suppose the opportunity cost to farmers of producing wheat is also $80 billion. Then in normal conditions, farmers just cover their opportunity cost.

Poor Harvest Suppose there is a bad growing season, resulting in a poor harvest. What happens to the price of wheat and the revenue of farmers? These questions are answered in Fig. 7.11(a). Supply decreases, and the momentary supply curve shifts leftward to MS_1, where 15 billion bushels of wheat are produced. With a decrease in supply, the price increases to $6 a bushel.

What happens to total farm revenue? It *increases* to $90 billion. A decrease in supply has brought an increase in price and an increase in farm revenue. It does so because the demand for wheat is *inelastic*. The percentage decrease in the quantity demanded is less than the percentage increase in price. You can verify this fact by noticing in Fig. 7.11(a) that the increase in revenue from the higher price ($30 billion light blue area) exceeds the decrease in revenue from the smaller quantity ($20 billion red area). Farmers are now making a revenue in excess of their opportunity cost.

Although total farm revenue increases when there is a poor harvest, some farmers, whose entire crop is

FIGURE 7.11

Harvests, Farm Prices, and Farm Revenue

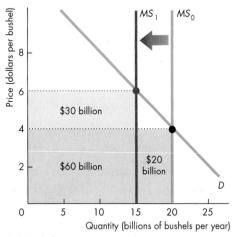

(a) Poor harvest: revenue increases

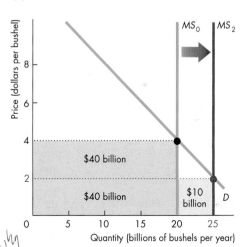

(b) Bumper harvest: revenue decreases

The demand curve for wheat is *D*. In normal times, the supply curve is MS_0 and 20 million bushels are sold for $4 a bushel. In part (a), a poor harvest decreases supply to MS_1. The price rises to $6 a bushel, and farm revenue increases to $90 billion—the $30 billion increase from the higher price (light blue area) exceeds the $20 billion decrease from the smaller quantity (red area). In part (b), a bumper harvest increases supply to MS_2. The price falls to $2 a bushel, and farm revenue decreases to $50 billion—the $40 billion decrease from the lower price (red area) exceeds the $10 billion increase from the increase in the quantity sold (light blue area).

wiped out, suffer a decrease in revenue. Others, whose crop is unaffected, make an enormous gain.

Bumper Harvest   Figure 7.11(b) shows what happens in the opposite situation, when there is a bumper harvest. Now supply increases to 25 billion bushels, and the momentary supply curve shifts rightward to MS_2. With the increased quantity supplied, the price falls to $2 a bushel. Farm revenue decreases to $50 billion. It does so because the demand for wheat is inelastic. To see this fact, notice in Fig. 7.11(b) that the decrease in revenue from the lower price ($40 billion red area) exceeds the increase in revenue from the increase in the quantity sold ($10 billion light blue area).

Elasticity of Demand   In the example we've just worked through, demand is inelastic. If demand is elastic, the price fluctuations go in the same directions as those we've worked out, but revenue fluctuates in the opposite direction. Bumper harvests increase revenue, and poor harvests decrease it. But the demand for most agricultural products is inelastic, and the case we've studied is the relevant one.

Because farm prices fluctuate, institutions have evolved to stabilize them. There are two types of institutions:

■ Speculative markets in inventories
■ Farm price stabilization policy

Speculative Markets in Inventories

Many goods, including a wide variety of agricultural products, can be stored. These inventories provide a cushion between production and consumption. If production decreases, goods can be sold from inventory; if production increases, goods can be put into inventory.

In a market that has inventories, we must distinguish production from supply. The quantity produced is not the same as the quantity supplied. The quantity supplied exceeds the quantity produced when goods are sold from inventory. And the quantity supplied is less than the quantity produced when goods are put into inventory. Supply therefore depends on the behavior of inventory holders.

The Behavior of Inventory Holders   Inventory holders speculate. They hope to buy at a low price and sell at a high price. That is, they hope to buy

goods and put them into inventory when the price is low and sell them from inventory when the price is high. They make a profit or incur a loss equal to their selling price minus their buying price and minus the cost of storage.

But how do inventory holders know when to buy and when to sell? How do they know whether the price is high or low? To decide whether a price is high or low, inventory holders forecast future prices. If the current price is above the forecasted future price, inventory holders sell goods from inventory. If the current price is below the forecasted future price, inventory holders buy goods to put into inventory. This behavior by inventory holders makes the supply perfectly elastic at the price forecasted by inventory holders.

Let's work out what happens to price and quantity in a market in which inventories are held when production fluctuates. Let's look again at the wheat market.

Fluctuations in Production   In Fig. 7.12 the demand curve for wheat is D. Inventory holders expect the future price to be $4 a bushel. The supply curve is S—supply is perfectly elastic at the price expected by inventory holders. Production fluctuates between Q_1 and Q_2.

When production fluctuates and there are no inventories, the price and the quantity fluctuate. We saw this result in Fig. 7.11. But if there are inventories, the price does not fluctuate. When production decreases to Q_1, or 15 billion bushels, inventory holders sell 5 billion bushels from inventory and the quantity bought by consumers is 20 billion bushels. The price remains at $4 a bushel. When production increases to Q_2, or 25 billion bushels, inventory holders buy 5 billion bushels and consumers continue to buy 20 billion bushels. Again, the price remains at $4 a bushel. Inventories reduce price fluctuations. In Fig. 7.12, the price fluctuations are entirely eliminated. When there are costs of carrying inventories and when inventories become almost depleted, some price fluctuations do occur, but these fluctuations are smaller than those occurring in a market without inventories.

Farm Revenue   Even if inventory speculation succeeds in stabilizing prices, it does not stabilize farm revenue. With the price stabilized, farm revenue fluctuates as production fluctuates. But now bumper harvests bring larger revenues than poor harvests do.

FIGURE 7.12

How Inventories Limit
Price Changes

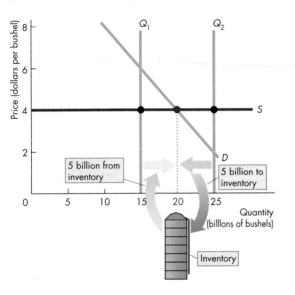

Inventory holders sell wheat from inventory if a poor harvest causes the price to rise above $4 a bushel and buy wheat to hold in inventory if a bumper harvest causes the price to fall below $4 a bushel, making supply (S) perfectly elastic. When production decreases to Q_1, 5 billion bushels are sold from inventory; when production increases to Q_2, 5 billion bushels are added to inventory. The price remains at $4 a bushel.

The reason is that now farmers, in effect, face a perfectly elastic demand for their output.

Farm Price Stabilization Policy

Most governments intervene in agricultural markets. The most extensive such intervention occurs in the European Union. But it also occurs in the United States, where it is designed to stabilize the prices of many agricultural products, such as grains, milk, eggs, tobacco, rice, peanuts, and cotton.

Governments intervene in agricultural markets in three ways. They:

■ Set production limits
■ Set price floors
■ Hold inventories

Production limits, which are called *quotas,* restrict the quantity produced and can result in the price exceeding the price in an unregulated market. Farmers benefit from quotas because the price rises above the minimum supply-price. But consumers lose and quotas create deadweight loss. Quotas exist mainly because of the power of the farm lobby.

Price floors, which are set above the equilibrium price, create surpluses. They work in a similar way to the minimum wage that we studied earlier. The minimum wage creates unemployment and price floors in agricultural markets create surpluses of food products. To make a price floor work, the government's price stabilization agency must buy the persistent surpluses. If the price is persistently greater than the equilibrium price, the government agency buys more than it sells and ends up with large inventory. Such has been the outcome in Europe, where they have "mountains" of butter and "lakes" of wine! The cost of buying and storing the inventory falls on taxpayers, and the main gainers are large, low-cost farms.

If the government price stabilization agency operates like a private inventory holder, it maintains the price close to the equilibrium price. It sells from inventory when price is above normal, and it buys for inventory when the price is below normal. But this type of intervention is not necessary because private trading can achieve the same outcome.

R E V I E W

■ The demand for most farm products is inelastic. With no inventories, a poor harvest increases price and increases farm revenue and a bumper harvest decreases price and decreases farm revenue.

■ Inventory holders who buy at a low price and sell at a high price reduce price fluctuations.

■ Farm price stabilization policies limit price fluctuations but create inefficiency and usually create surpluses.

◆ You now know how to use the demand and supply model to predict prices, to study government intervention in markets, and to study the sources and costs of inefficiency. Before you leave this topic, take a look at *Reading Between the Lines* on pp. 144–145 and see what is happening in the California housing market today.

Policy
WATCH

Rent Controls Today

THE NEW YORK TIMES, DECEMBER 31, 1995

California Begins Easing Its Once-Strict Laws on Rent Control

SANTA MONICA, Calif.—New Year's Day will bring a loosening of rent control in this bayside city and four other California cities, under a state law that takes effect on Monday.

Santa Monica, whose nearly 90,000 residents are nearly 80 percent renters, has offered cheap apartments with cool breezes and ocean views since voters approved a 1979 ordinance that controlled the rents of 31,600 apartments here.

Under this ordinance—one of the strictest in the nation—Santa Monica landlords could raise rents only once a year, and then by only half the inflation rate. This meant, landlords complained, that they were not getting a fair profit.

Under the new law, ... landlords will be able to raise rents on new tenants by 15 percent. Although landlords can take this increase only twice during the next three years, beginning in 1999 they can raise rents on vacant units to whatever the market will bear. ...

Joan McDowell, who lives in a $450-a-month, one-bedroom apartment just two blocks from the beach in Santa Monica, says rent control enabled her to stay in the Los Angeles area, where she has lived for most of her 67 years. "I never thought I could continue to live in Southern California because the cost of living was so high and I had to live on my retirement income," she said.

While landlords and tenant advocates rarely agree, they both say that Santa Monica apartments rent for $200 to $500 less than they would without rent control.

But landlords have long argued that rent control benefits upper-income renters, rather than those who need it, and discourages maintenance and new construction because of limited rental profits. ...

John M. Rodriguez, a landlord and vocal critic of rent control, says the new law will bring additional revenue for landlords, more construction and maintenance jobs for local residents, and more taxes for state and Federal coffers. Under rent control, he said, "We all lose."...

Essence of THE STORY

■ Santa Monica and four other California cities loosened rent controls on January 1, 1996.

■ Under the new law, landlords can raise rent by 15 percent twice through 1998 on new tenants. Starting in 1999, vacant apartment rent can be raised to whatever the market will bear.

■ Landlords and tenants agree that without rent control, rents would be $200 to $500 higher.

■ The new legislation is predicted to bring new construction to Santa Monica.

Economic

A N A L Y S I S

■ Figure 1 shows the market for rental units in Santa Monica. Under rent control, 31,600 units are available at a monthly rent of $1,000 (assumed).

■ The equilibrium rent with no rent control is $1,500 a month.

■ In Fig. 1, the rent ceiling is $500 a month below the unregulated market rent, which is the upper end of the range reported in the news article.

■ The rent ceiling is below the equilibrium rent, so there is a shortage of rental housing in Santa Monica.

■ With rent controls, landlords receive a producer surplus (the blue area) that is smaller than they would receive without rent controls.

■ With rent controls, renters receive a consumer surplus (the green area) that is larger than they would receive without rent controls.

■ But some would-be landlords and would-be renters bear a deadweight loss (the gray area).

■ Rent control is being relaxed only on units as they become vacant.

■ Figure 2 shows that as rents initially rise by 15 percent, the quantity of rental housing supplied increases—there is a movement along the supply curve of housing.

■ When rent controls are completely removed, the rent rises to $1,500 a month.

■ This situation is not likely to be the long-run equilibrium. As predicted by John Rodriguez in the news article, higher rents will bring more construction.

■ New construction will limit the rise in rents because it will shift the supply curve rightward.

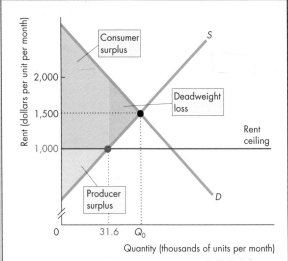

Figure 1 Rent ceilings

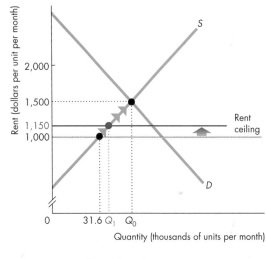

Figure 2 Ceiling relaxed

You're

THE VOTER

■ If you lived in a rental apartment in Santa Monica, would you favor or oppose the relaxation of rent control?

■ If you owned a rental apartment in Santa Monica, would you favor or oppose the relaxation of rent control?

■ If you owned a block of land on which apartments can be built in Santa Monica, would you favor or oppose the relaxation of rent control?

■ If you were the mayor of Santa Monica, would you favor or oppose the relaxation of rent control?

■ If you were a new resident of Santa Monica and were looking for your first home, would you favor or oppose to the relaxation of rent control?

■ All things considered, how would you vote on a rent control referendum and why?

SUMMARY

Key Points

Housing Markets and Rent Ceilings (pp. 128–131)

- A decrease in the supply of housing decreases short-run supply and increases the equilibrium rent.
- The higher rent increases the quantity of housing supplied in the short run and stimulates building in the long run. The rent decreases, and the quantity of housing increases.
- If a rent ceiling prevents the rent from increasing, the quantity supplied remains constant and there is a housing shortage, which creates wasteful search and black markets.

The Labor Market and the Minimum Wage (pp. 132–134)

- A decrease in the demand for low-skilled labor lowers the wage rate and reduces employment.
- The lower wage rate encourages people with low skill to acquire more skill, which decreases the supply of low-skilled labor. The wage rises gradually to its original level, and employment decreases.
- Imposing a minimum wage above the equilibrium wage creates unemployment and an increase in the amount of time people spend searching for a job.
- Minimum wages hit young people who have the fewest skills hardest.

Taxes (pp. 135–138)

- When a good or service is taxed, usually the price increases and the quantity bought decreases but the price increases by less than the tax. The buyer pays part of the tax and the seller pays part of the tax.
- The portion of the tax paid by the buyer and by the seller depends on the elasticity of demand and the elasticity of supply.
- The less elastic the demand and the more elastic the supply, the greater is the price increase, the smaller is the quantity decrease, and the larger is the portion of the tax paid by the buyer.

- If demand is perfectly elastic or supply is perfectly inelastic, the seller pays the entire tax. If demand is perfectly inelastic or supply is perfectly elastic, the buyer pays the entire tax.

Markets for Prohibited Goods (pp. 139–140)

- Penalties on sellers of an illegal good increase the cost of selling the good and decrease its supply. Penalties on buyers decrease their willingness to pay and decrease the demand for the good.
- The higher the penalties and the more effective the law enforcement, the smaller is the quantity bought. The price is higher or lower than the unregulated price, depending on whether the penalties on sellers or buyers are higher.
- A tax set at a sufficiently high rate will decrease the quantity of a drug consumed, but there will be a tendency for the tax to be evaded.

Stabilizing Farm Revenues (pp. 141–143)

- Farm revenues fluctuate because supply fluctuates.
- The demand for most farm products is inelastic, so a decrease in supply increases the price and increases farm revenue, while an increase in supply decreases price and decreases farm revenue.
- Inventory holders and government agencies act to stabilize farm prices and revenues.

Key Figures

Key Terms

QUESTIONS

1. What happens to the rent and to the quantity of housing available if an earthquake reduces the supply of housing? Trace the evolution of the rent and the quantity of housing rented over time.

2. What is a rent ceiling? In the situation described in question 1, how will things be different if a rent ceiling is imposed?

3. Describe what happens to the price and quantity in a housing market in which there is an increase in supply. Trace the evolution of the price and quantity in the market over time.

4. Describe what happens to the wage rate and quantity of low-skilled labor employed when there is a decrease in demand for labor. Trace the evolution of the wage rate and employment over time.

5. What is a price floor? In the situation described in question 4, how are things different if a minimum wage is introduced?

6. How does the imposition of the sales tax on a good influence the supply of and demand for that good? How does it influence the price of the good and the quantity bought?

7. How does a prohibition of the sale of a good affect the demand for and supply of the good? How does it affect the price of the good and the quantity bought?

8. How does a prohibition of the consumption of a good affect the demand for and supply of the good? How does it affect the price of the good and the quantity bought?

9. Explain the alternative ways in which the consumption of harmful drugs can be controlled. What are the arguments for and against each method?

10. Why do farm revenues fluctuate?

11. Do farm revenues increase or decrease when there is a bumper crop and there are no inventories? Why?

12. Explain why speculation can stabilize the price of a storable commodity but does not stabilize the revenues of the producers of such a commodity.

13. How can farm prices be stabilized? Is such stabilization profitable?

PROBLEMS

1. The figure shows the demand for and supply of rental housing in your town.

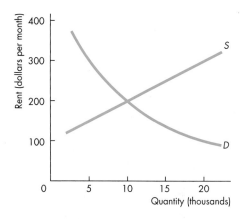

What are the equilibrium rent and the equilibrium quantity of rented housing?

2. A rent ceiling of $150 a month is imposed in the housing market in problem 1.
   a. What is the quantity of housing rented?
   b. What is the shortage of housing?
   c. What is the maximum price that demanders are willing to pay for the last unit available?

3. The demand for and supply of teenage labor are:

Wage rate (dollars per hour)	Quantity demanded	Quantity supplied
	(hours per month)	
2	3,000	1,000
3	2,500	1,500
4	2,000	2,000
5	1,500	2,500
6	1,000	3,000

   a. What is the equilibrium wage rate?
   b. What is the level of employment?
   c. What is the level of unemployment?
   d. If the government imposes a minimum wage of $3 an hour for teenagers, how many hours do teenagers work?
   e. If the government imposes a minimum wage of $5 an hour for teenagers, what are the employment and unemployment levels?

f.   If there is a minimum wage of $5 an hour and demand increases by 500 hours, what is the level of unemployment?

4. The demand and supply schedules for chocolate brownies are:

Price (cents per brownie)	Quantity demanded	Quantity supplied
	(millions per day)	
50	5	3
60	4	4
70	3	5
80	2	6
90	1	7

a.   If there is no tax on brownies, what is their price and how many are produced and consumed?

b.   If a tax of 20¢ a brownie is introduced, what happens to the price of a brownie and the number produced and consumed?

c.   How much tax does the government collect and who pays it?

5. Calculate the elasticity of demand in Fig. 7.11 if the price of wheat in normal conditions is $6 a bushel. Does its magnitude imply that farm revenues fluctuate in the same direction as price fluctuations or in the opposite direction?

6. On Turtle Island, the government is considering ways of stabilizing farm prices and farm revenues. Currently, the egg market is competitive, and the demand for and supply of eggs are:

Price (dollars per dozen)	Quantity demanded	Quantity supplied
	(dozens per week)	
1.20	3,000	500
1.30	2,750	1,500
1.40	2,500	2,500
1.50	2,250	3,500
1.60	2,000	4,500

a.   Calculate the competitive equilibrium price and the quantity bought and sold.

b.   The government introduces a floor price of $1.50 a dozen. Calculate the market price, the quantity of eggs bought and sold, and farm revenue. Calculate the surplus of eggs.

c.   Calculate the amount the government must spend on eggs to maintain the floor price.

CRITICAL THINKING

1. Study *Reading Between the Lines* on pp. 144–145 on the ending of rent controls in California and then answer the following questions:

a.   How do we know that the rent ceilings in Santa Monica are below the market rent?

b.   For how long has Santa Monica had rent controls?

c.   How do you think scarce housing resources are allocated among their competing uses in Santa Monica? Give some examples.

d.   What do you predict the scale of building activity has been in Santa Monica in recent years?

e.   Is John Rodriguez correct when he says: "We all lose"?

f.   Why do you think the voters of Santa Monica have tolerated rent ceilings for so long?

g.   Why do you think the voters of Santa Monica are willing to relax rent ceilings today?

h.   Why do you think rent ceilings are being relaxed only on vacant units?

2. The price of sugar in the United States is about twice the world market price. How do you think this high price is achieved? Who benefits from it? Who loses from it? Is there a deadweight loss? Use the theory you have learned in this chapter to make some predictions about the answers to these questions, and use your Web browser to get some facts about the market for sugar.

3. A cool Web site called The Tomato Page (http://www.tomato.org) reports that in California, "There are 250 growers producing fresh tomatoes on 40,000 acres, May through mid-November. Major growing regions include the San Joaquin, Salinas, and Imperial Valleys, and Orange and San Diego Counties. The typical 25 lb. box of tomatoes costs $4.50 to produce and market. The grower/shippers' selling price averages $5. In 1995, prices ranged from $3 to $12 per box depending on demand. The price to the grower often does not influence retail pricing. California growers do not receive any federal or state production subsidies. Tomatoes grown for fresh market are not used for processed products, like paste or sauce." Explain and critically evaluate this statement.

Part 3

A Closer Look at Demand and Supply

Making the Most of Life

Demand and supply are powerful forces. They shape the fortunes of families, businesses, nations, and empires in the same unrelenting way that the tides and winds shape rocks and coastlines. We've studied some of the effects of these forces. We've seen how they raise and lower prices, increase and decrease quantities bought and sold, cause revenues to fluctuate, and send resources to their most valuable uses. But we have not probed what lies beneath and shapes the forces of demand and supply. That is your next task. ◆ Behind the forces of demand and supply lie our choices. We choose the goods and services to buy and consume in order to get the most we can from our limited incomes. We choose the type of work to do and the hours to work in order to get the most we can from their limited time. People who run businesses choose the goods and services to produce and the labor and other resources to hire in order to make the maximum possible profit. ◆ In the next four chapters, we study how the choices people make determine demand and supply. In Chapters 8 and 9, you will study individual choices, and in Chapters 10 and 11, you will study business decisions. ◆ We begin, in Chapter 8, by learning about the marginal utility theory of human decisions.

This theory explains the consumption plans of individuals. It also explains how we allocate our time. It can even be used to explain other non-economic choices, such as whether to marry and how many children to have. In a sense, there are no non-economic choices. If there is scarcity, there must be choice; and economics studies all such choices. In Chapter 9, you can learn about a tool that enables us to make a map of people's likes and dislikes, a tool called an *indifference curve*. Indifference curves are considered an advanced topic, so this chapter is *strictly optional*. But the presentation of indifference curves in Chapter 9 is the clearest and most straightforward available, so if you want to learn about this tool, this chapter is the place to do so. ◆ In Chapter 10, we turn our attention to business decisions. You will discover why there are different types of businesses and how firms calculate their costs. In Chapter 11, you will study the relationship between a firm's production and its costs. ◆ But first, we'll spend a little time with Jeremy Bentham, a nineteenth century scholar who pioneered the use of the concept of utility to study human choices, and we'll talk with one of today's most influential students of human behavior, Gary Becker of the University of Chicago.

Understanding Human Behavior

The Economist: Jeremy Bentham

Jeremy Bentham (1748–1832), who lived in London, was the son and grandson of a lawyer and was himself trained as a barrister. But he rejected the opportunity to maintain the family tradition and instead spent his life as a writer, activist, and Member of Parliament, in the pursuit of rational laws that would bring the greatest happiness to the greatest number.

Bentham, whose embalmed body is preserved to this day in a glass cabinet at the University of London, was the first person to use the concept of utility to explain human choices. But in Bentham's day, the distinction between explaining and prescribing was not a sharp one, and Bentham was ready to use his ideas to tell people how they ought to behave. He was one of the first to propose pensions for the retired, guaranteed employment, minimum wages, and social benefits such as free education and free medical care.

> "...*it is the greatest happiness of the greatest number that is the measure of right and wrong.*"
>
> JEREMY BENTHAM
>
> *FRAGMENT ON GOVERNMENT*

The Issues and Ideas

The economic analysis of human behavior in the family, the workplace, the markets for goods and services, the markets for labor services, and financial markets is based on the idea that our behavior can be understood as a response to scarcity. Everything we do can be understood as a choice that maximizes total benefit subject to the constraints imposed by our limited resources and technology. If people's preferences are stable in the face of changing constraints, then we have a chance of predicting how they will respond to an evolving environment.

The economic approach explains the incredible change that has occurred during the past 100 years in the way women allocate their time as the consequence of changing constraints, not of changing attitudes. Technological advances have equipped the nation's farms and factories with machines that have increased the productivity of both women and men, thereby raising the wages they can earn. The increasingly technological world has increased the return to education for both women and men and has led to a large increase in high school and college graduates of both sexes. And equipped with an ever widening array of gadgets and appliances that cut the time taken to do household jobs, an increasing proportion of women have joined the labor force.

The economic explanation might not be correct, but it is a powerful one. And if it is correct, the changing attitudes are a consequence, not a cause, of the economic advancement of women.

THEN...

Economists explain people's actions as the consequences of choices that maximize total utility subject to constraints. In the 1890s, fewer than 20 percent of women chose market employment, and most of those who did had low-paying and unattractive jobs. The other 80 percent of women chose nonmarket work in the home. What were the constraints that led to these choices?

Today, one economist who stands out above all others and who stands on the shoulders of Jeremy Bentham is Gary Becker of the University of Chicago. Professor Becker has transformed the way we think about human choices. Before you begin your deeper look at demand and supply and the choices that people make, you can meet Professor Becker on the following pages.

...AND NOW

By 1997, more than 60 percent of women were in the labor force, and although many had low-paying jobs, women were increasingly found in the professions and in executive positions. What brought about this dramatic change compared with 100 years earlier? Was it a change in preferences or a change in the constraints that women face?

Talking with

Gary S. Becker is Professor of Economics and Sociology at the University of Chicago. Born in 1930 in Pottsville, Pennsylvania, he was an undergraduate at Princeton University and a graduate student at the University of Chicago. His graduate supervisor was Milton Friedman, and his Ph.D. thesis became the book *The Economics of Discrimination*, a work that profoundly changes the way we think about discrimination and economic ways of reducing it.

Professor Becker's other major book, *Human Capital*, first published in 1964, has become a classic and has influenced the thinking of the Clinton Administration on education issues. In 1992 he was awarded the Nobel Prize for Economic Science for his work on human capital.

Professor Becker has revolutionized the way we think about human decisions in all aspects of life. Michael Parkin talked with Professor Becker about his work, how it uses and builds on the work of Jeremy Bentham.

Why are you an economist?

When I went to Princeton, I was interested in mathematics, but I wanted to do something for society. I took economics in my freshman year by accident, and it was a lucky accident. I found economics to be tremendously exciting intellectually because it could be used to understand the difference between capitalism and socialism, what determined wages, and how people are taxed. This was so exciting to me that I didn't even worry about job opportunities at the time.

Can we really hope to explain all human choices by using models that were invented initially to explain and predict choices about the allocation of income among alternative consumer goods and services?

I think we can hope to explain all human choices. All choices involve making comparisons and assessing how to allocate our time between work, leisure, and taking care of children. These are choices that are not in principle very different from the type of choices involved in allocating income. Whether economists succeed at the goal of explaining everything, of course, remains to be seen. We certainly haven't done that yet, but I think we've made considerable progress in expanding our horizons with the theory of choice.

You are both a professor of economics and sociology. Do you see these same techniques that we've developed in economics being used to address questions that are the traditional domain of the sociologist? Or is sociology just a totally different discipline?

Sociology is a discipline with many different approaches. There is a small but growing and vocal group of sociologists who believe in what they call *rational choice theory*, which is the theory economists have used to explain choices in markets. My late colleague,

James Coleman, was the leader of that group. One of the issues they deal with is the influence of peers on behavior. For example, imagine that I am a teenager facing choices of getting involved with drugs or heavy drinking or smoking because of peer pressure. How would rational choice theorists incorporate this peer pressure into an analysis of these choices? The simple approach they take is that my utility, or pleasure, depends not only on what I'm consuming but also on what my peers are doing. If they're doing something very different from what I'm doing, that reduces my utility partly because I receive less respect from them and feel less part of the group.

Therefore when I am trying to get as much utility as possible, I take into account what my peers are doing. But since we're all doing that, this leads to some equilibrium in this peer market. Instead of us all behaving independently, we are all behaving interdependently. I think economists have given social structures such as peer pressure far too little attention. One of the things I learned during my association with Coleman and other sociologists is a better appreciation of the importance of social factors in individual behavior.

Can you identify the historical figures that have been most influential to your thinking and your career?

Economics is a cumulative field in which we build on the giants who went earlier, and we try to add a little bit. And then other people build on our generation's contributions. The view I take of the broad scope of the economic approach has had a number of major practitioners, including Jeremy Bentham, who stated and applied a very general view of utility-maximizing behavior to many problems, such

as the factors that reduce crime.

Other nineteenth century people like Wicksteed and Marshall highlighted the rational choice aspect of economics. In the eighteenth century, Adam Smith already applied economic reasoning to political behavior. My work on human capital was very much influenced by Irving Fisher, Alfred Marshall, Milton Friedman, and Ted Schultz. Very few people's work, certainly not mine, spring out of nowhere. They have continuity with the past. What we do is try to build on the work of past economists and do a little more and a little better than what they did.

> *Very few people's work, certainly not mine, spring out of nowhere. They have continuity with the past. What we do is try to build on the work of past economists and do a little more and a little better than what they did.*

How would you characterize the major achievements of the economics of human behavior? What questions, for example, would have convincing answers?

The area of law and economics has been very successful in analyzing criminal behavior. Work by many lawyers and economists, particu-

larly Judge Richard Posner and William Landes of the University of Chicago Law School, has produced many successful applications. The question that economics of crime seeks to answer is: What determines the amount of crime that we have and how effective are various actions that governments can take in reducing the amount of crime? This analysis discusses apprehending and punishing criminals, giving better education to people who might commit crimes, reducing unemployment, and so on. They have basically said that fundamentally, the factors determining criminal behavior are not so different from the factors determining whether people become professors or not. People make choices, and these choices are conditional on their expected benefits and the cost. You can affect the number of people who decide to enter criminal activities by affecting the benefits and costs. To the extent that people make these calculations, they are more likely to enter crime when benefits are high relative to the cost.

One way to affect costs is to make it more likely that if somebody commits a crime they'll be captured, apprehended, convicted, and punished. That raises the cost and reduces crime. I think now that people accept this conclusion for most crimes.

But the economic approach is not simply a law and order approach. It also says that if you can increase the attractiveness to people of working at legal activities rather than illegal or criminal activities, you will also have less crime. One way to increase the attractiveness is to make it easier for people to find jobs and to earn more by improving their skills, their education, and their training and also by improving the functioning of labor markets.

You've made a significant contribution to demographic economics. Nearly 40 years ago, you introduced the idea of children being durable goods. Can you talk about the evolution of this idea?
Demographers initially were extremely hostile to my point of view. However, I recently received the Irene Taeuber Award from the Population Association of America, their most prestigious demographic award. It was given to me in recognition of the value of the economic way of looking at demographic questions, including birth and marriage rates. Over time, the cumulative work of many economists working on population problems around the world made an impact.

The main payoffs from this work have been in our understanding of fertility. The conclusions from the economic approach are that the number of children people have is very much a function of two variables: costs and choices. Costs depend not only on how much food and shelter you give children, but also on the time of parents. In most societies, most of that time is the mother's time, which has a value. As we have become richer, and as women have become better educated and are working outside the home more, the cost to them of spending time on children has risen. As these costs have risen, families are deterred from having as many children as they had in the past. So one of the factors explaining the big decline in birth rates is the increasing costs of children.

The second variable that economists recognize is that families are making choices about the quality of children's lives in terms of their education, training, and health. In modern economies, this quality component has become very important because the emphasis in modern economies is on knowledge, technology, and skills. But there is a tradeoff. If you spend more on each child's skills, education, and training, you make children more costly and you are likely to have fewer children. Over the past 30 years, birth rates have been decreasing in most countries of the world, including India, China, parts of Asia, Latin America, some parts of Africa, Europe, and the United States.

How do you respond to people who feel that explaining choices such as how many children to raise is deeply personal and that it is therefore immoral to think of children in these terms?
I think morality is misplaced in this area. We are trying to understand very major changes in the world. There are about 15 countries of the world that now have birth rates well below replacement levels. If families continue with these rates, these populations will eventually decline—and decline rapidly. This includes Germany, Italy, Spain, Portugal, France, and Japan. It is important to understand why birth rates are going down. If this way of looking at it is a powerful tool for understanding why families have made these choices, then it would be immoral, I believe, to neglect this approach. If we are concerned about low birth rates, how can we go about raising them? Or if we want to understand what to expect in other countries that are experiencing significant economic development, we will miss out if we neglect an important set of considerations that help us to understand what's going on.

Is economics a subject that a young person can happily enter in 1998? What are the major incentives for pursuing economics as an undergraduate?
I would certainly encourage a young person to enter economics for several reasons. There are many employment opportunities in economics, and it is also valuable if you decide to go into other areas such as the law, business, or even medicine. Economic issues, including the budget deficit, entitlement programs, minimum wages, and how to subsidize the elderly, are extremely important public policy issues.

I want also to stress that economics is a wonderful intellectual activity. To be able to take this very mysterious world we live in and to illuminate parts of it, important parts of it, through the use of economics is enormously intellectually satisfying and challenging for an undergraduate or for anybody else. So I would say it's both practical and satisfying. Who can ask for a better combination?

> *There are about 15 countries of the world that now have birth rates well below replacement levels. If families continue with these rates, the populations will eventually decline—and decline rapidly.*

8

Utility and Demand

We need water to live. We don't need diamonds for much besides decoration. If the benefits of water far outweigh the benefits of diamonds, why, then, does water cost practically nothing while diamonds are terribly expensive? ◆ When the Organization of Petroleum Exporting Countries (OPEC) restricted its sale of oil in 1973, it created a dramatic rise in price, but people continued to use almost as much oil as they had before. Our demand for oil was price inelastic. But why? ◆ When the CD player was introduced in 1983, it cost more than $1,000, and consumers didn't buy very many. Since then, the price has decreased dramatically, and people are buying CD players in enormous quantities. Our demand for CD players is price elastic. What makes the demand for some things price elastic while the demand for others is price inelastic? ◆ Over the past 20 years, after the effects of inflation are removed, incomes in the United States have increased by 40 percent. Over that same period, expenditure on electricity has increased by more than 60 percent, while expenditure on transportation has increased by less than 20 percent. Thus the proportion of income spent on electricity has increased, and the proportion spent on transportation has decreased. Why, as incomes rise, does the proportion of income spent on some goods rise and that spent on others fall? ◆ In the preceding four chapters, we saw that demand has an important effect on the price of a good. But we did not analyze what exactly shapes a person's demand. This chapter examines household behavior and its influence on demand. It explains why demand for some goods is elastic and demand for other goods is inelastic. It also explains why the prices of some things, such as diamonds and water, are so out of proportion to their total benefits.

Water, Water, Everywhere

After studying this chapter, you will be able to:

■ Explain the household's budget constraint

■ Define total utility and marginal utility

■ Explain the marginal utility theory of consumer choice

■ Use marginal utility theory to predict the effects of changing prices and incomes

■ Explain the connection between individual demand and market demand

■ Explain the paradox of value

Household Consumption Choices

L A HOUSEHOLD'S CONSUMPTION CHOICES ARE determined by many factors, but we can summarize all of these factors under two concepts:

- Budget constraint
- Preferences

Budget Constraint

A household's consumption choices are constrained by the household's income and by the prices of the goods and services it buys. The household has a given amount of income to spend and cannot influence the prices of the goods and services it buys.

The limits to a household's consumption choices are described by its *budget line.* Let's consider Lisa's household. Lisa has an income of $30 a month, and she plans to buy only two goods: movies and soda. Movies cost $6 each; soda costs $3 a six-pack. If Lisa spends all her income, she will reach the limits to her consumption of movies and soda.

Figure 8.1 illustrates Lisa's possible consumption of movies and soda. Rows *a* through *f* in the table show six possible ways of allocating $30 to these two goods. For example, Lisa can see 2 movies for $12 and buy 6 six-packs for $18 (row *c*). Points *a* through *f* in the figure illustrate the possibilities presented in the table. The line passing through these points is Lisa's budget line.

Lisa's budget line is a constraint on her choices. It marks the boundary between what she can afford and what she can not afford. She can afford all the points on the line and inside it. She cannot afford the points outside the line. The constraint on her consumption depends on prices of movies and soda and on her income. The constraint changes when the price of movies or soda changes or her income changes.

Preferences

How does Lisa divide her $30 between these two goods? The answer depends on her likes and dislikes—her *preferences.* Economists use the concept of utility to describe preferences. The benefit or satisfaction that a person gets from the consumption of a good or service is called **utility** But what exactly is utility and in what units can we measure it? Utility is an abstract concept, and its units are arbitrary.

FIGURE 8.1

Consumption Possibilities

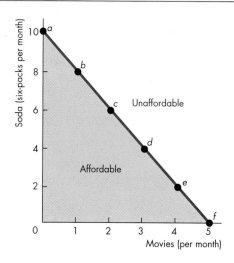

Possibility	Movies		Soda	
	Quantity	Expenditure (dollars)	Six-packs	Expenditure (dollars)
a	0	0	10	30
b	1	6	8	24
c	2	12	6	18
d	3	18	4	12
e	4	24	2	6
f	5	30	0	0

Rows *a* through *f* in the table show six possible ways that Lisa can allocate $30 to movies and soda. For example, Lisa can buy 2 movies and 6 six-packs (row *c*). The combination in each row costs $30. These possibilities are points *a* through *f* in the figure. The line through those points is a boundary between what Lisa can afford and what she cannot afford. Her choices must lie along the line *af* or inside the orange area.

Temperature—An Analogy Temperature is an abstract concept, and the units of temperature are arbitrary. You know when you feel hot, and you know when you feel cold. But you can't *observe* temperature. You can observe water turning to steam if it is hot enough or turning to ice if it is cold enough. And you can construct an instrument, called a thermometer, which can help you to predict when such changes will occur. The scale on the thermometer is what we call temperature. But the units in which we measure temperature are arbitrary. For example, we can accurately predict that when a Celsius thermometer shows a temperature of 0, water will turn to ice. But the units of measurement do not matter because this same event also occurs when a Fahrenheit thermometer shows a temperature of 32.

The concept of utility helps us make predictions about consumption choices in much the same way that the concept of temperature helps us make predictions about physical phenomena. Admittedly marginal utility theory is not as precise as the theory that enables us to predict when water will turn to ice or steam.

Let's now see how we can use the concept of utility to describe preferences.

Total Utility

Total utility is the total benefit that a person gets from the consumption of goods and services. Total utility depends on the level of consumption—more consumption generally gives more total utility. Table 8.1 shows Lisa's total utility from movies and soda. If she sees no movies, she gets no utility from movies. If she sees 1 movie in a month, she gets 50 units of utility. As the number of movies she sees in a month increases, her total utility increases; if she sees 10 movies a month, she gets 250 units of total utility. The other part of the table shows Lisa's total utility from soda. If she drinks no soda, she gets no utility from soda. As the amount of soda she drinks increases, her total utility increases.

Marginal Utility

Marginal utility is the change in total utility that results from a one-unit increase in the quantity of a good consumed. The table in Fig. 8.2 shows the calculation of Lisa's marginal utility of movies. When the number of movies she sees increases from 4 to 5 a month, her total utility from movies increases from 150 units to 175 units. Thus for Lisa, the marginal utility of seeing a fifth movie each month is 25 units. Notice that marginal utility appears midway between the quantities of movies. It does so because it is the *change* in consumption from 4 to 5 movies that produces the *marginal* utility of 25 units. The table displays calculations of marginal utility for each number of movies seen.

TABLE 8.1

Lisa's Total Utility from Movies and Soda

Movies		Soda	
Quantity per month	Total utility	Six-packs per month	Total utility
0	0	0	0
1	50	1	75
2	88	2	117
3	121	3	153
4	150	4	181
5	175	5	206
6	196	6	225
7	214	7	243
8	229	8	260
9	241	9	276
10	250	10	291
11	256	11	305
12	259	12	318
13	261	13	330
14	262	14	341

Figure 8.2(a) illustrates the total utility that Lisa gets from movies. The more movies Lisa sees in a month, the more total utility she gets. Figure 8.2(b) illustrates her marginal utility. This graph tells us that as Lisa sees more movies, the marginal utility that she gets from watching movies decreases. For example, her marginal utility decreases from 50 units from the first movie to 38 units from the second and 33 units from the third. We call this decrease in marginal utility as the quantity of the good consumed increases the principle of **diminishing marginal utility**.

Marginal utility is positive but diminishes as the consumption of a good increases. Why does marginal utility have these two features? In Lisa's case, she likes movies, and the more she sees the better. That's why marginal utility is positive. The benefit that Lisa gets from the last movie seen is its marginal utility. To see why marginal utility diminishes, think about the following two situations: In one, you've

FIGURE 8.2
Total Utility and Marginal Utility

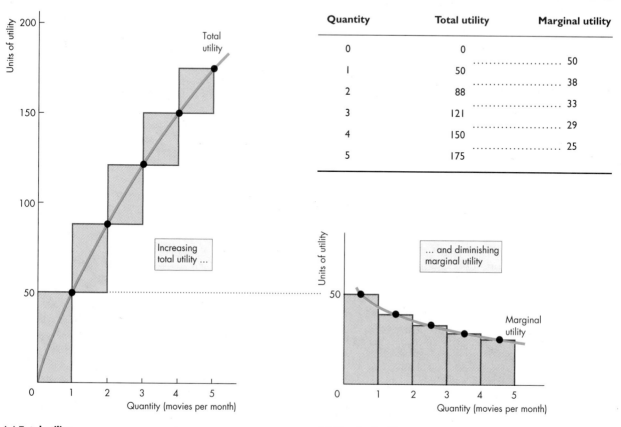

Quantity	Total utility	Marginal utility
0	0	
		50
1	50	
		38
2	88	
		33
3	121	
		29
4	150	
		25
5	175	

(a) Total utility

The table shows that as Lisa sees more movies her total utility from movies increases. The table also shows her marginal utility—the change in total utility resulting from seeing one additional movie. Marginal utility declines as consumption increases. The figure graphs Lisa's total utility and marginal

(b) Marginal utility

utility from movies. Part (a) shows her total utility. It also shows as a bar the extra total utility she gains from each additional movie—her marginal utility. Part (b) shows how Lisa's marginal utility from movies diminishes by placing the bars shown in part (a) side by side as a series of declining steps.

just been studying for 29 evenings. An opportunity arises to see a movie. The utility you get from seeing that movie is the marginal utility from seeing one movie in a month. In the second situation, you've been on a movie binge. For the past 29 nights, you have not even seen an assignment. You are up to your eyeballs in movies. You are happy enough to go to a movie once more. But the thrill that you get out of that thirtieth movie in 30 days is not very large. It is the marginal utility of the thirtieth movie in a month.

R E V I E W

- Consumption possibilities are limited by the consumer's income and the prices of goods.
- Consumers' preferences can be described by using the concept of utility.
- Marginal utility theory assumes that as more of a good is consumed, the total utility derived from that good increases but the marginal utility from it decreases.

Maximizing Utility

A HOUSEHOLD'S INCOME AND THE PRICES THAT it faces limit the household's consumption choices, and the household's preferences determine the utility that it can obtain from each consumption possibility. The key assumption of marginal utility theory is that the household chooses the consumption possibility that maximizes its total utility. This assumption of utility maximization is a way of expressing the fundamental economic problem—scarcity. People's wants exceed the resources available to satisfy those wants, so they must make hard choices. In making choices, they try to get the maximum attainable benefit—they try to maximize total utility.

Let's see how Lisa allocates $30 a month between movies and soda to maximize her total utility. We'll continue to assume that movies cost $6 each and soda costs $3 a six-pack.

The Utility-Maximizing Choice

The most direct way of calculating how Lisa spends her income to maximize her total utility is by making a table like Table 8.2. The rows of the table show the affordable combinations of movies and soda that lie along her budget line in Fig. 8.1. The table records three things: first, the number of movies seen and the total utility derived from them (the left side of the table); second, the number of six-packs consumed and the total utility derived from them (the right side of the table); and third, the total utility derived from both movies and soda (the center column).

The first row of Table 8.2 records the situation when Lisa watches no movies and buys 10 six-packs. In this case, Lisa gets no utility from movies and 291 units of total utility from soda. Her total utility from movies and soda (the center column) is 291 units. The rest of the table is constructed in the same way.

The consumption of movies and soda that maximizes Lisa's total utility is highlighted in the table. When Lisa sees 2 movies and buys 6 six-packs of soda, she gets 313 units of total utility. This is the best Lisa can do, given her preferences, given that she has only $30 to spend, and given the prices of movies and six-packs. If she buys 8 six-packs of soda, she can see only 1 movie. She gets 310 units of total utility, 3 less than the maximum attainable. If she sees 3 movies, she can drink only 4 six-packs. She gets 302 units of total utility, 11 less than the maximum attainable.

TABLE 8.2

Lisa's Affordable Combinations

| | Movies | | Total utility from movies and soda | Soda | |
	Quantity per month	Total utility		Total utility	Six-packs per month
a	0	0	291	291	10
b	1	50	310	260	8
c	2	88	313	225	6
d	3	121	302	181	4
e	4	150	267	117	2
f	5	175	175	0	0

We've just described Lisa's consumer equilibrium. A **consumer equilibrium** is a situation in which a consumer has allocated all his or her available income in the way that, given the prices of goods and services, maximizes his or her total utility. Lisa's consumer equilibrium is 2 movies and 6 six-packs.

In finding Lisa's consumer equilibrium, we measured her *total* utility from movies and soda. But there is a better way of determining a consumer equilibrium—one that does not involve measuring total utility at all. Let's look at this alternative.

Equalizing Marginal Utility per Dollar Spent

Another way to find out the allocation that maximizes a consumer's total utility is to make the marginal utility per dollar spent on each good equal for all goods. The **marginal utility per dollar spent** is the marginal utility obtained from the last unit of a good consumed divided by the price of the good. For example, Lisa's marginal utility from seeing the first movie is 50 units of utility. The price of a movie is $6, which means that when Lisa sees one movie the marginal utility per dollar spent on movies is 50 units divided by $6, or 8.33 units of utility per dollar.

Total utility is maximized when all the consumer's available income is spent and when the marginal utility per dollar spent is equal for all goods.

Lisa maximizes total utility when she spends all her income and consumes movies and soda such that

$$\frac{\text{Marginal utility from movies}}{\text{Price of a movie}} = \frac{\text{Marginal utility from soda}}{\text{Price of soda}}.$$

Call the marginal utility from movies MU_m, the marginal utility from soda MU_s, the price of a movie P_m, and the price of soda P_s. Then Lisa maximizes her utility when she spends all her income and when

$$\frac{MU_m}{P_m} = \frac{MU_s}{P_s}.$$

Let's use this formula to find Lisa's utility-maximizing consumption choice. Table 8.3 sets out Lisa's marginal utilities (which are calculated from Table 8.1) and her marginal utility per dollar spent on each good. For example, in row *b*, Lisa's marginal utility from movies is 50 units, and since movies cost $6 each, her marginal utility per dollar spent on movies is 8.33 units per dollar (50 units divided by $6). Each row exhausts Lisa's income of $30. You can see that Lisa's marginal utility per dollar spent on each good, like marginal utility itself, decreases as more of the good is consumed.

Lisa maximizes her total utility when the marginal utility per dollar spent on movies is equal to the marginal utility per dollar spent on soda—possibility *c*. Lisa consumes 2 movies and 6 six-packs.

Figure 8.3 shows why the rule "equalize marginal utility per dollar spent on all goods" works. Suppose that instead of 2 movies and 6 six-packs (possibility *c*), Lisa consumes 1 movie and 8 six-packs (possibility *b*). She then gets 8.33 units of utility per dollar spent on movies and 5.67 units per dollar spent on soda. Lisa can increase her total utility by buying less soda and seeing more movies. If she spends less on soda and more on movies, her total utility from soda decreases by 5.67 units per dollar and her total utility from movies increases by 8.33 units per dollar. Her total utility increases by 2.66 units per dollar.

TABLE 8.3
Equalizing Marginal Utilities per Dollar Spent

	Movies ($6 each)			Soda ($3 per six-pack)		
	Quantity	Marginal utility	Marginal utility per dollar spent	Six-packs	Marginal utility	Marginal utility per dollar spent
a	0			10	15	5.00
b	1	50	8.33	8	17	5.67
c	2	38	6.33	6	19	6.33
d	3	33	5.50	4	28	9.33
e	4	29	4.83	2	42	14.00
f	5	25	4.17	0		

FIGURE 8.3
Equalizing Marginal Utilities per Dollar Spent

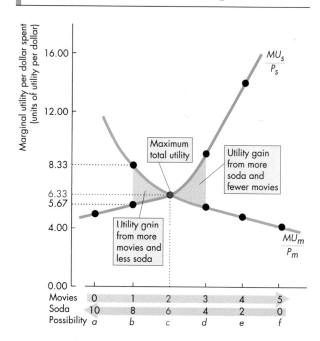

If Lisa consumes 1 movie and 8 six-packs (possibility *b*), she gets 8.33 units of utility from the last dollar spent on movies and 5.67 units of utility from the last dollar spent on soda. She can get more total utility by seeing one more movie. If she consumes 4 six-packs and 3 movies (possibility *d*), she gets 5.50 units of utility from the last dollar spent on movies and 9.33 units of utility from the last dollar spent on soda. She can increase her total utility by seeing one fewer movie. When Lisa's marginal utility per dollar spent on both goods is equal, her total utility is maximized.

Or suppose that Lisa consumes 3 movies and 4 six-packs (possibility *d*). In this situation, her marginal utility per dollar spent on movies (5.50) is less than her marginal utility per dollar spent on soda (9.33). Lisa can now increase her total utility by spending less on movies and more on soda.

The Power of Marginal Analysis The method we've just used to find Lisa's utility-maximizing choice of movies and soda is an example of the power of marginal analysis. By comparing the marginal gain from having more of one good with the marginal loss from having less of another good, Lisa is able to ensure that she gets the maximum attainable utility.

In the example, Lisa chooses the combination in which the marginal utilities per dollar spent on movies and soda are equal. Because we buy goods and services in indivisible lumps, the numbers don't always work out so precisely. But the basic approach always works.

The rule to follow is very simple: If the marginal utility per dollar spent on movies exceeds the marginal utility per dollar spent on soda, see more movies and buy less soda; if the marginal utility per dollar spent on soda exceeds the marginal utility per dollar spent on movies, buy more soda and see fewer movies.

More generally, if the marginal gain from an action exceeds the marginal loss, take the action. You have met this principle before, and you will meet it time and again in your study of economics. And you will find yourself using it when you make your own economic choices, especially when you must make a big decision.

Units of Utility In calculating Lisa's utility-maximizing choice in Table 8.3 and Fig. 8.3, we have not used the concept of total utility at all. All our calculations use marginal utility and price. By making the marginal utility per dollar spent equal for both goods, we know that Lisa maximizes her total utility.

This way of viewing maximum utility is important; it means that the units in which utility is measured do not matter. We could double or halve all the numbers measuring utility, or multiply them by any other positive number, or square them, or take their square roots. None of these transformations of the units used to measure utility makes any difference to the outcome. It is in this respect that utility is analogous to temperature. Our prediction about the freezing of water does not depend on the temperature scale; our prediction about the household's consumption choice does not depend on the units of utility.

REVIEW

- A consumer chooses the quantities of goods and services that maximize total utility.
- The consumer does so by spending all the available income and by making the marginal utility per dollar spent on each good equal.
- When marginal utilities per dollar spent are equal for all goods, a consumer cannot reallocate spending to get more total utility.

Predictions of Marginal Utility Theory

LET'S NOW USE MARGINAL UTILITY THEORY TO make some predictions. What happens to Lisa's consumption of movies and soda when their prices change and when her income changes?

To work out the effect of a change in price or income on the consumption choice: First, determine the combinations of movies and soda that just exhaust the new income at the new prices. Second, calculate the new marginal utilities per dollar spent. Third, determine the combination that makes the marginal utilities per dollar spent on movies and soda equal.

A Fall in the Price of Movies

Suppose that the price of a movie falls from $6 to $3. The rows of Table 8.4 show the combinations of movies and soda that exactly exhaust Lisa's $30 of income when movies cost $3 each and soda costs $3 a six-pack. Lisa's preferences do not change when prices change, so her marginal utility schedule remains the same as before. Now divide her marginal utility from movies by $3 to get the marginal utility per dollar spent on movies.

To find how Lisa responds to the fall in the price of a movie, compare her new utility-maximizing choice (Table 8.4) with her original choice (Table 8.3). Lisa sees more movies (up from 2 to 5 a month) and drinks less soda (down from 6 to 5 six-packs a month). That is, Lisa *substitutes* movies for soda. Figure 8.4 shows these effects. The fall in the price of a movie produces a movement along Lisa's demand curve for movies (part a) and shifts her demand curve for soda (part b).

TABLE 8.4

How a Change in Price of Movies Affects Lisa's Choices

Movies ($3 each)		Soda ($3 per six-pack)	
Quantity	Marginal utility per dollar spent	Six-packs	Marginal utility per dollar spent
0		10	5.00
1	16.67	9	5.33
2	**12.67**	8	5.67
3	11.00	7	6.00
4	9.67	**6**	**6.33**
5	8.33	5	8.33
6	7.00	4	9.33
7	6.00	3	12.00
8	5.00	2	14.00
9	4.00	1	25.00
10	3.00	0	

A Rise in the Price of Soda

Now suppose that the price of soda rises from $3 to $6 a six-pack. The rows of Table 8.5 show the combinations of movies and soda that exactly exhaust Lisa's $30 of income when movies cost $3 each and soda costs $6 a six-pack. Lisa's preferences don't change when the price of soda changes. Now divide Lisa's marginal utility from soda by $6 to get her marginal utility per dollar spent on soda.

To find the effect of the rise in the price of soda on Lisa's utility-maximizing choice, compare her new choice (Table 8.5) with her previous choice (Table 8.4). When the price of soda increases, Lisa drinks less soda (down from 5 to 2 six-packs a month) and sees more movies (up from 5 to 6 a month). That is, Lisa *substitutes* movies for soda. Figure 8.5 shows these effects. The rise in the price of soda produces a movement along Lisa's demand curve for soda (part a) and shifts her demand curve for movies (part b).

FIGURE 8.4

A Fall in the Price of Movies

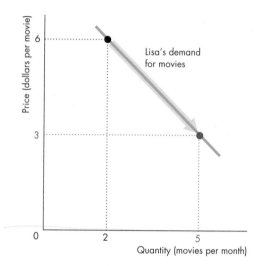

(a) Movies

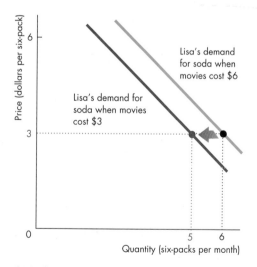

(b) Soda

When the price of a movie falls and the price of soda remains the same, the quantity of movies demanded by Lisa increases and, in part (a), Lisa moves along her demand curve for movies. Also, Lisa decreases her demand for soda and, in part (b), her demand curve for soda shifts leftward.

TABLE 8.5

How a Change in Price of
Soda Affects Lisa's Choices

Movies ($3 each)		Soda ($6 per six-pack)	
Quantity	Marginal utility per dollar spent	Six-packs	Marginal utility per dollar spent
0		5	4.17
2	12.67	4	4.67
4	9.67	3	6.00
6	7.00	2	7.00
8	5.00	1	12.50
10	3.00	0	

Marginal utility theory predicts these two results:

■ When the price of a good rises, the quantity demanded of that good decreases.

■ If the price of one good rises, the demand for another good that can serve as a substitute increases.

Does this sound familiar? It should. These predictions of marginal utility theory correspond to the assumptions that we made about demand in Chapter 4. There we *assumed* that the demand curve for a good slopes downward, and we *assumed* that a rise in the price of a substitute increases demand.

We have now seen that marginal utility theory predicts how the quantities of goods and services that people demand respond to price changes. The theory helps us to understand both the shape and the position of the demand curve and how the demand curve for one good shifts when the price of another good changes. Marginal utility theory also helps us to understand one further thing about demand: how it changes when income changes. Let's study the effects of a change in income on consumption.

FIGURE 8.5

A Rise in the Price of Soda

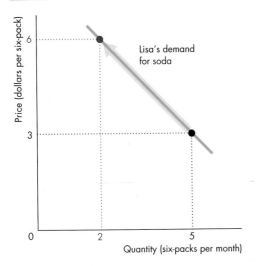

(a) Soda

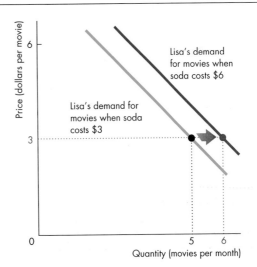

(b) Movies

When the price of soda rises and the price of movies remains the same, the quantity of soda demanded by Lisa decreases and, in part (a), Lisa moves along her demand curve for soda.

Also, Lisa increases her demand for movies and, in part (b), her demand curve for movies shifts rightward.

A Rise in Income

Let's suppose that Lisa's income increases to $42 a month and that a movie costs $3 and a six-pack costs $3. We saw in Table 8.4 that with these prices and with an income of $30 a month, Lisa sees 5 movies and drinks 5 six-packs a month. We want to compare this choice of movies and soda with Lisa's choice when her income is $42. Table 8.6 shows the calculations needed to make the comparison. With $42, Lisa can see 14 movies a month and buy no soda or buy 14 six-packs a month and see no movies or choose any combination of the two goods in the rows of the table. We calculate the marginal utility

per dollar spent in exactly the same way as we did before and find the quantities at which the marginal utilities per dollar spent on movies and on soda are equal. With an income of $42, the marginal utility per dollar spent on each good is equal when Lisa sees 7 movies and drinks 7 six-packs of soda a month.

By comparing this situation with that in Table 8.4, we see that with an additional $12 a month, Lisa buys 2 more six-packs and sees 2 more movies a month. Lisa's response arises from her preferences, as described by her marginal utilities. Different preferences would produce different quantitative responses. With a larger income, the consumer always buys more of a *normal* good and less of an *inferior* good. For Lisa, soda and movies are normal goods. When her income increases, Lisa buys more of both goods.

You have now completed your study of the marginal utility theory of a household's consumption choices. Table 8.7 summarizes the key assumptions, implications, and predictions of the theory.

TABLE 8.6

Lisa's Choices with an Income of $42 a Month

Movies ($3 each)		Soda ($3 per six-pack)	
Quantity	Marginal utility per dollar spent	Six-packs	Marginal utility per dollar spent
0		14	3.67
1	16.67	13	4.00
2	12.67	12	4.33
3	11.00	11	4.67
4	9.67	10	5.00
5	8.33	9	5.33
6	7.00	8	5.67
7	6.00	7	6.00
8	5.00	6	6.33
9	4.00	5	8.33
10	3.00	4	9.33
11	2.00	3	12.00
12	1.00	2	14.00
13	0.67	1	25.00
14	0.33	0	

So the more $ you have the less you appreciate things

TABLE 8.7

Marginal Utility Theory

Assumptions

■ A consumer derives utility from the goods consumed.

■ Each additional unit of consumption yields additional total utility; marginal utility is positive.

■ As the quantity of a good consumed increases, marginal utility decreases.

■ A consumer's aim is to maximize total utility.

Implication

Total utility is maximized when all the available income is spent and when the marginal utility per dollar spent is equal for all goods.

Predictions

■ Other things remaining the same, the higher the price of a good, the smaller is the quantity demanded (the law of demand).

■ The higher the price of a good, the greater is the quantity demanded of substitutes for that good.

■ The higher the consumer's income, the greater is the quantity demanded of normal goods.

Individual Demand and Market Demand

Marginal utility theory explains how an individual household spends its income and enables us to derive an individual household's demand curve. In earlier chapters, we used *market* demand curves. We can derive a *market* demand curve from individual demand curves. Let's see how.

The relationship between the total quantity demanded of a good and its price is called **market demand**. The market demand curve is what you studied in Chapter 4. The relationship between the quantity demanded of a good by a single individual and its price is called *individual demand*.

Figure 8.6 illustrates the relationship between individual demand and market demand. In this example, Lisa and Chuck are the only people. The market demand is the total demand of Lisa and Chuck. At $3 a movie, Lisa demands 5 movies a month and Chuck demands 2, so the total quantity demanded by the market is 7 movies a month. Lisa's demand curve for movies in part (a) and Chuck's in part (b) sum *horizontally* to give the market demand curve in part (c).

The market demand curve is the horizontal sum of the individual demand curves and is formed by adding the quantities demanded by each individual at each price.

Because marginal utility theory predicts that individual demand curves slope downward, it also predicts that market demand curves slope downward.

FIGURE 8.6

Individual and Market Demand Curves

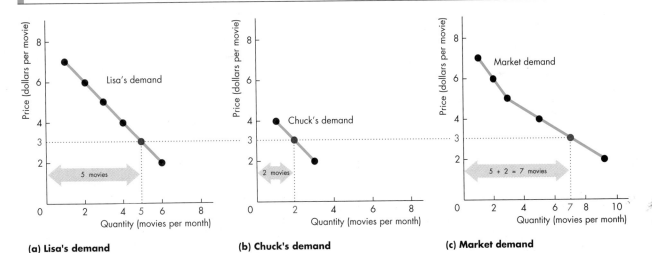

(a) Lisa's demand   **(b) Chuck's demand**   **(c) Market demand**

| Price | Quantity of movies demanded | | |
(dollars per movie)	Lisa	Chuck	Market
7	1	0	1
6	2	0	2
5	3	0	3
4	4	1	5
3	5	2	7
2	6	3	9

The table and the figure illustrate how the quantity of movies demanded varies as the price of a movie varies. In the table, the market demand is the sum of the individual demands. For example, at a price of $3, Lisa demands 5 movies and Chuck demands 2 movies, so the total quantity demanded in the market is 7 movies. In the figure, the market demand curve is the horizontal sum of the individual demand curves. Thus when the price is $3, the market demand curve shows that the quantity demanded is 7 movies, the sum of the quantities demanded by Lisa and Chuck.

Marginal Utility and the Real World

Marginal utility theory can be used to answer a wide range of questions about the real world. The theory sheds light on why the demand for CD players is price elastic while the demand for oil is price inelastic and why the demand for electricity is income elastic while the demand for transportation is income inelastic. Elasticities are determined by preferences. The feature of our preferences that determines elasticity is the step size with which marginal utility declines—the steepness of the marginal utility steps in Fig. 8.2(b).

If marginal utility declines in big steps, a small change in the quantity bought brings a big change in the marginal utility per dollar spent. So it takes a big change in price or income to bring a small change in the quantity demanded—demand is inelastic. Conversely, if marginal utility diminishes slowly, even a large change in the quantity bought brings a small change in the marginal utility per dollar spent. So it takes only a small change in price or income to bring a large change in quantity—demand is elastic.

But marginal utility theory can do much more than explain households' *consumption* choices. It can be used to explain *all* the choices made by households. One of these choices, the allocation of time between work in the home, office, or factory and leisure is the theme of the part opener on pp. 149–154.

REVIEW

- When the price of a good falls and the prices of other goods and a consumer's income remain the same, the consumer increases consumption of the good whose price has fallen and decreases demand for other goods.

- These changes result in a movement along the demand curve for the good whose price has changed and shifts in the demand curves for other goods whose prices have remained constant.

- When a consumer's income increases, the consumer can afford to buy more of all goods and the quantity bought increases for all *normal* goods.

Let's end this chapter by returning to a recurring theme throughout your study of economics: the concept of efficiency and the distinction between price and value.

Efficiency, Price, and Value

MARGINAL UTILITY THEORY HELPS US TO DEEPEN our understanding of the concept of efficiency and also helps us to see more clearly the distinction between *value* and *price*. Let's see how.

Consumer Efficiency and Consumer Surplus

When Lisa allocates her limited budget to maximize utility, she is using her resources efficiently. Any other allocation of her budget wastes some resources.

But when Lisa has allocated her limited budget to maximize utility, she is *on* her demand curve for each good. A demand curve is a description of the quantity demanded at each price when utility is maximized. When we studied efficiency in Chapter 6, we learned that a demand curve is also a willingness-to-pay curve. It tells us a consumer's *marginal benefit*—the benefit from consuming an additional unit of a good. You can now give the idea of marginal benefit a deeper meaning.

Marginal benefit is the maximum price that a consumer is willing to pay for an extra unit of a good or service when utility is maximized.

The Paradox of Value

For centuries, philosophers have been puzzled by a paradox that we raised at the start of this chapter. Water, which is essential to life itself, costs little, but diamonds, which are useless compared to water, are expensive. Why? Adam Smith tried to solve this paradox. But not until the theory of marginal utility had been developed could anyone give a satisfactory answer.

You can solve this puzzle by distinguishing between *total* utility and *marginal* utility. The total utility that we get from water is enormous. But remember, the more we consume of something, the smaller is its marginal utility. We use so much water that its marginal utility—the benefit we get from one more glass of water—diminishes to a small value. Diamonds, on the other hand, have a small total utility relative to water, but because we buy few diamonds, they have a high marginal utility. When a household has maximized its total utility, it has allocated its budget in the way that makes the marginal utility per dollar spent equal for all goods. That is, the marginal

FIGURE 8.7

The Paradox of Value

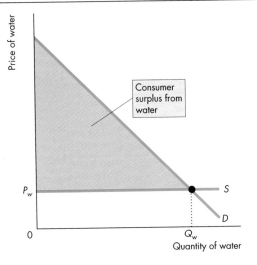

(a) Water

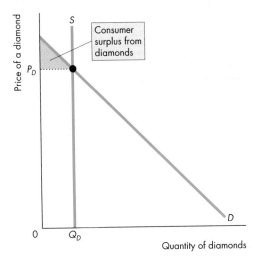

◆ **(b) Diamonds**

Part (a) shows the demand for water, D, and the supply of water, S. The supply is (assumed to be) perfectly elastic at the price P_W. At this price, the quantity of water consumed is Q_W and the consumer surplus from water is the large green triangle. Part (b) shows the demand for diamonds, D, and the supply of diamonds, S. The supply is (assumed to be) perfectly inelastic at the quantity Q_D. At this quantity, the price of a diamond is P_D and the consumer surplus from diamonds is the small green triangle. Water is valuable—has a large consumer surplus—but is cheap. Diamonds are less valuable than water—have a smaller consumer surplus—but are expensive.

utility from a good divided by the price of the good is equal for all goods. This equality of marginal utilities per dollar spent holds true for diamonds and water: Diamonds have a high price and a high marginal utility. Water has a low price and a low marginal utility. When the high marginal utility of diamonds is divided by the high price of diamonds, the result is a number that equals the low marginal utility of water divided by the low price of water. The marginal utility per dollar spent is the same for diamonds as for water.

Another way to think about the paradox of value uses *consumer surplus*. Figure 8.7 explains the paradox of value by using this idea. The supply of water (part a) is perfectly elastic at price P_W, so the quantity of water consumed is Q_W and the consumer surplus from water is the large green area. The supply of diamonds (part b) is perfectly inelastic at price Q_D, so the price of diamonds is P_D and the consumer surplus from diamonds is the small green area. Water is cheap but brings a large consumer surplus, while diamonds are expensive but bring a small consumer surplus.

REVIEW

- Along a demand curve, a consumer's choices are efficient.
- A low-priced good, such as water, has a small marginal utility but a large total utility and a large consumer surplus.
- A high-priced good, such as diamonds, has a large marginal utility but a small total utility and a small consumer surplus.

We've now completed our study of the marginal utility theory. And we've seen how the theory can be used to explain our real-world consumption choices. You can see the theory in action once again in *Reading Between the Lines* on pp. 168–169, where it is used to interpret some recent trends in student's choices about where to go to school.

The next chapter presents an alternative theory of household behavior. To help you see the connection between the two theories of consumer behavior, in the next chapter we'll continue with the same example. We'll meet Lisa again and discover another way of understanding how she gets the most out of her $30 a month.

Marginal Utility in Action

DETROIT FREE PRESS, DECEMBER 2, 1996

More Students Studying Abroad, Traveling Further

WASHINGTON—Rising numbers of U.S. college students are studying overseas, and many aren't going to the traditional universities in Europe, a survey found. They're venturing farther afield, to Africa, Australia, the Middle East.

The number of U.S. students studying abroad rose to 84,403 in 1994-95, 10.6 percent from the previous year, continuing a 10-year increase, a report released Sunday by the New York-based Institute of International Education said. ...

"As recently as a decade ago, studying abroad was considered a luxury," said Richard Krasno, the institute's president. "I think it's now considered a more instrumental part of undergraduate education."

He speculated that U.S. students are warming to the idea of studying abroad because they are exposed to other cultures on their own campuses. Many also recognize the importance of a second language and international experience in competing for good jobs, he said.

The number of study abroad programs at the University of Michigan has leapt from 30 in 1993 to 65 in 1996, said Jordan Pollack, assistant director of the Office of International Programs.

...

The school has programs in Senegal, Morocco and Ghana and students may soon be able to study in Egypt, Kuwait and Israel, Pollack said.

Besides trying to become more marketable in their job search, students are also looking for a sense of adventure, Pollack added. ...

A fast-growing economic market in China led to a 30-percent increase in U.S. students studying there in 1994-95, Krasno said. Costa Rica also reported a 30-percent increase, partly because many students recognize the advantage of knowing Spanish, Krasno added.

He said Australia is aggressively recruiting U.S. students. It reported a 42-percent rise in U.S. enrollees in 1994-95 with 3,346.

While these countries reported large percentage increases in U.S. students, Britain still hosted the most—19,410 students, or 23 percent of all study-abroad students. France, Spain and Italy ranked second, third and fourth with 7,000 to 7,900 students. ...

DETROIT FREE PRESS and wire services. Reprinted with permission.

Essence of THE STORY

■ The number of U.S. students studying abroad rose to 84,403 in 1994–95, up 10.6 percent from the previous year.

■ Many students seek the benefits of a second language and international experience when competing for good jobs.

■ The number of study abroad programs at the University of Michigan grew from 30 in 1993 to 65 in 1996.

■ China, Costa Rica, and Australia all show increases in the number of U.S. students who are studying at their universities.

■ Britain, France, Spain, and Italy are the most popular countries in which Americans study abroad.

Economic

A N A L Y S I S

■ You receive utility from being in school because some of what you do is fun and some of what you do will increase your future income and living standard.

■ But *where* you study also influences your utility. Some students prefer to study at home, and some prefer to go to a different state or country.

■ Over the past decade, increasing numbers of students have chosen to study abroad as Fig. I shows.

■ The news article reports that the growth has been most rapid in Australia, China, and Costa Rica.

■ You can understand students' choices about where to study by using the marginal utility theory.

■ Students allocate their budgets to maximize utility. And they achieve this outcome by making the marginal utility per dollar spent equal for all goods and services.

■ For most students, the marginal utility of studying in the United States is greater than the marginal utility of studying abroad.

■ But the price of studying in the United States is less than the price of studying abroad. For example, a term's tuition at the University of Michigan costs a Michigan resident $2,700, while at Oxford University in England it costs $9,500 (plus an airfare).

■ So most students choose to study in the United States.

■ But for some 84,000 students, the marginal utility of studying abroad is sufficiently large to overcome the price difference. For them, the marginal utility *per dollar spent* for studying abroad is larger than it is for studying in the United States.

■ But the country to which a student goes also depends on prices. If the cost of studying in a particular country rises, the marginal utility per dollar spent in that country decreases. So fewer students go to that country.

■ Figure 2 shows the power of prices in students' decisions about where to study. Generally, the greater the fall in price of studying abroad, the greater is the increase in the number of students who study abroad.

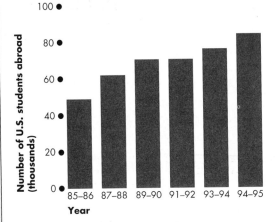

Figure 1 The trend

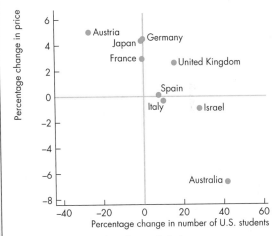

Figure 2 Changes in price and choice

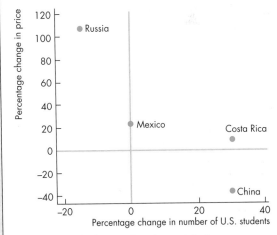

Figure 3 More changes in price and choice

■ But other factors also are at work. Four countries (shown in Fig. 3) have experienced a larger increase (or smaller decrease) in numbers than can be explained by the price changes.

SUMMARY

Key Points

Household Consumption Choices (pp. 156–158)

- A household's choices are determined by its consumption possibilities and preferences.
- A household's consumption possibilities are constrained by its income and by prices. Some combinations of goods are affordable, and some are not affordable.
- A household's preferences can be described by marginal utility.
- The key assumption of marginal utility theory is that the marginal utility of a good or service decreases as consumption of the good or service increases.
- Marginal utility theory assumes that people buy the affordable combination of goods and services that maximizes total utility.

Maximizing Utility (pp. 159–161)

- Total utility is maximized when all the available income is spent and when the marginal utility per dollar spent on each good is equal.
- If the marginal utility per dollar spent on good *A* exceeds that on good *B*, the consumer can increase total utility by buying more of good *A* and less of good *B*.

Predictions of Marginal Utility Theory (pp. 161–166)

- Marginal utility theory predicts the law of demand. That is, other things remaining the same, the higher the price of a good, the smaller is the quantity demanded of that good.
- Marginal utility theory also predicts that other things remaining the same, the higher the income of a consumer, the larger is the quantity demanded of a normal good.

- Market demand is the sum of all individual demands, and the market demand curve is found by summing horizontally all the individual demand curves.

Efficiency, Price, and Value (pp. 166–167)

- When a consumer maximizes utility, he or she is using resources efficiently.
- Marginal utility theory resolves the paradox of the relative value of water and diamonds.
- When we talk loosely about value, we are thinking of *total* utility or consumer surplus. But price is related to *marginal* utility.
- Water, which we consume in large amounts, has a high total utility and a large consumer surplus but has a low price and low marginal utility.
- Diamonds, which we consume in small amounts, have a low total utility and a small consumer surplus but have a high price and a high marginal utility.

Key Figures and Table

Key Terms

QUESTIONS

1. What is a household's budget constraint?

2. What determines a household's consumption possibilities?

3. What do we mean by utility?

4. Distinguish between total utility and marginal utility.

5. How does the marginal utility from a good change as:
   a. The household increases the amount of the good it consumes?
   b. The household decreases the amount of the good it consumes?

6. Susan is a consumer. When is Susan's total utility maximized?
   a. When she has spent all her income
   b. When she has spent all her income, and marginal utility is equal for all goods
   c. When she has spent all her income, and the marginal utility per dollar spent is equal for all goods

   Explain your answer.

7. What does the term "marginal utility per dollar spent" mean?

8. Explain what happens to the marginal utility per dollar spent on a good as:
   a. More dollars are spent on the good.
   b. Fewer dollars are spent on the good.

9. What does marginal utility theory predict about the effect of a change in price on the quantity of a good consumed?

10. What does marginal utility theory predict about the effect of a change in the price of one good on the consumption of another good?

11. What does marginal utility theory predict about the effect of a change in income on consumption of a good?

12. What is the relationship between individual demand and market demand?

13. How do we construct a market demand curve from individual demand curves?

14. Can a consumer use her budget more efficiently than when she is maximizing utility?

15. What is the paradox of value? How does marginal utility theory resolve it?

PROBLEMS

1. Calculate Lisa's marginal utility from soda from the numbers given in Table 8.1. Draw two graphs, one of her total utility and the other of her marginal utility from soda. Make your graphs look similar to those in Fig. 8.2.

2. Marcus enjoys rock CDs and spy novels. He obtains the following utility from each of these goods:

Quantity per month	Utility from rock CDs	Utility from spy novels
1	60	20
2	110	38
3	150	53
4	180	64
5	200	70
6	206	75
7	211	79
8	215	82
9	218	84

   a. Draw graphs showing Marcus's utility from rock CDs and from spy novels.
   b. Compare the two utility graphs. Can you say anything about Marcus's preferences?
   c. Draw graphs showing Marcus's marginal utility from rock CDs and from spy novels.
   d. What do the two marginal utility graphs tell you about Marcus's preferences?
   e. If rock CDs and spy novels both cost $10 each, and if Marcus has a monthly income of $60 to spend on these two goods, how does he spend it?

3. Max enjoys windsurfing and snorkeling. He obtains the following utility from each of these sports:

Hours per month	Utility from windsurfing	Utility from snorkeling
1	120	40
2	220	76
3	300	106
4	360	128
5	400	140
6	412	150
7	422	158
8	430	164

Max has $35 to spend. Equipment for wind-surfing rents for $10 an hour, while snorkeling equipment rents for $5 an hour.

a. Draw a graph of Max's consumption possi-bilities.

b. Draw graphs of Max's utility from wind-surfing and from snorkeling.

c. Compare the two utility graphs. Can you say anything about Max's preferences?

d. If Max has unlimited time available for his leisure pursuits, how long does he spend windsurfing and how long does he spend snorkeling?

4. Max's sister gives him $20 to spend on his leisure pursuits, so he now has $55 to spend. With this additional income, how long does Max choose to windsurf and how long does he choose to snorkel?

5. If Max has $55 to spend and the rent on wind-surfing equipment decreases to $5 an hour, how does Max now spend his time windsurfing and snorkeling?

6. Max takes a Club Med vacation, the cost of which includes unlimited sports activities. There is no extra charge for any equipment. Max decides to spend a total of six hours each day on windsurfing and snorkeling. How does Max allocate his six hours between windsurfing and snorkeling?

7. Still on his Club Med vacation, Max hears on the weather report that high winds and poor visibility will prevent all water sports during the afternoon. So he now plans to spend only four hours today on windsurfing and snorkeling. How does Max allocate his four hours between windsurfing and snorkeling?

8. Shirley's and Dan's demand schedules are:

Price (cents per carton)	Quantity demanded (cartons per week)	
	By Shirley	**By Dan**
10	12	6
30	9	5
50	6	4
70	3	3
90	1	2

If Shirley and Dan are the only two individuals, what is the market demand?

CRITICAL THINKING

1. Study *Reading Between the Lines* on pp. 168–169 on the trends in the number of Americans studying abroad and then answer the following questions:

a. What are some of the main sources of ben-efit or utility from studying abroad?

b. What are some of the main costs of study-ing abroad?

c. Use the marginal utility theory to explain the trend shown in Fig. 1 on p. 169.

d. Use the marginal utility theory to explain the patterns that are shown in Fig. 2 and Fig. 3 on p. 169.

e. Why do you think the number of students who study in Russia has increased by such a large percentage?

f. Why do you think the number of students who study in China has decreased by such a large percentage?

g. If China wanted to increase the number of American students enrolled in its univer-sities, how might it go about the task?

2. In recent years, bottled water, fruit drinks, and sports drinks—"new age drinks"—have become popular. Use the marginal utility theory you have learned in this chapter to explain the rise in popularity of new age drinks.

3. Why do you think the percentage of income spent on food has decreased while the percent-age of income spent on cars has increased dur-ing the past 50 years?

Use the marginal utility theory to explain these trends.

4. Smoking is banned on all airline flights in the United States and on most international flights.

a. What effect does this ban have on the util-ity of smokers?

b. How do you expect the ban to influence the decisions of smokers?

c. What effect does this ban have on the utility of nonsmokers?

d. How do you expect the ban to influence the decisions of nonsmokers?

Use marginal utility theory to explain your answers.

Possibilities, Preferences, and Choices

Like the continents floating on the earth's mantle, our spending patterns change steadily over time. On such subterranean movements, business empires rise and fall. Goods such as home videos and microwave popcorn now appear on our shopping lists, while 78 rpm phonograph records and horse-drawn carriages have disappeared. Miniskirts appear, disappear, and reappear in cycles of fashion. ◆ But the glittering surface of our consumption obscures deeper and slower changes in how we spend. In the last few years, we've seen a proliferation of gourmet food shops and designer clothing boutiques. Yet we spend a smaller percentage of our

Subterranean Movements

income today on food and clothing than we did in 1950. At the same time, the percentage of our income spent on vacations and medical care has grown steadily. Why does consumer spending change over the years? How do people react to changes in income and changes in the prices of the things they buy? ◆ Similar subterranean movements govern the way we spend our time. For example, the average workweek has fallen steadily from 70 hours a week in the nineteenth century to 35 hours a week today. Although the average workweek is now much shorter than it once was, far more people now have jobs. This change has been especially dramatic for women, who are much more likely to work outside the home than they were in previous generations. Why has the average workweek declined? And why do more women work? ◆ We're going to study a model of choice that predicts the effects of changes in prices and incomes on what people buy and how much work they do.

After studying this chapter, you will be able to:

- Calculate and graph a household's budget line

- Work out how the budget line changes when prices or income changes

- Make a map of preferences by using indifference curves

- Explain the choices that households make

- Predict the effects of price and income changes on consumption choices

- Predict the effects of wage changes on work-leisure choices

Consumption Possibilities

CONSUMPTION CHOICES ARE LIMITED BY INCOME and by prices. A household has a given amount of income to spend and cannot influence the prices of the goods and services it buys. The limits to a household's consumption choices are described by its **budget line**.

Let's look at Lisa's budget line.[1] Lisa has an income of $30 a month to spend. She buys two goods—movies and soda. Movies cost $6 each; soda costs $3 for a six-pack. Figure 9.1 shows alternative affordable ways for Lisa to consume movies and soda. Row *a* says that she can buy 10 six-packs of soda and see no movies, a combination of movies and soda that exhausts her monthly income of $30. Row *f* says that Lisa can watch 5 movies and drink no soda—another combination that exhausts the $30 available. Each of the other rows in the table also exhausts Lisa's income. (Check that each of the other rows costs exactly $30.) The numbers in the table define Lisa's consumption possibilities. We can graph Lisa's consumption possibilities as points *a* through *f* in Fig. 9.1.

Divisible and Indivisible Goods   Some goods—called divisible goods—can be bought in any quantity desired. Examples are gasoline and electricity. We can best understand household choice if we suppose that all goods and services are divisible. For example, Lisa can consume a half a movie a month *on the average* by seeing one movie every two months. When we think of goods as being divisible, the consumption possibilities are not just the points *a* through *f* shown in Fig. 9.1, but those points plus all the intermediate points that form the line running from *a* to *f.* Such a line is a budget line.

Lisa's budget line is a constraint on her choices. It marks the boundary between what is affordable and what is unaffordable. She can afford any point on the line and inside it. She cannot afford any point outside the line. The constraint on her consumption depends on prices and her income, and the constraint changes when prices or her income changes. Let's see how by studying the budget equation.

[1]If you have read the preceding chapter on marginal utility theory, you have already met Lisa. This tale of her thirst for soda and zeal for movies will sound familiar to you—up to a point. But in this chapter, we're going to use a different method for representing preferences—one that does not require us to resort to the idea of utility.

FIGURE 9.1
The Budget Line

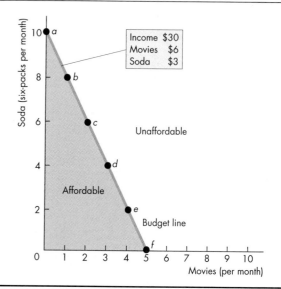

Consumption possibility	Movies (per month)	Soda (six-packs per month)
a	0	10
b	1	8
c	2	6
d	3	4
e	4	2
f	5	0

Lisa's budget line shows the boundary between what she can and cannot afford. The rows of the table list Lisa's affordable combinations of movies and soda when her income is $30, the price of soda is $3 a six-pack, and the price of a movie is $6. For example, row *a* tells us that Lisa exhausts her $30 income when she buys 10 six-packs and sees no movies. The figure graphs Lisa's budget line. Points *a* through *f* on the graph represent the rows of the table. For divisible goods, the budget line is the continuous line *af*. To calculate the equation for Lisa's budget line, start with expenditure equal to income:

$$\$3Q_s + \$6Q_m = \$30.$$

Divide by $3 to obtain

$$Q_s + 2Q_m = 10.$$

Subtract $2Q_m$ from both sides to obtain

$$Q_s = 10 - 2Q_m.$$

The Budget Equation

We can describe the budget line by using a *budget equation*. The budget equation starts with the fact that

Expenditure = Income.

Expenditure is equal to the sum of the price of each good multiplied by the quantity bought. For Lisa,

Expenditure = Price of soda × Quantity of soda

+ Price of movie × Quantity of movies.

Call the price of soda P_s, the quantity of soda Q_s, the price of a movie P_m, the quantity of movies Q_m, and income y. Using these symbols, Lisa's budget equation is

$$P_s Q_s + P_m Q_m = y.$$

Or, using the prices Lisa faces, $3 for a six-pack and $6 for a movie, and Lisa's income, $30, we get

$$\$3 Q_s + \$6 Q_m = \$30.$$

Lisa can choose any quantities of soda (Q_s) and movies (Q_m) that satisfy this equation. To find the relationship between these quantities, first divide both sides of the equation by the price of soda (P_s) to get

$$Q_s + \frac{P_m}{P_s} \times Q_m = \frac{y}{P_s}.$$

Now subtract the term (P_m/P_s) × Q_m from both sides of this equation to give

$$Q_s = \frac{y}{P_s} - \frac{P_m}{P_s} \times Q_m.$$

For Lisa, income (y) is $30, the price of a movie (P_m) is $6, and the price of a six-pack (P_s) is $3. So Lisa must choose the quantities of movies and soda to satisfy the equation

$$Q_s = \frac{\$30}{\$3} - \frac{\$6}{\$3} \times Q_m$$

or

$$Q_s = 10 - 2 Q_m.$$

To interpret the equation, go back to the budget line of Fig. 9.1 and check that the equation delivers that budget line. First set Q_m equal to zero. In this case, the budget equation tells us that Q_s, the quantity of soda, is y/P_s, which is 10 six-packs. This combination of Q_m and Q_s is the same as that shown in row *a* of the table in Fig. 9.1. Next set Q_m equal to 5.

Q_s is now equal to zero (row *f* of the table). Check that you can derive the other rows.

The budget equation contains two variables chosen by the household (Q_m and Q_s) and two variables (y/P_s and P_m/P_s) that the household takes as given. Let's look more closely at these variables.

Real Income A household's **real income** is the household's income expressed not as money but as a quantity of goods the household can afford to buy. Expressed in terms of soda, Lisa's real income is y/P_s. This quantity is the maximum number of six-packs that she can buy. It is equal to her money income divided by the price of soda. Lisa's income is $30 and the price of soda is $3 a six-pack, so her real income in terms of soda is 10 six-packs, which is shown in Fig. 9.1 as the point at which the budget line intersects the *y*-axis.

Relative Price A **relative price** is the price of one good divided by the price of another good. In Lisa's budget equation, the variable P_m/P_s is the relative price of a movie in terms of soda. For Lisa, P_m is $6 a movie and P_s is $3 a six-pack, so P_m/P_s is equal to 2 six-packs per movie. That is, to see one more movie, Lisa must give up 2 six-packs.

You've just calculated Lisa's opportunity cost of a movie. Recall that the opportunity cost of an action is the best alternative forgone. For Lisa to see 1 more movie a month, she must forgo 2 six-packs. You've also calculated Lisa's opportunity cost of soda. For Lisa to consume 2 more six-packs a month, she must give up seeing 1 movie. So her opportunity cost of 2 six-packs is 1 movie.

The relative price of a movie in terms of soda is the magnitude of the slope of Lisa's budget line. To calculate the slope of the budget line, recall the formula for slope (Chapter 2): Slope equals the change in the variable measured on the *y*-axis divided by the change in the variable measured on the *x*-axis as we move along the line. In Lisa's case (Fig. 9.1), the variable measured on the *y*-axis is the quantity of soda, and the variable measured on the *x*-axis is the quantity of movies. Along Lisa's budget line, as soda decreases from 10 to 0 six-packs, movies increase from 0 to 5. Therefore the magnitude of the slope of the budget line is 10 six-packs divided by 5 movies, or 2 six-packs per movie. The magnitude of this slope is exactly the same as the relative price we've just calculated. It is also the opportunity cost of a movie.

A Change in Prices When prices change, so does the budget line. The lower the price of the good measured on the horizontal axis, other things remaining the same, the flatter is the budget line. For example, if the price of a movie falls from $6 to $3, real income in terms of soda does not change but the relative price of a movie falls. The budget line rotates outward and becomes flatter as shown in Fig. 9.2(a). The higher the price of the good measured on the horizontal axis, other things remaining the same, the steeper is the budget line. For example, if the price of a movie rises from $6 to $12, the relative price of a movie increases. The budget line rotates inward and becomes steeper as shown in Fig. 9.2(a).

A Change in Income A change in *money income* changes real income but does not change the relative price. The budget line shifts, but its slope does not change. The bigger a household's money income, the bigger is real income and the farther to the right is the budget line. The smaller a household's money income, the smaller is real income and the farther to the left is the budget line. Figure 9.2(b) shows the effect of a change in money income on Lisa's budget line. The initial budget line is the same one that we began with in Fig. 9.1 when Lisa's income is $30. The new budget line shows the limits to Lisa's consumption if her income falls to $15 a month. The two budget lines have the same slope because they have the same relative price. The new budget line is closer to the origin than the initial one because Lisa's real income has decreased.

R E V I E W

▪ The budget line describes the limits to a household's consumption.

▪ The position of the budget line depends on real income, and its slope depends on the relative price.

▪ A change in the price of one good changes the relative price and changes the slope of the budget line.

▪ A change in money income changes real income and shifts the budget line, but its slope does not change.

We've studied the limits to what a household can consume. Let's now learn how we can describe preferences and make a map that contains a lot of information about a household's preferences.

FIGURE 9.2
Changes in Prices and Income

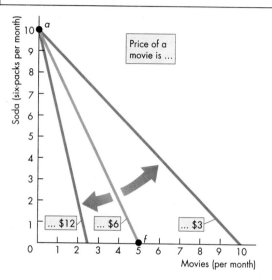

(a) A change in price

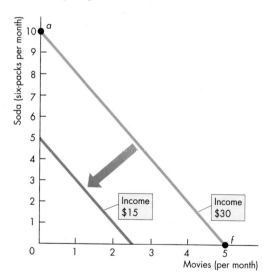

(b) A change in income

In part (a), the price of a movie changes. A fall in the price from $6 to $3 rotates the budget line outward and makes it flatter. A rise in the price from $6 to $12 rotates the budget line inward and makes it steeper.

In part (b), income falls from $30 to $15 while the prices of movies and soda remain constant. The budget line shifts leftward, but its slope does not change.

Preferences and Indifference Curves

YOU ARE GOING TO DISCOVER A VERY NEAT IDEA —that of drawing a map of a person's preferences. A preference map is based on the intuitively appealing assumption that people can sort all the possible combinations of goods into three groups: preferred, not preferred, and indifferent. To make this idea more concrete, let's ask Lisa to tell us how she ranks various combinations of movies and soda.

Figure 9.3(a) shows part of Lisa's answer. She tells us that she currently consumes 2 movies and 6 six-packs a month at point c. She then lists all the combinations of movies and soda that she says are equally acceptable to her as her current consumption. When we plot these combinations of movies and soda, we get the green curve in Fig. 9.3(a). This curve is the key element in a map of preferences and is called an indifference curve.

An **indifference curve** is a line that shows combinations of goods among which a consumer is *indifferent*. The indifference curve in Fig. 9.3(a) tells us that Lisa is just as happy to consume 2 movies and 6 six-packs a month at point c as to consume the combination of movies and soda at point g or at any other point along the curve.

Lisa also says that she prefers any combination of movies and soda in the yellow area above the indifference curve in Fig. 9.3(a) to any combination on the indifference curve. And she prefers any combination on the indifference curve to any combination in the gray area below the indifference curve.

The indifference curve in Fig. 9.3(a) is just one of a whole family of such curves. This indifference curve appears again in Fig. 9.3(b) labeled I_1. The curves labeled I_0 and I_2 are two other indifference curves. Lisa prefers any point on indifference curve I_2 to any point on indifference curve I_1, and she prefers any point on I_1 to any point on I_0. We refer to I_2 as being a higher indifference curve than I_1 and I_1 as being higher than I_0.

A preference map is a series of indifference curves that resemble the contour lines on a map. By looking at the shape of the contour lines on a map, we can draw conclusions about the terrain. Similarly, by looking at the shape of indifference curves, we can draw conclusions about a person's preferences.

Let's learn how to "read" a preference map.

FIGURE 9.3

A Preference Map

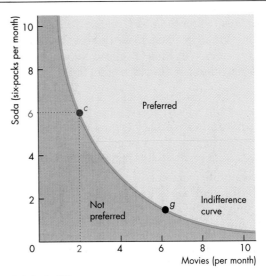

(a) An indifference curve

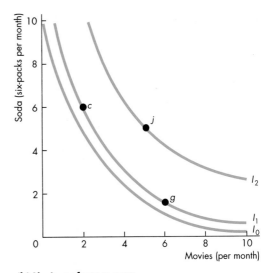

(b) Lisa's preference map

In part (a), Lisa consumes 6 six-packs of soda and 2 movies a month at point c. She is indifferent between all the points on the green indifference curve such as c and g. She prefers any point above the indifference curve (yellow area) to any point on it, and she prefers any point on the indifference curve to any point below it (gray area). A preference map is a number of indifference curves. Part (b) shows three—I_0, I_1, and I_2— that are part of Lisa's preference map. She prefers point j to point c or g, so she prefers any point on I_2 to any point on I_1.

Marginal Rate of Substitution

The **marginal rate of substitution** (*MRS*) is the rate at which a person will give up good *y* (the good measured on the *y*-axis) to get more of good *x* (the good measured on the *x*-axis) and at the same time remain indifferent (remain on the same indifference curve). The marginal rate of substitution is measured by the magnitude of the slope of an indifference curve.

- If the indifference curve is *steep*, the marginal rate of substitution is *high*. The person is willing to give up a large quantity of good *y* to get a small quantity of good *x* while remaining indifferent.

- If the indifference curve is *flat*, the marginal rate of substitution is *low*. The person is willing to give up only a small amount of good *y* to get a large amount of good *x* to remain indifferent.

Figure 9.4 shows you how to calculate the marginal rate of substitution. Suppose that Lisa consumes 6 six-packs and 2 movies at point *c* on indifference curve I_1. Her marginal rate of substitution is calculated by measuring the magnitude of the slope of the indifference curve at point *c*. To measure this magnitude, place a straight line against, or tangent to, the indifference curve at point *c*. Along that line, as soda consumption decreases by 10 six-packs, movie consumption increases by 5. So at point *c*, Lisa is willing to give up soda for movies at the rate of 2 six-packs per movie. Her marginal rate of substitution is 2.

Now, suppose that Lisa consumes 6 movies and $1\tfrac{1}{2}$ six-packs at point *g* in Fig. 9.4. Her marginal rate of substitution is now measured by the slope of the indifference curve at point *g*. That slope is the same as the slope of the tangent to the indifference curve at point *g*. Here, as soda consumption decreases by 4.5 six-packs, movie consumption increases by 9. So at point *g*, Lisa is willing to give up soda for movies at the rate of 1/2 six-pack per movie. Her marginal rate of substitution is 1/2.

As Lisa's consumption of movies increases and her consumption of soda decreases, her marginal rate of substitution diminishes. Diminishing marginal rate of substitution is the key assumption of consumer theory. The assumption of **diminishing marginal rate of substitution** is a general tendency for the marginal rate of substitution to diminish as the consumer moves along an indifference curve, increasing consumption of the good measured on the *x*-axis and decreasing consumption of the good measured on the *y*-axis.

FIGURE 9.4
The Marginal Rate of Substitution

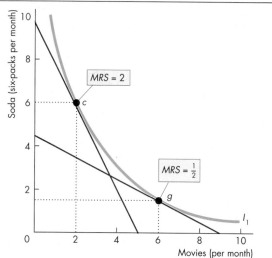

The magnitude of the slope of an indifference curve is called the marginal rate of substitution (MRS). The red line at point *c* tells us that Lisa is willing to give up 10 six-packs to see 5 movies. Her marginal rate of substitution at point *c* is 10 divided by 5, which equals 2. The red line at point *g* tells us that Lisa is willing to give up 4.5 six-packs to see 9 movies. Her marginal rate of substitution at point *g* is 4.5 divided by 9, which equals 1/2.

Your Own Diminishing Marginal Rate of Substitution   You may be able to appreciate why we assume the principle of a diminishing marginal rate of substitution by thinking about your own preferences. Imagine that in a week, you consume 10 six-packs of soda and no movies. Most likely you are willing to give up a lot of soda so that you can go to the movies just once. But now imagine that in a week, you consume 1 six-pack and 6 movies. Most likely you will now be willing to give up only a little soda to see a seventh movie. As a general rule, the greater the number of movies you see, the smaller is the quantity of soda you are willing to give up to see one additional movie.

The shape of a person's indifference curves incorporates the principle of the diminishing marginal rate of substitution because the curves are bowed toward the origin. The tightness of the bend of an indifference curve tells us how willing a person is to substitute one good for another while remaining indifferent. Let's look at some examples that make this point clear.

Degree of Substitutability

Most of us would not regard movies and soda as being close substitutes for each other. We probably have some fairly clear ideas about how many movies we want to see each month and how many cans of soda we want to drink. Nevertheless, to some degree, we are willing to substitute between these two goods. No matter how big a soda freak you are, there is surely some increase in the number of movies you can see that will compensate you for being deprived of a can of soda. Similarly, no matter how addicted you are to the movies, surely some number of cans of soda will compensate you for being deprived of seeing one movie. A person's indifference curves for movies and soda might look like those shown in Fig. 9.5(a).

Close Substitutes Some goods substitute so easily for each other that most of us do not even notice which we are consuming. The different brands of personal computers are an example. So long as it has an "Intel inside" and runs Windows, most of us don't

care whether our PC is a Dell, a Compaq, a Toshiba, or any of a dozen other brands. The same holds true for marker pens. Most of us don't care whether we use a marker pen from the campus bookstore or the local supermarket. When two goods are perfect substitutes for each other, their indifference curves are straight lines that slope downward, as Fig. 9.5(b) illustrates. The marginal rate of substitution is constant.

Complements Some goods cannot substitute for each other at all. Instead, they are complements. The complements in Fig. 9.5(c) are left and right running shoes. Indifference curves of perfect complements are L-shaped. One left running shoe and one right running shoe are as good as one left shoe and two right ones. Having two of each is preferred to having one of each, but having two of one and one of the other is no better than having one of each.

The extreme cases of perfect substitutes and perfect complements shown here don't often happen in reality. They do, however, illustrate that the shape of the indifference curve shows the degree of substitutability between two goods. The more perfectly substitutable

FIGURE 9.5
The Degree of Substitutability

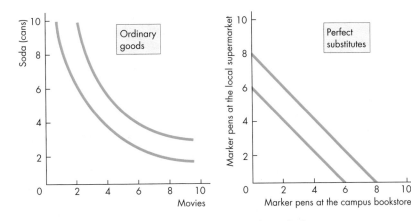
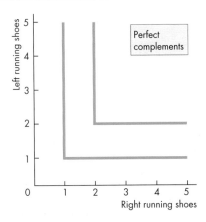

(a) Ordinary goods   **(b) Perfect substitutes**   **(c) Perfect complements**

The shape of the indifference curves reveals the degree of substitutability between two goods. Part (a) shows the indifference curves for two ordinary goods: movies and soda. To consume less soda and remain indifferent, one must see more movies. The number of movies that compensates for a reduction in soda increases as less soda is consumed. Part (b) shows the indifference curves for two perfect substitutes. For the

consumer to remain indifferent, one fewer marker pen from the local supermarket must be replaced by one extra marker pen from the campus bookstore. Part (c) shows two perfect complements—goods that cannot be substituted for each other at all. Having two left running shoes with one right running shoe is no better than having one of each. But having two of each is preferred to having one of each.

"With the pork I'd recommend an Alsatian white or a Coke."

Drawing by Weber; © 1988 The New Yorker Magazine, Inc.

the two goods, the more nearly are their indifference curves straight lines and the less quickly does the marginal rate of substitution fall. Poor substitutes for each other have tightly curved indifference curves, approaching the shape of those shown in Fig. 9.5(c).

As you can see in the cartoon, according to the waiter's preferences, Coke and Alsatian white wine are perfect substitutes and each is a complement with pork. We hope the customers agree with him.

REVIEW

- Preferences can be represented by a preference map that consists of a series of indifference curves.
- For most goods, indifference curves slope downward and are bowed toward the origin.
- The magnitude of the slope of an indifference curve is called the marginal rate of substitution.
- The marginal rate of substitution diminishes as a person moves along an indifference curve and consumes less of the good measured on the *y*-axis and more of the good measured on the *x*-axis.

The two components of the model of household choice are now in place: the budget line and the preference map. We will now use these components to work out the household's choice and to predict how choices change when prices and income change.

Predicting Consumer Behavior

WE ARE NOW GOING TO PREDICT THE QUANTITIES of movies and soda that Lisa *chooses* to buy. Figure 9.6 shows Lisa's budget line from Fig. 9.1 and her indifference curves from Fig. 9.3(b). We assume that Lisa consumes at her best affordable point, which is 2 movies and 6 six-packs—at point *c*. Here, Lisa:

- Is on her budget line
- Is on her highest attainable indifference curve
- Has a marginal rate of substitution between movies and soda equal to the relative price of movies and soda.

For every point inside the budget line, such as point *i*, there are points *on* the budget line that Lisa

---

FIGURE 9.6
The Best Affordable Point

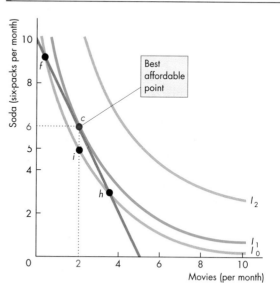

Lisa's best affordable point is *c*. At that point, she is on her budget line and also on the highest attainable indifference curve. At a point such as *h*, Lisa is willing to give up more movies in exchange for soda than she has to. She can move to point *i*, which is just as good as point *h* and have some unspent income. She can spend that income and move to *c*, a point that she prefers to point *i*.

prefers. For example, she prefers all the points on the budget line between *f* and *h* to point *i*. So she chooses a point on the budget line.

Every point on the budget line lies on an indifference curve. For example, point *h* lies on the indifference curve I_0. At point *h*, Lisa's marginal rate of substitution is less than the relative price. Lisa is willing to give up more movies in exchange for soda than the budget line says she must give up. So she moves along her budget line from *h* toward *c*. As she does so, she passes through a number of indifference curves (not shown in the figure) located between indifference curves I_0 and I_1. All of these indifference curves are higher than I_0, and therefore Lisa prefers any point on them to point *h*. But when Lisa gets to point *c*, she is on the highest attainable indifference curve. If she keeps moving along the budget line, she starts to encounter indifference curves that are lower than I_1. So Lisa chooses point *c*.

At the chosen point, the marginal rate of substitution (the magnitude of the slope of the indifference curve) equals the relative price (the magnitude of the slope of the budget line).

Let's use this model of household choice to predict the effects on consumption of changes in prices and income. We'll begin by studying the effect of a change in price.

A Change in Price

The effect of a change in price on the quantity of a good consumed is called the **price effect**. We will use Fig. 9.7(a) to work out the price effect of a fall in the price of a movie. We start with movies costing $6 each, soda costing $3 a six-pack, and Lisa's income at $30 a month. In this situation, she consumes 6 six-packs and 2 movies a month at point *c*.

Now suppose that the price of a movie falls to $3. With a lower price of a movie, the budget line rotates outward and becomes flatter. (Check back to Fig. 9.2(a) for a refresher on how a price change affects the budget line.) The new budget line is the dark orange one in Fig. 9.7(a).

Lisa's best affordable point is now point *j*, where she consumes 5 movies and 5 six-packs of soda. Lisa drinks less soda and watches more movies now that movies cost less. She cuts her soda consumption from 6 to 5 six-packs and increases the number of movies she sees from 2 to 5 a month. Lisa substitutes movies for soda when the price of a movie falls and the price of soda and her income remain constant.

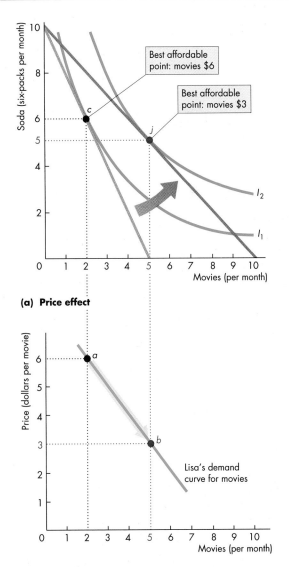

FIGURE 9.7

Price Effect and Demand Curve

(a) Price effect

(b) Demand curve

Initially, Lisa consumes at point *c* (part a). If the price of a movie falls from $6 to $3, she consumes at point *j*. The move from *c* to *j* is the price effect.

At a price of $6 a movie, Lisa sees 2 movies a month, at point *a* (part b). At a price of $3 a movie, she sees 5 movies a month, at point *b*. Lisa's demand curve traces out her best affordable quantity of movies as the price of a movie varies.

The Demand Curve In Chapter 4, we asserted that the demand curve slopes downward. We can now derive a demand curve from a consumer's budget line and indifference curves. By doing so, we can see that the law of demand and the downward-sloping demand curve are consequences of the consumer's choosing his or her best affordable combination of goods.

To derive Lisa's demand curve for movies, lower the price of a movie and find her best affordable point at different prices. We've just done this for two movie prices in Fig. 9.7(a). Figure 9.7(b) highlights these two prices and two points that lie on Lisa's demand curve for movies. When the price of a movie is $6, Lisa sees 2 movies a month at point *a*. When the price falls to $3, she increases the number of movies she sees to 5 a month at point *b*. The demand curve is made up of these two points plus all the other points that tell us Lisa's best affordable consumption of movies at each movie price, given the price of soda and Lisa's income. As you can see, Lisa's demand curve for movies slopes downward. The lower the price of a movie, the more movies she watches each month. This is the law of demand.

Next, let's examine how Lisa changes her consumption of movies and soda when her income changes.

A Change in Income

The effect of a change in income on consumption is called the **income effect**. Let's work out the income effect by examining how consumption changes when income changes and prices remain constant. Figure 9.8(a) shows the income effect when Lisa's income falls. With an income of $30 and with a movie costing $3 and soda $3 a six-pack, she consumes at point *j*—5 movies and 5 six-packs. If her income falls to $21, she consumes at point *k*—consuming 4 movies and 3 six-packs. When Lisa's income falls, she consumes less of both goods. Movies and soda are normal goods.

The Demand Curve and the Income Effect
A change in income leads to a shift in the demand curve, as shown in Fig. 9.8(b). With an income of $30 and a movie costing $3, Lisa is at point *b* on demand curve D_0, the same curve as in Fig. 9.7. But when her income falls to $21, Lisa sees only 4 movies at point *c*. With less income, she plans to see fewer movies at each price, so her demand curve shifts leftward to D_1.

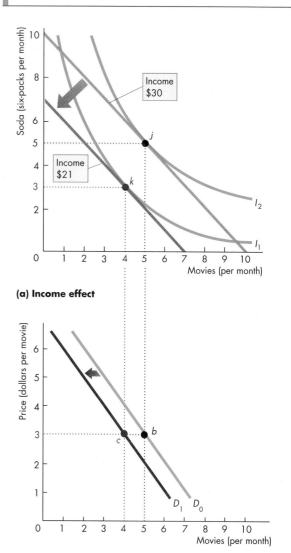

FIGURE 9.8

Income Effect and Change in Demand

(a) Income effect

(b) Demand curve

A change in income shifts the budget line and changes the best affordable point and changes consumption. In part (a), when Lisa's income decreases from $30 to $21, she consumes less of both movies and soda. In part (b), Lisa's demand curve for movies when her income is $30 is D_0. When Lisa's income decreases to $21, her demand curve for movies shifts leftward to D_1. Lisa's demand for movies decreases because she now sees fewer movies at each price.

Substitution Effect and Income Effect

For a normal good, a fall in price *always* increases the quantity bought. We can prove this assertion by dividing the price effect into two parts:

- Substitution effect
- Income effect

Figure 9.9(a) shows the price effect and Fig. 9.9(b) divides that price effect into its two parts.

Substitution Effect   The **substitution effect** is the effect of a change in price on the quantity bought when the consumer (hypothetically) remains indifferent between the original and the new situation. To work out Lisa's substitution effect, we imagine that when the price of a movie falls, we cut Lisa's income by enough to keep her on the same indifference curve as before.

When the price of a movie falls from $6 to $3, suppose (hypothetically) that we cut Lisa's income to $21. What's special about $21? It is the income that is just enough, at the new price of a movie, to keep Lisa's best affordable point on the same indifference curve as her original consumption point *c*. Lisa's budget line is now the light orange line shown in Fig. 9.9(b). With the lower price of a movie and the smaller income, Lisa's best affordable point is *k* on indifference curve I_1. The move from *c* to *k* isolates the substitution effect of the price change. The substitution effect of the fall in the price of a movie is an increase in the consumption of movies from 2 to 4. The direction of the substitution effect never varies: When the relative price of a good falls, the consumer substitutes more of that good for the other good.

Income Effect   To calculate the substitution effect, we gave Lisa a $9 pay cut. Now let's give Lisa her $9 back. The $9 increase in income shifts Lisa's budget line outward, as shown in Fig. 9.9(b). The slope of the budget line does not change because both prices remain constant. This change in Lisa's budget line is similar to the one illustrated in Fig. 9.8. As Lisa's budget line shifts outward, her best affordable point becomes *j* on indifference curve I_2. The move from *k* to *j* isolates the income effect of the price change. The income effect of the fall of the price of movies is the increase in the quantity of movies consumed from 4 to 5. As Lisa's income increases, she increases

FIGURE 9.9

Substitution Effect and Income Effect

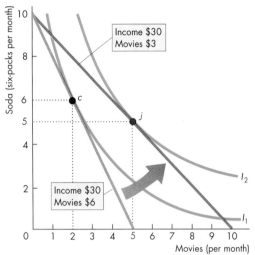

(a) Price effect

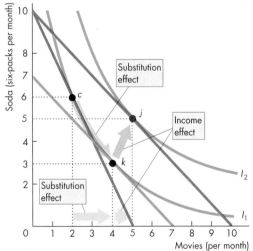

(b) Substitution effect and income effect

The price effect in part (a) can be separated into a substitution effect and an income effect in part (b). To isolate the substitution effect, we confront Lisa with the new price but keep her on her original indifference curve, I_1. The substitution effect is the move from *c* to *k*. To isolate the income effect, we confront Lisa with the new price of movies but increase her income so that she can move from the original indifference curve, I_1, to the new one, I_2. The income effect is the move from *k* to *j*.

her consumption of movies. For Lisa, movies are a normal good. For a normal good, the income effect reinforces the substitution effect.

Inferior Goods The example that we have just studied is that of a change in the price of a normal good. The effect of a change in the price of an inferior good is different. Recall that an inferior good is one whose consumption decreases as income increases. For an inferior good, the income effect is negative. Thus for an inferior good, a lower price does not always lead to an increase in the quantity demanded. The lower price has a substitution effect that increases the quantity demanded. But the lower price also has a negative income effect that reduces the demand for the inferior good. Thus the income effect offsets the substitution effect to some degree. If the negative income effect exceeded the positive substitution effect, the demand curve would slope upward. This case does not appear to occur in the real world.

Back to the Facts

We started this chapter by observing how consumer spending has changed over the years. The indifference curve model explains those changes. Spending patterns are determined by best affordable choices. Changes in prices and incomes change the best affordable choice and change consumption patterns.

R E V I E W

▪ A consumer buys the best affordable combination of goods and services.

▪ With this combination, all the consumer's income is spent (on the budget line) and the marginal rate of substitution (the magnitude of the slope of the indifference curve) equals the relative price (the magnitude of the slope of the budget line).

▪ A fall in price or an increase in income increases the quantity demanded for a normal good.

▪ The effect of a price change can be divided into a substitution effect and an income effect.

▪ For a normal good, the income effect reinforces the substitution effect. For an inferior good the income effect partly offsets the substitution effect.

The model of household choice can explain many other household choices. Let's look at one of them.

Work-Leisure Choices

HOUSEHOLDS MAKE MANY CHOICES OTHER THAN those about how to spend their income on the various goods and services available. We can use the model of consumer choice to understand many other household choices. Some of these are discussed in the part opener on pp. 149–154. Here we'll study a key choice: how much labor to supply.

Labor Supply

Every week, we allocate our 168 hours between working—called *labor*—and all other activities—called *leisure*. How do we decide how to allocate our time between labor and leisure? We can answer this question by using the theory of household choice.

The more hours we spend on *leisure*, the smaller is our income. The relationship between leisure and income is described by an *income-time budget line*. Figure 9.10(a) shows Lisa's income-time budget line. If Lisa devotes the entire week to leisure—168 hours—she has no income and is at point z. By supplying labor in exchange for a wage, she can convert hours into income along the income-time budget line. The slope of that line is determined by the hourly wage rate. If the wage rate is $5 an hour, Lisa faces the flattest budget line. If the wage rate is $10 an hour, she faces the middle budget line. And if the wage rate is $15 an hour, she faces the steepest budget line.

Lisa buys leisure by not supplying labor and by forgoing income. The opportunity cost of an hour of leisure is the hourly wage rate forgone.

Figure 9.10(a) also shows Lisa's indifference curves for income and leisure. Lisa chooses her best attainable point. This choice of income and time allocation is just like her choice of movies and soda. She gets onto the highest possible indifference curve by making her marginal rate of substitution between income and leisure equal to her wage rate. Lisa's choice depends on the wage rate she can earn. At a wage rate of $5 an hour, Lisa chooses point a and works 20 hours a week (168 minus 148) for an income of $100 a week. At a wage rate of $10 an hour, she chooses point b and works 35 hours a week (168 minus 133) for an income of $350 a week. And at a wage rate of $15 an hour, she chooses point c and works 30 hours a week (168 minus 138) for an income of $450 a week.

FIGURE 9.10
The Supply of Labor

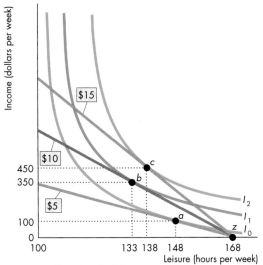

(a) Time allocation decision

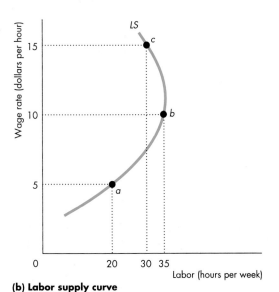

(b) Labor supply curve

In part (a), at a wage rate of $5 an hour, Lisa takes 148 hours of leisure and works 20 hours a week at point *a*. If the wage rate increases from $5 to $10, she decreases her leisure to 133 hours and increases her work to 35 hours a week at point *b*. But if the wage rate increases from $10 to $15, Lisa *increases* her leisure to 138 hours and *decreases* her work to 30 hours a week at point *c*. Part (b) shows Lisa's labor supply curve. Points *a*, *b*, and *c* on the supply curve correspond to Lisa's choices on her income-time budget lines in part (a).

The Labor Supply Curve

Figure 9.10(b) shows Lisa's labor supply curve. This curve shows that as the wage rate increases from $5 an hour to $10 an hour, Lisa increases the quantity of labor supplied from 20 hours a week to 35 hours a week. But when the wage rate increases to $15 an hour, she decreases her quantity of labor supplied to 30 hours a week.

Lisa's supply of labor is similar to that described for the economy as a whole at the beginning of this chapter. As wage rates have increased, work hours have decreased. At first, this pattern seems puzzling. We've seen that the hourly wage rate is the opportunity cost of leisure. So a higher wage rate means a higher opportunity cost of leisure. This fact on its own leads to a decrease in leisure and an increase in work hours. But instead, we've cut our work hours. Why? Because our incomes have increased. As the wage rate increases, incomes increase, so people demand more of all normal goods. Leisure is a normal good, so as incomes increase, people demand more leisure.

The higher wage rate has both a *substitution effect* and an *income effect*. The higher wage rate increases the opportunity cost of leisure and so leads to a substitution effect away from leisure. And the higher wage rate increases income and so leads to an income effect toward more leisure.

This theory of household choice can explain the facts about work patterns described at the beginning of this chapter. First, it can explain why the average workweek has fallen steadily from 70 hours in the nineteenth century to 35 hours today. The reason is that as wage rates have increased, although people have substituted work for leisure, they have also decided to use their higher incomes in part to consume more leisure. Second, the theory can explain why more women now have jobs in the labor market. The reason is that increases in their wage rates and improvements in their job opportunities have led to a substitution effect away from working at home and toward working in the labor market.

◆ This theory of household choice can also explain trends in the fast food industry, as you can see in *Reading Between the Lines* on pp. 186–187.

In the chapters that follow, we're going to study the choices made by firms. We'll see how, in the pursuit of profit, firms make choices that determine the supply of goods and services and the demand for productive resources.

Indifference Curves in Action

THE ADVOCATE, BATON ROUGE, NOVEMBER 7, 1996

Markets Need to Offer "Hassel-Free" Meals

BY TOMMY C. SIMMONS

The old question was "What's for dinner?"

The new question is "Who's fixing dinner?"

If supermarkets can capitalize on the growing market for home replacement meals—food to replace home-cooked meals—the answer to the second question will be Hi Nabor or Super Fresh, Calandro's, Delchamps, Schwegmann's, Kenilworth Supermarket, Albertson's or Winn-Dixie. Supermarkets and neighborhood grocery stores are poised to enter the next phase of food retailing which is likely to bring them into competition with restaurants, fast food chains and pizza delivery operations.

Ira Blumenthal, president of a food industry consulting and marketing firm based in Atlanta, was in Baton Rouge in October to talk with members of the Associated Grocers about trends in home dining. Grocery stores, he said, had better wake up and realize the world is changing.

Grocery stores aren't just competing with one another. They are also competing with convenience stores, restaurants, drive-through fast food outlets, pizza delivery chains and even video rental stores.

The customer profile that must be accommodated is the time-stressed, double-income family. What the wife/mother in this family is saying more often than not is "I don't feel like eating out, and I don't feel like cooking at home."

Carryout, home-cooked style food restaurants such as Boston Market, Eatzi's and Deli Central have been tremendously successful in major markets across the country because they have responded to that need for hassle-free, home-style food.

Grab and go is here and getting bigger.

Blumenthal urged grocers to embrace the concept of home meal replacement. Be inventive in responding to this need, he told the grocers. ...

To illustrate the changes in family dining, Blumenthal reminded the audience of grocers that 30 years ago eating out was a special event. Today, it is special to make a dish at home from scratch. ...

Reprinted with permission.

Essence of **THE STORY**

■ People are demanding hassle-free, home-style food in increasing quantity and variety.

■ Carryout, home-cooked-style food restaurants are on the increase because they are responding to the demand for hassle-free, home-style food.

■ Today, making a dish at home from scratch is a special event. Thirty years ago, it was the norm.

Economic

A N A L Y S I S

■ To prepare home-cooked meals, a household must use money to buy the ingredients and a lot of time.

■ The value of the time spent preparing meals is determined by the wage rate.

■ The total cost of home-cooked meals equals the cost of the ingredients plus the value of the time spent in the kitchen.

■ To serve carryout meals, a household must use money but almost no time.

■ Home-cooked food and fast food are substitutes, but they are not perfect substitutes. Indifference curves for these two types of food are bowed toward the origin and are I_0 and I_1 in Fig. 1.

■ Thirty years ago, a household's budget line for home-cooked food and fast food was the line ab in Fig. 1.

■ The household chose the best affordable point by consuming H_0 home-cooked food and F_0 fast food.

■ Today, wage rates are much higher than they were 30 years ago. So households can afford much more fast food today than they could 30 years ago.

■ Most of the cost of home-cooked food is the cost of time needed to prepare it. But the cost of time has increased by the same percentage as the rise in wages. So if a household consumes only home-cooked food, we'll assume that it cannot afford any more today than it could 30 years ago.

■ The budget line today is the line ac in Fig. 1.

■ Today, the best afford-able point is where the household consumes H_1 of home-cooked food and F_1 of fast food.

■ Because the value of time has increased, the relative price of fast food has fallen and people buy more fast food and less home-cooked food.

■ Is fast food an *inferior good*? Probably not. Figure 2 shows the substitution effect and the income effect.

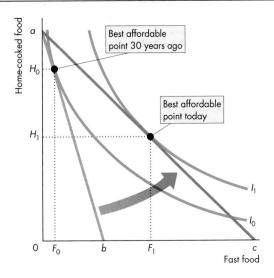

Figure 1 A price effect

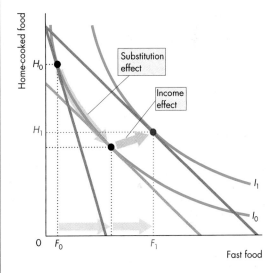

Figure 2 Substitution and income effect

■ We give the household a (hypothetical) cut in income to keep it on the same indifference curve as it was on 30 years ago. So the budget line is the pale orange line in Fig. 2. The household moves along indifference curve I_0 and consumes more fast food. This movement is the substitution effect.

■ We then reverse the (hypothetical) income cut, and the budget line moves outward with a constant relative price. The quantity of fast food increases. It is a normal good.

■ If wage rates continue to rise, the trend toward fast food will also continue.

S U M M A R Y

Key Points

Consumption Possibilities (pp. 174–176)

- The budget line is the boundary between what the household can and cannot afford given its income and the prices of goods.
- The point at which the budget line intersects the *y*-axis is the household's real income in terms of the good measured on that axis.
- The magnitude of the slope of the budget line is the relative price of the good measured on the *x*-axis in terms of the good measured on the *y*-axis.
- A change in price changes the slope of the budget line. A change in income shifts the budget line but does not change its slope.

Preferences and Indifference Curves (pp. 177–180)

- A consumer's preferences can be represented by indifference curves. An indifference curve joins all the combinations of goods among which the consumer is indifferent.
- A consumer prefers any point above an indifference curve to any point on it and any point on an indifference curve to any point below it.
- The magnitude of the slope of an indifference curve is called the marginal rate of substitution.
- The marginal rate of substitution diminishes as consumption of the good measured on the *y*-axis decreases and consumption of the good measured on the *x*-axis increases.

Predicting Consumer Behavior (pp. 180-184)

- A household consumes at its best affordable point. This point is on the budget line and on the highest attainable indifference curve and has a marginal rate of substitution equal to relative price.
- The effect of a price change (the price effect) can be divided into a substitution effect and an income effect.
- The substitution effect is the effect of a change in price on the quantity bought when the consumer (hypothetically) remains indifferent between the original and the new situation.
- The substitution effect always results in an increase in consumption of the good whose relative price has fallen.
- The income effect is the effect of a change in income on consumption.
- For a normal good, the income effect reinforces the substitution effect. For an inferior good, the income effect works in the opposite direction to the substitution effect.

Work-Leisure Choices (pp. 184–189)

- The indifference curve model of household choice enables us to understand how a household allocates its time between work and leisure.
- Work hours have decreased and leisure hours have increased because the income effect on the demand for leisure has been greater than the substitution effect.

Key Figures

Key Terms

QUESTIONS

1. What determines the limits to a household's consumption choices?
2. What is the budget line?
3. Derive the equation for the budget line and interpret it.
4. What determines the intercept of the budget line on the y-axis?
5. What do we call the intercept of the budget line on the y-axis? In what units is it measured?
6. What determines the intercept of the budget line on the x-axis?
7. What do we call the intercept of the budget line on the x-axis? In what units is it measured?
8. What determines the slope of the budget line?
9. How does the slope of the budget line change if the price of the good measured on the x-axis falls?
10. How does the slope of the budget line change if the price of the good measured on the x-axis rises?
11. How does the slope of the budget line change if the price of the good measured on the y-axis falls?
12. How does the slope of the budget line change if the price of the good measured on the y-axis rises?
13. What do all the points on an indifference curve have in common?
14. What is the marginal rate of substitution and how is it calculated?
15. What conditions are satisfied when a consumer makes the best affordable consumption choice?
16. What is the effect of a change in income on consumption?
17. What is the effect of a change in price on consumption?
18. Define and distinguish between the substitution effect and the income effect.
19. What is the opportunity cost of leisure?
20. Explain the shape of the labor supply curve.

PROBLEMS

1. Sara has an income of $12 a week. Popcorn costs $3 a bag, and cola costs $3 a can.
   a. What is Sara's real income in terms of cola?
   b. What is her real income in terms of popcorn?
   c. What is the relative price of cola in terms of popcorn?
   d. What is the opportunity cost of a can of cola?
   e. Calculate the equation for Sara's budget line (placing popcorn on the left side).
   f. Draw a graph of Sara's budget line with cola on the x-axis.
   g. In part (f), what is the slope of Sara's budget line? What is it equal to?
2. Sara's income and the prices she faces are the same as in problem 1. The indifference curves in the figure show her preferences.

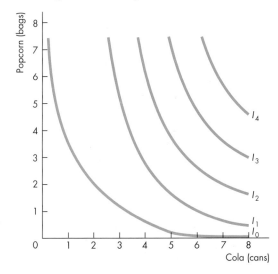

   a. What are the quantities of popcorn and cola that Sara buys?
   b. What is Sara's marginal rate of substitution of popcorn for cola at the point at which she consumes?
3. Now suppose that in the situation described in problem 1, the price of cola falls to $1.50 per can and the price of popcorn and Sara's income remain constant.

a. Find the new quantities of cola and pop-corn that Sara buys.
b. Find two points on Sara's demand curve for cola.
c. Find the substitution effect of the price change.
d. Find the income effect of the price change.
e. Is cola a normal good or an inferior good for Sara?
f. Is popcorn a normal good or an inferior good for Sara?

4. Jerry buys cookies that cost $1 each and comic books that cost $2 each, and he spends all his $40 income on these two goods. The figure illustrates Jerry's preferences.

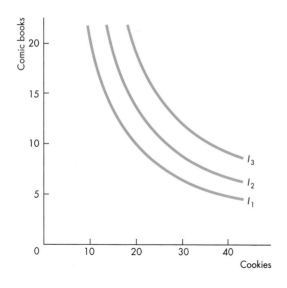

Jerry is confronted with some price changes. The price of a cookie falls to 50¢, and the price of a comic book rises to $3.

a. What is Jerry's initial consumption of cookies and comic books at the original prices?
b. Can Jerry buy his initial consumption at the new prices?
c. Will he want to?
d. If he changes his consumption, which good does he buy more of and which does he buy less of?
e. What is Jerry's consumption of cookies and comic books at the new prices?
f. Which situation does Jerry prefer: cookies at $1 and comic books at $2 or cookies at 50¢ and comic books at $3?

CRITICAL THINKING

1. Study *Reading Between the Lines* about the fast food industry on pp. 186–187, and then answer the following questions.
   a. What has happened to the relative price of home-cooked food and carryout food over the past 30 years?
   b. What do you think has happened to people's preferences for home-cooked food and carryout food over the past 30 years?
   c. Use the indifference curve model to explain the trends in the carryout industry during the past 30 years.
   d. What do you predict would happen to the carryout industry if wage rates fell?
   e. What do you predict would happen to the carryout industry if the farm price of food products increased sharply?

2. The sales tax is a tax on goods. Some people say that a consumption tax, a tax that is paid on both goods and services, would be better. If we replaced the sales tax with a consumption tax:
   a. What would happen to the relative price of floppy disks and haircuts?
   b. What would happen to the budget line that shows the quantities of floppy disks and haircuts you can afford to buy?
   c. How would you change your purchases of floppy disks and haircuts?
   d. Which type of tax is best for the consumer and why?

   Show in a figure the changes and show the substitution effect and the income effect.

3. Jim, a Generation-Xer, spends his income on apartment rent, food, clothing, and vacations. He gets a pay raise from $3,000 a month to $4,000 a month. At the same time, airfares and other vacation-related costs increase by 50 percent.
   a. How do you think Jim will change his spending pattern as a result of the changes in his income and prices?
   b. Can you say whether Jim is better off or worse off in his new situation?
   c. If all prices rise by 50 percent, how does Jim change his purchases? Can you now say whether he is better off or worse off?
   d. Show in a figure the changes in Jim's choices that the change in income and changes in prices induce.

10

Organizing Production

On a July day in 1977, a tiny new firm was born that grew into a giant—Apple Computer. But that day was not unusual. Every day, a new successful firm is born. Apple began its life when two Stanford University students produced the world's first commercially successful personal computer in a backyard garage. From that modest start, Apple has grown into a giant. ◆ Apple is one of some 20 million firms that operate in the United States today. They range from multinational giants, such as Apple and Sony, to small family restaurants and corner stores. Three quarters of all firms are operated by their owners, as Apple once was. But corporations (like Apple today) account for 86 percent of all business sales. What are the different forms a firm can take? Why do some remain small while others become giants? Why are most firms owner-operated? ◆ Firms spend billions of dollars on buildings and production lines and on developing and marketing new products. How does a firm get the funds needed to pay for all these activities? What do investors expect in return when they put funds into a firm? And how do we measure a firm's economic health? ◆ Most of the components of an IBM personal computer are made by other firms. Microsoft, not IBM, created the operating system for the PC. Microsoft has now outgrown IBM, and its products such as DOS and Windows have become household names. Why doesn't IBM make its own computer components? Why didn't it create its own operating system? Why did it leave these activities to other firms? How do firms decide what to make themselves and what to buy in the marketplace from other firms? ◆ In this chapter, we are going to learn about firms and the choices they make to cope with scarcity. We begin by studying the economic problems and choices that all firms face.

An Apple a Day

After studying this chapter, you will be able to:

■ Explain what a firm is and describe the economic problems that *all* firms face

■ Define and explain the principal-agent problem

■ Describe and distinguish among different forms of business organization

■ Explain how firms finance their operations

■ Calculate a firm's opportunity cost and economic profit

■ Explain why firms coordinate some economic activities and markets coordinate others

The Firm and Its Economic Problem

THERE ARE 20 MILLION FIRMS IN THE UNITED States, and they differ enormously in size and in the scope of what they do. What do they have in common? What is the distinguishing characteristic of a firm? What are the different ways in which firms are organized? Why are there different forms of organization? These are the questions we'll tackle first.

What Is a Firm?

A **firm** is an institution that hires productive resources and that organizes those resources to produce and sell goods and services. Firms exist because of scarcity. They help us to cope with the fundamental economic problem of scarcity, and they enable us to use our scarce resources efficiently. But each firm faces its own economic problem. That is, each firm must strive to get the most it can out of the scarce resources it controls. To do so, a firm must decide on the following:

- Which goods and services to produce and in what quantities

- Which of its inputs to produce itself and which to buy from other firms

- Which techniques of production to use

- Which productive resources to employ and in what quantities

- How to organize its management structure

- How to compensate its productive resources and suppliers

For the majority of firms, these decisions are made so that the firm makes the maximum possible profit. And for every firm, whether it is motivated by profit or some other goal, these decisions are made so that the firm produces its output at the lowest possible cost.

In the rest of this chapter and in Chapters 11 through 14, we are going to study the actions a firm must take to be efficient. And we are going to see how we can predict a firm's behavior by working out its efficient response to a change in its circumstances. But we are going to begin by looking a bit more closely at the fundamental problem the firm faces.

The fundamental problem for a firm is *organization*—the firm organizes the production of goods and services by combining and coordinating the productive resources it hires. Firms organize production by using a mixture of two systems:

- Command systems
- Incentive systems

Command Systems

A command system is a method of coordinating the productive resources that a firm hires that is based on a managerial hierarchy. A chief executive is at the top of the managerial ladder and directs the senior managers. The senior managers direct the middle managers, who in turn direct operations managers. This lowest level of management controls the workers who produce the goods and services. Commands pass downward through the managerial hierarchy, and information passes upward. Managers spend most of their time collecting and processing information about the performance of the people under their control and making decisions about commands to issue and how best to get those commands implemented.

The number of layers of management depends on the complexity of the business and on the technology available for managing information. In the smallest and simplest organizations, perhaps one or two layers of managers are all that are needed. But in large organizations that undertake complex tasks, several layers of management are found. The computer and information revolution of the 1980s and 1990s has decreased the number of layers needed and has brought a big shakeout of middle managers.

Despite the enormous efforts they make to be well informed, managers always have incomplete information about what is happening in the divisions of the firm under their control. It is for this reason that firms use incentive systems as well as command systems to organize production.

Incentive Systems

Incentive systems are market-like mechanisms that firms create inside their organizations. Such systems operate at all levels, from the chief executive down to the factory floor and the sales force. And they arise because a firm's owners and managers cannot know everything that is relevant to the efficient operation of their business. What did John Sculley (a former president of Apple Computer) contribute to the success and subsequent problems faced by Apple? What role did Lee Iaccoca play in the fortunes of Chrysler? These questions cannot be answered with certainty even long after the event. Yet Apple and Chrysler must put chief executive officers (CEOs) like these in charge of operations and give them *incentives* to succeed, even when the contribution they make cannot be measured directly.

At the bottom of the management ladder, some workers are more diligent than others, and it is often difficult for managers to know who is working and who is shirking. Did sales fall last month because the sales force slacked off or because of some other unknown factor? Again, firms must devise incentives to ensure that the sales force works effectively.

Because of incomplete information, firms do not simply demand productive resources and pay for them as if they were buying toothpaste at the drugstore. Instead, they enter into contracts and devise compensation packages that strengthen incentives and raise productivity. These contracts and compensation packages are called *agency relationships*, and they are an attempt to solve what is called the principal-agent problem.

The Principal-Agent Problem

The **principal-agent problem** is to devise compensation rules that induce an *agent* to act in the best interest of a *principal*. For example, the relationship between the stockholders of the Bank of America and the bank's managers is an agency relationship. The stockholders (the principals) must induce the managers (agents) to act in the stockholders' best interest. Another example of an agency relationship is that between Microsoft Corporation (a principal) and its programmers working on a new version of Windows (agents). Microsoft must induce the programmers to work in the best interest of the firm.

Coping with the Principal-Agent Problem

Agents, whether they are managers or workers, pursue their own goals and often impose costs on a principal. For example, the goal of a stockholder of the Bank of America (a principal) is to maximize the bank's profit. But the bank's profit depends on the actions of its managers (agents), who have their own goals. Perhaps a manager takes a customer to a ball game on the pretense that she is building customer loyalty, when in fact she is simply taking on-the-job leisure. This same manager is also a principal, and her tellers are agents. The manager wants the tellers to work hard and attract new customers so she can meet her operating targets. But the tellers enjoy conversations with each other and keep customers waiting in line. Nonetheless, the bank constantly strives to find ways of improving performance and increasing profits.

Just giving orders and having workers obey them cannot solve the principal-agent problem. In most firms, it isn't possible for the shareholders to monitor the managers or even for the managers to monitor the workers. To achieve their goal, the firm's owners (principals) must induce its managers (agents) to pursue the maximum possible profit. And the managers (principals) must induce the workers (agents) to work efficiently. Each principal attempts to do this by creating incentives that induce each agent to work in the interests of the principal. The three main ways of coping with the principal-agent problem are:

- Ownership
- Incentive pay
- Long-term contracts

3 kinds of incentive

Ownership   By assigning a manager or worker ownership (or part-ownership) of a business, it is sometimes possible to induce a job performance that increases a firm's profits. Part-ownership schemes for senior managers are quite common, but they are less common for workers. When United Airlines was running into problems a few years ago, it adopted this solution and made all its employees owners of the company.

Incentive Pay   Incentive pay schemes—pay related to performance—are very common. They are based on a wide variety of performance criteria. For example, managers often share in a firm's profits for meeting profit targets, and workers get bonuses for meeting production or sales targets.

Long-Term Contracts   Long-term contracts are a way of coping with the principal-agent problem because they tie the long-term fortunes of managers and workers (agents) to the success of the principal(s)—the owner(s) of the firm.

Examples of long-term contracts are multiyear employment contracts for CEOs and other senior managers. These contracts enable a management team to take a long-term view and devise strategies that might create large returns over a sustained period.

A further fundamental problem that all firms must cope with is uncertainty about the future.

Uncertainty About the Future

Firms' decisions are based on their expectations of the consequences of their actions. But expectations often turn out to be wrong. The main problem is that almost every firm must commit to a project and spend huge amounts on it *before* it knows whether it will be able to sell its output in sufficient quantities and at a sufficiently high price to cover its outlays. For example, 30 years ago, French and British airplane makers spent several years and millions of dollars building a supersonic transatlantic passenger plane—the Concorde. They expected to be able to sell enough of these technologically sophisticated airplanes to recover their cost. But it turned out that too few people value the Concorde's extra speed for it to generate sales revenues equal to its cost. On a smaller scale, millions of people try their luck at opening coffee shops and other small businesses. They spend several thousands of dollars setting up a business before they know how much revenue their business will earn. And many of them turn out to be too optimistic. The revenue falls short of the cost and the business fails.

The facts of incomplete information and uncertainty about the future give rise to different forms of business organization. Let's look at these different forms.

The Forms of Business Organization

The three main forms of business organization are:

- Proprietorship
- Partnership
- Corporation

Which form a firm takes influences its management structure, how it compensates productive resources, how much tax its owners pay, and who receives its profits and is liable for its debts if it goes out of business.

Proprietorship A *proprietorship* is a firm with a single owner—a proprietor—who has unlimited liability. *Unlimited liability* is the legal responsibility for all the debts of a firm up to an amount equal to the entire wealth of the owner. If a proprietorship cannot pay its debts, those to whom the firm owes money can claim the personal property of the owner. Corner stores, computer programmers, and artists are all examples of proprietorships.

The proprietor makes the management decisions and is the firm's sole residual claimant. A firm's *residual claimant* is the person who receives the firm's profits and is responsible for its losses. The profits of a proprietorship are part of the income of the proprietor. They are added to the proprietor's other income and taxed as personal income.

Partnership A *partnership* is a firm with two or more owners who have unlimited liability. Partners must agree on an appropriate management structure and on how to divide the firm's profits among themselves. As in a proprietorship, the profits of a partnership are taxed as the personal income of the owners. But each partner is legally liable for all the debts of the partnership (limited only by the wealth of an individual partner). Liability for the full debts of the partnership is called *joint unlimited liability*. Most law firms are partnerships.

Corporation A *corporation* is a firm owned by one or more limited liability stockholders. *Limited liability* means that the owners have legal liability only for the value of their initial investment. This limitation of liability means that if the corporation becomes bankrupt, the owners of the corporation, unlike the owners of a proprietorship or partnership, cannot be forced to use their personal wealth to pay the corporation's debts.

The stock of a corporation is divided into shares. A *share* is a fraction of the stock of a corporation. Shares in many corporations are bought and sold on stock markets such as the New York Stock Exchange.

Some corporations, no bigger than a proprietorship, have just one effective owner and are managed in the same way as a proprietorship. Large corporations have elaborate management structures headed by a CEO and senior vice-presidents responsible for such areas as production, finance, marketing, and research. These senior executives are in turn served by a series of specialists. Each layer in the management structure knows enough about what happens in the layer below it to exercise control, but the entire management consists of specialists who concentrate on a narrow aspect of the corporation's activities.

The corporation receives its financial resources from its owners—the stockholders—and by borrowing. Corporations sometimes borrow from banks, but they can also borrow directly from households by issuing bonds—loans on which they pay a fixed number of dollars of interest.

If a corporation makes a profit, the residual claimants to that profit are the stockholders, who receive dividends. If a corporation incurs a loss on such a scale that it becomes bankrupt, the banks and other corporations to whom the troubled corporation is in debt absorb the residual loss. The stockholders themselves, by virtue of their limited liability, are responsible for the debt of the corporation only up to the value of their initial investment.

The profits of a corporation are taxed independently of the incomes of its stockholders, so corporate profits are, in effect, taxed twice. After the corporation has paid tax on its profits, the stockholders themselves pay taxes on the income they receive as dividends on stocks. The stockholders also pay tax on capital gains when they sell a stock. A **capital gain** is the income received by selling a stock (or a bond) for a higher price than the price paid for it. Corporate stocks generate capital gains when a corporation retains some of its profit and reinvests it in profitable activities instead of paying dividends. So even retained earnings are effectively taxed twice because the capital gains they generate are taxed.

The Pros and Cons of the Different Types of Firms

Because each of the three main types of firms exists, each type obviously has advantages in particular situations. Each type also has its disadvantages, which explains why it has not driven out the other two. Table 10.1 summarizes these pros and cons.

TABLE 10.1

The Pros and Cons of Different Types of Firms

Proprietorship	Cons
■ Easy to set up	■ Bad decisions not checked by need for consensus
■ Simple decision making	■ Owner's entire wealth at risk
■ Profits taxed only once as owner's income	■ Firm dies with owner
	■ Capital is expensive
	■ Labor is expensive
Partnership	
■ Easy to set up	■ Achieving consensus may be slow and expensive
■ Diversified decision making	■ Owners' entire wealth at risk
■ Can survive withdrawal of partner	■ Withdrawal of partner may create capital shortage
■ Profits taxed only once as owners' incomes	■ Capital is expensive
Corporation	
■ Owners have limited liability	■ Complex management structure can make decisions slow and expensive
■ Large-scale, low-cost capital available	■ Profits taxed twice as company profit and as stockholders' income
■ Professional management not restricted by ability of owners	
■ Perpetual life	
■ Long-term labor contracts cut labor costs	

FIGURE 10.1

Relative Importance of the Three Main Types of Firms

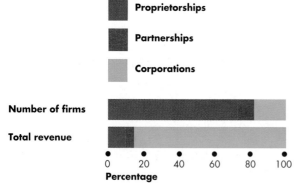

(a) Number of firms and total revenue

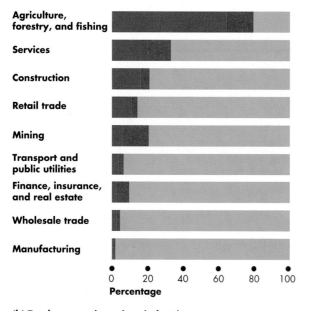

(b) Total revenue in various industries

Three quarters of all firms are proprietorships, almost one fifth are corporations, and only a twentieth are partnerships. Corporations account for 86 percent of business revenue (part a). But proprietorships and partnerships account for a significant percentage of business revenue in some industries (part b).

Source: U.S. Bureau of the Census *Statistical Abstract of the United States: 1995,* 115th ed. CD-ROM (Washington, DC: 1995): 544 and 671.

The Relative Importance of Different Types of Firms

Figure 10.1(a) shows the relative importance of the three main types of firms in the U.S. economy. The figure also shows that the revenue of corporations is much larger than that of the other types of firms. Although only 18 percent of all firms are corporations, they generate 86 percent of revenue.

Figure 10.1(b) shows the percentage of total revenue accounted for by the different types of firms in various industries. Proprietorships account for a large percentage of revenue in agriculture, forestry, and fishing and in the service sector. They also account for a large percentage in construction and retail trades. Partnerships are more prominent in agriculture, forestry, and fishing; services; mining; and finance, insurance, and real estate than in other sectors of the economy. Corporations are important in all sectors. In manufacturing, corporations have the field almost to themselves.

Why do corporations dominate the business scene? Why do the other forms of business survive? And why are proprietorships and partnerships more prominent in some sectors? The answer to these questions lies in the pros and cons of the different forms of business organization that are summarized in Table 10.1. Corporations dominate where a large amount of capital is used. But proprietorships dominate where flexibility in decision making is critical.

REVIEW

- A firm is any institution that hires productive resources and organizes the production and sale of goods and services.
- Firms strive to be efficient and most firms aim to maximize profit, but they face uncertainty and have incomplete information. To cope with these problems, firms enter into relationships—principal-agent relationships—with owners, managers, workers, and other firms and devise efficient legal structures and compensation schemes.
- Each main type of firm—proprietorship, partnership, and corporation—has its advantages and disadvantages, and each type plays a role in every sector of the economy.

Business Finance

EVERY YEAR, FIRMS RAISE BILLIONS OF DOLLARS to enable them to buy capital equipment and to finance their inventory holdings. For example, an airline might raise hundreds of millions of dollars to buy a bigger fleet of jets. A steel manufacturer might raise hundreds of millions of dollars to build a new plant. A software producer might raise millions of dollars to pay programmers to develop a new computer game. Let's see how firms raise funds.

How Firms Raise Funds

All firms get some of their funds from their owners. The owner's stake in a business is called **equity**. Firms also borrow some of the funds they need from banks. Proprietorships and partnerships raise additional funds by borrowing from friends. The more permanent structure of corporations gives them two ways of raising large amounts of money that are not generally available to unincorporated businesses. They are:

- Selling stock
- Selling bonds

Selling Stock

One major way in which a corporation can raise funds is by selling stock. Funds raised in this way are the corporation's *equity* because the stockholders of a corporation are its owners. They have bought shares of the corporation's stock.

Corporations sell shares of their stock, and these shares are regularly traded on stock exchanges. A *stock exchange* is an organized market for trading in stock. The biggest stock exchanges in the United States are the New York Stock Exchange (NYSE), the National Association of Securities Dealers Automated Quotations (NASDAQ), and the American Stock Exchange (ASE). Other major stock exchanges are in Boston, Philadelphia, Chicago, and San Francisco.

Figure 10.2 shows an example of a firm raising funds by selling stock. In February 1994, Reebok International Ltd. sold 3 million shares of stock for $33.125 a share, thereby raising $99,375,000. A firm that raises funds by selling stock is not obligated to

FIGURE 10.2

Selling Stock

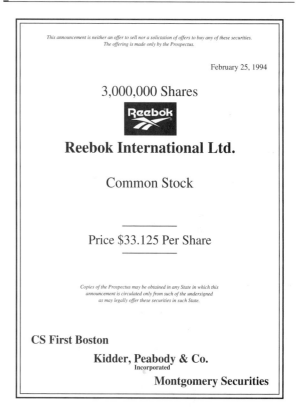

This announcement is neither an offer to sell nor a solicitation of offers to buy any of these securities. The offering is made only by the Prospectus.

February 25, 1994

3,000,000 Shares

Reebok

Reebok International Ltd.

Common Stock

Price $33.125 Per Share

Copies of the Prospectus may be obtained in any State in which this announcement is circulated only from such of the undersigned as may legally offer these securities in such State.

CS First Boston

Kidder, Peabody & Co.
Incorporated

Montgomery Securities

A share of the stock in a company entitles its holder to receive a dividend (if the directors vote to pay one). Reebok sold 3,000,000 shares of stock at $33.125 a share, thereby raising $99,375,000 of additional funds.

make dividend payments to its stockholders. But stockholders expect a dividend or a capital gain—otherwise, no one will buy the shares.

Selling Bonds

Firms borrow funds by selling bonds. A **bond** is a legally enforceable debt obligation to pay specified amounts of money at specified future dates. Usually, a bond specifies that a certain amount of money called the *redemption value* of the bond will be paid at a certain future date, called the *maturity date*. In addition, another amount will be paid each year between the date of sale of the bond and the maturity

So if people buy stocks why would firms sell bonds? And if firms sell bonds, why would people buy stock??

date. The amount of money paid each year is called the *coupon payment*.

Figure 10.3 gives an example of bond financing. On July 12, 1994, Kinpo Electronics Inc., a company based in Taiwan that plans to take on Apple Computer, Motorola, and Texas Instruments in a bid for the world market in personal digital assistants,

---

FIGURE 10.3

Selling Bonds

This announcement appears as a notice of record only.

Kinpo Electronics, Inc.

US $44,000,000

3 per cent. Bonds due 2001

Issue Price: 100 per cent.

Jardine Fleming

Indosucz Capital
J. Henry Schroder Wagg & Co. Limited

China Development Corporation
Swiss Bank Corporation

Capital Securities Hong Kong Limited
Droedner Bank

Nomura International
Morgan Stanley & Co.

Nikko Europe Plc

Finanical Advisor to the Company in the ROC
China Development Corporation

July 1994

A bond is an obligation to make coupon payments and a redemption payment. Kinpo, a producer of computer components and personal digital assistants, sold bonds to raise $44 million in 1994. The company promised to pay $3 per $100 borrowed each year as a coupon payment and to redeem the bonds in 2001.

---

raised $44 million by selling bonds. On that day, Kinpo committed itself to making a coupon payment of $1.32 million (the equivalent of an interest rate of 3 percent a year) on July 12 each year through 2001 and to repaying the $44 million on July 12, 2001. So the total amount that Kinpo committed to pay is $53.24 million, the $44 million borrowed plus $1.32 million a year for seven years.

When a firm makes a financing decision, it tries to minimize its cost of funds. If the cost of raising funds is lower from selling bonds than from any other source, the firm will choose this method of financing. But how does it decide how much to borrow? To answer this question, we need to understand a key principle of business and personal finance.

Discounting and Present Value

When a firm raises funds, it receives money in the current period and takes on an obligation to make a series of payments in *future* periods. For example, Kinpo received $44 million in 1994 and took on an obligation to pay out $53.24 million through 2001. But also when a firm raises funds, it does so because it plans to use them to generate a future net inflow of cash from its business operations. For example, Kinpo borrowed $44 million because it planned to use it to manufacture and sell computer components and products that would bring in some future revenue.

To decide whether to borrow and how much to borrow, a firm must somehow compare money today with money in the future. If you are given a choice between a dollar today and a dollar a year from today, you will choose a dollar today. A dollar today is worth more to you than a dollar in the future because you can invest today's dollar to earn interest. The same is true for a firm. To compare an amount of money in the future with an amount of money in the present, we calculate the present value of the future amount of money. The **present value** of a future amount of money is the amount that, if invested today, will grow to be as large as that future amount when the interest that it will earn is taken into account. Let's express this idea with an equation:

Future amount = Present value + Interest income.

The interest income is equal to the present value multiplied by the interest rate, r, so

Future amount = Present value + ($r \times$ Present value)

What's the dif. btw. "amount" & "value"?

*r × present value?
(yes, in decimal form)*

or

$$\text{Future amount} = \text{Present value} \times (1 + r).$$

If you have $100 today and the interest rate is 10 percent a year ($r = 0.1$), one year from today you will have $110—the original $100 plus $10 interest. Check that the above formula delivers that answer: $100 × 1.1 = $110.

The formula that we have just used calculates a future amount one year from today from the present value and an interest rate. To calculate the present value, we just work backward. Instead of multiplying the present value by $(1 + r)$, we divide the future amount by $(1 + r)$. That is,

$$\text{Present value} = \frac{\text{Future amount}}{(1 + r)}.$$

You can use this formula to calculate present value. Calculating present value is called discounting. **Discounting** is the conversion of a future amount of money to its present value. Let's check that we can use the present value formula by calculating the present value of $110 one year from now when the interest rate is 10 percent a year. You'll be able to guess that the answer is $100 because we just calculated that $100 invested today at 10 percent a year becomes $110 in one year. Thus it follows immediately that the present value of $110 in one year's time is $100. But let's use the formula. Putting the numbers into the above formula, we have

$$\text{Present value} = \frac{\$110}{(1 + 0.1)}$$

$$= \frac{\$110}{(1.1)} = \$100.$$

Calculating the present value of an amount of money one year from now is the easiest case. But we can also calculate the present value of an amount any number of years in the future. As an example, let's see how we calculate the present value of an amount of money that will be available two years from now.

Suppose that you invest $100 today for two years at an interest rate of 10 percent a year. The money will earn $10 in the first year, which means that by the end of the first year, you will have $110. If the interest of $10 is invested, then the interest earned in the second year will be a further $10 on the original $100 plus $1 on the $10 interest. Thus the total interest earned in the second year will be $11. The total interest earned overall will be $21 ($10 in the first year and $11 in the second year). After two years, you will have $121. From the definition of present value, you can see that the present value of $121 two years hence is $100. That is, $100 is the present amount that, if invested at an interest rate of 10 percent a year, will grow to $121 two years from now.

To calculate the present value of an amount of money two years in the future, we use the formula

$$\text{Present value} = \frac{\text{Amount of money two years in future}}{(1 + r)^2}.$$

Let's check that the formula works by calculating the present value of $121 two years in the future when the interest rate is 10 percent a year. Putting these numbers into the formula gives

$$\text{Present value} = \frac{\$121}{(1 + 0.1)^2}$$

$$= \frac{\$121}{(1.1)^2}$$

$$= \frac{\$121}{1.21}$$

$$= \$100.$$

We can calculate the present value of an amount of money any number of years in the future by using a formula based on the two that we've already used. The general formula is

$$\text{Present value} = \frac{\text{Amount of money } n \text{ years in future}}{(1 + r)^n}.$$

For example, if the interest rate is 10 percent a year, $100 to be received 10 years from now has a present value of $38.55. That is, if $38.55 is invested today at an interest rate of 10 percent, it will accumulate to $100 in 10 years. (You might check that calculation on your pocket calculator.)

You've seen how to calculate the present value of an amount of money one year in the future, two years in the future, and n years in the future. Most practical applications of present value calculate the present value of a sequence of future amounts of money that spread over several years. To calculate the present value of a sequence of amounts over several years, we use the formula you have learned and apply it to each year. We then sum the present values for each year to find the present value of the sequence of amounts.

Present Value and Marginal Analysis

The goal of the firm is to make the largest possible profit. To do so, it must use the resources it owns and hires as efficiently as possible. Being efficient in raising capital to finance its purchases of equipment and buildings is a key part of the firm's overall economic problem.

Firms use the concept of present value to achieve an efficient use of capital. They also use another fundamental principle that you've met repeatedly: They compare *marginal benefit* and *marginal cost*.

In making any decision, only the additional benefit—*marginal benefit*—and additional cost—*marginal cost*—that result from the decision are relevant. By evaluating the marginal benefit and marginal cost of borrowing, a firm is able to maximize its profit. Marginal benefit minus marginal cost is net benefit, and the present value of net benefit is called *net present value*.

The firm decides how much to borrow by calculating the net present value of borrowing one additional dollar—the marginal dollar borrowed. If the net present value of the marginal dollar borrowed is positive, then the firm can increase its profit by increasing the amount it borrows. That is, the marginal dollar borrowed brings in more revenue than it costs. If the net present value of the marginal dollar borrowed is negative, then the firm can increase its profit by *decreasing* its borrowing. When the present value of the marginal dollar borrowed is zero, then the firm cannot increase its profit—it is maximizing its profit.

R E V I E W

- Firms finance their purchases of capital equipment by selling bonds—promises of a fixed payment independent of the firm's profit—and selling stock—opportunities to share in the firm's profit.
- Firms borrow if doing so increases the net present value of their cash flow.

We've seen how firms pursue maximum profits by establishing appropriate types of business organizations and by raising funds in the most profitable way. But how do firms measure their performance? How do they calculate their costs and profits? These are the questions we now study.

Opportunity Cost and Economic Profit

A FIRM'S OPPORTUNITY COST OF PRODUCING A good is the best alternative action that the firm forgoes to produce it. Equivalently, it is the firm's best alternative use for the productive resources it employs to produce a good. Opportunity cost is a real alternative forgone. But so that we can compare the opportunity cost of one action with that of another action, we often express opportunity cost in units of money. Even though we express opportunity cost in money units, it is the real alternative forgone and not the money value of that alternative.

A firm's opportunity cost of production has two components:

- Explicit costs
- Implicit costs

Explicit Costs

Explicit costs are paid directly in money—*money costs*. It is easy to measure explicit costs, and accountants have developed routine methods of doing so.

A firm incurs explicit costs when it pays for a factor of production at the same time as it uses it. The money cost is the amount paid for the factor of production, but this same amount could have been spent on something else, so it is also the opportunity cost (expressed in dollars) of using this factor of production. For example, if a pizza restaurant hires a waiter, the wages paid are both the money cost and the opportunity cost of hiring the waiter—the firm pays the waiter at the same time as it uses the services of the waiter. Labor is the factor of production whose money cost typically equals its opportunity cost.

Implicit Costs

Implicit costs are measured in units of money, but they are not paid for directly in money. Like explicit costs, implicit cost are the value of forgone opportunities for the firm.

A firm incurs implicit costs when it uses the following productive resources:

- Capital
- Inventories
- Owner's resources

Cost of Capital

The cost of using capital is an implicit cost because a firm usually buys its capital and then uses the equipment over a future period. For example, GM buys an assembly line, pays for it this year, and uses it for several years. We need to calculate the opportunity cost of using the capital over its entire life. The opportunity cost of using capital has two components, econmomic depreciation and interest.

1. Economic depreciation
2. Interest

1. Economic Depreciation Depreciation is the change in the value of capital over a given period. **Economic depreciation** is change in the *market* value of capital over a given period. It is calculated as the market price of the capital at the beginning of the period minus its market price at the end of the period. For example, suppose that United Airlines has a jumbo jet that it could have sold on December 31, 1995, for $5 million. If it could sell the same airplane on December 31, 1996, for $4 million, the $1 million fall in the market value is the economic depreciation of the airplane during 1996. It is part of the opportunity cost of using the airplane during 1996.

2. Interest The funds used to buy capital could have been used for some other purpose. And in their next best alternative use, they would have yielded a return—an interest income. This forgone interest is part of the opportunity cost of using the capital. It is part of the opportunity cost regardless of whether the firm borrows the funds to buy its capital or uses its previous earnings. To see why, think about two cases: The firm borrows funds or it uses its previous earnings.

If a firm borrows funds, then it makes an explicit interest payment, so the interest is an explicit cost. If the firm uses its own funds, the opportunity cost is the amount that could have been earned by using those funds in their best alternative use. Suppose the best alternative is to put the money in a bank deposit. The interest forgone is part of the opportunity cost of using the capital.

Implicit Rental Rate To measure the opportunity cost of using capital, we calculate the sum of economic depreciation and interest costs. This opportunity cost is the income that the firm forgoes by using the assets itself and not renting them to another firm instead. When a firm uses its own assets, the firm implicitly rents the assets to itself. Because the firm implicitly rents assets to itself, it pays an **implicit rental rate** for their use.

People rent houses, apartments, cars, telephones, and videotapes. Firms rent photocopiers, earth-moving equipment, satellite launching services, and so on. If a piece of equipment is rented, an *explicit* cost is incurred. If a piece of equipment is bought and used by its owner rather than rented to someone else, an *implicit* rent is paid. The owner-user of a piece of equipment could have rented it to someone else instead. The income forgone is the opportunity cost of using the equipment. That opportunity cost is the *implicit* rental rate.

Market forces make the market rental rate equal to the implicit rental rate. If renting had a lower opportunity cost than buying, everyone would want to rent and no one would want to buy. So some renters would not be able to find anyone to rent from, and the market rent would rise. If renting had a higher opportunity cost than buying, everyone would want to buy and no one would want to rent. So owners would not be able to find anyone to rent to, and the market rent would fall. Only when the opportunity costs of renting and buying are equal is there no incentive to switch between buying and renting.

Sunk Cost A **sunk cost** is a cost that has been incurred and that cannot be reversed. Most capital expenditure is to some degree a sunk cost. If Ford wanted to sell an assembly line, it would be able to do so only for its scrap value, not the price it paid. The price Ford paid minus the scrap value of the assembly line is a sunk cost. Sunk cost is not an *opportunity cost*. Ford's opportunity cost of using its assembly line does *not* include the fall in value.

Accounting Measures Accountants measure depreciation, but they do not usually measure *economic depreciation*. Instead, they apply a conventional depreciation rate to the purchase value.

The conventions used are based on Internal Revenue Service rules and on standards established by the Financial Accounting Standards Board (FASB). For buildings, a conventional depreciation period is 20 years. Thus if a firm buys a new office building for $100,000, its accounts show one twentieth of that amount, $5,000, as a cost of production each year. At the end of the first year, the firm's accounts record the value of the building as $95,000 (the original cost minus the $5,000 depreciation). Different depreciation rates are used for different types of capital. For example, for cars and computers, the conventional depreciation period is 3 years.

These accounting measures of depreciation do not measure the economic depreciation component of the opportunity cost of using capital.

Cost of Inventories

Inventories are stocks of raw materials, semifinished goods, and finished goods held by firms. The opportunity cost of using an item from inventory is its current market price. Firms hold inventories to make the production process efficient. So when an item is taken out of inventory, it must be replaced by a new item. The cost of that new item is the opportunity cost of using the item taken from inventory. Another line of reasoning leads to the same conclusion. An alternative to *using* an item from inventory is to sell it for its current market price. So the opportunity forgone is the current market price.

To measure the cost of using inventories, accountants frequently use a method called FIFO, which stands for "First In, First Out." This method values an item taken from inventory at the price of oldest item in the inventory. An alternative accounting measure is called LIFO, which stands for "Last In, First Out." This method values an item taken from inventory at the price of the last one placed into the inventory. FIFO does not measure opportunity cost, but LIFO comes close to doing so.

Cost of Owner's Resources

The owner of a firm often puts a great deal of time and effort into organizing the firm. But the owner could have worked at some other activity and earned a wage. The opportunity cost of the owner's time spent working for the firm is the wage income forgone by not working in the best alternative job.

In addition to supplying labor to the firm, its owner also supplies *entrepreneurial ability*—the factor of production that organizes the business, makes business decisions, innovates, and bears the risk of running the business. These activities would not be undertaken without the expectation of a return. The expected return for supplying entrepreneurial ability is called **normal profit**. Normal profit is part of a firm's opportunity cost, because it is the cost of a forgone alternative. The forgone alternative is running another firm.

Usually, the owner of a firm withdraws cash from the business to meet living expenses. Accountants regard such withdrawals of cash as part of the owner's profit from the business rather than as part of the opportunity cost of the owner's time and entrepreneurial ability. But to the extent that they compensate for wages forgone and risk, they are part of the firm's opportunity cost.

Economic Profit

What is the bottom line—the profit or loss of the firm? A firm's **economic profit** is equal to its total revenue minus its opportunity cost. Its opportunity cost is the explicit and implicit costs of the best alternative actions forgone, including *normal profit*.

Economic profit is not the same as what accountants call profit. For the accountant, a firm's profit is equal to its total revenue minus its money cost and its conventional depreciation.

Opportunity Cost and Economic Profit: An Example

To help you get a clearer picture of the concepts of a firm's opportunity cost and economic profit, we'll look at a concrete example. And we'll contrast the economist's concepts of opportunity cost and economic profit with the accounting measures of cost and profit.

Rocky owns a shop that sells bikes. His revenue, cost, and profit appear in Table 10.2. The accountant's calculations of Rocky's cost are on the left side, and the economist's calculations of Rocky's opportunity cost are on the right.

Rocky sold $300,000 worth of bikes during the year. This amount appears as his total revenue in both the accountant's and the economist's statement. The wholesale cost of bikes was $150,000, he bought $20,000 worth of utilities and other services, and he paid out $50,000 in wages to his mechanic and sales clerk. Rocky also paid $12,000 in interest to the bank. All of the items just mentioned appear in both the accountant's and the economist's statement. The remaining items differ between the two statements; some notes at the foot of the table explain the differences.

TABLE 10.2

Rocky's Mountain Bikes' Revenue, Cost, and Profit Statement

The accountant	
Item	**Amount**
Total revenue	$300,000
Costs:	
Wholesale cost of bikes	150,000
Utilities and other services	20,000
Wages	50,000
Depreciation	22,000
Bank interest	12,000
Total cost	$254,000
Profit	$46,000

The economist	
Item	**Amount**
Total revenue	$300,000
Costs:	
Wholesale cost of bikes	150,000
Utilities and other services	20,000
Wages	50,000
Fall in market value of assets[a]	10,000
Rocky's wages (implicit)[b]	40,000
Bank interest	12,000
Interest on Rocky's money invested in firm (implicit)[c]	11,500
Normal profit (implicit)[d]	6,000
Opportunity cost	$299,500
Economic profit	$500

[a] The fall in the market value of the assets of the firm gives the opportunity cost of not selling them one year ago. That is part of the opportunity cost of using them for the year.
[b] Rocky could have worked elsewhere for $40 an hour, but he worked 1000 hours on the firm's business, which means that the opportunity cost of his time is $40,000.

[c] Rocky has invested $115,000 in the firm. If the current interest rate is 10% a year, the opportunity cost of those funds is $11,500.
[d] Rocky could avoid the risk of running his own business, and he would be unwilling to take on the risk for a return of less than $6,000. This is his *normal profit.* (The magnitude of normal profit is assumed.)

The accountant's depreciation calculation is based on conventional life assumptions for Rocky's capital. The economist calculates the cost of Rocky's time, funds invested in the firm, and risk-bearing and also calculates economic depreciation. The accountant says that Rocky's costs are $254,000 and his profit is $46,000. In contrast, the economist says that Rocky's year in business had an opportunity cost of $299,500 and yielded an economic profit of $500.

The accountant's calculation of Rocky's profit does not tell Rocky his economic profit because it omits some components of opportunity cost and measures others incorrectly. The economist's measure of economic profit tells Rocky how his business is doing compared with what he can normally expect. Any positive economic profit is good news for Rocky because his normal profit—the normal return to his entrepreneurial ability—is part of the opportunity cost of running his business.

R E V I E W

■ A firm's economic profit is equal to its total revenue minus its opportunity cost of production.

■ Opportunity cost measures cost as the value of the best alternative forgone. Money cost measures cost as the money spent to hire inputs.

■ The opportunity cost of capital, inventories, and the resources supplied directly by a firm's owner differ from the money cost of these items. Opportunity cost includes normal profit—the expected return for entrepreneurial services.

We are interested in measuring the opportunity cost of production, not for its own sake but so that we can compare the efficiency of alternative methods of production. What do we mean by efficiency?

Economic Efficiency

How DOES A FIRM CHOOSE AMONG ALTERNATIVE methods of production? What is the most efficient way of producing? There are two concepts of production efficiency: technological efficiency and economic efficiency. **Technological efficiency** occurs when it is not possible to increase output without increasing inputs. **Economic efficiency** occurs when the cost of producing a given output is as low as possible.

Technological efficiency is an engineering matter. Given what is technologically feasible, something can or cannot be done. Economic efficiency depends on the prices of the productive resources. Something that is technologically efficient may not be economically efficient. But something that is economically efficient is always technologically efficient. Let's study technological efficiency and economic efficiency by looking at an example.

Suppose that there are four methods of making TV sets:

a. *Robot production.* One person monitors the entire computer-driven process.

b. *Production line.* Workers specialize in a small part of the job as the emerging TV set passes them on a production line.

c. *Bench production.* Workers specialize in a small part of the job but walk from bench to bench to perform their tasks.

d. *Hand-tool production.* A single worker uses a few hand tools to make a TV set.

Table 10.3 sets out the amount of labor and capital required to make 10 TV sets a day by each of these four methods. Are all of these alternative methods technologically efficient? By inspecting the numbers in the figure, you will be able to see that method c is not technologically efficient. It requires 100 workers and 10 units of capital to produce 10 TV sets. Those same 10 TV sets can be produced by method b with 10 workers and the same 10 units of capital. Therefore method c is not technologically efficient.

Are any of the other methods not technologically efficient? The answer is no: Each of the other three methods is technologically efficient. Method a uses less labor and more capital than method b, and method d uses more labor and less capital than method b.

What about economic efficiency? Are all three methods economically efficient? To answer that question, we need to know the labor and capital costs. Let's suppose that labor costs $75 per person-day and that capital costs $250 per machine-day. Recall that economic efficiency occurs with the least expensive production process. Table 10.4(a) calculates the costs of using the four different methods of production. As you can see, the least expensive method of producing a TV set is b. Method a uses less labor but more capital. It costs much more to make a TV set by using method a than by using method b. Method d, the other technologically efficient method, uses much more labor and hardly any capital. Like method a, it costs far more to make a TV set by using method d than by using method b.

Method c is technologically inefficient. It is interesting to notice that although method c is technologically inefficient, it costs less to produce a TV set by using method c than it does by using methods a and d. But method b dominates method c. Because method c is not technologically efficient, there is always a method available that has a lower cost. That is, a method that is technologically inefficient is never economically efficient.

Although b is the economically efficient method in this example, method a or d could be economically efficient in other circumstances. Let's see when.

First, suppose that labor costs $150 a person-day and capital costs only $1 a machine-day. Table 10.4(b) now shows the costs of making a TV set. In this case, method a is economically efficient. Capital is now sufficiently cheap relative to labor that the

---

TABLE 10.3

Four Ways of Making
10 TV Sets a Day

| | | Quantities of inputs | |
	Method	Labor	Capital
a	Robot production	1	1,000
b	Production line	10	10
c	Bench production	100	10
d	Hand-tool production	1,000	1

TABLE 10.4

The Costs of Different Ways of Making 10 TV Sets a Day

(a) Four ways of making TVs

Method	Labor cost ($75 per day)		Capital cost ($250 per day)		Total cost	Cost per TV set
a	$75	+	$250,000	=	$250,075	$25,007.50
b	750	+	2,500	=	3,250	325.00
c	7,500	+	2,500	=	10,000	1,000.00
d	75,000	+	250	=	75,250	7,525.00

(b) Three ways of making TVs: High Labor Costs

Method	Labor cost ($150 per day)		Capital cost ($1 per day)		Total cost	Cost per TV set
a	$150	+	$1,000	=	$1,150	$115.00
b	1,500	+	10	=	1,510	151.00
d	150,000	+	1	=	150,001	15,000.10

(c) Three ways of making TVs: High Capital Costs

Method	Labor cost ($1 per day)		Capital cost ($1,000 per day)		Total cost	Cost per TV set
a	$1	+	$1,000,000	=	$1,000,001	$100,000.10
b	10	+	10,000	=	10,010	1,001.00
d	1,000	+	1,000	=	2,000	200.00

method that uses the most capital is the economically efficient method.

Now suppose that labor costs only $1 a day while capital costs $1,000 a day. Table 10.4(c) shows the costs in this case. As you can see, method *d*, which uses a lot of labor and little capital, is now the least expensive method of producing a TV set. Method *d* is now the economically efficient method.

From these examples, you can see that economic efficiency depends on the relative costs of resources. The higher the relative cost of a resource, the smaller is the quantity used of that resource and the greater is the quantity used of other resources.

A firm that does not use the economically efficient method of production does not maximize profit. Natural selection favors firms that are efficient and opposes firms that are not. In extreme cases, an inefficient firm goes out of business or is taken over by a firm that can see a way of lowering costs. Efficient firms are stronger and better able to survive temporary adversity than inefficient ones are.

R E V I E W

■ Technological efficiency occurs when a firm cannot increase production without using more productive resources.
■ Economic efficiency occurs when a firm cannot produce a given output at a lower cost.
■ Technological efficiency depends only on feasible production techniques, while economic efficiency depends on the costs of productive resources.
■ The lower the cost of capital relative to the cost of labor, the more capital and the less labor is employed to minimize cost.

Now that we've seen how firms achieve economic efficiency, let's use this key idea and return to an issue raised at the beginning of this chapter. Why do firms coordinate the production of some goods and services and why do firms and individuals use markets to coordinate some other productive activities?

Firms and Markets

AT THE BEGINNING OF THIS CHAPTER, WE defined a firm as an institution that hires productive resources and organizes them to produce and sell goods and services. To organize production, firms coordinate the economic decisions and activities of many individuals. But firms are not the only coordinators of economic decisions. You learned in Chapter 4 that markets also coordinate decisions. By adjusting prices, markets make the decisions of buyers and sellers consistent—make the quantities demanded equal to the quantities supplied for different goods and services.

Markets can coordinate production. An example of market coordination versus firm coordination is the production of a rock concert. A promoter hires a stadium, some stage equipment, audio and video recording engineers and technicians, some rock groups, a superstar, a publicity agent, and a ticket agent—all market transactions—and sells tickets to thousands of rock fans, audio rights to a recording company, and video and broadcasting rights to a television network—another set of market transactions. If rock concerts were produced like corn flakes, the firm producing them would own all the capital used (stadiums, stage, sound and video equipment) and would employ all the labor needed (singers, engineers, salespeople, and so on).

Another example of market coordination versus firm coordination is outsourcing. A firm uses outsourcing when it buys parts or products from another firm rather than making them itself. The major automakers use outsourcing for windshields and windows, gearboxes, tires, and many other car parts.

What determines whether a firm or markets coordinate a particular set of activities? How do firms decide whether to buy from another firm or manufacture an item themselves? The answer is cost. Taking account of the opportunity cost of time as well as the costs of the other inputs, people use the method that costs least. In other words, they use the economically efficient method.

Firms coordinate economic activity when they can perform a task more efficiently than markets. In such a situation, it is profitable to set up a firm. If markets can perform a task more efficiently than a firm can, people will use markets, and any attempt to set up a firm to replace such market coordination will be doomed to failure.

Why Firms?

There are four key reasons why, in many instances, firms are more efficient than markets as coordinators of economic activity. Firms can achieve:

- Lower transactions costs
- Economies of scale
- Economies of scope
- Economies of team production

Transactions Costs The idea that firms exist because there are activities in which they are more efficient than markets was first suggested by University of Chicago economist and Nobel Laureate Ronald Coase. Coase focused on the firm's ability to reduce or eliminate transactions costs. **Transactions costs** are the costs arising from finding someone with whom to do business, of reaching an agreement about the price and other aspects of the exchange, and of ensuring that the terms of the agreement are fulfilled. *Market* transactions require buyers and sellers to get together and to negotiate the terms and conditions of their trading. Sometimes, lawyers have to be hired to draw up contracts. A broken contract leads to still more expenses. A *firm* can lower such transactions costs by reducing the number of individual transactions undertaken.

Consider, for example, two ways of getting your creaking car fixed.

Firm coordination: You take the car to the garage. The garage owner coordinates parts and tools as well as the mechanic's time, and your car gets fixed. You pay one bill for the entire job.

Market coordination: You hire a mechanic who diagnoses the problems and makes a list of the parts and tools needed to fix them. You buy the parts from the local wrecker's yard and rent the tools from ABC Rentals. You hire the mechanic again to fix the problems. You return the tools and pay your bills—wages to the mechanic, rental to ABC, and the cost of the parts used to the wrecker.

What determines the method that you use? The answer is cost. Taking account of the opportunity cost of your own time as well as the costs of the other inputs that you would have to buy, you will use the method that costs least. In other words, you will use the economically efficient method.

The first method requires that you undertake only one transaction with one firm. It's true that the firm has to undertake several transactions—hiring the labor and buying the parts and tools required to do the job. But the firm doesn't have to undertake those transactions simply to fix your car. One set of such transactions enables the firm to fix hundreds of cars. Thus there is an enormous reduction in the number of individual transactions that take place if people get their cars fixed at the garage rather than going through an elaborate sequence of market transactions.

Economies of Scale   When the cost of producing a unit of a good falls as its output rate increases, economies of scale exist. Automakers, for example, experience economies of scale because as the scale of production increases, the firm can use cost-saving equipment and highly specialized labor. An automaker that produces only a few cars a year must use hand-tool methods that are costly. Economies of scale arise from specialization and the division of labor that can be reaped more effectively by firm coordination rather than market coordination.

compared to rising marginal cost).

Economies of Scope   A firm experiences **economies of scope** when it uses specialized (and often expensive) resources to produce a *range of goods and services.* For example, Microsoft hires specialist programmers, designers, and marketing experts and uses their skills across a range of software products. As a result, Microsoft coordinates the resources that produce software at a lower cost than an individual can who buys all these services in markets.

Team Production   A production process in which the individuals in a group specialize in mutually supportive tasks is *team production.* Sport provides the best example of team activity. Some team members specialize in pitching and some in batting, some in defense and some in offense. The production of goods and services offers many examples of team activity. For example, production lines in automobile and TV manufacturing plants work most efficiently when individual activity is organized in teams, each specializing in a small task. You can also think of an entire firm as being a team. The team has buyers of raw material and other inputs, production workers, and salespeople. There are even specialists within these various groups. Each individual member of the team specializes, but the value of the output of the team and the profit that it earns depend on the coordinated activities of all the team's members. The idea that firms arise as a consequence of the economies of

team production was first suggested by Armen Alchian and Harold Demsetz of the University of California at Los Angeles.

Because firms can economize on transactions costs, reap economies of scale, and organize efficient team production, it is firms rather than markets that coordinate most of our economic activity. But there are limits to the economic efficiency of firms. If a firm becomes too big or too diversified in the things that it seeks to do, the cost of management and monitoring per unit of output begins to rise, and at some point, the market becomes more efficient at coordinating the use of resources. IBM is an example of a firm that became too big to be efficient. In an attempt to restore efficient operations, IBM split up its large organization into a number of "Baby Blues," each of which specializes in a segment of the computer market.

Sometimes firms enter into long-term relationships with each other that effectively cut out ordinary market transactions and make it difficult to see where one firm ends and another begins. For example, GM has long-term relationships with suppliers of windows, tires, and other parts. Wal-Mart has long-term relationships with suppliers of the goods it sells in its stores. Such relationships make transactions costs lower than they would be if GM or Wal-Mart went shopping on the open market each time it wanted new supplies.

R E V I E W

- Economic activity can be coordinated either by firms or by markets.
- Whether a firm or markets coordinate production depends on cost.
- The main reasons a firms can often coordinate production at a lower cost than markets can are (1) they avoid or reduce some transactions costs, (2) they achieve economies of scale, (3) they achieve economies of scope, and (4) they achieve economies of team production.

◆ In the next four chapters, we are going to study more choices of firms. We will study their production decisions, how they minimize costs, how they choose the amounts of labor and capital to employ, how they set their prices, and what determines their profits.

Mergers, Markets, and Management Methods

THE NEW YORK TIMES, DECEMBER 16, 1996

The Aerospace Merger: The Heritage

By AGIS SALPUKAS

... By combining with the Boeing Company, McDonnell Douglas ... will end its rich but troubled history as an independent company that played a vital role in making the United States a powerhouse in military and commercial aircraft.

The military division was founded in 1939 by James S. McDonnell. ...

Douglas Aircraft, the commercial airplane branch, had its beginnings in 1920, founded by ... Donald W. Douglas. ...

But for all their achievements, the two companies that combined in 1967 to form McDonnell Douglas have endured some of the rockiest rides in corporate history since their merger. Numerous crises were often caused by the personalities and styles of the men that headed the company. ...

The seeds for McDonnell Douglas's decline, analysts say, were planted after the death of the two founders. ... Control was assumed ... by ... men very different from the founder known as Mr. Mac.

Mr. Mac took risks, believed in holding subordinates responsible and kept a careful eye so that even the most esoteric projects eventually made a profit. But the next genera-tion experimented with management methods that some analysts and former executives said led to a loss of mission and caused chaos in production and design. ...

After the death of the elder McDonnell ... [a] tendency grew to experiment with motiva-tion programs for managers and workers. Those often brought praise from the business press and consultants but began to sap the tough-minded, bottom-line focus of the past. ...

By the time John F. McDonnell took over in 1988, the company was reeling. It was heav-ily in debt, short of cash and so desperate that it sought a $1 billion loan from the Pentagon to tide it over. ... Turned down by the Pentagon ... Mr. McDonnell and his managers resorted to drastic cost-cutting. They shed 63,000 jobs in seven years, ending in the early 1990's.

... Mr. McDonnell was also enamored of new management theories. What was called a Total Quality Management System was put into place. The most startling result came in February 1989 when 5,200 man-agers of Douglas Aircraft were assembled and Mr. McDonnell told them they had lost their titles. ...

Such turmoil contributed to delays in delivering aircraft to airlines and, combined with the cuts in staff, made it difficult to come up with new designs. ...

Essence of THE STORY

■ In December 1996, Boeing and McDonnell Douglas merged.

■ McDonnell Douglas itself had a similar begin-ning when, in 1967, a military aircraft company founded in 1939 by James S. McDonnell merged with a commercial airplane company founded in 1920 by Donald W. Douglas.

■ McDonnell Douglas had a tumultuous history often caused by changes in management styles.

■ James S. McDonnell took risks but monitored employees closely and held them responsible for achieving profits.

■ The next generation experimented with incen-tive programs but paid less attention to profits.

■ In 1988, John F. McDonnell ran the com-pany and cut 63,000 jobs. In 1989, he reorganized its management structure.

■ The company began to miss delivery dates and had a hard time coming up with new designs.

Economic

A N A L Y S I S

■ Figure 1 shows the profits (measured by accountants but converted to 1992 dollars) of Boeing and McDonnell Douglas from 1980 through 1995.

■ You can see that Boeing's profits have consistently exceeded those of McDonnell Douglas.

■ Both company's profits took a dive in 1992, and McDonnell Douglas incurred a loss during that year and again in 1995.

■ Part of the difference in the performance of the two companies lies in the markets in which they sell. Boeing has been more successful in selling commercial aircraft, and McDonnell Douglas has been more successful in selling military aircraft.

■ The market for military aircraft shrank during the 1990s, and McDonnell Douglas's revenue fell.

■ Management methods and company organization also explain part of the difference in the success rates experienced by the two companies.

■ Figure 2 shows two management structures. Part (a) is a traditional management system. Managers supervise subordinates and report to superiors. Managers can hold subordinates responsible for achieving profitable outcomes. But in some cases, this management method is inflexible and inefficient.

■ Part (b), a more flexible management structure, is similar to what McDonnell Douglas adopted in 1989. It involves many principal-agent relationships.

■ But to succeed, a decentralized structure needs well-designed incentive plans that reward people for actions that result in profit. According to the news article, the arrangements at McDonnell Douglas after the death of the two founders did not have this focus.

■ The point of a merger is to create a bigger profit than the sum of the profits of the pre-merger companies.

■ Will the new enlarged Boeing plus McDonnell Douglas achieve this objective? No one knows. But investors expect the merger to be a success. We know this because the stock market price of Boeing jumped by 4 percent and that of McDonnell Douglas jumped by 20 percent the day after the merger was announced.

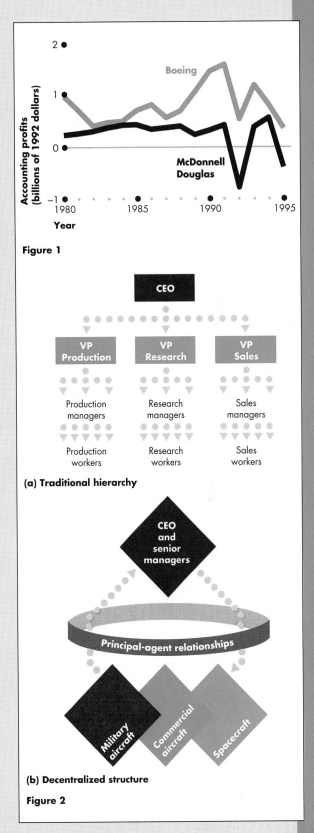

Figure 1

(a) **Traditional hierarchy**

(b) **Decentralized structure**

Figure 2

209

SUMMARY

Key Points

The Firm and Its Economic Problem (pp. 192–196)

- Firms hire and organize resources to produce and sell goods and services and maximize profit.
- Uncertainty and incomplete information place limits on what a firm can attain, and firms must devise incentive schemes that induce managers and workers to perform in ways that are consistent with the goal of maximum profit.
- The main forms of business organization are proprietorships, partnerships, and corporations. Each form has its advantages and disadvantages. Corporations produce most of the goods and services, but there are more proprietorships than any other type of firm.

Business Finance (pp. 197–200)

- Firms get funds from their owners and from the sale of stock and bonds. A firm gets its funds from the source that costs least.
- To make a financing decision, the firm uses the concept of the *net present value* of future amounts of money.
- A firm borrows the amount of funds for which the net present value of borrowing one additional dollar—the marginal dollar borrowed—is zero. At this amount of borrowing, the firm is maximizing its profit. (pp. 193–196)

Opportunity Cost and Economic Profit (pp. 200–203)

- Economic profit is total revenue minus opportunity cost.
- Opportunity cost is made up of explicit costs (money costs) and implicit costs. Implicit costs are opportunities forgone but not paid for directly in money. They arise from the use of capital, inventories, and the owner's own resources.
- The opportunity cost of the resources supplied by a firm's owner, including normal profit for supplying entrepreneurial ability, is part of a firm's costs.

Economic Efficiency (pp. 204–205)

- A method of production is technologically efficient when it is not possible to increase output without using more inputs.
- A method of production is economically efficient when the cost of producing a given output is as low as possible.

Firms and Markets (pp. 206–207)

- Firms coordinate economic activities when they can perform a task more efficiently—at lower cost—than markets can.
- Firms can often coordinate activities at a lower cost than a market can because they economize on transactions costs and achieve the benefits of economies of scale, economies of scope, and team production.

Key Figure and Tables

Key Terms

QUESTIONS

1. What is a firm and what is the fundamental economic problem that all firms face?
2. What factors make it difficult for a firm to get the most out of its resources?
3. What is a principal-agent relationship and why does it arise?
4. In what ways can a principal cope with the principal-agent problem?
5. What are the main forms of business organizations and the advantages and disadvantages of each?
6. What is the most common type of business and which type produces most of the economy's output?
7. What are the main ways in which firms can raise funds?
8. Describe and contrast a bond and a stock.
9. What do we mean by net present value?
10. What determines the value of a bond?
11. Explain how a firm uses marginal analysis when it makes a financing decision.
12. Distinguish between money cost and opportunity cost. What are the main items of opportunity cost that don't get counted as part of money cost?
13. Distinguish between implicit costs and explicit costs.
14. Distinguish between profit as defined by accountants, normal profit, and economic profit.
15. Distinguish between technological efficiency and economic efficiency and give an example of each concept of efficiency.
16. What do we mean by *coordination* of productive resources?
17. How might markets coordinate the production of a good or service?
18. Give some examples of goods or services that are produced by using mainly market coordination.
19. Why do firms, rather than markets, coordinate the resources that produce most goods and services?
20. Give some examples of transactions costs, economies of scale, economies of scope, and team production.

PROBLEMS

1. Soap Bubbles, Inc. has a bank loan of $1 million on which it is paying an interest rate of 10 percent a year. The firm's financial advisor suggests paying off the loan by selling bonds. To sell bonds valued at $1 million, Soap Bubbles, Inc. must offer the following deal: One year from today, pay the bond holders $9 for each $100 of bonds; two years from today, redeem the bonds for $114 per $100 of bonds.

   a. Does it pay Soap Bubbles to sell the bonds to repay the bank loan?

   b. What is the present value of the profit or loss that would result from repaying the bank loan and selling the bonds?

2. One year ago, Jack and Jill set up a vinegar-bottling firm (called JJVB). In that year:

   a. Jack and Jill put $50,000 of their own money into the firm.

   b. They bought equipment for $30,000 and an inventory of bottles and vinegar for $15,000.

   c. They hired one employee to help them for an annual wage of $20,000.

   d. JJVB's sales for the year were $100,000.

   e. Jack gave up his previous job, at which he earned $30,000, and spent all his time working for JJVB.

   f. Jill kept her old job, which paid $30 an hour, but gave up 10 hours of leisure each week (for 50 weeks) to work for JJVB.

   g. Other expenses of JJVB were $10,000 for the year.

   h. The inventory at the end of the year was worth $20,000.

   i. The market value of the equipment at the end of the year was $28,000.

   j. JJVB's accountant depreciated the equipment over 5 years.

   k. The interest rate was 5 percent a year.

      (i) Construct JJVB's profit and loss account as recorded by its accountant.

      (ii) Construct JJVB's profit and loss account based on opportunity cost rather than money cost concepts.

      (iii) What is JJVB's economic profit?

3. You operate your own gas station, and the following facts describe some aspects of your business:
   a. Your gas tanks hold 2 million gallons, and once a week, you get them filled to capacity.
   b. Your sell 2 million gallons of gas per week, and your sales are the same each day.
   c. You buy your gasoline from a wholesale company that charges you 20 cents per gallon.
   d. You sell gasoline for 60 cents per gallon.
   e. On each gallon you sell, you pay taxes to the government of 30 cents.
   f. Your wholesaler has tanks that hold a month's supply of gasoline.
   g. Your wholesaler gets its tanks filled once a month from the refinery.
   h. The refinery buys crude oil by the tanker load, and it agrees the price of each load as it leaves port in Saudi Arabia. The journey from Saudi Arabia takes two weeks.
   i. On the average, it takes two months for crude oil on a tanker in Saudi Arabia to become refined gasoline in your tanks.
   j. One day, the price of crude oil jumps by an amount that is equivalent to doubling the price you will pay your wholesaler. On the day after the price of crude oil has increased:
      (i) What is the opportunity cost of crude oil in Saudi Arabia?
      (ii) What is your wholesaler's opportunity cost of refined oil?
      (iii) What is your opportunity cost of selling a gallon from your inventory?
      (iv) When will your price change?
      Explain each part of your answer.

4. There are three methods that you can use to do your income tax return: a personal computer (PC), a pocket calculator, or a pencil and paper. With a PC, you complete the task in an hour; with a pocket calculator, it takes 12 hours; and with a pencil and paper, it takes two days. The PC and its software cost $1,000, the pocket calculator costs $10, and the pencil and paper cost $1.
   a. Which, if any, of the above methods is technologically efficient?
   b. Which of the above methods is economically efficient if your wage is $5 an hour?
   c. Which of the above methods is economically efficient if your wage is $50 an hour?
   d. Which of the above methods is economically efficient if your wage is $500 an hour?

CRITICAL THINKING

1. Study the news article about the 1996 Boeing and McDonnell Douglas merger in *Reading Between the Lines* on pp. 208–209 and then:
   a. Describe the profit record of the two companies since 1980.
   b. Think of some reasons why Boeing has consistently earned more than McDonnell Douglas has.
   c. Explain why the profits of both companies fell in 1992.
   d. Explain the principal-agent problem that companies like Boeing and McDonnell Douglas face.
   e. Explain how McDonnell Douglas tried to cope with its principal-agent problem.
   f. Find recent data on the stock price of Boeing and compare today's price with that on December 15, 1996, the date of the merger. Can you think of reasons for the change you have discovered?

2. It is January 1, 1998, and Michael Jordan is trying to decide which of two alternative contracts to accept. Contract A pays the following amounts:

On December 31,	Amount
1998	2,000,000
1999	2,500,000
2000	3,000,000
2001	3,500,000
2002	4,000,000
2003	4,500,000

Contract B pays $5,000,000 now (on January 1, 1998) and $14,500,000 on December 31, 2003. Michael Jordan's financial advisor points out that under both contracts, Michael Jordan collects $19,500,000. But he says Contract B is better because it puts $5 million in Michael Jordan's pocket right away. The interest rate is 10 percent a year. What is your advice?
   a. Is Michael Jordan better off with A or B?
   b. How would you convince Michael Jordan that his financial advisor is wrong?
   c. Thinking more broadly about the principal-agent problem, if you were offering Michael Jordan one of these contracts, which would you offer and why?

11

Output and Costs

Size does not guarantee survival in business. Of the 100 largest companies in the United States in 1917, only 21 still remained in that league in 1997. But remaining small does not guarantee survival either. Every year, millions of small businesses close down. Call a random selection of restaurants and fashion boutiques from *last* year's yellow pages and see how many have vanished. What does a firm have to do to be one of the survivors? ◆ Firms differ in lots of ways—from Mom-and-Pop's convenience store to multinational giants producing hi-tech goods. But regardless of their size or what they produce, all firms must decide how much to produce

Survival of the Fittest

and how to produce it. How do firms make these decisions? ◆ Most car makers in the United States can produce far more cars than they can sell. Why do car makers have expensive equipment lying around that isn't fully used? Many electric utilities in the United States don't have enough production equipment on hand to meet demand on the coldest and hottest days and have to buy power from other producers. Why don't such firms install more equipment so that they can supply the market themselves? ◆ We are going to answer these questions in this chapter. To do so, we are going to study the economic decisions of a small, imaginary firm—Swanky, Inc., a producer of knitted sweaters. The firm is owned and operated by Sidney. By studying Swanky's economic problems and the way Sidney solves them, we will be able to get a clear view of the problems that face all firms—small ones like Swanky as well as the giants.

After studying this chapter, you will be able to:

■ Explain what limits the profit a firm can make

■ Explain the relationship between a firm's output and costs in the short run when its capital is fixed

■ Derive a firm's short-run cost curves

■ Explain the relationship between a firm's output and costs in the long run when its capital changes

■ Derive a firm's long-run average cost curve

The Firm's Objective and Constraints

To UNDERSTAND AND PREDICT THE BEHAVIOR OF firms, we need to know what they are trying to achieve—what their objectives are—and the constraints they face. We'll begin by looking at what firms are trying to achieve.

The Objective: Profit Maximization

Individual firms and the entrepreneurs that run them have many different objectives. If you asked a group of entrepreneurs what their objectives were, you'd get lots of different answers. Some would talk about making a quality product, others about business growth, others about market share, and others about work force job satisfaction. All of these objectives might be pursued, but they are not the fundamental objective. They are means to a deeper objective—*profit maximization*.

The firm that we will study has a single objective: to maximize its profit. A firm that seeks to maximize profit is one that tries to use its scarce resources efficiently. It is also a firm that has the best chance of surviving in a competitive environment and of avoiding being taken over by another firm.

Two types of constraints limit the profit a firm can make. They are:

■ Market constraints
■ Technology constraints

Market Constraints

A firm's market constraints are the conditions under which it can buy its inputs and sell its output. On the output side, people have a limited demand for each good or service and will buy additional quantities only at lower prices. On the input side, people have a limited supply of the productive resources that they own and will supply additional quantities only at higher prices.

We'll study these market constraints on firms in Chapters 12 through 16. Swanky, the firm that we'll study in this chapter, is small and cannot influence the prices at which it sells its output or buys its inputs. For such a firm, the market constraints are a set of given prices.

Technology Constraints

A firm's technology constraints are the limits to the quantity of output that can be produced by using given quantities of inputs—productive resources. To maximize profit, a firm chooses a *technologically efficient* method of production. It does not use more inputs than necessary to produce a given output. Equivalently, it does not waste resources. But a firm must also choose the *economically efficient* technique—the technique that produces a given output at the lowest possible cost. (See Chapter 10, pp. 204–205.)

The possibilities that are open to a firm depend on the length of the planning period over which it is making its decisions. A firm that plans to change its output rate tomorrow has fewer options than one that plans to change its output rate six months from now. In studying the way a firm's technology constrains its actions, we distinguish between two planning horizons: the short run and the long run.

The Short Run and the Long Run

The **short run** is a period of time in which the quantity of at least one input is fixed and the quantities of the other inputs can be varied. The **long run** is a period of time in which the quantities of all inputs can be varied. Inputs whose quantity can be varied in the short run are called *variable inputs*. Inputs whose quantity cannot be varied in the short run are called *fixed inputs*.

There is no specific time that can be marked on the calendar to separate the short run from the long run. In some cases—for example, a laundromat or a copying service—the short run is a month or two. New premises can be rented and new machines can be installed quickly. In other cases—for example, an electric power company or a railroad company—the short run is several years. Bigger power generators and additional track and rolling stock take a few years to build.

In the short run, Swanky has a fixed amount of capital—knitting machines—so to vary its output in the short run, it must vary the quantity of labor that it employs. For Swanky, the knitting equipment is the fixed input and labor is the variable input. In the long run, Swanky can vary the quantity of both inputs—knitting machines and labor employed.

Let's look more closely at the short-run technology constraint.

Short-Run Technology Constraint

TO INCREASE OUTPUT IN THE SHORT RUN, A FIRM must increase the quantity of labor that it employs. We describe the relationship between output and the quantity of labor employed by using three related concepts:

- Total product
- Marginal product
- Average product

These product concepts can be illustrated either by product schedules or by product curves. Let's look first at the product schedules.

TABLE II.I

Total Product, Marginal Product, and Average Product

	Labor (workers per day)	Total product (sweaters per day)	Marginal product (sweaters per additional worker)	Average product (sweaters per worker)
a	0	0		
			4	
b	1	4		4.00
			6	
c	2	10		5.00
			3	
d	3	13		4.33
			2	
e	4	15		3.75
			1	
f	5	16		3.20

Total product is the total amount produced. Marginal product is the change in total product that results from a one-unit increase in labor. For example, when labor increases from 2 to 3 workers a day (row c to row d), total product increases from 10 to 13 sweaters. The marginal product of the third worker is 3 sweaters. Average product is total product divided by the quantity of labor employed. For example, the average product of 3 workers is 4.33 sweaters per worker (13 sweaters a day divided by 3 workers).

Product Schedules

Table 11.1 shows some data that describe Swanky's total product, marginal product, and average product. The numbers tell us how Swanky's production increases in the short run as more workers are employed. They also tell us about the productivity of labor.

Focus first on the columns headed "Labor" and "Total product." **Total product** is the total output produced. You can see from the numbers in these columns that as Swanky employs more labor, total product increases. For example, when Swanky employs 1 worker, total product is 4 sweaters a day, and when it employs 2 workers, total product is 10 sweaters a day. Each increase in employment brings an increase in total product.

Marginal product tells us by how much total product increases when employment increases. The **marginal product** of labor is the increase in total product that results from a one-unit increase in the quantity of labor employed. For example, in Table 11.1, when Swanky increases employment from 2 to 3 workers, the marginal product of the third worker is 3 sweaters—total product goes from 10 to 13 sweaters.

Average product tells how productive workers are on the average. The **average product** of labor is equal to total product divided by the quantity of labor employed. For example, in Table 11.1, the average product of 3 workers is 4.33 sweaters per worker—13 sweaters a day divided by 3 workers.

If you look closely at the numbers in Table 11.1, you can see some patterns. For example, as employment increases, marginal product at first increases and then begins to decrease. For example, marginal product increases from 4 sweaters a day for the first worker to 6 sweaters a day for the second worker and then decreases to 3 sweaters a day for the third worker. Average product also increases at first and then decreases. The relationships between employment and the three product concepts can be seen more clearly by looking at the product curves.

Product Curves

The product curves are graphs of the relationships between the quantity of labor employed and the three product concepts you've just studied. These curves show how total product, marginal product, and average product change as the quantity of labor employed changes. They also show the relationships among the three concepts. Let's look at the product curves.

Total Product Curve

Figure 11.1 shows Swanky's total product curve, *TP*. As employment increases, so does the number of sweaters knitted. Points *a* through *f* on the curve correspond to the same rows in Table 11.1.

The total product curve is similar to the *production possibility frontier* (explained in Chapter 3). It separates the attainable output levels from those that are unattainable. All the points that lie above the curve are unattainable. Points that lie below the curve, in the orange area, are attainable. But they are inefficient—they use more labor than is necessary to produce a given output. Only the points *on* the total product curve are technologically efficient.

Notice especially the shape of the total product curve. As employment increases from zero to 1 worker per day, the curve becomes steeper. Then, as employment continues to increase to 3, 4, and 5 workers a day, the curve becomes less steep. The steeper the slope of the total product curve, the greater is marginal product, as you are about to see.

FIGURE II.I
Total Product Curve

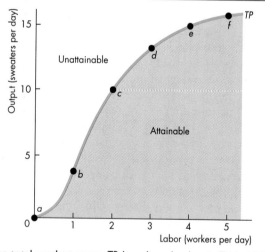

The total product curve, *TP*, based on the data in Table 11.1, shows how the quantity of sweaters produced changes as the quantity of labor employed changes. For example, 2 workers can produce 10 sweaters a day (point *c*). Points *a* through *f* on the curve correspond to the rows of Table 11.1. The total product curve separates attainable outputs from unattainable outputs. Points below the *TP* curve are inefficient.

Marginal Product Curve

Figure 11.2 shows Swanky's marginal product of labor. Part (a) reproduces the total product curve, which is the same as the total product curve in Fig. 11.1. Part (b) shows the marginal product curve, *MP*.

In part (a), the orange bars illustrate the marginal product of labor. The height of each bar measures marginal product. Marginal product is also measured by the slope of the total product curve. Recall that the slope of a curve is the change in the value of the variable measured on the *y*-axis—output—divided by the change in the variable measured on the *x*-axis—labor input—as we move along the curve. A one-unit increase in labor input, from 2 to 3 workers, increases output from 10 to 13 sweaters, so the slope from point *c* to point *d* is 3, the same as the marginal product that we've just calculated.

We've calculated the marginal product of labor for a series of unit increases in the quantity of labor. But labor is divisible into smaller units than one person. It is divisible into hours and even minutes. By varying the amount of labor in the smallest imaginable units, we can draw the marginal product curve shown in Fig. 11.2(b). The *height* of this curve measures the *slope* of the total product curve at a point. Part (a) shows that an increase in employment from 2 to 3 workers increases output from 10 to 13 sweaters (an increase of 3). The increase in output of 3 sweaters appears on the vertical axis of part (b) as the marginal product of going from 2 to 3 workers. We plot that marginal product at the midpoint between 2 and 3 workers. Notice that marginal product shown in Fig. 11.2(b) reaches a peak at 1 unit of labor, and at that point, marginal product is more than 6 sweaters. The peak occurs at 1 unit of labor because the total product curve is steepest at 1 unit of labor.

The total product and marginal product curves are different for different firms and different types of goods. Ford Motor Company's product curves are different from those of Jim's Burger Stand, which in turn are different from those of Sidney's sweater factory. But the shapes of the product curves are similar, because almost every production process has two features:

- Increasing marginal returns initially
- Diminishing marginal returns eventually

Increasing Marginal Returns If Swanky employs just one worker, that person must learn all the aspects of sweater production: running the knitting machines,

FIGURE 11.2
Marginal Product

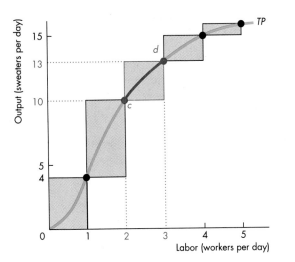

(a) Total product

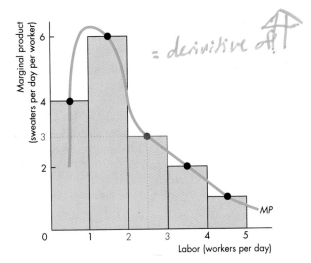

= derivitive of ↑

(b) Marginal product

Marginal product is illustrated by the orange bars. For example, when labor increases from 2 to 3, marginal product is the orange bar whose height is 3 sweaters. (Marginal product is shown midway between the labor inputs to emphasize that it is the result of *changing* inputs.) The steeper the slope of the total product curve (*TP*) in part (a), the larger is marginal product (*MP*) in part (b). Marginal product increases to a maximum (when 1 worker is employed in this example) and then declines—diminishing marginal product.

fixing breakdowns, packaging and mailing sweaters, buying and checking the type and color of the wool. All these tasks must be performed by that one person.

If Swanky hires a second person, the two workers can specialize in different parts of the production process. As a result, two workers produce more than twice as much as one. The marginal product of the second worker is greater than the marginal product of the first worker. Marginal returns are increasing.

Increasing marginal returns occur when the marginal product of an additional worker exceeds the marginal product of the previous worker. Increasing marginal returns arise from increased specialization and division of labor in the production process.

Diminishing Marginal Returns   Most production processes experience increasing marginal returns initially. But all production processes eventually reach a point of *diminishing* marginal returns. **Diminishing marginal returns** occur when the marginal product of an additional worker is less than the marginal product of the previous worker.

Diminishing marginal returns arise from the fact that more and more workers are using the same capital and working in the same space. As more workers are hired, there is less and less for the additional workers to do that is productive. For example, if Swanky hires a third worker, output increases but not by as much as it did when it hired the second worker. In this case, after two workers are hired, all the gains from specialization and the division of labor have been exhausted. By hiring a third worker, the factory produces more sweaters, but the equipment is being operated closer to its limits. There are even times when the third worker has nothing to do because the machines are running without the need for further attention. Hiring more and more workers continues to increase output but by successively smaller amounts. Marginal returns are diminishing. This phenomenon is such a pervasive one that it is called a "law"—"the law of diminishing returns." The **law of diminishing returns** states that

As a firm uses more of a variable input, with a given quantity of fixed inputs, the marginal product of the variable input eventually diminishes.

You are going to return to the law of diminishing returns when we study a firm's costs. But before we do that, let's look at the average product of labor and the average product curve.

Average Product Curve

Figure 11.3 illustrates Swanky's average product of labor, *AP*. It also shows the relationship between average product and marginal product, *MP*. Points *b* through *f* on the average product curve correspond to those same rows in Table 11.1. Average product increases from 1 to 2 workers (its maximum value at point *c*) but then decreases as yet more workers are employed. Notice also that average product is largest when average product and marginal product are equal. That is, the marginal product curve cuts the average product curve at the point of maximum average product. For employment levels at which marginal product exceeds average product, average product is increasing. For employment levels at which marginal product is less than average product, average product is decreasing.

The relationship between the average and marginal product curves is a general feature of the relationship between the average and marginal values of any variable. Let's look at a familiar example.

FIGURE 11.3

Average Product

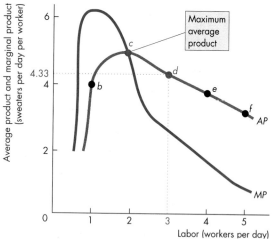

The figure shows the average product of labor (*AP*) and the connection between the average product and marginal product (*MP*). With 1 worker per day, marginal product exceeds average product, so average product is increasing. With 2 workers per day, marginal product equals average product, so average product is at its maximum. With more than 2 workers per day, marginal product is less than average product, so average product is decreasing.

Marginal Grade and Grade Point Average

To see the relationship between average product and marginal product, think about the similar relationship between Sidney's average grade and marginal grade over five semesters. (Suppose Sidney is a part-time student who takes just one course each semester.) In the first semester, Sidney takes calculus and his grade is a 2. This grade is his marginal grade. It is also his average grade—his GPA. In the next semester, Sidney takes French and gets a 3. French is Sidney's marginal course and his marginal grade is 3. His GPA rises to 2.5. Because his marginal grade exceeds his average grade, it pulls his average up. In the third semester, Sidney takes economics and gets a 4—his new marginal grade. Because his marginal grade exceeds his GPA, it again pulls his average up. Sidney's GPA is now 3, the average of 2, 3, and 4. In the fourth semester, he takes history and gets a 3. Because his marginal grade is equal to his average, his GPA does not change. In the fifth semester, Sidney takes English and gets a 2. Because his marginal grade, a 2, is below his average of 3, his GPA falls.

This everyday relationship between marginal and average values agrees with that between marginal and average product. Sidney's GPA increases when his marginal grade exceeds his GPA. His GPA falls when his marginal grade is below his GPA. And his GPA is constant when his marginal grade equals his GPA. The relationship between marginal product and average product is exactly the same as that between Sidney's marginal and average grades.

R E V I E W

- Initially, as the labor input increases, marginal product and average product might increase.

- But as the labor input increases further, marginal product eventually declines—the law of diminishing returns.

- When marginal product exceeds average product, average product increases; when marginal product is less than average product, average product decreases; and when marginal product equals average product, average product is at its maximum.

Swanky cares about its product curves because they influence its costs. Let's look at Swanky's costs.

Short-Run Cost

To produce more output in the short run, a firm must employ more labor, which means it must increase its costs. We describe the relationship between output and cost by using three cost concepts:

■ Total cost
■ Marginal cost
■ Average cost

Total Cost

A firm's **total cost** (TC) is the cost of all the productive resources it uses. Total cost includes the cost of land, capital, and labor. It also includes the cost of entrepreneurship, which is *normal profit* (see Chapter 10, p. 198). We divide total cost into total fixed cost and total variable cost.

Total fixed cost (TFC) is the cost of all the firm's fixed inputs. Because the quantity of a fixed input does not change as output changes, fixed cost is independent of the output level.

Total variable cost (TVC) is the cost of all the firm's variable inputs. Because to change its output, a firm must change the quantity of variable inputs, a variable cost is a cost that varies with the output level.

Total cost is the sum of total fixed cost and total variable cost. That is,

$$TC = TFC + TVC.$$

The table in Fig. 11.4 shows Swanky's total costs. With one knitting machine that costs $25 a day, TFC is $25. To produce more sweaters, Swanky hires more labor, which costs $25 a day. TVC, which increases as output increases, is the number of workers multiplied by $25. For example, to produce 13 sweaters a day, Swanky hires 3 workers and TVC is $75. TC is the sum of TFC and TVC, so to produce 13 sweaters a day, Swanky's total cost, TC, is $100. Check the calculations in each row of the table.

Figure 11.4 graphs Swanky's total cost curves. These curves graph total costs against output. The green total fixed cost curve (TFC) is a constant at $25. The purple total variable cost curve (TVC) and the blue total cost curve (TC) both increase with output. The vertical distance between the TVC and TC curves is total fixed cost as shown by the arrows.

Let's now look at Swanky's marginal cost.

FIGURE 11.4
Total Cost Curves

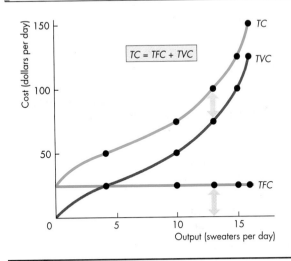

Labor (workers per day)	Output (sweaters per day)	Total fixed cost (TFC)	Total variable cost (TVC)	Total cost (TC)
		(dollars per day)		
a	0	0	25	0	25
b	1	4	25	25	50
c	2	10	25	50	75
d	3	13	25	75	100
e	4	15	25	100	125
f	5	16	25	125	150

Swanky rents its knitting machine for $25 a day. This amount is its total fixed cost. It hires workers at a wage rate of $25 a day, and this cost is Swanky's total variable cost. For example, if Swanky employs 3 workers, its total variable cost is (3 × $25), which equals $75. Total cost is the sum of total fixed cost and total variable cost. For example, when Swanky employs 3 workers, its total cost is $100—total fixed cost of $25 plus total variable cost of $75. The graph shows Swanky's total cost curves. Total fixed cost (TFC) is constant—it graphs as a horizontal line—and total variable cost (TVC) increases as output increases. Total cost (TC) also increases as output increases. The vertical distance between the total cost curve and the total variable cost curve is total fixed cost, as illustrated by the two arrows.

Marginal Cost

In Fig. 11.4, total variable cost and total cost increase at a decreasing rate at small levels of output and then begin to increase at an increasing rate as output increases. To understand these patterns in the changes in total cost, we need to use the concept of *marginal cost*.

A firm's **marginal cost** is the increase in total cost that results from a one-unit increase in output. We calculate marginal cost as the increase in total cost divided by the increase in output. The table in Fig. 11.5 shows this calculation. When, for example, output increases from 10 sweaters to 13 sweaters, total cost increases from $75 to $100. The change in output is 3 sweaters, and the change in total cost is $25. The marginal cost of one of those 3 sweaters is ($25 ÷ 3), which equals $8.33.

Figure 11.5 graphs the marginal cost data in the table as the red marginal cost curve, *MC*. This curve is U-shaped because when Swanky hires a second worker, marginal cost decreases, but when it hires a third, a fourth, and a fifth worker, marginal cost successively increases.

Marginal cost decreases at low outputs because of economies from greater specialization. It eventually increases because of *the law of diminishing returns*. The law of diminishing returns means that each additional worker produces a successively smaller addition to output. So to get an additional unit of output, ever more workers are required. Because more workers are required to produce one additional unit of output, the cost of the additional output—marginal cost—must eventually increase.

Marginal cost tells us how total cost changes as output changes. The final cost concept tells us what it costs, on the average, to produce a unit of output. Let's now look at Swanky's average costs.

Average Cost

There are three average costs:

1. Average fixed cost
2. Average variable cost
3. Average total cost

Average fixed cost (*AFC*) is total fixed cost per unit of output. **Average variable cost** (*AVC*) is total variable cost per unit of output. **Average total cost** (*ATC*) is total cost per unit output. The average cost concepts are calculated from the total cost concepts as follows:

$$TC = TFC + TVC.$$

Divide each total cost term by the quantity produced, *Q*, to give

$$\frac{TC}{Q} = \frac{TFC}{Q} + \frac{TVC}{Q}$$

or

$$ATC = AFC + AVC.$$

The table in Fig. 11.5 shows the calculation of average total cost. For example, when output is 10 sweaters, average fixed cost is ($25 ÷ 10), which equals $2.50, average variable cost is ($50 ÷ 10), which equals $5.00, and average total cost is ($75 ÷ 10), which equals $7.50. Note that average total cost is equal to average fixed cost ($2.50) plus average variable cost ($5.00).

Figure 11.5 shows the average cost curves. The green average fixed cost curve (*AFC*) slopes downward. As output increases, the same constant fixed cost is spread over a larger output. The blue average total cost curve (*ATC*) and the purple average variable cost curve (*AVC*) are U-shaped. The vertical distance between the average total cost and average variable cost curves is equal to average fixed cost—as indicated by the two arrows. That distance shrinks as output increases because average fixed cost declines with increasing output.

The marginal cost curve intersects the average variable cost curve and the average total cost curve at their minimum points. That is, when marginal cost is less than average cost, average cost is decreasing, and when marginal cost exceeds average cost, average cost is increasing. This relationship holds for both the *ATC* curve and the *AVC* curve and is another example of the relationship you saw in Figure 11.3 for average product and marginal product and in Sidney's course grades.

Why the Average Total Cost Curve Is U-Shaped

Average total cost, *ATC*, is the sum of average fixed cost, *AFC*, and average variable cost, *AVC*. So the shape of the *ATC* curve combines the shapes of the *AFC* and *AVC* curves. The U shape of the average

FIGURE 11.5
Marginal Cost and Average Costs

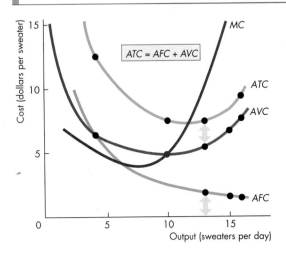

Marginal cost is calculated as the change in total cost divided by the change in output. When output increases from 4 to 10, an increase of 6, total cost increases by $25 and marginal cost is $25 ÷ 6, which equals $4.17. Each average cost concept is calculated by dividing the related total cost by output. When 10 sweaters are produced, AFC is $2.50 ($25 ÷ 10), AVC is $5.00 ($50 ÷ 10), and ATC is $7.50 ($75 ÷ 10).

The figure shows the marginal cost curve and the average cost curves. The marginal cost curve (MC) is U-shaped and intersects the average variable cost curve and the average total cost curve at their minimum points. Average fixed cost (AFC) decreases as output increases. The average total cost curve (ATC) and average variable cost curve (AVC) are U-shaped. The vertical distance between these two curves is equal to average fixed cost, as illustrated by the two arrows.

	Labor (workers per day)	Output (sweaters per day)	Total fixed cost (TFC)	Total variable cost (TVC)	Total cost (TC)	Marginal cost (MC) (dollars per additional sweater)	Average fixed cost (AFC)	Average variable cost (AVC)	Average total cost (ATC)
			(dollars per day)				(dollars per sweater)		
a	0	0	25	0	25		—	—	—
						.... 6.25			
b	1	4	25	25	50		6.25	6.25	12.50
						.... 4.17			
c	2	10	25	50	75		2.50	5.00	7.50
						.... 8.33			
d	3	13	25	75	100		1.92	5.77	7.69
						.... 12.50			
e	4	15	25	100	125		1.67	6.67	8.33
						.... 25.00			
f	5	16	25	125	150		1.56	7.81	9.38

total cost curve arises from the influence of two opposing forces:

■ Spreading fixed cost over a larger output
■ Eventually diminishing returns

When output increases, the firm spreads its fixed costs over a larger output and its average fixed cost decreases—its average fixed cost curve slopes downward.

Diminishing returns mean that as output increases, ever-larger amounts of labor are needed to produce an additional unit of output. So average

variable cost eventually increases, and the *AVC* curve eventually slopes upward.

The shape of the average total cost curve combines these two effects. Initially, as output increases, both average fixed cost and average variable cost decrease, so average total cost decreases and the *ATC* curve slopes downward. But as output increases further and diminishing returns set in, average variable cost begins to increase. Eventually, average variable cost increases more quickly than average fixed cost decreases, so average total cost increases and the *ATC* curve slopes upward.

Cost Curves and Product Curves

The technology that a firm uses determines its costs. Figure 11.6 shows the links between the firm's technology constraint (its product curves) and its cost curves. The upper part of the figure shows the average product curve and the marginal product curve—like those in Fig. 11.3(b). The lower part of the figure shows the average variable cost curve and the marginal cost curve—like those in Fig. 11.5.

The figure highlights the links between technology and costs. Over the output range in which marginal product and average product are rising, marginal cost and average variable cost are falling. Then, at the point of maximum marginal product, marginal cost is a minimum. At larger outputs, marginal product diminishes and marginal cost increases. But there is an intermediate range of output over which average product is still rising and average variable cost is falling. Then an output is reached at which average product is a maximum and average variable cost is a minimum. At larger outputs, average product diminishes and average variable cost increases.

Shifts in the Cost Curves

The position of a firm's short-run cost curves depends on two factors:

- Technology
- Prices of productive resources

Technology A technological change that increases productivity shifts the total product curve upward. It also shifts the marginal product curve and the average product upward. Because with a better technology, the same inputs can produce more output, technological change lowers costs and shifts the cost curves downward.

For example, advances in robot production techniques have increased productivity in the automobile industry. As a result, the product curves of Chrysler, Ford, and GM have shifted upward, and their cost curves have shifted downward. But the relationships between their product curves and cost curves have not changed. The curves are still linked in the way shown in Fig. 11.6.

Often a technological advance results in a firm using more capital, a fixed input, and less labor, a variable input. For example, today the telephone

FIGURE 11.6
Product Curves and Cost Curves

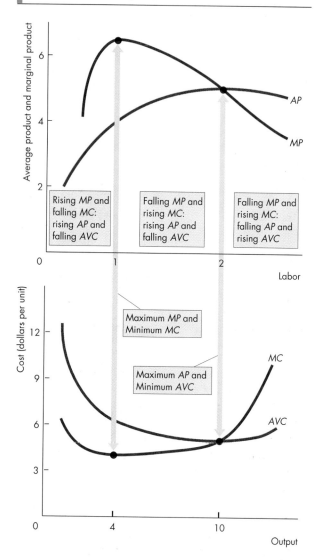

A firm's cost curves are linked to its product curves. Over the range of rising marginal product, marginal cost is falling. When marginal product is a maximum, marginal cost is a minimum. Over the range of rising average product, average *variable* cost is falling. When average product is a maximum, average variable cost is a minimum. Over the range of diminishing marginal product, marginal cost is rising. Over the range of falling average product, average *variable* cost is rising.

TABLE 11.2

A Compact Glossary of Costs

Term	Symbol	Definition	Equation
Fixed cost		Cost that is independent of the output level; cost of a fixed input	
Variable cost		Cost that varies with the output level; cost of a variable input	
Total fixed cost	TFC	Cost of the fixed inputs	
Total variable cost	TVC	Cost of the variable inputs	
Total cost	TC	Cost of all inputs	$TC = TFC + TVC$
Output (total product)	TP	Output produced	
Marginal cost	MC	Change in total cost resulting from a one-unit increase in total product	$MC = \Delta TC \div \Delta TP$
Average fixed cost	AFC	Total fixed cost per unit of output	$AFC = TFC \div TP$
Average variable cost	AVC	Total variable cost per unit of output	$AVC = TVC \div TP$
Average total cost	ATC	Total cost per unit of output	$ATC = AFC + AVC$

companies use computers to connect long-distance calls in place of the human operators they used in the 1980s. When such a technological change occurs, fixed costs increase and variable costs decrease. This change in the mix of fixed cost and variable cost means that at small output levels, average total cost might increase, while at large output levels, average total cost decreases.

Prices of Resources An increase in the price of a productive resource increases costs and shifts the cost curves. But how the curves shift depends on which resource price changes. An increase in rent or some other component of *fixed* cost shifts the fixed cost curves (*TFC* and *AFC*) upward and shifts the total cost and average total cost curves (*TC* and *ATC*) upward but leaves the variable cost curves (*AVC* and *TVC*) and the marginal cost curve (*MC*) unchanged. An increase in wages or some other component of variable cost shifts the variable curves (*TVC* and *AVC*) upward and shifts the (*MC*) upward but leaves the fixed cost curves (*AFC* and *TFC*) unchanged. So, for example, if a truck driver's wage rate increases, the variable cost and marginal cost of transportation services increase. If the interest expense paid by a trucking company increases, the fixed cost of transportation services increases.

You've now completed your study of short-run costs. All the concepts that you've met are summarized in a compact glossary in Table 11.2.

REVIEW

- A firm's short-run cost curves show the relationships between short-run cost and output.
- Marginal cost eventually increases because of *diminishing returns*—each additional worker produces a successively smaller addition to output.
- Average fixed cost decreases because as output increases, fixed costs are spread over a larger output.
- The average total cost curve is U-shaped because as output increases, it combines the influences of falling average fixed cost and eventually diminishing returns.

Long-Run Cost

L IN THE SHORT RUN, A FIRM CAN VARY THE quantity of labor but the quantity of capital is fixed. In the long run, a firm can vary both the quantity of labor and the quantity of capital. We are now going to see how costs vary when the quantities of labor and capital vary. That is, we are going to study a firm's long-run costs. **Long-run cost** is the cost of production when a firm uses the economically efficient quantities of labor and capital.

The behavior of long-run cost depends on the firm's **production function**, which is the relationship between the maximum output attainable and the quantities of both labor and capital.

The Production Function

Table 11.3 shows Swanky's production function. The table lists the total product for four different quantities of capital and five different quantities of labor. We'll identify the quantity of capital by the plant size. The numbers for Plant 1 are for a factory with one knitting machine—the case we've just studied. The other three plants have 2, 3, and 4 machines. If Swanky doubles its capital to 2 knitting machines, the various amounts of labor can produce the outputs shown in the second output column of the table. The last two columns show the outputs of yet larger quantities of capital.

Diminishing Returns   Diminishing returns occur with each quantity of capital as the quantity of labor increases. You can check that fact by calculating the marginal product of labor in plants with 2, 3, and 4 machines. At each plant size, as the quantity of labor increases, its marginal product (eventually) diminishes.

Diminishing Marginal Product of Capital
Diminishing returns also occur as the quantity of capital increases. You can check that fact by calculating the marginal product of capital at a given quantity of labor. The *marginal product of capital* is the change in total product divided by the change in capital when the quantity of labor is constant—equivalently, the change in output resulting from a one-unit increase in the quantity of capital. For example, if Swanky has 3 workers and increases its capital from 1 machine to 2 machines, output increases from 13 to 18 sweaters a day. The marginal product of capital is 5 sweaters per day. If Swanky increases the number of

---

TABLE 11.3

The Production Function

Labor (workers per day)	Output (sweaters per day)			
	Plant 1	Plant 2	Plant 3	Plant 4
1	4	10	13	15
2	10	15	18	21
3	13	18	22	24
4	15	20	24	26
5	16	21	25	27
Knitting machines (number)	1	2	3	4

The table shows the total product data for four quantities of capital. The greater the plant size, the larger is the total product for any given quantity of labor. But for a given plant size, the marginal product of labor diminishes. And for a given quantity of labor, the marginal product of capital diminishes.

---

machines from 2 to 3, output increases from 18 to 22 sweaters per day. The marginal product of the third machine is 4 sweaters per day, down from 5 sweaters per day for the second machine.

Let's now see what a firm's production function implies for its long-run costs.

Short-Run Cost and Long-Run Cost

Continue to assume that labor costs $25 per worker per day and capital costs $25 per machine per day. Using these input prices and the data in Table 11.3, we can calculate and graph the average total cost curves for factories with 1, 2, 3, and 4 knitting machines. We've already studied the costs of a factory with 1 machine in Figs. 11.4 and 11.5. In Fig. 11.7, the average total cost curve for that case is ATC_1. Figure 11.7 also shows the average total cost curve for a factory with 2 machines, ATC_2; with 3 machines, ATC_3; and with 4 machines, ATC_4.

You can see, in Fig. 11.7, that plant size has a big effect on the firm's average total cost. Two things stand out:

FIGURE 11.7
Short-Run Costs of Four Different Plants

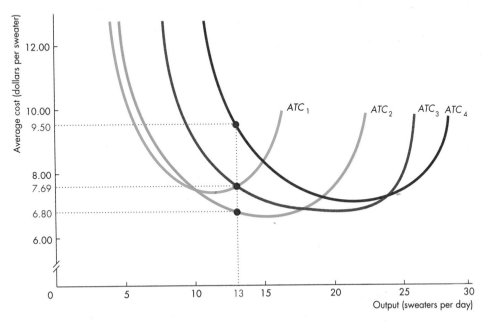

The figure shows short-run average total cost curves for four different quantities of capital. Swanky can produce 13 sweaters a day with 1 knitting machine on ATC_1 or with 3 knitting machines on ATC_3 for an average cost of $7.69 per sweater. Swanky can produce the same number of sweaters by using 2 knitting machines on ATC_2 for $6.80 per sweater or with 4 machines on ATC_4 for $9.50 per sweater. If Swanky produces 13 sweaters a day, the least-cost method—the long-run method—is with 2 machines on ATC_2.

- Each short-run average total cost curve is U-shaped.

- For each short-run average total cost curve, the larger the plant, the greater is the output at which average total cost is a minimum.

Each short-run average total cost curve is U-shaped because as the quantity of labor increases, its marginal product at first increases and then diminishes. These patterns in the marginal product of labor, which we examined in some detail for the case of the plant with 1 knitting machine on pp. 216–217, occur at all plant sizes.

A larger plant has a minimum average total cost at a greater output than a smaller plant because the larger plant has a higher fixed cost and therefore, for any given output level, a higher average total cost.

Which one of the short-run average cost curves Swanky operates on depends on its plant size. But in the long run, Swanky chooses its plant size. And which plant size it chooses depends on the output it plans to produce. The reason is that the average total cost of producing a given output depends on the plant size.

To see why, suppose that Swanky plans to produce 13 sweaters a day. With 1 machine, the average total

cost curve is ATC_1 (in Fig. 11.7) and the average total cost of 13 sweaters a day is $7.69 per sweater. With 2 machines, on ATC_2, the average total cost is $6.80 per sweater. With 3 machines, on ATC_3, the average total cost is $7.69 per sweater, the same as with 1 machine. Finally, with 4 machines, on ATC_4, the average total cost is $9.50 per sweater.

The economically efficient plant size for producing a given output is the one that has the lowest average total cost. For Swanky, the economically efficient plant to use to produce 13 sweaters a day is one with 2 machines.

In the long run, Swanky chooses its efficient plant size to minimize average total cost. When a firm is producing a given output at the least possible cost, it is operating on its *long-run average cost curve.*

The **long-run average cost curve** is the relationship between the lowest attainable average total cost and output when both capital and labor are varied. The long-run average cost curve is a planning curve. It tells the firm the plant size and the quantity of labor to use at each output to minimize cost.

Once the plant size is chosen, the firm operates on the short-run cost curves that apply to that plant size.

The Long-Run Average Cost Curve

Figure 11.8 shows Swanky's long-run average cost curve *LRAC*. This long-run average cost curve is derived from the short-run average total cost curves in Fig. 11.7. For output rates up to 10 sweaters a day, average total cost is the lowest on ATC_1. For output rates between 10 and 18 sweaters a day, average total cost is the lowest on ATC_2. For output rates between 18 and 24 sweaters a day, average total cost is the lowest on ATC_3. And for output rates in excess of 24 sweaters a day, average total cost is the lowest on ATC_4. The segment of each of the four average total cost curves along which average total cost is the lowest is highlighted in dark blue in Fig. 11.8. The scallop-shaped curve made up of these four segments is the long-run average cost curve.

Economies and Diseconomies of Scale

Economies of scale are present when, as output increases, long-run average cost decreases. When

economies of scale are present, the *LRAC* curve slopes downward. The *LRAC* curve in Fig. 11.8 shows that Swanky experiences economies of scale for outputs up to 15 sweaters a day. *Diseconomies of scale* are present when, as output increases, long-run average cost increases. When diseconomies of scale are present, the *LRAC* curve slopes upward. In Fig. 11.8, Swanky experiences diseconomies of scale at outputs greater than 15 sweaters a day. Economies and diseconomies of scale arise from returns to scale.

Returns to Scale

A change in scale occurs when there is an equal percentage change in the use of all the firm's inputs. For example, if Swanky increases its labor and capital from 1 worker and 1 machine to 2 workers and 2 machines, it doubles its scale. **Returns to scale** are the increases in output that result from increasing all inputs by the same percentage. There are three possible cases:

■ Constant returns to scale
■ Increasing returns to scale
■ Decreasing returns to scale

FIGURE II.8

Long-Run Average Cost Curve

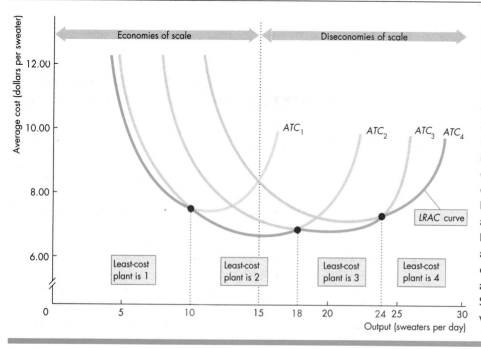

In the long run, Swanky can vary both capital and labor inputs. The long-run average cost curve, *LRAC*, traces the lowest attainable average total cost of production. Swanky produces on its long-run average cost curve if it uses 1 machine to produce up to 10 sweaters a day, 2 machines to produce between 10 and 18 sweaters a day, 3 machines to produce between 18 and 24 sweaters a day, and 4 machines to produce more than 24 sweaters a day. Within these ranges, Swanky varies its output by varying its labor input.

Constant Returns to Scale When the percentage increase in a firm's output is equal to the percentage increase in its inputs, the firm experiences **constant returns to scale**. If constant returns to scale are present and a firm doubles all its inputs, its output exactly doubles. Constant returns to scale occur if an increase in output is achieved by replicating the original production process. For example, General Motors can double its production of Cavaliers by doubling its production facility for those cars. It can build an identical production line and hire an identical number of workers. With the two identical production lines, GM produces exactly twice as many cars.

With constant returns to scale, long-run average cost is constant. There are neither economies of scale nor diseconomies of scale.

Increasing Returns to Scale When the percentage increase in the firm's output exceeds the percentage increase in its inputs, the firm experiences **increasing returns to scale**. If increasing returns to scale are present and a firm doubles all its inputs, its output more than doubles. Increasing returns to scale occur in production processes in which increased output enables a firm to increase the division of labor and to use more specialized labor and capital. For example, if GM produces only 100 cars a week, each worker and each machine must be capable of performing many different tasks. But if it produces 10,000 cars a week, each worker and each piece of equipment can be highly specialized. Workers specialize in a small number of tasks at which they become highly proficient. General Motors might use 100 times more capital and labor, but the number of cars produced increases more than a hundredfold. General Motors experiences increasing returns to scale.

With increasing returns to scale, long-run average cost falls. There are economies of scale.

Decreasing Returns to Scale When the percentage increase in the firm's output is less than the percentage increase in its inputs, the firm experiences **decreasing returns to scale**. If decreasing returns to scale are present and a firm doubles all its inputs, its output less than doubles. Decreasing returns to scale occur in all production processes at some output rate, but perhaps at a very large one.

One of the main reasons that decreasing returns arise is that management systems become stretched and inefficient. But this problem generally arises only at a very large scale.

With decreasing returns to scale, long-run average cost rises. There are diseconomies of scale.

Returns to Scale at Swanky Swanky's production function, shown in Table 11.3, displays both increasing returns to scale and decreasing returns to scale. When Swanky doubles its scale from 1 knitting machine and 1 worker to 2 knitting machines and 2 workers, the factory's output increases almost four-fold from 4 sweaters to 15 sweaters a day. If Swanky's inputs increase by another 50 percent to 3 knitting machines and 3 workers, output increases by less than 50 percent from 15 sweaters to 22 sweaters a day. Doubling Swanky's scale from 1 to 2 units of each input gives rise to increasing returns to scale, but the further increase from 2 to 3 units of each input gives rise to decreasing returns to scale.

You've now studied the principles of long-run cost. Let's use what you've learned to answer some questions about real businesses.

Producing Cars and Generating Electric Power At the beginning of this chapter, we noted that most car makers can produce more cars than they can sell. We posed the question: Why do car makers have expensive equipment lying around that isn't fully used? You can see the answer in the cost curves you've studied in this chapter. A car producer uses the plant size that minimizes the average total cost of producing the output that it can sell. But it experiences economies of scale. Its short-run average total cost curve looks like ATC_1. If it could sell more cars, average total cost would fall.

We also noted that many electric utilities don't have enough production equipment to meet demand on the coldest and hottest days and have to buy power from other producers. You can now see why this happens and why an electric utility doesn't build more generating capacity. A power producer uses the plant size that minimizes the average total cost of producing the output that it can sell on a normal day. But it experiences diseconomies of scale. Its short-run average total cost curve looks like ATC_4. With more capital, its average total costs of producing its normal output would be higher.

◆ You've now studied a firm's costs. You can apply what you've just learned in *Reading Between the Lines* on pp. 228–229, which looks at banks' cost curves for teller services. Your next task is to study the behavior of firms in markets for goods and services and learn how prices, outputs, and profits are determined.

Lowering the Cost of Banking

WINSTON-SALEM JOURNAL, MAY 30, 1996

ATM Fees Getting Many People's Goat

BY THE ASSOCIATED PRESS

Until two months ago, Marisa Gonzalez visited a bank automatic-teller machine two or three times a week.

The marketing manager at a Miami steamship company banks at a small credit union that doesn't have ATMs. She liked the convenient ATMs at Barnett Banks or SunTrust Banks, until they levied a $1.00 surcharge on ATM transactions by noncustomers.

Now Gonzalez goes just once a week to an ATM at her neighborhood supermarket and makes cash withdrawals stretch. "They put a sign up saying they wouldn't charge," Gonzalez said. "Now I make it a point to go there." ...

Surcharges are extra fees, on top of fees already charged, that any bank can now levy on transactions done with ATM cards not issued by that bank. They range from 50 cents to $2.00, with some as high as $10.00. ...

Few dispute that ATM transactions save banks money. Each one costs about 27 cents, compared with $1.07 for a teller transaction, says the Gemini Consulting firm in Morristown, N.J. Telephone, personal-computer and Internet transactions are cheaper still. But because they are so convenient, people use ATMs about twice as much as they had used tellers. ...

In 1995, the Federal Reserve found that, counting insurance and servicing costs, big banks—those with deposits exceeding $200 million—actually lose an average of $130 a month on every ATM they deploy. Smaller banks lose much more—up to $896.

Whether they are vastly profitable, merely profitable or outright unprofitable, banks are expanding their ATM reach.

NationsBank plans to increase its ATM network by 60 percent this year. ...

The Associated Press. Reprinted with permission.

Essence of **THE STORY**

■ Banks charge 50¢ to $10 on each ATM transaction that non-customers make.

■ Some small credit unions do not have ATMs. They use only tellers.

■ An ATM transaction costs a bank 27 cents; a teller transaction costs a bank $1.07.

■ Customers use ATMs twice as often as they previously used tellers.

■ Telephone, personal-computer, and Internet transactions are cheaper than ATM transactions.

■ Large banks lose an average of $130 a month on each ATM. Small banks lose an average of $896 a month on each ATM.

■ Regardless of the profitability of ATMs, banks are increasing the number of ATMs.

Economic

A N A L Y S I S

■ Banks levy surcharges on ATM transactions as a means of covering their costs.

■ ATM transactions use more capital and less labor than do teller transactions. The cost of the capital is a fixed cost, and the cost of the labor is a variable cost.

■ The average fixed cost of an ATM transaction exceeds the average fixed cost of a teller transaction.

■ The average variable cost of a teller transaction exceeds the average variable cost of an ATM transaction.

■ Average total cost, the sum of average fixed cost and average variable cost, are shown in the figure—ATC_T for teller transactions and ATC_A for ATM transactions.

■ Smaller banks do not have ATMs. The figure shows that with any number of transactions

up to Q a month, the bank's average total cost of a teller transaction is less than that of an ATM transaction.

■ But with more than Q transactions a month, the bank's average total cost of an ATM transaction is less than the cost of a teller transaction.

■ The monthly losses reported in the news article are accounting losses, not economic losses (see Chapter 10 pp. 201–203).

■ A bank's economic profit or loss is equal to its total revenue minus the opportunity cost of its services.

■ If it calculates cost as opportunity cost, a bank does not incur an economic loss when it offers ATM services. It is most likely that banks earn an economic profit. If they truly incurred a loss, they would get rid of their ATMs.

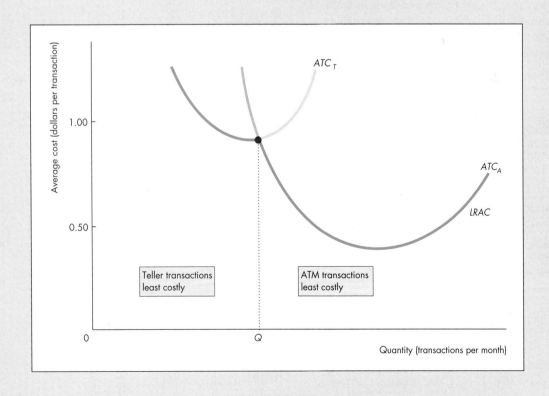

S U M M A R Y

Key Points

The Firm's Objective and Constraints (p. 214)

■ A firm's objective to maximize its profit is constrained by the demand for its product, the technology for producing its product, and the prices of its outputs.

■ In the short run, the quantity of at least one input—usually capital—is fixed, and the quantities of the other inputs—usually labor—can be varied. In the long run, the quantities of all inputs can be varied.

Short-Run Technology Constraint (pp. 215–218)

■ A total product curve shows how much output a firm can produce using a given quantity of capital and different quantities of labor.

■ Initially, the marginal product of labor increases as the quantity of labor increases, but eventually, marginal product diminishes—the law of diminishing returns.

■ Average product increases initially and eventually diminishes.

Short-Run Cost (pp. 219–223)

■ As output increases, total fixed cost is constant, and total variable cost and total cost increase.

■ As output increases, average fixed cost decreases.

■ As output increases, average variable cost, average total cost, and marginal cost decrease at small outputs and increase at large outputs. These cost curves are U-shaped.

Long-Run Cost (pp. 224–227)

■ Long-run cost is the cost of production when all inputs—labor and capital—have been adjusted to their economically efficient levels.

■ There is a set of short-run cost curves for each different plant size. There is one least-cost plant size for each output. The larger the output, the larger is the plant size that minimizes average total cost.

■ The long-run average cost curve traces out the lowest attainable average total cost at each output when both capital and labor inputs can be varied.

■ With economies of scale, the long-run average cost curve slopes downward. With diseconomies of scale, the long-run average cost curve slopes upward.

Key Figures and Table

Key Terms

QUESTIONS

1. Why do firms try to maximize profit?
2. What are the constraints on a firm's ability to maximize profit?
3. Distinguish between the short run and the long run.
4. What does a firm's total product curve show?
5. What does a firm's marginal product curve show?
6. What does a firm's average product curve show?
7. Explain the relationships between a firm's total product curve and its marginal product curve.
8. Explain the relationship between a firm's average product curve and its marginal product curve.
9. What is the law of diminishing returns? What does this law imply about the shapes of the total, marginal, and average product curves?
10. Why does the marginal product of labor first increase and eventually diminish?
11. Define total cost, total fixed cost, and total variable cost. What is the relationship among the three concepts of total cost?
12. Explain how the three total cost measures change as output increases.
13. Define marginal cost. Why does marginal cost eventually increase as output increases?
14. Define average total cost, average variable cost, and average fixed cost. What is the relationship among the three average cost concepts?
15. Explain how the three average cost measures change as output increases.
16. What is the relationship between average variable cost and marginal cost and between average total cost and marginal cost?
17. Explain the relationship between the average product curve and average variable cost curve and between the marginal product curve and the marginal cost curve.
18. What is the relationship between the long-run average cost curve and the short-run average total cost curves?
19. What effects do economies of scale and diseconomies of scale have on the shape of the long-run average cost curve?
20. Explain why returns to scale arise.

PROBLEMS

1. The table sets out the total product schedule of Rubber Duckies, Inc., a firm that makes rubber boats.

Labor (workers per week)	Output (rubber boats per week)
1	1
2	3
3	6
4	10
5	15
6	21
7	26
8	30
9	33
10	35

  a. Draw the total product curve.
  b. Calculate the average product of labor and draw the average product curve.
  c. Calculate the marginal product of labor and draw the marginal product curve.
  d. What is the relationship between average product and marginal product when Rubber Duckies produces fewer than 30 boats a week? Why?
  e. What is the relationship between average and marginal product when Rubber Duckies produces more than 30 boats a week? Why?

2. Suppose that the price of labor is $400 a week, the total fixed cost is $1,000 a week, and the total product schedule is the same as in problem 1.
  a. Calculate total cost, total variable cost, and total fixed cost for each level of output.
  b. Draw the total cost, total variable cost, and total fixed cost curves.
  c. Calculate average total cost, average fixed cost, average variable cost, and marginal cost at each level of output.
  d. Draw the following cost curves: average total cost, average variable cost, average fixed cost, and marginal cost.

3. Suppose that total fixed cost increases to $1,100 a week. What will now happen to the firm's short-run cost curves in problem 2?

4. Suppose that total fixed cost remains at $1,000 a week but that the price of labor increases to $450 a week. Using these new costs, rework problem 2.

5. Rubber Duckies, Inc., can buy an additional factory. If it does so and operates two factories, its total product schedule is:

Labor (workers per week)	Output (rubber boats per week)
1	2
2	6
3	12
4	20
5	30
6	42
7	52
8	60
9	66
10	70

The total fixed cost of operating its current factory is $1,000 a week, and the total fixed cost of operating the additional factory is also $1,000 a week. The wage rate is $400 a week.

a. Calculate the total cost for each of the outputs given for the new factory.

b. Calculate Rubber Duckies' average total cost of each output given.

c. Draw Rubber Duckies' long-run average cost curve.

d. Over what output range would it be efficient for Rubber Duckies to operate one factory?

e. Over what output range would it be efficient for Rubber Duckies to operate two factories?

CRITICAL THINKING

1. Study *Reading Between the Lines* on pp. 228–229 and then answer the following questions:

a. What is the main difference, from a cost point of view, between human tellers and ATMs?

b. Why do you think ATMs have become so popular?

c. Would it ever make sense for a bank in the United States not to use ATMs?

d. Do you predict that ATMs are as common in China as they are in the United States? Explain why they might not be as common.

e. Suppose the government put a tax on the banks for each ATM transaction but did not put on a similar tax for human teller transactions. How would the tax affect a bank's costs and cost curves? Would it change the number of ATMs and the number of tellers that banks hire? If so, how? Explain.

2. Suppose that AT&T replaces human telephone operators with computers that lower total cost but increase fixed cost.

a. Sketch the total cost curves for the original technology that uses human operators.

b. Sketch the average cost curves for the original technology that uses human operators.

c. Sketch the marginal cost curves for the original technology that uses human operators.

d. Sketch the total cost curves for the new technology that uses computers.

e. Sketch the average cost curves for the new technology that uses computers.

f. Sketch the marginal cost curves for the new technology that uses computers.

g. For a phone company whose output is small, which technology is more likely to be efficient?

h. How would you advise a telephone company as to whether it should use human operators or computers?

Managing Change

Our economy is constantly changing. Every year, new goods appear and old ones disappear. New firms are born and old ones die. This process of change is initiated and managed by firms operating in markets. When a new product is invented, just one or two firms sell it initially. For example when the personal computer first became available, there was an Apple or an IBM. The IBM-PC had just one operating system, DOS, made by Microsoft. The chip that runs an IBM-PC was and still is today made by one firm, Intel. These are examples of industries in which the producer has market power to determine the price of the product and the quantity produced. In the extreme case of a single producer that cannot be challenged by new competitors, we call the market a *monopoly*. ◆ But not all industries with just one producer are monopolies. In many cases, the firm that is first to produce a new good faces severe competition from new rivals. As more and more firms get into the business of producing a new good, an industry becomes competitive. Even with just two rivals, the industry changes its face in a dramatic way. We call this case *duopoly*. In duopoly the two firms must pay close attention to each other's production and prices and must predict the effects of their own actions on the actions of the other firm. We call this situation one of *strategic interdependence*. As the number of rivals grows, the industry becomes an *oligopoly*. In an oligopoly, a small number of firms must devise strategies and pay close attention to the strategies of their competitors. ◆ With the continued arrival of new firms in an industry, the market eventually becomes competitive. Competition might be limited because each firm produces its own special version or brand of a good. This case is called *monopolistic competition* because it has elements of both monopoly and competition. Or competition might be extreme, a case that we call *perfect competition*. ◆ Often, an industry that is competitive becomes less so as the bigger and more successful firms in the industry begin to swallow up the smaller firms, either by driving them out of business or by acquiring their assets. Through this process, an industry might return to oligopoly, or even monopoly. ◆ We begin, in Chapter 12, by studying competitive markets and learn how business decisions lead to the market supply curve. You will gain a deeper understanding of the forces at play that move resources to their highest value use and will begin to see the anatomy of the invisible hand. In Chapter 13, we jump to the opposite extreme of pure monopoly. Here, we learn how firms use market power to increase profits. Finally, in Chapter 14, we study the intermediate cases of monopolistic competition and oligopoly. ◆ But first, we'll spend some time with John von Neumann, who pioneered the idea of game theory as a tool to study strategic choices, and we'll also talk with one of today's students of market power and strategic thinking, Avinash Dixit of Princeton University.

Understanding Market Power

The Economist: John von Neumann

John von Neumann was one of the great minds of the twentieth century. Born in Budapest, Hungary, in 1903, Johnny, as he was known, showed early mathematical brilliance. His first mathematical publication was an article that grew out of a lesson with his tutor, which he wrote at the age of 18! But at the age of 25, in 1928, von Neumann published the article that began a flood of research on game theory—a flood that has still not ended today. In that article, he proved that in a zero-sum game (like sharing a pie), there exists a best strategy for each player.

Von Neumann invented and helped to build the first modern practical computer, and he worked on the "Manhattan Project," which developed the atomic bomb at Los Alamos, New Mexico, during World War II.

Von Neumann believed that the social sciences would progress only if they used mathematical tools. But he believed that they needed different tools than those developed from the physical sciences.

"Real life consists of bluffing, of little tactics of deception, of asking yourself what is the other man going to think I mean to do."

JOHN VON NEUMANN

told to Jacob Bronowski (in a London taxi) and reported in THE ASCENT OF MAN

The Issues and Ideas

It is not surprising that firms with market power will charge higher prices than those charged by competitive firms. But how much higher?

This question has puzzled generations of economists. Adam Smith said, "The price of a monopoly is upon every occasion the highest which can be got." But he was wrong. Antoine-Augustin Cournot (see p. 62) first worked out the price a monopoly will charge. It is not the "highest which can be got," but the price that maximizes profit. Cournot's work was not appreciated until almost a century later when Joan Robinson explained how a monopoly sets its price.

Questions about monopoly became urgent and practical during the 1870s, a time when rapid technological change and falling transportation costs enabled huge monopolies to emerge in the United States. Monopolies dominated oil, steel, railroads, tobacco, and even sugar. Industrial empires grew ever larger.

The success of the nineteenth century monopolies led to the creation of our antitrust laws—laws that limit the use of monopoly power. Those laws have been used to prevent monopolies from being set up and to break up existing monopolies. They were used during the 1960s to end a conspiracy between General Electric, Westinghouse, and other firms when they colluded to fix their prices instead of competing with each other. The laws were used during the 1980s to bring greater competition to long-distance telecommunication. But in spite of antitrust laws, near monopolies still exist. Among the most prominent today are those in computer chips and operating systems. Like their forerunners, today's near monopolies make huge profits. But unlike the situation in the nineteenth century, the technological change taking place today is strengthening the forces of competition. Today's information technologies are creating substitutes for services that previously had none. Direct satellite TV is competing with cable, and new phone companies are competing with the traditional phone monopolies.

THEN...

Ruthless greed, exploitation of both workers and customers—these are the traditional images of monopolies and the effects of their power. These images appeared to be an accurate description during the 1880s, when monopolies were at their peak of power and influence. One monopolist, John D. Rockefeller, Sr., built his giant Standard Oil Company, which, by 1879, was refining 90 percent of the nation's oil and controlling its entire pipeline capacity.

...AND NOW

In spite of antitrust laws that regulate monopolies, they still exist. One is the monopoly in cable television. In many cities, one firm decides which channels viewers will receive and the price they will pay. During the 1980s, with the advent of satellite technology and specialist cable program producers such as CNN and HBO, the cable companies expanded their offerings. At the same time, they steadily increased prices and their businesses became very profitable. But the very technologies that made cable television profitable are now challenging its market position. Direct satellite TV services are eroding cable's monopoly and bringing greater competition to this market.

Today, many economists who work on microeconomics use the ideas that John von Neumann pioneered. Game theory is the tool of choice. One economist who has made good use of this tool (and many other tools) is Avinash Dixit of Princeton University, whom you can meet on the following pages.

Talking with

Avinash K. Dixit is the Sherrerd University Professor of Economics at Princeton University. Born in 1944 in Bombay, India, he was an undergraduate at Cambridge University, England, and a graduate student at MIT.

Professor Dixit has worked on a wide range of economic problems, but his most widely known work is his 1991 book *Thinking Strategically* (with Barry J. Nalebuff), which became an international best-seller. This book explains how to use game theory in business, politics, and even social and family situations. Professor Dixit has also helped to explain how a firm establishes and maintains a dominant market position. Professor Dixit has revolutionized the way we think about irreversible decisions—decisions on which we can't go back or can reverse only at great cost. Michael Parkin talked with Professor Dixit about these issues.

Professor Dixit, what is game theory and how do economists use it?

Game theory is a framework for thinking about decisions when your best choice depends on what someone else is choosing and vice versa. Such interdependence is called strategic interaction. For example, a chess player making an opening move with the white pieces must calculate how the opponent with the black pieces will respond, knowing in turn that black is taking into account how white will respond at the next move, and so on. The outcome for each player depends on the actions of the other player, and each player makes his or her actions based on awareness of this interdependence.

Strategic interactions occur for either of two reasons. The first arises in small groups of people, firms, or nations where the choices of each have a significant impact on the others. The classic example in economics is an industry with a small number of firms, such as the U.S. auto industry. Before the 1970s, three major auto firms existed in the United States: General Motors, Ford, and Chrysler. Each firm had to decide which vehicles to produce, how to price them, and how many people to employ. While making these decisions, the firm also had to take into account the likely responses to these decisions by the other two firms. In international relations, war or peace among major powers hinges upon similar calculations by each nation's leaders of the interests and responses of others.

The second reason strategic interactions occur is if the market for a product or service extends over time or is of uncertain quality. Consider, for example, that someone is interested in having a home built and needs a contractor. He or she can choose from among many contractors, and a contractor can similarly choose from among numerous potential clients. But once a choice is made, the contractor and client become linked in a bilateral relationship. The builder might procrastinate or do a poor quality job, and the client might be slow with future payments. In anticipation of these problems, a contract is negotiated, monitored, and enforced.

We frequently play games in which the opponent is not another person but ourselves or, more accurately, our future self. Your future self is going to give in to temptations of the moment and do things you know would be really bad for you—eat more, exercise less, or study less diligently.

Can you give some everyday examples of how game theory helps a person to think strategically and make a better decision?
We frequently play games in which the opponent is not another person but ourselves or, more accurately, our future self. Your future self is going to give in to temptations of the moment and do things you know would be really bad for you—eat more, exercise less, or study less diligently. You can defeat this "opponent" by tak-ing actions right now that diminish your future self's freedom of action. For example, you could join a group where other members will pressure you into keeping your current good resolutions to diet and exercise and study. In game theory, such actions are called "commitments." Finding good devices of commitment is a very important kind of strategy we all have to practice in our daily lives.

Another very important class of games is that of "no-win" interactions, which are best avoided altogether or resolved by prior negotiation. In game theory, these interactions are typically "prisoners' dilemma" or "chicken" games, in which each person's pursuit of private advantage can lead to mutual harm. The nuclear arms race between the United States and the Soviet Union was the most dramatic example. Each country thought that a hundred more missiles would give it a decisive edge. The result of this thinking was very costly escalation of weapons with no net advantage to either country.

How do firms such as Microsoft and Intel use strategic thinking to dominate their markets?
Firms can become dominant or powerful in their markets for many reasons. First, a firm can be much better than others, producing a higher-quality product and selling it at a lower price. Second, a firm can take predatory strategic actions that increase and sustain its own dominance. For example, it can preemptively install capacity that exceeds what its current production would justify. This acts as a credible demonstration of its willingness to produce more and fight a price war and thereby deters other firms from entering or growing. And third, a product might have such strong economies of scale that the market is most efficiently served by just one firm, but which one emerges in this position can be a matter of historical accident. In practice, all three factors may be present—a firm may get an initial stroke of good luck, then use superior technology or management to lever it into a dominant position, and finally use predatory practices to preserve such a position.

All three factors operated in the computer industry. Both processor chips and operating systems have very large initial design costs but low costs of production or duplication of each copy thereafter. Thus we have good reasons to expect the markets to be dominated by one or a few firms. Which ones?

In the case of Microsoft and Intel, the fact that IBM chose them for its first PC clearly launched them into a favorable position. In the summer of 1980, IBM needed an operating system for their original personal computer. The obvious choice was CP-M, developed by Digital Research in California. The IBM team flew out to see Digital's chief, Gary Kildall. But he forgot the appointment and went flying in his small plane. In his absence, his wife wouldn't sign IBM's nondisclosure agreement. The IBM team left and then went on to Seattle to see Bill Gates, whose Basic language program they also wanted. Hearing that IBM needed an operating system, Gates bought one called QDOS—Quick and Dirty Operating System—from another local company, turned it into MS-DOS, and sold it to IBM as PC-DOS. The rest is history. This was a historical accident par excellence.

Microsoft and Intel made the most of the advantage they got from dealing with IBM. But the reason for their near-total dominance of the industry is a matter of controversy. The Microsoft-lovers argue that for the majority of business and home PC users, the company has delivered a good product at a good price. Microsoft-haters allege predation. They say Microsoft has used "unfair" strategies to make it impossible for others to compete. For example, Microsoft insists on contracts with suppliers of DOS-Windows PCs whereby the suppliers have to pay Microsoft a royalty for each unit they ship, whether or not it has a Microsoft operating system. I suspect there is some truth on both sides.

Can you explain your key insight about irreversible investment decisions?

If an action cannot be reversed, or can be reversed only at a great cost, you are more cautious about taking it. Two conditions create this scenario. The first is uncertainty. You can never be entirely sure what the future will bring, but the passage of time and active searching reveals further information. The second is a window of opportunity. Most decisions can be postponed.

Waiting gives you an "option" that is very similar to a financial option—the right but not the obligation to do something in the future if conditions are right then. You can either buy or sell stock at various times. If the future brings new information that shows the action be to undesirable, then the waiting has enabled you to avoid a mistake. If the new information reaffirms the desirability of the action, then you can go ahead, having lost only the benefit that would have flowed from the action for the few weeks' or months' delay.

Your choice of a major or of an area of specialization in graduate school is a good application of this principle. Nuclear physics may appear to be an attractive career at one point in time and finance or law at another, but conditions change. There is much to be said for acquiring a broad set of flexible skills of wide applicability while learning more about your own interests and the prospects of particular career paths and delaying irreversible specialization.

Who are the giant economists of the past whose ideas have been most fruitful in your work?

I have drawn inspiration and knowledge from the work of so many great economists that it is very difficult to pick one or two. But if forced, I would choose Paul Samuelson and Thomas Schelling. Samuelson's *Foundations of Economic Analysis* and *Economics* were the first two books I read on the subject, Samuelson was one of my teachers in graduate school, and almost all my research has been influenced by the fundamental principles and techniques of optimization and equilibrium that I learned from him.

Thomas Schelling's books, most particularly *The Strategy of Conflict* and *Micromotives and Macrobehavior*, have been immensely influential for my thinking. You can learn about the formalism of game theory from dry mathematical articles and books, but to appreciate the importance of game theory for almost all aspects of life—interactions in the family, social groups, business, and international relations—you have to read Schelling.

What is the case for majoring in economics today? What are the

profits from an economics degree? In very practical terms, an economics major is a good background for professional graduate training in law and business. But perhaps more important, economics is among the "broad set of flexible skills of wide applicability" that I recommended earlier. Economics teaches us the fundamentals of decision making—to

> *Economics teaches us the fundamentals of decision making—to be clear about objectives, recognize constraints and thereby opportunity costs, handle uncertainty, and know how to update information in the light of new observations.*

be clear about objectives, recognize constraints and thereby opportunity costs, handle uncertainty, and know how to update information in the light of new observations. The techniques that are used in such analysis—mathematics, probability, and statistics—are also useful for many other applications. Studying economics is buying an option that can be exercised later in many kinds of careers and many walks of life.

12

Competition

Ice cream is big business. In the United States in 1996, more than 2 million pounds were bought—an average of sixteen pounds per person—at a cost of more than $10 billion. Competition in the ice cream industry is fierce. National names such as Baskin-Robbins and Häagen-Dazs compete with Ben and Jerry's, Bart's, Annabel's, and hundreds of private label store brands for a place in a crowded market. New firms enter and try their luck while other firms are squeezed out of the business. How does competition affect prices and profits? What causes some firms to enter an industry and others to leave it? What are the effects on profits and prices of new firms entering and old firms leaving an industry? ◆ In 1996, on the average, seven million people were

Hot Rivalry in Ice Cream

unemployed. Of these, more than a million were unemployed because they had been laid off by firms seeking to trim their costs and avoid bankruptcy. Ice cream producers, computer makers, and firms in almost every sector of the economy laid off workers in 1996, even though the economy was expanding and the total number of jobs was growing. Why do firms lay off workers? When will a firm temporarily shut down, laying off its workers? ◆ Over the past few years, there has been a dramatic fall in the prices of personal computers. For example, a slow computer cost almost $4,000 a few years ago, and a fast one costs only $1,000 today. What goes on in an industry when the price of its output falls sharply? What happens to the profits of the firms producing such goods? ◆ Ice cream, computers, and most other goods are produced by more than one firm, and these firms compete with each other for sales. To study competitive markets, we are going to build a model of a market in which competition is as fierce and extreme as possible—more extreme than in the examples we've just considered. We call this situation "perfect competition."

After studying this chapter, you will be able to:

- Define perfect competition
- Explain how price and output are determined in a competitive industry
- Explain why firms sometimes shut down temporarily and lay off workers
- Explain why firms enter and leave an industry
- Predict the effects of a change in demand and of a technological advance
- Explain why perfect competition is efficient

Perfect Competition

PERFECT COMPETITION IS AN EXTREME FORM OF competition. **Perfect competition** arises when:

- There are many firms, each selling an identical product.
- There are many buyers.
- There are no restrictions on entry into the industry.
- Firms in the industry have no advantage over potential new entrants.
- Firms and buyers are well informed about the prices of the products of each firm in the industry.

An industry can have a large number of firms only if the demand for its product is large relative to the output level at which average total cost is a minimum. For example, the worldwide demand for corn, rice, and other basic grains is many thousands of times larger than the output that can be produced by a single farm at minimum average cost.

The conditions that define perfect competition imply that no firm can influence the price at which it sells its output. Firms in perfect competition are said to be price takers. A **price taker** is a firm that cannot influence the price of a good or service.

The key reason why a perfectly competitive firm is a price taker is that it produces a tiny proportion of the total output of a particular good and buyers are well-informed about the prices of other firms.

Imagine that you are a wheat farmer in Kansas. You have a thousand acres under cultivation—which sounds like a lot. But then you go on a drive, first heading west. The flat lands turn into rolling hills as you head toward the Rocky Mountains, but everywhere you look, you see thousands and thousands of acres of wheat. The sun goes down in the west behind millions of acres of golden plants. The next morning, it rises in the east above the same scene. Driving to Colorado, Oklahoma, Texas, and back up to Nebraska and the Dakotas reveals similar vistas. You also find unbroken stretches of wheat in Canada, Argentina, Australia, and Ukraine. Your thousand acres is a drop in the ocean.

Nothing makes your wheat any better than any other farmer's, and all the buyers of wheat know the price at which they can do business. If everybody else sells their wheat for $4 a bushel and you want $4.10, why would people buy from you? They can simply go to the next farmer, and the one after that, and the next

and buy all they need for $4. This price is determined in the market for wheat, and you are a *price taker*. A price taker faces a perfectly elastic demand curve.

The *market* demand for wheat is not perfectly elastic. The market demand curve is downward sloping, and its elasticity depends on the substitutability of wheat for other grains such as barley, rye, corn, and rice. But the demand for wheat from farm *A* is perfectly elastic because wheat from farm *A* is a *perfect substitute* for wheat from farm *B*.

Perfect competition does not occur frequently in the real world. But competition in many industries is so fierce that the model of perfect competition we're about to study is of enormous help in predicting the behavior of the firms in these industries. Ice cream making and retailing, farming, fishing, wood pulping and paper milling, the manufacture of paper cups and plastic shopping bags, grocery retailing, photo finishing, lawn service, plumbing, painting, dry cleaning, and the provision of laundry services are all examples of industries that are highly competitive.

Economic Profit and Revenue

A firm's goal is to maximize **economic profit**, which is equal to total revenue minus total cost. Total cost is the *opportunity cost* of production, and opportunity cost includes **normal profit**, which is the return that a firm's entrepreneur can obtain in the best alternative business. (For a refresher on these profit and cost concepts, review Chapter 10, pp. 200–203.)

Total revenue is the value of a firm's sales. It equals the price of the firm's output multiplied by the number of units of output sold (price × quantity). **Marginal revenue** is the change in total revenue divided by the change in quantity sold. That is, marginal revenue is the change in total revenue resulting from a one-unit increase in the quantity sold. In perfect competition, the price is constant when the quantity sold changes. So the change in total revenue resulting from a one-unit increase in the quantity sold equals price. Therefore, in perfect competition, marginal revenue equals price. **Average revenue** is total revenue divided by the total quantity sold—revenue per unit sold. Because total revenue equals price multiplied by quantity sold, average revenue (total revenue divided by quantity sold) equals price.

Figure 12.1 shows these revenue concepts for Swanky, Inc. The table shows three different quantities of sweaters sold. For a price taker, as the quantity sold varies, the price stays constant—in this example at $25 a sweater. Total revenue is equal to price multiplied by quantity sold. For example, if Swanky sells 8 sweaters, total revenue is 8 times $25, which equals $200. Marginal revenue is the change in total revenue resulting from a one-unit change in quantity. For example, when the quantity sold increases from 8 to 9, total revenue increases from $200 to $225, so marginal revenue is $25 a sweater. (Notice that in the table, marginal revenue appears *between* the lines for the quantities sold to remind you that marginal revenue results from the *change* in the quantity sold.) Average revenue is total revenue divided by quantity. Again, if Swanky sells 8 sweaters, average revenue is total revenue ($200) divided by quantity (8), which equals $25 a sweater.

Suppose that Swanky is one of a thousand similar small producers of sweaters. Figure 12.1(a) shows the demand and supply curves for the entire sweater industry. Demand curve D intersects supply curve S at a price of $25 a sweater and a quantity of 9,000 sweaters. Figure 12.1(b) shows Swanky's demand curve. Because the firm is a price taker, its demand curve is perfectly elastic—the horizontal line at $25. The figure also illustrates Swanky's average and marginal revenues. Because average revenue and marginal revenue equal price, the firm's demand curve is also its average revenue curve (AR) and its marginal revenue curve (MR). That is, the firm's demand curve tells us the revenue per sweater sold and the change in total revenue that results from selling one more sweater. Swanky's total revenue curve, TR (part c), shows the total revenue for each quantity sold. For example, when Swanky sells 9 sweaters, total revenue is $225 (point *a*). Because each additional sweater sold brings in a constant amount—$25—the total revenue curve is an upward-sloping straight line.

FIGURE 12.1

Demand, Price, and Revenue in Perfect Competition

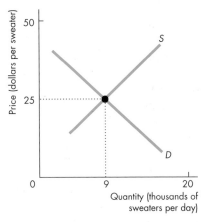

(a) Sweater industry

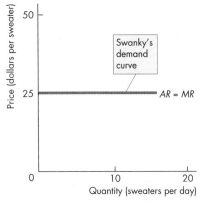

(b) Swanky's demand, average revenue and marginal revenue

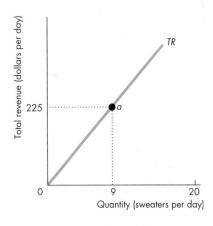

(c) Swanky's total revenue

Quantity sold (Q) (sweaters per day)	Price (P) (dollars per sweater)	Total revenue (TR = P × Q) (dollars)	Marginal revenue (MR = ΔTR/ΔQ) (dollars per additional sweater)	Average revenue (AR = TR/Q) (dollars per sweater)
8	25	200		25
			 25	
9	25	225		25
			 25	
10	25	250		25

The industry demand and supply curves determines the market price. In part (a), the price is $25 a sweater and 9,000 sweaters are bought and sold. Swanky faces a perfectly elastic demand curve at the market price of $25 a sweater, part (b). The table calculates Swanky's total revenue, marginal revenue, and average revenue. Part (b) shows that Swanky's demand curve is also its average revenue curve (AR) and marginal revenue curve (MR). Part (c) shows Swanky's total revenue curve (TR). Point *a* corresponds to the second row of the table.

The Firm's Decisions in Perfect Competition

Firms in a perfectly competitive industry face a given market price and have the revenue curves that you've studied. These revenue curves summarize the market constraint faced by a perfectly competitive firm.

Firms also have a technology constraint, which is described by the product curves (total product, average product, and marginal product) that you studied in Chapter 11. The technology available to the firm determines its costs, which are described by the cost curves (total cost, average cost, and marginal cost) that you also studied in Chapter 11.

The task of the competitive firm is to make the maximum economic profit possible, given the constraints it faces. To achieve this objective, a firm must make four key decisions: two in the short run and two in the long run.

Short-Run Decisions

The short run is a time frame in which each firm has a given plant and the number of firms in the industry is fixed. But many things can change in the short run, and the firm must react to these changes. For example, the price for which the firm can sell its output might have a seasonal fluctuation, or it might fluctuate with general business fluctuations.

The firm must react to such short-run price fluctuations and decide:

1. Whether to produce or to shut down
2. If the decision is to produce, what quantity to produce

Long-Run Decisions

The long run is a time frame in which each firm can change the size of its plant and decide whether to leave the industry. Other firms can decide to enter the industry. So in the long run, both the plant size of each firm and the number of firms in the industry can change. Also in the long run, the constraints facing firms can change. For example, the demand for the good can permanently fall, or technological advance can change the industry's costs.

The firm must react to such long-run changes and decide:

1. Whether to increase or decrease its plant size
2. Whether to stay in the industry or leave it

The Firm and the Industry in the Short Run and the Long Run

To study a competitive industry, we begin by looking at an individual firm's short-run decisions. We then see how the short-run decisions of all firms in a competitive industry combine to determine the industry price, output, and economic profit. Then we turn to the long run and study the effects of long-run decisions on the industry price, output, and economic profit. All the decisions we study are driven by a single objective: to maximize economic profit.

Profit-Maximizing Output

A perfectly competitive firm maximizes economic profit by choosing its output level. One way of finding the profit-maximizing output is to study a firm's total revenue and total cost and to find the output level at which total revenue exceeds total cost by the largest amount. Figure 12.2 shows how to do this for Swanky, Inc. The table lists Swanky's total revenue and total cost at different outputs, and part (a) of the figure shows Swanky's total revenue and total cost curves. These curves are graphs of the numbers shown in the first three columns of the table. The total revenue curve (*TR*) is the same as that in Fig. 12.1(c). The total cost curve (*TC*) is similar to the one that you met in Chapter 11. As output increases, so does total cost.

Economic profit equals total revenue minus total cost. The fourth column of the table in Fig. 12.2 shows Swanky's economic profit, and part (b) of the figure illustrates these numbers as Swanky's profit curve. This curve shows that Swanky makes an economic profit at outputs between 4 and 12 sweaters a day. At outputs less than 4 sweaters a day, Swanky incurs an economic loss. It also incurs an economic loss if output exceeds 12 sweaters a day. At outputs of 4 sweaters and 12 sweaters a day, total cost equals total revenue and Swanky's economic profit is zero. An output at which total cost equals total revenue is called a *break-even point*. The firm's economic profit is zero, but because normal profit is part of total cost, a firm makes normal profit at a break-even point. That is, at the break-even point, the entrepreneur makes an income equal to the best alternative return forgone.

Notice the relationship between the total revenue, total cost, and profit curves. Economic profit is measured by the vertical distance between the total revenue and total cost curves. When the total revenue

FIGURE 12.2

Total Revenue, Total Cost, and Economic Profit

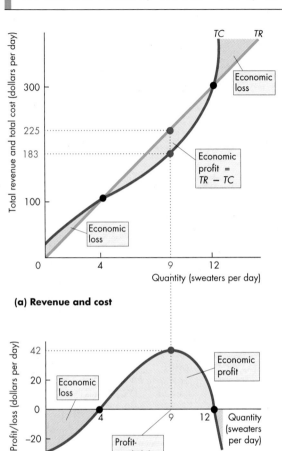

(a) Revenue and cost

(b) Economic profit and loss

Quantity (Q) (sweaters per day)	Total revenue (TR) (dollars)	Total cost (TC) (dollars)	Economic profit (TR − TC) (dollars)
0	0	22	−22
1	25	45	−20
2	50	66	−16
3	75	85	−10
4	100	100	0
5	125	114	11
6	150	126	24
7	175	141	34
8	200	160	40
9	225	183	42
10	250	210	40
11	275	245	30
12	300	300	0
13	325	360	−35

The table lists Swanky's total revenue, total cost, and economic profit. Part (a) graphs the total revenue and total cost curves. Economic profit, in part (a), is the height of the blue area between the total cost and total revenue curves. Swanky makes maximum economic profit, $42 a day ($225 − $183), when it produces 9 sweaters—the output at which the vertical distance between the total revenue and total cost curves is at its largest. At outputs of 4 sweaters a day and 12 sweaters a day, Swanky makes zero economic profit—these are break-even points. At outputs less than 4 and greater than 12 sweaters a day, Swanky incurs an economic loss. Part (b) shows Swanky's profit curve. The profit curve is at its highest when economic profit is at a maximum. The profit curve cuts the horizontal axis at the break-even points.

curve in part (a) is above the total cost curve, between 4 and 12 sweaters, the firm is making an economic profit and the profit curve in part (b) is above the horizontal axis. At the break-even point, where the total cost and total revenue curves intersect, the profit curve intersects the horizontal axis. The profit curve is at a maximum when *TR* exceeds *TC* by the largest amount. In this example, profit maximization occurs at an output of 9 sweaters a day. At this output, Swanky's economic profit is $42 a day.

Marginal Analysis

Another way of finding the profit-maximizing output is to use *marginal analysis* and compare marginal revenue, *MR*, with marginal cost, *MC*. As output increases, marginal revenue remains constant but marginal cost changes. At low output levels, marginal cost decreases, but it eventually increases. So where the marginal cost curve intersects the marginal revenue curve, marginal cost is rising.

If marginal revenue exceeds marginal cost (if *MR* > *MC*), then the extra revenue from selling one more unit exceeds the extra cost incurred to produce it. The firm makes an economic profit on the marginal unit, so its economic profit increases if output increases.

If marginal revenue is less than marginal cost (if *MR* < *MC*), then the extra revenue from selling one more unit is less than the extra cost incurred to produce it. The firm incurs an economic loss on the marginal unit, so its economic profit decreases if output increases and its economic profit increases if output decreases.

If marginal revenue equals marginal cost (if *MR* = *MC*), economic profit is maximized. The rule *MR* = *MC* is a prime example of marginal analysis. Let's check that this rule works to find the profit-maximizing output by returning to Swanky's sweater factory.

Look at Fig. 12.3. The table records Swanky's marginal revenue and marginal cost. Marginal revenue is a constant $25 a sweater. Over the range of outputs shown in the table, marginal cost increases from $19 a sweater to $35 a sweater as the number of sweaters a day increases.

Focus on the highlighted rows of the table. If Swanky increases output from 8 sweaters to 9 sweaters, marginal revenue is $25 and marginal cost is $23. Because marginal revenue exceeds marginal cost, economic profit increases. The last column of the table shows that economic profit increases from $40 to $42, an increase of $2. This economic profit from the ninth sweater is shown as the blue area in the figure.

If Swanky increases output from 9 sweaters to 10 sweaters, marginal revenue is still $25, but marginal cost is $27. Because marginal revenue is less than marginal cost, economic profit decreases. The last column of the table shows that economic profit decreases from $42 to $40. This loss from the tenth sweater is shown as the red area in the figure.

Swanky maximizes economic profit by producing 9 sweaters a day, the quantity at which marginal revenue equals marginal cost.

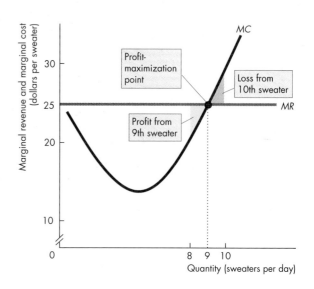

FIGURE 12.3

Profit-Maximizing Output

Quantity (Q) (sweaters per day)	Total revenue (TR) (dollars)	Marginal revenue (MR) (dollars per additional sweater)	Total cost (TC) (dollars)	Marginal cost (MC) (dollars per additional sweater)	Economic profit (TR – TC) (dollars)
7	175		141		34
		25		19	
8	200		160		40
		25		23	
9	225		183		42
		25		27	
10	250		210		40
		25		35	
11	275		245		30

Another way of finding the profit-maximizing output is to determine the output at which marginal revenue equals marginal cost. The table shows that if output increases from 8 to 9 sweaters, marginal cost is $23, which is less than the marginal revenue of $25. If output increases from 9 to 10 sweaters, marginal cost is $27, which exceeds the marginal revenue of $25. The figure shows that marginal cost and marginal revenue are equal when Swanky produces 9 sweaters a day. If marginal revenue exceeds marginal cost, an increase in output increases economic profit. If marginal revenue is less than marginal cost, an increase in output decreases economic profit. If marginal revenue equals marginal cost, economic profit is maximized.

The Firm's Short-Run Supply Curve

A perfectly competitive firm's short-run supply curve shows how the firm's profit-maximizing output varies as the market price varies, other things remaining the same. Figure 12.4 shows how to derive Swanky's supply curve. Part (a) shows Swanky's marginal cost and average variable cost curves, and part (b) shows its supply curve. There is a direct link between the marginal cost and average variable cost curves and the supply curve. Let's see what that link is.

Temporary Plant Shutdown   In the short run, a firm cannot avoid incurring its fixed cost. But it can avoid variable costs by temporarily laying off its workers and shutting down. If a firm shuts down, it produces no output and it incurs a loss equal to total fixed cost. This loss is the largest that a firm need incur. A firm shuts down if price falls below the minimum of average variable cost. The **shutdown point** is the output and price at which the firm just covers its total variable cost—point s in Fig. 12.4(a). If the price is $17, the marginal revenue curve is MR_0 and the profit-maximizing output is 7 sweaters a day at point s. But both price and average variable cost equal $17, so Swanky makes no economic profit on these 7 sweaters. Its economic loss equals its total fixed cost. At a price below $17, no matter what quantity Swanky produces, average *variable* cost exceeds price and the firm's loss exceeds fixed cost. At a price below $17, the firm shuts down.

The Short-Run Supply Curve   If the price is above minimum average variable cost, Swanky maximizes profit by producing the output at which marginal cost equals price. We can determine the quantity produced at each price from the marginal cost curve. At a price of $25, the marginal revenue curve is MR_1 and Swanky maximizes profit by producing 9 sweaters. At a price of $31, the marginal revenue curve is MR_2 and Swanky produces 10 sweaters.

Swanky's short-run supply curve, shown in Fig. 12.4(b), has two separate parts: First, at prices that exceed minimum average variable cost, the supply curve is the same as the marginal cost curve above the shutdown point (s). Second, at prices below minimum average variable cost, Swanky shuts down and produces nothing. Its supply curve runs along the vertical axis. At a price of $17, Swanky is indifferent between shutting down and producing 7 sweaters a day. Either way, it incurs a loss of $25 a day.

FIGURE 12.4

A Firm's Supply Curve

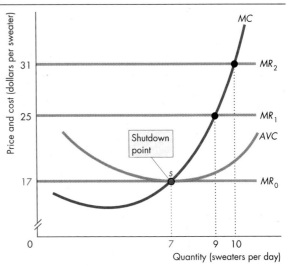

(a) Marginal cost and average variable cost

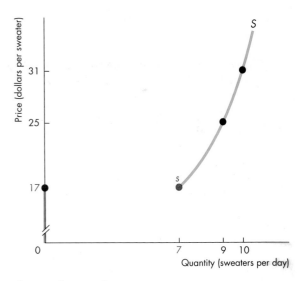

(b) Swanky's supply curve

Part (a) shows Swanky's profit-maximizing output at various market prices. At $25 a sweater, Swanky produces 9 sweaters. At $17 a sweater, Swanky produces 7 sweaters. At any price below $17 a sweater, Swanky produces nothing. Swanky's shutdown point is s. Part (b) shows Swanky's supply curve—the number of sweaters Swanky will produce at each price. It is made up of its marginal cost curve (part a) at all points above its average variable cost curve and the vertical axis at all prices below minimum average variable cost.

Short-Run Industry Supply Curve

The **short-run industry supply curve** shows the quantity supplied by the industry at each price when the plant size of each firm and the number of firms remain constant. The quantity supplied by the industry at a given price is the sum of the quantities supplied by all firms in the industry at that price.

Figure 12.5 shows the supply curve for the competitive sweater industry. In this example, the industry consists of 1,000 firms exactly like Swanky. At each price, the quantity supplied by the industry is 1,000 times the quantity supplied by a single firm.

The table in Fig. 12.5 shows the firm's and the industry's supply schedule and how the industry supply curve is constructed. At prices below $17, every firm in the industry shuts down; the quantity supplied by the industry is zero. At a price of $17, each firm is indifferent between shutting down and producing nothing or operating and producing 7 sweaters a day. Some firms will shut down, and others will supply 7 sweaters a day. The quantity supplied by each firm is *either* 0 or 7 sweaters, but the quantity supplied by the industry is *between* 0 (all firms shut down) and 7,000 (all firms produce 7 sweaters a day each).

To construct the industry supply curve, we sum the quantities supplied by the individual firms. Each of the 1,000 firms in the industry has a supply schedule like Swanky's. At prices below $17, the industry supply curve runs along the price axis. At a price of $17, the industry supply curve is horizontal—supply is perfectly elastic. As the price rises above $17, each firm increases its quantity supplied, and the quantity supplied by the industry increases by 1,000 times that of one firm.

R E V I E W

- In perfect competition, a firm is a price taker and its marginal revenue equals the market price.
- The lowest price at which a firm produces is equal to its minimum average variable cost.
- The firm's supply curve is its marginal cost curve at points above minimum average variable cost.
- The industry supply curve shows the sum of the quantities supplied by all the firms in the industry at each price.

FIGURE 12.5

Industry Supply Curve

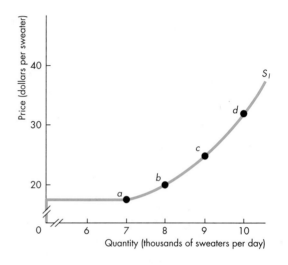

Price (dollars per sweater)	Quantity supplied by Swanky, Inc. (sweaters per day)	Quantity supplied by industry (sweaters per day)
a	17	0 or 7	0 to 7,000
b	20	8	8,000
c	25	9	9,000
d	31	10	10,000

The industry supply schedule is the sum of the supply schedules of all individual firms. An industry that consists of 1,000 identical firms has a supply schedule similar to that of the individual firm, but the quantity supplied by the industry is 1,000 times as large as that of the individual firm (see table). The industry supply curve is S_I. Points a, b, c, and d correspond to the rows of the table. At the shutdown price of $17, each firm produces either 0 or 7 sweaters per day, so the industry supply curve is perfectly elastic at the shutdown price.

So far, we have studied a single firm in isolation. We have seen that the firm's profit-maximizing actions depend on the market price, which the firm takes as given. But how is the market price determined? Let's find out.

Output, Price, and Profit in Perfect Competition

To DETERMINE THE MARKET PRICE AND THE quantity bought and sold in a perfectly competitive market, we need to study how market demand and market supply interact. We begin this process by studying a perfectly competitive market in the short run when the number of firms is fixed and each firm has a given plant size.

Short-Run Equilibrium

Industry demand and industry supply determine the market price and industry output. Figure 12.6(a) shows a short-run equilibrium. The supply curve S is the same as S_I in Fig. 12.5.

If demand is at the level shown by the demand curve D_1, the equilibrium price is $20. Although industry demand and supply determine this price, each firm takes the price as given and produces its

profit-maximizing output, which is 8 sweaters a day. Because the industry has 1,000 firms, industry output is 8,000 sweaters a day.

A Change in Demand

Changes in demand bring changes to short-run industry equilibrium. Figure 12.6(b) shows these changes.

If demand increases, the demand curve shifts rightward to D_2. The price rises to $25. At this price, each firm increases its output to maximize profit. The new output level is 9 sweaters a day for each firm and 9,000 sweaters a day for the industry.

If demand decreases, the demand curve shifts leftward to D_3. The price now falls to $17. At this price, each firm decreases its output to maximize profit. The new output level is 7 sweaters a day for each firm and 7,000 sweaters a day for the industry.

If the demand curve shifts farther leftward than D_3, the price remains constant at $17 because the industry supply curve is horizontal at that price. Some firms continue to produce 7 sweaters a day,

---

FIGURE 12.6
Short-Run Equilibrium

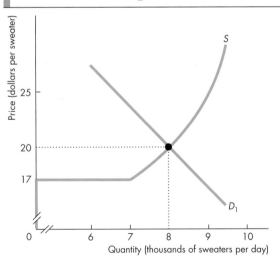

(a) Equilibrium

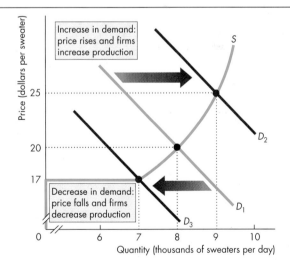

(b) Change in equilibrium

In part (a), the industry's supply curve is S. Demand is D_1, and the price is $20. At this price, each firm produces 8 sweaters a day and the industry produces 8,000 sweaters a day. In part (b), when demand increases to D_2, the price rises to $25 and

each firm increases its output to 9 sweaters a day. Industry output is 9,000 sweaters a day. When demand decreases to D_3, the price falls to $17 and each firm decreases its output to 7 sweaters a day. Industry output is 7,000 sweaters a day.

and others temporarily shut down. Firms are indifferent between these two activities, and, whichever they choose, they incur an economic loss equal to total fixed cost. The number of firms that continue to produce is just enough to satisfy the market demand at a price of $17.

Let's now look at the profits that firms make and the losses they can incur in a short-run equilibrium.

Profits and Losses in the Short Run

In short-run equilibrium, although the firm produces the profit-maximizing output, it does not necessarily end up making an economic profit. It might do so, but it might alternatively break even (with a normal profit) or incur an economic loss. To determine which of these outcomes occurs, we compare the firm's total revenue and total cost, or equivalently, we compare price with average total cost. If price equals average total cost, a firm breaks even—makes normal profit. If price exceeds average total cost, a firm makes an economic profit. If price is less than average total cost, a firm incurs an economic loss. Figure 12.7 shows these three possible short-run profit outcomes.

Three Possible Profit Outcomes In part (a), the price of a sweater is $20. Swanky produces 8 sweaters a day. Average total cost is also $20 a sweater, so Swanky makes normal profit and zero economic profit.

In part (b), the price of a sweater is $25. Profit is maximized when output is 9 sweaters a day. Here, price exceeds average total cost (ATC), so Swanky makes an economic profit. This economic profit is $42 a day. It is made up of $4.67 per sweater ($25.00 – $20.33) multiplied by the number of sweaters ($4.67 × 9 = $42). The blue rectangle shows this economic profit. The height of that rectangle is profit per sweater, $4.67, and the length is the quantity of sweaters produced, 9 a day, so the area of the rectangle measures Swanky's economic profit of $42 a day.

In part (c), the price of a sweater is $17. Here, price is less than average total cost and Swanky incurs an economic loss. Price and marginal revenue are $17 a sweater, and the profit-maximizing (in this case, loss-minimizing) output is 7 sweaters a day. Swanky's total revenue is $119 a day (7 × $17). Average total cost is $20.14 a sweater, so the economic loss is $3.14 per sweater ($20.14 – $17.00). This loss per sweater multiplied by the number of sweaters is $22 ($3.14 × 7 = $22). The red rectangle shows this

---

FIGURE 12.7

Three Possible Profit Outcomes in the Short Run

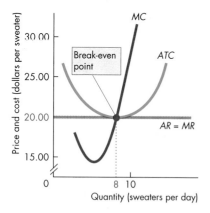

(a) Normal profit

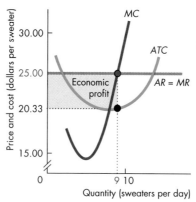

(b) Economic profit

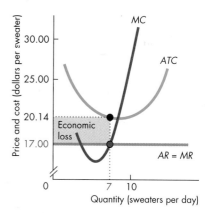

(c) Economic loss

In the short run, firms might break even (making a normal profit), make an economic profit, or incur an economic loss. If the price equals minimum average total cost, the firm breaks even and makes a normal profit (part a). If the price exceeds the average total cost of producing the profit-maximizing output, the firm makes an economic profit (the blue rectangle in part b). If the price is below minimum average total cost, the firm incurs an economic loss (the red rectangle in part c).

economic loss. The height of that rectangle is economic loss per sweater, $3.14, and the length is the quantity of sweaters produced, 7 a day, so the area of the rectangle measures Swanky's economic loss of $22 a day.

Long-Run Adjustments

In short-run equilibrium, a firm might make an economic profit, incur an economic loss, or break even (make normal profit). Although each of these three situations is a short-run equilibrium, only one of them is a long-run equilibrium. To see why, we need to examine the forces at work in a competitive industry in the long run.

In the long run, an industry adjusts in two ways:

■ Entry and exit
■ Changes in plant size

Let's look first at entry and exit.

Entry and Exit

In the long run, firms respond to economic profit and economic loss by either entering or exiting an industry. Firms enter an industry in which firms are making an economic profit, and they exit an industry in which firms are incurring an economic loss. Temporary economic profit or temporary economic loss, like the win or loss at a casino, do not trigger entry or exit. But the prospect of persistent economic profit or loss does.

Entry and exit influence price, the quantity produced, and economic profit. The immediate effect of these decisions is to shift the industry supply curve. If more firms enter an industry, supply increases and the industry supply curve shifts rightward. If firms exit an industry, supply decreases and the industry supply curve shifts leftward.

Let's see what happens when new firms enter an industry.

The Effects of Entry   Figure 12.8 shows the effects of entry. Suppose that all the firms in this industry have cost curves like those of Swanky in Fig. 12.7. At any price greater than $20, firms make an economic profit. At any price less than $20, firms incur an economic loss. And at a price of $20, firms make zero economic profit. Also suppose that the demand curve for sweaters is D. If the industry supply curve is S_1, sweaters sell for $23 and 7,000 sweaters a day are

produced. Firms in the industry make an economic profit. This economic profit is a signal for new firms to enter the industry. As these events unfold, supply increases and the industry supply curve shifts rightward to S_0. With the greater supply and unchanged demand, the market price falls from $23 to $20 a sweater and the quantity produced by the industry increases from 7,000 to 8,000 sweaters a day.

Industry output increases, but Swanky and the other firms in the industry *decrease* output! Because as the price falls, each firm moves down along its supply curve and produces less. But because the number of firms in the industry increases, the industry as a whole produces more.

Because price falls, each firm's economic profit decreases. When the price falls to $20, economic profit disappears and each firm makes a normal profit.

You have just discovered a key proposition:

As new firms enter an industry, the price falls and the economic profit of each existing firm decreases.

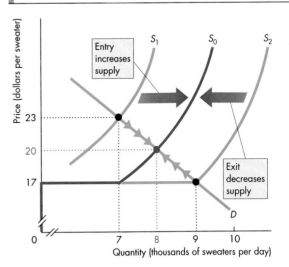

FIGURE 12.8

Entry and Exit

When new firms enter the sweater industry, the industry supply curve shifts rightward, from S_1 to S_0. The equilibrium price falls from $23 to $20, and the quantity produced increases from 7,000 to 8,000 sweaters. When firms exit the sweater industry, the industry supply curve shifts leftward, from S_2 to S_0. The equilibrium price rises from $17 to $20, and the quantity produced decreases from 9,000 to 8,000 sweaters.

An example of this process occurred during the 1980s in the personal computer industry. When IBM introduced its first PC, there was little competition and the price of a PC gave IBM a big profit. But new firms such as Compaq, NEC, Dell, and a host of others entered the industry with machines that were technologically identical to IBM's. In fact, they were so similar that they came to be called "clones." The massive wave of entry into the personal computer industry shifted the supply curve rightward and lowered the price and the economic profit for all firms.

Let's now look at the effects of exit.

The Effects of Exit   Figure 12.8 shows the effects of exit. Suppose that firms' costs and market demand are the same as before. But now suppose the supply curve is S_2. The market price is $17, and 9,000 sweaters a day are produced. Firms now incur an economic loss. This economic loss is a signal for some firms to exit the industry. As firms exit, the supply curve shifts leftward to S_0. With the decrease in supply, industry output decreases from 9,000 to 8,000 sweaters and the price rises from $17 to $20.

As the price rises, Swanky, like each other firm in the industry, moves up along its supply curve and increases output. That is, for each firm that remains in the industry, the profit-maximizing output increases. Because the price rises and each firm sells more, economic loss decreases. When the price rises to $20, each firm makes a normal profit.

You have just discovered a second key proposition:

As firms leave an industry, the price rises and the economic loss of each remaining firm decreases.

An example of a firm leaving an industry is International Harvester, a manufacturer of farm equipment. For decades, people associated the name "International Harvester" with tractors, combines, and other farm machines. But International Harvester wasn't the only maker of farm equipment. The industry became intensely competitive, and the firm began losing money.

International Harvester exited because it was incurring an economic loss. Its exit decreased supply and made it possible for the remaining firms in the industry to break even.

You've now seen how economic profits induce entry, which in turn lowers profits, and you've seen how economic losses induce exit, which in turn eliminates losses. Let's now look at changes in plant size.

Changes in Plant Size

A firm changes its plant size if, by doing so, it can lower its costs and increase its economic profit. You can probably think of lots of examples of firms changing their plant size.

One example that has almost certainly happened near your campus in recent years is a change in the plant size of Kinko's or similar copy shops. Another is the number if FedEx vans that you see on the streets and highways. Another is the number of square feet of retail space devoted to selling computers and video games. These are examples of firms increasing their plant size to seek larger profits.

There are also many examples of firms decreasing their plant size to avoid economic losses. One of these is Schwinn, the Chicago-based maker of bicycles. As competition from Asian bicycle makers became tougher, Schwinn cut back. Many firms have scaled back their operations—a process called *downsizing*—in recent years.

Figure 12.9 shows a situation in which Swanky can increase its profit by increasing its plant size. With its current plant, Swanky's marginal cost curve is MC_0 and its short-run average total cost curve is $SRAC_0$. The market price is $25 a sweater, so Swanky's marginal revenue curve is MR_0 and Swanky maximizes profit by producing 6 sweaters a day.

Swanky's long-run average cost curve is $LRAC$. By increasing its plant size—installing more knitting machines—Swanky can move along its long-run average cost curve. As Swanky increases its plant size, its short-run marginal cost curve shifts rightward.

Recall that a firm's short-run supply curve is linked to its marginal cost curve. As Swanky's marginal cost curve shifts rightward, so does its supply curve. If Swanky and the other firms in the industry increase their plants, the short-run industry supply curve shifts rightward and the market price falls. The fall in the market price limits the extent to which Swanky can profit from increasing its plant size.

Figure 12.9 also shows Swanky in a long-run competitive equilibrium. This situation arises when the market price has fallen to $20 a sweater. Marginal revenue is MR_1, and Swanky maximizes profit by producing 8 sweaters a day. In this situation, Swanky cannot increase its profit by changing its plant size. It is producing at minimum long-run average cost (point m on $LRAC$).

Because Swanky is producing at minimum long-run average cost, it has no incentive to change its plant

FIGURE 12.9

Plant Size and Long-Run Equilibrium

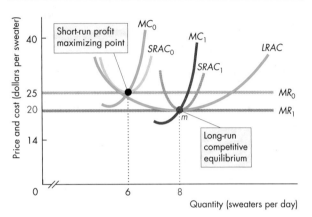

Initially, Swanky's plant has marginal cost curve MC_0 and short-run average total cost curve $SRAC_0$. The market price is \$25 a sweater, and Swanky's marginal revenue is MR_0. The short-run profit-maximizing quantity is 6 sweaters a day. Swanky can increase its profit by increasing its plant size. If all firms in the sweater industry increase their plant sizes, the short-run industry supply increases and the market price falls. In long-run equilibrium, a firm operates with the plant size that minimizes its average cost. Here, Swanky operates the plant with short-run marginal cost MC_1 and short-run average cost $SRAC_1$. Swanky is also on its long-run average cost curve $LRAC$ and produces at point m. Its output is 8 sweaters a day, and its average total cost equals the price of a sweater—\$20.

size. Either a bigger plant or a smaller plant has a higher long-run average cost. If Fig. 12.9 describes the situation of all firms in the sweater industry, the industry is in long-run equilibrium. No firm has an incentive to change its plant size. Also, because each firm is making zero economic profit (normal profit), no firm has an incentive to enter the industry or to leave it.

Long-Run Equilibrium

Long-run equilibrium occurs in a competitive industry when economic profit is zero (when firms earn normal profit). If the firms in a competitive industry are making an economic profit, new firms enter the

industry. If firms can lower their costs by increasing their plant size, they expand. Each of these actions increases industry supply, shifts the industry supply curve rightward, lowers the price falls, and decreases economic profit.

Firms continue to enter, and profit decreases as long as firms in the industry are earning positive economic profits. When economic profit has been eliminated, firms stop entering the industry. And when firms are operating with the least-cost plant size, they stop expanding.

If the firms in a competitive industry are incurring an economic loss, some firms exit the industry. If firms can lower their costs by decreasing their plant size, they downsize. Each of these actions decreases industry supply, shifts the industry supply curve leftward, raises the price falls, and increases economic profit (shrinks economic loss).

Firms continue to exit and profit increases as long as firms in the industry are incurring economic losses. When economic loss has been eliminated, firms stop exiting the industry. And when firms are operating with the least-cost plant size, they stop downsizing.

So in long-run equilibrium in a competitive industry, firms neither enter nor exit the industry and neither expand nor downsize. Each firm earns normal profit.

REVIEW

- A firm in perfect competition maximizes profit by producing the quantity at which marginal cost equals marginal revenue and price.
- Economic profits bring entry, which increases supply, lowers price, and decreases economic profit.
- Economic losses bring exit, which decreases supply, raises price, and increases economic profit.
- In long-run equilibrium, economic profit is zero and long-run average cost is at a minimum.

You've seen how a competitive industry adjusts toward its long-run equilibrium. But a competitive industry is rarely *in* a state of long-run equilibrium. It is constantly and restlessly evolving toward such an equilibrium. The constraints that firms in the industry face are constantly changing. The two most persistent sources of change are in tastes and technology. Let's see how a competitive industry reacts to such changes.

Changing Tastes and Advancing Technology

INCREASED AWARENESS OF THE HEALTH HAZARDS of smoking has caused a decrease in the demand for tobacco and cigarettes. The development of inexpensive car and air transportation has caused a huge decrease in the demand for long-distance trains and buses. Solid-state electronics have caused a large decrease in the demand for TV and radio repair. The development of good-quality inexpensive clothing has decreased the demand for sewing machines. What happens in a competitive industry when there is a permanent decrease in the demand for its products?

The development of the microwave oven has produced an enormous increase in demand for paper, glass, and plastic cooking utensils and for plastic wrap. The widespread use of the personal computer has brought a huge increase in the demand for floppy disks. What happens in a competitive industry when the demand for its product increases?

Advances in technology are constantly lowering the costs of production. New biotechnologies have dramatically lowered the costs of producing many food and pharmaceutical products. New electronic technologies have lowered the cost of producing just about every good and service. What happens in a competitive industry when technological change lowers its production costs?

Let's use the theory of perfect competition to answer these questions.

A Permanent Change in Demand

Figure 12.10(a) shows a competitive industry that initially is in long-run equilibrium. The demand curve is D_0, the supply curve is S_0, the market price is P_0, and industry output is Q_0. Figure 12.10(b) shows a single firm in this initial long-run equilibrium. The firm produces q_0 and makes a normal profit and zero economic profit.

Now suppose that demand decreases and the demand curve shifts leftward to D_1, as shown in part (a). The price falls to P_1, and the quantity supplied by the industry decreases from Q_0 to Q_1 as the industry slides down its short-run supply curve S_0. Part (b) shows the situation facing a firm. Price is now below the firm's minimum average total cost, so the firm incurs an economic loss. But to keep its loss to a

minimum, the firm adjusts its output to keep marginal cost equal to price. At a price of P_1, each firm produces an output of q_1.

The industry is now in short-run equilibrium but not long-run equilibrium. It is in short-run equilibrium because each firm is maximizing profit. But it is not in long-run equilibrium because each firm is incurring an economic loss—its average total cost exceeds the price.

The economic loss is a signal for some firms to leave the industry. As they do so, short-run industry supply gradually decreases and the supply curve gradually shifts leftward. As industry supply decreases, the price rises. At each higher price, a firm's profit-maximizing output is greater, so the firms remaining in the industry increase their output as the price rises. Each firm slides up its marginal cost or supply curve (part b). That is, as firms exit the industry, industry output decreases but the output of the firms that remain in the industry increases. Eventually, enough firms leave the industry for the industry supply curve to have shifted to S_1 (part a). At this time, the price has returned to its original level, P_0. At this price, the firms remaining in the industry produce q_0, the same quantity that they produced before the decrease in demand. Because firms are now making normal profits and zero economic profit, no firm wants to enter or exit the industry. The industry supply curve remains at S_1, and industry output is Q_2. The industry is again in long-run equilibrium.

The difference between the initial long-run equilibrium and the final long-run equilibrium is the number of firms in the industry. A permanent decrease in demand has decreased the number of firms. Each remaining firm produces the same output in the new long-run equilibrium as it did initially and earns a normal profit. In the process of moving from the initial equilibrium to the new one, firms incur economic losses.

We've just worked out how a competitive industry responds to a permanent *decrease* in demand. A permanent increase in demand triggers a similar response, except in the opposite direction. The increase in demand brings a higher price, economic profit, and entry. Entry increases industry supply and eventually lowers the price to its original level.

The demand for airline travel in the United States has increased permanently in recent years, and the deregulation of the airlines has freed up firms to seek profit opportunities in this industry. The result has been a massive rate of entry of new airlines. The

FIGURE 12.10

A Decrease in Demand

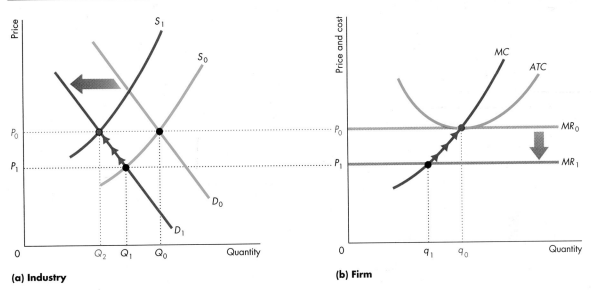

(a) Industry

(b) Firm

An industry starts out in long-run competitive equilibrium. Part (a) shows the industry demand curve D_0, the industry supply curve S_0, the equilibrium quantity Q_0, and the market price P_0. Each firm sells its output at price P_0, so its marginal revenue curve is MR_0 in part (b). Each firm produces q_0 and makes a normal profit. Demand decreases permanently from D_0 to D_1 (part a). The equilibrium price falls to P_1, each firm decreases its output to q_1 (part b), and industry output decreases to Q_1 (part a).

In this new situation, firms incur economic losses and some firms leave the industry. As they do so, the industry supply curve gradually shifts leftward, from S_0 to S_1. This shift gradually raises the market price from P_1 back to P_0. While the price is below P_0, firms incur economic losses and some firms leave the industry. Once the price has returned to P_0, each firm makes a normal profit. Firms have no further incentive to leave the industry. Each firm produces q_0, and industry output is Q_2.

---

process of competition and change in the airline industry is similar to what we have just studied (but with an increase in demand rather than a decrease in demand).

We've now studied the effects of a permanent change in demand for a good. To study these effects, we began and ended in a long-run equilibrium and examined the process that takes a market from one equilibrium to another. It is this process, not the equilibrium points, that describes the real world.

One feature of the predictions that we have just generated seems odd: In the long run, regardless of whether demand increases or decreases, the price returns to its original level. Is this outcome inevitable? In fact, it is not. It is possible for the long-run equilibrium price to remain the same, rise, or fall.

External Economies and Diseconomies

The change in the long-run equilibrium price depends on external economies and external diseconomies. **External economies** are factors beyond the control of an individual firm that lower its costs as the *industry* output increases. **External diseconomies** are factors outside the control of a firm that raise the firm's costs as industry output increases. With no external economies or external diseconomies, a firm's costs remain constant as the industry output changes.

Figure 12.11 illustrates these three cases and introduces a new supply concept: the long-run industry supply curve.

A **long-run industry supply curve** shows how the quantity supplied by an industry varies as the market price varies after all the possible adjustments have been made, including changes in plant size and the number of firms in the industry.

Part (a) shows the case we have just studied—no external economies or diseconomies. The long-run industry supply curve (LS_A) is perfectly elastic. In this case, a permanent increase in demand from D_0 to D_1 has no effect on the price in the long run. The increase in demand brings a temporary increase in price to P_S and a short-run quantity increase from Q_0 to Q_S. Entry increases short-run supply from S_0 to S_1, which lowers the price to its original level, P_0, and increases the quantity to Q_1.

Part (b) shows the case of external diseconomies. The long-run supply industry curve (LS_B) slopes upward. A permanent increase in demand from D_0 to D_1 increases the price in both the short run and the long run. As in the previous case, the increase in demand brings a temporary increase in price to P_S and a short-run quantity increase from Q_0 to Q_S. Entry increases short-run supply from S_0 to S_2, which lowers the price to P_2 and increases the quantity to Q_2.

One source of external diseconomies is congestion. The airline industry provides a good example. With bigger airline industry output, there is more congestion of airports and airspace, which results in longer delays and extra waiting time for passengers and airplanes. These external diseconomies mean that as the output of air transportation services increases (in the absence of technological advances), average cost increases. As a result, the long-run supply curve is upward sloping. So a permanent increase in demand brings an increase in quantity and a rise in the price. Technological advances decrease costs and *shift* the long-run supply curve downward. So even an industry that experiences external diseconomies might have falling prices over the long run.

Part (c) shows the case of external economies. In this case, the long-run industry supply curve (LS_C) slopes downward. A permanent increase in demand from D_0 to D_1 increases the price in the short run and lowers it in the long run. Again, the increase in demand brings a temporary increase in price to P_S and a short-run quantity increase from Q_0 to Q_S. Entry increases short-run supply from S_0 to S_3, which lowers the price to P_3 and increases the quantity to Q_3.

FIGURE 12.11
Long-Run Changes in Price and Quantity

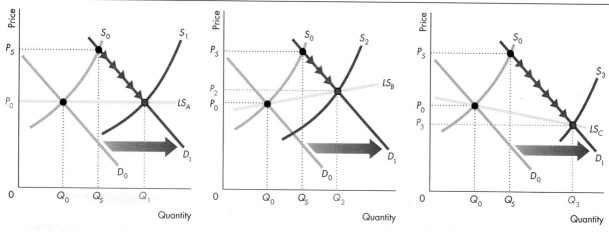

(a) Constant-cost industry

(b) Increasing-cost industry

(c) Decreasing-cost industry

Three possible changes in price and quantity occur in the long run. When demand increases from D_0 to D_1, entry occurs and the industry supply curve shifts from S_0 to S_1. In part (a), the long-run supply curve, LS_A, is horizontal. The quantity increases from Q_0 to Q_1, and the price remains constant at P_0. In part

(b), the long-run supply curve is LS_B; the price rises to P_2, and the quantity increases to Q_2. This case occurs in industries with external diseconomies. In part (c), the long-run supply curve is LS_C; the price falls to P_3, and the quantity increases to Q_3. This case occurs in an industry with external economies.

One of the best examples of external economies is the growth of specialist support services for an industry as it expands. As farm output increased in the nineteenth and early twentieth centuries, the services available to farmers expanded and average farm costs fell. For example, new firms specialized in the development and marketing of farm machinery and fertilizers. As a result, average farm costs decreased. Farms enjoyed the benefits of external economies. As a consequence, as the demand for farm products increased, the output increased but the price fell.

Over the long term, the prices of many goods and services have fallen, not because of external economies but because of technological change. Let's now study this influence on a competitive market.

Technological Change

Industries are constantly discovering lower-cost techniques of production. Most cost-saving production techniques cannot be implemented, however, without investing in new plant and equipment. As a consequence, it takes time for a technological advance to spread through an industry. Some firms whose plants are on the verge of being replaced will be quick to adopt the new technology, while other firms whose plants have recently been replaced will continue to operate with an old technology until they can no longer cover their average variable cost. Once average variable cost cannot be covered, a firm will scrap even a relatively new plant (embodying an old technology) in favor of a plant with a new technology.

New technology allows firms to produce at a lower cost. As a result, as firms adopt a new technology, their cost curves shift downward. With lower costs, firms are willing to supply a given quantity at a lower price, or, equivalently, they are willing to supply a larger quantity at a given price. In other words, industry supply increases, and the industry supply curve shifts rightward. With a given demand, the quantity produced increases and the price falls.

Two forces are at work in an industry undergoing technological change. Firms that adopt the new technology make an economic profit. So there is entry by new-technology firms. Firms that stick with the old technology incur economic losses. They either exit the industry or switch to the new technology.

As old-technology firms disappear and new-technology firms enter, the price falls and the quantity produced increases. Eventually, the industry arrives at a long-run equilibrium in which all the firms use the new technology and make a zero economic profit (a normal profit). Because in the long run competition eliminates economic profit, technological change brings only temporary gains to producers. But the lower prices and better products that technological advances bring are permanent gains for consumers.

The process that we've just described is one in which some firms experience economic profits and others experience economic losses. It is a period of dynamic change for an industry. Some firms do well, and others do badly. Often, the process has a geographical dimension—the expanding new-technology firms bring prosperity to what was once the boondocks, and traditional industrial regions decline. Sometimes, the new-technology firms are in a foreign country, while the old-technology firms are in the domestic economy. The information revolution of the 1990s has produced many examples of changes like these. Commercial banking, traditionally concentrated in New York, San Francisco, and other large cities, now flourishes in Charlotte, North Carolina, which has become the nation's number three commercial banking city. Television shows and movies, traditionally made in Los Angeles and New York, are now made in large numbers in Orlando, Florida. Technological advances are not confined to the information and entertainment industry. Even milk production is undergoing a major technological change because of genetic engineering.

R E V I E W

■ A decrease in demand in a competitive industry brings a fall in price, economic loss, and exit. Exit decreases industry supply, which brings a rise in price. In the long run, enough firms exit for those remaining to make a normal profit.

■ An increase in demand in a competitive industry brings a rise in price, economic profit, and entry. Entry increases industry supply, which brings a fall in price. In the long run, enough firms enter for the economic profit to decrease to zero and leave firms making a normal profit.

■ A new technology lowers costs, increases supply, and lowers price. Firms that adopt the new technology make an economic profit, and firms that do not use it incur an economic loss and exit. In the long run, all remaining firms adopt the new technology and make normal profit.

Competition and Efficiency

DOES A PERFECTLY COMPETITIVE INDUSTRY produce the right quantities of goods and services at the right prices? Is perfect competition efficient?

Efficiency

Resources are used efficiently when no one can become better off without someone else becoming worse off (see Chapter 6, pp. 112–113). If someone can become better off without anyone else becoming worse off, resources are not being used efficiently. For example, suppose a school has a computer that no one uses and that no one will ever use. Suppose also that the students in another school are clamoring for an extra computer. If the computer is reallocated from the first school to the second, some people are better off and no one is worse off.

Resources are used efficiently when there is:

1. Consumer efficiency
2. Producer efficiency
3. Exchange efficiency

Consumer Efficiency   Consumers allocate their budgets to get the most value possible out of them. **Consumer efficiency** is achieved when it is not possible for consumers to become better off—to increase utility—by reallocating their budgets.

Consumers have allocated their budgets efficiently when they have equalized the marginal utility from each dollar spent (see Chapter 8, pp. 159–161). This condition is met at all points along a household's demand curve. So, when a household is on its demand curve, it has achieved consumer efficiency.

If there are no *external benefits*, an entire market achieves consumer efficiency at any point on the *market* demand curve. **External benefits** are benefits that accrue to people other than the buyer of a good. For example, you might get pleasure (utility) from your neighbor's expenditure on her garden. Your neighbor buys the quantities of garden plants that maximize her utility, not hers plus yours.

In the absence of externalities, the market demand curve measures *marginal benefit*—the value that consumers place on one more unit of a good or service. So when consumers are on their demand curves, consumer efficiency is achieved.

Producer Efficiency   When firms cannot lower the cost of producing a given output by changing the resources they use, they have achieved producer efficiency. A firm achieves **producer efficiency** at any point on its marginal cost curve or, equivalently, on its supply curve.

If there are no *external costs*, a market achieves producer efficiency at any point on the *market* (or *industry*) supply curve. **External costs** are costs not borne by the producer of a good or service but borne by someone else. For example, a firm might lower its own costs by polluting. The cost of pollution is an external cost. Firms produce the output level that maximizes their own profit, and they do not count the cost of pollution as a charge against their profit.

In the absence of externalities, the market supply curve measures the opportunity cost that firms incur to produce the various quantities of a good or service and along the market supply curve, firms are maximizing profit. (Two separate conditions are met when producer efficiency is achieved: *technological efficiency*—maximum possible output from productive resources—and *economic efficiency*—resources are used in the combination that minimizes cost. See Chapter 10, pp. 204–205.)

Exchange Efficiency   When all the gains from trade have been realized, **exchange efficiency** is achieved. The gains from trade for consumers are measured by *consumer surplus*, which is the value that consumers place on a good minus the price paid for it. Consumer surplus is measured by the area between the demand curve and the price paid. (See Chapter 6, p. 115, for a more detailed explanation of consumer surplus.)

The gains from trade for producers are measured by *producer surplus*, which is the total revenue that producers receive for a good minus the opportunity cost of producing it. Opportunity cost equals marginal cost, and the competitive firm's marginal cost curve is its supply curve. Because producer surplus is total revenue minus opportunity cost, it is measured by the area between the price received and the supply curve.

The total gains from trade are the sum of consumer surplus and producer surplus.

An Efficient Allocation   Figure 12.12 shows an efficient allocation. Consumer efficiency is achieved at all points on the demand curve, D. Producer efficiency is achieved at all points on the supply curve, S. Exchange efficiency is achieved at the quantity Q^*

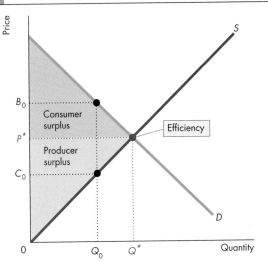

FIGURE 12.12

Efficiency of Competition

The efficient use of resources requires *consumer efficiency,* which occurs when consumers are on their demand curves; *producer efficiency,* which occurs when firms are on their supply curves; and *exchange efficiency,* which occurs when all the gains from trade have been realized. Resources are used efficiently at the quantity Q^* and the price P^*. With no external benefits and external costs, perfect competition achieves an efficient use of resources. If output is Q_0, some gains from trade are not realized. The cost of producing one more unit, C_0, is less than its marginal benefit, B_0. At the output Q_0, the sum of consumer and producer surplus is not maximized.

and price P^*. In this situation, the sum of producer surplus (blue area) and consumer surplus (green area) is maximized.

To see that the gains from trade cannot be increased, imagine that output is restricted to Q_0. The cost of producing one more unit is C_0, and the value placed on one more unit by consumers is B_0. Producers are willing to supply more of the good for a price lower than B_0. Consumers are willing to buy more of the good for a price higher than C_0. Everyone would like to trade more and get more consumer surplus and producer surplus. If output exceeded Q^*, the cost of producing one more unit would exceed the value placed on it. Only at Q^* does the value the consumer places on the last unit bought equal its cost of production and are the gains from trade maximized.

Efficiency of Perfect Competition

Perfect competition achieves efficiency if there are no external benefits and costs. In such a case, the benefits accrue to the buyers of the good and the costs are borne by its producer. In Fig. 12.12, the equilibrium quantity Q^* at the price P^* is efficient.

There are three main obstacles to efficiency:

1. Monopoly
2. Public goods
3. External costs and external benefits

Monopoly   Monopoly (Chapter 13) restricts output below its competitive level to raise price and increase profit. Government policies (Chapter 19) arise to limit such use of monopoly power.

Public goods   Goods such as national defense, the enforcement of law and order, the provision of clean drinking water, and the disposal of sewage and garbage are examples of goods and services in which there are public goods. Left to competitive markets, too small a quantity of them would be produced. Government institutions and policies (Chapter 18) help to overcome the problem of providing an efficient quantity of public goods.

External Costs and External Benefits   The production of steel and chemicals can generate air and water pollution and perfect competition might produce too large a quantity of these goods. Government policies (Chapter 20) attempt to cope with external costs and benefits.

◆ You've now completed your study of perfect competition. *Reading Between the Lines* on pp. 258–259 gives you an opportunity to use what you have learned to understand recent events in a highly competitive world market for steel.

Although many markets approximate the model of perfect competition, many do not. Your next task is to study markets at the opposite extreme of perfect competition—monopoly. Then, in Chapter 14, we'll study markets that lie between perfect competition and monopoly—monopolistic competition (competition with monopoly elements) and oligopoly (competition among a few producers). When you have completed this study, you'll have a tool kit that enables you to understand the variety of real-world markets.

Competition in Steel

The Wall Street Journal, July 18, 1996

U.S. Steelmakers Run Mills Close to Capacity But Still Earn Little

BY ERLE NORTON

The painful bloodletting of the 1980s left the titans of the American steel industry leaner and smarter. Or so it would seem.

Yet, despite strong demand and slowing imports, some major steelmakers are earning just a measly few bucks a ton. ...

Lester Telser, a University of Chicago economist, says steel, with its high fixed costs, has always been a troubled industry. ...

And big steelmakers' inability to make much money is raising questions about what will happen when demand dries up, as it inevitably will in such a cyclical business. ... And new competitors have emerged; among them are the minimills, which make steel fast and cheaply by melting steel scrap into thin slabs rather than, like integrated producers, starting out with raw materials - iron ore, coke and limestone.

Prof. Telser says the industry's situation won't improve without further bloodletting, with some major producers going under and with others merging and closing capacity. ...

Steelmakers say the low profits belie inherent strengths and a transformation of their operations. They have closed outdated plants and invested in winners. ...

Steel is a commodity: No matter how you roll it, cut it or coat it, it is much the same, although variations in quality are important to some customers. To most, all that matters is price. ...

...[T]o make operations even marginally profitable, big steelmakers must run full-out. It's like a car that is more efficient at 55 miles an hour than in stop-and-go traffic at 25. ...

Pricing is a problem industry-wide. The average price of steel fell 5.9% in the second quarter to $493 a ton from $524 a year earlier. ...

And the outlook isn't very cheery. ... [N]ew minimills are expected to add 15 million to 20 million tons of low-cost sheet steel product. ...

Two decades ago, the six major integrated steelmakers controlled two-thirds of the industry. Today, amid dozens of steelmakers, the Big Six control only a third of it. In addition to minimills, new players include mills discarded by the big producers and reincarnated as employee-owned companies or joint ventures with foreign companies. Sharon Steel Corp. in Sharon, Pa., was bankrupt twice and is back again as the Caparo Steel unit of British-based Caparo Group Ltd. ...

Essence of THE STORY

■ Despite strong demand, some steelmakers are earning small profits.

■ The price of steel fell during the second quarter of 1996 from $524 per ton to $493 per ton.

■ Firms that use new minimills, employee-owned firms, and firms in joint ventures with foreign companies have entered the market. Some firms have left the market.

Economic

A N A L Y S I S

■ The steel industry is experiencing technological change that is lowering the cost of production.

■ Producers that adopt the new technology make an economic profit. So more firms are entering the industry and using the new technology.

■ Producers that use the old technology have higher costs than the new producers. Some of them are incurring economic losses and exiting.

■ Parts (a) and (b) of the figure show the situation in the industry before the new-technology firms entered.

■ In part (a), the industry demand curve is D and the industry supply curve is S_0. The price is $524 a ton, and the quantity produced by the industry is Q_0.

■ Part (b) shows the cost curves of an old-technology steel producer. The marginal cost curve is MC_O, the marginal revenue curve is MR_O, and the average total cost curve is ATC_O. At a price of $524 a ton, the firm maximizes profit by producing q_0^O tons. Economic profit is zero.

■ Part (c) of the figure shows the average total cost curve, ATC_N, and the marginal cost curve, MC_N, for producing steel using new minimills.

■ At a price of $524 a ton, minimills can make an economic profit (price exceeds average total cost) so minimill firms enter the industry.

■ In part (a), as minimill producers enter the industry, supply increases and the industry supply curve shift rightward to S_1.

■ The price of steel falls. During the second quarter of 1996, the price fell from $524 per ton to $493 per ton, as shown in part (a).

■ The fall in price is bad news for the old-technology firms. They are now faced with marginal revenue curve MR_1 in part (b). With the lower price (marginal revenue), these firms maximize profit by cutting production to q_1^O tons. But they now incur an economic loss (the red rectangle).

■ In part (c), the new minimills continue to make an economic profit even at the lower price (the blue rectangle).

■ Because old-technology firms are incurring an economic loss, they will gradually exit the industry.

■ Because minimills are earning economic profit, they will continue to enter the industry.

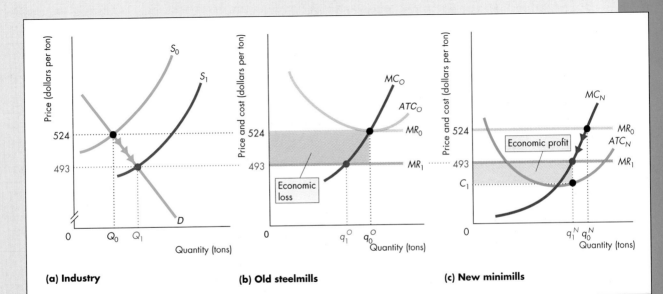

(a) Industry **(b) Old steelmills** **(c) New minimills**

SUMMARY

Key Points

Perfect Competition (pp. 240–246)

■ A perfectly competitive firm is a price taker.

■ The firm produces the output at which marginal revenue (price) equals marginal cost.

■ If price is less than minimum average variable cost, the firm temporarily shuts down.

■ A firm's supply curve is the upward-sloping part of its marginal cost curve above minimum average variable cost.

■ An industry supply curve shows the sum of the quantities supplied by each firm at each price.

Output, Price, and Profit in Perfect Competition (pp. 247–251)

■ Market demand and market supply determine price.

■ The firm produces the output at which price, which is marginal revenue, equals marginal cost.

■ In short-run equilibrium, a firm can make an economic profit, incur an economic loss, or break even.

■ Economic profit induces entry. Economic loss induces exit.

■ Entry and plant expansion increase supply and lower price and profit. Exit and plant contraction decrease supply and raise price and profit.

■ In long-run equilibrium, economic profit is zero (firms earn normal profit). There is no entry, exit, plant expansion, or plant contraction.

Changing Tastes and Advancing Technology (pp. 252–255)

■ A permanent decrease in demand leads to a smaller industry output and a smaller number of firms.

■ A permanent increase in demand leads to a larger industry output and a larger number of firms.

■ The long-run effect of a change in demand on price depends on whether there are external economies (price falls) or external diseconomies (price rises) or neither (price remains constant).

■ New technologies increase supply and in the long run lower the price and increase the quantity.

Competition and Efficiency (pp. 256–257)

■ Resources are used efficiently when no one can be better off without someone else being worse off.

■ Three conditions for the efficient use of resources—producer efficiency, consumer efficiency, and exchange efficiency—occur in perfect competition when there are no external costs and external benefits.

■ The two main obstacles to using resources efficiently are the existence of external costs and external benefits and monopoly.

Key Figures

Key Terms

QUESTIONS

1. What are the main features of a perfectly competitive industry?

2. Why can't a perfectly competitive firm influence the industry price?

3. List the four key decisions that a firm in a perfectly competitive industry has to make to maximize profit.

4. Why is marginal revenue equal to price in a perfectly competitive industry?

5. When will a perfectly competitive firm temporarily stop producing?

6. In a perfectly competitive industry, what is the connection between the firm's supply curve and its marginal cost curve?

7. In a perfectly competitive industry, what is the relationship between a firm's supply curve and the short-run industry supply curve?

8. When will firms enter an industry and when will they leave it?

9. What happens to the short-run industry supply curve when firms enter a competitive industry?

10. What is the effect of entry on the market price and quantity produced?

11. What is the effect of entry on economic profit?

12. Trace the effects of a permanent increase in demand on price, quantity sold, number of firms, and economic profit.

13. Trace the effects of a permanent decrease in demand on price, quantity sold, number of firms, and economic profit.

14. What are external economies and external diseconomies?

15. Under what circumstances will a perfectly competitive industry have
    a. A perfectly elastic long-run supply curve?
    b. An upward-sloping long-run supply curve?
    c. A downward-sloping long-run supply curve?

16. Under what circumstances are resources used efficiently?

17. What are external costs and external benefits?

18. What are the gains from trade?

19. What are the obstacles to efficiency?

PROBLEMS

1. Quick Copy is one of the many copy shops near the campus. The figure shows Quick Copy's cost curves.

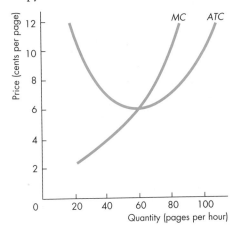

a. If the market price of copying one page is 10 cents, what is Quick Copy's profit-maximizing output?

b. Calculate Quick Copy's economic profit.

2. Pat's Pizza Kitchen is a price taker. It has the following hourly costs:

Output (pizzas per hour)	Total cost (dollars per hour)
0	10
1	21
2	30
3	41
4	54
5	69

a. If a pizza sells for $14, what is Pat's profit-maximizing output per hour? How much economic profit does Pat make?

b. What is Pat's shutdown point?

c. Derive Pat's supply curve.

d. What range of prices will cause Pat to leave the pizza industry?

e. What range of prices will cause other firms with costs identical to Pat's to enter the industry?

f. What is the long-run equilibrium price of a pizza?

3. The market demand schedule for cassettes is as follows:

Price (dollars per cassettes)	Quantity demanded (thousands of cassettes per week)
3.65	500
5.20	450
6.80	400
8.40	350
10.00	300
11.60	250
13.20	200
14.80	150

The market is perfectly competitive, and each firm has the following cost structure:

Output (cassettes per week)	Marginal cost (dollars per additional cassette)	Average variable cost	Average total cost
		(dollars per cassette)	
150	6.00	8.80	15.47
200	6.40	7.80	12.80
250	7.00	7.00	11.00
300	7.65	7.10	10.43
350	8.40	7.20	10.06
400	10.00	7.50	10.00
450	12.40	8.00	10.22
500	12.70	9.00	11.00

There are 1,000 firms in the industry.
a. What is the market price?
b. What is the industry's output?
c. What is the output of each firm?
d. What is the economic profit of each firm?
e. What is the shutdown point?
f. What is the long-run equilibrium price?
g. What is the number of firms in the long run?

4. The same demand conditions as those in problem 3 prevail, and there are still 1,000 firms in the industry, but fixed costs increase by $980.
a. What is the short-run profit-maximizing output for each firm?
b. Do firms enter or exit the industry?
c. What is the new long-run equilibrium price?
d. What is the new long-run equilibrium number of firms in the industry?

5. The same cost conditions as those in problem 3 prevail, and there are 1,000 firms in the industry, but a fall in the price of compact discs decreases the demand for cassettes, and the demand schedule becomes as follows:

Price (dollars per cassette)	Quantity demanded (thousands of cassettes per week)
2.95	500
4.13	450
5.30	400
6.48	350
7.65	300
8.83	250
10.00	200
11.18	150

a. What is the short-run profit-maximizing output for each firm?
b. Do firms enter or exit the industry in the long run?
c. What is the new long-run equilibrium price?
d. What is the new long-run equilibrium number of firms in the industry?

CRITICAL THINKING

1. After you have studied *Reading Between the Lines* on pp. 258–259, answer the following questions.
a. What were the main economic problems that faced U.S. steel producers during the 1980s?
b. What have the firms in the industry done in the face of these problems?
c. Why does Lester Telser say there must be more bloodletting in the industry? Do you agree with him? Why or why not?

2. Why have the prices of pocket calculators and VCRs fallen? What do you expect has happened to the costs and economic profits of the firms that make these products?

3. What has been the effect of an increase in world population on the wheat market and the individual wheat farmer?

4. How has the diaper service industry been affected by the decrease in the U.S. birth rate and the development of disposable diapers?

13

Monopoly

You have been reading a lot in this book about firms that want to maximize profit. But perhaps you've been looking around at some of the places where you do business and wondering whether they are really so intent on profit. After all, don't you get a student's discount when you get a haircut? Don't museums and movie theaters give discounts to students, too? And what about the airline that gives a discount for buying a ticket in advance? Are your barber and movie theater owner, as well as the museum and airline operators, simply generous folks to whom the model of profit-maximizing firms does not apply? Aren't they simply throwing profit away by cutting ticket prices and offering discounts?

The Profits of Generosity

◆ When you buy electric power, you don't shop around. You buy from your electric power utility, which is your only available supplier. If you live in New York City and want cable TV service, you have only one option: buy from Manhattan Cable. These are examples of a single producer of a good or service controlling its supply. Such firms are obviously not like firms in perfectly competitive industries. They don't face a market-determined price. They can choose their own price. How do such firms behave? How do they choose the quantity to produce and the price at which to sell it? How does their behavior compare with firms in perfectly competitive industries? Do such firms charge prices that are too high and that damage the interests of consumers? Do such firms bring any benefits? ◆ In this chapter, we study markets in which an individual firm can influence the quantity of goods supplied and exert an influence on price. We also compare the performance of a firm in such markets with that of a competitive market and examine whether monopoly is as efficient as competition.

After studying this chapter, you will be able to:

- ■ Define monopoly and explain the conditions under which it arises
- ■ Distinguish between price-discriminating monopoly and single-price monopoly
- ■ Explain how a single-price monopoly determines its price and output
- ■ Explain how a price-discriminating monopoly determines its price and output and how price discrimination increases profit
- ■ Compare the performance and efficiency of competition and monopoly
- ■ Define rent seeking and explain why it arises

How Monopoly Arises

THE SUPPLIERS OF LOCAL PHONE SERVICES, GAS, electricity, and water are monopolies. A **monopoly** is an industry that produces a good or service for which no close substitute exists and in which there is one supplier that is protected from competition by a barrier preventing the entry of new firms. In most places, the phone, gas, electricity, and water suppliers are local monopolies—monopolies restricted to a given location. Microsoft Corp., the software developer that created Windows, the operating system used by PCs, is an example of a global monopoly. A monopoly has two key features:

- No close substitutes
- Barriers to entry

No Close Substitutes

If a good has a close substitute, even though only one firm produces the good, that firm effectively faces competition from the producers of substitutes. Water supplied by a local public utility is an example of a good that does not have close substitutes. While it does have a close substitute for drinking—bottled spring water—it has no effective substitutes for showering or washing a car.

Monopolies are constantly under attack from new products and ideas that substitute for products produced by monopolies. For example, FedEx, UPS, the fax machine, and e-mail have weakened the monopoly of the U.S. Postal Service. Similarly, the satellite dish has weakened the monopoly of cable television companies.

But new products also are constantly creating monopolies. An example is Microsoft's monopoly in DOS during the 1980s and in the Windows operating system today.

Barriers to Entry

Barriers to entry are legal or natural constraints that protect a firm from potential competitors. A firm can sometimes create its own barrier to entry by acquiring a significant portion of a key resource. An example is DeBeers, a South African firm that controls more than 80 percent of the world's supply of natural diamonds.

But most monopolies arise from two other types of barrier: legal barriers and natural barriers.

Legal Barriers to Entry   Legal barriers to entry create legal monopoly. A **legal monopoly** is a market in which competition and entry are restricted by the granting of a public franchise, government license, patent, or copyright.

A *public franchise* is an exclusive right granted to a firm to supply a good or service. Examples are the U.S. Postal Service, which has the exclusive right to carry first-class mail. A *government license* controls entry into particular occupations, professions, and industries. Examples of this type of barrier to entry are medicine, law, dentistry, schoolteaching, architecture, and many other professional services. Licensing does not always create monopoly, but it does restrict competition.

A *patent* is an exclusive right granted to the inventor of a product or service. A *copyright* is an exclusive right granted to the author or composer of a literary, musical, dramatic, or artistic work. Patents and copyrights are valid for a limited time period that varies from country to country. In the United States, a patent is valid for 20 years. Patents encourage the *invention* of new products and production methods. They also stimulate *innovation*—the use of new inventions—by encouraging inventors to publicize their discoveries and offer them for use under license. Patents have stimulated innovations in areas as diverse as soybean seeds, pharmaceuticals, memory chips, and video games.

Natural Barriers to Entry   Natural barriers to entry create **natural monopoly**, which is an industry in which one firm can supply the entire market at a lower price than two or more firms can.

Figure 13.1 shows a natural monopoly in the distribution of electric power. Here, the demand curve for electric power is *D*, and the average total cost curve is *ATC*. Because average total cost decreases as output increases, economies of scale prevail over the entire length of the *ATC* curve. One firm can produce 4 million kilowatt-hours at 5 cents a kilowatt-hour. At this price, the quantity demanded is 4 million kilowatt-hours. So if the price was 5 cents, one firm could supply the entire market. If two firms shared the market, it would cost each of them 10 cents a kilowatt-hour to produce a total of 4 million kilowatt-hours. If four firms shared the market, it would cost each of them 15 cents a kilowatt-hour to produce a total of 4 million kilowatt-hours. So, in conditions like those shown in Fig. 13.1, one firm can supply the entire market at a lower cost than two or more firms can. The distribution of electric power is an example of natural monopoly. So is the distribution of water and gas.

Most monopolies are regulated in some way by government agencies. We will study such regulation in Chapter 19. Here we will study unregulated monopoly for two reasons. First, we can better understand why governments regulate monopolies and the effects of regulation if we also know how an unregulated monopoly behaves. Second, even in industries with more than one producer, firms often have a degree of monopoly power and the theory of monopoly sheds light on the behavior of such firms and industries.

A major difference between monopoly and competition is that a monopoly sets its own price. But it faces a market constraint. Let's see how the market limits a monopoly's pricing choices.

FIGURE 13.1
Natural Monopoly

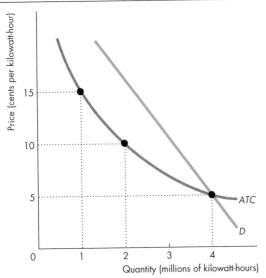

The demand curve for electric power is D, and the average total cost curve is ATC. Economies of scale exist over the entire ATC curve. One firm can distribute 4 million kilowatt-hours at a cost of 5 cents a kilowatt-hour. This same total output costs 10 cents a kilowatt-hour with two firms and 15 cents a kilowatt-hour with four firms. So one firm can meet the market demand at a lower cost than two or more firms can, and the market is a natural monopoly.

Monopoly Price-Setting Strategies

ALL MONOPOLIES FACE A TRADEOFF BETWEEN price and the quantity sold. To sell a larger quantity, the monopolist must charge a lower price. But there are two broad monopoly situations that create different tradeoffs. They are:

- Price discrimination
- Single price

Price Discrimination

Many firms price discriminate, and most are *not* monopolies. Airlines offer a dizzying array of different prices for the same trip. Pizza producers charge one price for a single pizza and almost give away a second pizza. These firms are practicing *price discrimination*. **Price discrimination** is the practice of selling different units of a good or service for different prices. Different customers might pay different prices (like airline passengers), or one customer might pay different prices for different quantities bought (like the bargain price for a second pizza).

When a firm price discriminates, it looks as if it is doing its customers a favor. In fact, it is charging the highest possible price for each unit sold and making the largest possible profit.

Not all monopolies can price discriminate. The main obstacle to price discrimination is resale by customers who buy for a low price. Because of resale possibilities, price discrimination is limited to monopolies that sell services that cannot be resold.

Single Price

DeBeers sells diamonds (of a given size and quality) for the same price to all its customers. If it tried to sell at a low price to some customers and at a higher price to others, only the low-price customers would buy. They would resell to those customers whom DeBeers wants to charge a high price.

DeBeers is a *single-price* monopoly. A **single-price monopoly** is a firm that must sell each unit of its output for the same price. All the firm's customers pay the same price for each unit they buy.

We'll look first at single-price monopoly because its key principle applies to the price discrimination.

Single-Price Monopoly

THE STARTING POINT FOR UNDERSTANDING HOW a single-price monopoly chooses its price and output is to work out the relationship between price and marginal revenue.

Price and Marginal Revenue

Because in a monopoly there is only one firm, the firm's demand curve is the market demand curve. Let's look at Bobbie's Barbershop, the sole supplier of haircuts in Cairo, Nebraska. The table in Fig. 13.2 shows Bobbie's demand schedule. At a price of $20, she sells no haircuts. The lower the price, the more haircuts per hour Bobbie can sell. For example, at $12, consumers demand 4 haircuts per hour (row *e*).

Total revenue (*TR*) is the price (*P*) multiplied by the quantity sold (*Q*). For example, in row *d*, Bobbie sells 3 haircuts at $14 each, so total revenue is $42. *Marginal revenue* (*MR*) is the change in total revenue (ΔTR) resulting from a one-unit increase in the quantity sold. For example, if the price falls from $16 (row *c*) to $14 (row *d*), the quantity sold increases from 2 to 3 haircuts. Total revenue rises from $32 to $42, so the change in total revenue is $10. Because the quantity sold increases by 1 haircut, marginal revenue equals the change in total revenue and is $10. Marginal revenue is placed between the two rows to emphasize that marginal revenue relates to the *change* in the quantity sold.

Figure 13.2 shows Bobbie's demand curve (*D*) and marginal revenue curve (*MR*) and also illustrates the calculation we've just made. Notice that at each level of output, marginal revenue is less than price— the marginal revenue curve lies below the demand curve. Why is marginal revenue less than price? The reason is that when the price is lowered to sell one more unit, two opposing forces affect total revenue. The lower price results in a revenue loss, and the increased quantity sold results in a revenue gain. For example, at a price of $16, Bobbie sells 2 haircuts (point *c*). If she lowers the price to $14, she sells 3 haircuts and has a revenue gain of $14 on the third haircut. But she now receives only $14 on the first two—$2 less than before. As a result, she loses $4 of revenue on the first 2 haircuts. To calculate marginal revenue, she must deduct this amount from the revenue gain of $14. So her marginal revenue is $10, which is less than the price.

FIGURE 13.2

Demand and Marginal Revenue

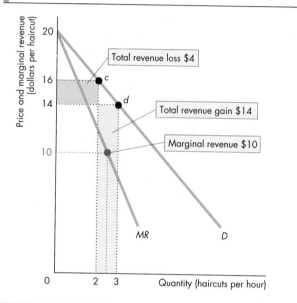

	Price (P) (dollars per haircut)	Quantity demanded (Q) (haircuts per hour)	Total revenue (TR = P × Q) (dollars)	Marginal revenue (MR = ΔTR/ΔQ) (dollars per additional haircut)
a	20	0	0	
				18
b	18	1	18	
				14
c	16	2	32	
				10
d	14	3	42	
				6
e	12	4	48	
				2
f	10	5	50	

The table shows Bobbie's demand schedule. Total revenue (*TR*) is price multiplied by quantity sold. For example, in row *c* the price is $16 a haircut, 2 haircuts are sold, and total revenue is $32. Marginal revenue (*MR*) is the change in total revenue that results from a one-unit increase in the quantity sold. For example, when the price falls from $16 to $14 a haircut, the quantity sold increases by 1 haircut and total revenue increases by $10. Marginal revenue is $10. The demand curve, *D*, and the marginal revenue curve, *MR*, are based on the numbers in the table and illustrate the calculation of marginal revenue when the price falls from $16 to $14.

Marginal Revenue and Elasticity

A single-price monopoly's marginal revenue is related to the *elasticity of demand* for its good. The demand for a good can be *elastic* (the elasticity of demand is greater than 1), *inelastic* (the elasticity of demand is less than 1), or *unit elastic* (the elasticity of demand is equal to 1). Demand is *elastic* if a 1 percent fall in price brings a greater than 1 percent increase in the quantity demanded. Demand is *inelastic* if a 1 percent fall in price brings a less than 1 percent increase in the quantity demanded. And demand is *unit elastic* if a 1 percent fall in price brings a 1 percent increase in the quantity demanded.

If demand is elastic, a fall in price brings an increase in total revenue—the increase in revenue from the increase in quantity sold outweighs the decrease in revenue from the lower price—and marginal revenue is positive. If demand is inelastic, a fall in price brings a decrease in total revenue—the increase in revenue from the increase in quantity sold is outweighed by the decrease in revenue from the lower price—and marginal revenue is negative. If demand is unit elastic, total revenue does not change—the increase in revenue from the increase in quantity sold offsets the decrease in revenue from the lower price—and marginal revenue is zero. (Chapter 5, pp. 94–95, explains the relationship between total revenue and elasticity more fully.)

Figure 13.3 illustrates the relationship between marginal revenue, total revenue, and elasticity. As the price of a haircut gradually falls from $20 to $10, the quantity of haircuts demanded increases from 0 to 5 an hour. Over this output range, marginal revenue is positive (part a), total revenue increases (part b), and the demand for haircuts is elastic. As the price falls from $10 to $0 a haircut, the quantity of haircuts demanded increases from 5 to 10 an hour. Over this output range, marginal revenue is negative (part a), total revenue decreases (part b), and the demand for haircuts is inelastic. When the price is $10 a haircut, marginal revenue is zero, total revenue is a maximum, and the demand for haircuts is unit elastic.

Monopoly Demand Is Always Elastic The relationship between marginal revenue and elasticity that you've just discovered implies that a profit-maximizing monopoly never produces an output in the inelastic range of its demand curve. If it did so, it could charge a higher price, produce a smaller quantity, and increase its profit. Let's now look more closely at a monopoly's price and output decision.

FIGURE 13.3

Marginal Revenue and Elasticity

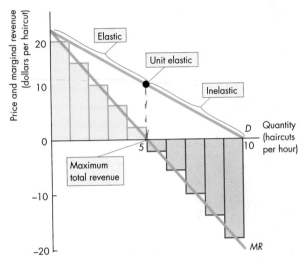

(a) Demand and marginal revenue curves

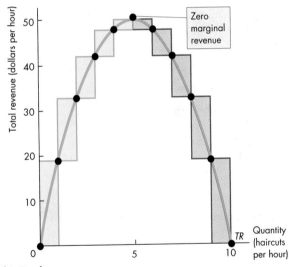

(b) Total revenue curve

Bobbie's demand curve (*D*) and marginal revenue curve (*MR*) are shown in part (a), and total revenue curve (*TR*) is shown in part (b). Over the range from 0 to 5 haircuts an hour, a price cut increases total revenue, so marginal revenue is positive, as shown by the blue bars. Demand is elastic. Over the range 5 to 10 haircuts an hour, a price cut decreases total revenue, so marginal revenue is negative, as shown by the red bars. Demand is inelastic. At 5 haircuts an hour, total revenue is maximized, and marginal revenue is zero. Demand is unit elastic.

Price and Output Decision

To determine the output level and price that maximize a monopoly's profit, we need to study the behavior of both revenue and costs as output varies. A monopoly and a competitive firm face the same types of technology and cost constraints. But they face different market constraints. The competitive firm is a price taker, whereas the monopoly's production decision influences the price it receives. Let's see how.

Bobbie's revenue, which we studied in Fig. 13.2, is shown again in Table 13.1. The table also contains information on Bobbie's costs and economic profit. Total cost (*TC*) rises as output increases, and so does total revenue (*TR*). Economic profit equals total revenue minus total cost. As you can see in the table, the maximum profit ($12) occurs when Bobbie sells 3 haircuts for $14 each. If she sells 2 haircuts for $16 each or 4 haircuts for $12 each, her economic profit will be only $8.

You can see why 3 haircuts is Bobbie's profit-maximizing output by looking at the marginal revenue and marginal cost columns. When Bobbie increases output from 2 to 3 haircuts, her marginal revenue is $10 and her marginal cost is $6. Profit increases by the difference—$4 an hour. If Bobbie

increases output yet further, from 3 to 4 haircuts, her marginal revenue is $6 and her marginal cost is $10. In this case, marginal cost exceeds marginal revenue by $4, so profit decreases by $4 an hour. When marginal revenue exceeds marginal cost, profit increases if output increases. When marginal cost exceeds marginal revenue, profit increases if output decreases. When marginal cost and marginal revenue are equal, profit is maximized.

The information set out in Table 13.1 is shown graphically in Fig. 13.4. Part (a) shows Bobbie's total revenue curve (*TR*) and total cost curve (*TC*). Economic profit is the vertical distance between *TR* and *TC*. Bobbie maximizes her profit at 3 haircuts an hour—economic profit is $42 minus $30, or $12.

A monopoly, like a competitive firm, maximizes profit by producing the output at which marginal cost equals marginal revenue. Figure 13.4(b) shows Bobbie's demand curve (*D*) and marginal revenue curve (*MR*) along with her marginal cost curve (*MC*) and average total cost curve (*ATC*). Bobbie maximizes her profit by doing 3 haircuts an hour. But what price does she charge for a haircut? To set the price, the monopolist uses the demand curve and finds the highest price at which it can sell the profit-maximizing output. In Bobbie's case, the highest price at which she can sell 3 haircuts an hour is $14.

TABLE 13.1

A Monopoly's Output and Price Decision

Price (P) (dollars per haircut)	Quantity demanded (Q) (haircuts per hour)	Total revenue (TR = P × Q) (dollars)	Marginal revenue (MR = ΔTR/ΔQ) (dollars per additional haircut)	Total cost (TC) (dollars)	Marginal cost (MC = ΔTC/ΔQ) (dollars per additional haircut)	Profit (TR − TC) (dollars)
20	0	0		20		−20
			·······18		········1	
18	1	18		21		−3
			·······14		········3	
16	2	32		24		+8
			·······10		········6	
14	**3**	**42**		**30**		**+12**
			·······6		·······10	
12	4	48		40		+8
			·······2		·······15	
10	5	50		55		−5

This table gives the information needed to find the profit-maximizing output and price. Total revenue (*TR*) equals price multiplied by the quantity sold. Profit equals total revenue minus total cost (*TC*). Profit is maximized when the price is $14 and 3 haircuts are sold. Total revenue is $42, total cost is $30, and economic profit is $12 ($42 − $30).

FIGURE 13.4

A Monopoly's
Output and Price

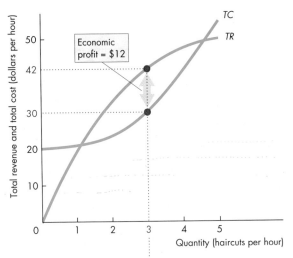

(a) Total revenue and total cost curves

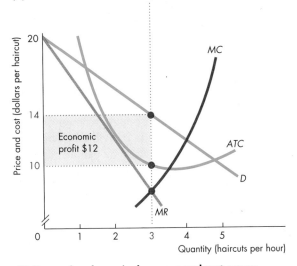

(b) Demand and marginal revenue and cost curves

In part (a), economic profit equals total revenue (*TR*) minus total cost (*TC*) and is maximized at 3 haircuts an hour. In part (b), economic profit is maximized when marginal cost (*MC*) equals marginal revenue (*MR*). The price is determined by the demand curve (*D*) and is $14. Economic profit, the blue rectangle, is $12—the profit per haircut ($4) multiplied by 3 haircuts.

All firms maximize profit by producing the output at which marginal revenue equals marginal cost. For a competitive firm, price equals marginal revenue, so price also equals marginal cost. For a monopoly, price exceeds marginal revenue, so price also exceeds marginal cost.

A monopoly charges a price that exceeds marginal cost, but does it always make an economic profit? In Bobbie's case, when she produces 3 haircuts an hour, her average total cost is $10 (read from the *ATC* curve) and her price is $14 (read from the *D* curve). Her profit per haircut is $4 ($14 minus $10). Bobbie's economic profit is shown by the blue rectangle, which equals the profit per haircut ($4) multiplied by the number of haircuts (3), for a total of $12.

If firms in a perfectly competitive industry make a positive economic profit, new firms enter. That does not happen in a monopolistic industry. Barriers to entry prevent new firms from entering. So in a monopolistic industry, a firm can make a positive economic profit and continue to do so indefinitely. Sometimes that profit is large, as in the international diamond business.

Bobbie makes a positive economic profit. But suppose that the owner of the shop that Bobbie rents increases Bobbie's rent. If Bobbie pays an additional $12 an hour, her fixed cost increases by $12 an hour. Her marginal cost and marginal revenue don't change, so her profit-maximizing output remains at 3 haircuts an hour. Her profit decreases by $12 an hour to zero. If Bobbie pays more than an additional $12 an hour for her shop rent, she incurs an economic loss. If this situation were permanent, Bobbie would go out of business. But entrepreneurs are a hardy lot, and Bobbie might find another shop where the rent is less.

REVIEW

- A monopoly maximizes profit by producing an output at which marginal cost equals marginal revenue.
- At the profit-maximizing output, the monopoly charges the highest price that consumers are willing to pay, which is determined by the demand curve.
- Because in a monopoly, price exceeds marginal revenue, price also exceeds marginal cost.
- A monopoly can make a positive economic profit even in the long run because of barriers to entry.

Price Discrimination

PRICE DISCRIMINATION—THE PRACTICE OF SELL-ing identical goods or services for different prices—is widespread. You encounter it when you travel, when you go to the movies, when you get your hair cut, when you buy pizza, and when you go to a museum or art gallery. Most firms that practice price discrimination are *not* monopolies. But monopolies price discriminate when they can do so.

Not all price *differences* are examples of price *discrimination*. Sometimes, goods that are similar but not identical have different costs and sell for different prices *because* they have different costs. For example, the marginal cost of producing electricity depends on the time of day. If an electric power company charges a higher price for consumption between 7:00 and 9:00 in the morning and between 4:00 and 7:00 in the evening than it does at other times of the day, this practice is not called price discrimination. Firms that practice price discrimination charge varying prices to consumers, not because the costs of producing the goods differ but because consumers have different elasticities of demand for the good.

At first sight, it appears that price discrimination contradicts the assumption of profit maximization. Why would a movie theater operator allow children to see movies at half price? Why would a hairdresser charge students and senior citizens less? Aren't these producers losing profit by being nice?

Deeper investigation shows that price discrimination pays. A monopoly has an incentive to try to find ways of discriminating among groups of consumers and charging each group the highest possible price. Some people may pay less with price discrimination, but others pay more. How do firms make more profit when they practice price discrimination?

Price Discrimination and Consumer Surplus

Demand curves slope down because the value that an individual places on a good falls as the quantity consumed of that good increases. When all the units consumed can be bought for a single price, consumers benefit. The benefit is the value the consumers get from each unit of the good minus the price actually paid for it. We call this benefit **consumer surplus**. (If you need to refresh your understanding of consumer surplus, flip back to Chapter 6, page 111.) Price discrimination can be seen as an attempt by a monopoly to capture the consumer surplus (or as much of the surplus as possible) for itself.

Discriminating Among Units of a Good

One form of price discrimination charges each single buyer a different price on each unit of a good bought. An example of this type of discrimination is a discount for bulk buying. The larger the order, the larger is the discount—and the lower is the price. This type of price discrimination works because each individual's demand curve slopes downward. Note that some discounts for bulk arise from lower costs of production for greater bulk. In these cases, such discounts are not price discrimination.

To extract every dollar of consumer surplus from every buyer, the monopoly would have to offer each individual customer a separate price schedule based on that customer's own demand curve. Clearly, such price discrimination cannot be carried out in practice because a firm does not have enough information about each consumer's demand curve.

Discriminating Among Individuals

Even when it is not possible to charge each individual a different price for each unit bought, it might still be possible to discriminate among individuals. This possibility arises from the fact that some people place a higher value on consuming one more unit of a good than do other individuals. By charging such an individual a higher price, the producer can obtain some of the consumer surplus that would otherwise accrue to their customers.

Discriminating Between Groups

Price discrimination often takes the form of discriminating between different groups of consumers on the basis of age, employment status, or some other easily distinguished characteristic. This type of price discrimination works only if each group has a different price elasticity of demand for the product. But this situation is a common one. For example, the elasticity of demand for air travel is lower for business travelers than for vacation travelers. For a business traveler, a trip is essential; for a vacation traveler, any of several different trips or even no vacation travel is a possibility. Let's see how an airline exploits the differences in demand by business and vacation travelers and increases its profit by price discriminating.

Global Air has a monopoly on an exotic route. Figure 13.5(a) shows the demand curve (*D*) and the marginal revenue curve (*MR*) for travel on this route. It also shows Global Air's marginal cost curve (*MC*). Marginal cost is constant, and fixed cost is zero. Global Air is a single-price monopoly and maximizes its profit by producing the output at which marginal revenue equals marginal cost. This output is 10,000 trips a year. The price at which Global can sell 10,000 trips is $1,500 per trip. Global Air's total revenue is $15 million a year. Its total cost is $10 million a year, so its economic profit is $5 million a year, as shown by the blue rectangle in part (a).

Global is struck by the fact that most of its customers are business travelers. Global knows that its exotic route is ideal for vacationers, but it also knows that to attract more of these travelers, it must offer a lower fare than $1,500. At the same time, Global knows that if it cuts the fare, it will lose revenue on its business travelers. So Global decides to price discriminate between the two groups.

Global's first step is to determine the demand curve of business travelers and the demand curve of vacation travelers. The market demand curve (in Fig. 13.5a) is the horizontal sum of the demand curves for these two types of traveler (see Chapter 8, p. 161). Global determines that the demand curve for business travel is D_B in Fig. 13.5(b) and the demand curve for vacation travel is D_V in Fig. 13.5(c). At the single fare of $1,500, the 10,000 trips that Global sells is made up of 6,000 to business travelers and 4,000 to vacation travelers. At $1,500 a trip, business travelers buy more trips than vacation travelers—there are 6,000 business trips and 4,000 vacation trips—but at this price, the demand for business travel is much less elastic than the demand for vacation travel. As the price decreases below $1,500, the demand for business travel becomes perfectly inelastic while the demand for vacation travel is more elastic.

Profiting by Price Discriminating

Global uses the profit-maximization rule: Produce the quantity at which marginal revenue equals marginal cost and set the price at the level the consumer is willing to pay. But now that Global has separated

---

FIGURE 13.5

A Single Price of Air Travel

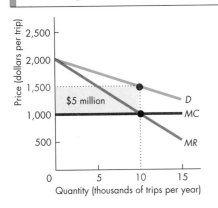

(a) All travelers

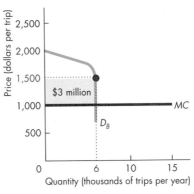

(b) Business travelers

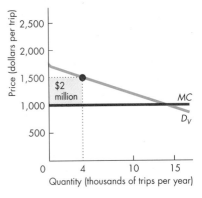

(c) Vacation travelers

Part (a) shows the demand curve (*D*), marginal revenue curve (*MR*), and marginal cost curve (*MC*) for a route on which Global Air has a monopoly. As a single-price monopoly, Global maximizes profit by selling 10,000 trips a year at $1,500 a trip. Its profit is $5 million, which is shown by the blue rectangle in

part (a). The demand curve in part (a) is the horizontal sum of the demand curves for business travel (D_B) in part (b) and the demand for vacation travel (D_V) in part (c). Global sells 6,000 trips to business travelers for a profit of $3 million and 4,000 trips to vacation travelers for a profit of $2 million.

its market into two parts, it has two marginal revenue curves. Global's marginal revenue curve for business travel is MR_B in Fig 13.6(a), and its marginal revenue curve for vacation travel is MR_V in Fig. 13.6(b).

In Fig. 13.6(a), marginal revenue from business travel equals the marginal cost of $1,000 at 5,000 trips a year. The price that business travelers are willing to pay for this quantity of trips is $1,700 a trip, up $200 from the current price. In Fig. 13.6(b), marginal revenue from vacation travel equals the marginal cost of $1,000 at 7,000 trips a year. The price that vacation travelers are willing to pay for 7,000 trips is $1,350 a trip.

If Global can charge its business travelers a fare of $1,700 and its vacation travelers $1,350, it can increase its sales from 10,000 to 12,000 trips a year and can increase its economic profit from $5 million a year to $5.95 million. On business travelers, it can make $3.5 million a year. This economic profit is shown by the blue rectangle in Fig. 13.6(a). On vacation travelers, Global can make $2.45 million a

year. The blue rectangle in Fig. 13.6(b) illustrates this economic profit.

How can Global get its business travelers to pay $1,700? If it offers fares to vacation travelers for $1,350, won't business travelers claim to be vacationers? Not with the deal that Global comes up with.

Global has noticed that its business travelers never make reservations more than three weeks in advance. It conducts a survey, which reveals that these travelers never know more than a month in advance when they will need to travel. Its survey also reveals that vacation travelers always know at least a month in advance of their travel plans. So Global offers a deal to all travelers: a basic fare of $1,700, but if a traveler buys a nonrefundable ticket one month in advance of the date of travel, the fare is discounted by $350 to $1,350. By price discriminating between business and vacation travelers, Global increases the quantity of trips to 12,000 and increases its profit by $0.95 million a year.

FIGURE 13.6
Price Discrimination

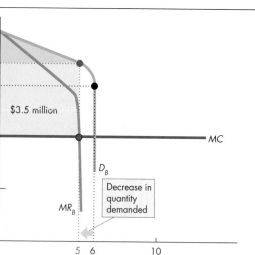

(a) Business travelers

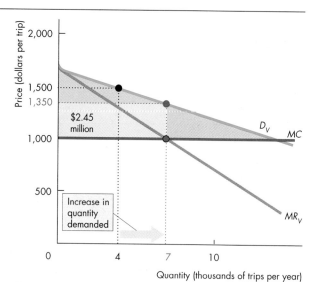

(b) Vacation travelers

The marginal revenue curve for business travel is (MR_B) in part (a), and that for vacation travel is (MR_V) in part (b). Global maximizes profit by making marginal revenue equal to marginal cost for each type of travel. By increasing the business fare to $1,700 and by cutting the vacation fare to $1,350, Global increases its

economic profit. It now sells 5,000 business trips for a profit of $3.5 million (the blue rectangle in part a) and 7,000 vacation trips for a profit of $2.45 million (the blue rectangle in part b), so its total profit increases from $5 million with no price discrimination to $5.95 million with discrimination.

More Perfect Price Discrimination

Global can do even better. Some of the business travelers are willing to pay more than $1,700 a trip. They make a consumer surplus, as shown by the green triangle in Fig. 13.6(a). Also, most of the vacation travelers who are paying $1,350 a trip are willing to pay more. They make a consumer surplus, as shown by the green triangle in Fig. 13.6(b). Further, some potential vacation travelers are not willing to pay $1,350 but are willing to pay at least $1,000. With a price of $1,000 a trip, these potential vacation travelers would make a consumer surplus equal to the orange triangle in Fig. 13.6(b).

Global gets creative. It comes up with a host of special deals. For higher prices, it offers priority reservations and frills to the business travelers. (These deals don't change Global's marginal cost.) It refines the list of restrictions on its discount fares and creates many different fare categories, the lowest of which has lots of restrictions but is $1,000 a trip.

The quantity of seats sold increases until Global is selling 20,000 trips a year, 6,000 to business travelers at various prices between $1,500 and almost $2,000 and 14,000 to vacationers at prices ranging between $1,000 and $1,700 a trip. Global is now almost a perfect price discriminator.

Perfect price discrimination captures the entire consumer surplus. Figure 13.7 shows Global as a perfect price discriminator.

Price Discrimination in Practice

You can now see why price discrimination is profitable. Global's special offer—"Normal fare: $1,700, 30-day advance purchase special: $1,350"—is no generous gesture. It is profit-maximizing behavior. The model of price discrimination that you have just studied explains a wide variety of familiar pricing practices, even by firms that are not pure monopolies.

FIGURE 13.7

Perfect Price Discrimination

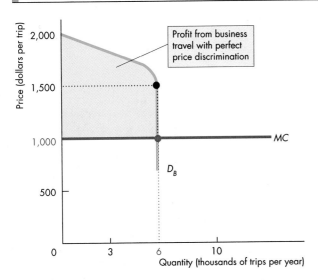

(a) Business travelers

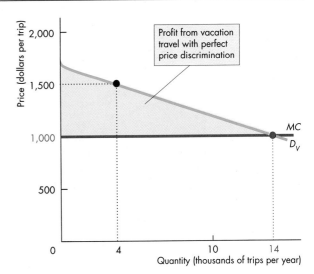

(b) Vacation travelers

By offering a wide array of special fares, restrictions, and deals, Global tries to perfectly price discriminate. If it succeeds, it sells 6,000 trips to business travelers and 14,000 trips to vaca-

tion travelers and it captures the entire consumer surplus. Its economic profit increases to the magnitude shown by the blue areas under the two demand curves.

For example, real airlines, not just the imaginary Global, offer lower fares for advance-purchase tickets than for last-minute travel. Last-minute travelers usually have a lower elasticity of demand than do vacation travelers who can plan ahead. Retail stores of all kinds hold seasonal "sales" when they reduce their prices, often by substantial amounts. These sales are a form of price discrimination. Each season, the newest fashions carry a high price tag, but retailers do not expect to sell all their stock at such high prices. At the end of the season, they sell off what is left at a discount. Thus such stores discriminate between buyers who have an inelastic demand (for example, those who want to be instantly fashionable) and buyers who have a more elastic demand (for example, those who pay less attention to up-to-the-minute fashion and more attention to price).

Limits to Price Discrimination

If price discrimination is profitable, why don't more firms do it? What limits price discrimination?

Profitable price discrimination can take place only under certain conditions. First, it is possible to price discriminate only if the good cannot be resold. If a good can be resold, then customers who get the good for the low price can resell it to someone who is willing to pay a higher price. Price discrimination breaks down. It is for this reason that price discrimination usually occurs in markets for services rather

than in markets for storable goods. One major exception, price discrimination in the sale of fashion clothes, works because at the end of the season when the clothes go on sale, the fashion plates are looking for next season's fashions. People buying on sale have no one to whom they can resell the clothes at a higher price.

Second, a price-discriminating monopoly must be able to identify groups with different elasticities of demand. The characteristics used for discrimination must also be within the law. These requirements usually limit price discrimination to cases based on age, employment status, or the timing of the purchase.

Despite these limitations, some firms use ingenious criteria for discriminating. For example, American Airlines discriminates between four different passenger groups on many of its international flights. The economy-class alternatives between New York and London in the summer of 1997 were:

- $2,364—no restrictions
- $959—7-day advance purchase
- $786—14-day advance purchase, mid-week only
- $713—21-day advance purchase, mid-week only

These different prices discriminate between different groups of customers with different elasticities of demand. The $2,364 fare is probably paid by last-minute business travelers who have a lower elasticity of demand, and the $713 fare is probably paid by vacationers who have a higher elasticity of demand.

Would it bother you to hear how little I paid for this flight?

From William Hamilton, "Voodoo Economics," ©1992 by The Chronicle Publishing Company, p.3. Reprinted with permission of Chronicle Books.

R E V I E W

- Price discrimination can increase a monopoly's profit.
- By charging the highest price for each unit of the good that each person is willing to pay, a monopoly perfectly price discriminates and captures all of the consumer surplus.
- Most price discrimination takes the form of discriminating among different groups of customers with different elasticities of demand.
- People with a lower elasticity of demand pay a higher price, and people with a higher elasticity of demand pay a lower price.

Next, we compare monopoly and competition.

Comparing Monopoly and Competition

TO COMPARE MONOPOLY AND COMPETITION, LET'S imagine an industry made up of a large number of identical competitive firms. We will work out what the price and quantity produced will be in that industry. Then we will imagine that a single firm buys out all the firms and creates a monopoly. We will then work out the price charged and quantity produced by the monopoly, first if it is a single-price monopoly and second if it is a price-discriminating monopoly.

Price and Output Comparison

Figure 13.8 shows the industry we'll study. The market demand curve is D, and the industry supply curve is S. In perfect competition, equilibrium occurs where the supply curve and the demand curve intersect.

In Perfect Competition   The quantity produced by the industry is Q_C, and the price is P_C. Each firm takes the price P_C and maximizes its profit by producing the output at which its own marginal cost equals the price. Because each firm is a small part of the total industry, there is no incentive for any firm to try to manipulate the price by varying its output.

With Single-Priced Monopoly   Now suppose that this industry is taken over by a single firm. No changes in production techniques occur, so the new combined firm has costs identical to those of the original firms. Recall that an industry supply curve is the sum of the supply curves of the firms in the industry and that a firm's supply curve is its marginal cost curve (see Chapter 12, pp. 246–247). So when the industry is taken over by a single firm, that firm's marginal cost curve is the competitive industry's supply curve. (The supply curve has also been labeled MC to remind you of this fact.)

The new single firm maximizes profit by producing Q_M, where marginal revenue equals marginal cost. Because the marginal revenue curve is below the demand curve, output Q_M is smaller than output Q_C. The monopoly charges the highest price for which output Q_M can be sold, and that price is P_M. We have just established that:

Compared to a perfectly competitive industry, a single-price monopoly restricts its output and charges a higher price.

With Perfect Price Discrimination   If a monopoly can perfectly price discriminate, it will charge a different price on each unit sold and increase output to Q_C. The highest price charged is P_A, and the lowest price charged is P_C, the price in a competitive market. The price P_A is the highest that is charged because at yet higher prices, nothing can be sold. The price P_C is the lowest charged because when a monopoly perfectly price discriminates, its demand curve is also its marginal revenue curve and at prices below P_C, marginal cost exceeds marginal revenue. We have just established a second key proposition:

The more perfectly the monopoly can price discriminate, the closer its output gets to the competitive output.

We've seen how the output and price of a monopoly compare with those in a competitive industry. Let's now compare the efficiency of the two types of markets.

FIGURE 13.8

Monopoly and Competition Compared

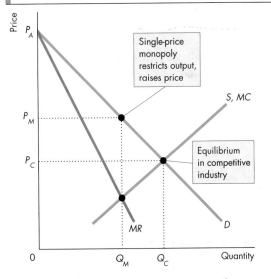

A competitive industry produces the quantity Q_C at price P_C. A single-price monopoly produces the quantity Q_M, and sells that quantity for the price P_M. A perfect price-discriminating monopoly produces Q_C and charges a different price for each unit sold. The prices charged range from P_A to P_C. Monopoly restricts output and raises the price. But the more perfectly a monopoly can price discriminate, the closer its output gets to the competitive output.

Efficiency Comparison

Whether monopoly is less efficient than competition depends on how successfully the monopoly can price discriminate. A single-price monopoly is inefficient, and a perfect price-discriminating monopoly is efficient. Let's look at these two cases.

Inefficiency of a Single-Price Monopoly Figure 13.9 compares perfect competition and a single-price monopoly. Under perfect competition (part a), consumers pay P_C for each unit bought. The maximum price that consumers are willing to pay for each unit is shown by the demand curve (D). This price measures the value of the good to the consumer. The value of a good minus its price is *consumer surplus*. (See Chapter 6, p. 115.) In Fig. 13.9(a), consumer surplus is shown by the green triangle.

A single-price monopoly in Fig. 13.9(b) restricts output to Q_M and sells that output for P_M. Consumer surplus decreases to the smaller green triangle. Consumers lose partly by having to pay more for the good and partly by getting less of it. But is the consumers' loss equal to the monopoly's gain? Is there simply a redistribution of the gains from trade? A closer look at Fig. 13.9(b) will convince you that there is a reduction in the gains from trade. Some of the loss in consumer surplus accrues to the monopoly—the monopoly gets the difference between the higher price (P_M) and P_C on the quantity sold (Q_M). So the monopoly takes the part of the consumer surplus shown by the blue rectangle. This portion of the loss of consumer surplus is not a loss to society. It is a redistribution from consumers to the monopoly.

What, though, has become of the rest of the consumer surplus? The answer is that because output has been restricted, it is lost. But more than that has been lost. The total loss resulting from the smaller monopoly output (Q_M) is the gray triangle in Fig. 13.9(b). The part of the gray triangle above P_C is the loss of consumer surplus, and the part of the triangle below P_C is a loss of producer surplus. **Producer surplus** is the difference between a producer's revenue and the opportunity cost of production (see Chapter 6, p. 117). It is calculated as the sum of the differences between price and the marginal cost of producing each unit of output. Under competition, the producer sells the output between Q_M and Q_C for a price of P_C. The marginal cost of producing each extra unit of output through that range is shown by the marginal cost (supply) curve. Thus the vertical distance

FIGURE 13.9

Inefficiency of Monopoly

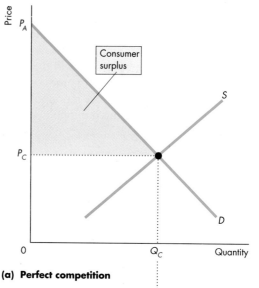

(a) Perfect competition

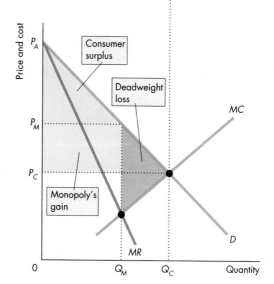

(b) Monopoly

In perfect competition (part a), the quantity Q_C is sold at the price P_C. Consumer surplus is the green triangle. In long-run equilibrium, firms' economic profits are zero and consumer surplus is maximized. A single-price monopoly (part b) restricts output to Q_M and increases the price to P_M. Consumer surplus is the green triangle. The monopoly takes the blue rectangle and creates a deadweight loss (the gray triangle).

between the marginal cost curve and price represents a producer surplus. Part of the producer surplus is lost when a monopoly restricts output to less than its competitive level, and this loss is the bottom half of the gray triangle in Fig.13.9(b).

But the entire gray triangle measures the total loss of both consumer and producer surplus. This loss is called the deadweight loss. **Deadweight loss** measures inefficiency as the reduction in consumer and producer surplus that occurs when output is either below or above its efficient level. The smaller output and higher price give the monopoly some of the consumer surplus. But the smaller output eliminates the producer surplus and the consumer surplus on the output that a competitive industry would have produced but that the monopoly does not.

Usually, a monopoly produces an output well below that at which average total cost is a minimum. It has far more capacity than it uses. But even if a monopoly produces the quantity at which average total cost is a minimum, which it might, the consumer does not have the opportunity of buying the good at a price equal to that cost. The price paid by the consumer always exceeds marginal cost.

Efficiency of Perfect Price Discrimination The deadweight loss if the monopoly practices perfect price discrimination is zero. A perfect price discriminator produces the same output as the competitive industry would. The price of the last item sold is P_C, the same as its marginal cost. Consumer surplus is zero, but deadweight loss is also zero. So perfect price discrimination achieves efficiency. But what about the distribution of the gains from trade?

Redistribution

Under perfect competition, the consumer surplus is the green triangle in Fig. 13.9(a). Because of free entry, the long-run equilibrium economic profit of each perfectly competitive firm is zero. We've just seen that the creation of monopoly reduces consumer surplus. Further, in the case of a single-price monopoly, a deadweight loss arises. But what happens to the distribution of surpluses between producers and consumers? The answer is that the monopoly always wins. In the case of a single-price monopoly (Fig. 13.9b), the monopoly gains the blue rectangle at the expense of the consumer, but it loses part of its producer surplus—its share of the deadweight loss. This

loss reduces its gain. But there is always a net gain for the monopoly and a net loss for the consumer. We also know that because there is a deadweight loss, the consumer loses more than the monopoly gains.

In the case of a perfectly price-discriminating monopoly, there is no deadweight loss but there is an even larger redistribution of the gains from trade away from consumers to the monopoly. In this case, the monopoly captures the entire consumer surplus, the green triangle in Fig. 13.9(a).

Because a single-price monopoly creates a deadweight loss, it is inefficient. It imposes a cost on society. The breakup of a monopoly might avoid this cost. And a considerable amount of law and regulation, which is described and explained in Chapter 19, is directed at this problem.

Because a monopoly creates economic profit in the long run, people devote a lot of effort to obtain monopoly rights. Let's look at this activity.

Rent Seeking

The activity of trying to obtain a monopoly from which an economic profit can be made is called **rent seeking**. The term *rent seeking* is used because *rent* (or *economic rent*) is a general term that includes consumer surplus, producer surplus, and economic profit. We've seen that a monopoly makes its economic profit by diverting part of the consumer surplus to itself. Thus the pursuit of an economic profit by a monopolist is rent seeking. It is the attempt to capture some consumer surplus.

Rent seekers pursue their goals in two main ways. They might:

- Buy a monopoly
- Create a monopoly

Buy a Monopoly This type of rent seeking is the searching out of existing monopoly rights that can be bought for a lower price than the monopoly's economic profit—that is, seeking to acquire existing monopoly rights. An example of this type of rent-seeking activity is the purchase of taxicab licenses. In some cities, taxicabs are regulated. The city restricts both the fares and the number of taxis that can operate. Operating a taxi results in economic profit or rent. A person who wants to operate a taxi must buy a license from someone who already has one.

But buying an existing monopoly does not ensure an economic profit. The reason is that there is freedom of entry into the activity of rent seeking. Rent seeking is like perfect competition. If an economic profit is available, a new entrant will try to get some of it. Competition among rent seekers pushes up the price that must be paid for a monopoly right to the point at which only a normal profit can be made by operating the monopoly. The economic profit—the rent—goes to the person who created the monopoly in the first place. For example, competition for the right to operate a taxi in New York City leads to a price of more than $100,000 for a taxi license, which is sufficiently high to eliminate long-run economic profit for the new taxi operator. But the person who acquired the right in the first place collects the economic rent. This type of rent seeking transfers wealth from the buyer to the seller of the monopoly.

Create a Monopoly   This type of rent-seeking activity takes the form of lobbying and seeking to influence the political process. Such influence is sometimes sought by making campaign contributions in exchange for legislative support or by indirectly seeking to influence political outcomes through publicity in the media or more direct contacts with politicians and bureaucrats. An example of a monopoly right created in this way is the government-imposed restrictions on the quantities of textiles that may be imported into the United States. Another is a regulation that limits the number of oranges that may be sold in the United States. These are regulations that restrict output and increase price.

This type of rent seeking is a costly activity that uses up scarce resources. In aggregate, firms spend billions of dollars lobbying Congress, state legislators, and local officials in the pursuit of licenses and laws that create barriers to entry and establish a monopoly right. Everyone has an incentive to rent seek, and because there are no barriers to entry into the rent-seeking activity, there is a great deal of competition for new monopoly rights.

What determines the value of the resources that a person will use to obtain a monopoly right? The answer is the monopoly's economic profit. If the value of resources spent trying to establish a monopoly exceeds the monopoly's economic profit, the net result is an economic loss. But as long as the value of the resources used to create a monopoly falls short of the monopoly's economic profit, there is an economic profit to be earned. With no barrier to entry into rent seeking, the value of the resources used up in rent seeking equals the monopoly's economic profit.

Because of rent seeking, monopoly imposes a social cost that exceeds the deadweight loss. That social cost equals the deadweight loss plus the value of resources used in rent seeking—the monopoly's entire economic profit because that is the value of the resources that it pays to use in rent seeking. Thus the social cost of monopoly is the deadweight loss plus the monopoly's economic profit.

Gains from Monopoly

So far, compared to perfect competition, monopoly has come out in a pretty bad light. If monopoly is so bad, why do we put up with it? Why don't we have laws that crack down on monopoly so hard that it never rears its head? We do indeed have laws that limit monopoly power (see Chapter 19). We also have laws that regulate those monopolies that exist. But monopoly is not all bad. Let's look at its potential advantages and some of the reasons for its existence.

The main reasons why monopoly might have some advantages are:

■ Economies of scale and economies of scope
■ Incentive to innovate

Economies of Scale and Scope   Economies of scale and scope can lead to *natural monopoly*. And as you saw at the beginning of this chapter, in a natural monopoly, a single firm can produce at a lower average cost than a larger number of firms can achieve.

A firm experiences *economies of scale* when an increase in its production of a good or service brings a decrease in the average total cost of producing it—see Chapter 11, pp. 226–227. *Economies of scope* arise when an increase in the *range of goods produced* brings a decrease in average total cost—see Chapter 10, p. 207. Economies of scope occur when different goods can share highly specialized (and usually very costly) technical inputs. For example, McDonald's can produce both hamburgers and french fries at an average total cost that is lower than what it would cost two separate firms to produce the two goods because at McDonald's hamburgers and french fries share the use of specialized food storage and preparation facilities. A firm that produces a wide range of products can hire specialist computer programmers, designers, and marketing experts whose skills can be used across the product range, thereby spreading their costs and lowering the average total cost of production of each of the goods.

Large-scale firms that have control over supply and can influence price—and that therefore behave like the monopoly firm that we've been studying in this chapter—can reap these economies of scale and scope. Small, competitive firms cannot. As a consequence, there are situations in which the comparison of monopoly and competition that we made earlier in this chapter is not a valid one. Recall that we imagined the takeover of a large number of competitive firms by a monopoly firm. But we also assumed that the monopoly would use exactly the same technology as the small firms and have the same costs. But if one large firm can reap economies of scale and scope, its marginal cost curve will lie below the supply curve of a competitive industry made up of thousands of small firms. It is possible for such economies of scale and scope to be so large as to result in a larger output and lower price under monopoly than a competitive industry would achieve.

Examples of industries in which economies of scale are so significant that they lead to a natural monopoly are becoming more rare. Public utilities such as gas, electric power, local telephone service, and garbage collection once were natural monopolies but no longer are. Water distribution though, remains a natural monopoly. There are many examples in which a combination of economies of scale and economies of scope arise. Some examples are the brewing of beer, the manufacture of refrigerators and other household appliances, the manufacture of pharmaceuticals, and the refining of petroleum.

Incentives to Innovate

Innovation is the first-time application of new knowledge in the production process. Innovation may take the form of developing a new product or a lower-cost way of making an existing product. Controversy has raged over whether large firms with monopoly power or small competitive firms lacking such monopoly power are the most innovative. It is clear that some temporary monopoly power arises from innovation. A firm that develops a new product or process and patents it obtains an exclusive right to that product or process for the term of the patent.

But does the granting of a monopoly, even a temporary one, to an innovator increase the pace of innovation? One line of reasoning suggests that it does. With no protection, an innovator is not able to enjoy the profits from innovation for very long. Thus the incentive to innovate is weakened. A contrary argument is that monopolies can afford to be lazy while competitive firms cannot. Competitive firms must strive to innovate and cut costs even though they know that they cannot hang onto the benefits of their innovation for long. But that knowledge spurs them on to greater and faster innovation.

The evidence on whether monopoly leads to greater innovation than competition is mixed. Large firms do more research and development than do small firms. But measuring research and development is measuring the volume of inputs into the process of innovation. What matters is not input but output. Two measures of the output of research and development are the number of patents and the rate of productivity growth. On these measures, there is no clear evidence that big is better. But there is a clear pattern in the process of diffusion of technological knowledge. After innovation, a new process or product spreads gradually through the industry, with large firms jumping on the bandwagon more quickly than the remaining small firms. Thus large firms speed the process of diffusion of technological advances.

REVIEW

- Comparing monopoly with perfect competition, monopoly produces a smaller quantity, which it sells for a higher price.
- A perfect price-discriminating monopoly produces the same quantity as in perfect competition but sells each unit for the highest price possible.
- Monopoly creates deadweight loss when it restricts the quantity produced below the competitive quantity.
- Monopoly redistributes economic gains away from consumers toward the monopoly.
- The full cost of monopoly includes the cost of rent seeking.
- Monopoly can be beneficial if it achieves economies of scale or scope or if it speeds innovation.

◆ You've now studied two market structures: perfect competition and monopoly. *Reading Between the Lines* on pp. 280–281 looks at monopoly in action. In the next chapter, we're going to study the ground between monopoly and competition. But you'll discover that the lessons you've learned from these two extreme market types are still relevant and help to understand how real-world markets work.

POLICY
WATCH

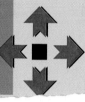

Monopoly in Action

The Wall Street Journal, OCTOBER 2, 1996

Microsoft Gives Technology Away to Beat Rival

BY BART ZIEGLER
AND DON CLARK

Microsoft Corp., which came to dominate the global software industry by imposing its standards on everyone else, will let a little-known industry group dictate the evolution of Internet technology the software giant invented.

After spending more than $100 million over seven years to develop key file-linking software, Microsoft yesterday agreed to cede control of the technology to the Open Group, a Cambridge, Mass., industry group that will now set the software's future design standards.

The unprecedented move involving Microsoft's ActiveX technology illustrates how much the global network has changed software-industry ground rules. Faced with competition from Netscape Communications Corp., which has a lead in Internet software, Microsoft apparently believes that only this dramatic gesture will allow its own products to thrive.

More than 100 software developers from more than 80 companies gathered in a Manhattan conference room yesterday to approve the transfer of the ActiveX technology. ...

But some observers say the technology transfer isn't altruistic. "Microsoft wouldn't be doing this if it didn't think it was in its best interests," said Jamie Lewis, president of Burton Group, a software consulting firm. Moreover, Microsoft can continue to make and sell its own enhancements to ActiveX, provided they meet the specifications that will be controlled by the Open Group.

Microsoft has been reinventing itself this year to focus its efforts on the network. Netscape dominates the market for Internet "browsers," the software needed to surf the World Wide Web, and also sells the special software used on the "server" computers that dish out Web pages. ...

But because Microsoft's ActiveX and the Netscape technologies are incompatible, software developers must choose one system or another.

Microsoft hopes that giving control of future ActiveX versions to the Open Group will make software vendors more willing to use the ActiveX approach. ...

John McCarthy, an analyst at Forrester Research Inc., observed that Microsoft's move illustrates how the company has used the threat of Internet competition to change its culture—and especially to open itself to new technologies from outside the company. While some Internet products bring no direct revenue to the company—because Microsoft is often giving them away—they provide additional reasons for customers to buy PCs, which may well come packaged with other Microsoft products that do benefit the company directly. ...

Essence of THE STORY

■ In the Internet software market, Microsoft Corp. faces stiff competition from Netscape Communications Corp.

■ Microsoft's ActiveX and Netscape's Internet software are incompatible. Software developers must choose one or the other.

■ Microsoft has given control of its Internet software, ActiveX, to the Open Group, an industry group that will set standards.

■ Microsoft hopes that this action will encourage developers to use ActiveX rather than Netscape's software.

■ Microsoft receives no direct revenue on some of its Internet products because it gives them away.

■ But these products encourage people to buy PCs, which come equipped with other Microsoft products that increase Microsoft's revenue.

Economic

A N A L Y S I S

■ Microsoft gets most of its market power from its Windows operating system.

■ The demand for Windows 95 depends on its value to users. And the lower the prices of programs that run in Windows 95, the greater is the demand for Windows 95.

■ Figure 1 shows the market for Microsoft's Windows 95 if users must pay for their web browser software. The demand curve is D and the marginal revenue curve is MR. The cost of developing Windows 95 was large, but the cost of installing a single copy is almost zero. So average total cost is ATC and marginal cost is MC.

■ Microsoft maximizes profit by producing at the point where marginal revenue equals marginal cost. In Fig. 1, the profit-maximizing quantity is Q_0 and the price is $60 a copy. (This assumed price is

that received by Microsoft. The *retail* price of Windows 95 is around $100.)

■ Microsoft's economic profit is shown by the blue rectangle in Fig. 1.

■ Netscape dominates the market for Internet browsers, and Fig. 2 shows Netscape's position in this market. The demand for browsers is D and the marginal revenue curve is MR. Like Windows 95, Navigator, Netscape's browser, was costly to develop and costs almost nothing to reproduce.

■ Netscape maximizes profit by selling the quantity Q_N of Navigator in Fig. 2. It charges $30 a copy. (This assumed price is what Netscape receives. The retail price of Navigator is around $50.)

■ To stimulate the demand for its products, Microsoft uses two marketing techniques.

■ First, it gives away its web browser, Explorer. This move probably doesn't cost Microsoft much. It could not sell Explorer for a higher price than the price of Navigator. And the demand for Explorer is probably quite small. So even if Microsoft restricted sales and charged the profit-maximizing price, it would not make much economic profit on this product.

■ By giving away Explorer, Microsoft increases the demand for Window 95.

■ If demand increases from D_0 to D_1, in Fig. 3, marginal revenue increases from MR_0 to MR_1. In this example, the profit maximizing price remains $60, but Microsoft sells more copies of Windows 95 and its average total cost is lower because average fixed cost falls as the quantity produced increases. Economic profit also increases.

■ Second, by giving away control over ActiveX, its own basic programming

language, Microsoft seeks to dominate a competing Netscape product.

■ It is rational for Microsoft to preserve its market power and to use up resources doing so.

You're

THE VOTER

■ Does Microsoft's position in the market for operating systems need government attention?

■ Can the free market deliver the efficient quantity of computer software?

■ How would you vote on a bill that requires Microsoft to give away copies of Windows 95 and any future operating system it develops?

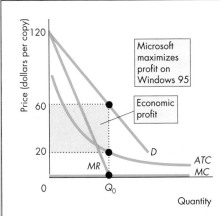

Figure 1   Windows 95

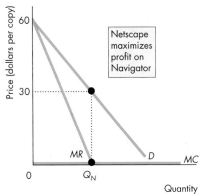

Figure 2   Netscape Navigator

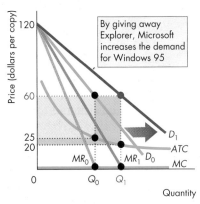

Figure 3   Windows 95 with free Explorer

SUMMARY

Key Points

How Monopoly Arises (pp. 264–265)

- A monopoly is an industry with a single supplier of a good or service that has no close substitutes and in which barriers to entry prevent competition.
- Barriers to entry may be legal or natural and can arise when a firm owns control of a resource.
- Legal barriers arise from public franchise, license, patent, and copyright.
- Natural barriers are created by economies of scale.

Monopoly Price-Setting Strategies (p. 265)

- A monopoly might be able to price discriminate when there is no resale possibility.
- Where resale is possible, a firm charges one price.

Single-Price Monopoly (pp. 266–269)

- A monopoly's demand curve is the market demand curve, and a single-price monopoly's marginal revenue is less than price.
- A monopoly maximizes profit by producing the output at which marginal revenue equals marginal cost and by charging the highest price that consumers are willing to pay for that output.

Price Discrimination (pp. 270–274)

- Price discrimination is an attempt by the monopoly to convert consumer surplus into economic profit.
- Perfect price discrimination extracts all the consumer surplus. Such a monopoly charges a different price for each unit sold and obtains the maximum price that each consumer is willing to pay for each unit bought.
- With perfect price discrimination, the monopoly produces the same output as would a perfectly competitive industry.
- A monopoly that discriminates between groups of customers produces the output for each group at which marginal cost equals marginal revenue and charges each group the most it is willing to pay.

Comparing Monopoly and Competition (pp. 275–279)

- A single-price monopoly charges a higher price and produces a smaller quantity than does a perfectly competitive industry.
- A perfect price-discriminating monopoly produces the competitive quantity and sells the last unit for the competitive price.
- A single-price monopoly restricts output and creates a deadweight loss. A perfect price-discriminating monopolist is efficient but captures all the surplus.
- Monopoly imposes costs that equal its deadweight loss plus the cost of the resources devoted to rent seeking.
- Monopolies with large economies of scale and scope can produce a larger quantity at a lower price than a competitive industry can achieve, and monopoly might be more innovative than competition.

Key Figures and Table

Key Terms

QUESTIONS

1. What is a monopoly? What are some examples of monopoly in your state?
2. What are barriers to entry? Give some examples of the various barriers to entry.
3. Distinguish between a legal monopoly and a natural monopoly. Give examples of each type.
4. Explain why a monopoly must lower its price to sell a larger quantity.
5. Explain why marginal revenue is always less than the price for a single-price monopoly.
6. Does a single-price monopoly operate on the inelastic part of its demand curve? Explain why it does or does not.
7. Explain how a single-price monopoly chooses its output and price.
8. Does a monopoly always make a positive economic profit in the short run? Explain why or why not.
9. Does a monopoly make zero economic profit in the long run? Explain why or why not.
10. Can any monopoly price discriminate? If yes, why? If no, why not?
11. Explain why a single-price monopoly produces a smaller output than an equivalent competitive industry.
12. Is a single-price monopoly as efficient as competition?
13. What are consumer surplus and producer surplus?
14. What is deadweight loss?
15. Show graphically the deadweight loss under perfect price discrimination.
16. Does a single-price monopoly make more efficient or less efficient use of resources than a perfect price-discriminating monopoly? Why?
17. Monopoly redistributes consumer surplus. Explain why the consumer loses more under perfect price discrimination than under single-price monopoly.
18. Explain why people engage in rent-seeking activities.
19. When taking account of the cost of rent seeking, what is the social cost of monopoly?
20. What are economies of scale and economies of scope? What effects, if any, do they have on the efficiency of monopoly?

PROBLEMS

1. The figure illustrates the situation facing the publisher of the only newspaper containing local news in an isolated community. Use the figure to answer the following questions.

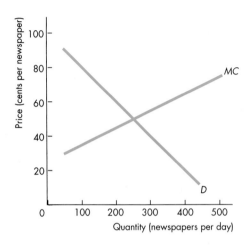

a. What quantity of newspapers will maximize the publisher's profit?
b. What price will the publisher charge for a daily newspaper?
c. What is the publisher's daily total revenue?
d. At the price charged for a newspaper, is the demand for newspapers elastic or inelastic? Why?

2. Refer to problem 1.
a. What is the efficient quantity of newspapers to print each day? Explain your answer.
b. Calculate the consumer surplus.
c. Calculate the deadweight loss created by the newspaper publisher.

3. Refer to the newspaper industry in problem 1. If this industry were efficient:
a. How many newspapers would be printed?
b. What would be the price of a newspaper?
c. What would be the consumer surplus?
d. What would be the deadweight loss?

4. Minnie's Mineral Springs, a single-price monopoly, faces the following demand schedule for bottled mineral water:

CHAPTER 13 MONOPOLY

Price (dollars per bottle)	Quantity demanded (bottles)
10	0
8	1
6	2
4	3
2	4
0	5

a. Calculate Minnie's total revenue schedule.
b. Calculate its marginal revenue schedule.
c. At what price is demand unit elastic?

5. Minnie's in problem 4 has the following total cost:

Quantity produced (bottles)	Total cost (dollars)
0	1
1	3
2	7
3	13
4	21
5	31

Calculate the profit-maximizing:
a. Output and price.
b. Marginal cost.
c. Marginal revenue.
d. Economic profit.
e. Does Minnie's use resources efficiently? Explain your answer.

6. Suppose that Minnie's can perfectly price discriminate. Calculate its profit-maximizing:
a. Output.
b. Total revenue.
c. Economic profit.
d. Does Minnie's use resources efficiently? Explain your answer.

7. What is the maximum price that someone would be willing to pay Minnie's for a license to operate its mineral spring?

8. The table sets out two demand schedules for round-trip flights between New York and Mexico City. Weekday travelers are those who make round-trips on weekdays and return within the same week. Weekend travelers are those who stay through the weekend. (The former tend to be business travelers, and the latter tend to be vacation travelers.)

Weekday travelers		Weekend travelers	
Price (dollars per round-trip)	Quantity demanded (thousands of round-trips)	Price (dollars per round-trip)	Quantity demanded (thousands of round-trips)
1,500	0		
1,250	5		
1,000	10		
750	15	750	0
500	15	500	5
250	15	250	10
0	15	0	15

The marginal cost of a round-trip is $500.
a. If a monopoly airline controls this route and charges a single price, what are the price and the number of passengers?
b. Is the market efficient? Explain your answer.
c. If the airline price discriminates between trips within a week and trips over a weekend, what are the prices for the two types of trips?

CRITICAL THINKING

1. Study *Reading Between the Lines* on pp. 280–281 and then answer the following questions.
   a. Bearing in mind the definition of a monopoly and the conditions that give rise to a monopoly, is it strictly correct to call Microsoft a monopoly?
   b. How would the arrival of a viable alternative operating system to Windows 95 affect Microsoft?
   c. Can you think of ways of intervening in the software industry to ensure that resources are allocated efficiently in that industry? (Think about price ceilings, price floors, taxes, and any other measures that strike you as being relevant.)
   d. "Anyone is free to buy stock in Microsoft, so everyone is free to share in Microsoft's economic profit and the bigger that economic profit, the better for all." Evaluate this statement.
   e. Why doesn't Microsoft buy Netscape?

14

Monopolistic Competition and Oligopoly

Every week, we receive a newspaper stuffed with supermarket fliers describing this week's "specials," providing coupons and other enticements, all designed to grab our attention and persuade us that A&P, Kroger, Safeway, Alpha Beta, Winn Dixie, Stop & Shop, Shop 'n' Save, and H.E.B.'s have the best deals in town. One claims the lowest price, another the best brands, yet another the best value for money even if its prices are not the lowest. How do firms locked in fierce competition with other firms set their prices, pick their products, and choose the quantities to produce? How are the profits of such firms affected by the actions of other

Fliers and War Games

firms? ◆ Until recently, only one firm made the chips that drive IBM and compatible PCs: Intel Corporation. During 1994, the prices of powerful personal computers based on Intel's fast Pentium chips collapsed. The reason: Intel suddenly faced competition

from new chip producers such as Advanced Micro Devices Inc. and Cyrix Corp. The price of Intel's Pentium processor, set at more than $1,000 when it was launched in 1993, fell to less than $200 by spring 1996, and the price of a Pentium-based computer fell to less than $2,000. How did competition among a small number of chip makers bring such a rapid fall in the price of chips and computers? ◆ The theories of monopoly and perfect competition do not predict the kind of behavior that we've just described. There are no fliers and coupons, best brands, or price wars in perfect competition because each firm produces an identical product and is a price taker. And there are none in monopoly because each monopoly firm has the entire market to itself. To understand coupons, fliers, and price wars, we need the richer models explained in this chapter.

After studying this chapter, you will be able to:

- Define monopolistic competition and oligopoly

- Explain how price and output are determined in a monopolistically competitive industry

- Explain why the price might be sticky in an oligopoly industry

- Explain how price and output are determined when an industry has one dominant firm and several small firms

- Use game theory to make predictions about price wars and competition among a small number of firms

Varieties of Market Structure

WE HAVE STUDIED TWO TYPES OF MARKET structure—perfect competition and monopoly. In perfect competition, a large number of firms produce identical goods, there are no barriers to entry, and each firm is a price taker. In the long run, there is no economic profit. In monopoly, a single firm is protected from competition by barriers to entry and makes an economic profit, even in the long run.

Many real-world industries lie somewhere between the extremes of perfect competition and monopoly, and two other market models are used to study the behavior of these industries. These models are:

1. Monopolistic competition
2. Oligopoly

Monopolistic competition is a market structure in which a large number of firms compete by making similar but slightly different products. Making a product slightly different from the product of a competing firm is called **product differentiation**. Because of product differentiation, a monopolistically competitive firm has an element of monopoly power. The firm is the sole producer of the particular version of the good in question. For example, in the market for microwave popcorn, only Nabisco makes Planters Premium Select. Only General Mills makes Pop Secret. And only American Popcorn makes Jolly Time. Each of these firms has a monopoly on a particular brand of microwave popcorn. Differentiated products are not necessarily different products. What matters is that consumers perceive them to be different. For example, the different brands of aspirin are chemically identical and differ only in their packaging.

Oligopoly is a market structure in which a small number of firms compete. Computer software, airplane manufacture, and international air transportation are examples of oligopolistic industries. Oligopolies might produce almost identical products, such as the oil and gasoline produced by Texaco and Exxon. Or they might produce differentiated products such as Chevrolet's Lumina and Ford's Taurus.

Many factors must be taken into account to determine which market structure describes a particular real-world market. But one of these factors is the extent to which the market is dominated by a small number of firms. To measure this feature of markets, economists use indexes called measures of concentration. Let's look at these measures.

Measures of Concentration

To tell how close to the competitive or monopolistic extreme an industry comes or where in between these extremes it lies, economists use two measures of concentration. They are:

1. The four-firm concentration ratio
2. The Herfindahl-Hirschman Index

The Four-Firm Concentration Ratio The **four-firm concentration ratio** is the percentage of the value of sales accounted for by the four largest firms in an industry. The range of the concentration ratio is from almost zero for perfect competition to 100 percent for monopoly. This ratio is the main measure used to assess market structure.

Table 14.1 shows two calculations of the four-firm concentration ratio, one for tires and one for printing. In this example, 14 firms produce tires. The biggest four have 80 percent of the sales, so the four-firm concentration ratio is 80 percent. In the printing industry, with 1,004 firms, the top four firms have only 0.5 percent of the sales, so the four-firm concentration ratio is 0.5 percent.

A low concentration ratio indicates a high degree of competition, and a high concentration ratio indicates an absence of competition. A monopoly has a concentration ratio of 100 percent—the largest (and only) firm has 100 percent of the sales.

A four-firm concentration ratio that exceeds 60 percent is regarded as an indication of a market that is highly concentrated and dominated by a few firms in an oligopoly. A ratio of less than 40 percent is regarded as an indication of a competitive market.

The Herfindahl-Hirschman Index The **Herfindahl-Hirschman Index**—also called the HHI—is the square of the percentage market share of each firm summed over the largest 50 firms (or summed over all the firms if there are fewer than 50) in a market. For example, if there are four firms in a market and the market shares of the firms are 50 percent, 25 percent, 15 percent, and 10 percent, the Herfindahl-Hirschman Index is

$$HHI = 50^2 + 25^2 + 15^2 + 10^2 = 3,450.$$

In perfect competition, the HHI is small. For example, if each of the largest 50 firms in an industry has a market share of 0.1 percent, the HHI is $0.1^2 \times 50 = 0.5$. In a monopoly, the HHI is 10,000—the firm has 100 percent of the market: $100^2 = 10,000$.

TABLE 14.1

Concentration Ratio Calculations

Tiremakers			**Printers**	
Firm	**Sales** (millions of dollars)		**Firm**	**Sales** (millions of dollars)
Top, Inc.	200		Fran's	2.5
ABC, Inc.	250		Ned's	2.0
Big, Inc.	150		Tom's	1.8
XYZ, Inc.	100		Jill's	1.7
Top 4 sales	700		Top 4 sales	8.0
Other 10 firms' sales	175		Other 1,000 firms' sales	1,592.0
Industry sales	**875**		Industry sales	**1,600.0**

Four-firm concentration ratios:

Tiremakers: $\dfrac{700}{875} \times 100 = 80\%$ Printers: $\dfrac{8}{1,600} \times 100 = 0.5\%$

The HHI became a popular measure of monopoly power during the 1980s, when the Justice Department used it to classify markets. If the HHI is less than 1,000, a market is regarded as being highly competitive. If the HHI lies between 1,000 and 1,800, it is moderately competitive. But if the HHI exceeds 1,800, a market is regarded as being concentrated. The Justice Department scrutinizes any merger of firms in a market in which the HHI exceeds 1,000 and is likely to challenge a merger if the HH1 exceeds 1,800.

Table 14.2 summarizes the characteristics of the different market types and their measures of concentration.

Limitations of Concentration Measures

Although concentration measures are useful, they must be supplemented by other information to determine a market's structure. There are three main problems:

- The geographical scope of the market
- Barriers to entry and firm turnover
- The correspondence between a market and an industry

Geographical Scope of Market   Concentration ratio data are based on a *national* view of the market. Many goods are sold in a national market, but some are sold in a *regional* market and some in a *global* one. The newspaper industry is an example of local markets. The concentration ratio for newspapers is not high, but there is a high degree of concentration in the newspaper industry in most cities. The automobile industry is an example of a global market. The biggest three U.S. car producers account for 92 percent of cars sold by U.S. producers, but they account for a smaller percentage of the total U.S. car market (including imports) and a smaller percentage of the global market for cars.

Barriers to Entry and Turnover   Concentration measures don't measure barriers to entry. Some industries are highly concentrated but have easy entry and an enormous amount of turnover of firms. For example, many small towns have few restaurants, but there are no restrictions on opening a restaurant and many firms attempt to do so.

Also, an industry might be competitive because of *potential entry*—because a few firms in a market face competition from many firms that can easily enter the market and will do so if economic profits are available.

TABLE 14.2

Market Structure

Characteristics	Perfect competition	Monopolistic competition	Oligopoly	Monopoly
Number of firms in industry	Many	Many	Few	One
Product	Identical	Differentiated	Either identical or differentiated	No close substitutes
Barriers to entry	None	None	Moderate	High
Firm's control over price	None	Some	Considerable	Considerable or regulated
Concentration ratio	0	Low	High	100
HHI	Less than 1,000	1,000 to 1,800	More than 1,800	10,000
Examples	Wheat, corn	Food, clothing	Automobiles, cereals	Local water supply

Market and Industry   To calculate concentration ratios, the Department of Commerce classifies each firm as being in a particular industry. But markets do not always correspond to industries.

First, markets are often narrower than industries. For example, the pharmaceutical industry, which has a low concentration ratio, operates in many separate markets for individual products—for example, measles vaccine and AIDS-fighting drugs. These drugs do not compete with each other, so this industry, which looks competitive, includes firms that are monopolies (or near monopolies) in markets for individual drugs.

Second, firms make many products. For example, Westinghouse makes electrical equipment and, among other things, gas-fired incinerators and plywood. So this one firm operates in at least three separate markets. But the Department of Commerce classifies Westinghouse as being in the electrical goods and equipment industry.

Third, firms switch from one market to another depending on profit opportunities. For example, Motorola, which today produces a wide variety of wireless communications products, has diversified from being a TV and computer chip maker. Motorola produces no TVs today. Publishers of newspapers, magazines, and textbooks are today rapidly diversifying into Internet and multimedia products.

Despite their limitations, combined with information about the geographical scope of the market, barriers to entry, and the extent to which large, multiproduct firms straddle a variety of markets, concentration ratios provide a basis for determining the degree of competition in an industry.

Concentration Measures for the U.S. Economy

Figure 14.1 shows a selection of concentration ratios and HHIs for the United States calculated by the Department of Commerce.

Industries that produce chewing gum, household laundry equipment, light bulbs, breakfast cereals, and motor vehicles have a high degree of concentration and are oligopolies. Industries that produce ice cream and milk and those that do commercial printing have low concentration measures and are highly competitive. Industries that produce pet food and cookies and crackers are moderately concentrated. These industries are examples of monopolistic competition.

FIGURE 14.1

Concentration Measures in the United States

The industries producing chewing gum, household laundry equipment, and lightbulbs are highly concentrated, while those producing commercial printing, ice cream, and milk are highly competitive. The industries producing pet food and cookies and crackers have an intermediate degree of concentration.

Source: U.S. Department of Commerce, *Concentration Ratios in Manufacturing,* Washington, D.C., 1996.

Market Structures in the U.S. Economy

Figure 14.2 shows the market structure of the U.S. economy and the trends in market structure between 1939 and 1980. (Comparable data for the 1980s and 1990s are not available.) Over this period, the U.S. economy became increasingly competitive.

In 1980, three quarters of the value of goods and services bought and sold in the United States was

FIGURE 14.2

The Market Structure of the U.S. Economy

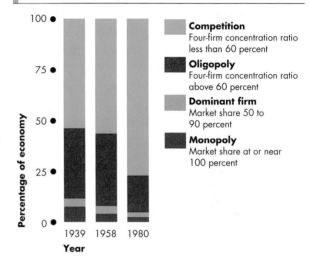

Three quarters of the U.S. economy is effectively competitive (perfect competition or monopolistic competition), one fifth is oligopoly, and the rest is monopoly. The economy became more competitive between 1939 and 1980. (Professor Shepherd, whose 1982 study remains the latest word on this topic, suspects that although some industries have become more concentrated, others have become less concentrated, so the net picture has probably not changed much since 1980.)

Source: William G. Shepherd, "Causes of Increased Competition in the U.S. Economy, 1939–1980," *Review of Economics and Statistics,* November 1982, pp. 613–626.

traded in markets that are essentially competitive— markets that have almost perfect competition or monopolistic competition. Monopoly and the dominance of a single firm accounted for about 5 percent of sales. Oligopoly, which is found mainly in manufacturing, accounted for about 18 percent of sales.

You now know the variety of market structures in our economy, and you know how we classify different types of firms and industries into these market types. You also know how we measure industrial concentration to determine the degree of competition and market power in different industries. In the rest of this chapter, we are going to study the two market types that lie between competition and monopoly. We'll begin with monopolistic competition. Then we'll study oligopoly.

Monopolistic Competition

MONOPOLISTIC COMPETITION ARISES IN AN industry in which:

- A large number of firms compete.
- Each firm produces a differentiated product, which is a close but not a perfect substitute for the products of the other firms.
- Firms are free to enter and exit.

Makers of running shoes, pizza producers, auto service stations, family restaurants, and realtors are all examples of firms that operate in monopolistic competition. In monopolistic competition, as in perfect competition, the industry consists of a large number of firms and each firm supplies a small part of the total industry output. Because each firm is small, no one firm can effectively influence what other firms do. If one firm changes its price, this action has no effect on the actions of the other firms.

Unlike perfect competition and like monopoly, a firm in monopolistic competition faces a downward-sloping demand curve. The reason is that the firm's product is differentiated from the products of its competitors. Some people will pay more for one variety of the product, so when its price rises, the quantity demanded falls but it does not (necessarily) fall to zero. For example, Adidas, Asics, Diadora, Etonic, Fila, New Balance, Nike, Puma, and Reebok all make differentiated running shoes. Other things remaining the same, if the price of Adidas running shoes rises and the prices of the other shoes remain constant, Adidas sells fewer shoes and the other producers sell more. But Adidas shoes don't disappear unless the price rises by a large amount. Because a firm in monopolistic competition faces a downward-sloping demand curve, it maximizes profit by choosing both its price and its output.

Like perfect competition and unlike monopoly, in monopolistic competition there is free entry and free exit. As a consequence, a firm in monopolistic competition cannot make an economic profit in the long run. When economic profit is being made, new firms enter the industry. This entry lowers prices and eventually eliminates economic profit. When economic losses are incurred, some firms leave the industry. This exit increases prices and profits and eventually eliminates the economic loss. In long-run equilibrium, firms neither enter nor leave the industry, and the firms in the industry make zero economic profit.

Price and Output in Monopolistic Competition

Figure 14.3 shows how a firm in a monopolistically competitive industry determines its price and output. Part (a) deals with the short run, and part (b) deals with the long run. Let's concentrate initially on the short run. The demand curve D shows the demand for the firm's own variety of the product. For example, it is the demand for Bayer aspirin rather than for painkillers in general or for McDonald's hamburgers rather than for hamburgers in general. The curve labeled MR is the marginal revenue curve associated with the demand curve. The figure also shows the firm's average total cost (ATC) and marginal cost (MC). The firm maximizes profit in the short run by producing output Q_S, where marginal revenue equals marginal cost, and charging the price P_S. The firm's average total cost is C_S, and the firm makes a short-run economic profit, as measured by the blue rectangle.

So far, the firm in monopolistic competition looks just like a monopoly. It produces the quantity at which marginal revenue equals marginal cost and then charges the highest price that buyers are willing to pay for that quantity, determined by the demand curve. The key difference between monopoly and monopolistic competition lies in what happens next.

There is no restriction on entry in monopolistic competition, so economic profit attracts new entrants. As new firms enter the industry, the firm's demand curve and marginal revenue curve start to shift leftward. At each point in time, the firm maximizes its short-run profit by producing the quantity at which marginal revenue equals marginal cost and by charging the highest price that buyers are willing to pay for this quantity. But as the demand curve shifts leftward, the profit-maximizing quantity and price fall.

Figure 14.3(b) shows the long-run equilibrium. The firm produces Q_L and sells it at a price of P_L. In this situation, the firm is making zero economic profit. There is no incentive for firms to enter or exit.

Excess Capacity A firm's *capacity* output is the output produced when average total cost is a minimum—the output at the bottom of the U-shaped ATC curve (Q_C in Fig. 14.3b). In monopolistic competition, in the long run, firms always have *excess capacity*. In Fig. 14.3(b), the firm produces Q_L and has excess capacity of $Q_C - Q_L$. That is, firms produce less output than that which minimizes average total

FIGURE 14.3

Monopolistic Competition

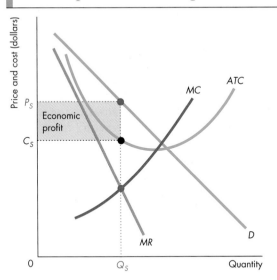

(a) Short run

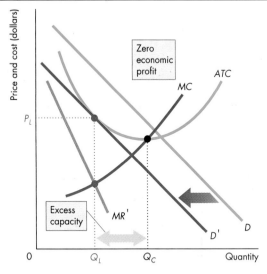

(b) Long run

Profit is maximized where marginal revenue equals marginal cost. Part (a) shows the short-run outcome. Profit is maximized by producing quantity Q_S and selling it for price P_S. Average total cost is C_S, and the firm makes an economic profit (the blue rectangle). Economic profit encourages new entrants in the long run.

Part (b) shows the long-run outcome. The entry of new firms decreases each firm's demand and shifts the demand curve and marginal revenue curve leftward. When the demand curve has shifted to D', the marginal revenue curve is MR' and the firm is in long-run equilibrium. The output that maximizes profit is Q_L, the price is P_L, and economic profit is zero. Because each firm produces less output than its capacity Q_C, it has excess capacity.

cost. As a consequence, the consumer pays a price that exceeds minimum average total cost. This result arises from the fact that the firm faces a downward-sloping demand curve. The demand curve slopes down because of product differentiation—because one firm's product is not a perfect substitute for another firm's product. So product differentiation creates excess capacity.

You can see the excess capacity in monopolistic competition all around you. Family restaurants (except for the truly outstanding ones) almost always have some empty tables. You can always get a pizza delivered in less than 30 minutes. It is rare that every pump at a gas station is in use with customers waiting in line. There is always an abundance of realtors ready to help find or sell a home.

These industries are all examples of monopolistic competition. The firms have excess capacity. They could sell more, but only by cutting their prices. They would then incur losses in the long run.

Monopolistic Competition and Efficiency

When we studied a perfectly competitive industry, we discovered that in some circumstances, such an industry allocates resources efficiently. A key feature of efficiency is that marginal benefit equals marginal cost. Price measures marginal benefit, so efficiency requires price to equal marginal cost. When we studied monopoly, we discovered that such a firm creates an inefficient use of resources because it restricts output to a level at which price exceeds marginal cost. In such a situation, the marginal benefit exceeds marginal cost and production is less than its efficient level. You've now discovered that monopolistic competition shares this feature with monopoly. Even though there is zero economic profit in long-run equilibrium, the monopolistically competitive industry produces an output at which price equals average total cost but exceeds marginal cost.

Because in monopolistic competition, price exceeds marginal cost, this market structure, like monopoly, is inefficient. The marginal cost of producing one more unit of output is less than the marginal benefit to the consumer, determined by the price the consumer is willing to pay. But the inefficiency of monopolistic competition arises from product differentiation—from product variety. Consumers value variety, but it is achievable only if firms make differentiated products. So the loss in efficiency that occurs in monopolistic competition must be weighed against the gain of greater product variety.

Innovation and Product Differentiation

Another source of gain from monopolistically competitive industries is product innovation. Monopolistically competitive firms are constantly seeking out new products that will provide them with a competitive edge, even if only temporarily. A firm that manages to introduce a new and differentiated variety will temporarily face a steeper demand curve than before and will be able to temporarily increase its price. It will make an economic profit. Eventually, new firms that make close substitutes for the new product will enter and compete away the economic profit arising from this initial advantage.

Selling Costs and Product Differentiation

Firms in monopolistic competition incur large selling costs in order to differentiate their products from those of other firms. Some product differentiation is achieved by designing and introducing products that are actually different from those of the other firms in the industry. But firms also attempt to differentiate the consumer's perception of the product. Marketing and advertising are the principal means whereby firms seek to achieve this end.

But selling costs increase a monopolistically competitive firm's costs above those of a competitive firm or a monopoly. A large and increasing proportion of the prices we pay covers the cost of selling a good, not the cost of making it. Selling costs include the cost of elaborately designed shopping malls; glossy catalogs and brochures; magazine and television advertising; and the salaries, airfares, and hotel bills of salespeople.

To the extent that selling costs provide consumers with services that they value and with information about the precise nature of the differentiation of products, they serve a useful purpose to the consumer and enable a better product choice to be made. But the opportunity cost of the additional services and information must be weighed against the gain to the consumer.

The bottom line on the question of efficiency of monopolistic competition is ambiguous. In some cases, the gains from extra product variety unquestionably offset the selling and marketing costs and the extra cost arising from excess capacity. The tremendous varieties of books and magazines, clothing, food, and drinks are examples of such gains. It is less easy to see the gains from being able to buy brand-name drugs that have a chemical composition identical to that of a generic alternative. But some people do willingly pay more for the brand-name alternative.

REVIEW

- In monopolistic competition, a large number of firms compete by producing differentiated products. Each firm faces a downward-sloping demand curve.
- Economic profit in the short run stimulates entry in the long run.
- In long-run equilibrium, price equals average total cost (economic profit is zero) and price exceeds marginal cost. The quantity produced is less than that which minimizes average total cost.
- The cost of monopolistic competition is excess capacity and high selling costs; the gain is a wide product variety.

You've seen that monopolistic competition is a blend of monopoly and competition. As in monopoly, each firm faces a downward-sloping demand curve and sets its price. But as in perfect competition economic profit triggers entry, so in long-run equilibrium, firms make normal profit.

Oligopoly, which we now study, is fundamentally different from the other market types because each firm must take account of its competitors' reactions to its own actions.

Oligopoly

IN OLIGOPOLY, A SMALL NUMBER OF PRODUCERS compete. The quantity sold by any one producer depends on that producer's price *and* on the other producers' prices and quantities sold.

To see the interplay between the firm's prices and sales, suppose you run one of the three gas stations in a small town. If you cut your price and your two competitors don't cut theirs, your sales increase, but the sales of the other two firms decrease. With lower sales, the other firms will most likely cut their prices too. If they do cut their prices, your sales and profits will take a tumble. So before deciding to cut your price, you try to predict how the other firms will react and you attempt to calculate the effects of those reactions on your own profit.

Several models have been developed to explain the prices and quantities in oligopoly markets. But no one theory has been found that can explain all the different types of behavior that we observe in such markets. The models fall into two broad groups: traditional models and game theory models. We'll look at examples of both types, starting with two traditional models.

The Kinked Demand Curve Model

The kinked demand curve model of oligopoly is based on the assumption that each firm believes that:

1. If it raises its price, others will not follow.
2. If it cuts its price, so will the other firms.

Figure 14.4 shows the demand curve (D) that a firm believes it faces. The demand curve has a kink at the current price, P, and quantity, Q. A small price rise above P brings a big decrease in the quantity sold. The other firms hold their current price and the firm has the highest price for the good, so it loses its market share. Even a large price cut below P brings only a small increase in the quantity demanded. In this case, other firms match the price cut, so the firm gets no price advantage over its competitors.

The kink in the demand curve creates a break in the marginal revenue curve (MR). To maximize profit, the firm produces the quantity at which marginal cost equals marginal revenue. That quantity, Q, is where the marginal cost curve passes through the gap ab in the marginal revenue curve. If marginal cost fluctuates

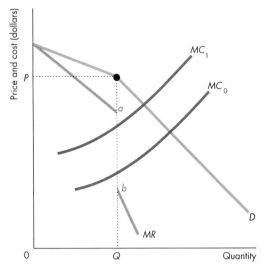

FIGURE 14.4

The Kinked Demand Curve Model

The price in an oligopoly market is P. Each firm believes it faces the demand curve D. A small price rise above P brings a big decrease in the quantity sold because other firms do not raise their prices. Even a big price cut below P brings only a small increase in the quantity sold because other firms also cut their prices. Because the demand curve is kinked, the marginal revenue curve, MR, has a break ab. Profit is maximized by producing Q. The marginal cost curve passes through the break in the marginal revenue curve. Marginal cost changes inside the range ab leave the price and quantity unchanged.

between a and b, like the marginal cost curves MC_0 and MC_1, the firm does not change its price or its output. Only if marginal cost fluctuates outside the range ab does the firm change its price and output. So the kinked demand curve model predicts that price and quantity are insensitive to small cost changes.

A problem with the kinked demand curve model is that the firms' beliefs about the demand curve are not always correct and firms can figure out that they are not correct. If marginal cost increases by enough to cause the firm to increase its price and if all firms experience the same increase in marginal cost, they all increase their prices together. The firm's belief that others will not join it in a price rise is incorrect. A firm that bases its actions on beliefs that are wrong does not maximize profit and might even end up incurring an economic loss.

Dominant Firm Oligopoly

A second traditional model explains a dominant firm oligopoly, which arises when one firm—the dominant firm—has a big cost advantage over the other firms and produces a large part of the industry output. The dominant firm sets the market price, and the other firms are price takers. Examples of dominant firm oligopoly are a large gasoline retailer or a big video rental store that dominates its local market.

To see how a dominant firm oligopoly works, suppose that 11 firms operate gas stations in a city. Big-G is the dominant firm. Figure 14.5 shows the market for gas in this city. In part (a), the demand curve D tells us the total quantity of gas demanded in the city at each price. The supply curve S_{10} is the supply curve of the 10 small suppliers.

Part (b) shows the situation facing Big-G. Its marginal cost curve is MC. Big-G's demand curve is XD,

and its marginal revenue curve is MR. Big-G's demand curve shows the excess demand not met by the 10 small firms. For example, at a price of $1 a gallon, the quantity demanded is 20,000 gallons, the quantity supplied by the 10 small firms is 10,000 gallons, and the excess quantity demanded is 10,000, measured by the distance ab in both parts of the figure.

To maximize profit, Big-G operates like a monopoly. It sells 10,000 gallons a week for a price of $1 a gallon. The 10 small firms take the price of $1 a gallon. They behave just like firms in perfect competition. The quantity of gas demanded in the entire city at $1 a gallon is 20,000 gallons, as shown in part (a). Of this amount, Big-G sells 10,000 gallons and the 10 small firms each sell 1,000 gallons.

The traditional theories of oligopoly do not enable us to understand all oligopoly markets, and in recent years, economists have developed new models based on game theory. Let's now learn about game theory.

FIGURE 14.5
A Dominant Firm Oligopoly

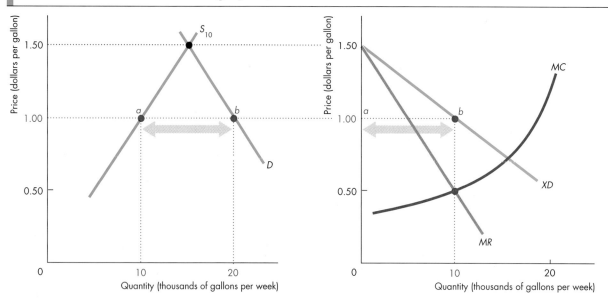

(a) Ten small firms and market demand

The demand curve for gas in a city is D in part (a). There are 10 small competitive firms that together have a supply curve of S_{10}. In addition, there is 1 large firm, Big-G, shown in part (b). Big-G faces the demand curve XD, determined as market demand D minus the supply of the other 10 firms S_{10}—the demand that is not satisfied by the small firms. Big-G's mar-

(b) Big-G's price and output decision

ginal revenue is MR, and its marginal cost is MC. Big-G sets its output to maximize profit by equating marginal cost, MC, and marginal revenue, MR. This output is 10,000 gallons per week. The price at which Big-G can sell this quantity is $1 a gallon. The other 10 firms take this price, and each firm sells 1,000 gallons per week.

Game Theory

THE MAIN TOOL THAT ECONOMISTS USE TO analyze *strategic behavior*—behavior that takes into account the expected behavior of others and the mutual recognition of interdependence—is called **game theory**. Game theory was invented by John von Neumann in 1937 and extended by von Neumann and Oskar Morgenstern in 1944. Today, it is one of the major research fields in economics.

Game theory seeks to understand oligopoly as well as other forms of economic, political, social, and even biological rivalries by using a method of analysis specifically designed to understand games of all types, including the familiar games of everyday life. We will begin our study of game theory, and its application to the behavior of firms, by thinking about familiar games.

What Is a Game?

What is a game? At first thought, the question seems silly. After all, there are many different games. There are ball games and parlor games, games of chance and games of skill. But what is it about all these different activities that make them games? What do all these games have in common? All games share three features:

- Rules
- Strategies
- Payoffs

Let's see how these common features of games apply to a game called "the prisoners' dilemma." This game, it turns out, captures some of the essential features of oligopoly, and it gives a good illustration of how game theory works and how it generates predictions.

The Prisoners' Dilemma

Art and Bob have been caught red-handed, stealing a car. Facing airtight cases, each will receive a sentence of two years for the crime. During his interviews with the two prisoners, the district attorney begins to suspect that he has stumbled on the two people who were responsible for a multimillion-dollar bank robbery some months earlier. But this is just a suspicion. The district attorney has no evidence on which he can convict them of the greater crime unless he can get them to confess. The district attorney decides to make the prisoners play a game with the following rules.

Rules   Each prisoner (player) is placed in a separate room and cannot communicate with the other player. Each is told that he is suspected of having carried out the bank robbery and that:

If both of them confess to the larger crime, each will receive a sentence of 3 years for both crimes.

If he alone confesses and his accomplice does not, he will receive an even shorter sentence of 1 year while his accomplice will receive a 10-year sentence.

Strategies   In game theory, **strategies** are all the possible actions of each player. Art and Bob each have two possible actions:

- Confess to the bank robbery
- Deny having committed the bank robbery

Payoffs   Because there are two players, each with two strategies, there are four possible outcomes:

1. Both confess.
2. Both deny.
3. Art confesses and Bob denies.
4. Bob confesses and Art denies.

Each prisoner can work out exactly what happens to him—his *payoff*—in each of these four situations. We can tabulate the four possible payoffs for each of the prisoners in what is called a payoff matrix for the game. A **payoff matrix** is a table that shows the payoffs for every possible action by each player for every possible action by each other player.

Table 14.3 shows a payoff matrix for Art and Bob. The squares show the payoffs for each prisoner—the red triangle in each square shows Art's, and the blue triangle shows Bob's. If both prisoners confess (top left), each gets a prison term of 3 years. If Bob confesses but Art denies (top right), Art gets a 10-year sentence and Bob gets a 1-year sentence. If Art confesses and Bob denies (bottom left), Art gets a 1-year sentence and Bob gets a 10-year sentence. Finally, if both of them deny (bottom right), neither can be convicted of the bank robbery charge, but both are sentenced for the car theft—a 2-year sentence.

Equilibrium   The equilibrium of a game occurs when player *A* takes the best possible action given the action of player *B* and player *B* takes the best possible action given the action of player *A*. In the case of the prisoners' dilemma, the equilibrium occurs when Art makes his best choice given Bob's choice and when Bob makes his best choice given Art's choice. Let's find the equilibrium of the prisoners' dilemma game.

First, look at the situation from Art's point of view. If Bob confesses, it pays Art to confess because in that case, he is sentenced to 3 years rather than 10 years. If Bob does not confess, it still pays Art to confess because in that case he receives 1 year rather than 2 years. So Art's best action is to confess.

Second, look at the situation from Bob's point of view. If Art confesses, it pays Bob to confess because in that case, he is sentenced to 3 years rather than 10 years. If Art does not confess, it still pays Bob to confess because in that case he receives 1 year rather than 2 years. So Bob's best action is to confess.

Because each player's best action is to confess, each does confess, each gets a 3-year prison term, and the district attorney has solved the bank robbery. This is the equilibrium of the game.

Nash Equilibrium   The equilibrium concept that we have used is called a **Nash equilibrium**; it is so named because it was first proposed by John Nash of Princeton University, who received the Nobel Prize for Economic Science in 1994.

The prisoners' dilemma has a special kind of Nash equilibrium called a dominant strategy equilibrium. A *dominant strategy* is a strategy that is the same regardless of the action taken by the other player. In other words, each player has a unique best action regardless of what the other player does. A **dominant strategy equilibrium** occurs when there is a dominant strategy for each player.

The Dilemma   Now that you have found the solution to the prisoners' dilemma, you can better see the dilemma. The dilemma arises as each prisoner contemplates the consequences of denying. Each prisoner knows that if both of them deny, they will receive only a 2-year sentence for stealing the car. But neither has any way of knowing that his accomplice will deny. Each poses the following questions: Should I deny and rely on my accomplice to deny so that we will both get only 2 years? Or should I confess in the hope of getting just 1 year (provided that my accomplice denies), knowing that if my accomplice does confess, we will both get 3 years in prison? The dilemma is resolved by finding the equilibrium of the game.

TABLE 14.3
Prisoners' Dilemma Payoff Matrix

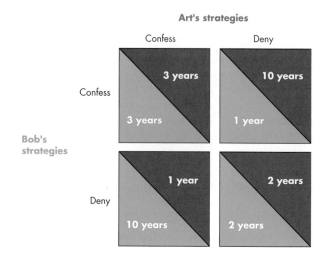

Each square shows the payoffs for the two players, Art and Bob, for each possible pair of actions. In each square, the red triangle shows Art's payoff and the blue triangle shows Bob's. For example, if both confess, the payoffs are in the top left square. The equilibrium of the game is for both players to confess, and each gets a 3-year sentence.

A Bad Outcome   For the prisoners, the equilibrium of the game, with each confessing, is not the best outcome. If neither of them confesses, each gets only 2 years for the lesser crime. Isn't there some way in which this better outcome can be achieved? It seems that there is not, because the players cannot communicate with each other. Each player can put himself in the other player's place, and so each player can figure out that there is a dominant strategy for each of them. The prisoners are indeed in a dilemma. Each knows that he can serve 2 years only if he can trust the other to deny. But each prisoner also knows that it is not in the other's best interest to deny. So each prisoner knows that he must confess, thereby delivering a bad outcome for both.

Let's now see how we can use the ideas we've just developed to understand a host of economic situations such as price fixing, price wars, and other aspects of the behavior of firms in oligopoly.

An Oligopoly Price-Fixing Game

To UNDERSTAND HOW OLIGOPOLIES FIX PRICES, we're going to study a special case of oligopoly called duopoly. **Duopoly** is a market structure in which two producers compete with each other. You can probably find some examples of duopoly in your city. Many cities have only two suppliers of milk, two local newspapers, two taxi companies, two car rental firms, two copy centers, or two college bookstores. But the main reason for studying duopoly is not its realism. It is because it captures the essence of oligopoly and yet is more revealing.

Our goal is to predict the prices charged and the quantities produced by the two firms. To pursue that goal, we're going to study the duopoly game.

Suppose that two firms, Trick and Gear, enter into a collusive agreement. A **collusive agreement** is an agreement between two (or more) producers to restrict output in order to raise prices and profits. Such an agreement is illegal in the United States and is undertaken in secret. A group of firms that has entered into a collusive agreement to restrict output and increase prices and profits is called a **cartel**. The strategies that firms in a cartel can pursue are to:

- Comply
- Cheat

Complying simply means sticking to the agreement. Cheating means breaking the agreement in a manner designed to benefit the cheating firm.

Because each firm has two strategies, there are four possible combinations of actions for the two firms:

- Both firms comply.
- Both firms cheat.
- Trick complies and Gear cheats.
- Gear complies and Trick cheats.

We'll begin by describing the cost and demand conditions in a duopoly industry.

Cost and Demand Conditions

Trick and Gear face identical costs and Fig. 14.6(a) shows their average total cost curve (*ATC*) and marginal cost curve (*MC*). Figure 14.6(b) shows the market demand curve for switchgears (*D*). Each firm produces an identical switchgear product, so one firm's switchgear is a perfect substitute for the other's. The price of each firm's product, therefore, is identical. And the higher the price, the smaller is the quantity demanded.

This industry is a natural duopoly. Two firms can produce this good at a lower cost than either one firm or three firms can. For each firm, average total cost is at its minimum when production is 3,000 units a week. And when price equals minimum average total cost, the total quantity demanded is 6,000 units a week. So two firms can just supply that quantity.

FIGURE 14.6
Costs and Demand

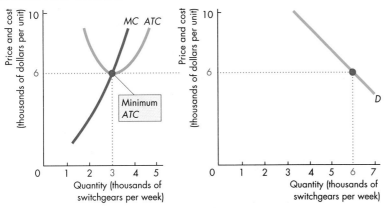

(a) Individual firm   **(b) Industry**

The average total cost curve for each firm is *ATC*, and the marginal cost curve is *MC* (part a). Minimum average total cost is at $6,000 a unit, and it occurs at an output of 3,000 units a week. Part (b) shows the industry demand curve. At a price of $6,000, the quantity demanded is 6,000 units per week. The two firms can produce this output at the lowest possible average cost. If the market had one firm, it would be profitable for another to enter. If the market had three firms, one would exit. There is room for just two firms in this industry. It is a natural duopoly.

Colluding to Maximize Profits

Let's begin by working out the payoffs to the two firms if they collude to make the maximum industry profit by acting like a monopoly. The calculations that the two firms will perform are exactly the same calculations that a monopoly performs. (You can refresh your memory of these calculations by looking at Chapter 13, pp. 268–269.) The only thing that the duopolists must do that is additional to what a monopolist must do is to agree on how much of the total output each of them will produce.

Figure 14.7 shows the price and quantity that maximize industry profit for the duopolists. Part (a) shows the situation for each firm, and part (b) shows the situation for the industry as a whole. The curve labeled MR is the industry marginal revenue curve. This marginal revenue curve is exactly like that of a single-price monopoly. The curve labeled MC_I is the industry marginal cost curve if each firm produces the same output. That curve is constructed by adding together the outputs of the two firms at each level of marginal cost. That is, at each level of marginal cost, industry output is twice as much as the output of each firm. Thus the curve MC_I in part (b) is twice as far to the right as the curve MC in part (a).

To maximize industry profit, the duopolists agree to restrict output to the rate that makes the industry marginal cost and marginal revenue equal. That output rate, as shown in part (b), is 4,000 switchgears a week.

The highest price for which the 4,000 switchgears can be sold is $9,000 each. This is the price that Trick and Gear agree to charge.

To hold the price at $9,000 a unit, production must not exceed 4,000 units a week. So Trick and Gear must agree on production levels for each of them that totals 4,000 units a week. Let's suppose that they agree to split the market equally so that each firm produces 2,000 switchgears a week. Because the firms are identical, this division is the most likely.

The average total cost (ATC) of producing 2,000 switchgears a week is $8,000, so the profit per unit is $1,000 and economic profit is $2 million (2,000 units × $1,000 per unit). The economic profit of each firm is represented by the blue rectangle in Fig. 14.7(a).

We have just described one possible outcome for a duopoly game: The two firms collude to produce the monopoly profit-maximizing output and divide that output equally between themselves. From the industry point of view, this solution is identical to a monopoly. A duopoly that operates in this way is indistinguishable from a monopoly. The economic profit that is made by a monopoly is the maximum total profit that can be made by colluding duopolists.

But with price greater than marginal cost, either firm might think of trying to increase profit by cheating on the agreement and producing more than the agreed amount. Let's see what happens if one of the firms does cheat in this way.

FIGURE 14.7
Colluding to Make Monopoly Profits

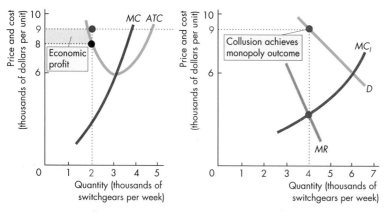

(a) Individual firm   **(b) Industry**

The industry marginal cost curve, MC_I (part b) is the horizontal sum of the two firms' marginal cost curves, MC (part a). The industry marginal revenue curve is MR. To maximize profit, the firms produce 4,000 units a week (the quantity at which marginal revenue equals marginal cost). They sell that output for $9,000 a unit. Each firm produces 2,000 units a week. Average total cost is $8,000 a unit, so each firm makes an economic profit of $2 million (blue rectangle)—2,000 units multiplied by $1,000 profit a unit.

One Firm Cheats on a Collusive Agreement

To set the stage for cheating on their agreement, Trick convinces Gear that demand has decreased and that it cannot sell 2,000 units a week. Trick tells Gear that it plans to cut its price in order to sell the agreed 2,000 units each week. Because the two firms produce an identical product, Gear matches Trick's price cut but still produces only 2,000 units a week.

In fact, there has been no decrease in demand. Trick plans to increase output, which it knows will lower the price, and Trick wants to ensure that Gear's output remains at the agreed level.

Figure 14.8 illustrates the consequences of Trick cheating. Suppose that Trick (the cheat) increases output to 3,000 units a week (part b). If Gear (the complier) sticks to the agreement to produce only 2,000 units a week (part a), total output is 5,000 a week, and given market demand in part (c), the price falls to $7,500 a unit.

Gear continues to produce 2,000 units a week at a cost of $8,000 a unit and incurs a loss of $500 a unit, or $1 million a week. This economic loss is the red rectangle in part (a). Trick produces 3,000 units a

week at an average total cost of $6,000. With a price of $7,500, Trick makes a profit of $1,500 a unit and therefore an economic profit of $4.5 million. This economic profit is the blue rectangle in part (b).

We've now described a second possible outcome for the duopoly game: One of the firms cheats on the collusive agreement. In this case, the industry output is larger than the monopoly output and the industry price is lower than the monopoly price. The total economic profit made by the industry is smaller than the monopoly economic profit. Trick (the cheat) makes an economic profit of $4.5 million, and Gear (the complier) incurs an economic loss of $1 million. The industry makes an economic profit of $3.5 million, which is $0.5 million less than the economic profit a monopoly would make. But the profit is distributed unevenly. Trick makes a bigger economic profit while Gear incurs an economic loss.

A similar outcome would arise if Gear cheated and Trick complied with the agreement. The industry profit and price would be the same, but in this case Gear (the cheat) would make an economic profit of $4.5 million and Trick (the complier) would incur an economic loss of $1 million.

Let's next see what happens if both firms cheat.

FIGURE 14.8

One Firm Cheats

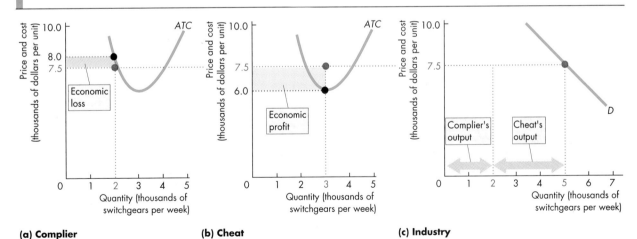

(a) Complier **(b) Cheat** **(c) Industry**

One firm, shown in part (a), complies with the agreement and produces 2,000 units. The other firm, shown in part (b), cheats on the agreement and increases its output to 3,000 units. Given the market demand curve, shown in part (c), and with a total production of 5,000 units a week, the price falls to

$7,500. At this price, the complier in part (a) incurs an economic loss of $1 million ($500 per unit × 2,000 units), shown by the red rectangle. In part (b), the cheat makes an economic profit of $4.5 million ($1,500 per unit × 3,000 units), shown as the blue rectangle.

Both Firms Cheat

Suppose that instead of just one firm cheating on the collusive agreement, both firms cheat. In particular, suppose that each firm behaves in exactly the same way as the cheating firm that we have just analyzed. Each tells the other that it is unable to sell its output at the going price and that it plans to cut its price. But because both firms cheat, each will propose a successively lower price. As long as price exceeds marginal cost, each firm has an incentive to increase its production—to cheat. Only when price equals marginal cost is there no further incentive to cheat. This situation arises when the price has reached $6,000. At this price, marginal cost equals price. Also, price equals minimum average total cost. At a price less than $6,000, each firm incurs an economic loss. At a price of $6,000, each firm covers all its costs and makes zero economic profit (makes normal profit). Also, at a price of $6,000, each firm wants to produce 3,000 units a week, so the industry output is 6,000 units a week. Given the demand conditions, 6,000 units can be sold at a price of $6,000 each.

Figure 14.9 illustrates the situation just described. Each firm, shown in part (a), produces 3,000 units a week, and at this output level, average total cost is a minimum ($6,000 per unit). The market as a whole, shown in part (b), operates at the point at which the demand curve (D) intersects the industry marginal cost curve. This marginal cost curve is constructed as the horizontal sum of the marginal cost curves of the two firms. Each firm has lowered its price and increased its output to try to gain an advantage over the other firm. Each has pushed this process as far as it can without incurring an economic loss.

We have now described a third possible outcome of this duopoly game: Both firms cheat. If both firms cheat on the collusive agreement, the output of each firm is 3,000 units a week and the price is $6,000. Each firm makes zero economic profit.

The Payoff Matrix

Now that we have described the strategies and payoffs in the duopoly game, let's summarize the strategies and the payoffs in the form of the game's payoff matrix and then calculate the equilibrium.

Table 14.4 sets out the payoff matrix for this game. It is constructed in exactly the same way as the payoff matrix for the prisoners' dilemma in Table 14.3. The squares show the payoffs for the two firms—Gear and Trick. In this case, the payoffs are profits. (In the case of the prisoners' dilemma, the payoffs were losses.)

The table shows that if both firms cheat (top left), they achieve the perfectly competitive outcome—each firm makes zero economic profit. If both firms comply (bottom right), the industry makes the monopoly profit and each firm earns an economic profit of $2 million. The top right and bottom left squares show what happens if one firm

---

FIGURE **14.9**

FIGURE 14.9
Both Firms Cheat

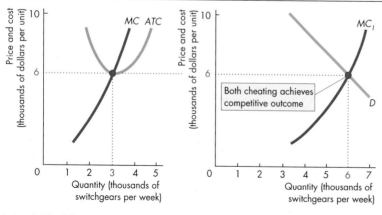

(a) Individual firm   **(b) Industry**

If both firms cheat by increasing production, the collusive agreement collapses. The limit to the collapse is the competitive equilibrium. Neither firm will cut price below $6,000 (minimum average total cost), for to do so results in economic losses. In part (a), both firms produce 3,000 units a week at an average total cost of $6,000 a unit. In part (b), with a total production of 6,000 units, the price falls to $6,000. Each firm now makes zero economic profit because price equals average total cost. The output and price are the ones that would prevail in a competitive industry.

TABLE 14.4
Duopoly Payoff Matrix

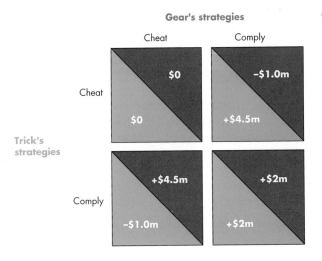

Each square shows the payoffs from a pair of actions. For example, if both firms comply with the collusive agreement, the payoffs are recorded in the bottom right square. The red triangle shows Gear's payoff, and the blue triangle shows Trick's. The equilibrium is a Nash equilibrium in which both firms cheat.

cheats while the other complies. The firm that cheats collects an economic profit of $4.5 million, and the one that complies incurs a loss of $1 million.

This duopoly game is like the prisoners' dilemma that we examined earlier in this chapter; it is a duopolists' dilemma.

Equilibrium of the Duopolists' Dilemma

What do the firms do? Do they comply or cheat? To answer these questions, we must find the equilibrium of the duopoly dilemma.

Look at things from Gear's point of view. Gear reasons as follows: Suppose that Trick cheats. If I comply, I will incur an economic loss of $1 million. If I also cheat, I will make zero economic profit. Zero is better than *minus* $1 million, so I'm better off if I cheat. Now suppose Trick complies. If I cheat, I will make an economic profit of $4.5 million; and if I comply, I will make an economic profit of $2 million. A $4.5 million profit is better than a $2 million

profit, so I'm better off if I cheat. So regardless of whether Trick cheats or complies, it pays Gear to cheat. Cheating is Gear's dominant strategy.

Trick comes to the same conclusion as Gear because the two firms face an identical situation. So both firms cheat. The equilibrium of the duopoly game is that both firms cheat. And although the industry has only two firms, the price and quantity are the same as in a competitive industry and each firm makes zero economic profit.

Although we have done this analysis for only two firms, it would not make any difference (other than to increase the amount of arithmetic) if we were to play the game with three, four, or more firms. In other words, although we have analyzed duopoly, the game theory approach can also be used to analyze oligopoly. The analysis of oligopoly is much harder, but the essential ideas that we have learned also apply to oligopoly.

Repeated Games

The games we've studied are played just once. In contrast, most real-world games get played repeatedly. This fact suggests that real-world duopolists might find some way of learning to cooperate so that their efforts to collude are more effective.

If a game is played repeatedly, one player has the opportunity to penalize the other player for previous "bad" behavior. If Gear cheats this week, perhaps Trick will cheat next week. Before Gear cheats this week, won't it take account of the possibility of Trick cheating next week? What is the equilibrium of this more complicated prisoners' dilemma game when it is repeated indefinitely?

Actually, there is more than one possible equilibrium. One is the Nash equilibrium that we have just analyzed. Both players cheat, and each makes zero economic profit forever. In such a situation, it will never pay one of the players to start complying unilaterally; because to do so would result in a loss for that player and a profit for the other. The price and quantity remain at the competitive levels forever. But another equilibrium, called a cooperative equilibrium, is possible. A **cooperative equilibrium** is an equilibrium in which the players make and share the monopoly profit.

A cooperative equilibrium may occur if each player knows that the other player will punish cheating. There are two extremes of punishment. The smallest penalty that one player can impose on the other is what is called "tit for tat." A *tit-for-tat strategy* is one in which a player cooperates in the current period if the other player cooperated in the previous period but cheats in the current period if the other player cheated in the previous period. The most severe form of punishment that one player can impose on the other arises in what is called a trigger strategy. A *trigger strategy* is one in which a player cooperates if the other player cooperates but plays the Nash equilibrium strategy forever thereafter if the other player cheats.

In the duopoly game between Gear and Trick, a tit-for-tat strategy keeps both players cooperating and earning monopoly profits. Let's see why.

If both firms stick to the collusive agreement in period 1, each makes an economic profit of $2 million. Suppose that Trick contemplates cheating in period 2. The cheating produces a quick $4.5 million economic profit and inflicts a $1 million economic loss on Gear. Adding up the profits over two periods of play, Trick comes out ahead by cheating ($6.5 million compared with $4 million if it did not cheat). The next period, Gear punishes Trick with its tit-for-tat response and cheats. But Trick must cooperate to induce Gear to cooperate again in period 4. Gear now makes an economic profit of $4.5 million, and Trick incurs an economic loss of $1 million. Adding up the profits over three periods of play, Trick would have made more profit by cooperating. In that case, its economic profit would have been $6 million compared with $5.5 million from cheating and generating Gear's tit-for-tat response.

What is true for Trick is also true for Gear. Because each firm makes a larger profit by sticking with the collusive agreement, both firms do so and the monopoly price, quantity, and profit prevail.

In reality, whether a cartel works like a one-play game or a repeated game depends primarily on the number of players and the ease of detecting and punishing cheating. The larger the number of players, the harder it is to maintain a cartel.

Games and Price Wars

The theory of price and output determination under duopoly can help us understand real-world behavior and, in particular, price wars. Some price wars can be interpreted as the implementation of a tit-for-tat strategy. We've seen that with a tit-for-tat strategy in place, firms have an incentive to stick to the monopoly price. But fluctuations in demand lead to fluctua-

tions in the monopoly price, and sometimes, when the price changes, it might seem to one of the firms that the price has fallen because the other has cheated. In this case, a price war will break out. The price war will end only when each firm has satisfied itself that the other is ready to cooperate again. There will be cycles of price wars and the restoration of collusive agreements. Fluctuations in the world price of oil can be interpreted in this way.

Some price wars arise from the entry of a small number of firms into an industry that had previously been a monopoly. Although the industry has a small number of firms, the firms are in a prisoners' dilemma, and they cannot impose effective penalties for price cutting. The behavior of prices and outputs in the computer chip industry during 1995 and 1996 can be explained in this way. Until 1995, the market for Pentium chips for IBM-compatible computers was dominated by one firm, Intel Corporation, which was able to make maximum economic profit by producing the quantity of chips at which marginal cost equaled marginal revenue. The price of Intel's chips was set to ensure that the quantity demanded equaled the quantity produced. Then in 1995 and 1996, with the entry of a small number of new firms, the industry became an oligopoly. If the firms had maintained Intel's price and shared the market, together they could have made economic profits equal to Intel's profit. But the firms were in a prisoners' dilemma. So prices tumbled closer to competitive levels.

R E V I E W

- A collusive agreement to restrict output and raise price creates a game like the prisoners' dilemma.
- Because price exceeds marginal cost, each firm can increase its profit at the expense of the other firm by cheating on the agreement and increasing production.
- If the game is played once, the agreement breaks down because the equilibrium strategy for each firm is to cheat.
- If the game is played repeatedly, punishment strategies such as tit for tat can be used that enable the agreement to persist.

The game theory approach can be extended to deal with a much wider range of choices that firms face. Let's look at some other oligopoly games.

Other Oligopoly Games

Firms must decide whether to mount expensive advertising campaigns; whether to modify their product; whether to make their product more reliable (the more reliable a product, usually, the more expensive it is to produce but the more people are willing to pay for it); whether to price discriminate and, if so, among which groups of customers and to what degree; whether to undertake a large research and development (R&D) effort aimed at lowering production costs; or whether to enter or leave an industry. All of these choices can be analyzed by using game theory. The basic method that you have studied can be applied to these problems by working out the payoff for each of the alternative strategies and then finding the equilibrium of the game.

We'll look at two examples: first an R&D game and second an entry-deterrence game.

An R&D Game

Disposable diapers were first marketed in 1966. The two market leaders from the start of this industry have been Procter & Gamble (makers of Pampers) and Kimberly-Clark (makers of Huggies). Procter & Gamble has about 40 percent of the total market, and Kimberly-Clark has about 33 percent. When the disposable diaper was first introduced in 1966, it had to be cost-effective in competition with reusable, laundered diapers. A costly research and development effort resulted in the development of machines that could make disposable diapers at a low enough cost to achieve that initial competitive edge. But as the industry has matured, a large number of firms have tried to get into the business and take market share away from the two industry leaders, and the industry leaders themselves have battled each other to maintain or increase their own market share.

During the early 1990s, Kimberly-Clark was the first to introduce Velcro closures. And in 1996, Procter & Gamble was the first to introduce "breathable" diapers into the U.S. market. The key to success in this industry (or any industry) is designing products that people value highly relative to the cost of producing them. The firm that develops the most highly valued product and also develops the least-cost technology for producing it gains a competitive edge, undercutting the rest of the market, increasing its market share, and

increasing its profit. But the research and development effort that must be undertaken to achieve product improvements and cost reductions is itself costly. This cost of research and development must be deducted from the profit resulting from the increased market share that lower costs achieve. If no firm does R&D, every firm can be better off, but if one firm initiates the R&D activity, all must follow.

Each firm is in a research and development dilemma situation that is similar to the game played by Art and Bob. Although the two firms play an ongoing game against each other, it has more in common with the one-play game than with a repeated game. The reason is that research and development is a long-term process. Effort is repeated, but payoffs occur only infrequently and with uncertainty.

Table 14.5 illustrates the dilemma (with hypothetical numbers) for the R&D game that Kimberly-Clark and Procter & Gamble are playing. Each firm

TABLE 14.5

Pampers Versus Huggies: An R&D Game

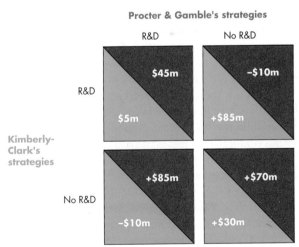

If both firms undertake R&D, their payoffs are those shown in the top left square. If neither firm undertakes R&D, their payoffs are in the bottom right square. When one firm undertakes R&D and the other one does not, their payoffs are in the top right and bottom left squares. The red triangle shows Procter & Gamble's payoff, and the blue triangle shows Kimberly-Clark's. The dominant strategy equilibrium for this game is for both firms to undertake R&D. The structure of this game is the same as that of the prisoners' dilemma.

has two strategies: to spend $25 million a year on R&D or to spend nothing on R&D. If neither firm spends on R&D, they make a joint profit of $100 million: $30 million for Kimberly-Clark and $70 million for Procter & Gamble (bottom right square of the payoff matrix). If each firm conducts R&D, market shares are maintained but each firm's profit is lower by the amount spent on R&D (top left square of the payoff matrix). If Kimberly-Clark pays for R&D but Procter & Gamble does not, Kimberly-Clark gains a large part of Procter & Gamble's market. Kimberly-Clark profits, and Procter & Gamble loses (top right square of the payoff matrix). Finally, if Procter & Gamble conducts R&D and Kimberly-Clark does not, Procter & Gamble gains market share from Kimberly-Clark, increasing its profit, while Kimberly-Clark incurs a loss (bottom left square).

Confronted with the payoff matrix in Table 14.5, the two firms calculate their best strategies. Kimberly-Clark reasons as follows: If Procter & Gamble does not undertake R&D, we will make $85 million if we do and $30 million if we do not; so it pays us to do R&D. If Procter & Gamble conducts R&D, we will lose $10 million if we don't and make $5 million if we do. Again, R&D pays off. Thus conducting R&D is a dominant strategy for Kimberly-Clark. It pays, regardless of Procter & Gamble's decision.

Procter & Gamble reasons similarly: If Kimberly-Clark does not undertake R&D, we will make $70 million if we follow suit and $85 million if we conduct R&D. It therefore pays to conduct R&D. If Kimberly-Clark does undertake R&D, we will make $45 million by doing the same and lose $10 million by not doing R&D. Again, it pays us to conduct R&D. So for Procter & Gamble, R&D is also a dominant strategy.

Because R&D is a dominant strategy for both players, it is the Nash equilibrium. The outcome of this game is that both firms conduct R&D. They make less profit than they would if they could collude to achieve the cooperative outcome of no R&D.

The real-world situation has more players than Kimberly-Clark and Procter & Gamble. A large number of other firms share a small portion of the market, all of them ready to eat into the market share of Procter & Gamble and Kimberly-Clark. So the R&D effort by these two firms not only serves the purpose of maintaining shares in their own battle, but also helps to keep barriers to entry high enough to preserve their joint market share.

Let's now study an entry-deterrence game in which a firm tries to prevent other firms from entering an industry. Such a game is played in a type of market called a contestable market.

Contestable Markets

A **contestable market** is a market in which one firm (or a small number of firms) operates but in which both entry and exit are free, so the firm (or firms) in the market faces competition from *potential* entrants. Examples of contestable markets are routes served by airlines and by barge companies that operate on the major waterways. These markets are contestable because even though only one or a few firms actually operate on a particular air route or river, other firms could enter those markets if an opportunity for economic profit arose and could exit those markets if the opportunity for economic profit disappeared. The potential entrance prevents the firm (or few firms) from making an economic profit.

If the HHI is used to determine the degree of competition, a contestable market appears to be uncompetitive. But a contestable market behaves as if it were perfectly competitive. You can see why by thinking about a game that we'll call an entry-deterrence game.

Entry-Deterrence Game

In the entry-deterrence game we'll study, there are two players. One player is Agile Air, the only firm operating on a particular route. The other player is Wanabe Inc., a potential entrant that is making a normal profit in its current business. The strategies for Agile Air are to set its price at the monopoly profit-maximizing level or at the competitive (zero economic profit) level. The strategies for Wanabe are to enter and set a price just below that of Agile or to not enter.

Table 14.6 shows the payoffs for the two firms. If Wanabe does not enter, Agile earns a normal profit by setting a competitive price or earns maximum monopoly profit (a positive economic profit) by setting the monopoly price. If Wanabe does enter and undercuts Agile's price, Agile incurs an economic loss regardless of whether it sets its price at the competitive or monopoly level. The reason is that Wanabe takes the market with the lower price, so Agile incurs a cost but has zero revenue. If Agile sets a competitive price, Wanabe earns a normal profit if it does not enter or incurs an economic loss if it enters and

TABLE 14.6

Agile Versus Wanabe: An Entry-Deterrence Game

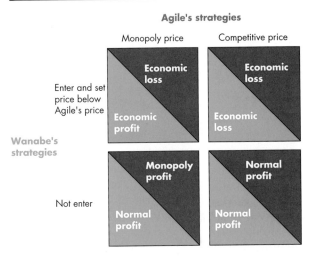

Agile's strategies

Agile is the only firm in a contestable market. If Agile sets the monopoly price, Wanabe earns an economic profit by entering and undercutting Agile's price or a normal profit by not entering. So if Agile sets the price at the monopoly level, Wanabe will enter. If Agile sets the competitive price, Wanabe earns a normal profit if it does not enter or incurs an economic loss if it does enter. So if Agile sets the price at the competitive level, Wanabe will not enter. With entry, Agile incurs an economic loss regardless of the price it sets. The Nash equilibrium of this game is for Agile to set the competitive price, for Wanabe not to enter, and for both firms to make normal profit.

undercuts Agile by setting a price that is less than average total cost. If Agile sets the monopoly price, Wanabe earns a positive economic profit by entering or a normal profit by not entering.

The Nash equilibrium for this game is a competitive price at which Agile Air earns a normal profit and Wanabe does not enter. If Agile sets the monopoly price, Wanabe would enter and, by undercutting Agile's price, would take all the business, leaving Agile with an economic loss equal to total cost. Agile avoids this outcome by sticking with the competitive price and deterring Wanabe from entering.

Limit Pricing   **Limit pricing** is the practice of charging a price below the monopoly profit-maximizing price and producing a quantity greater than that

at which marginal revenue equals marginal cost in order to deter entry. The game that we've just studied is an example of limit pricing, but the practice is more general. For example, a firm can use limit pricing to try to convince potential entrants that its own costs are so low that new entrants will incur an economic loss if they enter the industry. To see how this works, let's go back to Agile and Wanabe.

Wanabe knows the current market price but does not know Agile's costs and profit. It can infer those costs, though. Suppose Wanabe believes that marginal revenue is 50 percent of price. If the price is $100, then Wanabe estimates that marginal revenue is $50. Wanabe might assume that Agile is maximizing profit by setting marginal revenue equal to marginal cost. Given this assumption, Wanabe estimates Agile's marginal cost to be $50. If Wanabe's marginal cost is greater than $50, it can't compete with Agile, so it will drop the idea of entering this industry. But if its marginal cost is less than $50, it might be able to enter the industry and also drive Agile out.

Recognizing that Wanabe reasons in this way, Agile might decide to use limit pricing to send a false but possibly believable signal to Wanabe. Agile might cut its price to (say) $80 to make Wanabe believe that its marginal cost is only $40 (50 percent of $80). The lower Wanabe believes Agile's marginal cost to be, the less likely is Wanabe to enter. The strategic use of limit pricing makes it possible, in some situations, for a firm (or group of firms) to maintain a monopoly or collusive oligopoly and limit entry.

◆ The two market structures you've studied in this chapter—monopolistic competition and oligopoly—are the most common ones you encounter in real-world markets. *Reading Between the Lines* on pages 306–307 shows you that you can even find monopolistic competition on Broadway.

A key element in our study of markets for goods and services is the behavior of firms' costs. Costs are determined by technology and by the prices of productive resources. We have treated resource prices as given. We are now going to see how resource prices are themselves determined. Resource prices interact with the goods market that we have just studied in two ways. First, they determine the firm's production costs. Second, they determine household incomes and therefore influence the demand for goods and services. Resource prices also affect the distribution of income. We study each of these interactions in the next three chapters.

Monopolistic Competition on Broadway

The Wall Street Journal, May 23, 1996

How to Turn $4,000 into Many Millions: The Story of 'Rent'

BY JEFFREY A. TRACHTENBERG

NEW YORK—In November 1994, Jeffrey Seller, a young Broadway show booker, took his partner Kevin McCollum to lower Manhattan to see ... an unknown rock opera named "Rent." At the end of the first act, Mr. McCollum uttered four fateful words: "Get out the checkbook."

The two friends and a third partner ... went on to buy commercial rights to the show for just $4,000. ...

"Rent," Broadway's biggest artistic sensation in years, is also turning out to be a gold-plated business phenomenon. Sold out through the end of August at the Nederlander Theater, "Rent" booked $10 million in tickets sales in just nine weeks. If the theater stays 90% full, it will be pulling in annual ... operating profit, before taxes, of $8 million. ...

Whether "Rent" will prove to be a long-term hit among the tourists who keep big shows open for years is still a debated question on Broadway. Its subject matter is dark: An HIV-positive musician, his drug-addicted girlfriend and their friends attempt to survive on society's fringes.

Ted Chapin, who manages the Rodgers & Hammerstein Organiza-tion, ... says, "You can't get a ticket today, but let's wait for six months and see if it has legs.".…

With the cost of mounting a major Broadway show skyrocketing into the millions, most producers are only backing proven crowd-pleasers with familiar brand names. Five of Broadway's current 17 musicals are revivals, including "Show Boat," "Grease" and "How to Succeed in Business Without Really Trying." Another five—including "Miss Saigon," "Sunset Boulevard," and "Les Miserables"—are imports of British hits. Two of the only "new" shows this season are merely remakes of popular movies: "Big" and "Victor/Victoria."…

At [a cost of] $3.5 million, "Rent" is a relative bargain. "Victor/Victoria" cost $8.5 million. ... The "Rent" team kept costs down with a cast of 15 unknowns, only five musicians, and one stationary set largely construct-ed of scaffolding and junkyard-style fixtures. Total overhead amounts to about $275,000 a week. By compari-son "Victor/Victoria" has weekly over-head of $550,000. ...

As for Mr. Seller, the show's suc-cess has ensured that rent will never be a problem for him. ...

Essence of THE STORY

■ There are currently 17 different musicals playing on Broadway.

■ "Rent," a new Broadway hit, is sold out through the end of August. If the the-ater remains 90% full, the show will make an annual operating profit, before taxes, of $8 million.

■ Because of its subject matter, it is unknown whether or not "Rent" will prove to be a long-term hit.

■ The cost to produce "Rent" is $3.5 million; the cost to produce "Victor/ Victoria" is $8.5 million.

Economic

A N A L Y S I S

■ The market for musical plays on Broadway is a monopolistic competition. Seventeen different musical plays are currently running.

■ Figure 1 shows the market for "Rent" in the short run. The initial demand curve for "Rent" tickets is D_0, and the marginal revenue curve is MR_0.

■ The average total cost curve is ATC, and the marginal cost curve is MC. (These curves have the usual U shape because of marketing costs. Filling one more seat costs the amount that must be spent to persuade someone to sit in it.)

■ To maximize profit, "Rent" sells Q_0 tickets a year for a price (average) of P_0 per ticket. The intersection of the marginal revenue and marginal cost curves determines this profit-maximizing quantity.

■ "Rent" earns an economic profit, shown by the blue area.

■ A show such as "Victor/Victoria" with higher production costs than "Rent" would have an ATC curve above that of "Rent" and, depending on its demand curve, would probably make a smaller economic profit than "Rent."

■ According to the news article, "Rent" is operating at 90 percent of theater capacity. Operating below capacity is in the interest of a firm in monopolistic competition.

■ If "Rent" was operating at full capacity, it would be operating at the point where MC and ATC intersect. Excess capacity is Q_F minus Q_0.

■ The lifetime of "Rent" on Broadway is unknown. Its subject matter might not be popular enough to keep the demand curve at D_0. In addition, other musical plays might open on Broadway, decreasing demand for "Rent" tickets.

■ Figure 2 shows what will happen if the demand for "Rent" tickets decreases from D_0 to D_1; profit is maximized by selling Q_1 tickets. The price of a ticket will fall to P_1, which equals C_1. "Rent" will make normal profit, and it will continue to run as long as demand does not decrease any further.

■ Figure 3 shows the end of "Rent." Here, demand has fallen farther still, to D_2. Average total cost per ticket, C_2 exceeds the profit-maximizing price. So "Rent" now incurs an economic loss, and eventually the show closes.

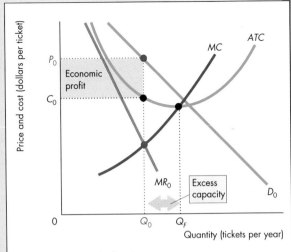

Figure 1 "Rent" in the short run

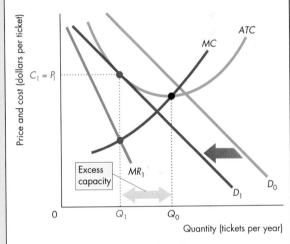

Figure 2 "Rent" earns normal profit

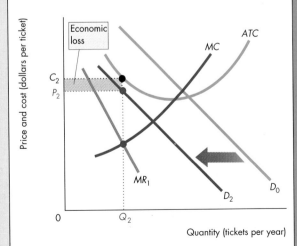

Figure 3 "Rent" exits

SUMMARY

Key Points

Varieties of Market Structure (pp. 286–289)

- Monopolistic competition occurs when a large number of firms compete with each other by making slightly different products.
- Oligopoly is a situation in which a small number of producers compete with each other.
- Monopoly power is measured by using the four-firm concentration ratio and the Herfindahl-Hirschman Index.

Monopolistic Competition (pp. 290–292)

- Under monopolistic competition, firms face downward-sloping demand curves and set prices.
- In long-run equilibrium, economic profit is zero and firms operate with excess capacity.
- Monopolistic competition is inefficient, but the inefficiency must be weighed against greater product variety.

Oligopoly (pp. 293–294)

- If rivals match price cuts but do not match price increases, firms face a kinked demand curve and a marginal cost curve with a break at the current quantity.
- Fluctuations in marginal cost inside the break in marginal revenue have no effects on either price or output.
- If one firm dominates a market, it acts like a monopoly and the small firms take its price as given and act like perfectly competitive firms.

Game Theory (pp. 295–296)

- Game theory is a method of analyzing strategic behavior.
- In the prisoners' dilemma game, two prisoners, each acting in his or her own best interest, end up not acting in their joint best interest.

An Oligopoly Price-Fixing Game (pp. 297–302)

- An oligopoly (duopoly) price-fixing game is like the prisoners' dilemma game.
- The firms might collude, one firm might cheat, or both firms might cheat.
- In a one-play game, both firms cheat and the industry output and price are the same as in perfect competition.
- In a repeated game, a tit-for-tat punishment strategy can produce a cooperative equilibrium in which price and output are the same as in a monopoly.

Other Oligopoly Games (pp. 303–305)

- A firm's decisions about whether to enter or leave an industry, how much to spend selling its product, whether to modify its product, and whether to undertake research and development can be studied by using game theory.

Key Figures and Tables

Key Terms

QUESTIONS

1. What are the main varieties of market structure? What are the main characteristics of each of those market structures?

2. Explain how a firm can differentiate its product.

3. What is a four-firm concentration ratio?

4. What is the Herfindahl-Hirschman Index and what does a large value of that index indicate?

5. Give some examples of U.S. industries that have a high concentration ratio and of U.S. industries that have a low concentration ratio.

6. What is the value of the four-firm concentration ratio for each market structure?

7. What is the value of the Herfindahl-Hirschman Index for each market structure?

8. How do monopolistic competition and perfect competition differ?

9. Is monopolistic competition efficient? Explain your answer.

10. Why might the demand curve facing an oligopoly be kinked, and what is marginal revenue at the kink?

11. In what circumstances might the dominant firm model of oligopoly be relevant?

12. List the key features that all games have in common.

13. What is the prisoners' dilemma?

14. What is a Nash Equilibrium?

15. What is a dominant strategy equilibrium?

16. What are the features of duopoly that make it reasonable to treat duopoly as a game between two firms?

17. What is meant by a repeated game?

18. Explain what a tit-for-tat strategy is.

19. What is a price war? What is the effect of a price war on the profit of the firms in the industry and on the profitability of the industry itself?

20. What is a contestable market? Will the Herfindahl-Hirschman Index reveal such a market? How does a contestable market operate?

21. What is limit pricing? How might a firm try to use limit pricing to increase its economic profit?

PROBLEMS

1. The figure shows the situation facing Lite and Kool Inc., a producer of running shoes.

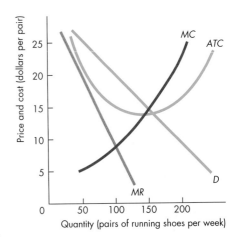

a. What quantity does Lite and Kool produce?

b. What price does it charge?

c. How much profit does it make?

2. A monopolistically competitive industry is in long-run equilibrium as illustrated in Fig. 14.3(b). Demand for the industry's product increases, increasing the demand for each firm's output. Using diagrams similar to those in Fig. 14.3, analyze the short-run and long-run effects on price, output, and economic profit of this increase in demand.

3. Another monopolistically competitive industry is in long-run equilibrium, as illustrated in Fig. 14.3(b), when it experiences a large increase in wages. Using diagrams similar to those in Fig. 14.3, analyze the short-run and long-run effects on price, output, and economic profit of this increase in wages.

4. A firm with a kinked demand curve experiences an increase in its variable cost. Explain the effects on the firm's price, output, and economic profit/loss.

5. An industry with one very large firm and 100 very small firms experiences an increase in the demand for its product. Use the dominant firm model to explain the effects on:

a. The price, output, and economic profit of the large firm.

b. The price, output, and economic profit of a typical small firm.

6. Describe the game known as the prisoners' dilemma. In describing the game:
   a. Make up a story that motivates the game.
   b. Work out a payoff matrix.
   c. Describe how the equilibrium of the game is arrived at.

7. Consider the following game. There are two players, and each is asked a question. They can answer the question honestly, or they can lie. If both answer honestly, each receives a payoff of $100. If one answers honestly and the other lies, the liar gains at the expense of the honest player. In that event, the liar receives a payoff of $500 and the honest player gets nothing. If both lie, then each receives a payoff of $50.
   a. Describe this game in terms of its players, strategies, and payoffs.
   b. Construct the payoff matrix.
   c. What is the equilibrium for this game?

8. Two firms, Soapy and Suddies Inc., are the only producers of soap powder. They collude and agree to share the market equally. If neither cheats on the agreement, each makes $1 million economic profit. If either firm cheats, the cheat increases its economic profit to $1.5 million while the firm that abides by the agreement incurs an economic loss of $0.5 million. Neither firm has any way of policing the other's actions.
   a. Describe the best strategy for each firm in a game that is played once.
   b. What is the economic profit for each firm if both cheat?
   c. Construct the payoff matrix of a game that is played just once.
   d. What is the equilibrium if the game is played once?
   e. If this duopolist game can be played many times, describe some of the strategies that each firm might adopt.

CRITICAL THINKING

1. Study *Reading Between the Lines* on pp. 306–307 and then answer the following questions.
   a. Why are Broadway musicals an example of monopolistic competition?

   b. How are the price of a ticket and ticket sales determined for a single musical like *Rent*?
   c. Why can't a musical earn an economic profit in the long run?
   d. What is the role of advertising and other selling costs in promoting a musical?
   e. Could the producers of musicals collude to increase their profits? Explain the difficulties they face, the benefits they would receive, and the costs to the consumer from such an action.

2. Netscape and Microsoft each develop their own versions of an amazing new Web browser that allows advertisers to target consumers with great precision. Also, the new browser is easier and more fun to use than existing browsers. Each firm is trying to decide whether to sell the browser for $30 or to give it away free. Giving the browser away gets more people using it and brings in more advertising revenue, but selling it brings in a lot of revenue also. If one firm gives the browser away, the other firm will not be able to sell any because the two browsers have exactly the same features. In this event, the firm that tries to sell the browser will lose the development cost. The table shows the payoffs (economic profit) from the two strategies for the firms.

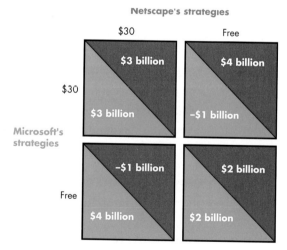

   a. Find the best strategy for each firm and explain why it is best.
   b. What is the economic profit of each firm?

3. Why do Coca-Cola Co. and PepsiCo spend huge amounts on advertising? Do they benefit? Does the consumer benefit? Explain your answer.

Part 5 Resource Markets

For Whom?

During the past thirty years, the rich have been getting richer and the poor poorer. This trend is new. From the end of World War II until 1965, the poor got richer at a faster pace than the rich and the gap between rich and poor narrowed a bit. What are the forces that generate these trends? To answer this question, we study resource markets—markets that determine the prices and quantities used of our productive resources. ◆ The three categories of resources are human, capital, and natural. Human resources include labor, human capital, and entrepreneurship. The income of labor and human capital depends on wage rates and employment levels, which are determined in labor markets. The income from capital depends on interest rates and on the amount of capital, which are determined in capital markets. The income from natural resources depends on prices and quantities determined in natural resource markets. Only the return to entrepreneurship is not determined directly in a market. That return is normal profit plus economic profit, and it depends on how successful each entrepreneur is in the business that he or she runs. ◆ The chapters in this part study the forces at play in resource markets and explain how those forces have led to changes in the distribution of income. ◆ Chapter 15 presents an overview of all the resource markets and explains how the demand for resources results from the profit-maximizing decisions of firms. You've already studied these decisions from a different angle. You've seen how firms choose their profit-maximizing output and, except in the case of perfect competition, the profit-maximizing price. Here, you study the implications of the profit-maximizing output decision for the demand for productive resources. Chapter 15 also explains how resource supply decisions are made and how equilibrium determines resource prices and incomes. You'll discover that some of the biggest incomes earned by superstars are a surplus that we call *economic rent*. ◆ We use the labor market as the main example in Chapter 15. But we also look at some special features of capital markets and natural resource markets. ◆ In Chapter 16, we look more closely at the labor market and study the main sources of differences among people's wages. ◆ Then, in Chapter 17, we study the distribution of income. Here, we come right back to the fundamentals of economics. We answer one of the big questions: Who gets to consume the goods and services that are produced? ◆ But first, we'll spend some time with one of the pioneering thinkers about resources in general and the interplay and conflict between the demands of humans and the resources available. He is Thomas Robert Malthus, and his work first gave rise to economics being called the dismal science. Also, we will talk with Claudia Goldin, a professor of economics at Harvard University, who has made important contributions to our understanding of modern labor markets.

Running Out?

The Economist:
Thomas Robert Malthus

Thomas Robert Malthus (1766–1834), an English parson and economist, was an extremely influential social scientist. In his best-selling *Essay on the Principle of Population*, published in 1798, he predicted that population growth would outstrip food production and said that wars, famine, and disease were inevitable unless population growth was held in check by what he called "moral restraint." By "moral restraint" he meant marrying at a late age and living a celibate life. He married at the age of 38 a wife of 27, marriage ages that he recommended for others. Malthus's ideas were regarded as too radical in their day. But they had a profound influence on Charles Darwin, who got the key idea that led him to the theory of natural selection from reading the *Essay on Population*. And David Ricardo and the classical economists were strongly influenced by Malthus's ideas. Modern-day Malthusians believe that his basic idea was right and that it applies not only to food but also to every natural resource.

> *"The passion between the sexes has appeared in every age to be so nearly the same, that it may always be considered, in algebraic language as a given quantity."*
>
> THOMAS ROBERT MALTHUS
>
> *AN ESSAY ON THE PRINCIPLE OF POPULATION*

The Issues
and Ideas

Is there a limit to economic growth, or can we expand production and population without effective limit? Thomas Malthus gave one of the most influential answers to these questions in 1798. He reasoned that population, unchecked, would grow at a geometric rate—1, 2, 4, 8, 16, … while the food supply would grow at an arithmetic rate—1, 2, 3, 4, 5, … To prevent the population from outstripping the available food supply, there would be periodic wars, famines, and plagues. In Malthus's view, only what he called moral restraint could prevent such periodic disasters.

As industrialization proceeded through the nineteenth century, Malthus's idea came to be applied to all natural resources, especially those that are exhaustible. A modern-day Malthusian, ecologist Paul Ehrlich, believes that we are sitting on a "population bomb" and that the government must limit both population growth and the resources that may be used each year.

In 1931, Harold Hotelling developed a theory of natural resources with different predictions from those of Malthus. The Hotelling Principle is that the relative price of an exhaustible natural resources will steadily rise, bringing a decline in the quantity used and an increase in the use of substitute resources.

Julian Simon, a contemporary

economist, has challenged both the Malthusian gloom and the Hotelling Principle. He believes that people are the "ultimate resource" and predicts that a rising population lessens the pressure on natural resources. A bigger population provides a larger number of resourceful people who can work out more efficient ways of using scarce resources. As these solutions are found, the prices of exhaustible resources actually fall. To demonstrate his point, in 1980, Simon bet Ehrlich that the prices of five metals—copper, chrome, nickel, tin, and tungsten—would fall during the 1980s. Simon won the bet!

THEN...

No matter whether it is agricultural land, an exhaustible natural resource, or the space in the center of Chicago, and no matter whether it is 1998 or, as shown below, 1892, there is a limit to what is available, and we persistently push against that limit. Economists see urban congestion as a consequence of the value of doing business in the city center relative to the cost. They see the price mechanism, bringing ever-higher rents and prices of raw materials, as the means of allocating and rationing scarce natural resources. Malthusians, in contrast, explain congestion as the consequence of population pressure, and they see population control as the solution.

HUNT.

...AND NOW

In Tokyo, the pressure on space is so great that in some residential neighborhoods, a parking space costs $1,700 a month. To economize on this expensive space—and to lower the cost of car ownership and hence boost the sale of cars— Honda, Nissan, and Toyota, three of Japan's big car producers, have developed a parking machine that enables two cars to occupy the space of one. The most basic of these machines costs a mere $10,000 less than 6 months' parking fees.

Malthus developed his ideas about population growth in a world in which women played a limited role in the economy. Malthus did not consider the opportunity cost of women's time as a factor to be considered in predicting trends in the birth rate and population growth. But today, the opportunity cost of women's time is a crucial factor because of the expanded role that women play in the labor force. One woman who has made significant contributions to our knowledge of labor markets and the role of women in those markets is Claudia Goldin of Harvard University. You can meet Professor Goldin on the following pages.

Born in New York City, **Claudia Goldin** was an undergraduate at Cornell University and a graduate student at the University of Chicago, where she obtained her Ph.D. in 1972. Now Professor of Economics at Harvard University and Program Director at the National Bureau of Economic Research, Dr. Goldin is one of the world's foremost scholars. Her work combines economic history and labor economics and has investigated a wide range of important problems such as slavery in the American south, strategic factors in American economic development during the nineteenth century, and the evolution of labor markets during the twentieth century. She has studied the effects of technological change and the role of women in the labor market. Not only a brilliant research economist, Professor Goldin has received honors for her undergraduate teaching.

Michael Parkin talked with Professor Goldin about her research and about the problems facing U.S. labor markets in the 1990s.

Professor Goldin, why and how did you get into economics?

I entered Cornell University from the Bronx High School of Science intending to be a microbiologist, but I first wanted to acquire a strong liberal arts education. Economics appealed to me because of its rigor, its internal consistency, and, most of all, its relevance. But only after I took economics from Fred Kahn (who later, as head of the Civil Aeronautics Board, deregulated the airline industry) did I decide to major in the subject. I traded the laboratory of the scientist for that of the social scientist. Ours, I should add, is more challenging because we have to devise controlled experiments from already existing data.

In 1896, 18 percent of women were in the labor force; in 1996, 58 percent were in the labor force. What have been the driving forces behind this substantial change?

In 1896, most of the 18 percent were young, single, foreign-born, and black. Women generally worked for pay only before they married, although black women and poor women worked regardless of their marital status and age. In 1896, fewer than 5 percent of all married women were in the paid labor force. Therefore the question is why have married and adult women entered the labor force in such large numbers in the past 100 years. Contrary to popular opinion, the first large increase in married women's employment did not occur during the resurgence of feminism in the late 1960s, nor did it occur among the younger age groups. The large initial movement into the labor force occurred during the 1940s and 1950s among women older than 40 years. A host of long-run factors had been operating to reduce the time demands of women in their homes. These include the markedly reduced birth rate and the appearance of market goods substituting for those produced within the home, such as factory-made bread and clothing.

> *"I traded the laboratory of the scientist for that of the social scientist."*

How do you explain the timing and the extent of the explosion in women's employment?

It was rooted in two changes earlier in the century. Between 1915 and 1930, the proportion of all Americans graduating from high school vastly increased, and at the same time, there was a surge in the demand for educated labor in the burgeoning clerical and sales sectors. Young women entered these jobs in droves in the 1920s but generally exited when they married. After World War II, rising wages and an increased demand for labor drew these women back

> *"...the first large increase in married women's employment did not occur during the resurgence of feminism in the late 1960s..."*

into the labor force. Younger married women were raising the baby boom of the 1950s and were less willing to trade the household for the marketplace. The shift of

employment from manufacturing to office and sales work from 1920 to 1950 was an important factor in enabling adult and married women to work for pay. And the generation of older women in the 1950s, who had the requisite education for these jobs, was ripe for this monumental change in employment. They, not the young women of their era, were the real pioneers in women's employment. But the trailblazers did not view these changes as part of a larger social movement.

In the 1970s and 1980s, younger women greatly increased their participation in the labor force, and in the 1980s, even women with infants expanded their employment. In short, rising real wages, falling relative prices of market substitutes for home-produced goods, a declining demand for goods within the home, and a shift of jobs from blue collar to white collar led women to enter the labor force. But the timing of the changes suggests that various norms and institutional rigidities had to be broken down for the long-run forces to operate. These were accomplished first during the 1940s and 1950s.

What have we learned from your work and the work of other labor economists about the sources of persistent wage differences between men and women?

From the mid-1950s to 1980, the ratio of female to male full-time, weekly (median) earnings was constant at about 0.60. Women as a group made little if any noticeable progress relative to men. But from 1981 to the present, the ratio increased by approximately 16 percentage points to 0.76. The analysis of the period of stability and the subsequent period of a narrowing gap reveals much about the sources of gender differences in

earnings. The factors that economists group under the heading of "human capital" are most relevant. When working women's job experience and education advanced on those of men, their relative earnings increased, and when these factors remained constant compared with those of men, women's relative earnings were stable. The aspirations and expectations of teenaged girls are another factor. These young women formed far more realistic expectations in the 1970s than in the 1960s, when they severely underestimated their future participation in the labor force. Young women today are in a much better position to prepare themselves for a lifetime of labor market work than were their elders. We also know that in the 1980s, the returns to education and job experience increased for women relative to men. We aren't certain why this has been the case. Some of the increase could be due to better education or women's greater willingness to undertake more demanding jobs. But we cannot dismiss the notion that the labor market became more gender-neutral in the 1980s, and we also cannot dismiss the role of policy interventions in making it so.

What trend do we observe in the wage differences between blacks and whites?

Similar forces have operated over the long run to narrow differences in earnings between white and black males and between white and black females. In 1940, the ratio of the earnings of black men to white men was astoundingly low—0.43—but by 1980, it was 0.73. Among college graduate men about 35 years old, the increase was even greater—from 0.45 in 1940 to 0.81 in 1980. On the average, black women have made greater progress relative to white women than have black men relative to white men.

What caused these extraordinary changes?

There were two compelling factors—educational changes, including advances in the quality of the education of black Americans, and the movement of blacks from the low-wage South to the higher-wage North. But there were critical junctures in this history. Two occurred during World Wars I and II and led to the greater integration of blacks into the white-dominated manufacturing sector and to an enormous migration to the North. The third occurred during the mid-1960s, when the Civil Rights Act led to further inroads by blacks into the higher-wage manufacturing sector. Unfortunately, some of the gains made since World War I were reversed in the 1980s. I don't mean that we have turned the clock back with regard to education and prejudice. The 1980s were a period of widening inequality in which the lower-educated and the manufacturing sector in particular lost a tremendous amount of ground, and black Americans are still disproportionately represented in these two groups.

What have been the main effects of affirmative action programs? Have they helped or hindered the progress of women and minorities?

Affirmative action is a complex doctrine under which federal contractors, that is, firms that sell goods or services to the federal government, have target levels for the hiring and promotion of women and minorities. There are direct effects from affirmative action programs and, possibly, indirect effects. Most scholarly work has been focused on the direct effects and finds that affirmative action programs have increased the employment and

earnings of minorities. There is little evidence, however, that the programs have served to increase the employment and earnings of women. The indirect effects are more difficult to quantify.

Let's look at the economics profession, for example. Far fewer women than men major in economics, so it isn't surprising that women are vastly underrepresented as teachers and researchers in the field. If we want to know whether having more women economics professors would encourage more female undergraduates to major in economics—that is, if there is a "role model effect"—we could test whether female enrollments increase when women teach the basic economics courses, such as principles. If so, we can make a case for affirmative action as a means of increasing the pool of candidates for a field and thus increasing the future employment of the group even in the absence of further affirmative action. Another possible indirect effect has been the subject of considerable controversy and forms the basis of the conservative attack on the programs. It is that women and minorities get hired or promoted under affirmative action when they should not have been. Such actions will then reinforce discriminatory views of women and minorities as being incompetent at particular jobs and can, in addition, make both groups more complacent and less competitive. I know of no hard evidence to substantiate such claims.

What are the most important labor market problems that we don't understand and that the next generation of economists will work on and possibly solve?

A pressing problem today is why the wage structure and distribution of earnings widened so substantially during the past 10 or 15

years. We need to know more about the interaction among education, inherent ability, and new technologies, such as the computer revolution. What makes some individuals more able to adapt while others are left behind? What types of educational and training interventions will help workers make the transition?

The labor market isn't yet structured or ready for the egalitarian family.

Returning to gender differences in the workplace, I wonder whether the gap in earnings can ever be eliminated, given the structure of jobs and the division of labor in the home. If women are still expected to raise children and do a disproportionate share of household work, they will not advance with men in the labor market. Even if individual husbands and wives would like to create the egalitarian home, the husband is likely to confront considerable problems if he asks his employer for family leave, shorter hours, or a flexible schedule, even at greatly reduced pay. The labor market isn't yet structured or ready for the egalitarian family. I see this restructuring of the workplace as a major issue facing the next generation of labor economists.

15

Demand and Supply in Resource Markets

It may not be your birthday, and even if it is, chances are you are spending most of it working. But at the end of the week or month (or, if you're devoting all your time to college, when you graduate), you will receive the *returns* from your labor. Those returns vary a lot. Pedro Lopez, who spends his chilly winter days in a small container suspended from the top of Chicago's John Hancock Tower cleaning windows, makes a happy return of $12 an hour. Dan Rather, who puts on a 30-minute news show each weekday evening, makes a very happy return of $3.6 million a year. Students working at what

Many Happy Returns

have been called "McJobs"—serving fast food or laboring in the fields of southern California—earn just a few dollars an hour. Why aren't *all* jobs well paid? ◆ Most of us have little trouble spending our pay. But most of us do manage to save some of what we earn. What determines the amount of saving that people do and the returns they make on that saving? How do the returns on saving influence the allocation of savings across the many industries and activities that use our capital resources? ◆ Some people receive income from supplying land, but the amount earned varies enormously with the land's location and quality. For example, an acre of farmland in Iowa rents for about $1,000 a year, while a block on Chicago's "Magnificent Mile" rents for several million dollars a year. What determines the rent that people are willing to pay for different blocks of land? Why are rents so enormously high in big cities and so relatively low in the great farming regions of the nation? ◆ In this chapter we study the markets for productive resources—labor, capital, land, and entrepreneurship—and learn how their prices and people's incomes are determined.

After studying this chapter, you will be able to:

■ Explain how firms choose the quantities of labor, capital, and natural resources to employ

■ Explain how people choose the quantities of labor, capital, natural resources, and entrepreneurship to supply

■ Explain how wages, interest, natural resource prices, and normal profit are determined in competitive resource markets

■ Explain the concept of economic rent and distinguish between economic rent and opportunity cost

Resource Prices and Incomes

GOODS AND SERVICES ARE PRODUCED BY USING the four economic resources—*labor, capital, land,* and *entrepreneurship.* (These resources are defined in Chapter 3, p. 42.) Incomes are determined by *resource prices*—the *wage* rate for labor, the *interest* rate for capital, the *rental* rate for land, and the rate of *normal profit* for entrepreneurship—and the quantities of resources used.

In addition to the four resource incomes, a residual income, *economic profit* (or *economic loss*) is paid to (or borne by) firms' owners. For a small firm, the owner is usually the entrepreneur. For a large corporation, the owners are the stockholders, who supply capital.

An Overview of a Competitive Resource Market

We're going to learn how competitive resource markets determine the prices, quantities used, and incomes of productive resources. The tool that we use is the demand and supply model. The quantity demanded of a resource depends on its price, and the law of demand applies to resources just as it does to goods and services. The lower the price of a resource, other things remaining the same, the greater is the quantity demanded. Figure 15.1 shows the demand curve for a resource as the curve labeled *D*.

The quantity supplied of a resource also depends on its price. With a possible exception that we'll identify later in this chapter, the law of supply applies to resources. The higher the price of a resource, other things remaining the same, the greater is the quantity supplied of the resource. Figure 15.1 shows the supply curve of a resource as the curve labeled *S*.

The equilibrium resource price is determined at the point of intersection of the demand and supply curves. In Fig. 15.1, the price is *PR* and the quantity used is *QR*.

The income earned by the resource is its price multiplied by the quantity used. In Fig. 15.1, the resource income equals the area of the blue rectangle. This income is the total income received by the resource. Each person who supplies the resource receives the resource price multiplied by the quantity supplied by that person. Changes in demand and supply change the equilibrium price and quantity and change income.

An increase in demand shifts the demand curve rightward and increases price, quantity, and income. An increase in supply shifts the supply curve rightward and decreases price. The quantity used increases, and the income of the resource can increase, decrease, or remain constant. The change in income that results from an increase in supply depends on the elasticity of demand for the resource. If demand is elastic, income rises; if demand is inelastic, income falls; and if demand is unit elastic, income remains constant (see Chapter 5, pp. 98–99).

The rest of this chapter explores the influences on the demand for and supply of productive resources. It also studies the influences on the elasticities of supply and demand for resources. These elasticities have major effects on resource prices, quantities used, and incomes.

We begin with the market for labor. But most of what we learn about the labor market also applies to the other resource markets that we study later in the chapter.

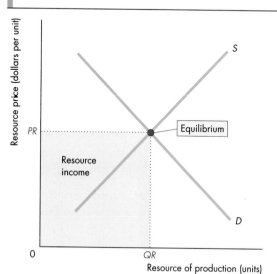

FIGURE 15.1

Demand and Supply in a Resource Market

The demand curve for a productive resource (D) slopes downward, and the supply curve (S) slopes upward. Where the demand and supply curves intersect, the resource price (PR) and the quantity of a resource used (QR) are determined. The resource income is the product of the resource price and the quantity of the resource, as represented by the blue rectangle.

Labor Markets

FOR MOST OF US, THE LABOR MARKET IS OUR ONLY source of income. And in recent years, many people have had a tough time. But over the years, both wages and the quantity of labor have moved steadily upward. Figure 15.2(a) shows the record since 1960. Using 1992 dollars to remove the effects of inflation, the average real wage rate per hour of work increased by 80 percent from $10 in 1960 to more than $18 in 1995. Over the same period, the quantity of labor employed increased by 70 percent from 127 billion hours in 1960 to 216 billion hours in 1995.

Figure 15.2(b) shows why these trends occurred. The demand increased from LD_{60} to LD_{95} and this increase was much larger than the increase in supply from LS_{60} to LS_{95}.

A lot of diversity lies behind the average wage rate and the aggregate quantity of labor. During the 1980s and 1990s, some wages have grown much more rapidly than the average and others have fallen. To understand the trends in the labor market, we must probe the forces that influence the demand for labor and the supply of labor. This chapter studies these forces (and Chapter 16 takes a deeper look at them). We begin on the demand side of the labor market.

The Demand for Labor

The demand for labor is a derived demand. A **derived demand** is a demand for a productive resource, which is *derived* from the demand for the goods and services produced by the resource. The derived demand for labor (and the other resources demanded by firms) is driven by the firm's objective, which is to maximize profit.

You learned in Chapters 12, 13, and 14 that a profit-maximizing firm produces the output at which marginal cost equals marginal revenue. This principle holds true for all firms, regardless of whether they operate in perfect competition, monopolistic competition, oligopoly, or monopoly.

A firm that maximizes profit hires the quantity of labor that can produce the profit-maximizing output. What is that quantity of labor? And how does it change as the wage rate changes? We can answer these questions by comparing the *marginal* revenue earned by hiring one more worker with the *marginal* cost of that worker. Let's look first at the marginal revenue side of this comparison.

FIGURE 15.2

Labor Market Trends in the United States

(a) Labor and wage rate

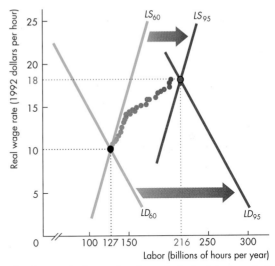

(b) Changes in demand and supply in the labor market

Between 1960 and 1995, the real wage rate increased by **80** percent and the quantity of labor employed increased by **70** percent. Part (a) shows these trends. Each dot in part (b) shows the real wage rate and the quantity of labor in each year from 1960 to 1995. Part (b) shows how changes in demand and supply have generated the trends. The demand for labor increased from LD_{60} to LD_{95}, and the supply of labor increased from LS_{60} to LS_{95}. Demand increased by more than supply, so both the wage rate and the quantity of labor employed increased.

Source: Economic Report of the President, 1997 and author's assumptions.

Marginal Revenue Product

The change in total revenue that results from employing one more unit of labor is called the **marginal revenue product** of labor. Table 15.1 shows you how to calculate marginal revenue product for a perfectly competitive firm.

The first two columns show the total product schedule for Max's Wash 'n' Wax car wash service. (Look back at p. 216 for a quick refresher on this concept.) The numbers tell us how the number of car washes per hour varies as the quantity of labor varies.

The third column shows the *marginal product of labor*—the change in output that results from a one-unit increase in the quantity of labor employed. (Look back at p. 217 for a quick refresher on this concept.)

The car wash market is perfectly competitive, and the (assumed) market price $4 a wash. Given this information, we can now calculate *marginal revenue product* (fourth column). It equals marginal product multiplied by price. For example, the marginal product of hiring a second worker is 4 car washes an hour, and because the price of a car wash is $4, the marginal revenue product of the second worker is $16 (4 washes at $4 each).

The last two columns show an alternative way to calculate marginal revenue product. Total revenue is equal to output multiplied by price. For example, two workers produce 9 washes per hour, which means that they generate a total revenue of $36 (9 washes at $4 each). One worker produces 5 washes per hour, which means that he or she generates a total revenue of $20 (5 washes at $4 each). Marginal revenue product, shown in the sixth column, is the change in total revenue from hiring one more worker. When the second worker is hired, total revenue increases from $20 to $36, an increase of $16. So the marginal revenue product of the second worker is $16, which agrees with our previous calculation.

Diminishing Marginal Revenue Product As the quantity of labor increases, its marginal revenue product diminishes. For a firm in perfect competition, marginal revenue product diminishes because, although price is constant, marginal product diminishes. For a monopoly (or in monopolistic competition or oligopoly), the marginal revenue product of labor diminishes for a second reason. When more labor is hired and more output is produced, the firm must cut its price to sell the extra output. So marginal product *and* marginal revenue decrease, both of which bring decreasing marginal revenue product.

TABLE 15.1

Marginal Revenue Product at Max's Wash 'n' Wax

	Quantity of labor (L) (workers)	Output (Q) (car washes per hour)	Marginal product (MP = ΔQ/ΔL) (additional washes per worker)	Marginal revenue product (MRP = P × MP) (additional dollars per worker)	Total revenue (TR = P × Q) (dollars)	Marginal revenue product (MRP = ΔTR/ΔL) (additional dollars per worker)
a	0	0			0	
			5	20		20
b	1	5			20	
			4	16		16
c	2	9			36	
			3	12		12
d	3	12			48	
			2	8		8
e	4	14			56	
			1	4		4
f	5	15			60	

Max operates in a perfectly competitive car wash market and can sell any quantity of washes at $4 a wash. To calculate marginal revenue product, first work out marginal product (column 3) and multiply it by price. For example, the marginal product of the second worker is 4 washes and the price of a wash is $4, so the marginal revenue product of the second worker (in column 4) is $16. Alternatively, work out total revenue (in column 5). If Max hires 1 worker (row b), output is 5 washes an hour and total revenue is $20. If he hires 2 workers (row c), output is 9 washes an hour and total revenue is $36. By hiring the second worker, total revenue rises by $16—the marginal revenue product of labor is $16.

The Labor Demand Curve

Figure 15.3 shows how the labor demand curve is derived from the marginal revenue product curve. The *marginal revenue product curve* graphs the marginal revenue product of a resource at each quantity of the resource hired. Figure 15.3(a) illustrates the marginal revenue product curve for workers employed by Max. The horizontal axis measures the number of workers that Max hires, and the vertical axis measures the marginal revenue product of labor. The blue bars show the marginal revenue product of labor as Max employs more workers. These bars correspond to the numbers in Table 15.1. The curve labeled *MRP* is Max's marginal revenue product curve.

A firm's demand for labor curve is its marginal revenue product curve. Figure 15.3(b) shows Max's demand for labor curve (*D*). The horizontal axis measures the number of workers hired—the same as in part (a). The vertical axis measures the wage rate in dollars per hour. The demand for labor curve is exactly the same as the firm's marginal revenue product curve. When Max employs 3 workers an hour, his marginal revenue product is $10 an hour, as in Fig. 15.3(a); and at a wage rate of $10 an hour, Max hires 3 workers an hour, as in Fig. 15.3(b).

Why is the demand for labor curve identical to the marginal revenue product curve? Because the firm hires the profit-maximizing quantity of labor. If the cost of hiring one more worker—the wage rate—is less than the additional revenue that the worker brings in, then the firm can increase its profit by employing one more worker. Conversely, if the cost of hiring one more worker is greater than the additional revenue that the worker brings in—the wage rate exceeds the marginal revenue product—then the firm can increase its profit by employing one worker less. But if the cost of hiring one more worker is equal to the additional revenue that the worker brings in—the wage rate equals the marginal revenue product—then the firm cannot increase its profit by changing the number of workers it employs. The firm is making the maximum possible profit. Thus the quantity of labor demanded by the firm is such that the wage rate equals the marginal revenue product of labor.

When we studied firms' output decisions, we discovered that a condition for maximum profit is that marginal revenue equals marginal cost. We've now discovered another condition for maximum profit: Marginal revenue product of a resource equals the resource's price. Let's study the connection between these two conditions.

FIGURE 15.3

The Demand for Labor at Max's Wash 'n' Wax

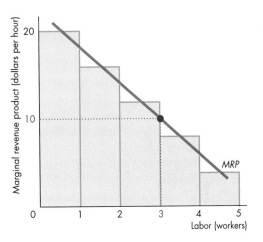

(a) Marginal revenue product

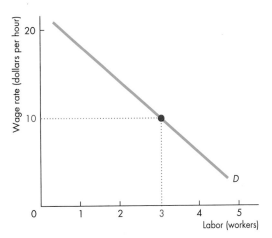

(b) Demand for labor

Max's Wash 'n' Wax operates in a perfectly competitive car wash market and can sell any quantity of washes at $4 a wash. The blue bars in part (a) represent the firm's marginal revenue product of labor. They are based on the numbers in Table 15.1. The orange line is the firm's marginal revenue product of labor curve. Part (b) shows Max's demand for labor curve. This curve is identical to Max's marginal revenue product curve. Max demands the quantity of labor that makes the wage rate, which is the marginal cost of labor, equal to the marginal revenue product of labor.

Two Conditions for Profit Maximization

The concept of *marginal revenue product* sounds a bit like the concept of *marginal revenue*. These two concepts are related, but they are not the same. Marginal revenue product is the extra revenue generated by employing one extra unit of labor; marginal revenue is the extra revenue generated by selling one additional unit of output.

When a firm produces the output that maximizes profit, marginal revenue equals marginal cost. Also, the firm is employing the amount of labor that makes the marginal revenue product of labor equal to the wage rate. These two conditions for maximum profit are equivalent, as Table 15.2 shows.

You've now derived the law of demand as it applies to the labor market. And you've discovered that the same principles that apply to the demand for goods and services apply here as well. The demand for labor curve slopes downward. Other things remaining the same, the lower the wage rate (the price of labor), the greater is the quantity of labor demanded.

Let's now study the influences that change the demand for labor and shift the demand for labor curve.

Changes in the Demand for Labor

The position of a firm's demand for labor curve depends on three factors:

1. The price of the firm's output
2. The prices of other productive resources
3. Technology

The higher the price of a firm's output, the greater is the quantity of labor demanded by the firm, other things remaining the same. The price of output affects the demand for labor through its influence on marginal revenue product. A higher price for the firm's output increases marginal revenue, which, in turn, increases the marginal revenue product of labor. A change in the price of a firm's output leads to a shift in the firm's demand for labor curve. If the price of the firm's output increases, the demand for labor increases and the demand for labor curve shifts rightward.

The other two influences affect the *long-run demand for labor*, which is the relationship between the wage rate and the quantity of labor demanded when all resources can be varied. In contrast, the *short-run demand for labor* is the relationship between the

---

TABLE 15.2

Two Conditions for Maximum Profit

SYMBOLS

Marginal product	**MP**
Marginal revenue	**MR**
Marginal cost	**MC**
Marginal revenue product	**MRP**
Resource price	**PR**

TWO CONDITIONS FOR MAXIMUM PROFIT

1.   **MR = MC**   2.   **MRP = PR**

EQUIVALENCE OF CONDITIONS

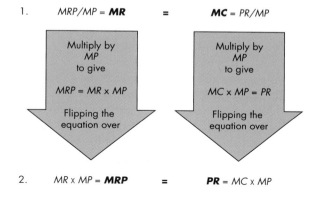

1. $MRP/MP =$ **MR** $=$ **MC** $= PR/MP$

Multiply by MP to give

$MRP = MR \times MP$

Flipping the equation over

Multiply by MP to give

$MC \times MP = PR$

Flipping the equation over

2. $MR \times MP =$ **MRP** $=$ **PR** $= MC \times MP$

The two conditions for maximum profit are marginal revenue (MR) equals marginal cost (MC) and marginal revenue product (MRP) equals the price of the resource (PR). These two conditions are equivalent because marginal revenue product (MRP) equals marginal revenue (MR) multiplied by marginal product (MP) and the resource price (PR) equals marginal cost (MC) multiplied by marginal product (MP).

---

wage rate and the quantity of labor demanded when the quantities of the other resources are fixed and labor is the only variable resource. A change in the relative price of productive resources—such as the relative price of labor and capital—leads to a substitution away from the resource whose relative price has increased and toward the resource whose relative price has decreased. So if the price of using capital decreases relative to that of using labor, the firm substitutes capital for labor and increases the quantity of capital demanded.

But the demand for labor might increase or decrease. If the lower price of capital increases the scale of production by enough, the demand for labor increases. Otherwise the demand for labor decreases.

Finally, a new technology that changes the marginal product of labor changes the demand for labor. For example, the electronic telephone exchange has decreased the demand for telephone operators. This same new technology has increased the demand for telephone engineers. Again, these effects are felt in the long run when the firm adjusts all its resources and incorporates new technologies into its production process. Table 15.3 summarizes the influences on a firm's demand for labor.

We saw in Fig. 15.2 that the demand for labor has increased over time and the demand curve has shifted rightward. We can now give some of the reasons for this increase in demand. The main factors are advances in technology and investment in new capital that increase the marginal product of labor. Both of these factors have increased the demand for labor.

Market Demand

So far, we've studied the demand for labor by an individual firm. The market demand for labor is the total demand by all firms. The market demand for labor curve is derived (similarly to the market demand curve for any good or service) by adding together the quantities demanded by all firms at each wage rate. Because a firm's demand for labor curves slopes downward, so does the market demand curve.

Elasticity of Demand for Labor

The elasticity of demand for labor measures the responsiveness of the quantity of labor demanded to the wage rate. This elasticity tells us how labor income changes when the supply of labor changes. An increase in the supply of labor (other things remaining the same) brings a lower wage rate. If the demand for labor is inelastic, the increase in supply decreases labor income. But if demand for labor is elastic, an increase in supply brings a lower wage rate and increases labor income. And if the demand for labor is unit elastic, a change in supply leaves labor income unchanged.

The demand for labor is less elastic in the short run, when only labor can be varied, than in the long run, when labor and other resources can be varied. The elasticity of demand for labor depends on:

■ The labor intensity of the production process
■ The elasticity of demand for the good
■ The substitutability of capital for labor

Labor Intensity   The more labor intensive the production process, the more elastic is the demand for labor. A labor-intensive production process is one that uses a lot of labor and little capital. Home building is an example. The greater the degree of labor intensity, the more elastic is the demand for labor. To see why, first suppose wages are 90 percent of total cost. A 10 percent increase in the wage rate increases total cost by 9 percent. Firms will be sensitive to such a large change in total cost, so if wages increase, firms will decrease the quantity of labor demanded by a relatively large amount. But if wages are 10 percent of

---

TABLE 15.3

A Firm's Demand for Labor

THE LAW OF DEMAND
(Movements along the demand curve for labor)

The quantity of labor demanded by a firm

Decreases if:	*Increases if:*
■ The wage rate increases	■ The wage rate decreases

CHANGES IN DEMAND
(Shifts in the demand curve for labor)

A firm's demand for labor

Decreases if:	*Increases if:*
■ The firm's output price decreases	■ The firm's output price increases
■ A new technology decreases the marginal product of labor	■ A new technology increases the marginal product of labor

(Changes in the prices of other resources have an ambiguous effect on the demand for labor.)

total cost, a 10 percent increase in the wage rate increases total cost by only 1 percent. Firms will be less sensitive to this increase in cost, so if wages increase in this case, firms will decrease the quantity of labor demanded by a relatively small amount.

The Elasticity of Demand for the Good   The greater the elasticity of demand for the good, the larger is the elasticity of demand for the labor used to produce it. An increase in the wage rate increases marginal cost and decreases the supply of the good. The decrease in the supply of the good increases the price of the good and decreases the quantity demanded of the good and the quantities of the resources used to produce it. The greater the elasticity of demand for the good, the larger is the decrease in the quantity demanded of the good and so the larger is the decrease in the quantities of the productive resources used to produce it.

The Substitutability of Capital for Labor   The more easily capital can be substituted for labor in production, the more elastic is the long-run demand for labor. For example, it is easy to substitute robots for assembly line workers in car factories and grape-picking machines for labor in vineyards. So the demand for these types of labor is more elastic. At the other extreme, it is difficult (but possible) to substitute computers for newspaper reporters, bank loan officers, and teachers. So the demand for these types of labor is less elastic.

Let's now turn from the demand side of the labor market to the supply side and examine the decisions that people make about how to allocate time between working and other activities.

The Supply of Labor

People can allocate their time to two broad activities: labor supply and leisure. (Leisure is a catch-all. It includes all activities other that supplying labor.) For most people, leisure is more enjoyable than supplying labor. We'll look at Jill's labor supply decision. Like most people, Jill enjoys her leisure time, and she would be pleased if she didn't have to spend her weekends working a supermarket checkout line.

But Jill has chosen to work weekends. The reason is that she is offered a wage rate that exceeds her *reservation wage*. Jill's reservation wage is the lowest wage at which she is willing to supply labor. If the wage rate exceeds her reservation wage, she supplies some labor.

But how much labor does she supply? The quantity of labor that Jill supplies depends on the wage rate.

Substitution Effect   Other things remaining the same, the higher the wage rate she is offered, at least over a range, the greater is the quantity of labor that Jill supplies. The reason is that Jill's wage rate is her *opportunity cost of leisure*. If she quits work an hour early to catch a movie, the cost of that extra hour of leisure is the wage rate that Jill forgoes. The higher the wage rate, the less willing is Jill to forgo the income and take the extra leisure time. This tendency for a higher wage rate to induce Jill to work longer hours is a *substitution effect*.

But there is also an *income effect* that works in the direction opposite to that of the substitution effect.

Income Effect   The higher Jill's wage rate, the larger is her income. A larger income, other things remaining the same, induces Jill to increase her demand for most goods. Leisure is one of those goods. Because an increase in income creates an increase in the demand for leisure, it also creates a decrease in the quantity of labor supplied.

Backward-Bending Supply of Labor Curve   As the wage rate rises, the substitution effect brings an increase in the quantity of labor supplied while the income effect brings a decrease in the quantity of labor supplied. At low wage rates, the substitution effect is larger than the income effect, so as the wage rate rises, people supply more labor. But as the wage rate continues to rise, the income effect eventually becomes larger than the substitution effect and the quantity of labor supplied decreases. The labor supply curve is *backward bending*.

Figure 15.4(a) shows the labor supply curves for Jill, Jack, and Kelly. Each labor supply curve is backward bending, but the three people have different reservation wage rates.

Market Supply   The market supply of labor curve is the sum of the individual supply curves. Figure 15.4(b) shows the market supply curve (S_M) derived from the supply curves of Jill, Jack, and Kelly (S_A, S_B, S_C) in Fig. 15.4(a). At a wage rate less than $1 an hour, no one supplies any labor. At a wage rate of $1 an hour, Jill works but Jack and Kelly don't. As the wage rate increases and reaches $7 an hour, all three of them are working. The market supply curve S_M eventually bends backward, but it has a long upward-sloping section.

FIGURE 15.4

The Supply of Labor

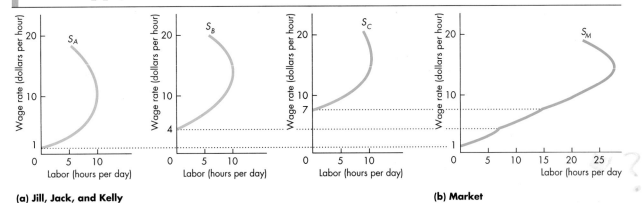

(a) Jill, Jack, and Kelly

(b) Market

Part (a) shows the labor supply curves of Jill (S_A), Jack (S_B), and Kelly (S_C). Each person has a reservation wage below which he or she will supply no labor. As the wage rate rises, the quantity of labor supplied increases to a maximum. If the wage continues to rise, the quantity of labor supplied begins to decrease.

Each person's supply curve eventually bends backward. Part (b) shows how, by adding the quantities of labor supplied by each person at each wage rate, we derive the market supply curve of labor (S_M). The market supply curve has a long upward-sloping region before it bends backward.

Changes in the Supply of Labor   The supply of labor changes when influences other than the wage rate changes. The key factors that change the supply of labor and that over the years have increased it are:

- Adult population
- Capital in home production

An increase in the adult population increases the supply of labor. Also, an increase in the capital in home production (of meals, laundry services, and cleaning services) increases the supply of labor. These factors have increased the supply of labor and shifted the labor supply curve rightward.

Let's now build on what we've learned about the demand for labor and the supply of labor and study labor market equilibrium and the trends in wage rates and employment.

Labor Market Equilibrium

Wages and employment are determined by equilibrium in the labor market. You saw, in Fig. 15.2, that the wage rate and employment have both increased over the years. You can now explain why.

Trends in the Demand for Labor   The demand for labor has *increased* because of technological

change and the demand for labor curve has shifted steadily rightward.

Many people are surprised that technological change *increases* the demand for labor. They see new technologies *destroying jobs*, not creating them. Downsizing has become a catchword of the nineties as the computer and information age has taken hold and eliminated millions of "good" jobs, even those of managers. So how can it be that technological change *creates* jobs and increases the demand for labor?

Technological change destroys some jobs and creates others. But it creates more jobs than it destroys, and *on the average* the new jobs pay more than the old ones did. But to benefit from the advances in technology, people must acquire new skills and change their jobs. For example, during the past fifteen years, the demand for typists has fallen almost to zero. But the demand for people who can type (on a computer rather than a typewriter) and do other things as well has increased. And the output of these people is worth more that that of a typist. So the demand for people who have typing (and other) skills has increased.

Trends in the Supply of Labor   The supply of labor has increased because of population growth and increase in capital in home production. The mechanization of home production of fast-food preparation services (the freezer and the microwave oven) and laundry services (the automatic washer and dryer and steam irons) have decreased the time spent on activities that once were full-time jobs and have lead to a large increase in the supply of labor. As a result, the supply labor curve has shifted steadily rightward, but at a slower pace than the shift in the demand curve.

Trends in Equilibrium   Because technological advances have increased demand by more than population growth and increases in capital in home production have increased supply, both wages and employment have increased. But not everyone has shared in the advancing prosperity that comes from higher wage rates. Some groups have been left behind, and some have even seen their wage rates fall. Why?

Two key reasons can be identified. First, technological change affects the marginal productivity of different groups in different ways. High-skilled computer-literate workers have benefited from the information revolution while low-skilled workers have suffered. The demand for the services of the first group has increased, and the demand for the services of the second group has decreased. (Draw a supply and demand figure, and you will see that these changes widen the wage difference between the two groups.) Second, international competition has lowered the marginal revenue product of low-skilled workers and so decreased the demand for their labor. We look further at skill differences in Chapter 16 and at trends in the distribution of income in Chapter 17.

R E V I E W

- Wage rates and employment are determined by demand and supply in the labor market.

- The quantity of labor demanded is greater, the lower the wage rate (because the marginal revenue product of labor diminishes). An increase in the price of the good produced increases the demand for labor.

- The quantity of labor supplied is greater, the higher the wage rate (but labor supply curves eventually bend backward). Population growth and an increase in capital in home production increase the supply of labor.

- Wages and employment have increased because the demand for labor has increased faster than supply.

Capital Markets

CAPITAL MARKETS ARE THE **CHANNELS THROUGH** which firms obtain *financial* resources to buy *physical* capital resources. These financial resources come from saving. The *price of capital*, which adjusts to make the quantity of capital supplied equal to the quantity demanded, is the interest rate.

For most of us, capital markets are where we make our biggest ticket transactions. We borrow in a capital market to buy a home. And we lend in capital markets to build up a fund on which to live when we retire. Do the rates of return in capital markets increase as wage rates do? Figure 15.5(a) answers this question by showing the record since 1960. Measuring the interest rate as the *real* interest rate, which means we subtract the loss in the value of money from inflation, the rate of return has fluctuated. It averaged around 3 percent a year during the 1960s, became negative during the 1970s, climbed to 8 percent during the 1980s, and steadied at around 5 percent during the 1990s. Over the same period, the quantity of capital employed increased steadily. In 1995, it stood at around $20 trillion (1992 dollars), up by 166 percent from its 1960 level.

Figure 15.5(b) shows why these trends occurred. Demand increased from KD_{60} to KD_{95}, and this increase was similar to the increase in supply from KS_{60} to KS_{95}. To understand the trends in the capital market, we must again probe the forces of demand and supply. Many of the ideas you've already met in your study of demand and supply in the labor market apply to the capital market as well. But there are some special features of capital. Its main special feature is that in the capital market, people must compare *present* costs with *future* benefits. Let's discover how these comparisons are made by studying the demand for capital.

The Demand for Capital

A firm's demand for *financial* capital stems from its demand for *physical* capital, and the amount that a firm plans to borrow in a given time period is determined by its planned investment—purchases of new capital. This decision is driven by its attempt to maximize profit. As a firm increases the quantity of capital employed, other things remaining the same, the marginal revenue product of capital eventually diminishes. To maximize profit, a firm increases its plant size and

FIGURE 15.5

Capital Market Trends in the United States

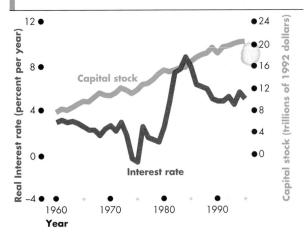

(a) Capital stock and interest rate

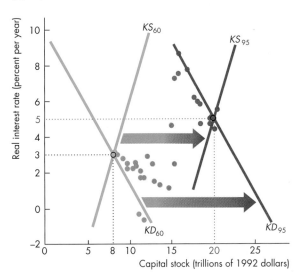

(b) Changes in demand and supply in the capital market

The real interest rate (the interest rate minus the inflation rate) fluctuated between a negative return in 1974 and 1975 and a high of almost 9 percent a year in 1984. It was steady at 3 percent a year during the 1960s and 5 percent a year during the 1990s. During the same period, the quantity of capital employed increased by 166 percent. Part (a) shows these trends. Each dot in part (b) shows the real interest rate and capital stock in a particular year. Part (b) shows how changes in demand and supply have generated the trends. The demand for capital increased from KD_{60} to KD_{95}, and the supply of capital increased from KS_{60} to KS_{95}.

uses more capital if the marginal revenue product of capital exceeds the cost of capital. But the marginal revenue product comes in the future, and capital must be paid for in the present. So the firm must convert expected *future* marginal revenue products into a *present value* so that it can be compared with the price of a new piece of capital equipment. Chapter 10 (pp. 198–200) explains the concept of present value.

The Net Present Value of a Computer   Let's see how a firm decides how much capital to buy by calculating the present value of a new computer.

Tina runs Taxfile, Inc., a firm that sells advice to taxpayers. Tina is considering buying a new computer that costs $10,000. The computer has a life of two years, after which it will be worthless. If Tina buys the computer, she will pay $10,000 now and she expects to generate business that will bring in an additional $5,900 at the end of each of the next two years.

To calculate the present value, PV, of the marginal revenue product of a new computer, Tina uses the formula:

$$PV = \frac{MRP_1}{(1 + r)} + \frac{MRP_2}{(1 + r)^2}.$$

Here, MRP_1 is the marginal revenue product received by Tina at the end of the first year. It is converted to a present value by dividing it by $(1 + r)$, where r is the interest rate (expressed as a proportion). The term MRP_2 is the marginal revenue product received at the end of the second year. It is converted to a present value by dividing it by $(1 + r)^2$.

If Tina can borrow or lend at an interest rate of 4 percent a year, the present value of her marginal revenue product is given by

$$PV = \frac{\$5,900}{(1 + 0.04)} + \frac{\$5,900}{(1 + 0.04)^2}$$

$$PV = \$5,673 + \$5,455$$

$$PV = \$11,128.$$

The present value (PV) of $5,900 one year in the future is $5,900 divided by 1.04 (4 percent as a proportion is 0.04). The present value of $5,900 two years in the future is $5,900 divided by $(1.04)^2$. Tina works out those two present values and then adds them to get the present value of the future flow of marginal revenue product, which is $11,128.

Table 15.4, parts (a) and (b), summarize the data and the calculations we've just made. Review these calculations and make sure you understand them.

How does interest work for Tina?

TABLE 15.4

Net Present Value of an Investment—Taxfile, Inc.

(a) Data

Price of computer	$10,000
Life of computer	2 years
Marginal revenue product	$5,900 at end of each year
Interest rate	4% a year

(b) Present value of the flow of marginal revenue product

$$PV = \frac{MRP_1}{(1 + r)} + \frac{MRP_2}{(1 + r)^2}$$

$$= \frac{\$5,900}{1.04} + \frac{\$5,900}{(1.04)^2}$$

$$= \$5,673 + \$5,455$$

$$= \$11,128.$$

(c) Net present value of investment

NPV = PV of marginal revenue product – Cost of computer

$$= \$11,128 - \$10,000$$

$$= \$1,128.$$

Tina's Decision to Buy   Tina decides whether to buy the computer by comparing the present value of its future flow of marginal revenue product with its purchase price. She makes this comparison by calculating the net present value (*NPV*) of the computer. **Net present value** is the present value of the future flow of marginal revenue product generated by the capital minus the cost of the capital. If the net present value is positive, the firm buys additional capital. If the net present value is negative, the firm does not buy additional capital. Table 15.4(c) shows the calculation of Tina's net present value of a computer. The net present value is $1,128—greater than zero—so Tina buys the computer.

Tina can buy any number of computers that cost $10,000 and have a life of two years. But like all other factors of production, capital is subject to diminishing marginal returns. The greater the amount of capital employed, the smaller is its marginal revenue product. So if Tina buys a second computer or a third one, she gets successively smaller marginal revenue products from the additional machines.

Table 15.5(a) sets out Tina's marginal revenue products for one, two, and three computers. The marginal revenue product of one computer (the case just reviewed) is $5,900 a year. The marginal revenue product of a second computer is $5,600 a year, and the marginal revenue product of a third computer is $5,300 a year. Table 15.5(b) shows the calculations of the present values of the marginal revenue products of the first, second, and third computers.

You've seen that with an interest rate of 4 percent a year, the net present value of one computer is positive. At an interest rate of 4 percent a year, the present value of the marginal revenue product of a second computer is $10,562, which exceeds its price by $562. So Tina buys a second computer. But at an interest rate of 4 percent a year, the present value of the marginal revenue product of a third computer is $9,996, which is $4 less than the price of the computer. So Tina does not buy a third computer.

A Change in the Interest Rate   We've seen that at an interest rate of 4 percent a year, Tina buys two computers but not three. Suppose that the interest rate is 8 percent a year. In this case, the present value of the first computer is $10,521 (see Table 15.5b), so Tina still buys one machine because it has a positive net present value. At an interest rate of 8 percent a year, the net present value of the second computer is $9,986, which is less than $10,000, the price of the computer. So at an interest rate of 8 percent a year, Tina buys only one computer.

Suppose that the interest rate is even higher, 12 percent a year. In this case, the present value of the marginal revenue product of one computer is $9,971 (see Table 15.5b). At this interest rate, Tina buys no computers.

These calculations trace Taxfile's demand schedule for capital, which shows the value of computers demanded by Taxfile at each interest rate. Other things remaining the same, as the interest rate rises, the quantity of capital demanded decreases. The higher the interest rate, the smaller is the quantity of *physical* capital demanded. But to finance the purchase of *physical* capital, firms demand *financial* capital. So the higher the interest rate, the smaller is the quantity of *financial* capital demanded.

TABLE 15.5

Taxfile's Investment Decision

(a) Data

Price of computer	$10,000
Life of computer	2 years
Marginal revenue product:	
Using 1 computer	$5,900 a year
Using 2 computers	$5,600 a year
Using 3 computers	$5,300 a year

(b) Present value of the flow of marginal revenue product

If r = 0.04 (4% a year):

Using 1 computer: $PV = \dfrac{\$5,900}{1.04} + \dfrac{\$5,900}{(1.04)^2} = \$11,128.$

Using 2 computers: $PV = \dfrac{\$5,600}{1.04} + \dfrac{\$5,600}{(1.04)^2} = \$10,562.$

Using 3 computers: $PV = \dfrac{\$5,300}{1.04} + \dfrac{\$5,300}{(1.04)^2} = \$9,996.$

If r = 0.08 (8% a year):

Using 1 computer: $PV = \dfrac{\$5,900}{1.08} + \dfrac{\$5,900}{(1.08)^2} = \$10,521.$

Using 2 computers: $PV = \dfrac{\$5,600}{1.08} + \dfrac{\$5,600}{(1.08)^2} = \$9,986.$

If r = 0.12 (12% a year):

Using 1 computer: $PV = \dfrac{\$5,900}{1.12} + \dfrac{\$5,900}{(1.12)^2} = \$9,971.$

Demand Curve for Capital

The quantity of capital demanded by a firm depends on the marginal revenue product of capital and the interest rate. A firm's demand curve for capital shows the relationship between the quantity of capital demanded by the firm and the interest rate, other things remaining the same. The market demand curve (as in Fig. 15.5b) shows the relationship between the total quantity of capital demanded and the interest rate, other things remaining the same.

Changes in the Demand for Capital   Figure 15.5(b) shows that the demand for capital has increased steadily over the years. The demand for capital changes when expectations about the future marginal revenue product of capital change. An increase in the expected marginal revenue product of capital increases the demand for capital. The two main factors that change the marginal revenue product of capital and bring changes in the demand for capital are:

1. Population growth
2. Technological change

An increase in the population increases the demand for all goods and services and so increases the demand for the capital that produces them. Advances in technology increase the demand for some types of capital and decrease the demand for other types. For example, the development of diesel engines for railroad transportation decreased the demand for steam engines and increased the demand for diesel engines. In this case, the railroad industry's overall demand for capital did not change much. In contrast, the development of desktop computers increased the demand for office computing equipment, decreased the demand for electric typewriters, and increased the overall demand for capital in the office.

Let's now turn to the supply side of the capital market.

The Supply of Capital

The quantity of capital supplied results from people's saving decisions. The main factors that determine saving are:

- Income
- Expected future income
- Interest rate

Income   Saving is the act of converting *current* income into *future* consumption. Usually, the higher a person's income, the more he or she plans to consume both in the present and in the future. But to increase *future* consumption, the person must save. So, other things remaining the same, the higher a person's income, the more he or she saves. The relationship between saving and income is remarkably stable. Most people save a constant proportion of each additional dollar of income.

Expected Future Income Because a major reason for saving is to increase future consumption, the amount that a person saves depends not only on the person's current income but also on his or her *expected future income*. If a person's current income is high and expected future income is low, he or she will have a high level of saving. But if a person's current income is low and expected future income is high, he or she will have a low (perhaps even negative) level of saving.

Young people (especially students) usually have low current incomes compared with their expected future income. To smooth out consumption over their lifetime, young people consume more than they earn and incur debts. Such people have a negative amount of saving. In middle age, most people's incomes reach their peak. At this stage in life, saving is at its maximum. After retirement, people spend part of the wealth they have accumulated during their working lives.

Interest Rate A dollar saved today grows into a dollar plus interest tomorrow. The higher the interest rate, the greater is the amount that a dollar saved today becomes in the future. Thus the higher the interest rate, the greater is the opportunity cost of current consumption. With a higher opportunity cost of current consumption, people cut their consumption and increase their saving.

Supply Curve of Capital

The supply curve of capital (like that in Fig. 15.5b) shows the relationship between the quantity of capital supplied and the interest rate, other things remaining the same. An increase in the interest rate brings an increase in the quantity of capital supplied and a movement along the supply curve. The supply of capital is inelastic in the short run but probably quite elastic in the long run. The reason is that in any given year, the total amount of saving is small relative to the stock of capital in existence. So even a large change in the amount of saving brings only a small change in the quantity of capital supplied.

Changes in the Supply of Capital The main influences on the supply of capital are the size and age distribution of the population and the level of income.

Other things remaining the same, an increase in the population or an increase in income brings an increase in the supply of capital. Also, other things remaining the same, the larger the proportion of middle-aged people, the larger is the amount of saving. The reason is that middle-aged people do most of the saving as they build up a pension fund to provide a retirement income. Any one of the factors that increases the supply of capital shifts the supply curve of capital rightward.

Let's now use what we've learned about the demand for and supply of capital and see how the interest rate is determined.

The Interest Rate

Saving plans and investment plans are coordinated through capital markets, and the real interest rate adjusts to make these plans compatible.

Figure 15.6 shows the capital market. Initially, the demand for capital is KD_0 and the supply of capital is KS_0. The equilibrium real interest rate is 6 percent a year, and the quantity of capital is $10 trillion. If the interest rate exceeds 6 percent a year, the quantity of capital supplied exceeds the quantity of capital demanded and the interest rate falls. And if the interest rate is less than 6 percent a year, the quantity of capital demanded exceeds the quantity of capital supplied and the interest rate rises.

Over time, both the demand for capital and the supply of capital increase. The demand curve shifts rightward to KD_1, and the supply curve also shifts rightward to KS_1. Both curves shift because the same forces influence both. Population growth increases both demand and supply. Technological advances increase demand and bring higher incomes, which in turn increase supply. Because both demand and supply increase over time, the quantity of capital trends upward and the real interest rate has no trend.

Although the real interest rate does not follow a rising or falling trend, it does fluctuate, as you can see in Fig. 15.5(a). The reason is that the demand for capital and the supply of capital do not change in lockstep. Sometimes rapid technological change brings an increase in the demand for capital *before* it brings rising incomes that increase the supply of capital. When this sequence of events occurs, the real interest rate rises. The 1990s appear to be such a time, as you can see in Fig. 15.5(a).

At other times, the demand for capital grows slowly or even decreases temporarily. In this situation, supply outgrows demand and the real interest rate falls. Figure 15.5(a) shows that 1975 was one of these times.

FIGURE 15.6
Capital Market Equilibrium

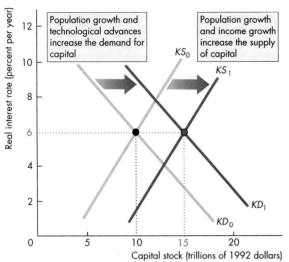

Initially, the demand for capital is KD_0 and the supply of capital is KS_0. The equilibrium interest rate is 6 percent a year, and the capital stock is $10 trillion. Over time, demand and supply increase, to KD_1 and KS_1. The capital stock increases, but the real interest rate remains constant. Demand and supply increase because they are influenced by common factors.

R E V I E W

■ The real interest rate and the capital stock are determined by the demand for capital and the supply of capital.

■ The demand for capital is derived from the marginal revenue product of capital. Firms compare the *present value* of expected marginal revenue product with the cost of a piece of capital. The lower the interest rate, the greater is the quantity of capital demanded. The demand for capital increases because of technological change and fluctuates because expectations fluctuate.

■ The supply of capital arises from saving decisions. The higher the interest rate, the greater is the quantity of capital supplied. The supply of capital increases because of income growth and population growth.

The lessons that we've just learned about capital markets can be used to understand the prices of exhaustible natural resource prices. Let's see how.

Land and Exhaustible Natural Resource Markets

LAND IS THE QUANTITY OF NATURAL RESOURCES. All natural resources are called *land,* and they fall into two categories:

■ Nonexhaustible
■ Exhaustible

Nonexhaustible natural resources are natural resources that can be used repeatedly. Examples are land (in its everyday sense), rivers, lakes, rain, and sunshine.

Exhaustible natural resources are natural resources that can be used only once and that cannot be replaced once they have been used. Examples are coal, natural gas, and oil—the so-called hydrocarbon fuels.

The demand for natural resources as inputs into production is based on the same principle of marginal revenue product as the demand for labor (and the demand for capital). But the supply of natural resources is special. Let's look first at the supply of nonexhaustible natural resources.

The Supply of Land (Nonexhaustible Natural Resources)

The quantity of land and other nonexhaustible natural resources available is fixed. The quantity supplied cannot be changed by individual decisions. People can vary the amount of land they own. But when one person buys some land, another person sells it. The aggregate quantity of land supplied of any particular type and in any particular location is fixed, regardless of the decisions of any individual. This fact means that the supply of each particular piece of land is perfectly inelastic. Figure 15.7 illustrates such a supply. Regardless of the rent available, the quantity of land supplied on Chicago's "Magnificent Mile" is a fixed number of square feet.

Because the supply of land is fixed regardless of its price, price is determined by demand. The greater the demand for a specific piece of land, the higher is its price.

Expensive land can be, and is, used more intensively than inexpensive land. For example, high-rise buildings enable land to be used more intensively. However, to use land more intensively, it has to be

FIGURE 15.7

The Supply of Land

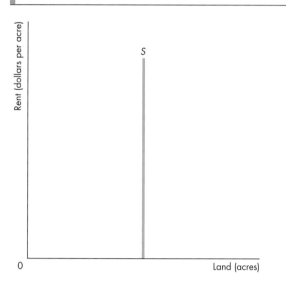

The supply of a given piece of land is perfectly inelastic. No matter what the rent, no more land than the quantity that exists can be supplied.

combined with another productive resource—capital. Increasing the amount of capital per block of land does not change the supply of land itself.

Although the supply of each type of land is fixed and its supply is perfectly inelastic, each individual firm, operating in competitive land markets, faces an elastic supply of land. For example, Fifth Avenue in New York City has a fixed amount of land, but Doubleday, the bookstore, could rent some space from Saks, the department store. Each firm can rent the quantity of land that it demands at the going rent, as determined in the marketplace. Thus provided that land markets are competitive, firms are price takers in these markets, just as they are in the markets for other productive resources.

The Supply of Exhaustible Natural Resources

To understand the supply of an exhaustible natural resource, we must distinguish between three supply concepts: the *stock* supply, the *known stock* supply, and the *flow* supply that is used in production.

1. The *stock* supply of a natural resource is the quantity in existence at a given time. This supply is perfectly inelastic, just like land. No matter what its price, the quantity cannot be changed at that given time.

2. The *known stock* supply is the quantity of a natural resource that has been discovered. This supply is elastic. If the price of a natural resource rises, other things remaining the same, the known quantity increases. The reason is that the higher price strengthens the incentive to widen the search for additional reserves. The known supply increases over time—the supply curve shifts rightward—because advances in technology enable ever less accessible sources to be discovered.

3. The *flow* supply is the quantity of a natural resource that is offered for use during a given time period. This supply is *perfectly elastic* at a price that equals the present value of next period's expected price.

The Flow Supply of Exhaustible Natural Resources

Why is the flow supply of an exhaustible natural resource *perfectly elastic* at a price that equals the present value of next period's expected price? It is because *not* supplying the resource means holding it and selling it later. If next year's *expected* price exceeds this year's price by a percentage that exceeds the interest rate, it pays to hold onto the resource and sell it next year rather than this year. The reason is that the rate of return from holding the resource exceeds the interest rate. Equivalently, if this year's price is less than the *present value* of next year's expected price, it pays to hold onto the resource and sell it next year rather than this year. This year's price is too low relative to next year's expected price.

Similarly, if this year's price exceeds the *present value* of next year's expected price, it pays to sell the resource now rather than wait until next year. This year's price is high relative to next year's expected price.

But if this year's price equals the *present value* of next year's expected price, it makes no difference whether the owner of a resource sells it now or next year. A dollar today is worth the same as the present value of a dollar plus the interest on a dollar a year from today. Because the two amounts are equal, a resource owner is indifferent between supplying and not supplying. Supply is perfectly elastic at the present value of next period's expected price.

Because supply is perfectly elastic at the present value of next period's expected price, the actual price of the natural resource also equals the present value of next period's expected price. Figure 15.8 shows the equilibrium in the market for oil.

The idea that the price of an exhaustible natural resource is *expected* to rise at a rate equal to the interest rate is called the *Hotelling Principle*. It was first realized by Harold Hotelling, a mathematician and economist at Columbia University. But as Fig. 15.9 shows, prices do not follow the path predicted by the Hotelling Principle. Why do natural resource prices sometimes fall rather than follow their expected path and increase over time?

The key reason is that the future is unpredictable. Expected technological change is reflected in the price of a natural resource. But a previously unexpected new technology that leads to the discovery of, or to the more efficient use of an exhaustible natural resource causes its price to fall.

FIGURE 15.9

Falling Resource Prices

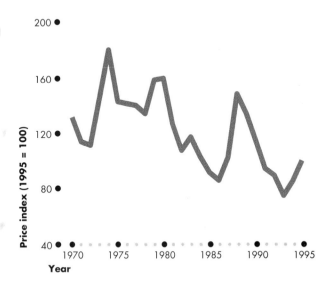

The prices of metals (here an average of the prices of aluminum, copper, iron ore, lead, manganese, nickel, silver, tin, and zinc) have tended to fall over time, not rise as predicted by the Hotelling Principle. The reason is that advances in technology have decreased the cost of extracting resources and greatly increased the exploitable known reserves.

Source: International Financial Statistics (various issues). Washington, D.C.: International Monetary Fund.

FIGURE 15.8

An Exhaustible Natural Resource Market

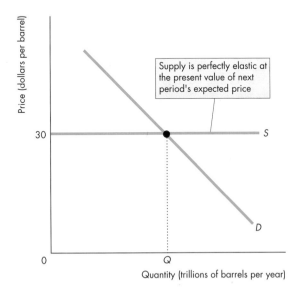

The supply of an exhaustible natural resource is perfectly elastic at the *present value* of next period's expected price. The demand for an exhaustible natural resource is determined by its marginal revenue product. The price is determined by supply and equals the *present value* of next period's expected price.

R E V I E W

- The supply of land (and other nonexhaustible natural resources) is inelastic. Price is determined by demand.

- The flow supply of an exhaustible natural resource is perfectly elastic at a price equal to the present value of the expected future price.

- The price of an exhaustible natural resource is expected to rise at a rate equal to the interest rate.

- Exhaustible resource prices fluctuate and even fall because of unpredictable technological change.

People supply resources to earn an income. But some people earn enormous incomes. Are such incomes necessary to induce people to work and supply other resources? Let's now answer this question.

Income, Economic Rent, and Opportunity Cost

YOU'VE NOW SEEN HOW RESOURCE PRICES ARE determined by the interaction of demand and supply. And you've seen that demand is determined by marginal productivity and supply is determined by the resources available and by peoples' choices about their use. The interaction of demand and supply in resource markets determines who receives a large income and who receives a small income.

Large and Small Incomes

National news anchors earn large incomes because they have a high marginal revenue product—reflected in the demand for their services—and the supply of people with the combination of talents needed for this kind of job is small—reflected in the supply. Equilibrium occurs at a high wage rate and a small quantity employed.

People who do McJobs earn a low wage rate because they have a low marginal revenue product—reflected in the demand—and many people are able and willing to supply their labor for these jobs. Equilibrium occurs at a low wage rate and a large quantity employed.

If the demand for news anchors increases, their incomes increase by a large amount and the number of news anchors barely changes. If the demand for workers in McJobs increases, the number of people doing these jobs increases by a large amount and the wage rate barely changes.

Another difference between a news anchor and a fast-food cook is that if the news anchor were hit with a pay cut, she would probably still supply her services, but if a fast-food cook were hit with a pay cut, he would probably quit. This difference arises from the interesting distinction between economic rent and opportunity cost.

Economic Rent and Opportunity Cost

The total income of a productive resource is made up of its economic rent and its opportunity cost. **Economic rent** is the income received by the owner of a resource over and above the amount required to induce that owner to offer the resource for use. Any

productive resource can receive an economic rent. The income required to induce the supply of a productive resource is the opportunity cost of using a productive resource—the value of the resource in its next best use.

Figure 15.10(a) illustrates the way in which a resource income has an economic rent and an opportunity cost component. The figure shows the market for a productive resource. It could be *any* productive resource—labor, capital, or land—but we'll suppose it is labor. The demand curve is D, and its supply curve is S. The wage rate is W, and the quantity employed is C. The income earned is the sum of the yellow and green areas. The yellow area below the supply curve measures opportunity cost, and the green area above the supply curve but below the resource price measures economic rent.

To see why the area below the supply curve measures opportunity cost, recall that a supply curve can be interpreted in two different ways. It shows the quantity supplied at a given price, and it shows the minimum price at which a given quantity is willingly supplied. If suppliers receive only the minimum amount required to induce them to supply each unit of the productive resource, they will be paid a different price for each unit. The prices will trace the supply curve, and the income received is entirely opportunity cost—the yellow area in Fig. 15.10(a).

The concept of economic rent is similar to the concept of consumer surplus that you met in Chapter 6 (p. 115). Recall that consumer surplus is the maximum price someone is willing to pay, as indicated by the demand curve, minus the price paid. In a parallel sense, economic rent is the price a person receives for the use of a resource minus the minimum price at which a given quantity of the resource is willingly supplied.

Economic rent is not the same thing as the "rent" that a farmer pays for the use of some land or the "rent" that you pay for your apartment. Everyday "rent" is a price paid for the services of land or a building. *Economic rent* is a component of the income received by any productive resource.

The portion of the income of a productive resource that consists of economic rent depends on the elasticity of the supply of the productive resource. When the supply of a productive resource is perfectly inelastic, its entire income is economic rent. Most of Garth Brooks's and Pearl Jam's income is economic rent. Also, a large part of the income of a major league baseball player is economic rent. When the supply of a productive resource is perfectly elastic, none of its income is economic rent. Most

FIGURE 15.10
Economic Rent and Opportunity Cost

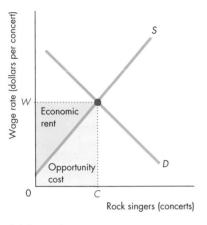

(a) General case

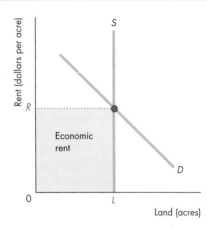

(b) All economic rent

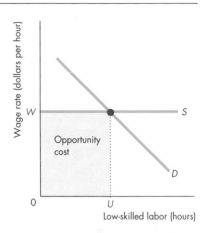

(c) All opportunity cost

When a resource supply curve slopes upward—the general case—as in part (a), part of the resource income is economic rent (green) and part is opportunity cost (yellow). When the supply of a productive resource is perfectly inelastic (the sup- ply curve is vertical), as in part (b), the entire resource income is economic rent. When the supply of the productive resource is perfectly elastic, as in part (c), the resource's entire income is opportunity cost.

of the income of a baby-sitter is opportunity cost. In general, when the supply curve is neither perfectly elastic nor perfectly inelastic, like that illustrated in Fig. 15.10(a), some part of the resource income is economic rent and the other part is opportunity cost.

Figures 15.10(b) and (c) show the other two possibilities. Part (b) shows the market for a particular parcel of land in New York City. The quantity of land is fixed in size at L acres. Therefore the supply curve of the land is vertical—perfectly inelastic. No matter what the rent on the land is, there is no way of increasing the quantity that can be supplied. Suppose that the demand curve in Fig. 15.10(b) shows the marginal revenue product of this block of land. Then it commands a rent of R. The entire income accruing to the owner of the land is the green area in the figure. This income is *economic rent.*

Figure 15.10(c) shows the market for a productive resource that is in perfectly elastic supply. An example of such a market might be that for low-skilled labor in a poor country such as India or China. In those countries, large amounts of labor flock to the cities and are available for work at the going wage rate (in this case, W). Thus in these situations, the supply of labor is almost perfectly elastic.

The entire income earned by this labor is opportunity cost. They receive no economic rent.

◇ We've now studied the markets for productive resources, and we've seen how the returns to these productive resources are determined. We've seen how the interaction of demand and supply determines wage rates, interest rates, and natural resource prices. We've also seen how changes in demand and supply bring changes in resource prices and incomes. We've seen the crucial role played in determining the demand for a productive resource by the resource's marginal revenue product, and we've seen why some resources receive large incomes and others receive small incomes. Finally, we've distinguished between economic rent and opportunity cost. *Reading Between the Lines* on pp. 336–337 shows you the concept of economic rent in action at the Chicago Bulls.

The next chapter studies labor markets more closely and explains differences in wage rates among high-skilled and low-skilled workers, males and females, and racial and ethnic minorities. Chapter 17 looks at how the market economy distributes income and at efforts by governments to redistribute income and to modify the market outcome.

A Superstar Labor Market

CHICAGO TRIBUNE, July 13, 1996

The Signing

BY TERRY ARMOUR

It was quite simple.

All Bulls Chairman Jerry Reinsdorf had to do was decide how much Michael Jordan was worth to his team and to the city, let Jordan know and hope Jordan would be satisfied with the numbers.

The ball then would be in Jordan's court. If Jordan liked what he saw, he would stick around.

That's just how easily things worked out leading up to Friday when Jordan agreed to a one-year deal. ... Financial details weren't disclosed but Jordan is believed to have settled for close to $30 million. ...

The deal ultimately came down to how much Jordan, the world's most famous athlete, is worth to the franchise and the league as a whole.

Jordan's net worth is estimated to be near $200 million, with most of his money coming from endorsements. Since Jordan entered the NBA in 1984, NBA licensing has jumped from $44 million annually to $3 billion, with the Bulls the top-selling team in merchandise since 1990. Yet Jordan's basketball salary was just $3.85 million last season in the final year of an eight-year pact that paid him $24 million.

When Jordan first threw out the figure of $36 million in May for the Bulls to keep him in Chicago over the next two seasons, he added he simply hoped to get what Reinsdorf believed he was worth. Jordan, after all, did help build the two-year-old United Center. ...

Jordan must have been happy with Reinsdorf's numbers, which leave him as the NBA's highest-paid player. ...

"Michael asked for a one-year contract because he never wants to play if he is unable to meet his own standards," Reinsdorf said. "This way, Michael and the Bulls will be able to discuss what is appropriate after each subsequent season. Michael's desire for a one-year contract is refreshing in this era where athletes often seek to be paid beyond their productive years. ..."

Essence of THE STORY

■ Jerry Reinsdorf, Chicago Bulls chairman, offered Michael Jordan a contract based on Jordan's worth to the team. Jordan believed that he was worth $36 million over two seasons.

■ The one-year contract is estimated to be worth close to $30 million.

■ Since Jordan entered the NBA in 1984, NBA licensing has increased from $44 million to $3 billion annually. The Bulls have been the top-selling team in merchandise since 1990.

■ During the 1995–1996 season, Jordan's basketball salary was $3.85 million, the last year of an eight-year contract that paid a total of $24 million.

■ Reinsdorf is pleased that Jordan is interested in signing a one-year deal and renegotiating next year according to his on-court performance. Reinsdorf believes that other athletes seek to be paid beyond their productive years.

Economic

A N A L Y S I S

■ Michael Jordan is a special productive resource. The supply of Michael Jordan's services is limited because he is uniquely talented and other people cannot replicate all the things he does.

■ Figure I shows the supply curve, S, of Michael Jordan's services. At a very low wage rate, he supplies no labor. As the wage rate increases, the quantity of labor that he supplies increases up to a maximum amount H. No matter how much he is offered, he cannot work more than H hours a year.

■ Figure I also shows the demand curve, D_0, for Michael Jordan's services in 1988, when he signed an eight-year contract with the Bulls.

■ The demand for Michael Jordan's services is determined by his marginal revenue product.

■ Because Michael Jordan fills the United Center for all Bulls home games and increases sales of Bulls merchandise, his marginal revenue product is enormous.

■ In 1988, the market for Michael Jordan's services was in equilibrium at a wage rate of $3.85 million a year.

■ Most of this income was economic rent. It was not the opportunity cost of Michael Jordan's services.

■ Over the next seven years, merchandise from the Bulls has become the NBA's top seller largely because of Michael Jordan's popularity. His marginal revenue has increased.

■ Figure 2 shows that by 1996, Michael Jordan's marginal revenue product had increased to $30 million a year and the demand for his services increased to D_1.

■ But Michael Jordan's contract gave him only $3.85 million, so the Bulls collected most of the economic rent.

■ When Michael Jordan signed a new contract for 1997, he negotiated a wage of $30 million dollars a year, which gave him all the economic rent. Figure 3 shows this outcome.

■ By agreeing to determine next year's wage based on this year's on-court performance, a player such as Michael Jordan might increase his income. He has an even stronger incentive to perform well. And a better performance brings a bigger attendance,

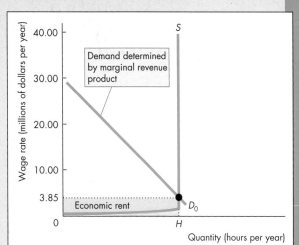
Figure 1 Michael Jordan's eight-year contract

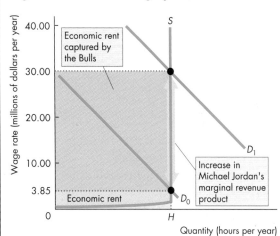
Figure 2 Last year of eight-year contract

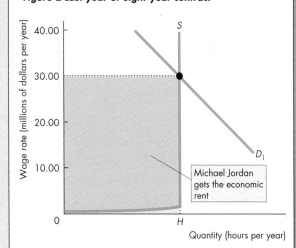
Figure 3 Michael Jordan's 1997 contract

greater merchandise sales—greater marginal revenue product for Michael Jordan.

■ Players who are in the declining performance years resist such pay deals because their marginal revenue products are falling. So they try to capture some economic rent while they are playing well.

337

SUMMARY

Key Points

Resource Prices and Incomes (p. 318)

- An increase in the demand for a productive resource increases the resource's price and total income; a decrease in the demand for a productive resource decreases its price and total income.

- An increase in the supply of a productive resource increases the quantity used but decreases price and might increase or decrease its total income, depending on whether demand is elastic or inelastic.

Labor Markets (pp. 319–326)

- The demand for labor is determined by the marginal revenue product of labor.

- The demand for labor increases because of technological change and capital accumulation.

- The elasticity of demand for labor depends on the labor intensity of production, the elasticity of demand for the product, and the ease with which labor can be substituted for capital.

- The quantity of labor supplied increases as the real wage rate increases, but at high wage rates, the supply curve eventually bends backwards.

- The supply of labor increases as the population increases and with increases in capital in home production.

- Real wages and employment increase because demand increases by more than supply.

Capital Markets (pp. 326–331)

- To make an investment decision, a firm compares the *present value* of the expected marginal revenue product of capital with the price of capital.

- Population growth and technological change increase the demand for capital.

- The higher the interest rate, the greater are the amount of saving and quantity of capital supplied.

- The supply of capital increases as incomes increase.

- Capital market equilibrium determines interest rates.

Land and Exhaustible Natural Resource Markets (pp. 331–333)

- The demand for natural resources is determined by its marginal revenue product.

- The supply of land is inelastic.

- The supply of exhaustible natural resources is perfectly elastic at a price equal to the present value of the expected future price.

- The price of exhaustible natural resources is expected to rise at a rate equal to the interest rate but fluctuates and sometimes falls.

Incomes, Economic Rent, and Opportunity Cost (pp. 334–335)

- Economic rent is the income received by a resource owner over and above the amount needed to induce the owner to supply the productive resource for use.

- The rest of a resource's income is opportunity cost.

- When the supply of a resource is perfectly inelastic, its entire income is made up of economic rent; when supply is perfectly elastic, the entire income is made up of opportunity cost.

Key Figures and Tables

Key Terms

QUESTIONS

1. Define marginal revenue product and distinguish between marginal revenue product and marginal revenue.
2. Why does marginal revenue product of a resource decline as the quantity of the resource employed increases?
3. What is the relationship between the demand curve for a productive resource and its marginal revenue product curve? Why?
4. Show that the condition for maximum profit in the goods market—marginal cost equals marginal revenue—is equivalent to the condition for maximum profit in the resource market—marginal revenue product equals marginal cost of resource (equals resource price in a competitive resource market).
5. Review the main influences on the demand for a productive resource—the influences that shift the demand curve for a resource.
6. What determines the short-run and the long-run elasticity of demand for labor?
7. What determines the supply of labor?
8. Why might the supply of labor curve bend backward at a high enough wage rate?
9. Explain why wage rates and employment increase over time.
10. What is present value and how is it calculated?
11. What determines the supply of capital?
12. How are interest rates determined?
13. Why is the price of a block of land determined by its marginal revenue product?
14. Why is the price of an exhaustible natural resource determined by the present value of its expected future price?
15. Why do national news anchors receive large incomes and fast-food cooks such low ones?
16. Define economic rent and opportunity cost and distinguish between these two components of income.
17. Suppose that a productive resource is in perfectly inelastic supply. If the marginal revenue product of the resource decreases, what happens to the price, quantity used, income, opportunity cost, and economic rent of the resource?

PROBLEMS

1. The figure illustrates the market for blueberry pickers:

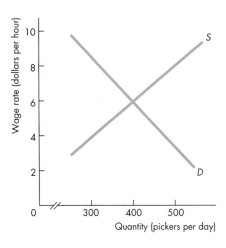

a. What is the wage rate paid to blueberry pickers?
b. How many blueberry pickers get hired?
c. What is the income received by blueberry pickers?
d. What is the marginal revenue product of blueberry pickers?
e. If the price of blueberries is $1 a carton, what is the marginal product of the last picker hired?
2. In problem 1, show on the figure the pickers'
a. Economic rent.
b. Opportunity cost.
3. In problem 1, if the demand for blueberry pickers increases by 100 pickers a day,
a. What is the increase in the wage rate paid to the pickers?
b. How many additional pickers get hired?
c. What is the total income paid to pickers?
d. What now is the pickers' economic rent?
e. What now is the pickers' opportunity cost?
4. Wanda owns a fish shop. She employs students to sort and pack the fish. Students can pack the following amounts of fish in an hour:

Number of students	Quantity of fish (pounds)
1	20
2	50
3	90
4	120
5	145
6	165
7	180
8	190

a. Draw the marginal product curve of these students.
b. If Wanda can sell her fish for 50¢ a pound, draw the marginal revenue product curve.
c. Draw Wanda's demand for labor curve.
d. If all fish shops in Wanda's area pay their packers $7.50 an hour, how many students will Wanda employ?

5. The price of fish falls to 33.33¢ a pound, and fish packers' wages remain at $7.50 an hour.
a. What happens to Wanda's marginal product curve?
b. What happens to her marginal revenue product curve?
c. What happens to her demand for labor curve?
d. What happens to the number of students that she employs?

6. Fish packers' wages increase to $10 an hour, but the price of fish remains at 50¢ a pound.
a. What happens to the marginal revenue product curve?
b. What happens to Wanda's demand curve?
c. How many students does Wanda employ?

7. Using the information provided in problem 4, calculate Wanda's marginal revenue and marginal cost, marginal revenue product, and marginal cost of labor. Show that when Wanda is making maximum profit, marginal cost equals marginal revenue and marginal revenue product equals the marginal cost of labor.

8. You are given the following information about the labor market in an isolated town in the Amazon rain forest: Everyone works for logging companies, but there are many logging companies in the town. The market for logging workers is perfectly competitive. The town's labor supply is given as follows:

Wage rate (cruzeiros per hour)	Quantity of labor supplied (hours)
200	120
300	160
400	200
500	240
600	280
700	320
800	360

The market demand for labor from all the logging firms in the town is as follows:

Wage rate (cruzeiros per hour)	Quantity of labor demanded (hours)
200	400
300	360
400	320
500	280
600	240
700	200
800	160

a. What is the equilibrium wage rate, and how many hours of labor are employed?
b. What is total labor income?
c. How much of that labor income is economic rent and how much is opportunity cost? (You may find it easier to answer this question by drawing graphs of the demand and supply curves and then finding the economic rent and opportunity cost as areas on the graph in a manner similar to what was done in Fig. 15.10.)

CRITICAL THINKING

1. Study *Reading Between the Lines* on pp. 336–337 and answer the following questions:
a. Does Michael Jordan earn more or less than his opportunity cost?
b. Why doesn't Michael Jordan earn his opportunity cost?
c. Why do some players want long-term contracts?
d. Why do some team managers want long-term contracts?

As you well know, college is not just a party. Those exams and problem sets require a lot of time and effort. Are they worth the sweat that goes into them? What is the payoff? Is it sufficient to make up for the years of tuition, room and board, and lost wages? (You could, after all, be working for pay now instead of slogging through this economics course.) ◆ Many workers belong to labor unions. Usually, union workers earn a higher wage than nonunion workers in comparable jobs. Why? How are unions able to get higher wages for their members than the wages that nonunion workers are paid? ◆ Among the most visible and persistent differences in earnings are those between men and women and between whites and

minorities. White men, on the average, earn incomes that are one third higher than the incomes earned by black men and white women. Black men and white women earn more, in descending order, than Hispanic men, black women, and Hispanic women, who earn only 58 cents for each dollar earned

The Sweat of Our Brows

by the average white man. Certainly, a lot of individuals defy the averages. But why do minorities and women so consistently earn less than white men? Is it because of discrimination and exploitation? Or is it because of economic factors? Or is it a combination of the two? ◆ Equal pay legislation has resulted in comparable-worth programs that try to ensure that jobs of equivalent value receive the same pay regardless of the pay set by the market. Can comparable-worth programs bring economic help to women and minorities? ◆ We hear a lot these days about immigration. How does immigration affect the economic well-being of both immigrants and native Americans? ◆ In this chapter, we answer questions such as these by continuing our study of labor markets. We study the effects of education and training, labor unions, gender and race, comparable-worth laws, and immigration.

After studying this chapter, you will be able to:

■ Explain why college graduates earn more, on the average, than high school graduates

■ Explain why union workers earn higher wages than nonunion workers

■ Explain why, on the average, men earn more than women and whites earn more than minorities

■ Predict the effects of a comparable-worth program

■ Explain the effects of immigration on the wages of immigrants and native Americans

Skill Differentials

EVERYONE IS SKILLED BUT THE VALUE THE market places on different types of skills varies a great deal so that differences in skills lead to large differences in earnings. For example, a clerk in a law firm earns less than a tenth of the earnings of the attorney he assists. An operating room assistant earns less than a tenth of the earnings of the surgeon she works with. Differences in skills arise partly from differences in education and partly from differences in on-the-job training. Differences in earnings between workers with varying levels of education and training can be explained by using a model of competitive labor markets. In the real world, there are many different levels and varieties of education and training. To keep our analysis as clear as possible, we'll study a model economy with two different skill levels and two types of labor: high-skilled labor and low-skilled labor. We'll study the demand for and supply of these two types of labor and see why there is a difference in their wages and what determines that difference. Let's begin by looking at the demand for the two types of labor.

The Demand for High-Skilled and Low-Skilled Labor

High-skilled workers can perform a variety of tasks that low-skilled workers would perform badly or perhaps could not even perform at all. Imagine an untrained, inexperienced person performing surgery or piloting an airplane. High-skilled workers have a higher marginal revenue product than low-skilled workers. As we learned in Chapter 15, a firm's demand for labor curve is the same as the marginal revenue product of labor curve.

Figure 16.1(a) shows the demand curves for high-skilled (D_H) and low-skilled labor (D_L). At any given level of employment, firms are willing to pay a higher wage rate to a high-skilled worker than to a low-skilled worker. The gap between the two wage rates measures the marginal revenue product of skill—for example, at an employment level of 2,000 hours, firms are willing to pay $12.50 for a high-skilled worker and only $5 for an low-skilled worker, a difference of $7.50 an hour. Thus the marginal revenue product of skill is $7.50 an hour.

The Supply of High-Skilled and Low-Skilled Labor

Skills are costly to acquire. Furthermore, a worker usually pays the cost of acquiring a skill before benefiting from a higher wage. For example, attending college usually leads to a higher income, but the higher income is not earned until after graduation. These facts imply that the acquisition of a skill is an investment. To emphasize the investment nature of acquiring a skill, we call that activity an investment in human capital. **Human capital** is the accumulated skill and knowledge of human beings.

The opportunity cost of acquiring a skill includes actual expenditures on such things as tuition and room and board and also a cost in the form of lost or reduced earnings while the skill is being acquired. When a person goes to school full time, that cost is the total earnings forgone. However, some people acquire skills on the job. Such skill acquisition is called on-the-job training. Usually, a worker undergoing on-the-job training is paid a lower wage than one doing a comparable job but not undergoing training. In such a case, the cost of acquiring the skill is the difference between the wage paid to a person not being trained and that paid to a person being trained.

Supply Curves of High-Skilled and Low-Skilled Labor The position of the supply curve of high-skilled workers reflects the cost of acquiring the skill. Figure 16.1(b) shows two supply curves: one for high-skilled workers and the other for low-skilled workers. The supply curve for high-skilled workers is S_H, and that for low-skilled workers is S_L.

The high-skilled workers' supply curve lies above the low-skilled workers' supply curve. The vertical distance between the two supply curves is the compensation that high-skilled workers require for the cost of acquiring the skill. For example, suppose that the quantity of low-skilled labor supplied is 2,000 hours at a wage rate of $5 an hour. This wage rate compensates the low-skilled workers mainly for their time on the job. Consider next the supply of high-skilled workers. To induce 2,000 hours of high-skilled labor to be supplied, firms must pay a wage rate of $8.50 an hour. This wage rate for high-skilled labor is higher than that for low-skilled labor because high-skilled labor must be compensated not only for the time on the job but also for the time and other costs of acquiring the skill.

FIGURE 16.1

Skill Differentials

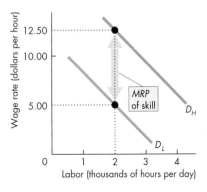

(a) Demand for high-skilled and low-skilled labor

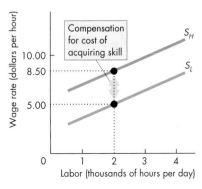

(b) Supply of high-skilled and low-skilled labor

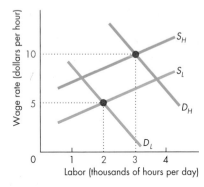

(c) Markets for high-skilled and low-skilled labor

Part (a) illustrates the marginal revenue product of skill. Low-skilled workers have a marginal revenue product that gives rise to the demand curve marked D_L. High-skilled workers have a higher marginal revenue product than low-skilled workers. Therefore the demand curve for high-skilled workers, D_H, lies to the right of D_L. The vertical distance between these two curves is the marginal revenue product of the skill.

Part (b) shows the effects of the cost of acquiring skills on the supply curves of labor. The supply curve for low-skilled

workers is S_L. The supply curve for high-skilled workers is S_H. The vertical distance between these two curves is the required compensation for the cost of acquiring a skill.

Part (c) shows the equilibrium employment and the wage differential. Low-skilled workers earn a wage rate of $5 an hour, and 2,000 hours of low-skilled labor are employed. High-skilled workers earn a wage rate of $10, and 3,000 hours of high-skilled labor are employed. The wage rate for high-skilled workers always exceeds that for low-skilled workers.

Wage Rates of High-Skilled and Low-Skilled Labor

To work out the wage rates of high-skilled and low-skilled labor, we have to bring together the effects of skill on the demand and supply of labor.

Figure 16.1(c) shows the demand curves and the supply curves for high-skilled and low-skilled labor. These curves are exactly the same as those plotted in parts (a) and (b). Equilibrium occurs in the market for low-skilled labor where the supply and demand curves for low-skilled labor intersect. The equilibrium wage rate is $5 an hour, and the quantity of low-skilled labor employed is 2,000 hours. Equilibrium in the market for high-skilled workers occurs where the supply and demand curves for high-skilled workers intersect. The equilibrium wage rate is $10 an hour, and the quantity of high-skilled labor employed is 3,000 hours.

As you can see in part (c), the equilibrium wage rate of high-skilled labor is higher than that of low-skilled labor. This outcome occurs for two reasons: First, high-skilled labor has a higher marginal revenue product than low-skilled labor, so at a given wage rate, the quantity of high-skilled labor demanded exceeds that of low-skilled labor. Second, skills are costly to acquire, so at a given wage rate, the quantity of high-skilled labor supplied is less than that of low-skilled labor. The wage differential (in this case, $5 an hour) depends on both the marginal revenue product of the skill and the cost of acquiring it. The higher the marginal revenue product of the skill, the larger is the vertical distance between the demand curves. The more costly it is to acquire a skill, the larger is the vertical distance between the supply curves. The higher the marginal revenue product of the skill and the more costly it is to acquire, the larger is the wage differential between high-skilled and low-skilled workers.

Do Education and Training Pay?

Figure 16.2 shows that there are large and persistent differences in earnings based on the degree of education and training. This figure also highlights the second main source of earnings differences: age. Age is strongly correlated with experience and the degree of on-the-job training a person has had. So as a person gets older, up to middle age, earnings increase.

Rates of return on high school and college education have been estimated to be in the range of 5 to 10 percent a year after allowing for inflation, which suggest that a college degree is a better investment than almost any other that a person can undertake.

Education is an important source of earnings differences. But there are others, and one of them is labor unions. Let's see how unions affect wages and why union wages tend to exceed nonunion wages.

FIGURE 16.2
Education and Earnings

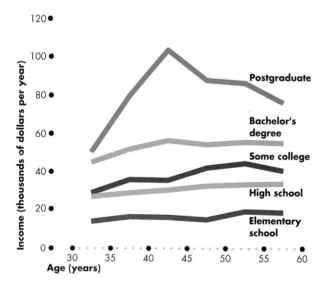

Earnings of male employees at various ages and with varying school levels are shown. Earnings increase with length of education. For postgraduates, earnings peak in the middle forties. For other groups, earnings peak in the middle fifties. These differences show the importance of experience and education in influencing skill differentials.

Source: U.S. Bureau of the Census, *Money Income in the United States 1995* and *Current Population Reports Consumer Income*, Series P-60, (1996).

Union-Nonunion Wage Differentials

WAGE DIFFERENTIALS CAN ARISE FROM MONOPOLY power in the labor market. Just as monopoly producers can restrict output and raise price, so a monopoly owner of a resource can restrict supply and raise the price of the resource.

The main source of monopoly power in the labor market is the labor union. A **labor union** is an organized group of workers whose purpose it is to increase wages and influence other job conditions for its members. The union seeks to restrict competition and, as a result, increases the price at which labor is traded.

There are two main types of union: craft unions and industrial unions. A **craft union** is a group of workers who have a similar range of skills but work for many different firms in many different industries and regions. Examples are the carpenters' union and the electrical workers union (IBEW). An **industrial union** is a group of workers who have a variety of skills and job types but work for the same industry. The United Auto Workers (UAW) and the United Steelworkers of America (USWA) are industrial unions.

Most unions are members of the AFL-CIO. The AFL-CIO was created in 1955 when two labor organizations combined: the American Federation of Labor (AFL), which was founded in 1886 to organize craft unions, and the Congress of Industrial Organizations (CIO), founded in 1938 to organize industrial unions. The AFL-CIO provides many services to member unions, such as training union organizers and acting as a national voice in the media and in the political arena.

Unions vary enormously in size. Craft unions are the smallest, and industrial unions are the biggest. Figure 16.3 shows the 12 largest unions in the United States—measured by number of members. Union strength peaked in the 1950s, when 35 percent of the nonagricultural work force belonged to unions. That percentage has declined steadily since 1955 and is now only 12 percent. Changes in union membership, however, have been uneven. Some unions have declined dramatically, while others, especially those in the government sector such as the American Federation of State, County and Municipal Employees, have increased in strength.

Union organization is based on a subdivision known as the local. The *local* is a subunit of a union that organizes the individual workers. In craft unions,

FIGURE 16.3

Unions with the Largest Membership

Each of the 12 largest labor unions in the United States, shown here, has more than 350,000 members.

Source: U.S. Bureau of the Census, *Statistical Abstract of the United States: 1996,* 116th edition, p. 436, Table 682.

the local is based on a geographical area; in industrial unions, the local is based on a plant or an individual firm.

There are three possible forms of organization for a local: an open shop, a closed shop, or a union shop. An *open shop* is an arrangement in which workers can be employed without joining the union—there is no union restriction on who can work in the "shop." A *closed shop* is an arrangement in which only union members can be employed by a firm. Closed shops have been illegal since the passage of the Taft-Hartley Act in 1947. A *union shop* is an arrangement in which a firm can hire nonunion workers, but in order for such workers to remain employed, they must join the union within a brief period specified by the union.

Union shops are illegal in the 20 states that have passed right-to-work laws. A *right-to-work law* allows an individual to work at any firm without joining a union.

Unions negotiate with employers or their representatives in a process called **collective bargaining**. The main weapons available to the union and the employer in collective bargaining are the strike, the lockout, and the use of replacement workers. A *strike* is a group decision to refuse to work under prevailing conditions. A *lockout* is a firm's refusal to operate its plant and employ its workers. Each party uses the threat of a strike, lockout, or the use of replacement workers to try to get an agreement in its own favor. Sometimes, when the two parties in the collective bargaining process cannot agree on the wage rate or other conditions of employment, they agree to submit their disagreement to binding arbitration. *Binding arbitration* is a process in which a third party—an arbitrator—determines wages and other employment conditions on behalf of the negotiating parties.

Although they are not labor unions in a legal sense, professional associations act similarly to labor unions. A *professional association* is an organized group of professional workers such as lawyers, dentists, or physicians (an example of which is the American Medical Association—AMA). Professional associations control entry into the professions and license practitioners, ensuring the adherence to minimum standards of competence. But they also influence the compensation and other labor market conditions of their members.

Union's Objectives and Constraints

A union has three broad objectives that it strives to achieve for its members:

1. To increase compensation
2. To improve working conditions
3. To expand job opportunities

Each of these objectives contains a series of more detailed goals. For example, in seeking to increase members' compensation, a union operates on a variety of fronts: wage rates, fringe benefits, retirement pay, and such things as vacation allowances. In seeking to improve working conditions, a union is concerned with occupational health and safety as well as the environmental quality of the workplace. In seeking to expand job opportunities, a union tries to get greater job security for existing union members and to find ways of creating additional jobs for them.

A union's ability to pursue its objectives is restricted by two sets of constraints—one on the supply side of the labor market and the other on the demand side. On the supply side, the union's activities are limited by how well it can restrict nonunion workers from offering their labor in the same market as union labor. The larger the fraction of the work force controlled by the union, the more effective the union can be in this regard. It is difficult for unions to operate in markets where there is an abundant supply of willing nonunion labor. For example, the market for farm labor in southern California is very tough for a union to organize because of the ready flow of nonunion, often illegal, labor from Mexico. At the other extreme, unions in the construction industry can better pursue their goals because they can influence the number of people who can obtain skills as electricians, plasterers, and carpenters. The professional associations of dentists and physicians are best able to restrict the supply of dentists and physicians. These groups control the number of qualified workers by controlling either the examinations that new entrants must pass or entrance into professional degree programs.

On the demand side of the labor market, the union faces a tradeoff that arises from firms' profit maximizing decisions. Because labor demand curves slope downward, anything a union does that increases the wage rate or other employment costs decreases the quantity of labor demanded.

Despite the difficulties they face, unions do operate in competitive labor markets. Let's see how they do so.

Unions in a Competitive Labor Market

When a union operates in an otherwise competitive labor market, it seeks to increase wages and other compensation and to limit employment reductions by increasing demand for the labor of its members. That is, the union tries to take actions that shift the demand curve for its members' labor rightward.

Figure 16.4 illustrates a competitive labor market that a union enters. The demand curve is D_C, and the supply curve is S_C. Before the union enters the market, the wage rate is $7 an hour and 100 hours of labor are employed.

Now suppose that a union is formed to organize the workers in this market. The union can attempt to increase wages in this market in two ways. It can

FIGURE 16.4

A Union in a Competitive Labor Market

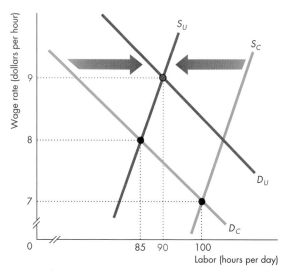

In a competitive labor market, the demand curve is D_C and the supply curve is S_C. Competitive equilibrium occurs at a wage rate of $7 an hour with 100 hours employed. By restricting employment below the competitive level, the union shifts the supply of labor to S_U. If the union can do no more than that, the wage rate will increase to $8 an hour, but employment will fall to 85 hours. If the union can increase the demand for labor (by increasing the demand for the good produced by union members or by raising the price of substitute labor) and shift the demand curve to D_U, then it can increase the wage rate still higher, to $9 an hour, and achieve employment of 90 hours.

try to restrict the supply of labor or it can try to stimulate the demand for labor. First, look at what happens if the union has sufficient control over the supply of labor to be able to artificially restrict that supply below its competitive level—to S_U. If that is all the union is able to do, employment falls to 85 hours of labor and the wage rate rises to $8 an hour. The union simply picks its preferred position along the demand curve that defines the tradeoff it faces between employment and wages.

You can see that if the union can only restrict the supply of labor, it raises the wage rate but decreases the number of jobs available. Because of this outcome unions try to increase the demand for labor and shift the demand curve rightward. Let's see what they might do to achieve this outcome.

How Unions Try to Change the Demand for Labor

Unless a union can take actions that change the demand for the labor that it represents, it has to accept the fact that a higher wage rate can be obtained only at the price of lower employment.

The union tries to operate on the demand for labor in two ways. First, it tries to make the demand for union labor less elastic. Second, it tries to increase the demand for union labor. Making the demand for labor less elastic does not eliminate the tradeoff between employment and wages, but it does make the tradeoff less unfavorable. If a union can make the demand for labor less elastic, it can increase the wage rate at a lower cost in terms of lost employment opportunities. But if the union can increase the demand for labor, it might even be able to increase both the wage rate and the employment opportunities of its members.

Some of the methods used by a union to increase the demand for the labor of its members are to:

- Increase the marginal product of union members
- Encourage import restrictions
- Support minimum wage laws
- Support immigration restrictions
- Increase demand for the good produced

Unions try to increase the marginal product of their members, which in turn increases the demand for their labor, by organizing and sponsoring training schemes, by encouraging apprenticeship and other on-the-job training activities, and by professional certification.

One of the best examples of import restrictions is the support by the United Auto Workers union (UAW) for import restrictions on foreign cars.

Unions support minimum wage laws to increase the cost of employing low-skilled labor. An increase in the wage rate of low-skilled labor leads to a decrease in the quantity demanded of low-skilled labor and to an increase in demand for high-skilled union labor, a substitute for low-skilled labor.

Restrictive immigration laws decrease the supply and increase the wage rate of low-skilled workers. As a result, the demand for high-skilled union labor increases.

Because the demand for labor is a derived demand, an increase in the demand for the good produced increases the demand for union labor. The best examples of attempts by unions in this activity are in the textile and auto industries. The garment workers' union urges us to buy union-made clothes, and the UAW asks us to buy only American cars made by union workers.

Figure 16.4 illustrates the effects of an increase in the demand for the labor of a union's members. If the union can also take steps that increase the demand for labor to D_U, it can achieve an even bigger increase in the wage rate with a smaller fall in employment. By maintaining the restricted labor supply at S_U, the union increases the wage rate to $9 an hour and achieves an employment level of 90 hours of labor.

Because a union restricts the supply of labor in the market in which it operates, its actions increase the supply of labor in nonunion markets. Workers who can't get union jobs must look elsewhere for work. This increase in supply in nonunion markets lowers the wage rate in those markets and further widens the union-nonunion differential.

The Scale of Union-Nonunion Wage Differentials

We have seen that unions can influence the wage rate by restricting the supply of labor and increasing the demand for labor. How much of a difference to wage rates do unions make in practice?

Union wage rates are, on the average, 30 percent higher than nonunion wage rates. In mining and financial services, union and nonunion wages are similar. In services, manufacturing, and transportation, the differential is between 11 and 19 percent. In wholesale and retail trades, the differential is 28 percent, and in construction, it is 65 percent.

But these union-nonunion wage differentials don't give a true measure of the effects of unions. In some industries, union wages are higher than nonunion wages because union members do jobs that involve greater skill. Even without a union, those workers receive a higher wage. To calculate the effects of unions, we have to examine the wages of unionized and nonunionized workers who do nearly identical work. The evidence suggests that after allowing for skill differentials, the union-nonunion wage differential lies between 10 percent and 25 percent. For example, airline pilots who belong to the Air Line

Pilots' Association earn about 25 percent more than nonunion pilots with the same level of skill.

Let's now turn our attention to the case in which employers have considerable influence in the labor market.

Monopsony

A **monopsony** is a market in which there is a single buyer. This market type is unusual but it does exist. With the growth of large-scale production over the last century, large manufacturing plants such as coal mines, steel and textile mills, and car manufacturers became the major employer in some regions, and in some places a single firm employed almost all the labor. Today, in some parts of the country, managed health-care organizations are the major employer of health-care professionals. These firms have monopsony power.

In monopsony, the employer determines the wage rate and pays the lowest wage at which it can attract the labor it plans to hire. A monopsony makes a bigger profit than a group of firms that compete with each other for their labor. Let's find out how they achieve this outcome.

Like all firms, a monopsony has a downward-sloping marginal revenue product curve, which is *MRP* in Fig. 16.5. This curve tells us the extra revenue the monopsony receives by selling the output produced by an extra hour of labor. The supply of labor curve is *S*. This curve tells us how many hours are supplied at each wage rate. It also tells us the minimum wage for which a given quantity of labor is willing to work

A monopsony recognizes that to hire more labor, it must pay a higher wage; equivalently, by hiring less labor, it can pay a lower wage. Because a monopsony controls the wage rate, the marginal cost of labor exceeds the wage rate. The marginal cost of labor is shown by the curve *MCL*. The relationship between the marginal cost of labor curve and the supply curve is similar to the relationship between the marginal cost and average cost curves that you studied in Chapter 11. The supply curve is like the average cost of labor curve. In Fig. 16.5, the firm can hire 49 hours of labor for a wage rate of just below $4.90 an hour. The firm's total labor cost is $240. But suppose that the firm hires 50 hours of labor. It can hire the 50th hour of labor for $5 an hour. The total cost of labor is now $250 an hour. So, hiring the 50th hour of labor increases the cost of labor from $240 to $250, which

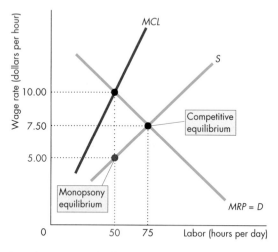

FIGURE 16.5

A Monopsony Labor Market

A monopsony is a market structure in which there is a single buyer. A monopsony in the labor market has marginal revenue product curve *MRP* and faces a labor curve *S*. The marginal cost of labor curve is *MCL*. Making the marginal cost of labor equal to marginal revenue product maximizes profit. The monopsony hires 50 hours of labor and pays the lowest wage for which that labor will work, which is $5 an hour.

is a $10 increase. The marginal cost of labor is $10 an hour. The curve *MCL* shows the $10 marginal cost of hiring the 50th hour of labor.

To calculate the profit-maximizing quantity of labor to hire, the firm sets the marginal cost of labor equal to the marginal revenue product of labor. That is, the firm wants the cost of the last worker hired to equal the extra total revenue brought in. In Fig. 16.5, this outcome occurs when the monopsony employs 50 hours of labor. What is the wage rate that the monopsony pays? To hire 50 hours of labor, the firm must pay $5 an hour, as shown by the supply of labor curve. So each worker is paid $5 an hour. But the marginal revenue product of labor is $10 an hour, which means that the firm makes an economic profit of $5 on the last hour of labor that it hires. Compare this outcome with that in a competitive labor market. If the labor market shown in Fig. 16.5 were competitive, equilibrium would occur at the point of intersection of the demand curve and the supply curve. The wage rate would be $7.50 an hour, and 75 hours of labor a day would be employed. So, compared with a competitive labor market, a monopsony decreases both the wage rate and the level of employment.

The ability of a monopsony to lower the wage rate and employment level and make an economic profit depends on the elasticity of the labor supply. The more elastic the supply of labor, the less opportunity a monopsony has to cut wages and employment and make an economic profit.

Monopsony Tendencies   Today, monopsony is rare. Workers can commute long distances to a job, so most people have more than one potential employer. But firms that are dominant employers in isolated communities do face an upward-sloping supply of labor curve and so have a marginal cost of labor that exceeds the wage rate. But in such situations, there is also, usually, a union. Let's see how unions and monopsonies interact.

Monopsony and Unions   When we studied monopoly in Chapter 13, we discovered that a single seller in a market is able to determine the price in that market. We have just studied monopsony—a market with a single buyer—and discovered that in such a market, the buyer is able to determine the price. Suppose that a union starts to operate in a monopsony labor market. A union is like a monopoly. It controls the supply of labor and acts like a single seller of labor. If the union (monopoly seller) faces a monopsony buyer, the situation is one of **bilateral monopoly**. In bilateral monopoly, the wage rate is determined by bargaining between the two sides. Let's study the bargaining process.

In Fig. 16.5, if the monopsony is free to determine the wage rate and the level of employment, it hires 50 hours of labor for a wage rate of $5 an hour. But suppose that a union represents the workers and can, if necessary, call a strike. Also suppose that the union agrees to maintain employment at 50 hours but seeks the highest wage rate the employer can be forced to pay. That wage rate is $10 an hour. That is, the wage rate equals the marginal revenue product of labor. It is unlikely that the union will get the wage rate up to $10 an hour. But it is also unlikely that the firm will keep the wage rate down to $5 an hour. The monopsony firm and the union bargain over the wage rate, and the result is an outcome between $10 an hour (the maximum that the union can achieve) and $5 an hour (the minimum that the firm can achieve).

The actual outcome of the bargaining depends on the costs that each party can inflict on the other as a result of a failure to agree on the wage rate. The firm can lock out its workers and threaten to use replacement workers, and the workers can shut the plant by striking. Each party knows the other's strength and knows what it will lose if it does not agree to the other's demands. If the two parties are equally strong and they realize it, they will split the difference and agree to a wage rate of $7.50 an hour. If one party is stronger than the other—and both parties know that—the agreed wage will favor the stronger party. Usually, an agreement is reached without a strike or a lockout. The threat—knowledge that such an event can occur—is usually enough to bring the bargaining parties to an agreement. But when a strike or lockout does occur, it is often because one party has misjudged the costs each party can inflict on the other.

Minimum wage laws have interesting effects in monopsony labor markets. Let's study these effects.

Monopsony and the Minimum Wage

In a competitive labor market, a minimum wage that exceeds the equilibrium wage decreases employment (see Chapter 7, pp. 132–134). In a monopsony labor market, a minimum wage can *increase* both the wage rate and employment. Let's see how.

Figure 16.6 shows a monopsony labor market in which the wage rate is $5 an hour and 50 hours of labor are employed. A minimum wage law is passed that requires employers to pay at least $7.50 an hour. The monopsony in Fig. 16.6 now faces a perfectly elastic supply of labor at $7.50 an hour up to 75 hours. Above 75 hours, a higher wage than $7.50 an hour must be paid to hire additional hours of labor. Because the wage rate is a fixed $7.50 an hour up to 75 hours, the marginal cost of labor is also constant at $7.50 up to 75 hours. Beyond 75 hours, the marginal cost of labor rises above $7.50 an hour. To maximize profit, the monopsony sets the marginal cost of labor equal to its marginal revenue product. That is, the monopsony hires 75 hours of labor at $7.50 an hour. The minimum wage law has made the supply of labor perfectly elastic and made the marginal cost of labor the same as the wage rate up to 75 hours. The law has not affected the supply of labor curve or the marginal cost of labor at employment levels above 75 hours. The minimum wage law has succeeded in raising the wage rate by $2.50 an hour and increasing the amount of labor employed by 25 hours a day.

FIGURE 16.6
Minimum Wage in Monopsony

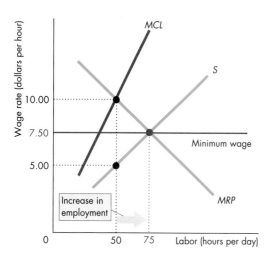

In a monopsony labor market, the wage rate is $5 an hour and 50 hours are hired. If a minimum wage law increases the wage rate to $7.50 an hour, employment increases to 75 hours.

R E V I E W

■ Earnings differences based on skill or education arise because higher skill brings higher marginal revenue product and skills are costly to acquire.

■ Union wages are higher than nonunion wages because a union restricts the supply of labor and influences the marginal revenue product of its members.

■ A monopsony, a single buyer, pays a lower wage than a competitive firm and makes a larger profit. A minimum wage law can increase both the wage rate and level of employment in a monopsony market.

You now understand two sources of wage differentials: skill differentials and the actions of labor unions. These two sources of wage differences are easy to see and to analyze. The third source of wage differentials, sex and race, is harder to explain but it is the most sensitive of the sources of income differentials.

Wage Differentials Between Sexes and Races

THE OBJECTIVE OF THIS SECTION IS TO SHOW you how to use economic analysis to address a controversial and emotionally charged issue. Figure 16.7 gives a quick view of the earnings differences that exist between the sexes and the races and also shows how those differences have evolved since 1955. The wages of each race and sex group are expressed as a percentage of the wages of white men. In 1995, the most recent year for which we have data, these percentages ranged from 73 for white women and black men to 54 for women of Hispanic origin.

Why do the differentials shown in Fig. 16.7 exist? Do they arise because there is discrimination against women and members of minority races, or is there some other explanation? These controversial questions generate an enormous amount of passion. It is not my

FIGURE 16.7
Sex and Race Differentials

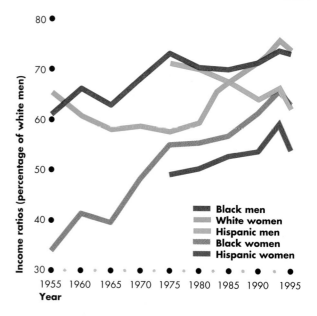

Wages of different race and sex groups are shown as percentages of white male wages. These differentials have persisted over many years, but their magnitudes have changed.

Source: U.S. Bureau of the Census, *Statistical Abstract of the United States: 1996,* 116th edition (CD-ROM), Table 663.

intention to make you angry, but that might happen as an unintended consequence of this discussion.

We are going to examine four possible explanations for earnings differences:

- Job types
- Discrimination
- Differences in human capital
- Differences in the degree of specialization

Job Types

Some of the sex differences in wages arise because men and women do different jobs and the jobs that men do are better paid. But today, greater numbers of women are entering jobs such as those of bus driver, police officer, and construction worker, traditionally done by men. The trend is strongest in professions such as architecture, medicine, law, and accounting. The percentage of enrollments in university courses in these subjects for women has increased from less than 20 percent in 1970 to as high as 50 percent today.

But many women and minorities earn less than white men even when they do the same job. One possible reason is discrimination. Let's see how discrimination might affect wage rates.

Discrimination

Suppose that black females and white males have identical abilities as investment advisors. Figure 16.8 shows the supply curves of black females, S_{BF} (in part a), and of white males, S_{WM} (in part b). The marginal revenue product of investment advisors, as shown by the two curves labeled *MRP* in parts (a) and (b), is the same for both groups.

If everyone is free of prejudice about race and sex, the market determines a wage rate of $40,000 a year for both groups of investment advisors. But if the customers of investment houses are prejudiced against women and minorities, this prejudice is reflected in wages and employment.

Suppose that the marginal revenue product of the black females, when discriminated against, is MRP_{DA}, where *DA* stands for "discriminated against." Suppose that the marginal revenue product for white males, the group discriminated in favor of, is MRP_{DF}, where *DF* stands for "discriminated in favor of." With these marginal revenue product curves, black females earn $20,000 a year, and only 1,000 will work as investment advisors. White males earn $60,000 a year, and 3,000 of them will work as investment advisors.

FIGURE 16.8

Discrimination

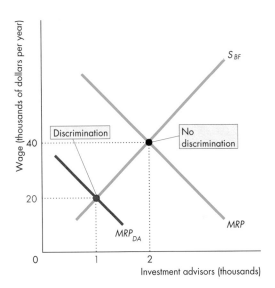

(a) Black females

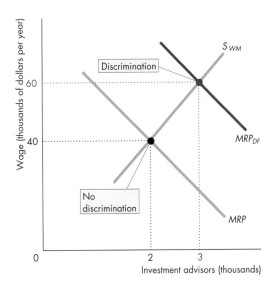

(b) White males

With no discrimination, the wage rate is $40,000 a year and 2,000 of each group are hired. With discrimination against blacks and women, the marginal revenue product curve in part (a) is MRP_{DA} and in part (b) it is MRP_{DF}. The wage rate for black women falls to $20,000 a year, and only 1,000 are employed. The wage rate for white men rises to $60,000 a year, and 3,000 are employed.

Economists disagree about whether prejudice actually causes wage differentials, and one line of reasoning suggests that it does not. In the example you've just studied, customers who buy from white men pay a higher service charge for investment advice than do the customers who buy from black women. This price difference acts as an incentive to encourage people who are prejudiced to buy from the people against whom they are prejudiced. This force could be so strong as to eliminate the effects of discrimination altogether. Suppose, as is true in manufacturing, that a firm's customers never meet its workers. If such a firm discriminates against women or minorities, it cannot compete with firms that hire these groups because its costs are higher than those of the nonprejudiced firms. So only those firms that do not discriminate survive in a competitive industry.

Let's now turn to the third source of wage differences: differences in human capital.

Differences in Human Capital

The more human capital a person possesses, the more that person earns, other things being equal. We measure human capital by using three indicators, which are:

1. Years of schooling
2. Years of work experience
3. Number of job interruptions

A larger proportion of men (25 percent) than women (20 percent) have completed 4 years of college. And a larger proportion of whites (24 percent) than blacks (13 percent) have completed a BA degree or higher. These differences in education levels among the sexes and the races are becoming smaller. But they have not yet been eliminated.

The more years of work and the fewer job interruptions a person has had, the higher is the person's wage, other things being equal. Interruptions to a career reduce the effectiveness of job experience and bring lower incomes. Historically, job interruptions are more serious for women than for men because women's careers have been interrupted for bearing and rearing children. This factor is a possible source of lower wages, on the average, for women. But maternity leave and day-care facilities are making career interruptions for women less common.

A final source of earnings differences, the relative degree of specialization of women and men, affects women's incomes adversely.

Differences in the Degree of Specialization

Couples must choose how to allocate their time between working for a wage and doing jobs in the home such as cooking, cleaning, shopping, organizing vacations and, most important, bearing and rearing children. Let's look at the choices of Bob and Sue.

Bob might specialize in earning an income and Sue in taking care of the home. Or Sue might specialize in earning an income and Bob in taking care of the home. Or both of them might earn an income and share home production jobs.

The allocation they choose depends on their preferences and on the earning potential of each of them. The choice of an increasing number of households is for each person to diversify between earning an income and doing some home chores. But in most households, Bob will specialize in earning an income and Sue will both earn an income and take care of the home. It seems likely that with this allocation, Bob will earn more than Sue. If Sue devotes time and effort to ensuring Bob's mental and physical well-being, the quality of Bob's market labor will be higher than if he were diversified. If the roles were reversed, Sue would be able to supply market labor that earns more than Bob.

To test whether the degree of specialization accounts for earnings differentials between the sexes, economists have studied two groups: "never married" men and "never married" women. The available evidence suggests that, on the average, when they have the same amount of human capital—measured by years of schooling, work experience, and career interruptions—the wages of these two groups are not significantly different.

R E V I E W

- Wage differences between the sexes and the races might arise from differences in job types, discrimination, and differences in human capital.
- Wage differences between the sexes might also arise from differences in the degree of specialization.

Because labor markets bring unequal incomes, governments intervene in these markets to modify the wages and employment levels that they determine. One potentially far-reaching intervention is comparable-worth laws. Let's see how these laws work.

Comparable-Worth Laws

CONGRESS PASSED THE EQUAL PAY ACT IN 1963 and the Civil Rights Act in 1964. These acts require equal pay for equal work. They are attempts to remove the most blatant forms of discrimination between men and women and between whites and minorities. But many people believe that these acts do not go far enough. In their view, getting paid the *same* wage for doing the *same* job is just the first step that has to be taken. What's important is that jobs that are *comparable*—require the same levels of skills and responsibilities—receive the *same* wages, regardless of whether the jobs are done by men or women or by blacks or whites. Paying the same wage for different jobs that are judged to be comparable is called *comparable worth*.

Figure 16.9 shows how comparable-worth laws work. Part (a) shows the market for oil rig operators, and part (b) shows the market for school teachers. The marginal revenue product curves (MRP_R and MRP_T) and the supply curves (S_R and S_T) are shown for each type of labor. Competition generates a wage rate W_R for oil rig operators and W_T for teachers.

Suppose it is decided that these two jobs are of comparable worth and that the courts enforce a wage rate of W_C for both groups. What happens? First, there is a shortage of oil rig operators. Oil rig companies are able to hire only S_R workers at the wage rate W_C. They cut back their production or build more expensive labor-saving oil rigs. Also the number of teachers employed decreases. But this decrease occurs because school boards demand fewer teachers. At the higher wage W_C, school boards demand only D_T teachers. The quantity of teachers supplied is S_T, and the difference between S_T and D_T is the number of unemployed teachers looking for jobs. These teachers eventually accept nonteaching jobs (which they don't like as much as teaching jobs), quite likely at a lower rate of pay than that of teachers.

Although comparable-worth laws can eliminate wage differences, they can do so only by incurring costly unintended consequences. They limit job

FIGURE 16.9
The Problem with Comparable Worth

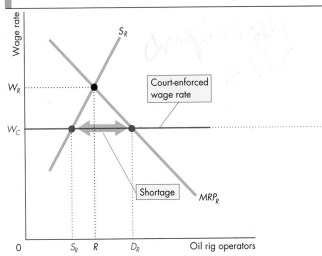

(a) Market for oil rig operators

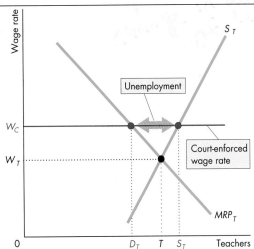

(b) Market for teachers

Part (a) shows the demand for and supply of oil rig operators, MRP_R and S_R, and part (b) shows the demand for and supply of school teachers, MRP_T and S_T. The competitive equilibrium wage rate for oil rig operators is W_R, and that for teachers is W_T. If an evaluation of the two jobs finds that they have comparable worth and rules that the wage rate W_C be paid to both types of workers, such a wage creates a shortage of oil rig operators and a surplus of teachers. Oil producers search for labor-saving ways of producing oil (that are more expensive), and teachers search for other jobs (that are less desirable to them and probably are less well paid).

opportunities and create unemployment among workers whose wages they raise. And they make it hard for employers to hire workers whose wages are held down. Only in the rare case of a monopsonistic labor market does equalizing wage rates not create permanent surpluses and shortages of skills. In this situation, a comparable-worth law works in a similar way to a minimum wage law.

Effective Wage Policies

We have now surveyed the major sources of wage differentials, and one stands out: the level of education. People with postgraduate degrees earn much more than college graduates, who in turn earn much more than high school graduates, who in turn earn more than people who have not completed high school. This source of differences in earnings is the main one on which an effective policy can operate.

By pursuing the most effective education available in grade school, high school, and college and university, people can equip themselves with human capital that brings significantly higher earnings. But in today's rapidly changing world, education and human capital accumulation must be an ongoing enterprise. The most successful workers are those who are able to repeatedly retool and actively embrace each new technological advance. The least successful are those who get locked into a particular technology and are unable or unwilling to adapt when that technology becomes redundant.

So an effective wage policy is one that emphasizes the importance of ongoing education and training.

R E V I E W

- Comparable-worth laws require equal pay for work requiring same levels of skill and responsibility.
- These laws can eliminate wage differences but only by creating shortages of labor whose market wage is high and surpluses of labor whose market wage is low.
- Effective policies to eliminate wage differentials focus on encouraging people to acquire human capital.

We're now going to turn to the final topic of this chapter: immigration.

Immigration

SIXTY MILLION PEOPLE, OR 1.2 PERCENT OF THE world's current population, have migrated from the country in which they were born. And close to one third of these immigrants live in the United States.[1] We'll study four questions about U.S. immigration:

- How many people immigrate into the United States, where do they come from, and what skills do they bring?
- How does immigration affect employment and wage rates of native-born Americans?
- How do new immigrants perform in the United States?
- What are the effects of immigrants on the government budget?

Scale, Origin, and Skills of U.S. Immigrants

Almost 800,000 legal immigrants have arrived in the United States during each of the last few years. More than a quarter of these new immigrants, plus a further 200,000 to 300,000 a year, have come from Mexico.

The scale and pattern of immigration have changed over the years. Figure 16.10(a) shows that immigration was huge during the late nineteenth century and the first 30 years of the twentieth century. It fell during the 1930s and 1940s but built up again after World War II. By the 1980s, a new large wave of immigration was under way.

Figure 16.10(b) shows that before World War II, most immigration was either directly from Europe or indirectly from Europe via Canada. But gradually, over the decades, Asia, Mexico, and other American countries replaced Europe and Canada as the places of origin of new immigrants.

The skills that immigrants bring with them vary enormously. But the averages are interesting and important. We can measure skills of immigrants in two ways, by earnings and education levels. Based on earnings, newly arrived immigrants are less productive, on the average, than native Americans. And over the years, they have been getting less skilled relative

---

[1] This section on immigration draws extensively on George J. Borjas, "The Economics of Immigration," *Journal of Economic Literature,* Vol. XXXII (December 1994). pp. 1667–1717.

FIGURE 16.10

The Scale and Sources of U.S. Immigration

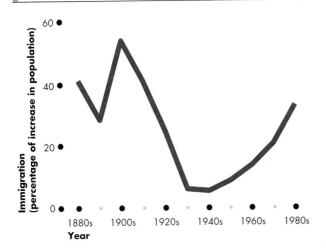

(a) Amount of immigration

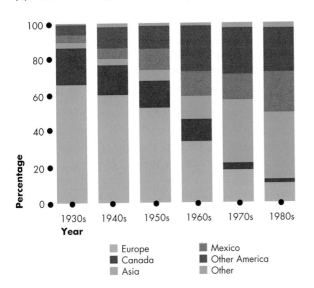

(b) Region of origin of immigrants

Part (a) shows the scale of immigration into the United States, decade by decade, since the 1880s. After a big wave during the 50 years to 1930, immigration decreased. A new wave began after World War II, which continued to rise through the 1980s. Before 1930, almost all the immigrants came from Europe. But over the years, Asia and other American countries have replaced Europe as the main source of new immigrants.

to native Americans. New immigrants who arrived during the 1960s earned 17 percent less than comparable Americans. Those who arrived during the 1970s earned 28 percent less than native Americans. And those who arrived during the 1980s earned 32 percent less than native Americans. Based on education levels, immigrants are also becoming less skilled, relative to native Americans. The percentage of immigrants who have not completed high school has decreased, but only slightly, and stands at almost 40 percent. In contrast, the high school dropout rate for native Americans has decreased from 40 percent in 1970 to less than 15 percent today.

At the other end of the education spectrum, the percentage of immigrants who are college graduates has increased somewhat, but the percentage of native American college graduates has increased faster.

To summarize the anatomy of U.S. immigrants: They are increasingly from Asia and Latin America, and their skill level is lower than that of native Americans and has been getting relatively lower.

Immigrants and the Labor Market

Immigration increases the supply of labor. By so doing, it lowers the wage rates of existing workers. At the same time, it decreases the supply of labor and raises wage rates in the country the immigrants are leaving. Figure 16.11 shows these effects in the labor markets of the United States (part a) and Mexico (part b). The demand for labor in the United States is LD_{US}, and in Mexico, it is LD_M. Before immigration takes place, 125 million workers in the United States earn $15 an hour and 50 million workers in Mexico earn $1 an hour. (The numbers are hypothetical.)

With free movement, Mexicans enter the United States as long as, by doing so, they can increase their incomes. In this example, the labor force of the United States increases to 150 million and the wage rate falls to $8 an hour. In Mexico, the labor force decreases to 25 million and the wage rate rises to $8 an hour. When the wage rates are the same, there is no incentive for anyone to migrate between the two countries.

The outcome shown in Fig. 16.11 would be unlikely to occur because people would not vote for an open border immigration law. Instead, we vote for immigration laws that prevent the free movement of people and so prevent the outcome shown in Fig. 16.11.

But does immigration move wage rates in the directions shown in the figure? Does it lower the wages of existing workers? The answer is ambiguous.

FIGURE 16.11

Immigration and the Labor Market

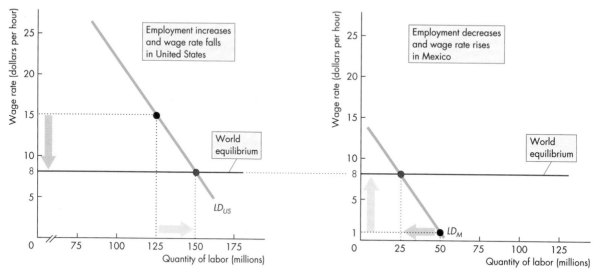

(a) The U.S. labor market

(b) The Mexican labor market

Part (a) shows the labor market in the United States. The demand for labor is LD_{US}, and with 125 million workers, the wage rate is $15 an hour. Part (b) shows the labor market in Mexico. The demand for labor is LD_M, and with 50 million workers, the wage rate is $1 an hour. With free movement of people between the two countries, people leave Mexico and migrate to the United States. Employment increases and the wage rate falls in the United States, and employment decreases and the wage rate rises in Mexico. The world equilibrium occurs when the wage rate is equal in the two countries, at $8 an hour.

It might lower wages. But it might raise them. Either way, the effect is probably small.

According to George Borjas, a leading authority on this topic, immigration might be partly responsible for the fall in the earnings of low-skilled Americans during the 1980s.

There are several reasons why immigration does not have the dramatic effect on domestic wages that Fig. 16.11 shows. First, immigrants bring not only a supply of labor but also a demand for goods and services. Consequently, firms expand and the demand for labor increases. This increase in the demand for labor limits the extent to which the wage rate falls. Second, some immigrants bring capital with them. This additional capital is invested in businesses and brings an increase in the demand for labor. Third, immigrants are not necessarily *substitutes* for domestic labor. They might be *complements* with it. For example, a shortage of low-skilled labor might cause a firm to close down and lay off its high-skilled workers.

Immigration might restore the ability of the firm to operate profitably and enable it to hire again.

For these three reasons, the effect of immigration of wage rates is smaller than the direct effect shown in Fig. 16.11.

Let's next look at the economic fortunes of the immigrants themselves.

How Do New Immigrants Perform in the United States?

We've seen that when a new immigrant arrives in the United States, he or she earns less, on the average, than similarly qualified native Americans. We've also seen that this earnings gap has been widening and is today close to one third. But what happens to immigrants in the years that follow their arrival?

The answer depends on when the immigrant arrived, the number of years elapsed since arriving, the ethnicity, and the language skills of the immigrant.

As a rule, immigrants' earnings grow more rapidly than the earnings of native Americans. That is, there is a tendency for immigrants' earnings to converge on and even to surpass the earnings of similar native Americans. But this tendency was stronger in the past than it is today. By 1990, immigrants who had arrived in the United States before 1970 had, on the average, reached income levels equal to those of native Americans. Those who had arrived before 1950 had income levels that averaged 26 percent *more* than the incomes of native Americans.

For more recent immigrant groups, there is still a tendency for incomes to grow faster than those of non-immigrants. But the starting gap is now so wide and the speed of convergence so slow that many new immigrants will never earn as much as their native equivalents.

This tendency for the immigrant to perform less well than a native American is more pronounced among Hispanic immigrants than among other ethnic groups. But it is also present among Asian immigrants.

Because the immigrant groups that perform least well are from countries in which English is not a major language, language skills might be playing a role. Studies of the influence of language on earnings agree with this suspicion. It has been estimated that immigrants who are proficient in the English language earn 17 percent more, on the average, than immigrants who are not proficient in English. This estimate, combined with the fact that an increasing percentage of immigrants have no English, explains some of the tendency for the most recent wave of immigrants to converge to non-immigrant earnings levels at a slower speed than that of earlier waves.

If the current group of immigrants might not catch up with the earnings of native Americans, what are the prospects for their children? Will they complete the convergence process? We do not know enough to be able to answer this question. But we do know that there is a strong correlation between the earnings of new immigrant families and the earnings of their children. Because of this correlation, there is a possiblity that convergence will continue to be slow.

Immigrants and the Government Budget

Since the mid-1960s, the United States has created a huge social welfare safety net. Do immigrants benefit more from our social programs than they contribute to them?

Immigrants have qualified for welfare assistance in increasing numbers over the past 20 years. In 1970, 6 percent of all native households and 5.9 percent of all immigrant households received some form of welfare. By 1990, these percentages were 7.4 for native households and 9.1 for immigrant households. Partly as a reaction to this trend, Congress passed legislation making it more difficult for immigrants to qualify for welfare and this new law might change the trend.

But there are huge differences in the extent to which different groups of immigrants use welfare. Those who rely most heavily on it are new immigrants from Cambodia, Laos, the Dominican Republic, and Vietnam.

But immigrants pay taxes. And their total tax payments are much greater than their welfare receipts. Data from the 1990 Census tell us that immigrants pay $85 billion in taxes and receive $24 billion in welfare benefits. Immigrants also impose other hard-to-quantify costs on the government, so we cannot say for sure what the net cost of benefit of immigration is for the government's budget.

REVIEW

- During recent years, the United States has received a new wave of immigrants, mainly from Asia, Mexico, and other American countries.
- Immigration lowers wages, but the effect is a small one.
- Immigrants have lower wages than others on arrival but have more rapid wage growth. In recent years, immigrants have fewer skills, lower wages, and slower convergence of earnings and rely more on welfare than earlier waves of immigrants.

◆ *Reading Between the Lines* on pages 358–359 returns to the U.S. labor markets and looks at a current trend away from long-term employment contracts toward temporary contracts. It looks at the effects of this trend on wages and the response of unions to the trend.

In the next chapter, we're going to examine the distributions of income and wealth that result from the operation of labor markets and the markets for other productive resources.

Policy
WATCH

Labor Markets in Action

The Wall Street Journal, December 2, 1996

Temp Workers May Be Able to Join Unions

BY GLENN BURKINS

WASHINGTON–The National Labor Relations Board is poised to make it easier for the growing number of temporary workers to join labor unions.

Current rules that make it "virtually impossible" for temps to join unions alongside an employer's permanent staff are based on a "flimsy premise" says NLRB Chairman William B. Gould IV.

Today and tomorrow, the board will hear arguments in cases in which the unionization of temporary workers is at issue. ...

Business groups warn of repercussions–and a probable court fight–if the regulations are changed. "If you start messing around in this area," says Dan Yager, general counsel for the Labor Policy Association, a business lobbying group, "clearly it's going to discourage the use of temporary workers."

The issue has taken on greater significance with the changes in the temporary-staffing industry. The Labor Department says about 2.2 million people worked as temporary employees last year, up from just 417,000 in 1982.

Once limited mainly to clerical workers, temporary agencies today offer a wide range of occupations. Factory workers, engineers, architects, computer programmers, designers and even lawyers can be hired through temporary agencies. ...

Despite the industry's growth, the labor laws that govern temporary workers have not changed, critics say. For example, if temporary workers are sent into a unionized company, they are prohibited from joining that company's bargaining unit without first getting consent from both the company and the temporary agency that sent them. ...

As employers have slashed their payrolls, unions have accused some of hiring temporary workers to avoid paying benefits to permanent staffs. Stephen Lerner, assistant organizing director at the AFL-CIO, calls it a "moral issue," as well as a legal issue. The current rule, he says, allows employers to "do a half-step" and duck their responsibility for workers.

Mr. Gould, the NLRB chairman, says the rule also has had the unintended effect of widening the economic gap among American workers. "The whole nature of the employment relationship is changing," he says. ...

Essence of THE STORY

- In 1996, there were 2.2 million people temporary employees, up from 417,000 in 1982.

- Factory workers, engineers, architects, computer programmers, designers, and lawyers can be hired through temporary agencies.

- Temporary employees may not join a union without the consent of both the firm that employs them and the agency that placed them.

- The National Labor Relations Board seeks to end this arrangement.

- Unions accuse some companies of hiring temporary workers to avoid paying the benefits they pay to union employees.

Economic

A N A L Y S I S

■ Figure 1 shows how the market for temporary labor has grown between 1982 and 1996.

■ In 1982, the demand for temporary labor was D_{82} and the supply was S_{82}. The equilibrium real wage rate was W_a, and 417,000 temporary workers were employed.

■ Between 1982 and 1996, there was a large increase in the demand for temporary labor and the demand curve shifted rightward to D_{96}.

■ Unions believe that some of this increased demand occurred because temporary labor costs less than union labor.

■ At the same time that demand increased, corpo-

rate downsizing created an increase in the supply of temporary labor. The supply curve has shifted rightward from S_{82} to S_{96}.

■ In 1996, the equilibrium real wage rate had risen to W_b (an assumption) and temporary employment had increased to 2.2 million workers.

■ Temporary workers compete with union workers. Figure 2 shows what is happening in the market for union workers.

■ With no competition from temporary workers, the demand for union labor is D_0. The supply of union labor is S_0. The equilibrium real wage rate is W_0, which is greater than W_b, the wage rate of temporary labor. The

quantity of union labor is Q_0. The union wage is W_0.

■ But the unions are under competitive pressure from temporary labor. The increase in the availability of temporary labor at a relatively low real wage rate has decreased the demand for union labor. The demand curve has shifted leftward to D_1.

You're

THE VOTER

■ Should temporary workers be permitted, barred from, or required to join a union that represents a firm's permanent workers?

■ Draft a short bill for Congress on this matter and explain why your draft bill should become law.

■ At this lower demand, the quantity of union labor decreases to Q_1 at the union wage W_0.

■ If the unions can get temporary workers to become members and if they can increase the wage rates of these workers, the demand for permanent union labor will increase and union membership will increase.

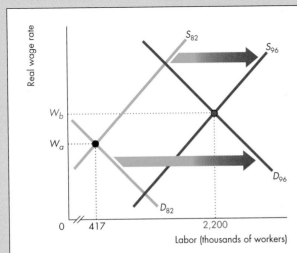

Figure 1 Temporary workers

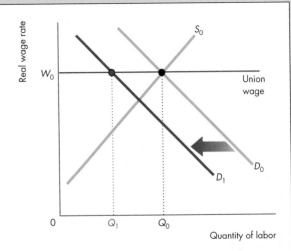

Figure 2 Union workers

SUMMARY

Key Points

Skill Differentials (pp. 342–344)

▪ Skill differentials arise from differences in marginal revenue products and because skills are costly to acquire.

▪ Wage rates of high-skilled and low-skilled labor are determined by demand and supply in the two labor markets.

Union-Nonunion Wage Differentials (pp. 344–350)

▪ Labor unions influence wages by controlling the supply of labor.

▪ In competitive labor markets, unions obtain higher wages only at the expense of lower employment, but they try to influence the demand for labor.

▪ In a monopsony a union can increase the wage rate without sacrificing employment.

▪ Bilateral monopoly occurs when a union confronts a single buyer of labor. The wage rate is determined by bargaining between the two parties.

▪ Union workers earn 10 to 25 percent more than comparable nonunion workers.

Wage Differentials Between Sexes and Races (pp. 350–352)

▪ Earnings differentials between men and women and between whites and minorities arise from differences in types of jobs, discrimination, differences in human capital, and differences in degree of specialization.

▪ Well-paid jobs are more likely to be held by white men than by women and minorities. But discrimination is hard to measure objectively.

▪ Historically, white males have had more human capital than other groups. Human capital differences arising from schooling differences have been falling but they have not been eliminated.

▪ Differentials based on work experience have kept women's pay below that for men because women's careers have traditionally been interrupted more frequently than those of men. This difference is smaller today than in the past.

▪ Differentials arising from different degrees of specialization are probably important and might persist. Men have traditionally been more specialized in market activity, on the average, than women.

Comparable-Worth Laws (pp. 353–354)

▪ Comparable-worth laws determine wages by using objective characteristics rather than what the market will pay to assess the value of different types of jobs.

▪ Determining wages through comparable worth will result in a decrease in the number of people employed in jobs on which the market places a lower value and shortages of workers that the market values more highly.

Immigration (pp. 354–357)

▪ U.S. immigration has followed waves. A big increase occurred during the 1970s and 1980s. The origin of immigrants has shifted from Europe to Asia and Latin America. Immigrants have become less skilled than in the past.

▪ Immigration lowers wage rates but only slightly.

▪ Immigrants enter with low earnings but in the past their earnings have converged on those of native Americans. This convergence has slowed. Immigrants now use welfare more than in the past.

Key Figures

Key Terms

QUESTIONS

1. What is human capital? How is it acquired?
2. Explain why the demand curve for high-skilled labor lies to the right of the demand curve for low-skilled labor.
3. Explain why the supply curve for high-skilled labor lies to the left of the supply curve for low-skilled labor.
4. What is the influence of education and on-the-job training on earnings?
5. Explain why high-skilled workers are paid more than low-skilled workers.
6. What is a labor union? What are the main types of labor unions?
7. What is collective bargaining? What are the main weapons available to a union and an employer?
8. How does a labor union try to influence wages?
9. What can a union do in a competitive labor market?
10. How might a union increase the demand for its members' labor?
11. Explain why the elasticity of supply of labor influences how much the union can raise the wage rate paid to union members.
12. What is monopsony? Where in the United States might a monopsony exist?
13. Explain why the supply of labor facing a monopsony is not the marginal cost of labor.
14. Explain why a monopsony maximizes its profit by paying labor a wage rate that is less than the marginal revenue product of labor.
15. Under what circumstances will the introduction of a minimum wage increase employment?
16. How big are the union-nonunion wage differentials in the United States today?
17. What are the four main reasons why sex and race differentials in earnings exist?
18. Is the wage differential between men and women all due to discrimination? Explain your answer.
19. What is a comparable-worth law?
20. How do comparable-worth laws work and what are their predicted effects?
21. Describe the main trends in U.S. immigration.
22. How might immigration influence wage rates?
23. Describe the path of wages of an immigrant in the years after arriving in the United States.

PROBLEMS

1. The figure shows the demand for and supply of low-skilled labor.

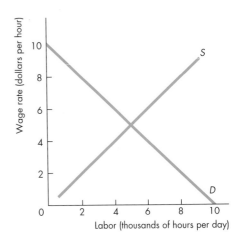

a. What is the wage rate of low-skilled labor?
b. What is the quantity of low-skilled labor employed?

2. The workers in problem 1 can be trained—can obtain a skill—and their marginal productivity doubles. (The marginal product at each employment level is twice the marginal product of a low-skilled worker.) But the compensation for the cost of acquiring skill adds $2 an hour to the wage that must be offered to attract the high-skilled labor. What is:
a. The wage rate of high-skilled labor?
b. The quantity of high-skilled labor employed?

3. Suppose in problems 1 and 2 that high-skilled workers become unionized and the union restricts the amount of high-skilled labor to 5,000 hours. What is:
a. The wage rate of high-skilled workers?
b. The wage differential between low- and high-skilled workers?

4. If the government in problem 1 introduces a minimum wage rate of $6 an hour for low-skilled workers
a. What is the wage rate paid to low-skilled workers?
b. How many hours of low-skilled labor gets hired each day?

5. In an isolated part of the Amazon Basin, a gold-mining company faces the labor market illustrated in the figure. The gold mine is a monopsony.

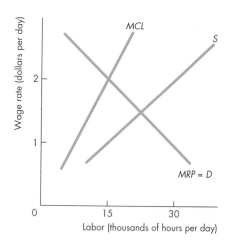

a. What wage rate does the company pay?

b. How many hours of labor does the gold mine hire?

c. What is the marginal revenue product of the last hour of labor?

d. How does the gold mine maximize its profit when it does not pay its workers their marginal revenue product?

e. If the world price of gold increases, what happens to the wage rate paid and the number of workers hired?

6. If the government in problem 5 imposes a minimum wage rate of $1.50 a day,

a. What wage rate does the gold mine pay?

b. Does the gold mine increase or decrease the number of hours of labor it hires?

7. Explain how the arrival of new immigrants influences the supply of labor and the wage rate.

a. Use a diagram similar to that in Fig. 16.11 to show the effects on both the supply of labor and the demand for labor of immigration.

b. Why might the demand for labor be affected as well as the supply?

CRITICAL THINKING

1. Study *Reading Between the Lines* on pp. 358–359 and then answer the following questions:

a. Why do business groups oppose making it easier for temporary workers to join unions?

b. Why do unions favor making it easier for temporary workers to join unions?

c. What do you think temporary workers will do if they are permitted to join unions? Will there be a flood or a trickle of people joining? Why?

d. Why has there been a trend toward hiring temporary workers? Do you predict the trend will become stronger or weaker? Explain.

⊕ 2. Visit the World Wide Web site of the AFL-CIO at http://www.aflcio.org/ (or use the link on the Parkin Web site) and click on the "Don't Buy List." Choose an item on this list that interests you and explain why the AFL-CIO is recommending a boycott of this item. Explain how not buying this item increases either the wage rate or the employment level of union members.

⊕ 3. Visit the World Wide Web site of the Bureau of Labor Statistics (BLS) at http://stats.bls.gov/blshome.html (or use the link on the Parkin Web site) and obtain data for the past three months on usual weekly earnings and the level of employment.

a. What has happened to earnings and employment during the past three months?

b. Try to explain the changes by using the tools of demand and supply.

4. "Wages should be determined on the basis of what is fair." Debate this proposition. Set out the cases for and against. Then determine and explain your verdict.

5. "Education is the key to overcoming earnings inequality." Debate this proposition. Set out the cases for and against. Then determine and explain your verdict.

6. Explain why we have laws that limit immigration. Who benefits from these laws?

7. Suppose that all nations agreed to permit the free movement of people. Which nations would be the biggest suppliers of immigrants? Which nations would attract most immigrants? Describe the world economy 10 years after the start of this process.

17

Inequality, Redistribution, and Health Care

Fifty-three stories above Manhattan is a penthouse with unobstructed views of Central Park, the Hudson River, and the city skyline. Its price? $4 million. "Now, you can be one of the enviable few to fly Around the World by Supersonic Concorde ... for just $32,000 per person," trumpets an advertisement in *The New Yorker*. Not quite within view of the $4 million penthouse, but not far from it, is Fort Washington Armory in Upper Manhattan. What was opened as a temporary shelter in 1981 permanently houses close to

Riches and Rags

1,000 men who sleep in one football-field-sized room. These men live on the edge of despair and in fear of AIDS and other life-threatening diseases. ◆ Why are some people exceedingly rich while others are very poor and own almost nothing? Are the rich getting richer and the poor getting poorer? Does the information we have about the inequality of income and wealth in the United States paint an accurate picture or a misleading one? How do taxes and social security, welfare, and health-care programs influence economic inequality? ◆ In this chapter, we study economic inequality—its extent, its sources, and its potential remedies. We look at taxes and government programs that redistribute incomes and study their effects on economic inequality in the United States. We also study the different ways in which health care can be delivered and their effects on economic efficiency and equality. Let's begin by looking at some facts about economic inequality.

After studying this chapter, you will be able to:

- Describe the inequality in income and wealth in the United States

- Explain why wealth inequality is greater than income inequality

- Explain how economic inequality arises

- Explain the effects of taxes and social security and welfare programs on economic inequality

- Explain the effects of health-care reform on economic inequality

Economic Inequality in the United States

WE CAN STUDY INEQUALITY BY LOOKING AT either the distribution of income or the distribution of wealth. A family's income is the amount that it receives in a given period of time. A family's wealth is the value of the things it owns at a point in time. We can measure income inequality by looking at the percentage of total income received by a given percentage of families. And we can measure wealth inequality by looking at the percentage of total wealth owned by a given percentage of families.

In 1995, the average U.S. family income, before tax and not counting government transfers, was close to $45,000. But there was considerable inequality around that number. The poorest 20 percent of families received only 3.7 percent of total income. The next poorest 20 percent of families received 9.1 percent of total income. The richest 20 percent of families received almost 48.7 percent of total income.

The wealth distribution shows even greater inequality. Average family wealth in 1992 was $193,000. But the range was enormous. The poorest 90 percent of families owned about one third of total wealth. The next 9 percent owned another third of total wealth. And the wealthiest 1 percent of families owned the remaining one third of total wealth.

Lorenz Curves

Figure 17.1 shows the distributions of income and wealth. The table divides families into five groups, called *quintiles*, ranging from the lowest income (row *a*) to highest income (row *e*), and shows the percentages of income of each group. For example, row *a* tells us that the lowest quintile receives 3.7 percent of total income. The table also shows the *cumulative* percentages of families and income. For example, row *b* tells us that the lowest two quintiles (lowest 40 percent) of families receive 12.8 percent of total income (3.7 percent for the lowest quintile and 9.1 percent for the next lowest). The data on cumulative income shares are illustrated by a Lorenz curve. A **Lorenz curve** graphs the cumulative percentage of income against the cumulative percentage of families.

If income were distributed equally to every family, the cumulative percentages of income received by the cumulative percentages of families would fall along the straight line labeled "Line of equality." The

FIGURE 17.1

Lorenz Curves for Income and Wealth

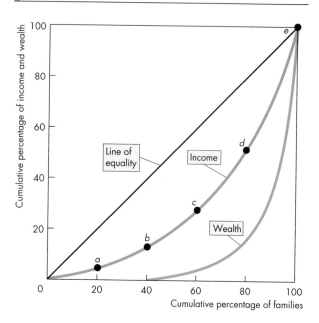

Families		Income		Wealth	
Percentage	Cumulative percentage	Percentage	Cumulative percentage	Percentage	Cumulative percentage
a Lowest 20	20	3.7	3.7	0	0
b Second 20	40	9.1	12.8	0	0
c Third 20	60	15.2	28.0	4	4
d Fourth 20	80	23.3	51.3	11	15
e Highest 20	100	48.7	100.0	85	100

The cumulative percentages of income and wealth are graphed against the cumulative percentage of families. If income and wealth were distributed equally, each 20 percent of families would have 20 percent of the income and wealth—the line of equality. Points *a* through *e* on the Lorenz curve for income correspond to the rows of the table. The Lorenz curves show that income and wealth are unequally distributed and that wealth is more unequally distributed than income.

Sources: U.S. Bureau of the Census, Current Population Reports, P-60-193, *Money Income in the United States (With Separate Data on Valuation of Noncash Benefits)* (Washington, D.C., U.S. Government Printing Office, 1996), and Robert D. Avery and Arthur B. Kennickell, "Measurement of Household Saving Obtained from First Differencing Wealth Estimates" (Washington, D.C.: Federal Reserve Board, February 1990).

actual distribution of income is shown by the Lorenz curve labeled "Income."

Figure 17.1 also shows a Lorenz curve for wealth. This curve is based on the distribution described in the table. The wealthiest 20 percent of families own 85 percent of total wealth. The second wealthiest own 11 percent, and the third wealthiest own 4 percent.

The Lorenz curve shows the degree of inequality. The closer the Lorenz curve is to the line of equality, the more equal is the distribution. As you can see from the two Lorenz curves in Fig. 17.1, the Lorenz curve for wealth is much farther away from the line of equality than the Lorenz curve for income is, so the distribution of wealth is much more unequal than the distribution of income.

Inequality over Time

Figure 17.2 shows how the distribution of income has changed since 1970.

- The share of income received by the richest 20 percent of households has increased.
- The share of income received by all four other groups of households has decreased.

The higher-income groups have gained because rapid technological change has increased the return to education. The lower income groups have suffered for a variety of reasons; one is increased international mobility and competition that is keeping down the wages of the low skilled. The trends visible in Fig. 17.2 are real, but they are exaggerated somewhat after 1989 and more so in 1994 by a change in the method of measuring large incomes.

Who Are the Rich and the Poor?

What are the characteristics of poor and rich families? The lowest-income household in the United States today is likely to be a black woman over 65 years of age who lives alone somewhere in the South and has fewer than eight years of elementary school education. The highest-income household in the United States today is likely to be a college-educated white married couple between 45 and 54 years of age living together with two children in the Northeast.

These snapshot profiles are the extremes in Fig. 17.3. That figure illustrates the importance of the education of householder, size of household, marital status, age of householder, race, and region of residence in influencing the size of a family's income.

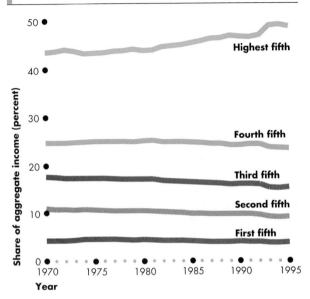

FIGURE 17.2

Trends in the Distribution of Income: 1950–1995

The distribution of income in the United States became more unequal between 1970 and 1995. The percentage of income earned by the highest fifth increased steadily through the 1970s and 1980s and sharply during the 1990s.

Source: U.S. Bureau of the Census, *Current Population Reports*, P-60-193, *Money Income in the United States (With Separate Data on Valuation of Noncash Benefits)*, and *Current Population Reports*, *Consumer Income*, P-60-168 (Washington, D.C., U.S. Government Printing Office, 1990 and 1996).

The range of variation associated with education is the largest. On the average, people who have not completed grade 9 earn $14,275 a year, while people with a bachelor's degree or more earn an average of $57,440 a year. Four-person households have incomes that average more than $46,757 while one-person households have an average income of $16,222. Single females, on the average, have incomes of $14,948 a year, while married couples earn an average joint income of $45,041 a year. The oldest and youngest households have lower incomes than middle-aged households. Black families have an average income of $21,027, while white families have an average income of almost $34,028. Finally, incomes are lowest in the South and highest in the Northeast; those in the West are fairly close to those in the Northeast, and incomes in the Midwest lie midway between those in the West and those in the South.

Does this account for cost of living? Salaries are in NYC than Macon, GA.

FIGURE 17.3

The Distribution of Income by Selected
Family Characteristics in 1994

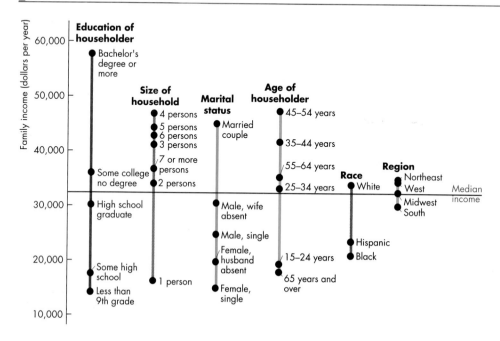

Education is the single biggest factor affecting family income distribution, but size of household, marital status, and age of householder are also important. Race and region of residence also play a role.

Source: U.S. Bureau of the Census, *Statistical Abstract of the United States: 1996*, 116th edition, Table 711.

Poverty

Families at the low end of the income distribution are so poor that they are considered to be living in poverty. **Poverty** is a state in which a family's income is too low to be able to buy the quantities of food, shelter, and clothing that are deemed necessary. Poverty is a relative concept. Millions of people living in Africa and Asia survive on incomes of less than $400 a year. In the United States, the poverty level is calculated each year by the Social Security Administration. In 1995, the poverty level for a four-person family was an income of $15,569. In that year, 39.5 million Americans were in families that had incomes below the poverty level. Many of these families benefited from Medicare and Medicaid, two government programs that benefit the poorest families and lift some of them above the poverty level.

The distribution of poverty by race is very unequal: 12 percent of white families, 31 percent of

Hispanic-origin families, and 33 percent of black families are below the poverty level. Poverty is also influenced by family status. Almost 40 percent of families in which the householder is a female and no husband is present are below the poverty level, while 12 percent of other families are.

R E V I E W

- Income and wealth are distributed unequally, but wealth is distributed more unequally than income.
- Between 1970 to 1995, the distribution of income became more unequal. The share of income received by the richest 20 percent increased.
- The main influences on a family's income, in decreasing order of importance, are education of householder, household size, marital status, age of householder, race, and region of residence.

Comparing Like with Like

To DETERMINE THE DEGREE OF INEQUALITY, we compare one person's economic situation with another person's. But what is the correct measure of a person's economic situation? Is it income or is it wealth? And is it *annual* income, the measure we've used so far in this chapter, or income over a longer time period—for example, over a family's lifetime?

Wealth Versus Income
is a job an asset?

Wealth is a stock of assets, and income is the flow of earnings that results from the stock of wealth. Suppose that a person owns assets worth $1 million—has a wealth of $1 million. If the rate of return on assets is 5 percent a year, then this person receives an income of $50,000 a year from those assets. We can describe this person's economic condition by using either the wealth of $1 million or the income of $50,000. When the rate of return is 5 percent a year, $1 million of wealth equals $50,000 of income in perpetuity. Wealth and income are simply different ways of looking at the same thing.

But in Fig. 17.1, the distribution of wealth is much more unequal than the distribution of income. Why? It is because the wealth data measure tangible assets and exclude the value of human capital while the income data measure income from both tangible assets and human capital.

Table 17.1 illustrates the consequence of omitting human capital from the wealth data. Lee has twice the wealth and twice the income of Peter. But Lee's human capital is less than Peter's—$200,000 compared with $499,000. And Lee's income from human capital of $10,000 is less than Peter's income from human capital of $24,950. Lee's nonhuman capital is larger than Peter's—$800,000 compared with $1,000. And Lee's income from nonhuman capital of $40,000 is larger than Peter's income from nonhuman capital of $50.

The national wealth and income surveys record their incomes of $50,000 and $25,000, respectively, which indicate that Lee is twice as well off as Peter. And they record their tangible assets of $800,000 and $1,000, respectively, which indicate that Lee is 800 times as wealthy as Peter. Because the national survey of wealth excludes human capital, the income distribution is a more accurate measure of economic inequality than the wealth distribution.

TABLE 17.1
Capital, Wealth, and Income

	Lee		Peter	
	Wealth	**Income**	**Wealth**	**Income**
Human capital	200,000	10,000	499,000	24,950
Nonhuman capital	800,000	40,000	1,000	50
Total	$1,000,000	$50,000	$500,000	$25,000

When wealth is measured to include the value of human capital as well as nonhuman capital, the distribution of income and the distribution of wealth display the same degree of inequality.

Annual or Lifetime Income and Wealth?

A typical family's income changes over time. It starts out low, grows to a peak when the family's workers reach retirement age, and then falls after retirement. Also, a typical family's wealth changes over time. Like income, it starts out low, grows to a peak at the point of retirement, and falls after retirement.

Suppose we look at three families that have identical lifetime incomes. One family is young, one is middle aged, and one is retired. The middle-aged family has the highest income and wealth, the retired family has the lowest, and the young family falls in the middle. The distributions of annual income and wealth in a given year are unequal, but the distributions of lifetime income and wealth are equal. So some of the measured inequality arises from the fact that different families are at different stages in the life cycle. Inequality of annual incomes overstates the degree of lifetime inequality.

R E V I E W

- The distribution of income is a more accurate indicator of the degree of inequality than the distribution of wealth because the wealth data exclude human capital.
- The distribution of lifetime income is a more accurate indicator of the degree of inequality than the distribution of annual income because income varies over a family's life cycle.

Let's look at the sources of economic inequality.

Resource Prices, Endowments, and Choices

A FAMILY'S INCOME DEPENDS ON THREE THINGS:

- Resource prices
- Resource endowments
- Choices

The distribution of income depends on the distribution of these three things across the population. The first two are outside our individual control and are determined by market forces and by history. From the viewpoint of each one of us, they appear to be determined by luck. The last item is under individual control. We make choices that influence our incomes. Let's look at the three factors that influence incomes.

Resource Prices

Everyone faces the same interest rates in capital markets, but people face differing wage rates in the labor market. And the labor market is the biggest single source of income for most people. To what extent do variations in wage rates account for the unequal distribution of income? The answer is that they do to some extent, but wage differences cannot account for all the inequality. High-skilled workers earn about 3.5 times as much as low-skilled workers. Highly paid professionals earn about 3 times as much as high-skilled workers. So the highest-paid professionals earn around 10 times what the least skilled are paid. *More*.

Differences in resource endowments are another. *($6/hr → $250/hr)*

Resource Endowments

There is a large amount of variety in a family's endowments of capital and of human abilities. Differences in capital make a big contribution to differences in incomes. But so do differences in ability.

Physical and mental abilities (some inherited, some learned) have a normal, or bell-shaped, distribution—like the distribution of heights. The distribution of ability across individuals is a major source of inequality in income and wealth. But it is not the only source. If it were, the distributions of income and wealth would look like the bell-shaped curve that describes the distribution of heights. In fact, these distributions are skewed toward high incomes and

look like the curve in Fig. 17.4. This figure shows income on the horizontal axis and the percentage of families receiving each income on the vertical axis. In 1995, the median household income—the income that separates households into two groups of equal size—was $31,241. The most common income—called the mode income—is less than the median income. The mean income—also called the average income—is greater than the median income and in 1995 was $44,938. A skewed distribution like the one shown in Fig. 17.4 is one in which many more families have incomes below the average than above it, a large number of families have low incomes, and a small number of families have high incomes. The distribution of (nonhuman) wealth has a shape similar to that of the distribution of income but is even more skewed.

The skewed distribution of income cannot be explained by the bell-shaped distribution of individual abilities. It results from the choices that people make.

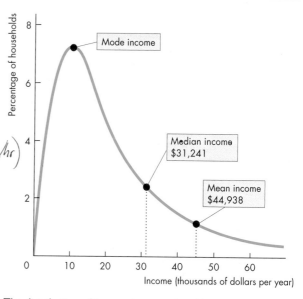

FIGURE 17.4

The Distribution of Income

The distribution of income is unequal and is not symmetric around the mean income. There are many more families with incomes below the mean income than above it. Also, the distribution has a long, thin upper tail representing a small number of families who earn very large incomes.

Choices

While many poor families feel trapped and do not have many options open to them, a family's income and wealth depend partly on the choices that its members make. You are going to discover that the choices people make exaggerate the differences among them and make the distribution of income more unequal than the distribution of abilities, as well as making the distribution of income skewed.

Wages and the Supply of Labor   Other things remaining the same, the quantity of labor that a person supplies usually increases as that person's wage rate increases. A person who has a low wage rate chooses to work fewer hours than a person who has a high wage rate. *Salaries?*

Because the quantity of labor supplied increases as the wage rate increases, the distribution of income is more unequal than the distribution of hourly wages and skewed, like the one shown in Fig. 17.4. People whose wage rates are below the average tend to work fewer hours than the average, and their incomes bunch together below the average. People whose wage rates are above the average tend to work more hours than the average, and their incomes stretch out above the average.

Saving and Bequests   Another choice that results in unequal distributions in income and wealth is the decision to save and make bequests. A *bequest* is a gift from one generation to the next. The higher a family's income, the more that family tends to save and accumulate wealth across generations.

Saving and bequests are not inevitably a source of increased inequality. If a family saves to redistribute an uneven income over the life cycle and enable consumption to be constant, the act of saving decreases the degree of inequality. If a lucky generation that has a high income saves a large amount and makes a bequest to a generation that is unlucky, this act of saving also decreases the degree of inequality. But two features of bequests make intergenerational transfers of wealth a source of increased inequality:

■ Debts cannot be bequeathed
■ Mating is assortative

Debts Cannot Be Bequeathed   Although a person may die with debts that exceed assets—with negative wealth—debts cannot be forced onto other family members. Because a zero inheritance is the smallest inheritance that anyone can receive, bequests can only add to future generations' wealth and income potential.

Most people inherit nothing or a very small amount. A few people inherit enormous fortunes. As a result, bequests make the distribution of income persistently more unequal than the distribution of ability and job skills. A family that is poor in one generation is more likely to be poor in the next. A family that is wealthy in one generation is likely to be wealthy in the next. But there is a tendency for income and wealth to converge, across generations, to the average. Although there can be long runs of good luck or bad luck, or good judgment or bad judgment, such long runs are uncommon across generations. But a feature of human behavior slows the convergence of wealth to the average and makes inequalities persist—assortative mating.

Assortative Mating   *Assortative mating* is the tendency for people to marry within their own socioeconomic class. In the vernacular, "like attracts like." Although there is a good deal of folklore that "opposites attract," perhaps such Cinderella tales appeal to us because they are so rare in reality. Marriage partners tend to have similar socioeconomic characteristics. Wealthy individuals seek wealthy partners. The consequence of assortative mating is that inherited wealth becomes more unequally distributed.

REVIEW

■ Income inequality arises from unequal wage rates, unequal endowments, and choices.

■ Wage rates are unequal because of differences in skills or human capital.

■ Endowments are unequal and have a bell-shaped distribution.

■ The distribution of income is skewed because people with higher wage rates tend to work longer hours and so make a disproportionately larger income.

■ The distribution of wealth is skewed because people with higher incomes save more, bequeath more to the next generation, and marry people with similar wealth.

We've now examined why inequality exists. Next, we're going to see how taxes and government programs redistribute income and wealth.

Income Redistribution

THE THREE MAIN WAYS IN WHICH GOVERNMENTS in the United States redistribute income are:

- Income taxes
- Income maintenance programs
- Subsidized services

Income Taxes

Income taxes may be progressive, regressive, or proportional. A **progressive income tax** is one that taxes income at a marginal rate that increases with the level of income. The term "marginal," applied to income tax rates, refers to the fraction of the last dollar earned that is paid in taxes. A **regressive income tax** is one that taxes income at a marginal rate that decreases with the level of income. A **proportional income tax** (also called a *flat-rate income tax*) is one that taxes income at a constant rate, regardless of the level of income.

The tax rates that apply in the United States are composed of two parts: federal and state taxes. Some cities, such as New York City, also have an income tax. There is variety in the detailed tax arrangements in the individual states, but the tax system, at both the federal and state levels, is progressive. The poorest working families receive money from the government through an earned income tax credit. The middle-income families pay 15 percent of each additional dollar they earn, and successively richer families pay 28 percent, 31 percent, 36 percent, and 39.6 percent of each additional dollar earned.

Income Maintenance Programs

Three main types of programs redistribute income by making direct payments (in cash, services, or vouchers) to people in the lower part of the income distribution. They are:

- Social security programs
- Unemployment compensation
- Welfare programs

Social Security   The main social security program is OASDHI—Old Age, Survivors, Disability, and Health Insurance. Monthly cash payments to retired or disabled workers or their surviving spouses and children are paid for by compulsory payroll taxes on both employers and employees. In 1994, total social security expenditure was $317 billion, and 43 million people received an average monthly social security check of $737.

The other component of social security is Medicare, which provides hospital and health insurance for the elderly and disabled.

Unemployment Benefits   To provide an income to unemployed workers, every state has established an unemployment insurance program. Under these programs, a tax is paid based on the income of each covered worker and such a worker receives a benefit when he or she becomes unemployed. The details of the benefits vary from state to state.

Welfare Programs   The purpose of welfare is to provide incomes to needy people who do not qualify for social security or unemployment benefits. They are:

1. Supplementary Security Income (SSI) program, designed to help the neediest elderly, disabled, and blind people
2. Temporary Assistance for Needy Families (TANF) program, designed to help families who have inadequate financial resources
3. Food Stamp program, designed to help the poorest families obtain a basic diet
4. Medicaid, designed to cover the costs of medical care for families receiving help under the SSI and TANF programs

Subsidized Services

A great deal of redistribution takes place in the United States through the provision of subsidized services—services provided by the government at prices far below the cost of production. The taxpayers who consume these goods and services receive a transfer in kind from the taxpayers who do not consume them. The two most important areas in which this form of redistribution takes place are education—both kindergarten through grade 12 and college and university—and health care.

In 1995, students enrolled in the University of California system paid annual tuition fees of around $3,000. The cost of one year's education at the University of California at Berkeley or San Diego in 1993 was more than $15,000. So families with a member enrolled in these institutions received a benefit from the government of more than $12,000 a year.

Government provision of health-care services has grown to equal the scale of private provision. Programs such as Medicaid and Medicare bring high-quality and high-cost health care to millions of people who earn too little to buy such services themselves.

The Scale of Income Redistribution

A family's income in the absence of government redistribution is called *market income*. We can measure the scale of income redistribution by calculating the percentage of market income paid in taxes and the percentage received in benefits at each income level. The data available include redistribution through taxes and cash and noncash benefits to welfare recipients. They do not include the value of subsidized services such as college, which might decrease the total amount of redistribution from the rich to the poor.

Figure 17.5 shows the scale of redistribution. The blue Lorenz curve describes the market distribution of income. It is the same as that in Fig. 17.1. The red Lorenz curve shows the distribution of income after all taxes and benefits including Medicaid and Medicare benefits. The distribution after taxes and benefits is much less unequal than the market distribution. The lowest 20 percent of households receive only 3.7 percent of market income but 13 percent of income after taxes and benefits. The highest 20 percent of households receive 48.7 percent of market income but only 31 percent of income after taxes. Redistribution increases the share of total income received by the lowest 60 percent of households. It decreases the share of total income received by the highest 40 percent of households.

Another measure of the scale of redistribution is provided by the sources of income at different points of the income distribution. The poorest 20 percent of households receive more than 70 percent of their income from the government. The second 20 percent receive 43 percent of their income from the government. In contrast, the richest 20 percent receive almost nothing from the government but receive a third of their income from capital—interest and dividends from financial assets. The proportion of income from capital for the other 80 percent of families is remarkably constant at about 8 percent.

FIGURE 17.5

Income Redistribution

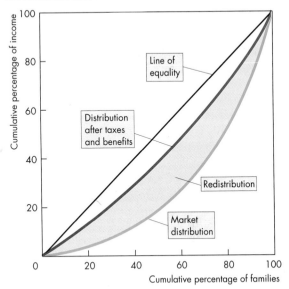

Taxes and income maintenance programs reduce the degree of inequality that the market generates. In 1995, the 20 percent of families with the lowest incomes received net benefits that increased their share of total income from 3.7 percent to 13 percent. The 20 percent of families with the highest incomes paid taxes that decreased their share of total income from 48.7 percent to 31 percent of total income.

Sources: U.S. Bureau of the Census, Current Population Reports, P-60-193, *Money Income in the United States (With Separate Data on Valuation of Noncash Benefits),* (Washington, D.C., U.S. Government Printing Office, 1996), and the author's calculations.

The Big Tradeoff

The redistribution of income creates what has been called the **big tradeoff**, a tradeoff between equity and efficiency. The big tradeoff arises because redistribution uses scarce resources and weakens incentives.

A dollar collected from a rich person does not translate into a dollar received by a poor person. Some of it gets used up in the process of redistribution. Tax-collecting agencies such as the Internal Revenue Service and welfare-administering agencies (as well as tax accountants and lawyers) use skilled labor, computers, and other scarce resources to do their work. The bigger the scale of redistribution, the greater is the opportunity cost of administering it.

But the cost of collecting taxes and making welfare payments is a small part of the total cost of redistribution. A bigger cost arises from the inefficiency—deadweight loss—of taxes and benefits. Greater equality can be achieved only by taxing productive activities such as work and saving. Taxing people's income from their work and saving lowers the after-tax income they receive. This lower income makes them work and save less, which in turn result in smaller output and less consumption not only for the rich who pay the taxes but also for the poor who receive the benefits.

It is not only taxpayers who face weaker incentives to work. Benefit recipients also face weaker incentives. In fact, under the welfare arrangements that prevailed before the 1996 reforms, the weakest incentives to work were those faced by families that benefited from welfare. When a welfare recipient got a job, benefits were withdrawn and eligibility for programs like Medicaid ended so that the family in effect paid a tax of more than 100 percent on its earnings. This arrangement locked poor families in a welfare trap.

So the scale and methods of income redistribution must pay close attention to the incentive effects of taxes and benefits. Let's look at the way lawmakers are tackling the "big tradeoff" today.

Welfare Reform

A major welfare reform occurred in 1996 with the passage of the Personal Responsibility and Work Opportunities Reconciliation Act, which President Clinton signed into law in August 1996. This act eliminated Aid to Families with Dependent Children (AFDC) and created Temporary Assistance for Needy Families (TANF).

Until 1996, AFDC was the major source of incomes for low-income families. By the mid-1990s, this program was costing the federal government more than $22 billion a year and the cost was rising. The main source of the high and rising cost is a large and growing number of single mothers. By the early 1990s, more than 30 percent of births were to single mothers and a large number of these women have not completed high school and have limited earning potential. AFDC was an open-ended federal entitlement program, which means that anyone who qualifies for benefits can receive them. The program also provided almost no incentive for benefit recipients to find work and end their reliance on welfare.

The new TANF program contrasts with AFDC in three main ways. First, TANF is a block grant paid to the states, not an open-ended entitlement paid directly to individuals. Second, an adult member of a family receiving assistance must either work or perform community service. Third, there is a five-year limit for assistance (with exemption for some existing welfare recipients).

These measures go a long way toward removing some of the most serious sources of inefficiency in the redistribution system in the United States. But they don't go as far as some economists want to go. Let's look at a more radical reform of welfare, the negative income tax.

Negative Income Tax

A negative income tax is *not* on the political agenda. But it is popular among economists, and it is the subject of several real-world experiments.

A **negative income tax** gives every family a *guaranteed minimum annual income* and taxes *all* income above the guaranteed minimum at a fixed *marginal tax rate*. Suppose the guaranteed minimum annual income is $10,000 and the marginal tax rate is 25 percent. A family with no market income receives the $10,000 guaranteed minimum income from the government. This family "pays" income tax of *minus* $10,000, hence the name *negative* income tax. A family with a market income of $40,000 also receives the $10,000 guaranteed minimum income from the government. But it also pays $10,000—25 percent of its market income—to the government. So this family pays no income tax. It has the break-even income. Families with a market income of between zero and $40,000 "pay" a negative income tax. They receive more from the government than they pay. A family with a market income of $60,000 receives the $10,000 guaranteed minimum income from the government, but it pays $15,000—25 percent of its market income—to the government. So this family pays income tax of $5,000. All families with incomes greater than $40,000 pay income tax to the government.

Figure 17.6 illustrates a negative income tax and compares it with our pre-1996 arrangements. In both parts of the figure, the horizontal axis measures *market income* and the vertical axis measures income *after* taxes are paid and benefits are received. The 45° line shows the hypothetical case of "no redistribution."

FIGURE 17.6

Comparing Traditional Programs and a Negative Income Tax

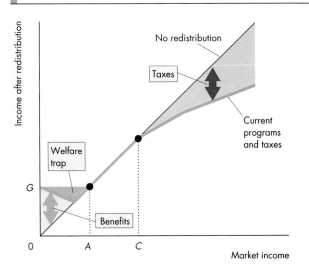

(a) Current redistribution arrangements

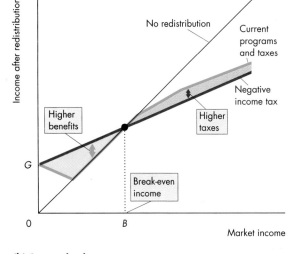

(b) A negative income tax

Part (a) shows traditional redistribution arrangements—the blue curve. Benefits of *G* are paid to those with no income. As incomes increase from zero to *A*, benefits are withdrawn, *lowering* income after redistribution below *G* and creating a welfare trap—the gray triangle. As incomes increase from *A* to *C*, there is no redistribution. As incomes increase above *C*, income taxes are paid at successively higher rates.

In part (b), a negative income tax gives a guaranteed annual income of *G* and decreases benefits at the same rate as the tax rate on incomes. The red line shows how market incomes translate into income after redistribution. Families with market incomes below *B*, the break-even income, receive net benefits. Those with market incomes above *B* pay net taxes.

Part (a) shows traditional redistribution arrangements—the blue curve. Benefits of *G* are paid to those with no income. As incomes increase from zero to *A*, benefits are withdrawn. This arrangement creates a *welfare trap*, shown as the gray triangle. It does not pay a person to work if the income he or she can earn is less than *A*. Over the income range *A* to *C*, each additional dollar of market income increases income after redistribution by a dollar. At incomes greater than *C*, income taxes are paid and at successively higher rates, so income after redistribution is smaller than market income.

Part (b) shows the negative income tax. The guaranteed annual income is *G*, and the break-even income is *B*. Families with market incomes below *B* receive an additional net benefit (blue area), and those with incomes above *B* pay additional taxes (red area). A negative income tax removes the welfare trap and gives greater encouragement to low-income

families to seek more employment, even at a low wage. It also overcomes many of the other problems arising from existing income maintenance programs.

R E V I E W

- Governments redistribute income in the United States by using income taxes and income maintenance programs and providing goods and services below cost.
- The poorest 20 percent of families receive almost two thirds of their income from the government.
- Welfare reform seeks to strengthen the incentive to work.

Health and the cost of health care are major sources of inequality, and we now study the economics of health care and health-care reform.

Health-Care Reform

EXPENDITURE PER PERSON ON HEALTH CARE IS greater in the United States than in any other country. Also, the percentage of total income spent on health care in the United States exceeds that of any other country. An American who has a good job and the comprehensive health insurance that goes with it enjoys a high degree of security and receives the highest-quality health care. Let's look at the scale of spending on health care and at who does the spending.

Total spending on health care in the United States was 14 percent of total income in 1995. The government meets 45 percent of the total health-care cost, and this share has increased from 26 percent in 1965, as Fig. 17.7 shows. The government's share of the cost is made up of its expenditures on Medicare and Medicaid ($263 billion in 1996) and the premiums it pays to private health-care insurance companies for government employees. The other 50 percent of the cost of health care is met by private health-care insurance (up from 32 percent of total payments in 1965 to 35 percent in 1994) and by direct payments by patients (*down* from 42 percent of total payments in 1965 to 20 percent in 1994).

Despite our large commitment of resources and our high quality of care, many people perceive health care in the United States to be in crisis. Why? There are two main problem areas:

1. Health-care costs appear to be out of control.
2. Private health-care insurance does not cover everyone.

Let's take a closer look at these problems.

FIGURE 17.7

Who Pays for Health Care?

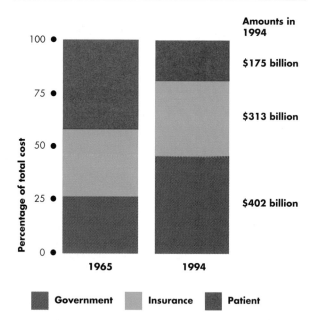

Government pays 45 percent of the total cost of health care, up from 26 percent in 1965. The direct payments by patients declined from 42 percent of the total in 1965 to 20 percent in 1994.

Source: U.S. Bureau of the Census, Statistical Abstract of the United States: 1996, 116th edition, Table 154.

Problem of Health-Care Costs

Health-care costs have increased more rapidly than consumer prices, on the average, as Fig. 17.8 shows. Two separate factors create the gap between the rate of increase in health-care costs and average price increases—the health-care cost gap.

First, health care is a labor-intensive personal service with limited scope for labor-saving technological change. Health-care labor costs—wage rates of medical workers from surgeons to janitors—generally increase at a faster rate than do average prices, and because there is limited scope for labor-saving changes in health-care technology, these higher labor costs are reflected in higher costs for the final health-care product.

Second, the main effect of the technological change that does take place in health care is to improve the quality of the product. For example, the applications of computer technology and advances in drugs have broadened the range of conditions that can be treated. But the cost of using new technologies to treat previously untreatable conditions steadily rises. Both sources of the health-care cost gap can be expected to persist.

Figure 17.9 shows the market for health care. Initially (say in 1980), the demand curve was D_0, the supply curve was S_0, the quantity was Q_0, and the price was P_0. Increasing incomes, longer life spans, and advances in the medical conditions that can be treated increase the demand for health-care

FIGURE 17.8

FIGURE 17.8
The Rising Cost of Health Care

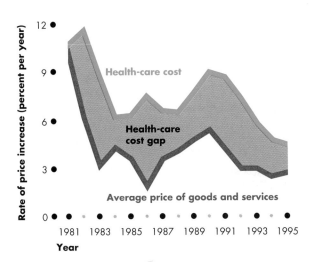

The cost of health care has increased much faster than the average price of other goods and services. The reasons are that health care is a labor-intensive industry—a personal service industry—so labor costs increase and quality improvements have changed the nature of the product and increased its cost.

Source: Economic Report of the President, 1995.

FIGURE 17.9
The Market for Health Care

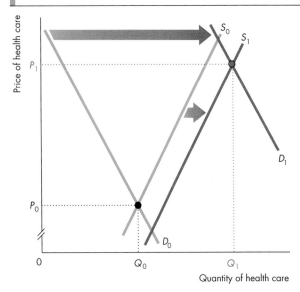

Initially (say in 1980), demand was D_0, supply was S_0, the quantity was Q_0, and the price was P_0. Increasing incomes and technological advances that expand the range of conditions that can be treated increase demand and shift the demand curve rightward to D_1. Advancing technology also increases supply, but increasing wages and more costly equipment and drugs counteract this increase in supply. The net result is that the supply curve shifts rightward to S_1. The quantity increases by a moderate amount, to Q_1, and the price increases steeply, to P_1.

services, and the demand curve shifts rightward from D_0 to D_1. Technological advances in health care have increased supply of health-care services. But the increase in supply is smaller than the increase in demand because some factors have worked to decrease supply. One of these factors is the increasing wage rates of health-care workers; another is the increasing cost of ever more sophisticated health-care technologies. The net effect of the positive and negative influences on supply is a rightward shift in the supply curve to S_1. The quantity of health care has increased to Q_1—and the price has risen to P_1—a relatively large increase.

The forces at work that produce the changes shown in Fig. 17.9 do not appear to be temporary, and they may be expected to bring similar changes in the future.

Health-Care Insurance

In 1994, 51 percent of the health-care dollar was spent on 8 percent of the population. A further 32 percent was spent on 20 percent of the population. Health-care spending on the healthiest 72 percent of the population was 17 percent of total health-care cost.

Because the costs are high and the frequency of use is low, most people choose to finance their health care by insurance. But health-care insurance, like all types of insurance, faces two problems: *moral hazard* and *adverse selection*.[1] Moral hazard in health insurance is the tendency for people who are covered by

---

[1] These problems and other aspects of insurance are explained more fully in Chapter 21, pp. 455–456.

insurance to use more health services or to be less careful about avoiding health risks than they otherwise would. Adverse selection in health insurance is the tendency for people who know they have a greater chance than the average of falling ill to be the ones most likely to buy health insurance.

For example, a person might buy insurance only a few days before going on a ski trip to Colorado (adverse selection). Covered by insurance, this person makes a faster run down the ski slope, knowing that the cost of fixing a broken ankle will be borne, in part, by the insurance company (moral hazard).

But the main adverse selection and moral hazard problems do not arise from reckless young skiers. They arise from the decisions of cautious physicians who elect to perform tests and procedures that are demanded by equally cautious patients only because someone else is paying for them.

Insurance companies set their premium levels sufficiently high to cover claims arising from people who have been adversely selected and who face moral hazard. But to attract profitable business from low-risk customers, insurance companies give preference to the healthy and employed. They also limit the coverage of preexisting conditions and claims arising from major illness. The result is that many people are uninsured or are insured for minor problems but not for catastrophic illness.

Reform Proposals

Health-care reform is a major political issue. Almost always, when some feature of the economy is not working the way people want it to, some people reach the conclusion that the government must step in to deal with the problem and others reach the opposite conclusion and identify existing government intervention as the source of the problem. So it is with health care. We'll end our brief study of the economics of health care by examining a range of alternative proposals for improving the performance of the health-care sector.

A Bigger Role for Government?   Many Democrats want a universal health-care system similar to the one proposed by President Clinton in 1993. The main features of President Clinton's health-care reform plan were the following:

1. Insurance companies would be required to offer a comprehensive package of health-care benefits to every citizen on equal terms and not reject any applicant.
2. People would be free to choose their doctor and their health plan.
3. Cost would be contained through increased competition and efficiency and by capping insurance premium increases.
4. Contributions to the cost of health care would be collected from everyone (with limited exceptions).

If insurance companies were required to provide universal coverage, their ability to select customers based on health risk would be removed. The result would be better insurance for those who were previously excluded but higher insurance premiums for those who had qualified for insurance under the previous rules.

It is possible that some one-time cost savings might be achieved from more efficient administration of the insurance and health-care industries. For example, simplifying the administration of claims and reducing fraud—two measures featured in the plan—might decrease costs. But the scope for such cost cuts is limited. It was estimated (by President Clinton's economic advisors) that administration costs are 25 percent of hospital costs and that fraud accounts for 10 percent of total health-care costs. Decreasing these components of health-care cost is likely to bring some benefit. But it cannot stop the process of rising prices.

If a premium cap—a spending ceiling—is imposed on insurance premiums, the total cost of health care might be limited. But spending ceilings create shortages. The quantity of health care demanded will exceed the quantity supplied. In this situation, some method other than the price mechanism will ration the scarce resources of health care. One possible device is a queue—a waiting line for services. The evidence from Britain and Canada, two countries that ration health-care services by waiting lines, is that the people who are likely to wait longest and get the worst deal are those whom the current scheme serves least well.

Make the Private Health-Care Market Work Better?   Many Republicans want to scale back the federal government's funding of health-care services. Proposals have been made to cut the projected increase by $270 billion from Medicare over a seven-year period. People who can afford to buy their own health care would no longer be eligible for Medicare, and people would be given incentives to switch from high-cost fee-for-service providers to lower-cost managed-care providers.

The hope is that by cutting the scale of public expenditure, health-care costs would rise less quickly. There is evidence that this is a realistic hope. Removing the effects of inflation, the cost of Medicaid and Medicare has increased more than fourfold since 1970, while the cost of private health care has less than doubled.

By providing tax incentives that encourage employers to buy medical insurance, the government has made the private part of health care less efficient. Although *employers* buy medical insurance, it is the *employees* who pay for it. The compensation package, which consists of wages plus medical insurance, is determined by the forces of demand and supply. The amount that employers spend buying medical insurance is subtracted from the total compensation to determine the amount to be paid as wages.

But the income tax laws interact with employer-provided medical insurance to create a big problem. Employees pay income tax on their wages but not on the value of their medical insurance. So suppose a firm and its workers are negotiating a new compensation package. Will wages rise by $100 per employee, or will medical insurance premiums rise by $100 per employee to improve the quality of medical insurance? (Improved medical insurance might take the form of a lower deductible or a wider coverage.)

If a firm's labor cost is going to increase by $100 per employee, the firm doesn't care whether it pays the $100 in higher wages or in improved health insurance. But the employees care. Because wages are taxed, an extra $100 in wages translates into around $60 in disposable income. So employees must compare the value of improved health insurance that costs $100 with an additional $60 of disposable income. If the value employees place on improved medical insurance that costs $100 exceeds $60, they will opt for the insurance rather than the higher wages. If employers were not permitted to shelter employees from income tax in this way, wages would be higher and people would decide for themselves how much medical insurance coverage to buy.

There would be a strengthened incentive to buy insurance at a lower cost with a larger deductible and smaller range of coverage. With a larger deductible, people would have a stronger incentive to economize on medical treatments and the moral hazard and adverse selection problems would be lessened.

But the fundamental problem is that rising health-care costs stem from forces that are going to persist. Advances in health-care technology can be expected to keep the demand for health care increasing briskly. And the increasing cost of applying new medical technologies and steadily rising wage rates for skilled health-care workers can be expected to keep supply growing more slowly than demand. The result: The price that balances the quantities demanded and supplied will continue to increase faster than the average rise in prices.

REVIEW

- Health-care costs are high and rising, and many people lack health-care insurance.
- Health-care costs increase more quickly than average prices because health care is a labor-intensive personal service and it experiences continuous improvements in product quality.
- Health-care insurance (like all types of insurance) faces *moral hazard* and *adverse selection* problems.
- Health-care reform plans call for either more government intervention—such as universal coverage and a ceiling on insurance premiums—or less government intervention—such as ending tax incentives for employers to provide medical insurance.

◆ We've examined economic inequality in the United States, and we've seen that there is a large amount of inequality across families and individuals. Some of that inequality arises from comparing families at different stages in the life cycle. But even if we take a lifetime view, inequality remains. Some of that inequality arises from differences in wage rates. And economic choices accentuate those differences.

We've also seen that inequality has been increasing. *Reading Between the Lines* on pages 378–379 looks at the widening gap between the rich and the poor in California.

We've seen that actions in the political marketplace redistribute income to alleviate the worst aspects of poverty. Our next task is to look more fully at the ways in which government actions modify the outcome of the market economy. We look at sources of market failure and the ways in which government actions aim to overcome it. We also look at what is called the political marketplace and the potential for it to fail too.

Policy
WATCH

The Changing Income Distribution

LOS ANGELES TIMES, JULY 15, 1996

Income Gap Is Growing, Study Reports

BY CARLA HALL

The gap between rich and poor in California has been steadily widening in the last three decades, as the rich got a little richer and the poor got a lot poorer, according to a study released today by a new California think tank.

Though California's gap has generally mirrored the national income gap, "it has exceeded the nation in the last seven years—which is not something to be proud of," said Deborah Reed, principal author of "The Distribution of Income in California."

"This particular gap is bad because it represents a decline in the income of the poor," said Reed, a labor economist and research fellow at the Public Policy Institute of California. ...

The study, which covers the years from 1967 to 1994, does not follow specific people, so it does not conclude that people who were poor in 1967 are necessarily poorer today. ...

The study examined 26 indicators of income, including household income (which includes all sources of money coming into the home, not just wages) and wages earned by men.

In 1967, it says, annual household income for a family of four at the 10th percentile—meaning households that rank below 90% of households in the state—was $14,782, expressed in 1994 dollars. In 1994, a household at the 10th percentile has an income of $11,205—a decline of 24%.

On the other end, at the 90th percentile, household income was $81,308 in 1967 and $110,106 in 1994—a rise of 35%.

More dramatic is the difference in earnings by men.

A male wage earner at the 10th percentile in 1967 earned $9,291. In 1994, he earned $6,000—a drop of 35%.

Men at the 90th percentile in 1967 earned $54,903. In 1994, they earned $65,000. That's an increase of 18%. ...

The study does not identify why the gap has increased but suggests that the recession, defense cutbacks, immigration and the effect of technology on workers are factors. ...

Essence of THE STORY

■ The gap between rich and poor in California has widened over the last 30 years.

■ A family of four whose income is in the lowest 10 percent of the population earned $14,782 (1994 dollars) in 1967 and $11,205 in 1994.

■ A family of four whose income is in the highest 10 percent of the population earned $81,308 (1994 dollars) in 1967 and $110,106 in 1994.

■ A male wage earner whose earnings are in the lowest 10 percent of the population earned $9,291 (1994 dollars) in 1967 and $6,000 in 1994.

■ A male wage earner whose earnings are in the highest 10 percent of the population earned $54,903 (1994 dollars) in 1967 and $65,000 in 1994.

■ Recession, defense cutbacks, immigration, and technology are all suggested as possible reasons for the increase in the earnings gap.

Economic

A N A L Y S I S

■ The changes in relative incomes in California are greater than those for the United States as a whole, but the entire nation has experienced a change in the same direction as that in California.

■ Figure 1 shows the market for low-skilled male labor in California, using the numbers in the news article. The supply curve in 1967 was S_{67}, and the demand curve was D_{67}. The market is in equilibrium at quantity Q_0 and annual wages of $9,291.

■ Between 1967 and 1994 the supply of low-skilled labor increased. The reason is the population increased. Some of this population increase resulted from immigration from Latin America. The supply curve shifted right to S_{94}.

■ The demand for low-skilled labor also increased but by a small amount. The increase in demand was kept small because advances in technology displaced low-skilled labor with machines. The demand curve shifted rightward to D_{94}.

■ In 1994, the low-skilled labor market is in equilibrium at a wage of $6,000 a year.

■ Figure 2 shows the market for high-skilled labor, using the numbers in the news article.

■ The technological advances that decreased the demand for low-skilled labor increased the demand for high-skilled labor. The demand curve shifted rightward from D_{67} to D_{94}.

■ The supply of high-skilled labor also increased, because of the population and the number of people completing college increased. But the increase in supply was smaller than the increase in demand. The supply curve shifted rightward from S_{67} to S_{94}.

■ The equilibrium wage rate of high-skilled labor increased from $54,903 to $65,000 a year.

■ The wage gap between the two groups will begin to narrow again only if either low-skilled labor acquires more skill or further technological change increases the demand for low-skilled labor.

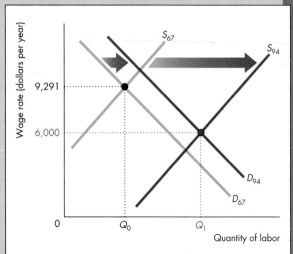

Figure 1 Lowest 10 percent

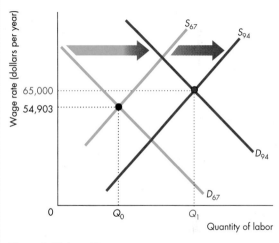

Figure 2 Highest 10 percent

You're

THE VOTER

■ What policies do you think the California state government should take to deal with the situation described in this news article? Set out your policy proposals in the form of a memo to the Governor of California.

■ What policies do you think the federal government should take to deal with the situation described in this news article? Set out your policy proposals in the form of a memo to your Senator.

SUMMARY

Key Points

Economic Inequality in the United States (pp. 364–366)

■ The richest 1 percent of Americans own almost one third of the total wealth in the country.

■ Income is distributed less unevenly than wealth. Throughout the 1970s, 1980s, and 1990s, inequality increased.

■ The poorest people in the United States are single black women with less than eight years of schooling who live in the South. The richest people live in the Northeast and are college-educated, middle-aged, white families in which husband and wife live together.

Comparing Like with Like (p. 367)

■ The distribution of wealth exaggerates the degree of inequality because it excludes human capital.

■ The distributions of annual income and wealth exaggerate lifetime inequality because they do not take the life cycle into account.

Resource Prices, Endowments, and Choices (pp. 368–369)

■ Differences in income and wealth arise from differences in resource prices, endowments, and choices.

■ People who face high wage rates generally work longer than those who face low wage rates, so the distribution of income becomes more unequal and more skewed than the distribution of wage rates.

Income Redistribution (pp. 370–373)

■ Governments redistribute income through income taxes, income maintenance programs, and provision of subsidized services.

■ Income taxes are progressive.

■ Redistribution creates a "big tradeoff" between equity and efficiency, which arises because the process of redistribution uses resources and weakens incentives to work and save.

■ Traditional income maintenance programs create a welfare trap that discourages work, so poverty is persistent. Reforms seek to lessen the severity of the welfare trap. A more radical negative income tax reform would encourage people on welfare to find work.

Health-Care Reform (pp. 374–377)

■ Total spending on health care in the United States is 14 percent of total income (45 percent met by the government, 35 percent by private insurance payments, and 20 percent by direct payments by patients.)

■ Health-care costs have increased more rapidly than consumer prices.

■ Health-care insurance faces moral hazard—the tendency for people who are insured to take greater risks—and adverse selection—the tendency for people with the greatest chance of making an insurance claim to be the ones who buy insurance.

■ Some people suggest that health-care reform requires universal comprehensive health insurance and ceilings on insurance premiums, while others say that market forces need strengthening.

Key Figures

Key Terms

QUESTIONS

1. Which of the following describes the distributions of personal income and wealth in the United States today?
   a. The distributions of income and wealth are best represented by normal or bell-shaped curves.
   b. More than 50 percent of the population is wealthier than the average.
   c. More than 50 percent of the population is poorer than the average.

2. What is a Lorenz curve? How does a Lorenz curve illustrate inequality? Explain how the Lorenz curves for the distributions of income and wealth in the United States differ from each other.

3. Which is more unequally distributed, income or wealth? In answering this question, pay careful attention both to the way in which income and wealth are measured by official statistics and to the fundamental concepts of income and wealth.

4. How has the distribution of income in the United States changed over the past 20 years? Which groups have received a larger share of total income and which have received a smaller share?

5. What is wrong with the way in which the official statistics measure the distribution of wealth?

6. Explain why the work/leisure choices made by individuals can result in a distribution of income that is more unequal than the distribution of ability. If ability is distributed normally (bell-shaped), will the resulting distribution of income also be bell-shaped?

7. Explain how bequests and assortative mating influence the distribution of income and wealth.

8. What are the three main ways in which governments redistribute income in the United States?

9. What is a negative income tax and why don't we have one?

10. What are the main health-care problems facing Americans today?

11. What are the main arguments of people who want less government expenditure on health care?

PROBLEMS

1. You are given the following information about income and wealth shares in an economy:

	Income shares (percent)	Wealth shares (percent)
Lowest 20%	5	0
Second 20%	11	1
Third 20%	17	3
Fourth 20%	24	11
Highest 20%	43	85

   a. Draw the Lorenz curves for income and wealth for this economy.
   b. Explain which of the two variables—income or wealth—is more unequally distributed.
   c. Compare the distributions of income and wealth in this economy with those in the United States. Is U.S. income distributed more equally or less equally than in the economy described in the table?

2. Imagine an economy with five people who are identical in all respects. Each lives for 70 years. For the first 14 of those years, they earn no income. For the next 35 years, they work and earn $30,000 a year from their work. For their remaining years, they are retired and have no income from labor. To make the arithmetic easy, let's suppose that the interest rate in this economy is zero; the individuals consume all their income during their lifetime and at a constant annual rate. What are the distributions of income and wealth in this economy if the individuals have the following ages:
   a. All are 45
   b. 25, 35, 45, 55, 65

   Is case (a) one of greater inequality than case (b)?

3. An economy consists of 10 people, each of whom has the following labor supply schedule:

Wage rate (dollars per hour)	Hours worked per day
1	0
2	1
3	2
4	3
5	4

The people differ in ability and earn different wage rates. The distribution of *wage rates* is as follows:

Wage rate (dollars per hour)	Number of people
1	1
2	2
3	4
4	2
5	1

a. Calculate the average wage rate.
b. Calculate the ratio of the highest to the lowest wage rate.
c. Calculate the average daily income.
d. Calculate the ratio of the highest to the lowest daily income.
e. Sketch the distribution of hourly wage rates.
f. Sketch the distribution of daily incomes.
g. What important lesson is illustrated by this problem?

4. The table shows the distribution of market income in an economy.

Percentage of families	Income (millions of dollars)
Lowest 20%	5
Second 20%	10
Third 20%	18
Fourth 20%	28
Highest 20%	39

a. Draw the Lorenz curve for this economy.
b. Is the distribution of income in this economy more unequal or less unequal than in the United States?

5. The government in the economy in problem 4 redistributes income by collecting the income taxes and paying the benefits shown in the following table:

Percentage of families	Income taxes (percent of income)	Benefits (millions of dollars)
Lowest 20%	0	10
Second 20%	10	8
Third 20%	15	3
Fourth 20%	20	0
Highest 20%	30	0

a. Draw the Lorenz curve for this economy after taxes and benefits.
b. Is the scale of redistribution of income in this economy greater or smaller than in the United States?

CRITICAL THINKING

1. Study *Reading Between the Lines* on pp. 378–379, and then:
   a. Describe the main facts about the changes in the distribution of income in California reported in the news article.
   b. Compare the situation in California with that in the rest of the country.
   c. How do you think the tax system and the welfare system change the situation described in the news article?
   d. How would a negative income tax modify the outcome described in the article?

2. Visit the World Wide Web site of the U.S. Census Bureau at http://www.census.gov/hhes/www/income.html or use the link at the Parkin Web site and obtain data on poverty and income distribution for your own state (or county if the data are available). Then:
   a. Describe the main facts about poverty and the distribution of income in your state (county).
   b. Compare the situation in your state (county) with that in the rest of the country.
   c. Why do you think your state (county) is performing better/worse than the nation as a whole?

3. Describe and evaluate the Personal Responsibility and Work Opportunity Reconciliation Act of 1996. In what ways do you think the 1996 law improves on the programs that it replaces? You can get as much detail on the 1996 law as you wish from the World Wide Web site of the National Governors' Association http://www.nga.org/.

http://hepg.awl.com/parkin/econ100

Part 6 Market Failure and Government

We, the People, ...

Thomas Jefferson knew that creating a government of the people, by the people, and for the people was a huge enterprise and one that could easily go wrong. Creating a constitution that made despotic and tyrannical rule impossible was relatively easy. The founding fathers did their best to practice sound economics. They designed a sophisticated system of incentives—of carrots and sticks—to make the government responsive to public opinion and to limit the ability of individual special interests to gain at the expense of the majority. But they were not able to create a constitution that effectively blocks the ability of special interest groups to capture the consumer and producer surpluses that result from specialization and exchange. ◆ We have created a system of government to deal with four economic problems. The market economy would produce too small a quantity of those public goods and services that we must consume together, such as national defense and air-traffic control. It enables monopoly to restrict production and charge too high a price. It produces too large a quantity of some goods and services the production of which creates pollution. And it generates a distribution of income and wealth that most people believe is too unequal. So, we need a government to help cope with these economic problems. But as the founding fathers knew would happen, when governments get involved in the economy, people try to steer the government's actions in directions that bring personal gains at the expense of the general interest. ◆ The next four chapters study the variety of situations in which the market has a hard time coping with scarcity. Chapter 18 previews the entire range of problems and studies one of them, public goods, more deeply. Chapter 19 studies antitrust law and the regulation of natural monopoly. And Chapter 20 deals with externalities. It examines the external costs imposed by pollution and the external benefits that come from education and research. It describes some of the ways in which externalities can be dealt with. You will discover that one way of coping with externalities is to strengthen the market and "internalize them" rather than to intervene in the market. Chapter 21 is different from the other three. It looks at the problems of uncertainty and incomplete information and the problems that markets have in the face of these problems. But it also shows you that the market does cope with these problems remarkably well. ◆ Before you begin these chapters, spend a few minutes with an economist who has thought a great deal about the issues you will study here, Ronald Coase. Also, meet Walter Williams of George Mason University.

Understanding Externalities

The Economist:
Ronald Coase

Ronald Coase (1910–), was born in England and educated at the London School of Economics, where he was deeply influenced by his teacher, Arnold Plant, and by the issues of his youth: Communist central planning versus free markets.

Professor Coase has lived in the United States since 1951. He first visited America as a 20-year-old on a traveling scholarship during the depths of the Great Depression. It was on this visit, and before he had completed his bachelor's degree, that he conceived the ideas that 60 years later were to earn him the 1991 Nobel Prize for Economic Science. He discovered and clarified the significance of transaction costs and property rights for the functioning of the economy. Ronald Coase has revolutionized the way we think about property rights and externalities and has opened up the growing field of law and economics.

"The question to be decided is: is the value of fish lost greater or less than the value of the product which contamination of the stream makes possible?"

RONALD H. COASE

THE PROBLEM OF SOCIAL COST

The Issues
and Ideas

As knowledge accumulates, we are becoming more sensitive to environmental externalities. We are also developing more sensitive methods of dealing with them. But all the methods involve a public choice.

Urban smog, which is both unpleasant and dangerous to breathe, forms when sunlight reacts with emissions from automobile tailpipes. Because of this external cost of auto exhaust, we set emission standards and tax gasoline. Emission standards increase the cost of a car, and gasoline taxes increase the cost of the marginal mile traveled. The higher costs decrease the quantity demanded of road transportation and so decrease the amount of pollution it creates. Is the value of cleaner urban air worth the higher cost of transportation? The public choices of voters, regulators, and lawmakers answer this question.

Acid rain, which imposes a cost on everyone who lives in its path, falls from sulfur-laden clouds produced by electric utility smokestacks. This external cost is being tackled with a market solution. This solution is marketable permits, the price and allocation of which are determined by the forces of supply and demand. Private choices determine the demand for pollution permits, but a public choice determines the supply.

As cars stream onto an urban freeway at morning rush hour, the highway clogs and becomes an expensive parking lot. Each rush hour traveler imposes external costs on all the others. Today, road users bear private congestion costs but do not face a share of the external congestion costs they create. But a market solution to this problem is now technologically feasible. It is a solution that charges road users a fee similar to a toll that varies with time of day and degree of congestion. Confronted with the social marginal cost of their actions, each road user makes a choice and the market for highway space is efficient. Here, a public choice to use a market solution leaves the final decision about the degree of congestion to private choices.

THEN...

Chester Jackson, a Lake Erie fisherman, recalls that when he began fishing on the lake, boats didn't carry drinking water. Fishermen drank from the lake. Speaking after World War II, Jackson observed, "Can't do that today. Those chemicals in there would kill you." Farmers used chemicals, such as the insecticide DDT that got carried into the lake by runoff. Industrial waste and trash were also dumped in the lake in large quantities. As a result, Lake Erie became badly polluted during the 1940s and became incapable of sustaining a viable fish stock.

...AND NOW

Today, Lake Erie supports a fishing industry, just as it did in the 1930s. No longer treated as a garbage dump for chemicals, the lake is regenerating its ecosystem. Fertilizers and insecticides are now recognized as products that have potential externalities, and their external effects are assessed by the Environment Protection Agency before new versions are put into widespread use. Dumping industrial waste into rivers and lakes is now subject to much more stringent regulations and penalties. Lake Erie's externalities have been dealt with by one of the methods available: government regulation.

Many economists today work on problems of public policy and the problems of government intervention in the economy. One of these economists is Walter Williams of George Mason University, whom you can meet on the following pages.

Talking with

Walter E. Williams is Professor of Economics at George Mason University in Fairfax, Virginia. Born in Philadelphia, Pennsylvania, in 1936, Professor Williams was an undergraduate at California State University at Los Angeles and a graduate student at UCLA, where he obtained his Ph.D. in 1972.

Professor Williams's research covers a wide area, but his major work is on labor markets, discrimination, and market failure. He has lectured throughout the world, including the University of Capetown during the 1980s, where he learned firsthand the lessons of apartheid. Professor Williams is a member of the prestigious Mont Pelerin Society, an international organization of free market economists. Its membership includes six Nobel Laureates: Milton Friedman, Friedrich Hayek, George Stigler, James Buchanan, Gary Becker, and Ronald Coase.

Michael Parkin talked with Professor Williams about his work, how it connects with the ideas of other great economists, and the insights they offer us in facing today's problems.

Professor Williams, what attracted you to economics?

Like many undergraduate students of the 1960s, I was concerned with public policy that focused on the betterment of mankind and tackled issues such as urban decay, poverty, unemployment, and discrimination. At the time, it seemed that social sciences like sociology and psychology were the ideal tools to analyze these important social issues. That was until by pure chance a particular sociology class was filled, and so I substituted an introductory economics class. As a consequence of not being good at the deductive logic of economics, plus several classroom disputes with the professor on topics such as income distribution and racial discrimination, I wound up getting a "D." However, I was sufficiently interested in economics that I took two economics classes the following semester, earning an "A" in both. Ultimately, I changed my major to economics and earned a B.A. from California State University at Los Angeles and later earned a Ph.D. in Economics from UCLA.

You and I first met in Capetown, South Africa, in 1980, when we were both visiting professors at the University of Capetown. What are the big economic lessons that the experience of South Africa teaches about the proper role of government in economic life?

When we first met in Capetown, apartheid was very much a part of South Africa. I was very impressed with the economic lessons of apartheid, so much so that I ultimately wrote a book in 1992 entitled *South Africa's War Against Capitalism*. The biggest lesson from South Africa's experience is that the free market does not confer privileges based on race. The free market instead uses economic factors such as prices and productivity. If people wish to indulge their preferences for noneconomic factors such as race, sex, and nationality, the free market exacts a price. South African whites knew this very well and found that if they wanted privileges, they needed the extensive government apparatus of coercion and control that became known as apartheid. Labor laws such as those that reserved certain jobs for whites stand as unambiguous evidence that the market would not discriminate in employment to the extent whites wished. If it would have, there would have been no need for racially restrictive laws.

> *The biggest lesson from South Africa's experience is that the free market cannot be trusted to confer privileges based on race. The free market instead uses economic factors such as prices and productivity.*

What do you identify as the major sources of market failure that need government action today?
Many alleged instances of "market failure" are the result of ill-defined property rights. That is surely the case in instances of air and water pollution. In those instances, a case can be made for efficient government intervention. Government can ban the polluting activity, assign pollution taxes, or assign pollution rights that can be bought and sold in the market. Many economists agree that the last is a more efficient method of dealing with the external costs of pollution. We should also recognize that government decision makers do not hold property rights to the resources they control. Since they are not residual claimants to either the costs or benefits they create, we cannot expect to see the kinds of forces, such as the threat of bankruptcy, that create the kind of operational efficiency we see in the market. In other words, since a politician's personal wealth is not at stake, when he makes decisions, he will be far more shortsighted than his counterpart in the private sector.

Has deregulation of telecommunications and air transportation done its job? Has deregulation brought problems that were not expected?
By any objective measure, the deregulation of the telecommunications and transportation industries has done its job. Consumers pay lower prices and receive higher quality and a more varied set of services than was the case before deregulation. Deregulation of airlines led to cheaper fares, which in turn led to more Americans traveling by air. To the extent that statistics show that air travel is far safer than highway travel, the deregulation has actually saved thousands of lives. With the deregulation of the telephone industry, we see the greater use of services such as faxes, modems, electronic transactions, and the Internet that would have been impossible with the regulatory heavy hand of government. The remaining problem in these industries is that deregulation has not gone far enough: in the case of transportation, privatization of the airports and air traffic control, and in the case of telecommunications, complete auctioning of the airwaves to new and existing firms in the communications industry.

Do we have a monopoly problem in the new information industries? Microsoft? Intel? The Internet? Why and what do we need to do about it?
Often a monopoly is the most efficient method of organization. Monopolies are not inherently good or bad. After all, the institution of marriage is essentially one of a monopolistic structure: It hopes to limit competition. Obviously, the participants guess there are some gains from limited competition. If you read the Ten Commandments, you will see that the first two, presumably the most important, are: Thou shalt have none other gods before me, and thou shalt not make any graven image. In other words, there cannot be any substitutes for God— surely a monopoly arrangement!

Monopoly is a problem when government creates monopolies, whether the monopoly is private or public. Classic government-created monopolies are those in education, postal services, and rail services that limit consumer choices and are not subject to the corrective forces of the marketplace when they do not serve their customers properly. Such insulation does not apply in the cases of Microsoft and Intel.

What are the main forms of discrimination that economic policy can correct and what is your assessment of the progress made in the United States during the past decade?
First, we need to come up with an operational and useful definition of discrimination. I think discrimination can be best described solely as the act of choice. Scarcity implies choice. When one chooses one activity or person, he or she must necessarily choose against some other activity or person. For example, when the student chooses to major in economics, he or

she must necessarily choose—or discriminate—against other majors. When someone chooses a spouse, he or she must discriminate against other potential spouses.

When one modifies the word "discrimination" with the word "sex" or "race," one is merely specifying an attribute upon which a choice is made. What most people call discrimination is more properly called preference indulgence. As such, the preference for Burgundy wine over Bordeaux wine does not conceptually differ from a person's preference for a white spouse, white employee, or white renter. In other words, there are no commonly accepted criteria to say whether the preference for one good or set of physical attributes is better or more righteous than another.

Preference indulgence becomes a moral and economic problem when government is used. For example, any principle of liberty suggests that a person has the right to sell his house to whomever he pleases, but that principle does not allow him to use state coercion to force his neighbor to act likewise. When there is public provision of a good such as schools, libraries, or golf courses, that fact implies that every member of the public has the right to use the good in question. While racial or sexual preference indulgence may be offensive, the true test of one's commitment to freedom of association does not come when we permit people to associate as we see fit. The true test of that commitment comes when we allow people to associate in ways we deem offensive.

The best thing that government can do in the area of racial or sex discrimination is not to subsidize it through laws that regulate prices such as minimum wages and rent control and other regula-tory laws such as occupational and business licensure. Minimum wages deny people the right to bid lower prices for their labor services. Rent control laws deny them the right to bid higher prices for rental services. Licensure laws allow incumbent practitioners to establish arbitrary, capricious, legally binding occupational and business entry standards.

The power to bid lower prices for what one sells or higher prices for what one buys is the most effective way for people deemed less preferred—minorities, women, and foreigners—to compete with others. Price controls prevent that competition. Similarly, voluntary mutually satisfactory exchange permits effective competition with people deemed more preferred.

Who are the great economists of the past who have inspired you most? What principal idea has proved crucial in your own thinking?
Frederic Bastiat's works, *The Law* and *Economic Sophisms*, have been my major sources of inspiration. But Friedrich Hayek's many works have played a major part as well. Both shared the vision that the uglier portions of mankind's history features arbitrary abuse and control by a powerful government. If liberty is to emerge and survive, government must be limited to the legitimate and moral functions of government. For the most part, those functions lie principally in the areas of protection of the individual from coercion by others and the protection of his property, including his person. Evidence shows that where individuals have a greater measure of liberty, there is a higher level of prosperity and wealth accumulation. But prosperity and wealth should be viewed as a secondary benefit of liberty. Liberty is morally superior, and its primary benefit lies in its respect for the individual.

> *Evidence shows that where individuals have a greater measure of liberty, there is a higher level of prosperity and wealth accumulation.*

What do you say to an undergraduate who wants to know whether it is worth majoring in economics?
Economics is a way of thinking and, as such, a powerful tool of analysis that has broad application. Economic theory can be usefully applied in any discussion where there is an issue of benefits versus the cost of human action. Economists have a broad range of employment choices from working in business, government, research, and educational institutions. Moreover, among social scientists, economists tend to be the more highly paid.

> *Economists have a broad range of employment choices from working in business, government, research, and educational institutions.*

Market Failure and Public Choice

In 1996, the federal, state, and local governments in the United States employed more than 19 million people and spent $2.4 trillion. Independent government agencies employed yet another million people. Do we need this much government? Is government, as conservatives sometimes suggest, too big? Is government "the problem"? Or, despite its enormous size, is government too small to do all the things it must attend to? Is government, as liberals sometimes suggest, not contributing enough to economic life? ◆ Government touches many aspects of our lives. It is present at our birth, supporting the hospitals in which we are born and helping to train the doctors and nurses who deliver us. It is present throughout our education, supporting schools and colleges and helping to train our teachers. It is present throughout our working lives, taxing our incomes, regulating our work environment, and paying us benefits when we are unemployed. It is present throughout our retirement, paying us a small income and, when we die, taxing our bequests. And government provides services such as the enforcement of law and order and the provision of national defense. But the government does not make all our choices. We decide what work to do, how much to save, and what to spend our income on. Why does the government participate in some aspects of our lives but not others? ◆ Almost everyone, from the poor single mother to the wealthy taxpayer, grumbles about government services. Why is the bureaucracy so unpopular? And what determines the scale on which public services are provided? ◆ We begin our study of governments and markets by describing the government sector and explaining how, in the absence of a government, the market economy fails to achieve an efficient allocation of resources. We also explain how the scale of government is determined.

Government— the Solution or the Problem?

After studying this chapter, you will be able to:

- Explain how the economic role for government arises from market failure and inequality

- Distinguish between public goods and private goods and explain the free-rider problem

- Explain how the quantity of public goods is determined

- Explain why most of the government's revenue comes from income taxes and why income taxes are progressive

- Explain why some goods are taxed at a much higher rate than others

The Economic Theory of Government

THE ECONOMIC THEORY OF GOVERNMENT SEEKS to predict the economic actions that governments take and the consequences of those actions. Governments exist to help people cope with scarcity and provide a nonmarket mechanism for allocating scarce resources. Four economic problems that governments help people cope with are:

- Public goods
- Monopoly
- Externalities
- Economic inequality

Public Goods

Some goods and services are consumed either by everyone or by no one. Examples are national defense, law and order, and sewage and waste disposal services. National defense systems cannot isolate individuals and refuse to protect them. Airborne diseases from untreated sewage do not favor some people and hit others. A good or service that is consumed either by everyone or by no one is called a **public good**.

The market economy fails to deliver the efficient quantity of public goods because of a free-rider problem. Everyone tries to free ride on everyone else because the good is available to all whether they pay for it or not. We'll study public goods and the free-rider problem later in this chapter.

Monopoly

Monopoly and *rent seeking* prevent the allocation of resources from being efficient. Every business tries to maximize profit, and when a monopoly exists, it can increase profit by restricting output and increasing price. Until fairly recently, for example, AT&T had a monopoly on long-distance telephone services, and the quantity of long-distance services was much smaller and the price much higher than they are today. Since the breakup of AT&T, the quantity of long-distance calls has exploded.

Some monopolies arise from *legal barriers to entry*—barriers to entry created by governments—but a major activity of government is to regulate

monopoly and to enforce laws that prevent cartels and other restrictions on competition. We study these regulations and laws in Chapter 19.

Externalities

An **externality** is a cost or benefit that arises from an economic transaction and that falls on people who do not participate in that transaction. For example, when a chemical factory (legally) dumps its waste into a river and kills the fish, it imposes an external cost on the members of a fishing club who fish downstream. External costs and benefits are not usually taken into account by the people whose actions create them. For example, when the chemical factory decides whether to dump waste into the river, it does not take the fishing club's views into account. When a homeowner fills her garden with spring bulbs, she generates an external benefit for all the passersby. In deciding how much to spend on this lavish display, she takes into account only the benefits accruing to herself. We study externalities in Chapter 20.

These three problems from which government economic activity arises create an *inefficient* use of resources, a situation called **market failure.** When market failure occurs, the market produces too many of some goods and services and too few of some others. In these cases, the cost of producing a good does not equal the value people place on it. By reallocating resources, it is possible to make some people better off while making no one worse off. So some government activity is an attempt to modify the market outcome so as to moderate the effects of market failure.

Economic Inequality

Government economic activity also arises because an unregulated market economy delivers what most people regard as an unfair distribution of income. To lessen the degree of inequality, governments tax some people and pay benefits to others. You studied inequality and redistribution in Chapter 17. In this chapter, we look further at taxes and try to explain why the income tax is progressive and why some goods are taxed at extremely high rates.

Before we begin to study each of these problems from which government activity arises, let's look at the arena in which governments operate—the "political marketplace."

Public Choice and the Political Marketplace

Government is a complex organization made up of millions of individuals, each with his or her *own* economic objective. Government policy is the outcome of the choices made by these individuals. To analyze these choices, economists have developed a *public choice theory* of the political marketplace. The actors in the political marketplace are:

- Voters
- Politicians
- Bureaucrats

Figure 18.1 illustrates the choices and interactions of these actors. Let's look at each in turn.

Voters　Voters are the consumers in the political marketplace. In markets for goods and services, people express their preferences by their willingness to pay. In the political marketplace, they express their preferences by their votes, campaign contributions, and lobbying activity. Public choice theory assumes that people support the policies they believe will make them better off and oppose the policies they believe will make them worse off. It is voters' *perceptions* rather than reality that guide their choices.

Politicians　Politicians are the entrepreneurs of the political marketplace. Public choice theory assumes that the objective of a politician is to get elected and to remain in office. Votes to a politician are like economic profit to a firm. To get enough votes, politicians propose policies that they expect will appeal to a majority of voters.

Bureaucrats　Bureaucrats are the hired officials in government departments. They are the producers or firms in the political marketplace. Public choice theory assumes that bureaucrats aim to maximize their own utility and that to achieve this objective, they try to maximize the budget of their department.

The bigger the budget of a department, the greater is the prestige of its chief and the larger is the opportunity for promotion for people farther down the bureaucratic ladder. So all the members of a department have an interest in maximizing the department's budget. To maximize their budgets, bureaucrats devise programs that they expect will appeal to politicians and they help politicians to explain their programs to voters.

FIGURE 18.1
The Political Marketplace

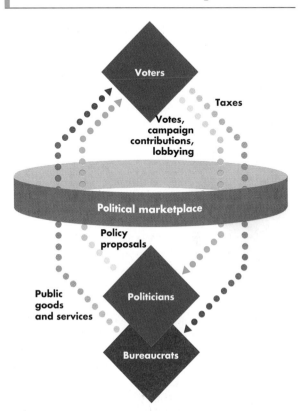

Voters express their demands for policies by voting, making campaign contributions, and lobbying. Politicians propose policies to appeal to a majority of voters. Bureaucrats try to maximize the budgets of their departments. A political equilibrium emerges in which no group can improve its position by making a different choice.

Political Equilibrium

Voters, politicians, and bureaucrats make choices to best further their own objectives. But each group is constrained by the preferences of the other groups and by what is technologically feasible. The outcome that results from the choices of voters, politicians, and bureaucrats is a **political equilibrium**, which is a situation in which all their choices are compatible and in which no group can improve its position by making a different choice. Let's see how voters, politicians, and bureaucrats interact to determine the quantity of public goods.

Public Goods and the Free-Rider Problem

WHY DOES THE GOVERNMENT PROVIDE GOODS and services such as national defense and public health? Why don't we buy our national defense from North Pole Protection, Inc., a private firm that competes for our dollars in the marketplace in the same way that McDonald's and Coca-Cola do? The answer to these questions lies in the free-rider problem created by public goods. Let's explore this problem. We begin by looking at the nature of a public good.

Public Goods

A *public good* is a good or service that can be consumed simultaneously by everyone and from which no one can be excluded. The first feature of a public good is called nonrivalry. A good is *nonrival* if the consumption by one person does not decrease the consumption by another person. An example is watching a television show. The opposite of nonrival is rival. A good is *rival* if the consumption by one person decreases the consumption by another person. An example is eating a hotdog.

The second feature of a public good is that it is nonexcludable. A good is *nonexcludable* if it is impossible, or extremely costly, to prevent someone from benefiting from a good. An example is national defense. It would be difficult to exclude someone from being defended. The opposite of nonexcludable is excludable. A good is *excludable* if it is possible to prevent a person from enjoying the benefits of a good. An example is cable television. Cable companies can ensure that only those people who have paid the fee receive programs.

Figure 18.2 classifies goods according to these two criteria and gives examples of goods in each category. National defense is a *pure* public good. One person's consumption of the security provided by our national defense system does not decrease the security of someone else—defense is nonrival. And the military cannot select those whom it will protect and those whom it will leave exposed to threats—defense is nonexcludable.

Many goods have a public element but are not pure public goods. An example is a highway. A highway is nonrival until it becomes congested. One more car on a highway with plenty of space does not

FIGURE 18.2
Public Goods and Private Goods

	Rival	Nonrival
Excludable	**Pure private goods** Food Car House	**Excludable and nonrival** Cable television Bridge Highway
Non-excludable	**Nonexcludable and rival** Fish in the ocean Air	**Pure public goods** Lighthouse National defense

A pure public good (bottom right) is one for which consumption is nonrival and from which it is impossible to exclude a consumer. Pure public goods pose a free-rider problem. A pure private good (top left) is one for which consumption is rival and from which consumers can be excluded. Some goods are nonexcludable but are rival (bottom left), and some goods are nonrival but are excludable (top right).

Source: Adapted from and inspired by E. S. Savas, *Privatizing the Public Sector,* Chatham House Publishers, Inc., Chatham, NJ, 1982, p. 34.

reduce anyone else's consumption of transportation services. But once the highway becomes congested, one extra vehicle lowers the quality of the service available to everyone else—it becomes rival like a private good. Also, users can be excluded from a highway by tollgates. Another example is fish in the ocean. Ocean fish are rival because a fish taken by one person is not available for anyone else. Ocean fish are also nonexcludable because it is difficult to prevent people from catching them.

The Free-Rider Problem

Public goods create a free-rider problem. A **free rider** is a person who consumes a good without paying for it. Public goods create a *free-rider problem* because the quantity of the good that a person is able to consume is not influenced by the amount the person pays for the good. So no one has an incentive to pay for a public good. Let's look more closely at the free-rider problem by studying an example.

The Benefit of a Public Good

Suppose that for its defense, a country must launch some surveillance satellites. The benefit provided by a satellite is the *value* of its services. The value of a *private* good is the maximum amount that a *person* is willing to pay for one more unit, which is shown by the person's demand curve. The value of a *public* good is the maximum amount that all the *people* are willing to pay for one more unit of it.

To calculate the value placed on a public good, we use the concepts of total benefit and marginal benefit. *Total benefit* is the dollar value that a person places on a given level of provision of a public good. The greater the quantity of a public good, the larger is a person's total benefit. *Marginal benefit* is the increase in total benefit that results from a one-unit increase in the quantity of a public good.

Figure 18.3 shows the marginal benefit that arises from defense satellites for a society with just two members, Lisa and Max. Lisa's and Max's marginal benefits are graphed as MB_L and MB_M, respectively, in parts (a) and (b) of the figure. The marginal benefit from a public good is similar to the marginal utility from a private good—its magnitude diminishes as the quantity of the good increases. For Lisa, the marginal benefit from the first satellite is $80, and from the second it is $60. By the time 4 satellites are deployed, Lisa's marginal benefits is zero. For Max, the marginal utility from the first satellite is $50, and from the second it is $40. By the time 4 satellites are deployed, Max perceives only $10 worth of marginal benefit.

Part (c) shows the economy's marginal benefit curve, *MB*. An individual's marginal benefit curve for a public good is similar to the individual's demand curve for a private good. But the economy's marginal benefit curve for a public good is different from the market demand curve for a private good. To obtain the market demand curve for a private good, we sum the quantities demanded by all individuals at each price—we sum the individual demand curves horizontally (see Chapter 8, p. 165). But to find the economy's marginal benefit curve of a public good, we sum the marginal benefits of each individual at each quantity—we sum the individual marginal benefit curves *vertically*. The resulting marginal benefit for the economy made up of Lisa and Max is the economy's marginal benefit curve graphed in part (c)—the curve *MB*. Lisa's marginal benefit from the first satellite gets added to Max's marginal benefit from the first satellite because they *both* enjoy security from the first satellite.

FIGURE 18.3

Benefits of a Public Good

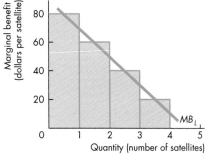

(a) Lisa's marginal benefit

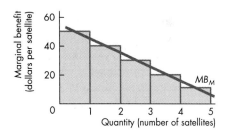

(b) Max's marginal benefit

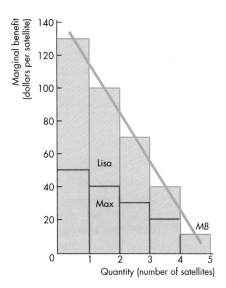

(c) Economy's marginal benefit

The marginal benefit to the economy at each quantity of the public good is the sum of the marginal benefits of all individuals. The marginal benefit curves are MB_L for Lisa, MB_M for Max, and *MB* for the economy.

The Efficient Quanitity of a Public Good

An economy with two people would not buy any satellites—because the total benefit falls far short of the cost. But an economy with 250 million people might. To determine the efficient quantity, we need to take the cost as well as the benefit into account.

The cost of a satellite is based on technology and the prices of the resources used to produce it (just like the cost of producing sweaters, which you studied in Chapter 11).

Figure 18.4 sets out the benefits and costs. The second and third columns of the table show the total and marginal benefits. The next two columns show the total and marginal cost of producing satellites. The final column shows net benefit. Total benefit, *TB*, and total cost, *TC*, are graphed in part (a) of the figure.

The efficient quantity is the one that maximizes *net benefit*—total benefit minus total cost—and occurs when 2 satellites are provided.

The fundamental principles of marginal analysis that you have used to explain how consumers maximize utility and how firms maximize profit can also be used to calculate the efficient scale of provision of a public good. Figure 18.4(b) shows this alternative approach. The marginal benefit curve is *MB*, and the marginal cost curve is *MC*. When marginal benefit exceeds marginal cost, net benefit increases if the quantity produced increases. When marginal cost exceeds marginal benefit, net benefit increases if the quantity produced decreases. Marginal benefit equals marginal cost with 2 satellites. So making marginal cost equal to marginal benefit maximizes net benefit and uses resources efficiently.

Private Provision

We have now worked out the quantity of satellites that maximizes net benefit. Would a private firm—North Pole Protection, Inc.—deliver that quantity? It would not. To do so, it would have to collect $15 billion to cover its costs—or $60 from each of the 250 million people in the economy. But no one would have an incentive to buy his or her share of the satellite system. Everyone would reason as follows: The number of satellites provided by North Pole Protection, Inc., is not affected by my $60. But my own private consumption is greater if I free ride and do not pay my share of the cost of the satellite system. If I do not pay, I enjoy the same level of security and

I can buy more private goods. Therefore I will spend my $60 on other goods and free ride on the public good. This is the free rider problem.

If everyone reasons the same way, North Pole Protection has zero revenue and so provides no satellites. Because two satellites is the efficient level, private provision is inefficient.

Public Provision

Suppose there are two political parties, the Hawks and the Doves, that agree with each other on all issues except for the quantity of satellites. The Hawks would like to provide 4 satellites at a cost of $50 billion, with benefits of $50 billion and a net benefit of zero, as shown in Fig. 18.4. The Doves would like to provide 1 satellite at a cost of $5 billion, a benefit of $20 billion, and a net benefit of $15 billion—see Fig. 18.4.

Before deciding on their policy proposals, the two political parties do a "what-if" analysis. Each party reasons as follows. If each party offers the satellite program it wants—Hawks 4 satellites and Doves 1 satellite—the voters will see that they will get a net benefit of $15 billion from the Doves and zero net benefit from the Hawks, and the Doves will win the election.

Contemplating this outcome, the Hawks realize that their party is too hawkish to get elected. They figure that they must scale back their proposal to 2 satellites. At this level of provision, total cost is $15 billion, total benefit is $35 billion, and net benefit is $20 billion. If the Doves stick with 1 satellite, the Hawks will win the election.

But contemplating this outcome, the Doves realize that they must match the Hawks. They too propose to provide 2 satellites on exactly the same terms as the Hawks. If the two parties offer the same number of satellites, the voters are indifferent between the parties. They flip coins to decide their votes, and each party receives around 50 percent of the vote.

The result of the politicians' "what-if" analysis is that each party offers 2 satellites, so regardless of who wins the election, this is the quantity of satellites installed. And this quantity is efficient. It maximizes the perceived net benefit of the voters. Thus in this example, competition in the political marketplace results in the efficient provision of a public good. But for this outcome to occur, voters must be well informed and evaluate the alternatives. But as you will see below, they do not always have an incentive to achieve this outcome.

FIGURE 18.4

The Efficient Quantity of a Public Good

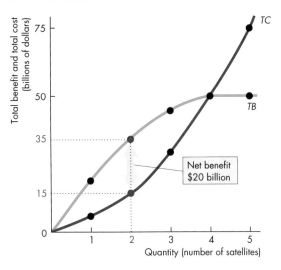

(a) Total benefit and total cost

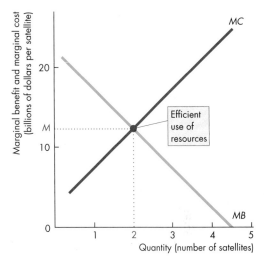

(b) Marginal benefit and marginal cost

Quantity (number of satellites)	Total benefit (billions of dollars)	Marginal benefit (billions of dollars per satellite)	Total cost (billions of dollars)	Marginal cost (billions of dollars per satellite)	Net benefit (billions of dollars)
0	0		0		0
		20		5	
1	20		5		15
		15		10	
2	35		15		20
		10		15	
3	45		30		15
		5		20	
4	50		50		0
		0		25	
5	50		75		−25

Net benefit—the vertical distance between total benefit, *TB*, and total cost, *TC*—is maximized when 2 satellites are installed (part a) and where marginal benefit, *MB*, equals marginal cost, *MC* (part b). The Doves would like to provide 1

satellite, and the Hawks would like to provide 4. But each party recognizes that its only hope of being elected is to provide 2 satellites—the quantity that maximizes net benefit and so leaves no room for the other party to improve on.

The Principle of Minimum Differentiation In the example we've just studied, both parties propose identical policies. This tendency toward identical policies is an example of the **principle of minimum differentiation**, which is the tendency for competitors to make themselves identical to appeal to the maximum number of clients or voters. This principle not only describes the behavior of political

parties but also explains why fast food restaurants cluster in the same block and even why new auto models share similar features. If McDonald's opens a restaurant in a new location, it is likely that Burger King will open next door to McDonald's rather than a mile down the road. If Chrysler designs a new van with a sliding door on the driver's side, most likely Ford will too.

The Role of Bureaucrats

We have analyzed the behavior of politicians but not that of the bureaucrats who translate the choices of the politicians into programs and who control the day-to-day activities that deliver public goods. Let's now see how the economic choices of bureaucrats influence the political equilibrium.

To do so, we'll stick with the previous example. We've seen that competition between two political parties delivers the efficient quantity of satellites. But will the Defense Department—the Pentagon—cooperate and accept this outcome?

Suppose the objective of the Pentagon is to maximize the defense budget. With 2 satellites being provided at minimum cost, the defense budget is $15 billion (see Fig. 18.4). To increase its budget, the Pentagon might do two things. First, it might try to persuade the politicians that 2 satellites cost more than $15 billion. As Fig. 18.5 shows, if possible, the Pentagon would like to convince Congress that 2 satellites cost $35 billion—the entire benefit. Second, and pressing its position even more strongly, the Pentagon might argue for more satellites. It might press for 4 satellites and a budget of $50 billion. In this situation, total benefit and total cost are equal and net benefit is zero.

The Pentagon wants to maximize its budget, but won't the politicians prevent it from doing so because the Pentagon's preferred outcome costs votes? They will if voters are well informed and know what is best for them. But voters might be rationally ignorant. In this case, well-informed interest groups might enable the Pentagon to achieve its objective.

Rational Ignorance

A principle of public choice theory is that it is rational for a voter to be ignorant about an issue unless that issue has a perceptible effect on the voter's income. **Rational ignorance** is the decision *not* to acquire information because the cost of doing so exceeds the expected benefit. For example, each voter knows that he or she can make virtually no difference to the defense policy of the U.S. government. Each voter also knows that it would take an enormous amount of time and effort to become even moderately well informed about alternative defense technologies. So voters remain relatively uninformed about the technicalities of defense issues. (Though we are using

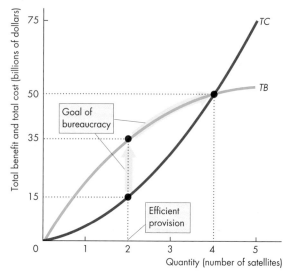

FIGURE 18.5

Bureaucratic Overprovision

The goal of a bureaucracy is to maximize its budget. A bureaucracy that maximizes its budget will seek to increase its budget so that its total cost equals total benefit and then to use its budget to expand output and expenditure. Here, the Pentagon tries to get $35 billion to provide 2 satellites. It would like to increase the quantity of satellites to 4 with a budget of $50 billion.

defense policy as an example, the same applies to all aspects of government economic activity.)

All voters are consumers of national defense. But not all voters are producers of national defense. Only a small number are in this latter category. Voters who own or work for firms that produce satellites have a direct personal interest in defense because it affects their incomes. These voters have an incentive to become well informed about defense issues and to operate a political lobby aimed at furthering their own interests. In collaboration with the defense bureaucracy, these voters exert a larger influence than do the relatively uninformed voters who only consume this public good.

When the rationality of the uninformed voter and special interest groups are taken into account, the political equilibrium provides public goods in excess of the efficient quantity. So in the satellite example, 3 or 4 satellites might be installed rather than the efficient quantity, which is 2 satellites.

Two Types of Political Equilibrium

We've seen that two types of political equilibrium are possible: efficient and inefficient. These two types of political equilibrium correspond to two theories of government:

- Public interest theory
- Public choice theory

Public Interest Theory   Public interest theory predicts that governments make choices that achieve efficiency. This outcome occurs in a perfect political system in which voters are fully informed about the effects of policies and refuse to vote for outcomes that can be improved upon.

Public Choice Theory   Public choice theory predicts that governments make choices that result in inefficiency. This outcome occurs in political markets in which voters are rationally ignorant and base their votes only on issues that they know affect their own net benefit. Voters pay more attention to their interests as producers than their interests as consumers, and public officials also act in their own best interest. The result is *government failure* that parallels market failure.

Why Government Is Large and Grows

Now that we know how the quantity of public goods is determined, we can explain part of the reason for the growth of government. Government grows, in part, because the demand for some public goods increases at a faster rate than the demand for private goods. There are two possible reasons for this growth:

- Voter preferences
- Inefficient overprovision

Voter Preferences   The growth of government can be explained by voter preferences in the following way. As voters' incomes increase (as they usually do in most years), the demand for many public goods increases more quickly than income. (Technically, the *income elasticity of demand* for many public goods is greater than 1—see Chapter 5, pp. 111–112.) Many (and the most expensive) public goods are in this category. They include transportation systems such as highways, airports, and air-traffic control systems; public health; education; and national defense. If

politicians did not support increases in expenditures on these items, they would not get elected.

Inefficient Overprovision   Inefficient overprovision might explain the *size* of government but not its *growth rate*. It (possibly) explains why government is *larger* than its efficient scale, but it does not explain why governments use an increasing proportion of total resources.

Voters Strike Back

If government grows too large, relative to what voters are willing to accept, there might be a voter backlash against government programs and a large bureaucracy. The electoral success of the Republicans in 1994 and the embracing of small government by President Clinton during the 1996 election campaign might be interpreted as such a backlash.

Another way that voters—and politicians—can try to counter the tendency of bureaucrats to expand their budgets is to privatize the *production* of public goods. Government *provision* of a public good does not automatically imply that a government-operated bureau must *produce* the good. Garbage collection (public good) is often done by a private firm, and experiments are being conducted with private fire departments and even private prisons.

R E V I E W

- Private provision of a public good creates a free-rider problem and provides less than the efficient quantity of the good.
- Competition between politicians for votes can achieve an efficient quantity of a public good, provided that voters are well informed.
- If consumers of a public good are less well informed than producers of that good, bureaucrats supported by well-informed voters have a larger influence than uninformed voters and the quantity of public goods exceeds the efficient quantity.

We've now seen how voters, politicians, and bureaucrats interact to determine the quantity of a public good. But public goods are paid for with taxes. Taxes also redistribute income. How does the political marketplace determine the scale and variety of taxes that we pay?

Taxes

TAXES GENERATE THE FINANCIAL RESOURCES that governments use to provide voters with public goods and other benefits. Five types of taxes are used:

- Income taxes
- Payroll taxes
- Sales taxes
- Property taxes
- Excise taxes

Figure 18.6 shows the relative amounts raised by these five types of tax in 1996. Income taxes are the biggest tax source and raised 46 percent of tax revenues in 1996. Payroll taxes that contribute to Social Security are the next biggest revenue source, and they raised 30 percent of total taxes in 1996. State sales taxes and local government property taxes each raise about 10 percent of total taxes. Finally, excise taxes raise a small amount of government revenue. Although they raise a small amount of revenue, excise taxes have a big impact on some markets, as you'll discover later in this chapter. Let's take a closer look at each type of tax.

FIGURE 18.6
Government Tax Revenues

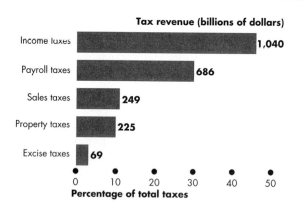

Almost a half of government revenues comes from income taxes. Almost a third comes from payroll taxes (Social Security contributions). Excise taxes bring in a small amount of revenue, but these taxes have big effects on a small number of markets.

Source: Survey of Current Business, U.S. Department of Commerce, Washington D.C., 1996.

Income Taxes

Income taxes are paid on personal incomes and corporate profits. In 1996, the personal income tax raised $660 billion for the federal government and another $140 billion for state and local governments. Corporate profits taxes raised $200 billion for the federal government and $40 billion for the state governments. We'll look first at the effects of personal income taxes and then at corporate profits taxes.

Personal Income Tax The amount of income tax that a person pays depends on her or his *taxable income,* which equals total income minus a *personal exemption* and a *standard deduction* or other allowable deductions. In 1996, the personal exemption was $2,550 and the standard deduction was $4,000 for a single person. So for such a person, taxable income equals total income minus $6,550.

The *tax rate* (percent) depends on the income level and for a single person increases according to the scale:

$0 to $24,000	15 percent
$24,000 to $58,150	28 percent
$58,150 to $121,300	31 percent
$121,300 to $263,750	36 percent
Over $263,750	39.6 percent

The percentages in this list are marginal tax rates. A **marginal tax rate** is the percentage of an additional dollar of income that is paid in tax. For example if taxable income increases from $24,000 to $24,001, the additional tax paid is 15 cents and the marginal tax rate is 15 percent. If income increases from $263,750 to $263,751, the additional tax paid is 39.6 cents and the marginal tax rate is 39.6 percent.

The **average tax rate** is the percentage of income that is paid in tax. The average tax rate is less than the marginal tax rate. For example, suppose a single person earns $50,000 in a year. Taxable income is $50,000 minus $6,550 deductions, which equals $43,450. On the first $24,000, the tax rate is 15 percent ($3,600), and on the remaining $19,450 of taxable income, the tax rate is 28 percent ($5,446). Total taxes equal $3,600 plus $5,446, which is $9,046, or 18.1 percent of income. The average tax rate is 18.1 percent.

If the average tax rate increases as income increases, the tax is a **progressive tax**. The personal income tax is a progressive tax. To see this feature of the income tax, calculate another average tax rate. For example, for someone whose income is $100,000 a year, the average rate is 24.1 percent ($6,550 at zero plus $24,000 at 15 percent plus $34,150 at 28 percent plus $35,300 at 31 percent).

A progressive tax contrasts with a **proportional tax**, which has the same average tax rate at all income levels and a **regressive tax**, which has a decreasing average tax rate as income increases.

The Effect of Income Taxes   Figure 18.7 shows how the income tax affects labor markets. Part (a) shows the market for low-wage workers and part (b) shows the market for high-wage workers. These labor markets are competitive, and with no income taxes, they work just like all the other competitive markets you have studied. The demand curves are *LD*, and the supply curves are *LS* (in both parts of the figure). Both groups work 40 hours a week. Low-wage workers earn $9.50 an hour, and high-wage workers earn $175 an hour. What happens when an income tax is introduced?

If low-wage workers are willing to supply 40 hours a week for $9.50 an hour when there is no tax, then they are willing to supply that same quantity in the face of a 15 percent tax only if the wage rises to $11.18 an hour. That is, they want to get the $9.50 an hour they received before plus the 15 percent tax that they now must pay to the government. So the supply of labor decreases because the amount received from work is lowered by the amount of income tax paid. The acceptable wage rate at each level of employment rises by the amount of the tax that must be paid. For low-wage workers who face a tax rate of 15 percent, the supply curve shifts to *LS + tax*. The equilibrium wage rate rises to $10 an hour, but the after-tax wage rate falls to $8.50 an hour. Employment falls to 36 hours a week.

For high-wage workers who face a tax rate of 39.6 percent, the supply curve shifts to *LS + tax*. The equilibrium wage rate rises to $200 an hour, and the after-tax wage rate falls to $121 an hour. Employment falls to 32 hours a week. The decrease in employment of high-wage workers is larger than that of low-wage workers because of the differences in the marginal tax rates they each face.

FIGURE 18.7

The Effects of Income Taxes

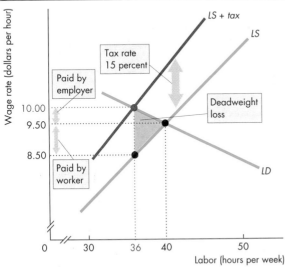

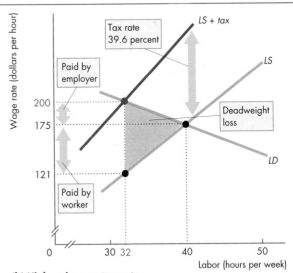

(a) Lowest income tax rate

(b) Highest income tax rate

The demand for labor is *LD*, and with no income taxes, the supply of labor is *LS* (both parts). In part (a), low-wage workers earn $9.50 an hour and each works 40 hours a week. In part (b), high-wage workers earn $175 an hour and each works 40 hours a week. An income tax decreases the supply of labor and the labor supply curve shifts leftward. For low-wage workers in part (a), whose marginal tax rate is 15 per-

cent, supply decreases to *LS + tax*. Employment falls to 36 hours a week. For high-wage workers in part (b), whose marginal tax rate is 39.6 percent, supply decreases to *LS + tax*. Employment falls to 32 hours a week. The deadweight loss from the high marginal tax rate on high-wage workers is much larger than that from the low marginal tax rate on low-wage workers.

Notice that the income tax is paid by both the employer and the worker. In the case of low-wage workers, the employer pays an extra 50 cents an hour and the worker pays $1 an hour. In the case of high-wage workers, employers pay an extra $25 an hour and workers pay $54 an hour. The exact split depends on the elasticities of demand and supply.

Notice also the difference in the *deadweight loss* for the two groups. (Check Chapter 6 pp. 120–121 if you need a refresher on the concept of deadweight loss.) The deadweight loss is much larger for the high-wage workers than for the low-wage workers.

Why Do We Have a Progressive Income Tax?

We have a progressive income tax because it is part of the political equilibrium. A majority of voters support it, so politicians who also support it get elected.

The economic model that predicts progressive income taxes is called the *median voter* model. The core idea of the median voter model is that political parties pursue policies that are most likely to attract the support of the median voter. The median voter is the one in the middle—one half of the population lies on one side and one half on the other. So a political party must win the support of the median voter if it is to win an election. Let's see how the median voter model predicts a progressive income tax.

Imagine that government programs benefit everyone equally and are paid for by a proportional income tax. Everyone pays the same percentage of their income. In this situation, there is a redistribution from high-income voters to low-income voters. Everyone benefits equally, but because high-income voters have larger incomes, they pay larger taxes.

Is this situation the best one possible for the median voter? It is not. Suppose that instead of using a proportional tax, the marginal tax rate is lowered for low-income voters and increased for high-income voters—a progressive tax. Low-income voters are now better off, and high-income voters are worse off. Low-income voters will support this change, and high-income voters will oppose it. But there are many more low-income voters than high-income voters, so the low-income voters win.

The median voter is a low-income voter. In fact, because the distribution of income is skewed, the median voter has a smaller income than the average income (see Fig. 17.4 on pp. 368). This fact raises an interesting question: Why doesn't the median voter support taxes that skim off all income above the average and redistribute it to everyone with a below-average income. This tax would be so progressive that

it would result in equal incomes after taxes and transfers were paid.

The answer is that such high taxes would discourage effort and saving to the point that the median voter would be worse off with such a radical redistribution than under the arrangements that prevail today.

Let's now look at corporate profits taxes.

Corporate Profits Tax   In popular discussions of taxes, corporate profits taxes are seen as a free source of revenue for the government. Taxing people is bad, but taxing corporations is just fine.

It turns out that taxing corporations is very inefficient. We use an inefficient tax because it redistributes income in favor of the median voter, just like the income tax. Let's see why taxing corporate profits is inefficient.

First, the tax is misnamed. It is only partly a tax on economic profit. It is mainly a tax on the income from capital. Taxing the income from capital works like taxing the income from labor except for two critical differences: The supply of capital is highly (perhaps perfectly) elastic, and the quantity of capital influences the productivity of labor and wage income. Because the supply of capital is highly elastic, the tax is fully borne by firms and the quantity of capital decreases. With a smaller capital stock than we would otherwise have, the productivity of labor and incomes are lower than they would otherwise be.

Payroll Taxes

Payroll taxes are the contributions paid by employers and employees to provide social security benefits, unemployment compensation, and health and disability benefits to workers (see Chapter 17, pp. 370–373).

Unions lobby to get employers to pay a bigger share of these taxes, and employer's organizations lobby to get workers to pay a bigger share of them. But this lobbying effort is not worth much. For who *really* pays these taxes depends in no way on who writes the checks. It depends on the elasticities of demand for and supply of labor.

Figure 18.8 shows you why. In both parts of the figure, the demand curve LD and the supply curve LS are identical. With no payroll taxes, the quantity of labor employed is QL^* and the wage rate is W^*.

A payroll tax is now introduced. In part (a) the employee pays the tax, and in part (b) the employer pays. When the employee pays, supply decreases and the supply of labor curve shifts leftward to $LS + tax$. The vertical distance between the supply curve LS, and the new supply curve $LS + tax$ is the amount of the tax. The wage rate rises to WC, the after-tax wage rate falls to WT, and employment decreases to QL_0.

When the employer pays (in part b), demand decreases and the demand for labor curve shifts leftward to $LD - tax$. The vertical distance between the demand curve LD and the new demand curve $LD - tax$ is the amount of the tax. The wage rate falls to WT, but the cost of labor rises to WC, and employment decreases to QL_0.

So regardless of which side of the market is taxed, the outcome is identical. If the demand for labor is perfectly inelastic or if the supply of labor is perfectly elastic, the employer pays the entire tax. And if the demand for labor is perfectly elastic or if the supply of labor is perfectly inelastic, the employee pays the entire tax. These cases are exactly like those for the sales tax that you studied in Chapter 7 on pp. 135–138.

Sales Taxes

Sales taxes are the taxes levied by state governments on a wide range of goods and services. We have studied the effects of these taxes in Chapter 7. There is one feature of these taxes, though, that we need to note. They are *regressive*. The reason they are regressive is that saving increases with income and sales taxes are paid only on the part of income that is spent.

Suppose, for example, that the sales tax is 8 percent. A family with an income of $20,000 that spends all its income pays $1,600 in sales tax. Its average tax rate is 8 percent. A family with an income of $100,000 that spends $60,000 and saves $40,000 pays sales taxes of $4,800 (8 percent of $60,000). So this family's average tax rate is 4.8 percent.

If the sales tax is regressive, why is it supported by the median voter? It is the entire tax code that matters, not an individual tax. So a regressive sales tax is voted for only as part of an overall tax regime that is progressive.

Property Taxes

Property taxes are collected by local governments and are used to provide local public goods. A **local public good** is a public good that is consumed by all the people who live in a particular area. Examples of local public goods are parks, museums, and safe neighborhoods.

FIGURE 18.8

Payroll Taxes

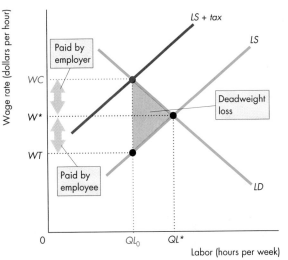

(a) Tax on employees

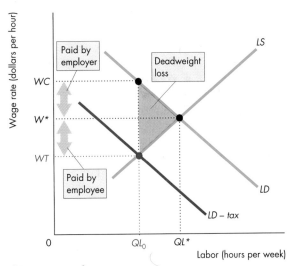

(b) Tax on employers

The labor demand curve is LD, and the supply curve is LS. With no payroll taxes, the quantity of labor employed is QL^* and the wage rate is W^* (in both parts). In part (a), employees pay a payroll tax. Supply decreases, and the supply of labor curve shifts leftward to $LS + tax$. The wage rate rises to WC, the after-tax wage rate falls to WT, and employment decreases to QL_0. In part (b), employers pay a payroll tax. Demand decreases, and the demand for labor curve shifts leftward to $LD - tax$. The wage rate falls to WT, but the cost of labor rises to WC and employment decreases to QL_0. The outcome is identical in both cases.

There is a much closer connection between property taxes paid and benefits received than in the case of federal and state taxes. This close connection makes property taxes similar to a price for local services. Because of this connection, property taxes change both the demand for and supply of property in a neighborhood. A higher property tax lowers supply, but improved local public goods increase demand. So some neighborhoods have high taxes and high-quality local government services, and other neighborhoods have low taxes and low-quality services. Both can exist in the political equilibrium.

Excise Taxes

An **excise tax** is a tax on the sale of a particular commodity. The total amount raised by these taxes is small, but they have a big impact on some markets. Let's study the effects of an excise tax by considering the tax on gasoline shown in Fig. 18.9. The demand curve for gasoline is D, and the supply curve is S. If there is no tax on gasoline, its price is 60¢ a gallon and 400 million gallons of gasoline a day are bought and sold.

Now suppose that a tax is imposed on gasoline at the rate of 60¢ a gallon. As a result of the tax, the supply of gasoline decreases and the supply curve shifts leftward. The magnitude of the shift is such that the vertical distance between the original and the new supply curve is the amount of the tax. The new supply curve is the red curve, S + tax. The new supply curve intersects the demand curve at 300 million gallons a day and $1.10 a gallon. This situation is the new equilibrium after the imposition of the tax.

The excise tax creates a deadweight loss made up of the loss of consumer surplus and the loss of producer surplus. The dollar value of that loss is $30 million a day. Because 300 million gallons of gasoline are sold each day and the tax is 60¢ a gallon, total revenue from the gasoline tax is $180 million a day (300 million gallons multiplied by 60¢ a gallon). So to raise tax revenue of $180 million dollars a day by using the gasoline tax, a deadweight loss of $30 million a day—one sixth of the tax revenue—is incurred.

One of the main influences on the deadweight loss arising from an excise tax is the elasticity of demand for the commodity. The demand for gasoline is fairly inelastic. As a consequence, when a tax is imposed, the quantity demanded falls by a smaller percentage than the percentage rise in price.

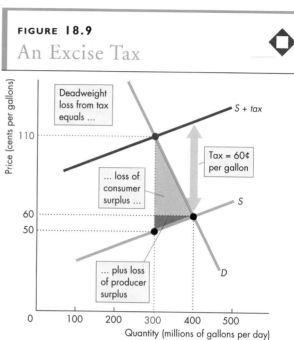

FIGURE 18.9
An Excise Tax

The demand curve for gasoline is D, and the supply curve is S. In the absence of any taxes, gasoline will sell for 60¢ a gallon and 400 million gallons a day will be bought and sold. When a tax of 60¢ a gallon is imposed, the supply curve shifts leftward to become the curve S + tax. The new equilibrium price is $1.10 a gallon, and 300 million gallons a day are bought and sold. The excise tax creates a deadweight loss represented by the gray triangle. The tax revenue collected is 60¢ a gallon on 300 million gallons, which is $180 million a day. The deadweight loss from the tax is $30 million a day. That is, to raise tax revenue of $180 million a day, a deadweight loss of $30 million a day is incurred.

To see the importance of the elasticity of demand, let's consider a different commodity—orange juice. So that we can make a quick and direct comparison, let's assume that the orange juice market is exactly as big as the market for gasoline. Figure 18.10 illustrates this market. The demand curve for orange juice is D, and the supply curve is S. Orange juice is not taxed, and so the price of orange juice is 60¢ a gallon— where the supply curve and the demand curve intersect—and the quantity of orange juice is 400 million gallons a day.

Now suppose that the government contemplates abolishing the gasoline tax and taxing orange juice instead. The demand for orange juice is more elastic than the demand for gasoline. It has many good substitutes in the form of other fruit juices. The

FIGURE 18.10

Why We Don't Tax Orange Juice

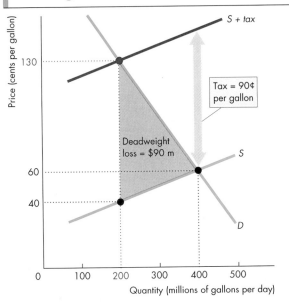

The demand curve for orange juice is *D*, and the supply curve is *S*. The equilibrium price is 60¢ a gallon, and 400 million gallons of juice a day are traded. To raise $180 million of tax revenue, a tax of 90¢ a gallon will have to be imposed. The introduction of this tax shifts the supply curve to *S + tax*. The price rises to $1.30 a gallon, and the quantity bought and sold falls to 200 million gallons a day. The deadweight loss is represented by the gray triangle and equals $90 million a day. The deadweight loss from taxing orange juice is much larger than that from taxing gasoline (Fig. 18.9) because the demand for orange juice is much more elastic than the demand for gasoline. Items that have a low elasticity of demand are taxed more heavily than items that have a high elasticity of demand.

government wants to raise $180 million a day so that its total revenue is not affected by this tax change. The government's economists, armed with their statistical estimates of the demand and supply curves for orange juice that appear in Fig. 18.10, work out that a tax of 90¢ a gallon will do the job. With such a tax, the supply curve shifts leftward to become the curve labeled *S + tax*. This new supply curve intersects the demand curve at a price of $1.30 a gallon and at a quantity of 200 million gallons a day. The price at which suppliers are willing to produce 200 million gallons a day is 40¢ a gallon. The government collects

a tax of 90¢ a gallon on 200 million gallons a day, so it collects a total revenue of $180 million a day—exactly the amount that it requires.

But what is the deadweight loss in this case? The answer can be seen by looking at the gray triangle in Fig. 18.10. The magnitude of that deadweight loss is $90 million. Notice how much bigger the deadweight loss is from taxing orange juice than from taxing gasoline. In the case of orange juice, the deadweight loss is one half the revenue raised, while in the case of gasoline, it is only one sixth. What accounts for this difference? The supply curves are identical in each case, and the examples were also set up to ensure that the initial no-tax prices and quantities were identical. The difference between the two cases is the elasticity of demand: In the case of gasoline, the quantity demanded falls by only 25 percent when the price almost doubles. In the case of orange juice, the quantity demanded falls by 50 percent when the price only slightly more than doubles.

You can see why taxing orange juice is not on the political agenda of any of the major parties. Vote-seeking politicians seek out taxes that benefit the median voter. Other things being equal, this means that they try to minimize the deadweight loss of raising a given amount of revenue. Equivalently, they tax items with poor substitutes more heavily than items with close substitutes.

REVIEW

- Income taxes decrease employment and create deadweight losses. They are progressive because such taxes benefit the median voter.
- Who pays a payroll tax (and any other tax) depends on the elasticities of demand and supply.
- Property taxes change both demand and supply and can create neighborhoods with high taxes and high services and with low taxes and low services.
- Excise taxes are imposed at high rates on goods that have a low elasticity of demand.

◆ *Reading Between the Lines* on pages 404–405 looks at one example of the types of question you've studied in this chapter, the public provision of space launches. It asks whether NASA is an efficient bureaucracy and whether a private space program would be more efficient. In the next two chapters, we are going to look at government economic actions in the face of monopolies and externalities.

Private Space

The Wall Street Journal, July 2, 1996

10—9—8 ... Privatized Space Program Is Near

By Jeff Cole

After 35 years, the U.S. government wants someone else to send people into orbit, but this flight toward privatization of the space program is shaping up to be a rocky ride. ...

Proponents of privatization say it would lower costs and allow the U.S. to keep its competitive edge in the space race. Aerospace companies are expected to quickly take over the shuttling of astronauts and payloads into space, with an eye toward grabbing profits from satellite communications, space labs, exploration and even tourism.

Toward that end, the right price will be as essential as astronauts with the Right Stuff. Advanced ships that are fully reusable—as opposed to more generations of "expendable" rockets—seem to hold the key to sharply lower launch costs. ...

It currently costs about $10,000 a pound to launch the shuttle, satellites and other payloads into orbit; with the next-generation shuttle, those costs are projected to drop to below $1,000 a pound—perhaps eventually as low as $100 a pound.

Not surprisingly, some entrenched middle managers at NASA are vehemently opposed to the privatizing initiatives, officials of that agency concede, and are only grudgingly letting go of the control they have exercised since 1958. Despite such internal resistance, however, it is NASA's chief, former TRW Inc. space executive Daniel Goldin, who has provided much of the impetus toward cutting space-launch costs through privatization.

Mr. Goldin holds both industry and government culpable for what he sees as American's weakness in space-launch markets. ... American rockets remain costly and are "inferior" to those of foreign rivals such as disposable-rocket market leader Arianespace SA of Europe, said the administrator in a speech this year that shocked many industry executives in the crowd. ...

Essence of THE STORY

■ Supporters of a private space industry say that privatization will lower costs and keep the United States in the competitive space race.

■ It is predicted that private aerospace companies will produce the next generation of rockets, leading to launch costs of $100 a pound. The current cost is $10,000 a pound.

■ Middle managers at NASA are opposed to privatization and fear losing control of their industry.

■ NASA's chief says that U.S. rockets are currently costly and inferior to foreign rockets. He favors privatization.

Economic

A N A L Y S I S

■ Yoda, Obi-Wan Kenobi, and Luke Skywalker (three of the leading characters in *Star Wars*) did not embark on their planet-trotting lives as employees of a NASA.

■ George Lucas's imaginative vision makes an economic point. Space is not a public good. It is a location in which both public and private activities take place side by side.

■ During the 35 years that the United States has been in space, it has been dominated by two public goods and one private good.

■ The public goods are national defense and scientific knowledge. The private good is telecommunication (both audio and video).

■ Until now, all three goods have been produced by NASA, a government agency.

■ There is no compelling reason why NASA must launch communications satellites. In fact, there is a competitive global market in launches that includes China, Russia, and Europe.

■ Further, many public goods are produced privately. Examples are highways, legal services, and public health services. Also, private firms produce weapons for national defense as well as the equipment that NASA uses.

■ But NASA itself could be disbanded. The Pentagon could manage space defense projects. And private firms such as AT&T, Time Warner, Lockheed Martin, and Boeing could produce and sell all the private goods associated with space.

■ Figures 1 and 2 compare NASA and private production of space launches. In both figures, the total benefit of space launches is *TB*, and the total cost is *TC*. The efficient quantity is *Q*.

■ In Fig. 1, NASA maximizes its budget. It provides Q_N launches at a cost of B_N. This outcome is the most costly that voters will tolerate.

■ In Fig. 2, private firms and buyers trade in a competitive (global) market. The equilibrium quantity produced is *Q*. The firms' costs are *C*—opportunity cost including normal profit.

■ Consumers receive a total benefit *B* and the net benefit equal to the total benefit minus total cost, as shown in Fig 2.

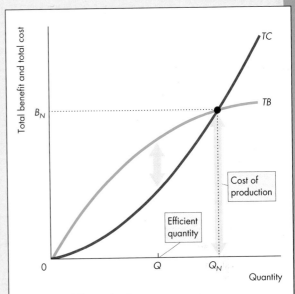

Figure 1 Public production

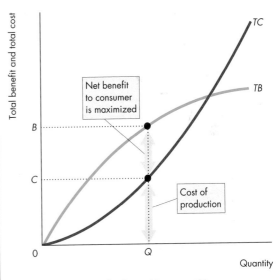

Figure 2 Private production with competition

■ NASA's middle managers oppose a competitive market because it will decrease their budget and job prospects. NASA's senior managers support privatization because they see it as the only way to survive in what has already become a competitive world market.

405

SUMMARY

Key Points

The Economic Theory of Government
(pp. 390–391)

- Government exists to provide public goods, regulate monopoly, cope with externalities, and reduce economic inequality.
- Public choice theory explains how voters, politicians, and bureaucrats interact in a political marketplace.

Public Goods and the Free-Rider Problem
(pp. 392–397)

- A public good is a good or service that is consumed by everyone and that is *nonrival* and *nonexcludable*.
- A public good creates a *free-rider* problem—no one has an incentive to pay their share of the cost of providing a public good.
- The efficient level of provision of a public good is that at which net benefit is maximized. Equivalently, it is the level at which marginal benefit equals marginal cost.
- Competition between political parties, each of which tries to appeal to the maximum number of voters, can lead to the efficient scale of provision of a public good and to both parties proposing the same policies—the principle of minimum differentiation.
- Bureaucrats try to maximize their budgets, and if voters are rationally ignorant, producer interests may result in voting to support taxes that provide public goods in quantities that exceed those that maximize net benefit.

Taxes (pp. 398–403)

- Government revenue comes from income taxes, payroll taxes, sales taxes, property taxes, and excise taxes.
- Income taxes decrease the level of employment and create a deadweight loss.

- Taxes can be progressive (the average tax rate rises with income), proportional (the average tax rate is constant), or regressive (the average tax rate falls with income).
- Income taxes are progressive because this arrangement is in the interest of the median voter.
- Payroll taxes are paid by the employer and the employee (and sales taxes are paid by the buyer and the seller) in amounts that depend on the elasticities of demand and supply.
- Property taxes change both demand and supply and can result in neighborhoods with high taxes and high-quality services and with low taxes and low-quality services.
- Excise taxes at high rates on commodities such as gasoline create a smaller deadweight loss than would taxes on commodities with more elastic demands.

Key Figures

Figure 18.3   Benefits of a Public Good, 393
Figure 18.4   The Efficient Quantity of a Public Good, 395
Figure 18.5   Bureaucratic Overprovision, 396
Figure 18.7   The Effects of Income Taxes, 399
Figure 18.8   Payroll Taxes, 401
Figure 18.9   An Excise Tax, 402

Key Terms

Average tax rate, 398
Excise tax, 402
Externality, 390
Free rider, 392
Local public good, 401
Marginal tax rate, 398
Market failure, 390
Political equilibrium, 391
Principle of minimum differentiation, 395
Progressive tax, 398
Proportional tax, 399
Public good, 390
Rational ignorance, 396
Regressive tax, 399

QUESTIONS

1. What are the four economic problems that governments can help to cope with?
2. What is market failure and from what does it arise?
3. What is a public good? Give three examples.
4. What is the free-rider problem and how does government help to overcome it?
5. What is an externality?
6. Why is economic inequality a problem?
7. Describe the three actors in the political marketplace.
8. Describe the economic functions of voters and explain how they make their economic choices.
9. Describe the economic functions of politicians and explain how they make their economic choices.
10. Describe the economic functions of bureaucrats and explain how they make their economic choices.
11. What is meant by political equilibrium?
12. How is the marginal benefit of a public good determined for an individual?
13. How is the marginal benefit of a public good determined for a society?
14. How is the efficient provision of a public good determined?
15. Can a political system deliver the efficient quantity of a public good?
16. What is the principle of minimum differentiation?
17. How does the principle of minimum differentiation explain political parties' policy platforms?
18. Explain why the quantity of a public good might exceed its efficient scale.
19. Why is it rational for voters to be ignorant?
20. What are the sources of revenue for governments in the United States and what is the biggest revenue source?
21. What are the main effects of income taxes and why are they progressive?
22. Who pays payroll and sales taxes?
23. Why don't we tax orange juice?

PROBLEMS

1. You are given the following information about a sewage disposal system that a city of 1 million people is considering installing:

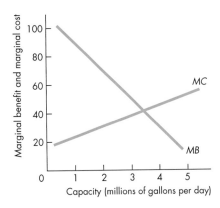

a. What is the capacity that achieves maximum net benefit?
b. How much will each person have to pay in taxes to pay for the efficient capacity level?
c. What is the political equilibrium if voters are well informed?
d. What is the political equilibrium if voters are rationally ignorant and bureaucrats achieve the highest attainable budget?

2. An economy has two groups of people, A and B. The population consists of 80 percent A types and 20 percent B types. A-types have a perfectly elastic supply of labor at a wage rate of $10 an hour. B-types have a perfectly inelastic supply of labor, and their equilibrium wage rate is $100 an hour.

a. What kinds of tax arrangements do you predict this economy will adopt?
b. Analyze the labor market in this economy and explain what will happen to the wage rates and employment levels of the two groups when the taxes you predict in your answer to part (a) are introduced.
c. How would this economy change if the proportion of A-types was 20 percent and the proportion of B-types was 80 percent?

3. In a competitive labor market:

Wage Rate (dollars per hour)	Quantity demanded (hours per week)	Quantity supplied (hours per week)
20	0	50
16	15	40
12	30	30
8	45	20
4	60	10
0	75	0

a. What are the equilibrium wage rate and hours of work done?
b. If a $4 payroll tax is imposed on employers:
   (i)   What is the new wage rate?
   (ii)   What is the new number of hours worked?
   (iii) What is the after-tax wage rate?
   (iv)   What is the tax revenue?
   (v)   What is the deadweight loss?
c. If a $4 payroll tax is imposed on employees:
   (i)   What is the new wage rate?
   (ii)   What is the new number of hours worked?
   (iii) What is the after-tax wage rate?
   (iv)   What is the tax revenue?
   (v)   What is the deadweight loss?
d. Compare the situations in parts (b) and (c) and explain the similarities and differences in the two situations.

4. In a competitive market for cookies:

Price (dollars per pound)	Quantity demanded (pounds per month)	Quantity supplied (pounds per month)
10	0	36
8	3	30
6	6	24
4	9	18
2	12	12
0	15	0

a. Find the equilibrium price and quantity.
b. If cookies are taxed 10 percent:
   (i)   What is the new price of cookies?
   (ii)   What is the new quantity bought?
   (iii) What is the tax revenue?
   (iv)   What is the deadweight loss?

CRITICAL THINKING

1. Study *Reading Between the Lines* on pp. 404–405 and then answer the following:
   a. What is the distinction between public provision and public production of a public good?
   b. Give some examples of public provision of a public good and private provision of a public good.
   c. What is the case for NASA being the sole provider of space launches in the United States?
   d. If AT&T wants to place a new communications satellite in orbit, must it use NASA or does it have other options?
   e. Can you think of any reasons why there might be a free-rider problem in space?
   f. Can you think of any externalities (either external costs or external benefits) that arise from economic activities in space that result in an inefficient use of resources?
   g. Do there appear to be any monopoly problems in space that result in an inefficient use of resources?
   h. Who owns space? Is there a property rights problem in space?
   i. Is the current amount of space exploration and economic activity too little or too much relative to the efficient quantity?

2. Your local city council is contemplating upgrading its system for controlling traffic signals. The council believes that by installing computers, it can improve the speed of the traffic flow. The bigger the computer the council buys, the better job it can do. The mayor and the other elected officials who are working on the proposal want to determine the scale of the system that will win them the most votes. The city bureaucrats want to maximize the budget. Suppose that you are an economist who is observing this public choice. Your job is to calculate the quantity of this public good that uses resources efficiently.
   a. What data would you need to reach your own conclusions?
   b. What does the public choice theory predict will be the quantity chosen?
   c. How could you, as an informed voter, attempt to influence the choice?

Regulation and Antitrust Law

When you consume water, cable TV, or local phone service you usually buy from a regulated monopoly. Why are the industries that produce these goods and services regulated? How are they regulated? Do the regulations work in the public interest—the interest of all consumers and producers—or do they serve special interests— the interests of particular groups of consumers or producers? ◆ Cable TV has been on a regulatory roller coaster. It was initially regulated, but in 1984 it was deregulated. After deregulation, the profits of cable TV firms soared, and in 1992, Congress re-regulated the industry. Why was cable deregulated and then re-regulated? ◆ Some years ago,

Public Interest or Special Interests?

PepsiCo and 7-Up wanted to merge. Coca-Cola and Dr Pepper also wanted to merge. But the federal government blocked these mergers, citing its antitrust laws. It used these same laws to break up the American Telephone and Telegraph Company (AT&T). This action brought competition into the market for long-distance telephone service by encouraging new firms such as MCI and Sprint to enter the market. The government has also used its antitrust laws to punish Archer Daniels Midland for price fixing and to determine whether Boeing and McDonnell Douglas may merge their aircraft-building businesses. What are antitrust laws? How have they evolved over the years? How are they used today? Do they serve the public interest of consumers or the special interests of producers? ◆ This chapter studies government regulation. It draws on your earlier study of how markets work and on your knowledge of consumer surplus and producer surplus. It shows how consumers and producers can redistribute the gains from trade in the political marketplace, and it identifies who stands to win and who stands to lose from government intervention.

After studying this chapter, you will be able to:

■ Define regulation and antitrust law

■ Distinguish between the public interest and capture theories of regulation

■ Explain how regulation affects prices, outputs, profits, and the distribution of the gains from trade between consumers and producers

■ Explain how antitrust law has been applied in a number of landmark cases

■ Explain how antitrust law is used today

Market Intervention

THE GOVERNMENT INTERVENES IN MONOPOLISTIC and oligopolistic markets to influence prices, quantities produced, and the distribution of the gains from economic activity. It intervenes in two main ways:

- Regulation
- Antitrust law

Regulation

Regulation consists of rules administered by a government agency to influence economic activity by determining prices, product standards and types, and the conditions under which new firms may enter an industry. To implement its regulations, the government establishes agencies to oversee the regulations and ensure their enforcement. The first national regulatory agency to be set up in the United States was the Interstate Commerce Commission (ICC), established in 1887. Over the years since then, up to the late 1970s, regulation of the economy grew until, at its peak, almost a quarter of the nation's output was produced by regulated industries. Regulation applied to banking and financial services, telecommunications, gas and electric utilities, railroads, trucking, airlines and buses, many agricultural products, and even haircutting and braiding. Since the late 1970s, there has been a tendency to deregulate the U.S. economy.

Deregulation is the process of removing restrictions on prices, product standards and types, and entry conditions. In recent years, deregulation has occurred in domestic air transportation, telephone service, interstate trucking, and banking and financial services. Cable TV was deregulated in 1984 but re-regulated in 1992.

Antitrust Law

An **antitrust law** is a law that regulates and prohibits certain kinds of market behavior, such as monopoly and monopolistic practices. Antitrust law is enacted by Congress and enforced through the judicial system. Lawsuits under the antitrust laws may be initiated either by government agencies or by injured private parties.

The main thrust of antitrust law is the prohibition of monopoly practices of restricting output to achieve higher prices and profits. The first antitrust law—the Sherman Act—was passed in 1890. Successive acts and amendments have strengthened and refined the body of antitrust law. Antitrust law (like all law) depends as much on the decisions of the courts and of the Supreme Court as on the statutes passed by Congress. Over the 100 years since the passage of the Sherman Act, there have been some interesting changes in the court's interpretation of the law and in how vigorously the law has been enforced. We'll study these later in this chapter.

To understand why the government intervenes in the markets for goods and services and to work out the effects of its interventions, we need to identify the gains and losses that government actions can create. These gains and losses are the consumer surpluses and producer surpluses associated with different output levels and prices. We first study the economics of regulation.

Economic Theory of Regulation

THE ECONOMIC THEORY OF REGULATION IS part of the broader theory of public choice that is explained in Chapter 18. Here, we apply public choice theory to regulation. We'll examine the demand for government actions, the supply of those actions, and the political equilibrium that emerges.

Demand for Regulation

People and firms demand regulation that makes them better off. They express this demand through political activity—voting, lobbying, and making campaign contributions. But engaging in political activity is costly, so people demand political action only if the benefit that they individually receive from such action exceeds their individual costs in obtaining it. The four main factors that affect the demand for regulation are:

1. Consumer surplus per buyer
2. Number of buyers
3. Producer surplus per firm
4. Number of firms

The larger the consumer surplus per buyer that results from regulation, the greater is the demand for regulation by buyers. Also, as the number of buyers increases, so does the demand for regulation. But numbers alone do not necessarily translate into an effective political force. The larger the number of buyers, the greater is the cost of organizing them, so the demand for regulation does not increase proportionately with the number of buyers.

The larger the producer surplus per firm that arises from a particular regulation, the larger is the demand for that regulation by firms. Also, as the number of firms that might benefit from some regulation increases, so does the demand for that regulation. But again, large numbers do not necessarily mean an effective political force. The larger the number of firms, the greater is the cost of organizing them.

For a given consumer or producer surplus, the smaller the number of households or firms that share the surplus, the larger is the demand for the regulation that creates the surplus.

Supply of Regulation

Politicians and bureaucrats supply regulation. According to public choice theory, politicians choose policies that appeal to a majority of voters, thereby enabling themselves to achieve and maintain office. Bureaucrats support policies that maximize their budgets (see Chapter 18, p. 396). Given these objectives of politicians and bureaucrats, the supply of regulation depends on the following three factors:

1. Consumer surplus generated per buyer
2. Producer surplus generated per firm
3. The number of voters benefited

The larger the consumer surplus per buyer or producer surplus per firm generated and the larger the number of people affected by a regulation, the greater is the tendency for politicians to supply that regulation. If regulation benefits a large number of people by enough for it to be noticed and if the recipients know the source of the benefits, that regulation appeals to politicians and is supplied. If regulation benefits a *small* number of people by a large amount per person, that regulation also appeals to politicians, provided that its costs are spread widely and are not easily identified. If regulation benefits a large number of people but by too small an amount

per person to be noticed, that regulation does not appeal to politicians and is not supplied.

Political Equilibrium

In equilibrium, the regulation that exists is such that no interest group finds it worthwhile to use additional resources to press for changes and no group of politicians finds it worthwhile to offer different regulations. Being in a political equilibrium is not the same thing as everyone being in agreement. Lobby groups will devote resources to trying to change regulations that are already in place. Others will devote resources to maintaining the existing regulations. But no one will find it worthwhile to *increase* the resources they are devoting to such activities. Also, political parties might not agree with each other. Some support the existing regulations, and others propose different regulations. In equilibrium, no one wants to change the proposals that they are making.

What will a political equilibrium look like? The answer depends on whether the regulation serves the public interest or the interest of the producer. Let's look at these two possibilities.

Public Interest Theory The **public interest theory** is that regulations are supplied to satisfy the demand of consumers and producers to maximize total surplus—that is, to attain allocative efficiency. The public interest theory implies that the political process relentlessly seeks out deadweight loss and introduces regulations that eliminate it. For example, where monopoly practices exist, the political process will introduce price regulations to ensure that outputs increase and prices fall to their competitive levels.

Capture Theory The **capture theory** is that the regulations are supplied to satisfy the demand of producers to maximize producer surplus—that is, to maximize economic profit. The key idea of the capture theory is that the cost of regulation is high and only those regulations that increase the surplus of small, easily identified groups and that have low organization costs are supplied by the political process. Such regulations are supplied even if they impose costs on others, provided that those costs are spread thinly and widely enough that they do not decrease votes.

The predictions of the capture theory are less clear-cut than those of the public interest theory. The capture theory predicts that regulations benefit cohesive interest groups, which have large and visible benefits and imposes small costs on everyone else. Those costs per person are so small that no one finds it worthwhile to incur the cost of organizing an interest group to avoid them.

Whichever theory of regulation is correct, according to public choice theory, the political system delivers amounts and types of regulations that best further the electoral success of politicians. Because producer-oriented and consumer-oriented regulation are in conflict with each other, the political process can't satisfy both groups in any particular industry. Only one group can win. This makes the regulatory actions of government a bit like a unique product—for example, a painting by Leonardo da Vinci. There is only one original, and it will be sold to just one buyer. Normally, a unique commodity is sold at auction; the highest bidder takes the prize. Equilibrium in the regulatory process is similar: The suppliers satisfy the demands of the highest bidder. If the producer demand offers a bigger return to the politicians, either directly through votes or indirectly through campaign contributions, then the producers' interests will be served. If the consumer demand translates into a larger number of votes, then the consumers' interests will be served by regulation.

R E V I E W

■ The demand for regulation is expressed by consumers and producers who spend scarce resources voting, lobbying, and campaigning for regulations that best further their own interests.

■ Regulation is supplied by politicians and bureaucrats. Politicians choose actions that appeal to a majority of voters, and bureaucrats choose actions that maximize their budgets.

■ The regulation that exists is the political equilibrium that balances the opposing demand and supply forces. The political equilibrium either achieves efficiency—the public interest theory—or maximizes producer surplus—the capture theory.

We have now completed our study of the *theory* of regulation in the marketplace. Let's turn our attention to the regulations that exist in our economy today. Which theory of regulation best explains these real-world regulations? Which regulations are in the public interest and which are in the interest of producers?

Regulation and Deregulation

THE PAST 20 YEARS HAVE SEEN DRAMATIC changes in the way in which the U.S. economy is regulated by government. We're going to examine some of these changes. To begin, we'll look at what is regulated and also at the scope of regulation. Then we'll turn to the regulatory process and examine how regulators control prices and other aspects of market behavior. Finally, we'll tackle the more difficult and controversial questions: Why do we regulate some things but not others? Who benefits from the regulations that we have—consumers or producers?

The Scope of Regulation

The first federal regulatory agency, the Interstate Commerce Commission (ICC), was set up in 1887 to control prices, routes, and the quality of service of interstate railroads. Its scope later covered trucking lines, bus lines, water carriers, and, in more recent years, oil pipelines. Following the establishment of the ICC, the federal regulatory environment remained static until the years of the Great Depression. Then, in the 1930s, more agencies were established—the Federal Power Commission, the Federal Communications Commission, the Securities and Exchange Commission, the Federal Maritime Commission, the Federal Deposit Insurance Corporation, and, in 1938, the Civil Aeronautical Agency, which was replaced in 1940 by the Civil Aeronautics Board. There was a further lull until the establishment during the 1970s of the Copyright Royalty Tribunal and the Federal Energy Regulatory Commission. In addition to these, there are many state and local regulatory commissions.

In the mid-1970s, almost one quarter of the economy was subject to some form of regulation. Heavily regulated industries—those subject both to price regulation and to regulation of entry of new firms—were electricity, natural gas, telephones, airlines, highway freight services, and railroads.

Regulation reached its peak in 1977. Since then, there has been a gradual process of deregulation. Deregulation has had the most significant impact in the telecommunication, banking and financial services, railroad, bus, trucking, and airline industries.

What exactly do regulatory agencies do? How do they regulate?

The Regulatory Process

Though regulatory agencies vary in size and scope and in the detailed aspects of economic life that they control, all agencies have features in common.

First, the bureaucrats who are the key decision makers in a regulatory agency are appointed by the administration or Congress in the case of federal agencies and by state and local governments. In addition, all agencies have a permanent bureaucracy made up of experts in the industry being regulated and often recruited from the regulated firms. Agencies have financial resources, voted by Congress or state or local legislatures, to cover the costs of their operations.

Second, each agency adopts a set of practices or operating rules for controlling prices and other aspects of economic performance. These rules and practices are based on well-defined physical and financial accounting procedures that are relatively easy to administer and to monitor.

In a regulated industry, individual firms are usually free to determine the technology that they will use in production. But they are not free to determine the prices at which they will sell their output, the quantities that they will sell, or the markets that they will serve. The regulatory agency grants certification to a company to serve a particular market and with a particular line of products, and it determines the level and structure of prices that will be charged. In some cases, the agency also determines the quantity that firms may produce.

To analyze the way in which regulation works, it is convenient to distinguish between the regulation of natural monopoly and the regulation of cartels. Let's begin with the regulation of natural monopoly.

Natural Monopoly

Natural monopoly was defined in Chapter 13 (p. 264) as an industry in which one firm can supply the entire market at a lower cost than two or more firms can. As a consequence, a natural monopoly experiences economies of scale, no matter how large its output rate. Examples of natural monopolies include local distribution of cable television signals, electricity and gas, and urban rail services. It is much more expensive to have two or more competing sets of

wires, pipes, and train lines serving every neighborhood than it is to have a single set. (What is a natural monopoly changes over time as technology changes. With the introduction of fiber-optic cables, telephone companies and cable television companies can compete with each other in both markets, so what was once a natural monopoly is gradually becoming a more competitive industry. Direct satellite TV is also beginning to break the cable monopoly.)

Let's consider the example of cable TV, which is shown in Fig. 19.1. The demand curve for cable TV is *D*. The cable TV company's marginal cost curve is *MC*. That marginal cost curve is (assumed to be)

FIGURE 19.1

Natural Monopoly: Marginal Cost Pricing

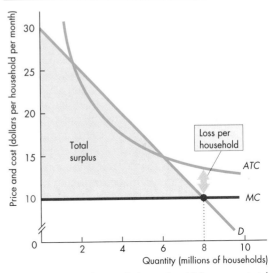

A natural monopoly is an industry in which average total cost is falling even when the entire market demand is satisfied. A cable TV operator faces the demand curve *D*. The firm's marginal cost is constant at $10 per household per month, as shown by the curve labeled *MC*. Fixed costs are large, and the average total cost curve, which includes average fixed cost, is shown as *ATC*. A marginal cost pricing rule that maximizes total surplus sets the price at $10 a month, with 8 million households being served. The resulting consumer surplus is shown as the green area. The firm incurs a loss on each household, indicated by the red arrow. To remain in business, the firm must price discriminate, use a two-part tariff, or receive a subsidy.

horizontal at $10 per household per month—that is, the cost of providing each additional household with a month of cable programming is $10. The cable company has a heavy investment in satellite receiving dishes, cables, and control equipment and so has high fixed costs. These fixed costs are part of the company's average total cost curve, shown as *ATC*. The average total cost curve slopes downward because as the number of households served increases, the fixed cost is spread over a larger number of households. (To refresh your memory on the average total cost curve, take a quick look at Chapter 11, pp. 220–221.)

Regulation in the Public Interest How will cable TV be regulated according to the public interest theory? In the public interest theory, regulation maximizes total surplus, which occurs if marginal cost equals price. As you can see in Fig. 19.1, that outcome occurs if the price is regulated at $10 per household per month and if 8 million households are served. Such a regulation is called a marginal cost pricing rule. A **marginal cost pricing rule** sets price equal to marginal cost. It maximizes total surplus in the regulated industry.

A natural monopoly that is regulated to set price equal to marginal cost incurs an economic loss. Because its average total cost curve is falling, marginal cost is below average total cost. Because price equals marginal cost, price is below average total cost. Average total cost minus price is the loss per unit produced. It's pretty obvious that a cable TV company that is required to use a marginal cost pricing rule will not stay in business for long. How can a company cover its costs and, at the same time, obey a marginal cost pricing rule?

One possibility is price discrimination (see Chapter 13, pp. 270–274). Another possibility is to use a two-part price (called a *two-part tariff*). For example, local telephone companies can charge consumers a monthly fee for being connected to the telephone system and then charge a price equal to marginal cost for each local call. A cable TV operator can charge a one-time connection fee that covers its fixed cost and then charge a monthly fee equal to marginal cost.

But a natural monopoly cannot always cover its costs in these ways. If a natural monopoly cannot cover its total cost from its customers and if the government wants it to follow a marginal cost pricing rule, the government must give the firm a subsidy. In such a case, the government raises the revenue for the subsidy by taxing some other activity. But as we saw

in Chapter 18, taxes themselves generate deadweight loss. Thus the deadweight loss resulting from additional taxes must be subtracted from the efficiency gained by forcing the natural monopoly to adopt a marginal cost pricing rule.

It is possible that deadweight loss will be minimized by permitting the natural monopoly to charge a higher price than marginal cost rather than by taxing some other sector of the economy to subsidize the natural monopoly. Such a pricing arrangement is called an average cost pricing rule. An **average cost pricing rule** sets price equal to average total cost. Figure 19.2 shows the average cost pricing solution. The cable TV operator charges $15 a month and serves 6 million households. A deadweight loss arises, which is shown by the gray triangle in the figure.

Capturing the Regulator What does the capture theory predict about the regulation of this industry? According to the capture theory, regulation serves the

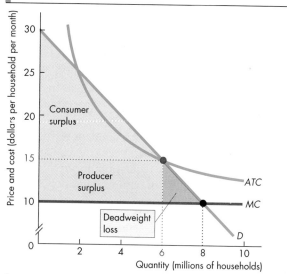

FIGURE 19.2

Natural Monopoly:
Average Cost Pricing

Average cost pricing sets price equal to average total cost. The cable TV operator charges $15 a month and serves 6 million households. In this situation, the firm breaks even—average total cost equals price. Deadweight loss, shown by the gray triangle, is generated. Consumer surplus is reduced to the green area.

interests of the producer, which means maximizing profit. To work out the price that achieves this goal, we need to look at the relationship between marginal revenue and marginal cost. A monopoly maximizes profit by producing the output at which marginal revenue equals marginal cost. The monopoly's marginal revenue curve in Fig. 19.3 is the curve *MR*. Marginal revenue equals marginal cost when output is 4 million households. The monopoly charges a price of $20 a month and makes the profit shown by the blue area. Thus a regulation that best serves the interest of the producer will set the price at this level.

But how can a producer go about obtaining regulation that results in this monopoly profit-maximizing outcome? To answer this question, we need to look at the way in which agencies determine a regulated price. A key method used is called rate of return regulation.

FIGURE 19.3

Natural Monopoly: Profit Maximization

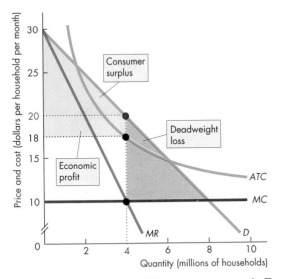

The cable TV operator would like to maximize profit. To do so, marginal revenue (*MR*) is made equal to marginal cost. At a price of $20 a month, 4 million households buy cable service. Consumer surplus is reduced to the green triangle. The deadweight loss increases to the gray triangle. The monopoly makes the profit shown by the blue rectangle. If the producer can capture the regulator, the outcome will be the situation shown here.

Rate of Return Regulation **Rate of return regulation** determines a regulated price by setting the price at a level that enables the regulated firm to earn a specified target percent return on its capital. The target rate of return is determined with reference to what is normal in competitive industries. This rate of return is part of the opportunity cost of the natural monopolist and is included in the firm's average total cost. By examining the firm's total cost, including the normal rate of return on capital, the regulator attempts to determine the price at which average total cost is covered. Thus rate of return regulation is equivalent to average cost pricing.

In Fig. 19.2, average cost pricing results in a regulated price of $15 a month with 6 million households being served. Thus rate of return regulation, based on a correct assessment of the producer's average total cost curve, results in a price that favors the consumer and does not enable the producer to maximize monopoly profit. The special interest group will have failed to capture the regulator, and the outcome will be closer to that predicted by the public interest theory of regulation.

But there is a feature of many real-world situations that the above analysis does not take into account: the ability of the monopoly firm to mislead the regulator about its true costs.

Inflating Costs The managers of a firm might be able to inflate the firm's costs by spending part of the firm's revenue on inputs that are not strictly required for the production of the good. By this device, the firm's apparent costs exceed the true costs. On-the-job luxury in the form of sumptuous office suites, limousines, free baseball tickets (disguised as public relations expenses), company jets, lavish international travel, and entertainment are all ways in which managers can inflate costs.

If the cable TV operator manages to inflate its costs and persuade the regulator that its true average total cost curve is that shown as *ATC (inflated)* in Fig. 19.4, then the regulator, applying the normal rate of return principle, will regulate the price at $20 a month. In this example, the price and quantity will be the same as those under unregulated monopoly. It might be impossible for firms to inflate their costs by as much as the amount shown in the figure. But to the extent that costs can be inflated, the apparent average total cost curve lies somewhere between the true *ATC* curve and *ATC (inflated)*. The greater the ability of the firm to pad its costs in this way, the

FIGURE 19.4

Natural Monopoly: Inflating Costs

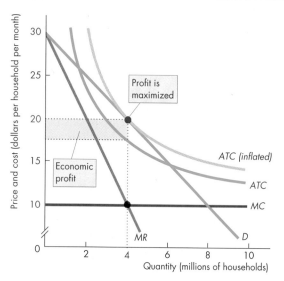

If the cable TV operator is able to inflate its costs to *ATC (inflated)* and persuade the regulator that these are genuine minimum costs of production, rate of return regulation results in a price of $20 a month—the profit-maximizing price. To the extent that the producer can inflate costs above average total cost, the price rises, output falls, and deadweight loss increases. The profit is captured by the managers, not the shareholders (owners) of the firm.

more closely its profit (measured in economic terms) approaches the maximum possible. The shareholders of this firm don't receive this economic profit because it gets used up in baseball tickets, luxury offices, and the other actions taken by the firm's managers to inflate the company's costs.

Incentive Regulation Schemes   Partly for the reasons we've just examined, rate of return regulation is increasingly being replaced by incentive regulation schemes. An **incentive regulation scheme** is a type of regulation that gives a firm an incentive to operate efficiently and keep costs under control. Today, a majority of states have adopted incentive regulation schemes for telecommunications rather than traditional rate of return regulation. These new schemes take two main forms: price caps (adopted in

California, New Jersey, Oregon, and Rhode Island) and earnings sharing plans (adopted in Colorado, Connecticut, Florida, Georgia, Kentucky, Tennessee, and Texas). Under a price cap regulation, the regulators set the maximum price that may be charged and hold that price cap for a number of years. If profits are considered too high, the price cap will be lowered. Under earnings-sharing regulation, if profits rise above a certain level, they must be shared with the firm's customers. There is some evidence that under these types of regulations, local telephone companies are attempting to cut costs.

Public Interest or Capture?

It is not clear whether actual regulation produces prices and quantities that more closely correspond with the predictions of capture theory or with public interest theory. One thing is clear, however. Price regulation does not require natural monopolies to use the marginal cost pricing rule. If it did, most natural monopolies would make losses and receive hefty government subsidies to enable them to remain in business. But there are even exceptions to this conclusion. For example, many local telephone companies do appear to use marginal cost pricing for local telephone calls. They cover their total cost by charging a flat fee each month for being connected to their telephone system but then permitting each call to be made at its marginal cost—zero or something very close to it.

A test of whether natural monopoly regulation is in the public interest or the interest of the producer is to examine the rates of return earned by regulated natural monopolies. If those rates of return are significantly higher than those in the rest of the economy, then, to some degree, the regulator might have been captured by the producer. If the rates of return in the regulated monopoly industries are similar to those in the rest of the economy, then we cannot tell for sure whether the regulator has been captured or not, for we cannot know the extent to which costs have been inflated by the managers of the regulated firms.

Table 19.1 shows rates of return in regulated natural monopolies as well as the economy's average rate of return. In the 1960s, rates of return in regulated natural monopolies were somewhat below the economy average; in the 1970s, those returns exceeded the economy average. Overall, the rates of return achieved by regulated natural monopolies were not

TABLE 19.1

Rates of Return in Regulated Monopolies

Industry	Years 1962–69	1970–77
Electricity	3.2	6.1
Gas	3.3	8.2
Railroad	5.1	7.2
Average of above	3.9	7.2
Economy average	6.6	5.1

Source: Paul W. MacAvoy, *The Regulated Industries and the Economy* (New York: W.W. Norton, 1979), 49–60.

very different from those in the rest of the economy. We can conclude from these data either that natural monopoly regulation does, to some degree, serve the public interest or that natural monopoly managers inflate their costs by amounts sufficiently large to disguise the fact that they have captured the regulator and that the public interest is not being served.

A final test of whether regulation of natural monopoly is in the public interest or the producers' interest is to study the changes in consumer surplus

TABLE 19.2

Gains from Deregulating Natural Monopolies

Industry	Consumer surplus	Producer surplus	Total surplus
	(billions of 1990 dollars)		
Railroads	8.5	3.2	11.7
Telecommunications	1.2	0.0	1.2
Cable television	0.8	0.0	0.8
Total	10.5	3.2	13.7

Source: Clifford Winston, "Economic Deregulation: Days of Reckoning for Microeconomists," *Journal of Economic Literature*, XXXI, September 1993, pp. 1263–1289, and the author's calculations.

and producer surplus following deregulation. Microeconomists have researched this issue and Table 19.2 summarizes their conclusions. In the case of railroad deregulation, which occurred during the 1980s, both consumers and producers gained, and by large amounts. The gains from deregulation of telecommunications and cable television were smaller and accrued only to consumers. These findings suggest that railroad regulation hurt everyone, while regulation of telecommunications and cable television hurt only consumers.

We've now examined the regulation of natural monopoly. Let's next turn to regulation in oligopolistic industries—the regulation of cartels.

Cartel Regulation

A *cartel* is a collusive agreement among a number of firms that is designed to restrict output and achieve a higher profit for the cartel's members. Cartels are illegal in the United States and in most other countries. But international cartels can sometimes operate legally, such as the international cartel of oil producers known as OPEC (the Organization of Petroleum Exporting Countries).

Illegal cartels can arise in oligopolistic industries. An oligopoly is a market structure in which a small number of firms compete with each other. We studied oligopoly (and duopoly—two firms competing for a market) in Chapter 14. There we saw that if firms manage to collude and behave like a monopoly, they can set the same price and sell the same total quantity as a monopoly firm would. But we also discovered that in such a situation, each firm will be tempted to cheat, increasing its own output and profit at the expense of the other firms. The result of such cheating on the collusive agreement is the unraveling of the monopoly equilibrium and the emergence of a competitive outcome with zero economic profit for producers. Such an outcome benefits consumers at the expense of producers.

How is oligopoly regulated? Does regulation prevent monopoly practices or does it encourage those practices?

According to the public interest theory, oligopoly is regulated to ensure a competitive outcome. Consider, for example, the market for trucking tomatoes from the San Joaquin Valley to Los Angeles, illustrated in Fig. 19.5. The market demand curve for trips is *D*. The industry marginal cost curve—and the competitive supply curve—is *MC*. Public interest regulation will regulate the price of a trip at $20, and there will be 300 trips a week.

How would this industry be regulated according to the capture theory? Regulation that is in the producer interest will maximize profit. To find the outcome in this case, we need to determine the price and quantity when marginal cost equals marginal revenue. The marginal revenue curve is *MR*. So marginal cost equals marginal revenue at 200 trips a week. The price of a trip is $30.

One way of achieving this outcome is to place an output limit on each firm in the industry. If there are 10 trucking companies, an output limit of 20 trips per company ensures that the total number of trips in a week is 200. Penalties can be imposed to ensure that no single producer exceeds its output limit.

FIGURE 19.5
Collusive Oligopoly

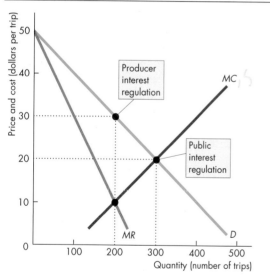

Ten trucking firms transport tomatoes from the San Joaquin Valley to Los Angeles. The demand curve is *D*, and the industry marginal cost curve is *MC*. Under competition, the *MC* curve is the industry supply curve. If the industry is competitive, the price of a trip will be $20 and 300 trips will be made each week. Producers will demand regulation that restricts entry and limits output to 200 trips a week, where industry marginal revenue (*MR*) is equal to industry marginal cost (*MC*). This regulation raises the price to $30 a trip and results in each producer making maximum profit—as if it is a monopoly.

All the firms in the industry would support this type of regulation because it helps to prevent cheating and to maintain a monopoly outcome. Each firm knows that without effectively enforced production quotas, every firm has an incentive to increase output. (For each firm, price exceeds marginal cost, so a greater output brings a larger profit.) So each firm wants a method of preventing output from increasing above the industry profit-maximizing level, and the quotas enforced by regulation achieve this end. With this type of cartel regulation, the regulator enables a cartel to operate legally and in its own best interest.

What does cartel regulation do in practice? Although there is disagreement about the matter, the consensus view is that regulation tends to favor the producer. Trucking (when it was regulated by the Interstate Commerce Commission), taxicabs (regulated by cities), and airlines (when they were regulated by the Civil Aeronautics Board) are specific examples in which profits of producers increased as a result of regulation. In some cases—and trucking is one of these—the work force, through unionization, also managed to take a large part of the producer surplus.

Some further evidence in support of the conclusion that regulation sometimes increases profit is presented in Table 19.3. If regulation ensures a competitive outcome, rates of return in a regulated oligopoly will be no higher than those in the economy as a whole. As the numbers in Table 19.3 show, rates of return in airlines and trucking were close to twice the economy average rate of return in the 1960s. In the 1970s, the rate of return in trucking remained higher than the economy average (although by a smaller margin than had prevailed in the 1960s). Airline

TABLE 19.3
Rates of Return in Regulated Oligopolies

Industry	Years	
	1962–69	1970–77
Airlines	12.8	3.0
Trucking	13.6	8.1
Economy average	6.6	5.1

Source: Paul W. MacAvoy, *The Regulated Industries and the Economy* (New York: W.W. Norton, 1978), 49–60.

rates of return in the 1970s fell to below the economy average. The overall picture that emerges from examining data on rates of return is mixed. The regulation of oligopoly does not always result in higher profit, but there are many situations in which it does.

Further evidence on oligopoly regulation can be obtained from the performance of prices and profit following deregulation. If, following deregulation, prices and profit fall, then, to some degree, the regulation must have been serving the interest of the producer.

In contrast, if, following deregulation, prices and profits remain constant or increase, then the regulation may be presumed to have been serving the public interest. Because there has been a substantial amount of deregulation in recent years, we can use this test of oligopoly regulation to see which of the two theories better fits the facts.

The evidence is mixed, but in the cases of the airlines and trucking, the two main oligopolies that have been deregulated, prices fell and there was a large increase in the volume of business. Table 19.4 summarizes the estimated effects of deregulation of airlines and trucking on consumer surplus, producer surplus, and total surplus. Most of the gains were in consumer surplus. In the case of the airlines, there was a gain in producer surplus as well.

But the table shows that in the trucking industry, producer surplus decreased by almost $5 billion a year. This outcome implies that the regulation benefited the producer by restricting competition and enabling prices to exceed their competitive levels.

Making Predictions

Most industries have a few producers and many consumers. In these cases, public choice theory predicts that regulation will protect producer interests because a small number of people stand to gain a large amount and so they will be fairly easy to organize as a cohesive lobby. Under such circumstances, politicians will be rewarded with campaign contributions rather than votes. But there are situations in which the consumer interest has prevailed. There are also cases in which the balance has switched from producer to consumer, as seen in the deregulation process that began in the late 1970s.

Deregulation raises some hard questions for economists seeking to understand and make predictions about regulation. Why were the transportation and telecommunication sectors deregulated? If producers gained from regulation and if the producer lobby was strong enough to achieve regulation, what happened during the 1970s to change the equilibrium to one in which the consumer interest prevailed?

Part of the answer is that economists become more confident and vocal in predicting gains from deregulation. Regulation had become very costly to consumers, and the potential benefits to them from deregulation were estimated to be so large that the cost of organizing the consumer voice became a price worth paying.

One factor that increased the cost of regulation borne by consumers and brought deregulation in the transportation sector was the large increase in energy prices in the 1970s. These price hikes made route regulation by the ICC extremely costly and changed the balance in favor of consumers in the political equilibrium.

Technological change was the main factor at work in the telecommunication sector. New satellite-based, computer-controlled long-distance technologies enabled smaller producers to offer low-cost services. These producers wanted a share of the business—and profit—of AT&T. Furthermore, as communication technology improved, the cost of communication fell and the cost of organizing larger groups of consumers also fell.

If this line of reasoning is correct, we can expect to see more consumer-oriented regulation in the future. In practice, more consumer-oriented regulation often means deregulation—removing the regulations that are already in place to serve the interests of producer groups.

TABLE 19.4

Gains from Deregulating Oligopolies

Industry	Consumer surplus	Producer surplus	Total surplus
		(billions of 1990 dollars)	
Airlines	11.8	4.9	16.7
Trucking	15.4	−4.8	10.6
Total	27.2	0.1	27.3

Source: Clifford Winston, "Economic Deregulation: Days of Reckoning for Microeconomists," *Journal of Economic Literature*, XXXI, September 1993, pp. 1263–1289, and the author's calculations.

REVIEW

- Regulation of a natural monopoly in the public interest sets price equal to marginal cost or, to avoid a tax-financed subsidy, sets price equal to average total cost.
- In practice, natural monopolies face either rate of return regulation or incentive regulation schemes.
- With rate of return regulation, firms have an incentive to inflate costs and move as closely as possible to the profit-maximizing output. Incentive regulation—price caps and earnings sharing—encourages cost cutting.
- Cartel regulation that establishes output levels for each firm can help perpetuate a cartel and work against the public interest.

Let's now leave regulation and turn to the other method of intervention in markets: antitrust law.

Antitrust Law

ANTITRUST LAW PROVIDES AN ALTERNATIVE WAY in which the government may influence the marketplace. As in the case of regulation, antitrust law can be formulated in the public interest, to maximize total surplus, or in private interests, to maximize the surpluses of particular special interest groups such as producers.

Landmark Antitrust Cases

The antitrust laws themselves are brief and easily summarized. The first antitrust law, the Sherman Act, was passed in 1890 in an atmosphere of outrage and disgust at the actions and practices of J.P. Morgan, John D. Rockefeller, and W.H. Vanderbilt—the so-called "robber barons." Ironically, the most lurid stories of the actions of these great American capitalists are not of their monopolization and exploitation of consumers but of their sharp practices against each other. Nevertheless, monopolies did emerge—for example, the spectacular control of the oil industry by John D. Rockefeller. The Sherman Act had little effect. But in 1914, the antitrust laws were strengthened. The Clayton Act supplemented the Sherman Act, and the

TABLE 19.5

Antitrust Laws

Name of law	Year passed	What the law prohibits
Sherman Act	1890	■ Combination, trust, or conspiracy to restrict interstate or international trade ■ Monopolization or attempt to monopolize interstate or international trade
Clayton Act Robinson-Patman Amendment Cellar-Kefauver Amendment	1914 1936 1950	■ Price discrimination if the effect is to substantially lessen competition or create monopoly and if such discrimination is not justified by cost differences ■ Contracts that force other goods to be bought from same firm ■ Acquisition of competitors' shares or assets ■ Interlocking directorships among competing firms
Federal Trade Commission Act	1914	■ Unfair methods of competition and unfair or deceptive business practices

Federal Trade Commission, an agency charged with enforcing the antitrust laws, was set up. Table 19.5 gives a summary of the main antitrust laws.

The real force of any law arises from its interpretation. Interpretation of the antitrust laws has ebbed and flowed. At times, it has appeared to favor producers, and at other times, consumers. Let's see how.

Table 19.6 summarizes the landmark antitrust cases. The first cases were those of the American Tobacco Company and Standard Oil Company, decided in 1911. These two companies were found guilty of violations under the Sherman Act and ordered to divest themselves of large holdings in other companies. The breakup of John D. Rockefeller's Standard Oil Company resulted in the creation of the oil companies that today are household names, such as Amoco, Chevron, Exxon, and Sohio.

In finding these companies to be in violation of the provisions of the Sherman Act, the Supreme

TABLE 19.6

Landmark Antitrust Cases

Case	Year	Verdict and consequence
American Tobacco Co. and *Standard Oil Co.*	1911	*Guilty:* Ordered to divest themselves of large holdings in other companies; "rule of reason" enunciated—only *unreasonable* combinations guilty under Sherman Act.
U.S. Steel Co.	1920	*Not guilty:* Although U.S. Steel had a very large market share (near monopoly), mere "size alone is not an offense"; application of the "rule of reason."
Socony-Vacuum Oil Co.	1940	*Guilty:* Combination was formed for purpose of price fixing; no consideration of "reasonableness" applied.
Alcoa	1945	*Guilty:* Too big—had too large a share of the market; end of "rule of reason."
General Electric, Westinghouse, and others	1961	*Guilty:* Price-fixing conspiracy; executives fined and jailed.
Brown Shoe	1962	*Guilty:* Ownership of Kinney, a retail chain, reduced competition; ordered to sell Kinney (Brown supplied 8 percent of Kinney's shoes, and Kinney sold 2 percent of nation's shoes).
Von's Grocery	1965	*Guilty:* Merger of two supermarkets in Los Angeles would restrain competition (the merged firm would have had 7 $\frac{1}{2}$ percent of the L.A. market).
IBM	1982	*Case dismissed* as being "without merit."
AT&T	1983	*Agreement* between AT&T and government that the company would divest itself of all local telephone operating companies—80 percent of its assets.

Court enunciated the "rule of reason." The rule of reason states that monopoly arising from mergers and agreements among firms is not necessarily illegal. Only if there is an unreasonable restraint of trade does the arrangement violate the provisions of the Sherman Act. The rule of reason was widely regarded as removing the force of the Sherman Act itself. This view was reinforced in 1920 when U.S. Steel Company was acquitted of violations under the act even though it had a very large (more than 50 percent) share of the U.S. steel market. Applying the "rule of reason," the court declared that "size alone is not an offense."

Matters remained much as they were in 1920 until 1940, when the *Socony-Vacuum Oil Company* case resulted in the first chink in the armor of the "rule of reason." The court found Socony-Vacuum Oil Company guilty because a combination had been formed for the purpose of price fixing. The court ruled that no consideration of reasonableness should be applied to such a case. If the purpose of the agreement was price fixing, the automatic interpretation was to be that the agreement was unreasonable.

The "rule of reason" received its death blow in the *Alcoa* case, decided in 1945. Alcoa was judged to be in violation of the law because it was too big. It had too large a share of the aluminum market. A relatively tough interpretation of the law continued through the late 1960s. In 1961, General Electric, Westinghouse, and other electrical component manufacturers were found guilty of a price-fixing conspiracy. This case was the first one in which the executives (rather than the company itself) were fined and also jailed.

Tough antimerger decisions were taken in 1962 against Brown Shoe and in 1965 against Von's Grocery. In the first of these cases, Brown Shoe was required to divest itself of ownership of the Kinney shoe retail chain. This case is an example of the court ruling that a vertically integrated firm is capable of restraining competition. *Vertical integration* is the merger of two or more firms operating at different stages in a production process of a single good or service. For example, the merger of a firm that produces raw materials, a firm that converts those raw materials into a manufactured good, and a firm that retails the finished product creates a vertically integrated firm. The vertically integrated Brown Shoe and Kinney retail chain was ordered to be broken up even though Brown supplied only 8 percent of Kinney's shoes and Kinney sold only 2 percent of the nation's shoes.

Von's Grocery is an example of a horizontally integrated firm. *Horizontal integration* is a merger of two or more firms providing essentially the same product or service. In the *Von's Grocery* case, the court ruled that the combination of two supermarkets in Los Angeles would restrict competition even though the combined sales of the two firms would have been only 7 1/2 percent of total supermarket sales in the Los Angeles area.

Three Recent Antitrust Cases

Three recent antitrust cases have arisen in the high-technology computer and telecommunications industries.

The IBM Case In the late 1960s, IBM was charged with anticompetitive practices. At that time, IBM faced little competition in the market for mainframe computers (the large computers used by banks, insurance companies, and universities and other research institutions). But it faced fierce competition from firms that produced peripherals such as tape drives and disk drives that were compatible with IBM's own peripherals. IBM reacted to this competition by cutting its prices on peripherals to the point at which its competitors could not cover their costs, while maintaining high prices on its computers. After 13 years of litigation, the IBM case was dismissed by the Department of Justice in 1982 as being "without merit." The entry of new firms during the 1970s had created a highly competitive market in both mainframe and microcomputers and substantially weakened the original case against IBM.

The AT&T Case In 1974, AT&T was charged with violating the Sherman Act and accused of actions aimed at maintaining a monopoly in long-distance and local telephone communications. This case was resolved by an agreement between AT&T and the Department of Justice under which AT&T gave up its regional telephone business (which broke up into regional companies, known as "baby Bells") and competed in its long-distance business with new carriers such as MCI and Sprint. But it was technological

changes in telecommunications as much as the law that made this outcome feasible.

The Microsoft Case In 1993, the Department of Justice began to study Microsoft. Microsoft's competitors claimed that the company monopolized the market for PC operating systems (DOS and Windows) because of "per-processor" contracts. Under these contracts, computer makers paid Microsoft a royalty on every computer shipped, regardless of whether the computers had Microsoft software installed on them. This practice made it difficult for producers of other operating systems to compete with Microsoft. It has also been claimed that Microsoft frustrates competitors of its applications programs (such as word processors and spreadsheets) by giving other developers of applications an incomplete description of the code needed to work properly with Windows.

More recently, Netscape has complained because Microsoft's web browser, Internet Explorer, which competes with Netscape's browser, Navigator, is available at a zero price. Microsoft says it is giving consumers greater value. Microsoft will be the subject of ongoing study by the Justice Department.

Current Mergers Rules

Today, the Department of Justice uses guidelines to determine which mergers it will examine and possibly block based on the Herfindahl-Hirschman index (HHI), which is explained in Chapter 14 (p. 286). A market in which the HHI is less than 1,000 is regarded as competitive. An index between 1,000 and 1,800 indicates a moderately concentrated market, and a merger in this market that would increase the index by 100 points is challenged by the Department of Justice. An index above 1,800 indicates a concentrated market, and a merger in this market that would increase the index by 50 points is challenged. Figure 19.6(a) summarizes these guidelines.

The Department of Justice used these guidelines in analyzing two proposed mergers in the market for carbonated soft drinks. In 1986, PepsiCo announced its intention to buy 7-Up for $380 million. A month later, Coca-Cola said it would buy Dr Pepper for $470 million. Whether this market is concentrated depends on how it is defined. The market for all soft drinks, which includes carbonated drinks marketed by these four companies plus fruit juices and bottled water, has an HHI of 120, so it is highly competitive. But the

FIGURE 19.6

The HHI Merger Guidelines

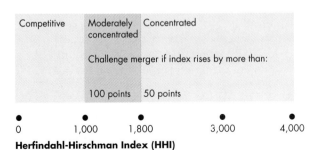

(a) The merger guidelines

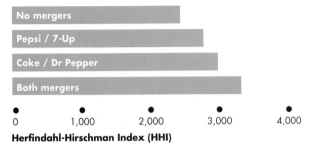

(b) Product mergers in soft drinks

The Justice Department scrutinizes proposed mergers if the HHI exceeds 1,000. Proposed mergers between producers of carbonated soft drinks were blocked in 1986 by application of these guidelines.

market for carbonated soft drinks is highly concentrated. Coca-Cola has a 39 percent share, PepsiCo has 28 percent, Dr Pepper is next with 7 percent, then comes 7-Up with 6 percent. One other producer, RJR, has a 5 percent market share. So the five largest firms in this market have an 85 percent market share. If we assume that the other 15 percent of the market consists of 15 firms, each with a 1 percent market share, the Herfindahl-Hirschman index is:

$$\text{HHI} = 39^2 + 28^2 + 7^2 + 6^2 + 5^2 + 15 = 2,430.$$

With an HHI of this magnitude, a merger that increases the index by 50 points is examined by the Department of Justice. Figure 19.6(b) shows how the HHI would have changed with the mergers. The PepsiCo and 7-Up merger would have increased the index by more than 300 points, the Coca-Cola and

Dr Pepper merger would have increased it by more than 500 points, and both mergers together would have increased the index by almost 800 points. The Justice Department decided to define the market narrowly and, with increases of these magnitudes, blocked the mergers.

Public or Special Interest?

It is clear from the historical contexts in which antitrust law has evolved that its intent has been to protect and pursue the public interest and restrain the profit-seeking and anticompetitive actions of producers. But it is also clear from the above brief history of antitrust legislation and cases that from time to time the interest of the producer has had an influence on the way in which the law has been interpreted and applied. Nevertheless, the overall thrust of antitrust law appears to have been directed toward achieving efficiency and therefore to serving the public interest.

There is a key difference between the ways in which antitrust law and regulation are administered. Regulation is administered by a bureaucracy. Antitrust law is interpreted and enforced by the legal process—the courts. Economists are now beginning to extend theories of public choice to include an economic analysis of the law and the way in which the courts interpret the law. It is interesting to speculate that the legal institutions that administer antitrust law are more sensitive to the public interest than the bureaucratic institutions that administer regulations.

◆ In this chapter, we've seen how the government intervenes in markets to affect prices, quantities, the gains from trade, and the division of those gains between consumers and producers when there is monopoly or oligopoly. We've seen that there is a conflict between the pursuit of the public interest— achieving efficiency—and the pursuit of the special interests of producers—maximizing producer surplus or economic profit. The political and legal arenas are the places in which these conflicts are resolved.

We've reviewed the public interest and capture theories of government regulation. And we've seen that regulators do sometimes get captured by the regulated and work against the interest of consumers. But this outcome does not always occur. In *Reading Between the Lines*, on pages 424–425, you can see a recent example of antitrust law being used to penalize price fixing in an attempt to protect the public interest.

Policy
WATCH

Price Fixing

THE NEW YORK TIMES, OCTOBER 15, 1996

Archer Daniels Agrees to Big Fine for Price Fixing

By KURT EICHENWALD

The Archer Daniels Midland Company, long one of the country's most powerful corporations, agreed to plead guilty to conspiring with competitors to fix the prices of two agricultural products and pay $100 million in fines, the company announced yesterday.

The fine is by far the largest ever obtained by the Justice Department in a criminal price-fixing case, eclipsing the next highest by almost seven times. ...

In the plea, Archer Daniels—a food processing giant that advertises itself as the "Supermarket to the World"—will admit that it fixed prices of lysine, a feed additive, and citric acid, an organic acid used in various foods and beverages.

Under the deal, Archer Daniels will pay $70 million in fines for fixing lysine prices and $30 million for the citric acid case. ...

"The $100 million fine is shareholder assets that are being squandered to pay for criminal activity that never should have occurred," said James E. Burton, chief executive of the California Public Employees Retirement System, one of the nation's largest pension funds and an investor in Archer Daniels. ...

The company's financial power means that Archer Daniels will be able to pay its $100 million in fines—as well as another $90 million it has agreed to pay to settle class action suits relating to the investigation—without feeling much pain. The company has more than $1.3 billion in cash and liquid securities on hand; its profits last year approached $700 million and its businesses continue to boom. ...

Essence of THE STORY

■ Archer Daniels Midland (ADM) paid fines totaling $100 million for fixing the prices of lysine and citric acid.

■ The fine is seven times larger than the previous largest.

■ One large investor in ADM complained that the fine was squandering shareholder assets.

■ With $1.3 billion in cash and liquid assets and a profit of close to $700 million a year, ADM was easily able to pay the fine.

Economic

A N A L Y S I S

■ Here, we'll focus on fixing the price of lysine, for which ADM paid a $70 million fine.

■ First, a few technical facts. Lysine is an amino acid that is essential in the diets of most animals.

■ Animal food such as soybeanmeal contain lysine, but corn is deficient in lysine. So animals can be fed soybeanmeal or corn supplemented with lysine.

■ Now to the economics. Cost-conscious farmers use the least-cost diet. They buy lysine only if corn plus lysine costs less than soybeanmeal. So the price of lysine cannot rise much above the gap between the price of soybeanmeal and the price of corn.

■ The figure shows the (worldwide) market for lysine. The demand curve, D, is highly elastic because lysine competes with soybeanmeal.

■ The marginal cost of lysine is MC. In a competitive market, the marginal cost curve is the supply curve, S.

■ Equilibrium in a competitive market occurs at the quantity Q_C and the price P_C.

■ If the producers of lysine collude to fix the price, and if they act like a monopoly, their marginal revenue curve is MR in the figure.

■ To maximize economic profit, the firms fix the price at P_M, the highest price at which they can sell Q_M, the quantity at which marginal revenue equals marginal cost. The firms allocate the total output Q_M among themselves.

■ This action brings gains to producers—their economic profit increases by the blue area in the figure.

■ This action imposes costs on consumers because it decreases consumer surplus and also creates deadweight loss, the gray area in the figure.

■ The fine imposed on ADM decreases its profit and returns some of the loss to the taxpayers (consumers).

■ Some ADM stockholders say that their assets are being used to pay the fine. This claim is not exactly correct. The illegal price fixing increased ADM's profit, which boosted its share price and benefited its stockholders. The fine corrects this situation.

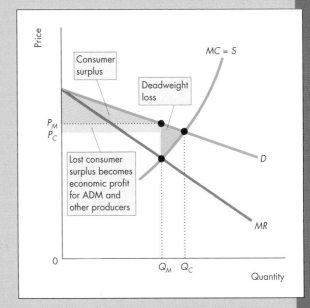

■ It is not known if the fine is large enough to wipe out the gains from price fixing or to leave ADM and its stockholders with a net gain from illegal actions.

■ But what is known is that the deadweight loss from price fixing is lost forever. No fine can restore this loss.

You're

THE VOTER

■ The largest fine for price fixing before the ADM fine was $15 million, imposed on Dyno Nobel for price fixing. Is the ADM fine is too large, too small, or about right? Explain.

■ Price fixing is punishable by fines or by possibly jailing the people found responsible. This news article reports only the fine on ADM. But in January 1997, a Chicago federal grand jury indicted three former top executives of ADM, along with a Japanese executive, for conspiring to fix prices and allocate sales in the worldwide market for lysine. How would you use economic reasoning to decide which penalty is likely to be more effective (a) to deter price fixing and (b) to compensate those who lose from it?

SUMMARY

Key Points

Market Intervention (p. 410)

- The government intervenes to regulate monopolistic and oligopolistic markets in two ways: regulation and antitrust law.

- In the United States, both of these methods are widely used. We seek to understand the reasons for and the effects of regulation.

Economic Theory of Regulation (pp. 410–412)

- Consumers and producers express their demands for regulation by voting, lobbying, and making campaign contributions.

- The larger the surplus per person generated by a regulation, the greater the number of gainers, and the smaller the number of losers, the larger is the demand for the regulation.

- Regulation is supplied by politicians, who pursue their own best interest.

- The larger the surplus per person generated and the larger the number of people who benefit from it, the larger is the supply of regulation.

- Public interest theory predicts that regulation will maximize total surplus. Capture theory predicts that producer surplus will be maximized.

Regulation and Deregulation (pp. 412–420)

- Federal regulation began in 1887 (with the Interstate Commerce Commission) and expanded until the mid-1970s. Since then, transportation, telecommunication, and financial sectors have been deregulated.

- Regulation is conducted by regulatory agencies controlled by politically appointed bureaucrats and staffed by a permanent bureaucracy of experts.

- Regulated firms must comply with rules about price, product quality, and output levels.

- Both natural monopoly and cartel regulation has left regulated firms earning profit levels similar to those in the rest of the economy.

- Deregulation has brought gains for both consumers and producers.

Antitrust Law (pp. 420–423)

- Antitrust law is an alternative way in which the government can control monopoly and monopolistic practices.

- The first antitrust law, the Sherman Act, was passed in 1890. The law was strengthened in 1914 when the Clayton Act was passed and the Federal Trade Commission was created.

- The first landmark cases (against the American Tobacco Company and Standard Oil Company) established the "rule of reason," that monopoly arising from mergers is illegal only if there is an unreasonable restraint of trade; size alone is not illegal.

- The "rule of reason" was abandoned in a case against Alcoa in 1945, and a tougher interpretation of the law continued through the late 1960s.

- Today, the Department of Justice uses guidelines to determine which mergers to examine and possibly block based on the Herfindahl-Hirschman Index.

- The intent of antitrust law is to protect the public interest. This intent has been served most of the time.

Key Figures and Tables

Key Terms

QUESTIONS

1. What are the two main ways in which the government can intervene in monopolistic and oligopolistic markets?

2. Why do consumers demand regulation? In what kinds of industries would their demands for regulation be greatest?

3. Why do producers demand regulation? In what kinds of industries would their demands for regulation be greatest?

4. Explain the public interest and capture theories of the supply of regulation. What does each theory imply about the behavior of politicians?

5. How is oligopoly regulated in the United States? In whose interest is it regulated?

6. What are the main antitrust laws in force in the United States today?

7. What is the "rule of reason"? When was this rule formulated? How has it been applied? When was it abandoned?

8. What are the landmark antitrust cases?

9. Describe the issues and outcome of the American Tobacco and Standard Oil cases?

10. What was the main difference between the American Tobacco and Standard Oil cases on the one hand and the U.S. Steel case on the other hand?

11. What was special about the Alcoa case that makes it a landmark case?

12. Describe the case against IBM. How was the case settled?

13. Describe the case against AT&T. How was the case settled?

14. Describe the case against Microsoft. Is Microsoft a monopoly?

15. How does the Department of Justice decide whether to challenge and possibly seek to block a merger?

16. What was the problem with mergers in the soft drink industry recently?

PROBLEMS

1. Elixir Springs, Inc., is an unregulated natural monopoly that bottles Elixir, a unique health product with no substitutes. The total fixed cost incurred by Elixir Springs is $150,000, and its marginal cost is 10¢ a bottle. The demand for Elixir is as shown in the figure.

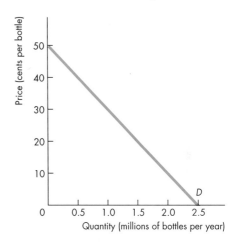

   a. What is the price of a bottle of Elixir?
   b. How many bottles does Elixir Springs sell?
   c. Does Elixir Springs maximize total surplus or producer surplus?

2. The government regulates Elixir Springs in problem 1 by imposing a marginal cost pricing rule.
   a. What is the price of a bottle of Elixir?
   b. How many bottles does Elixir Springs sell?
   c. What is Elixir Springs' producer surplus?
   d. What is the consumer surplus?
   e. Is the regulation in the public interest or in the private interest?

3. The government regulates Elixir Springs in problem 1 by imposing an average cost pricing rule.
   a. What is the price of a bottle of Elixir?
   b. How many bottles does Elixir Springs sell?
   c. What is Elixir Springs' producer surplus?
   d. What is the consumer surplus?
   e. Is the regulation in the public interest or in the private interest?

4. The value of the capital invested in Elixir Springs in problem 1 is $750,000. The government introduces a rate of return regulation requiring the firm to sell its water for a price that gives it a rate of return of 5 percent on its capital.
   a. What is the price of a bottle of Elixir?
   b. How many bottles does Elixir Springs sell?
   c. What is Elixir Springs' producer surplus?
   d. What is the consumer surplus?
   e. Is the regulation in the public interest or in the private interest?

5. Faced with the rate of return regulation of problem 4, Elixir Springs inflates its costs by paying a special bonus to its owner that it counts as a cost.
   a. Counting the bonus as part of the producer surplus, what is the size of the bonus that maximizes producer surplus and that makes the measured rate of return equal to 6 percent as required by the regulation?
   b. How many bottles does Elixir Springs sell?
   c. What is Elixir Springs' producer surplus?
   d. What is the consumer surplus?
   e. Is the regulation in the public interest or in the private interest?

6. Explain the difference between regulation and antitrust law. What types of situations does each apply to? Give an example of the use of each.

CRITICAL THINKING

1. After you have studied *Reading Between the Lines* on pp. 424–425, answer the following questions.
   a. To what charges did Archer Daniels Midland plead guilty?
   b. Why is price fixing a problem? Who gains and who loses?
   c. Why is it likely that the demand for lysine is highly elastic? What effect does the elasticity of demand have on a firm's ability to increase price in a price-fixing agreement?
   d. What is citric acid used for? Is it likely that the demand for citric acid is highly elastic?
   e. Critically evaluate the claim of James E. Burton.
   f. Try to think of some different ways in which price fixing can be prevented. Use economic reasoning to explain why each method you have thought of will work.

2. Why might the Department of Justice be interested in and concerned about the practices of Microsoft?

3. Based on your own observations as a consumer of long-distance telephone services, how do you think deregulation is working in this market? What are the major innovations that have occurred in recent years that have benefited the consumer?

4. Visit the U.S. Department of Justice on the World Wide Web (http://www.usdoj.gov) and go to the page on press releases for February 1997. Read the press release on price fixing by California crab fishermen.
   a. Explain how the price of crabs was fixed.
   b. Explain what the Department of Justice did about the problem.

20

Externalities, the Environment, and Knowledge

We burn huge quantities of fossil fuels—coal, natural gas, and oil—that cause acid rain and possibly global warming. The persistent and large-scale use of chlorofluorocarbons (CFCs) may have caused irreparable damage to the earth's ozone layer, thereby exposing us to additional ultraviolet rays, which increase the incidence of skin cancer. We dump toxic waste into rivers, lakes, and oceans. These environmental issues are simultaneously everybody's problem and nobody's problem. What, if anything, can government do to protect our environment? How can government action help us to take account of the damage that we cause others every time we turn on our heating or air conditioning systems? ◆ Almost every day, we hear about a new discovery—in medicine, engineering, chemistry, physics, or even economics. The advance of knowledge seems boundless. And more and more people are learning more and more of what is already known. The stock of knowledge—what is known and how many people know it—is increasing, apparently without bound. We are getting smarter. But is our stock of knowledge advancing fast enough? Are we spending enough on research and development? Do we spend enough on education? Do enough people remain in school for long enough? Would we be better off if we spent more on research and education? ◆ In this chapter, we study the problems that arise because many of our actions create externalities. They affect other people, for ill or good, in ways that we do not usually take into account when we make our own economic choices. We study two big areas—the environment and the accumulation of knowledge—in which these problems are especially important. Externalities are a major source of *market failure*. When market failure occurs, we must either live with the inefficiency it creates or try to achieve greater efficiency by making some *public choices*. This chapter studies these choices. It begins by looking at external costs that affect the environment.

Greener and Smarter

After studying this chapter, you will be able to:

■ Explain how property rights can sometimes overcome externalities

■ Explain how emission charges, marketable permits, and taxes can be used to achieve efficiency in the face of external costs

■ Explain how subsidies can be used to achieve efficiency in the face of external benefits

■ Explain how scholarships, below-cost tuition, and research grants make the quantity of education and invention more efficient

■ Explain how patents increase efficiency

Economics of the Environment

ENVIRONMENTAL PROBLEMS ARE NOT NEW, AND they are not restricted to rich industrial countries. Preindustrial towns and cities in Europe had severe sewage disposal problems that created cholera epidemics and plagues that killed tens of millions of people. Nor is the desire to find solutions to environmental problems new. The development in the fourteenth century of pure water supplies and of garbage and sewage disposal are examples of early contributions to improving the quality of the environment.

Popular discussions of the environment usually pay little attention to economics. They focus on physical aspects of the environment, not costs and benefits. A common assumption is that if people's actions cause *any* environmental degradation, those actions must cease. In contrast, an economic study of the environment emphasizes costs and benefits. An economist talks about the efficient amount of pollution or environmental damage. This emphasis on costs and benefits does not mean that economists, as citizens, do not share the same goals as others and value a healthy environment. Nor does it mean that economists have the right answers and everyone else has the wrong ones (or vice versa). Economics provides a set of tools and principles that clarify the issues. It does not provide an agreed list of solutions. The starting point for an economic analysis of the environment is the demand for a healthy environment.

The Demand for Environmental Quality

The demand for a clean and healthy environment is greater today than it has ever been. We express our demand for a better environment in several ways. We join organizations that lobby for environmental regulations and policies. We vote for politicians who support the environmental policies that we want to see implemented. (All politicians at least pay lip service to the environment today.) We buy "green" products and avoid hazardous products, even if we pay a bit more to do so. And we pay higher housing costs and commuting costs to live in pleasant neighborhoods.

The demand for a cleaner and healthier environment has grown for two main reasons. First, as our incomes increase, we demand a larger range of goods and services, and one of these "goods" is a high-quality environment. We value clean air, unspoiled natural scenery, and wildlife, and we are willing and able to pay for them.

Second, as our knowledge of the effects of our actions on the environment grows, we are able to take measures that improve the environment. For example, now that we know how sulfur dioxide causes acid rain and how clearing rain forests destroys natural stores of carbon dioxide, we are able, in principle, to design measures that limit these problems.

Let's look at the range of environmental problems that have been identified and the actions that create those problems.

The Sources of Environmental Problems

Environmental problems arise from pollution of the air, water, and land, and these individual sources of pollution interact through the *ecosystem*.

Air Pollution   Figure 20.1(a) shows the five economic activities that create most of our air pollution. It also shows the relative contributions of each activity. More than two thirds of air pollution comes from road transportation and industrial processes. Only one sixth arises from electric power generation.

A common belief is that air pollution is getting worse. On many fronts, as we will see later in this chapter, *global* air pollution *is* getting worse. But air pollution in the United States is getting less severe for most substances. Figure 20.1(b) shows the trends in the concentrations of six air pollutants. While lead has been almost eliminated from our air and sulfur dioxide, carbon monoxide, and suspended particulates have been reduced substantially, levels of other pollutants have remained more stable.

While the facts about the sources and trends in air pollution are not in doubt, there is considerable disagreement in the scientific community about the *effects* of air pollution. The least controversial problem is *acid rain,* which is caused by sulfur dioxide and nitrogen oxide emissions from coal- and oil-fired generators of electric utilities. Acid rain begins with air pollution, and it leads to water pollution and damages vegetation.

More controversial are airborne substances (suspended particulates) such as lead from leaded gasoline. Some scientists believe that in sufficiently large concentrations, these substances (189 of which have

FIGURE 20.1

Air Pollution

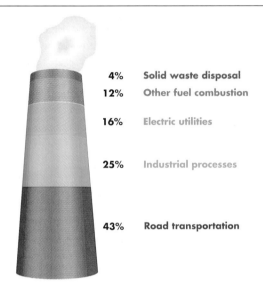

4% Solid waste disposal

12% Other fuel combustion

16% Electric utilities

25% Industrial processes

43% Road transportation

(a) Sources of emission

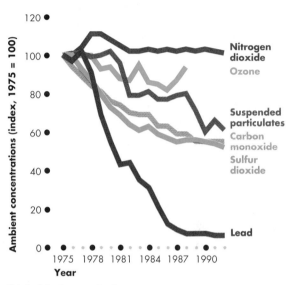

(b) Ambient concentrations

Part (a) shows that road transportation is the largest source of air pollution, followed by industrial processes and electric utilities. Part (b) shows that lead has almost been eliminated from our air and concentrations of carbon monoxide, sulfur dioxide, and suspended particulates have decreased. But nitro-

gen dioxide and ozone have persisted at close to their 1975 levels.

Source: U.S. Environmental Protection Agency, *National Air Quality and Emissions Trends Report,* 1995.

currently been identified) cause cancer and other life-threatening conditions.

Even more controversial is *global warming,* which some scientists believe results from the carbon dioxide emissions of road transportation and electric utilities, methane created by cows and other livestock, nitrous oxide emissions of electric utilities and from fertilizers, and chlorofluorocarbons (CFCs) from refrigeration equipment and (in the past) aerosols. The earth's average temperature has increased over the past 100 years, but most of the increase occurred *before* 1940. Determining what causes changes in the earth's temperature and separating out the effect of carbon dioxide and other factors are proving to be very difficult.

Equally controversial is the problem of *ozone layer depletion.* There is no doubt that a hole in the ozone layer exists over Antarctica and that the ozone layer protects us from cancer-causing ultraviolet rays from the sun. But how our industrial activity influences the ozone layer is simply not understood at this time.

One air pollution problem has almost been eliminated: lead from gasoline. In part, this happened because the cost of living without leaded gasoline, it turns out, is not high. But sulfur dioxide and the so-called greenhouse gases are a much tougher problem to tackle. Their alternatives are costly or have environmental problems of their own. The major sources of these pollutants are road vehicles and electric utilities. Road vehicles can be made "greener" in a variety of ways. One is with new fuels—some alternatives being investigated are alcohol, natural gas, propane and butane, and hydrogen. Another way of making cars and trucks "greener" is to change the chemistry of gasoline. Refiners are working on reformulations of gasoline that cut tailpipe emissions. Similarly, electric power can be generated in cleaner ways by harnessing solar power, tidal power, or geothermal power. Technically possible, these methods are more costly than conventional carbon-fueled generators. Another alternative is nuclear power. This method is good for air pollution but bad for land and water pollution because there is no known safe method of disposing of spent nuclear fuel.

Water Pollution The largest sources of water pollution are the dumping of industrial waste and treated sewage in lakes and rivers and the runoff from fertilizers. A more dramatic source is the accidental spilling of crude oil into the oceans such as the *Exxon Valdez* spill in Alaska in 1989 and an even larger spill in the Russian Arctic in 1994. The most frightening is the dumping of nuclear waste into the ocean by the former Soviet Union.

There are two main alternatives to polluting the waterways and oceans. One is the chemical processing of waste to render it inert or biodegradable. The other, in wide use for nuclear waste, is to use land sites for storage in secure containers.

Land Pollution Land pollution arises from dumping toxic waste products. Ordinary household garbage does not pose a pollution problem unless dumped garbage seeps into the water supply. This possibility increases as less-suitable landfill sites are used. It is estimated that 80 percent of existing landfills will be full by 2010. Some regions (New York, New Jersey, and other East Coast states) and some countries (Japan and the Netherlands) are seeking less costly alternatives to landfill, such as recycling and incineration. Recycling is an apparently attractive alternative, but it requires an investment in new technologies to be effective. Incineration is a high-cost alternative to landfill, and it produces air pollution. These alternatives are not free, and they become efficient only when the cost of using landfill is high.

We've seen that the demand for a high-quality environment has grown, and we've described the range of environmental problems. Let's now look at the ways in which these problems can be handled. We'll begin by looking at property rights and how they relate to environmental externalities.

Absence of Property Rights and Environmental Externalities

Externalities arise because of an *absence* of property rights. **Property rights** are social arrangements that govern the ownership, use, and disposal of factors of production and goods and services. In modern societies, a property right is a legally established title that is enforceable in the courts.

Property rights are absent when externalities arise. No one owns the air, the rivers, and the oceans. So it is no one's private business to ensure that these resources are used in an efficient way. In fact, there is an incentive to use them more than if there were property rights.

Figure 20.2 show an environmental externality in the absence of property rights. A chemical factory upstream from a fishing club must decide how to dispose of its waste.

The factory's marginal benefit curve, *MB*, tells us the benefit to the factory of an additional ton of waste dumped into the river. The *MB* curve is also the firm's demand curve for the use of the river, which is a productive resource. The demand for a resource slopes downward because of the law of diminishing returns (see Chapter 15, pp. 320–321).

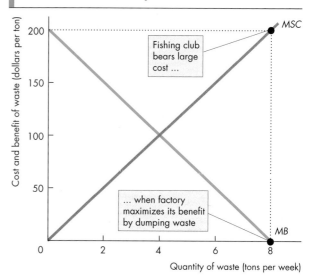

FIGURE 20.2
An Externality

A chemical factory's marginal benefit from dumping its waste into a river is MB, and a fishing club's marginal cost of having waste dumped is MSC. With no property rights, the factory maximizes total benefit by dumping 8 tons a week, the quantity at which the marginal benefit of dumping equals the marginal cost (zero). With this quantity of waste, the fishing club bears a marginal cost of $200 per ton. This outcome is inefficient because marginal social cost exceeds marginal benefit.

Marginal social cost is the marginal cost incurred by the producer of a good—marginal private cost—plus the marginal cost imposed on others—the external cost. The factory bears no cost of dumping. All the costs are borne by the fishing club. The marginal social cost curve, *MSC*, tells us the cost borne by the club when one additional ton of waste is dumped into the river. Marginal cost increases as the quantity dumped increases.

If no one owns the river, the factory dumps the amount of waste that maximizes *its own* total benefit. Its marginal cost is zero (along the *x*-axis), so it dumps 8 tons a week, the quantity that makes marginal benefit zero. The marginal social cost of the waste, which is borne by the fishing club, is $200 a ton. Marginal cost exceeds marginal benefit, so the outcome is inefficient.

Property Rights and the Coase Theorem

Sometimes it is possible to correct an externality by establishing a property right where one does not currently exist. For example, suppose that the chemical factory owns the river. The fishing club must pay the factory for the right to fish in the river. But the price that the club is willing to pay depends on the number and quality of fish, which in turn depend on how much waste the factory dumps in the river. The greater the amount of pollution, the smaller is the amount the fishing club is willing to pay for the right to fish. The chemical factory is now confronted with the cost of its pollution decision. It might still decide to pollute, but if it does, it faces the opportunity cost of its actions—forgone revenue from the fishing club.

Alternatively, suppose that the fishing club owns the river. Now the factory must pay a fee to the fishing club for the right to dump its waste. The more waste it dumps (equivalently, the more fish it kills), the more it must pay. Again, the factory faces an opportunity cost for the pollution it creates.

Does it matter how property rights are assigned? Does it matter whether the polluter or the victim of the pollution owns the resource that might be polluted? At first thought, ownership seems crucial. And until 1960, that is what everyone thought—including economists who had thought about the problem for longer than a few minutes. But in 1960, Ronald Coase had a remarkable insight, now called the Coase theorem. The **Coase theorem** is the proposition

that if property rights exist and transactions costs are low, private transactions are efficient. Equivalently, with property rights and low transactions costs, there are no externalities. All the costs and benefits are taken into account by the transacting parties. So it doesn't matter how the property rights are assigned.

Figure 20.3 illustrates the Coase theorem. As before, the demand curve for dumping waste is the factory's marginal benefit curve, *MB*. This curve tells us what the factory is willing to pay to dump. With property rights in place, the *MSC* curve is the fishing club's supply curve of river use to the firm. It tells us what the club's members must be paid if they are to put up with inferior fishing and supply the firm with a permit to dump.

The efficient level of waste is 4 tons a week. At this level, the club bears a cost of $100 for the last

FIGURE 20.3

The Coase Theorem

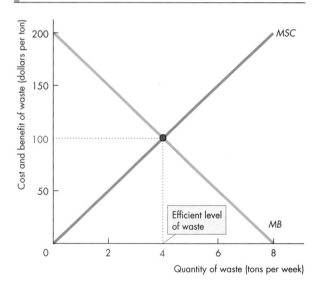

Pollution of a river imposes a marginal social cost, *MSC*, on the victim and provides a marginal benefit, *MB*, to the polluter. The efficient amount of pollution is the quantity that makes marginal benefit equal to marginal social cost—in this example, 4 tons per week. If the polluter owns the river, the victim will pay $400 a week ($100 a ton × 4 tons a week) to the polluter for the assurance that pollution will not exceed 4 tons a week. If the victim owns the river, the polluter will pay $400 for pollution rights to dump 4 tons a week.

ton dumped into the river, and the factory gets a benefit of that amount. If waste disposal is restricted below 4 tons a week, an increase in waste disposal benefits the factory more than it costs the club. The factory can pay the club to put up with more waste disposal, and both the club and the factory can gain. If waste disposal exceeds 4 tons a week, an increase in waste disposal costs the club more than it benefits the factory. The club can now pay the factory to cut its waste disposal, and again, both the club and the factory can gain. Only when the level of waste disposal is 4 tons a week can neither party do any better. This is the efficient level of waste disposal.

The amount of waste disposal is the same regardless of who owns the river. If the factory owns it, the club pays $400 for fishing rights and for an agreement that waste disposal will not exceed 4 tons a week. If the club owns the river, the factory pays $400 for the right to dump 4 tons of waste a week. In both cases, the amount of waste disposal is the efficient amount.

Property rights work if transactions costs are low. The factory and the fishing club can negotiate the deal that produces the efficient outcome. But in many situations, transactions costs are high and property rights cannot be enforced. Imagine the transactions costs if the 50 million people who live in the northeastern part of the United States and Canada tried to negotiate an agreement with the 20,000 factories that emit sulfur dioxide and cause acid rain! In this type of case, governments use alternative methods of coping with externalities. They use:

1. Emission charges
2. Marketable permits
3. Taxes

In the United States, the federal government has established an agency, the Environmental Protection Agency (EPA), to coordinate and administer the nation's environment policies. Let's look at the tools available to the EPA and see how they work.

Emission Charges

Emission charges are a method of using the market to achieve efficiency, even in the face of externalities. The government (or the regulatory agency established by the government) sets the emission charges, which are, in effect, a price per unit of pollution. The more pollution a firm creates, the more it pays in emission

charges. This method of dealing with environmental externalities has been used only modestly in the United States, but it is common in Europe. For example, in France, Germany, and the Netherlands, water polluters pay a waste disposal charge.

To work out the emission charge that achieves efficiency, the regulator must determine the marginal social cost and marginal *social* benefit of pollution. **Marginal social benefit** is the marginal benefit received by the buyer of a good—marginal private benefit—plus the marginal benefit to others—the external benefit. To achieve efficiency, the price per unit of pollution must be set to make the marginal social cost of the pollution equal to its marginal social benefit.

Figure 20.4 illustrates an efficient emissions charge. The marginal benefit of pollution is *MB* and accrues to the polluters—there is no *external* benefit. The marginal social cost of pollution is *MSC* and is

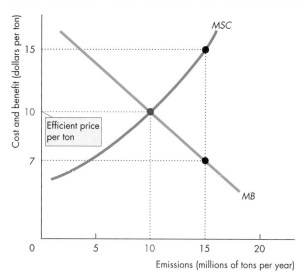

Electric utilities obtain marginal benefits from sulfur dioxide emissions of *MB*, and everyone else bears a marginal social cost of *MSC*. The efficient level of pollution—10 million tons a year in this example—is achieved by imposing an emission charge on the utilities of $10 a ton. If the emission charge is set too low, at $7 a ton, the resulting amount of pollution is greater than the efficient amount—at 15 million tons a year in this example. In this case, the marginal social cost is $15 a ton and it exceeds the marginal benefit of $7 a ton.

entirely an external cost. The efficient level of sulfur dioxide emissions is 10 million tons a year, which is achieved with an emission charge of $10 per ton. At this price, polluters do not find it worthwhile to buy the permission to pollute in excess of 10 million tons a year.

In practice, it is hard to determine the marginal benefit of pollution. And the people who are best informed about the marginal benefit, the polluters, have an incentive to mislead the regulators about the benefit. As a result, if a pollution charge is used, the most likely outcome is for the price to be set too low. For example, in Fig. 20.4, the price might be set at $7 per ton. At this price, polluters find it worthwhile to pay for 15 million tons a year. At this level of pollution, the marginal social cost is $15 a ton, and the amount of pollution exceeds the efficient level.

One way of overcoming excess pollution is to impose a quantitative limit. The most sophisticated way of doing this is with quantitative limits that firms can buy and sell—with marketable permits. Let's look at this alternative.

Marketable Permits

Instead of imposing emission charges on polluters, each potential polluter might be given a pollution limit. To achieve efficiency, marginal benefit and marginal cost must be assessed just as in the case of emission charges. Provided that these benefit-cost calculations are correct, the same efficient outcome can be achieved with quantitative limits as with emission charges. But in the case of quantitative limits, a cap must be set for each polluter. To set these caps at their efficient levels, the marginal benefit of *each* producer must be assessed. If firm *H* has a higher marginal benefit than firm *L*, an efficiency gain can be achieved by decreasing the cap of firm *L* and increasing that of firm *H*. It is virtually impossible to determine the marginal benefits of each firm, so in practice, quantitative restrictions cannot be allocated to each producer in an efficient way.

Marketable permits are a clever way of overcoming the need for the regulator to know every firm's marginal benefit schedule. Each firm can be allocated a permit to emit a certain amount of pollution, and firms may buy and sell such permits. Firms that have low marginal benefits from sulfur dioxide emissions will be willing to sell their permits to other firms that have a high marginal benefit. If the market in permits is competitive, the price at which firms trade permits makes the marginal benefit of pollution equal for all firms. And if the correct number of permits has been allotted, the outcome can be efficient.

The Market for Emissions in the United States
Markets for emission permits have operated in the United States since the Environmental Protection Agency first implemented air quality programs following the passage of the Clean Air Act in 1970.

Trading in lead pollution permits became common during the 1980s, and this marketable permit program has been rated a success. It enabled lead to be virtually eliminated from the atmosphere of the United States (see Figure 20.1b). But this success might not easily translate to other situations because lead pollution has some special features. First, most lead pollution came from a single source, leaded gasoline. Second, lead in gasoline is easily monitored. Third, the objective of the program was clear: eliminate lead in gasoline.

The EPA is now considering using marketable permits to promote efficiency in the control of chlorofluorocarbons, the gases that are believed to damage the ozone layer.

Taxes and External Costs

Taxes can be used to provide incentives for producers or consumers to cut back on an activity that creates external costs. To see how taxes work, consider the market for transportation services.

The costs borne by the producers of transportation services are not the only costs. External costs arise from the airborne particulates and greenhouse gases caused by vehicle emissions. Further, one person's decision to use a highway imposes congestion costs on others. These costs also are external costs. When all the external marginal costs are added to the marginal cost faced by the producer, we obtain the marginal social cost of transportation.

Figure 20.5 shows the market for transportation services. The demand curve, *D*, is also the marginal benefit curve, *MB*. This curve tells us how much consumers value each different quantity of transportation services. The curve *MC* measures the marginal *private* cost of producing transportation services—the costs directly incurred by the producers of these services. The curve *MSC* measures the marginal *social* cost, which sums the external costs and private costs.

FIGURE 20.5

Taxes and Pollution

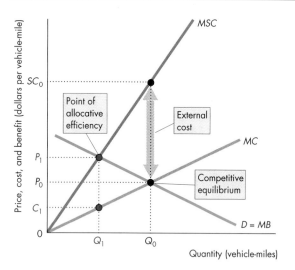

The demand curve for road transportation services is also the marginal benefit curve ($D = MB$). The marginal private cost curve is MC. If the market is unregulated, output is Q_0 vehicle-miles and the price is P_0 per vehicle-mile. Marginal social cost is SC_0 per vehicle-mile. Because of congestion and pollution, the marginal social cost exceeds the marginal private cost. Marginal social cost is shown by curve MSC. If the government imposes a tax so that producers of transportation services must pay the marginal social cost, the MSC curve becomes the relevant marginal cost curve for suppliers' decisions. The price increases to P_1 per vehicle-mile, and the quantity decreases to Q_1 vehicle-miles. Allocative efficiency is achieved.

If the transportation market is competitive and unregulated, the equilibrium will be at the price P_0 and quantity Q_0. Road users will balance their own marginal cost, MC, against their own marginal benefit, MB, and travel Q_0 vehicle-miles at a price (and cost) of P_0 per mile. At this scale of transportation services, the marginal social cost is SC_0. The marginal social cost minus the marginal private cost, $SC_0 - P_0$, is the marginal cost imposed on others—the marginal external cost.

Suppose the government taxes road transportation and that it sets the tax equal to the external marginal cost. By imposing such a tax, the government makes the suppliers of transportation services incur a marginal cost equal to the marginal social cost. That

is, the marginal private cost plus the tax equals the marginal social cost. The market supply curve is now the same as the MSC curve. The price rises to P_1 per vehicle-mile, and at this price, people travel Q_1 vehicle-miles. The marginal cost of the resources used in producing Q_1 vehicle-miles is C_1, and the marginal external cost is P_1 minus C_1. That marginal external cost is paid by the consumer through the tax.

The situation at the price P_1 and the quantity Q_1 is efficient. At a quantity greater than Q_1, marginal social cost exceeds marginal benefit, so net benefit increases by decreasing the quantity of transportation services. At a quantity less than Q_1, marginal benefit exceeds marginal social cost, so net benefit increases by increasing the quantity of transportation services.

A Carbon Fuel Tax? A tax can be imposed on any activity that creates external costs. For example, we could tax *all* air-polluting activities. Because the carbon fuels that we use to power our vehicles and generate our electric power are a major source of pollution, why don't we have a broad-based tax on all activities that burn carbon fuel and set the tax rate high enough to give a large reduction in carbon emissions?

The question becomes even more pressing when we consider not only the current levels of greenhouse gases but also their projected future levels. In 1995, annual carbon emissions worldwide were a staggering 6.8 billion tons. By 2050, with current policies, that annual total is predicted to be 24 billion tons.

Uncertainty About Global Warming Part of the reason we do not have a high, broad-based, carbon fuel tax is that the scientific evidence that carbon emissions produce global warming is not accepted by everyone. Climatologists are uncertain about how carbon emissions translate into atmospheric concentrations—about how the *flow* of emissions translates into a *stock* of pollution. The main uncertainty arises because carbon drains from the atmosphere into the oceans and vegetation at a rate that is not well understood. Climatologists are also uncertain about the connection between carbon concentration and temperature. And economists are uncertain about how a temperature increase translates into economic costs and benefits. Some economists believe that the costs and benefits are almost zero, while others believe that a temperature increase of 5.4 degrees Fahrenheit by 2050 will reduce the total output of goods and services by 20 percent.

Present Cost and Future Benefit   Another factor weighing against a large change in fuel use is that the costs would be borne now, while the benefits, if any, would accrue many years in the future. To compare future benefits with current costs, we must use an interest rate. If the interest rate is 1 percent a year, a dollar today becomes $2.70 in 100 years. If the interest rate is 5 percent a year, a dollar today becomes more than $131.50 in 100 years. So at an interest rate of 1 percent a year, it is worth spending $1 million in 1997 on pollution control to avoid $2.7 million in environmental damage in 2097. At an interest rate of 5 percent a year, it is worth spending $1 million today only if this expenditure avoids $131.5 million in environmental damage in 2097.

Because large uncertain future benefits are needed to justify small current costs, a general tax on carbon fuels is not a high priority on the political agenda.

International Factors   A final factor against a large change in fuel use is the international pattern of the use of carbon fuels. Right now, carbon pollution comes in even doses from the industrial countries and the developing countries. But by 2050, three quarters of the carbon pollution will come from the developing countries (if the trends persist).

One reason for the high pollution rate in some developing countries (notably China, Russia, and other Eastern European countries) is that their governments *subsidize* the use of coal or oil. These subsidies lower producers' marginal costs and encourage the use of fuels. The result is that the quantity of carbon fuels consumed exceeds the efficient quantity—and by a large amount. It is estimated that by 2050, these subsidies will induce annual global carbon emissions of some 10 billion tons—about two fifths of total emissions. If the subsidies were removed, global emissions in 2050 would be 10 billion tons a year less.

A Global Warming Dilemma

With the high output rate of greenhouse gases in the developing world, the United States and the other industrial countries are faced with a global warming dilemma (like the prisoners' dilemma in Chapter 14, pp. 295–296). Decreasing pollution is costly and might bring benefits. But the benefits depend on all countries taking action to limit pollution. If one country acts alone, it bears the cost of limiting pollution and gets almost no benefits. So it is worthwhile

taking steps to limit global pollution only if all nations act together.

Table 20.1 shows the global warming dilemma faced by the United States and the developing countries. The numbers are hypothetical. Each country (we'll call the developing countries a country) has two possible policies: to control carbon emissions or to pollute. If each country pollutes, it receives a zero net return (by assumption), shown in the top left square in the table. If both countries control emissions, each pays the cost and gets the benefit. Its net return is $25 billion, as shown in the bottom right square of the table. If the United States controls emissions but the developing countries do not, the United States alone bears the cost and all countries enjoy a lower level of pollution. In this example, the United States pays $50 billion more than it benefits and the developing countries benefit by $50 billion more than they pay, as shown in the top right corner of the table. Finally, if the developing countries control emissions and the United States does not, the developing countries bear the cost and the United States

TABLE 20.1

A Global Warming Dilemma

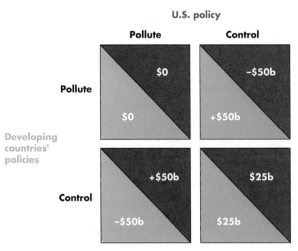

If the United States and developing countries both pollute, the top left square shows their payoffs. If both countries control pollution, the bottom right square shows their payoffs. When one country pollutes and the other one does not, the top right and bottom left squares show their payoffs. The outcome of this game is for both countries to pollute. The structure of this game is the same as that of the prisoners' dilemma.

shares the gains. The developing countries lose $50 billion and the United States gains this amount, as shown in the bottom left corner of the table.

Confronted with these possible payoffs, the United States and the developing countries decide their policies. Each country reasons as follows: If the other country does not control emissions, we break even if we pollute and we lose $50 billion if we control our emissions. Conclusion: Each country is better off individually by polluting. So no one controls emissions, and pollution continues unabated.

Treaties and International Agreements

To break the dilemma, international agreements—treaties—might be negotiated. But such treaties must have incentives for countries to comply with their agreements. Otherwise, even with a treaty, the situation remains as we've just described and illustrated in Table 20.1.

One such international agreement is the *climate convention* that came into effect on March 21, 1994. This convention is an agreement among 60 countries to limit their output of greenhouse gases. But the convention does not have economic teeth. The poorer countries are merely asked to list their sources of greenhouse gases. The rich countries must show how, by 2000, they will return to their 1990 emissions levels.

REVIEW

- When externalities are present, the market allocation is not efficient.
- If an externality can be eliminated by assigning property rights, an efficient allocation can be achieved.
- If the government levies emission charges on firms, imposes pollution limits, or imposes taxes equivalent to marginal external cost, it induces them to produce the efficient quantity of pollution, even in the face of externalities.
- When an externality goes beyond the scope of one country, effective international cooperation is necessary to achieve an efficient outcome.

Economics of Knowledge

KNOWLEDGE, THE THINGS PEOPLE KNOW AND understand, has a profound effect on the economy. The economics of knowledge is an attempt to understand that effect. It is also an attempt to understand the process of knowledge accumulation and the incentives people face to discover, to learn, and to pass on what they know to others. It is an economic analysis of the scientific and engineering processes that lead to the discovery and development of new technologies. And it is a study of the education process of teaching and learning.

You can think of knowledge as being both a consumer good and a factor of production. The demand for knowledge—the willingness to pay to acquire knowledge—depends on the marginal benefit it provides to its possessor. As a consumer good, knowledge provides utility, and this is one source of its marginal benefit. As a factor of production—part of the stock of capital—knowledge increases productivity, and this is another source of its marginal benefit.

Knowledge clearly creates benefits for its possessor. It might also create external benefits. When children learn the basics of reading, writing, and numbers in grade school, they are equipping themselves to be better citizens, better able to communicate and interact with each other. The process continues through high school and college. But when people make decisions about how much schooling to undertake, they undervalue the external benefits that it creates.

External benefits also arise from research and development activities that lead to the creation of new knowledge. Once someone has worked out how to do something, others can copy the basic idea. They do have to work to copy an idea, so they face an opportunity cost. But they do not usually have to pay the person who made the discovery to use it. When Isaac Newton worked out the formulas for calculating the rate of response of one variable to another—calculus—everyone was free to use his method. When a spreadsheet program called VisiCalc was invented, others were free to copy the basic idea. Lotus Corporation developed its 1-2-3 and later Microsoft created Excel, and both became highly successful, but they did not pay for the key idea first used in VisiCalc. When the first shopping mall was built and found to be a successful way of arranging retailing, everyone was free to copy the idea, and malls spread like mushrooms.

When people make decisions about the quantity of education to undertake or the amount of research and development to do, they balance the *private* marginal costs against the private marginal benefits. They undervalue the external benefits. As a result, if we were to leave education and research and development to unregulated market forces, we would get too little of these activities. To deliver them in efficient quantities, we make public choices through governments to modify the market outcome.

Three devices that governments can use to achieve an efficient allocation of resources in the presence of the external benefits from education and research and development are:

- Subsidies
- Below-cost provision
- Patents and copyrights

Subsidies

A **subsidy** is a payment made by the government to producers that depends on the level of output. By subsidizing private activities, government can in principle encourage private decisions to be taken in the public interest. A government subsidy program might alternatively enable private producers to capture resources for themselves. Although subsidies cannot be guaranteed to work successfully, we'll study an example in which they do achieve their desired goal.

Figure 20.6 shows how subsidizing education can increase the amount of education undertaken and achieve allocative efficiency. Suppose that the marginal cost of producing a student-year of college education is a constant $20,000. We'll assume that all these costs are borne by the colleges and that there are no external costs. The marginal social cost is the same as the colleges' marginal cost and is shown by the curve *MC = MSC*. The maximum price that students (or parents) are willing to pay for an additional year of college determines the marginal private benefit curve and the demand curve for education. That curve is *MPB = D*. In this example, a competitive market in private college education results in 20 million students being enrolled in college with tuition at $20,000 a year.

Suppose that the external benefit—the benefit derived by people other than those who receive the education—results in marginal social benefits described by the curve *MSB*. Allocative efficiency occurs when

marginal social cost equals marginal social benefit. In the example in Fig. 20.6, this equality occurs when 40 million students are enrolled in college. One way of getting 40 million students in college is to subsidize private colleges. In the example, a subsidy of $15,000 per student per year paid to the colleges does the job. With a subsidy of $15,000 and a marginal cost of $20,000, colleges earn an economic profit if the annual tuition exceeds $5,000. Competition among the colleges would drive the tuition down to $5,000, and at this price, 40 million students would enroll in college. So a subsidy can achieve an efficient outcome.

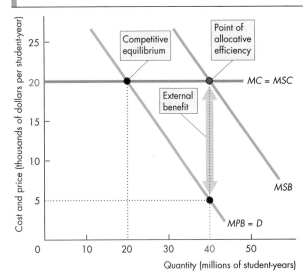

FIGURE 20.6

The Efficient Quantity of Education

The demand curve for education measures the marginal private benefit of education (*MPB = D*). The curve *MC* shows the marginal cost of education—in this example, $20,000 per student-year. If education is provided in a competitive market, tuition is $20,000 a year and 20 million students enroll. Education produces an external benefit, and adding the external benefit to the marginal private benefit gives marginal social benefit, *MSB*. Education has no external costs, so *MC* is also the marginal social cost of education, *MSC*. Allocative efficiency is achieved if the government provides education services to 40 million students a year, which is achieved by either subsidizing private colleges or providing education below cost in public colleges. In this example, students pay an annual tuition of $5,000 and the government pays a subsidy of $15,000.

The lessons in this example can be applied to stimulating the rate of increase in the stock of knowledge—research and development. By subsidizing these activities, the government can move the allocation of resources toward a more efficient outcome. The mechanism that the government uses for this purpose is a research and development grant. In 1997, through the National Science Foundation, the government made research and development grants to universities and federally funded research and development centers of more than $2.5 billion.

Another way to achieve an efficient amount of education or research and development is through public provision below cost.

Below-Cost Provision

Instead of subsidizing private colleges, the government can establish its own colleges (public colleges) that provide schooling below cost. And instead of subsidizing research and development in industry and the universities, the government can establish its own research facilities and make discoveries available to others. Let's see how this approach works by returning to the example in Fig. 20.6.

By establishing public colleges with places for 40 million students, the government can supply the efficient quantity of college education. To ensure that this number of places is taken up, the public colleges would charge a tuition, in this example, of $5,000 a student per year. The government provides this tuition below its marginal cost of $20,000 a student per year. At this price, the number of people who choose to attend college makes the marginal social benefit of education equal to its marginal social cost.

We've now looked at two examples of how government action can help market participants take account of the external benefits deriving from education to achieve an outcome different from that of a private unregulated market. In reality, governments use both methods of encouraging an efficient quantity of education. They subsidize private colleges and universities, and they run their own institutions and sell their services at below cost. But in education, the public sector is by far the larger. In research and development, subsidies to the private sector are far larger than the government direct provision.

Patents and Copyrights

Knowledge may well be the only factor of production that does not display *diminishing marginal productivity*.

More knowledge (about the right things) makes people more productive. And there seems to be no tendency for the additional productivity from additional knowledge to diminish.

For example, in just 15 years, advances in knowledge about microprocessors have given us a sequence of processor chips that has made our personal computers increasingly powerful. Each advance in knowledge about how to design and manufacture a processor chip has brought apparently ever-larger increments in performance and productivity. Similarly, each advance in knowledge about how to design and build an airplane has brought apparently ever larger increments in performance: Orville and Wilbur Wright's "Flyer 1" was a one-seat plane that could hop a farmer's field. The Lockheed Constellation was an airplane that could fly 120 passengers from New York to London, but with two refueling stops in Newfoundland and Ireland. The latest version of the Boeing 747 can carry 400 people nonstop from Los Angeles to Sydney or New York to Tokyo (flights of 7,500 miles that take 13 1/2 hours). Similar examples can be found again and again in fields as diverse as agriculture, biogenetics, communications, engineering, entertainment, medicine, and publishing.

A key reason why the stock of knowledge increases without diminishing returns is the sheer number of different techniques that can in principle be tried. Paul Romer explains this fact with an amazing example. Suppose, says Romer,

> that to make a finished good, 20 different parts have to be attached to a frame, one at a time. A worker could proceed in numerical order, attaching part one first, then part two. ... Or the worker could proceed in some other order, starting with part 10, then adding part seven. ... With 20 parts, a standard (but incredible) calculation shows that there are about 10^{18} different sequences one can use for assembling the final good. This number is larger than the total number of seconds that have elapsed since the big bang created the universe, so we can be confident that in all activities, only a very small fraction of the possible sequences have ever been tried.[1]

---

[1]From Paul Romer, "Ideas and Things," in *The Future Surveyed*, supplement to *The Economist*, 11 September, 1993, pp. 71–72. © 1993 The Economist Newspaper Group, Inc. Reprinted with permission. Further reproduction prohibited. The "standard calculation" that Romer refers to is the number of ways of selecting

Think about all the processes, all the products, and all the different bits and pieces that go into each, and you can see that we have only begun to scratch around the edges of what is possible.

Because knowledge is productive and creates external benefits, it is necessary to use public policies to ensure that those who develop new ideas face incentives that encourage an efficient level of effort. The main way of creating the right incentives is to provide the creators of knowledge with property rights in their discoveries—called **intellectual property rights**. The legal device for creating intellectual property rights is the patent or copyright. A **patent** or **copyright** is a government-sanctioned exclusive right granted to the inventor of a good, service, or productive process to produce, use, and sell the invention for a given number of years. A patent enables the developer of a new idea to prevent, for a limited number of years, others from benefiting freely from an invention. But to obtain the protection of the law, an inventor must make knowledge of the invention public.

Although patents encourage invention and innovation, they do so at an economic cost. While a patent is in place, its holder is a monopolist. And monopoly is another type of market failure. To maximize profit, a monopoly (patent holder) produces the quantity at which marginal cost equals marginal revenue. The monopoly sets the price above marginal cost and equal to the highest price at which the profit-maximizing quantity can be sold. In this situation, consumers value the good more highly (are willing to pay more for one more unit of it) than its marginal cost. So the quantity of the good available is less than the efficient quantity.

But without a patent, the effort to develop new goods, services, or processes is diminished and the flow of new inventions is slowed. So the efficient outcome is a compromise that balances the benefits of more inventions against the cost of temporary monopoly power in newly invented activities.

---

and arranging in order 20 objects from 20 objects—also called the number of permutations of 20 objects 20 at a time. This number is *factorial* 20, or 20! = 20 × 19 × 18 × ... × 2 × 1 = $10^{18.4}$. A standard theory (challenged by observations made by the Hubbel space telescope in 1994) is that a big bang started the universe 15 billion years, or $10^{17.7}$ seconds, ago. Although $10^{18.4}$ and $10^{17.7}$ look similar, $10^{18.4}$ is *five* times as large as $10^{17.7}$, so if you started trying alternative sequences at the moment of the big bang and took only one second per trial, you would still have tried only one fifth of the possibilities. Amazing?

REVIEW

- Knowledge is a consumer good and a factor of production that creates external benefits.

- External benefits arise both from education—passing on existing knowledge to others—and from research and development—creating new knowledge.

- Three devices used by governments to achieve an efficient stock of knowledge are subsidies, below-cost provision, and patents and copyrights.

- Subsidies or below-cost provision can deliver an efficient amount of education.

- Knowledge does not seem to have diminishing returns, so incentives must exist to encourage the development of new ideas.

- Patents and copyrights can stimulate research, but they create a temporary monopoly, so the gain from more knowledge must be balanced against the loss from monopoly.

◆ *Reading Between the Lines* on pages 442–443 looks at the challenge to intellectual property rights presented by digital information technologies. As you study this problem, try to reflect on all the topics you've learned about in your study of *microeconomics*. You've learned how all economic problems arise from scarcity, that scarcity forces choices, and that choice implies cost—opportunity cost. Prices (*relative prices*) are opportunity costs and are determined by the interactions of buyers and sellers in markets. People choose what to buy and what resources to sell to maximize utility. Firms choose what to sell and what resources to buy to maximize profit. People and firms interact in markets. But the resulting equilibrium might be inefficient and might be viewed as creating too much inequality. By providing public goods, redistributing income, curbing monopoly power, and coping with externalities, public choice modifies the market outcome.

The next chapter studies some problems for the market economy that arise from uncertainty and incomplete information. But unlike the cases we've studied here, the market does a good job of coping with these problems, as you're about to discover.

Policy
WATCH

Protecting Intellectual Property Rights

THE NEW YORK TIMES, DECEMBER 2, 1996

160 Nations to Weigh Revisions of International Copyright Laws

By PETER H. LEWIS

Copyright laws are under technological siege. Intended to insure both a financial return to those who create everything from poetry to computer software and reasonable public access to such material, the current laws may be unequal to the task.

Copies of the latest Madonna song, a computer spreadsheet or a telephone directory can all be duplicated and distributed on the Internet at the click of a computer mouse, often with little regard for the legal rights of the owners of their copyrights.

Now, for the first time in the age of the personal computer and the Internet, copyright experts from 160 countries are gathering in Switzerland today to begin to write new international treaties protecting intellectual property in the digital age. ...

Delegates to the World Intellectual Property Organization diplomatic conference in Geneva, ... hope to agree on one or more global pacts to update copyright laws for an era in which anything that can be copyrighted can be digitized, and anything that can be digitized can be distributed almost instantly around the world.

The United States ... delegation, led by Bruce Lehman, the Commissioner of Patents and Trademarks, will offer three proposals to protect literary and artistic works, music recordings and data bases from unauthorized use. ...

Supporters of the American proposals say ... that changes in international copyright law are needed to halt the growing international trend to pirate billions of dollars worth of intellectual property. Without stronger protections, they argue, there will be no incentive to develop new material to sate the appetite of the emerging global information infrastructure. ...

"The central premise of the Administration is that creators of intellectual property will be wary of the electronic marketplace unless the law gives them protection, but I would differ," said Richard B. Hovey, director of the Digital Equipment Corporation's corporate technology and strategy group.

Mr. Hovey said his company and others are already developing hardware and software methods for preventing unauthorized duplication, transmission or playback of copyrighted materials, including not just text and graphics, but also video, audio and multimedia. ...

Essence of **THE STORY**

■ Copyright laws, which are intended to give a financial return to creators, authors, and inventors, are difficult to enforce in the digital information age.

■ Music, literary works, and other material can be duplicated and distributed on the Internet.

■ Changes in international copyright law are required to stop growing international pirating of billions of dollars worth of intellectual property.

■ Without stronger protection, there will be no incentive to develop new material.

■ Copyright experts from 160 countries gathered in Switzerland to write new international treaties that protect intellectual property.

■ Digital Equipment Corporation is trying to use new technologies to create tools that prevent unauthorized duplication and that protect inventors and authors without a change in the law.

Economic

A N A L Y S I S

■ A copyright gives the inventor of a good, service, or productive process the exclusive right to produce, use, and sell the invention for a given number of years.

■ During the life of the copyright, the inventor is a monopolist.

■ Figure 1 shows what happens when copyright law is violated. It uses the example of a recording of a Madonna song. The demand for a copy of the song is shown by the demand curve, D.

■ The marginal cost of making one more copy of the Madonna song is constant and is shown by the marginal cost curve MC.

■ If people freely copy the Madonna song, the marginal cost curve becomes the supply curve in a competitive market.

■ The number of copies made is Q_C, and the price is P_C, which equals marginal cost.

■ This outcome appears to be efficient. Marginal cost equals marginal benefit, and the gains from trade are maximized.

■ But this outcome is not efficient. In fact, it is not

even feasible because Madonna has no incentive to record her songs. Without Madonna, there is nothing to copy. The quantity is zero, and the consumer surplus is zero.

■ An enforced copyright law can improve on this situation. Figure 2 shows you how. Again, the demand curve is D, and the marginal cost curve is MC.

■ By being granted a copyright on her song, Madonna becomes a monopolist. Madonna's marginal revenue curve is MR, and she maximizes profit by authorizing Q_{CR} copies to be made, which sell for P_{CR}.

■ The market appears to be inefficient because a deadweight loss, the gray area in Fig. 2, is created.

■ This deadweight loss is unavoidable. But in the long run, it disappears when the life of the copyright ends and the market becomes competitive.

■ The blue area in Fig. 2 shows Madonna's economic profit during the life of her copyright. It is this gain that encourages her to sing and create material that is worth copying.

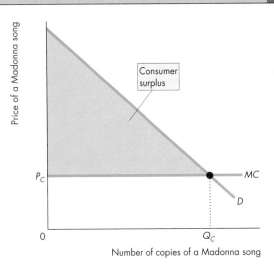

Figure 1 When copyright law is violated

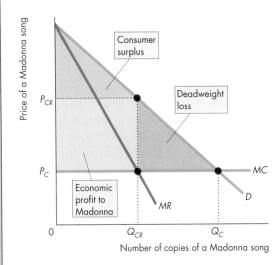

Figure 2 How a copyright works

You're

THE VOTER

■ How would you write the copyright law?

■ How many years' protection would you give the inventor or creator of a new good or service such as a Madonna song?

■ How would you suggest that violators of copyright law be penalized? Use economic reasoning and the concept of efficiency to develop your answers.

443

SUMMARY

Key Points

Economics of the Environment (pp. 430–438)

- Popular discussion of the environment frames the debate in terms of right and wrong, but economists emphasize costs and benefits and a need to find a way to balance the two.

- The demand for environmental policies has grown because incomes and awareness of the connection between actions and the environment have grown.

- Air pollution arises from road transportation, electric utilities, and industrial processes. In the United States, the trends in most types of air pollution are downward.

- Externalities (environmental and others) arise when property rights are absent. Sometimes it is possible to overcome an externality by assigning a property right.

- The Coase theorem states that if property rights exist and transactions costs are low, private transactions are efficient—there are no externalities. In this case, the same efficient amount of pollution is achieved regardless of *who* has the property right—the polluter or the victim.

- When property rights cannot be assigned, governments might overcome environmental externalities by using emission charges, marketable permits, or taxes.

- Marketable permits were used successfully to virtually eliminate lead from our air.

- Global externalities, such as greenhouse gases and substances that deplete the earth's ozone layer, can be overcome only by international action. Each country acting alone has insufficient incentive to act in the interest of the world as a whole. But there is a great deal of scientific uncertainty and disagreement about the effects of greenhouse gases and ozone depletion, and in the face of this uncertainty, international resolve to act is weak.

- The world is locked in a type of prisoners' dilemma game, in which it is in every country's self-interest to let other countries carry the costs of environmental policies.

Economics of Knowledge (pp. 438–441)

- Knowledge is both a consumer good and a factor of production that creates external benefits.

- External benefits from education—passing on existing knowledge to others—arise because the basic reading, writing, and number skills equip people to interact and communicate more effectively.

- External benefits from research and development—creating and applying new knowledge—arise because once someone has worked out how to do something, others can copy the basic idea.

- To enable the efficient amount of education and innovation to take place, we make public choices through governments to modify the market outcome.

- Three devices are available to governments: subsidies, below-cost provision, and patents and copyrights.

- Subsidies to private schools or the provision of public education below cost can achieve an efficient provision of education.

- Patents and copyrights create intellectual property rights and increase the incentive to innovate. But they do so by creating a temporary monopoly, the cost of which must be balanced against the benefit of more inventive activity.

Key Figures

Key Terms

QUESTIONS

1. What are externalities? Give some examples of positive and negative externalities.
2. Why is an external cost a problem?
3. Why does the existence of external costs and external benefits lead to market failure?
4. How can external benefits pose an economic problem?
5. Describe the sources of air pollution and how they have changed since 1975.
6. Why has the demand for a better environment increased?
7. Describe the various types of pollution and identify their sources.
8. What are the main economic activities that cause air pollution?
9. What do property rights have to do with externalities?
10. State the Coase theorem. Under what conditions does the Coase theorem apply?
11. Explain why property rights assigned to either the polluter or the victim of pollution give an efficient amount of pollution if transactions costs are low.
12. What is an emission charge and how does it work?
13. What is a marketable pollution permit and how does it work?
14. How might a tax be used to overcome an external cost?
15. What are the pros and cons of a high, broad-based carbon tax and why don't we have such a tax?
16. Explain how the Environmental Protection Agency regulates the quality of air in the United States.
17. Which countries have high pollution rates?
18. Why do some countries have high pollution rates?
19. Is the efficient rate of pollution zero? Explain your answer.
20. What is the global warming dilemma?
21. What are the externalities problems posed by knowledge?
22. Why do we have free schooling?
23. What is a patent and how does it work?

PROBLEMS

1. A trout farmer and a pesticide maker are located next to each other on the side of a lake. The pesticide maker can dispose of waste by dumping it into the lake or by trucking it to a safe land storage place. The marginal cost of trucking is a constant $100 a ton. The trout farmer's total cost depends on how much waste the pesticide maker dumps into the lake and is as follows:

Quantity of waste (tons per week)	Trout farmer's total cost (dollars per week)
0	0
1	50
2	125
3	225
4	350
5	500
6	675
7	875

  a. What is the efficient amount of waste to be dumped into the lake?
  b. If the trout farmer owns the lake, how much waste will be dumped and how much will the pesticide maker pay to the farmer for each ton dumped?
  c. If the pesticide maker owns the lake, how much waste will be dumped and how much will the farmer pay to the factory to rent space on the lake?

2. Using the information given in problem 1, suppose that no one owns the lake and that the government introduces a pollution tax.
  a. What is the tax per ton of waste dumped that will achieve an efficient outcome?
  b. Explain the connection between the answer to this problem and the answer to problem 1.

3. Using the information given in problem 1, suppose that no one owns the lake and that the government issues marketable pollution permits to both the farmer and the factory. Each may dump the same amount of waste in the lake, and the total that may be dumped is the efficient amount.

a. What is the quantity that may be dumped into the lake?

b. What is the market price of a permit? Who buys and who sells?

c. What is the connection between the answer to this problem and the answers to problems 1 and 2?

4. The marginal cost of educating a student is $4,000 a year and is constant. The figure shows the marginal private benefit curve.

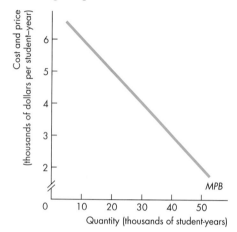

a. With no government involvement and if the schools are competitive, how many students are enrolled and what is the tuition?

b. The external benefit from education is $2,000 per student year and is constant. If the government provides the efficient amount of education, how many school places does it offer and what is the tuition?

CRITICAL THINKING

1. After you have studied *Reading Between the Lines* on pp. 442–443, answer the following questions:

   a. Do copyright laws create an efficient or an inefficient outcome?

   b. What are the pros and cons of a long copyright period?

   c. How could a further technological advance that makes unauthorized copying impossible change copyright law? Who would need protecting from whom in this situation?

2. Since its foundation 25 years ago, Greenpeace has fought for a cleaner and safer environment. What impact has Greenpeace had on the environment? Has pollution been eliminated? If not, why not?

3. To decrease the amount of overfishing in New Zealand waters, the New Zealand government has introduced private property rights with an allocation of Individual Transferable Quotas (ITQs). To check out the effects of this system, visit the Web site of the Fraser Institute at http://www.fraserinstitute.ca and read the article "ITQs in New Zealand: Bureaucratic Management Versus Private Property. The Score After Ten Years."

   a. Would the introduction of ITQs in the United States help to replenish U.S. fish stocks?

   b. Explain why ITQs give an incentive to not overfish.

   c. Who would oppose ITQs and why?

4. President Clinton wants stronger tax incentives to encourage more people to go to college and to remain in college longer. What are the economic arguments in favor of such a change in incentives? What are the arguments against it? Where do you come out on this issue and why?

http://hepg.awl.com/parkin/econ100

21

Uncertainty and Information

Life is like a lottery. You work hard in school, but what will the payoff be? Will you get an interesting, high-paying job or a miserable, low-paying one? You set up a small summer business and work hard at it. But will you make enough income to keep you in school next year or will you get wiped out? How do people make a decision when they don't know its consequences? ◆ As you drive across an intersection on a green light, you see a car on your left that's still moving. Will it stop or will it run the red light? You buy insurance against such a risk, and insurance companies gain from your business. Why are we willing to buy insurance at prices that leave insurance companies with a gain? ◆ Buying a new car—or a used car—is fun, but it's also scary. You could get stuck with a lemon. And cars are not unique. Just about every complicated product you buy could be defective. How do car dealers and retailers induce us to buy what might turn out to be a lemon? ◆ People keep some of their wealth in the bank, some in mutual funds, some in bonds, and some in stocks. Some of these ways of holding wealth have a high return, and some have a low return. Why don't people put all their wealth in the place that has the highest return? Why does it pay to diversify? ◆ In this chapter, we answer questions such as these. In doing so, we will extend and enrich the models of markets that we studied in earlier chapters. We'll begin by explaining how people make decisions when they're uncertain about the consequences. We'll see how it pays to buy insurance, even if its price leaves the insurance company with a profit. We'll explain why we use scarce resources to generate and disseminate information. And we'll look at transactions in a variety of markets in which uncertainty and the cost of acquiring information play important roles. ◆ A recurring theme of economics is that markets help people to use their scarce resources efficiently. Uncertainty and incomplete information are possible reasons why markets might fail to achieve efficiency. But markets do an amazing job of coping with these problems.

Lotteries and Lemons

After studying this chapter, you will be able to:

- Explain how people make decisions when they are uncertain about the consequences

- Explain why people buy insurance and how insurance companies make a profit

- Explain why buyers search and sellers advertise

- Explain how markets cope with private information

- Explain how people use financial markets to lower risk

Uncertainty and Risk

ALTHOUGH WE LIVE IN AN UNCERTAIN WORLD, we rarely ask what uncertainty is. Yet to explain how we make decisions and do business with each other in an uncertain world, we need to think more deeply about uncertainty. What exactly is uncertainty? We also live in a risky world. Is risk the same as uncertainty? Let's begin by defining uncertainty and risk and distinguishing between them.

Uncertainty is a situation in which more than one event may occur but we don't know which one. For example, when farmers plant their crops, they are uncertain about the weather during the growing season.

In ordinary speech, risk is the probability of incurring a loss (or some other misfortune). In economics, **risk** is a situation in which more than one outcome may occur and the *probability* of each possible outcome can be estimated. A *probability* is a number between 0 and 1 that measures the chance of some possible event occurring. A 0 probability means the event will not happen. A probability of 1 means the event will occur for sure—with certainty. A probability of 0.5 means that the event is just as likely to occur as not. An example is the probability of a tossed coin falling heads. In a large number of tosses, about half of them will be heads and the other half tails.

Sometimes, probabilities can be measured. For example, the probability that a tossed coin will come down heads is based on the fact that in a large number of tosses, half are heads and half are tails; the probability that an automobile in Chicago in 1998 will be involved in an accident can be estimated by using police and insurance records of previous accidents; the probability that you will win a lottery can be estimated by dividing the number of tickets you have bought by the total number of tickets bought.

Some situations cannot be described by using probabilities based on past observed events. These situations may be unique events, such as the introduction of a new product. How much will sell and at what price? Because the product is new, there is no previous experience on which to base a probability. But the questions can be answered by looking at past experience with *similar* new products, supported by some judgments. Such judgments are called *subjective probabilities*.

Regardless of whether the probability of some event occurring is based on actual data or judgments—or even guesses—we can use probability to study the way in which people make decisions in the face of uncertainty. The first step in doing this is to describe how people assess the cost of risk.

Measuring the Cost of Risk

Some people are more willing to bear risk than others, but almost everyone prefers less risk to more, other things remaining the same. We measure people's attitudes toward risk by using their utility of wealth schedules and curves. The **utility of wealth** is the amount of utility a person attaches to a given amount of wealth. The greater a person's wealth, other things remaining the same, the higher is the person's total utility. Greater wealth brings higher total utility, but as wealth increases, each additional unit of wealth increases total utility by a smaller amount. That is, the *marginal utility of wealth diminishes*.

Figure 21.1 sets out Tania's utility of wealth schedule and curve. Each point *a* through *e* on Tania's utility of wealth curve corresponds to the row of the table identified by the same letter. You can see that as her wealth increases, so does her total utility of wealth. You can also see that her marginal utility of wealth diminishes. When wealth increases from $3,000 to $6,000, total utility increases by 20 units, but when wealth increases by a further $3,000 to $9,000, total utility increases by only 10 units.

We can use Tania's utility of wealth curve to measure her cost of risk. Let's see how Tania evaluates two summer jobs that involve different amounts of risk.

One job, working as a painter, pays enough for her to save $5,000 by the end of the summer. There is no uncertainty about the income from this job and hence no risk. If Tania takes this job, by the end of the summer her wealth will be $5,000. The other job, working as a telemarketer selling subscriptions to a magazine, is risky. If she takes this job, her wealth at the end of the summer depends entirely on her success at selling. She might be a good salesperson or a poor one. A good salesperson makes $9,000 in a summer, and a poor one makes $3,000. Tania has never tried telemarketing, so she doesn't know how successful she'll be. She assumes she has an equal chance—a probability of 0.5—of making either $3,000 or $9,000. Which outcome does Tania

FIGURE **21.1**
The Utility of Wealth

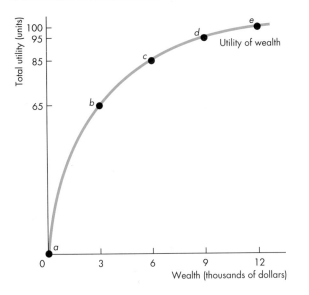

	Wealth (thousands of dollars)	Total utility (units)	Marginal utility (units)
a	0	0	
			65
b	3	65	
			20
c	6	85	
			10
d	9	95	
			5
e	12	100	

The table shows Tania's utility of wealth schedule, and the figure shows her utility of wealth curve. Utility increases as wealth increases, but the marginal utility of wealth diminishes.

prefer, $5,000 for sure from the painting job or a 50 percent chance of either $3,000 or $9,000 from the telemarketing job?

When there is uncertainty, people do not know the *actual* utility they will get from taking a particular action. But it is possible to calculate the utility they *expect* to get. **Expected utility** is the average utility arising from all possible outcomes. So, to choose her summer job, Tania calculates the expected utility from each job. Figure 21.2 shows how she does this.

FIGURE **21.2**
Choice Under Uncertainty

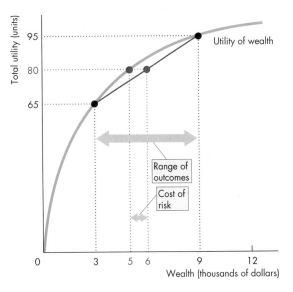

If Tania's wealth is $5,000 and she faces no risk, her utility is 80 units. If she faces an equal probability of having $9,000 with a utility of 95 or $3,000 with a utility of 65, her expected wealth is $6,000. But her expected utility is 80 units—the same as with $5,000 and no uncertainty. Tania is indifferent between these two alternatives. Tania's extra $1,000 of expected wealth is just enough to offset her extra risk.

If Tania takes the painting job, she has $5,000 of wealth and 80 units of utility. There is no uncertainty, so her expected utility equals her actual utility—80 units. But suppose she takes the telemarketing job. If she makes $9,000, her utility is 95 units, and if she makes $3,000, her utility is 65 units. Tania's *expected income* is the average of these two outcomes and is $6,000—($9,000 × 0.5) + ($3,000 × 0.5). This average is called a *weighted average*, the weights being the probabilities of each outcome (both 0.5 in this case). Tania's *expected utility* is the average of these two possible total utilities and is 80 units—(95 × 0.5) + (65 × 0.5).

Tania chooses the job that maximizes her expected utility. In this case, the two alternatives give the same expected utility—80 units—so she is indifferent between them. She is equally likely to take either job. The difference between Tania's expected wealth of $6,000 from the risky job and $5,000 from the no-risk job—$1,000—is just large enough to off-set the additional risk that Tania faces.

The calculations that we've just done enable us to measure Tania's cost of risk. The cost of risk is the amount by which expected wealth must be increased to give the same utility as a no-risk situation. In Tania's case, the cost of the risk arising from an uncertain income of $3,000 or $9,000 is $1,000.

If the amount Tania can make from painting remains at $5,000 and the expected income from telemarketing also remains constant while its range of uncertainty increases, Tania will take the painting job. To see this conclusion, suppose that good tele-marketers make $12,000 and poor ones make nothing. The average income from telemarketing is unchanged at $6,000, but the range of uncertainty has increased. The table in Fig. 21.1 shows that Tania gets 100 units of utility from a wealth of $12,000 and zero units of utility from a wealth of zero. Thus in this case, Tania's expected utility from telemarketing is 50 units—$(100 \times 0.5) + (0 \times 0.5)$. Because the expected utility from telemarketing is now less than that from painting, she chooses painting.

Risk Aversion and Risk Neutrality

There is a huge difference between Bill Parcells, coach of the New York Jets, who favors a cautious running game and Jim Kelly, former quarterback of the Buffalo Bills, who favored a risky passing game. They have different attitudes toward risk. Bill is more *risk averse* than is Jim. Tania is also *risk averse*. The shape of the utility of wealth curve tells us about the attitude toward risk—about the person's degree of *risk aversion*. The more rapidly a person's marginal utility of wealth diminishes, the more risk-averse that person is. You can see this fact best by considering the case of *risk neutrality*. A risk-neutral person cares only about *expected wealth* and doesn't mind how much uncertainty there is.

Figure 21.3 shows the utility of wealth curve of a risk-neutral person. It is a straight line, and the marginal utility of wealth is constant. If this person has an expected wealth of $6,000, expected utility is 50 units regardless of the range of uncertainty around that average. An equal probability of having $3,000 or $9,000 gives the same expected utility as a certain $6,000. When Tania's risk increased to this range, she needed an extra $1,000. This person does not. Even if the range of risk becomes $0 to $12,000, the risk-neutral person still gets the same expected utility as a certain $6,000 gives. Most real people are risk averse,

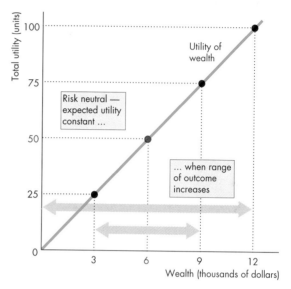

FIGURE 21.3
Risk Neutrality

People's dislike of risk implies a diminishing marginal utility of wealth. A (hypothetical) risk-neutral person has a linear utility of wealth curve and a constant marginal utility of wealth. For a risk-neutral person, expected utility does not depend on the range of uncertainty, and the cost of risk is zero.

and their utility of wealth curves look like Tania's. But the case of risk neutrality illustrates the importance and the consequences of the shape of the utility of wealth curve for a person's degree of risk aversion.

REVIEW

- Faced with uncertain outcomes, people take the actions that maximize expected utility.
- The cost of risk can be measured as the amount by which expected wealth must be increased to give the same expected utility as in a no-risk situation.
- The cost of risk depends on the degree of *risk aversion*. The greater the degree of risk aversion, the greater is the cost of risk.
- For a *risk-neutral* person, risk is costless.

Most people are risk averse. Let's now see how insurance enables them to reduce the risk they face.

Insurance

ONE WAY OF REDUCING THE RISK WE FACE IS TO buy insurance. How does insurance reduce risk? Why do people buy insurance? And what determines the amount we spend on insurance? Before we answer these questions, let's look at the insurance industry in the United States today.

Insurance Industry in the United States

We spend close to 15 percent of our income, on the average, on private insurance. That's as much as we spend on housing and more than we spend on cars and food. In addition, we buy insurance through our taxes in the form of social security and unemployment insurance. When we buy private insurance, we enter into an agreement with an insurance company to pay an agreed price—called a *premium*—in exchange for benefits to be paid to us if some specified event occurs. The three main types of insurance we buy are:

■ Life insurance

■ Health insurance

■ Property and casualty insurance

Life Insurance Life insurance reduces the risk of financial loss in the event of death. Almost 80 percent of households in the United States have life insurance, and the average amount of coverage is $110,000 per household. More than 2,400 companies supply life insurance, and the total premiums paid in a year are more than $450 billion. As you can see in Fig. 21.4, life insurance has been the greatest source of private insurance business in recent years.

Health Insurance Health insurance reduces the risk of financial loss in the event of illness. It can provide funds to cover both lost earnings and the cost of medical care. Private health insurance is growing rapidly and is profitable. Figure 21.4 shows that it is almost as large as life insurance.

Property and Casualty Insurance Property and casualty insurance reduces the risk of financial loss in the event of an accident involving damage to persons or property. It includes auto insurance—its biggest component—workers' compensation; fire, earthquake, and professional malpractice insurance;

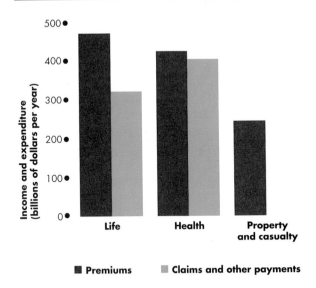

FIGURE 21.4

The Insurance Industry

■ Premiums   ■ Claims and other payments

Total expenditure on private insurance is more than a trillion dollars a year. Most is spent on life insurance and health insurance.

Source: U.S. Bureau of the Census, *Statistical Abstract of the United States 1995*, 115th edition (Washington, D.C., 1995), Tables 150, 840, 841, and 843–845 and the author's assumptions and calculations.

and a host of smaller items. Figure 21.4 shows that we spend almost $250 billion a year on these types of insurance.

How Insurance Works

Insurance works by pooling risks. It is possible and profitable because people are risk averse. The probability of any one person having a serious auto accident is small, but the cost of an accident to the person involved is enormous. For a large population, the probability of one person having an accident is the proportion of the population that does have an accident. Because this probability can be estimated, the total cost of accidents can be predicted. An insurance company can pool the risks of a large population and share the costs. It does so by collecting premiums from everyone and paying out benefits to those who suffer a loss. If the insurance company does its calculations correctly, it collects at least as much in premiums as it pays out in benefits and operating costs.

To see why people buy insurance and why it is profitable, let's consider an example. Dan has the utility of wealth curve shown in Fig. 21.5. He owns a car worth $10,000, and that is his only wealth. If there is no risk of his having an accident, his utility will be 100 units. But there is a 10 percent chance (a probability of 0.1) that he will have an accident within a year. Suppose Dan does not buy insurance. If he does have an accident, his car is worthless, and with no insurance, he has no wealth and no utility. Because the probability of an accident is 0.1, the probability of *not* having an accident is 0.9. Dan's expected wealth, therefore, is $9,000 ($10,000 × 0.9 + $0 × 0.1), and his expected utility is 90 units (100 × 0.9 + 0 × 0.1).

Given his utility of wealth curve, Dan has 90 units of utility if his wealth is $7,000 and he faces no uncertainty. That is, Dan's utility of a guaranteed wealth of $7,000 is the same as his utility of a 90 percent chance of having wealth of $10,000 and a 10 percent chance of having nothing. If the cost of an insurance policy that pays out in the event of an accident is less than $3,000 ($10,000 – $7,000), Dan will buy the policy. Thus Dan has a demand for auto insurance at premiums less than $3,000.

Suppose there are lots of people like Dan, each with a $10,000 car and each with a 10 percent chance of having an accident within the year. If an insurance company agrees to pay each person who has an accident $10,000, the company will pay out $10,000 to one tenth of the population, or an average of $1,000 per person. This amount is the insurance company's minimum premium for such insurance. It is less than the value of insurance to Dan because Dan is risk averse. He is willing to pay something to reduce the risk he faces.

Now suppose that the insurance company's operating expenses are a further $1,000 and that it offers insurance for $2,000. The company now covers all its costs—the amounts paid out to policyholders for their losses plus the company's operating expenses. Dan—and all the other people like him—will maximize their utility by buying this insurance.

FIGURE 21.5
The Gains from Insurance

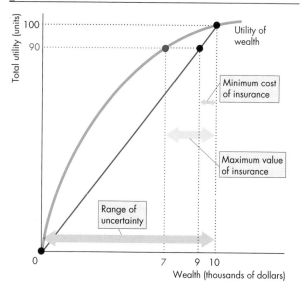

Dan has a car valued at $10,000 that gives him a utility of 100 units, but there is a 0.1 probability that he will have an accident, making his car worthless (wealth and utility equal to zero). With no insurance, his expected wealth is $7,000 and his expected utility is 90 units. He is willing to pay up to $3,000 for insurance. An insurance company (with no operating expenses) can offer insurance to Dan and the rest of the community for $1,000. Hence there is a potential gain from insurance for both Dan and the insurance company.

REVIEW

- Americans spend 15 percent of their income, on the average, on life, health, and property and casualty insurance.
- Insurance works by pooling risks. Every insured person pays in, but only those who suffer a loss are compensated.
- Insurance is worth buying and is profitable because people are risk averse and are willing to pay for lower risk.

Much of the uncertainty we face arises from ignorance. We just don't know all the things we could benefit from knowing. But knowledge or information is not free. And government intervention is of little use in dealing with this problem. Governments usually are even less well informed than buyers and sellers. Faced with incomplete information, we must make decisions about how much information to acquire. Let's now study the choices we make about obtaining information and how markets cope with incomplete information.

Information

WE SPEND A HUGE QUANTITY OF OUR SCARCE resources on economic information. **Economic information** includes data on the prices, quantities, and qualities of goods and services and resources.

In the models of perfect competition, monopoly, and monopolistic competition, information is free. Everyone has all the information he or she needs. Households are completely informed about the prices of the goods and services they buy and the factors of production they sell. Similarly, firms are completely informed about consumers' preferences and about the prices and products of other firms.

In contrast, information is scarce in the real world. If it were not, we wouldn't need *The Wall Street Journal* and CNN. And we wouldn't need to shop around for bargains or spend time looking for a job. The opportunity cost of economic information—the cost of acquiring information on prices, quantities, and qualities of goods and services and resources—is called **information cost**.

The fact that many economic models ignore information costs does not make these models useless. They give us insights into the forces generating trends in prices and quantities over periods long enough for information limits not to be important. But to understand how markets work hour by hour and day by day, we must take information problems into account. Let's look at some of the consequences of information cost.

Searching for Price Information

When many firms sell the same good or service, there is a range of prices and buyers want to find the lowest price. But searching takes time and is costly. So buyers must balance the expected gain from further search against the cost of further search. To perform this balancing act, buyers use a decision rule called the *optimal-search rule*—or *optimal-stopping rule*. The optimal-search rule is:

- Search for a lower price until the expected marginal benefit of additional search equals the marginal cost of search.
- When the expected marginal benefit from additional search is less than or equal to the marginal cost, stop searching and buy.

To implement the optimal-search rule, each buyer chooses her or his own reservation price. The buyer's **reservation price** is the highest price that the buyer is willing to pay for a good. The buyer will continue to search for a lower price if the lowest price so far found exceeds the reservation price but will stop searching and buy if the lowest price found is less than or equal to the reservation price. At the buyer's reservation price, the expected marginal benefit of search equals the marginal cost of search.

Figure 21.6 illustrates the optimal-search rule. Suppose you've decided to buy a used Mazda Miata. Your marginal cost of search is $\$C$ per dealer visited and is shown by the horizontal orange line in the figure. This cost includes the value of your time, which is the amount that you could have earned by working instead of cruising around used car lots, and the amount spent on transportation and advice. Your expected marginal benefit of visiting one more dealer

FIGURE 21.6
Optimal-Search Rule

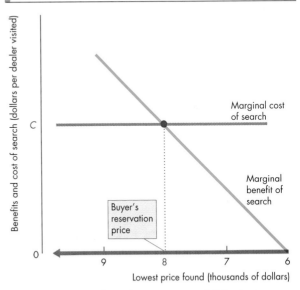

The marginal cost of search is constant at $\$C$. As the lowest price found (measured from right to left on the horizontal axis) declines, the expected marginal benefit of further search diminishes. The lowest price found at which the marginal cost equals the expected marginal benefit is the reservation price. The optimal-search rule is to search until the reservation price is found and then buy at that lowest found price.

depends on the lowest price that you've found. The lower the price you've already found, the lower is your expected marginal benefit of visiting one more dealer, as shown by the blue curve in the figure.

The price at which expected marginal benefit equals marginal cost is your reservation price—$8,000 in the figure. If you find a price equal to or below your reservation price, you stop searching and buy. If you find a price that exceeds your reservation price, you continue to search for a lower price. Individual shoppers differ in their marginal cost of search and so have different reservation prices. As a result, identical items can be found selling for a range of prices.

A Real Car Shopping Trip   Real car shoppers are confronted with a much bigger problem than the one we've just studied. There are many more dimensions of the car they are looking for than its price. They could spend almost forever gathering information about the alternatives. But at some point in their search, they decide they've done enough looking and make a decision to buy. Your imaginary shopping trip to buy a used Mazda Miata rationalizes their decision. Real shoppers think, "The benefits I expect from further search are insufficient to make it worth going on with the process." They don't do the calculations we've just done—at least, not explicitly—but their actions can be explained by those calculations. But buyers are not alone in creating information. Sellers do a lot of it too—in the form of advertising. Let's see what the effects of advertising are.

Advertising

Advertising constantly surrounds us—on television, radio, and billboards and in newspapers and magazines—and costs billions of dollars. How do firms decide how much to spend on advertising? Does advertising create information, or does it just persuade us to buy things we don't really want? What does it do to prices?

Advertising for Profit Maximization   A firm's advertising decision is part of its overall profit-maximization strategy. Firms in perfect competition don't advertise because everyone has all the information there is. But firms selling differentiated products in monopolistic competition and firms locked in the struggle of survival in oligopoly advertise a lot.

The amount of advertising undertaken by firms in monopolistic competition is such that the marginal revenue product of advertising equals its marginal cost. The amount of advertising undertaken by firms in oligopoly is determined by the game they are playing. If that game is a *prisoners' dilemma*, they might spend amounts that lower their combined profits, but they can't avoid advertising without being wiped out by other firms in the industry.

Persuasion or Information   Much advertising is designed to persuade us that the product being advertised is the best in its class. For example, the Pepsi advertisement tells us that Pepsi is really better than Coke. The Coca-Cola advertisement tells us that Coke is really better than Pepsi. But advertising also informs. It provides information about the quality and price of a good or service.

Does advertising mainly persuade or mainly inform? The answer varies for different goods and different types of markets. Goods whose quality can be assessed *before* they are bought are called *search goods*. Typically, the advertising of search goods mainly informs—gives information about price, quality, and location of suppliers. Examples of such goods are gasoline, basic foods, and household goods. Goods whose quality can be assessed only *after* they are bought are called *experience goods*. Typically, the advertising of experience goods mainly persuades—encourages the consumer to buy now and make a judgment later about quality, based on experience with the good. Examples of such goods are cigarettes, alcoholic beverages, and perfume.

Because most advertising involves experience goods, it is likely that advertising is more often persuasive rather than merely informative. But persuasive advertising doesn't necessarily harm the consumer. It might result in lower prices.

Advertising and Prices   Does advertising increase the price of the good advertised? Your immediate response is "Of course it does!" But this conclusion is not always correct. Advertising can lower prices for two different reasons. First, *informative advertising* can lower prices because it increases competition by telling potential buyers about alternative sources of supply. Second, if advertising enables firms to increase their output and reap economies of scale, it is possible that the price of the good will be lower with advertising than without it, provided that there is sufficient competition to prevent firms from restricting output.

REVIEW

- Information on the prices, quantities, and qualities of goods and services and factors of production—economic information—is scarce, and people economize on its use.

- Buyers searching for price information stop when they find a price at or below their reservation price, the price that makes the expected marginal benefit of search equal the marginal cost of search.

- Sellers advertise to inform potential buyers of the good or to persuade them to buy it.

- Advertising can increase competition and may raise or lower the price of the advertised good.

Private Information

SO FAR WE HAVE LOOKED AT SITUATIONS IN which information is available to everyone and can be obtained with an expenditure of resources. But not all situations are like this. For example, someone might have private information. **Private information** is information that is available to one person but too costly for anyone else to obtain.

Private information affects many economic transactions. One is your knowledge about your driving. You know much more than your auto insurance company does about how carefully and defensively you drive. Another is your knowledge about your work effort. You know far more than your employer about how hard you work. Yet another is your knowledge about the quality of your car. You know whether it's a lemon. But the person to whom you are about to sell it does not and can't find out until after he or she has purchased it from you.

Private information creates two problems:

1. Moral hazard
2. Adverse selection

Moral hazard exists when one of the parties to an agreement has an incentive *after the agreement is made* to act in a manner that brings additional benefits to himself or herself at the expense of the other party. Moral hazard arises because it is too costly for the injured party to monitor the actions of the advantaged party. For example, Jackie hires Mitch as a salesperson and pays him a fixed wage regardless of

his sales. Mitch faces a moral hazard. He has an incentive to put in the least possible effort, benefiting himself and lowering Jackie's profits. For this reason, salespeople are usually paid by a formula that makes their income higher the greater is the volume (or value) of their sales.

Adverse selection is the tendency for people to enter into agreements in which they can use their private information to their own advantage and to the disadvantage of the less informed party. For example, if Jackie offers salespeople a fixed wage, she will attract lazy salespeople. Hardworking salespeople will prefer *not* to work for Jackie because they can earn more by working for someone who pays by results. The fixed-wage contract adversely selects those with private information (knowledge about their work habits) who can use that knowledge to their own advantage and to the disadvantage of the other party.

A variety of devices have evolved that enable markets to function in the face of moral hazard and adverse selection. We've just seen one, the use of incentive payments for salespeople. Let's look at some more and also see how moral hazard and adverse selection influence three real-world markets:

- The market for used cars
- The market for loans
- The market for insurance

The Market for Used Cars

When a person buys a car, it might turn out to be a lemon. If the car is a lemon, it is worth less to the buyer and to everyone else than if it has no defects. Does the used car market have two prices reflecting these two values—a low price for lemons and a higher price for cars without defects? It does not. To see why, let's look at a used car market, first with no dealer warranties and second with warranties.

Used Cars Without Warranties To make the points as clearly as possible, we'll make some extreme assumptions. There are just two kinds of cars: lemons and those without defects. A lemon is worth $1,000 both to its current owner and to anyone who buys it. A car without defects is worth $5,000 to its current and potential future owners. Whether a car is a lemon is private information that is available only to the current owner. Buyers of used cars can't tell whether they are buying a lemon until *after* they have bought the car and learned as much about it as its current owner knows. There are no dealer warranties.

Because buyers can't tell the difference between a lemon and a good car, they are willing to pay only one price for a used car. What is that price? Are they willing to pay $5,000, the value of a good car? They are not, because there is at least some probability that they are buying a lemon worth only $1,000. If buyers are not willing to pay $5,000 for a used car, are the owners of good cars willing to sell? They are not, because a good car is worth $5,000 to them, so they hang onto their cars. Only the owners of lemons are willing to sell—as long as the price is $1,000 or higher. But, reason the buyers, if only the owners of lemons are selling, all the used cars available are lemons, so the maximum price worth paying is $1,000. Thus the market for used cars is a market for lemons, and the price is $1,000.

Moral hazard exists in the car market because sellers have an incentive to claim that lemons are good cars. But, given the assumptions in the above description of the car market, no one believes such claims. Adverse selection exists, resulting in only lemons actually being traded. The market for used cars is not working well. Good used cars just don't get bought and sold, but people want to be able to buy and sell good used cars. How can they do so? The answer is by introducing warranties into the market.

Used Cars with Warranties   Buyers of used cars can't tell a lemon from a good car, but car dealers sometimes can. For example, they might have regularly serviced the car. They know, therefore, whether they are buying a lemon or a good car and can offer $1,000 for lemons and $5,000 for good cars.[1] But how can they convince buyers that it is worth paying $5,000 for what might be a lemon? The answer is by giving a guarantee in the form of a warranty. The dealer *signals* which cars are good ones and which are lemons. A **signal** is an action taken outside a market that conveys information that can be used by that market. There are many examples of signals, one of which is students' grades. Your grade acts as a *signal* to potential employers.

In the case of the used cars, dealers take actions in the market for car repairs that can be used by the market for cars. For each good car sold, the dealer gives a warranty. The dealer agrees to pay the costs of repairing the car if it turns out to have a defect. Cars with a warranty are good; cars without a warranty are lemons.

Why do buyers believe the signal? It is because the cost of sending a false signal is high. A dealer who gives a warranty on a lemon ends up paying the high cost of repairs—and risks gaining a bad reputation. A dealer who gives a warranty only on good cars has no repair costs and a reputation that gets better and better. It pays to send an accurate signal. It is rational, therefore, for buyers to believe the signal. Warranties break the lemon problem and enable the used car market to function with two prices, one for lemons and one for good cars.

The Market for Loans

The market for bank loans is one in which private information plays a crucial role. Let's see how.

The quantity of loans demanded by borrowers depends on the interest rate. The lower the interest rate, the greater is the quantity of loans demanded—the demand curve for loans is downward-sloping. The supply of loans by banks and other lenders depends on the cost of lending. This cost has two parts. One is interest, and this interest cost is determined in the market for bank deposits—the market in which the banks borrow the funds that they lend. The other part of the cost of lending is the cost of bad loans—loans that are not repaid—called the default cost. The interest cost of a loan is the same for all borrowers. The default cost of a loan depends on the quality of the borrower.

Suppose that borrowers fall into two classes: low-risk and high-risk. Low-risk borrowers seldom default on their debts and then only for reasons beyond their control. For example, a firm might borrow to finance a project that fails and be unable to repay the bank. High-risk borrowers take high risks with the money they borrow and frequently default on their loans. For example, a firm might borrow to speculate in high-risk mineral prospecting that has a very small chance of paying off.

If banks can separate borrowers into risk categories, they supply loans to low-risk borrowers at one interest rate and to high-risk borrowers at another, higher interest rate. Real banks do this as much as possible. But they cannot always separate their borrowers. They have no sure way of knowing whether they are lending to a low-risk or a high-risk borrower.

---

[1] In this example, to keep the numbers simple, we'll ignore dealers' profit margins and other costs of doing business and suppose that dealers buy cars for the same price as they sell them. The principles are the same with dealers' profit margins.

So the banks charge the same interest rate to both low-risk and high-risk borrowers. If they offered loans to everyone at the low-risk interest rate, borrowers would face moral hazard and the banks would attract a lot of high-risk borrowers—adverse selection. Most borrowers would default, and the banks would incur economic losses. If the banks offered loans to everyone at the high-risk interest rate, most low-risk borrowers, with whom the banks would like to do profitable business, would be unwilling to borrow.

Faced with moral hazard and adverse selection, banks use *signals* to discriminate between borrowers, and they *ration* or limit loans to amounts below the amounts demanded. To restrict the amounts they are willing to lend to borrowers, banks use signals such as length of time in a job, ownership of a home, marital status, age, and business record.

Figure 21.7 shows how the market for loans works in the face of moral hazard and adverse selection. The demand for loans is D, and the supply is S. The supply curve is horizontal—perfectly elastic supply—because it is assumed that banks have access to a large quantity of funds that have a constant marginal cost of r. With no loan limits, the interest rate is r and the quantity of loans is Q. Because of moral hazard and adverse selection, the banks set loan limits based on signals and restrict the total loans to L. At the interest rate r, there is an excess demand for loans. A bank cannot increase its profit by making more loans because it can't identify the type of borrower taking the loans. Because the signals used mean that more high-risk borrowers are unsatisfied than low-risk borrowers, it is likely that additional loans will be biased toward high-risk (and high-cost) borrowers.

The Market for Insurance

People who buy insurance face a moral hazard problem, and insurance companies face an adverse selection problem. The moral hazard problem is that a person with insurance coverage for a loss has less incentive than an uninsured person to avoid such a loss. For example, a business with fire insurance has less incentive to take precautions against fire, such as installing a fire alarm or sprinkler system, than a business with no fire insurance does. The adverse selection problem is that people who face greater risks are more likely to buy insurance. For example, a person with a family history of serious illness is more likely to buy health insurance than is a person with a family history of good health.

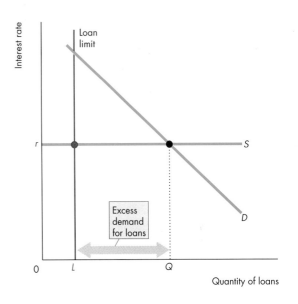

FIGURE 21.7
The Market for Loans

If a bank supplied loans on demand at the going interest rate r, the quantity of loans would be Q, but most of the loans would be taken by high-risk borrowers. Banks use signals to distinguish between low-risk and high-risk borrowers, and they limit the total loans to L and ration them. Banks have no incentive to increase interest rates and increase the quantity of loans because the additional loans would be to high-risk borrowers.

Insurance companies have an incentive to find ways around the moral hazard and adverse selection problems. By doing so, they can lower premiums and increase the amount of business they do. Real-world insurance markets have developed a variety of devices for overcoming or at least moderating these private information problems. Let's see how signals work in markets for insurance by looking at the example of auto insurance.

One of the clearest signals a person can give an auto insurance company is her or his driving record. Suppose that Dan is a good driver and rarely has an accident. If he can demonstrate to the insurance company that his driving record is impeccable over a long enough period, then the insurance company will recognize him as a good driver. Dan will work hard at establishing a reputation as a good driver because he will be able to get his insurance at a lower price.

If all drivers, good and bad alike, can establish good records, then simply having a good record will not convey any information. For the signal to be informative, it must be difficult for bad drivers to fake low risk by having a good record. The signals used in car insurance are the "no-claim" bonuses that drivers accumulate when they do not make an insurance claim.

Another device that insurance companies use is the deductible. A deductible is the amount of a loss that the insured person agrees to bear. For example, most auto insurance policies have the insured person paying the first few hundred dollars worth of damage. The premium varies with the deductible, and the decrease in the premium is more than proportionate to the increase in the deductible. By offering insurance with full coverage—no deductible—on terms that are attractive only to the highest-risk people and by offering coverage with a deductible on more favorable terms that are attractive to other people, insurance companies can do profitable business with everyone. High-risk people choose policies with low deductibles and high premiums; low-risk people choose policies with high deductibles and low premiums.

R E V I E W

- Private information creates moral hazard and adverse selection.
- In markets for cars, loans, and insurance, methods such as warranties, loan limits, and no-claim bonuses and deductibles have been devised to limit the problems caused by private information.

Managing Risk in Financial Markets

RISK IS A DOMINANT FEATURE OF MARKETS FOR stocks and bonds—indeed for any asset whose price fluctuates. One thing people do to cope with risky asset prices is diversify their asset holdings.

Diversification to Lower Risk

The idea that diversification lowers risk is very natural. It is just an application of not putting all one's eggs into the same basket. How exactly does diversification reduce risk? The best way to answer this question is to consider an example.

Suppose there are two risky projects that you can undertake. Each involves investing $100,000. The two projects are independent of each other, but they both promise the same degree of risk and return.

On each project, you will either make $50,000 or lose $25,000, and the chance that either of these will happen is 50 percent. The expected return on each project is ($50,000 × 0.5) + (–$25,000 × 0.5), which is $12,500. But because the two projects are completely independent, the outcome of one project in no way influences the outcome of the other.

Undiversified Suppose you risk everything, investing the $100,000 in either Project 1 or Project 2. You will either make $50,000 or lose $25,000. Because the probability of each of these outcomes is 50 percent, your expected return is the average of these two outcomes—an expected return of $12,500. But in this case in which only one project is chosen, there is no chance that you will actually make a return of $12,500.

Diversified Suppose instead that you diversify by putting 50 percent of your money into Project 1 and 50 percent into Project 2. (Someone else is putting up the other money in these two projects.) Because the two projects are independent, you now have *four* possible returns:

1. Lose $12,500 on each project, and your return is –$25,000.
2. Make $25,000 on Project 1 and lose $12,500 on Project 2, and your return is $12,500.
3. Lose $12,500 on Project 1 and make $25,000 on Project 2, and your return is $12,500.
4. Make $25,000 on each project, and your return is $50,000.

Each of these four possible outcomes is equally probable—each has a 25 percent chance of occurring. You have lowered the chance that you will earn $50,000, but you have also lowered the chance that you will lose $25,000. And you have increased the chance that you will actually make your expected return of $12,500. By diversifying your portfolio of assets, you have reduced its riskiness while maintaining an expected return of $12,500.

If you are risk averse—if your utility of wealth curve looks like Tania's, which you studied earlier in this chapter—you'll prefer the diversified portfolio to the one that is not diversified. That is, your *expected utility* with a diversified set of assets is greater.

A common way to diversify is to buy stocks in different corporations. Let's look at the market in which these stocks are traded.

The Stock Market

The prices of the stocks are determined by demand and supply. But demand and supply in the stock market is dominated by one thing: the expected future price. If the price of a stock today is higher than the expected price tomorrow, people will sell the stock today. If the price of a stock today is less than its expected price tomorrow, people will buy the stock today. As a result of such trading, today's price equals tomorrow's expected price, and so today's price embodies all the relevant information that is available about the stock. A market in which the actual price embodies all currently available relevant information is called an **efficient market**.

In an efficient market, it is impossible to forecast changes in price. Why? If your forecast is that the price is going to rise tomorrow, you will buy now. Your action of buying today is an increase in demand today and increases *today's* price. It's true that your action—the action of a single trader—is not going to make much difference to a huge market like the New York Stock Exchange. But if traders in general expect a higher price tomorrow and they all act today on the basis of that expectation, then today's price will rise. It will keep on rising until it reaches the expected future price, because only at that price do traders see no profit in buying more stock today.

There is an apparent paradox about efficient markets. Markets are efficient because people try to make a profit. They seek a profit by buying at a low price and selling at a high price. But the very act of buying and selling to make a profit means that the market price moves to equal its expected future value. When it has done that, no one, not even those who are seeking to profit, can *predictably* make a profit. Every profit opportunity seen by traders leads to an action that produces a price change that removes the profit opportunity for others. Even the probability of an intergalactic attack on New York City is taken into account in determining stock market prices—see the cartoon.

"Drat! I suppose the market has already discounted this, too."

Drawing by Lorenz; © 1986 The New Yorker Magazine, Inc.

Thus an efficient market has two features:

1. Its price equals the expected future price and embodies all the available information.
2. No forecastable profit opportunities are available.

The key thing to understand about an efficient market such as the stock market is that if something can be anticipated, it will be, and the anticipation of a future event will affect the *current* price of a stock.

Volatility in Stock Prices If the price of a stock equals its expected future price, why is the stock market so volatile? It is volatile because expectations are volatile. They depend on the information available. As new information becomes available, stock traders form new expectations about the future state of the economy and, in turn, new expectations of future stock prices. New information comes randomly, so prices change randomly.

◆ We've seen how people cope with uncertainty and how markets work when there are information problems. *Reading Between the Lines* on pages 460–461 looks one more time at the problem of picking a portfolio and at differences of opinion about how to go about this task.

The next part of this book studies *macroeconomics*. It builds on what you learned in Chapter 3 about production possibilities and shows how economic growth expands these possibilities. It also studies fluctuations in production, employment, and prices.

A Tradeoff Between Risk and Return

The Wall Street Journal, May 31, 1996

Risk Aversion as a Behavioral Problem

BY JAMES S. HIRSCH

CAMBRIDGE, Mass.—Why do smart investors make dumb decisions? Because they are human beings—prisoners of passion who are bound to make irrational choices.

So say a bunch of behavior experts who gathered here recently for a two-day conference at the Harvard Faculty Club. ... 50 money managers and academics plunged into "behavioral economics," the study of how people deal with money and finance.

We're not too rational, was the general conclusion. Budgets and balance sheets play secondary roles in our investment decisions. ...

... [S]ome money managers who attended the conference ... were bargain-hunting "value" investors, contrarian spirits who argue that stocks should be purchased when they're cheap ... .

The forum's embrace of this value investing ... flows from a central tenet of behavioral economics. According to this view, most investors are dazzled by sexy names or shiny products, and they incorrectly believe that past growth rates will predict future performance. They shun old maids but, in doing so, leave behind a lot of Cinderellas.

It's a recipe for safety—and mediocrity—says Christopher Browne, a partner at Tweedy, Browne Co. in New York. ...

Richard Thaler, professor of economics at the University of Chicago, said that since 1926 the average inflation-adjusted return on stocks has been about 7%, while the average for Treasury bills has been about 1%. But several studies show that investors lack faith in stocks. In a survey between 1991 and 1995, Greenwich Associates, a research firm in Greenwich, Conn., found that 1,592 corporate and public pension funds and endowments had about 53% of their money in stocks. The rest went for bonds, guaranteed investment contracts and other low-yielding assets. "A policy for cowards," Prof. Thaler said. ...

Essence of THE STORY

■ Since 1926, the average inflation-adjusted return on stocks has been about 7 percent, while the average for Treasury bills has been about 1 percent.

■ Between 1991 and 1995 (according to a survey), corporate and public pension funds held 53 percent of their money in stocks and the remaining 47 percent in low-yielding safer investments.

■ Some investors say that stocks should be bought only when they are cheap.

■ Other investors say that the stocks to buy are those with a proven track record of growth.

Economic

A N A L Y S I S

■ Figure 1 shows a risky investment strategy. The investor's utility of wealth curve shows that this investor is risk averse.

■ The investor has wealth of W_0. If this wealth is held in cash, the investor faces no risk and gets no return. Total utility is U_0.

■ The risky investment strategy is to buy low-priced, bargain stocks that have no proven track record.

■ The best possible outcome is a big return that generates wealth of W_1. If this outcome occurs, the investor has a total utility of U_1.

■ But the worst outcome is that these stocks become worthless. In this case, the investor has zero wealth and zero utility (at the origin of Fig. 1).

■ Suppose these two outcomes are the only possible ones and that they are equally likely. Then the investor has a 50 percent chance of doubling her wealth and a 50 percent chance of being wiped out. Expected utility is the average of the utilities in each case and is U_x.

■ Figure 2 shows a cautious investment strategy.

Instead of buying risky stocks, the investor buys some stocks with "proven track records" along with some safe Treasury bills.

■ The best possible outcome is a modest return that generates wealth of W_2. If this outcome occurs, the investor has a total utility of U_2.

■ But the worst outcome is that this portfolio earns nothing. It does not become worthless though. In this case, the investor has the same wealth and utility that she started out with, W_0 and U_0.

■ Again, suppose these two outcomes are the only possible ones and that they are equally likely. Expected utility is the average of the utilities in each case and is U_x in Fig. 2.

■ In Fig. 1, expected utility U_x is less than the original utility U_0, so the investor expects to be worse off if she buys the risky portfolio. In Fig. 2, expected utility U_x is greater than the original utility U_0, so the investor expects to be better off if she buys the cautious portfolio.

■ Although the potential gain with bargain stocks is greater than the potential

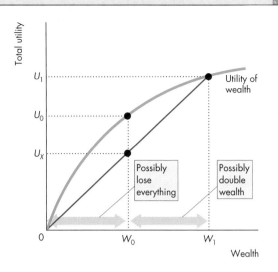

Figure 1 Risky strategy

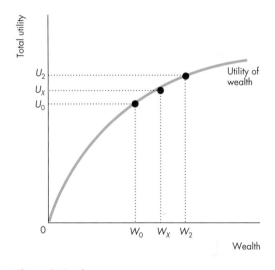

Figure 2 Cautious strategy

gain of a portfolio that combines safer stocks and bonds, the risk-averse investor prefers the safer portfolio.

■ Richard Thaler notes that historically, the return on stocks has been greater than that on bonds and Treasury bills.

■ This observation is correct over long periods, but not over short periods.

■ An investor who is concerned about risk and returns over a short period might rationally buy lower-return bonds. Such behavior might be described as "a recipe for safety and mediocrity" or a "policy for cowards," but it cannot be described as being irrational.

SUMMARY

Key Points

Uncertainty and Risk (pp. 448–450)

■ Uncertainty is a situation in which more than one event may occur but we don't know which one.

■ Risk is uncertainty with probabilities attached to outcomes.

■ A person's attitude toward risk, called the degree of risk aversion, is described by a utility of wealth schedule and curve.

■ Faced with uncertainty, people choose the action that maximizes expected utility.

Insurance (pp. 451–452)

■ We spend 15 percent of our income on insurance to reduce the risk we face.

■ The three main types of insurance are life, health, and property and casualty.

■ By pooling risks, insurance companies can reduce the risks people face (from insured activities) at a lower cost than the value placed on the lower risk.

Information (pp. 453–455)

■ Buyers search for the least-cost source of supply and stop when the expected marginal benefit of search equals the marginal cost of search.

■ The price at which the search stops is less than or equal to the buyer's reservation price.

■ Advertising provides information, and it might increase prices or decrease them.

■ Advertising can lower prices because it increases competition or extends economies of scale.

Private Information (pp. 455–458)

■ Private information is one person's knowledge that is too costly for anyone else to discover.

■ Private information creates the problems of moral hazard (the use of private information to the advantage of the informed and the disadvantage

of the uninformed) and adverse selection (the tendency for people to enter into agreements in which they can use their private information to their own advantage and to the disadvantage of the less informed party).

■ Devices that enable markets to function in the face of moral hazard and adverse selection are incentive payments, guarantees such as warranties, rationing, and signals.

Managing Risk in Financial Markets (pp. 458–459)

■ Risk can be reduced by diversifying asset holdings, thereby combining the returns on projects that are independent of each other.

■ A common way to diversify is to buy stocks in different corporations. Stock prices are determined by the expected future price of the stock.

■ Expectations about future stock prices are based on all the information that is available and regarded as relevant.

■ A market in which the price equals the expected price is an efficient market.

Key Figures

Key Terms

QUESTIONS

1. Distinguish between uncertainty and risk.

2. How do we measure a person's attitude toward risk? How do these attitudes vary from one person to another?

3. What is a risk-neutral person and what does such a person's utility of wealth curve look like?

4. What is risk aversion and how could you tell which of two people are the more risk averse by looking at their utility of wealth curves?

5. Why do people buy insurance and why do insurance companies make a profit?

6. Why is information valuable?

7. What determines the amount of searching you do for a bargain?

8. Why do firms advertise?

9. Does advertising always increase prices? Why might it lower them?

10. What are moral hazard and adverse selection and how do they influence the way markets for loans and insurance work?

11. What is a lemon and how does the lemon problem arise?

12. Explain how the used car market works.

13. Why do firms give guarantees such as warranties?

14. Why do banks limit the amounts they are willing to lend?

15. How do deductibles make insurance more efficient and enable insurance companies to discriminate between high-risk and low-risk customers?

16. What is diversification?

17. What is the most common way of diversifying assets?

18. How does diversification lower risk?

19. How is a stock price determined and what role does the expected future price play?

20. What is an efficient market? What types of markets are efficient?

PROBLEMS

1. The figure shows Lee's utility of wealth curve.

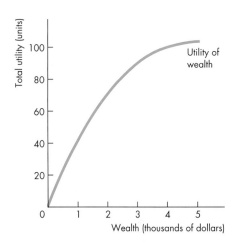

Lee is offered a job as a salesperson in which there is a 50 percent chance she will make $4,000 a month and a 50 percent chance she will make nothing.

a. What is Lee's expected income from taking this job?

b. What is Lee's expected utility from taking this job?

c. How much (approximately) would another firm have to offer Lee with certainty to persuade her not to take the risky sales job?

2. The figure shows Colleen's utility of wealth curve.

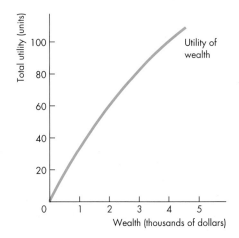

Colleen is offered the same kind of sales job as Lee in problem 1—a 50 percent chance of making $4,000 a month and a 50 percent chance of making nothing.
  a. What is Colleen's expected income from taking this job?
  b. What is Colleen's expected utility from taking this job?
  c. Explain who is more likely to be willing to take this risky job, Lee or Colleen.

3. Jimmy and Zenda have the following utility of wealth schedules:

Wealth (dollars)	Jimmy's total utility (units)	Zenda's total utility (units)
0	0	0
100	200	512
200	300	640
300	350	672
400	375	678
500	387	681
600	393	683
700	396	684

Who is more risk averse, Jimmy or Zenda?

4. Suppose that Jimmy and Zenda in problem 3 have $400 each and that each sees a business project that involves committing the entire $400 to the project. They reckon that the project could return $600 (a profit of $200) with a probability of 0.85 or $200 (a loss of $200) with a probability of 0.15. Who goes for the project and who hangs onto the initial $400?

5. In problem 3, who is more likely to buy insurance, Jimmy or Zenda, and why?

CRITICAL THINKING

1. Study *Reading Between the Lines* on pp. 460–461 and then answer the following questions:
  a. Why is it rational to buy low-yielding Treasury bills?
  b. Who will make more money on the average, the buyer of a stock that might double in value or become worthless with equal probabilities or the person who simply holds cash? Given these two possibilities, what does a risk-averse person do?
  c. Why do pension funds hold a mixture of stocks and bonds?

2. Why do you think it is not possible to buy insurance against having to put up with a low-paying, miserable job? Explain why a market in insurance of this type would not work.

3. Although you can't buy insurance against the risk of being sold a lemon, the market does give you some protection. How? What are the main ways in which markets overcome the lemon problem?

4. Grades send signals to potential employers. Are you better served by a professor who demands high standards for an A or by one who always ensures that 20 percent of the class gets an A?

5. A new wonder drug is discovered by Merck that is expected to bring big profits. Describe in detail what happens in the stock market and how these actions influence the price of Merck's stock. Why would people diversify rather than put all their wealth into Merck's stock?

Part 7

Macroeconomic Overview

The Big Picture

Macroeconomics is a large and controversial subject. It is interlaced with political ideological disputes. And it is a field in which charlatans as well as serious thinkers have much to say. This page is a map that will guide you through this challenging but interesting terrain of macroeconomics and help you to keep the big picture in view. ◆ There is no better place to begin than with the core questions of macroeconomics, which are what causes:

- Economic growth
- Business cycles
- Unemployment
- Inflation

The three chapters in this part provide a first take on these questions. ◆ In Chapter 22, you will learn some facts about economic growth, business cycles, unemployment, and inflation in the United States and around the world. ◆ In Chapter 23, you will learn how we measure the economy's output and prices. These measures are used to calculate the rate of economic growth, business cycle fluctuations, and inflation. You'll discover that making these measurements is not straightforward and that small measurement errors can have a big effect on our perceptions about how we are doing. ◆ In Chapter 24, you will study the macroeconomic version of supply and demand—*aggregate supply* and *aggregate demand*. The aggregate supply–aggregate demand model is the big picture model. It explains both the long-term trends in economic growth and inflation and the short-term business cycle fluctuations in production, jobs, and inflation. ◆ The chapters that follow look behind aggregate supply and aggregate demand. First, in Chapters 25 through 27, you will study long-run aggregate supply and long-term growth. This material is so central to the oldest question in macroeconomics that some professors like students to jump into it right away *before* studying aggregate supply and aggregate demand. Second, in Chapters 28 through 32, you will study aggregate demand and the sources of fluctuations in production and prices and long-term trends in inflation. This material is central to the macroeconomics that Keynes developed, and some people like to study it before aggregate supply and long-term growth. Third, in Chapters 33 and 34, you will study the alternative theories of the business cycle and the problems of stabilizing the economy and achieving faster growth. ◆ Before beginning your study of macroeconomics, we'll spend a few minutes with the economist who developed the subject— John Maynard Keynes. We'll also talk with one of today's macroeconomic revolutionaries, Robert E. Lucas, Jr., of the University of Chicago.

Macroeconomic Revolutions

The Economist: John Maynard Keynes

John Maynard Keynes, born in England in 1883, was one of the outstanding minds of the twentieth century. He wrote on probability as well as economics, represented Britain at the Versailles peace conference at the end of World War I, was a master speculator on international financial markets (an activity he conducted from bed every morning and which made and lost him several fortunes), and played a prominent role in creating the International Monetary Fund. He was a member of the Bloomsbury Group, a circle of outstanding artists and writers that included E. M. Forster, Bertrand Russell, and Virginia Woolf. Keynes was a controversial and quick-witted figure. A critic once complained that Keynes had changed his opinion on some matter, to which Keynes retorted, "When I discover I am wrong, I change my mind. What do you do?"

> "... The ideas of economists and political philosophers, both when they are right and when they are wrong, are more powerful than is commonly understood. Indeed the world is ruled by little else."
>
> JOHN MAYNARD KEYNES
>
> THE GENERAL THEORY OF EMPLOYMENT, INTEREST, AND MONEY

The Issues and Ideas

During the Industrial Revolution, as technological change created new jobs and destroyed old ones, people began to wonder whether the economy could create enough jobs and sufficient demand to buy all the things that the new industrial economy could produce.

Jean-Baptiste Say argued that production creates incomes that are sufficient to buy everything that is produced—supply creates its own demand—an idea that came to be called *Say's Law*.

Say and Keynes would have had a lot to disagree about. Jean-Baptiste Say, born in Lyon, France, in 1767 (he was 9 years old when Adam Smith's *The Wealth of Nations* was published), suffered the wrath of Napoleon for his views on government and the economy. In today's America, Say would be leading the Republican charge for a smaller and leaner government. Say was the most famous economist of his era on both sides of the Atlantic. His book, *Traité d'économie politique* (*A Treatise on Political Economy*), published in 1803, became a best selling university economics textbook in both Europe and America.

As the Great Depression of the 1930s became more severe and more prolonged, Say's Law looked less and less relevant. John Maynard Keynes revolutionized macroeconomic thinking by turning Say's Law on its head, arguing that production does not depend on supply. Instead, it depends on what people are willing to buy—on demand. Or as Keynes put it, production depends on *effective demand*. It is possible, argued Keynes, for people to refuse to spend all of their incomes. If businesses fail to spend on new capital the amount that people plan to save, demand might be less than supply. In this situation, resources might go unemployed and remain unemployed indefinitely.

The influence of Keynes persists even today, more than 60 years after the publication of his main work. But during the past 20 years, Nobel Laureate Robert E. Lucas, Jr., with significant contributions from a list of outstanding macroeconomists too long to name, has further revolutionized macroeconomics. Today, we know a lot about economic growth, unemployment, inflation, and business cycles. And we know how to use fiscal policy and monetary policy to improve macroeconomic performance. But we don't yet have all the answers. Macroeconomics remains a field of lively controversy and exciting research.

THEN...

In 1776, James Hargreaves, an English weaver and carpenter, developed a simple hand-operated machine called a spinning jenny (pictured here). Using this machine, a person could spin 80 threads at once. Thousands of hand-wheel spinners, operators of machines that could spin only one thread, lost their jobs. They protested by wrecking spinning jennies. In the long run, the displaced hand-wheel spinners found work, often in factories that manufactured the machines that had destroyed their previous jobs. From the earliest days of the Industrial Revolution to the present day, people have lost their jobs as new technologies have automated what human effort had previously been needed to accomplish.

...AND NOW

Advances in computer technology have made it possible for us to dial our own telephone calls to any part of the world and get connected in a flash. A task that was once performed by telephone operators, who made connections along copper wires, is now performed faster and more reliably by computers along fiber-optic cables. Just as the Industrial Revolution transformed the textile industry, so today's Information Revolution is transforming the telecommunications industry. In the process, the mix of jobs is changing. There are fewer jobs for telephone operators but more jobs for telephone systems designers, builders, managers, and marketers. In the long run, as people spend the income they earn in their changing jobs, supply creates its own demand, just as Say predicted. But does supply create its own demand in the short run, when displaced workers are unemployed?

Keynes and Robert E. Lucas, Jr., would have had plenty of disagreements too. Lucas, of the University of Chicago, has lead a revolution in macroeconomics that has enabled economists to build model (artificial) economies that display properties similar to those of the actual economy and to use these models to study the effects of alternative policies on macroeconomic performance. A cornerstone of the new macroeconomics is the idea of "rational expectations": People use all the available information to make economic forecasts. This information includes economists' theories about how the economy works. Lucas, like Say, believes that it is easier for government intervention to do harm than good. Said Lucas, "I don't want to manage the U.S. economy. And I don't think anybody else should take the job either." You can meet Professor Lucas on the following pages.

Robert E. Lucas, Jr., is a professor of economics at the University of Chicago, a position he has held since 1975. Professor Lucas was born in Yakima, Washington, in 1937. He earned his B.A. and his Ph.D. from the University of Chicago in 1959 and 1963, respectively.

In 1995, Professor Lucas received the Nobel Prize for Economic Science for his work on developing the theory of rational expectations. Challenging the Keynesian theories of economic fluctuations, this new macroeconomic theory is based on the hypothesis that people and businesses make rational decisions based on rational expectations and markets reconcile individual decisions by balancing supply and demand, even in a recession.

Michael Parkin spoke with Professor Lucas about rational expectations macroeconomics, his views of economic policy, and the legacy of Keynes.

Why are you an economist?

I grew up in a family where everyone talked about politics and economics every night at dinner. So I've been concerned with social questions as long as I can remember. My experience as an undergraduate history major confirmed my belief in the importance of economic forces.

You applied the idea of rational expectations to macroeconomics and to expectations about inflation. How has that hypothesis changed the way we think about things?

It ties down a loose end that shouldn't have been there. Any important economic decision depends on what you think about the future. Rational expectations is a way of dealing with that.

What do you see as the chief criticism of the rational expectations hypothesis?

Here's the genuine difficulty people have with the idea. You would never discover the idea of rational expectations by introspection. Rational expectations describes something that has to be true of the outcome of a much more complicated underlying process. But it doesn't describe the actual thought process people use in trying to figure out the future. Our behavior is adaptive. We try some mode of behavior. If it's successful, we do it again. If not, we try something else. Rational expectations describes the situation when you've got it right.

Can you give an example?

In economics, we're mostly concerned about repetitive events and decisions of some consequence. Our capitalist economy has been operating under pretty much the same laws for 200 years now. People aren't reacting to every monetary contraction as if it's the first time it ever happened: That is just inconceivable. I think people have developed certain ways of living with regular events as best they can.

> *People aren't react-ing to every mone-tary contraction as if it's the first time it ever happened.*

One of the most significant developments in macroeconomics in recent years has been real business cycle theory. How do you evaluate this approach?

Real business cycle theory asks what the time path of the economy's GDP or employment would be under the best possible macroeconomic policy. The early authors of this approach asked themselves what fraction of the actual variation in GDP you could account for if you restricted yourself to the fluctuations in the rate of technological change. Their initial answer was: All of it, that there is nothing left over for traditional macroeconomic theory to account for. I don't think that can be right.

For example, you can't account for something like the events of 1929 to 1933, when real output fell by a quarter in four years, as if it resulted from the changes in the rate at which technology was decaying. The Depression didn't occur because production techniques got worse. But real business cycle theory has shown us that real forces are much more important than we had thought and that the questions addressed by traditional macroeconomics are not as important as we once thought. That's the important message.

How can we introduce monetary forces into a macroeconomic model that at the same time pays serious attention to real forces, one that shows fluctuations in price as well as in output?

This question is the subject of my Nobel Lecture, "Monetary Neutrality." I think it is the central question of macroeconomics, but it remains unresolved today, as it did when David Hume first addressed it in the eighteenth century.

Your early work focused primarily on short-term macroeconomic problems. For the past 10 years, you've increasingly devoted your life to thinking about long-term growth. Why has your work changed in that direction?

When I began taking economics courses in the early 1960s, the Great Depression of the 1930s was a key topic of discussion for all my professors. The study of macroeconomics was, at that time, the study of how to prevent depressions and how to get out of them. The United States has not had a serious depression since the 1930s, and we should not be surprised that macroeconomic study has switched from a depression focus to a growth focus. If you ask what determines our income today relative to what it was in the 1960s, 99 percent of the answer is economic growth.

> *If you ask what determines our income today relative to what it was in the 1960s, 99 percent of the answer is economic growth.*

What can we bring to the study of growth today that Smith couldn't bring to it when he tried to figure out what caused the wealth of nations.

When Adam Smith wrote about the wealth of nations, he was thinking about a world in which no country had ever experienced sustained growth in living standards. Some countries had higher *levels* of income than others, and Smith was interested in understanding why those differences existed. But Smith never observed or imagined a country where production could grow at 3 percent per year for a century and more. Smith also lacked good data, by modern standards. We now have tremendous data sets on income and the growth of income for the richest and poorest countries. During the past 10 years, growth theory has evolved from being the study of the United States, the United Kingdom, and a few other very wealthy economies to being the comparative study of rich and poor economies. The hope is that the same general theoretical principles will apply to both.

There's about a 25 to 1 difference between the United States and India in per capita production. How do you explain that difference?

Only a small fraction can be explained by the differences in physical capital. U.S. workers have better equipment than Indian workers, and that's certainly a factor in making them more productive, but a much more important factor is human capital. The level of education and training of the U.S. worker is much higher than the typical Indian worker. Once human capital is introduced—and placed at the center of growth theory—a lot of things start falling into place and it becomes much easier to understand the enormous differences in incomes.

The countries of East Asia are catching up with those of Europe and North America. The Industrial Revolution has opened them up to trade with the more advanced countries of the world. East Asia is experiencing annual growth rates of 6 to 8 percent. Nothing like that ever occurred in the United States or the United Kingdom, the countries that were leaders from the start of the Industrial Revolution. East Asian countries are rapidly learning technology that took decades to produce.

I'm not that big on the distinction. I think of myself as a monetarist. But the term does refer to several different things. One aspect of what people call monetarism is just an emphasis on the quantity of some money as a determinant of prices and of economic activity. In some ways, I think that revolution has been so successful that it doesn't seem like a revolution any more. In this day and age, no one talks about the price level, exchange rates, or interest rates without talking about the quantity of money. In that sense, we're all monetarists. The second aspect of monetarism is a hostility toward

the government's continual management of the economy. The role of government, in a monetarist perspective, is to make its own behavior on fiscal or monetary policy simple and predictable and then just to let the system operate without fine tuning. That view, I think, is absolutely right.

Economics is a great major. … economics is a good pre–almost anything major.

I was a deficit alarmist in the early years of the Reagan administration because I thought the deficits would be inflationary. Well, that just hasn't happened. I've become more sympathetic to people like Larry Kotlikoff, who argued that

the deficit just doesn't measure anything we care about, since things like future social security liabilities are arbitrarily excluded.

Keynes' influence was almost entirely political. He wrote *The General Theory* in the 1930s at a time when many of the major countries were in the process of moving away from liberal democracy and capitalism toward fascism in Germany and Italy and toward Communism in Russia. These countries appeared to deal better with the depression of the 1930s than countries like ours that stayed with liberal institutions. Keynes' message in *The General Theory* is that we can deal with depressions within the framework of a basically capitalistic economy and liberal democratic institutions. This is an important message to get across.

The intellectual forefathers of modern macroeconomics are, for me, the classical economists, Smith and Ricardo, the neoclassical work of Marshall, and the generation of our teachers, Arrow, Friedman, and Samuelson.

Economics is a great major. I feel economics is a good pre–almost anything major. Most of the economics majors at the University of Chicago will go to law school, professional school, or work for a while. Our students have a lot of electives to choose from; they have a broad, liberal arts education.

Chapter 22

A First Look at Macroeconomics

During the past 100 years, the quantity of goods and services produced in the nation's farms, factories, shops, and offices has expanded more than twentyfold. As a result, we have a much higher living standard than our grandparents had. Will production always expand? Will your world be more prosperous than today's? ◆ For most of us, a high standard of living means finding a good job. What kind of job will you find when you graduate? Will you have lots of choice, or will you face a labor market with a high unemployment rate in which jobs are hard to find? ◆ A high standard of living means being able to afford to buy life's necessities and some fun. If prices rise too quickly, some people get left behind and must trim what they buy. Prices have increased slowly over the past few years. But can we count on them

What Will Your World Be Like?

rising slowly in the future? What will the dollar buy next year? What will it buy in 10 years when you are paying off your student loan? And what will it buy in 50 years when you are spending your life's savings in retirement? ◆ Every year since 1970, the government has spent more than it has raised in taxes. And most years, we have imported more goods and services from the rest of the world than we have exported to it. We have experienced large and persistent government and international deficits. How will these deficits affect your future? ◆ To keep production expanding and prevent an economic slowdown, the federal government and the Federal Reserve Board—the nation's financial managers—take policy actions. What kinds of actions do they take? How do their actions influence production, jobs, prices, and the ability of Americans to compete in the global marketplace? ◆ These are the questions of macroeconomics. The macroeconomic events through which we are now living are tumultuous and exciting. With what you learn in these chapters, you will be able to understand these events, the policy challenges they bring, and the political debate they stir. You will be able to prepare yourself better for your world, the economic world that you will enter when you graduate and in which you will earn your living.

After studying this chapter, you will be able to:

- Describe the origins of macroeconomics and the problems it deals with

- Describe the long-term trends and short-term fluctuations in economic growth, unemployment, inflation, and government and international deficits

- Explain why economic growth, unemployment, inflation, and deficits matter

- Identify the macroeconomic policy challenges and describe the tools available for meeting them

Origins and Issues of Macroeconomics

ECONOMISTS BEGAN TO STUDY LONG-TERM economic growth, inflation, and international payments as long ago as the 1750s, and this work was the origin of macroeconomics. But modern macroeconomics did not emerge until the **Great Depression**, a decade (1929–1939) of high unemployment and stagnant production throughout the world economy. In the Depression's worst year, 1933, the production of U.S. farms, factories, shops, and offices was only 70 percent of its 1929 level and 25 percent of the labor force was unemployed. These were years of human misery on a scale that is hard to imagine today. They were also years of extreme pessimism about the ability of the market economy to work properly. Many people believed that private ownership, free markets, and democratic political institutions could not survive.

The science of economics had no solutions to the Great Depression. The major alternative system of central planning and socialism seemed increasingly attractive. It was in this climate of economic depression and political and intellectual turmoil that modern macroeconomics emerged with the publication in 1936 of John Maynard Keynes' *The General Theory of Employment, Interest, and Money* (see p. 466).

Short-Term Versus Long-Term Goals

Keynes' theory was that depression and high unemployment result from insufficient private spending and that to cure these problems, the government must increase its spending. Keynes' focused primarily on the *short term*. He wanted to cure an immediate problem almost regardless of the *long-term* consequences of the cure. "In the long run," said Keynes, "we're all dead."

But Keynes believed that after his cure for depression had restored the economy to a normal condition, the long-term problems of inflation and slow economic growth would return. And he suspected that his cure for depression, increased government spending, might trigger inflation and might lower the long-term growth rate of production. With a lower long-term growth rate, the economy would create fewer jobs. If this outcome did occur, a policy aimed at lowering unemployment in the short run might end up increasing it in the long run.

By the late 1960s and through the 1970s, Keynes' predictions became a reality. Inflation increased, economic growth slowed down, and in some countries, unemployment became persistently high. The causes of these developments are complex. But they point to an inescapable conclusion: The long-term problems of inflation, slow growth, and persistent unemployment and the short-term problems of depression and economic fluctuations intertwine and are most usefully studied together. So although macroeconomics was reborn during the Great Depression, it has now returned to its older tradition. Today, macroeconomics studies long-term economic growth and inflation as well as short-term business fluctuations and unemployment.

The Road Ahead

There is no unique way to study macroeconomics. Because its rebirth was a product of depression, the common practice for many years was to pay most attention to short-term output fluctuations and unemployment but to never completely lose sight of the long-term issues. When a rapid inflation emerged during the 1970s, this topic returned to prominence. During the 1980s, when long-term growth slowed in the United States and other rich industrial countries but exploded in East Asia, economists redirected their energy toward economic growth. During the 1990s, as information technologies continue to shrink the globe, the international dimension of macroeconomics has become more prominent. The result of these developments is that modern macroeconomics is a broad subject that studies all the issues we've just identified: long-term economic growth, unemployment, and inflation. It also studies two new problems: the government budget and international deficits.

Over the past 40 years, economists have developed a clearer understanding of the forces that determine macroeconomic performance and have devised policies that they hope will improve this performance. Your main goal is to become familiar with the theories of macroeconomics and the policies they make possible. To set you on your path toward this goal, we're going to take a first look at economic growth, unemployment, inflation, and deficits and learn why these macroeconomic phenomena merit our attention.

Economic Growth

YOUR PARENTS ARE RICHER THAN YOUR GRANDparents were when they were young. But are you going to be richer than your parents? And are your children going to be richer than you? The answers depend on the rate of economic growth.

Economic growth is the expansion of the economy's production possibilities. It can be pictured as an outward shift of the production possibility frontier (*PPF*)—see Chapter 3, pp. 49–50.

We measure economic growth by the increase in real gross domestic product. **Real gross domestic product** (also called **real GDP**) is the value of the total production of all the nation's farms, factories, shops, and offices linked back to the prices of a single year. Real GDP in the United States is currently linked back to the prices of 1992 (called 1992 dollars). We link back to the dollar prices of a single year to eliminate the influence of *inflation*—the increase in prices—and determine how much production has grown from one year to another. (Real GDP is explained more fully in Chapter 23 on pp. 502–503.)

Real GDP is not a perfect measure of total production because it does not include everything that is produced. It excludes the things we produce for ourselves at home (preparing meals, doing laundry, house painting, gardening, and so on). It also excludes production that people hide to avoid taxes or because it is illegal—the underground economy. But despite its shortcomings, real GDP is the best measure of total production available. Let's see what it tells us about economic growth in the United States.

Economic Growth in the United States

Figure 22.1 shows real GDP in the United States since 1960 and highlights two features of economic growth:

- The growth of potential GDP
- Fluctuations of real GDP around potential GDP

The Growth of Potential GDP   When all the economy's resources are fully employed, the value of production is called **potential GDP**. Real GDP fluctuates around potential GDP, and the rate of long-term economic growth is measured by the growth rate of potential GDP. It is shown by the steepness of the potential GDP line (the black line) in Fig. 22.1.

During the 1960s, real GDP grew at an unusually rapid rate of 4.4 percent a year. But the growth rate of output per person slowed during the 1970s, a phenomenon called the **productivity growth slowdown**. Faster growth might have returned during the late 1980s and 1990s, but it is too soon to be certain about this possibility.

Why did the productivity growth slowdown occur? This question is controversial. One possible cause is a sharp rise in the relative price of energy. How this factor might have slowed productivity growth is explored in Chapter 27 on pp. 595–596. Whatever its cause, the productivity growth slowdown means that we all have smaller incomes today than we would have had if the economy had continued to grow at its 1960s rate.

Let's now look at GDP fluctuations.

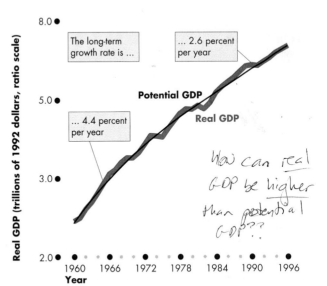

FIGURE 22.1

Economic Growth in the United States

The long-term economic growth rate, measured by the growth of potential GDP, was 4.4 percent a year during the 1960s but slowed to 2.6 percent a year during the mid-1970s. Growth has remained slower into the 1990s. Real GDP fluctuates around potential GDP.

Source: U.S. Department of Commerce, *National Income and Product Accounts of the United States.*

Fluctuations Around Potential GDP   Real GDP fluctuates around potential GDP in a business cycle. A **business cycle** is the periodic but irregular up-and-down movement in production. It is measured by fluctuations in real GDP around potential GDP. When real GDP is less than potential GDP, some resources are underused. For example, some labor is unemployed and capital is underutilized. When real GDP is greater than potential GDP, resources are being *overused*. Many people work longer hours than they are willing to put up with in the long run, capital is worked so intensively that it is not maintained in prime working order, delivery times lengthen, bottlenecks occur, and backorders increase.

Business cycles are not regular, predictable, or repeating cycles like the phases of the moon. Their timing changes unpredictably. But cycles do have some things in common. Every business cycle has two phases:

1. A recession
2. An expansion

and two turning points:

1. A peak
2. A trough

Figure 22.2 shows these features of the most recent business cycle in the United States. A **recession** is a period during which real GDP decreases—the growth rate of real GDP is negative—for at least two successive quarters. The most recent recession, which is highlighted in the figure, began in the third quarter of 1990 and ended in the first quarter of 1991. This recession lasted for three quarters. An **expansion** is a period during which real GDP increases. The most recent expansion began in the second quarter of 1991 and was still in progress during 1997. An earlier expansion ended with the onset of recession in the third quarter of 1990.

When a business cycle expansion ends and a recession begins, the turning point is called a *peak*. The most recent peak occurred in the second quarter of 1990. When a business cycle recession ends and a recovery begins, the turning point is called a *trough*. The most recent trough occurred in the first quarter of 1991.

FIGURE 22.2

The Most Recent U.S. Business Cycle

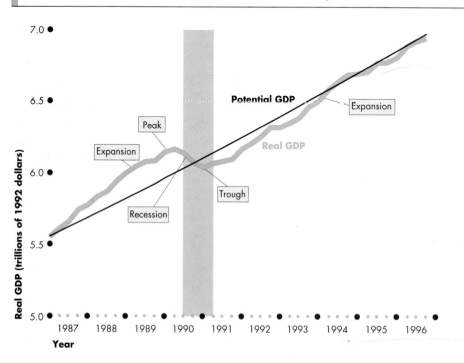

A business cycle has two phases: recession and expansion. The most recent recession (highlighted) ran from the third quarter of 1990 through the first quarter of 1991. Then a new expansion began in the second quarter of 1991. A business cycle has two turning points, a peak and a trough. In the most recent business cycle, the peak occurred in the second quarter of 1990 and the trough occurred in the first quarter of 1991.

The Recent Recession in Historical Perspective

The recession of 1990–1991 seemed severe while we were passing through it, but compared with earlier recessions, it was mild. You can see how mild it was by looking at Fig. 22.3, which shows a longer history of U.S. economic growth. The biggest decrease in real GDP occurred during the Great Depression of the 1930s. A large decrease also occurred in 1946 and 1947, immediately after World War II. In more recent times, severe recessions occurred during the mid-1970s, following oil price hikes by the Organization of Petroleum Exporting Countries (OPEC), and during the early 1980s.

Each of these economic downturns was more severe than that in 1990–1991. But you can see that the Great Depression was much more severe than anything that followed it. This episode was so extreme that we don't call it a recession. We call it a *depression*.

This last truly great depression occurred before governments started taking policy actions to stabilize the economy. It also occurred before the birth of modern macroeconomics. Is the absence of another great depression a sign that macroeconomics has contributed to economic stability? Some people believe it

is. Others doubt it. We'll evaluate these opinions on a number of occasions in this book.

We've looked at real GDP growth and fluctuations in the United States. But is the U.S. experience typical? Do other countries share our experience? Let's see whether they do.

Economic Growth Around the World

A country might have a rapid growth rate of real GDP, but it might also have a rapid population growth rate. To compare growth rates over time and across countries, we use the growth rate of real GDP *per person*. Real GDP per person is real GDP divided by the population. For example, U.S. real GDP in 1996 was $6,903 billion (1992 dollars), and the population of the United States was 265.5 million. So U.S. real GDP per person was $6,903 billion divided by 265.5 million, which equals $26,000.

Figure 22.4 shows real GDP per person between 1960 and 1996 for three of the world's largest economies: the United States, Japan, and Germany.

FIGURE 22.3

Long-Term Economic Growth in the United States

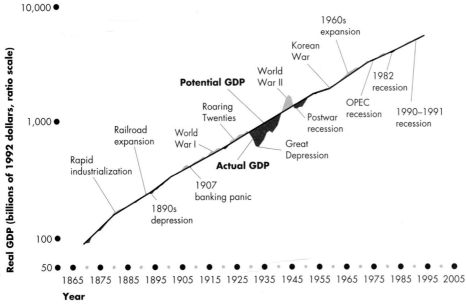

The thin black line shows potential GDP. Along this line, real GDP grew at an average rate of 3.3 percent a year between 1870 and 1994. The blue areas show when real GDP was above potential GDP, and the red areas show when it was below potential GDP. During some periods, such as World War II, real GDP expanded quickly. During other periods, such as the Great Depression and more recently in 1975 (following the OPEC oil price hike), 1982, and 1990–1991, real GDP declined.

Sources: 1869–1928, Christina D. Romer, "The Prewar Business Cycle Reconsidered: New Estimates of Gross National Product, 1869–1908," *Journal of Political Economy* 97, (1989) 1–37. 1929–1996, U.S. Department of Commerce, *National Income and Product Accounts of the United States.*

In these countries, three features of the paths of real GDP per person stand out:

- Similar productivity growth slowdowns
- Similar business cycles
- Different long-term trends in potential GDP

Similar Productivity Growth Slowdowns   U.S. real GDP per person grew at a rate of 2.9 percent a year during the 1960s but slowed to 1.3 percent a year during the 1970s and 1980s and 0.9 percent a year during the 1990s. In Germany, the growth of real GDP per person slowed from 3.5 percent a year during the 1960s to 2 percent a year during the 1970s and 1980s and 1 percent a year during the 1990s. In Japan, the slowdown was more spectacular, from 8.5 percent a year during the 1960s to 3.1 percent a year during the 1970s and 1980s and 1.5 percent a year during the 1990s.

The slowdown experienced by the United States, Japan, and Germany was experienced by most other industrial countries. Exceptions were the major oil-producing nations.

Similar Business Cycles   The three big economies have also experienced similar business cycles. Each economy had an expansion running from the early or mid-1960s through 1973, a recession from 1973 to 1975, an expansion through 1979, another recession in the early 1980s, and a long expansion through the rest of the 1980s.

Like the common productivity growth slowdown, this common business cycle is also shared by most economies around the world.

Different Long-Term Trends in Potential GDP
Perhaps the most striking feature of Fig. 22.4 is the variation in the long-term growth rates of the three big economies. In 1960, real GDP per person was $9,900 in the United States, $6,600 in Germany, and $3,000 in Japan. So in round numbers, in 1960, Germany produced twice as much per person as Japan, and the United States produced three times as much per person as Japan.

But during the 1960s, Japan's production streaked upward like a rocket leaving Cape Canaveral. When U.S. long-term growth of real GDP per person was

FIGURE 22.4

Economic Growth in Three Large Economies

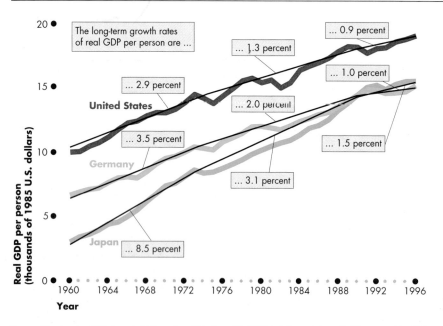

Economic growth in three large economies, the United States, Germany, and Japan, has followed a similar pattern. The growth rate in all three countries slowed during the 1970s, and each country has had similar business cycles. But Japan has grown fastest, and Germany too has grown faster than the United States.

Sources: The data for 1960 through 1992 are from "The Penn World Table," *Quarterly Journal of Economics,* May 1991, pp. 327–368. New computer disk supplement (Mark 5.6a). The data use comparable international relative prices converted to 1985 U.S. dollars. The data for 1993-1996 are from *International Financial Statistics* (Washington, D.C.: International Monetary Fund, 1997).

2.9 percent a year, Germany achieved a rate of 3.5 percent a year, and Japan achieved an astonishing 8.5 percent a year. These differences in the long-term growth trend survived the productivity growth slowdown. After the slowdown, even though Japan's growth rate more than halved, its growth of real GDP per person still exceeded the U.S. rate before the slowdown.

Because it has achieved such a high growth rate, Japan has narrowed the gap between its own level of real GDP per person and that of the United States and has overtaken Germany.

Figure 22.5 compares the growth of the U.S. economy with that of several other countries and regions since 1978. Among the industrial countries (the red bars), Japan has grown the fastest and the European Union has grown the slowest. The U.S. growth rate has been toward the low end of the range for industrial countries. The developing countries and the countries in transition to a market economy (the green bars) have experienced a wide range of growth rates. The most rapid growth has occurred in Asia, where the average growth rate has exceeded 7 percent a year—three times the U.S. growth rate. The slowest growth has been in Russia and the other countries of Central and Eastern Europe, where production has shrunk. Africa has also grown slowly. With the exception of these regions, growth rates in the developing countries have exceeded that of the United States.

Benefits and Costs of Economic Growth

What are the benefits and costs of economic growth? Does it matter whether the long-term growth rate slows as it did during the 1970s?

The main benefit of long-term economic growth is expanded consumption possibilities, including more health care for the poor and elderly, more cancer and AIDS research, more space research and exploration, better roads, and more and better housing. We can even have cleaner lakes, more trees, and cleaner air by devoting more resources to environmental problems.

When the long-term growth rate slows, some of these benefits are lost, and the loss can be large. For example, if long-term growth had not slowed in the United States during the 1970s, real GDP in 1996 would have been $8,650 billion, or $32,600 per

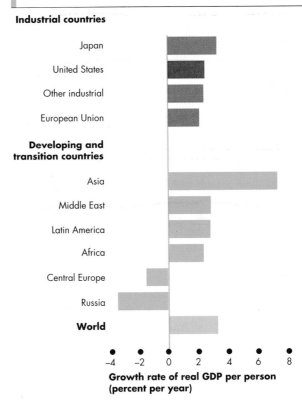

FIGURE 22.5

Growth Rates Around the World

Between 1978 and 1996, the growth rate of real GDP has been lower in the United States than in some other industrial countries. The developing countries of Asia have had the most rapid growth rates and those of Africa, Central and Eastern Europe, and Russia have had the slowest growth.

Source: World Economic Outlook (Washington D.C.: International Monetary Fund, October 1996), pp. 167, 173–176.

person. Instead, it was $6,903 billion, or $26,000 per person. So if the long-term trend of the 1960s had persisted, as a nation we would have had $1,750 billion more to spend. Each person (on the average) would have had $6,600 more. If the government had taken one third of this extra income, it could have provided more health care, education, day-care services, highways, space stations, and a super-collider with no decrease in its provision of other goods and services, and its budget would be in a huge surplus. At the same time, you might have had another $4,400 a year to spend on whatever pleased you.

The main cost of economic growth is forgone consumption. To sustain a high growth rate, resources must be devoted to advancing technology and accumulating capital rather than to producing goods and services for current consumption. This cost cannot be avoided. But it brings the benefit of greater consumption in the future.

Two other possible costs of faster growth are a more rapid depletion of exhaustible natural resources such as oil and natural gas and increased pollution of the air, rivers, and oceans. But neither of these two costs is inevitable. The technological advances that bring economic growth help us to economize on natural resources and to clean up the environment. For example, more efficient auto engines cut the gasoline use and tailpipe emissions.

A fourth possible cost of faster growth is more frequent job changes and more frequent moves from one region of the country to another. For example, during the 1990s, the South (Sun Belt) expanded and people migrated there from the Northeast and Midwest (the Rust Belt).

The pace of economic growth is determined by the choices that people make to balance the benefits and costs of economic growth. You'll study these choices and their consequences in Chapters 26 and 27.

REVIEW

- Economic growth is the expansion of production possibilities. The long-term trend in economic growth is measured by the growth rate of potential GDP.
- Long-term growth in the United States and other countries slowed during the 1970s and 1980s.
- Real GDP growth fluctuates in a business cycle. An *expansion* to a *peak* is followed by a *recession*, *trough,* and a new *expansion.*
- The main benefit of economic growth is expanded consumption possibilities. The main costs are less *current* consumption, possibly resource depletion and environmental pollution, and rapid changes in jobs and locations.

We've seen that real GDP grows and that it fluctuates over the business cycle. The business cycle brings fluctuations in the number of jobs available and in unemployment. Let's now examine these core macroeconomic problems.

Jobs and Unemployment

WHAT KIND OF LABOR MARKET WILL YOU ENTER when you graduate? Will there be plenty of good jobs to choose from, or will there be so much unemployment that you will be forced to take a low-paying job that doesn't use your education? The answer depends, to a large degree, on the total number of jobs available and on the unemployment rate.

Jobs

The U.S. economy is an incredible job-creating machine. In 1996, 127 million people had jobs. That number is 20 million more than in 1985 and 23 million more than in 1975. Every year, on the average, the U.S. economy creates an *additional* 1.8 million jobs.

When President Clinton took office in 1993, he predicted that 8 million jobs would be created during his four-year term. In an average four-year period, the economy creates 7.2 million jobs, so President Clinton was ambitious. As it turns out, the businesses of the United States created 8.2 million jobs during these four years.

The pace of job creation and destruction fluctuates over the business cycle. More jobs are destroyed than created during a recession, so the number of jobs decreases. But more jobs are created than destroyed during an expansion, so the number of jobs increases. For example, during the recession of 1990–1991, the number of jobs fell by more than 1 million, but through the expansion that followed, 2 million jobs were created each year. During the expansion of the 1980s, jobs were created at an even faster pace of 2.5 million jobs each year.

Unemployment

Not everyone who wants a job can find one. On any one day in a normal or average year, seven million people are unemployed, and during a recession or depression, unemployment rises above this level. For example, in the recession of 1991, almost nine million people were looking for jobs.

A person is defined as being **unemployed** if he or she does not have a job but is available for work, is willing to work, and has made some effort to find work within the previous four weeks. The sum of the people who are unemployed and the people who are employed is called the **labor force**. The **unemployment rate** is the percentage of the people in the labor force who are unemployed. (The concepts of the labor force and unemployment are explained more fully in Chapter 25 on pp. 544–545.)

The unemployment rate is not a perfect measure of the underutilization of labor for two main reasons. First, it excludes discouraged workers. A **discouraged worker** is a person who does not have a job, is available for work, and is willing to work but who has given up the effort to find work. Many people switch between the unemployment and discouraged worker categories in both directions every month. Second, the unemployment rate measures unemployed people rather than unemployed labor hours. As a result, the unemployment rate excludes part-time workers who want full-time jobs.

Despite these two limitations, the unemployment rate is the best available measure of underused labor resources. Let's look at some facts about unemployment.

Unemployment in the United States

Figure 22.6 shows the unemployment rate in the United States from 1929 through 1996. Three features stand out. First, during the Great Depression of the 1930s, the unemployment rate climbed to an all-time high of 25 percent in 1933 and remained high throughout the 1930s. After 1934, the official rate probably overstates unemployment because it counts as unemployed the people who had make-work jobs created by governments.

Second, although in recent years we have not experienced anything as devastating as the Great Depression, we have seen some high unemployment rates during recessions. Figure 22.6 highlights three of them—the OPEC recession of the mid-1970s, the 1982 recession, and the 1990–1991 recession.

Third, unemployment never falls to zero. In the period since the Great Depression, the average unemployment rate has been close to 6 percent.

How does U.S. unemployment compare with unemployment in other countries?

FIGURE 22.6
Unemployment in the United States

Unemployment is a persistent feature of economic life, but its rate varies. At its worst—during the Great Depression—25 percent of the labor force was unemployed. Even in recent recessions, the unemployment rate climbed toward 10 percent. Between the late 1960s and 1982, there was a general tendency for the unemployment rate to increase. The unemployment rate has remained below its peak during the 1982 recession and has fallen during the 1990s.

Source: *Economic Report of the President, 1997.*

Unemployment Around the World

Figure 22.7 shows the unemployment rate in Canada, Western Europe, and Japan and compares those unemployment rates with that of the United States. Over the period shown in this figure, U.S. unemployment averaged 7 percent, much higher than Japanese unemployment, which averaged 2.5 percent, but lower than Canadian unemployment, which averaged 9.6 percent, and European unemployment, which averaged 8.1 percent.

U.S. unemployment fluctuates over the business cycle. It increases during a recession and decreases during an expansion. Like U.S. unemployment, Canadian and European unemployment increase during recessions and decrease during expansions. The cycles in Canadian unemployment are similar to those in U.S. unemployment, but the European cycle is out of phase with the U.S. cycle. Also, European unemployment was on a rising trend through the 1980s. In contrast with the other countries, Japanese unemployment has remained remarkably stable.

We've looked at some facts about unemployment in the United States and in other countries. Let's now look at some of the consequences of unemployment that make it the serious problem that it is.

Why Unemployment Is a Problem

Unemployment is a serious economic, social, and personal problem for two main reasons:

- Lost production and incomes
- Lost human capital

Lost Production and Incomes The loss of a job brings an immediate loss of income and production. These losses are devastating for the people who bear them and make unemployment a frightening prospect for everyone. Unemployment insurance creates a safety net, but it does not provide the same living standard as having a job provides.

Lost Human Capital Prolonged unemployment can permanently damage a person's job prospects. For example, a manager loses his job when his employer downsizes. Short of income, he becomes a taxi driver. After a year in this work, he discovers that he can't compete with new MBA graduates. He eventually gets hired as a manager but in a small firm and at a low wage. He has lost some of his human capital.

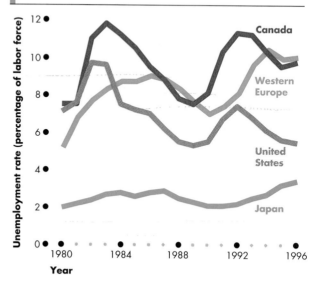

FIGURE 22.7

Unemployment in Industrial Economies

The unemployment rate in the United States has been lower than that in Canada and Western Europe but higher than that in Japan. The cycles in Canadian unemployment are similar to those in the United States. Western European unemployment has a cycle that is out of phase with the U.S. unemployment cycle. Unemployment in Japan has drifted upward in recent years.

Source: Economic Report of the President, 1997.

The costs of unemployment are spread unequally, which makes unemployment a highly charged political problem, as well as a serious economic problem.

REVIEW

- On the average, the U.S. economy creates 1.8 million additional jobs a year.
- The unemployment rate fluctuates over the business cycle and never disappears.
- Unemployment brings a loss of income, production, and human capital. The costs fall unevenly and make unemployment a social and political problem.

Let's now turn to the third major problem: inflation.

Inflation

PRICES ON THE AVERAGE CAN BE RISING, FALLING, or stable. **Inflation** is a process of rising prices. We measure the *inflation rate* as the percentage change in the *average* level of prices or the **price level**. A common measure of the price level is the *Consumer Price Index* (CPI). The CPI tells us how the average price of all the goods and services bought by a typical urban household changes from month to month. (The CPI is explained in Chapter 23, p. 501).

So that you can see in a concrete way how the inflation rate is measured, let's do a calculation. In December 1996, the CPI was 158.6, and in December 1995, it was 153.5, so the inflation rate during 1996 was

$$\text{Inflation} = \frac{158.6 - 153.5}{153.5} \times 100$$

$$= 3.3\%.$$

Inflation in the United States

Figure 22.8 shows the U.S. inflation rate from 1960 through 1996. You can see from this figure that during the early 1960s, the inflation rate was between 1 and 2 percent a year. Inflation began to increase in the late 1960s at the time of the Vietnam War. But the largest increases occurred in 1974 and 1980, years in which the actions of the Organization of Petroleum Exporting Countries (OPEC) resulted in exceptionally large increases in the price of oil. Inflation was brought under control in the early 1980s when Federal Reserve chairman Paul Volcker pushed interest rates up and people cut back on their spending. Since 1983, inflation has been relatively mild, and during the 1990s, its rate has fallen yet further.

The inflation rate rises and falls over the years, but it rarely becomes negative. If the inflation rate is negative, the price *level* is falling and we have **deflation**. Since the 1930s, the price level has generally risen—the inflation rate has been positive. Thus even when the inflation rate is low, as it was in 1961 and 1986, the price level is rising.

FIGURE 22.8

Inflation in the United States

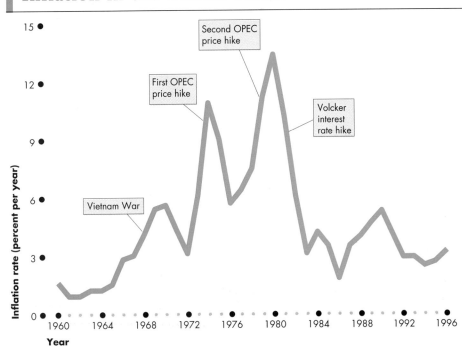

Inflation is a persistent feature of economic life in the United States. The inflation rate was low in the first half of the 1960s, but it increased during the Vietnam War years. It increased further with the OPEC oil price hikes but eventually declined in the early 1980s because of policy actions taken by the Federal Reserve. Since 1983, inflation has been mild, and during the 1990s, it has fallen further.

Source: Economic Report of the President, 1997.

Inflation Around the World

Figure 22.9 shows inflation around the world since 1970. It also shows the U.S. inflation rate in a broader perspective. Part (a) shows that the U.S. inflation rate has been similar to that of other industrial countries. You can also see that all the industrial countries shared the burst of double-digit inflation during the 1970s and the fall in inflation during the 1980s. Part (b) shows that the average inflation rate of industrial countries has been very low compared with that of the developing counties. Among the developing countries, the most extreme inflation in recent times has occurred in the former Yugoslavia, where its rate has exceeded 6,000 percent per year.

Is Inflation a Problem?

If inflation were predictable, it would not be much of a problem. But inflation is not predictable. Unpredictable inflation makes the economy behave a bit like a casino in which some people gain and some lose and no one can predict where the gains and losses will fall. Gains and losses occur because of unpredictable changes in the value of money. Money is used as a measuring rod of value in the transactions that we undertake. Borrowers and lenders, workers and employers, all make contracts in terms of money. If the value of money varies unpredictably over time, then the amounts *really* paid and received—the quantity of goods that the money will buy—also fluctuate unpredictably. Measuring value with a measuring rod whose units vary is a bit like trying to measure a piece of cloth with an elastic ruler. The size of the cloth depends on how tightly the ruler is stretched.

In a period of rapid, unpredictable inflation, resources get diverted from productive activities to forecasting inflation. It becomes more profitable to forecast the inflation rate correctly than to invent a new product. Doctors, lawyers, accountants, farmers—just about everyone—can make themselves better off, not by specializing in the profession for which they have been trained but by spending more of their time dabbling as amateur economists and inflation forecasters and managing their investment portfolios.

From a social perspective, this diversion of talent resulting from inflation is like throwing scarce resources onto the garbage heap. This waste of resources is a cost of inflation.

FIGURE 22.9

Inflation Around the World

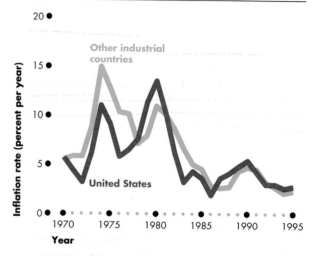

(a) The United States and other industrial countries

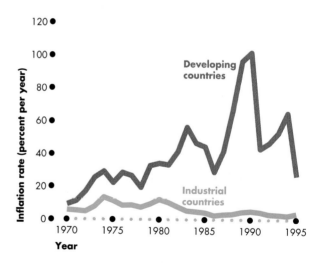

(b) Industrial countries and developing countries

Inflation in the United States is similar to that in the other industrial countries. Compared with the developing countries, inflation in the United States and the other industrial countries is low.

Source: International Financial Statistics Yearbook 1996, (Washington, D.C.: International Monetary Fund, 1996).

The most serious type of inflation is called *hyperinflation*—an inflation rate that exceeds 50 percent a month. At the height of a hyperinflation, workers are often paid twice a day because money loses its value so quickly. As soon as workers are paid, they rush out to spend their wages before they lose too much value.

Hyperinflation is rare but there have been some spectacular examples of it. Several European countries experienced hyperinflation during the 1920s after World War I and again during the 1940s after World War II. But hyperinflation is more than just a historical curiosity. It occurs in today's world. In 1994, the African nation of Zaire had a hyperinflation that peaked at a *monthly* inflation rate of 76 percent. Also in 1994, Brazil almost reached the hyperinflation stratosphere with a monthly inflation rate of 40 percent. A cup of coffee that cost 15 cruzeiros in 1980 cost 22 *billion* cruzeiros in 1994.

Inflation imposes costs, but getting rid of inflation is also costly. Policies that lower the inflation rate increase the unemployment rate. Most economists think the increase in the unemployment rate that accompanies a fall in the inflation rate is temporary. But some economists say that higher unemployment is a permanent cost of low inflation. The cost of lowering inflation must be evaluated when an anti-inflation policy is pursued. You will learn more about inflation and the costs of curing it in Chapter 32.

REVIEW

- Inflation is a process of rising prices and a falling value of money.
- Inflation is a serious problem because its rate is usually unpredictable.
- Unpredictable inflation brings unpredictable gains and losses to borrowers and lenders, workers and employers, and it diverts resources from producing goods and services to forecasting inflation.
- Anti-inflation polices bring a temporary but costly increase in unemployment.

Now that we've studied economic growth and fluctuations, unemployment, and inflation, let's turn to the fourth macroeconomic problem: deficits. What happens when a government spends more than it collects in taxes? And what happens when a nation buys more from other countries that it sells to them? Do governments and nations face the problem that you and I would face if we spent more than we earned? Do they run out of funds? Let's look at these questions.

Deficits

DEFICITS GENERATE A LOT OF ANXIETY AND MEDIA discussion. Two deficits in particular are never far from the headlines. They are:

- Government budget deficit
- International deficit

Government Budget Deficit

If the federal government spends more than it collects in taxes, it has a deficit—a **government budget deficit**. In the United States, the federal government has had a deficit every year since 1970. How big is the government budget deficit? Is it getting bigger, or is it being brought under control?

Figure 22.10(a) answers these questions. It shows the federal government budget deficit since 1960. So that we can compare the deficit in one year with that in another year, we measure it as a percentage of GDP. The concept of GDP (which is explained more fully in Chapter 23, pp. 492-500) equals total income in the economy. So you can think of the deficit as a percentage of GDP as the number of cents of deficit per dollar of income earned by an average person.

You can see that every year since 1970, the government has had a deficit. That deficit swelled to almost 5 percent of GDP in 1975 and again in 1983 and 1992. Throughout the 1980s and 1990s, the deficit had never been less than 2 percent of GDP until 1996, when it fell to 1.7 percent of GDP. Since 1992, the government budget deficit has been shrinking. But it has shrunk before. Has the deficit now finally been brought under control, or will it swell again as it has done before? In Chapter 29, we'll study the policies that have lowered the deficit in recent years.

International Deficit

When we import goods and services from the rest of the world, we make payments to foreigners. When we export goods and services to the rest of the world, we receive payments from foreigners. If our imports exceed our exports, we have an international deficit.

Figure 22.10(b) shows the history of the international deficit of the United States since 1960. The figure shows the balance on the **current account**, which includes our exports minus our imports but

FIGURE 22.10

Government Budget and International Deficits

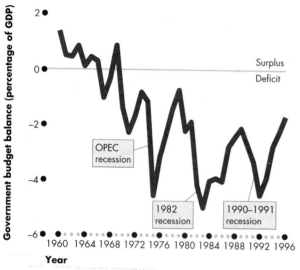

(a) U.S. government budget deficit

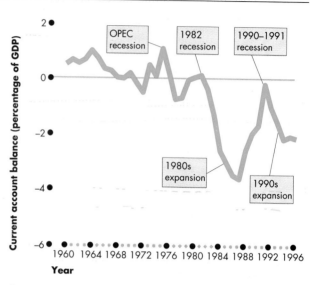

(b) U.S. international deficit

In part (a), the federal government's deficit increased as a percentage of GDP before 1982 and shrank after 1982. In part (b), the U.S. international deficit (measured by the current account) was generally in surplus until the 1980s. During

the expansion of the 1980s, a large international deficit emerged. The deficit almost disappeared during the 1990–1991 recession, but it reappeared during the 1990s expansion.

Sources: The government budget balance is the U.S. federal government's budget deficit, *Economic Report of the President*, 1997. The international balance is the current account balance, *Survey of Current Business*, U.S. Department of Commerce, March 1997.

also takes interest payments paid to and received from the rest of the world into account. To compare one year with another, the figure shows the current account as a percentage of GDP. The U.S. current account deficit has fluctuated, and since 1980, it has ranged from close to zero to almost 4 percent of GDP. Our imports have usually exceeded our exports.

Do Deficits Matter?

Why do deficits cause anxiety? What happens when a government cannot cover its spending with taxes or when a country buys more from other countries than it sells to them?

If you spend more than you earn, you have a deficit. And to cover your deficit, you have to borrow. But when you borrow, you must pay interest on your debt. Just like you, if a government or a nation

has a deficit, it must borrow. And like you, the government and the nation must pay interest on their debts.

Whether borrowing and paying out huge amounts of interest are a good idea depends on what the borrowed funds are used for. If you borrow to finance a vacation, you must eventually tighten your belt, cut spending, and repay your debt as well as pay interest on the debt. But if you borrow to invest in a business that earns a large profit, you might be able to repay your debt and pay the interest on it while continuing to increase your spending. It is the same with a government and a nation. A government or a nation that borrows to increase its consumption might be heading for trouble later. But a government or a nation that borrows to buy assets that earn a profit might be making a sound investment.

You will learn more about government budget deficits in Chapter 29 and about the international current account deficit in Chapter 36.

R E V I E W

- When government spending exceeds tax receipts, a government has a budget deficit.
- The U.S. government has had a persistent deficit since 1970.
- When imports exceed exports, a nation has an international deficit.
- The United States has had a fluctuating international deficit during the 1980s and 1990s.

Macroeconomic Policy Challenges and Tools

FROM THE TIME OF ADAM SMITH'S *THE WEALTH of Nations* in 1776 until the publication of Keynes' *General Theory of Employment, Interest, and Money* in 1936, it was widely believed that the only economic role for government was to enforce property rights. The economy behaves best, it was believed, if the government leaves people free to pursue their own best interests. The macroeconomics of Keynes challenged this view. Keynes' central point was that the economy will not fix itself and that government actions are needed to achieve and maintain full employment. The U.S. government declared full employment as a policy goal soon after World War II ended.

Policy Challenges and Tools

Today, the five widely agreed challenges for macroeconomic policy are to:

1. Boost economic growth
2. Stabilize the business cycle
3. Reduce unemployment
4. Keep inflation low
5. Reduce the government and international deficits

But how can we do all these things? What are the tools available to pursue the macroeconomic policy challenges? Macroeconomic policy tools are divided into two broad categories:

- Fiscal policy
- Monetary policy

Fiscal Policy   Making changes in taxes and government spending is called **fiscal policy**. This range of policy actions is under the control of the federal government. Fiscal policy can be used to try to boost long-term growth by creating incentives that encourage saving, investment and technological change. Fiscal policy can also be used to try to smooth out the business cycle. When the economy is in a recession, the government might cut taxes or increase its spending. Conversely, when the economy is in a rapid expansion, the government might increase taxes or cut its spending in an attempt to slow real GDP growth and prevent inflation from increasing. Fiscal policy is discussed in Chapter 29.

Montary Policy   Changing interest rates and the amount of money in the economy is called **monetary policy**. These actions are under the control of the Federal Reserve (the Fed). The principal aim of monetary policy is to keep inflation in check. To achieve this objective, the Fed prevents money from expanding too rapidly. Monetary policy can also be used to smooth the business cycle. When the economy is in recession, the Fed might lower interest rates and inject money into the economy. And when the economy is in a rapid expansion, the Fed might increase interest rates in an attempt to slow real GDP growth and prevent the inflation from increasing. Monetary policy is discussed in Chapters 30 and 31.

R E V I E W

- The macroeconomic policy challenges are to boost economic growth, stabilize the business cycle, reduce unemployment, keep inflation low, and reduce the government and international deficits.
- To meet these challenges, the government uses fiscal policy (taxes and government spending) and the Fed uses monetary policy (interest rates and money supply).

◈ In your study of macroeconomics, you will learn what is currently known about the causes of economic growth, business cycles, unemployment, inflation, and government and international deficits and about the policy choices and challenges that the government and the Fed face. *Reading Between the Lines* on pp. 486–487 looks at the state of the U.S. macroeconomy in 1996 and examines the long expansion, falling unemployment, and low inflation of the 1990s.

Economy Watching

THE RECORD, HACKENSACK, NJ, DECEMBER 29, 1996

Count on Economists to Coo Over the Nation's Numbers

BY MARTIN CRUTSINGER
THE ASSOCIATED PRESS

Washington—Economists, normally staid practitioners of what is called "the dismal science," are sounding downright giddy these days. The object of their delight, the good old U.S. economy.

No less an authority than Alan Greenspan, the Federal Reserve chairman, described the economy as fundamentally the best he has seen in three decades.

Searching for their own superlatives, some private economists have taken to calling this the "nirvana economy," a state of perfect economic bliss.

And as they prepare their outlooks for the new year, they're predicting the good times will continue to roll in 1997, with no threat of recession to disrupt an economic expansion that is already the third longest in U.S. history. ...

Finishing up its sixth year of uninterrupted growth, the current recovery's growth rates have not been stellar. But its slow, steady growth has avoided past boom-bust cycles in which overly rapid growth created inflation and forced the Federal Reserve to raise interest rates, triggering a recession. ...

While President Clinton cited his stewardship of the economy as a principal reason for his reelection, economists generally give most of the credit to Greenspan and his colleagues at the Fed.

In 1995, the central bank raised interest rates, trying to dampen growth to keep inflation from veering out of control. The effort succeeded and produced the so-called soft landing in which growth slowed enough to keep inflation in check but without a recession.

Economists believe 1997 will in many ways be a replay of 1996: moderate growth will keep inflation levels low and let the Fed stay on the sidelines for another year. ...

The last downturn ended in March 1991 and economists believe the current expansion should continue for some time to come. If it lasts until the end of 1998, it will surpass the long expansion of the 1980s. Some economists think 2000 could be the danger point for a downturn, noting that the country has been in recession in the last four years ending in a zero, 1960, 1970, 1980, and 1990.

Essence of THE STORY

■ Alan Greenspan, chairman of the Federal Reserve, describes the economy as the best he has experienced in three decades.

■ By 1997, the economy had expanded for six years—the third longest expansion in U.S. history.

■ If the 1990s expansion lasts until the end of 1998, it will surpass the long expansion of the 1980s.

■ Some people say that 2000 could be the danger point for a downturn, because the U.S. economy has been in recession in the last four years ending in a zero—1960, 1970, 1980, and 1990.

Unemployment @ 5.5% since '95

Economic

A N A L Y S I S

■ Figure I shows the expansions in real GDP since 1921. The longest expansion lasted for almost 10 years during the 1960s. The second longest lasted for almost 8 years during the 1980s. The 1990s expansion is the third longest since World War II.

■ Figure 2 shows the 1990s expansion. Real GDP started out below potential GDP in the recession of 1990-1991. Real GDP expanded and, by mid-1994, was close to potential GDP. Both real GDP and potential GDP have grown at a similar rate since 1994.

■ Figure 3 shows the unemployment rate during the 1990s expansion. Unemployment peaked in 1992 and fell quickly through 1994. It has been steady at around 5.5 since 1995.

■ Figure 4 shows the inflation rate during the 1990s expansion. Beginning at almost 5 percent a year, the inflation rate has fallen to around 2 percent a year, its lowest level since the 1960s.

■ Expansions that last as long as the 1990s expansion are rare, and the current expansion will at some time come to an end.

■ The news article says that some people expect the next recession to occur in 2000 because "the country has been in recession in the last four years ending in a zero, 1960, 1970, 1980, and 1990."

■ There is nothing in the causes of recessions to think that timing of these four earlier recessions were anything other than coincidences.

■ The next recession will begin when some *currently unforeseeable* event brings a cut in spending and a surge in layoffs. In the past, such events have occurred on the average every 4 years but with a range that runs from 1 year to 10 years.

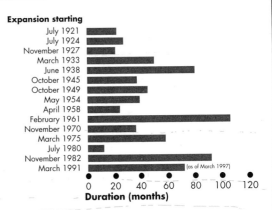

Figure 1 Expansion since 1921

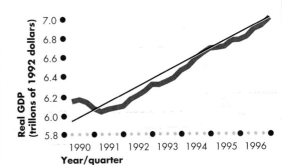

Figure 2 Real GDP

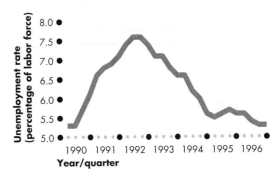

Figure 3 Unemployment

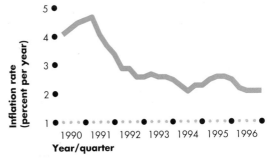

Figure 4 Inflation

SUMMARY

Key Points

Origins and Issues of Macroeconomics (p. 472)

■ Macroeconomics studies economic growth and fluctuations, unemployment, inflation, and deficits.

Economic Growth (pp. 473–478)

■ Economic growth is the expansion of potential GDP. Real GDP fluctuates around potential GDP in a business cycle.

■ Countries have similar productivity growth slowdowns and business cycles but different long-term trends in potential GDP.

■ The main benefit of long-term economic growth is higher future consumption, and the main cost is lower current consumption.

Jobs and Unemployment (pp. 478–480)

■ The U.S. economy creates 1.8 million jobs a year, but unemployment persists.

■ Unemployment increases during a recession and decreases during an expansion. The U.S. unemployment rate is lower than that in Canada and Western Europe but higher than that in Japan.

■ Unemployment can permanently damage a person's job prospects.

Inflation (pp. 481–483)

■ Inflation, a process of rising prices, is measured by the percentage change in the CPI.

■ Inflation is a problem because it lowers the value of money and makes money less useful as a measuring rod of value.

Deficits (pp. 483–485)

■ When government spending exceeds tax receipts, the government has a budget deficit.

■ When imports exceed exports, a nation has an international deficit.

■ Deficits are financed by borrowing.

Macroeconomic Policy Challenges and Tools (p. 485)

■ The macroeconomic policy challenge is to use fiscal policy and monetary policy to boost long-term growth, stabilize the business cycle, lower unemployment, tame inflation, and prevent large deficits.

Key Figures

Key Terms

QUESTIONS

1. What is economic growth and how is the long-term economic growth rate measured?

2. Is real GDP an ideal measure of total production? Explain why or why not.

3. Distinguish between actual real GDP and potential GDP.

4. Describe the productivity growth slowdown that occurred in the United States and other countries during the 1970s.

5. What is a business cycle? Describe its phases.

6. In what phase of the business cycle was the U.S. economy during 1975? 1980? 1985? 1995?

7. What are the benefits of long-term economic growth?

8. What are the costs of long-term economic growth?

9. What is unemployment?

10. Describe the main features of unemployment in the United States since 1930.

11. What does the unemployment rate tell us about the underutilization of labor? Explain your answer.

12. What are the main costs of unemployment?

13. Why is unemployment a serious problem?

14. Compare the unemployment rate in the United States since 1980 with that in Canada.

15. What is inflation? How is it measured?

16. What are some of the costs of inflation?

17. Compare inflation in the United States since 1970 with inflation in other industrial countries.

18. Why is inflation a problem?

19. What determines a government's budget deficit? How has the federal government's budget deficit evolved since 1970?

20. What is a country's international deficit? How has the U.S. international deficit changed since 1970?

21. What are the main challenges and tools of macroeconomic policy?

22. Distinguish between fiscal policy and monetary policy.

PROBLEMS

1. Obtain data on the growth rates of real GDP for the United States, Canada, Japan, the European Union, and the developing countries of Africa, Asia, the Middle East and Europe, and the Western Hemisphere since 1977. You will find the data in the most recent issue of the *Economic Report of the President* or by using the Parkin Web Link. Use what you have discovered to answer the following questions:
   a. Which region of the world has grown fastest during the past 20 years?
   b. In which regions is production shrinking rather than growing?
   c. Describe the growth of Japan in recent years and compare it with that in the United States.
   d. Compare the growth rates of the four big economies in the European Union (France, Germany, Italy, and the United Kingdom). Which has the fastest growth rate over the 1990s?

2. Study the figure, which shows real GDP in Mexico, and then answer the following questions:
   a. How many recessions did Mexico experience during this period?
   b. In which quarters, if any, did Mexico experience a business cycle peak?

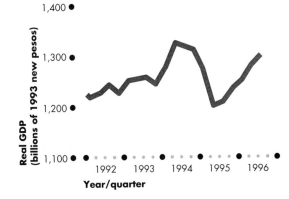

   c. In which quarters, if any, did Mexico experience a business cycle trough?
   d. In which quarters, if any, did Mexico experience an expansion?

http://hepg.awl.com/parkin/econ100

e.   In which years was economic growth in Mexico positive?

f.   In which years was economic growth in Mexico negative?

3.   Obtain data on unemployment rates in the United States and other major industrial countries. You can find the data in the *Monthly Labor Review* or from the Parkin Web Link.

a.   Compare the behavior of unemployment in the United States with that in the other countries.

b.   Which country had the lowest and which the highest unemployment rate in 1995?

c.   Which country had the lowest and which the highest teenage unemployment rate in 1995?

d.   Draw a graph and determine whether the unemployment rates move up and down together. Which country or countries stand out as having an especially low unemployment rate.

4.   Use the data in the Variable Graphing tool in the *Economics in Action* tutorial software to answer the following questions:

a.   Which country had the highest real GDP growth rate: the United States, Canada, France, or Japan?

b.   Which country had the highest unemployment rate: the United States, Canada, Sweden, or Japan?

c.   Which country had the lowest inflation rate: the United States, Canada, France, or Japan?

d.   Which country had the largest government budget deficit: the United States, Australia, Ireland, or Japan?

e.   Which countries, if any, that feature in the *Economics in Action* macroeconomics data set did not have a recession during the 1990s?

5.   Obtain data on the Consumer Price Index in your home city (or the nearest city for which you can get the data). You can find the data in the *CPI Detailed Report* (monthly) or from the Parkin Web Link. Then answer the following questions:

a.   Has your local CPI been higher or lower than the U.S. average CPI?

b.   Has your local inflation rate been higher or lower than the U.S. average inflation rate?

c.   Can you think of an explanation for what you've discovered?

6.   Obtain data on the federal government budget deficit as a percentage of GDP since the Great Depression. You can find the data in the *Economic Report of the President* (annual) or from the Parkin Web Link. Then answer the following questions:

a.   In how many years since 1934 has the federal government had a budget surplus?

b.   In which years were government budget deficits at their highest levels?

c.   Can you detect a trend in the deficit since World War II?

d.   Can you find periods in which the deficit was decreasing?

e.   In which earlier period did the deficit behave in a way similar to its behavior during the 1990s?

7.   Obtain data on the United States current account deficit and the current account deficits or surpluses of Japan and Canada. You can find these data from the Parkin Web Link:

a.   Do Japan and Canada have deficits or surpluses during the 1990s?

b.   When the U.S. deficit increases, what happens to the deficit or surplus in Canada and Japan?

c.   Can you think of reasons for the relationships you describe in your answer to b?

CRITICAL THINKING

1.   Study *Reading Between the Lines* on pp. 486–487 and then answer the following questions:

a.   When did the most recent expansion begin?

b.   How long has the most recent expansion lasted? Is it an unusually long expansion? Compare its length with that of other expansions since World War II and before World War II?

c.   Can you think of convincing reasons why the 1990s expansion has been a long one?

d.   Alan Greenspan was pleased with the economy in 1996. What actions do you think he should be considering taking to keep the economy expanding with low inflation?

23

Measuring GDP, Inflation, and Economic Growth

When Motorola contemplates spending $1 billion developing a wireless communications system in China, it pays close attention to forecasts of China's real GDP. When AT&T plans to expand its fiber-optics network, it uses forecasts of long-term growth in the U.S. economy. The outcomes of many business decisions turn on the quality of forecasts of economic conditions. ◆ A key input for making economic forecasts is gross domestic product, or GDP, which is like a barometer of a nation's economy. Economists pore over the numbers, looking at past trends and seeking patterns that might give a glimpse of the future. How do economic statisticians add up all the production of the country to arrive at the number called GDP? What exactly *is* GDP? ◆ Most of the time, our economy grows, but sometimes it shrinks. To reveal the rate of growth (or shrinkage), we must remove the effects of inflation on GDP and assess how *real* GDP is changing. How do we remove the inflation component of GDP to reveal real GDP? ◆ From economists to home makers, all types of people pay close attention to another economic barometer, the Consumer Price Index, or CPI. The Department of Labor publishes new figures each month, and analysts in newspapers and on TV quickly leap to conclusions about the causes of recent changes in prices and the prospects for future changes. How does the government determine the CPI? How well does it measure a consumer's living costs and the inflation rate? ◆ Some countries are rich, while others are poor and only now are in the process of developing their industries and reaching their productive potential. How do we compare incomes in one country with incomes in another? How can we make international comparisons of GDP? ◆ In this chapter, you are going to find out how economic statisticians measure real GDP and the price level. You are also going to learn how they use these measures to assess the economic growth rate and the inflation rate and to compare macroeconomic performance across countries.

Economic Barometers

After studying this chapter, you will be able to:

- Explain why aggregate income, expenditure, and product are equal

- Explain how GDP is measured

- Explain how the Consumer Price Index (CPI) and the GDP deflator are measured

- Explain the shortcomings of the CPI and the GDP deflator as measures of inflation

- Explain how *real* GDP is measured

- Explain the shortcomings of real GDP growth as a measure of improvements in living standards

Gross Domestic Product

WHAT EXACTLY IS GDP, HOW IS IT CALCULATED, what does it mean, and why do we care about it? You are going to discover the answers to these questions in this chapter. First, what *is* GDP? **GDP**, or **gross domestic product**, is the value of the *aggregate* production of goods and services in a country during a given time period—usually a year. The GDP of the United States, which measures the value of aggregate production in the United States during a year, was $7,576 billion in 1996.

How is GDP calculated? In a nutshell, GDP is calculated by valuing everything that is produced and adding all the values together. But precisely *what* is valued and *how* it is valued? To answer these questions, you need to understand two fundamental principles of economic accounting:

- The distinction between flows and stocks
- The equality of income, expenditure, and the value of production

Flows and Stocks

To keep track of our personal economic transactions and the economic transactions of a country, we distinguish between flows and stocks. A **flow** is a quantity per unit of time. The water that is running from an open faucet into a bathtub is a flow. So are the number of CDs that you buy during a month and the amount of income that you earn during a month. GDP is a flow. It is the value of the goods and services produced in a country *during a given time period*.

A **stock** is a quantity that exists at a point in time. The water in a bathtub is a stock. So are the number of CDs that you own and the amount of money in your savings account.

Capital and Investment The key macroeconomic stock is capital. **Capital** is the plant, equipment, buildings, and inventories of raw materials and semifinished goods that are used to produce other goods and services. The amount of capital in the economy exerts a big influence on GDP. Two flows change the stock of capital: investment and depreciation. Investment is the purchase of new capital. It increases the stock of capital. (Investment includes additions to inventories.) **Depreciation** is the decrease in the stock of capital that results from wear and tear and obsolescence.

Another name for depreciation is *capital consumption*. The total amount spent on adding to the stock of capital and on replacing depreciated capital is called **gross investment**. The amount spent on adding to the stock of capital is called **net investment**. Net investment equals gross investment minus depreciation.

Figure 23.1 illustrates these concepts. On January 1, 1997, Tom's Tapes, Inc. had 3 machines. This quantity was its initial capital. During 1997, Tom's scrapped an older machine. This quantity is its depreciation. After depreciation, Tom's stock of capital was down to 2 machines. But also during 1997, Tom's bought 2 new machines. This amount is its gross investment. By December 31, 1997, Tom's Tapes had 4 machines, so its capital had increased by 1 machine. This amount is Tom's net investment. Tom's net investment equals its gross investment (the

FIGURE 23.1
Capital and Investment

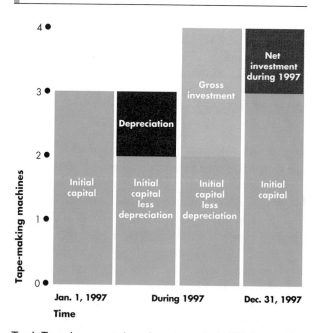

Tom's Tapes has a capital stock at the end of 1997 that equals its capital stock at the beginning of the year plus its net investment. Net investment is equal to gross investment less depreciation. Tom's gross investment is the 2 new machines bought during the year, and its depreciation is the 1 machine that Tom's scrapped during the year.

purchase of 2 new machines) minus its depreciation (1 machine scrapped).

The example of Tom's Tapes factory can be applied to the economy as a whole. The nation's capital stock decreases because capital depreciates and increases because of gross investment. The change in the nation's capital stock from one year to the next equals its net investment.

Wealth and Saving   Another macroeconomic stock is **wealth**, which is the value of all the things that people own. What people *own*, a stock, is related to what they *earn*, a flow. People *earn* an *income*, which is the amount they receive during a given time period from supplying the services of resources. Income can be either consumed or saved. **Consumption expenditure** is the amount spent on consumption goods and services. **Saving** is the amount of income remaining after meeting consumption expenditures. Saving adds to wealth, and dissaving (negative saving) decreases wealth.

For example, suppose that at the end of the school year, you have $250 in a savings account and some textbooks that are worth $300. That's all you own. Your wealth is $550. Suppose that you take a summer job and earn an income of $5,000. You are extremely careful and spend only $1,000 through the summer on consumption goods and services. At the end of the summer, when school starts again, you have $4,250 in your savings account. Your wealth is now $4,550. Your wealth has increased by $4,000, which equals your saving of $4,000. Your saving of $4,000 equals your income of $5,000 minus your consumption expenditure of $1,000.

National wealth and national saving work just like this personal example. The wealth of a nation at the start of a year equals its wealth at the start of the previous year plus its saving during the year. Its saving equals its income minus its consumption expenditure.

We'll make the idea of the nation's income and consumption expenditure more precise a bit later in this chapter. Before doing so, let's see what the stocks and flows that we've just learned about imply for the recurring theme of macroeconomics: short-term fluctuations in actual real GDP and long-term growth in potential GDP.

The Short Term Meets the Long Term   You saw in Chapter 22 that potential GDP grows incessantly, year after year. You also saw that actual real GDP grows and fluctuates around potential GDP. The

stocks and flows that you've just studied influence *both* the long-term growth in potential GDP and the short-term fluctuations in actual GDP. One of the reasons why potential GDP grows is that the capital stock grows. One of the reasons that real GDP fluctuates is that investment fluctuates. So capital and investment as well as wealth and saving are part of the key to understanding the growth of potential GDP and the fluctuations of real GDP.

The flows of investment and saving together with the flows of income and consumption expenditure interact in a circular flow of income and expenditure. In this circular flow, income equals expenditure, which also equals the value of production. This amazing equality is the foundation on which a nation's economic accounts are built and from which its GDP is measured.

Investment saving income expenditure

Income, Expenditure, and the Value of Production

To see that for the economy as a whole, income equals expenditure and also equals the value of production, we study the circular flow of income and expenditure.

Figure 23.2 illustrates the circular flow of income and expenditure. In the figure, the economy consists of four sectors: households, firms, governments, and the rest of the world (the purple diamonds). It has three types of markets: resource markets, goods (and services) markets, and financial markets. Focus first on households and firms.

Households and Firms   Households sell and firms buy the services of labor, capital, land, and entrepreneurship in resource markets. For these resource services, firms pay income to households: wages for labor services, interest for the use of capital, rent for the use of land, and profits for entrepreneurship. Firms' retained earnings—profits that are not distributed to households—are also part of the household sector's income. You can think of retained earnings as being income that households save and lend back to firms. Figure 23.2 shows the *aggregate income* received by all households in payment for the services of resources by the blue dots labeled *Y*.

Firms sell and households buy consumer goods and services—such as popcorn and soda, movies and chocolate bars, microwave ovens and inline skates, dental and dry cleaning services—in the markets for goods and services. The total payment that households make for these goods and services is *consumption*

FIGURE 23.2
The Circular Flow of Income and Expenditure

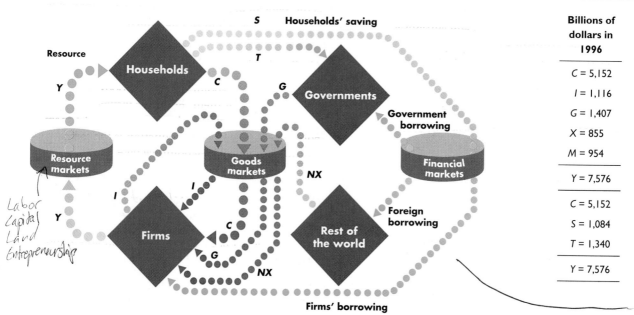

Billions of dollars in 1996	
$C = 5,152$	
$I = 1,116$	
$G = 1,407$	
$X = 855$	
$M = 954$	
$Y = 7,576$	
$C = 5,152$	
$S = 1,084$	
$T = 1,340$	
$Y = 7,576$	

In the circular flow of income and expenditure, households receive incomes (Y) from firms (blue flow) and make consumption expenditures (C); firms make investment expenditures (I); governments purchase goods and services (G); the rest of the world purchases net exports (NX)—(red flows). Aggregate income (blue flow) equals aggregate expenditure (red flows). Households' saving (S) and net taxes (T) leak from the circular flow. Firms borrow to finance their investment expenditures, and governments and the rest of the world borrow to finance their deficits or lend their surpluses (green flows). The table gives the values for the flows in 1996. Net exports (NX) is exports (X) minus imports (M).

Source: U.S. Department of Commerce, *Survey of Current Business* (March 1997).

expenditure. Figure 23.2 shows consumption expenditure by the red dots labeled C.

Firms buy and sell new capital equipment in the goods market. For example, IBM sells 1,000 PCs to General Motors, or Boeing sells an airplane to United Airlines. Some of what firms produce might not be sold at all and is added to inventory. For example, if GM produces 1,000 cars and sells 950 of them, the other 50 cars remain unsold and GM's inventory of cars increases by 50. When a firm adds unsold output to inventory, we can think of the firm as buying goods from itself. The purchase of new plant, equipment, and buildings and the additions to inventories are *investment.*

Figure 23.2 shows investment by the red dots labeled I. Notice that in the figure, investment flows from firms through the goods markets and back to firms. Some firms produce capital goods, and other

firms buy them (and firms "buy" inventories from themselves).

Firms finance their investment by borrowing from households in financial markets. Households' saving flows into financial markets, and firms' borrowing flows out of financial markets. Figure 23.2 shows these flows by the green dots labeled "Households' saving" or S and "Firms' borrowing." These flows are neither income nor expenditure. Income is a payment for the services of a resource, and expenditure is a payment for goods or services.

Governments   Governments buy goods and services, called **government purchases**, from firms. In Fig. 23.2 these government purchases are shown as the red flow G. Governments use taxes to pay for their purchases. Figure 23.2 shows taxes as net taxes by the green dots labeled T. **Net taxes** are equal to taxes paid to governments minus transfer payments received from governments and minus interest payments from the government on its debt. *Transfer payments* are cash transfers from governments to households and firms such as social security benefits, unemployment compensation, and subsidies.

When government purchases (G) exceed net taxes (T), the government has a budget deficit, which it finances by borrowing in financial markets (shown by the green dots labeled "Government borrowing.")

Rest of World Sector   Firms export goods and services to the rest of the world and import goods and services from the rest of the world. The value of exports minus the value of imports is called **net exports**. Figure 23.2 shows net exports by the red flow *NX*.

If the value of exports exceeds the value of imports, net exports are positive and flow from the rest of the world to firms. But if the value of exports is less than the value of imports, net exports are negative and flow from firms to the rest of the world.

If net exports are positive, the rest of the world is in deficit and we are in surplus. To finance its deficit, the rest of the world borrows from the domestic economy or sells domestic assets that it owns. For example, Korean Airlines can borrow in New York to finance the purchase of new airplanes from Boeing. These transactions take place in financial markets, and they are shown by the green flow labeled "Foreign borrowing."

If net exports are negative, we are in deficit and the rest of the world is in surplus. To finance our deficit, we borrow from the rest of the world or we sell foreign assets that we own. For example, a California winemaker might borrow in Frankfurt, Germany, to finance the purchase of a German-made grape-picking machine. Again, these transactions take place in financial markets. To illustrate this case in Fig. 23.2, we would reverse the directions of the flows of net exports and foreign borrowing.

To help you keep track of the different types of flows that make up the circular flow of income and expenditure, the flows are color-coded in Fig. 23.2. The red flows are expenditures on goods and services, the blue flow is income, and the green flows are financial transfers. The expenditure flows (red flows) are consumption expenditure, investment, government purchases, and net exports. The income flow (blue flow) is aggregate income. The financial transfers (green flows) are saving, net taxes, govern-

ment borrowing, foreign borrowing, and firms' borrowing.

Gross Domestic Product   Gross domestic product is the value of *aggregate production* in a country during a year. Production can be valued in two ways:

1. By what buyers pay for it
2. By what it costs producers to make it

From the viewpoint of buyers, goods are worth the prices paid for them. From the viewpoint of producers, goods are worth what it costs to make them. Fortunately, the value of production is the same regardless of which viewpoint we take. Let's see why.

Expenditure Equals Income   The total amount that buyers pay for the goods and services produced is *aggregate expenditure*. Let's focus on aggregate expenditure in Fig. 23.2. The expenditures on goods and services are shown by the red flows. Firms' revenues from the sale of goods and services equal consumption expenditure (C) plus investment (I) plus government purchases of goods and services (G) plus net exports (NX). The sum of these four flows is equal to aggregate expenditure on goods and services.

The total amount it costs producers to make goods and services is equal to the incomes paid for resource services. This amount is shown by the blue flow in Fig. 23.2.

The sum of the red flows equals the blue flow. The reason is that everything a firm receives from the sale of its output is paid out as incomes to the owners of the resources that it employs. That is,

$$Y = C + I + G + NX,$$

or aggregate income (Y) equals aggregate expenditure ($C + I + G + NX$).

The buyers of aggregate production pay an amount equal to aggregate expenditure, and the sellers of aggregate production pay an amount equal to aggregate income. Because aggregate expenditure equals aggregate income, these two methods of valuing aggregate production give the same answer. So

Aggregate production, or GDP, equals aggregate expenditure and equals aggregate income.

The circular flow of income and expenditure is the foundation on which the national economic accounts are built. It is used to provide the two approaches to measuring GDP. And it is used to create other accounts that help us to keep track of the flows of saving and investment, the government's budget, and the balance of our exports and imports.

Let's look next at how the circular flows you've just studied enable us to keep track of how investment is financed.

How Investment Is Financed

Investment, which adds to the stock of capital, is one of the determinants of the rate at which production grows. Investment is financed by:

- National saving
- Borrowing from the rest of the world

National Saving　The amount of saving by households and businesses plus government saving is called **national saving**. Saving by households and businesses, S, equals income minus taxes minus consumption expenditure. Government saving equals net taxes minus government purchases of goods and services, $(T - G)$. If the government has a budget surplus, $(T - G)$ is positive and this surplus is a source of finance for investment. But if the government has a budget deficit, $(T - G)$ is negative and part of saving is used to finance the government deficit. So

$$\text{National saving} = S + (T - G).$$

Borrowing from the Rest of the World　If we spend more on foreign goods and services than the rest of the world spends on ours, we must borrow from the rest of the world to pay the difference. That is, if the value of our imports (M) exceeds the value of our exports (X), we must borrow from the rest of the world an amount equal to $(M - X)$. In this case, part of the rest of the world's saving finances our negative net exports and frees up an equal amount of national saving to finance investment in the United States. Conversely, if foreigners spend more on U.S.-made goods and services than we spend on theirs, foreigners must borrow from us to pay the difference. That is, part of U.S. national saving flows to the rest of the world and is not available to finance U.S. investment.

In 1996, U.S. investment was $1,116 billion. This investment was financed by $1,017 billion of national saving and $99 billion of funds borrowed from the rest of the world.

Let's now see how the Department of Commerce uses the circular flows to measure GDP.

Measuring U.S. GDP

TO MEASURE GDP, THE DEPARTMENT OF Commerce uses two approaches:

- Expenditure approach
- Income approach

The Expenditure Approach

The *expenditure approach* measures GDP by using data on consumption expenditure, investment, government purchases, and net exports. Table 23.1 shows this approach. The first column gives the terms used in the *National Income and Product Accounts of the United States* (published by the Department of Commerce). The next column gives the symbol we've used in our GDP equations. GDP using the expenditure approach is the sum of personal consumption expenditures (C), gross private domestic investment (I), government purchases of goods and services (G), and net exports of goods and services (NX).

Personal consumption expenditures are the expenditures by households on goods and services produced in the United States and in the rest of the world. They include goods such as CDs and books and services such as banking and legal advice. They do *not* include the purchase of new homes, which is counted as part of investment.

TABLE 23.1

GDP: The Expenditure Approach

Item	Symbol	Amount in 1996 (billions of dollars)	Percentage of GDP
Personal consumption expenditures	C	5,152	68.0
Gross private domestic investment	I	1,116	14.7
Government purchases of goods and services	G	1,407	18.6
Net exports of goods and services	NX	–99	–1.3
Gross domestic product	Y	7,576	100.0

The expenditure approach measures GDP by adding personal consumption expenditures (C), gross private domestic investment (I), government purchases of goods and services (G), and net exports (NX). In 1996, GDP measured by the expenditure approach was $7,576 billion. Two thirds of aggregate expenditure is on personal consumption goods and services.

Source: U.S. Department of Commerce, *Survey of Current Business* (March 1997).

Gross private domestic investment is expenditure on capital equipment and buildings by firms and expenditure on new homes by households. It also includes the change in business inventories.

Government purchases of goods and services are the purchases of goods and services by all levels of government. This item includes expenditures on national defense and garbage collection. But it does *not* include *transfer payments*. These payments, such as medical aid and social security benefits, are not purchases of goods and services. They are transfers of funds from government to households.

Net exports of goods and services are the value of exports minus the value of imports. This item includes computers that IBM sells to Volkswagen, the German car producer, (a U.S. export) and Mazda RX7s that your local dealer buys from Japan (a U.S. import).

Table 23.1 shows the relative importance of the four items of aggregate expenditure. The largest component is personal consumption expenditures, and the smallest is net exports (negative in 1996).

Expenditures Not in GDP Aggregate expenditure, which equals GDP, does not include all the things that people and businesses buy. To distinguish total expenditure on GDP from other items of spending, we call the expenditure included in GDP *final expenditure*. Spending that is not part of final expenditure and not part of GDP include the purchase of:

- Intermediate goods and services
- Used goods
- Financial assets

Intermediate goods and services are the goods and services that firms buy from each other and use as inputs in the goods and services that they eventually sell to final users. When Dell Corp. buys computer chips from Intel Corp., it buys an intermediate good. A Dell computer is a final good, but an Intel chip is an intermediate good. To count the expenditure on intermediate goods and services as well as the expenditure on the final good involves counting the same thing twice—called *double counting*.

A good can sometimes be an intermediate good and sometimes a final good. For example, the ice cream that you buy on a hot summer day is a final good, but the ice cream that a diner buys and uses to make sundaes is an intermediate good. Whether a good is intermediate or final depends on what it is used for, not on what it is.

Expenditure on *used goods* is not part of GDP because these goods were counted as part of GDP in the period in which they were produced and in which they were new goods. For example, a 1990 automobile was part of GDP in 1990. If the car is traded on the used car market in 1997, the amount paid for the car is not part of GDP in 1997.

Firms often sell *financial assets* such as bonds and stocks to finance purchases of newly produced capital goods. The expenditure on newly produced capital goods is part of GDP, but the expenditure on financial securities is not. GDP includes the amount spent on new capital, not the amount spent on pieces of paper.

Let's look at the second way of measuring GDP, the income approach.

The Income Approach

The *income approach* measures GDP by summing the incomes that firms pay households for the resources they hire—wages for labor, interest for capital, rent for land, and profits for entrepreneurship. Let's see how the income approach works.

The *National Income and Product Accounts* divide incomes into five categories:

1. Compensation of employees
2. Net interest
3. Rental income
4. Corporate profits
5. Proprietors' income

Compensation of employees is the payment for labor services. It includes net wages and salaries (called "take-home pay") that workers receive plus taxes withheld on earnings plus fringe benefits such as social security and pension fund contributions.

Net interest is the interest households receive on loans they make minus the interest households pay on their own borrowing.

Rental income is the payment for the use of land and other rented inputs. It includes payments for rented housing and imputed rent for owner-occupied housing. (Imputed rent is an estimate of what home-owners would pay to rent the housing they own and use themselves. By including this item in the national income accounts, we measure the total value of housing services, whether they are owned or rented.)

Corporate profits are the profits of corporations. Some of these profits are paid to households in the form of dividends, and some are retained by corporations as undistributed profits. They are all income.

Proprietors' income is a mixture of the previous four items. It is difficult to split the income earned by the owner-operator of a business into compensation for labor, payment for the use of capital, and profit, so the national income accounts lump all these items into a single category.

Table 23.2 shows these five incomes and their relative magnitudes. Compensation of employees is the largest income category.

The sum of these five categories of incomes is called *net domestic income at factor cost.* The term *factor cost* is used because *factor of production* is another name for a productive resource. But *net domestic income at factor cost* is not GDP. We must make two further adjustments to get to GDP, one from *factor cost* to *market prices* and another from *net* product to *gross* product.

Factor Cost to Market Prices When we add up all the final expenditures on goods and services, we arrive at a total called *domestic product at market prices.* These expenditures are valued at the market prices that people pay for the various goods and services. Another way of valuing goods and services is at factor cost. *Factor cost* is the value of a good or service measured by adding together the costs of all the resources used to produce it. If the only economic transaction were between households and firms—if there were no government taxes or subsidies—the market price and factor cost values would be the same. But the presence of indirect taxes and subsidies makes these two methods of valuation differ.

An *indirect tax* is a tax paid by consumers when they buy goods and services. (In contrast, a *direct tax* is a tax on income.) State sales taxes and taxes on alcohol, gasoline, and tobacco products are indirect

[handwritten note: what loans do households make?]

TABLE 23.2

GDP: The Income Approach

Item	Amount in 1996 (billions of dollars)	Percentage of GDP
Compensation of employees	4,449	58.7
Net interest	405	5.4
Rental income	127	1.7
Corporate profits	650	8.6
Proprietors' income	518	6.8
Indirect taxes *less* Subsidies	569	7.5
Capital consumption (depreciation)	858	11.3
Gross domestic product	7,576	100.0

The sum of all incomes plus indirect taxes less subsidies equals net domestic income. GDP equals net domestic income plus capital consumption (depreciation). In 1996, GDP measured by the income approach was $7,576 billion.

Source: U.S. Department of Commerce, *Survey of Current Business* (March 1997).

taxes. Because of indirect taxes, consumers pay more for some goods and services than producers receive. Market price exceeds factor cost. For example, if the sales tax is 7 percent, when you buy a $1 chocolate bar you pay $1.07. The factor cost of the chocolate bar including profit is $1. The market price is $1.07.

A *subsidy* is a payment by the government to a producer. Payments made to grain growers and dairy farmers are subsidies. Because of subsidies, consumers pay less for some goods and services than producers receive. Factor cost exceeds market price.

To get from factor cost to market price, we add indirect taxes and subtract subsidies. Making this adjustment brings us one step closer to GDP, but it does not quite get us there. We must make one further adjustment.

Net Domestic Product to Gross Domestic Product What do the words *gross* and *net* mean? *Gross* means *before* subtracting *depreciation*—the decrease in the value of the capital stock that results from wear and tear and obsolescence. *Net* means *after* subtracting depreciation.

Gross investment is a component of aggregate expenditure. So total expenditure includes depreciation and is a gross measure. The *net profit* of businesses—profit *after* subtracting depreciation—is a component of aggregate incomes. So total income excludes depreciation and is a net measure.

To get *gross* domestic product from the income approach, we must add depreciation to aggregate income.

Table 23.2 summarizes these calculations and shows how the income approach leads to the same estimate of GDP as the expenditure approach after the adjustments that we've just described have been made.

Valuing the Output of Industries

The methods used to measure GDP can also be used to measure the contribution that an industry makes to GDP. But to measure the value of production of an individual industry, we count only the value added by that industry. **Value added** is the value of a firm's production minus the value of the *intermediate goods* that the firm buys from other firms. Equivalently, it is the sum of the incomes (including profits) paid to the resources used by the firm.

Figure 23.3 illustrates value added by looking at the brief life of a loaf of bread. It starts with the

farmer, who grows the wheat. The farmer hires labor, capital, and land and pays wages, interest, and rent for these resources. The farmer also earns a profit. The entire value of the wheat produced is the farmer's value added. The miller buys wheat from the farmer and turns it into flour. The miller hires labor and capital, pays wages and interest, and earns a profit. The miller has now added value to the wheat bought from the farmer. The baker buys flour from the miller. The price of the flour includes the value added by both the farmer and the miller. The baker adds more value by turning the flour into bread. The grocer buys the bread from the baker. The price paid by the grocer includes the value added by the farmer, the miller, and the baker. At this stage, the value of the loaf is its *wholesale* value. The grocer adds further value by

FIGURE 23.3

Value Added and
Final Expenditure

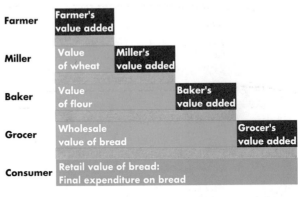

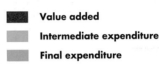

Value added

Intermediate expenditure

Final expenditure

A consumer's expenditure on bread (the green bar) is equal to the sum of the value added at each stage in its production (the red bars). The blue bars illustrate intermediate expenditure. Intermediate expenditure, for example the amount paid by the baker for the purchase of flour from the miller, equals the value added by the farmer and the miller. So to include intermediate expenditure and final expenditure double counts some value added.

making the loaf available in a convenient place and time. The consumer buys the bread for a price—its *market price*—that includes the value added by the farmer, the miller, the baker, and the grocer.

Final Goods and Intermediate Goods To value output, we count only *value added* because the sum of the value added at each stage of production equals expenditure on the *final good*. By using value added, we avoid double counting. In the above example, the only thing that has been produced and consumed is a loaf of bread—shown by the green bar in Fig. 23.3. The value added at each stage is shown by the red bars, and the sum of the red bars equals the green bar. The transactions involving intermediate goods,

shown by the blue bars, are not part of value added and are not counted as part of the value of output or of GDP.

Aggregate Expenditure, Income, and GDP

You've seen that aggregate expenditure equals aggregate income. And you've seen that the Department of Commerce uses both aggregate expenditure and aggregate income to measure GDP. Why does it use two approaches when they are supposed to be the same? The answer is that although the two concepts of the value of aggregate production are identical, the actual measurements, which are based on samples of information, give slightly different answers. The expenditure approach uses data from surveys of retail stores, house building, and business investment, the accounts of the federal, state, and local government, customs records, and many other sources. The income approach uses data supplied by the Internal Revenue Service. None of these sources gives a complete coverage of all the items that make up aggregate expenditure and aggregate income. So by using the two approaches, the Department of Commerce can check one aggregate against the other. The small discrepancy between the approaches is used to adjust both approaches to make them equal.

Figure 23.4 shows this equality between the approaches to measuring GDP and summarizes the expenditure, income, and product concepts.

FIGURE 23.4

Aggregate Expenditure, Output, and Income

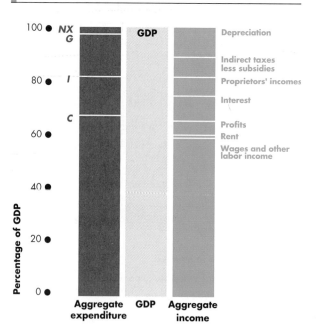

The red bar illustrates the components of aggregate expenditure as well as their relative magnitudes. Net exports, the smallest component, is shown here as a positive quantity, but in some years it is negative. The green bar illustrates the components of aggregate income and their relative magnitudes. The figure illustrates the equality between aggregate expenditure, aggregate income, and GDP (the yellow bar).

R E V I E W

■ The *expenditure approach* to measuring GDP sums consumption expenditure, investment, government purchases, and net exports.
■ The *income approach* to measuring GDP sums wages, interest, rent, and profits.
■ To value the production of an industry, we calculate the value added of that industry.

So far, in our study of GDP and its measurement, we've been concerned with the dollar value of GDP and its components. But the dollar value of GDP can change either because prices change or because there is a change in the volume of goods and services produced—a change in *real* GDP. Let's now see how we measure the price level and distinguish between the dollar value and the real value of GDP.

The Price Level and Inflation

THE PRICE LEVEL IS THE AVERAGE LEVEL OF PRICES measured by a *price index*. The **inflation rate** is the percentage change in the price level from one year to the next. The two main price indexes that are used in the United States today are:

- The Consumer Price Index
- The GDP deflator

Let's see how the two price indexes are calculated.

The Consumer Price Index

The **Consumer Price Index (CPI)** measures the average level of prices of the goods and services that a typical urban family buys. The Bureau of Labor Statistics (BLS) publishes the CPI every month. To construct the CPI, the BLS first selects a base period (currently the three-year period 1982–1984) and surveys consumer spending patterns to determine the "basket" of goods and services that people bought in the base period. That basket contains around 400 different goods and services.

Then, every month, the BLS sends a team of observers to more than 50 urban centers in the United States to record the prices of the 400 items. The CPI is calculated by valuing the basket at the current month's prices and expressing its value as a percentage of the value of the same basket in the base period.

Table 23.3 shows an example of the CPI calculation. The basket contains 5 pounds of oranges, 6 haircuts, and 100 bus rides. The table shows the prices in the base period and total expenditure. A typical consumer buys 5 pounds of oranges at $0.80 a pound and spends $4 on oranges. Expenditure on haircuts and bus rides is worked out in the same way. Total expenditure is the sum of expenditures on the three goods, which is $210.

To calculate the CPI for the current period, we need only discover the prices of the goods in the current period. We do not need to know the quantities bought. Suppose that the prices are those shown in Table 23.3 under "Current period." We can now calculate the current period's value of the basket. For example, the current price of oranges is $1.20 per pound, so the current period's value of the oranges in the basket (5 pounds) is 5 multiplied by $1.20, which is $6. The quantities of haircuts and bus rides are valued at this period's prices in a similar way. The total value of the basket in the current period is $231.

The CPI is the ratio of the current period's value of the basket to the base period's value, multiplied by 100. In Table 23.3, the CPI is 110 in the current period. The current period's price of the basket is 10 percent higher than it was in the base period.

TABLE 23.3
The CPI: A Simplified Calculation

Base-period basket	Base period Price	Base period Expenditure	Current period Price	Current period Expenditure
5 pounds of oranges	$ 0.80/pound	$ 4	$ 1.20/pound	$ 6
6 haircuts	$ 11.00 each	$ 66	$ 12.50 each	$ 75
100 bus rides	$ 1.40 each	$ 140	$ 1.50 each	$ 150
Total expenditure		$210		$231
CPI	$\frac{\$210.00}{\$210.00} \times 100 = 100$		$\frac{\$231.00}{\$210.00} \times 100 = 110$	

A fixed basket of goods—5 pounds of oranges, 6 haircuts, and 100 bus rides—is valued in the base period at $210. Prices change, and that same basket is valued at $231 in the current period. The CPI is equal to the current-period value of the basket divided by the base-period value of the basket, multiplied by 100. In the base period the CPI is 100, and in the current period the CPI is 110.

The GDP Deflator

The **GDP deflator** measures the average level of prices of all the goods and services that are included in GDP.

To calculate the GDP deflator, we use the formula

$$\text{GDP deflator} = \frac{\text{Nominal GDP}}{\text{Real GDP}} \times 100.$$

In this formula, **nominal GDP** is GDP valued in the current year's prices. It is the dollar value of GDP. **Real GDP** is GDP in a base year (currently 1992) scaled up by the growth rate of real GDP since the base year. But how do we calculate real GDP growth? Let's find out.

Real GDP Growth: A Chain-Weighted Measure

The **chain-weighted output index** is an index number that measures the growth rate of real GDP. To learn how to calculate such an index, let's study an imaginary economy that produces only oranges and video games. Table 23.4 lists the quantities produced and prices of these goods in 1992 and 1993.

Our goal is to calculate a chain-weighted output index that compares the 50 oranges and 5 video games produced in 1992 with the 45 oranges and 7 video games produced in 1993. To make a comparison, we must value the items using prices. But we have two sets of price: 1992 and 1993 prices. The chain-weighted output index uses *both* sets of prices.

TABLE 23.4

Calculating a Chain-Weighted Output Index

Item	1992 quantities	1992 prices	1992 quantities valued at 1992 prices	1993 prices	1992 quantities valued at 1993 prices
Oranges	50	$1.00	$50	$2.00	$100
Video games	5	$10.00	$50	$8.00	$40
Totals			A = $100		D = $140

Item	1993 quantities	1992 prices	1993 quantities valued at 1992 prices	1993 prices	1993 quantities valued at 1993 prices
Oranges	45	$1.00	$45	$2.00	$90
Video games	7	$10.00	$70	$8.00	$56
Totals			B = $115		E = $146

Output index $\qquad C = B \div A = 1.150 \qquad\qquad F = E \div D = 1.043$

Chain-weighted output index (geometric mean of C and $F = \sqrt{1.150 \times 1.043}$) = 1.095

Growth rate in 1993 using chain-weighted output index $\qquad$ 9.5 percent

---

In 1992, an imaginary economy produces 50 oranges at $1 each and 5 video games at $10 each and in 1993, the economy produces 45 oranges at $2 each and 7 video games at $8 each. Nominal GDP in 1992 is $100 (A in the table). The value of the 1993 quantities in the 1992 prices is $115 (B in the table). Output valued in 1992 prices has grown by 15 percent (B is 15 percent larger than A).

Nominal GDP in 1993 is $146 (E in the table). The value of 1992 quantities in the 1993 prices is $140 (D in the table). Output valued in 1993 prices has grown by 4.3 percent (E is 4.3 percent larger than D). The chain-weighted output index is the geometric mean of the two indexes C and F and is 1.095. Real GDP in 1993 is equal to real GDP in 1992 multiplied by 1.095. The growth rate in 1993 is 9.5 percent.

The calculations needed are the following:

- Nominal GDP in 1992 (total expenditure on oranges and video games during 1992), which is $100 (*A* in the table).
- The value of output in 1993 using the 1992 prices, which is $115 (*B*).
- An output index for 1993, which equals the value of output in 1993 using 1992 prices divided by nominal GDP in 1992. That index is 1.150 (*C*).
- Nominal GDP in 1993, which is $146 (*E*).
- The value of output in 1992 using the 1993 prices, which is $140 (*D*).
- A second output index for 1993, which equals nominal GDP in 1993 divided by the value of output in 1992 using 1993 prices. That index is 1.043 (*F*).
- The chain-weighted index for 1993, which is the *geometric means* of the two output indexes for 1993. (A geometric mean is a special kind of average that is used for calculating average growth rates. For two numbers it is the square root of their product.) In the table, this index is 1.095, which means that the growth rate of real GDP in 1993 is 9.5 percent.

The calculation is repeated every year and always uses data for the current year and the previous year. Real GDP is calculated by applying the current year's growth rate to the previous year's real GDP. Each year is chained to the base year by a series of "links," each of which uses information from only the year in question and the previous year. So unlike the CPI, the weights for the GDP deflator are constantly changing.

Back to the GDP Deflator With an estimate of real GDP, we can now calculate the GDP deflator. Let's use the numbers we've calculated in Table 23.4 in the formula for the GDP deflator. Nominal GDP is $146 and real GDP is $109.5, so the GDP deflator is

$$\text{GDP deflator} = \frac{\$146}{\$109.5} \times 100 = 133.3.$$

A GDP deflator of 133.3 tells us that the price level in the current year is 33.3 percent higher than the price level in the base year. In the base year, nominal GDP equals real GDP and the GDP deflator is 100.

You can think of nominal GDP as a balloon that is blown up by growing production and rising prices. In Fig. 23.5, the GDP deflator lets the inflation air out of the nominal GDP balloon—the contribution of

FIGURE 23.5

The U.S. GDP Balloon

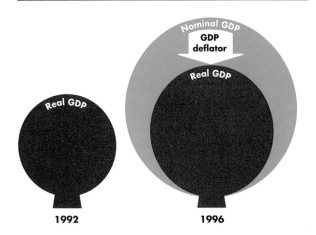

Part of the rise in GDP comes from inflation and part from increased production—an increase in real GDP. The GDP deflator lets some air out of the GDP balloon so that we can see the extent to which production has grown.

Source: *Economic Report of the President,* 1997.

rising prices—so that we can see what has happened to *real* GDP. The red balloon for 1992 shows real GDP in that year. The green balloon shows *nominal* GDP in 1996. The red balloon for 1996 shows real GDP for that year. To see real GDP in 1996, we *deflate* nominal GDP using the GDP deflator.

R E V I E W

- We measure the price level by using the CPI and the GDP deflator.
- The CPI measures the average price of a fixed basket of goods and services that a typical family buys.
- The GDP deflator measures the average price of the changing basket of goods and services that make up GDP.
- The GDP deflator is calculated as nominal GDP divided by real GDP (multiplied by 100). Real GDP is measured by using a chain-linked output index that uses the prices of the current year and the previous year.

The Biased CPI

A MAJOR PURPOSE OF THE CPI IS TO MEASURE inflation, and the measure is put to practical use. For example, it is used to determine cost of living adjustments to Social Security payments and changes in tax brackets—the income ranges over which different income tax rates apply. The data generated by the CPI survey are also used, along with other information, in the calculations of real GDP, nominal GDP, and the GDP deflator.

Measuring the inflation rate accurately is of crucial importance. A 1 percent upward bias in the estimated inflation rate translates into a 1 percent downward bias in the estimated growth rate of real GDP.

How good a measure of inflation is the CPI? Does a 2.7 percent increase in the CPI mean that the cost of living has increased by 2.7 percent? Does a 3 percent increase in the GDP deflator mean that the prices of the goods and services that make up real GDP have increased by 3 percent?

Despite the importance of getting the numbers right, the CPI and the GDP deflator give different views of the inflation rate, and neither index is a perfect measure. Figure 23.6 shows the difference in the two measures. The average inflation rate over the period shown is 4.9 percent a year for the CPI and 4.8 percent a year for the GDP deflator, but the CPI fluctuates more than the GDP deflator. Worse, *both* measures of inflation probably overstate the inflation rate.

The Sources of Bias

The main sources of bias in the CPI are:

- New goods bias
- Quality change bias
- Commodity substitution bias
- Outlet substitution bias

New Goods Bias New goods keep replacing old goods. For example, PCs have replaced typewriters. If you want to compare the price level in 1997 with that in 1977, you somehow have to compare the price of a computer today with that of a typewriter in 1977. Because PCs are more expensive than typewriters, the arrival of these new goods puts an upward bias into the estimate of the price level.

FIGURE 23.6
Two Measures of Inflation

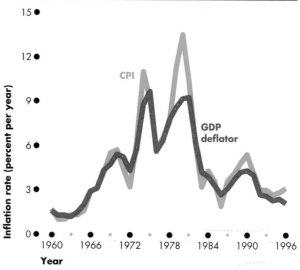

The CPI and the GDP deflator have similar averages over the period shown here—4.9 percent a year for the CPI and 4.8 percent a year for the GDP deflator—but the CPI fluctuates more than the GDP deflator, and both measures probably overstate the inflation rate.

Source: Economic Report of the President, 1997.

Quality Change Bias Most goods undergo constant quality improvement. Cars, VCRs, TVs, computers, CD players, and even textbooks get better year after year. Improvements in quality sometimes bring higher prices. But such price increases are not inflation. For example, suppose that a 1997 car is 5 percent better and costs 5 percent more than a 1995 car. Adjusted for the quality change, the price of the car has been constant. But in calculating the CPI, the price of the car will be counted as having increased by 5 percent.

Commodity Substitution Bias A change in the CPI measures the percentage change in the price of a *fixed* basket of goods and services. But changes in relative prices lead consumers to seek less costly items and to substitute such items in place of items whose prices have increased. For example, if the price of beef rises but the price of chicken remains constant, consumers substitute chicken for beef—they increase their consumption of chicken and decrease their consumption of beef. They might consume the same number of calories and the same amount of protein and get the same (or very similar) enjoyment from their food. The cost of the protein that people are actually buying has not changed, but the CPI records that it has increased because it does not take such a substitution into account.

Outlet Substitution Bias   People do not only change the items they buy when relative prices change. They also change their shopping patterns. With higher prices, people use discount stores more frequently and convenience stores less frequently. This phenomenon is called *outlet substitution*. By being careful to find the least-cost outlets, consumers can cut the prices they pay. And when prices rise, the incentive to seek lower-cost outlets increases. The CPI surveys do not monitor the outlet substitutions that people make.

Because of the four sources of bias, the Consumer Price Index, which is based on a fixed basket, overstates the effects of a given price change on the price level and therefore on the inflation rate.

To reduce the bias problems, the Bureau of Labor Statistics revises the basket used for calculating the CPI about every 10 years. The current plan is to revise the CPI in 1998 by using a basket of goods and services based on spending patterns in 1993–1995. The BLS also uses some sophisticated statistical techniques to reduce the biases.

The Magnitude of the Bias

How big is the bias in the measurement of the CPI? This question was tackled in 1996 by a Congressional Advisory Commission on the Consumer Price Index chaired by Michael Boskin, an economics professor at Stanford University. This commission said that the CPI overstates inflation by 1.1 percentage points a year. That is, if the CPI reports that inflation is 3.1 percent a year, most likely inflation is actually 2 percent a year.

Is the GDP Deflator Biased?

The GDP deflator is calculated from nominal GDP and the chain-linked estimate of real GDP growth. In principle, real GDP includes new goods and quality improvements. It is also based on people's actual expenditures and so reflects substitutions of both commodities and retail outlets. So in principle, the GDP deflator is not subject to the biases of the CPI. But in practice, the GDP deflator suffers from some of the CPI's problems. To arrive at its estimate of real GDP, the Commerce Department does not directly measure the physical quantities produced. Instead, it estimates quantities by dividing expenditures by price indexes. And one of these price indexes is the CPI. So the biased CPI injects a bias into the GDP deflator.

Some Consequences of the Bias

The bias in the CPI has three main consequences. It:

- Distorts private contracts
- Increases government outlays
- Biases estimates of real earnings

Many private agreements, such as wage contracts, are linked to the CPI. For example, a firm and its workers might agree to a three-year wage deal that increases the wage rate by 2 percent a year *plus* the percentage increase in the CPI. Such a deal ends up giving the workers more real income than the firm intended.

Close to a third of federal government outlays are linked directly to the CPI. And while a bias of 1 percent a year seems small, accumulated over a decade, it adds up to almost a trillion dollars of additional expenditures.

According to official government statistics, since 1973, real hourly earnings in manufacturing industries have *fallen* by 13 percent. If the CPI is adjusted for the bias estimated by the Boskin Commission, this picture is transformed into one in which real earnings have *increased* by 13 percent!

REVIEW

- The arrival of new goods, quality changes, commodity substitution, and outlet substitution make the CPI a biased measure of the price level.
- It is estimated that the CPI overstates the inflation rate by 1.1 percentage points per year.
- The CPI is an input into the calculation of the GDP deflator, so it too is biased.

You now know some limitations of the price level. Let's next look at the limitations of the real GDP data.

The Limitations of Real GDP

ESTIMATES OF REAL GDP AND THE REAL GDP growth rate are used for three main purposes:

- Economic welfare comparisons
- International comparisons of GDP
- Business cycle assessment and forecasting

Although real GDP is used for these three purposes, it is not a perfect measure for any of them. We'll look at how real GDP is used and its limitations in each of the three cases.

Economic Welfare

Economic welfare is a comprehensive measure of the general state of economic well-being. Real GDP growth is one indicator of an improvement in economic welfare. Today, with a real GDP per person in the United States of about $25,000, we are much better off than we were in 1960, when real GDP per person was $12,500. But are we twice as well off? Does real GDP give us a full and accurate measure of economic welfare? It does not. The reason is that economic welfare depends on many other factors that are not measured by real GDP (or that are not measured accurately by real GDP). Some of these factors are:

- Overadjustment for inflation
- Household production
- Underground economic activity
- Health and life expectancy
- Leisure time
- Environment quality
- Political freedom and social justice

Overadjustment for Inflation   You've seen that the price indexes used to measure inflation give an upward-biased estimate of true inflation. They give a downward-biased estimate of the growth rate of real GDP. When car prices rise because cars have gotten better (safer, more fuel efficient, more comfortable), the CPI and the GDP deflator count the price increase as inflation. So what is really an increase in production is counted as an increase in price rather than an increase in real GDP. It is deflated away by the wrongly measured higher price level. The magnitude of this bias is less than the bias in the CPI

(less than 1.1 percentage points a year), but its exact magnitude is not known.

Household Production   An enormous amount of production takes place every day in our homes. Changing a light bulb, cutting the grass, washing the car, growing vegetables, and teaching a child to catch a ball are all examples of productive activities that do not involve market transactions and are not counted as part of GDP.

Household production has become much more capital intensive over the years. As a result, less labor is used in household production than in earlier periods. For example, a microwave meal that takes just a few minutes to prepare uses a great deal of capital and almost no labor. Because we use less labor and more capital in household production, it is not easy to work out whether household production has increased or decreased over time. But it is likely that market production counted in GDP has increasingly replaced household production. Two trends point in this direction. One is the trend in the number of people who hold jobs, which has increased from 60 percent in 1970 to 67 percent in 1996. The other is the trend in the purchase of traditionally home-produced goods and services in the market. For example, more and more families now eat in fast food restaurants—one of the fastest-growing industries in the United States—and use day-care services. This trend means that an increasing proportion of food preparation and child care that used to be part of household production is now measured as part of GDP.

Underground Economic Activity   The *underground economy* is the part of the economy that is purposely hidden from the view of the government so as to avoid taxes and regulations or because the goods and services being produced are illegal. Because underground economic activity is unreported, it is omitted from GDP.

The underground economy is easy to describe, even if it is hard to measure. It includes the production and distribution of illegal drugs, production that uses illegal labor that is paid less than the minimum wage, and jobs done for cash to avoid paying income taxes. This last category might be quite large and includes tips earned by cab drivers, hairdressers, and hotel and restaurant workers.

Estimates of the scale of the underground economy range between 9 and 30 percent of GDP ($630 billion to $2,100 billion) in the United States and much more in some countries. It is particularly large in some Eastern European countries that are making a transition from Communist economic planning to a market economy.

Provided that the underground economy is a reasonably stable proportion of the total economy, the growth rate of real GDP still gives a useful estimate of changes in economic welfare. But sometimes production shifts from the underground to the rest of the economy, and sometimes it shifts the other way. The underground economy expands relative to the rest of the economy if taxes become especially high or if regulations become especially restrictive. And the underground economy shrinks relative to the rest of the economy if the burdens of taxes and regulations are eased. During the 1980s, when tax rates were cut, there was an increase in the reporting of previously hidden income, and tax revenues increased. So some part (but probably a very small part) of the expansion of real GDP during the 1980s represented a shift from the underground economy rather than an increase in production.

Health and Life Expectancy Good health and a long life—the hopes of everyone—do not show up in real GDP, at least not directly. A higher real GDP does enable us to spend more on medical research, health care, a good diet, and exercise equipment. And as real GDP has increased, our life expectancy has lengthened—from 70 years at the end of World War II to approaching 80 years today. Infant deaths and death in childbirth, two fearful scourges of the nineteenth century, have almost been eliminated.

But we face new health and life expectancy problems every year. AIDS, drug abuse, and violence are taking young lives at a rate that causes serious concern. When we take these negative influences into account, we see that real GDP growth overstates the improvements in economic welfare.

Leisure Time Leisure time is an economic good that adds to our economic welfare. Other things being equal, the more leisure we have, the better off we are. Our time spent working is valued as part of GDP, but our leisure time is not. Yet from the point of view of economic welfare, that leisure time must be at least as valuable to us as the wage that we earn on the last hour worked. If it were not, we would work instead of taking the leisure. Over the years, leisure time has steadily increased. The workweek has become shorter, more people take early retirement, and the number of vacation days has increased.

These improvements in economic well-being are not reflected in GDP.

Environment Quality The quality of the environment is directly affected by economic activity. The burning of hydrocarbon fuels is the most visible activity that damages our environment. But it is not the only example. The depletion of exhaustible resources, the mass clearing of forests, and the pollution of lakes and rivers are other major environmental consequences of industrial production.

Resources that are used to protect the environment are valued as part of GDP. For example, the value of catalytic converters that help to protect the atmosphere from automobile emissions are part of GDP. But if we did not use such pieces of equipment and instead polluted the atmosphere, we would not count the deteriorating air that we were breathing as a negative part of GDP.

An industrial society possibly produces more atmospheric pollution than an agricultural society does. But such pollution does not always increase as we become wealthier. One of the things that wealthy people value is a clean environment, and they devote resources to protecting it. Compare the pollution that was discovered in East Germany in the late 1980s with pollution in the United States. East Germany, a relatively poor country, polluted its rivers, lakes, and atmosphere in a way that is unimaginable in the United States or in wealthy West Germany. *But because it was poor, or because it was compt?*

Political Freedom and Social Justice Most people value political freedoms such as those provided by the U.S. Constitution. And they value social justice or fairness—equality of opportunity and of access to social security safety nets that protect people from the extremes of misfortune.

A country might have a very large real GDP per person but have limited political freedom and equity. For example, a small elite might enjoy political liberty and extreme wealth while the vast majority are effectively enslaved and live in abject poverty. Such an economy would generally be regarded as having less economic welfare than one that had the same amount of real GDP but in which political freedoms were enjoyed by everyone. Today, China has rapid real GDP growth but limited political freedoms, while Russia has a decreasing real GDP and an emerging democratic political system. Economists have no easy way to determine which of these countries is better off.

The Bottom Line Do we get the wrong message about changes (or differences) in economic welfare by looking at changes (or differences) in real GDP? The influences omitted from real GDP are probably important and could be large. Developing countries have a larger underground economy and a larger amount of household production than do developed countries. So as an economy develops and grows, part of the apparent growth might reflect a switch from underground to regular production and from home production to market production. This measurement error overstates the rate of economic growth and the improvement in economic welfare.

Other influences on living standards include the amount of leisure time available, the quality of the environment, the security of jobs and homes, the safety of city streets, and so on. It is possible to construct broader measures that combine the many influences that contribute to human happiness. Real GDP will be one element in those broader measures, but it will by no means be the whole of them.

International Comparisons of GDP

All the problems we've just reviewed affect economic welfare of every country, so to make international comparisons of economic welfare, factors additional to real GDP must be used. But real GDP comparisons are a major component of international welfare comparisons, and two special problems arise in making these comparisons. First, the real GDP of one country must be converted into the same currency units as the real GDP of the other country. Second, the same prices must be used to value the goods and services in the countries being compared. Let's look at these two problems by using a striking example, a comparison of the United States and China.

In 1992 (the most recent year for which we can make this comparison), real GDP per person in the United States was $24,408. The official Chinese statistics published by the International Monetary Fund (IMF) say that real GDP per person in China in 1992 was 2,028 yuan. (The yuan is the currency of China.) On the average, during 1992, $1 U.S. was worth 5.762 yuan. If we use this exchange rate to convert Chinese yuan into U.S. dollars, we get a value of $352.

The official comparison of China and the United States makes China look extremely poor. In 1992, real GDP per person in the United States was 69 times that in China.

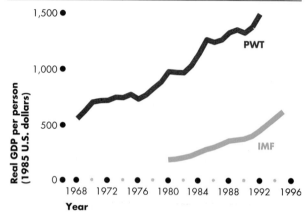

FIGURE 23.7

Two Views of Real GDP in China

According to the official statistics of the International Monetary Fund (IMF) and the World Bank, China is a poor developing country. But according to an alternative view, Penn World Table (PWT), which is based on purchasing power prices, China has a real GDP more than 6 times the official view and has the world's third largest total production.

Sources: *International Financial Statistics Yearbook* 1994, (Washington, D.C.: International Monetary Fund, *World Development Report, 1994,* (Washington, D.C.: World Bank, 1994); "The Penn World Table: An Expanded Set of International Comparisons, 1950–1988," *Quarterly Journal of Economics,* May 1991, pp. 327–368; new computer diskette, Mark 5.6a, January 15, 1995; and the author's calculations.

Figure 23.7 shows the official story of real GDP in China between 1968 and 1992. But Fig. 23.7 also shows another story. It shows an estimate of real GDP per person in China that is much larger than the official measure. Let's see how this alternative measurement is made.

GDP in the United States is measured by using prices that prevail in the United States. China's GDP is measured by using prices that prevail in China. But the relative prices in the two countries are very different. Some goods that are expensive in the United States cost very little in China. These items get a small weight in China's real GDP. If, instead of using China's prices, all the goods and services produced in China are valued at the prices prevailing in the United States, then a more valid comparison can be made of GDP in the two countries. Such a comparison uses prices called *purchasing power parity prices.*

Robert Summers and Alan Heston, economists in the Center for International Comparisons at the University of Pennsylvania, have used purchasing power parity prices to construct real GDP data for more than 100 countries. These data, which are published in the Penn World Table (PWT), tell a remarkable story about China. The PWT data use 1985 as the base year, so they are measured in 1985 dollars. According to the Penn World Table, in 1992, real GDP per person in the United States was 12 times that of China, not the 69 times shown in the official data.

Figure 23.7 shows the PWT view of China and compares it with the official view. The difference in the two views arises from the prices used. The official statistics use Chinese prices, while the PWT data use purchasing power parity prices.

Despite large differences in estimates of the *level* of China's real GDP, there is much less doubt about its growth rate. The economy of China is expanding at an extraordinary rate, and it is for this reason that most businesses are paying a great deal of attention to the prospects of expanding their activities in China and the other Asian economies.

U.S. real GDP is measured quite reliably. But China's is not. The alternative measures of China's real GDP are somewhat unreliable, and the truth about GDP in China is not known.

Business Cycle Assessment and Forecasting

When the Fed decides to raise interest rates to slow an expansion that it believes is too strong, it looks at the latest estimates of real GDP and inflation. But we've seen that the inflation rate is biased. Does this bias hamper our ability to isolate the phases of the business cycle? It does not. The reason is that the bias in the CPI does not change over the business cycle. The CPI is inaccurate by a similar amount every year. So while inflation mismeasurement leads to wrong estimates of long-term real GDP growth, it does not cause a wrong assessment of the phase of the business cycle.

The fluctuations in economic activity measured by real GDP tell a reasonably accurate story about the phase of the business cycle that the economy is in. When real GDP grows, the economy is in a business cycle expansion, and when real GDP shrinks (for two quarters), the economy is in a recession. Also, as real GDP fluctuates, so do employment and unemployment.

But real GDP fluctuations probably exaggerate or overstate the fluctuations in total production and economic welfare. The reason is that when business activity slows down in a recession, household production increases and so does leisure time. When business activity speeds up in an expansion, household production and leisure time decrease. Because household production and leisure time increase in a recession and decrease in an expansion, real GDP fluctuations tend to overstate the fluctuations in total production and in economic welfare. But the directions of change of real GDP, total production, and economic welfare are probably the same.

R E V I E W

- Real GDP is not an accurate measure of economic welfare because it undervalues quality improvements, omits some production, and ignores indicators of economic welfare such as health and life expectancy, leisure time, the environment, and political freedom.
- To make international comparisons of real GDP, we must use purchasing power parity prices.
- Real GDP understates the long-term growth rate and overstates business cycle fluctuations.

◆ In Chapter 22 we studied the macroeconomic performance of the United States in recent years—the growth and fluctuations in real GDP, unemployment, inflation, and deficits. We've now studied the methods used to measure some of these indicators of macroeconomic performance. We've seen how real GDP and the price level are measured, and we've seen what these measures mean.

In Chapter 24, we study *aggregate* demand and *aggregate* supply. This aggregate model parallels the demand and supply model of a single market. And it serves as an overview and backdrop against which to place your study of economic growth, unemployment, and inflation. An understanding of this model will help you to find your way through what can sometimes seem like a macroeconomic maze.

Before you embark on this next topic, spend a few minutes with *Reading Between the Lines* on pp. 510-511, which explores the consequences of the bias in the CPI for the measurement of real GDP and real hourly earnings. You'll be surprised by the numbers.

Policy
WATCH Correcting the CPI Bias

Essence of
THE STORY

THE NEW YORK TIMES, DECEMBER 1, 1996

Sorry, Wrong Numbers So Maybe It Wasn't the Economy

By FLOYD NORRIS

Economic statistics are thrust into the news every day, with a portentous exactitude that can send Wall Street soaring or reeling, influence Government policy, even sway elections. Did consumer prices rise one-tenth of a percent more than was expected? Was economic growth a half percentage point less than people had been hoping?

But what if the statistics are wrong? And what if they are consistently wrong in the same direction? Over time, that can produce a very distorted picture of the economy, with unfortunate effects brought about not by the economy but by our perceptions of it and with those perceptions having effects of their own. ...

This week a commission headed by Michael Boskin, the Stanford economist and former adviser to President Bush, will report to the Senate Finance Committee that inflation, as measured by the Consumer Price Index, has been rising at a far slower pace than we had thought. Economists who have studied the issue now generally agree that inflation has been overstated, although some

argue that the error is relatively small and may not make a significant difference.

The commission was appointed last year because of serious doubts about how changes in benefits and tax brackets, which have a major effect on the deficit, are calculated. A conclusion that the Consumer Price Index [CPI] has been overstated could lead to efforts to reduce the automatic increases in certain benefits, notably Social Security. That's sure to provoke a fight.

But perhaps even more important are changes that may be necessary in our view of the economy for the last two decades. For much of that time, even as America came roaring back into a preeminent position in technological leadership and the stock market zoomed, economists have been looking at statistics that showed a weak economy. And politicians have been trying to address public angst over economic decline. ...

Leonard Nakamura, an economist with the Federal Reserve Bank of Philadelphia, is known for his work on inflation. ... His estimates of the overstatement are among the largest ... at about 1.25 percent annually in the mid-1970s, rising to about 2.75 percent now. ...

■ Economic statistics can influence stock markets and government policy and, if inaccurate, economic statistics can produce a distorted picture of the economy.

■ In December 1996, a commission headed by Michael Boskin reported to the Senate Finance Committee that the CPI overstates the inflation rate.

■ Economists generally agree that the CPI overstates the inflation rate but are uncertain about the magnitude of the overstatement.

■ For the last 20 years, technology has advanced and the stock prices have increased, but economic statistics have shown slow economic growth.

■ Leonard Nakamura, an economist at the Federal Reserve Bank of Philadelphia, says the economic statistics are wrong and that inflation has been overstated—by 1.25 percent a year during the mid-1970s to 2.75 percent a year in 1996.

Economic

A N A L Y S I S

■ Leonard Nakamura, a research economist at the Federal Reserve Bank of Philadelphia, believes that inflation has been over-stated for at least 20 years. He says that the overstate-ment was approximately 1.25 percent annually dur-ing the mid-1970s, rising to approximately 2.75 percent annually by the mid-1990s.

■ Figure 1 shows Mr. Nakamura's estimate of the Consumer Price Index. His index equals 100 in 1975. According to Mr. Nakamura, the price level doubled between 1975 and 1996, not tripled as has been reported in the official data.

■ If we accept Mr. Nakamura's revised price level, we must change other economic indicators that are expressed in con-stant dollars.

■ Figure 2 shows the implications of Mr. Nakamura's assumptions for real GDP. Using his new inflation figures, real GDP has increased by twice as much as reported in the official data.

■ Figure 3 shows the impact of the new view of prices on real hourly earnings. The official view is that since 1975, real hourly earnings have *decreased* by 9 percent. The new view is that real hourly earnings have *increased* by 35 percent!

■ Mr. Nakamura's views are toward the upper end of the range of what economists believe, but they are not outrageous. He could be correct. If he is correct, the U.S. econo-my is in even better shape than Alan Greenspan, President Clinton, and many other leading public commentators dared to believe.

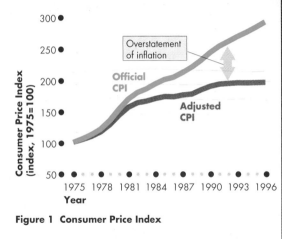

Figure 1 Consumer Price Index

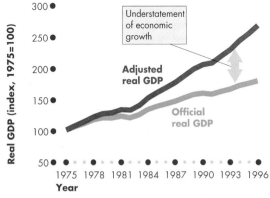

Figure 2 Real GDP

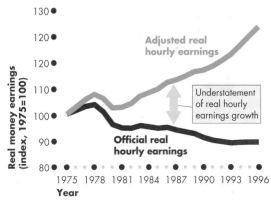

Figure 3 Hourly earnings

You're

THE VOTER

■ As a taxpayer and voter, do you care whether the government's economic statistics are accurate?

■ Try to think of reasons why is matters *to you* that the official statistics are accurate?

■ Would you be willing to see government funds diverted from some existing use and spent on data gathering and processing to get better measures of prices, real GDP, and real earnings?

SUMMARY

Key Points

Gross Domestic Product (pp. 492–496)

- Gross domestic product (GDP) is the value of total production in a country during a given period.
- GDP is calculated by using the circular flow of income and expenditure.
- Aggregate expenditure on goods and services equals aggregate income and GDP.

Measuring U.S. GDP (pp. 496–500)

- Because aggregate expenditure, aggregate income, and the value of aggregate production are equal, we can measure GDP by using the expenditure approach or the income approach.
- The expenditure approach sums consumption expenditure, investment, government purchases of goods and services, and net exports.
- The income approach sums wages, interest, rent, and profit.

The Price Level and Inflation (pp. 501–503)

- Inflation is measured by the rate of change of the CPI or the GDP deflator.
- The price level is measured by the Consumer Price Index (CPI) and the GDP deflator.
- The CPI measures the average price of goods and services typically consumed by American families.
- The GDP deflator measures the average price of all goods and services that make up GDP.

The Biased CPI (pp. 504–505)

- The CPI gives an upward-biased measure of inflation because some goods disappear and new goods become available, and the quality of many goods and services improves over time.
- The CPI is further biased because it ignores the fact that as relative prices change, consumers substitute less expensive items for more expensive items.
- The size of the bias might be large.

The Limitations of Real GDP (pp. 506–509)

- Real GDP is not a perfect measure of aggregate production or economic welfare because it excludes quality improvements, household production, the underground economic activity, health and life expectancy, leisure time, environmental quality, and political freedom and social justice.
- The growth rate of real GDP gives a good indication of the phases of the business cycle.

Key Figures and Tables

Key Terms

QUESTIONS

1. Distinguish between a stock and a flow.

2. What are the main macroeconomic stocks? What are the flows that change them?

3. List the components of aggregate expenditure.

4. What are the components of aggregate income?

5. Why does aggregate income equal aggregate expenditure and the value of output (GDP)?

6. Distinguish between government purchases of goods and services and transfer payments.

7. Explain the expenditure approach to measuring GDP.

8. Explain the income approach to measuring GDP.

9. Explain how real GDP and the growth rate of real GDP are calculated.

10. Distinguish between expenditure on final goods and expenditure on intermediate goods?

11. What is value added? How is it calculated?

12. What are the two main price indexes used to measure the price level?

13. How is the Consumer Price Index calculated?

14. How is the GDP deflator calculated?

15. How is real GDP calculated?

16. How is the growth rate of real GDP calculated?

17. Is the CPI biased? If so, how?

18. Is real GDP a good measure of economic welfare? If not, why not?

19. Is the growth of real GDP a good measure of the growth of real economic activity?

20. Compare the fluctuations of real GDP with the phases of the business cycle.

PROBLEMS

1. The figure at the bottom of the page shows the flows of income and expenditure on Lotus Island during 1996. The amounts are thousands of dollars.

   Calculate Lotus Island's
   a. Aggregate expenditure.
   b. Aggregate income.
   c. GDP.
   d. Government budget deficit.
   e. Household saving.
   f. Government saving.
   g. Foreign borrowing.
   h. National saving.

2. Use the figure at the bottom of the page to calculate:
   a. Firms' borrowing.
   b. Government borrowing.
   c. Rest of the world's borrowing.

3. Cindy, the owner of The Great Cookie, spends $100 on eggs, $50 on flour, $45 on milk, $10 on utilities, and $60 on wages to produce 200 great cookies. Cindy sells her cookies for $1.50

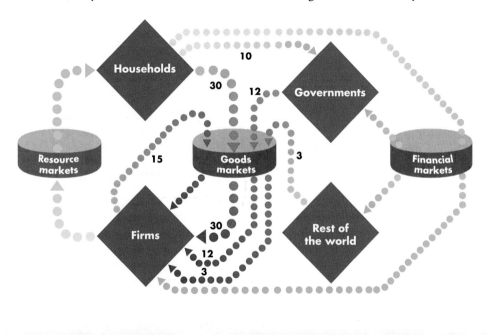

each. Calculate the value added per cookie at The Great Cookie.

4. Bananaland produces only two goods: bananas and sunscreen. The quantities of these goods produced and their prices in 1996 and 1997 are:

Good	1996 quantity	1997 quantity
Bananas	1,000 pounds	1,100 pounds
Sunscreen	500 gallons	525 gallons

Good	1996 price	1997 price
Bananas	$2 per pound	$3 per pound
Sunscreen	$10 per gallon	$8 per gallon

Calculate
a. Bananaland's GDP in 1996 and 1997.
b. The chain-weighted output index in 1997.
c. The growth rate of real GDP in 1997.
d. Real GDP in 1997 in 1996 dollars.
e. The GDP deflator in 1997.
f. The inflation rate in 1997.

5. A typical family living on Sandy Island consumes only apple juice, bananas, and cloth. In the base year the typical family spent $40 on apple juice, $45 on bananas, and $25 on cloth. Prices in the base year were $4 a gallon for apple juice, $3 a pound for bananas, and $5 a yard for cloth. In the current year, apple juice costs $3 a gallon, bananas cost $4 a pound, and cloth costs $7 a yard. Calculate:
a. The basket used in the CPI.
b. The Consumer Price Index in the current year.
c. The inflation rate between the base year and the current year.

CRITICAL THINKING

1. Study *Reading Between the Lines* on pp. 510–511 and then answer the following questions:
a. How large does Mr. Nakamura believe the bias in the CPI to be?
b. How does Mr. Nakamura's estimate of the CPI bias compare with that of the Boskin commission?
c. Write a brief description of the U.S. economy since 1975 based on the view of the official statistics and based on the view of Mr. Nakamura.
d. If Mr. Nakamura's view of the economy is correct, how different does economic growth look during the terms of Presidents Carter, Reagan, Bush, and Clinton compared with each other and compared with the official data?
e. Should social security benefits be linked to the measured CPI or to an estimate of the true CPI?
f. What difference, if any, do you think there would be in the distribution of income between workers and business owners if the bias in the CPI had been discovered 10 years ago?

🌐 2. Use the link on the Parkin Web site to visit the Federal Reserve Economic Data (FRED) Web site at the Federal Reserve Bank of St. Louis. There you can obtain the latest data on real GDP, nominal GDP, and the GDP deflator as well as the data for the previous year.
a. What was the GDP deflator in the most recent year?
b. What was the GDP deflator in the previous year?
c. What is the inflation rate as measured by the GDP deflator between these two years?
d. What was real GDP in the most recent year?
e. What was real GDP in the previous year?
f. What is the real GDP growth rate between these two years?
g. Check that, for the data you have obtained, nominal GDP divided by real GDP equals the deflator.

Chapter 24

Aggregate Supply and Aggregate Demand

During the past 30 years, U.S. real GDP has more than doubled. In fact, a doubling of real GDP every 30 years has been routine. What forces drive our economy to grow? ◆ At the same time that real GDP has grown, we've experienced first a rise and then a fall in inflation. In 1967, U.S. prices were rising at a rate of 3 percent a year. In 1981, the peak inflation year, prices increased by 10 percent. Today, the inflation rate stands at about 2.5 percent a year. The result of all this inflation is that you need $400 today to buy what $100 bought in 1967. What causes inflation? And why did its rate explode during the 1970s? ◆ Our economy does not expand at a constant pace. Instead, it ebbs and flows over the business cycle. For example, we had a recession during 1990

What Makes Our Garden Grow?

and early 1991. For half a year, real GDP decreased. Then began a long period of expansion that was still in progress in mid-1997. What makes real GDP grow at an uneven pace? Why does growth sometimes speed up, and why does real GDP sometimes shrink? ◆ When economic growth speeds up in Asia and Europe, we benefit because we sell more goods and services abroad. And when economic growth slows in the rest of the world, we suffer because the demand for our goods and services decreases. But some influences on our economy are home made and stem from the actions of the government and the Federal Reserve Board (the Fed) in Washington. How do events in the rest of the world and the policy actions of the government and the Fed affect production and prices? ◆ To answer these questions, we need a *model* of real GDP and the price level. Our main task in this chapter is to study such a model: the *aggregate supply–aggregate demand model.* Our second task is to use the aggregate supply–aggregate demand (or *AS-AD*) model to answer the questions we've just posed. You'll discover that this model enables us to understand the forces that make our economy expand, that bring inflation, and that cause business cycle fluctuations. You will also find that this model is a useful tool with which to organize your entire study of macroeconomics.

After studying this chapter, you will be able to:

- Explain what determines aggregate supply

- Explain what determines aggregate demand

- Explain macroeconomic equilibrium

- Explain the effects of changes in aggregate supply and aggregate demand on economic growth, inflation, and business cycles

- Explain U.S. economic growth, inflation, and business cycles by using the *AS-AD* model.

Aggregate Supply

THE AGGREGATE SUPPLY–AGGREGATE DEMAND model enables us to understand three features of macroeconomic performance:

- Growth of potential GDP
- Inflation
- Business cycle fluctuations

The model uses the concepts of *aggregate* supply and *aggregate* demand to determine *real GDP* and the *price level* (the *GDP deflator*). We begin by looking at the fundamental limits to production that influence aggregate supply.

Aggregate Supply Fundamentals

The *quantity of real GDP supplied* (Y) depends on just three factors:

- The quantity of labor (N)
- The quantity of capital (K)
- The state of technology (T)

The influence of these three factors on the quantity of real GDP supplied is described by the **aggregate production function**, which is written as the equation:

$$Y = F(N, K, T).$$

In words, the quantity of real GDP supplied is determined by (is a function F of) the quantities of labor and capital and of the state of technology. The larger N, K, or T, the greater is Y.

At any given time, the quantity of capital and the state of technology are fixed. They depend on decisions that were made in the past. The population is also fixed. But the quantity of labor is not fixed. It depends on decisions made by people and firms about the supply of and demand for labor.

Firms demand labor only if it is profitable to do so. And the lower the wage rate, which is the cost of labor, the greater is the quantity of labor demanded. People supply labor only if doing so is the most valuable use of their time. And the higher the wage rate, which is the return to labor, the greater is the quantity of labor supplied. The wage rate that makes the quantity of labor demanded equal to the quantity of labor supplied is the equilibrium wage rate. At this wage rate, there is **full employment.**

Even at full employment, there are always some people looking for jobs and some firms looking for people to hire. The reason is that there is constant turnover in the labor market. Every day, some jobs are destroyed as businesses reorganize or fail. Some jobs are created as new businesses start up or existing ones expand. Some workers decide, for any of a thousand personal reasons, to quit their jobs. And other people decide to start looking for a job. This constant churning in the labor market prevents unemployment from ever disappearing. At full employment, the unemployment rate is called the **natural rate of unemployment**. In 1997, the natural rate of unemployment is about 5.5 percent.

The quantity of real GDP supplied when unemployment is at its natural rate and there is full employment is **potential GDP**. Potential GDP depends on the full-employment quantity of labor, the quantity of capital, and the state of technology.

Over the business cycle, employment fluctuates around full employment and real GDP fluctuates around potential GDP. You saw these fluctuations in Chapter 22 (Figs. 22.2 and 22.3 on pp. 474–475).

To study the economy at full employment and over the business cycle, we distinguish two time frames for aggregate supply:

- Long-run aggregate supply
- Short-run aggregate supply

Long-Run Aggregate Supply

The economy is constantly bombarded by events that move real GDP away from potential GDP and, equivalently, that move the unemployment rate away from full employment. Following such an event, forces operate to take real GDP back toward potential GDP and restore full employment. The **macroeconomic long run** is a time frame that is sufficiently long for these forces to have done their work so that real GDP equals potential GDP and full employment prevails.

The **long-run aggregate supply curve** is the relationship between the quantity of real GDP supplied and the price level in the long run when real GDP equals potential GDP. Figure 24.1 shows this relationship as the vertical line labeled *LAS*. Along the long-run aggregate supply curve, as the price level changes, real GDP remains at potential GDP, which in Fig. 24.1 is $7 trillion. The long-run aggregate

FIGURE 24.1

Long-Run Aggregate Supply

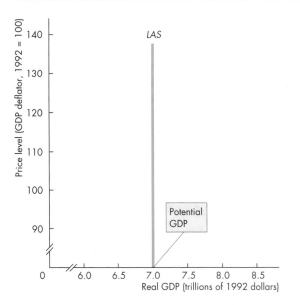

The long-run aggregate supply (*LAS*) curve shows the relationship between potential GDP and the price level. Potential GDP is independent of the price level, so the *LAS* curve is vertical at potential GDP.

supply curve is always vertical and is located at potential GDP.

The long-run aggregate supply curve is vertical because potential GDP is independent of the price level. The reason for this independence is that a movement along the *LAS* curve is accompanied by a change in *two* sets of prices: the prices of goods and services—the price level—and the prices of productive resources. A 10 percent increase in the prices of goods and services is matched by a 10 percent increase in wage rates and other resource prices. That is, the price level, wage rate, and other resource prices all change by the same percentage, and *relative prices* and the *real wage rate* remain constant. When the price level changes but relative prices and the real wage rate remain constant, real GDP also remains constant.

Production at a Pepsi Plant You can see why real GDP remains constant when all prices change by the same percentage by thinking about production

decisions at a Pepsi bottling plant. The plant is producing the quantity of Pepsi that maximizes profit. The plant can increase production, but only by incurring a higher *marginal cost* (see Chapter 3, pp. 42–43). So the firm has no incentive to change production.

Short-Run Aggregate Supply

The **macroeconomic short run** is a period during which real GDP has fallen below or risen above potential GDP. At the same time, the unemployment rate has risen above or fallen below the natural rate.

The **short-run aggregate supply curve** is the relationship between the quantity of real GDP supplied and the price level in the short run when the money wage rate, other resource prices, and potential GDP remain constant. Figure 24.2 shows a short-run aggregate supply curve as the upward-sloping curve labeled *SAS*. This curve is based on the short-run aggregate supply schedule, and each point on the aggregate supply curve corresponds to a row of the aggregate supply schedule. For example, point *a* on the short-run aggregate supply curve and row *a* of the schedule tell us that if the price level is 100, the quantity of real GDP supplied is $6 trillion.

At point *c*, the price level is 110 and the quantity of real GDP supplied is $7 trillion, which equals potential GDP. If the price level is higher than 110, real GDP exceeds potential GDP; if the price level is below 110, real GDP is less than potential GDP.

Back at the Pepsi Plant You can see why the short-run aggregate supply curve slopes upward by returning to the Pepsi bottling plant. The plant produces the quantity that maximizes profit. If the price of Pepsi rises and wage rates and other costs don't change, the *relative price* of Pepsi rises and the firm has an incentive to increase its production. The higher relative price of Pepsi covers the higher marginal cost of producing more Pepsi, so the firm increases production.

Similarly, if the price of Pepsi falls and wage rates and other costs don't change, the lower relative price is not sufficient to covers the marginal cost of Pepsi, so the firm decreases production.

Again, what's true for Pepsi bottlers is true for the producers of all goods and services. So when the price level rises and the money wage rate and other resource prices remain constant, the quantity of real GDP supplied increases.

FIGURE 24.2

Short-Run
Aggregate Supply

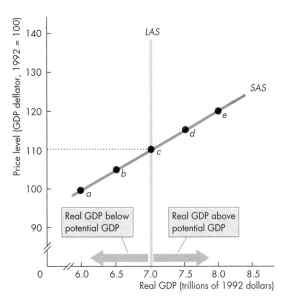

	Price Level (GDP deflator)	Real GDP (trillions of 1992 dollars)
a	100	6.0
b	105	6.5
c	110	7.0
d	115	7.5
e	120	8.0

The short-run aggregate supply (SAS) curve shows the relationship between the quantity of real GDP supplied and the price level when the money wage rate, other resource prices, and potential GDP are constant. The short-run aggregate supply curve SAS is based on the schedule in the table. The short-run aggregate supply curve is upward-sloping because firms' costs increase as the rate of output increases, so a higher price is needed, relative to the prices of productive resources, and bring forth an increase in the quantity produced. On the SAS curve, when the price level is 110, real GDP equals potential GDP. If the price level is greater than 110, real GDP exceeds potential GDP; if the price level is below 110, real GDP is less than potential GDP.

Movements Along the *LAS* and *SAS* Curves

Figure 24.3 summarizes what you've just learned about the *LAS* and *SAS* curves. When the price level, the money wage rate, and other resource prices rise by the same percentage, relative prices remain constant and real GDP remains at potential GDP. There is a *movement along* the *LAS* curve.

When the price level rises but the money wage rate and other resource prices remain constant, the quantity of real GDP supplied increases and there is a *movement along* the *SAS* curve.

Let's next study the influences that bring changes in aggregate supply.

Changes in Aggregate Supply

You've just seen that a change in the price level brings a movement along the aggregate supply curves but it does not change aggregate supply. Aggregate supply changes when influences on production plans other than the price level change. Let's begin by looking at factors that change potential GDP.

Changes in Potential GDP When potential GDP changes, both long-run aggregate supply and short-run aggregate supply change. Potential GDP changes for three reasons:

1. Change in the full-employment quantity of labor
2. Change in the quantity of capital
3. Advance in technology.

Change in the Full-Employment Quantity of Labor A Pepsi bottling plants that employs 100 workers bottles more Pepsi than an otherwise identical plant that employs 10 workers. The same is true for the economy as a whole. The larger the quantity of labor employed, the greater is GDP.

Over time, potential GDP increases because the labor force increases. But (with constant capital and technology) *potential* GDP increases only if the full-employment quantity of labor increases. Fluctuations in employment over the business cycle bring fluctuations in real GDP. But these changes in real GDP are fluctuations around potential GDP. They are not changes in potential GDP and long-run aggregate supply.

FIGURE 24.3

Movements Along the Aggregate Supply Curves

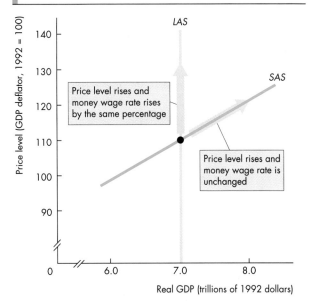

A rise in the price level with no change in the money wage rate and other resource prices brings an increase in the quantity of real GDP supplied and a movement along the short-run aggregate supply curve. A rise in the price level with equal percentage rises in the money wage rate and other resource prices keeps the quantity of real GDP supplied constant and brings a movement along the long-run aggregate supply curve.

Change in the Quantity of Capital A Pepsi plant with two production lines bottles more Pepsi than does an otherwise identical plant that has only one production line. For the economy as a whole, the larger the quantity of capital, the more productive is the labor force and the greater is its potential GDP. Potential GDP per person in the capital-rich United States is vastly greater than that in capital-poor China and Russia.

Capital includes *human capital*. One Pepsi plant is managed by an economics major with an MBA and has a labor force with an average of 10 years experience. This plant produces a much larger output than an otherwise identical plant that is managed by someone with no business training or experience and that has a young labor force that is new to bottling.

The first plant has a greater amount of human capital than the second. For the economy as a whole, the larger the quantity of *human capital*—the skills that people have acquired in school and through on-the-job training—the greater is potential GDP.

Advance in Technology A Pepsi plant that has pre–computer age machines produces less than one that uses the latest robot technology. Technological change enables firms to produce more from any given amount of inputs. So even with fixed quantities of labor and capital, improvements in technology increase potential GDP.

Technological advances are by far the most important source of increased production over the past two centuries. Because of technological advances, one farmer in the United States today can feed 100 people, and one auto worker can produce almost 14 cars and trucks in a year.

Figure 24.4 shows the effect of a change in potential GDP. Initially, the long-run aggregate supply curve is LAS_0 and the short-run aggregate supply curve is SAS_0. If an increase in the quantity of capital or a technological advance increases potential GDP to $8 trillion, long-run aggregate supply increases and the long-run aggregate supply curve shifts rightward to LAS_1. Short-run aggregate supply also increases, and the short-run aggregate supply curve shifts rightward to SAS_1.

You've seen how a change in potential GDP changes aggregate supply. Let's now look at the effects of changes in money wages and other resource prices.

Changes in Money Wages and Other Resource Prices A change in the money wage rate or in the money prices of any other resources, such as the price of oil, changes short-run aggregate supply but does not change long-run aggregate supply.

Money wages and resource prices affect short-run aggregate supply through their influence on firms' costs. The higher the money wage rate and other resource prices, the higher are firms' costs and the smaller is the quantity that firms are willing to supply at each price level. Thus an increase in the money wage rate and other resource prices decreases short-run aggregate supply.

Changes in the money wage rate and other resource prices do not change long-run aggregate supply. The reason is that along the long-run aggregate supply curve, any change in the money wage rate or other resource price is accompanied by an equal percentage change in the price level. With no change

FIGURE 24.4

A Change in Potential GDP

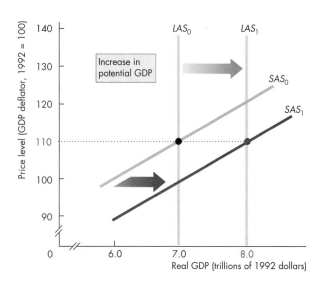

An increase in potential GDP increases both long-run aggregate supply and short-run aggregate supply and shifts both aggregate supply curves rightward, from LAS_0 to LAS_1 and from SAS_0 to SAS_1.

FIGURE 24.5

A Change in the Money Wage Rate

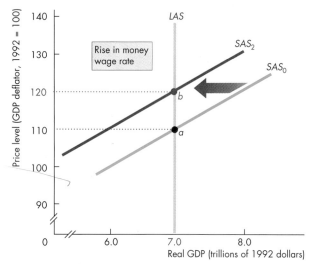

A rise in the money wage rate decreases short-run aggregate supply and shifts the short-run aggregate supply curve leftward from SAS_0 to SAS_2. A rise in the money wage rate does not change potential GDP, so the long-run aggregate supply curve does not shift.

in *relative* prices, firms have no incentive to change production and potential GDP remains constant.

Figure 24.5 shows the effect on aggregate supply of an increase in the money wage rate (or an increase in the money price of other resources). Initially, the short-run aggregate supply curve is SAS_0. A rise in the money wage rate *decreases* short-run aggregate supply and shifts the short-run aggregate supply curve leftward to SAS_2.

The vertical distance between the original SAS curve and the new SAS curve is determined by the percentage change in the money wage rate. That is, the percentage increase in the price level between point a and point b equals the percentage increase in the money wage rate.

Because potential GDP does not change when the money wage rate changes, long-run aggregate supply does not change. The long-run aggregate supply curve remains at LAS.

REVIEW

- A change in the price level that is accompanied by an equal percentage change in the money wage rate keeps real GDP at potential GDP and brings a movement along the LAS curve.
- An increase in the price level with no change in the money wage rate brings an increase in the quantity of real GDP supplied and a movement along the SAS curve.
- An increase in potential GDP increases both long-run aggregate supply and short-run aggregate supply and shifts the LAS curve and the SAS curve rightward.
- An increase in the money wage rate decreases short-run aggregate supply but leaves long-run aggregate supply unchanged. The SAS curve shifts leftward.

Aggregate Demand

THE QUANTITY OF REAL GDP DEMANDED IS THE sum of the real consumption expenditure (C), investment (I), government purchases (G), and exports (X) minus imports (M). That is,

$$Y = C + I + G + X - M.$$

The *quantity of real GDP demanded* is the total amount of final goods and services produced in the United States that people, businesses, governments, and foreigners plan to buy. What determines these buying plans?

Buying plans depend on many factors. Some of the main ones are:

- The price level
- Expectations
- Fiscal policy and monetary policy
- The world economy

We first focus on the relationship between the quantity of real GDP demanded and the price level, and to study this relationship, we hold constant all other influences on buying plans. We then ask: How does the quantity of real GDP demanded vary as the price level varies?

The Aggregate Demand Curve

Other things remaining the same, the higher the price level, the smaller is the quantity of real GDP demanded. This relationship between the quantity of real GDP demanded and the price level is called **aggregate demand**. Aggregate demand is described by an *aggregate demand schedule* and an *aggregate demand curve*.

Figure 24.6 shows an aggregate demand curve (AD) and an aggregate demand schedule. Each point on the AD curve corresponds to a row of the schedule. For example, point c' on the AD curve and row c' of the schedule tell us that if the price level is 110, the quantity of real GDP demanded is $7 trillion.

The aggregate demand curve slopes downward for two reasons:

- Wealth effect
- Substitution effects

FIGURE 24.6

Aggregate Demand

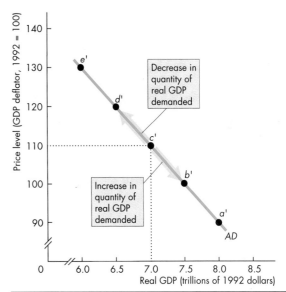

	Price Level (GDP deflator)	Real GDP (trillions of 1992 dollars)
a'	90	8.0
b'	100	7.5
c'	110	7.0
d'	120	6.5
e'	130	6.0

The aggregate demand curve (*AD*) shows the relationship between the quantity of real GDP demanded and the price level. The aggregate demand curve is based on the schedule in the table. Each point a' through e' on the curve corresponds to the row in the table identified by the same letter. Thus when the price-level is 110, the quantity of real GDP demanded is $7.0 trillion, shown by point c' in the figure.

Wealth Effect When the price level rises but other things remain the same, *real* wealth decreases. Real wealth is the amount of money in the bank, bonds, stocks, and other assets that people own, measured not in dollars but in terms of the goods and services that this money, bonds, and stock will buy.

People save and hold money, bonds, and stocks for many reasons. One reason is to build up funds for college expenses. Another reason is to build up enough funds to meet possible medical or other big bills. But the biggest reason is to build up enough funds to provide a retirement income.

If the price level rises, real wealth decreases. People then try to restore their wealth. To do so, they must increase saving and, equivalently, decrease consumption. Such a decrease in consumption is a decrease in the quantity of real GDP demanded.

Maria's Wealth Effect   You can see how the wealth effect works by thinking about Maria's buying plans. Maria lives in Belgrade, Serbia. She has worked hard all summer and saved 20,000 dinars (the dinar is the currency of Serbia), which she plans to spend attending graduate school when she's finished her economics degree. So Maria's wealth is 20,000 dinars. Maria has a part-time job, and her income from this job pays her current expenses. The price level in Serbia rises by 100 percent, and now Maria needs 40,000 dinars to buy what 20,000 once bought. To try to make up some of the fall in value of her savings, Maria saves even more and cuts her current spending to the bare minimum.

Substitution Effects   When the price level rises and other things remain the same, interest rates rise. The full reason why is explained in Chapter 32 on pp. 728–729. But the basic reason is easy to see. A rise in the price level decreases the real value of the money in people's pockets and bank accounts. With a smaller amount of real money around, banks and other lenders can get a higher interest rate on loans. But faced with higher interest rates, people and businesses delay plans to buy new capital and consumer durable goods and cut back on spending.

This substitution effect involves substituting goods in the future for goods in the present and is called an *intertemporal* substitution effect—a substitution across time. Saving increases to increase future consumption.

To see this intertemporal substitution effect more clearly, think about your own plan to buy a new computer. At an interest rate of 5 percent a year, you might borrow $2,000 and buy the new machine you've been researching. But at an interest rate of 10 percent a year, you might decide the payments would be too high. You don't abandon your plan to buy the computer, but you decide to delay your purchase.

A second substitution effect works through international prices. When the U.S. price level rises and other things remain the same, some of those other things are the prices in other countries. So a rise in the U.S. price level makes U.S.-made goods and services more expensive relative to foreign-made goods and services. This change in relative prices encourages people to spend less on U.S.-made items and more on foreign-made items. For example, if the U.S. price level rises relative to the Canadian price level, Canadians buy fewer U.S.-made cars (U.S. exports decrease) and Americans buy more Canadian-made cars (U.S. imports increase).

Maria's Substitution Effects   In Belgrade, Serbia, Maria makes some substitutions. She was planning on trading in her old motor scooter and getting a new one. But with a higher price level, and faced with higher interest rates, she decides to make her old scooter last one more year. Also, with the prices of Serbian goods sharply increasing, Maria substitutes a low cost dress made in Malaysia for the Serbian-made dress she had originally planned to buy.

Changes in the Quantity of Real GDP Demanded When the price level changes and other things remain the same, the quantity of real GDP demanded changes. Such a change is shown by a movement along the aggregate demand curve. The arrows in Fig. 24.6 illustrate changes in the quantity of real GDP demanded.

We've now seen how the quantity of real GDP demanded changes when the price level changes. How do other influences on buying plans affect aggregate demand?

Changes in Aggregate Demand

A change in any factor that influences buying plans other than the price level brings a change in aggregate demand. The main factors are:

- Expectations
- Fiscal policy and monetary policy
- The world economy

Expectations   Expectations about future incomes, inflation, and profits influence buying plans today. An increase in expected future income increases the amount of consumption goods (especially big-ticket items like cars) that people plan to buy today and increases aggregate demand.

An increase in the expected future inflation rate increases aggregate demand because people decide to buy more goods and services at today's relatively lower prices. An increase in expected future profit increases the investment that firms plan to undertake today and increases aggregate demand.

Fiscal Policy and Monetary Policy The government's attempt to influence the economy by setting and changing taxes, transfer payments, and government purchases is called **fiscal policy**. A decrease in taxes or an increase in transfer payments—unemployment benefits, social security benefits, and welfare payments—with no change in government purchases increases aggregate demand. Both of these influences operate by increasing households' *disposable* income. **Disposable income** is aggregate income minus taxes plus transfer payments. The greater the disposable income, the greater is the quantity of consumption goods and services that households plan to buy and the greater is aggregate demand.

Government purchases of goods and services are one component of aggregate demand. So if taxes and transfer payments don't change but the government plans to buy more spy satellites and highways, aggregate demand increases.

Monetary policy consists of changes in interest rates and in the quantity of money in the economy. The quantity of money is determined by the Fed and by the banks (in a process described in Chapters 30 and 31). An increase in the quantity of money in the economy increases aggregate demand. To see why money affects aggregate demand, imagine that the Fed borrows the army's helicopters, loads them with millions of new $10 bills, and sprinkles them like confetti across the nation. People gather the newly available money and plan to spend some of it. So the quantity of goods and services demanded increases. But people don't plan to spend all the new money. They plan to save some of it and lend it to others through the banks. Interest rates fall, and with lower interest rates, people plan to buy more consumer durables and firms plan to increase their investment.

The World Economy Two main world economy influences on aggregate demand are the foreign exchange rate and foreign income. The *foreign exchange rate* is the amount of a foreign currency that you can buy with a U.S. dollar. Other things

FIGURE 24.7
Changes in Aggregate Demand

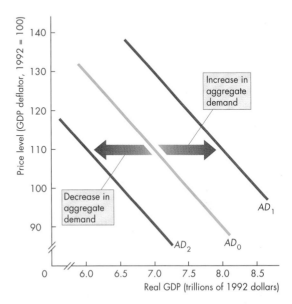

Aggregate demand

Decreases if

- Expected future incomes, inflation, or profits decrease

- Fiscal policy decreases government purchases, increases taxes, or decreases transfer payments

- Monetary policy decreases the quantity of money and increases interest rates

- The exchange rate increases or foreign income decreases

Increases if

- Expected future incomes, inflation, or profits increase

- Fiscal policy increases government purchases, decreases taxes, or increases transfer payments

- Monetary policy increases the quantity of money and decreases interest rates

- The exchange rate decreases or foreign income increases

remaining the same, a rise in the foreign exchange rate decreases aggregate demand. To see how the foreign exchange rate influences aggregate demand, suppose that $1 exchanges for 100 Japanese yen. A Fujitsu phone (made in Japan) costs 12,500 yen, and an equivalent Motorola phone (made in the United States) costs $110. In U.S. dollars, the Fujitsu phone costs $125, so people around the world buy the cheaper U.S. phone. Now suppose the exchange rate rises to 125 yen. At 125 yen per dollar, the Fujitsu phone costs $100 and is now cheaper than the Motorola phone. People will switch from the U.S. phone to the Japanese phone. U.S. exports will decrease and U.S. imports will increase, so U.S. aggregate demand will decrease.

An increase in foreign income increases U.S. exports and increases U.S. aggregate demand. For example, an increase in income in Japan and Germany increases the purchases of U.S.-made goods and services that Japanese and German consumers and producers plan to make.

Shifts of the Aggregate Demand Curve   When aggregate demand changes, the aggregate demand curve shifts. Figure 24.7 shows two changes in aggregate demand and summarizes the factors bringing about such changes.

The aggregate demand curve shifts rightward, from AD_0 to AD_1, when expected future incomes, inflation, or profits increase, government purchases on goods and services increase, taxes are cut, transfer payments increase, the quantity of money increases and interest rates fall, the foreign exchange rate falls, or foreign income increases. The aggregate demand curve shifts leftward, from AD_0 to AD_2, when expected future incomes, inflation, or profits decrease, government purchases of goods and services decrease, taxes increase, transfer payments decrease, the quantity of money decreases and interest rates rise, the foreign exchange rate rises, or foreign income decreases.

REVIEW

■ The aggregate demand curve shows the relationship between the price level and the quantity of real GDP demanded, other things remaining the same.

■ When the price level rises, the quantity of real GDP demanded decreases because real wealth decreases, interest rates rise, and the prices of domestic goods and services increase relative to those of foreign goods and services.

■ Changes in expectations, fiscal policy, monetary policy, and the world economy change aggregate demand and shift the aggregate demand curve.

Macroeconomic Equilibrium

THE PURPOSE OF THE AGGREGATE SUPPLY–aggregate demand model is to explain changes in real GDP and the price level. To achieve this purpose, we combine aggregate supply and aggregate demand and determine macroeconomic equilibrium. There is a macroeconomic equilibrium for each of the time frames for aggregate supply: a long-run equilibrium and a short-run equilibrium. Long-run equilibrium is the state toward which the economy is heading. Short-run equilibrium is the normal state of the economy as it fluctuates around potential GDP.

We'll begin our study of macroeconomic equilibrium by looking first at the short run.

Short-Run Macroeconomic Equilibrium

The aggregate demand curve tells us the quantity of real GDP demanded at each price level, and the short-run aggregate supply curve tells us the quantity of real GDP supplied at each price level. **Short-run macroeconomic equilibrium** occurs when the quantity of real GDP demanded equals the quantity of real GDP supplied. That is, short-run equilibrium occurs at the point of intersection of the AD curve and the SAS curve. Figure 24.8 shows such an equilibrium at a price level of 110 and real GDP of $7 trillion (points c and c').

To see why this position is the equilibrium, think about what happens if the price level is something other than 110. Suppose, for example, that the price level is 120 and that real GDP is $8 trillion (at point e) on the SAS curve. The quantity of real GDP demanded is less than $8 trillion, so firms are unable to sell all their output. Unwanted inventories pile up, and firms cut both production and prices. Production and prices are cut until firms can sell all their output. This situation occurs only when real GDP is $7 trillion and the price level is 110.

Now suppose the price level is 100 and real GDP is $6 trillion (at point a) on the SAS curve. The quantity of real GDP demanded exceeds $6 trillion, so firms are unable to meet the demand for their output. Inventories decrease, and customers clamor for goods and services. So firms increase production and raise prices. Production and prices increase until firms can

FIGURE 24.8
Short-Run Equilibrium

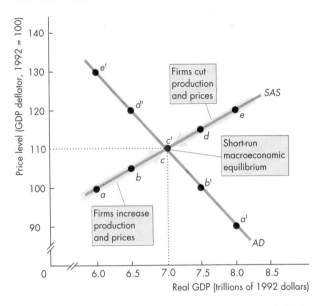

Short-run macroeconomic equilibrium occurs when real GDP demanded equals real GDP supplied—at the intersection of the aggregate demand curve (*AD*) and the short-run aggregate supply curve (*SAS*). Here, such an equilibrium occurs at points *c* and *c'*, where the price level is 110 and real GDP is $7 trillion. If the price level is 120 and real GDP is $8 trillion (point *e*), firms will not be able to sell all their output. They will decrease production and cut prices. If the price level is 100 and real GDP is $6 trillion (point *a*), people will not be able to buy all the goods and services they demand. Firms will increase production and raise their prices. Only when the price level is 110 and real GDP is $7 trillion can firms sell all that they produce and people buy all that they demand. This is the short-run macroeconomic equilibrium.

Long-Run Macroeconomic Equilibrium

Long-run macroeconomic equilibrium occurs when real GDP equals potential GDP—equivalently, when the economy is on its *long-run* aggregate supply curve. Figure 24.9 shows long-run equilibrium, which occurs at the intersection of the aggregate demand curve and the long-run aggregate supply curve (the blue curves). Long-run equilibrium comes about because the money wage rate adjusts. Potential GDP and aggregate demand determine the price level, and the price level influences the money wage rate. In long-run equilibrium, the money wage rate has adjusted to put the (green) short-run aggregate supply through the long-run equilibrium point.

We'll look at this adjustment process later in this chapter. But first, let's use the *AS-AD* model to study economic growth and inflation.

FIGURE 24.9
Long-Run Equilibrium

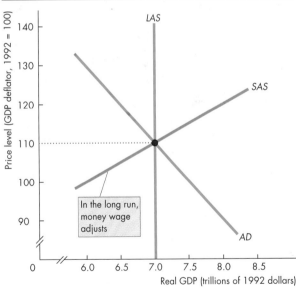

In long-run macroeconomic equilibrium, real GDP equals potential GDP. So long-run equilibrium occurs where the aggregate demand curve intersects the long-run aggregate demand curve. In the long run, aggregate demand determines the price level and has no effect on real GDP. The money wage rate adjusts in the long run so that the *SAS* curve intersects the *LAS* curve at the long-run equilibrium price level.

meet demand. This situation occurs only when real GDP is $7 trillion and the price level is 110.

In short-run equilibrium, the money wage rate is fixed. It does not adjust to bring full employment. So in the short run, real GDP can be greater than or less than potential GDP. But in the long run, the money wage rate does adjust and real GDP moves toward potential GDP. We are going to study this adjustment process. But first, let's look at the economy in long-run equilibrium.

Economic Growth and Inflation

Economic growth occurs because, over time, the quantity of labor grows, capital is accumulated, and technology advances. These changes increase potential GDP and shift the long-run aggregate supply curve rightward. Figure 24.10 shows such a shift. The growth rate of potential GDP is determined by the pace at which labor grows, capital is accumulated, and technology advances.

Inflation occurs when, over time, aggregate demand increases by more than long-run aggregate supply. That is, inflation occurs if the aggregate demand curve shifts rightward by more than the rightward shift in the long-run aggregate supply curve. Figure 24.10 shows such shifts.

If aggregate demand increased at the same pace as long-run aggregate supply, we would experience real GDP growth with no inflation.

FIGURE 24.10

Economic Growth and Inflation

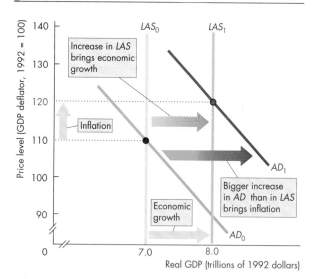

Economic growth is the persistent increase in potential GDP. Economic growth is shown as an ongoing rightward movement in the *LAS* curve. Inflation is the persistent rise in the price level. Inflation occurs when aggregate demand increases by more than the increase in long-run aggregate supply.

In the long run, the main influence on aggregate demand is the growth rate of the quantity of money. At times when the quantity of money increases rapidly, aggregate demand increases quickly and the inflation rate is high. When the growth rate of the quantity of money slows, other things remaining the same, the inflation rate eventually decreases.

Our economy experiences growth and inflation, like that shown in Fig. 24.10. But it does not experience *steady* growth and *steady* inflation. Real GDP fluctuates around potential GDP in a business cycle, and inflation also fluctuates. When we study the business cycle, we ignore economic growth. By doing so, we can see the business cycle more clearly.

Business Cycles

The business cycle occurs because aggregate demand and short-run aggregate supply fluctuate but the money wage rate does not adjust quickly enough to keep real GDP at potential GDP. Figure 24.11 shows three types of short-run equilibrium.

In part (a) there is a below full-employment equilibrium. A **below full-employment equilibrium** is a macroeconomic equilibrium in which potential GDP exceeds real GDP. The amount by which potential GDP exceeds real GDP is called a **recessionary gap**. This name reminds us that a gap has opened up between potential GDP and real GDP either because the economy has experienced a recession or because real GDP, while growing, has grown more slowly than potential GDP.

The below full-employment equilibrium shown in Fig. 24.11(a) occurs where the aggregate demand curve AD_0 intersects short-run aggregate supply curve SAS_0 at a real GDP of $6.8 trillion and a price level of 110. The recessionary gap is $0.2 trillion. The U.S. economy was in a situation similar to that shown in Fig. 24.11(a) in the early 1980s and again in the early 1990s. In those years, real GDP was less than potential GDP.

Figure 24.11(b) is an example of *long-run equilibrium* in which real GDP equals potential GDP. In this example, the equilibrium occurs where the aggregate demand curve AD_1 intersects the short-run aggregate supply curve SAS_1 at an actual and potential GDP of $7 trillion. The U.S. economy was in a situation such as that shown in Fig. 24.11(b) in mid-1996.

Figure 24.11(c) shows an above full-employment equilibrium. An **above full-employment equilibrium** is a macroeconomic equilibrium in which real

GDP exceeds potential GDP. The amount by which real GDP exceeds potential GDP is called an **inflationary gap**. This name reminds us that a gap has opened up between real GDP and potential GDP and that this gap creates inflationary pressure.

The above full-employment equilibrium shown in Fig. 24.11(c) occurs where the aggregate demand curve AD_2 intersects the short-run aggregate supply curve SAS_2 at a real GDP of $7.2 trillion and a price level of 110. There is an inflationary gap of $0.2

trillion. The U.S. economy was in a situation similar to that depicted in part (c) in 1988–1990.

The economy moves from one type of equilibrium to another as a result of fluctuations in aggregate demand and in short-run aggregate supply. These fluctuations produce fluctuations in real GDP and the price level. Figure 24.11(d) shows how real GDP fluctuates around potential GDP.

Let's now look at some of the sources of these fluctuations around potential GDP.

FIGURE 24.11

The Business Cycle

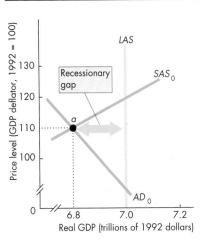

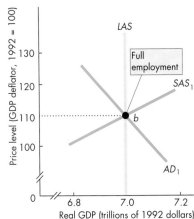

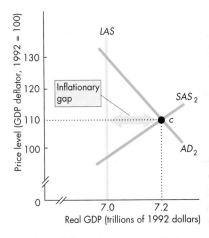

(a) Below full-employment equilibrium

(b) Long-run equilibrium

(c) Above full-employment equilibrium

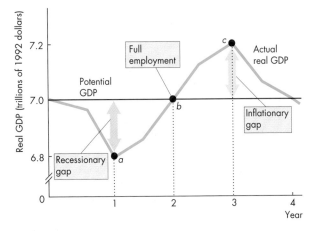

(d) Fluctuations in real GDP

Part (a) shows a below full-employment equilibrium in year 1; part (b) shows a long-run equilibrium in year 2; part (c) shows an above full-employment equilibrium in year 3. Part (d) shows how real GDP fluctuates around potential GDP in a business cycle. In year 1, there is a recessionary gap and the economy is at point *a* (in parts a and d). In year 2, there is long-run equilibrium and the economy is at point *b* (in parts b and d). In year 3, there is an inflationary gap and the economy is at point *c* (in parts c and d).

Fluctuations in Aggregate Demand

One reason real GDP fluctuates around potential GDP is that aggregate demand fluctuates. Let's see what happens when aggregate demand increases.

Figure 24.12(a) shows an economy in long-run equilibrium. The aggregate demand curve is AD_0, the short-run aggregate supply curve is SAS_0, and the long-run aggregate supply curve is LAS. Real GDP equals potential GDP at $7 trillion, and the price level is 110.

Now suppose that the world economy expands and that the demand for U.S.-made goods increases in Japan and Europe. The increase in U.S. exports increases aggregate demand, and the aggregate demand curve shifts rightward from AD_0 to AD_1 in Fig. 24.12(a).

Faced with an increase in demand, firms increase production and raise prices. Real GDP increases to $7.5 trillion, and the price level rises to 115. The economy is now in an above full-employment equilibrium. Real GDP exceeds potential GDP, there is an inflationary gap.

The increase in aggregate demand has increased the prices of all goods and services. Faced with higher prices, firms have increased their output rates. At this stage, prices of goods and services have increased but wage rates have not changed. (Recall that as we move along a short-run aggregate supply curve, wage rates are constant.)

The economy cannot produce in excess of potential GDP forever. Why not? What are the forces at work that bring real GDP back to potential GDP?

Because the price level has increased and wage rates are unchanged, workers have experienced a fall in the buying power of their wages and firms' profits have increased. In these circumstances, workers demand higher wages and firms, anxious to maintain their employment and output levels, meet those demands. If firms do not raise wage rates, they will either lose workers or have to hire less productive ones.

As wage rates rise, the short-run aggregate supply curve begins to shift leftward. In Fig. 24.12(b), the short-run aggregate supply curve moves from SAS_0

FIGURE 24.12

An Increase in Aggregate Demand

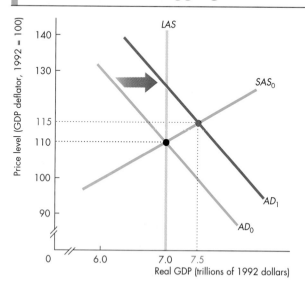

(a) Short-run effect

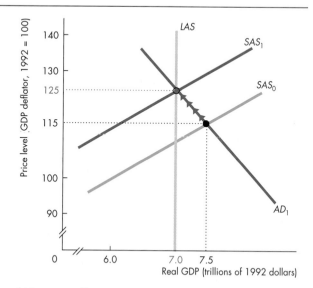

(b) Long-run effect

An increase in aggregate demand shifts the aggregate demand curve from AD_0 to AD_1. In the short-run equilibrium, real GDP is $7.5 trillion and the price level rises to 115 in part (a). In this situation, there is an inflationary gap. The money wage rate rises, and the short-run aggregate supply curve shifts

leftward from SAS_0 to SAS_1 in part (b). As it shifts, it intersects the aggregate demand curve AD_1 at higher price levels and lower real GDP levels. Eventually, the price level rises to 125 and real GDP decreases to $7.0 trillion—potential GDP.

toward SAS_1. The rise in wages and the shift in the SAS curve produce a sequence of new equilibrium positions. Along the adjustment path, real GDP falls and the price level rises. The economy moves up along its aggregate demand curve as shown by the arrowheads in the figure.

Eventually, wage rates rise by the same percentage as the price level. At this time, the aggregate demand curve AD_1 intersects SAS_1 at a new long-run equilibrium. The price level has risen to 125, and real GDP is back where it started, at potential GDP.

A decrease in aggregate demand has similar but opposite effects to those of an increase in aggregate demand. That is, a decrease in aggregate demand shifts the aggregate demand curve leftward. Real GDP decreases to less than potential GDP, and a recessionary gap emerges. Firms cut prices. The lower price level increases the purchasing power of wages and increases firms' costs relative to their output prices because wages remain unchanged. Eventually, the slack economy leads to falling wage rates and the short-run aggregate supply curve shifts rightward. But wage rates change slowly, so real GDP slowly returns to potential GDP and the price level falls slowly.

Let's now work out how real GDP and the price level change when aggregate supply changes.

Fluctuations in Aggregate Supply

Fluctuations in short-run aggregate supply can bring fluctuations in real GDP around potential GDP. Suppose that initially real GDP equals potential GDP. Then there is a large but temporary rise in the price of oil. What happens to real GDP and the price level?

Figure 24.13 answers this question. The aggregate demand curve is AD_0, the short-run aggregate supply curve is SAS_0, and the long-run aggregate supply curve is LAS. Equilibrium real GDP is $7 trillion, which equals potential GDP, and the price level is 110. Then the price of oil rises. Faced with higher energy and transportation costs, firms decrease production. Short-run aggregate supply decreases, and the short-run aggregate supply curve shifts leftward to SAS_1. The price level rises to 120, and real GDP decreases to $6.5 trillion. Because real GDP decreases, the economy experiences recession. Because the price level increases, the economy experiences inflation. A combination of recession and inflation, called *stagflation*, actually occurred in the United States in the mid-1970s and early 1980s. But events like this are not common.

FIGURE 24.13

A Decrease in Aggregate Supply

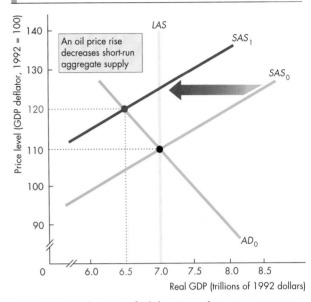

An increase in the price of oil decreases short-run aggregate supply and shifts the short-run aggregate supply curve from SAS_0 to SAS_1. Real GDP decreases from $7.0 trillion to $6.5 trillion, and the price level rises from 110 to 120. The economy experiences both recession and inflation—stagflation.

REVIEW

- Increases in long-run aggregate supply bring economic growth, and bigger increases in aggregate demand than in LAS bring inflation.
- There are three types of short-run macroeconomic equilibrium: (1) below full-employment equilibrium (potential GDP exceeds real GDP and there is a recessionary gap); (2) long-run equilibrium (real GDP equals potential GDP); and (3) above full-employment equilibrium (real GDP exceeds potential GDP and there is an inflationary gap).
- Fluctuations in aggregate demand and short-run aggregate supply bring fluctuations in real GDP around potential GDP.

Let's put our new knowledge of aggregate supply and aggregate demand to work and see how we can explain recent U.S. macroeconomic performance.

U.S. Economic Growth, Inflation, and Cycles

THE ECONOMY IS CONTINUALLY CHANGING. IF you imagine the economy as a video, then an aggregate supply–aggregate demand figure such as Fig. 24.13 is a freeze-frame. We're going to run the video (instant replay) but keep our finger on the freeze-frame button and look at some important parts of the previous action. Let's run the video from 1960.

Figure 24.14 shows the state of the economy in 1960 at the point of intersection of its aggregate demand curve AD_{60} and short-run aggregate supply curve SAS_{60}. Real GDP was $2.3 trillion, and the GDP deflator was 23.3 (about a fifth of its 1996 level). In 1960, real GDP equaled potential GDP—the economy was on LAS_{60}.

By 1996, the economy had reached the point marked by the intersection of aggregate demand curve AD_{96} and short-run aggregate supply curve SAS_{96}. Real GDP was $7 trillion, and the GDP

deflator was 111. Also in 1996, the economy was on LAS_{96}, with real GDP equal to potential GDP.

The path traced by the blue and red dots in Fig. 24.14 has three key features:

- Economic growth
- Inflation
- Business cycles

Economic Growth

Over the years, real GDP grows—shown in Fig. 24.14 by the rightward movement of the points. The faster real GDP grows, the larger is the horizontal distance between successive dots in the figure. The forces that generate economic growth are those that increase potential GDP. Potential GDP grows because the quantity of labor grows, we accumulate physical and human capital, and our technologies advance.

These forces that bring economic growth were stronger during the 1960s and mid-1980s than at other times. During the 1970s, growth was slow.

FIGURE 24.14

Aggregate Supply and Aggregate Demand: 1960–1996

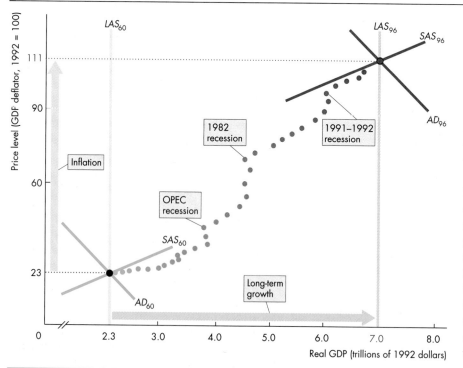

Each point shows the GDP deflator and real GDP in a given year. In 1960, these variables were determined by the aggregate demand curve AD_{60} and the short-run aggregate supply curve SAS_{60}. Each point is generated by the gradual shifting of the AD and SAS curves. By 1996, the curves were AD_{96} and SAS_{96}. Real GDP grew, and the price level increased. Real GDP grew quickly and inflation was moderate in the 1960s; real GDP growth sagged in 1974–1975 and again in 1982. Inflation was rapid in the 1970s but slowed after the 1982 recession. The period from 1982 to 1989 was one of strong, persistent expansion. A recession began in 1991, and a further expansion then followed.

Inflation

The price level rises over the years—shown in Fig. 24.14 by the upward movement of the points. The larger the rise in the price level, the larger is the vertical distance between successive dots in the figure. The main force generating the persistent increase in the price level is a tendency for aggregate demand to increase at a faster pace than the increase in long-run aggregate supply. All of the factors that increase aggregate demand and shift the aggregate demand curve influence the pace of inflation. But one factor—the growth of the quantity of money—is the main source of *persistent* increases in aggregate demand and persistent inflation.

Business Cycles

Over the years, the economy grows and shrinks in cycles—shown in Fig. 24.14 by the wavelike pattern made by the points, with the recessions highlighted. The cycles arise because both the expansion of short-run aggregate supply and the growth of aggregate demand do not proceed at a fixed, steady pace. Although the economy has cycles, recessions do not usually follow quickly on the heels of their predecessors; "double-dip" recessions like the one in the cartoon are rare.

The Evolving Economy: 1960–1996

During the 1960s, real GDP growth was rapid and inflation was low. This was a period of rapid increases in aggregate supply and of moderate increases in aggregate demand.

The mid-1970s were years of rapid inflation and recession—of stagflation. The major source of these developments was a series of massive oil price increases that shifted the short-run aggregate supply curve leftward and rapid increases in the quantity of money that shifted the aggregate demand curve rightward. Recession occurred because the short-run aggregate supply curve shifted leftward at a faster pace than the aggregate demand curve shifted rightward.

The rest of the 1970s saw high inflation—the price level increased quickly—and only moderate growth in real GDP. By 1980, inflation was a major problem and the Fed decided to take strong action against it. It permitted interest rates to rise to previously unknown levels. Consequently, aggregate demand decreased. By 1982, the decrease in aggregate demand put the economy in a deep recession.

"Please stand by for a series of tones. The first indicates the official end of the recession, the second indicates prosperity, and the third the return of the recession."

Drawing by Mankoff; © 1991 The New Yorker Magazine, Inc.

During the years 1982 to 1990, capital accumulation and steady technological advance resulted in a sustained rightward shift of the long-run aggregate supply curve. Wage growth was moderate, and the short-run aggregate supply curve also shifted rightward. Aggregate demand growth kept pace with the growth of aggregate supply. Sustained but steady growth in aggregate supply and aggregate demand kept real GDP growing and inflation steady. The economy moved from a recession with real GDP less than potential GDP in 1981 to above full-employment in 1990. It was in this condition when a decrease in aggregate demand led to the 1991 recession. The economy again embarked on a path of expansion through 1996. The expansion took real GDP back to potential GDP and returned employment to full employment.

◆ The aggregate supply–aggregate demand model explains economic growth, inflation, and the business cycle. The model is a useful one because it enables us to keep our eye on the big picture. But it lacks detail. It does not tell us as much as we need to know about the deeper forces that lie behind aggregate supply and aggregate demand. The chapters that follow begin to fill in the details. We begin with the supply side and study the forces that make our economy grow. But before you embark on this next stage, take a look at *Reading Between the Lines* on pages 532–533, which gives you a look at the U.S. economy in 1997.

Policy
WATCH

Aggregate Supply and Aggregate Demand in Action

THE WASHINGTON POST, JULY 17, 1996

Apply 1 Stock Drop and Watch the Economy Cool

BY JOHN M. BERRY

The 6.5 percent slide in stock prices this month could turn out to be a cloud with a silver lining.

That decline, a direct sign of weaker corporate earnings, could be a bit of a blow to consumers' confidence and dampen their spending somewhat in coming months, a number of analysts said.

Normally, such developments wouldn't be regarded as good news at all. But with economic growth running at a 4 percent pace recently, unemployment at its lowest level in six years and many investors braced for a Federal Reserve boost in short-term interest rates to head off any rise in inflation, a little cooling could be just what the doctor ordered.

Some investors appear to be interpreting the market's drop in exactly that fashion. Interest rates soared early this month when the Labor Department said payroll jobs had increased briskly in June, the unemployment rate had fallen to 5.3 percent and average hourly earnings had jumped 0.8 percent. Since then, the drop in stock prices and some other favorable news—including a report yesterday that consumer prices rose a scant 0.1 percent last month—have unwound much of the earlier rise in rates. ...

In a revised forecast, the administration predicted the economy would grow 2.6 percent from last year's fourth quarter to this year's, rather than the 2.2 percent expected at the beginning of this year. Nevertheless, the higher figure still assumes that growth will slow down in the second half of the year and that the unemployment rate will move back up to 5.6 percent. The forecast for consumer price inflation was revised upward slightly, from 3.1 percent to 3.2 percent.

Reprinted with permission.

- In mid-1996, real GDP was growing at a rate of 4 percent a year. The unemployment rate was at its lowest in six years.

- Investors expected the Fed to raise interest rates to check inflation.

- The Fed had raised interest rates in early July when the unemployment rate fell to 5.3 percent and wages increased by 0.8 percent.

- But stock prices fell in mid-July 1996.

- The lower stock prices might be sign of lower profits and might weaken consumer confidence and decrease consumer spending.

- Interest rates decreased with the news of the stock price drop and the announcement of a 0.1 percent increase in consumer prices.

Economic

A N A L Y S I S

■ Figure 1 shows that real GDP was above potential GDP at the end of 1994—an inflationary gap—below potential GDP at the end of 1995 and beginning of 1996—a recessionary gap—and equal to potential GDP in 1996. (Potential GDP is the author's estimate.)

■ Figure 2 shows that inflation increased in 1995 and decreased in 1996.

■ The increase in the inflation rate during 1995 was caused by the 1994 inflationary gap. The decrease in the inflation rate during late 1995 and 1996 was caused by the recessionary gap present during those years.

■ Figure 3 shows the U.S. economy in 1997 and explains the fears expressed in the news article in terms of the aggregate supply–aggregate demand model.

■ In the second quarter of 1996, real GDP was $6.9 trillion and the price level was 110.

■ You can see these values at the intersection of the aggregate demand curve AD_{96} and the short-run aggregate supply curve SAS_{96}.

■ The economy is at full-employment equilibrium. Real GDP equals potential GDP on the long-run aggregate supply curve LAS_{96}.

■ Many people feared that aggregate demand was growing quickly in 1996 and that, with no action from the Fed, the aggregate demand curve might shift rightward to AD'.

■ If the aggregate demand curve did shift rightward to AD', an inflationary gap would emerge and the inflation rate would begin to rise again.

■ And if an inflationary gap is expected, it is a good bet that the Fed will increase interest rates in an attempt to hold aggregate demand growth back.

■ But if households expect lower future incomes because business profits are down, perhaps aggregate demand growth will slow with no action by the Fed.

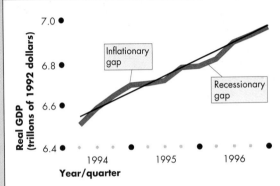

Figure 1 Real GDP

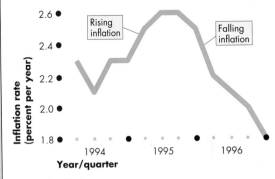

Figure 2 Inflation

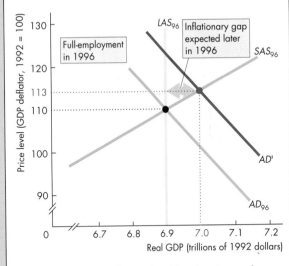

Figure 3 Aggregate demand and aggregate supply

You're

THE VOTER

■ During a two-week period in July 1996, the Fed first increased and then decreased interest rates. How do you think the economy responds to this type of action by the Fed?

■ Would you support an increase in interest rates to keep inflation in check?

■ Would you support a decrease in interest rates to lower unemployment?

SUMMARY

Key Points

Aggregate Supply (pp. 516–520)

■ In the long run, the quantity of real GDP supplied is potential GDP, which is independent of the price level. The long-run aggregate supply curve is vertical.

■ In the short run, the money wage rate is constant, so a rise in the price level increases the quantity of real GDP supplied. The short-run aggregate supply curve is upward sloping.

■ A change in potential GDP changes both long-run and short-run aggregate supply. A change in the money wage rate or resource prices changes only short-run aggregate supply.

Aggregate Demand (pp. 521–524)

■ A rise in the price level decreases the quantity of real GDP demanded, other things remaining the same.

■ The reason is that the higher price level decreases the quantity of *real* wealth, raises the interest rate, and raises the cost of domestic goods compared with foreign goods.

■ Changes in expected future incomes, profits, and inflation, changes in fiscal policy and monetary policy, and changes in world real GDP and the foreign exchange rate change aggregate demand.

Macroeconomic Equilibrium (pp. 524–529)

■ In the short run, real GDP and the price level are determined by aggregate demand and short-run aggregate supply.

■ In the long run, real GDP equals potential GDP and aggregate demand determines the price level and the money wage rate.

■ Economic growth occurs because potential GDP increases.

■ Inflation occurs because aggregate demand grows more quickly than potential GDP.

■ Business cycles occur because aggregate demand and aggregate supply fluctuate.

U.S. Economic Growth, Inflation, and Cycles (pp. 530–531)

■ U.S. potential GDP grew fastest during the 1960s and mid-1980s and slowest during the 1970s.

■ U.S. inflation persists because aggregate demand grows faster than potential GDP.

■ U.S. business cycles occur because aggregate supply and aggregate demand change at an uneven pace.

Key Figures

Key Terms

QUESTIONS

1. What are the three factors that determine the quantity of real GDP supplied?
2. What is the relationship between potential GDP and full employment?
3. Name and distinguish between two macroeconomic time frames and two concepts of aggregate supply.
4. Distinguish between movements along the short-run and the long-run aggregate supply curves.
5. Consider the following events:
   a. Potential GDP increases
   b. The money wage rate rises
   c. The price level rises
   d. The money wage rate and the price level rise by the same percentages
   Say which of these events, if any, change:
   (1) Long-run aggregate supply but not short-run aggregate supply.
   (2) Short-run aggregate supply but not long-run aggregate supply.
   (3) Both short-run aggregate supply and long-run aggregate supply.
   Also say which of these events, if any, bring a movement along
   (4) The long-run aggregate supply curve.
   (5) The short-run aggregate supply curve.
   (6) Both the short-run and long-run aggregate supply curves.
6. Distinguish between aggregate demand and the quantity of real GDP demanded.
7. Which of the following do not affect aggregate demand?
   a. Quantity of money
   b. Interest rates
   c. Technological change
   d. Human capital
8. Define short-run macroeconomic equilibrium.
9. Distinguish between a recessionary equilibrium and full-employment equilibrium.
10. Work out the short-run and long-run effects of an increase in the quantity of money on the price level and real GDP.
11. Work out the short-run effect of an increase in the price of oil on the price level and real GDP.
12. What are the main factors generating growth, inflation, and cycles in the U.S. economy?

PROBLEMS

1. The following events occur that influence the economy of Toughtimes:
   - A deep recession hits the world economy.
   - Oil prices rise sharply.
   - Businesses expect huge losses in the near future.
   a. Use the *AS–AD* model to explain the separate effects of each event on real GDP and the price level in Toughtimes, starting from long-run equilibrium.
   b. Use the *AS–AD* model to explain the combined effects of these events on real GDP and the price level in Toughtimes, starting from long-run equilibrium.
   c. Explain what the Toughtimes government or central bank can do to overcome the problems faced by the economy.

2. The following events occur that influence the economy of Coolland:
   - The world economy experiences a strong expansion.
   - Businesses expect huge profits in the near future.
   - The Coolland government cuts its purchases of goods and services.
   a. Use the *AS–AD* model to explain the separate effects of each event on real GDP and the price level in Coolland, starting from long-run equilibrium.
   b. Use the *AS–AD* model to explain the combined effects of these events on real GDP and the price level in Coolland, starting from long-run equilibrium.
   c. Explain why the Coolland government or Fed might want to take action to influence the Coolland economy.

3. The economy of Mainland has the following aggregate demand and supply schedules:

Price level	Real GDP demanded	Real GDP supplied in the short run
	(trillions of 1992 dollars)	
90	4.5	3.5
100	4.0	4.0
110	3.5	4.5
120	3.0	5.0
130	2.5	5.5
140	2.0	6.0

a. Plot the aggregate demand curve and short-run aggregate supply curve in a figure.
b. What are the values of real GDP and the price level in Mainland in a short-run macroeconomic equilibrium?
c. Mainland's potential GDP is $5.0 trillion. Plot the long-run aggregate supply curve in the same figure in which you answered part (a).

🖳 4. In problem 3, aggregate demand increases by $1 trillion. What are the changes in real GDP and the price level in the short run?

🖳 5. In problem 3, aggregate supply decreases by $1 trillion. What is the new short-run macroeconomic equilibrium?

6. In the economy shown in the figure below, short-run aggregate supply is SAS_0 and aggregate demand is AD_0. Then some events change aggregate demand and the aggregate demand curve shifts rightward to AD_1. Later, some further events change aggregate supply, and the short-run aggregate supply curve shifts leftward to SAS_1.

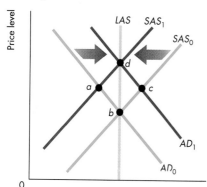

a. What is the initial equilibrium point?
b. What is the equilibrium point after the change in aggregate demand?
c. What is the equilibrium point after the change in aggregate supply?
d. What events could have changed aggregate demand from AD_0 to AD_1?
e. What events could have changed aggregate supply from SAS_0 to SAS_1?
f. After the increase in aggregate demand but before the decrease in aggregate supply, is the real GDP greater than or less than potential GDP?

CRITICAL THINKING

1. After you have studied the account of the U.S. economic expansion during the 1990s in *Reading Between the Lines* on pp. 532–533:
   a. Describe the main features of the economy in 1996 that worried economists.
   b. In which periods was there a recessionary gap and in which was there an inflationary gap?
   c. Use the *AS-AD* model to show the economy in 1996 if the Fed increased interest rates by too much and created a recession.
   d. Use the *AS-AD* model to show the economy in 1996 if the Fed cut interest rates to stimulate aggregate demand and avoid a recession.

🖳 2. You are the President's economic advisor and have the following forecasts of aggregate demand and aggregate supply for next year:

Price level	Real GDP demanded	Real GDP supplied	Potential GDP
	(trillions of 1992 dollars)		
100	8.3	5.3	7
105	7.8	6.3	7
110	7.3	7.3	7
115	6.8	8.3	7

This year, real GDP is $6.8 trillion, potential GDP is also $6.8 trillion, and the price level is 107. The President wants answers to the following questions:
   a. What is your forecast of next year's real GDP?
   b. What is your forecast of next year's price level?
   c. What is your forecast of the inflation rate?
   d. What is your forecast of the growth rate of real GDP?
   e. What is your forecast of the growth rate of potential GDP?
   f. Will there be a recessionary gap or an inflationary gap? By how much?

3. Carefully draw some figures similar to those in this chapter and use the information in question 2 to explain:
   a. What policy actions can bring real GDP to potential GDP.
   b. What the inflation rate is if aggregate demand is changed by policy to achieve potential GDP.

Expanding the Frontier

Economics is about how we cope with scarcity. We cope by making choices that balance marginal benefits and marginal costs so that we use our scarce resources efficiently. ◆ These choices determine how much work we do, how hard we work at school to learn the mental skills that form our human capital and that determine the kinds of jobs we get and the incomes we earn, and how much we save for future big ticket expenditures. These choices also determine how much businesses and governments spend on new capital—on auto assembly lines, computers and fiber cables for improved Internet services, shopping malls, highways, bridges, and tunnels—and how intensively existing capital and natural resources are used and therefore how quickly they wear out or are used up. Most significant of all, these choices determine the problems that scientists, engineers, and other inventors work on to develop new technologies. ◆ All the choices we've just described determine two vital measures of economic performance:

■ Real GDP
■ Economic growth

Real GDP is determined by the quantity of labor, the quantity of capital, and the state of technological knowledge. And economic growth—the growth rate of real GDP—is determined by growth in the quantity of labor, capital accumulation, and technological advances. ◆ Economic growth, maintained at a steady rate over a number of decades, is the single most powerful influence on any society. It brings a transformation that continues to amaze thoughtful people. Economic growth, maintained at a rapid rate, can transform a society in years, not decades. Such transformations are taking place right now in many Asian countries. These transformations are economic miracles. ◆ The three chapters in this part study the miracle of rapid economic growth and the forces that shape our capacity to produce goods and services. ◆ In Chapter 25, you will learn about our choices in the labor market that determine the quantity of labor and the levels of employment and unemployment. ◆ In Chapter 26, you will study the process of capital accumulation and the saving and investment decisions that govern it. You'll discover that some countries don't save enough to pay for the capital they accumulate and others save more than they need. And you'll see how international capital markets move savings to where they can obtain the highest possible return. ◆ In Chapter 27, you will study economic growth. You will learn about some economic miracles and some problems, especially the problem of the growth slowdown in the United States during the 1970s and 1980s. ◆ But first, we'll spend some time with Joseph Schumpeter and Paul Romer, two economists who have revolutionized the way we think about economic growth.

Economic Growth

The Economist:
Joseph Schumpeter

Joseph Schumpeter, the son of a textile factory owner, was born in Austria in 1883. He moved from Austria to Germany during the tumultuous 1920s when those two countries experienced hyperinflation. And in 1932, in the depths of the Great Depression, he came to the United States and became a professor of economics at Harvard University.

This creative economic thinker wrote on economic growth and development, business cycles, political systems, and economic biography. He was a person of strong opinions who expressed them strongly and delighted in verbal battles.

Schumpeter has become the unwitting founder of modern growth theory. He saw the development and diffusion of new technologies by profit-seeking entrepreneurs as the source of economic progress. But he saw economic progress as a process of creative destruction—the creation of new profit opportunities and the destruction of currently profitable businesses. For Schumpeter, economic growth and the business cycle were a single phenomenon.

When Schumpeter died in 1950, he had achieved his self-expressed life's ambition: He was regarded as the world's greatest economist.

"Economic progress, in capitalist society, means turmoil."

JOSEPH SCHUMPETER

CAPITALISM, SOCIALISM AND

DEMOCRACY

The Issues
and Ideas

Technological change, capital accumulation, and population growth all interact to produce economic growth. But what is cause and what is effect, and can we expect productivity and income per person to keep growing?

The classical economists of the eighteenth and nineteenth centuries believed that technological advances and capital accumulation were the engines of growth. But they also believed that no matter how successful people were at inventing more productive technologies and investing in new capital, they were destined to live at the subsistence level. These economists based their conclusion on the belief that productivity growth causes population growth, which in turn causes productivity to decline. These classical economists believed that whenever economic growth raises incomes above the subsistence level, the population will increase. And they went on to reason that the increase in population brings diminishing returns that lower productivity. As a result, incomes must always return to the subsistence level. Only when incomes are at the subsistence level is population growth held in check.

A new approach, called neoclassical growth theory, was developed by Robert Solow of MIT during the 1950s. Solow, who was one of Schumpeter's students, received the Nobel Prize for Economic Science for this work.

Solow challenged the conclusions of the classical economists. But the new theories of economic growth developed during the 1980s and 1990s went further. They stand the classical belief on its head. Today's theory of population growth is that rising income slows the population growth rate because it increases the opportunity cost of having children and lowers the opportunity cost of investing in children and equipping them with more human capital, which makes them more productive. Productivity and income grow because technology advances and the scope for further productivity growth, which is stimulated by the search for profit, is practically unlimited.

Flemish farmers in the fifteenth century. With newly developed horse-drawn plows, harrows, and planters, farmers could plant more wheat than they could harvest. But despite big efforts, no one had been able to make a machine that could replicate the swing of a scythe. Then in 1831, 22-year-old Cyrus McCormick built a machine that worked. It scared the horse that pulled it, but it did in a matter of hours what three men could accomplish in a day. Technological change has increased productivity on farms and brought economic growth. Do the facts about productivity growth mean that the classical economists, who believed that diminishing returns would push us relentlessly back to a subsistence living standard, were wrong?

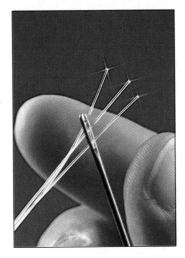

increase agricultural productivity. In the foreseeable future, we might have superconductors that revolutionize the use of electric power, virtual reality theme parks and training facilities, pollution-free hydrogen cars, wristwatch telephones, and optical computers that we can talk to. With these new technologies, our ability to create yet more dazzling technologies increases. Technological change begets technological change in an (apparently) unending process and makes us ever more productive and brings ever higher incomes.

THEN ...

In 1830, a strong and experienced farm worker could harvest three acres of wheat in a day. The only capital employed was a scythe to cut the wheat, which had been used since Roman times, and a cradle on which the stalks were laid, which had been invented by

... AND NOW

Today's technologies are expanding our horizons beyond the confines of our planet and are expanding our minds. Geosynchronous satellites bring us global television, voice and data communication, and more accurate weather forecasts, which incidentally

The revolution in the way economists think about economic growth has been led by Paul Romer, a professor of economics at Stanford University, whom you can meet on the following pages.

Talking with

Paul Romer is Professor of Economics at the Graduate School of Business at Stanford University and the Royal Bank Fellow of the Canadian Institute for Advanced Research. Born in 1955 in Denver, Colorado, he earned his B.S. in Mathematics (1977) and his Ph.D. in Economics (1983) from the University of Chicago.

Professor Romer has transformed the way economists think about economic growth. He believes that sustained economic growth arises from competition among firms. Firms try to increase their profits by devoting resources to creating new products and developing new ways of making existing products.

Michael Parkin talked with Professor Romer about his work, how he was influenced by Joseph Schumpeter and Robert Solow, and the insights economic growth offers us.

Professor Romer, why did you decide to become an economist?

As an undergraduate, I studied math and physics and was interested in becoming a cosmologist. During my senior year, I concluded that job prospects in physics were not very promising, so I decided to go to law school. I was an undergraduate at the University of Chicago, where the law and economics movement first emerged. In the fall of my senior year, I took my first economics course to prepare for law school. My economics professor, Sam Peltzman, presented a simple piece of economic analysis that changed my life. He argued that the demand for economists was likely to grow for decades. The government, which employs economists, would grow in size. Businesses that deal with the government would want their own economists. The legal profession that serves businesses would also need more economists. Because of all these demands, many students would want to take economics courses. This meant that there would be many job openings for economists at universities. Moreover, he claimed, being a professor of economics was a lot like being a cosmologist and far more fun than being a lawyer. I could take fragmentary bits of evidence and try to make sense of them using mathematical equations. So I tore up my law school applications, applied to graduate school in economics, and never looked back.

What are the truly important lessons we've learned about the causes of economic growth?

As a physics major, I felt that the description economists used for growth violated a basic law of physics: the conservation of mass. Economists seemed to be saying that GDP, the output of a nation, was a bunch of stuff that was "produced" and that the quantity of stuff produced has grown steadily over time and will continue to do so. But this can't be right. We have the same amount of stuff, or elements from the periodic table, that we had 100,000 years ago because there are many more people now. In terms of kilograms of matter per person, we know that we are vastly poorer than our ancestors were 100,000 years ago. Yet we clearly have a higher standard of living. How could this be? This basic question indicates that thinking about growth as a production process that generates stuff is a dead-end. Instead, economic growth has to be about rearranging the fixed amount of matter that we have to work with and making new combinations that seem a lot more valuable. The key insight is that economic growth comes from increases in value, not increases in the amount of matter.

Can you give us an example of what you mean by an increase in value?

For tens of thousands of years, we treated iron oxide, ordinary rust, like dirt. When we lived in caves, we learned how to use it as a pigment for decorating cave walls. We took the low-value dirt and put it to the higher-valued use of making cave paintings. Later, we learned how to extract the iron from iron ore to make bridges and rails. Later still, we learned how to arrange the iron atoms together with carbon atoms and make steel. Recently, we learned how to take iron oxide and put it on magnetic tape and use it to store sound and pictures. The iron, oxygen, and carbon atoms have always been here. We have a higher standard of living because we have learned how to take these atoms and arrange them in ways that we find more valuable.

What kind of policy implications does this kind of thinking lead to?

Policy makers must encourage institutions to become more efficient at discovering new recipes to rearrange matter. Consider the transistor as an example. We take silicon and mix it with a few impurities and some metal in just the right way, and we get a computer chip worth thousands of times what the raw ingredients were worth. Research grants, subsidies for education, and institutions like the nonprofit private university encourage the production of new recipes or ideas. But so

> *We take silicon and mix it with a few impurities and some metal in just the right way, and we get a computer chip worth thousands of times what the raw ingredients were worth.*

do venture capitalists who help new-technology startups, competitive markets that allow the firms with better instructions or ideas to quickly displace existing firms, and labor laws that let inefficient firms lay off workers when more efficient new firms come on the scene. We must let firms like Digital Electronics or Wang Computers shrink, maybe even fail, if we want to make room for new firms like Intel to enter the scene and thrive.

Were the classical economists wrong in their view that population growth and diminishing returns are the dominant long-term influences on production and incomes? Or is the current global population explosion part of a process that will ultimately prove them correct?

Classical economists like Malthus and Ricardo were right when they argued that we have a fixed amount of natural resources to work with. Malthus pointed out that resource scarcity will lead to falling standards of living if we continue to work with the same set of recipes or instructions for using our resources. Where he went wrong was in assuming that there was little scope for us to find new recipes for taking resources such as land, water, carbon dioxide, nitrogen, and sunshine and converting them into carbohydrates and proteins that we can eat.

The classical economists got half of the story right. We do live in a world with scarce resources. What they missed was the other half. There is an incomprehensibly large number of different formulas or recipes we can use to recombine these scarce resources into things we value, such as protein or entertainment.

Scarcity is a very important part of economics and our lives. For example, we know that there is an absolute limit on the number of people who can live on the earth. One way or another, we know that the rate of population growth will slow down. It's only a question of how and when. But will this ultimately lead to a period when standards of living fall as Malthus predicted? I doubt it. As countries get rich, population growth slows. As a larger fraction of the worldwide population becomes educated, these people will help us to discover new things, like plants that are more efficient at taking carbon dioxide out of the atmosphere, wires that are superconductors at high temperatures, and more efficient distribution systems. With these discoveries, standards of living for all humans will continue to improve.

During the past decade, China and several other economies in East Asia have experienced rapid, unheralded growth rates. Why?
These countries took some of the recipes, formulas, and instructions for generating value that already existed in the advanced countries of the world and put them to use within their borders. It's the same process that the Japanese followed after the Meiji restoration at the end of the last century. These countries noticed that other people in the world knew a lot about how to create value and realized that by trading with the people who possessed all this knowledge, they could share in the gains.

What lessons from East Asia can, in principle, be applied in Africa and Central Europe?
The basic insight is that there are huge potential gains from trade. Poor countries can supply their natural and human resources. Rich countries can supply their know-how. When these are combined, everyone can be better off. The challenge is for a country to arrange its laws and institutions so that both sides can profitably engage in trade. If there are barriers to trade or if the government cannot protect basic property rights and prevent crime, trade can't take place. For example, the Japanese have been able to borrow many ideas about manufacturing and design and even to improve on some of these ideas. But because they have barriers that limit entry of foreign firms into the retail sector, they still waste vast quantities of resources on a very inefficient distribution system.

What does today's thinking about economic growth owe to the work of Joseph Schumpeter and Robert Solow?
Schumpeter worked at a time before most economists had learned to work with equations. He coined the phrase "creative destruction," which describes the process by which companies like Wang shrink or go out of business when new firms come in. He also described in words how important monopoly profits are in the process of innovation. There were many other economists, including Alfred Marshall, who described these same issues in verbal terms and also struggled with the challenge of expressing these ideas in terms of equations.

Robert Solow was part of the post–World War II generation of economists who truly mastered the use of equations and wrote eloquently using both words and equations. As a result, his ideas have been far more influential than Schumpeter's. Many economists in the 1950s were trying to get a grasp on the economic effects of knowledge, formulas, recipes, and instructions. Solow called these things "technology" and gave us a wonderfully concise and workable way to think about how technology interacts with other economic inputs such as capital and labor. He also linked the methods that he and several economists were using to measure technology with this framework for thinking about the behavior of the economy as a whole. His work on growth was a masterful piece of invention, synthesis, and exposition.

In the last 15 years, economists have taken the mathematical framework that Solow gave us and extended it to bring in some of the elements that Schumpeter described in words, things like creative destruction and monopoly power. One of the great things about ideas is that they build on each other. In Isaac Newton's famous phrase, those of us working on growth today are "able to see farther because we stand on the shoulders of giants." Newton was another person who was pretty good with equations and could also turn a good phrase.

If you can learn how to write readable prose and use the basic tools of mathematics, you can do almost anything in today's world.

Is economics a worthwhile subject to major in today? What can a person do with an economics degree?
Economics is an excellent training ground for developing mathematical and verbal skills. But students should supplement the courses in economics with courses in mathematics and science that force them to practice working with equations, graphs, and numbers. In learning a skill, there is no substitute for practice. Innate ability is far less important than most students think.

They should also take courses that force them to write, revise, and edit. I took an English course in college that taught me the basics of how to edit, and it is one of the best investments I made. You can't tell what you will end up doing or what skills you will need later in life. But if you can learn how to write readable prose and use the basic tools of mathematics, you can do almost anything in today's world.

Chapter 25

Employment and Unemployment

Vital Signs

Each month, we chart the course of the unemployment rate as a measure of U.S. economic health. How do we measure unemployment? What does it tell us? Is it a reliable vital sign for the economy? ◆ June 1992 was a month in which unemployment peaked at almost 10 million. How can such a large number of people be unemployed? How do people become unemployed? Do most of them get fired, or do most quit their jobs to look for better ones? How long do spells of unemployment last for most people—a week, two weeks, or several months? And how does the length of unemployment spells vary over the business cycle?◆ You probably know that unemployment is more common among young people than among older people. It is also more common among minorities than among whites. Why are some groups more frequently unemployed than others? ◆ We also chart every month the number of people working. This number fluctuates as the unemployment rate fluctuates, but it also trends upward. At the start of 1997, more than 127 million people in the United States had jobs. What does this vital sign tell us about the health of the U.S. economy? Does the number of jobs grow quickly enough to keep pace with increases in the population? ◆ Yet other signs of economic health are the hours people work and the wages they receive. Are work hours growing as quickly as the number of people with jobs? Are most of the new jobs full time or part time? Also, are most new jobs high-wage or low-wage jobs? ◆ These are the questions we study in this chapter. You will discover that a lot of ideas that people have about the U.S. labor market are just plain wrong. The economy has created millions of jobs, including good jobs that pay high wages and provide good benefits. But most people have seen a slowdown in their rate of wage increase, and many have seen their wages fall. We begin by looking at the key labor market indicators and the way they are measured.

After studying this chapter, you will be able to:

- Define the unemployment rate, the labor force participation rate, the employment-to-population ratio, and aggregate hours

- Describe the trends and fluctuations in the indicators of labor market performance

- Describe the sources of unemployment, its duration, and the groups that are most affected by it

- Explain how employment and wage rates are determined by demand and supply in the labor market

Employment and Wages

THE QUANTITY OF REAL GDP SUPPLIED DEPENDS on the quantities of labor and capital and on the state of technology. And potential GDP depends on the quantity of capital and the state of technology and on the quantity of labor employed at *full employment*. In this chapter, we study the forces that determine the quantity of labor employed and the concept of full employment. We begin by learning how the state of the labor market is observed and measured.

Population Survey

Every month, the U.S. Census Bureau surveys 60,000 households and asks a series of questions about the age and job market status of its members. This survey is called the Current Population Survey. The Census Bureau uses the answers to describe the anatomy of the labor force.

Figure 25.1 shows the population categories used by the Census Bureau and the relationships among the categories. It divides the population into two groups: the working-age population and others who are too young to work or who live in institutions and are unable to work. The **working-age population** is the total number of people aged 16 years and over who are not in jail, hospital, or some other form of institutional care. The Census Bureau divides the working-age population into two groups: those in the labor force and those not in the labor force. It also divides the labor force into two groups: the employed and the unemployed. So the **labor force** is the sum of the employed and the unemployed.

To be counted as employed in the Current Population Survey, a person must have either a full-time job or a part-time job. To be counted as *un*employed, a person must be available for work and must be in one of three categories:

1. Without work but has made specific efforts to find a job within the previous four weeks
2. Waiting to be called back to a job from which he or she has been laid off
3. Waiting to start a new job within 30 days

Anyone surveyed who satisfies one of these three criteria is counted as unemployed. People in the working-age population who are neither employed nor unemployed are classified as not in the labor force.

FIGURE 25.1

Population Labor Force Categories

The population is divided into the working-age population and the young and institutionalized. The working-age population is divided into the labor force and those not in the labor force. The labor force is divided into the employed and the unemployed.

Source: Economic Report of the President, 1997.

In 1996, the population of the United States was 265.5 million. There were 64.9 million people under 16 years of age or living in institutions. The working-age population was 200.6 million. Of this number, 66.7 million were not in the labor force. Most of these people were in school full time or had retired from work. The remaining 133.9 million people made up the U.S. labor force. Of these, 126.7 million were employed and 7.2 million were unemployed.

Three Labor Market Indicators

The Census Bureau calculates three indicators of the state of the labor market, which are shown in Fig. 25.2. They are:

■ The unemployment rate
■ The labor force participation rate
■ The employment-to-population ratio

The Unemployment Rate The amount of unemployment is an indicator of the extent to which people who want jobs can't find them. The **unemployment rate** is the percentage of the people in the labor force who are unemployed. That is,

$$\text{Unemployment rate} = \frac{\text{Number of people unemployed}}{\text{Labor force}} \times 100,$$

and

$$\text{Labor force} = \text{Number of people employed} + \text{Number of people unemployed}.$$

In 1996, the number of people employed was 126.7 million and the number unemployed was 7.2 million. By using the above equations, you can verify that the labor force was 133.9 million (126.7 million plus 7.2 million) and the unemployment rate was 5.4 percent (7.2 million divided by 133.9 million, multiplied by 100).

Figure 25.2. shows the unemployment rate (orange line) and two other labor market indicators between 1960 and 1996. The average unemployment rate has been 6 percent, and it reached peak values during the OPEC recession and the recessions of 1982 and 1990–1991.

The Labor Force Participation Rate The number of people who join the labor force is an indicator of the willingness of people of working age to take jobs. The **labor force participation rate** is the percentage of the working-age population who are members of the labor force. That is,

$$\text{Labor force participation rate} = \frac{\text{Labor force}}{\text{Working-age population}} \times 100.$$

In 1996, the labor force was 133.9 million and the working-age population was 200.6 million. By using the above equation, you can calculate the labor force participation rate. It was 66.7 percent (133.9 million divided by 200.6 million, multiplied by 100).

The labor force participation rate (graphed in red and plotted on the left scale) has followed an upward trend and has increased from 59 percent during the early 1960s to 67 percent during the 1990s. It has also had some mild fluctuations. They result from unsuccessful job seekers becoming discouraged

FIGURE 25.2

Employment, Unemployment, and the Labor Force: 1960–1996

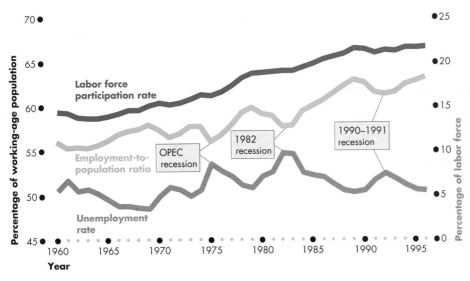

The unemployment rate increases in recessions and decreases in expansions. The labor force participation rate and the employment-to-population ratio have upward trends and fluctuate with the business cycle. The employment-to-population ratio fluctuates more than the labor force participation rate and reflects cyclical fluctuations in the unemployment rate. Fluctuations in the labor force participation rate arise mainly because of discouraged workers.

Source: *Economic Report of the President,* 1997.

workers. **Discouraged workers** are people who are available and willing to work but have not made specific efforts to find a job within the previous four weeks. These workers often temporarily leave the labor force during a recession and reenter during an expansion and become active job seekers.

The Employment-to-Population Ratio The number of people of working age who have jobs is an indicator of both the availability of jobs and the degree of match between people's skills and jobs. The **employment-to-population ratio** is the percentage of people of working age who have jobs. That is,

$$\text{Employment-to-population ratio} = \frac{\text{Number of people employed}}{\text{Working-age population}} \times 100.$$

In 1996, employment was 126.7 million and the working-age population was 200.6 million. By using the above equation, you can calculate the employment-to-population ratio. It was 63.2 percent (126.7 million divided by 200.6 million, multiplied by 100).

The employment-to-population ratio (graphed in blue and plotted against the left scale) has increased from 55 percent during the early 1960s to 63 percent during the 1990s. The increase in the employment-to-population ratio means that the U.S. economy has created jobs at a faster rate than the working-age population has grown. This labor market indicator also fluctuates, and its fluctuations coincide with but are opposite to those in the unemployment rate. It falls during a recession and increases during an expansion.

Why have the labor force participation rate and the employment-to-population ratio increased? The main reason is an increase in the number of women in the labor force. Figure 25.3 shows this increase. Between 1960 and 1996, the female labor force participation rate increased from 38 percent to 59 percent. Shorter work hours, higher productivity, and an increased emphasis on white-collar jobs have expanded the job opportunities and wages available to women. At the same time, technological advances have increased productivity in the home and freed up women's time to take jobs outside the home.

Figure 25.3 also shows another remarkable trend in the U.S. labor force: The labor force participation rate and the employment-to-population ratio for men have *decreased*. Between 1960 and 1996, the male labor force participation rate decreased from

FIGURE 25.3

The Changing Face of the Labor Market

The upward trends in the labor force participation rate and the employment-to-population ratio are accounted for mainly by the increasing participation of women in the labor market. The male labor force participation rate and employment-to-population ratio have decreased.

Source: *Economic Report of the President*, 1997.

83 percent to 75 percent. It has decreased because increasing numbers of men are remaining in school longer and because some are retiring earlier.

Aggregate Hours

The three labor market indicators that we've just examined are useful signs of the health of the economy and directly measure what matters to most people: jobs. But they don't tell us the quantity of labor used to produce GDP, and we cannot use them to calculate the productivity of labor. The productivity of labor is significant because it influences the wages people earn.

The reason why the number of people employed does not measure the quantity of labor employed is that jobs are not all the same. People in part-time jobs might work just a few hours a week. People in full-time jobs work around 35 to 40 hours a week.

And some people regularly work overtime. For example, a 7-11 store might hire six students who work for three hours a day each. Another 7-11 store might hire two full-time workers who work nine hours a day each. The number of people employed in these two stores is eight, but the total hours worked by six of the eight is the same as the total hours worked by the other two. To determine the total amount of labor used to produce GDP, we measure labor in hours rather than in jobs. **Aggregate hours** are the total number of hours worked by all the people employed, both full time and part time, during a year.

Figure 25.4(a) shows aggregate hours in the U.S. economy from 1960 to 1996. Like the employment-to-population ratio, aggregate hours have an upward trend. But aggregate hours have not grown as quickly as have the number of people employed. Between 1960 and 1996, the number of people employed in the U.S. economy increased by 90 percent. During that same period, aggregate hours increased by only 70 percent. Why the difference? Because average hours per worker decreased.

Figure 25.4(b) shows average hours per worker. After hovering at almost 39 hours a week during the early 1960s, average hours per worker decreased to about 34 hours a week during the 1990s. This shortening of the average workweek has arisen partly because of a decrease in the average hours worked by full-time workers but mainly because the number of part-time jobs has increased faster than the number of full-time jobs.

Fluctuations in aggregate hours and average hours per worker line up with the business cycle. Figure 25.4 highlights the past three recessions, during which aggregate hours decreased and average hours per worker decreased more quickly than trend.

Wage Rates

The **real wage rate** is the quantity of goods and services that an hour's work can buy. It is equal to the money wage rate (dollars per hour) divided by the price level. If we use the GDP deflator to measure the price level, the real wage rate is expressed in 1992 dollars because the GDP deflator is 100 in 1992. The real wage is a significant economic variable because it measures the reward for labor.

What has happened to the real wage rate in the United States? Figure 25.5 answers this question. It shows four measures of the average hourly real wage rate in the U.S. economy between 1960 and 1996.

FIGURE 25.4

Aggregate Hours: 1960–1996

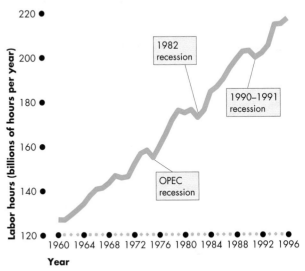

(a) Aggregate hours

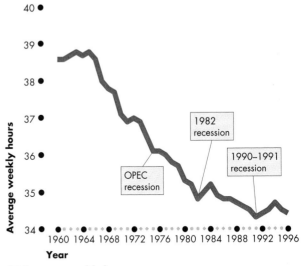

(b) Average weekly hours per person

Aggregate hours (part a) measure the total labor used to produce real GDP more accurately than does the number of people employed because an increasing proportion of jobs are part time. Between 1960 and 1996, aggregate hours increased by an average of 1.5 percent a year. Fluctuations in aggregate hours coincide with business cycle fluctuations. Aggregate hours have increased at a slower rate than the number of jobs because the average workweek has shortened (part b).

Source: Economic Report of the President, 1997, and the author's calculations.

FIGURE 25.5

Real Wage Rates: 1960–1996

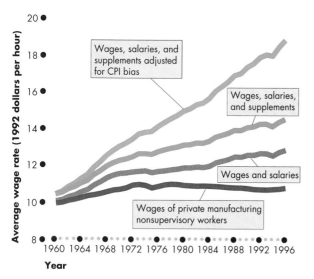

The average hourly real wage rate of private manufacturing nonsupervisory workers peaked in 1978 and then fell through 1993. Broader measures of the average hourly real wage rate increased. All the official measures show a productivity growth slowdown during the 1970s. An unofficial view is that inflation has been overestimated by 1.1 percent a year and the real wage rate has increased at roughly a constant rate.

Source: Economic Report of the President, 1997, and the author's calculations and assumptions.

The first measure of the real wage rate is the Department of Labor's calculation of the average hourly earnings of private manufacturing nonsupervisory workers. This measure increased to a maximum of $11.16 in 1978 (in 1992 dollars) and then followed a fifteen-year downward trend.

The second measure of the real wage rate is calculated by dividing total wages and salaries in the national income accounts by aggregate hours. This measure is broader than the first and includes the incomes of all types of labor, whether their rate of pay is calculated by the hour or not. This broader measure did not follow a downward trend, but its growth rate slowed during the mid-1970s and remained low through the early 1980s. It then speeded up during the late 1980s and 1990s.

An increasing proportion of labor compensation takes the form of fringe benefits such as pension contributions and the payment by employers of health insurance premiums. Figure 25.5 shows a third measure of the hourly real wage rate that reflects this trend. It is *total labor compensation*—wages, salaries, and benefits—divided by aggregate hours. This measure is the most comprehensive one available, and it shows that the real wage rate has increased. But it also shows that no matter how we measure the wage rate, the productivity growth slowdown also slowed real wage rate growth.

The decline in the average wage rate of manufacturing nonsupervisory workers and the slowdown in the growth rate of the broader measures of the average wage rate coincide with the *productivity growth slowdown* that you saw in Chapter 22. This productivity growth slowdown is the main reason for this behavior of average real wage rates. But whether this slowdown actually occurred depends on what actually happened to the price level. The three measures of real wages that we've just described are based on the official measure of inflation. If inflation has been overestimated by the 1.1 percent that the Boskin Commission (see Chapter 23, p. 505) estimates it has, then real wages have grown at a constant rate, as shown by the fourth line in Fig. 25.5.

R E V I E W

- The labor force participation rate and the employment-to-population ratio have an upward trend; the unemployment rate and employment-to-population ratio fluctuate with the business cycle.

- The female labor force participation rate has increased, but the male labor force participation rate has decreased.

- Aggregate hours have not grown as quickly as the number of people employed because the average workweek has shortened.

- Average hourly real wage rates have grown, but their growth rate slowed with the productivity growth slowdown of the 1970s.

Potential GDP depends on the full-employment quantity of labor. But at full employment, there is always some unemployment. Let's take a closer look at unemployment and see what determines its rate.

Unemployment and Full Employment

HOW DO PEOPLE BECOME UNEMPLOYED, HOW long do they remain unemployed, and who is at greatest risk to become unemployed? Let's answer these questions by looking at the anatomy of unemployment.

The Anatomy of Unemployment

People become unemployed if they:

1. Lose their jobs and search for another job
2. Leave their jobs and search for another job
3. Enter or reenter the labor force to search for a job

People end a spell of unemployment if they:

1. Are hired or recalled
2. Withdraw from the labor force

People who are laid off, either permanently or temporarily, from their jobs are called **job losers**. Some job losers become unemployed, but some immediately withdraw from the labor force. People who voluntarily quit their jobs are called **job leavers**. Like job losers, some job leavers become unemployed and search for a better job, while others withdraw from the labor force temporarily or permanently retire from work. People who enter or reenter the labor force are called **entrants** and **reentrants**. Entrants are mainly people who have just left school. Some entrants get a job right away and are never unemployed, but many spend time searching for their first job, and during this period they are unemployed. Reentrants are people who have previously withdrawn from the labor force. Most of these people are formerly discouraged workers. Figure 25.6 shows these labor market flows.

Let's see how much unemployment arises from the three different ways in which people can become unemployed.

The Sources of Unemployment Figure 25.7 shows unemployment by reason for becoming unemployed. Job losers are the biggest source of unemployment. Also, their number fluctuates a great deal. In the recession of 1990–1991, on any given day, more

FIGURE 25.6

Labor Market Flows

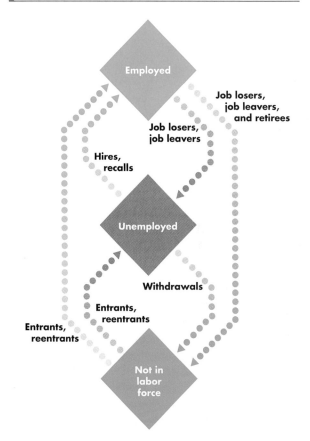

Unemployment results from employed people losing or leaving their jobs (job losers and job leavers) and from people entering the labor force (entrants and reentrants). Unemployment ends because people get hired or recalled or because they withdraw from the labor force.

than 5 million of the 9.4 million people who were unemployed were job losers. In contrast, in the peak year of 1989, fewer than 3 million of the 6.5 million people who were unemployed were job losers.

Entrants and reentrants also are a large component of the unemployed, and their number fluctuates mildly. On any given day, between 2.5 million and 3 million unemployed people are entrants and reentrants.

Job leavers are the smallest and most stable source of unemployment. On any given day, fewer than 1 million people are unemployed because they

FIGURE 25.7
Unemployment by Reasons

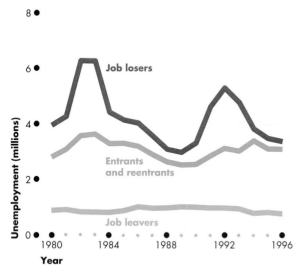

Everyone who is unemployed is either a job loser, a job leaver, or an entrant or reentrant into the labor force. Most of the unemployment that exists results from job loss. The number of job losers fluctuates more closely with the business cycle than do the numbers of job leavers and entrants and reentrants. Entrants and reentrants are the second most commonly unemployed people. Their number fluctuates with the business cycle because of discouraged workers. Job leavers are the least common unemployed people.

Source: Economic Report of the President, 1997.

FIGURE 25.8
Unemployment by Duration

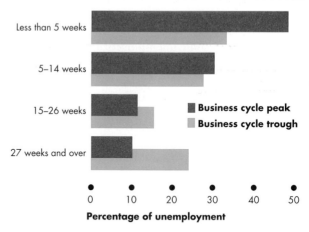

In the business cycle peak of 1989, when the unemployment rate was 5.3 percent, 49 percent of unemployment lasted for less than 5 weeks and 30 percent lasted for 5 to 14 weeks. So 79 percent of unemployment lasted for less than 15 weeks, and 21 percent lasted for 15 weeks or more. In the business cycle trough of 1983, when the unemployment rate was 9.7 percent, 33 percent of unemployment lasted for less than 5 weeks and 27 percent lasted for 5 to 14 weeks. So 60 percent of unemployment lasted for less than 15 weeks, and 40 percent lasted for 15 weeks or more.

Source: Economic Report of the President, 1997.

are job leavers. The number of job leavers is remarkably constant, although to the extent that it fluctuates, it does so in line with the business cycle: A slightly larger number of people leave their jobs in good times than in bad times.

The Duration of Unemployment   Some people are unemployed for a week or two, and others are unemployed for periods of a year or more. The longer the spell of unemployment, the greater the personal cost to the unemployed. The average duration of unemployment varies over the business cycle. Figure 25.8 compares the duration of unemployment in a business cycle peak in 1989, when the unemployment rate was low with that at the business cycle trough of 1983 when the unemployment rate was high. In 1989, when the unemployment rate hit a low of 5.3 percent, almost 50 percent of the unemployed were in that state

for less than 5 weeks and only 21 percent of the unemployed were jobless for longer than 15 weeks. In 1983, when unemployment reached a high of 9.7 percent, only 33 percent of the unemployed found a new job in less than 5 weeks and 40 percent were unemployed for more than 15 weeks. At both low and high unemployment rates, about 30 percent of the unemployed take between 5 weeks and 14 weeks to find a job.

The Demographics of Unemployment   Figure 25.9 shows unemployment for different demographic groups. The figure shows that high unemployment rates occur among young workers and also among blacks. In the business cycle trough in 1992, the unemployment rate of black teenagers was almost 40 percent. Even in 1996, when the unemployment rate was 5.4 percent, the rates for black teenagers barely fell. The unemployment rates for white teenagers are less than half those of black teenagers.

FIGURE 25.9

Unemployment by Demographic Group

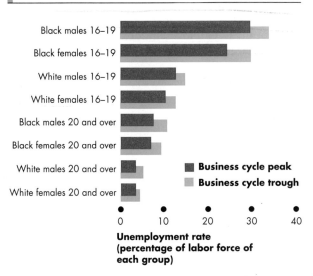

Black teenagers experience unemployment rates that average three times those of white teenagers, and the unemployment rates of teenagers are much higher than those of people aged 20 years and over. Even in a business cycle trough, when unemployment is at its highest rate, only 6 percent of whites aged 20 years and over are unemployed.

Source: Economic Report of the President, 1997.

The racial differences also exist for workers aged 20 years and over. The highest unemployment rates that whites 20 years and over experience are less than the lowest rates experienced by the other groups.

Why are unemployment rates of teenagers so high? There are three reasons. First, young people are still in the process of discovering what they are good at and trying different lines of work. So they leave their jobs more frequently than older workers do. Second, firms sometimes hire teenagers on a short-term or trial basis. So the rate of job loss is higher for teenagers than for other people. Third, most teenagers are not in the labor force but are in school. This fact means that the percentage of the teenage population that is unemployed is much lower than the percentage of the teenage labor force that is unemployed. In 1996, for example, 1,306,000 teenagers were unemployed and 6,499,000 were employed, and the teenage unemployment rate (all races) was 20 percent. But 11,000,000 teenagers were

in school. The ratio of teenage unemployment to the teenage population is less than 7.5 percent. That is, 20 percent of the teenage labor force or 7.5 percent of the teenage population is unemployed.

Types of Unemployment

Unemployment is classified into three types that are based on its causes. They are:

- Frictional
- Structural
- Cyclical

Frictional Unemployment **Frictional unemployment** is the unemployment that arises from normal labor turnover—from people entering and leaving the labor force and from the ongoing creation and destruction of jobs. Frictional unemployment is a permanent and healthy phenomenon in a dynamic, growing economy.

The unending flow of people into and out of the labor force and the processes of job creation and job destruction create the need for people to search for jobs and for businesses to search for workers. Always there are businesses with unfilled jobs and people seeking jobs. Look in your local newspaper, and you will see that there are always some jobs being advertised. Businesses don't usually hire the first person who applies for a job, and unemployed people don't usually take the first job that comes their way. Instead, both firms and workers spend time searching out what they believe will be the best match available. By this process of search, people can match their own skills and interests with the available jobs and find a satisfying job and income. While these unemployed people are searching, they are frictionally unemployed.

The amount of frictional unemployment depends on the rate at which people enter and reenter the labor force and on the rate at which jobs are created and destroyed. During the 1970s, the amount of frictional unemployment increased as a consequence of the postwar baby boom that began during the late 1940s. By the late 1970s, the baby boom had created a bulge in the number of people leaving school. As these people entered the labor force, the amount of frictional unemployment increased.

The amount of frictional unemployment is influenced by unemployment benefits. The greater the number of unemployed people covered by unemployment insurance and the more generous the unemployment benefit they receive, the longer is the average time taken in job search and the greater is the amount of frictional unemployment. In the United States in 1996, 36 percent of the unemployed received unemployment benefits. And the average benefit check was $160 a week. Canada and Western Europe have more generous benefits than those in the United States and have higher unemployment rates.

But surely their jobs, once found, are better for them

Structural Unemployment **Structural unemployment** is the unemployment that arises when changes in technology or international competition change the skills needed to perform jobs or change the locations of jobs. Structural unemployment usually lasts longer than frictional unemployment because workers must usually retrain and possibly relocate to find a job. For example, when a steel plant in Gary, Indiana, is automated, some jobs in that city are destroyed. Meanwhile, new jobs for security guards, life-insurance salespeople, and retail clerks are created in Chicago, Indianapolis, and other cities. The unemployed former steelworkers remain unemployed for several months until they move, retrain, and get one of these jobs. Structural unemployment is painful, especially for older workers for whom the best available option might be to retire early but with a lower income than they had expected.

At some times, the amount of structural unemployment is modest. At other times, it is large, and at such times, structural unemployment can become a serious long-term problem. It was especially large during the late 1970s and early 1980s. During those years, oil price hikes and an increasingly competitive international environment destroyed jobs in traditional U.S. industries, such as auto and steel, and created jobs in new industries, such as electronics and bioengineering, as well as in banking and insurance. Structural unemployment was also present during the early 1990s as many businesses and governments "downsized."

Cyclical Unemployment **Cyclical unemployment** is the fluctuating unemployment over the business cycle. Cyclical unemployment increases during a recession and decreases during an expansion. An auto worker who is laid off because the economy is in a recession and who gets rehired some months later when the expansion begins has experienced cyclical unemployment.

Figure 25.10, illustrates cyclical unemployment in the United States between 1980 and 1996. Part (a)

shows the fluctuations of real GDP around potential GDP. Part (b) shows fluctuations in the unemployment rate around a line labeled "Natural rate of unemployment." The **natural rate of unemployment** is the unemployment rate when there is no cyclical unemployment or, equivalently, when all the unemployment is frictional and structural. The divergence of the unemployment rate from the natural rate is cyclical unemployment. Notice that cyclical unemployment is *negative* at a business cycle peak. Total unemployment is less than the sum of frictional and structural unemployment.

In Fig. 25.10, the unemployment rate fluctuates around the natural rate of unemployment (part b) just as real GDP fluctuates around potential GDP (part a). When the unemployment rate equals the natural rate of unemployment, real GDP equals potential GDP. When the unemployment rate is less than the natural rate of unemployment, real GDP is greater than potential GDP. And when the unemployment rate is greater than the natural rate of unemployment, real GDP is less than potential GDP.

Full Employment

There is always *some* unemployment—someone looking for a job or laid off and waiting to be recalled. So what do we mean by *full employment?* **Full employment** occurs when the unemployment rate equals the natural rate of unemployment.

There can be a lot of unemployment at full employment, and the term "full employment" is an example of a technical economic term that does not correspond with everyday language. The term "natural rate of unemployment" is another example of a technical economic term that does not correspond with everyday language. For most people—especially for unemployed workers—there is nothing *natural* about unemployment.

So why are do economists call a situation with a lot of unemployment one of full employment? And why is the unemployment at full employment "natural"?

The reason is that the complex machine that we call the U.S. economy undergoes constant changes in its players, structure, and direction. This process of change creates frictions and dislocations that are unavoidable. And they create unemployment.

In 1996, the U.S. economy employed 127 million people. More than 2.5 million retired during

FIGURE 25.10

Unemployment and
Real GDP

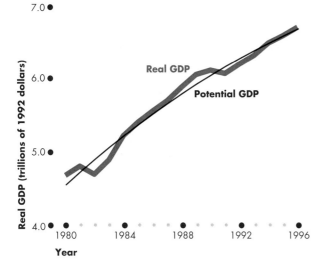

(a) Real GDP

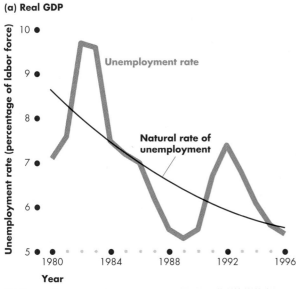

(b) Unemployment rate

As real GDP fluctuates around potential GDP (part a), the unemployment rate fluctuates around the natural rate of unemployment (part b). In the deep recession of 1982, unemployment reached almost 10 percent. In the milder recession of 1990–1991, the unemployment rate peaked at less than 8 percent. The natural rate of unemployment decreased during the 1980s and 1990s.

Source: Economic Report of the President, 1997, and the author's assumptions.

that year, and more than 3 million new workers entered the labor force. All these people worked in some 20 million businesses, some of which downsized and failed and others of which expanded. All these people and businesses produced goods and services valued at almost $7 trillion. The amount of unemployment that arises from the frictions and structural changes is "natural" unemployment.

There is not much controversy about the existence of a natural rate of unemployment. Nor is there much controversy that it fluctuates. The natural rate of unemployment arises from the existence of frictional and structural unemployment, and it fluctuates because the frictions and the amount of structural change fluctuate. But there is controversy about the magnitude of the natural rate of unemployment and the extent to which it fluctuates. Some economists believe that the natural rate of unemployment fluctuates frequently and that at times of rapid demographic and technological change, its rate can be high. Others think that it changes slowly.

In Fig. 25.10(b), the natural rate of unemployment is 8.5 percent in 1980 and it falls steadily through the 1980s and 1990s to less than 6 percent by 1996. This estimate of the natural rate of unemployment in the United States is one that many, but not all economists would accept.

REVIEW

- The people who become unemployed are job losers, job leavers, and labor force entrants or reentrants.

- Unemployment can be *frictional* (normal labor market turnover), *structural* (a long-lasting decline in a region or industry), or *cyclical* (in line with the business cycle).

- When all the unemployment is frictional and structural (when there is no cyclical unemployment), the unemployment rate equals the *natural rate of unemployment*.

- When the unemployment rate is equal to the *natural rate of unemployment*, there is full employment.

We're now going to turn from describing to *explaining* the trends and fluctuations in employment, wage rates, and unemployment. We begin by explaining the trends in employment and wage rates.

Explaining Employment and Wage Rates

WE CAN UNDERSTAND THE AMOUNT OF EMPLOY-ment and the wage rate by applying the model of demand and supply to the labor market.

Demand and Supply in the Labor Market

Figure 25.11 illustrates the U.S. labor market at the beginning of 1995, when there was full employment. The *x*-axis measures the quantity of labor employed as *aggregate hours*—billions of hours per year. The *y*-axis measures the real wage rate. The figure has two curves: a labor demand curve and a labor supply curve. In the labor market, firms demand labor and households supply labor.

The **labor demand curve** shows the quantity of labor that firms plan to hire at each possible real wage rate. The lower the real wage rate, the greater is the quantity of labor that firms plan to hire. That is, the labor demand curve slopes downward, just like the demand curves you studied in Chapter 4 (on p. 70). The reason why the quantity of labor demanded depends on the *real* wage rate is that firms care only about the amount they pay for labor relative to the amount they get for their output. If money wages and prices change in the same proportion, the quantity of labor that firms plan to hire is unaffected.

The **labor supply curve** shows the quantity of labor that households plan to supply at each possible real wage rate. The higher the real wage rate, the greater is the quantity of labor that households plan to supply. That is, the labor supply curve slopes upward like the supply curves in Chapter 4 (on pp. 74–75). The reason why the quantity of labor supplied depends on the *real* wage rate is that households care only about the amount they are paid for their labor relative to the price they must pay for the things they buy. If money wages and prices change in the same proportion, the quantity of labor that households plan to supply is unaffected.

The reason why the quantity of labor demanded increases as the real wage rate decreases—why the labor demand curve slopes downward—is that firms strive to maximize profit. If the wage rate at which firms can hire labor falls relative to the price they can get for their output, the real wage rate decreases and

FIGURE 25.11

The Labor Market

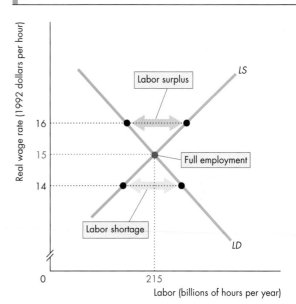

The labor demand curve, *LD*, shows the aggregate hours of labor that firms plan to hire at each real wage rate. The labor supply curve, *LS*, shows the aggregate hours that households plan to work at each real wage rate. In equilibrium, the real wage rate is $15 an hour and 215 billion hours of labor are employed.

they have an incentive to expand production and hire more labor. The reason why the quantity of labor supplied increases as the real wage rate increases— why the labor supply curve slopes upward—is that households strive to use their scarce time in the most efficient way. If the wage rate they are offered rises relative to the prices they must pay for goods and services, the real wage rate increases and they have a stronger incentive to work.

Labor demand and labor supply determine the level of employment, unemployment, and real wage rate. In Fig. 25.11, at wage rates below $15 an hour, for example at $14 an hour, there is a labor shortage. People find jobs easily, but businesses are short of labor. But this situation doesn't last long. Firms offer higher wage rates to attract labor, and the real wage rate rises toward the equilibrium of $15 an hour.

At wage rates above $15 an hour, for example at $16 an hour, there is a labor surplus. People have a hard time finding jobs, and businesses can easily hire all the labor they want. Firms now offer lower wages, and the real wage rate falls toward the equilibrium wage rate of $15 an hour.

At a wage rate of $15 an hour, the quantity demanded equals the quantity supplied. There is neither a shortage nor a surplus of labor.

The Trends in Employment and Wage Rates

We can use the model of labor demand and labor supply to understand the long-term trends in aggregate hours and real wage rates. We saw in Fig. 25.4 that aggregate hours have increased steadily over the years. In 1960, aggregate hours were 125 billion, and in 1996, they were 218 billion. We also saw in Fig. 25.5 that the real wage rate has increased. The economy-wide average real wage rate including supplements increased from $11 an hour in 1960 to $15 an hour in 1996.

Figure 25.12 shows how these changes came about. In 1960, the labor demand curve was LD_{60} and the labor supply curve was LS_{60}. The equilibrium real wage rate was $11 an hour, and 125 billion hours of labor were employed.

Throughout the period since 1960, labor has become more and more productive. The reason is that capital per worker has increased and technology has advanced. We will explore these reasons for this increased productivity in Chapter 27. But regardless of the reasons, the effect of an increase in labor productivity is an increase in the demand for labor. If an hour of labor can produce more output, firms are willing to pay a higher wage rate to hire that hour of labor. This increase in demand is shown by a rightward shift in the labor demand curve from LD_{60} to LD_{96}.

At the same time as labor became more productive and the demand for it increased, the population grew and so did the working-age population. With a larger working-age population, the supply of labor increased. This increase is shown by the rightward shift in the labor supply curve from LS_{60} to LS_{96}.

To predict the effects of an increase in *both* demand and supply, we need to know which had the larger increase. In this case, the increase in the demand for labor was larger than the increase in supply. As a result, both the quantity of labor employed and the average real wage rate increased.

FIGURE 25.12

Explaining Labor
Market Trends

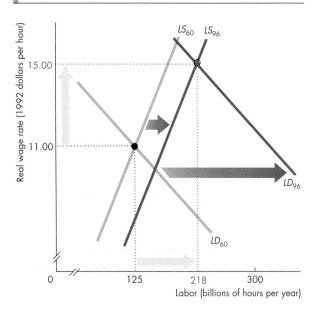

In 1960, the labor demand curve was LD_{60} and the labor supply curve was LS_{60}. The equilibrium real wage rate was $11 an hour, and 125 billion hours of labor were employed. Over the years, advances in technology increased the productivity of labor and increased the demand for labor. The demand curve shifted rightward to LD_{96}. At the same time, an increase in the working-age population increased the supply of labor and the labor supply curve shifted rightward to LS_{96}. But the labor supply curve shifted by less than the labor demand curve. Because both labor demand and labor supply increased, the quantity of labor employed increased. And because labor demand increased by more than labor supply, the real wage rate increased.

Changes in the Distribution of Jobs and Wage Rates

When we looked at the trends in wage rates, we saw that while total hourly compensation has grown, the average hourly wage rates of manufacturing non-supervisory workers has decreased. These changes have brought relative economic hardship to a large number of families. Why have these changes in wage rates occurred?

Figure 25.13 helps us to answer this question. It shows how structural change has increased some wages and employment opportunities and decreased others. The figure describes the U.S. labor market during the 1980s and 1990s. Part (a) shows the labor market in manufacturing industries—those that produce goods—and part (b) shows the labor market in service industries. In each part, the y-axis measures the real wage rate and the x-axis measures the quantity of labor in terms of workers, not hours.

In 1980, the labor supply curve in manufacturing was LS_M and in services it was LS_{80}. The labor demand curve in each sector was LD_{80}. In manufacturing, the average real wage rate was $12.60 an hour and 20 million people had jobs. In services, the average real wage rate was $10.00 an hour and 18 million people had jobs.

During the 1980s and through 1996, technological change and international competition brought a decrease in the demand for labor in manufacturing. The demand curve shifted leftward to become LD_{96} in part (a). With no change (assumed) in supply, the real wage rate fell to $11.80 and the number of people with jobs in manufacturing decreased to 18 million. The 2 million people who lost their jobs had to search for a job in the service industries.

The same technological change and international competition that destroyed jobs in manufacturing created jobs in services. The demand for labor in services increased, and the labor demand curve shifted rightward. By 1996, the demand curve had become LD_{96} in part (b).

As people who had lost their jobs in manufacturing looked for jobs in services and as the growing population entered the labor market, the supply of labor in services increased. The labor supply curve shifted rightward. By 1996, the supply curve had become LS_{96} in part (b).

The increase in labor supply was smaller than the increase in labor demand. As a result, the real wage rate increased to $10.80 and the number of people with jobs in services increased to 30 million.

The changes that we've just looked at break the labor market into just two sectors. In reality, it has many sectors and reallocations of labor take place among the many sectors. Even while the total number of jobs in services was increasing, some service jobs were being destroyed. For example, jobs for directory assistance operators and television service engineers virtually disappeared, while jobs for telephone sales persons and ATM service engineers increased.

FIGURE 25.13

Labor Force Reallocation

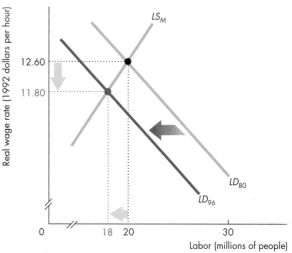

(a) Manufacturing

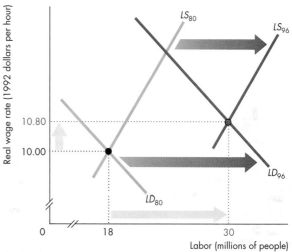

(b) Services

Between 1980 and 1996, the demand for labor in manufacturing decreased (part a) and the labor demand curve shifted leftward from LD_{80} to LD_{96}. In services (part b), the demand for labor increased and the demand curve shifted rightward from LD_{80} to LD_{96}. In manufacturing, the supply of labor was constant (an assumption) at LS_M, but in services the supply of labor increased and the supply curve shifted rightward from LS_{80} to LS_{96}. In manufacturing, employment and the real wage rate decreased. In services, demand increased by more than supply, so both employment and the real wage rate increased.

- The labor demand curve shows the quantity of labor that firms plan to hire at each real wage rate. The labor demand curve slopes downward because a fall in the real wage rate gives firms a stronger incentive to increase production and hire more labor.
- The labor supply curve shows the quantity of labor that households plan to supply at each real wage rate. The labor supply curve slopes upward because a rise in the real wage rate gives households a stronger incentive to work.
- Labor demand and labor supply curves interact to determine the level of employment and the real wage rate.
- Both the real wage rate and employment have increased because labor demand and labor supply have increased but labor demand has increased by more than labor supply.

We've now studied the main trends in employment and wage rates, and we have seen how the demand and supply model can help us to understand those trends. Our next task is to explain unemployment.

Explaining Unemployment

WE'VE DESCRIBED HOW PEOPLE BECOME unemployed—they lose jobs, leave jobs, and enter or reenter the labor force—and we've classified unemployment—it can be frictional, structural, and cyclical. But describing and classifying unemployment do not *explain* it. Why is there always some unemployment? Why does its rate fluctuate? Why was the unemployment rate lower during the 1960s than during the 1980s and early 1990s?

If we want to design policies that can reduce unemployment, we must answer these questions. We must understand the forces that generate unemployment and that cause its rate to change. Unemployment is ever present, and its rate fluctuates for three reasons:

- Job search
- Job rationing
- Sticky wages

Job Search

Job search is the activity of people looking for acceptable vacant jobs. There might be as many jobs as there are people looking for jobs, but there are always some people who have not yet found suitable jobs. The reason is that the labor market is in a constant state of change. Jobs are destroyed and created as businesses fail and new businesses start up and as new technologies and new markets evolve. In the process, people lose jobs. Other people enter or reenter the labor market. Still other people leave their jobs to look for better ones, and others retire. This constant churning in the labor market means that there are always some people looking for jobs, and these people are the unemployed. Job search takes place even when the quantity of labor demanded equals the quantity supplied. In this situation, some people have not yet found a job and some jobs have not yet been filled.

Job search explains frictional, structural, and cyclical unemployment. All three types of unemployment occur because job losers, job leavers, and labor force entrants and reentrants don't know about all the jobs available to them, so they must take time to *search* for an acceptable one. This search takes time, and the average amount of time varies. When there is a small amount of structural change and when the economy is close to a business cycle peak, search times are low and the unemployment rate is low. But when structural change is rapid and when the economy is in a recession, search times increase and the unemployment rate increases.

Although job search is cyclical, it also has slower changes that bring changes in the natural rate of unemployment. The main sources of these slower changes are:

- Demographic change
- Unemployment benefits
- Structural change

Demographic Change An increase in the proportion of the population that is of working age brings an increase in the entry rate into the labor force and an increase in the unemployment rate. This factor has been important in the U.S. labor market in recent years. The bulge in the birth rate that occurred in the late 1940s and early 1950s increased the proportion of new entrants into the labor force during the 1970s and brought an increase in the unemployment rate.

As the birth rate declined, the bulge moved into higher age groups and the proportion of new entrants declined during the 1980s. During this period, the natural rate of unemployment decreased.

Another demographic trend is an increase in the number of households with two paid workers. When unemployment comes to one of these workers, it is possible, with income still flowing in, to take longer to find a new job. This factor might have increased frictional unemployment.

Unemployment Benefits   The length of time that an unemployed person spends searching for a job depends, in part, on the opportunity cost of job search. With no income during a period of unemployment, an unemployed person faces a high opportunity cost of job search. In this situation, search is likely to be short and an unattractive job is likely to be accepted as a better alternative to continuing a costly search process. With generous unemployment insurance benefits, the opportunity cost of job search is low. In this situation, search is likely to be prolonged. An unemployed worker will hold out for the ideal job.

The opportunity cost of job search fell during the late 1960s and 1970s as unemployment benefits were extended to larger groups. As a result, the natural rate of unemployment increased during those years.

Structural Change   Labor market flows and unemployment are influenced by the pace and direction of technological change. Sometimes, technological change brings a *structural slump*, a condition in which some industries die and some regions suffer while other industries are born and other regions flourish. When these events occur, labor turnover is high—the flows between employment and unemployment increase and the pool of those unemployed increases. The decline of industries in the "Rust Belt" and the rapid expansion of industries in the "Sun Belt" illustrate the effects of technological change and were a source of the increase in unemployment during the 1970s and early 1980s. The analysis of the changes in the reallocation of the U.S. labor force from manufacturing to services (Fig. 25.13) is also an example of the effects of technological change. While these changes were taking place, the natural rate of unemployment increased.

Job search unemployment is present even when the quantity of labor demanded equals the quantity supplied. The other possible explanations of unemployment are based on the view that the quantity of labor demanded does not always equal the quantity supplied.

Job Rationing

Job rationing is the practice of paying employed people a wage that creates an excess supply of labor and a shortage of jobs and increases the natural rate of unemployment. When there is job rationing, there are fewer available jobs than there are people looking for jobs. Three reasons why jobs might be rationed are:

- Efficiency wages
- Insider interest
- The minimum wage

Efficiency Wages   Some firms can increase their labor productivity by paying wages above the competitive wage rate. The higher wage attracts a higher quality of labor, encourages greater work effort, and cuts down on the firm's labor turnover rate and recruiting costs. But the higher wage also adds to the firm's costs. So a firm offers a wage rate that balances productivity gains and additional costs. The wage rate that maximizes profit is called the **efficiency wage**.

The efficiency wage might be higher than the competitive equilibrium wage. The wage cannot be lower than the competitive wage because competition for labor would bid the wage up. With an efficiency wage above the competitive wage, some labor is unemployed and employed people have an incentive to perform well to avoid being fired.

Insider Interest   Why don't firms cut their wage costs by offering jobs to unemployed workers for a lower wage rate than that paid to existing workers? One explanation, called **insider-outsider theory**, is that to be productive, new workers—outsiders—must receive on-the-job training from existing workers—insiders. If insiders train outsiders who are paid a lower wage, the insiders' bargaining position is weakened. So insiders will train outsiders only if everyone receives the same rate of pay.

When bargaining for a pay deal, unions represent the interests of insiders only. The agreed-on wage exceeds the competitive wage and there are always outsiders who are unable to find work. So the pursuit of rational self-interest by insiders is a further reason why the natural rate of unemployment is not zero.

The Minimum Wage   A minimum wage is a wage rate legislated by the federal government. The minimum wage is usually set at a rate that is higher than what the market would determine. As a result, the quantity of labor supplied exceeds the quantity demanded. The minimum wage explains why the unemployment rate of young people is high.

Job rationing is a possible reason why the natural rate of unemployment is high. It is a source of persistent and possibly large amount of frictional unemployment. The distinction between unemployment that arises from job search and that which arises from job rationing can be illustrated by musical chairs. If there are equal numbers of chairs (jobs) and players (people who want jobs), when the music stops and everyone searches for a chair, everyone finds one. If there are more players than chairs, when the music stops and everyone searches for a chair, some players can't find one. The chairs are rationed.

Job rationing is a source of long-term frictional unemployment. The final explanation of unemployment—sticky wages—is one reason why unemployment is cyclical.

FIGURE 25.14

Sticky Wages and Unemployment ◆

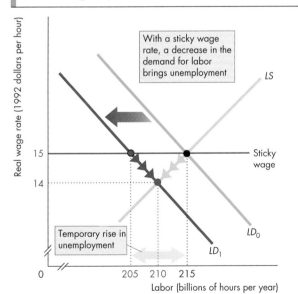

When the demand for labor is LD_0 and the supply of labor is LS, employment is 215 billion hours and the real wage rate is $15 an hour. The demand for labor decreases and the demand curve shifts leftward to LD_1, but the real wage rate is sticky at $15 an hour. Employment decreases to 205 billion hours, and there is a surplus of 10 billion hours—10 billion hours of labor are unemployed. Eventually, the real wage rate falls to $14 an hour and employment increases to 210 billion hours.

Sticky Wages

Wages do not change as often as prices do. So if the demand for labor decreases, the equilibrium real wage rate falls, but the actual real wage rate does not change immediately. Rather, it gradually falls toward its new equilibrium, and it takes some time to get there. During this process of gradual wage adjustment, there is a surplus of labor and unemployment is temporarily high.

Figure 25.14 illustrates this type of unemployment. Initially, the demand for labor is LD_0 and the supply of labor is LS. The equilibrium level of employment is 215 billion hours, and the real wage rate is $15 an hour. The demand for labor then decreases, and the demand curve shifts leftward to LD_1. But the real wage rate is temporarily sticky at $15 an hour. At this real wage rate and in the new conditions, firms are willing to hire only 205 billion hours of labor. So there is a surplus of 10 billion hours and unemployment is created.

Eventually, as prices and wages change, the real wage rate falls to its equilibrium level. In this example, when the real wage rate has fallen to $14 an hour, the quantity of labor demanded equals the quantity supplied and the surplus of labor vanishes.

REVIEW

■ Unemployment is always present because of job search.

■ The natural rate of unemployment depends on the age distribution of the population, unemployment benefits, and structural change.

■ Some unemployment results from job rationing and sticky wages.

◆ You have now completed your study of labor markets. Before you leave this topic, take a look at *Reading Between the Lines* on pp. 560–561, which examines how the computer and information revolution of the 1980s and 1990s has changed wages and employment.

You now know how the quantity of labor is determined. Your next task is to study the factors that influence the quantity of capital. Capital is accumulated as a result of saving and investment decisions. We study these decisions in Chapter 26.

Policy
WATCH

Technological Change and Jobs

THE DALLAS MORNING NEWS, AUGUST 8, 1996

July Job Cuts Rise 80 Percent

Despite labor shortages in some industries, announced job cuts in July continued to surge, Challenger, Gray & Christmas, Inc. said Wednesday.

The Chicago-based outplacement firm's latest report on layoffs said last month's total of job cuts was 41,843, up 79.7 percent from 23,283 in July 1995, and up 4.2 percent from 40,163 in June of this year.

July represented the largest number of job cuts since January, when AT&T announced massive job cuts.

The firm said that from January through July, job cuts averaged 44,622 per month, 32.6 percent higher than the monthly average of 33,654 for the same period in 1995. The monthly job cut average for the first seven months of 1993, the largest job cut year of the decade, was 50,516.

On average, there were 2,096 job cuts per business day between Jan. 2 and July 31, the firm said.

The increase in July job cuts comes on the heels of stunning figures from the first half of the year which showed job cuts rising sharply from 1995. Including the July data, the total for the first seven months of this year was 312,356, 32.5 percent higher than 235,582 in the same period last year. The total 12-month figure in 1995 was 439,882.

The tally of jobs lost in July was boosted by Digital Equipment Corp. and Allied-Signal Inc., which announced 7,000 and 6,100 job cuts, respectively, Challenger said.

The industry hardest hit in July was the computer industry, with 8,804 casualties.

■ Job cuts surged in July 1996, despite labor shortages in some industries.

■ According to a Chicago-based placement firm, job cuts increased by 79.7 percent from July 1995 to July 1996.

■ Job cuts in the first seven months of 1996 numbered 312,356, an increase of 32.5 percent over the same period in 1995.

■ The number of job cuts in July was partially attributable to 7,000 job cuts at Digital Equipment Corp. and 6,100 job cuts at AlliedSignal Inc.

■ Hardest hit in July was the computer industry, which cut 8,804 jobs.

Economic

A N A L Y S I S

■ Most of the job cuts reported in the news article create *structural* unemployment.

■ Figure I shows the rate of job destruction in U.S. manufacturing industries during the 1980s. These data are compiled infrequently and are not yet available for the 1990s. But the 1980s data tell us a lot.

■ The rate of job destruction fluctuates with the business cycle. But on the average, about I percent of jobs get destroyed each month.

■ Much of the job destruction arises because technological advances enable companies to produce more output with fewer workers. This process has been going on almost uninterrupted since the Industrial Revolution around 1760.

■ With a normal rate of job destruction, more than a million people would lose their jobs during July 1996.

■ The announced job cutbacks reported in this news article (and frequently reported in the media) are a tiny proportion of total job losses.

The reported job cuts are the losses in big companies that are shedding labor in large numbers.

■ Most job losses and most new jobs that are created are unreported because they happen in small companies.

■ Job cuts are serious for the people whom they affect. But they would be even more serious if jobs were not being created in even larger numbers.

■ Figure I also shows the rate of job creation and the net change in the number of jobs in manufacturing. In most years, more jobs were destroyed than created in the manufacturing industries. But (not shown in the figure) more jobs were created in services than the number lost in manufacturing.

■ Technological change creates more jobs than it destroys. It increases the productivity of labor and leads to an increase in the demand for labor.

■ Figure 2 shows the total amount of job creation and job destruction in manufacturing during the 1980s and the relationship between this number and the unemployment rate. It shows that the total amount of job creation and job destruction fluctuates in line with fluctuations in the unemployment rate.

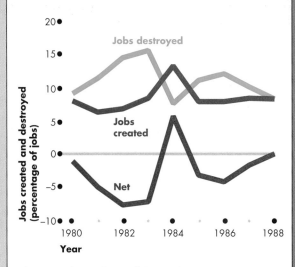

Figure 1 Job creation and destruction rates

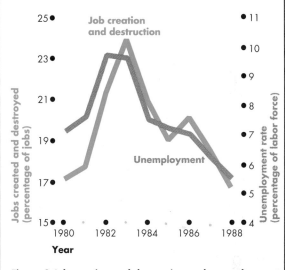

Figure 2 Job creation and destruction and unemployment

You're

THE VOTER

■ What policy actions, if any, can the government take to protect people from job losses?

■ List all the policy actions you can think of, and attach to each policy its pros and cons.

SUMMARY

Key Points

Employment and Wages (pp. 544–548)

- The labor force participation rate and the employment-to-population ratio have an upward trend, and fluctuate with the business cycle.
- The labor force participation rate has increased for females and decreased for males.
- Aggregate hours have an upward trend, and they fluctuate with the business cycle.
- Based on the CPI, real hourly wage rates in manufacturing fell after 1973. Broader real wage measures did not fall, but their growth rates slowed.

Unemployment and Full Employment (pp. 549–553)

- People are constantly entering and leaving the state of unemployment.
- The duration of unemployment fluctuates over the business cycle. But the demographic patterns of unemployment are constant.
- Unemployment can be frictional, structural, and cyclical.
- When all the unemployment is frictional and structural, unemployment is at its natural rate and there is *full employment*. The natural rate of unemployment fluctuates because of fluctuations in frictional and structural unemployment.

Explaining Employment and Wage Rates (pp. 554–557)

- The higher the real wage rate, the smaller is the quantity of labor demanded and the greater is the quantity of labor supplied.
- Labor demand and labor supply determine the level of employment and the real wage rate.
- The average real wage rate and employment increase because labor demand increases by more than labor supply.
- Labor demand increases because capital accumulation and technological change make labor more productive. Labor supply increases because the working-age population grows.

Explaining Unemployment (pp. 557–559)

- Unemployment arises from job search, job rationing, and sticky wages.
- Job search unemployment changes slowly because of changes in demographic trends, unemployment benefits, and the pace of structural change.
- Job rationing can arise from efficiency wages, insider interest, and the minimum wage.

Key Figures

Key Terms

QUESTIONS

1. What are the categories that the Census Bureau uses in its monthly survey to classify the population?
2. Define the unemployment rate, the labor force participation rate, and the employment-to-population ratio.
3. What do the unemployment rate, the labor force participation rate, and the employment-to-population ratio tell us about labor market performance?
4. What are discouraged workers? Does the official unemployment measure include them?
5. Define aggregate hours. Why might aggregate hours be a more accurate measure of the quantity of labor than the number of people employed?
6. Name four measures of the average hourly real wage rate and describe how each one changed between 1970 and 1996. Which of them increased fastest?
7. How do people become unemployed? What is the most common way and what is the one that fluctuates most?
8. How does the duration of unemployment vary over the business cycle?
9. Which groups of the population experience the highest unemployment rates?
10. Distinguish between frictional, structural, and cyclical unemployment.
11. What is the natural rate of unemployment, what is full employment, and how are the two related?
12. What is the relationship between the unemployment rate and real GDP over the business cycle?
13. Explain how demand and supply in the labor market determine the level of employment and the real wage rate.
14. What are the main changes in demand and supply in the labor market that have brought employment growth?
15. What are the main changes in demand and supply in the labor market that have brought a slowdown in the rate of increase in real wage rates and a fall in some real wage rates?
16. What are the three main explanations of unemployment?

PROBLEMS

1. The Census Bureau measured the following numbers in December 1996: labor force, 135 million; employment, 127.9 million; working-age population, 201.6 million. Calculate for that month the:
   a. Unemployment rate.
   b. Labor force participation rate.
   c. Employment-to-population ratio.
2. During 1996, the working-age population increased by 2.1 million, employment increased by 2.8 million, and the labor force increased by 2.6 million. What happened to the level of unemployment and what do you believe happened to the number of discouraged workers?
3. In January 1996, the unemployment rate was 5.7 percent. In December 1996, the unemployment rate was 5.3 percent. What do you believe happened in 1996 to the numbers of:
   a. Job losers?
   b. Job leavers?
   c. Labor force entrants and reentrants?
4. The labor market in an economy is described by the figure. Initially, demand is LD_0, but then it decreases to LD_1.

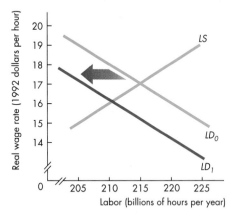

   a. What, initially, are the employment hours and real wage rate?
   b. What factors could have changed to decrease the demand for labor?
   c. When the demand for labor decreases, does the supply of labor change? Explain your answer
   d. When the demand for labor decreases, does the quantity of labor supplied change? Explain your answer.

e. When the demand for labor decreases, what are the new level of employment hours and the new real wage rate if wages are flexible?

5. Suppose that the labor market shown in the figure in problem 4 is that in manufacturing. Suppose that the labor market for services is exactly like that for manufacturing except that the demand for labor increases by exactly the same amount as the decrease in demand in manufacturing.
   a. Draw the new demand curve and answer the same questions as in problem 4.
   b. What do you predict will happen to the unemployment rate during the time the labor markets for manufacturing and services adjust to the changes in demand?

6. Suppose in problem 4 that when the demand for labor decreases, the real wage rate is sticky and does not change.
   a. What is the level of employment hours?
   b. What is the quantity of employment hours supplied?
   c. What is the number of hours that are unemployed?
   d. During the time that the real wage rate is stuck above its equilibrium level, is the unemployment rate greater than, less than, or equal to the natural rate of unemployment?

7. You are told the following facts about the economy of Big Time: All the people work in either fishing, Big Time's traditional economic activity, or video game production, Big Time's newfound bonanza industry. The working-age population is growing by 1 million people a year and the number of jobs is growing by 1.2 million a year. But jobs in fishing are disappearing at a rate of 2 million a year, and jobs are being created in video game production at a rate of 3.2 million a year. What do you predict is happening to wage rates, employment, and unemployment in Big Time both in total and in its two industries. Draw two labor market figures, one for the fishing industry and one for the video games industry, and show how the demand and supply curves are shifting and how wage rates and employment levels are changing.

⊕ http://hepg.awl.com/parkin/econ100

CRITICAL THINKING

1. Study *Reading Between the Lines* on pp. 560–561 and then answer the following questions:
   a. What types of jobs have been destroyed and created in the United States in the past 15 years?
   b. What types of businesses create and destroy jobs? Do all the jobs created get reported in the newspapers? Explain why or why not.
   c. What information would you need that is not supplied in the news article to determine whether the job losses reported will create frictional, structural, or cyclical unemployment?
   d. Which fluctuates most, the rate of job creation or the rate of job destruction?

⊕ 2. Visit the Web site of the Bureau of Labor Statistics at http://stats.bls.gov and click on the "Regional Information" button. You will see a map that enables you to find labor market data for your own region.
   a. What have been the trends in employment, unemployment, and labor force participation in your own region during the past two years?
   b. Based on what you know about your own region, how would you set about explaining these trends?
   c. Try to identify those industries that have expanded most and those that have shrunk.
   d. What are the problems with your own regional labor market that you think need state government action to resolve?
   e. What actions do you think your state government must take to resolve them? Answer this question by using the demand and supply model of the labor market and predict the effects of the actions you prescribe.
   f. Compare the labor market performance of your own region with that of the nation as a whole.
   g. If your region is performing better than the national average, to what do attribute the success? If your region is performing worse than the national average, to what do attribute its problems? What federal actions are needed in your regional labor market?

26

Capital, Investment, and Saving

The 1996 Olympic Games in Atlanta were watched, as they happened, by more than two billion people (two fifths of the world's population). This media event was made possible by an enormous investment in a global video network. An even larger investment in a vast network of computers, telecommunications equipment, and databases enables a grade school student in Alice Springs, Australia, to click her mouse button and surf the Internet or send an e-mail message to her "pen-friend" in Akron, Ohio. How do businesses make the investment decisions that create the amazing tools that are building a global village? ◆ Each one of us decides how much income to save and how much to spend on consumption goods and services. Some of us spend everything we earn and can't wait for the next payday to come around. Others of us save large amounts of income. How do people make their saving decisions? ◆ Investment and saving decisions combine to determine interest rates and the long-term growth of potential GDP. Fluctuations in investment create cycles in real GDP. How do investment and saving decisions influence the interest rate you pay on your credit card balance and the interest rate you'll pay when you take a mortgage to buy a home? How do they influence the size of your pension when you retire? ◆ In this chapter, we study the decisions that determine the amount of capital in the economy and the return—the interest rate—that capital earns. When you have completed your study of this topic, you will be ready to learn about the forces that make potential GDP grow, which are explained in Chapter 27. ◆ We begin by looking at some facts about investment, capital, and interest rates in the United States and around the world.

Building the Global Village

After studying this chapter, you will be able to:

- Describe the growth and fluctuations of investment and the capital stock

- Describe the fluctuations in the real interest rate

- Explain how investment decisions are made

- Explain how household saving decisions are made

- Explain how investment and saving determine the real interest rate

- Explain how government influences the real interest rate, saving, and investment

- Explain how international borrowing and lending are determined

Capital and Interest

THE TOTAL QUANTITY OF PLANT, EQUIPMENT, buildings, and inventories is the economy's **capital stock**. The purchase of new capital, called **gross investment**, increases the capital stock, and the wearing out and scrapping of existing capital, called **depreciation**, decreases the capital stock. The capital stock increases by the amount of **net investment,** which equals gross investment minus depreciation. (See Chapter 23, p. 492.)

Figure 26.1 shows investment and capital in the United States from 1970 through 1996. In part (a), you can see that gross investment has grown and fluctuated. In the recession years (1975, 1982, and 1991), gross investment decreased, and in the expansion years, it grew quickly. Part of gross investment replaces worn-out capital. The green line labeled "Replacement investment" in Fig. 26.1(a) shows this amount. This component of investment has grown steadily, and it does not fluctuate much.

Figure 26.1(a) also shows net investment, the addition to the capital stock. Net investment has fluctuated like gross investment. In the recession years, net investment falls. It was $0.2 trillion in 1991, a recession year, but was almost $0.5 trillion in 1996, an expansion year.

Figure 26.1(b) shows how the capital stock has changed over the years. It has grown every year and increased from about $8 trillion in 1970 to almost $17 trillion in 1996. The growth of the capital stock slowed during the recessions, but the growth rate has always been positive.

The reason why the capital stock has grown every year is that net investment has been positive. The reason why the fluctuations in the growth rate of the capital stock are small is that net investment is small relative to the capital stock. When net investment decreases during a recession, the capital stock almost stops growing. When net investment increases during an expansion, the capital stock grows at about 3 percent a year. On the average, the capital stock has grown at around 2.5 percent a year.

Figure 26.1 shows both private and government investment and the privately owned and government-owned capital stock. Private investment is business investment plus investment in new homes and additions to inventories. Government investment is the part of government purchases that creates *social infrastructure capital.* The most basic component of social

FIGURE 26.1

Investment and the Capital Stock: 1970–1996

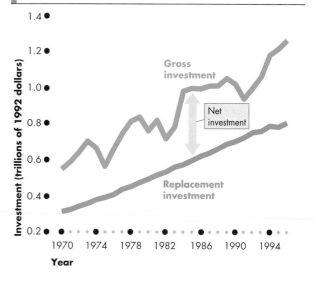

(a) Investment

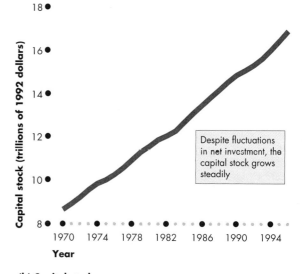

(b) Capital stock

Net investment fluctuates between less than $0.2 trillion a year in a recession and almost $0.5 trillion a year in an expansion. The capital stock has grown steadily to almost $17 trillion in 1996.

Source: U.S. Department of Commerce, *National Income and Product Accounts of the United States* and *The Capital Stock of the United States,* and author's assumptions and calculations.

infrastructure capital is the courts and the justice system that establish and enforce property rights. Without this social infrastructure our economy could not have developed. Other social infrastructure capital, for example, highways, dams and canals, schools, and state universities, increase potential GDP. National defense capital is also included in government investment.

Investment Around the World

Figure 26.2 compares investment in the United States with that in other parts of the world. Here, investment includes both business investment and government investment. And so that we can make comparisons, we measure investment as a percentage of GDP—called the investment rate.

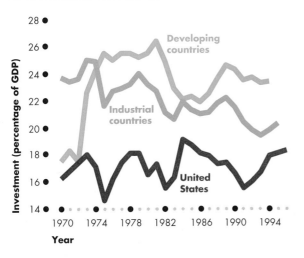

FIGURE 26.2

Investment in the United States and World: 1970–1995

Here, investment includes business investment and government investment. Investment in the United States fluctuates between 15 percent and 19 percent of GDP. The United States has invested a smaller percentage of GDP than many other countries have. Since 1975, the developing countries have invested a larger percentage of GDP than have the industrial countries.

Sources: U.S. Department of Commerce, *National Income and Product Accounts of the United States* and *International Financial Statistics, Yearbook*, 1996.

Figure 26.2 shows that the investment rate in the United States has fluctuated and, throughout the period shown in the figure, has been less than the investment rate in the other industrial countries and the developing countries. The industrial countries are Canada, Japan, Australia, New Zealand, and 18 rich countries in Western Europe. The developing countries comprise the rest of the world.

Investment in the industrial countries has fluctuated and has been on a downward trend. Investment in the developing countries has fluctuated and has followed two distinct trends: an upward trend from 1970 through 1981 and a downward trend through the 1980s. Since 1975, the investment rate in the developing countries has exceeded that in the industrial countries.

Within the developing economies, those in Asia (such as China, Korea, Taiwan, and Malaysia) have the highest investment rates and those in Africa and Central and South America have the lowest investment rates. But most of these countries have higher investment rates than that of the United States.

Interest Rates

When we studied labor in Chapter 25, we discovered that both the quantity of labor and the real wage rate per hour of labor have increased over the years. We've seen that the capital stock has grown steadily over time. But what has happened to the return on capital? Has it grown also? To find out, we must first define the return on capital.

The return on capital is the **real interest rate**, which is equal to the *nominal* interest rate adjusted for inflation. The nominal interest rate is the interest rate expressed in terms of money.

The real interest rate is approximately equal to the nominal interest rate minus the inflation rate. But the exact calculation allows for the change in the purchasing power of the interest as well as the amount of the loan.[1]

Suppose the nominal interest rate is 6 percent a year and there is no inflation. The real interest rate is also 6 percent a year. Now suppose the inflation rate is 4 percent a year. In this situation, prices are rising and

---

[1] To calculate the real interest rate, subtract the inflation rate from the nominal interest rate and divide that number by (1 + Inflation rate/100). If the nominal interest rate is 10.24 percent and the inflation rate is 4 percent, the real interest rate is (10.24 − 4)÷(1 + 0.04) = 6 percent.

money is losing value at a rate of 4 percent a year. If the real interest rate remains at 6 percent a year, the nominal interest rate must rise to 10.24 percent a year.

To see why the nominal interest rate is 10.24 percent when inflation is 4 percent and the real interest rate is 6 percent, think about the following example. You borrow $1,000 for one year. If the real interest rate is 6 percent a year, the people who loaned you the money must be able to buy goods and services valued in today's prices at $1,060 when you repay them. But after a year in which prices rise by 4 percent, they need $1,102.40 to buy goods and services that today cost $1060. So if you pay them $1,102.40, you are paying them only $1,060 in today's prices and the *real* interest paid is $60—6 percent a year.

In the world economy, there are thousands of different interest rates. The real interest rate at which homebuyers and risky businesses can borrow is higher than the rate at which large corporations can borrow. And large corporations pay a higher interest rate than the U.S. government pays. But all real interest rates tend to move up and down together.

One real interest rate that fluctuates with many others is the real interest rate at which big U.S. corporations borrow. This rate is higher than that at which the U.S government can borrow but lower than the rate that you must pay on a bank loan or credit card balance. But it moves up and down in the same way as all these other interest rates.

Figure 26.3 shows the real interest rate paid by big U.S. corporations from 1970 through 1996. The average real interest rate during these years is 4 percent a year. The real interest rate does not rise steadily like the real wage rate rises. It fluctuates around a constant level.

Four subperiods are striking:

1. The 1970s—low (and negative in 1975)
2. Between 1980 and 1985—increased to exceed 8 percent
3. Between 1985 and 1989—decreased to about 5 percent
4. The 1990s—steady between 4 percent and 6 percent

The 1970s were years of economic turmoil that resulted from huge oil price hikes. The 1980s began with a deep recession but then went into a long expansion. The 1990s also began in recession and then had a long expansion. We'll learn in this chapter *why* these events influenced the real interest rate.

FIGURE 26.3

The Real Interest Rate

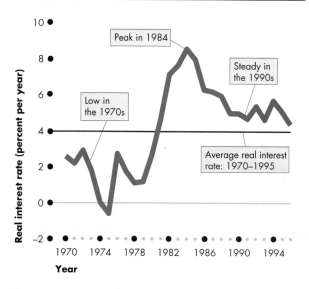

The real interest rate (here, the rate at which big U.S. corporations can borrow) was low during the 1970s and negative in 1975. It increased strongly between 1980 and 1984 and then decreased through 1989. It has been relatively steady at between 4 percent and 6 percent a year during the 1990s.

Source: Economic Report of the President, 1996, and the author's calculations.

REVIEW

- Net investment (gross investment minus depreciation) increases the capital stock.
- Net investment fluctuates but is usually positive, so the capital stock grows every year. Fluctuations in the growth of the capital stock are small because net investment is small relative to the capital stock.
- Government purchases include investment in social infrastructure capital.
- The U. S. investment rate (the percentage of GDP invested) is less than the rate in many other countries, especially the developing countries.
- The return on capital is the real interest rate.

How do businesses make investment decisions and what determines their demand for investment? We answer those questions next.

Investment Decisions

INVESTMENT CONSISTS OF PRIVATE INVESTMENT and government investment. We'll look at the role of government later in this chapter and first focus on private investment decisions.

How does Chrysler decide how much to spend on a new car assembly plant? How does AT&T decide how much to spend on fiber-optic cables? Business investment decisions are influenced by:

■ The expected profit rate
■ The real interest rate

To decide whether to invest in a new assembly line, Chrysler compares the expected profit rate with the real interest rate. The real interest rate is the opportunity cost of an investment. Let's look more closely at the expected profit rate and the real interest rate.

The Expected Profit Rate

Other things remaining the same, the greater the expected profit rate from new capital, the greater is the amount of investment.

Imagine that Chrysler is trying to decide whether to build a new $100 million automobile assembly line that will produce cars for one year and then be scrapped. Chrysler expects a net revenue of $120 million from operating the plant. Net revenue is equal to total revenue from sales minus the cost of labor and materials. The firm's expected profit from this assembly line is $20 million, which equals $120 million (net revenue) minus $100 million (cost of the plant). The expected *profit rate* is 20 percent a year—($20 million ÷ $100 million) × 100.

Of the many influences on the expected profit rate, the three that stand out are:

1. The phase of the business cycle
2. Advances in technology
3. Taxes

The phase of the business cycle influences the expected profit rate because sales fluctuate over the business cycle. In an expansion, an increase in sales brings a higher profit rate. In a recession, a decrease in sales brings a lower profit rate.

As technologies advance, profit expectations change. When a new technology first becomes available, firms expect to be on a learning curve and so expect a modest profit rate from the new technology. But as firms gain experience with a new technology, they expect costs to fall and the profit rate to increase.

It is the *after-tax* profit rate that a firm receives, so changes in tax rates influence the firm's after-tax profit rate. Firms go to extreme lengths to avoid taxes, and for multinational firms, the decision about *where* to invest often turns on the effect of taxes on profit.

The Real Interest Rate

Other things remaining the same, the lower the real interest rate, the greater is the amount of investment.

The funds used to finance investment might be borrowed, or they might be the financial resources of the firm's owners (the firm's retained earnings). But regardless of the source of the funds, the opportunity cost of the funds is the real interest rate. The real interest paid on borrowed funds is an obvious cost. The real interest rate is also the cost of using retained earnings because these funds could be loaned to another firm. The real interest income forgone is the opportunity cost of using retained earnings to finance an investment project.

In the Chrysler example, the expected profit rate is 20 percent a year. So it is profitable for Chrysler to invest as long as the real interest rate is less than 20 percent a year. That is, at real interest rates below 20 percent a year, Chrysler will build this assembly line, and at real interest rates in excess of 20 percent a year, it will not. Some projects are profitable at higher real interest rates, but other projects are profitable only at low real interest rates. Consequently, the higher the real interest rate, the smaller is the number of projects that are worth undertaking and the smaller is the amount of investment.

We summarize the influences on investment decisions in an investment demand curve.

Investment Demand

If the real interest rate rises, other things remaining the same, investment decreases. The table in Fig. 26.4 shows an example of this relationship. It lists the levels of investment that occur at three real interest rates and with three expected profit rates. The relationship between investment and the real interest rate, other things remaining the same, is called **investment demand**.

Figure 26.4(a) shows an investment demand curve when the expected profit rate is average. Each point (*a* through *c*) corresponds to a row in the table. If the real interest rate is 6 percent a year, investment is $1 trillion. A change in the real interest rate brings a movement along the investment demand curve. If the real interest rate rises to 8 percent a year, investment decreases to $0.8 trillion; there is a movement up the investment demand curve. If the real interest rate falls to 4 percent a year, investment increases to $1.2 trillion; there is a movement down the investment demand curve.

Figure 26.4(b) shows how investment demand depends on the expected rate of profit. When firms expect an average profit rate, the investment demand curve is ID_0, the same as in part (a). But when the expected profit rate increases, investment demand increases and the investment demand curve shifts rightward to ID_1. When the expected profit rate decreases, investment demand decreases and the investment demand curve shifts leftward to ID_2. Fluctuations in the expected profit rate are the main source of fluctuations in investment demand.

Let's now see how the investment demand curve helps us to understand the changes in investment in the United States.

FIGURE 26.4

Investment Demand

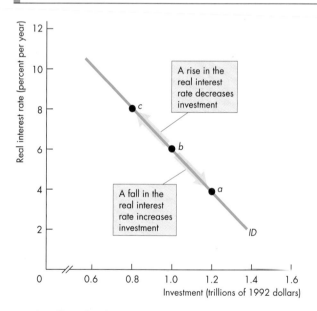

(a) The effect of a change in the real interest rate

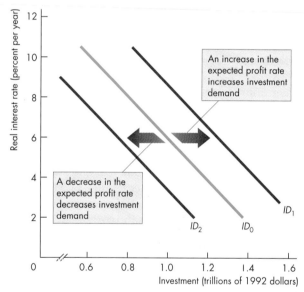

(b) The effect of a change in the expected profit rate

Real interest rate (percent per year)	Investment (trillions of 1992 dollars) Expected profit rate		
	Low	**Average**	**High**
a 4	1.0	1.2	1.4
b 6	0.8	1.0	1.2
c 8	0.6	0.8	1.0

The table shows the level of investment for three different expected profit rates—low, average, and high—and three different interest rates. When the real interest rate is 6 percent a year and the expected profit rate is average, investment is $1.0 trillion. Part (a) shows the investment demand curve, *ID*, for an average expected profit rate. A change in the interest rate brings a movement along the investment demand curve. In part (b), a high expected profit rate shifts the curve rightward to ID_1 and a low expected profit rate shifts it leftward to ID_2.

Investment Demand in the United States

Investment fluctuates because of fluctuations in the real interest rate and in the expected profit rate. Figure 26.5 shows the relative importance of these two factors in the United States. The dots in the figure show the gross investment and the real interest rate in the United States each year from 1981 to 1996. The figure also shows two U.S. investment demand curves—ID_0 and ID_1.

During the early 1980s, the investment demand curve was ID_0. Rising interest rates in 1982 brought a decrease in investment and a movement along the investment demand curve. The expected profit rate increased during the expansion in 1983 and 1984, and investment demand increased. This increase is shown by the rightward shift in the investment demand curve to ID_1. During the late 1980s, the expected profit rate decreased and the investment demand curve began to shift leftward. By 1991, the investment demand curve had shifted leftward back to ID_0. The expected profit rate increased again in the expansion of 1992–1994, and investment demand increased. Investment increased further in 1995 and 1996 as a lower real interest rate brought a movement along the investment demand curve ID_1.

You can see in Fig. 26.5 that investment fluctuates for two reasons: The real interest rate changes, which brings movements along an investment demand curve, and the expected profit rate changes, which shifts the investment demand curve.

FIGURE 26.5

Investment Demand in the United States

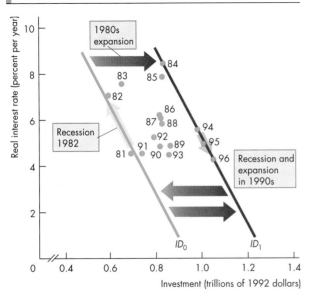

The blue dots show gross investment and the real interest rate in the United States for each year between 1981 and 1996. When the expected profit rate was low in the recession of the early 1980s, the investment demand curve was ID_0. As the real interest rate increased, investment decreased in 1982. During the 1980s, the expected profit rate increased and the investment demand curve shifted rightward. By 1984, it had shifted to ID_1. When the expected profit rate decreased in the late 1980s and the recession of 1991, the investment demand curve shifted leftward to ID_0. Then as the expected profit rate increased again through 1994, the investment demand curve shifted rightward to ID_1. As the real interest rate fell during 1995 and 1996, investment increased. Both swings in the expected profit rate and changes in interest rates bring fluctuations in gross investment.

Source: U.S. Department of Commerce, *National Income and Product Accounts of the United States,* and the author's assumptions.

R E V I E W

■ Investment depends on the expected profit rate and the real interest rate.

■ Other things remaining the same, if the real interest rate falls, investment increases and if the real interest rate rises, investment decreases. A change in the interest rate brings a movement along the investment demand curve.

■ When the expected profit rate increases, the investment demand curve shifts rightward; when the expected profit rate decreases, the *ID* curve shifts leftward.

■ Changes in the real interest rate and the expected profit rate play a role in creating fluctuations in U.S. investment, but changes in the expected profit rate have the larger effect.

Next, we study the decisions that create the funds that finance investment: saving and consumption decisions.

Saving Decisions

PRIVATE INVESTMENT IS FINANCED BY NATIONAL saving and by borrowing from the rest of the world (see Chapter 23, p. 496). **National saving** is the sum of private saving and government saving. We first study private saving. Later in the chapter, we'll see how government actions influence the saving decisions.

Households must decide how to allocate their *disposable income* between saving and consumption. Of the many factors that influence a household's saving decision, the more important ones are:

- The real interest rate
- Disposable income
- Purchasing power of net assets
- Expected future income

The Real Interest Rate

Other things remaining the same, the lower the real interest rate, the smaller is the amount of saving and the greater is the amount of consumption. The real interest rate is the opportunity cost of consumption. A dollar consumed is a dollar not saved, so the interest that could have been earned on that saving is forgone. This opportunity cost arises regardless of whether a person is a lender or a borrower. For a lender, saving less this year means receiving less interest next year. For a borrower, saving less this year means paying less off a loan this year and paying more interest next year.

You can see why the real interest rate influences saving by thinking about student loans. If the real interest rate on student loans jumped to 20 percent a year, students would save more (buying cheaper food and finding lower-rent accommodations) to pay off their loans as quickly as possible. If the real interest rate on student loans fell to 1 percent a year, students would save less and take larger loans.

Disposable Income

The greater a household's disposable income, other things remaining the same, the greater is its saving. For example, a student works during the summer and earns a disposable income of $10,000. She spends the entire $10,000 on consumption during the year and saves nothing. When she graduates as an economics

major, her disposable income jumps to $20,000 a year. She now saves $4,000 and spends $16,000 on consumption. The increase in disposable income of $10,000 has increased saving by $4,000.

Purchasing Power of Net Assets

A household's assets are what it *owns*, and its debts are what it *owes*. A household's *net assets* are its assets minus its debts. The purchasing power of a household's net assets is the *real* value of its net assets. It is the quantity of goods and services that its net assets can buy. The greater the purchasing power of a household's net assets, other things remaining the same, the less is its saving.

Patty is a department store executive who earns a disposable income of $30,000 a year. She has been saving and now has $15,000 in the bank and no debts. Patty's colleague, Tony, also earns a disposable income of $30,000, but he has no money in the bank. Patty decides that this year, she will take a vacation and save only $1,000 each year. But Tony decides to skip a vacation and save $5,000.

Expected Future Income

The lower a household's expected future income, other things remaining the same, the greater is its saving. That is, if two households have the same disposable income in the current year, the household with the larger expected future income will spend a larger portion of current disposable income on consumption goods and services.

Look at Patty and Tony again. Patty has just been promoted and will receive a $10,000 pay raise next year. Tony has just been told that he will be laid off at the end of the year. On receiving this news, Patty buys a new car—increases her consumption expenditure—and Tony sells his car and takes the bus—decreases his consumption expenditure.

Every young household expects to have a higher future income for some years and then to have a lower income during retirement. Because of this pattern of income over the life cycle, young people save a small amount, middle-aged people save a lot, and retired people gradually spend their accumulated savings.

We've studied households' saving decisions so that we can see how their saving decisions interact with firms' investment decisions to determine the real interest rate, investment, and saving. The next step is to learn about the saving supply curve.

Saving Supply

If the real interest rate rises, other things remaining the same, saving increases. The relationship between saving and the real interest rate, other things remaining the same, is called **saving supply**.

Figure 26.6 illustrates saving supply. The table shows a saving supply schedule, and the graph shows the saving supply curve. The points *a* through *c* on the saving supply curve *SS* in Fig. 26.6(a) correspond to the rows of the table. For example, point *b* indicates that when the real interest rate is 6 percent a year, saving is $1.0 trillion. If the real interest rate

rises from 6 percent a year to 8 percent a year, saving increases from $1 trillion to $1.1 trillion and there is a movement along the saving supply curve from *b* to *c*. If the real interest rate falls from 6 percent a year to 4 percent a year, saving decreases from $1 trillion to $0.9 trillion and there is a movement along the saving supply curve from *b* to *a*.

Along the saving supply curve, all other influences on saving remain the same. A change in any influence on saving other than the real interest rate changes saving supply and shifts the saving supply curve. An increase in disposable income, a decrease in the purchasing power of net assets, or a decrease

---

FIGURE 26.6

Saving Supply

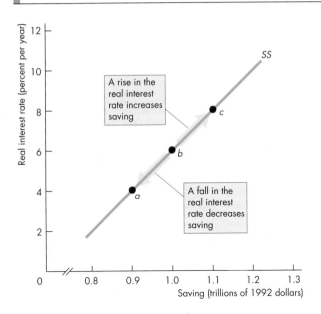

(a) The effect of a change in the real interest rate

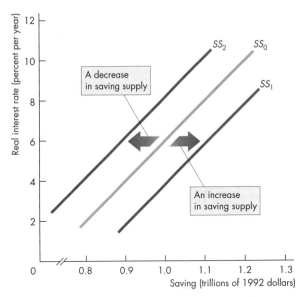

(b) The effects of other influences on saving

The table shows saving at three real interest rates. Part (a) shows the saving supply curve. Along the saving supply curve, the real interest rate changes but all other influences on saving remain the same. In part (b) an increase in disposable income (or a decrease in the purchasing power of net assets or a decrease in expected future income) increases saving and shifts the saving supply curve rightward from SS_0 to SS_1. A decrease in disposable income (or an increase in the purchasing power of net assets or an increase in expected future income) decreases saving and shifts the saving supply curve leftward from SS_0 to SS_2.

	Real interest rate (percent per year)	Saving (trillions of 1992 dollars)
a	4	0.9
b	6	1.0
c	8	1.1

in expected future income increases saving supply and shifts the saving supply curve rightward from SS_0 to SS_1. Changes in these factors in the opposite direction decrease saving and shift the saving supply curve leftward from SS_0 to SS_2.

Let's now see how the saving supply curve helps us to understand changes in saving in the United States.

Saving Supply in the United States

All the influences on saving that we have isolated—the real interest rate, disposable income, the purchasing power of net assets, and expected future income—combine to determine fluctuations in saving in the United States.

Figure 26.7 shows the U.S. saving supply curve. Each point identified by a blue dot represents saving and the real interest rate for a particular year. In 1970, the saving supply curve was SS_0. The curve indicates that when the real interest rate rises, saving increases. But a large change in the real interest rate brings a small change in saving.

Over time, the saving supply curve has shifted rightward because disposable income has increased. Between 1970 and 1974, the saving supply curve shifted rightward to SS_1. But from 1974 through 1983, saving supply did not change much. A rising expected future income encouraged consumption rather than saving. But saving increased during these years because the real interest rate increased, and there was a movement along the saving supply curve SS_1.

During the rest of the 1980s, rising disposable income increased saving supply again and the saving supply curve shifted rightward. By 1996, it had shifted to SS_2.

Changes in other influences have decreased saving. During the 1980s, the purchasing power of net assets and expected future incomes both increased. With a booming stock market and increasing personal wealth, people saved less. Expectations of continued rapid economic expansion, which increased expected future incomes, reinforced the effect of increasing personal wealth. The result was an increase in consumption expenditure that almost equaled the increase in disposable income and a tiny increase in saving.

We've now studied the decisions that determine investment and saving and seen that both sets of decisions depend on the real interest rate. Next, we're going to see how the real interest rate, investment, and saving are simultaneously determined.

FIGURE 26.7

Saving Supply in the United States: 1970–1996

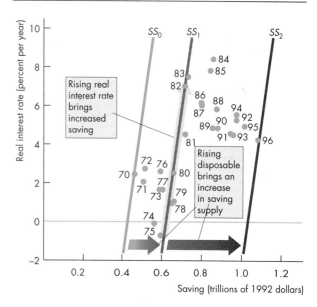

Each blue dot represents saving and the real interest rate for a particular year from 1970 through 1996. The blue curve SS_0 is an estimate of the saving supply curve for 1970. As disposable income increased, saving supply increased and the saving supply curve shifted rightward through SS_1 to SS_2. Saving supply did not change much between 1974 and 1983 because a rising stock market and rising expected future income encouraged consumption and discouraged saving.

Source: U.S. Department of Commerce, *National Income and Product Accounts of the United States*, and the author's assumptions.

REVIEW

■ Saving decisions are influenced by the real interest rate, disposable income, the purchasing power of net assets, and expected future income.

■ The saving supply curve is the relationship between saving and the real interest rate, other things remaining the same. The higher the real interest rate, the greater is the level of saving, other things remaining the same.

■ The U.S. saving supply curve shifted rightward during the 1970s and between 1990 and 1996; but during the early 1980s, saving stagnated.

Equilibrium in the World Economy

WE ARE NOW GOING TO SEE HOW INVESTMENT decisions and saving decisions determine the real interest rate. To do so, we study the economy of the entire world. The reason is that there is a single world capital market. Capital is free to roam the globe and seek the highest possible real rate of return. In 1996, for example, $244 billion of private funds flowed into the developing countries, $52 billion of which flowed into China. So the saving of one country is not always used to finance the investment of that country.

Real interest rates are not the same in every country because some countries are riskier than others. The riskier countries have higher real interest rates. But interest rates move up and down together. If two countries with equal risk had different interest rates, people would want to borrow in the country with a low interest rate and lend in the country with a high interest rate. But no one would want to lend in the country with a low interest rate, so its interest rate would rise. And no one would want to borrow in the country with a high interest rate, so its interest rate would fall. Interest rates would quickly become equal in the two countries. The real interest rate in the world economy is determined by global investment and global saving.

Determining the Real Interest Rate

In Fig. 26.8 the world investment demand curve is *ID* and the world saving supply curve is *SS*. The higher the real interest rate, the greater is the amount of saving and the smaller is the amount of investment.

In the figure, when the real interest rate exceeds 6 percent a year, saving exceeds investment. Borrowers have an easy time finding the loans they want, but lenders are unable to lend all the funds they have available. The real interest rate falls, and as it does so, investment increases and saving decreases. The interest rate continues to fall until saving equals investment.

Alternatively, when the interest rate is less than 6 percent a year, saving is less than investment. Borrowers can't find the loans they want, but lenders are able to lend all the funds they have available. So the real interest rate rises. As the real interest rate rises, investment decreases and saving increases. The interest rate continues to rise as long as saving exceeds investment.

FIGURE 26.8

Equilibrium in the World Capital Market

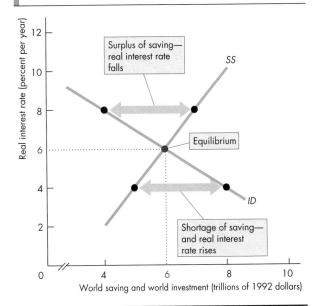

Real interest rate (percent per year)	Investment	Saving
	(trillions of 1992 dollars)	
a 4	8	5
b 6	6	6
c 8	4	7

The table shows world investment and saving at three interest rates, and the figure shows the world investment demand curve, *ID*, and world saving supply curve, *SS*. If the real interest rate is 4 percent a year, investment exceeds saving. There is a shortage of saving, and the real interest rate rises. If the real interest rate is 8 percent a year, investment is less than saving. There is a surplus of saving, and the real interest rate falls. When the real interest rate is 6 percent a year, investment equals saving. There is neither a shortage nor a surplus of saving, and the real interest rate is at its equilibrium level.

The real interest rate changes and is pulled toward an equilibrium level. In Fig. 26.8, this equilibrium is 6 percent a year. At this interest rate, there is neither a surplus nor a shortage of saving. Investors can get the funds they demand, and savers can lend all the funds they have available. The plans of savers and investors are consistent with each other.

Let's use the global saving supply and investment demand curves to explain changes in the real interest rate in the world economy.

Explaining Changes in the Real Interest Rate

In 1996, the real interest rate paid on long-term loans by the biggest and safest U.S. corporations was about 4 percent a year. It was much more than 4 percent a year for homebuyers and risky businesses. Twelve years earlier, in 1984, the real interest rate was more than twice its 1996 level. In that year, it reached a peak level for big companies of 8.4 percent a year. In contrast, 20 years earlier in 1975, the real interest rate was *negative*. Big companies could borrow at about 9 percent a year, and the inflation rate was about 10 percent a year. So the real interest rate was close to *minus* 1 percent a year.

Figure 26.9 explains why these changes in the real interest rate occurred. Each dot represents world investment and world saving and the real interest rate for a particular year. In 1973 (in part a), the saving supply curve was SS_{73} and the investment demand curve was ID_{73}. The real interest rate was 2 percent a year, and the amount of saving and investment in the world economy was $3.7 trillion.

In 1973, a huge rise in the price of oil increased the incomes and saving of oil producers and exporters.

FIGURE 26.9

Explaining Changes in the Real Interest Rate

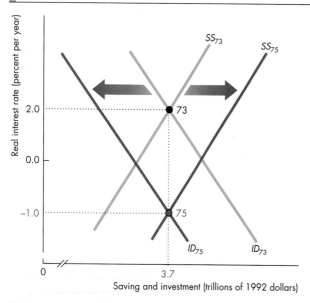

(a) Onset of growth slowdown

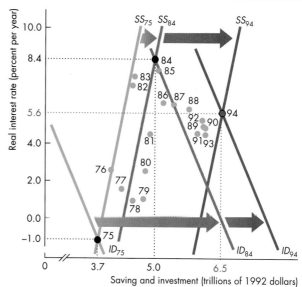

(b) 1975–1994

In 1973 (part a), world saving supply was SS_{73} and world investment demand was ID_{73}. The real interest rate was 2 percent a year. A large increase in the world price of oil increased world saving supply and decreased world investment demand. By 1975, world saving supply was SS_{75} and world investment demand was ID_{75}, and the real interest rate was negative. By 1984 (part b), a strong economic expansion was under way and investment demand had increased to ID_{84}, but saving supply had not increased by much and was SS_{84}. The real interest rate increased and reached a peak of 8.4 percent in 1984. During the rest of the 1980s, saving supply increased by more than investment demand, and by 1994, the saving supply curve was SS_{94} and the investment demand curve was ID_{94}. The real interest rate had fallen to 5.6 percent a year.

Sources: "The Penn World Table: An Expanded Set of International Comparisons, 1950–1988," *Quarterly Journal of Economics,* May 1991, pp. 327–368, New computer diskette, Mark 5.6a, *International Financial Statistics, Yearbook,* 1996, *Economic Report of the President,* 1997, and the author's assumptions and calculations.

By 1975, the world saving supply curve had shifted rightward to SS_{75}. Oil users and importers faced steep cost increases and a collapse of profits, which decreased investment demand. The world investment demand curve shifted leftward to ID_{75}. So by 1975, world saving supply had increased, world investment demand had decreased, and the real interest rate fell to –1 percent a year.

Figure 26.9(b) takes up the story at this point. Gradually, investment demand recovered and, except for severe recession in 1982, increased each year. By 1984, the investment demand curve had shifted rightward to ID_{84}. Through these same years, saving supply increased slowly. In 1984, the saving supply curve was similar to that in 1977. The reasons for slow saving growth are complex. But one factor at work, which we examine later in this chapter, was the emergence of large government deficits, which must be subtracted from private saving to determine total saving. The combination of a large increase in investment demand and a small increase in saving supply increased the real interest rate to 8.4 percent a year in 1984, and world investment and world saving increased to $5 trillion.

The rest of the 1980s and the 1990s saw a continued growth in the supply of saving relative to the increase in investment demand. By 1994, the investment demand curve had shifted rightward to ID_{94} and the saving supply curve had shifted to SS_{94}. As a result of these changes, the real interest rate fell to 5.6 percent a year.

R E V I E W

■ The real interest rate is determined by world saving supply and world investment demand.

■ A world oil price explosion of 1973–1974 increased saving supply and decreased investment demand. The real interest rate fell to a low point.

■ The 1980s expansion increased investment demand, but saving supply grew by less and the real interest rate rose.

■ During the late 1980s, investment demand increased less than saving supply and the real interest rate fell.

So far in our study of investment, saving, and the real interest rate, we've ignored government saving. Let's now bring government saving into the picture.

The Role of Government

PART OF THE CAPITAL STOCK ARISES FROM government investment. And investment is financed by total saving, which is made up of private saving plus government saving. So government actions influence investment, saving, and the real interest rate. To complete our study of the forces that determine the quantity of capital and the real interest rate, we must investigate the role played by governments.

But because the real interest rate is determined in the *world* capital market, it is the *aggregate* investment and saving of all governments that matters, not the investment and saving of one individual government.

Most governments are tiny, and many U.S. corporations have a bigger impact on the world capital market than some governments do. Even the biggest governments make a relatively small difference to the world capital market. For example, the net saving of the U. S. government, which is one of the largest, is around 3 percent of world saving.

But governments in aggregate are large. World aggregate government net saving is close to 20 percent of total saving. And the direction of that saving is negative. Government saving is *negative*!

Let's see why government saving is negative and how government investment and saving influence total investment, saving, and the real interest rate.

Government Budgets

You learned in Chapter 23 (p. 495) that GDP equals the sum of consumption expenditure, C, investment, I, government purchases G, and net exports. We'll ignore net exports for the moment and consider only a closed economy (such as the world economy). So in a closed economy,

$$GDP = C + I + G.$$

GDP also equals the sum of consumption expenditure, saving, S, and net taxes, T. That is,

$$GDP = C + S + T.$$

By combining these two ways of looking at GDP, you can see that

$$I = S + T - G.$$

■ If net taxes, *T*, exceed government purchases, *G*, the government has a budget surplus and government saving is positive.

■ If government purchases exceed net taxes, the government has a budget deficit and government saving is negative.

When the government has a budget surplus, it contributes toward financing investment. Its saving must be added to private saving. But when the government has a budget deficit, it competes with businesses for private saving. In this situation, government saving must be subtracted from private saving.

Government saving can influence the world capital market in two ways, one direct and one indirect. We'll begin with the direct effect.

Direct Effect of Government Saving

The direct influence of government arises because government saving is part of total saving. So we must add government saving and private saving together to determine total saving. Figure 26.10 shows the effects of governments that have a large deficit. The investment demand curve, *ID*, is the same as the one you met in Fig. 26.8. The *private* saving supply curve, *PSS*, shows the relationship between private saving and the real interest rate. The saving supply curve *SS* shows the sum of private saving and government saving.

The horizontal distance between the private saving curve and the saving supply curve is government saving. In this example, government saving is a negative $2 trillion. That is, the governments of all the nations have a total budget deficit of $2 trillion. (This number is larger than the actual deficit in the world economy in the mid-1990s.)

The effect of government negative saving, which is also called *dissaving*, is to increase the real interest rate and to decrease investment. In this example, the real interest rate rises from 6 percent a year to 7.3 percent a year, and investment decreases from $6 trillion to $4.7 trillion.

Investment does not decrease by the full amount of the government deficit because the higher real interest rate induces an increase in private saving. In this example, private saving increases by $0.7 to $6.7 trillion. In reality, the increase in private saving might be quite small, at least in the short term.

The tendency for a government budget deficit to decrease investment is called a **crowding-out effect**. By raising the real interest rate, the government

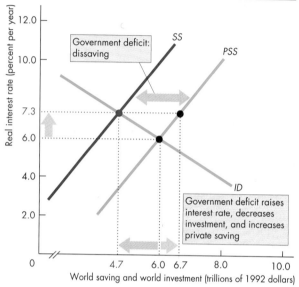

FIGURE 26.10

A Crowding-Out Effect

The world investment demand curve is *ID*, and the world private saving supply curve, *PSS*. With balanced government budgets, the real interest rate is 6 percent a year and investment equals saving at $6 trillion a year. A government budget deficit is negative government saving (dissaving). We subtract the government deficit from private saving to determine the saving supply curve *SS*. The real interest rate rises, investment decreases (is crowded out) and private saving increases.

deficit crowds out private investment and slows the rate of economic growth.

A government surplus has the opposite effect: It increases saving, lowers the real interest rate, and stimulates investment and economic growth.

We've just studied the direct effect of government saving on the world capital market. But there is an indirect effect that we must also take into account.

Indirect Effect of Government Saving

Government saving has an indirect effect on the world capital market because it influences private saving. In the crowding-out story we've just told, the *quantity of private saving* changes because the real interest rate changes. There is a movement along the *PSS* curve. But private saving supply does not change. That is, the *PSS* curve does not shift. The indirect effect arises from the possibility that a change in government saving changes private saving supply and shifts the *PSS* curve. In an extreme version of this effect, private saving changes to offset the government deficit and the deficit has no effect on the real interest rate or investment. Let's look at this extreme case.

The Barro-Ricardo Effect So named because it was first suggested by the English economist David Ricardo in the eighteenth century and refined by Robert J. Barro of Harvard University during the 1980s, the Barro-Ricardo effect holds that a government budget deficit has no effect on the real interest rate or investment. Another way of stating this view is that financing government purchases by taxes or by borrowing is equivalent.

The reasoning behind the Barro-Ricardo effect is the following. A government that runs a deficit must sell bonds to pay for the goods and services that are not paid for by taxes. And the government must pay interest on those bonds. It must also collect more taxes *in the future* to pay the interest on the larger quantity of bonds that are outstanding. Taxpayers are rational and have good foresight. They can see that their taxes will be higher in the future so their disposable income will be smaller. With a smaller expected future disposable income, saving increases. And if taxpayers want to neutralize the effects of the government deficit on their own consumption plans, they increase their saving by the same amount that the government is dissaving through its deficit.

Figure 26.11 shows this outcome. The private saving supply curve initially is PSS_0. The government has a balanced budget—neither a deficit nor a surplus—so saving supply is also PSS_0. With investment demand *ID*, the equilibrium real interest rate is 6 percent a year and investment and saving are $6 trillion.

Governments now run deficits that total $2 trillion. But these deficits induce an increase in private saving. Here, the increase is the full amount of the government deficit. So the private saving supply curve shifts rightward to PSS_1. Total saving supply remains at PSS_0, so the real interest rate remains at 6 percent a year. Investment also remains at $6 trillion a year. Private saving increases to $8 trillion.

The outcome shown in Fig. 26.11 is extreme and probably does not actually occur. Taxpayers probably respond in the *direction* suggested by Ricardo and Barro but not in the *amount* they suggest. So the effect of government deficits probably lies between the two cases shown in Figs. 26.10 and 26.11. That

FIGURE 26.11

A Barro-Ricardo Effect

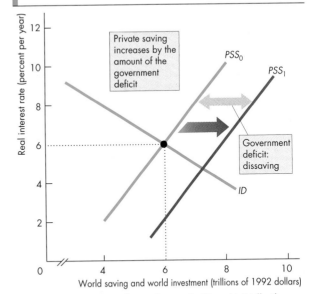

The world investment demand curve is *ID*, and initially, the world private saving supply curve, PSS_0. With balanced government budgets, the real interest rate is 6 percent a year and investment equals saving at $6 trillion a year. Government budget deficits induce an increase in private saving. The *PSS* curve shifts rightward to PSS_1, and the real interest rate, investment, and *total* saving remain constant.

is, a government deficit increases the real interest rate and partly crowds out investment, but it also induces a partial increase in private saving in anticipation of lean times later when the tax bill rises to pay the interest on a rising debt.

Government Deficits Today

Government deficits have been large in recent years and have probably been responsible for the high real interest rates of the 1990s. Figure 26.12 shows the deficits of the United States, the industrial countries, and the developing countries from 1988 through 1995 and projected deficits for 1996 and 1997.

During the early 1990s, deficits in the United States and the other industrial countries increased to more than 4 percent of GDP. For the world as a whole, a deficit of this magnitude exceeds $1 trillion. But after 1993, government deficits in the industrial countries decreased.

FIGURE 26.12
Government Deficits

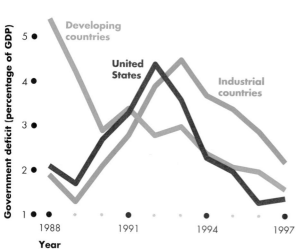

The government deficit of the United States increased through 1992 and then decreased. The other industrial countries followed a similar pattern but peaked in 1993. The deficit of the developing countries has been on a downward trend throughout the period shown here.

Source: *World Economic Outlook* (Washington D.C.: International Monetary Fund, October 1996).

Government deficits in the developing countries have fallen steadily, and by 1992, they represented a smaller percentage of GDP than the deficits of the industrial countries. Developing countries have decreased their deficits because doing so has been a condition for receiving loans from their banks, most notably the World Bank. (The World Bank is an international organization that finances development projects in developing countries and that uses funds paid to it by the industrial countries.)

During the 1990s, real interest rates are higher than average. The basic reason is that investment demand is high relative to saving supply. The 1990s is a time when investment opportunities are large and saving rates are low compared with average times. Figure 26.3 shows that real interest rates averaged 4 percent between 1970 and 1995. But even this number is above the long-term average, which over the past 100 years is 2 percent a year. If government deficits continue to decrease, real interest rates will also decrease (other things remaining the same).

REVIEW

■ Total saving equals private saving plus government saving. Government saving equals net taxes minus government purchases.

■ A government budget deficit decreases total saving, increases the real interest rate, decreases investment, and increases private saving.

■ In the mid-1990s, government deficits were large but decreasing.

So far, we've looked at investment and saving in the world economy. Next we look at the national economy.

Saving and Investment in the National Economy

SAVING SUPPLY AND INVESTMENT DEMAND IN THE world economy determine the world real interest rate. At the equilibrium real interest rate, world saving equals world investment.

Although saving equals investment in the world economy, it does not necessarily do so in a national economy. In a nation, investment is financed by *national* saving plus borrowing from the rest of the world (see Chapter 23, p. 496). Nations in which investment exceeds national saving borrow from the rest of the world, and nations in which national saving exceeds investment lend to the rest of the world. For the world as a whole, international borrowing equals international lending.

But as you also learned in Chapter 23, a nation's international lending equals its net exports. So a nation that has a net export surplus is also one that lends to the rest of the world. A nation whose imports exceed its exports has negative net exports and borrows from the rest of the world. Whether a nation has a surplus or deficit in its international trade depends on whether its national saving exceeds or falls short of its investment.

Let's take a closer look at the role played by national saving and investment decisions and see how they determine international borrowing. There are two channels of influence to consider.

First, each nation contributes to world saving and investment and so influences the world real interest rate. The larger the country, the greater is that influence. For example, investment and saving decisions in the United States, the European Union, and Japan have a big impact on world investment demand and world saving supply. So they have a big influence on the world real interest rate. The investment and saving of other nations individually have a small impact on world investment demand and world saving supply. So they have a negligible influence on the world real interest rate.

Second, a nation's saving and investment decisions, along with the world real interest rate, determine the amount the nation borrows from or lends to the rest of the world. They also, equivalently, determine a nation's net exports.

Figure 26.13 shows the determination of a nation's international borrowing and net exports. The nation's investment demand curve is *ID*, and its saving supply curve (including any government saving) is *SS*. The world real interest rate is 6 percent a year. At this real interest rate, investment is $1.5 trillion and saving is $1.0 trillion. International borrowing fills the gap between investment and saving. In the example in Fig. 26.13, investment exceeds saving, so the nation borrows from the rest of the world. If, at the world real interest rate, saving exceeds investment, the nation lends to the rest of the world.

Government Saving and International Borrowing

The greater the amount of government saving, other things remaining the same, the greater is national saving. And the greater the national saving, the smaller is international borrowing (or the larger is international lending). An increase in the government deficit decreases national saving and increases international borrowing.

You can now see why U.S. net exports have been negative for the past 20 years. It is because U.S. national saving has been less than investment. Government dissaving (a government budget deficit) has contributed to the shortfall. A low private saving rate has also contributed.

You can also see that one popular view about the U.S. budget deficit is incorrect. Because the capital market is a global market and the U.S. government is a small player, the U.S. government deficit cannot cause much damage to growth by crowding out investment. But it does damage the growth of U.S disposable incomes because it increases international borrowing and increases the interest payments that we must make to the rest of the world.

FIGURE 26.13

Saving, Investment, and International Borrowing

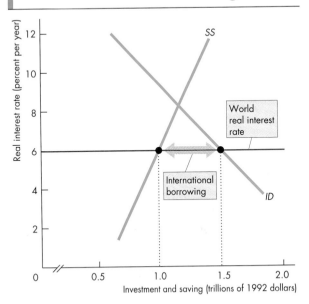

A nation's investment demand curve is *ID*, and its saving supply curve (including government saving) is *SS*. The world real interest rate is 6 percent a year. At this interest rate, investment, which is $1.5 trillion, exceeds saving, which is $1.0 trillion. The nation borrows $0.5 trillion from the rest of the world.

REVIEW

◼ If investment exceeds saving at the world real interest rate, net exports are negative and the nation borrows from the rest of the world.

◼ An increase in the government deficit increases international borrowing, but it does not crowd out investment.

◆ In this chapter, we've seen that the quantity of capital depends on investment and saving; and we've seen how the real interest rate is determined in the world capital market. Your next task is to see how technological change brings capital accumulation and economic growth.

Before embarking on this task, take a look at *Reading Between the Lines* on pp. 582–583, which examines the private saving performance of the United States in recent years.

Policy
WATCH

Saving in the United States

WINSTON-SALEM JOURNAL, OCTOBER 6, 1996

Seniors Aren't As Thrifty As Believed

BY STEVEN PEARLSTEIN
THE WASHINGTON POST

For some time, the economist's mantra has gone something like this: A falling savings rate has led to falling investment, and falling investment has led to slow erosion in the average American's standard of living.

But what accounts for this declining savings rate, which has fallen from more than 11 percent of household income in the 1950s and '60s to less than 4 percent in the 1990s?

During the 1980s, one favorite explanation was that profligate baby boomers were spending on BMWs, expensive suits and high-priced houses. ...

But a controversial new study by Laurence Kotlikoff of Boston University, John Sabelhaus of the Congressional Budget Office and Jagadeesh Gokhale of the Federal Reserve Bank of Cleveland concludes that it is really grandma and grandpa who have been living high on the hog.

In 1960, the typical 70-year-old American spent about 71 cents for every dollar spent by a 30-year-old.

By the late 1980s, it was the oldster who was the bigger spender, shelling out $1.18 for every dollar spent by the typical 30-year-old.

One obvious reason for this shift was the dramatic increase in health-care spending. ...

But even with medical costs factored out, the analysts still found that seniors have been on a spending spree these past 30 years. ...

[Gokhale, Kotlikoff and Sabelhaus] concluded that the elderly have been garnering an ever-increasing share of the country's resources and have been spending that increase rather than saving it.

The transfer of wealth and income from young to old—what economists call intergenerational transfers—has been well documented. ... The primary factors there are Social Security and Medicare benefits, the values of which have been rising faster than the incomes of working Americans. ...

In a world where people receive entitlements for life, they are more likely to spend down their savings knowing they can always fall back on annuities if they live longer than average and draw down their entire savings. ...

Of course, Social Security, Medicare and private pensions have been around for a long time. But whereas these annuities represented 16 percent of income received by the elderly in 1960, they represent 40 percent of the income received by the elderly today. ...

Essence of THE STORY

■ Household saving has fallen from 11 percent of income during the 1950s and 1960s to less than 4 percent during the 1990s.

■ In 1960, seniors spent 71 cents for every dollar spent by younger adults. By the late 1980s, seniors spent $1.18 for every dollar spent by younger adults.

■ In 1960, 16 percent of seniors' income came from Social Security and Medicare. Now the amount is 40 percent.

■ When people expect to receive pensions and benefits throughout their lives, they spend more and save less.

Economic

A N A L Y S I S

■ Figure 1 shows two measures of personal saving in the United States. The left scale (red line) shows national saving as a percentage of gross national product. The right scale (blue line) shows personal saving as a percentage of disposable income.

■ Both measures show a similar downward trend. But this trend raises two questions: What caused it, and what are its consequences?

■ Private saving depends on the real interest rate, disposable income, the purchasing power of net assets, and expected future income.

■ Figure 2 shows the private saving supply curve in 1963, PSS_{63}. The real interest rate was 3 percent a year and the average family saved $2,000 (measured in terms of 1992 prices), which is a point on PSS_{63}.

■ Disposable income in the United States has increased over the last 30 years.

■ Other things remaining the same, the increase in disposable income increases saving. By 1992, the increase in disposable income might have shifted the saving supply curve rightward to PSS'_{92}.

■ But the average family saved only $1,200 in 1992. And the real interest rate in that year was 5 percent, a higher rate than in 1962.

■ So the private saving supply curve in 1992 had actually shifted leftward to PSS_{92}. The 1992 saving per family of $1,200 at the real interest rate of 5 percent a year is a point on this curve.

■ The main factor that decreased saving, according to the research reported in the news article, is the increase in Social Security and Medicare. These programs give people a higher expected income during retirement and induce them to save less and consume more.

■ What are the consequences of decreased saving?

■ The United States is a large part of the world, so lower U.S. saving means a significant decrease in world saving and a higher real interest rate.

■ It also means a larger amount of U.S. borrowing from the rest of the world and imports that exceed exports.

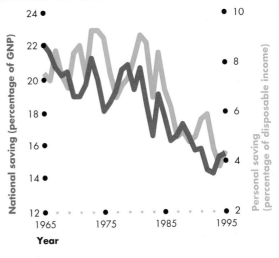

Figure 1 Saving rates

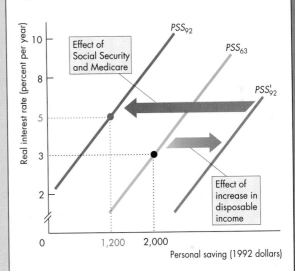

Figure 2 Saving supply curves

You're

THE VOTER

■ What do you think the federal government should do about the low U.S. saving rate?

■ If the study reported in the news article is correct, cutting Social Security and Medicare would increase private saving. What are the pros and cons of making such cuts?

■ What, if any, tax reforms would increase saving?

■ Would you vote for tax incentives, a cut in Social Security, neither, or both? Explain why.

583

SUMMARY

Key Points

Capital and Interest (pp. 566–568)

- The capital stock grows steadily because net investment is usually positive.
- The return on capital is the real interest rate—the nominal interest rate adjusted for inflation.

Investment Decisions (pp. 569–571)

- Other things remaining the same, the lower the real interest rate or the higher the expected profit rate, the greater is the amount of investment.
- Investment demand is the relationship between investment and the real interest rate, other things remaining the same. Investment demand changes when the expected profit rate changes.

Saving Decisions (pp. 572–574)

- Other things remaining the same, the higher the real interest rates, the greater is saving.
- Saving supply is the relationship between saving and the real interest rate, other things remaining the same.
- Saving supply changes when disposable income, the purchasing power of net assets, expected future income changes.

Equilibrium in the World Economy (pp. 575–577)

- Because capital is free to move internationally to seek the highest possible real rate of return, the real interest rate is determined in a global market.
- The equilibrium real interest rate makes world saving equal to world investment.

The Role of Government (pp. 577–580)

- National saving equals private saving plus government saving.
- Government saving equals net taxes minus government purchases.

- A government budget deficit might increase the real interest rate and crowd out private investment.
- A government budget deficit might also increase private saving supply because it decreases expected future disposable income.

Saving and Investment in the National Economy (pp. 580–581)

- In the national economy, foreign borrowing fills the gap between national saving and investment.
- An increase in the government budget deficit decreases national saving and increases foreign borrowing, but it does not decrease investment.

Key Figures

Key Terms

QUESTIONS

1. Which component of gross investment fluctuates the most, net investment or replacement investment?
2. Why does the capital stock grow smoothly when net investment fluctuates?
3. What is the real interest rate?
4. Describe how the real interest rate has changed since 1975.
5. What determines investment?
6. Why does a fall in the real interest rate increase investment?
7. How is investment influenced by the expected rate of profit?
8. What is the investment demand curve, what brings a movement along the investment demand curve, and what makes it shift?
9. What have been the main changes in investment demand in the United States in recent years?
10. What are the main influences on saving?
11. Why does a rise in the real interest rate increase saving?
12. How do disposable income, the purchasing power of net assets, and expected future income influence saving?
13. What is the saving supply curve, what brings a movement along the saving supply curve, and what makes it shift?
14. What have been the main changes in saving supply in the United States in recent years?
15. Explain how the real interest rate is determined.
16. What have been the main influences on the real interest rate during the 1980s and 1990s?
17. How does government saving influence national saving?
18. How does government saving influence the real interest rate, investment, and private saving?
19. What happens to the real interest rate, investment, and private saving if government deficits around the world increase?
20. What determines U.S. international borrowing?
21. How does a government budget deficit in the United States influence investment, saving, and U.S. international borrowing?

PROBLEMS

1. A cellular phone assembly plant costs $10 million and has a life of one year. The firm will have to hire labor at a cost of $3 million and buy parts and fuel at a cost of a further $3 million. If the firm builds the plant, it will be able to produce cellular telephones that will sell for $17 million. Does it pay the firm to invest in this new production line at the following real interest rates:
   a. 5 percent a year?
   b. 10 percent a year?
   c. 15 percent a year?
2. Suppose the phone producer in problem 1 expects its total revenue to increase to $17.5 million with unchanged costs. What now is the highest real interest rate at which it will undertake the investment? How does the firm's investment demand curve change as a result of an increase in its expected profit rate?
3. In 1997, the Batman family (Batman and Robin) had a disposable income of $50,000, net assets of $100,000, and an expected future income of $50,000 a year. At an interest rate of 4 percent a year, the Batmans would save $10,000. At an interest rate of 6 percent a year, they would save $12,500. And at an interest rate of 8 percent a year, they would save $15,000.
   a. Draw a graph of the Batman family's saving supply curve for 1997.
   b. In 1998, everything remained the same as the year before except that the Batmans expected their future income to rise to $60,000 a year. Show the influence of this change on the Batman family's saving supply curve.
   c. In 1999, everything remained the same as the year before except that the Batmans disposable income increased to the $60,000 a year they expected it would the year before. The Batmans now expect their income to remain at $60,000 a year. Show the influence of this change on the Batman family's saving supply curve.
   d. In 2000, the stock market boomed and the Batmans' assets increased by 50 percent. Show the influence of this change on the Batman family's saving supply curve.

4. The year is 3053. The economy of Alpha Centura, still isolated from all other planets, has the following saving supply and investment demand:

Real interest rate (percent per year)	Saving	Investment (trillions of 3050 zips)
4	2	7
5	6	6
6	10	5
7	14	4
8	18	3

Alpha Centura's government budget is balanced.
a. What is the equilibrium real interest rate?
b. What is equilibrium investment?
c. What is equilibrium saving?

5. The government of Alpha Centura spends big on a space program and incurs a deficit of 5 trillion zips. The Alpha Centurans have not heard of Ricardo and keep spending as if there were no government deficit.
a. What is the new equilibrium real interest rate?
b. What is the new equilibrium investment and saving?

6. Alpha Centura's space program pays off. The Alpha Centurans and Earth people discover each other and begin to pursue intergalactic economic trade, borrowing, and lending. The real interest rate on Earth is 5 percent a year. On Alpha Centura, it is the number you calculated for problem 5.
a. Which planet borrows from the other?
b. Do investment and saving on Alpha Centura increase or decrease?
c. Do investment and saving on Earth increase or decrease?

7. Suppose that before Alpha Centura and Earth discover each other, the Alpha Centurans begin to realize that the government deficit is going to mean that their taxes will rise. They discover and apply the Barro-Ricardo principle.
a. What happens to their saving supply curve?
b. What happens to their investment demand curve?
c. What happens to the real interest rate and investment?

CRITICAL THINKING

1. Study *Reading Between the Lines* on pp. 582–583 and then answer the following questions:
   a. What has happened to the saving rate in the United States during the past 30 years?
   b. How does the saving behavior of older Americans compare with that of younger Americans?
   c. What are the main reasons you can think of that might account for the patterns that you describe in your answers to parts (a) and (b)?
   d. What are the likely effects of a decrease in U.S. saving supply? Explain the effects on national saving, investment, the world real interest rate, and U.S. international borrowing and lending.
   e. If the U.S. saving rate increases during the 2000s, how will that change influence the U.S. and world quantity of capital by 2010?

2. Suppose the U.S. government cuts the tax rate on business profits.
   a. How do you think this tax cut will influence firm's investment plans?
   b. How will the tax cut influence private saving decisions?
   c. How will the tax cut influence the real interest rate?
   d. How will the tax cut influence U.S. international borrowing?
   For each part, draw a figure to illustrate the effects. Then go on to think about and answer the following questions:
   e. Who would benefit from such a tax cut?
   f. Who would pay for such a tax cut?
   g. On balance, do you favor or oppose such a tax cut? Why?

3. Use the latest *World Economic Outlook*, published twice a year by the International Monetary Fund, to get data on government budget deficits. (The data are *not* on the IMF World Wide Web site.)
   a. What are the trends in deficits? Are they the same as or different from those in Fig. 26.12 on p. 580?
   b. What influence do you expect the deficits to have on the real interest rate and investment next year?

Chapter 27

Economic Growth

Real GDP per person in the United States has doubled between 1960 and 1996. If you live in a dorm, chances are it was built during the 1960s and equipped with two electricity outlets, one for a desk lamp and one for a bedside lamp. Today, with the help of a power bar (or two), your room bulges with a television and VCR, CD player, microwave, refrigerator, coffee maker, toaster, computer—and the list goes on. What has brought about this growth in production and incomes? What can be done to speed up economic growth? ◆ We see greater extremes of economic growth if we look at modern Asia. On the banks of the Li River in Southern China, Songman Yang breeds cormorants, amazing birds that he trains to fish

Transforming People's Lives

and to deliver their catch to a basket on his simple bamboo raft. Songman's work, the capital equipment and technology he uses, and the income he earns are similar to those of his ancestors going back some 2,000 years. Yet all around Songman, in China's bustling villages, towns, and cities, people are partici-

pating in an economic miracle. They are creating businesses, investing in new technologies, developing local and global markets, and experiencing income growth of more than 6 percent a year. Similar rapid economic growth is taking place in Hong Kong, South Korea, and Taiwan. In these countries, real GDP has doubled *three times*—an eightfold increase—between 1960 and 1996. Why have incomes in these Asian economies grown so rapidly? What makes an economic miracle? ◆ In this chapter, we study the forces that make real GDP grow, that make some countries grow faster than others, and that make our own growth rate sometimes slow down and sometimes speed up. We'll also look at policies for achieving faster economic growth.

After studying this chapter, you will be able to:

- Describe the long-term growth trends in the United States and other countries and regions

- Identify the main sources of long-term of real GDP growth

- Explain the productivity growth slowdown in the United States during the 1970s

- Explain the rapid economic growth rates being achieved in East Asia

- Explain the theories of economic growth

- Describe the policies that might be used to speed up economic growth

Long-Term Growth Trends

THE LONG-TERM GROWTH TRENDS THAT WE
study in this chapter are the trends in *potential GDP*.
We are interested in long-term growth primarily
because it brings rising incomes *per person*. So we begin
by looking at some facts about the level and growth
rate of real GDP per person in the United States and
around the world. Let's look first at real GDP per person in the United States over the past hundred years.

Growth in the U.S. Economy

Figure 27.1 shows real GDP per person in the United
States for the hundred years from 1896 to 1996. The
average growth rate over this period is 2 percent a year.
But the long-term growth rate has varied from a low
of 1.1 percent a year between 1973 and 1984 to a high
of 3 percent a year during the 1920s and the 1960s.

Figure 27.1 shows you the recent productivity
growth slowdown in a longer perspective. It also shows
that productivity growth slowdowns have occurred
before. The early years of the 1900s and the mid-1950s
had even slower growth than we have today. The
rapid growth of the 1960s was not unusual either.
The decade of the 1920s was a period of similarly
rapid growth.

In the middle of the graph are two extraordinary
events: the Great Depression of the 1930s and World
War II of the 1940s. The fall in real GDP during the
Depression and the bulge during the war obscure any
changes in the long-term growth trend that might
have occurred within these years. But between 1930
and 1950, averaging out the Depression and the war,
the long-term growth rate was 2.2 percent a year.

A major goal of this chapter is to explain why our
economy grows and why the long-term growth rate
varies. A related goal is to explain variations in the
economic growth rate across countries. Let's look at
some facts about these variations.

FIGURE 27.1

A Hundred Years of Economic Growth in the United States

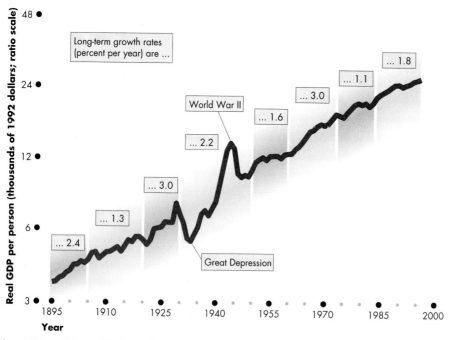

During the 100 years from 1896 to 1996, real GDP per person in the United States grew by 2 percent a year, on the average. The growth rate was above average during the 1920s and 1960s, and it was below average in 1903–1920, the 1950s, and 1973–1996.

Source: Christina D. Romer "The Prewar Business Cycle Reconsidered: New Estimates of Gross National Product, 1869–1908," *Journal of Political Economy* Vol. 97 (1989);
National Income and Product Accounts of the United States; Historical Statistics of the United States Colonial Times to 1957 (U.S. Department of Commerce, 1960); and
Economic Report of the President, 1997.

Real GDP Growth in the World Economy

Figure 27.2 shows real GDP growth in the United States and in some other countries since 1960. The data shown in this figure are in 1985 dollars. Part (a) looks at the richest countries. The United States has the highest real GDP per person, and Canada has the second highest. But up to 1989, Canada grew faster than the United States and so was catching up.

Until 1985, the third richest countries were France, Germany, Italy, and the United Kingdom. Figure 27.2(a) shows them as Europe Big 4. But in 1985, the fastest-growing rich country, Japan, caught up with Europe Big 4. All the countries shown in Fig. 27.2(a) are catching up with the United States. Japan has caught up most, Canada has got closest, and Europe Big 4 has caught up least.

Not all countries are growing faster than, and catching up with, the United States. Figure 27.2(b) looks at some of these. Africa and Central and South America were stagnating, not growing, during the 1980s. As a result, the gap between them and the United States widened. Western Europe other than the Big 4 countries grew during the 1970s and 1980s but at a rate that was roughly equal to that of the United States. So the gap remained constant. The former Communist countries of Central Europe grew faster than the United States until the late 1980s and then stagnated.

The data used in Fig. 27.2 are not currently available beyond 1992. But other data (not shown in Fig. 27.2) suggest that after 1992, real GDP per person shrank in some of the countries of Central Europe as they went through a process of traumatic political change.

FIGURE 27.2

Economic Growth Around the World: Catch-Up or Not?

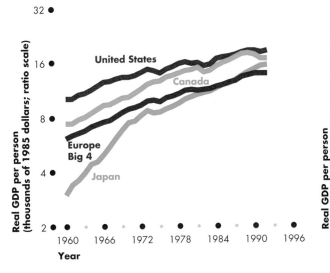

(a) Catch up?

(b) No catch up?

Real GDP per person has grown throughout the world economy. Among the rich industrial countries (part a), real GDP growth has been faster in Canada, the big four Western European countries (France, Germany, Italy, and the United Kingdom), and Japan than in the United States and they are catching up. The most spectacular growth was in Japan during the 1960s. The income level in Canada has also become closest to the U.S. income level. Among a wider range of countries (part b), there is less sign of convergence. The gaps between the income levels of the United States, other Western European countries, Central Europe, Central and South America, and Africa have remained remarkably constant.

Source: Robert Summers and Alan Heston, New Computer Diskette (Mark 5.6a), January 15, 1995 , distributed by the National Bureau of Economic Research to update "The Penn World Table: An Expanded Set of International Comparisons, 1950–1988," *Quarterly Journal of Economics,* May 1991, 327–368.

Taking both parts of Fig. 27.2 together, we can see that the catch-up in real GDP per person that is visible in part (a) is not a global phenomenon. Some rich countries are catching up with the United States, but the gaps between the United States and many poor countries are not closing.

Another group of countries that in 1960 had low levels of real GDP per person are catching up with the United States in a dramatic way. These are Hong Kong, Singapore, Taiwan, and Korea. Figure 27.3 shows how these countries are catching up with the United States. The figure also shows that China is catching up, but more slowly and from a very long way behind. In 1960, China's real GDP per person was one twentieth that of the United States, but by 1990, it was one twelfth.

The four small Asian countries shown in Fig. 27.3 are like fast trains running on the same track at similar speeds and with a roughly constant gap between them. Hong Kong is the lead train and runs about 12 years in front of Korea, which is the last train. Real GDP per person in Korea in 1990 was similar to that in Hong Kong in 1978, 12 years earlier. During the 30 years between 1960 and 1990, Hong Kong transformed itself from a poor developing country into one of the world's richest countries.

China is now doing what Hong Kong has done. If China continues its rapid growth, the world economy will become a dramatically different place. Because China is equivalent to more than 200 countries the size of Hong Kong. Whether China will continue on its current path of rapid growth is impossible to predict.

FIGURE 27.3
Catch-Up in Asia

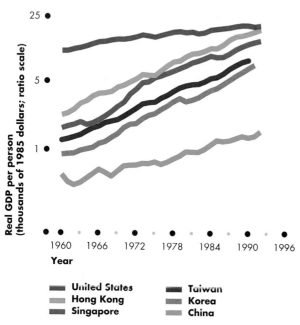

The clearest examples of catch-up have occurred in five economies in Asia. Starting out in 1960 with incomes as little as one tenth of that in the United States, four Asian economies (Hong Kong, Singapore, Taiwan, and Korea) have substantially narrowed the gap on the United States. And from being a very poor developing country in 1960, China's income level now exceeds the income level that Hong Kong had in 1960. China is growing at a rate that is enabling it to continue to catch up with the United States.

Source: Robert Summers and Alan Heston, New Computer Diskette (Mark 5.5), June 15 1993, distributed by the National Bureau of Economic Research to update "The Penn World Table (Mark 5): An Expanded Set of International Comparisons, 1950–1988," *Quarterly Journal of Economics*, May 1991, 327–368.

REVIEW

■ Over the hundred years between 1896 and 1996, real GDP per person in the United States grew at an average rate of 2 percent a year. Slow growth occurred during the early 1900s, mid-1950s, and 1973–1996, and rapid growth occurred during the 1920s and 1960s.

■ Some rich countries are catching up with the United States, but the gaps between the United States and many poor countries are not closing.

■ Hong Kong, Korea, Singapore, and Taiwan are catching up fastest. China is also catching up but more slowly and from a long way behind.

The facts about economic growth in the United States and around the world raise some big questions that we're now going to answer. We'll study the causes of economic growth in three stages. First, we'll look at the preconditions for growth and the activities that sustain it. Second, we'll learn how economists measure the relative contributions of the sources of growth—an activity called *growth accounting*. Third, we'll study three theories of economic growth that seek to explain how the influences on growth interact to determine the growth rate. Let's take our first look at the causes of economic growth.

The Causes of Economic Growth: A First Look

MOST HUMAN SOCIETIES HAVE LIVED FOR centuries and even thousands of years like Songman Yang, with no economic growth. The key reason is that they have lacked some fundamental social institutions and arrangements that are essential preconditions for economic growth. Let's see what these preconditions are.

Preconditions for Economic Growth

The most basic precondition for economic growth is an appropriate *incentive* system. Three institutions are crucial to the creation of incentives. They are:

1. Markets
2. Property rights
3. Monetary exchange

Markets enable buyers and sellers to get information and to do business with each other, and market prices send signals to buyers and sellers that create incentives to increase or decrease the quantities demanded and supplied. Markets enable people to specialize and trade and to save and invest. But for markets to work, we need property rights and monetary exchange.

Property rights are the social arrangements that govern the ownership, use, and disposal of resources and goods and services. They include the rights to physical property (land, buildings, and capital equipment), to financial property (claims by one person against another), and to intellectual property (such as inventions). Clearly established and enforced property rights give people an assurance that a capricious government will not confiscate their income or savings.

Monetary exchange facilitates transactions of all kinds, including the orderly transfer of private property from one person to another. Property rights and monetary exchange create incentives for people to specialize and trade, to save and invest, and to discover new technologies.

No unique political system is necessary to deliver the preconditions for economic growth. Liberal democracy, founded on the fundamental principle of the rule of law, is the system that does the best job. It provides a solid base on which property rights can be established and enforced. But authoritarian political systems have sometimes provided an environment in which economic growth has occurred.

Early human societies, based on hunting and gathering, did not experience economic growth because they lacked these preconditions. Economic growth began when societies evolved the three key institutions that create incentives. But the presence of an incentive system and the institutions that create it does not guarantee that economic growth will occur. It permits economic growth but does not make that growth inevitable.

The simplest way in which growth happens when the appropriate incentive system exists is that people begin to specialize in the activities at which they have a comparative advantage and trade with each other. You saw in Chapter 3 how everyone can gain from such activity. By specializing and trading, everyone can acquire goods and services at the lowest possible cost. Equivalently, people can obtain a greater volume of goods and services from their labor.

As an economy moves from one with little specialization to one that reaps the gains from specialization and exchange, its production and consumption grow. Real GDP per person increases, and the standard of living rises.

But for growth to be persistent, people must face incentives that encourage them to pursue three activities that generate ongoing economic growth. These activities are:

- Saving and investment in new capital
- Investment in human capital
- Discovery of new technologies

These three sources of growth, which interact with each other, are the primary sources of the extraordinary growth in productivity during the past 200 years. Let's look at each in turn.

Saving and Investment in New Capital

Saving and investment in new capital increase the amount of capital per worker and increase real GDP per hour of labor—labor productivity. Labor productivity took the most dramatic upturn when the amount of capital per worker increased during the Industrial Revolution. Production processes that use hand tools can create beautiful objects, but production methods that use large amounts of capital per worker, such as auto plant assembly lines, are much more productive.

The accumulation of capital on farms, in textile factories, in iron foundries and steel mills, in coal mines, on building sites, in chemical plants, in auto plants, in banks and insurance companies, and in shopping malls has added incredibly to the productivity of our economy. The next time you see a Western movie, look carefully at the small amount of capital around. Try to imagine how productive you would be in such circumstances compared with your productivity today.

Investment in Human Capital

Human capital—the accumulated skill and knowledge of human beings—is the most fundamental source of economic growth. It is a source of both increased productivity and technological advance.

The development of one of the most basic human skills, writing, was the source of some of the earliest major gains in productivity. The ability to keep written records made it possible to reap ever-larger gains from specialization and exchange. Imagine how hard it would be to do any kind of business if all the accounts, invoices, and agreements existed only in people's memories.

Later, the development of mathematics laid the foundation for the eventual extension of knowledge about physical forces and chemical and biological processes. This base of scientific knowledge was the foundation for the technological advances of the Industrial Revolution 200 years ago and of today's Information Revolution.

But much human capital that is extremely productive is much more humble. It takes the form of millions of individuals learning and repetitively doing simple production tasks and becoming remarkably more productive in the tasks.

One carefully studied example illustrates the importance of this kind of human capital. Between 1941 and 1944 (during World War II), U.S. shipyards produced some 2,500 units of a cargo ship, called the Liberty Ship, to a standardized design. In 1941, it took 1.2 million person-hours to build a ship. By 1942, it took 600,000, and by 1943, it took only 500,000. Not much change occurred in the capital employed during these years. But an enormous amount of human capital was accumulated. Thousands of workers and managers learned from experience and accumulated human capital that more than doubled their productivity in two years.

Discovery of New Technologies

Saving and investment in new capital and the accumulation of human capital have made a large contribution to economic growth. But the contribution of technological change—of the discovery and the application of new technologies and new goods—has made an even greater contribution.

People are many times more productive today than they were a hundred years ago. We are not more productive because we have more steam engines per person and more horse-drawn carriages per person. Rather, it is because we have the engines and transportation equipment that use technologies that were unknown a hundred years ago and that are more productive than the old technologies were. Technological change makes an enormous contribution to our increased productivity. It arises from formal research and development programs and from informal trial and error, and it involves discovering new ways of getting more out of our resources.

To reap the benefits of technological change, capital must increase. Some of the most powerful and far-reaching fundamental technologies are embodied in human capital—for example, language, writing, and mathematics. But most technologies are embodied in physical capital. For example, to reap the benefits of the internal combustion engine, millions of horse-drawn carriages and horses had to be replaced by automobiles; more recently, to reap the benefits of computerized word processing, millions of typewriters had to be replaced by PCs and printers.

REVIEW

- Economic growth cannot occur without institutions that create incentives to specialize and exchange, save and invest, and develop new technologies.
- The most significant sources of economic growth are saving and investment in new capital, the growth of human capital, and the discovery of new technologies. These sources interact: Human capital creates new technologies, which are embodied in both human and physical capital.

What is the quantitative contribution of the sources of economic growth? To answer this question, economists use growth accounting.

Growth Accounting

THE QUANTITY OF REAL GDP SUPPLIED (Y)
depends on three factors:

1. The quantity of labor (N)
2. The quantity of capital (K)
3. The state of technology (T)

The purpose of **growth accounting** is to calculate
how much real GDP growth results from growth of
labor and capital and how much is attributable to
technological change.

The key tool of growth accounting is the
aggregate production function, which is
written as the equation:

$$Y = F(N, K, T).$$

In words, the quantity of real GDP supplied is determined by (is a function F of) the quantities of labor
and capital and of the state of technology. The larger
N, K, or T, the greater is Y. And the faster N and K
grow and the faster T advances, the faster Y grows.

So understanding what makes labor and capital
grow and technology advance is the key to understanding economic growth. Labor growth depends primarily
on population growth. And the growth rate of capital
and the pace of technological advance determine the
growth rate of labor productivity.

Labor Productivity

Labor productivity is real GDP per hour of work. It
is calculated by dividing real GDP by aggregate labor
hours. That is, labor productivity equals Y divided by N.

Labor productivity determines how much income
an hour of labor generates. Figure 27.4 shows labor productivity for the period 1960–1996. You can see in this
figure that productivity growth was most rapid during
the 1960s and that it slowed down in 1973. You can also
see that it speeded up again after 1983, but not to the
pace of the 1960s.

Why did productivity grow fastest during the
1960s? Why did it slow down during the 1970s and
then speed up again during the 1980s? Growth
accounting answers these questions by dividing the

FIGURE 27.4
Real GDP per Hour of Work

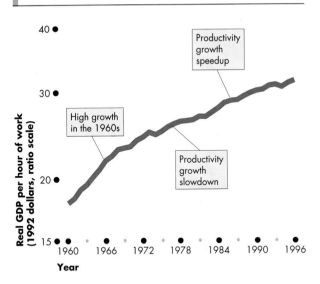

Real GDP divided by aggregate hours equals real GDP per
hour of work, which is a broad measure of productivity.
During the 1960s, the productivity growth rate was high. It
slowed during the 1970s and speeded up again after 1983.

Sources: U.S. Department of Commerce, *National Income and Product Accounts of
the United States* (Washington, D.C.: U.S. Government Printing Office); U.S.
Department of Labor, *Current Population Survey* (Washington, D.C.: U.S.
Government Printing Office).

growth in labor productivity into two components
and then measuring the contribution of each. The
components are:

■ Growth in capital per hour of work
■ Technological change

Technological change includes everything that
contributes to labor productivity growth that is not
included in growth in capital per hour. In particular,
it includes human capital growth. Human capital
growth and technological change are intimately
related. Technology advances because knowledge
advances. And knowledge is part of human capital.
So "technological change" is a broad catchall concept.

The analytical engine of growth accounting is a
relationship called the productivity function. Let's
learn about this relationship and see how it is used.

The Productivity Function

The **productivity function** is a relationship that shows how real GDP per hour of labor changes as the amount of capital per hour of labor changes with a given state of technology. Figure 27.5 illustrates the productivity function. Capital per hour of work is measured on the *x*-axis, and real GDP per hour of work is measured on the *y*-axis. The figure shows *two* productivity functions. One is the curve labeled PF_0, and the other is the curve labeled PF_1.

An increase in the quantity of capital per hour of labor increases real GDP per hour of labor, which is shown by a movement along a productivity function. For example, on PF_0, when capital per hour of labor is $30, real GDP per hour of labor is $20. If capital per hour of labor increases to $60, real GDP per hour of labor increases to $25.

Technological change increases the amount of GDP per hour of labor that can be produced by a given amount of capital per hour of labor. It is shown by an upward shift of the productivity function. For example, if capital per hour of work is $30 and a technological change increases real GDP per hour of work from $20 to $25, the productivity function shifts upward from PF_0 to PF_1 in Fig. 27.5. Similarly, if capital per hour of work is $60, the same technological change increases real GDP per hour of work from $25 to $32 and shifts the productivity function upward from PF_0 to PF_1.

To calculate the contributions of capital growth and technological change to productivity growth, we need to know the shape and slope of the productivity function. The shape of the productivity function reflects a fundamental economic law—the law of diminishing returns. The **law of diminishing returns** states that as the quantity of one input increases with the quantities of all other inputs remaining the same, output increases but by ever smaller increments. For example, in a factory that has a given amount of capital, as more labor is hired, production increases. But each *additional* hour of labor produces less *additional* output than the previous hour produced. Two typists working with one computer type fewer than twice as many pages per day as one typist working with one computer.

Applied to capital, the law of diminishing returns states that if a given number of hours of labor use more capital (with the same technology), the *additional* output that results from the *additional* capital gets smaller as the amount of capital increases. One typist working with two computers types fewer than

FIGURE 27.5

How Productivity Grows

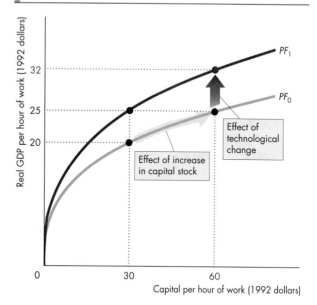

Productivity is measured by real GDP per hour of work, and it can grow for two reasons: (1) Capital per hour of work increases, and (2) technological advances occur. The productivity function, PF_0, shows the effects of an increase in capital per hour of work on productivity. Here, when capital per hour of work increases from $30 to $60, real GDP per hour of work increases from $20 to $25 along the productivity curve PF_0. Technological advance shifts the productivity function upward. Here, an advance in technology shifts the productivity function from PF_0 to PF_1. With this technological advance, real GDP per hour of work increases from $25 to $32 when there is $60 of capital per hour of work.

twice as many pages per day as one typist working with one computer. More generally, one hour of labor working with $60 of capital produces less than twice the output of one hour of labor working with $30 of capital. But how much less? The answer is given by the *one third rule*.

The One Third Rule   Robert Solow of MIT estimated a production function from U.S. data. He discovered that on the average, with no change in technology, a 1 percent increase in capital per hour of labor brings a *one third of 1 percent* increase in real GDP per hour of labor. This one third rule is used to calculate the contributions of an increase in capital per hour of work and technological change to the growth of real GDP. Let's do such a calculation.

Suppose that capital per hour of work grows by 3 percent a year and real GDP per hour of work grows by 2.5 percent a year. The one third rule tells us that capital growth has contributed one third of 3 percent, which is 1 percent. The rest of the 2.5 percent growth of real GDP comes from technological change. That is, technological change has contributed 1.5 percent, which is the 2.5 percent growth of real GDP per hour of work minus the estimated 1 percent contribution of capital growth.

Accounting for the Productivity Growth Slowdown and Speedup

We can use the one third rule to study U.S. productivity growth and the productivity growth slowdown. Figure 27.6 tells the story, starting in 1960.

1960 to 1973 In 1960, capital per hour of work was $49 and real GDP per hour of work was $18 at the point marked 60 on PF_0. During the next 13 years, real GDP per hour of work expanded by 39 percent to $25. At the same time, capital per hour of work increased by 24 percent to $61. With no change in technology, the economy would have moved to point a on PF_0 in Fig. 27.6, where real GDP per hour of work has increased by 8 percent ($1/3$ of 24 percent). But rapid technological change shifted the productivity curve upward to PF_1, and the economy moved to the point marked 73 on that curve.

1973 to 1983 During the 10 years from 1973 to 1983, real GDP per hour of work expanded by 8 percent to $27. At the same time, capital per hour of work increased by 15 percent to $70. With no change in technology, the economy would have moved to point b on PF_1 in Fig. 27.6, where real GDP per hour of work has increased by 5 percent ($1/3$ of 15 percent). But a tiny amount of technological change shifted the productivity curve upward to PF_2, and the economy moved to the point marked 83 on that curve.

We've now isolated the reason for the productivity growth slowdown. It occurred because the contribution of technological change to real GDP growth slowed.

1983 to 1995 During the 12 years from 1983 to 1996, real GDP per hour of work expanded by 18.5 percent to $32. At the same time, capital per hour of work increased by 11 percent to $78. With no change

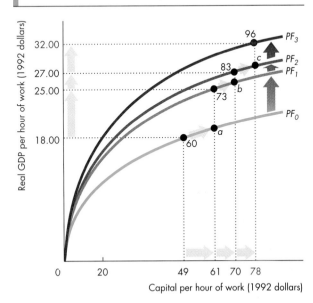

FIGURE 27.6

Growth Accounting and the Productivity Growth Slowdown

Between 1960 and 1973, which was a period of rapid productivity growth, capital per hour of work increased from $49 to $61, and technological progress shifted the productivity function upward from PF_0 to PF_1. Between 1973 and 1983, when potential GDP grew slowly, capital per hour of work increased from $61 to $70 and the productivity function barely shifted to PF_2. The effect of technological change was offset by oil price shocks. Between 1983 and 1995, capital per hour of work increased from $70 to $78 and technological progress shifted the productivity function upward from PF_2 to PF_3. Although productivity growth was not as rapid as in the 1960s, the productivity growth rate did increase.

Sources: U.S. Department of Commerce, National Income and Product Accounts of the United States (Washington, D.C.: U.S. Government Printing Office); U.S. Department of Labor, Current Population Survey (Washington, D.C.: U.S. Government Printing Office); and the author's calculations.

in technology, the economy would have moved to point c on PF_2 in Fig. 27.6, where real GDP per hour of work has increased by 3.7 percent ($1/3$ of 11 percent). But a return of more rapid technological change shifted the productivity curve upward to PF_3, and the economy moved to the point marked 96 on that curve. Although technological change resumed, its pace was slower than during the 1960s.

Technological Change During the Productivity Growth Slowdown

Technological change did not stop during the productivity growth slowdown. On the contrary, there was a lot of it. But the technological change that occurred did not increase productivity. Instead, it was directed toward coping with two other problems. They are:

■ Energy price shocks
■ The environment

Energy Price Shocks Energy prices increased sharply in 1973–1974 and again in 1979–1980. One effect of higher energy prices was an increase in the rate at which gas-guzzling automobiles, airplanes, and heating systems were scrapped. This effect would be shown as a leftward movement along the productivity function as capital per hour of labor decreases. But another effect of increases in oil prices is that technological change is directed toward saving energy rather than enhancing productivity. For example, airplanes became more fuel efficient, but they didn't operate with smaller crews. Real GDP per gallon of fuel increased a lot, but real GDP per hour of labor increased slowly.

The Environment The 1970s saw an expansion of laws and resources devoted to protecting the environment and improving the quality of the workplace. The benefits of these actions—cleaner air and water and safer factories—are not counted as real GDP. So the growth of these benefits is not measured as part of productivity growth. If these items were included in real GDP, the productivity function would have shifted upward during the 1970s and the growth slowdown would have been less severe.

R E V I E W

■ Growth accounting isolates the contributions of capital growth and technological change to productivity growth by using the *one third* rule—a 1 percent increase in capital per hour of work brings a one third of 1 percent increase in real GDP per hour of work.

■ The productivity growth slowdown of the 1970s occurred because technological change made almost no contribution to productivity growth.

Growth Theory

WE'VE SEEN THAT REAL GDP GROWS WHEN THE quantities of labor and capital grow and when technology (which includes human capital) advances. Does this mean that the growth of labor and capital and technological advances *cause* economic growth? It might. But there are other possibilities. *One* of these factors might be the cause of real GDP growth and the others the *effect*. We must try to discover how the influences on economic growth interact with each other to make some economies grow quickly and others grow slowly. And we must probe the reasons why a country's long-term growth rate sometimes speeds up and sometimes slows.

We're going to look at three theories of economic growth. All three theories contain some germs of truth—some fundamental insights into the process of economic growth. But none gives a firm and sure answer to the basic questions of what causes growth and makes growth rates vary. The three theories are:

■ Classical growth theory
■ Neoclassical growth theory
■ New growth theory

Classical Growth Theory

Classical growth theory is the view that real GDP growth is temporary and that when real GDP per person rises above the subsistence level, a population explosion eventually brings real GDP per person back to the subsistence level. Adam Smith, Thomas Robert Malthus, and David Ricardo, the leading economists of the late eighteenth century and early nineteenth century, were the first to suggest this theory, but the theory is most closely associated with the name of Malthus and is sometimes called the *Malthusian theory*.

Many people today are Malthusians. They point to the world population explosion—5 billion today and (they predict) 11 billion by 2200—and speculate that we will run out of resources and return to a primitive standard of living if we do not take action to contain the population growth.

To understand classical growth theory, let's transport ourselves back to the world of 1776, when Adam Smith is first explaining the idea. Most of the 2.5 million people who live in the newly independent

United States of America work on farms or on their own land and perform their tasks using simple tools and animal power. They earn about 2 shillings (a little less than $12 dollars in today's money) for working a ten-hour day. Then advances in farming technology bring new types of plows and seeds that increase farm productivity. As farm productivity increases, farm production increases and some farm workers move from the land to the cities, where they get work producing and selling the expanding range of farm equipment. Incomes rise, and the people seem to be prospering. But will the prosperity last? Classical growth theory says it will not.

Figure 27.7 illustrates the start of growth according to the classical growth theory. Before growth begins, the economy is in the situation shown in the figure. The labor demand curve is LD_0, and the labor supply curve is LS_0. There is equilibrium in the labor market: The quantity of labor demanded equals the quantity supplied at a real wage rate of 2 shillings a day, and 2 million people are employed. (We will use constant 1776 prices in this example to keep it in its historical context.)

Advances in technology—in both agriculture and industry—lead to investment in new capital, which makes labor more productive. More and more businesses start up and try to hire the now more productive labor. So the demand for labor increases and the labor demand curve shifts rightward to LD_1. With this greater demand for labor, the real wage rate rises to 4 shillings a day, and this higher wage rate brings an increase in the quantity of labor supplied (a movement along the labor supply curve). In the new situation, 3 million people are employed.

At this stage, economic growth has occurred and everyone has benefited from it. Real GDP has increased, and the real wage rate has increased. But the classical economists believe that this new situation can't last because it will induce a population explosion.

Classical Theory of Population Growth   The classical theory of population growth is based on the idea of a subsistence real wage rate. The **subsistence real wage rate** is the minimum real wage rate needed to maintain life. By its definition, if the actual real wage rate is less than the subsistence real wage rate, some people cannot survive and the population decreases. But in classical theory, whenever the real wage rate exceeds the subsistence real wage rate, the population grows. This assumption, combined with diminishing returns to labor, has a very dismal implication—one that resulted in economics being called the *dismal science*. This implication is that no matter how much investment and technological change occurs, real wage rates are always pushed back toward the subsistence level.

Figure 27.8 shows this process. Here, the subsistence real wage rate is (by assumption) 2 shillings a day. The actual real wage rate, at the intersection of LS_0 and LD_1, is 4 shillings a day. Because the actual real wage rate exceeds the subsistence real wage rate, the population grows and the labor supply increases. The labor supply curve shifts rightward to LS_1. As it does so, the real wage rate falls and the quantity of labor demanded increases. Eventually, in the absence of further technological change, the economy comes to rest at the subsistence real wage rate of 2 shillings a day, and 5 million people are employed.

FIGURE 27.7
Classical Growth Begins

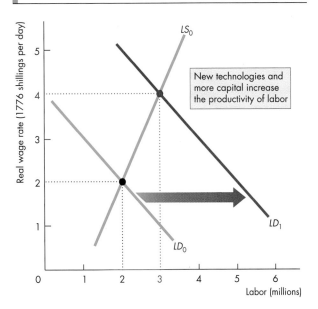

Initially, the demand for labor is LD_0, and the supply of labor is LS_0. There are 2 million people employed, and they earn 2 shillings (1776 shillings) a day. An advance in technology and an increase in capital increase the productivity of labor, and the demand for labor increases to LD_1. The real wage rate rises to 4 shillings a day, and the quantity of labor supplied increases to 3 million.

FIGURE 27.8

A Dismal Outcome

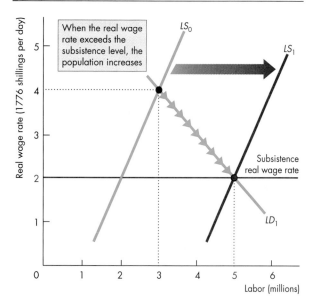

When the real wage rate is above the subsistence real wage rate, which in this example is 2 shillings a day, the population begins to increase. With an increase in population the supply of labor increases, and the labor supply curve shifts rightward to LS_1. As it does so, the real wage rate falls and the quantity of labor employed increases. The population stops growing when the real wage rate is back at the subsistence level.

The economy has grown, real GDP has increased, but a larger population is earning only the subsistence real wage rate.

The Modern Theory of Population Growth

When the classical economists were developing their ideas about population growth, a population explosion was under way. In Britain and other Western European countries, improvements in diet and hygiene had lowered the death rate while the birth rate remained high. For several decades, population growth was extremely rapid. For example, after being relatively stable for several centuries, the population of Britain increased by 40 percent between 1750 and 1800 and by a further 50 percent between 1800 and 1830. At the same time, an estimated 1 million people (about 20 percent of the 1750 population) left Britain for America and Australia before 1800, and

outward migration continued on a similar scale through the nineteenth century. Population growth on this scale alarmed Malthus and the other classical economists and was the empirical basis for their theory of population growth.

But eventually, the birth rate fell, and while the population continued to increase, its rate of increase was moderate. This slowdown in the population growth rate seemed to make the classical theory increasingly less relevant. It also eventually led to the development of a modern economic theory of population growth.

The population growth rate is influenced by economic factors. Key among them is the opportunity cost of women's time. As women's wage rates have increased and their job opportunities have expanded, the opportunity cost of having children has increased. Faced with a higher opportunity cost, families have chosen to have a smaller number of children and the birth rate has fallen. Also, the death rate has fallen as greater investment has been made in advances in medicine.

If there is a connection between income levels and population growth, it is the opposite of that feared by the classical economists. As incomes rise, the population growth rate falls. This historical trend not only contradicts the views of the classical economists but it also calls into question the modern doomsday conclusion that we will be one day swamped with too many people for the planet to feed.

But despite the influence of economic factors on population growth, the influence is weak. And to a good approximation, the rate of population growth is independent of the rate of economic growth.

Neoclassical Growth Theory

Neoclassical growth theory is the proposition that that real GDP per person grows because technological change induces saving and investment. Technological change is the fundamental cause of growth. Robert Solow of MIT suggested this theory during the 1950s. In the neoclassical theory, the rate of technological change influences the rate of economic growth, but economic growth does not influence the pace of technological change. It is assumed that technological change results from chance. When we get lucky, we have rapid technological change, and when bad luck strikes, the pace of technological advance slows.

At the heart of the neoclassical growth theory is the stock of capital per unit of labor and the *productivity function*—the relationship between capital per unit of labor and output per unit of labor. To keep things as simple as possible, the theory assumes that people work a fixed number of hours and that everyone works. So labor equals population. Also, the population grows at a constant rate. The model then can concentrate on the effects of technological change on saving, investment, and real GDP per person.

Zero Growth   Suppose that initially real GDP per person is constant. The quantity of capital is worth $10 trillion (1992 dollars). Each year, 10 percent of the capital stock wears out and is replaced. Investment and saving are $1 trillion. This amount is just sufficient to replace capital that wears out, so the quantity of capital remains constant at $10 trillion. With a constant labor force (which we are assuming), constant capital, and no technological change, real GDP is constant. There is no growth in this economy.

Saving and Investment   Figure 27.9 shows the investment demand curve and saving supply in the economy we've just described. (For a refresher on investment demand and saving supply, check back to Chapter 26, pp. 569–574.) The downward-sloping investment demand curve is ID_0. Along this curve, as the real interest rate falls, other things remaining the same, investment increases. The upward-sloping saving supply curve is SS_0. Along this curve, as the real interest rate rises, other things remaining the same, the supply of saving increases.

The real interest rate adjusts to achieve equilibrium. In Fig. 27.9, on ID_0 and SS_0, investment equals saving at a real interest rate of 4 percent a year with saving and investment equal to $1 trillion.

A Technological Advance   Now suppose that a technological advance occurs. This advance increases the productivity of capital and increases the expected profit rate. So businesses increase their investment demand. The investment demand curve shifts rightward to ID_1. The greater investment demand raises the real interest rate to 6 percent a year, and the higher real interest rate brings forth an increase in saving—a movement along the saving supply curve SS_0. Investment increases to $1.5 trillion.

Real GDP per person is now growing. Investment exceeds the amount needed to replace capital

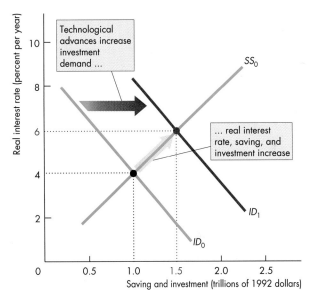

FIGURE 27.9

Neoclassical Growth Begins

In neoclassical growth theory, economic growth results from technological change. Initially, investment demand is ID_0 and saving supply is SS_0. Investment is $1 trillion a year, and the real interest rate is 4 percent a year. This investment level replaces worn out capital and the quantity of capital is constant, so real GDP is also constant. A technological advance increases expected profits and increases investment demand. Investment demand increases to ID_1. The real interest rate rises to 6 percent a year, and investment increases to $1.5 trillion. As a result, the quantity of capital and real GDP begin to grow.

that is wearing out, so the quantity of capital increases. And with an increasing quantity of capital, real GDP increases.

Saving and Investment in the Growing Economy   Now that real GDP is growing, rising disposable income and a rising capital stock induce changes in saving and investment—cause shifts in the saving supply curve and the investment demand curve.

We cannot keep track of all these changes by using the investment demand–saving supply figure. Instead, we look at the demand for the entire stock of capital and the supply of the stock of capital. (Investment demand is the demand for *newly produced* capital in a given time period. Saving supply is the supply of funds to buy newly produced capital in a given time period.)

Figure 27.10 shows the demand for the stock of capital KD_0. This demand curve slopes downward. The lower the real interest rate, the greater is the quantity of capital demanded.

At a given moment, the supply of capital is given. It is the vertical line KS_0. In the long run, the supply of capital depends on saving decision. The neoclassical theory holds that if the real interest rate exceeds a target rate, the supply of capital increases; if the real interest rate is less that a target rate, the supply of capital decreases; and if the real interest rate equals a target rate, the supply of capital is constant. In Fig. 27.10, the target real interest rate is 4 percent a year and the long-run capital supply curve is LKS.

Initially, equilibrium is at point *a*, where KD_0 and KS_0 intersect and where the real interest rate is 4 percent a year—its target rate. The capital stock is $10 trillion. Neoclassical growth begins from this point.

A technological advance now increases the productivity of capital and the demand for capital curve shifts rightward to KD_1. The expected rate of profit increases, which brings an increase in investment demand (shown in Fig. 27.9). With higher investment, the supply of capital increases and the KS curve begins to shift rightward. As it does so, the real interest rate falls.

Zero Growth Again

The capital stock continues to increase and the real interest rate continues to fall until the economy reaches point *b* in Fig. 27.10. Here the real interest rate is back at its long-run target rate of 4 percent a year and the capital stock has grown to $20 trillion. With no further capital growth, real GDP stops growing, and in the absence of another technological advance, growth has ended. In this new zero-growth situation, investment and saving are $2 trillion—just sufficient to replace 10 percent of the larger capital stock that wears out each year.

Throughout the process you've just studied, real GDP grows, but the growth rate gradually decreases and eventually growth ends. Ongoing exogenous technology advances are constantly increasing the demand for capital, raising the real interest rate, and inducing saving. The process that we've just examined repeats as long as technology advances, creating an ongoing process of long-term economic growth. The growth rate fluctuates because technological progress occurs at a variable rate.

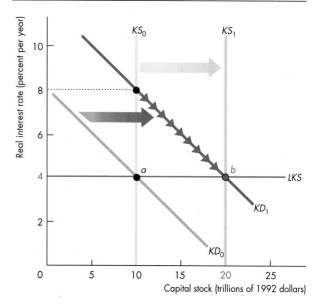

FIGURE 27.10

Neoclassical Growth Ends

The demand for the stock of capital initially is KD_0. The capital stock is fixed in the short run and initially is KS_0. The long-run supply of capital is LKS. A technological advance increases the productivity of capital and increases the demand for capital to KD_1. The real interest rate rises. But so do investment and saving. The capital stock also increases. As the capital stock increases, the KS curve shifts rightward toward KS_1. The real interest rate falls. When the real interest rate has fallen to its long-run target rate, the supply of capital stops increasing, the capital stock is constant at $20 trillion, and growth ends.

Problem with Neoclassical Growth Theory

All economies have access to the same technologies, and capital is free to roam the globe seeking the highest available rate of return. So neoclassical growth theory implies that growth rates and income levels per person around the globe converge. While there is some sign of convergence among the rich countries (shown in Fig. 27.2a), convergence is slow and it does not appear to be imminent for all countries (as we saw in Fig. 27.2b).

New growth theory attempts to overcome this shortcoming of neoclassical growth theory. It also attempts to explain how the rate of technological change is determined.

New Growth Theory

New growth theory holds that real GDP per person grows because of the choices that people make in the pursuit of profit and that growth can persist indefinitely.

The theory begins with two facts about market economies:

- Discoveries result from choices and actions.
- Discoveries bring profit, and competition destroys profit.

Discoveries and Choices   When people discover a new product or technique, they think of themselves as being lucky. They are right. But the pace at which new discoveries are made—the pace at which technology advances—is not determined by chance. It depends on how many people are looking for a new technology and how intensively they are looking.

Discoveries and Profits   Profit is the spur to technological change. The forces of competition squeeze profits, so to increase profit, people constantly seek either lower-cost methods of production or new and better products for which people are willing to pay a higher price. Inventors can maintain a profit for several years by taking out a patent or copyright. But eventually, a new discovery is copied and profits disappear.

Two further facts play a key role in the new growth theory:

- Discoveries can be used by many people at the same time.
- Physical activities can be replicated.

Discoveries Used by All   Once a profitable new discovery has been made, everyone can use it. And one person's use of a new discovery does not prevent others from using it. This fact means that as the benefits of a new discovery spread, free resources become available. These resources are free because nothing is given up when they are used. They have a zero opportunity cost.

Replicating Activities   Production activities can be replicated. For example, there might be two, three, or fifty-three identical firms making fiber-optic cable using an identical assembly line and production technique. If one firm increases output, that firm experiences diminishing returns. But the economy can increase the output of fiber-optic cable by adding another identical factory, and the economy does not experience diminishing returns.

The implication of this simple and appealing idea is astonishing. Unlike neoclassical theory, with its diminishing returns to capital, which eventually lowers the real interest rate to the target real interest rate, new growth theory has no such mechanism. Real GDP per person increases and does so indefinitely as long as people can undertake research and development that yields a higher return than the target real interest rate.

New growth theory sees the economy as a kind of perpetual motion mechanism. Economic growth is driven by our insatiable wants that lead us to pursue profit and innovate. The result of this process is new and better products. But new and better products result in new firms starting up and old firms going out of business. In this process, jobs are created and destroyed. The outcome is new and better jobs, more leisure, and more consumption. All this adds up to a higher standard of living. But our insatiable wants are still there, so the process continues, going round and round a circle of wants, profits, innovation, new products, and higher living standards.

The growth rate depends on people's ability to innovate and the rate of return to innovation. Over the years, this ability has changed. The invention of language and writing (the two most basic human capital tools), and later the development of the scientific method and the establishment of universities and research institutions, brought a huge increase in the rate of return to innovation. Today, a deeper understanding of genes is bringing profit in a growing biotechnology industry. And astonishing advances in computer technology are creating an explosion of profit opportunities in a wide range of new information age industries.

Figure 27.11 shows how the new growth theory works. Like Fig. 27.10, it shows the demand for and supply of the *stock* of capital. But unlike Fig. 27.10, here the marginal product of capital does not diminish as the quantity of capital increases. The demand curve for capital is horizontal at the real interest rate equal to the expected rate of profit.

The supply of capital is fixed in the short run and is shown by a vertical supply curve such as KS_0. The long-run capital supply curve is horizontal at the target real interest rate and is LKS.

Initially, the rate of return on capital is 2 percent a year, so the demand for capital is shown by the line KD_0 in Fig. 27.11. This rate of return is below the

FIGURE 27.11
New Growth Theory

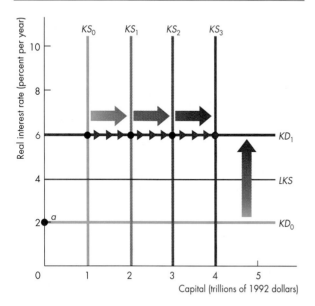

In new growth theory, economic growth results from technological change. The returns to capital do not diminish, and growth proceeds indefinitely. Initially, the rate of return on capital is 2 percent a year and the demand for capital is KD_0. The stock of capital is zero, and the economy is stuck at point a. The development of the scientific method increases the rate of return on capital to 6 percent a year and the demand for capital increases to KD_1. With a real interest rate greater than the target real interest rate, saving increases and the supply of capital increases. The capital supply curve shifts rightward successively through KS_1, KS_2, KS_3, and so on. As capital grows, real GDP grows but the real interest rate does not fall because there are no diminishing returns. Real GDP growth continues indefinitely.

target real interest rate, so no one has an incentive to save. The economy is stuck at point a.

The development of basic human capital tools such as mathematics and physics increases the return to capital and innovation and the demand for capital curve shifts upward to KD_1. The return to saving and investment now exceeds the target real interest rate. So investment and saving increase and the quantity of capital grows. As it does so, the supply of capital curve shifts rightward through KS_1, KS_2, KS_3, and so on. The capital stock grows, real GDP grows, and the rate of return on capital does not diminish.

Economic growth continues indefinitely as long as the real interest rate exceeds the target real interest rate.

Figure 27.11 shows the process we've just described. The target real interest rate is 4 percent a year, and the rate of return on capital is 6 percent a year. With positive saving, the capital supply curve shifts rightward indefinitely. The speed with which it shifts rightward depends on the extent to which the real interest rate exceeds the target real interest rate. The higher the real return on capital, the more the real interest rate exceeds that target real interest rate, and the faster the capital supply curve shifts rightward. So the faster the economy grows.

Sorting Out the Theories

Which theory is correct? Probably none is exactly correct. But they all teach us something of value. The classical theory reminds us that our physical resources are limited and that with no advances in technology, we must eventually hit diminishing returns. Neoclassical theory reaches essentially the same conclusion, but not because of a population explosion. Instead, it emphasizes potentially diminishing returns to capital and reminds us that we cannot necessarily keep growth going just by accumulating capital. New growth theory emphasizes the possible capacity of human resources to innovate at a pace that offsets diminishing returns.

R E V I E W

- Economic growth arises from increases in the capital stock, and advances in technology (which includes improvements in human capital).
- In classical growth theory, population explosions keep returning real GDP per person to the subsistence level because of diminishing returns to labor.
- In neoclassical growth theory, growth results from technological advances determined by chance.
- In new growth theory, the pursuit of profit brings persistent innovation and increased capital does not bring diminishing returns.

Your final task in this chapter is to examine the policy actions that might be taken to speed up the growth rate.

Achieving Faster Growth

To ACHIEVE FASTER ECONOMIC GROWTH, WE MUST either increase the growth rate of capital per hour of work or increase the pace of technological advance (which includes improving human capital).

The main suggestions for achieving these objectives are:

■ Stimulate saving
■ Stimulate research and development
■ Target high-technology industries
■ Encourage international trade
■ Improve the quality of education

Stimulate Saving   Saving finances investment, which brings capital accumulation and economic growth. So stimulating saving can stimulate economic growth. China, Hong Kong, Japan, Korea, Singapore, and Taiwan have the highest growth rates. They also have the highest saving rates. Some countries of Africa have the lowest growth rates. They also have the lowest saving rates. The saving rates in the United States and the other rich countries are modest.

The most obvious way in which saving could be increased is by providing tax incentives. Some incentives already exist, but more effective measures are possible. For example, instead of taxing incomes (which means taxing both consumption and saving), we could tax only consumption. Such a tax would encourage additional saving and most likely increase the economy's growth rate.

Stimulate Research and Development   Patents protect inventors and provide incomes that give incentives to research and development. But everyone can use the fruits of *basic* research and development efforts. For example, VisiCalc invented the basic idea of the spreadsheet. It did not take long for Lotus Corporation to use this idea and create the famous and immensely productive 1-2-3. And soon after, Microsoft Corporation created a Lotus 1-2-3 look-alike, Excel. Because basic inventions can be copied, the inventor's profit is limited, and the resources that a firm will allocate to making an invention or innovation are also limited. For this reason, the free market allocates too few resources to basic research.

This situation is one in which government subsidies might help. By using public funds to finance basic research and development that bring public benefits, it might be possible to encourage an efficient level of research. However, this solution is not fool-proof. The main problem is that some mechanism must be designed for allocating the public funds. At present, universities and public research institutions such as NASA are the main channels through which public funds get used to finance research.

Target High-Technology Industries   Some people argue that by providing public funds to high-technology firms and industries, a country can become the first to exploit a new technology and can earn above-average profits for a period while others are busy catching up. This strategy is risky and just as likely to use resources inefficiently as to speed growth.

Encourage International Trade   Free international trade stimulates growth by extracting all the available gains from specialization and exchange. It is no accident that the fastest-growing nations today are those with the fastest-growing international trade—both exports and imports.

Improve the Quality of Education   Education, like basic research, brings benefits beyond those valued by the people who receive the education. And by its nature, education is a good the value of which people only appreciate fully *after* receiving it. So the free market produces too little education. By funding basic education and by ensuring high standards in basic skills such as language, mathematics, and science, governments can contribute to a nation's growth potential. Education can also be stimulated and improved by using tax incentives to encourage an increased scale of private provision.

◆ Economic growth is the single most decisive factor in influencing a country's living standard, but it is not the only one. Another is the extent to which the country fully employs its scarce resources, especially its labor. In recent years, the United States has enjoyed full employment and steady growth. But the business cycle is almost certainly not dead. And unemployment has become a severe problem for many countries. In Part 9, we study the fluctuations of real GDP and employment and unemployment around their long-term trends. But before embarking on this new topic, take a look at *Reading Between the Lines* on pages 604–605 and see how the Internet is contributing to the growth of our economy today.

Growth in the Virtual Economy

The Wall Street Journal, October 17, 1996

The Internet Economy

BY TAKUMA AMANO AND
ROBERT BLOHM

Belying the pessimism of limits-to-growth advocates, the U.S. economy grew at a seemingly robust annualized rate of 4.8% in this year's second quarter despite frequently reported downsizings or restructurings of U.S. corporations—even causing the Federal Reserve Board to consider tightening monetary policy. This healthy economic growth and a declining unemployment rate haven't been accompanied by inflationary pressure; the most recent annual increase of the producer price index was just 2.6%.

While President Clinton takes credit for this happy turn of events, and Bob Dole pooh-poohs it, what both men overlook is that the single most important factor behind this economic performance is the Internet. Conceived by the Defense Department in the mid-1960s and beefed up by the Reagan administration to provide massive computing capability for Star Wars and backup in case of war, the Internet was accessible until the end of the 1980s only by a limited number of government and academic users.

With the end of the Cold War, the advantages of the Internet for individual users soon became apparent and a new products market developed—both for Internet access, browsers and search and directory guides, such as Netscape and Yahoo!, and for computer networking equipment, like the electronic message switching systems and routers of Cisco Systems Inc. ...

Beyond the development of physical capital, there is also the development of metaphysical capital ... in the form of the new entrepreneurial talent being created by folks whose creative lives have become enmeshed in the Web. Once, a substantial percentage of young graduates with degrees in science and engineering would start their careers in defense-related industries. Now many go directly into young software and hardware companies.

The Internet market represents a successful shift of this country's most important economic resource—the human brain—to the highest value-added sector of the economy, demonstrating the optimum resource allocation inherent in our free market. ...

Barring another oil crisis, or excessive government spending, the Internet market will continue pushing the U.S. economy into a growth era qualitatively different from the past ...

Essence of THE STORY

- During the second quarter of 1996, the Internet was the single most important source of strong U.S. economic growth.

- A few years ago, new science and engineering graduates found jobs in defense-related industries. Today, many get jobs in the computer industry.

- The market economy is moving human capital to its highest-valued use.

- The Internet will move the U.S. economy into a new growth era.

Economic

A N A L Y S I S

■ The growth of the Internet and the World Wide Web has been remarkable.

■ Figure 1 shows this growth. Measured by the number of host computers, the Internet grew from 1.3 million hosts at the end of 1992 to 9.5 million at the end of 1995, a growth rate of 5.7 percent *per month*.

■ The World Wide Web has grown even faster, from nothing in 1993 to more than half a million sites at the end of 1996, a growth rate of 22.7 percent *per month*! At this growth rate, the Web more than doubles in size every three months.

■ The news article says that the growth of the Internet is the main source of economic growth in the United States. But this claim is probably too strong. Let's see why.

■ Figure 2 shows real GDP from 1986 to 1996. The growth rate of real GDP was 2.19 percent a year between 1986 and 1992 (before the Web). It was 2.45 percent a year between 1993 and 1996 (after the Web).

■ Although real GDP growth increased slightly after 1993, there is no sign

that potential GDP growth increased. It might have done, but it is too early to tell because of the business cycle. In 1992, the economy was still recovering from the 1990–1991 recession and the unemployment rate was more than 7 percent. By 1996, the unemployment rate had fallen to 5.5 percent. We will not be able to say whether the *growth rate* of potential GDP has increased until we can see the current business cycle in a longer-term perspective.

■ Although we cannot determine whether the *growth rate* of potential GDP growth has increased, it is undeniable that the Internet has had a positive effect on the *level* of potential GDP.

■ The new technologies that are making the Internet grow are available for everyone to use. The opportunity cost of using these technologies is low.

■ Also, these forms of capital probably are not yet experiencing diminishing returns and perhaps will not do so for a long time.

■ It is possible that these new technologies have increased the rate of profit. If they have done so,

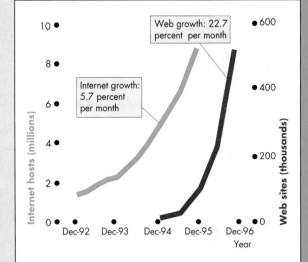

Figure 1 Growth of the Internet

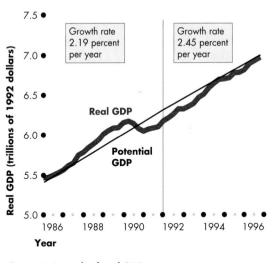

Figure 2 Growth of real GDP

they might have created a new growth environment in which the U.S. economy will expand at a more rapid rate than previously.

■ The evidence is not yet present in the GDP data. But real GDP growth might understate the true growth rate.

SUMMARY

Key Points

Long-Term Growth Trends (pp. 588–590)

- Between 1896 to 1996, real GDP per person in the United States grew at an average rate of 2 percent a year. Growth was fastest during the 1920s and 1960s.

- The real GDP gaps between the United States and Africa as well as Central and South America have widened. The gaps between the United States and Hong Kong, Korea, Taiwan, and China have narrowed.

The Causes of Economic Growth: A First Look (pp. 591–592)

- Economic growth occurs when an *incentive* system, which is created by markets, property rights, and monetary exchange, encourages saving, investment in physical and human capital, and the discovery of new technologies.

Growth Accounting (pp. 593–596)

- Growth accounting measures the contributions of capital accumulation and technological change to productivity growth.

- Growth accounting uses the productivity function and the *one third rule*: a 1 percent increase in capital per hour of work brings a one third of 1 percent increase in real GDP per hour of work.

- During the productivity growth slowdown of the 1970s, technological change made almost no contribution to real GDP growth.

Growth Theory (pp. 596–602)

- In classical theory, when the real wage rate exceeds the *subsistence* real wage rate, a population explosion brings diminishing returns to labor and real GDP per person returns to the subsistence level.

- In neoclassical growth theory, when the capital stock increases, the return to capital diminishes. Without technological change, growth ends.

- In new growth theory, the growth rate depends on the benefits and costs of developing new technologies.

- In new growth theory, the return to capital does not diminish when the capital stock increases.

Achieving Faster Growth (p. 603)

- To achieve faster economic growth, we must increase the growth of capital per hour of work or increase the pace of technological advance.

- It might be possible to achieve faster growth by stimulating saving, subsidizing research and development, targeting (and possibly subsidizing) high-technology industries, and encouraging more international trade and more education.

Key Figures

Key Terms

<table>
<tr><td colspan="2">

QUESTIONS

</td></tr>
</table>

<table>
<tr><td>

PROBLEMS

</td></tr>
</table>

1. What was the average growth rate of real GDP per person in the United States between 1896 and 1996?

2. Which countries have grown fastest and which have grown slowest?

3. Have levels of real GDP per person across countries converged?

4. What are the three necessary preconditions for economic growth to occur?

5. What three activities can create ongoing economic growth?

6. Explain how economic growth can occur even in the absence of investment and new technologies.

7. What is growth accounting?

8. What is the main concept used in growth accounting?

9. How are the effects of capital accumulation and technological change separated by growth accounting techniques?

10. What is the one third rule and how is it used?

11. Explain the main sources of economic growth in the United States.

12. What were the main sources of the productivity growth slowdown in the United States during the 1970s?

13. Why did technological advances not increase productivity during the 1970s?

14. What are the main theories of economic growth?

15. What are the key assumptions of classical growth theory?

16. What are the key assumptions of neoclassical growth theory?

17. What are the key assumptions of new growth theory?

18. Contrast neoclassical growth theory and new growth theory.

19. What are the main policy actions that governments might take to increase the growth rate?

1. The following information has been discovered about the economy of Longland: The economy's productivity function is:

Capital per hour of work (1992 dollars per hour)	Real GDP per hour of work (1992 dollars per hour)
10	3.80
20	5.40
30	6.80
40	8.00
50	9.00
60	9.80
70	10.40
80	10.80

Does this economy conform to the one third rule? If so, explain why. If not, explain why not and also explain what rule, if any, it does conform to.

2. The figure illustrates the productivity function of Lotus Land in 1989 and 1996.

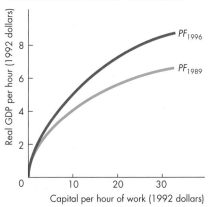

In 1989, capital per hour of work was $10, and in 1996 it was $25.

a. Does Lotus Land experience diminishing returns? Explain why or why not.

b. Use growth accounting to find the contribution of the change in capital between 1989 and 1996 to the growth of productivity in Lotus Land.

c. Use growth accounting to find the contribution of technological change between 1989 and 1996 to the growth of productivity in Lotus Land.

🖥 3. The following information has been discovered about the economy of Cape Despair. The subsistence real wage rate is $7 an hour. When the real wage rate rises above this level, the population grows; and when the real wage rate falls below this level, the population falls. With its current population, the demand and supply schedules for labor in Cape Despair are:

Real wage rate (1992 dollars per hour)	Quantity of labor demanded (billions of hours per year)	Quantity of labor supplied (billions of hours per year)
3	8	4
5	7	5
7	6	6
9	5	7
11	4	8
13	3	9
15	2	10
17	1	11

Initially, the labor force of Cape Despair is constant, and the real wage is at its subsistence level. Then a technological advance increases the amount that firms are willing to pay for labor by $2 at each level of employment.

a. What are the initial level of employment and real wage rate in Cape Despair?

b. What happens to the real wage rate immediately following the technological advance?

c. What happens to the population growth rate following the technological advance?

d. What is the employment level when Cape Despair returns to a long-run equilibrium?

4. Martha's Island is an economy that behaves according to the neoclassical growth model. The target real interest rate on capital is 3 percent a year. A technological advance increases the demand for capital and raises the interest rate to 5 percent a year. Describe what happens on Martha's Island.

🖥 5. Romeria is a country that behaves according to the predictions of new growth theory. The target real interest rate on capital is 3 percent a year. A technological advance increases the demand for capital and raises the interest rate to 5 percent a year. Describe what happens in Romeria and contrast it with the events in Martha's Island.

🌐 http://hepg.awl.com/parkin/econ100

CRITICAL THINKING

1. After studying *Reading Between the Lines* on pp. 604–605, answer the following questions:

a. How quickly is the Internet growing compared with the growth of real GDP?

b. Are the measures of growth of the Internet and the World Wide Web in Fig. 1 comparable with the measure of the growth of real GDP in Fig. 2? (Think about what real GDP measures.)

c. What information would you need about Internet growth to determine how quickly its output is increasing?

d. Suppose that the Internet really does increase the growth rate of potential GDP. What, according to each of the three economic growth theories—classical, neoclassical, and new—will happen in the longer term?

e. Which of the three economic growth theories—classical, neoclassical, and new—does the author of the news article seem to believe is relevant in the United States today?

🌐 2. Visit the Penn World Table Web site (linked from the Parkin site) and obtain data on real GDP per person for the United States, China, South Africa, and Mexico since 1960.

a. Draw a graph of the data.

b. Which country has the lowest real GDP per person and which has the highest?

c. Which country has experienced the fastest growth rate since 1960 and which the slowest?

d. Explain why the growth rates in these four countries are ranked on the order you have discovered.

e. Return to the Penn World Table Web site and obtain data for four other countries that interest you. Describe and explain the patterns that you find for these countries.

3. Write a memo to your Congress member in which you set out the policies you believe the U.S. government must follow to speed up the growth rate of real GDP in the United States.

4. Is faster economic growth always a good thing? Argue the case for faster growth and for slower growth and then reach a conclusion on whether growth should be increased or decreased.

Part 9 Aggregate Demand and Inflation

Money Chasing Goods

Aggregate demand fluctuations bring recessions and expansions. If aggregate demand expands more rapidly than long-run aggregate supply, we get inflation. So understanding the forces that determine aggregate demand helps us to understand both the business cycle and inflation. ◆ It took economists a long time to achieve this knowledge, and we still don't know enough about aggregate demand to be able to forecast it more than a few months ahead. But we do know the basic factors that influence aggregate demand. And we know a lot about how those factors interact to send shock waves rippling through the economy. ◆ Fundamentally, aggregate demand is a monetary phenomenon. The quantity of money is the single most significant influence on aggregate demand. This insight was first outlined more than 200 years ago by David Hume, a Scottish philosopher and close friend of Adam Smith. Said Hume, "In every Kingdom into which money begins to flow in greater abundance than formerly, every thing takes a new face: labor and industry gain life; the merchant becomes more enterprising, the manufacturer more diligent and skilful, and even the farmer follows his plow with greater alacrity and attention." Milton Friedman and other economists known as *monetarists* also emphasize the central role of money. Money lies at the center of Keynes' theory of aggregate demand as well. But Keynes also called attention to the power of independent changes in government purchases, taxes,

and business investment to influence aggregate demand. In the modern world, we also recognize the effect of changes in exports on aggregate demand. ◆ The chapters in this part explain the factors that influence aggregate demand and help you to understand how they interact to bring multiplier effects on aggregate expenditure. Chapter 28 explains the effects of changes in business investment and the multiplier effect it has on consumption expenditure and aggregate expenditure. This chapter also explain how changes in business inventories trigger changes in production and incomes. Chapter 29 looks at fiscal policy and applies the model of Chapter 28 to study the effects of changes in government purchases and taxes. Chapter 30 brings money into the picture and explains exactly what money is and how banks create it. Chapter 31 shows you how the Fed controls the quantity of money and thereby influences interest rates and expenditure. Chapter 32 returns to the aggregate supply–aggregate demand framework and explains inflation. It shows you how the trends in inflation are determined by the trend in the money supply and how fluctuations in aggregate demand bring fluctuations in inflation, employment and unemployment. ◆ Before you begin your study of aggregate demand and inflation, we'll spend some time with Milton Friedman, an economist who has advanced our knowledge in this field. And we'll talk with one of today's leading macroeconomists, Bennett McCallum of Carnegie Mellon University.

Money and Inflation

The Economist: Milton Friedman

Milton Friedman was born into a poor immigrant family in New York City in 1912. He was an undergraduate at Rutgers and graduate student at Columbia University during the Great Depression. Today, Professor Friedman is a Senior Fellow at the Hoover Institution at Stanford University. But his reputation was built between 1946 and 1983, when he was a leading member of the "Chicago School," an approach to economics developed at the University of Chicago and based on the views that free markets allocate resources efficiently and that stable and low money supply growth delivers macroeconomic stability.

Friedman has advanced our understanding of the forces that determine aggregate demand and clarified the effects of the quantity of money. For this work, he was awarded the (much overdue in the opinion of his many admirers) 1977 Nobel Prize for Economic Science.

By reasoning from basic economic principles, Friedman predicted that persistent demand stimulation would *not* increase output but *would* cause inflation. When output growth slowed and inflation broke out in the 1970s, Friedman seemed like a prophet and, for a time, his policy prescription, known as "monetarism," was embraced around the world.

> *"Inflation is always and everywhere a monetary phenomenon."*
>
> MILTON FRIEDMAN
>
> THE COUNTER-REVOLUTION IN MONETARY THEORY

The Issues and Ideas

The combination of history and economics has taught us a lot about the causes of inflation. Severe inflation—hyperinflation—arises from a breakdown of the normal fiscal policy processes at times of war or political upheaval. Tax revenues fall short of government spending, and newly printed money fills the gap between them. As inflation increases, the quantity of money needed to make payments increases, and a shortage of money can even result. So the rate of money growth increases yet further, and prices rise yet faster. Eventually, the monetary system collapses. Such was the experience of Germany during the 1920s and Brazil during the 1990s.

In earlier times, when commodities were used as money, inflation resulted from the discovery of new sources of money. The most recent occurrence of this type of inflation was at the end of the nineteenth century when gold, then used as money, was discovered in Australia, the Klondike, and South Africa.

In modern times, inflation has resulted from increases in the money supply that has accommodated increases in costs. The most dramatic of such inflations occurred during the 1970s when the Fed and other central banks around the world accommodated oil price increases.

To avoid inflation, money supply growth must be held in check. But at times of severe cost pressure, central banks feel a strong tug in the direction of avoiding recession and accommodating the cost pressure.

Yet some countries have avoided inflation more effectively than others have. One source of success is central bank independence. In low-inflation countries such as Germany and Japan, the central bank decides how much money to create and at what level to set interest rates and does not take instructions from the government. In high-inflation countries, such as the United Kingdom and Italy, the central bank takes direct orders from the government about interest rates and money supply growth. The architects of a new monetary system for the European Community have noticed this connection between central bank independence and inflation, and they are modeling the European Central Bank on Germany's Bundesbank.

THEN...

When inflation is especially rapid, as it was in Germany in 1923, money becomes almost worthless. In Germany at that time, bank notes were more valuable as fire kindling than as money, and the sight of people burning Reichmarks was a common one. To avoid having to hold money for too long, wages were paid and spent twice a day. Banks took deposits and made loans, but at interest rates that compensated both depositors and the bank for the falling value of money—interest rates that could exceed 100 percent a month.

The price of a dinner would increase during the course of an evening, making lingering over coffee a very expensive pastime.

...AND NOW

In 1994, Brazil had a computer-age hyperinflation, an inflation rate that was close to 50 percent a month. Banks installed ATMs on almost every street corner and refilled them several times an hour. Brazilians tried to avoid holding

currency. As soon as they were paid, they went shopping and bought enough food to get them through to the next payday. Some shoppers filled as many as six carts on a single monthly trip to the supermarket. Also, instead of using currency, Brazilians used credit cards whenever possible. But they paid their card balances off quickly because the interest rate on unpaid balances was 50 percent a month. Only at such a high interest rate did it pay banks to lend to cardholders, because banks themselves were paying interest rates of 40 percent a month to induce depositors to keep their money in the bank.

> **Many economists today are working on aggregate demand and inflation. One distinguished contributor, whom you can meet on the following pages, is Bennett McCallum of Carnegie Mellon University.**

Talking with

Bennett T. McCallum is
**Professor of Economics at
Carnegie Mellon University. He was
born in Poteet, Texas, in 1935. As
an undergraduate, he attended
Rice University, where he earned a
degree in chemical engineering in
1958. He earned an MBA from
Harvard Business School in 1963
and a Ph.D. in economics from Rice
University in 1969.**

**Professor McCallum's research
interests include monetary theory
and policy, macroeconomic dynam-
ics, and applied econometrics.
Much of his research is aimed
toward improving monetary policy,
and Professor McCallum's advice is
sought by central banks around the
world. He has recently spent time
at the Reserve Bank of New
Zealand as well as the central bank
of the Phillipines.**

**Michael Parkin talked with
Professor McCallum about his
work, how it connects with the
work of other great economists,
and his insights on monetary policy.**

**Professor McCallum, how did you
become interested in Economics?**

I majored in chemical engineering in
college and later worked for three years
as a process design engineer for a petro-
chemical firm in Houston, Texas.
Then, at my wife's urging, I earned an
MBA at Harvard University. While
attending Harvard, I took as many economics, statistics, and operations
research courses as possible. I enjoyed
these courses and, as a result, decided
to enroll in a Ph.D. program in economics.

What I found attractive about economics is its fascinating—even beautiful—theoretical structure combined
with its emphasis on thinking analytically about public policy issues. The
usual noneconomist approach to policy
issues that one gets from the media and
other sources seems to consist mostly
of moralizing on the basis of the effects
that a policy might have on some particular social group, which is very different from thinking analytically.

**Many economists of your generation
were heavily influenced by John
Maynard Keynes. Looking back now on
the work of Keynes, what do you think
his legacy amounts to?**

Keynes was by all accounts an exceptionally brilliant person and very good
at his chosen subject of economics.
But he was principally interested in
the practical side of economics and
government policy. During World War
II, for instance, he contributed greatly
to Britain's wartime finance policy and
to the design of the Bretton Woods
system that governed international
monetary relations from 1945 to 1971.
Thus for Keynes, economic theory was
something that he did to persuade others of insights that he had. As a consequence, his theoretical work was, in
my opinion, badly flawed. His famous
General Theory contains numerous theoretical mistakes. It nevertheless did
make a big contribution to the way

> *What I found attractive about economics is its fascinating—even beautiful—theoretical structure combined with its emphasis on thinking analytically about public policy issues.*

that economic analysis is done, primarily by helping to persuade economists to be interested in short-run rather than just long-run analysis. That was actually a major reorientation in thinking. It was like saying, "Hey, guys, let's pay attention to short-run effects. They're important."

Immediately following Keynes, economists began to emphasize that we can and should use fiscal policy to manipulate aggregate demand. What do we actually know about the ability of governments to manipulate aggregate expenditure using fiscal policy?

If there is a major sustained increase in government spending, starting from a deep recession such as in the 1930s, there will be major effects, as in 1940 to 1944. But if resources are fully employed, then the main real effect will be to shift consumption to the government from households and businesses. If, instead, the government imposes a tax change that's financed by bonds, by borrowing more or less, then the effects will be smaller. From a business cycle point of view, the most important fiscal policy considerations involve the automatic stabilizers, since, at least in the United States, the legislature typically isn't able to take actions promptly enough to be very helpful for any particular economic boom or slump.

What do we know about the Fed's ability to manipulate aggregate expenditure by using monetary policy?

The Fed can act much more quickly, and changes in its policy stance almost certainly affect nominal expenditures, or GDP in dollar terms. In other words, when the central bank pursues a more expansionary policy, the rate of aggregate expenditures will increase. But that is in money terms. What the real effects are depends on how wage and price adjustments occur, and our understanding in that respect is very far from complete. Indeed, my opinion is that the most serious weakness in our understanding of macro and monetary issues is the mechanism by which changes in monetary policy affect real variables such as employment or price-level-adjusted GDP. Although there is a lot of good work going on right now, we don't have agreement on the nature of the wage and price adjustment process.

Can we continue to use monetary policy to prevent inflation? If we can, how? And is Greenspan's current monetary policy on the right track?

Certainly monetary policy can be used to prevent inflation. You just cannot have a serious long-lasting inflation unless the central bank is creating money rapidly. As for gauging whether monetary policy is tight or not, I think the best single measure is the rate of growth of the monetary base, by which we mean currency plus bank reserves.

As for recent federal reserve policy, I think it's been quite good over the period since Greenspan became chairman, but nevertheless, I think that the United States would benefit from legislation stating that the prevention of inflation is the Fed's main objective. Currently, the law fails to state the main responsibility of the Fed. Although Greenspan has been quite consistent on this dimension himself, it's not a good idea to have a system that relies so much on the judgments of a single person. The next Fed chairman might not be so reasonable. Legislation clearly mandating prevention of inflation as the Fed's main responsibility would make it more difficult for Congress to pressure the Fed toward other objectives, which are less suitable.

What should the Fed be doing to minimize the risk of inflation and recession?

There's no question that Fed policies have substantial effects on output and employment, but these effects are temporary. From my perspective, the extent to which the Fed can usefully contribute to reducing cyclical fluctuation is rather limited. So I think the Fed should try to keep total spending, one measure of which would be nominal GDP, growing smoothly at a rate that is basically noninflationary. For example, if the objective is to keep inflation at about 2 percent per year, then the Fed ought to keep nominal GDP growing rather smoothly at about 4 1/2 percent (since real GDP will in any case grow at about 2 1/2 percent, on the average).

In conducting this policy, in which the Fed tightens or loosens depending on whether nominal GDP is growing faster or slower than 4 1/2 percent, you have to use some measure to determine whether you are in fact tightening or loosening, and I would favor looking at the growth rate of the monetary base. Now the Fed does not do that; instead, it looks at the federal funds interest rate. The problem with that approach is that from the perspective of short-run analysis, a high interest rate means tight money, but from the perspective of long-run analysis, a high interest rate reflects loose money (fast money growth). So gauging monetary conditions on the basis of an interest rate is a rather tricky and difficult thing to do. That's why I would prefer to look at a very narrow, controllable monetary measure, such as the monetary base.

What is your assessment of the U.S. deficit? Are deficits inflationary?
Government deficits per se are not all that important at the macroeconomic level. More important is the extent of goods and services that are consumed by the government, rather than the private sector. Deficits are going to be inflationary if the central bank responds to them by creating money in an attempt to keep interest rates from rising. This often happens, especially in countries with poorly developed tax systems. But in the United States, the Fed has not been printing money to finance the deficit. Instead, the Fed has forced the Treasury to finance the deficit by borrowing from the public. So we've not had an accommodating policy from the Fed, and as a result, we've not had much inflation. Much the same has been true in Europe and in many of the developed economies over the last 10 to 15 years.

Who historically are the big contributors to our understanding of aggregate fluctuations? Who are

today's big contributors?
There were several macroeconomists who took John Maynard Keynes' general body of reasoning and his idea of focusing on short-run phenomena and made something fairly coherent out them. Economists such as Patinkin, Modigliani, and Hicks developed Keynesian economics as opposed to thoughts that Keynes had himself begun with. What about before Keynes? His teacher, Alfred Marshall, viewed the generation of business cycles in a manner rather consistent with Keynes' views, but he did not give so much attention to that topic. Irving Fisher believed that if you stabilized price levels, it would tend to prevent the problems that create recessions. Marshall believed fairly much the same thing.

Robert Lucas has been easily the most productive economist of the last 25 years, certainly in the area of macroeconomics. Although his information-based theory of fluctuations has not prevailed, he nevertheless set the tone and direction for today's research.

There are two important lessons from Lucas's work. First, is the basic idea of rational expectations—that although people can't forecast the future perfectly, they can and do strive to avoid systematic expectational errors. This implies that in designing macroeconomic policy, governments should not rely on the presumption that people are going to make the same mistakes over and over again. The second main lesson from Lucas's work is that we should focus on long-run and long-lasting effects of policy actions rather than the temporary, short-term effects emphasized by the Keynesian approach of the 1950s and 1960s. We should try to design good institutions and good rules for policy making rather than

being distracted by the alleged crisis of the day. In these teachings, as in many other ways, Lucas was further developing the general approach of Milton Friedman.

Is an economics major a good thing to pursue at the end of the twentieth century?
Although only a small fraction of students studying economics will go on to become professional economists, it's an excellent subject to take for preparing for other careers—including business and the law—because of the disciplined, analytical thinking that it teaches.

I'm of the belief that an undergraduate should take subjects that are interesting to him or her. Find something that's enjoyable to you, that you're interested in, and then work hard on that. It doesn't have to be economics. What's unfortunate is for students to just go through the paces while they're undergraduates and miss the opportunity to gain a foundation in some field that will allow them to start off on an intellectually satisfying life.

> *I'm of the belief that an undergraduate should take subjects that are interesting to him or her. Find something that's enjoyable to you, that you're interested in, and then work hard on that.*

Expenditure Multipliers

In the Red Rocks Amphitheater in Denver, Bonnie Raitt sings into a microphone in a barely audible whisper. Moving to a louder passage, she increases the volume of her voice and now, through the magic of electronic amplification, booms across the stadium, drowning out every other sound. ◆ Dennis Archer, the mayor of Detroit, and a secretary are being driven to a business meeting along one of the city's less well-repaired highways. (There are some badly potholed highways in Detroit.) The car's wheels are bouncing and vibrating over some of the worst highways in the nation, but its passengers are completely undisturbed and the secretary's notes are written without a ripple, thanks to the car's efficient

Amplifier or Shock Absorber?

shock absorbers. ◆ Investment and exports fluctuate like the volume of Bonnie Raitt's voice and the uneven surface of a Detroit highway. How does the economy react to those fluctuations? Does it react like Dennis Archer's limousine, absorbing the shocks and providing a smooth ride for the economy's passengers? Or does it behave like Bonnie Raitt's amplifier, blowing up the fluctuations and spreading them out to affect the many millions of participants in an economic rock concert? ◆ You will explore these questions in this chapter. You will learn how a recession or a recovery begins when a change in investment or exports triggers a larger change in *aggregate* expenditure and real GDP—like Bonnie Raitt's amplifier. You will also learn how imports and income taxes have lowered the power of the amplifier. Finally, you will discover that in contrast to the initial amplification effect, the economy's shock absorbers, which are price and wage changes, pull real GDP back toward potential GDP. ◆ To achieve these objectives, we use a model called the *aggregate expenditure model*. This model explains changes in aggregate expenditure in a very short time frame during which prices do not change.

After studying this chapter, you will be able to:

- Explain how expenditure plans are determined

- Explain how real GDP is determined when the price level is fixed

- Explain the multiplier

- Explain how imports and taxes influence the multiplier

- Explain how recessions and expansions begin

- Explain the relationship between aggregate expenditure and aggregate demand

- Explain how the multiplier gets smaller as the price level changes

Fixed Prices and Expenditure Plans

MOST FIRMS ARE LIKE YOUR LOCAL SUPERMARKET. They set their prices, advertise their products and services, and sell the quantities their customers are willing to buy. If firms persistently sell a greater quantity than they plan to and are constantly running out of inventory, they eventually raise their prices. And if firms persistently sell a smaller quantity than they plan to and have inventories piling up, they eventually cut their prices. But in the very short term, their prices are fixed. They hold the prices they have set, and the quantities they sell depend on demand, not supply.

The Aggregate Implications of Fixed Prices

Fixed prices have two immediate implications for the economy as a whole:

1. Because each firm's price is fixed, the *price level* is fixed.
2. Because demand determines the quantities that each firm sells, *aggregate demand* determines the aggregate quantity of goods and services sold, which equals real GDP.

So to understand the fluctuations in real GDP when the price level is fixed, we must understand aggregate demand fluctuations. The aggregate expenditure model explains fluctuations in aggregate demand by identifying the forces that determine expenditure plans.

Expenditure Plans

The components of aggregate expenditure are:

- Consumption expenditure
- Investment
- Government purchases of goods and services
- Net exports (exports *minus* imports)

These four components of aggregate expenditure sum to real GDP (see Chapter 23, pp. 493–495). **Aggregate planned expenditure** is equal to *planned* consumption expenditure plus *planned* investment plus *planned* government purchases plus *planned* exports minus *planned* imports.

In the very short term, *planned* investment, *planned* government purchases, and *planned* exports are fixed. But *planned* consumption expenditure and *planned* imports are not fixed. They depend on the level of real GDP itself.

A Two-Way Link Between Aggregate Expenditure and GDP   Because real GDP influences consumption expenditure and imports, and because consumption expenditure and imports are components of aggregate expenditure, there is a two-way link between aggregate expenditure and GDP. Other things remaining the same,

- An increase in real GDP increases aggregate planned expenditure
- An increase in aggregate expenditure increases real GDP

You are going to learn how this two-way link between aggregate expenditure and real GDP determines real GDP when the price level is fixed. The starting point is to consider the first piece of the two-way link: the influence of real GDP on planned consumption expenditure and saving.

Consumption Function and Saving Function

Consumption and saving are influenced by several factors. The more important ones are:

- Real interest rate
- Disposable income
- Purchasing power of net assets
- Expected future income

Chapter 26 (see p. 572) explains how consumption and saving are influenced by these factors. Here, we are going to focus on the relationship between consumption and disposable income when the other factors (the real interest rate, the purchasing power of net assets, and expected future income) are constant. The reason for this focus is that disposable income and consumption are interrelated. Each influences the other.

Consumption and Saving Plans   The table in Fig. 28.1 shows an example of the relationship among planned consumption expenditure, planned saving, and disposable income. It lists the consumption expenditure and the saving that people plan to undertake at each level of disposable income. Notice that at each level of disposable income, consumption expenditure plus saving always equals disposable income. The reason is that households can only consume or save their disposable income. So planned consumption plus planned saving always equals disposable income.

The relationship between consumption expenditure and disposable income, other things remaining the same, is called the **consumption function.** The relationship between saving and disposable income, other things remaining the same, is called the **saving function**. Let's begin by studying the consumption function.

FIGURE 28.1

Consumption Function and Saving Function

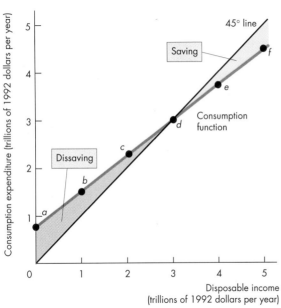

(a) Consumption function

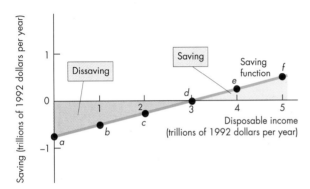

(b) Saving function

	Disposable income	Planned consumption expenditure	Planned saving
		(trillions of 1992 dollars per year)	
a	0	0.75	−0.75
b	1	1.50	−0.50
c	2	2.25	−0.25
d	3	3.00	0
e	4	3.75	0.25
f	5	4.50	0.50

The table shows consumption expenditure and saving plans at various levels of disposable income. Part (a) of the figure shows the relationship between consumption expenditure and disposable income (the consumption function). The height of the consumption function measures consumption expenditure at each level of disposable income. Part (b) shows the relationship between saving and disposable income (the saving function). The height of the saving function measures saving at each level of disposable income. Points a through f on the consumption and saving functions correspond to the rows of the table. The height of the 45° line in part (a) measures disposable income. So, along the 45° line, consumption expenditure equals disposable income. Consumption expenditure plus saving equals disposable income. When the consumption function is above the 45° line, saving is negative (dissaving occurs). When the consumption function is below the 45° line, saving is positive. At the point where the consumption function intersects the 45° line, all disposable income is consumed and saving is zero.

Consumption Function   Figure 28.1(a) shows a consumption function. The *y*-axis measures consumption expenditure, and the *x*-axis measures disposable income. Along the consumption function, the points labeled *a* through *f* correspond to the rows of the table. For example, point *e* shows that when disposable income is $4 trillion, consumption expenditure is $3.75 trillion. Along the consumption function, as disposable income increases, consumption expenditure also increases.

At point *a* on the consumption function, consumption expenditure is $0.75 trillion even though disposable income is zero. This consumption expenditure is called *autonomous consumption*, and it is the amount of consumption expenditure that would take place in the short run, even if people had no current income. Consumption expenditure in excess of this amount is called *induced consumption*, which is expenditure that is induced by an increase in disposable income.

45° Line   Figure 28.1(a) also contains a 45° line, the height of which measures disposable income. At each point on this line, consumption expenditure equals disposable income. In the range over which the consumption function lies above the 45° line—between *a* and *d*—consumption expenditure exceeds disposable income. In the range over which the consumption function lies below the 45° line—between *d* and *f*—consumption expenditure is less than disposable income. And at the point at which the consumption function intersects the 45° line—at point *d*—consumption expenditure equals disposable income.

Saving Function   Figure 28.1(b) shows a saving function. The *x*-axis is exactly the same as that in part (a). The *y*-axis measures saving. Again, the points marked *a* through *f* correspond to the rows of the table. For example, point *e* shows that when disposable income is $4 trillion, saving is $0.25 trillion. Along the saving function, as disposable income increases, saving also increases. At disposable income less than $3 trillion (point *d*), saving is negative. Negative saving is called *dissaving*. At disposable income greater than $3 trillion, saving is positive, and at $3 trillion, saving is zero.

Notice the connection between the two parts of Fig. 28.1. When consumption expenditure exceeds disposable income in part (a), saving is negative in part (b). When disposable income exceeds consumption expenditure in part (a), saving is positive in part (b). And when consumption expenditure equals disposable income in part (a), saving is zero in part (b).

When saving is negative (when consumption expenditure exceeds disposable income), past savings are used to pay for current consumption. Such a situation cannot last forever, but it can occur if disposable income falls temporarily.

Marginal Propensities to Consume and Save

The extent to which consumption expenditure changes when disposable income changes depends on the marginal propensity to consume. The **marginal propensity to consume** (*MPC*) is the fraction of a *change* in disposable income that is consumed. It is calculated as the *change* in consumption expenditure (ΔC) divided by the *change* in disposable income (ΔYD) that brought it about. That is,

$$MPC = \frac{\Delta C}{\Delta YD}.$$

In the table in Fig. 28.1, when disposable income increases from $3 trillion to $4 trillion, consumption expenditure increases from $3 trillion to $3.75 trillion. The $1 trillion increase in disposable income increases consumption expenditure by $0.75 trillion. The *MPC* is $0.75 trillion divided by $1 trillion, which equals 0.75.

The **marginal propensity to save** (*MPS*) is the fraction of a *change* in disposable income that is saved. It is calculated as the *change* in saving (ΔS) divided by the *change* in disposable income (ΔYD) that brought it about. That is,

$$MPS = \frac{\Delta S}{\Delta YD}.$$

In the table in Fig. 28.1, an increase in disposable income from $3 trillion to $4 trillion increases saving from zero to $0.25 trillion. The $1 trillion increase in disposable income increases saving by $0.25 trillion. The *MPS* is $0.25 trillion divided by $1 trillion, which equals 0.25.

The marginal propensity to consume plus the marginal propensity to save always equals 1. They sum to 1 because consumption expenditure and saving exhaust disposable income. Part of each dollar increase in disposable income is consumed, and the remaining part is saved. You can see that these two marginal propensities sum to 1 by using the equation

$$\Delta C + \Delta S = \Delta YD.$$

Divide both sides of the equation by the change in disposable income to obtain

$$\frac{\Delta C}{\Delta YD} + \frac{\Delta S}{\Delta YD} = 1.$$

$\Delta C/\Delta YD$ is the *marginal propensity to consume* (*MPC*), and $\Delta S/\Delta YD$ is the *marginal propensity to save* (*MPS*), so

$$MPC + MPS = 1.$$

Slopes and Marginal Propensities

The slopes of the consumption function and the saving function are the marginal propensities to consume and save. Figure 28.2(a) shows the *MPC* as the slope of the consumption function. A $1 trillion increase in disposable income from $3 trillion to $4 trillion is the base of the red triangle. The increase in consumption expenditure that results from this increase in income is $0.75 trillion and is the height of the triangle. The slope of the consumption function is given by the formula "slope equals rise over run" and is $0.75 trillion divided by $1 trillion, which equals 0.75—the *MPC*.

Figure 28.2(b) shows the *MPS* as the slope of the saving function. A $1 trillion increase in disposable income from $3 trillion to $4 trillion (the base of the red triangle) increases saving by $0.25 trillion (the height of the triangle). The slope of the saving function is $0.25 trillion divided by $1 trillion, which equals 0.25—the *MPS*.

Other Influences on Consumption Expenditure and Saving

You've seen that a change in disposable income leads to changes in consumption expenditure and saving. A change in disposable income brings movements along the consumption function and saving function.

FIGURE **28.2**

Marginal Propensities to Consume and Save

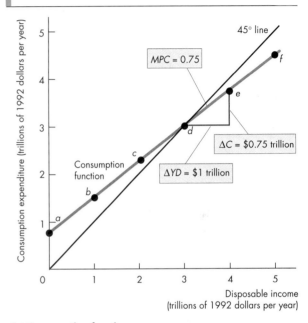

(a) Consumption function

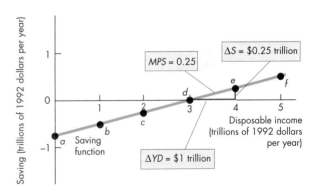

(b) Saving function

The marginal propensity to consume, *MPC*, is equal to the change in consumption expenditure divided by the change in disposable income, other things remaining the same. It is measured by the slope of the consumption function. In part (a), the *MPC* is 0.75. The marginal propensity to save, *MPS*, is equal to the change in saving divided by the change in disposable income, other things remaining the same. It is measured by the slope of the saving function. In part (b), the *MPS* is 0.25.

Along the consumption function and saving function, all other influences on consumption expenditure and saving (such as the real interest rate, expected future income, and the purchasing power net assets) are fixed. A change in any of these other influences shifts both the consumption function and the saving function.

When the real interest rate falls or when the purchasing power of net assets or expected future income increases, consumption expenditure increases and saving decreases. Figure 28.3 shows the effects of these changes on the consumption function and the saving function. The consumption function shifts upward from CF_0 to CF_1, and the saving function shifts downward from SF_0 to SF_1. Such shifts commonly occur during the expansion phase of the business cycle because, at such times, expected future income increases.

When the real interest rate rises or when the purchasing power of net assets or expected future income decreases, consumption expenditure decreases and saving increases. Figure 28.3 also shows the effects of these changes on the consumption function and the saving function. The consumption function shifts downward from CF_0 to CF_2, and the saving function shifts upward from SF_0 to SF_2. Such shifts often occur when a recession begins because at such a time, expected future income decreases.

We've studied the theory of the consumption function. Let's now see how that theory applies to the U.S. economy.

The U.S. Consumption Function

Figure 28.4 shows the U.S. consumption function. Each point identified by a blue dot represents consumption expenditure and disposable income for a particular year. (The dots are for the years 1970–1996, and the even-numbered years are identified in the figure.) The line labeled CF_0 is an estimate of the U.S. consumption function in 1970, and the line labeled CF_1 is an estimate of the U.S. consumption function in 1996.

The slope of the consumption function in Fig. 28.4 is 0.75, which means that a $1 trillion increase in disposable income brings a $0.75 trillion increase in consumption expenditure. This slope, which is an estimate of the marginal propensity to consume, is an assumption that is in the middle of the range of values that economists have estimated for the marginal propensity to consume.

FIGURE 28.3

Shifts in the Consumption and Saving Functions

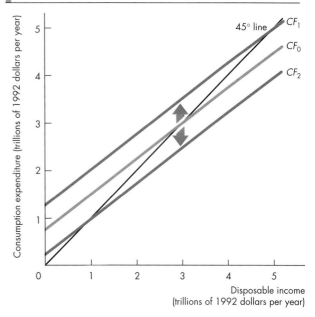

(a) Consumption function

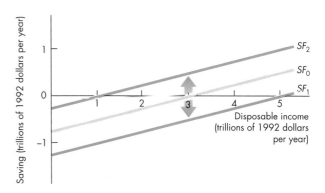

(b) Saving function

A fall in the real interest rate, an increase in the purchasing power of net assets, or an increase in expected future income increases consumption expenditure and decreases saving. It shifts the consumption function upward from CF_0 to CF_1 and shifts the saving function downward from SF_0 to SF_1. A rise in the real interest rate or a decrease in either the purchasing power of net assets or expected future income shifts the consumption function downward from CF_0 to CF_2 and shifts the saving function upward from SF_0 to SF_2.

The consumption function shifts upward over time as other influences on consumption expenditure. Of these other influences, the real interest rate and the purchasing power of net assets fluctuate and so bring upward and downward shifts in the consumption function. But rising expected future income brings a steady upward shift in the consumption function. As the consumption function shifts upward, autonomous consumption expenditure increases.

Consumption as a Function of Real GDP

You've seen that consumption expenditure changes when disposable income changes. Disposable income changes when either real GDP changes or net taxes change. If tax rates don't change, real GDP is the only influence on disposable income. So consumption depends not only on disposable income but also on real GDP. We use this link between consumption and real GDP to determine equilibrium expenditure. But before we do so, we need to look at one further component of aggregate expenditure: imports. For like consumption expenditure, imports also are influenced by real GDP.

Import Function

U.S. imports are determined by many factors, but in the short run, one factor dominates: U.S. real GDP. Other things remaining the same, the greater the U.S. real GDP, the larger is the quantity of U.S. imports.

The relationship between imports and real GDP is determined by the marginal propensity to import. The **marginal propensity to import** is the fraction of an increase in real GDP that is spent on imports. It is calculated as the change in imports divided by the change in real GDP that brought it about, other things remaining the same. For example, if a $1 trillion increase in real GDP increases imports by $0.25 trillion, the marginal propensity to import is 0.25.

In recent years, since the North American Free Trade Agreement was implemented, U.S. imports have surged. For example, in 1996, real GDP increased by $300 billion and imports increased by $60 billion. Assuming that other factors had a negligible influence on imports in 1996, the marginal propensity to import in that year was 0.2. The U.S. marginal propensity to import has been increasing.

FIGURE 28.4

The U.S. Consumption Function

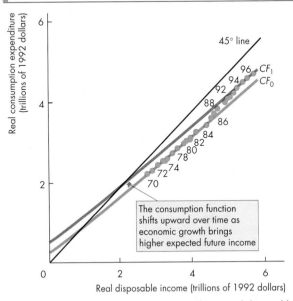

Each blue dot shows consumption expenditure and disposable income for a particular year. The lines CF_0 and CF_1 are estimates of the U.S. consumption function in 1970 and 1996, respectively. Here, the (assumed) marginal propensity to consume is 0.75.

REVIEW

- Consumption expenditure and imports are influenced by real GDP.
- The marginal propensity to consume is the proportion of an increase in disposable income that is consumed.
- The effects of real GDP on consumption expenditure and imports are determined by the marginal propensity to consume and the marginal propensity to import.

Real GDP influences consumption and imports. But consumption and imports along with investment, government purchases, and exports influence real GDP. Your next task is to study this second piece of the two-way link between aggregate expenditure and real GDP and see how all the components of aggregate planned expenditure interact to determine real GDP.

Real GDP with a Fixed Price Level

YOU ARE NOW GOING TO DISCOVER HOW AGGREGATE expenditure plans interact to determine real GDP when the price level is fixed. First we will study the relationship between aggregate planned expenditure and real GDP. Second, we'll learn about the key distinction between *planned* expenditure and *actual*

expenditure. And third, we'll study equilibrium expenditure, a situation in which aggregate planned expenditure and actual expenditure are equal.

The relationship between aggregate planned expenditure and real GDP can be described by either an aggregate expenditure schedule or an aggregate expenditure curve. The *aggregate expenditure schedule* lists aggregate planned expenditure generated at each level of real GDP. The *aggregate expenditure curve* is a graph of the aggregate expenditure schedule.

FIGURE 28.5

Aggregate Planned Expenditure

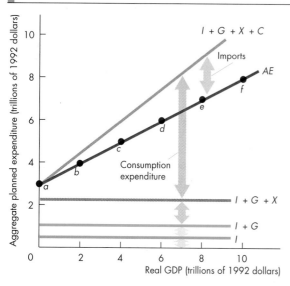

The aggregate expenditure schedule shows the relationship between aggregate planned expenditure and real GDP. Aggregate planned expenditure is the sum of planned consumption expenditure, investment, government purchases of goods and services, and exports minus imports. For example, in row *b* of the table, when real GDP is $2 trillion, planned consumption expenditure is $2.25 trillion, planned investment is $0.5 trillion, planned government purchases of goods and services are $0.55 trillion, planned exports are $1.2 trillion, and planned imports are $0.5 trillion. Thus when real GDP is $2 trillion, aggregate planned expenditure is $4 trillion ($2.25 + $0.5 + $0.55 + $1.2 − $0.5). The schedule shows that aggregate planned expenditure increases as real GDP increases. This relationship is graphed as the aggregate expenditure curve *AE*, the line *af*. The components of aggregate expenditure that increase with real GDP are consumption expenditure and imports. The other components—investment, government purchases, and exports—do not vary with real GDP.

		Planned expenditure					Aggregate planned expenditure $(AE = C + I + G + X - M)$
	Real GDP (Y)	Consumption expenditure (C)	Investment (I)	Government purchases (G)	Exports (X)	Imports (M)	
				(trillions of 1992 dollars)			
a	0	0.75	0.5	0.55	1.2	0.0	3
b	2	2.25	0.5	0.55	1.2	0.5	4
c	4	3.75	0.5	0.55	1.2	1.0	5
d	6	5.25	0.5	0.55	1.2	1.5	6
e	8	6.75	0.5	0.55	1.2	2.0	7
f	10	8.25	0.5	0.55	1.2	2.5	8

Aggregate Planned Expenditure and Real GDP

The table in Fig. 28.5 sets out an aggregate expenditure schedule together with the components of aggregate planned expenditure. To calculate aggregate planned expenditure at a given real GDP, we add the various components together. The first column of the table shows real GDP, and the second column shows the consumption expenditure generated by each level of real GDP. A $2 trillion increase in real GDP generates a $1.50 trillion increase in consumption expenditure—the *MPC* is 0.75.

The next two columns show investment and government purchases of goods and services. Investment depends on the real interest rate and the expected rate of profit (see Chapter 26, p. 569). At a given point in time, these factors generate a particular level of investment. Suppose this level of investment is $0.5 trillion. Also, suppose that government purchases of goods and services are $0.55 trillion.

The next two columns show exports and imports. Exports are influenced by events in the rest of the world, prices of foreign-made goods and services relative to the prices of similar U.S.-made goods and services, and foreign exchange rates. But exports are not directly affected by real GDP in the United States. Exports are a constant $1.2 trillion. Imports increase as real GDP increases. A $2 trillion increase in real GDP generates a $0.5 trillion increase in imports—the marginal propensity to import is 0.25.

The final column shows aggregate planned expenditure—the sum of planned consumption expenditure, investment, government purchases of goods and services, and exports minus imports.

Figure 28.5 plots an aggregate expenditure curve. Real GDP is shown on the *x*-axis, and aggregate planned expenditure is shown on the *y*-axis. The aggregate expenditure curve is the red line *AE*. Points *a* through *f* on that curve correspond to the rows of the table. The *AE* curve is a graph of aggregate planned expenditure (the last column) plotted against real GDP (the first column).

Figure 28.5 also shows the components of aggregate expenditure. The constant components—investment (*I*), government purchases of goods and services (*G*), and exports (*X*)—are shown by the horizontal lines in the figure. Consumption expenditure (*C*) is the vertical gap between the lines labeled *I* + *G* + *X* and *I* + *G* + *X* + *C* .

To construct the *AE* curve, subtract imports (*M*) from the *I* + *G* + *X* + *C* line. Aggregate expenditure is expenditure on U.S.-made goods and services. But the components of aggregate expenditure—*C*, *I*, and *G*—include expenditure on imported goods and services. For example, a student's purchase of a new motor bike is part of consumption expenditure. But if that motor bike is a Honda made in Japan, expenditure on it must be subtracted from consumption expenditure to find out how much is spent on goods and services produced in the United States—on U.S. real GDP. Money paid to Honda for motor bike imports from Japan does not add to aggregate expenditure on U.S.-made goods and services.

Figure 28.5 shows that aggregate planned expenditure increases as real GDP increases. But as real GDP increases, only some of the components of aggregate planned expenditure increase. These components are consumption expenditure and imports. The sum of the components of aggregate expenditure that vary with real GDP is called **induced expenditure**. The sum of the components of aggregate expenditure that are not influenced by real GDP is called **autonomous expenditure**. The components of autonomous expenditure are investment, government purchases, exports, and autonomous consumption—that part of consumption expenditure that does not vary with real GDP. That is, autonomous expenditure is equal to the level of aggregate planned expenditure when real GDP is zero. In Fig. 28.5, autonomous expenditure is $3 trillion. And as real GDP increases from zero to $2 trillion, aggregate expenditure increases from $3 trillion to $4 trillion. Induced expenditure is $1 trillion—$4 trillion minus $3 trillion.

The aggregate expenditure curve summarizes the relationship between aggregate *planned* expenditure and real GDP. But what determines the point on the aggregate expenditure curve at which the economy operates? What determines *actual* aggregate expenditure?

Actual Expenditure, Planned Expenditure, and Real GDP

Actual aggregate expenditure is always equal to real GDP, as we saw in Chapter 23 (p. 495). But aggregate *planned* expenditure is not necessarily equal to actual aggregate expenditure and therefore is not necessarily equal to real GDP. How can actual expenditure and planned expenditure differ from each other? Why don't expenditure plans get implemented? The main reason is that firms might end up with more inventories than planned or with less inventories than planned. People carry out their consumption expenditure plans, the government implements its planned purchases of goods and services, and net exports are as planned. Firms carry out their plans to purchase new buildings, plant, and equipment. But one component

of investment is the change in firms' inventories of goods. If aggregate planned expenditure is less than real GDP, firms don't sell all the goods they produce and they end up with inventories they hadn't planned. If aggregate planned expenditure exceeds real GDP, firms sell more than they produce and inventories decrease below the level that firms had planned.

FIGURE 28.6

Equilibrium Expenditure

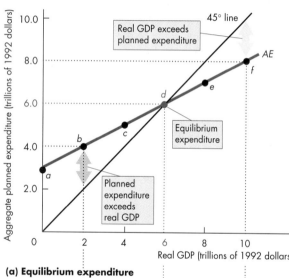

(a) Equilibrium expenditure

(b) Unplanned inventory changes

	Real GDP (Y)	Aggregate planned expenditure (AE)	Unplanned inventory change (Y – AE)
		(trillions of 1992 dollars)	
a	0	3	–3
b	2	4	–2
c	4	5	–1
d	6	6	0
e	8	7	1
f	10	8	2

The table shows expenditure plans at different levels of real GDP. When real GDP is $6 trillion, aggregate planned expenditure equals real GDP. Part (a) of the figure illustrates equilibrium expenditure, which occurs when aggregate planned expenditure equals real GDP at the intersection of the 45° line and the AE curve. Part (b) of the figure shows the forces that bring about equilibrium expenditure. When aggregate planned expenditure exceeds real GDP, inventories decrease— for example, point b in both parts of the figure. Firms increase production, and real GDP increases. When aggregate planned expenditure is less than real GDP, inventories increase—for example, point f in both parts of the figure. Firms decrease production, and real GDP decreases. When aggregate planned expenditure equals real GDP, there are no unplanned inventory changes and real GDP remains constant at equilibrium expenditure.

Equilibrium Expenditure

Equilibrium expenditure is the level of aggregate expenditure that occurs when aggregate *planned* expenditure equals real GDP. It is a level of aggregate expenditure and real GDP at which everyone's spending plans are fulfilled. When the price level is fixed, equilibrium expenditure determines real GDP. When aggregate planned expenditure and actual aggregate expenditure are unequal, a process of convergence toward equilibrium expenditure occurs. And throughout this convergence process, real GDP adjusts. Let's examine equilibrium expenditure and the process that brings it about.

Figure 28.6(a) illustrates equilibrium expenditure. The table sets out aggregate planned expenditure at various levels of real GDP. These values are plotted as points *a* through *f* along the *AE* curve. The 45° line shows all the points at which aggregate planned expenditure equals real GDP. Thus where the *AE* curve lies above the 45° line, aggregate planned expenditure exceeds real GDP; where the *AE* curve lies below the 45° line, aggregate planned expenditure is less than real GDP; and where the *AE* curve intersects the 45° line, aggregate planned expenditure equals real GDP. Point *d* illustrates equilibrium expenditure. At this point, real GDP is $6 trillion.

Convergence to Equilibrium

What are the forces that move aggregate expenditure toward its equilibrium level? To answer this question, we must look at a situation in which aggregate expenditure is away from its equilibrium level. Suppose that in Fig. 28.6, real GDP is $2 trillion. With real GDP at $2 trillion, actual aggregate expenditure is also $2 trillion. But aggregate *planned* expenditure is $4 trillion (point *b* in Fig. 28.6a). Aggregate planned expenditure exceeds *actual* expenditure. When people spend $4 trillion and firms produce goods and services worth $2 trillion, firms' inventories fall by $2 trillion (point *b* in Fig. 28.6b). Because the change in inventories is part of investment, *actual* investment is $2 trillion less than *planned* investment.

Real GDP doesn't remain at $2 trillion for very long. Firms have inventory targets based on their sales. When inventories fall below target, firms increase production to restore inventories to the target level. To increase inventories, firms hire additional labor and increase production. Suppose that they increase production in the next period by $2 trillion. Real GDP increases by $2.0 trillion to $4.0 trillion. But again, aggregate planned expenditure exceeds real GDP. When real GDP is $4.0 trillion, aggregate planned expenditure is $5 trillion (point *c* in Fig. 28.6a). Again, inventories decrease, but this time by less than before. With real GDP of $4.0 trillion and aggregate planned expenditure of $5 trillion, inventories decrease by $1 trillion (point *c* in Fig. 28.6b). Again, firms hire additional labor, and production increases; real GDP increases yet further.

The process that we have just described—planned expenditure exceeds real GDP, inventories decrease, and production increases to restore the level of inventories—ends when real GDP has reached $6 trillion. At this real GDP, there is an equilibrium. There are no unplanned inventory changes, and firms do not change their production.

You can do an experiment similar to the one we've just done but starting with a level of real GDP greater than equilibrium expenditure. In this case, planned expenditure is less than actual expenditure, inventories pile up, and firms cut production. As before, real GDP keeps on changing (decreasing this time) until it reaches its equilibrium level of $6.0 trillion.

R E V I E W

- Equilibrium expenditure occurs when aggregate planned expenditure equals real GDP.
- Equilibrium expenditure results from an adjustment in real GDP.
- If real GDP and aggregate expenditure are less than their equilibrium levels, an unplanned fall in inventories leads firms to increase production and real GDP increases.
- If real GDP and aggregate expenditure are greater than their equilibrium levels, an unplanned rise in inventories leads firms to decrease production and real GDP decreases.

We've learned that when the price level is fixed, real GDP is determined by equilibrium expenditure. And we have seen how unplanned changes in inventories and the production response they generate bring a convergence toward equilibrium. We're now going to study *changes* in equilibrium and discover an economic amplifier called the *multiplier*.

The Multiplier

INVESTMENT AND EXPORTS CAN CHANGE FOR
many reasons. A fall in the real interest rate might
induce firms to increase their planned investment.
A wave of innovation, such as occurred with the
spread of multimedia computers in the 1990s,
might increase expected future profits and lead firms
to increase their planned investment. An economic
boom in Western Europe and Japan might lead to a
large increase in their expenditure on U.S.-produced
goods and services—on U.S. exports. These are all
examples of increases in autonomous expenditure.

When autonomous expenditure increases, aggregate expenditure increases, and so does equilibrium
expenditure and real GDP. But the increase in real
GDP is *larger* than the change in autonomous expenditure. The **multiplier** is the amount by which a
change in autonomous expenditure is magnified or
multiplied to determine the change in equilibrium
expenditure and real GDP.

It is easiest to get the basic idea of the multiplier
if we work with an example economy in which there
are no income taxes and no imports. So we'll first
assume that these factors are absent. Then, when you
understand the basic idea, we'll bring these factors
back into play and see what difference they make to
the multiplier.

The Basic Idea of the Multiplier

Suppose that investment increases. The additional
expenditure by businesses means that aggregate expenditure and real GDP increase. The increase in real
GDP increases disposable income and with no income
taxes, real GDP and disposable income increase by
the same amount. The increase in disposable income
brings an increase in consumption expenditure. And
the increased consumption expenditure adds even
more to aggregate expenditure. Real GDP and disposable income increase further, and so does consumption expenditure. The initial increase in investment
brings an even bigger increase in aggregate expenditure because it induces an increase in consumption
expenditure. The magnitude of the increase in aggregate expenditure that results from an increase in autonomous expenditure is determined by the *multiplier.*

The table in Fig. 28.7 sets out aggregate planned
expenditure. Initially, when real GDP is $5 trillion,

aggregate planned expenditure is $5.25 trillion.
For each $1 trillion increase in real GDP, aggregate
planned expenditure increases by $0.75 trillion. This
aggregate expenditure schedule is shown in the figure
as the aggregate expenditure curve AE_0. Initially,
equilibrium expenditure is $6 trillion. You can see
this equilibrium in row *b* of the table and in the figure where the curve AE_0 intersects the 45° line at the
point marked *b*.

Now suppose that autonomous expenditure
increases by $0.5 trillion. What happens to equilibrium
expenditure? You can see the answer in Fig. 28.7.
When this increase in autonomous expenditure is
added to the original aggregate planned expenditure,
aggregate planned expenditure increases by $0.5
trillion at each level of real GDP. The new aggregate
expenditure curve is AE_1. The new equilibrium
expenditure, highlighted in the table (row *d'*), occurs
where AE_1 intersects the 45° line and is $8 trillion
(point *d'*). At this real GDP, aggregate planned
expenditure equals real GDP.

The Multiplier Effect

In Fig. 28.7, the increase in autonomous expenditure
of $0.5 trillion increases equilibrium expenditure by
$2 trillion. That is, the change in autonomous expen-
diture leads, like Bonnie Raitt's music-making equipment, to an amplified change in equilibrium expenditure. This amplified change is the *multiplier effect*—
equilibrium expenditure increases by *more than* the
increase in autonomous expenditure. The multiplier
is greater than 1.

Initially, when autonomous expenditure
increases, aggregate planned expenditure exceeds
real GDP. As a result, inventories decrease. Firms
respond by increasing production so as to restore
their inventories to the target level. As production
increases, so does real GDP. With a higher level of
real GDP, *induced expenditure* increases. Thus equilibrium expenditure increases by the sum of the
initial increase in autonomous expenditure and the
increase in induced expenditure. In this example,
induced expenditure increases by $1.5 trillion, so
equilibrium expenditure increases by $2 trillion.

Although we have just analyzed the effects of
an *increase* in autonomous expenditure, the same
analysis applies to a decrease in autonomous expenditure. If initially the aggregate expenditure curve is
AE_1, equilibrium expenditure and real GDP are $8

FIGURE 28.7
The Multiplier

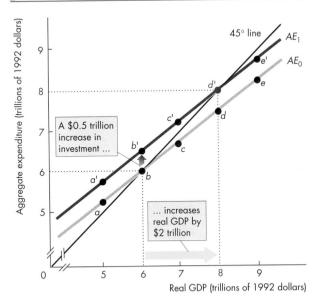

Real GDP (Y)	Aggregate planned expenditure		
		Original (AE₀)	New (AE₁)
		(trillions of 1992 dollars)	
5	a	5.25	a'	5.75
6	b	6.00	b'	6.50
7	c	6.75	c'	7.25
8	d	7.50	d'	8.00
9	e	8.25	e'	8.75

A $0.5 trillion increase in autonomous expenditure shifts the AE curve upward by $0.5 trillion from AE₀ to AE₁. Equilibrium expenditure increases by $2 trillion, from $6 trillion to $8 trillion. The increase in equilibrium expenditure is 4 times the increase in autonomous expenditure, so the multiplier is 4.

Why Is the Multiplier Greater Than 1?

We've seen that equilibrium expenditure increases by more than the increase in autonomous expenditure. This makes the multiplier greater than 1. How come? Why does equilibrium expenditure increase by more than the increase in autonomous expenditure?

The multiplier is greater than 1 because of induced expenditure—an increase in autonomous expenditure *induces* further increases in expenditure. If General Motors spends $10 million on a new car assembly line, aggregate expenditure and real GDP immediately increase by $10 million. But that is not the end of the story. Engineers and construction workers now have more income, and they spend part of the extra income on cars, microwave ovens, vacations, and a host of other goods and services. Real GDP now rises by the initial $10 million plus the extra consumption expenditure induced by the $10 million increase in income. The producers of cars, microwave ovens, vacations, and other goods now have increased incomes, and they, in turn, spend part of the increase in their incomes on consumption goods and services. Additional income induces additional expenditure, which creates additional income.

We have seen that a change in autonomous expenditure has a multiplier effect on real GDP. But how big is the multiplier effect?

The Size of the Multiplier

Suppose that the economy is in a recession. Profit prospects start to look better, and firms are making plans for large increases in investment. The world economy is also heading toward expansion, and exports are increasing. The question on everyone's lips is: How strong will the expansion be? This is a hard question to answer. But an important ingredient in the answer is working out the size of the multiplier.

The *multiplier* is the amount by which a change in autonomous expenditure is multiplied to determine the change in equilibrium expenditure that it generates. To calculate the multiplier, we divide the change in equilibrium expenditure by the change in autonomous expenditure. Let's calculate the multiplier for the example in Fig. 28.7. Initially, equilibrium expenditure is $6 trillion. Then autonomous expenditure increases by $0.5 trillion, and equilibrium expenditure increases by $2 trillion to $8 trillion.

trillion. A decrease in autonomous expenditure of $0.5 trillion shifts the aggregate expenditure curve downward by $0.5 trillion to AE₀. Equilibrium expenditure decreases from $8 trillion to $6 trillion. The decrease in equilibrium expenditure ($2 trillion) is larger than the decrease in autonomous expenditure that brought it about ($0.5 trillion). The multiplier is 4.

The multiplier is

$$\text{Multiplier} = \frac{\text{Change in equilibrium expenditure}}{\text{Change in autonomous expenditure}}$$

$$= \frac{\$2 \text{ trillion}}{\$0.5 \text{ trillion}} = 4.$$

The Multiplier and the Marginal Propensity to Consume and Save

What determines the magnitude of the multiplier? The answer is the marginal propensity to consume. The larger is the marginal propensity to consume, the larger is the multiplier. To see why, let's do a calculation.

Aggregate expenditure and real GDP change because consumption expenditure changes and investment changes. The change in real GDP (ΔY) equals the change in consumption expenditure (ΔC) plus the change in investment (ΔI). That is,

$$\Delta Y = \Delta C + \Delta I.$$

But the change in consumption expenditure is determined by the change in real GDP and the marginal propensity to consume. It is

$$\Delta C = MPC \times \Delta Y.$$

Now substitute $MPC \times \Delta Y$ for ΔC in the previous equation to give

$$\Delta Y = (MPC \times \Delta Y) + \Delta I.$$

Now, solve for ΔY as

$$(1 - MPC) \times \Delta Y = \Delta I.$$

and rearranging gives

$$\Delta Y = \frac{\Delta I}{\left(1 - MPC\right)}.$$

Finally, divide both sides of the previous equation by ΔI to give

$$\text{Multiplier} = \frac{\Delta Y}{\Delta I} = \frac{1}{(1 - MPC)}.$$

Using the numbers for Fig. 28.7, the MPC is 0.75 so the multiplier is

$$\text{Multiplier} = \frac{1}{(1 - 0.75)} = \frac{1}{0.25} = 4.$$

There is another formula for the multiplier. Because the marginal propensity to consume (MPC) plus the marginal propensity to save (MPS) sum to 1, the term $(1 - MPC)$ equals MPS. Therefore another formula for the multiplier is

$$\text{Multiplier} = \frac{1}{MPS}.$$

Again using the numbers in Fig. 28.7, we have

$$\text{Multiplier} = \frac{1}{0.25} = 4.$$

Because the marginal propensity to save (MPS) is a fraction—a number between 0 and 1—the multiplier is greater than 1.

Figure 28.8 illustrates the multiplier process. In round 1, autonomous expenditure increases by $0.5 trillion (shown by the green bar). At this time, induced expenditure does not change, so aggregate expenditure and real GDP increase by $0.5 trillion. In round 2, the larger real GDP induces more consumption expenditure. Induced expenditure increases by 0.75 times the increase in real GDP, so the increase in real GDP of $0.5 trillion induces a further increase in expenditure of $0.375 trillion. This change in induced expenditure (the green bar in round 2), when added to the previous increase in expenditure (the blue bar in round 2), increases aggregate expenditure and real GDP by $0.875 trillion. The round 2 increase in real GDP induces a round 3 increase in expenditure. The process repeats through successive rounds. Each increase in real GDP is 0.75 times the previous increase. The cumulative increase in real GDP gradually approaches $2 trillion.

So far, we've ignored imports and income taxes. Let's now see how these two factors influence the multiplier.

Imports and Income Taxes

The multiplier is determined, in general, not only by the marginal propensity to consume but also by the marginal propensity to import and by the marginal tax rate. Imports make the multiplier smaller than it otherwise would be. To see why, think about what

FIGURE 28.8

The Multiplier Process

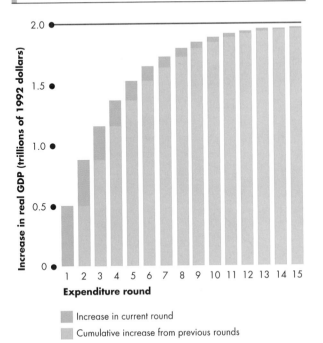

Increase in current round

Cumulative increase from previous rounds

Autonomous expenditure increases in round 1 by $0.5 trillion. As a result, real GDP increases by the same amount. With a marginal propensity to consume of 0.75, each additional dollar of real GDP induces an additional 0.75 of a dollar of aggregate expenditure. The round 1 increase in real GDP induces an increase in consumption expenditure of $0.375 trillion in round 2. At the end of round 2, real GDP has increased by $0.875 trillion. The extra $0.375 trillion of real GDP in round 2 induces a further increase in consumption expenditure of $0.281 trillion in round 3. Real GDP increases yet further to $1.156 trillion. This process continues with real GDP increasing by ever-smaller amounts. When the process comes to an end, real GDP has increased by a total of $2 trillion.

happens following an increase in investment. An increase in investment increases real GDP, which in turn increases consumption expenditure. But part of the increase in investment and consumption expenditure is expenditure on imported goods and services, not U.S.-produced goods and services. Only expenditure on U.S.-produced goods and services increases U.S. real GDP. The larger the marginal propensity to import, the smaller is the change in U.S. real GDP.

Income taxes also make the multiplier smaller than it otherwise would be. Again, think about what happens following an increase in investment. An increase in investment increases real GDP. But because income taxes increase, disposable income increases by less than the increase in real GDP. Consequently, consumption expenditure increases by less than it would do if taxes had not changed. The larger is the marginal tax rate, the smaller is the change in disposable income and real GDP.

The marginal propensity to import and the marginal tax rate together with the marginal propensity to consume determine the multiplier. And their combined influence depends on the slope of the *AE* curve. The multiplier is equal to 1 divided by 1 minus the slope of the *AE* curve. Figure 28.9 compares two situations. In Fig. 28.9(a), there are no imports and no taxes. The slope of the *AE* curve equals the marginal propensity to consume, which is 0.75, and the multiplier is 4. In Fig. 28.9(b), imports and income taxes decrease the slope of the *AE* curve to 0.5. In this case, the multiplier is 2.

Over time, the value of the multiplier changes as tax rates change and as the marginal propensity to consume and the marginal propensity to import change. These ongoing changes make the multiplier hard to predict. But they do not change the fundamental fact that an initial change in autonomous expenditure leads to a magnified change in aggregate expenditure and real GDP.

Now that we've studied the multiplier and the factors that influence its magnitude, let's use what we've learned to gain some insights into business cycle turning points.

Business Cycle Turning Points

At business cycle turning points, the economy moves from expansion to recession or from recession to expansion. Economists understand these turning points as seismologists understand earthquakes. They know quite a lot about the forces and mechanisms that produce them, but they can't predict them. The forces that bring business cycle turning points are the swings in autonomous expenditure such as investment and exports. The mechanism that gives momentum to the economy's new direction is the multiplier. Let's use what we've now learned to examine these turning points.

FIGURE **28.9**

The Multiplier and the Slope of the *AE* Curve

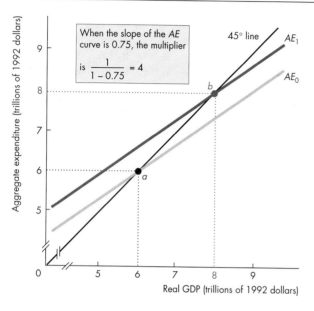

(a) Multiplier is 4

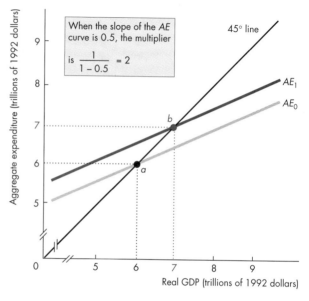

(b) Multiplier is 2

Imports and income taxes make the *AE* curve less steep and reduce the value of the multiplier. In part (a), with no imports and income taxes, the slope of the *AE* curve is 0.75 (the marginal propensity to consume) and the multiplier is 4. But with imports and income taxes, the slope of the *AE* curve is less than the marginal propensity to consume. In part (b), the slope of the *AE* curve is 0.5. In this case, the multiplier is 2.

An Expansion Begins   An expansion is triggered by an increase in autonomous expenditure that increases aggregate planned expenditure. At the moment the economy turns the corner into expansion, aggregate planned expenditure exceeds real GDP. In this situation, firms see their inventories taking an unplanned dive. The expansion now begins. To meet their inventory targets, firms increase production, and real GDP begins to increase. This initial increase in real GDP brings higher incomes that stimulate consumption expenditure. The multiplier process kicks in, and the expansion picks up speed.

A Recession Begins   The process we've just described works in reverse at a business cycle peak. A recession is triggered by a decrease in autonomous expenditure that decreases aggregate planned expenditure. At the moment the economy turns the corner into recession, real GDP exceeds aggregate planned expenditure. In this situation, firms see unplanned inventories piling up. The recession now begins. To reduce their inventories, firms cut production, and real GDP begins to decrease. This initial decrease in real GDP brings lower incomes that cut consumption expenditure. The multiplier process reinforces the initial cut in autonomous expenditure, and the recession takes hold.

The Next U.S. Recession?   Since 1991, the U.S. economy has been in a business cycle expansion. The last real GDP trough was in the first quarter of 1991. The science of macroeconomics cannot predict when the next recession will begin. A recession seemed possible in 1995 following a rapid buildup of inventories during 1994. But firms planned this inventory buildup. At the beginning of 1997, there was still no immediate prospect of the next recession. But it will surely come. And when it does, the mechanism you've just studied will operate.

REVIEW

■ A change in autonomous expenditure changes real GDP by an amount determined by the multiplier.

■ The multiplier is larger, the greater the marginal propensity to consume, the smaller the marginal propensity to import, and the smaller the marginal tax rate.

■ Fluctuations in autonomous expenditure bring business cycle turning points.

The economy's potholes are changes in investment and exports. And the economy does not operate like the shock absorbers on Dennis Archer's car. While the price level is fixed, the effects of the economic potholes are not smoothed out. Instead, they are amplified like Bonnie Raitt's voice. But we've considered only the adjustments in spending that occur in the very short term when the price level is fixed. What happens after a long enough time lapse for the price level to change? Let's answer this question.

The Multiplier and the Price Level

WHEN FIRMS CAN'T KEEP UP WITH SALES AND their inventories fall below target, they increase production, but at some point, they raise their prices. Similarly, when firms find unwanted inventories piling up, they decrease production, but eventually, they cut their prices. So far, we've studied the macroeconomic consequences of firms changing their production levels when their sales change, but we haven't looked at the effects of price changes. When individual firms change their prices, the economy's price level changes.

To study the simultaneous determination of real GDP and the price level, we use the *aggregate supply–aggregate demand model*, which is explained in Chapter 24. But to understand how aggregate demand adjusts, we need to work out the connection between the aggregate supply–aggregate demand model and the equilibrium expenditure model that we've used in this chapter.

The key to understanding the relationship between these two models is the distinction between the aggregate *expenditure* and aggregate *demand* and the related distinction between the aggregate *expenditure curve* and the aggregate *demand curve*.

Aggregate Expenditure and Aggregate Demand

The aggregate expenditure curve is the relationship between the aggregate planned expenditure and real GDP, all other influences on aggregate planned expenditure remaining the same. The aggregate demand curve is the relationship between the aggregate quantity of goods and services demanded and the price level, all other influences on aggregate demand remaining the same. Let's explore the links between these two relationships.

Aggregate Expenditure and the Price Level

When the price level changes, aggregate planned expenditure changes and the quantity of real GDP demanded changes. The aggregate demand curve slopes downward. Why? There are two main reasons:

1. Wealth effect
2. Substitution effects

Wealth Effect   Other things remaining the same, the higher the price level, the smaller is the purchasing power of people's assets. For example, suppose you have $100 in the bank and the price level is 110. If the price level rises to 130, your $100 buys fewer goods and services. You are less wealthy. With less wealth, you will probably want to try to spend a bit less and save a bit more. Aggregate planned expenditure is lower the higher the price level, other things remaining the same.

Substitution Effects   A rise in the price level today, other things remaining the same, makes current goods and services more costly relative to future goods and services and results in a delay in purchases—an *intertemporal substitution*. A rise in the price level, other things remaining the same, makes U.S.-produced goods more expensive relative to foreign-produced goods and services and increases imports and decreases exports—an *international substitution*.

When the price level rises, each of these effects reduces aggregate planned expenditure at each level of real GDP. As a result, when the price level rises, the aggregate expenditure curve shifts downward. A fall in the price level has the opposite effect. When the price level falls, the aggregate expenditure curve shifts upward.

Figure 28.10(a) shows the shifts of the *AE* curve. When the price level is 110, the aggregate expenditure curve is *AE₀*, which intersects the 45° line at point *b*. Equilibrium expenditure is $7 trillion. If the price level increases to 130, the aggregate expenditure curve shifts downward to *AE₁*, which intersects the 45° line at point *a*. Equilibrium expenditure is $6 trillion. If the price level decreases to 90, the aggregate expenditure curve shifts upward to *AE₂*, which intersects the 45° line at point *c*. Equilibrium expenditure is $8 trillion.

We've just seen that when the price level changes, other things remaining the same, the aggregate expenditure curve shifts and the equilibrium expenditure changes. And when the price level changes, other things remaining the same, there is a movement along the aggregate demand curve. Figure 28.10(b) shows these movements along the aggregate demand curve. At a price level of 110, the aggregate quantity of goods and services demanded is $7 trillion—point *b* on the aggregate demand curve *AD*. If the price level rises to 130, the aggregate quantity of goods and services demanded decreases to $6 trillion. There is a movement along the aggregate demand curve to point *a*. If the price level falls to 90, the aggregate quantity of goods and services demanded increases to $8 trillion. There is a movement along the aggregate demand curve to point *c*.

Each point on the aggregate demand curve corresponds to a point of equilibrium expenditure. The equilibrium expenditure points *a*, *b*, and *c* in Fig. 28.10(a) correspond to the points *a*, *b*, and *c* on the aggregate demand curve in Fig. 28.10(b).

When the price level changes, other things remaining the same, the aggregate expenditure curve shifts and there is a movement along the aggregate demand curve. When any other influence on aggregate planned expenditure changes, *both* the aggregate expenditure curve and the aggregate demand curve shift. For example, an increase in investment or in exports increases both aggregate planned expenditure and aggregate demand and shifts both the *AE* curve and the *AD* curve. Figure 28.11 illustrates the effect of such an increase.

Initially, the aggregate expenditure curve is *AE₀* in part (a) and the aggregate demand curve is *AD₀* in part (b). The price level is 110, real GDP is $7 trillion, and the economy is at point *a* in both parts of the figure. Now suppose that investment increases by $1 trillion. At a constant price level of 110, the aggregate expenditure curve shifts upward to *AE₁*. This curve intersects the 45° line at an equilibrium

FIGURE 28.10

Aggregate Demand

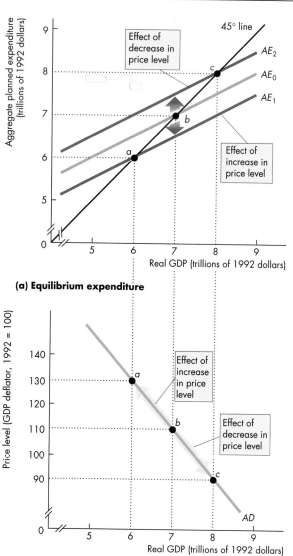

(a) Equilibrium expenditure

(b) Aggregate demand

A change in the price level shifts the *AE* curve and results in a *movement along* the *AD* curve. When the price level is 110, the *AE* curve is *AE₀*, and equilibrium expenditure is **$7 trillion** at point *b*. When the price level rises to 130, the *AE* curve is *AE₁*, and equilibrium expenditure is **$6 trillion** at point *a*. When the price level falls to 90, the *AE* curve is *AE₂*, and equilibrium expenditure is **$8 trillion** at point *c*. Points *a*, *b*, and *c* on the *AD* curve in part (b) correspond to the equilibrium expenditure points *a*, *b*, and *c* in part (a).

FIGURE 28.11

A Change in
Aggregate Demand

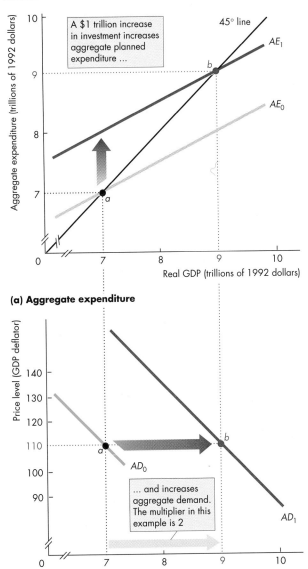

(a) Aggregate expenditure

(b) Aggregate demand

The price level is 110. When the aggregate expenditure curve is AE_0 (part a), the aggregate demand curve is AD_0 (part b). An increase in autonomous expenditure shifts the AE curve upward to AE_1. In the new equilibrium, real GDP is $9 trillion (at b). Because the quantity of real GDP demanded at a price level of 110 increases to $9 trillion, the AD curve shifts rightward to AD_1.

expenditure of $9 trillion (point b). This equilibrium expenditure of $9 trillion is the aggregate quantity of goods and services demanded at a price level of 110, as shown by point b in part (b). Point b lies on a new aggregate demand curve. The aggregate demand curve has shifted rightward to AD_1.

But how do we know by how much the AD curve shifts? The multiplier determines the answer. The larger the multiplier, the larger is the shift in the aggregate demand curve that results from a given change in autonomous expenditure. In this example, the multiplier is 2. A $1 trillion increase in investment produces a $2 trillion increase in the aggregate quantity of goods and services demanded at each price level. That is, a $1 trillion increase in autonomous expenditure shifts the aggregate demand curve rightward by $2 trillion.

A decrease in autonomous expenditure shifts the aggregate expenditure curve downward and shifts the aggregate demand curve leftward. You can see these effects by reversing the change that we've just studied. Suppose that the economy is initially at point b on the aggregate expenditure curve AE_1 and the aggregate demand curve AD_1. A decrease in autonomous expenditure shifts the aggregate planned expenditure curve downward to AE_0. The aggregate quantity of goods and services demanded falls from $9 trillion to $7 trillion, and the aggregate demand curve shifts leftward to AD_0.

Let's summarize what we have just discovered:

If some factor other than a change in the price level increases autonomous expenditure, the AE curve shifts upward and the AD curve shifts rightward.

The size of the AD curve shift depends on the change in autonomous expenditure and the multiplier.

Equilibrium GDP and the Price Level

In Chapter 24, we learned that aggregate demand and short-run aggregate supply determine equilibrium real GDP and the price level. We've now put aggregate demand under a more powerful microscope and have discovered that a change in investment (or in any component of autonomous expenditure) changes aggregate demand and shifts the aggregate demand curve. The magnitude of the shift depends on the multiplier. But whether a change in autonomous expenditure results ultimately in a change in real GDP, a change in the price level, or a combination of the two depends on aggregate supply. There are two time frames to consider, the short run and the long run. First we'll see what happens in the short run.

An Increase in Aggregate Demand in the Short Run

Figure 28.12 describes the economy. In part (a), the aggregate expenditure curve is AE_0, and equilibrium expenditure is $7 trillion—point a. In part (b), aggregate demand is AD_0, and the short-run aggregate supply curve is SAS. (Look at Chapter 24 if you need to refresh your understanding of this curve.) Equilibrium is at point a, where the aggregate demand and short-run aggregate supply curves intersect. The price level is 110, and real GDP is $7 trillion.

Now suppose that investment increases by $1 trillion. With the price level fixed at 110, the aggregate expenditure curve shifts upward to AE_1. Equilibrium expenditure increases to $9 trillion—point b in part (a). In part (b), the aggregate demand curve shifts rightward by $2 trillion, from AD_0 to AD_1. How far the aggregate demand curve shifts is determined by the multiplier when the price level is fixed. But with this new aggregate demand curve, the price level does not remain fixed. The price level rises, and as it does so the aggregate expenditure curve shifts downward. The short-run equilibrium occurs when the aggregate expenditure curve has shifted downward to AE_2 and the new aggregate demand curve, AD_1, intersects the short-run aggregate supply curve. Real GDP is $8.6 trillion, and the price level is 116 (at point c).

When price level effects are taken into account, the increase in investment still has a multiplier effect on real GDP, but the effect is smaller than it would be if the price level were fixed. The steeper the slope of the short-run aggregate supply curve, the larger is the increase in the price level and the smaller is the multiplier effect on real GDP.

An Increase in Aggregate Demand in the Long Run

Figure 28.13 illustrates the long-run effect of an increase in aggregate demand. In the long run, real GDP equals potential GDP and there is full employment. Potential GDP is $7 trillion, and the long-run aggregate supply curve is LAS. Initially, the economy is at point a (parts a and b).

FIGURE 28.12

The Multiplier in the Short Run

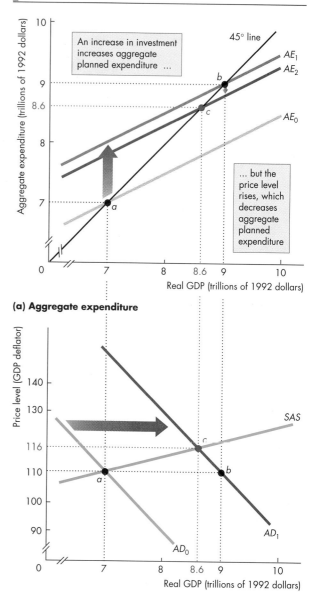

(a) Aggregate expenditure

(b) Aggregate demand

An increase in investment shifts the AE curve from AE_0 to AE_1 (part a) and the AD curve from AD_0 to AD_1 (part b). The price level does not remain at 110 but rises. The higher price level shifts the AE curve downward from AE_1 to AE_2. The economy moves to point c in both parts. In the short run, the multiplier effect is smaller than when the price level is fixed.

FIGURE 28.13

The Multiplier
in the Long Run

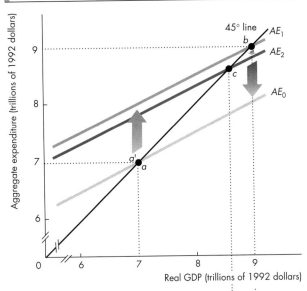

(a) Aggregate expenditure

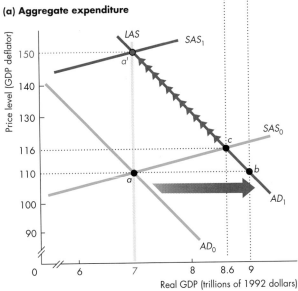

(b) Aggregate demand

Starting from point *a*, an increase in investment shifts the *AE* curve to *AE*₁ and the *AD* curve to *AD*₁. In the short run, the economy moves to point *c*. In the long run, the money wage rate rises, the *SAS* curve shifts to *SAS*₁, the *AE* curve shifts back to *AE*₀, the price level rises, and real GDP falls. The economy moves to point *a'*, and in the long run, the multiplier is zero.

Investment increases by \$1 trillion. The aggregate expenditure curve shifts to AE_1 and the aggregate demand curve shifts to AD_1. With no change in the price level, the economy would move to point *b* and real GDP would increase to \$9 trillion. But in the short run, the price level rises to 116 and real GDP increases to only \$8.6 trillion. With the higher price level, the *AE* curve shifts from AE_1 to AE_2. The economy is now in a short-run equilibrium at point *c*. Real GDP is now above potential GDP. The labor force is more than fully employed, and shortages of labor increase the money wage rate. The higher money wage rate increases costs, which decreases short-run aggregate supply and shifts the *SAS* curve leftward to SAS_1. The price level rises further, and real GDP decreases. There is a movement along AD_1, and the *AE* curve shifts downward from AE_2 toward AE_0. When the money wage rate and the price level have increased by the same percentage, real GDP is again equal to potential GDP and the economy is at point *a'*. In the long run, the multiplier is zero.

R E V I E W

- A change in the price level shifts the *AE* curve and brings a movement along the *AD* curve.
- A change in autonomous expenditure that is not caused by a change in the price level shifts both the *AE* curve and the *AD* curve, and the multiplier determines the magnitude of the shift in the *AD* curve.
- In the short run, the increase in real GDP that results from an increase in autonomous expenditure is smaller than the increase in aggregate demand.
- In the long run, an increase in aggregate demand leaves real GDP unchanged but increases the price level. In the long run, the multiplier is zero.

You are now ready to build on what you've learned about expenditure fluctuations and study the roles of fiscal policy and monetary policy in smoothing the business cycle. In Chapter 29, we study fiscal policy—government purchases, taxes, and the deficit—and in Chapters 30 and 31, we study monetary policy—interest rates and the quantity of money. But before you leave the current topic, look at *Reading Between the Lines* on pages 636–637 and see the model you've studied in this chapter in action in the U.S. economy.

Recession Watch

THE SEATTLE TIMES, DECEMBER 22, 1996

Polishing Up Those Forecasts

BY STEPHEN H. DUNPHY

This is the time of year when economists around the nation put the finishing touches on their forecasts for next year. ...

The consensus seems to be that the economy will experience slow growth next year with an outside chance of tipping into an outright recession. Most economists are pegging growth at about 2 percent to 2.5 percent for the year.

That's now being called a soft landing, engineered by the Federal Reserve. Of course, that used to be called a growth recession in which the economy grew, but not fast enough to create many new jobs. Soft landing sounds better than growth recession, but it is all the same.

Some signs are pointing toward a business slowdown. Among them: a bigger-than-expected drop in home construction, tepid retail revenue, falling auto sales, declining industrial home production and a slump in U.S. exports. Boeing sales could help that latter category as its production lines gear up for the recent spurt in orders.

Here is what economists watch for as danger signs of recession:

—A spike in inflation brought on by shortages in energy or labor. Oil prices have risen in recent months, but that remains a volatile commodity. Tight labor conditions in many regions—including the Seattle area—are threatening to push wages higher.

This is the area to watch: Most recessions in recent years have come from the Fed raising interest rates to slow or stop inflation.

—Inventory buildups. If sales slow, goods begin to build up on the shelf. That leads to production cuts and job losses. But some economists say "just-in-time" manufacturing techniques make inventories less important.

Business inventories rose less than 1 percent in the third quarter, while sales rose more than 1 percent. That suggests underlying economic conditions are still solid.

—Unexpected jolts. Something unexpected could trigger a recession. The Gulf War had that effect. Ditto the Arab oil embargo. There is nothing on the horizon now.

"We do believe that growth has slowed," said economists for DRI/McGraw Hill, a major economic forecasting company. "But the economy is not shifting into recession. ...

Reprinted with permission.

Essence of **THE STORY**

■ The consensus among economists (at the end of 1996) is that real GDP will grow by 2 percent to 2.5 percent during 1997.

■ The chance of a recession is seen as small.

■ Decreases in home construction, auto sales, industrial production, and U.S. exports and slow retail sales all point to a slowdown.

■ Danger signs of a recession include a spike in inflation brought on by shortages of labor and inventory buildups.

■ In 1997, there are signs of a labor shortage, but inventories have not built up.

Economic

A N A L Y S I S

■ Inventory investment fluctuates, and when recession begins, an *unplanned* inventory buildup occurs.

■ But not all increases in inventories are unplanned.

■ Figure 1 shows the changes in inventories between 1990 and 1996. The last recession, in 1990–1991, was preceded by an unplanned increase in inventories. But the most recent large increase in inventories, in 1994, was planned and did not lead to recession.

■ Figure 1 also shows that inventories increased during 1996. We do not know whether this increase is unplanned or planned.

■ Planned inventory changes are part of planned investment and so are part of aggregate planned expenditure.

■ Figure 2 shows two possible scenarios for 1997. In the first scenario, aggregate planned expenditure is AE_{97}. At point a, AE_{97} intersects the 45° line and aggregate planned expenditure equals real GDP at $7 trillion, which (we'll assume) equals potential GDP.

■ Figure 2(b) shows the relationship between real GDP and unplanned inventory changes as the line labeled UI_{97}. At the equilibrium real GDP of $7 trillion, shown at point a', there is no unplanned change in inventory.

■ In the second scenario, aggregate planned expenditure decreases and the AE curve shifts downward to AE'. The new equilibrium occurs at point b.

■ In Fig. 2(b), the unplanned inventory curve shifts to UI'.

■ With real GDP at $7 trillion, there is now an unplanned increase in inventories, shown in Fig. 2(b).

■ Firms decrease production, and real GDP decreases. In Fig. 2(a), the economy moves to point b.

■ Unplanned inventory changes return to zero when aggregate planned expenditure equals real GDP, at point b' in Fig. 2(b).

■ At the beginning of 1997, no events had occurred to make the second outcome predictable.

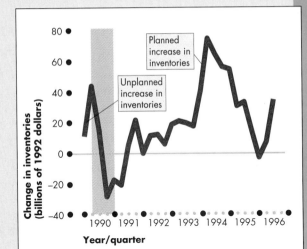

Figure 1 Change in inventories

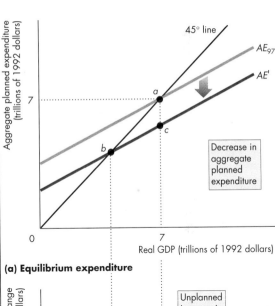

(a) Equilibrium expenditure

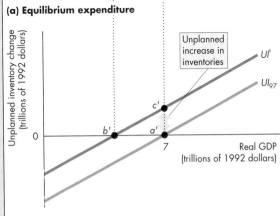

(b) Unplanned inventory changes

Figure 2 Equilibrium expenditure

Key Points

Fixed Prices and Expenditure Plans
(pp. 616–621)

- When the price level is fixed, expenditure plans determine real GDP.
- Consumption expenditure is determined by disposable income, and the marginal propensity to consume (*MPC*) determines the change in consumption expenditure brought about by a change in disposable income. Real GDP determines disposable income.
- Imports are determined by real GDP, and the marginal propensity to import determines the change in imports brought about by a change in real GDP.

Real GDP with a Fixed Price Level
(pp. 622–625)

- Aggregate *planned* expenditure depends on real GDP.
- Equilibrium expenditure occurs when aggregate planned expenditure equals actual expenditure and real GDP.

The Multiplier (pp. 626–631)

- The multiplier is the magnified effect of a change in autonomous expenditure on real GDP.
- The multiplier is influenced by the marginal propensity to consume, the marginal propensity to import, and the marginal income tax rate.

The Multiplier and the Price Level
(pp. 631–635)

- The aggregate demand curve is the relationship between the quantity of real GDP demanded and the price level, other things remaining the same.
- The aggregate expenditure curve is the relationship between aggregate planned expenditure and real GDP, other things remaining the same.

- At a given price level, there is a given aggregate expenditure curve. A change in the price level changes aggregate planned expenditure and shifts the aggregate expenditure curve. A change in the price level also creates a movement along the aggregate demand curve.
- A change in autonomous expenditure that is not caused by a change in the price level shifts the aggregate expenditure curve and shifts the aggregate demand curve. The magnitude of the shift of the aggregate demand curve depends on the multiplier and on the change in autonomous expenditure.
- The multiplier decreases as the price level changes, and in the long run the multiplier is zero.

Key Figures

Key Terms

QUESTIONS

1. What is the main influence on consumption expenditure and saving in the short term?

2. What are the consumption function and the saving function? What is the relationship between them?

3. What is the marginal propensity to consume? Why is it less than 1?

4. Explain the relationship between the marginal propensities to consume and to save.

5. What determines the slope of the consumption function?

6. What is the marginal propensity to import?

7. What are the aggregate expenditure schedule and the aggregate expenditure curve?

8. Distinguish between induced expenditure and autonomous expenditure.

9. How is equilibrium expenditure determined?

10. Explain how a recovery gets going when aggregate planned expenditure exceeds real GDP.

11. Explain why an increase in autonomous expenditure shifts the aggregate expenditure curve.

12. What is the multiplier?

13. Explain the multiplier process.

14. What determines the size of the multiplier?

15. Explain the influences of the marginal propensity to consume, imports, and taxes on the size of the multiplier.

16. Describe the relationship between the aggregate expenditure curve and the aggregate demand curve.

17. Explain why the aggregate expenditure curve shifts downward when the price level increases.

18. What happens to the aggregate expenditure curve and the aggregate demand curve when the price level changes and everything else is constant?

19. Explain why an increase in autonomous expenditure increases aggregate demand.

20. Explain why the multiplier is larger when the price level is fixed than when it changes.

21. Explain why the multiplier is zero in the long run.

PROBLEMS

1. You are given the following information about the economy of Heron Island:

Disposable income (millions of dollars per year)	Consumption expenditure (millions of dollars per year)
0	5
10	10
20	15
30	20
40	25

Calculate Heron Island's
a. Marginal propensity to consume.
b. Saving at each level of disposable income.
c. Marginal propensity to save.

2. Turtle Island has no imports or exports, the people of Turtle Island pay no incomes taxes, and the price level is fixed. The figure illustrates the components of aggregate planned expenditure on Turtle Island.

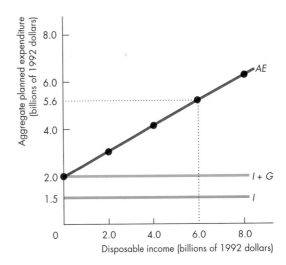

On Turtle Island, what is:
a. Autonomous expenditure?
b. The marginal propensity to consume?
c. Aggregate planned expenditure when real GDP is $6 billion?
d. If real GDP is $4 billion, what is happening to inventories?

e. If real GDP is $6 billion, what is happening to inventories?

f. What is the multiplier?

3. You are given the following information about the economy of Zeeland: Autonomous consumption expenditure is $100 billion, and the marginal propensity to consume is 0.9. Investment is $460 billion, government purchases of goods and services are $400 billion, and net taxes are a constant $400 billion—they do not vary with income.

a. What is the consumption function?

b. What is the equation that describes the aggregate expenditure curve?

c. Calculate equilibrium expenditure.

d. If investment falls to $360 billion, what is the change in equilibrium expenditure and what is the size of the multiplier?

4. Suppose that in problem 3, the price level is 100 and real GDP equals potential GDP.

a. If investment increases by $100 billion, what happens to the quantity of real GDP demanded?

b. In the short run, does equilibrium real GDP increase by more than, less than, or the same amount as the increase in the quantity of real GDP demanded?

c. In the long run, does equilibrium real GDP increase by more than, less than, or the same amount as the increase in the quantity of real GDP demanded?

d. In the short run, does the price level in Zeeland rise, fall, or remain unchanged?

e. In the long run, does the price level in Zeeland rise, fall, or remain unchanged?

CRITICAL THINKING

1. Study *Reading Between the Lines* on pp. 636–637, and then answer the following questions:

a. The 1994 investment in inventories seems to have been a *planned* investment. What are the implications of a planned investment in business inventories for real GDP, aggregate expenditure, and inventory investment? Use a figure similar to Fig. 2 on p. 637 to answer this question.

b. The 1990 investment in inventories seems to have been an *unplanned* investment. What are the implications of an unplanned investment in business inventories for real GDP, aggregate expenditure, and inventory investment? Use a figure similar to Fig. 2 on p. 637 to answer this question.

c. What do you think will happen to real GDP, aggregate expenditure, and inventory investment in 1997? What clues do you get from the news article?

d. Is a buildup of business inventories a cause or a consequence of recession?

2. Visit the Penn World Table Web site (linked from the Parkin site) and obtain data on real GDP per person and consumption as a percentage of real GDP for the United States, China, South Africa, and Mexico since 1960.

a. In a spreadsheet, multiply your real GDP data by the consumption percentage and divide by 100 to obtain data on real consumption expenditure per person.

b. Make graphs like Fig. 28.4 that show the relationship between consumption and real GDP for these four countries.

c. Based on the numbers you've obtained, in which country do you expect the multiplier to be largest (other things being equal)?

d. What other data would you need in order to calculate the multipliers for these countries?

e. You are a research assistant in the office of the President's Council of Economic Advisors. You've been asked to draft a note for the President that explains the power and limitations of the multiplier. The President wants only 250 words of crisp, clear, jargon-free explanation together with a lively example.

In 1997, the federal government planned to spend $1,631 billion, or 23 cents of every dollar that Americans earn. What are the effects of government spending on the economy? Does it create jobs? Or does it destroy them? And does a dollar spent by the government on goods and services have the same effect as a dollar spent by someone else? ◆ Although the federal government planned to *spend* 23 cents of every dollar earned, it did not plan to tax us by that amount. Its plans were for tax revenues of $1,505 billion or 21 cents of every dollar earned. What are the effects of taxes on the economy? Do taxes harm employment and economic growth? ◆ The plan to have tax revenues fall short of expenditures is not new on Capitol Hill. The last time the federal

Balancing Acts on Capitol Hill

government budget was in surplus was 1969. Over the 28 years since then, and using constant 1992 dollars, the federal government's debt has increased from $1,000 billion to $3,500 billion. If these numbers are too big to mean anything, divide them by the U.S. population to find *your* share. Government

debt per person was more than $13,000 in 1997. Does it matter if the government doesn't balance its books? What are the effects of an ongoing government deficit and accumulating debt? Does it slow economic growth? Does it impose a burden on future generations—on you and your children? What must be done to balance the budget? Can spending cuts do it? Or must taxes be increased? Or can spending be cut so severely that taxes can also be cut? ◆ These are the fiscal policy issues that you will study in this chapter. We'll begin by describing the federal budget and the process of creating it. We'll also look at the recent history of the budget. We'll then use the multiplier analysis of Chapter 28 and the aggregate supply–aggregate demand model of Chapter 24 to study the effects of the budget on the economy.

After studying this chapter, you will be able to:

- Describe the federal budget process
- Describe the recent history of federal expenditures, tax revenues, and the budget deficit
- Distinguish between automatic and discretionary fiscal policy
- Define and explain the fiscal policy multipliers
- Explain the effects of fiscal policy in the short run and in the long run
- Distinguish between and explain the demand-side and supply-side effects of fiscal policy

The Federal Budget

THE ANNUAL STATEMENT OF THE EXPENDITURES and tax revenues of the government of the United States together with the laws and regulations that approve and support those expenditures and taxes make up the **federal budget**. The federal budget has two purposes:

1. To finance the activities of the federal government
2. To stabilize the economy

The first purpose of the federal budget was its only purpose before the Great Depression years of the 1930s. The second purpose of the federal budget arose as a reaction to the Great Depression. The use of the federal budget to achieve macroeconomic objectives such as full employment, sustained economic growth, and price level stability is called **fiscal policy**. It is on this second purpose that we focus in this chapter.

The Institutions and Laws

Fiscal policy is made by the President and Congress on an annual time line that is shown in Figure 29.1.

The Roles of the President and Congress The President *proposes* a budget to Congress each February and, after Congress has passed the budget acts in September, either signs those acts into law or vetoes them. Until recently, the President approved or vetoed an entire budget bill. The President did not have veto power to eliminate specific items in a budget bill and approve others—a *line-item veto*. Many state governors have long had a line-item veto, and the President of the United States received this power in 1996. But a court challenge has put the veto in doubt. Although the President proposes and ultimately approves the budget, the task of making the tough decisions on spending and taxes rests with Congress.

Congress begins its work on the budget with the President's proposal. The House of Representatives and the Senate develop their own budget ideas in their respective House and Senate Budget Committees. Formal conferences between the two houses eventually resolve differences of view, and a series of spending acts and an overall budget act are usually passed by both houses before the start of the fiscal year. A *fiscal year* is a year that runs from October 1 to September

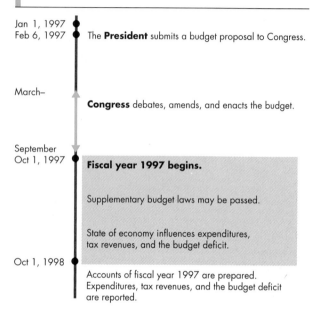

FIGURE 29.1

The Federal Budget Time Line in 1997–98

Jan 1, 1997
Feb 6, 1997 — The **President** submits a budget proposal to Congress.

March– — **Congress** debates, amends, and enacts the budget.

September
Oct 1, 1997 — **Fiscal year 1997 begins.**

Supplementary budget laws may be passed.

State of economy influences expenditures, tax revenues, and the budget deficit.

Oct 1, 1998 — Accounts of fiscal year 1997 are prepared. Expenditures, tax revenues, and the budget deficit are reported.

The federal budget process begins with the President's proposals in February. Congress debates and amends these proposals and enacts a budget before the start of the fiscal year on October 1. The President signs the budget acts into law but may exercise a line-item veto. Throughout the fiscal year, Congress might pass supplementary budget laws. The budget outcome is calculated after the end of the fiscal year.

30 in the next calendar year. *Fiscal 1997* is the fiscal year that *begins* on October 1, 1997.

During a fiscal year, Congress often passes supplementary budget laws, and the budget outcome is influenced by the evolving state of the economy. For example, if a recession begins, tax revenues fall and welfare payments increase.

The Employment Act of 1946 Fiscal policy operates within the framework of the landmark **Employment Act of 1946**, in which Congress declared that

> it is the continuing policy and responsibility of the Federal Government to use all practicable means … to coordinate and utilize all its plans, functions, and resources … to promote maximum employment, production, and purchasing power.

This act recognized a role for government actions to keep unemployment low, keep the economy expanding, and keep inflation in check. The *Full Employment and Balanced Growth Act of 1978*, more commonly known as the *Humphrey-Hawkins Act*, went further than the 1946 employment act and set a specific target of 4 percent for the unemployment rate. Most economists regard this target as unattainable and it has no operational significance. Under the 1946 Act, the President must describe the current economic situation and the policies he believes are needed in an annual *Economic Report of the President*, which is written by the Council of Economic Advisers.

The Council of Economic Advisers   The President's **Council of Economic Advisers** (CEA) was established in 1946 by the Employment Act. The Council consists of a Chair and two other members, all of whom are economists on leave from their regular university or public service jobs. Members typically serve for two to three years. In 1997, the Chair of President Clinton's Council of Economic Advisers was Janet Yellen of the University of California at Berkeley, and the two members were Jeffrey A. Frankel, also of Berkeley, and Alicia H. Munnell. The

main work of the Council is to monitor the economy and to keep the President and the public well informed about the current state of the economy and the best available forecasts of where it is heading. This economic intelligence activity is one source of data that informs the budget-making process.

Let's look at the most recent federal budget.

Highlights of the 1997 Budget

Table 29.1 shows the main items in the federal budget proposed by President Clinton in 1997. The numbers are projected amounts for the fiscal year beginning on October 1, 1997—fiscal 1997. Notice the three main parts of the table: *Tax revenues* are the government's receipts, *expenditures* are the government's outlays, and the *deficit* is the amount by which the government's expenditures exceed its tax revenues.

Tax Revenues   Tax revenues were projected to be $1,505 billion in fiscal 1997. These revenues come from four sources:

1. Personal income taxes
2. Social insurance taxes
3. Corporate income taxes
4. Indirect taxes

The largest source of revenue is *personal income taxes*, which in 1997 were expected to be $673 billion. These are the taxes paid by individuals on their incomes. The second largest source is *social insurance taxes*. These are the taxes paid by workers and their employers to finance the government's social security programs. Third in size are *corporate income taxes*. These are the taxes paid by companies on their profits. Finally, the smallest source of revenue comes from *indirect taxes*. These are taxes on the sale of gasoline, alcoholic drinks, and a few other items.

Expenditures   Expenditures are classified in three categories:

1. Transfer payments
2. Purchases of goods and services
3. Debt interest

The largest item of expenditure, *transfer payments*, are payments to individuals, businesses, other levels of government, and the rest of the world.

TABLE 29.1
Federal Budget in Fiscal 1997

Item	Projections (billions of dollars)	
Tax Revenues	**1,505**	
Personal income taxes		673
Social insurance taxes		536
Corporate income taxes		176
Indirect taxes		120
Expenditures	**1,631**	
Transfer payments		1,060
Purchases of goods and services		324
Debt interest		247
Deficit	**126**	

Source: *Economic Report of the President*, 1997, Table B-78.

In 1997, this item was expected to be $1,060 billion. It includes Social Security benefits, Medicare and Medicaid, unemployment checks, welfare payments, farm subsidies, grants to state and local governments, aid to developing countries, and dues to international organizations such as the United Nations. Transfer payments, especially those on Medicare and Medicaid, are sources of persistent growth in government expenditures and are a major source of political debate.

Purchases of goods and services are expenditures on final goods and services, and in 1997, they were expected to total $324 billion. These expenditures, which include those on national defense, the NASA space program, research on cures for AIDS and other diseases, computers for the Internal Revenue Service, government cars and trucks, federal highways, and dams, have decreased in recent years. This component of the federal budget is included in *government purchases of goods and services* that appears in the circular flow of expenditure and income and in the National Income and Product Accounts (see Chapter 23, pp. 496–497).

Debt interest is the interest on the government debt. In 1997, this item was expected to be $247 billion—some 15 percent of total expenditure. This interest payment is large because the government has a debt of almost $4 trillion, which has arisen from large and persistent budget deficits.

Deficit The government's budget balance is

Budget balance = Tax revenues – Expenditures.

If tax revenues exceed expenditures, the government has a **budget surplus**. If expenditures exceed tax revenues, the government has a **budget deficit**. If tax revenues equal expenditures, the government has a **balanced budget**. In fiscal 1997, with projected expenditures of $1,631 billion and tax revenues of $1,505 billion, the government projected a budget deficit of $126 billion.

Big numbers like these are hard to visualize and hard to compare over time. To get a better sense of the magnitude of taxes, spending, and the deficit, we often express them as percentages of GDP. Expressing them this way lets us to see how large the government is relative to the size of the economy and also helps us to study *changes* in the scale of government over time.

How typical is the federal budget of 1997? Let's look at its recent history.

The Budget in Historical Perspective

Figure 29.2 shows the government's tax revenues, expenditures, and budget deficit since 1978. Throughout this period, there was a budget deficit.

FIGURE 29.2
The Budget Deficit

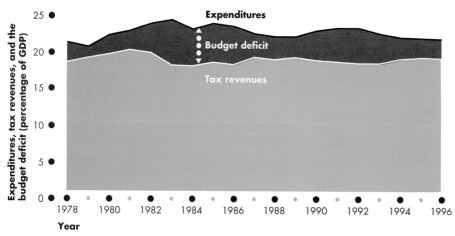

The figure records the federal government's expenditures, tax revenues, and budget deficit from 1978 to 1996. During the late 1970s, the deficit was small and decreasing, but during the 1980s, it became large and persisted. The budget deficit arose from the combination of a decrease in tax revenues and an increase in expenditures.

Source: *Economic Report of the President*, 1997.

The deficit was small and decreasing between 1978 and 1979, but it then increased and reached a peak in 1983 of 6.3 percent of GDP. It declined from 1983 through 1989 but averaged more than 4 percent of GDP through the entire decade of the 1980s. The deficit climbed again during the 1990–1991 recession and then decreased during the 1990s expansion.

Why did the government deficit grow in the early 1980s and remain high? The immediate answer is that expenditures increased and tax revenues decreased. But which components of expenditures increased and which sources of tax revenues decreased? Let's look at tax revenues and expenditures in a bit more detail.

Tax Revenues   Figure 29.3(a) shows the components of tax revenues as percentages of GDP between 1978 and 1996. Total tax revenues increased between 1978 and 1981 and then declined through 1986. Most of the decline was in corporate and personal

---

FIGURE **29.3**

Federal Government Tax Revenues and Expenditures

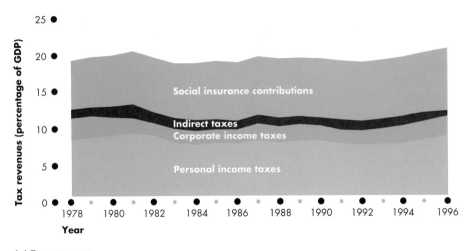

(a) Tax revenues

Part (a) shows the four components of government tax revenues: personal income taxes, corporate income taxes, indirect taxes, and social insurance contributions. Revenues from personal and corporate income taxes declined during the early 1980s, remained fairly steady from 1983 to 1991, and then increased. The other two components of tax revenues remained steady.

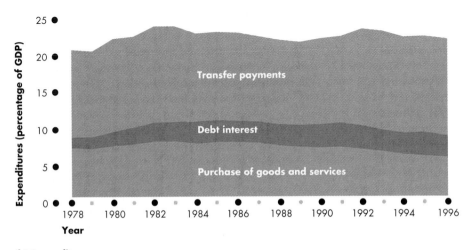

(b) Expenditures

Part (b) shows three components of government expenditures: purchases of goods and services, debt interest, and transfer payments. Purchases of goods and services fluctuated but did not increase. Transfer payments fluctuated most and did increase, especially during the early 1980s and in 1991–1992. Debt interest increased steadily during the 1980s and 1990s as the budget deficit fed on itself.

Source: Economic Report of the President, 1997.

income taxes, and the decline resulted from tax cuts passed in the Economic Recovery Tax Act of 1981. From 1986 through 1991, tax revenues did not change much as a percentage of GDP. But they increased after 1992 through 1996.

Expenditures   Figure 29.3(b) shows the components of government expenditures as percentages of GDP, between 1978 and 1996. Total expenditures decreased between 1978 and 1979 and then increased sharply between 1979 and 1983. Expenditures then declined slightly through 1989 before increasing again until 1992. After 1992, total expenditures decreased. Both purchases of goods and services and transfer payments fluctuated. The item that increased most persistently was debt interest. To understand why, we need to see the connection between the deficit and government debt.

Deficit and Debt   The government borrows to finance its deficit. And **government debt** is the total amount of government borrowing. It is the sum of past deficits minus the sum of past surpluses. When the government has a deficit, its debt increases. Once a persistent deficit emerged during the 1980s, the deficit began to feed on itself. The deficit led to increased borrowing; increased borrowing led to larger interest payments; and larger interest payments led to a larger deficit. That is the story of the increasing deficit of the 1980s.

   Figure 29.4 shows the history of government debt since 1945. At the end of World War II, debt (as a percentage of GDP) was at an all-time high of 114 percent. Huge wartime deficits had increased debt to the point that it exceeded real GDP. Postwar budget surpluses lowered the debt to GDP ratio through 1974, by which time it stood at 24 percent, its lowest point since World War II. Small deficits increased the debt to GDP ratio slightly through the 1970s, and large deficits increased it dramatically between 1981 and 1986. During the late 1980s, the ratio continued to increase but at a more moderate rate. It grew quickly again during the 1990–1991 recession, but the debt to GDP ratio fell when the economy recovered during 1993 and 1995.

Debt and Capital   When individuals and businesses incur debts, they usually do so to buy capital—assets that yield a return. In fact, the main point of debt is to enable people to buy assets that will earn a return that exceeds the interest paid on the debt.

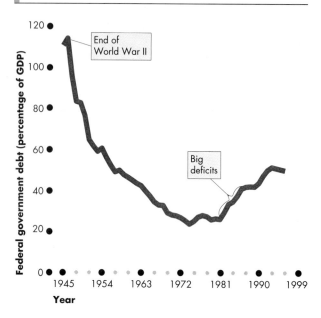

FIGURE 29.4
The Federal Government Debt

Federal government debt (the accumulation of past budget deficits less past budget surpluses) was more than 100 percent of GDP at the end of World War II. Debt as a percentage of GDP fell through 1974 but then started to increase. After a further brief decline during the late 1970s, it exploded during the 1980s and continued to increase through 1993.

Source: Economic Report of the President, 1997.

The government is similar to individuals and businesses in this regard. Much government expenditure is on public assets that yield a return. Highways, major irrigation schemes, public schools and universities, public libraries, and the stock of national defense capital all yield a social rate of return that probably far exceeds the interest rate that the government pays on its debt.

   But total government debt, which is almost $4 trillion, is more than twice the value of the public capital stock. So some government debt has been incurred to finance public consumption expenditure. This expenditure does not have an ongoing social return.

   How does the U.S. government deficit compare with deficits in other countries?

The Budget Deficit in Global Perspective

Is the United States unusual in running a budget deficit? Do other countries have budget deficits or do they have budget surpluses? Figure 29.5 answers these questions. Almost all countries have budget deficits in today's world. To make the deficits comparable across countries, we measure the deficits as percentages of GDP. The biggest deficits relative to GDP are found in Japan, the Middle East, and the countries of Central Europe that are making a transition from a heavily regulated economy to a market economy. The smallest deficits relative to GDP are found in the developing countries of the Western Hemisphere. The U.S. budget deficit is *smaller* than that of most countries. It is smaller than Japan's and the average of the rich industrial countries in Europe.

State and Local Budgets

The *total government* sector of the United States includes state and local governments as well as the federal government. In 1997, when federal government expenditures were $1,631 billion, state and local expenditures were $1,050 billion. Most of these expenditures were on public schools, colleges, and universities ($350 billion), local police and fire services, and roads.

It is the total government sector that influences the aggregate economy. But state and local budgets are not designed, as the federal budget is, with the specific goal of stabilizing the aggregate economy. On the contrary, sometimes, when the aggregate economy needs an injection of additional expenditures, state and local governments cut their expenditures and deficits. Such changes in expenditures occurred during the 1990–1991 recession when many states both cut their expenditures and increased taxes.

FIGURE 29.5
Government Deficits Around the World in 1996

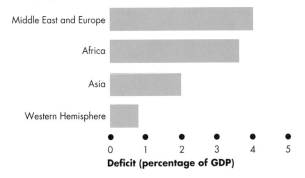

Governments in most countries have budget deficits. The largest ones are in Japan, the Middle East, and Europe, and the smallest are in the developing countries in the Western Hemisphere—Central and South America. The U.S. federal government deficit is at the low end of the scale.

Source: World Economic Outlook (Washington, D.C.: International Monetary Fund, May 1996), Tables A14 and A19.

R E V I E W

- Fiscal policy is created by Congress and the President and is a key tool designed to influence employment and economic activity.
- Each year, the budget is proposed by the President in February and amended and enacted by Congress. The fiscal year begins on October 1.
- For many years, the federal government has run a budget deficit and federal debt has grown.

Now that you know what the federal budget is and what the main items of revenue and expenditure are, it is time to study the *effects* of fiscal policy. We'll begin by learning about its effects on expenditure plans when the price level is fixed. You will see that fiscal policy has multiplier effects like the expenditure multipliers explained in Chapter 28. Then we'll study the influences of fiscal policy on both aggregate demand and aggregate supply and look at its short-run and long-run effects on real GDP and the price level.

Fiscal Policy Multipliers

FISCAL POLICY ACTIONS CAN BE EITHER AUTOMATIC or discretionary. **Automatic fiscal policy** is a change in fiscal policy that is triggered by the state of the economy. For example, an increase in unemployment triggers an *automatic* increase in payments to the unemployed. A fall in incomes triggers an *automatic* decrease in tax receipts. That is, this type of fiscal policy adjusts automatically. **Discretionary fiscal policy** is a policy action that is initiated by an act of Congress. It requires a change in tax laws or in some spending program. For example, an increase in the income tax rate and an increase in defense spending are discretionary fiscal policy actions. That is, discretionary fiscal policy is a deliberate policy action.

We begin by studying the effects of *discretionary* changes in government spending and taxes. To focus on the essentials, we'll initially study a model economy that is simpler than the one in which we live. In our model economy, there is no international trade and the taxes are all lump sum. **Lump-sum taxes** are taxes that do not vary with real GDP. The government fixes them, and they change when the government changes them. But they do not vary automatically with the state of the economy.

The main example of a lump-sum tax is the *property tax*. This tax varies across individuals and depends on the value of the property a person occupies. But unlike the income tax, it does not change simply because a person's income changes.

We use lump-sum taxes in our model economy because they make the principles we are studying easier to understand. Once we've grasped the principles, we'll explore our real economy with its international trade and income taxes—taxes that *do* vary with real GDP.

Like our real economy, the model economy we study is bombarded by spending fluctuations. Business investment in new building, plant and equipment, and inventories fluctuates because of swings in profit expectations and interest rates. These fluctuations set up multiplier effects that start a recession or an expansion. If a recession takes hold, unemployment increases and incomes fall. If an expansion becomes too strong, inflationary pressures build up. To minimize the effects of these swings in spending, the government might change either its purchases of goods and services or taxes. By changing either of these items, the government can influence aggregate expenditure and real GDP. But it also changes its budget deficit or surplus. An alternative fiscal policy action is to change both purchases and taxes together so that the budget balance does not change. We are going to study the initial effects of these discretionary fiscal policy actions in the very short run when the price level is fixed. Each of these actions creates a multiplier effect on real GDP. These multipliers are:

- The government purchases multiplier
- The lump-sum tax multiplier

The Government Purchases Multiplier

The **government purchases multiplier** is the magnification effect of a change in government purchases of goods and services on equilibrium expenditure and real GDP.

Government purchases are a component of aggregate expenditure. So when government purchases change, aggregate expenditure and real GDP change. The change in real GDP induces a change in consumption expenditure, which brings a further change in aggregate expenditure. A multiplier process ensues. This multiplier process is like the one described in Chapter 28 (pp. 626–631). Let's look at an example.

Cape Canaveral Multiplier Before the National Aeronautics and Space Administration (NASA) built a major space launching facility at Cape Canaveral in Florida in the 1960s, the Cape was a quiet place. The injection of government purchases to build the space launching and research facility created jobs in the region. Because construction workers and NASA workers spent most of their incomes locally, consumption expenditure increased. Retail stores and hotels and motels opened and hired yet more people and, in the process, created yet bigger incomes. These incomes were also spent in the area, so spending and incomes rose still further. Eventually, expenditures and incomes stopped rising but remained at their new higher levels.

The Size of the Multiplier Table 29.2 illustrates the government purchases multiplier with a numerical example. The first column lists various possible levels of real GDP. Our task is to find equilibrium expenditure and the change in real GDP when government purchases change. The second column shows taxes.

TABLE 29.2

The Government Purchases Multiplier

	Real GDP (Y)	Taxes (T)	Disposable income (Y – T)	Consumption expenditure (C)	Investment (I)	Initial government purchases (G)	Initial aggregate planned expenditure (AE = C + I + G)	New government purchases (G')	New aggregate planned expenditure (AE' = C + I + G')
					(trillions of dollars)				
a	5.0	0.5	4.5	3.75	1.0	0.5	5.25	1.0	5.75
b	6.0	0.5	5.5	4.50	1.0	0.5	6.00	1.0	6.50
c	7.0	0.5	6.5	5.25	1.0	0.5	6.75	1.0	7.25
d	8.0	0.5	7.5	6.00	1.0	0.5	7.50	1.0	8.00
e	9.0	0.5	8.5	6.75	1.0	0.5	8.25	1.0	8.75

They are fixed at $0.5 trillion, regardless of the level of real GDP. (This is an assumption that keeps your attention on the key idea and makes the calculations easier to do.) The third column calculates disposable income. Because taxes are a lump sum, disposable income equals real GDP minus the $0.5 trillion of taxes. For example, in row *b*, real GDP is $6 trillion and disposable income is $5.5 trillion. The next column shows consumption expenditure. In this example, the *marginal propensity to consume* is 0.75. That is, a $1 increase in disposable income brings a 75-cent increase in consumption expenditure. Check this fact by calculating the increase in consumption expenditure when disposable income increases by $1 trillion from row *b* to row *c*. Consumption expenditure increases by $0.75 trillion. The next column shows investment, which is a constant of $1 trillion. The next column shows the initial level of government purchases, which is $0.5 trillion. Aggregate planned expenditure is the sum of consumption expenditure, investment, and government purchases.

Equilibrium expenditure and real GDP occur when aggregate planned expenditure equals actual expenditure. In this example, equilibrium expenditure is $6 trillion (highlighted in row *b* of the table.)

The final two columns of the table show what happens when government purchases increase by $0.5 trillion to $1 trillion. Aggregate planned expenditure increases by $0.5 trillion at each level of real GDP. At the initial real GDP of $6 trillion (row *b*), aggregate planned expenditure increases to $6.5 trillion.

Because aggregate planned expenditure now exceeds real GDP, inventories decrease and firms increase production. Output, incomes, and expenditure increase. Increased incomes induce a further increase in expenditure. But the induced increase in aggregate planned expenditure is less than the increase in income, and eventually a new equilibrium is reached. The new equilibrium is at a real GDP of $8 trillion (highlighted in row *d*).

A $0.5 trillion increase in government purchases has increased equilibrium expenditure and real GDP by $2 trillion. Therefore the government purchases multiplier is 4. The size of the multiplier depends on the marginal propensity to consume, which in this example is 0.75. The following formula shows the connection between the government purchases multiplier and the marginal propensity to consume (*MPC*):

$$\text{Government purchase multiplier} = \frac{1}{1 - MPC}.$$

Let's check this formula by using the numbers in the above example. The marginal propensity to consume is 0.75, so the government purchases multiplier is 4.

Figure 29.6 illustrates the government purchases multiplier. Initially, aggregate planned expenditure is shown by the curve labeled AE_0. The points on this curve, labeled *a* through *e*, correspond with the rows of Table 29.2. This aggregate expenditure curve intersects the 45° line at the equilibrium level of real GDP, which is $6 trillion.

FIGURE 29.6
The Government Purchases Multiplier

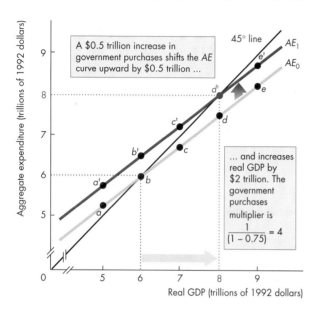

A $0.5 trillion increase in government purchases shifts the AE curve upward by $0.5 trillion ...

... and increases real GDP by $2 trillion. The government purchases multiplier is $\dfrac{1}{(1 - 0.75)} = 4$

Initially, the aggregate expenditure curve is AE_0 and real GDP is $6 trillion (at point b). An increase in government purchases of $0.5 trillion increases aggregate planned expenditure at each level of real GDP by $0.5 trillion. The aggregate expenditure curve shifts upward from AE_0 to AE_1—a parallel shift. At the initial real GDP of $6 trillion, aggregate planned expenditure is now $6.5 trillion. Because aggregate planned expenditure is greater than real GDP, real GDP increases. The new equilibrium is reached when real GDP is $8 trillion—the point at which the AE_1 curve intersects the 45° line (at d'). In this example, the government purchases multiplier is 4.

When government purchases increase by $0.5 trillion, the aggregate expenditure curve shifts upward by that amount to AE_1. With this new aggregate expenditure curve, equilibrium real GDP increases to $8 trillion. The increase in real GDP is 4 times the increase in government purchases. The government purchases multiplier is 4.

You've seen that in the very short term, when the price level is fixed, an increase in government purchases increases real GDP. But to produce more output, more people must be employed. So in the short term, an increase in government purchases can create jobs.

Increasing its purchases of goods and services is one way in which the government can try to stimulate the economy. A second way in which the government might act to increase real GDP in the very short run is by decreasing lump-sum taxes. Let's see how this action works.

The Lump-Sum Tax Multiplier

The **lump-sum tax multiplier** is the magnification effect of a change in lump-sum taxes on equilibrium expenditure and real GDP. An *increase* in taxes *decreases* disposable income, which *decreases* consumption expenditure. The amount by which consumption expenditure initially changes is determined by the marginal propensity to consume. In our example, the marginal propensity to consume is 0.75, so a $1 tax cut increases disposable income by $1 and increases aggregate expenditure initially by 75 cents.

This initial change in aggregate expenditure has a multiplier just like the government purchases multiplier. We've seen that the government purchases multiplier is $1/(1 - MPC)$. Because a tax *increase* leads to a *decrease* in expenditure, the lump-sum tax multiplier is *negative*. And because a change in lump-sum taxes changes aggregate expenditure initially by only MPC multiplied by the tax change, the lump-sum tax multiplier is equal to

$$\text{Lump-sum tax multiplier} = \frac{-MPC}{1 - MPC}.$$

In our example, the marginal propensity to consume is 3/4, so the lump-sum tax multiplier is

$$\text{Lump-sum tax multiplier} = \frac{-\dfrac{3}{4}}{1 - \dfrac{3}{4}} = -3.$$

Figure 29.7 illustrates the lump-sum tax multiplier. Initially, the aggregate expenditure curve is AE_0, and equilibrium expenditure is $8 trillion. Taxes increase by $1 trillion, and disposable income falls by that amount. With a marginal propensity to consume of 3/4, aggregate expenditure decreases initially by $0.75 trillion and the aggregate expenditure curve shifts downward by that amount to AE_1. Equilibrium expenditure and real GDP fall by $3 trillion to $5 trillion. The lump-sum tax multiplier is −3.

FIGURE 29.7

The Lump-Sum Tax Multiplier

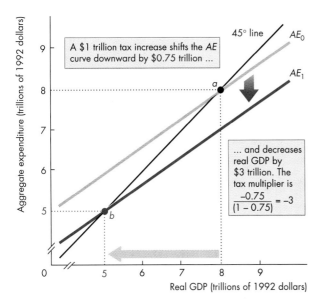

Initially, the aggregate expenditure curve is AE_0 and equilibrium expenditure is $8 trillion. The marginal propensity to consume is 0.75. Lump-sum taxes increase by $1 trillion, so disposable income falls by $1 trillion. The decrease in aggregate expenditure is found by multiplying this change in disposable income by the marginal propensity to consume and is $1 trillion x 0.75 = $0.75 trillion. The aggregate expenditure curve shifts *downward* by this amount to AE_1. Equilibrium expenditure decreases by $3 trillion, from $8 trillion to $5 trillion. The lump-sum tax multiplier is –3.

Lump-Sum Transfer Payments   The lump-sum tax multiplier also tells us the effects of a change in lump-sum transfer payments. Transfer payments are like negative taxes, so an increase in transfer payments works like a decrease in taxes. Because the tax multiplier is negative, a decrease in taxes increases expenditure. An increase in transfer payments also increases expenditure. So the lump-sum transfer payments multiplier is positive. It is

$$\text{Lump-sum transfer} \atop \text{payments multiplier} = \frac{MPC}{1 - MPC}.$$

Induced Taxes and Entitlement Spending

In the examples we've studied so far, taxes are lump-sum taxes. But in reality, net taxes (taxes minus transfer payments) vary with the state of the economy.

On the revenue side of the budget, tax laws define tax *rates* to be paid, not tax *dollars* to be paid. Tax *dollars* paid depend on tax *rates* and incomes. But incomes vary with real GDP, so tax *revenues* depend on real GDP. Taxes that vary with real GDP are called **induced taxes.** When the economy expands, induced taxes increase because real GDP increases. When the economy is in a recession, induced taxes decrease because real GDP decreases.

On the outlay side of the budget, the government creates programs that entitle suitably qualified people and businesses to receive benefits. The spending on such programs is called **entitlement spending,** and it results in transfer payments that depend on the economic state of individual citizens and businesses. When the economy is in a recession, unemployment is high, the number of people experiencing economic hardship increases, and a larger number of firms and farms experience hard times. Entitlement spending increases. When the economy expands, entitlement spending decreases.

Induced taxes and entitlement payments decrease the multiplier effects of changes in government purchases and lump-sum taxes. The reason is that they weaken the link between real GDP and disposable income and so dampen the effect of a change in real GDP on consumption expenditure. When real GDP increases, induced taxes increase and entitlement payments decrease, so disposable income does not increase by as much as the increase in real GDP. As a result, consumption expenditure does not increase by as much as it otherwise would have done and the multiplier effect is reduced.

The extent to which induced taxes and entitlement payments decrease the multiplier depends on the *marginal tax rate*. The marginal tax rate is the proportion of an additional dollar of real GDP that flows to the government in net taxes (taxes minus transfer payments). The higher the marginal tax rate, the larger is the proportion of an additional dollar of real GDP that is paid to the government and the smaller is the induced change in consumption expenditure. The smaller the change in consumption expenditure induced by a change in real GDP, the smaller is the multiplier effect of a change in government purchases or lump-sum taxes.

International Trade and Fiscal Policy Multipliers

Not all expenditure in the United States is on U.S.-produced goods and services. Some of it is on imports—on foreign-produced goods and services. Imports affect the fiscal policy multipliers in exactly the same way that they influence the investment multiplier, as explained in Chapter 28 (see pp. 628–629), and there is no new principle involved. The extent to which an additional dollar of real GDP is spent on imports is determined by the *marginal propensity to import*. Expenditure on imports does not generate U.S. real GDP and does not lead to an increase in U.S. consumption expenditure. The larger the marginal propensity to import, the smaller is the increase in consumption expenditure induced by an increase in real GDP and the smaller are the government purchases and lump-sum tax multipliers.

So far, we've studied *discretionary* fiscal policy. Let's now look at *automatic* stabilizers.

Automatic Stabilizers

Automatic stabilizers are mechanisms that stabilize real GDP without explicit action by the government. Their name is borrowed from engineering and conjures up images of shock absorbers, thermostats, and sophisticated devices that keep airplanes and ships steady in turbulent air and seas. Automatic fiscal stabilizers are a consequence of income taxes and transfer payments that automatically fluctuate with real GDP. If real GDP begins to decrease, tax revenues fall and transfer payments rise. These changes in taxes and transfer payments affect the economy and the government's budget deficit. Let's study the budget deficit over the business cycle.

Budget Deficit Over the Business Cycle Figure 29.8 shows the business cycle and fluctuations in the budget deficit since 1975. Part (a) shows the fluctuations of real GDP around potential GDP. Part (b) shows the federal budget deficit. Both parts highlight recessions by shading those periods. By comparing the two parts of the figure, you can see the relationship between the business cycle and the budget deficit. As a rule, when the economy is in the expansion phase of a business cycle, the budget deficit declines. (In the figure, a declining deficit means a deficit that is getting closer to zero.) As the expansion slows before the recession begins, the budget deficit

FIGURE 29.8

The Business Cycle and the Budget Deficit

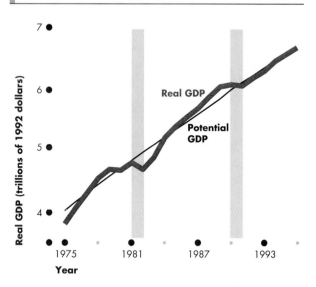

(a) Growth and recessions

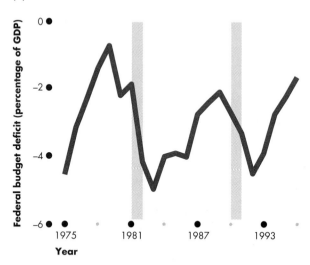

(b) Federal budget deficit

As real GDP fluctuates around potential GDP (part a), the budget deficit fluctuates (part b). During a recession (shaded years), tax revenues decrease, transfer payments increase, and the budget deficit increases. The deficit also increases *before* a recession as real GDP growth slows and *after* a recession before real GDP growth speeds up.

Source: Economic Report of the President, 1997, and the author's calculations.

increases. It continues to increase during the recession and for a further period after the recession is over. Then, when the expansion is well under way, the budget deficit declines again.

The budget deficit fluctuates with the business cycle because both tax revenues and expenditures fluctuate with real GDP. As real GDP increases during an expansion, tax revenues increase and transfer payments decrease, so the budget deficit automatically decreases. As real GDP decreases during a recession, tax revenues decrease and transfer payments increase, so the budget deficit automatically increases.

Fluctuations in investment and exports have a multiplier effect on real GDP. But automatic fluctuations in tax revenues (and the budget deficit) act as an automatic stabilizer. They decrease the swings in disposable income and make the multiplier effect smaller. They dampen both expansions and recessions.

Balanced Budget Amendment Some economists and politicians want to introduce a **balanced budget amendment** that requires the federal budget to be balanced. And such an amendment came close to passing during 1996.

A law that requires the federal budget to be balanced is probably infeasible. The budget might be balanced on the average over a number of years and perhaps balanced over a business cycle. But the budget is an annual event, and it is impossible, even if it were desirable, to balance the budget year by year. Most revenues and a large part of expenditures are determined not only by laws but also by the state of the economy. Further, a budget that was balanced every year would not have the automatic stabilizing properties that a cyclically unbalanced budget has.

Because the budget deficit increases when the economy is in recession and decreases when the economy is in an expansion, economists have developed a modified deficit concept called the cyclically adjusted deficit. The **cyclically adjusted deficit** is the budget deficit that would occur if the economy were at full employment.

The Cyclically Adjusted Deficit The cyclically adjusted deficit is a measure for judging whether the budget deficit is cyclical or structural. The budget deficit is cyclical only if it is present because real GDP is below potential GDP. In this state, taxes are temporarily low and transfer payments are temporarily high. The budget deficit is structural—there is a **structural deficit**—if government expenditures

exceed tax revenues when real GDP equals potential GDP. The two terms "cyclically adjusted deficit" and "structural deficit" are equivalent.

Figure 29.9 illustrates the deficit and the concept of the structural deficit. The blue curve shows government expenditures. The expenditures curve slopes downward because the higher the level of real GDP, the lower is the level of transfer payments, so the lower is the level of government expenditures. The green curve shows tax revenues. The tax revenues curve slopes upward because most components of tax revenues increase as incomes and real GDP increase.

FIGURE 29.9

Cyclical and Structural Deficits

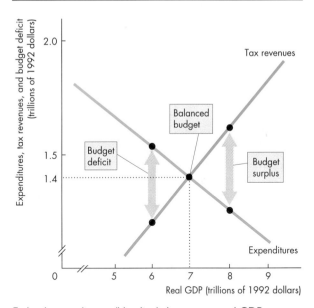

Federal expenditures (blue line) decrease as real GDP increases because transfer payments decrease. Tax revenues (green line) increase as real GDP increases because most taxes are linked to income and expenditures. If real GDP is $7 trillion, the government has a *balanced budget*. If real GDP is less than $7 trillion, expenditures exceed tax revenues and the government has a budget deficit. If real GDP exceeds $7 trillion, expenditures are less than tax revenues and the government has a budget surplus. If potential GDP is $7 trillion, there is no structural deficit—the budget deficits and surpluses are cyclical. But if potential GDP is less than $7 trillion, there is a structural deficit.

In Fig. 29.9, if real GDP is $7 trillion, the government has a *balanced budget*. Expenditures and tax revenues each equal $1.4 trillion. If real GDP is less than $7 trillion, expenditures exceed tax revenues and there is a budget deficit. And if real GDP is greater than $7 trillion, expenditures are less than tax revenues and there is a budget surplus.

To determine whether there is a structural deficit, we need to know potential GDP. First, suppose that potential GDP is $7 trillion. In this case, the structural deficit is zero. As real GDP fluctuates over the business cycle, the budget fluctuates around zero and alternates between a surplus and a deficit.

Second, suppose that potential GDP is $6 trillion. In this case, the budget is in deficit at full employment: There is a structural deficit. In a recession, the deficit increases, and in an expansion, the deficit decreases. But even at the peak of a business cycle, the budget might still be in deficit. The deficit cycles with the business cycle, but it rarely, perhaps never, gets into surplus. The deficit in this example behaves like the U.S. deficit shown in Fig. 29.8.

Finally, suppose that potential GDP is $8 trillion. In this case, the budget is in surplus at full employment: There is a structural surplus. In a recession, the surplus decreases, and in an expansion, the surplus increases. Even at the trough of a business cycle, there might still be a surplus. The government budget balance cycles with the business cycle, but the budget rarely, perhaps never, goes into deficit.

R E V I E W

- When the price level is fixed, a change in government purchases or lump-sum taxes has a multiplier effect on real GDP.
- The multiplier effect of a change in government purchases is greater than that of a change in lump-sum taxes because a dollar of taxes initially changes aggregate expenditure by less than a dollar.
- The presence of income taxes and international trade reduces the fiscal policy multipliers.
- Income taxes and entitlement programs work as automatic stabilizers to dampen the business cycle.

Your next task is to see how, with the passage of more time and with some price level adjustments, these multiplier effects change.

Fiscal Policy Multipliers and the Price Level

WE'VE SEEN HOW REAL GDP RESPONDS TO changes in fiscal policy when the price level is fixed and all the adjustments that take place are in spending, income, and production. The period over which this response occurs is very short. Once production starts to change, regardless of whether it increases or decreases, prices also start to change. The price level and real GDP change together, and the economy moves to a new short-run equilibrium.

To study the simultaneous changes in real GDP and the price level that result from fiscal policy, we use the aggregate supply–aggregate demand model of Chapter 24. In the long run, both the price level and the money wage rate respond to fiscal policy. As these further changes take place, the economy gradually moves toward a new long-run equilibrium. We also use the aggregate supply–aggregate demand model to study these adjustments.

We begin by looking at the effects of fiscal policy on aggregate demand and the aggregate demand curve.

Fiscal Policy and Aggregate Demand

You learned about the relationship between aggregate demand, aggregate expenditure, and equilibrium expenditure in Chapter 28. You are now going to use what you learned there to work out what happens to aggregate demand, the price level, real GDP, and jobs when fiscal policy changes. We'll start by looking at the effects of a change in fiscal policy on aggregate demand.

Figure 29.10 shows the effects of an increase in government purchases on aggregate demand. Initially, the aggregate expenditure curve is AE_0 in part (a), and the aggregate demand curve is AD_0 in part (b). The price level is 110, real GDP is $7 trillion, and the economy is at point a in both parts of the figure. Now suppose that government purchases increase by $0.5 trillion. At a constant price level of 110, the aggregate expenditure curve shifts upward to AE_1. This curve intersects the 45° line at an equilibrium expenditure of $9 trillion at point b. This amount is the aggregate quantity of goods and services demanded at a price level of 110, as shown by point b in part (b). Point b

FIGURE **29.10**

Government Purchases and Aggregate Demand

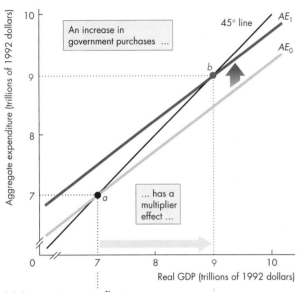

(a) Aggregate expenditure

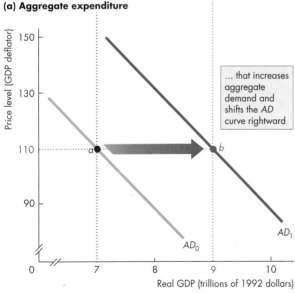

(b) Aggregate demand

The price level is 110, aggregate planned expenditure is AE_0 (part a), and aggregate demand is AD_0 (part b). An increase in government purchases shifts the AE curve to AE_1 and equilibrium real GDP increases to $9 trillion. The aggregate demand curve shifts rightward to AD_1.

lies on a new aggregate demand curve. The aggregate demand curve has shifted rightward to AD_1.

The government purchases multiplier determines the distance by which the aggregate demand curve shifts rightward. The larger the multiplier, the larger is the shift in the aggregate demand curve resulting from a given change in government purchases. In this example, a $0.5 trillion increase in government purchases produces a $2 trillion increase in the aggregate quantity of goods and services demanded at each price level. The multiplier is 4. So the $0.5 trillion increase in government purchases shifts the aggregate demand curve rightward by $2 trillion.

Figure 29.10 shows the effects of an increase in government purchases. But a similar effect occurs for *any* expansionary fiscal policy. An **expansionary fiscal policy** is an increase in government purchases or a decrease in tax revenues. But the distance the AD curve shifts is smaller for a tax cut than for a government purchases increase of the same size.

Figure 29.10 can also be used to illustrate the effects of a **contractionary fiscal policy**—a decrease in government purchases or an increase in tax revenues. In this case, start at point b in each part of the figure and decrease government purchases or increase taxes. Aggregate demand decreases from AD_1 to AD_0.

Equilibrium GDP and the Price Level in the Short Run We've seen how an increase in government purchases increases aggregate demand. Let's now see how it changes real GDP and the price level. Figure 29.11(a) describes the economy. Aggregate demand is AD_0, and the short-run aggregate supply curve is SAS. (Check back to Chapter 24 if you need to refresh your understanding of the SAS curve.) Equilibrium is at point a, where the aggregate demand and short-run aggregate supply curves intersect. The price level is 110, and real GDP is $7 trillion.

An increase in government purchases of $0.5 trillion shifts the aggregate demand curve rightward from AD_0 to AD_1. While the price level is fixed at 110, the economy moves toward point b and real GDP increases toward $9 trillion. But during the adjustment process, the price level does not remain constant. It gradually rises, and the economy moves along the short-run aggregate supply curve to the point of intersection of the short-run aggregate supply curve and the new aggregate demand curve—point c. The price level rises to 126, and real GDP increases to only $8.6 trillion.

FIGURE 29.11

Fiscal Policy, Real GDP, and the Price Level

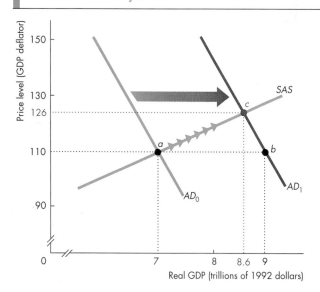

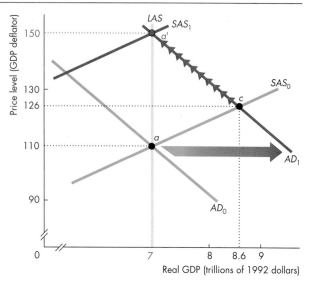

(a) Fiscal policy with unemployment

An increase in government purchases shifts the AD curve from AD_0 to AD_1. With a fixed price level, the economy would have moved to point b. But the price level rises, and in the short run, the economy moves to point c. The price level increases to 126, and real GDP increases to $8.6 trillion.

(b) Fiscal policy with full employment

At point c, real GDP exceeds potential GDP and unemployment is below the natural rate. The wage rate rises, and short-run aggregate supply decreases. The SAS curve shifts leftward to SAS_1, and in the long run, the economy moves to point a'. The price level rises to 150, and real GDP returns to $7 trillion.

When we take the price level effect into account, the increase in government purchases still has a multiplier effect on real GDP, but the effect is smaller than it would be if the price level remained constant. Also, the steeper the slope of the short-run aggregate supply curve, the larger is the increase in the price level, the smaller is the increase in real GDP, and the smaller is the government purchases multiplier. But the multiplier is not zero.

In the long run, real GDP equals potential GDP—the economy is at full-employment equilibrium. When real GDP equals potential GDP, an increase in aggregate demand has the same short-run effect as we've just worked out, but its long-run effect is different. The increase in aggregate demand raises the price level, but in the long run, it leaves real GDP unchanged at potential GDP.

To study this case, let's see what happens if the government embarks on an expansionary fiscal policy when real GDP equals potential GDP.

Fiscal Expansion at Potential GDP

Suppose that real GDP is equal to potential GDP, which means that unemployment is equal to the natural rate of unemployment. But suppose also that the unemployment rate and the natural rate are high and that most people, including the government, mistakenly think that the unemployment rate exceeds the natural rate. In this situation, the government tries to lower the unemployment rate by using an expansionary fiscal policy.

Figure 29.11(b) shows the effect of an expansionary fiscal policy when real GDP equals potential GDP. In this example, potential GDP is $7 trillion. Aggregate demand increases, and the aggregate demand curve shifts rightward from AD_0 to AD_1. The short-run equilibrium, point c, is an above full-employment equilibrium. The labor force is more than fully employed, and there are shortages of labor. Wage rates begin to increase. Higher wage rates increase costs, and short-run aggregate supply decreases. The *SAS* curve begins to shift leftward from SAS_0 to SAS_1. The economy moves up the aggregate demand curve AD_1 toward point a'.

Eventually, when all adjustment to wage rates and the price level have been made, the price level is 150 and real GDP is again at potential GDP of $7 trillion. The multiplier in the long run is zero. There has been a temporary decrease in the unemployment rate during the process you've just looked at, but not a permanent decrease. But the price level rise is permanent.

Limitations of Fiscal Policy

Because the short-run fiscal policy multipliers are not zero, expansionary fiscal policy can be used to increase real GDP and decrease the unemployment rate in a recession. Contractionary fiscal policy can also be used if the economy is overheating to decrease real GDP and help to keep inflation in check. But the use of fiscal policy is limited by two factors.

First, the legislative process is slow, which means that it is difficult to take fiscal policy actions in a timely way. The economy might be able to benefit from fiscal stimulation right now, but it will take Congress many months, perhaps more than a year, to act. By the time the action is taken, the economy might need an entirely different fiscal medicine.

Second, it is not always easy to tell whether real GDP is below (or above) potential GDP. A change in aggregate demand can move real GDP away from potential GDP, or a change in aggregate supply can change real GDP and change potential GDP. This difficulty is a serious one because, as you've seen, fiscal stimulation at full employment leads to a rise in the price level and has no long-run effect on real GDP.

R E V I E W

- Changes in the price level decrease the effect of the fiscal policy multiplier on real GDP.
- In the long run, when real GDP equals potential GDP, fiscal policy influences only the price level. The multiplier effect on real GDP is zero.

So far in this chapter, we've ignored any potential effects of fiscal policy on aggregate supply. Yet many economists believe the supply-side effects of fiscal policy are large. Let's now look at these effects.

Fiscal Policy and Aggregate Supply

DURING THE 1980S, WHEN RONALD REAGAN WAS President, a group of economists known as *supply-siders* became prominent. Supply-siders believed that tax cuts would strengthen incentives and increase aggregate supply. Their ideas were called "voodoo economics" by George Bush, and many other people are skeptical about supply-siders' claims. But these claims remain part of the political debate today. They are the main rationale for a flat tax that some economists and politicians have advocated.

Using the concepts of the *AS-AD* model, the supply-siders' claim is that tax cuts increase potential GDP. Is this claim correct?

There is no disagreement among economists that taxes create disincentives and decrease potential GDP. The disagreements are about numbers. Supply-siders say the effects are large. Others suspect that the effects are small, possibly too small to bother about.

Let's study the effects of taxes on potential GDP and then see how the supply effects and demand effects together influence real GDP and the price level.

Fiscal Policy and Potential GDP

Potential GDP depends on the full-employment quantity of labor, the quantity of capital, and the state of technology. Taxes can influence all three of these factors. The main tax to consider is the income tax. By taxing the incomes people earn when they work or save, the government weakens the incentives to work and save. The result is a smaller quantity of labor and capital and a lower potential GDP. Also, the income tax weakens the incentive to develop new technologies that increase income. So the pace of technological change might be slowed, which slows the growth rate of potential GDP. Let's look at the effect of the income tax on both the quantity of labor and the quantity of capital.

Labor and the Income Tax The quantity of labor is determined by demand and supply in the labor market (see Chapter 25, pp. 554–555). Figure 29.12(a) shows a labor market. The demand for labor is *LD*, and the supply is *LS*. With no income tax, this labor market achieves equilibrium at a real wage rate of $14 an hour and 230 billion hours of labor per year are employed.

FIGURE 29.12
Supply-Side Effects of the Income Tax

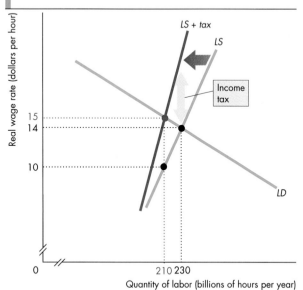

(a) The labor market

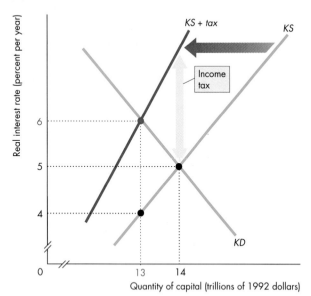

(b) The capital market

In part (a), the income tax shifts the supply of labor curve, *LS*, leftward to *LS + tax*. The before-tax wage rate rises, the after-tax wage rate falls, and the quantity of labor employed decreases. In part (b), the income tax shifts the supply of capital curve, *KS*, leftward to *KS + tax*. The before-tax interest rate rises, the after-tax interest rate falls, and the quantity of capital decreases. With less labor and less capital, potential GDP falls.

Now suppose an income tax is introduced. The income tax weakens the incentive to work and decreases the supply of labor. The supply curve shifts leftward to *LS + tax*. With this new lower supply of labor, the *before-tax* wage rate rises to $15 an hour and the quantity of labor employed decreases to 210 billion hours a year. The before-tax wage rate rises, but the *after-tax* wage rate falls. In Fig. 29.12(a), it falls to $10 an hour.

Capital and the Income Tax The quantity of capital is determined by demand and supply in the capital market (see Chapter 26, pp. 575–577). Figure 29.12(b) shows the capital market. The demand for capital is *KD*, and the supply is *KS*. With no income tax, the capital market achieves equilibrium at a real interest rate of 5 percent a year and $14 trillion of capital is available.

Now consider the effects of a tax on income from capital. The income tax, which weakens the incentive to save, decreases the supply of capital. The supply curve shifts leftward to *KS + tax*. The *before-tax* interest rate rises to 6 percent a year and the quantity of capital decreases to $13 trillion. The before-tax interest rate rises, but the *after-tax* interest rate falls. In Fig. 29.12, it falls to 4 percent a year.

Potential GDP and *LAS* Because the income tax decreases the equilibrium quantities of labor and capital, it also decreases potential GDP. But potential GDP determines long-run aggregate supply. So the income tax decreases long-run aggregate supply and shifts the *LAS* curve leftward.

Supply Effects and Demand Effects

Let's now bring the supply effects and demand effects of fiscal policy together. Figure 29.13(a) shows the most likely effects of a tax cut. The tax cut increases aggregate demand and shifts the *AD* curve rightward, just as before. But a tax cut that increases the incentive to work and save also increases aggregate supply. It shifts the long-run and short-run aggregate supply curves rightward. Here we focus on the short-run and show the effect on the *SAS* curve, which shifts rightward to *SAS₁*. In this example, the tax cut has a large effect on aggregate demand and a small effect on aggregate supply. The aggregate demand curve shifts rightward by a larger amount than the rightward shift in the short-run aggregate supply curve. The outcome is a rise in the price level and an increase in real GDP.

FIGURE 29.13

Two Views of the Supply-Side Effects of Fiscal Policy

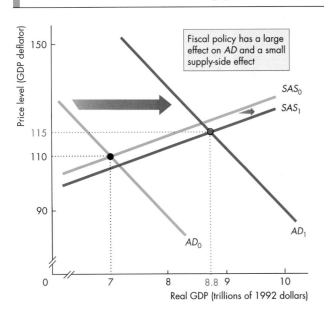

(a) The traditional view

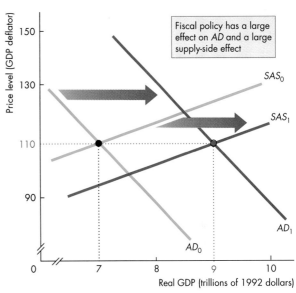

(b) The supply-side view

A tax cut increases aggregate demand and shifts the AD curve rightward from AD_0 to AD_1 (both parts). Such a policy change also has a supply-side effect. If the supply-side effect is small, the SAS curve shifts rightward from SAS_0 to SAS_1 in part (a). The demand-side effect dominates the supply-side effect, real GDP increases, and the price level rises.

If the supply-side effect of a tax cut is large, the SAS curve shifts to SAS_1 in part (b). In this case, the supply-side effect is as large as the demand-side effect. Real GDP increases, and the price level remains constant. But if the supply-side effect were larger than the demand-side effect, the price level would actually fall.

But notice that the price level rises by *less* and real GDP increases by *more* than would occur if there were no supply-side effects.

Figure 29.13(b) shows the effects that supply-siders believe to occur. A tax cut still has a large effect on aggregate demand, but it has a similarly large effect on aggregate supply. The aggregate demand curve and the short-run aggregate supply curve shift rightward by similar amounts. In this particular case, the price level remains constant and real GDP increases. A slightly larger increase in aggregate supply would have brought a fall in the price level, a possibility that some supply-siders believe could occur.

The general point that everyone agrees with is that a tax cut that strengthens incentives increases real GDP by more and is less inflationary than an equal-sized expansionary fiscal policy that does not change incentives or that weakens them.

REVIEW

■ The income tax has incentive effects on the supply of labor and the supply of capital, and a cut in the income tax rate increases potential GDP.

■ A tax cut increases both aggregate supply and aggregate demand. There is disagreement about which effect is larger. A tax cut increases real GDP, but it can either raise or lower the price level.

◆ You've seen how fiscal policy influences the way real GDP fluctuates and how it influences potential GDP. *Reading Between the Lines* on pp. 660–661 looks further at the 1997 budget and President Clinton's fiscal policy. Your next task is to study monetary policy. We begin in the next chapter by describing the monetary system of a modern economy.

Policy
WATCH

Deficit Reduction

LOS ANGELES TIMES, FEBRUARY 7, 1997

Clinton's Budget Plan

BY ART PINE

WASHINGTON—Never mind balancing the budget by fiscal year 2002, as President Clinton and top congressional leaders are promising. The real question is, what about 2003 and beyond? ...

That issue is troubling government and private budget analysts as political leaders from both parties rally around Clinton's newfound willingness—and that of Republican congressional leaders—to eliminate the federal budget deficit five years from now. ...

Revised estimates by the Congressional Budget Office show that lawmakers will have to cut only $154 billion more to erase the deficit that year—far less than the $285 billion forecast a year ago. Much of the $154-billion cut will come from lower interest rates.

The real problem will come after 2002—especially in 2008 and beyond, analysts said, when members of the baby-boom generation start to reach retirement age and the cost of Medicare, Medicaid and Social Security begins to explode.

Robert D. Reischauer, a Brookings Institution budget expert who headed the CBO from 1989 to 1995, warned that, unless lawmakers soon begin to make far more sweeping long-term changes than Clinton is asking, the deficit will come back quickly after 2002 with a vengeance.

CBO figures show that, barring a major restructuring of Medicare, Medicaid and Social Security, the budget deficit could mushroom from zero in 2002 to 4.5% of the gross domestic product—the output of the U.S. economy—by 2010 and 9.5% by 2025. (It was 1.4% in fiscal 1996.) ...

Moreover, analysts said that Medicare, Medicaid and Social Security are not the only big federal spending programs Congress needs to tackle to put the nation's fiscal house in order for the longer run. Another is defense, which many budget experts regard as a time bomb. ...

Finally, Brookings' Reischauer warned that, without major changes in Medicare and Social Security, the cutbacks in the remainder of the domestic budget—from environmental spending to highway programs—will have to be so deep that it is simply unrealistic to count on them. ...

To avoid widening the deficit after 2002, Congress must either slash spending on Medicare, Medicaid and Social Security or raise taxes to a level that is likely to be politically unacceptable. ...

Essence of THE STORY

■ President Clinton and Republican Congress leaders want to eliminate the federal budget deficit by 2002.

■ Congressional Budget Office (CBO) figures show that without a restructuring of Medicare, Medicaid, and Social Security, the budget deficit could grow from zero in 2002 to 4.5 percent of GDP by 2010 and 9.5 percent by 2025. The budget deficit was 1.4 percent of GDP in 1996.

■ To avoid a growing deficit after 2002, Congress must either reduce spending or raise taxes.

■ Some budget experts say the budget cannot be balanced after 2002 unless Medicare and Medicaid are overhauled.

Economic

A N A L Y S I S

■ Figure 1 shows two federal deficit projections, one before and one after the 1997 proposed budget. With no changes, the deficit would have fallen slightly from 1.5 percent of GDP in 1997 to 1.0 percent of GDP in 2002. The changes proposed in the 1997 budget eliminate the deficit by 2002.

■ Figure 1 also shows that compared with the projection made a year earlier, the deficit does not change in 1997 and 1998 and that in 1999, it falls by only 0.2 percent of GDP ($22 billion). The big reductions occur in 2000, 2001, and 2002.

■ Figure 1 also shows that most of the deficit reduction planned comes from spending cuts. There is a small decrease in debt interest and, in 2002, a one-time revenue from selling rights to broadcasters and mobile phone companies to use the airwaves.

■ Figure 2 shows what the government says will happen in 2000. Potential GDP will be $7.5 trillion and the long-run aggregate supply curve will be LAS_0. The short-run aggregate supply curve will be SAS_0

and the aggregate demand curve will be AD_0. Real GDP will be $7.5 trillion and the price level will be 122.

■ The decreases in spending on defense, Medicare, and Medicaid in 2000 will decrease aggregate planned expenditure and, with a multiplier effect, will decrease aggregate demand.

■ The aggregate demand curve shifts leftward to AD_1. With no other changes in planned expenditure in 2000, the economy would move to below full employment at point *a*.

■ The government forecasts that private spending will increase and keep aggregate demand at AD_0, so full employment will prevail despite the government cuts.

■ The government's forecasts for 2001 and 2002 are similar. That is, despite cuts in government purchases, increases in private expenditure will maintain full employment.

■ The forecasts for beyond 2003 are for a rise in the deficit unless taxes rise or social programs are radically restructured.

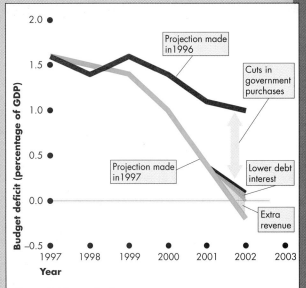

Figure 1 The projections

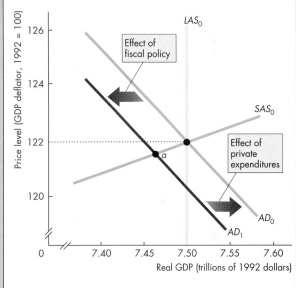

Figure 2 *AS–AD* in 2000

You're

THE VOTER

■ Do you think the deficit should be eliminated more quickly or more slowly than the government plans?

■ Do you think the deficit should be eliminated with greater tax increases than spending cuts?

■ What do you believe are the options after 2002 in light of the predictions about the growth of Medicaid and Medicare spending reported in the news article?

SUMMARY

Key Points

The Federal Budget (pp. 642–647)

- The federal budget finances the activities of the government and is used to stabilize real GDP.
- Federal tax revenues come from personal income taxes, social insurance taxes, corporate income taxes, and indirect taxes. Federal expenditures include transfer payments, purchases of goods and services, and debt interest.
- When government expenditures exceed tax revenues, the government has a budget deficit.

Fiscal Policy Multipliers (pp. 648–654)

- Fiscal policy actions are discretionary or automatic.
- The government purchases multiplier equals $1/(1 - MPC)$. The lump-sum tax multiplier equals $-MPC/(1 - MPC)$. The transfer payments multiplier is equal in magnitude to the lump-sum tax multiplier but is positive.
- Income taxes and entitlement payments bring fluctuations in tax revenues and transfer payments over the business cycle and act as automatic stabilizers.

Fiscal Policy Multipliers and the Price Level (pp. 654–657)

- An expansionary fiscal policy increases aggregate demand and shifts the aggregate demand curve rightward. It increases real GDP and raises the price level. (A contractionary fiscal policy has the opposite effects.)
- Price level changes dampen fiscal policy multiplier effects.
- At potential GDP, an expansionary fiscal policy raises the price level and in the long run leaves real GDP unchanged. The fiscal policy multipliers in the long run are zero.

Fiscal Policy and Aggregate Supply (pp. 657–659)

- Fiscal policy has supply-side effects because the increases in taxes weaken the incentives to work, save, and invest.
- A tax cut increases both aggregate demand and aggregate supply. It increases real GDP but has an ambiguous effect on the price level.

Key Figures

Key Terms

QUESTIONS

1. Describe the main purposes of the federal budget.

2. Describe the process that creates a federal budget.

3. List the four main sources of federal tax revenues and the three main components of federal expenditures.

4. List the main changes in taxes and government expenditures that are associated with the increase in the federal government deficit during the 1980s.

5. Compare the U.S. federal deficit with deficits in other regions and countries.

6. Explain the link between the deficit and government debt.

7. How has the federal government debt as a percentage of GDP changed since 1945?

8. Distinguish between automatic and discretionary fiscal policy.

9. Explain why an increase in government purchases has a multiplier effect on real GDP when the price level is fixed.

10. Explain why the lump-sum tax multiplier is smaller than the government purchases multiplier.

11. Explain why real GDP increases when both taxes and government purchases increase by the same amount.

12. Explain how induced taxes and entitlement spending influence the fiscal policy multipliers.

13. Explain how international trade influences the fiscal policy multipliers.

14. Explain how the deficit fluctuates over the business cycle and define the structural deficit.

15. Explain how the multiplier effect is modified in the short run when the price level begins to change.

16. Explain what happens following an increase in government purchases if real GDP equals potential GDP.

PROBLEMS

1. In the economy of Zapland, the marginal propensity to consume is 0.9, investment is $50 billion, government purchases of goods and services are $40 billion, and lump-sum taxes are $40 billion. Zapland has no exports and no imports.
   a. The government cuts its purchases of goods and services to $30 billion. What is the change in equilibrium expenditure?
   b. What is the value of the government purchases multiplier?
   c. The government continues to purchase $40 billion worth of goods and services and cuts lump-sum taxes to $30 billion. What is the change in equilibrium expenditure?
   d. What is the value of the lump-sum tax multiplier?
   e. The government simultaneously cuts both its purchases of goods and services and lump-sum taxes to $30 billion. What is the change in equilibrium expenditure?

2. Suppose that the price level in the economy of Zapland as described in problem 1 is 100. The economy is also at full employment.
   a. If the government of Zapland increases its purchases of goods and services by $10 billion, what happens to the quantity of real GDP demanded?
   b. How does Zapland's aggregate demand curve change? Draw a two-part diagram that is similar to Fig. 29.10 to illustrate the change in both the *AE* curve and the *AD* curve.
   c. In the short run, does equilibrium real GDP increase by more than, less than, or the same amount as the increase in the quantity of real GDP demanded?
   d. In the long run, does equilibrium real GDP increase by more than, less than, or the same amount as the increase in the quantity of real GDP demanded?
   e. In the short run, does the price level in Zapland rise, fall, or remain unchanged?
   f. In the long run, does the price level in Zapland rise, fall, or remain unchanged?

3. In the figure below, aggregate demand is initially AD_0 and short-run aggregate supply is initially SAS_0. A tax cut increases aggregate demand to AD_1. This same tax cut influences incentives and increases aggregate supply. At first, there is no supply-side effect. Then short-run aggregate supply increases to SAS_1. Eventually, short-run aggregate supply increases to SAS_2.

Use the letters in the figure and the values on the axes to trace the path of the economy and to answer the following questions.

a. What are the initial equilibrium values of real GDP and the price level before the tax cut occurs?

b. What is the immediate effect of the tax cut before its supply-side effects begin to occur?

c. How do real GDP and the price level change when short-run aggregate supply increases to SAS_1?

d. How do real GDP and the price level change when short-run aggregate supply increases to SAS_2?

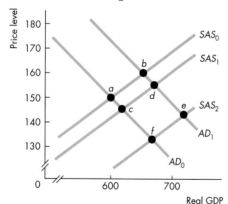

CRITICAL THINKING

1. Study *Reading Between the Lines* on pp. 660–661 and then:

a. Describe the plan to eliminate the federal budget deficit by 2002.

b. Explain what the Congressional Budget Office is predicting about the budget after 2002.

c. Lay out the options for keeping the budget balanced after 2002.

d. Explain why lower government expenditures are not predicted to lower real GDP. What else is expected to occur that will enable full employment to be maintained?

e. Suppose the government was to cut spending even more than planned and turn its deficit into a surplus. What do you predict would be the short-run and long-run effects of such an action?

2. Thinking about the supply-side effects of tax cuts:

a. What would be the main effects of lower income tax rates on potential GDP?

b. How would lower income taxes influence the real wage rate and the real interest rate?

c. What are the main costs of lower income taxes?

3. Visit the Web site of National Center for Policy Analysis Idea House at http://www.public-policy.org/~ncpa/pi/taxes/tax71.html and click on Dick Armey Flat Tax and Jerry Brown's Tax Plan. When you've studied these two pages, answer the following questions:

a. What are the main features of the plans?

b. What do you predict would be the main effects of each proposal?

c. Which proposal appeals more to you and why?

4. Visit the U.S. government budget Web site at http://cher.eda.doc.gov/BudgetFY97/index.html. Use the information that you can find at this site to compare the levels of government expenditure in the main industrial countries. Then use the fiscal policy multiplier analysis that you've learned about in this chapter to predict which countries have the strongest automatic stabilizers and which have the weakest. Explain the reasons for your predictions.

Money, like fire and the wheel, has been around for a very long time. An incredible array of items have served as money. Wampum (beads made from shells) was used by North American Indians, whale's teeth were used by Fijians, and tobacco was used by early American colonists. Cakes of salt served as money in Ethiopia and Tibet. Today, when we want to buy something, we use coins or bills, write a check, or present a credit card. Tomorrow, we'll use a "smart card" that keeps track of spending and that our pocket computer can read. Are all these things money? ◆ When we deposit some coins or notes into a bank, is that still money? And what happens when the bank lends the money in our deposit account to someone else? How can we get our money back if it's been lent out? Does lending by banks create money—out of thin air? ◆ In the

Money Makes the World Go Around

1970s, you had either a savings deposit that earned interest or a checking deposit that did not. Today, there are accounts that provide the convenience of a checking deposit and the income of a savings deposit. Why were these new kinds of bank deposits introduced? ◆ During the 1970s, the quantity of money in the United States increased quickly, but during the 1980s and 1990s, it increased at a slower pace. In Russia and in some Latin American countries, the quantity of money is increasing at an extremely rapid pace. In Switzerland and Germany, the quantity of money has increased at a slower pace. Does the rate of increase in the quantity of money matter? What are the effects of an increasing quantity of money on our economy? ◆ In this chapter, we'll study that useful invention: money. We'll look at its functions and the way it is measured in the United States today. We'll explain how banks and other financial institutions create money. Finally, we'll examine the effects of money on the economy.

After studying this chapter, you will be able to:

■ Define money and describe its functions

■ Explain the economic functions of banks and other financial institutions

■ Describe the financial innovations of the 1980s and 1990s

■ Explain how banks create money

■ Explain why the quantity of money is an important economic magnitude

■ Explain the quantity theory of money

What Is Money?

W̲HAT DO WAMPUM, TOBACCO, AND NICKELS AND dimes have in common? Why are they all examples of money? To answer these questions, we need a definition of money. **Money** is any commodity or token that is generally acceptable as the means of payment. A **means of payment** is a method of settling a debt. When a payment has been made, there is no remaining obligation between the parties to a transaction. So what wampum, tobacco, and nickels and dimes have in common is that they have served (or still do serve) as the means of payment. But money has three other functions:

- Medium of exchange
- Unit of account
- Store of value

Medium of Exchange

A *medium of exchange* is an object that is generally accepted in exchange for goods and services. Money acts as such a medium. Without money, it would be necessary to exchange goods and services directly for other goods and services—an exchange called **barter**. For example, if you want to buy a hamburger, you offer the paperback novel you've just finished reading in exchange for it. Barter requires a *double coincidence of wants*, a situation that occurs when Erika wants to buy what Kazia wants to sell and Kazia wants to buy what Erika wants to sell. To get your hamburger, you must find someone who's selling hamburgers and who wants your paperback novel. Money guarantees that there is a double coincidence of wants because people with something to sell will always accept money in exchange for it. Money acts as a lubricant that smoothes the mechanism of exchange.

Unit of Account

A *unit of account* is an agreed measure for stating the prices of goods and services. To get the most out of your budget, you have to figure out whether seeing one more movie is worth its opportunity cost. But that cost is not dollars and cents. It is the number of ice-cream cones, sodas, and cups of coffee that you must give up. It's easy to do such calculations when

all these goods have prices in terms of dollars and cents (see Table 30.1). If a movie costs $6 and a six-pack of soda costs $3, you know right away that seeing one movie costs you 2 six-packs of soda. If jelly beans are 50¢ a pack, a movie costs 12 packs of jelly beans. You need only one calculation to figure out the opportunity cost of any pair of goods and services.

But imagine how troublesome it would be if your local movie theater posted its price as 2 six-packs of soda, and if the convenience store posted the price of a six-pack of soda as 2 ice-cream cones, and if the ice-cream shop posted the price of a cone as 3 packs of jelly beans, and if the candy store priced a pack of jelly beans as 2 cups of coffee! Now how much running around and calculating do you have to do to figure out how much that movie is going to cost you

---

TABLE 30.1

The Unit of Account Function of Money Simplifies Price Comparisons

Good	Price in money units	Price in units of another good
Movie	$6.00 each	2 six-packs of soda
Soda	$3.00 per six-pack	2 ice-cream cones
Ice cream	$1.50 per cone	3 packs of jelly beans
Jelly beans	$0.50 per pack	2 cups of coffee
Coffee	$0.25 per cup	1 local phone call

Money as a unit of account: The price of a movie is $6 and the price of a cup of coffee is 25¢, so the opportunity cost of a movie is 24 cups of coffee ($6.00 ÷ 25¢ = 24).

No unit of account: You go to a movie theater and learn that the price of a movie is 2 six-packs of soda. You go to a candy store and learn that a pack of jelly beans costs 2 cups of coffee. But how many cups of coffee does seeing a movie cost you? To answer that question, you go to the convenience store and find that a six-pack of soda costs 2 ice-cream cones. Now you head for the ice-cream shop, where an ice-cream cone costs 3 packs of jelly beans. Now you get out your pocket calculator: 1 movie costs 2 six-packs of soda, or 4 ice-cream cones, or 12 packs of jelly beans, or 24 cups of coffee!

in terms of the soda, ice cream, jelly beans, or coffee that you must give up to see it? You get the answer for soda right away from the sign posted on the movie theater. But for all the other goods you're going to have to visit many different stores to establish the price of each commodity in terms of another and then calculate prices in units that are relevant for your own decision. Cover up the column labeled "price in money units" in Table 30.1 and see how hard it is to figure out the number of local phone calls it costs to see one movie. It's enough to make a person swear off movies! How much simpler it is if all the prices are expressed in dollars and cents.

Store of Value

Any commodity or token that can be held and exchanged later for goods and services is called a *store of value*. Money acts as a store of value. If it did not, it would not be acceptable in exchange for goods and services. The more stable the value of a commodity or token, the better it can act as a store of value, and the more useful it is as money. No store of value is completely safe. The value of a physical object, such as a house, a car, or a work of art, fluctuates over time. The value of commodities and tokens used as money also fluctuate, and when there is inflation, they persistently fall in value.

Money in the United States Today

In the United States today, money consists of:

■ Currency
■ Deposits at banks and other financial institutions

Currency   The bills and coins that we use in the United States today are known as **currency**. Bills are money because the government declares them so with the words "This note is legal tender for all debts, public and private." You can see these words on every dollar bill.

Deposits   Deposits at banks and other financial institutions such as savings and loan associations (S&Ls) are also money. Deposits are money because they can be converted into currency and because they are used to settle debts.

Official Measures of Money   The two main official measures of money in the United States today are known as M1 and M2. Figure 30.1 shows the items that make up these two measures. **M1** consists of currency and traveler's checks plus checking deposits owned by individuals and businesses. M1 does *not* include currency held by banks, and it does not include currency and checking deposits owned by the U.S. government. **M2** consists of M1 plus savings deposits, time deposits, money market mutual funds, and other deposits. (There is a third official measure of money, M3, which consists of M2 plus large-scale time deposits and term deposits.)

FIGURE 30.1
Two Measures of Money

	$ billions
M2	$3,826
Money market mutual funds and other deposits	$529
Time deposits	$949
Savings deposits	$1,271
M1	$1,077
Checking deposits	$673
Currency and traveler's checks	$404

M1	■ Currency held outside banks and traveler's checks
	■ Checking deposits at commercial banks, S&Ls, savings banks, and credit unions

M2	■ M1
	■ Savings deposits
	■ Time deposits
	■ Money market mutual funds and other deposits

Source: Economic Report of the President, 1997.

Are M1 and M2 Really Money?   Money is the means of payment. So the test of whether an asset is money is whether it serves as a means of payment. Currency passes the test. But what about deposits? Checking deposits are money because they can be transferred from one person to another by writing a check. Such a transfer of ownership is equivalent to handing over currency. Because M1 consists of currency plus checking deposits and each of these is a means of payment, *M1 is money.*

But what about M2? Some of the savings deposits in M2 are just as much a means of payment as the checking deposits in M1. You can use the ATM at the grocery store checkout or gas station and transfer funds directly from your saving account to pay for your purchase. But other saving deposits are not means of payment. These deposits are known as *liquid assets.* **Liquidity** is the property of being instantly convertible into a means of payment with little loss in value. Because most of the deposits in M2 are quickly and easily converted into currency or checking deposits, they are operationally similar to M1, but they are not means of payment.

Deposits Are Money but Checks Are Not   In defining money, we include, along with currency, deposits at banks and other financial institutions. But we do not count the checks that people write as money. Why are deposits money and checks not?

To see why deposits are money but checks are not, think about what happens when Colleen buys some roller blades for $200 from Rocky's Rollers. When Colleen goes to Rocky's shop, she has $500 in her deposit account at the Laser Bank. Rocky has $1,000 in his deposit account—at the same bank, as it happens. The total deposits of these two people is $1,500. Colleen writes a check for $200. Rocky takes the check to the bank right away and deposits it. Rocky's bank balance rises from $1,000 to $1,200, and Colleen's balance falls from $500 to $300. The total deposits of Colleen and Rocky are still the same as before: $1,500. Rocky now has $200 more, and Colleen has $200 less than before.

This transaction has transferred money from Colleen to Rocky. The check itself was never money. There wasn't an extra $200 worth of money while the check was in circulation. The check instructs the bank to transfer money from Colleen to Rocky.

In the example, Colleen and Rocky use the same bank. The same story, but with additional steps, describes what happens if Colleen and Rocky use

different banks. Rocky's bank credits the check to Rocky's account and then takes the check to a check-clearing center. The check is then sent to Colleen's bank, which pays Rocky's bank $200 and then debits Colleen's account $200. This process can take a few days, but the principles are the same as when two people use the same bank.

Credit Cards Are Not Money   So checks are not money. But what about credit cards? Isn't having a credit card in your wallet and presenting the card to pay for your roller blades the same thing as using money? Why aren't credit cards somehow valued and counted as part of the quantity of money?

When you pay by check, you are frequently asked to prove your identity by showing your driver's license. It would never occur to you to think of your driver's license as money. It's just an ID card. A credit card is also an ID card but one that lets you take a loan at the instant you buy something. When you sign a credit card sales slip, you are saying, "I agree to pay for these goods when the credit card company bills me." Once you get your statement from the credit card company, you must make the minimum payment due (or clear your balance). To make that payment, you need money—you need to have currency or a checking deposit to pay the credit card company. So although you use a credit card when you buy something, the credit card is not the *means of payment,* and it is not money.

R E V I E W

- Money is the means of payment and has three functions: medium of exchange, unit of account, and store of value.
- A commodity can serve as money, but modern societies use currency and deposits.
- The main component of money in the United States today is deposits at banks and other financial institutions.
- Checks and credit cards are not money.

We've seen that the main component of money in the United States is deposits at banks and other financial institutions. Let's take a closer look at these institutions.

Financial Intermediaries

A FIRM THAT TAKES DEPOSITS FROM HOUSEHOLDS and firms and makes loans to other households and firms is called a **financial intermediary**. The deposits of four types of financial intermediaries make up the nation's money:

- Commercial banks
- Savings and loan associations
- Savings banks and credit unions
- Money market mutual funds

Commercial Banks

A **commercial bank** is a firm, licensed by the Comptroller of the Currency (in the U.S. Treasury) or by a state agency to receive deposits and make loans. Close to 13,000 commercial banks operate in the United States today. A commercial bank's business is summarized in its balance sheet.

A bank's *balance sheet* lists its assets, liabilities, and net worth. *Assets* are what the bank *owns*, *liabilities* are what the bank *owes*, and *net worth*, which is equal to assets minus liabilities, is the value of the bank to its stockholders—its owners. A bank's balance sheet is described by the equation

Liabilities + Net worth = Assets.

Among a bank's liabilities are the deposits that are part of the nation's money. Your deposit at the bank is a liability to your bank (and an asset to you) because the bank must repay your deposit (and sometimes the interest on it too) whenever you decide to take your money out of the bank.

Profit and Prudence: A Balancing Act The aim of a bank is to maximize the net worth of its stockholders. To achieve this objective, the interest rate at which a bank lends exceeds that rate at which it borrows. But a bank must perform a delicate balancing act. Lending is risky, and the more a bank ties up its deposits in high-risk, high-interest rate loans, the bigger is its chance of not being able to repay its depositors. And if depositors perceive a high risk of not being repaid, they withdraw their funds and create a crisis for the bank. So a bank must be prudent in the way it uses its deposits, balancing security for the depositors against profit for its stockholders.

Reserves and Loans To achieve security for its depositors, a bank divides its funds into two parts: reserves and loans. **Reserves** are cash in a bank's vault plus its deposits at Federal Reserve banks. (We'll study the Federal Reserve banks in Chapter 31.) The cash in a bank's vaults is a reserve to meet its depositor's demand for currency. It keeps the ATM replenished every time you and your friends have raided it for cash for a midnight pizza. The account of a bank at the Federal Reserve is similar to your own bank account. Commercial banks use these accounts to receive and make payments. A commercial bank deposits cash into or draws cash out of its account at the Federal Reserve and writes checks on that account to settle debts with other banks.

If a bank kept all its deposits as reserves, it wouldn't make any profit. In fact, it keeps only a small fraction of its funds in reserves and lends the rest. A bank has three types of assets. They are as follows:

1. *Liquid assets* are U.S. government Treasury bills and commercial bills. These assets are the banks' first line of defense if they need cash. They can be sold and instantly converted into cash with virtually no risk of loss. Because liquid assets are virtually risk free, they have a low interest rate.

2. *Investment securities* are longer-term U.S. government bonds and other bonds. These assets can be sold quickly and converted into cash but at prices that fluctuate. Because their prices fluctuate, these assets are riskier than liquid assets, but they also have a higher interest rate.

3. *Loans* are commitments of fixed amounts of money for agreed-upon periods of time. Most banks' loans are made to corporations to finance the purchase of capital equipment and inventories and to households—personal loans—to finance consumer durable goods, such as cars or boats. The outstanding balances on credit card accounts are also bank loans. Loans are the riskiest assets of a bank because they cannot be converted into cash until they are due to be repaid. And some borrowers default and never repay. Because they are the riskiest of a bank's assets, they also carry the highest interest rate.

Commercial bank deposits are one component of the nation's money. But other financial intermediaries also take deposits that form part—an increasing part—of the nation's money. The largest of these other financial intermediaries are the S&Ls.

Savings and Loan Associations

A **savings and loan association** (S&L) is a financial intermediary that receives checking deposits and savings deposits and that makes personal, commercial, and home-purchase loans.

Savings Banks and Credit Unions

A **savings bank** is a financial intermediary owned by its depositors that accepts savings deposits and makes mostly home-purchase loans. Savings banks perform functions similar to those of S&Ls. The key difference is that savings banks, also called *mutual* savings banks, are owned by their depositors.

A **credit union** is a financial intermediary owned by its depositors that accepts savings deposits and makes mostly consumer loans. The key difference between a savings bank and a credit union is that a credit union is owned by a social or economic group such as a firm's employees.

Money Market Mutual Funds

A **money market mutual fund** is a financial institution that obtains funds by selling shares and uses these funds to buy highly liquid assets such as U.S. Treasury bills. Money market mutual fund shares act like the deposits at commercial banks and other financial intermediaries. Shareholders can write checks on their money market mutual fund accounts. But there are restrictions on most of these accounts. For example, the minimum deposit accepted might be $2,500, and the smallest check a depositor is permitted to write might be $500.

The Economic Functions of Financial Intermediaries

All financial intermediaries make a profit from the spread between the interest rate they pay on deposits and the interest rate at which they lend. Why can financial intermediaries get deposits at a low interest rate and lend at a higher one? What services do they perform that make their depositors willing to put up with a low interest rate and their borrowers willing to pay a higher one?

Financial intermediaries provide four main services that people are willing to pay for:

■ Creating liquidity
■ Minimizing the cost of obtaining funds
■ Minimizing the cost of monitoring borrowers
■ Pooling risk

Creating Liquidity   Financial intermediaries create liquidity. *Liquid* assets are those that are easily and with certainty convertible into money. Some of the liabilities of financial intermediaries are themselves money; others are highly liquid assets that are easily converted into money.

Financial intermediaries create liquidity by borrowing short and lending long. Borrowing short means taking deposits but standing ready to repay them on short notice (and on even no notice in the case of checking deposits). Lending long means making loan commitments for a prearranged, and often quite long, period of time. For example, when a person makes a deposit with a savings and loan association, that deposit can be withdrawn at any time. But the S&L makes a lending commitment for perhaps more than 20 years to a homebuyer.

Minimizing the Cost of Borrowing   Finding someone from whom to borrow can be a costly business. Imagine how troublesome it would be if there were no financial intermediaries. A firm that was looking for $1 million to buy a new production plant would probably have to hunt around for several dozen people from whom to borrow in order to acquire enough funds for its capital project. Financial intermediaries lower those costs. The firm needing $1 million can go to a single financial intermediary to obtain those funds. The financial intermediary has to borrow from a large number of people, but it's not doing that just for this one firm and the million dollars it wants to borrow. The financial intermediary can establish an organization that is capable of raising funds from a large number of depositors and can spread the cost of this activity over a large number of borrowers.

Minimizing the Cost of Monitoring Borrowers   Lending money is a risky business. There's always a danger that the borrower may not repay. Most of the money lent gets used by firms to invest in projects that they hope will return a profit. But sometimes those hopes are not fulfilled. Checking up on the activities of a borrower and ensuring that the best possible decisions are being made for making a profit and avoiding a loss are costly and specialized activities. Imagine how costly it would be if each household that lent money to a firm had to incur the costs of monitoring that firm directly. By depositing funds with a financial intermediary, households avoid those costs. The financial intermediary performs the monitoring activity by using specialized resources that have a much lower cost than what each household would incur if it had to undertake the activity individually.

Pooling Risk   As we noted above, lending money is risky. There is always a chance of not being repaid—of default. Lending to a large number of different individuals can reduce the risk of default. In such a situation, if one person defaults on a loan, it is a nuisance but not a disaster. In contrast, if only one person borrows and that person defaults on the loan, the entire loan is a write-off. Financial intermediaries enable people to pool risk in an efficient way. Thousands of people lend money to any one financial intermediary, and, in turn, the financial intermediary re-lends the money to hundreds, perhaps thousands, of individual firms. If any one firm defaults on its loan, that default is spread across all the depositors with the intermediary, and no individual depositor is left exposed to a high degree of risk.

R E V I E W

- Money consists of currency (including travelers' checks) and deposits owned by individuals and businesses. M1 is currency plus checking deposits. M2 is M1 plus savings deposits, small time deposits, and money market mutual funds.
- Most of the nation's money consists of deposits in commercial banks, savings and loan associations, savings banks, credit unions, and money market mutual funds.
- The main economic functions of financial intermediaries are to create liquidity, to minimize the cost of obtaining funds and of monitoring borrowers, and to pool risk.

We are interested in banks and other financial intermediaries because they create money. But these firms are highly regulated, and this regulation limits their ability to create money. So next, we'll examine these regulations. We'll also look at the deregulation and innovation that have occurred in the financial sector during the past 20 years.

Financial Regulation, Deregulation, and Innovation

FINANCIAL INTERMEDIARIES ARE HIGHLY REGULATED institutions. But regulation is not static, and in the 1980s, some important changes in their regulation as well as deregulation took place. Also, the institutions are not static. In their pursuit of profit, they constantly seek lower-cost ways of obtaining funds, monitoring borrowers, pooling risk, and creating liquidity. They also are inventive in seeking ways to avoid the costs imposed on them by financial regulation. Let's look at regulation, deregulation, and innovation in the financial sector in recent years.

Financial Regulation

Financial intermediaries face two types of regulation:

- Deposit insurance
- Balance sheet rules

Deposit Insurance   The deposits of most financial intermediaries are insured by the Federal Deposit Insurance Corporation (FDIC). The FDIC is a federal agency that receives its income from compulsory insurance premiums paid by commercial banks and other financial intermediaries. The FDIC operates two separate insurance funds: the Bank Insurance Fund (BIF), which insures deposits in commercial banks, and the Saving Association Insurance Fund (SAIF), which insures the deposits of S&Ls, savings banks, and credit unions. Each of these funds insures deposits of up to $100,000.

The existence of deposit insurance provides protection for depositors in the event that a financial intermediary fails. But it also limits the incentive for the owner of a financial intermediary to make safe investments and loans. Some economists believe that deposit insurance played an important role in creating a crisis for S&Ls during the 1980s. Depositors did not worry about risk because their deposits were insured. The S&L owners made high-risk loans because they knew they were making a one-way bet. If their loans paid off, they made a high rate of return. If they failed and could not meet their obligations to the depositors, the insurance fund would step in. Bad loans were good business!

Because of this type of problem, all financial intermediaries face regulation of their balance sheets.

Balance Sheet Rules The most important balance sheet regulations are:

- Capital requirements
- Reserve requirements
- Deposit rules
- Lending rules

Capital requirements are the minimum amount of an owner's own financial resources that must be put into an intermediary. This amount must be sufficiently large to discourage owners from making loans that are too risky.

Reserve requirements are rules setting out the minimum percentages of deposits that must be held in currency or other safe, liquid assets. These minimum percentages vary across the different types of intermediaries and deposits; they are largest for checking deposits and smallest for long-term savings deposits.

Deposit rules are restrictions on the different types of deposits that an intermediary can accept. These are the rules that historically have created the sharpest distinctions between the various institutions. For example, in the past, commercial banks provided checking accounts while other institutions provided only savings accounts.

Lending rules are restrictions on the proportions of different types of loans that an intermediary may make. Like deposit rules, these rules also helped to create sharp distinctions between the various institutions. Before 1980, commercial banks were the only intermediaries that were permitted to make commercial loans, and S&Ls and savings banks were restricted to making mostly mortgage loans to home buyers.

To enable S&Ls and savings banks to compete with commercial banks for funds, a ceiling was imposed on the interest rates that banks could pay on deposits. This interest ceiling regulation was known as *Regulation Q*. Also, commercial banks were not permitted to pay interest on checking deposits.

Deregulation in the 1980s

In 1980, Congress passed the Depository Institutions' Deregulation and Monetary Control Act (DIDMCA). The DIDMCA removed many of the distinctions between commercial banks and other financial intermediaries. It permitted nonbank financial intermediaries to compete with commercial banks in a wider range of lending business. At the same time it permitted the payment of interest on checking deposits so that NOW accounts and ATS accounts could be offered by all deposit-taking institutions—banks and nonbanks.[1] It also extended the powers of the Federal Reserve to place reserve requirements on all depository institutions. Despite the general direction of deregulation, this move brought a greater measure of central control over the financial system than had previously existed and represented a strengthening of the Fed's control.

The ability of S&Ls and savings banks to compete for lending business with commercial banks was further strengthened in 1982 with the passage of the Garn-St. Germain Depository Institutions Act. This legislation further eased restrictions on the scale of commercial lending that S&Ls and savings banks could undertake.

Another important regulatory change occurred in 1986: the abolition of Regulation Q. With the abolition of Regulation Q, a fiercely competitive environment was created. This environment encouraged rapid innovation in the types of deposits offered and rapid growth in money market mutual funds.

Financial Innovation

The development of new financial products—of new ways of borrowing and lending—is called **financial innovation**. The aim of financial innovation is to lower the cost of deposits or to increase the return from lending or, more simply, to increase the profit from financial intermediation. There are three main influences on financial innovation:

- Economic environment
- Technology
- Regulation

The pace of financial innovation was remarkable during the 1980s and 1990s, and all three of these forces played a role.

---

[1] A NOW account is a Negotiable Order of Withdrawal account; "negotiable order of withdrawal" is another name for a check. An ATS account is an Automatic-Transfer Savings account—a savings account that is linked to a checking account. Funds are automatically tranferred between the two accounts.

Economic Environment Some of the innovation was a response to high inflation and high interest rates. An important example is the development of variable interest rate mortgages. Traditionally, house purchases have been financed by mortgage loans at a guaranteed interest rate. Rising interest rates brought rising borrowing costs for S&Ls, and because they were committed to fixed interest rates on their mortgages, the industry incurred severe losses. The creation of variable interest rate mortgages has taken some of the risk out of long-term lending for house purchases.

Technology Other financial innovations resulted from technological change, most notably that associated with the decreased cost of computing and long-distance communication. The spread in the use of credit cards and the development of international financial markets—for example, the increased importance of Eurodollars—are consequences of technological change.[2]

Regulation A good deal of financial innovation takes place to avoid regulation. For example, Regulation Q, which prevented banks from paying interest on checking deposits, gave the impetus to devising new types of deposits on which checks could be written and interest paid, thereby getting around the regulation.

Deregulation, Innovation, and Money

Deregulation and financial innovation that have led to the development of new types of deposit accounts have brought important changes in the composition of the nation's money. In 1960, M1 consisted of only currency and checking deposits at commercial banks. In the 1990s, other new types of checking deposits have expanded while traditional checking deposits have declined. Similar changes have taken place in the composition of M2. Savings deposits have declined, while time deposits and money market mutual funds have expanded.

---

[2] Eurodollars are U.S. dollar bank accounts held in other countries, mainly in Europe. They were "invented" during the 1960s when the Soviet Union wanted the security and convenience of holding funds in U.S. dollars but were unwilling to place deposits in U.S. banks.

> ## R E V I E W
>
> - Financial intermediaries are required to insure their deposits, and their lending is regulated.
> - The 1980s saw a wave of financial deregulation that blurred the distinction between commercial banks and other financial institutions.
> - Financial intermediaries constantly seek new ways of making a profit and react to the changing economic environment, new technologies, and regulations.
> - Deregulation and innovation have brought new types of deposits that changed the composition of the nation's money.

We're now ready to learn how banks create money. In the following section, we'll use the term *banks* to refer to all the depository institutions whose deposits are part of the money supply. Let's see how money gets created.

How Banks Create Money

BANKS CREATE MONEY. BUT THIS DOESN'T MEAN that they have smoke-filled back rooms in which counterfeiters are busily working. Remember, most money is deposits, not currency. What banks create is deposits, and they do so by making loans. But the amount of deposits they can create is limited by their reserves.

Reserves: Actual and Required

We've seen that banks don't have $100 in bills for every $100 that people have deposited with them. In fact, a typical bank today has reserves of $6.00 for every $100 of deposits. No need for panic. These reserve levels are adequate for ordinary business needs.

The fraction of a bank's total deposits that are held in reserves is called the **reserve ratio**. The reserve ratio changes when a bank's customers make a deposit or withdrawal. Making a deposit increases the reserve ratio, and making a withdrawal decreases the reserve ratio.

The **required reserve ratio** is the ratio of reserves to deposits that banks are required, by regulation, to hold. A bank's *required reserves* are equal to its deposits multiplied by the required reserve ratio. Actual reserves minus required reserves are **excess reserves**. Whenever banks have excess reserves, they are able to create money.

To see how banks create money, we'll look at two model banking systems. In the first, there is only one bank; in the second, there are many banks.

Creating Deposits by Making Loans in a One-Bank Economy

In the model banking system that we'll study first, there is only one bank and its required reserve ratio is 25 percent. That is, for each dollar deposited, the bank keeps 25¢ in reserves and lends the rest. The balance sheet of One-and-Only Bank is shown in Fig. 30.2(a). On January 1, its deposits are $400 million and its reserves are 25 percent of this amount—$100 million. Its loans are equal to deposits minus reserves and are $300 million.

The story begins with Al Capone, who has decided to end his career of crime. He has been holding all his money in currency and has a nest egg of $1 million. On January 2, Al decides to put his $1 million on deposit at the One-and-Only Bank. On the day that Al makes his deposit, the One-and-Only Bank's balance sheet changes. The new situation is shown in Fig. 30.2(b). The bank now has $101 million in reserves and $401 million in deposits. It still has loans of $300 million.

The bank now has *excess reserves*. With reserves of $101 million, the bank would like to have deposits of $404 million and loans of $303 million. Because it is the One-and-Only Bank, the manager knows that the reserves will remain at $101 million. That is, she knows that when she makes a loan, the amount lent remains on deposit at the One-and-Only Bank. She knows, for example, that all the suppliers of Sky's-the-Limit Construction are also depositors of One-and-Only. So she knows that if she makes the loan that Sky's-the-Limit has just requested, the deposit she lends will never leave One-and-Only. When Sky's-the-Limit uses part of its new loan to pay $100,000 to I-Dig-It Excavating Company for some excavations, the One-and-Only Bank simply moves the funds from Sky's-the-Limit's checking account to I-Dig-It's checking account.

So on January 3, the manager of One-and-Only calls Sky's-the-Limit's accountant and offers to lend the maximum that she can. How much does she lend? She lends $3 million. By lending $3 million, One-and-Only's balance sheet changes to the one shown in Fig. 30.2(c). Loans increase by $3 million to $303 million. The loan shows up in Sky's-the-Limit's deposit initially, and total deposits increase to $404 million—$400 million plus Al Capone's deposit of $1 million plus the newly created deposit of $3 million. The bank now has no excess reserves and has reached the limit of its ability to create money.

FIGURE 30.2

Creating Money at the One-and-Only Bank

(a) Balance sheet on January 1

Assets (millions of dollars)		Liabilities (millions of dollars)	
Reserves	$100	Deposits	$400
Loans	$300		
Total	$400	Total	$400

(b) Balance sheet on January 2

Assets (millions of dollars)		Liabilities (millions of dollars)	
Reserves	$101	Deposits	$401
Loans	$300		
Total	$401	Total	$401

(c) Balance sheet on January 3

Assets (millions of dollars)		Liabilities (millions of dollars)	
Reserves	$101	Deposits	$404
Loans	$303		
Total	$404	Total	$404

In part (a) the One-and-Only Bank has deposits of $400 million, loans of $300 million, and reserves of $100 million. The bank's required reserve ratio is 25 percent. When the bank receives a deposit of $1 million (part b), it has excess reserves. It lends $3 million and creates a further $3 million of deposits. Deposits increase by $3 million, and loans increase by $3 million (in part c).

The Deposit Multiplier

The **deposit multiplier** is the amount by which an increase in bank reserves is multiplied to calculate the increase in bank deposits. That is,

$$\text{Deposit multiplier} = \frac{\text{Change in deposits}}{\text{Change in reserves}}.$$

In the example we've just worked through, the deposit multiplier is 4. The $1 million increase in reserves created a $4 million increase in deposits. The deposit multiplier is linked to the required reserve ratio by the following equation

$$\text{Deposit multiplier} = \frac{1}{\text{Required reserve ratio}}.$$

In the example the required reserve ratio is 25 percent, or 0.25. That is,

$$\text{Deposit multiplier} = \frac{1}{0.25}$$

$$= 4.$$

Creating Deposits by Making Loans with Many Banks

If you told the loans officer at your own bank that she creates money, she wouldn't believe you. Bankers see themselves as lending the money they receive from others, not creating money. But in fact, even though each bank lends only what it receives, the banking *system* creates money. To see how, let's look at another example.

Figure 30.3 is going to keep track of what is happening in the process of money creation by a banking system in which each bank has a required reserve ratio of 25 percent. The process begins when Art decides to decrease his currency holding and put $100,000 on deposit. Now Art's bank has $100,000 of new deposits and $100,000 of additional reserves. With a required reserve ratio of 25 percent, the bank keeps $25,000 on reserve and lends $75,000 to Amy. Amy writes a check for $75,000 to buy a copy-shop franchise from Barb. At this point, Art's bank has a new deposit of $100,000, new loans of $75,000, and new reserves of $25,000. You can see this situation in Fig. 30.3 as the first row of the "running tally."

For Art's bank, that is the end of the story. But it's not the end of the story for the entire banking system. Barb deposits her check for $75,000 in another bank, which has an increase in deposits and reserves of $75,000. This bank puts 25 percent of its increase in deposits ($18,750) into reserve and lends $56,250 to Bob. And Bob writes a check to Carl to pay off a business loan. The current state of play is seen in the second row of the "running tally" in Fig. 30.3. Now total bank reserves have increased by $43,750 ($25,000 plus $18,750), total loans have increased by $131,250 ($75,000 plus $56,250), and total deposits have increased by $175,000 ($100,000 plus $75,000).

When Carl takes his check to his bank, its deposits and reserves increase by $56,250, $14,063 of which it keeps in reserve and $42,187 of which it lends. This process continues until there are no excess reserves in the banking system. But the process takes a lot of further steps. One additional step is shown in Fig. 30.3. The figure also shows the final tallies—reserves increase by $100,000, loans increase by $300,000, and deposits increase by $400,000.

The sequence in Fig. 30.3 is the first four stages of the process. To figure out the entire process, look closely at the numbers in the figure. At each stage, the loan is 75 percent (0.75) of the previous loan and the deposit is 0.75 of the previous deposit. Call that proportion L ($L = 0.75$). The complete sequence is

$$1 + L + L^2 + L^3 + \dots.$$

Remember, L is a fraction, so at each stage in this sequence the amount of new loans gets smaller. The total number of loans made at the end of the process is the above sum, which is[3]

$$\frac{1}{(1 - L)}.$$

---

[3] Both here and in the expenditure multiplier process in Chapter 28, the sequence of values is called a convergent geometric series. To find the sum of a series such as this, begin by calling the sum S. Then write out the sum as

$$S = 1 + L + L^2 + L^3 + \dots.$$

Multiply by L to get

$$LS = L + L^2 + L^3 + \dots$$

and then subtract the second equation from the first to get

$$S(1 - L) = 1$$

or

$$S = \frac{1}{(1 - L)}.$$

FIGURE 30.3

The Multiple Creation of Bank Deposits

The sequence

Deposit
$100,000

Reserve
$25,000   Loan
$75,000

Deposit
$75,000

Reserve
$18,750   Loan
$56,250

Deposit
$56,250

Reserve
$14,063   Loan
$42,187

Deposit
$42,187

Reserve
$10,547   Loan
$31,640

and
so on ...

The running tally

Reserves	Loans	Deposits
$25,000	$75,000	$100,000
$43,750	$131,250	$175,000
$57,813	$173,437	$231,250
$68,360	$205,077	$273,437
•	•	•
•	•	•
▼	▼	▼
$100,000	$300,000	$400,000

When a bank receives deposits, it keeps 25 percent in reserves and lends 75 percent. The amount lent becomes a new deposit at another bank. The next bank in the sequence keeps 25 percent and lends 75 percent, and the process continues until the banking system has created enough deposits to eliminate its excess reserves. The running tally tells us the amounts of deposits and loans created at each stage. At the end of the process, an additional $100,000 of reserves creates an additional $400,000 of deposits.

If we use the numbers from the example, the total increase in deposits is

$100,000 + 75,000 + 56,250 + 42,190 + ...

$$= \$100,000\,(1 + 0.75 + 0.5625 + 0.4219 + ...)$$

$$= \$100,000\,(1 + 0.75 + 0.75^2 + 0.75^3 + ...)$$

$$= \$100,000 \times \frac{1}{(1 - 0.75)}$$

$$= \$100,000 \times \frac{1}{(0.25)}$$

$$= \$100,000 \times 4$$

By using the same method, you can check that the totals for reserves and loans are the ones shown in Fig. 30.3.

So even though each bank lends only the money it receives, the banking system as a whole does create money by making loans. The amount created is exactly the same in a multibank system as in a one-bank system.

The Deposit Multiplier in the United States

The deposit multiplier in the United States works in the same way as the deposit multiplier we've just worked out for a model economy. But the deposit multiplier in the United States differs from the one we've just calculated for three reasons. First, the required reserve ratio of U.S. banks is smaller than the 25 percent we used here. Second, U.S. banks sometimes choose to hold excess reserves. Third, not all the loans made by banks return to them in the form of reserves. Some of the loans remain outside the banks and are held as currency. The smaller required reserve ratio makes the U.S. multiplier larger than the multiplier in the above example. But the other two factors make the U.S. multiplier smaller.

R E V I E W

■ Banks create deposits by making loans, and their reserves and the required reserve ratio determine the amount they can lend.

■ Each time a bank makes a loan, both deposits at other banks and required reserves increase.

■ When deposits are at a level that makes required reserves equal to actual reserves, the banks have reached the limit of their ability to create money.

■ A change in reserves brings about a multiple change in deposits, and the deposit multiplier equals 1 divided by the required reserve ratio.

Now that we know what money is and how banks create it, let's see how the amount of money created by the banks influences the economy. We'll discover that this influence is powerful.

Money, Real GDP, and the Price Level

YOU NOW KNOW THAT IN A MODERN ECONOMY such as that of the United States today, most of the money is bank deposits. You've seen that banks actually create money by making loans. Does the quantity of money created by the banking and financial system matter? What effect does money have? Does it matter whether the quantity of money increases quickly or slowly? In particular, how does the quantity of money influence real GDP, the price level, and the inflation rate?

We're going to answer these questions first by using the aggregate supply–aggregate demand model, which explains how money affects real GDP and the price level in the short run. Then we're going to study a theory called the quantity theory of money, which explains how money growth influences inflation in the long run. We'll also look at some historical and international evidence on the relationship between money growth and inflation.

The Short-Run Effects of a Change in the Quantity of Money

Figure 30.4 illustrates the *AS-AD* model that explains how real GDP and the price level are determined in the short run. (For a full explanation of the *AS-AD* model, see Chapter 24, pp. 516–529.) We are going to use this model to study the short-run effects of a change in the quantity of money on real GDP and the price level. Potential GDP is $7 trillion, and the long-run aggregate supply curve is *LAS*. The short-run aggregate supply curve is *SAS*. Initially, the aggregate demand curve is AD_0. Equilibrium real GDP is $6.8 trillion, and the price level is 107 at the intersection of the *AD* curve and the *SAS* curve.

FIGURE 30.4

Short-Run Effects of Change in Quantity of Money

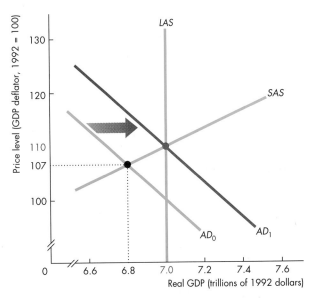

Real GDP is less than potential GDP. An increase in the quantity of money increases aggregate demand and shifts the aggregate demand curve rightward from AD_0 to AD_1. The price level rises to 110, and real GDP expands to $7 trillion. The increase in the quantity of money increases real GDP to potential GDP.

Banks, flush with excess reserves, make loans, and the loans create money. This increase results from the process of money creation we've just studied. With more money in their bank accounts and more loans, people plan to increase their consumption expenditure and businesses plan to increase their investment. Aggregate demand increases, and the aggregate demand curve shifts rightward to AD_1. A new equilibrium emerges at the intersection point of AD_1 and SAS. Real GDP expands to $7 trillion, and the price level rises to 110. Real GDP now equals potential GDP, and there is full employment. This increase in the quantity of money has increased both real GDP and the price level.

Now imagine the reverse situation. Real GDP is initially $7 trillion, and the price level is 110 at the intersection point of AD_1 and SAS. The quantity of money *decreases*. With *less* money in their bank accounts, people and businesses plan to decrease their expenditures. Aggregate demand decreases, and the aggregate demand curve shifts leftward to AD_0. A recession occurs as real GDP shrinks to $6.8 trillion, and the price level falls to 107.

These influences of the quantity of money on real GDP and the price level are *short-run* effects. In the long run, a change in the quantity of money, perhaps surprisingly, has no effect on real GDP. All its effects are on the price level. Let's see why this outcome occurs.

The Long-Run Effects of a Change in the Quantity of Money

Figure 30.5 explains how real GDP and the price level are determined in both the short run and the long run. Again, potential GDP is $7 trillion and the long-run aggregate supply curve is LAS. The short-run aggregate supply curve is SAS_1. Initially, the aggregate demand curve is AD_1. Equilibrium real GDP is $7 trillion, and the price level is 110. So real GDP equals potential GDP, and there is full employment.

Now suppose the quantity of money increases. Aggregate demand increases, and the aggregate demand curve shifts rightward to AD_2. The new short-run equilibrium is at the intersection point of AD_2 and SAS_1. The price level rises to 113, and real GDP expands to $7.2 trillion. This short-run adjustment has put real GDP above potential GDP and has decreased unemployment below the natural rate. A

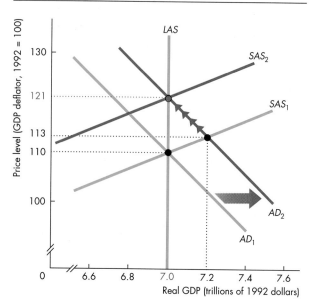

FIGURE 30.5

Long-Run Effects of
Change in Quantity of Money

Real GDP equals potential GDP. An increase in the quantity of money shifts the aggregate demand curve from AD_1 to AD_2. In the short run, the price level rises to 113, and real GDP increases to $7.2 trillion. Real GDP exceeds potential GDP, and the money wage rate rises. Short-run aggregate supply decreases, and the SAS curve shifts leftward from SAS_1 to SAS_2. Real GDP returns to potential GDP, and the price level rises to 121. In the long run, the increase in the quantity of money increases the price level and has no effect on real GDP.

shortage of labor makes the money wage rate rise. As the money wage rate rises, short-run aggregate supply decreases and the SAS curve shifts leftward toward SAS_2. As short-run aggregate supply decreases, the price level rises to 121 and real GDP decreases back to potential GDP at $7 trillion.

Thus from one full-employment equilibrium to another, an increase in the quantity of money increases the price level and has no effect on real GDP. This relationship between the quantity of money and the price level at full employment is made more precise by the quantity theory of money, which tells us about the quantitative link between money growth and inflation.

The Quantity Theory of Money

The **quantity theory of money** is the proposition that in the long run, an increase in the quantity of money brings an equal percentage increase in the price level. The original basis of the quantity theory of money is a concept known as *the velocity of circulation* and an equation called *the equation of exchange*.

The **velocity of circulation** is the average number of times a dollar of money is used annually to buy the goods and services that make up GDP. GDP is equal to the price level (P) multiplied by real GDP (Y); that is,

$$GDP = PY.$$

Call the quantity of money M. The velocity of circulation, V, is determined by the equation

$$V = PY/M.$$

For example, if GDP is $6.0 trillion and the quantity of money is $3 trillion, the velocity of circulation is

2. On the average, each dollar of money circulates twice in its use to purchase the final goods and services that make up GDP; that is, each dollar of money is used twice in a year to buy GDP.

Figure 30.6 shows the history of the velocity of circulation of both M1 and M2, the two main official definitions of money. You can see that the velocity of circulation of M1 increased between 1945 and 1980 and fluctuated through the 1980s and 1990s. In contrast, the velocity of circulation of M2 has been remarkably stable. The reason why the velocity of M1 has increased is that deregulation and financial innovation have created new types of deposits and payments technologies that are substitutes for M1. As a result, the quantity of M1 per dollar of GDP has decreased, and equivalently, the velocity of circulation of M1 has increased. The reason why the velocity of M2 has been almost constant is that the new types of deposits that have replaced M1 are part of M2. So the ratio of M2 to GDP and the velocity of circulation of M2 have been much more stable.

FIGURE 30.6

The Velocity of Circulation in the United States: 1930–1996

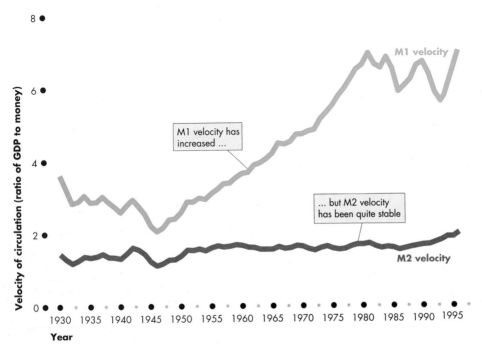

The velocity of circulation of M1 has increased over the years because financial innovation has developed M1 substitutes. The velocity of circulation of M2 has been relatively stable because the M1 substitutes that have resulted from financial innovation are new types of deposits that are part of M2.

The **equation of exchange** states that the quantity of money (M) multiplied by the velocity of circulation (V) equals GDP, or

$$MV = PY.$$

Given the definition of the velocity of circulation, this equation is always true—it is true by definition. With M equal to $3 trillion and V equal to 2, MV is equal to $6.0 trillion, the value of GDP.

The equation of exchange becomes the quantity theory of money by making two assumptions:

1. The velocity of circulation is not influenced by the quantity of money.
2. Potential GDP is not influenced by the quantity of money.

If these two assumptions are true, the equation of exchange tells us that a change in the quantity of money brings about an equal proportional change in the price level. You can see why by solving the equation of exchange for the price level. Dividing both sides of the equation by real GDP (Y) gives

$$P = (V/Y)M.$$

In the long run, real GDP (Y) equals potential GDP, so if potential GDP and velocity are not influenced by the quantity of money, the relationship between the change in the price level (ΔP) and the change in the quantity of money (ΔM) is

$$\Delta P = (V/Y)\,\Delta M.$$

Divide this equation by the previous one, $P = (V/Y)M$, to get

$$\Delta P/P = \Delta M/M.$$

($\Delta P/P$) is the proportional increase in the price level, and ($\Delta M/M$) is the proportional increase in the quantity of money. So this equation is the quantity theory of money: In the long run, the percentage increase in the price level equals the percentage increase in the quantity of money.

The Quantity Theory and the AS-AD Model

The quantity theory of money can be interpreted in terms of the AS-AD model. The aggregate demand curve is a relationship between the quantity of real GDP demanded (Y) and the price level (P), other things remaining constant. We can obtain such a relationship from the equation of exchange,

$$MV = PY.$$

Dividing both sides of this equation by real GDP (Y) gives

$$P = MV/Y.$$

This equation may be interpreted as describing an aggregate demand curve. In Chapter 24 (pp. 521–522), you saw that the aggregate demand curve slopes downward: As the price level increases, the quantity of real GDP demanded decreases. The above equation also shows such a relationship between the price level and the quantity of real GDP demanded. For a given quantity of money (M) and a given velocity of circulation (V), the higher the price level (P), the smaller is the quantity of real GDP demanded (Y).

In general, when the quantity of money changes, the velocity of circulation might also change. But the quantity theory asserts that velocity is not influenced by the quantity of money. If this assumption is correct, an increase in the quantity of money increases aggregate demand and shifts the aggregate demand curve upward by the same amount as the percentage change in the quantity of money.

The quantity theory of money also asserts that real GDP, which in the long run equals potential GDP, is not influenced by the quantity of money. This assertion is true in the AS-AD model in the long run when the economy is on its long-run aggregate supply curve. Figure 30.5 shows the quantity theory result in the AS-AD model. Initially, the economy is on the long-run aggregate supply curve LAS and at the intersection of the aggregate demand curve AD_1 and the short-run aggregate supply curve SAS_1. A 10 percent increase in the quantity of money shifts the aggregate demand curve from AD_1 to AD_2. This shift, measured by the vertical distance between the two demand curves, is 10 percent. In the long run, wages rise (also by 10 percent) and shift the SAS curve leftward to SAS_2. A new long-run equilibrium occurs at the intersection of AD_2 and SAS_2. Real GDP remains at potential GDP of $7 trillion, and the price level rises to 121. The new price level is 10 percent higher than the initial one ($121 - 110 = 11$, which is 10 percent of 110).

So the AS-AD model predicts the same outcome as the quantity theory of money. The AS-AD model also predicts a less precise relationship between the quantity of money and the price level in the short run than in the long run. For example, Fig. 30.4 shows that if we start out at a below-full employment equilibrium, an increase in the quantity of money increases real GDP. In this case, a 10 percent increase in the money supply increases the price level from 107 to 110—a 2.8 percent increase. That is, the price level increases by a smaller percentage than the percentage increase in the quantity of money.

How good a theory is the quantity theory of money? Let's answer this question by looking at the relationship between money and the price level, both historically and internationally.

Historical Evidence on the Quantity Theory of Money

The percentage increase in the price level is the inflation rate, and the percentage increase in the quantity of money is the money supply growth rate. So the quantity theory predictions can be cast in terms of money growth and inflation. The quantity theory predicts that at a given level of potential GDP and in the long run, the inflation rate will equal the money growth rate. But over time, potential GDP expands. Taking this expansion into account, the quantity theory predicts that in the long run, the inflation rate will equal the money growth rate minus the growth rate of potential GDP.

We can test the quantity theory of money by looking at the historical relationship between money growth and inflation in the United States. Figure 30.7 shows two views of this relationship for the years between 1930 and 1996. In both parts of the figure, the inflation rate is the percentage change in the GDP deflator, and the two alternative money growth rates are based on M1 and M2. Part (a) shows year-to-year changes in money and the price level. These changes show the short-run relationship between money growth and inflation. Part (b) shows decade average changes. These changes average out the year-to-year fluctuations and enable us to see the long-run relationship between the variables. If the quantity theory is a reasonable guide to reality, there should be a strong correlation between inflation and money growth in the decade average data and a weak correlation in the year-to-year data.

The data are broadly consistent with the quantity theory. The money growth rate and the inflation rate are correlated, but the relationship is not precise. During World War II, money growth increased sharply while inflation remained low. After the war, inflation exploded while money growth remained

steady. Between 1950 and 1995, the inflation rate fluctuated less than the fluctuations in the money growth rate. The year-to-year fluctuations in money growth and inflation, which contain short-run influences (in part a), show a weak correlation, and the decade average fluctuations in money growth and inflation (in part b) show a stronger correlation.

International Evidence on the Quantity Theory of Money

Another way to test the quantity theory of money is to look at the cross-country relationship between money growth and inflation. Figure 30.8 shows this relationship for 60 countries during the 1980s. By looking at a decade average, we again are smoothing out the short-run effects of money growth and focusing on the long-run effects. There is in these data an unmistakable tendency for high money growth to be associated with high inflation. The evidence is strongest for the high-inflation countries, which are shown in Fig. 30.8(a), but it is also present for the low-inflation countries, which are shown in Fig. 30.8(b).

Correlation, Causation, and Other Influences

Both the historical evidence for the United States and the international data tell us that in the long run, money growth and inflation are correlated. But the correlation between money growth and inflation does not tell us that money growth causes inflation. Money growth might cause inflation; inflation might cause money growth; or some third variable might simultaneously cause inflation and money growth.

According to the quantity theory and according to the *AS-AD* model, causation runs from money growth to inflation. But neither theory denies the possibility that at different times and places, causation might run in the other direction or that some third factor might be the root cause of both rapid money growth and inflation. One possible third factor is a large and persistent government budget deficit that gets financed by creating money.

But some occasions give us an opportunity to test our assumptions about causation. One of these is World War II and the years immediately following it. Rapid money growth during the war years was accompanied by controls that held prices down dur-

FIGURE 30.7

Money Growth and Inflation in the United States

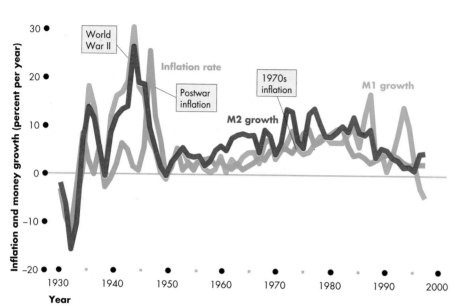

(a) Year-to-year change in money supply and the price level

Year-to-year fluctuations in money growth and inflation (part a) are loosely correlated, but decade average fluctuations in money growth and inflation (part b) are closely correlated. The burst of postwar inflation was caused by rapid money growth during World War II, and the rise in inflation during the 1970s was caused by more rapid money growth during the 1960s.

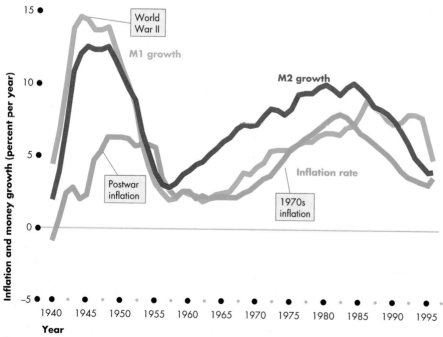

(b) Decade average change in money supply and the price level

Sources: *Historical Statistics of the United States, Economic Report of the President,* 1996, and the author's calculations.

FIGURE 30.8

Money Growth and Inflation in the World Economy

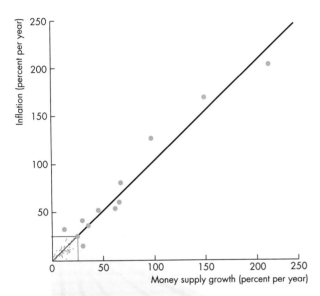

(a) All countries

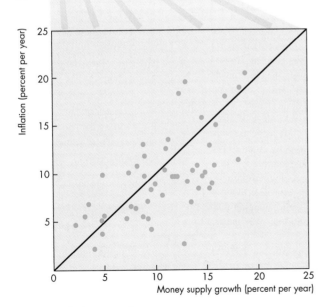

(b) Low-inflation countries

Inflation and money growth in 60 countries (in part a) and low-inflation countries (in part b) show a clear positive relationship between money growth and inflation.

Source: Federal Reserve Bank of St. Louis, Review, May/June 1988, p. 15.

ing the war but allowed them to rise immediately after the war. The inflationary consequences of wartime money growth was delayed by price controls but not removed. It is inconceivable that this was an example of reverse causation—of postwar inflation causing wartime money growth. Another is the late 1960s and 1970s. Rapid money growth that began during the 1960s almost certainly caused the high and persistent inflation of the 1970s. The combination of historical and international correlations between money growth and inflation and independent evidence about the direction of causation leads to the conclusion that the quantity theory is correct in the long run. It explains the long-term fundamental source of inflation. But the quantity theory is not correct in the short run. To understand the short-term fluctuations in inflation, the joint effects of a change in the quantity of money on real GDP, the velocity of circulation, and the price level must be explained. The *AS-AD* model provides this explanation. It also points to the possibility of other factors that influence both aggregate supply and aggregate demand influencing the inflation rate independently of the money growth rate in the short run.

R E V I E W

- The quantity of money influences the price level and real GDP.
- In the short run, an increase in the quantity of money increases aggregate demand and increases both the price level and real GDP.
- In the long run, when real GDP equals potential GDP, an increase in the quantity of money brings an equal percentage increase in the price level (the quantity theory of money).
- The long-run historical and international evidence on the relationship between money growth and inflation supports the quantity theory.

◆ Before you leave the subject of this chapter, look at *Reading Between the Lines* on pp. 684–685 and see how rapid money growth has brought inflation in Serbia. In the next chapter, we'll learn how the Fed influences the quantity of money and interest rates in its attempt to steer the course of the economy. Then, in Chapter 32, we'll return to the problem of inflation and explore more deeply its causes and consequences and ways of keeping it under control.

The Quantity Theory in Action

THE NEW YORK TIMES, DECEMBER 15, 1996

Serbia Tries to Buy Social Peace with Back Pay

By CHRIS HEDGES

BELGRADE, Serbia, Dec. 14—Business is brisk on the corner of Goce Delceva and Bulever Lenjina streets. And when business here prospers, the rest of Serbia suffers.

"We can't sell German marks fast enough," said Predrag Aleksic, who stood with a cluster of nine other black market money vendors.

"People cash their pension or salary checks at the bank and come out here to get at least some of it in foreign currency. We are seeing more and more new dinar bills, which means our Government is probably printing lots of money."

Serbia's economy, in a tailspin following decades of Communism and years of mismanagement and sanctions, seems headed for a new crisis.

After a year of relative stability, the local currency, the dinar, has begun to plummet in value. The Government of President Slobodan Milosevic, in an apparent bid to mute public unrest over the government's cancellation of election results, which has triggered huge demonstrations on the streets here every day for the last three weeks, has promised to pay pensions, salaries, student grants and social welfare payments that have been in arrears.

But economists say that to carry out this program, which requires hundreds of million of dollars, the government has begun to print money without the reserves to back it.

They also worry that the infusion of cash into the shaky economy has already triggered a devaluation that may snowball into hyperinflation by next year. ...

This morning, as tens of thousands of students and opposition politicians again marched through central Belgrade, lines of elderly pensioners, many in threadbare coats, gathered at a branch of Jugobanka in the city's New Belgrade section. Most worked for three or four decades in state-owned companies and now live on pensions of less than $100 a month.

For the first time in 12 months, these men and women received full pension checks today, although the payment covered only the month of October. The Government has promised to pay all pension payments for this year by the end of this month. ...

Economists fear that the days of disastrous hyperinflation in 1993, which saw the value of the currency drop by 10 or 20 percent in a single day, could return. ...

Street vendors, who clogged the sidewalks selling everything from eggs to videotapes outside the Merkator shopping mall, said sales had fallen by half over the last month.

"People aren't buying," said Nikola Suskavcevic, as he stood next to an array of cheap household goods spread out over the hood of his small car. "Everyone is scared about what will happen next." ...

Essence of THE STORY

■ The government of Serbia is creating money at a rapid rate and prices are rising rapidly.

■ To avoid losses, people cash their checks at the bank and then sell their dinars for foreign currency on the black market.

■ The government has promised to pay arrears of pensions, salaries, student grants, and social welfare, but economists say the government will create the money to make these payments.

■ People fear that injecting even more money into the economy will cause hyperinflation.

Economic

A N A L Y S I S

■ Current economic data for Serbia are not available. But data for Yugoslavia (of which present day Serbia is a part) are.

■ Figure I shows the inflation rate in Yugoslavia from 1986 through 1992 and the money supply growth rate through 1990. (Note that these growth rates are *thousands* of percent per year!)

■ Hyperinflation is defined as an inflation rate greater than 50 percent per month or 12,875 percent per year. Serbia doesn't have hyperinflation, but its inflation rate is high.

■ Figure I shows that money growth and inflation tend to move in a similar direction.

■ The quantity theory of money can be used to explain the movements in money growth and inflation.

■ The table contains some relevant data: inflation rate, real GDP growth, money growth, and the change in velocity for 1986, 1987, and 1988. (These are the last three years for which we have GDP data for this country.)

■ Velocity changes, but on the average, over a number of years, it is remarkably stable. Also, real GDP growth does not change much. But as the money supply growth rate changes, so also does the inflation rate change.

■ Between 1985 and 1988, money growth and inflation were 136 percent a year each and real GDP and velocity barely changed. With numbers like these, it is clear that money growth generates inflation.

■ When inflation is as high and variable as it has been in Serbia, money ceases to work well as a medium of exchange, a unit of account, or a store of value.

■ So people don't want to hold Serbian dinars. They prefer to hold German

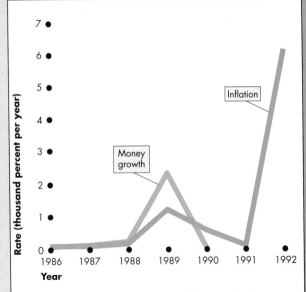

Figure I **Inflation and money growth in Yugoslavia**

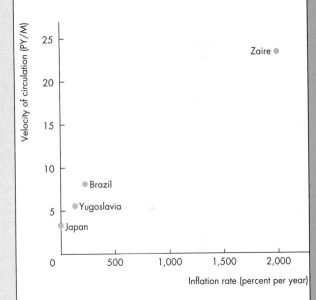

Figure 2 **Inflation and velocity**

marks, a currency that has stable buying power. So the velocity of circulation of dinars is high.

■ The higher the inflation rate, the more quickly people try to spend their income and the higher is the velocity of circulation. Figure 2 shows that in low-inflation Japan, the velocity is

less than in Yugoslavia. And in high-inflation Brazil and hyperinflation Zaire, the velocity is greater than in Yugoslavia.

■ Serbian money growth occurs not because the government is trying to cause inflation but because it has no way of financing its deficit other than by money printing.

	Inflation rate	Real GDP growth	Money growth	Change in velocity
	(percent per year)			
1986	88.4	3.5	110.4	−7.3
1987	125.0	−1.0	99.5	11.7
1988	211.8	−2.0	215.1	−3.0
Average	**136.4**	**0.1**	**136.5**	**0.1**

Source: International Financial Statistics Yearbook, 1995, (Washington D.C.: International Monetary Fund).

SUMMARY

Key Points

What Is Money? (pp. 666–668)

- Money is the means of payment, a medium of exchange, a unit of account, and a store of value.
- M1 consists of currency, travelers' checks, and checking deposits), and M2 consists of M1 plus savings deposits, time deposits, and money market mutual funds.

Financial Intermediaries (pp. 669–671)

- Commercial banks, S&Ls, savings banks, credit unions, and money market mutual funds are financial intermediaries whose liabilities are money.
- Financial intermediaries provide four main economic services: They create liquidity, minimize the cost of obtaining funds, minimize the cost of monitoring borrowers, and pool risks.

Financial Regulation, Deregulation, and Innovation (pp. 671–673)

- Financial regulation to protect depositors includes deposit insurance, minimum capital rules, and required reserves.
- Deregulation during the 1980s removed the distinctions between banks and nonbank intermediaries.
- The search for profit leads to the creation of new types of deposits and loans, which change the composition of the nation's money supply.

How Banks Create Money (pp. 673–677)

- Banks create money by making loans.
- The total quantity of deposits that can be supported by a given amount of reserves (the deposit multiplier) is determined by the required reserve ratio.

Money, Real GDP, and the Price Level (pp. 677–683)

- An increase in the quantity of money increases aggregate demand and, in the short run, increases both the price level and real GDP.
- In the long run, an increase in the quantity of money bring increases in the price level and no change in real GDP.
- Like the AS–AD model, the quantity theory of money predicts no long-run relationship between money and real GDP.

Key Figures

Key Terms

QUESTIONS

1. What is money? What are its functions?

2. What are the two main measures of money in the United States today?

3. Why aren't checks money?

4. Why aren't credit cards money?

5. What is a financial intermediary?

6. What are the types of financial intermediaries in the United States whose deposits are part of the nation's money?

7. What are the economic functions of financial intermediaries?

8. How do banks make a profit and how do they create money?

9. Describe the main types of financial regulation that a financial intermediary faces.

10. Describe the deregulation of financial intermediaries that took place in the 1980s.

11. What is financial innovation? Explain the financial innovation that took place in the 1980s.

12. Define the deposit multiplier.

13. Explain why the deposit multiplier equals 1 divided by the required reserve ratio.

14. What does the aggregate supply–aggregate demand model predict about the effects of a change in the quantity of money on the price level and real GDP when the economy is initially
   a. In a recession?
   b. At full employment?

15. What is the equation of exchange and the velocity of circulation? What assumptions are necessary to make the equation of exchange the quantity theory of money?

16. What is the U.S. historical evidence on the quantity theory of money?

17. What is the international evidence on the quantity theory of money?

PROBLEMS

1. In the United States today, money includes which of the following items?
   a. Federal Reserve banknotes in the Bank of America's cash machines
   b. Your Visa card
   c. The quarters inside public phones
   d. U.S. dollar bills in your wallet
   e. The check you have just written to pay for your rent
   f. The loan you took out last August to pay for your school fees

2. Which of the following items are money? Which are deposit money?
   a. Checking deposits at Citicorp
   b. IBM stock held by individuals
   c. The Susan B. Anthony dollar coin
   d. U.S. government securities
   e. NOW accounts
   Explain your answer by referring to the three basic functions of money.

3. Sara withdraws $1,000 from her savings account at the Lucky S&L, keeps $50 in cash, and deposits the balance in her checking account at the Bank of America. What is the immediate change in M1 and M2?

4. The commercial banks in Desertland have:

Reserves	$250 million
Loans	$1,000 million
Deposits	$2,000 million
Total assets	$2,500 million

   a. Construct the commercial banks' balance sheet. If you are missing any assets, call them "other assets"; if you are missing any liabilities, call them "other liabilities."
   b. Calculate the banks' reserve ratio.
   c. If banks hold no excess reserves, calculate the deposit multiplier.

5. An immigrant arrives in New Transylvania with $1,200. The $1,200 is put into a bank deposit. All the banks in New Transylvania have a required reserve ratio of 10 percent.
   a. What is the initial increase in the quantity of money of New Transylvania?

b. What is the initial increase in the quantity of bank deposits when the immigrant arrives?

c. How much does the immigrant's bank lend out?

d. Set out the transactions that take place and calculate the amount lent and the amount of deposits created if all the funds lent are returned to the banking system in the form of deposits.

e. By how much has the quantity of money increased after the banks have made 20 loans?

f. What is the total increase in the quantity of money, in bank loans, and in bank deposits?

6. Quantecon is a country in which the quantity theory of money operates. The country has a constant population, capital stock, and technology. In year 1, real GDP was $400 million, the price level was 200, and the velocity of circulation of money was 20. In year 2, the quantity of money was 20 percent higher than in year 1.

a. What was the quantity of money in year 1?

b. What was the quantity of money in year 2?

c. What was the price level in year 2?

d. What was the level of real GDP in year 2?

e. What was the velocity of circulation in year 2?

CRITICAL THINKING

1. Study *Reading Between the Lines* on pp. 684–685 and then answer the following questions:

a. How has Serbia coped with the problem of finding a stable unit of account?

b. What has happened to the velocity of circulation of money in Serbia?

c. How do people protect themselves from a falling value of money in Serbia?

d. Why has Serbia's inflation rate been higher than its money supply growth rate in some years? Does this fact contradict the quantity theory of money?

2. Rapid inflation in Brazil caused the cruzeiro to lose its ability to function as money. Which of these commodities do you think would be most likely to take the place of the cruzeiro in the Brazilian economy?

a. Tractor parts

b. Packs of cigarettes

c. Loaves of bread

d. Impressionist paintings

e. Baseball trading cards

3. Visit Mark Bernkopf's Central Banking Resource Center on the World Wide Web at http://adams.patriot.net/~bernkopf/ (or use the link on the Parkin Web site) and read the short article on Electronic Cash. Also read "The End of Cash" by James Gleick (first published in the *New York Times Magazine*, June 16, 1996). Then answer the following questions:

a. What is e-cash?

b. Mark Bernkopf asks: "Will 'e-cash' enable private currencies to overturn the ability of governments to make monetary policy?" What do you think?

c. When you buy an item on the Internet and pay by using a form of e-cash, are you using money? Explain why or why not.

d. In your opinion, is the concern about e-cash a real concern or hype?

31

Monetary Policy

In 1987, William Greider's *Secrets of the Temple: How the Federal Reserve Runs the Country* made the *New York Times* best-seller list. This book was popular partly because it was (and is) a good read and partly because it let its reader in on some secrets—the secrets of the mysterious Fed. What exactly is the Fed? What tools does it possess? And how does it use them? ◆ One thing the Fed does is to manage the nation's money. The amount of money in existence is surprisingly large. An unknown quantity of U.S. bills circulates abroad, especially in Russia and the rest of Eastern Europe. But there are enough coins and bills circulating in the United States today for every person to have a wallet stuffed with more than $1,000. In addition, enough money is deposited in banks and other financial institutions for every person to have a deposit of more than $12,500. What determines the amount of currency and bank deposits in existence? How does the Fed change the amount of money floating around the economy? And why do individuals and businesses hold so much money? ◆ Through

Temple of Secrets

1996, interest rates were remarkably stable. But toward the year's end, more and more people began to wonder when the Fed would push them upward, and by how much. Then, in March 1997, the Fed finally acted and increased interest rates. But was that the only interest rate increase we would see in 1997? Or would there be more interest rate increases? And how does the Fed change interest rates? How do interest rates influence the economy? How do higher interest rates keep inflation in check? ◆ In this chapter, you will learn about the Fed and monetary policy. You will learn how the Fed influences interest rates and how interest rates influence the economy. You'll discover that interest rates depend, in part, on the amount of money in existence. You will also discover how the Fed influences the quantity of money to influence interest rates as it attempts to smooth the business cycle and keep inflation in check.

After studying this chapter, you will be able to:

- Describe the structure of the Federal Reserve System (the Fed)

- Describe the tools used by the Fed to conduct its monetary policy

- Explain what an open market operation is and how it works

- Explain how an open market operation changes the money supply

- Explain what determines the demand for money

- Explain how the Fed influences interest rates

- Explain how interest rates influence the economy

The Federal Reserve System

THE CENTRAL BANK OF THE UNITED STATES IS the **Federal Reserve System**. A **central bank** is a bank's bank and a public authority that regulates a nation's financial institutions and markets. As the banks' bank, the Fed provides banking services to commercial banks such as Citibank and the Bank of America. A central bank is not a citizens' bank. That is, the Fed does not provide general banking services for businesses and individual citizens.

The Fed conducts the nation's **monetary policy**, which means that it adjusts the quantity of money in circulation. The Fed's goals are to keep inflation in check, maintain full employment, moderate the business cycle, and contribute toward achieving long-term growth. Complete success in the pursuit of these goals is impossible, and the Fed's more modest goal is to improve the performance of the economy and to get closer to the goals than a "hands off" approach would achieve. Whether the Fed succeeds in improving economic performance is a matter on which there is a range of opinion.

This chapter examines the tools available to the Fed in its conduct of monetary policy and looks at the effects of the Fed's actions on the economy. We begin by describing the structure of the Fed.

The Structure of the Federal Reserve System

The key elements in the structure of the Federal Reserve System are:

- The Board of Governors
- The Regional Federal Reserve Banks
- The Federal Open Market Committee

The Board of Governors The Board of Governors has seven members, who are appointed by the President of the United States and confirmed by the Senate, each for a 14-year term. The terms are staggered so that one seat on the board becomes vacant every two years. The President appoints one of the board members as Chairman for a term of four years, which is renewable.

The Federal Reserve Banks There are 12 Federal Reserve banks, one for each of 12 Federal Reserve districts shown in Fig. 31.1. Each Federal Reserve bank has nine directors, three of who are appointed by the Board of Governors and six of who are elected by the commercial banks in the Federal Reserve district. The directors of the regional Federal Reserve banks appoint the bank's president, and the Board of Governors approves this appointment.

The Federal Reserve Bank of New York (known as the New York Fed) occupies a special place in the Federal Reserve System because it implements some of the Fed's most important policy decisions.

The Federal Open Market Committee The **Federal Open Market Committee** (FOMC) is the main policy-making organ of the Federal Reserve System. The FOMC consists of the following voting members:

- The chairman and other six members of the Board of Governors
- The president of the Federal Reserve Bank of New York
- The presidents of the other regional Federal Reserve banks (of whom, on a yearly rotating basis, only four vote)

The FOMC meets approximately every six weeks to review the state of the economy and to decide the actions to be carried out by the New York Fed.

The Fed's Power Center

A description of the formal structure of the Fed gives the impression that power in the Fed resides with the Board of Governors. In practice, it is the chairman of the Board of Governors who has the largest influence on the Fed's monetary policy actions, and some remarkable individuals have held this position. One of these is Paul Volcker, who was appointed in 1979 by President Carter and reappointed in 1983 by President Reagan. Volcker eradicated inflation but helped to create one of the most severe postwar recessions. Another is Alan Greenspan, who was appointed by President Reagan in 1987 and reappointed by President Bush in 1992 and again for another term by President Clinton in 1996.

The chairman's power and influence stem from three sources. First, it is the chairman who controls the agenda and who dominates the meetings of the FOMC. Second, day-to-day contact with a large staff of economists and other technical experts provides the chairman with detailed background briefings on monetary policy issues. Third, the chairman is the spokesperson for the Fed and the Fed's

FIGURE 31.1

The Federal Reserve System

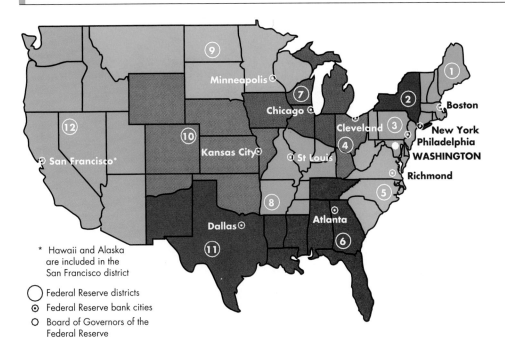

Minneapolis

Chicago

Cleveland

Kansas City

St Louis

Dallas

Atlanta

Boston

New York

Philadelphia

WASHINGTON

Richmond

San Francisco*

* Hawaii and Alaska
are included in the
San Francisco district

◯ Federal Reserve districts
◉ Federal Reserve bank cities
○ Board of Governors of the
Federal Reserve

The nation is
divided into 12
Federal Reserve
districts, each having
a Federal Reserve
bank. (Some of the
larger districts also
have branch banks.)
The Board of
Governors of the
Federal Reserve
System is located
in Washington, D.C.

Source: *Federal Reserve Bulletin,* published monthly.

main point of contact with the President and government and with foreign central banks and governments.

The Fed's Policy Tools

The Federal Reserve System has many responsibilities, but we'll examine its single most important one: regulating the amount of money floating around in the United States. How does the Fed control the money supply? It does so by adjusting the reserves of the banking system. It is also by adjusting the reserves of the banking system and by standing ready to make loans to banks that the Fed is able to prevent bank failures. The Fed uses three main policy tools to achieve its objectives:

- Required reserve ratios
- Discount rate
- Open market operations

Required Reserve Ratios All depository institutions in the United States are required to hold a minimum

percentage of deposits as reserves. This minimum percentage is known as a *required reserve ratio.* The Fed determines a required reserve ratio for each type of deposit. In 1997, banks were required to hold minimum reserves equal to 3 percent of checking deposits up to $49 million and 10 percent of these deposits in excess of $49 million. The required reserves on other types of deposits were zero.

Discount Rate The **discount rate** is the interest rate at which the Fed stands ready to lend reserves to commercial banks. A change in the discount rate is proposed to the FOMC by the Board of Directors of at least one of the 12 Federal Reserve banks and is approved by the Board of Governors.

Open Market Operations An **open market operation** is the purchase or sale of government securities—U.S. Treasury bills and bonds—by the Federal Reserve System in the open market. When the Fed conducts an open market operation, it makes a transaction with a bank or some other business but it does not transact with the federal government.

The structure and policy tools of the Federal Reserve System are summarized in Fig. 31.2. To understand how open market operations work, we need to know about the Fed's balance sheet.

The Fed's Balance Sheet

The balance sheet of the Federal Reserve System for December 1996 is set out in Table 31.1. The assets on the left side are what the Fed owns, and the liabilities on the right side are what it owes. The Fed's three main assets are:

1. Gold and foreign exchange
2. U.S. government securities
3. Loans to banks

The Fed's holdings of gold and foreign exchange are its international reserves. Most of the Fed's foreign exchange consists of deposits by the Fed at other central banks. The Fed's holdings of U.S. government securities are the backing for dollar bills and banks' deposits at the Fed. The Fed sometimes makes loans to banks on which the Fed charges them the discount rate. (These loans were negligible in December 1996.)

The Fed's two main liabilities are:

1. Federal Reserve notes in circulation
2. Banks' deposits

The Federal Reserve notes in circulation are the dollar bills that we use in our daily transactions. Some of these bills are in circulation with the public; others are in the tills and vaults of banks and other financial institutions. Banks' deposits are the deposits of commercial banks, which are part of the reserves of those banks.

You might be wondering why Federal Reserve notes are considered a liability of the Fed. When bank notes were invented, they gave their owner a claim on the gold reserves of the issuing bank. Such notes were *convertible paper money*. The holder of such a note could convert the note on demand into gold (or some other commodity such as silver) at a guaranteed price. Thus when a bank issued a note, it was holding itself liable to convert that note into gold or silver. Modern bank notes are nonconvertible. A *nonconvertible note* is a bank note that is not convertible into any commodity and that obtains its value by government fiat—hence the term "fiat money." Such notes are the legal liability of the bank that issues them, and they are backed by holdings of securities and loans. Federal Reserve notes are backed by the Fed's holdings of U.S. government securities.

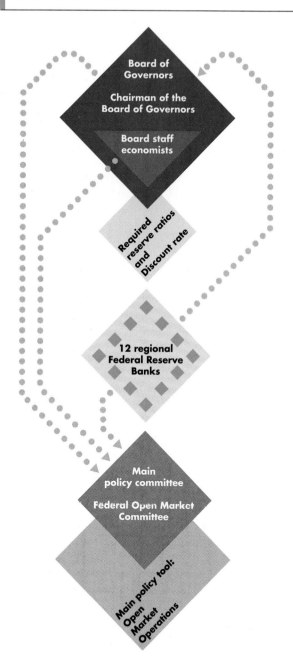

FIGURE 31.2

The Structure of the Fed

The Board of Governors sets required reserve ratios and, on the proposal of the 12 Federal Reserve banks, sets the discount rate. The Board of Governors and presidents of the regional Federal Reserve banks sit on the FOMC to determine open market operations.

TABLE 31.1

The Fed's Balance Sheet, December 1996

Assets (billions of dollars)		Liabilities (billions of dollars)	
Gold and foreign exchange	21	Federal Reserve notes	427
U.S. government securities	460	Banks' deposits	25
Loans to banks	0	Other liabilities (net)	29
Total assets	481	Total liabilities	481

Source: Federal Reserve Bulletin (March 1997).

The Fed's liabilities, together with coins in circulation (coins are issued by the Treasury and are not liabilities of the Fed), make up the monetary base. That is, the **monetary base** is the sum of Federal Reserve notes, coins, and banks' deposits at the Fed. The monetary base is so called because it acts like a base that supports the nation's money supply. The larger the monetary base, the greater is the quantity of money.

R E V I E W

- The Federal Reserve System is the central bank of the United States.
- A central bank conducts a nation's monetary policy and supervises the financial system.
- The Fed's policy tools are required reserve ratios, the discount rate, and open market operations.
- The Board of Governors sets required reserve ratios.
- It also sets the discount rate on the recommendation of the regional Federal Reserve banks.
- The Federal Open Market Committee (FOMC) determines open market operations.

Next, we're going to see how the Fed controls the money supply. We'll see how the Fed's monetary policy instruments change the monetary base and how changes in the monetary base change the quantity of money in circulation.

Controlling the Money Supply

THE FED CONSTANTLY MONITORS AND ADJUSTS the quantity of money in the economy. To change the quantity of money, the Fed can use any of its three tools: required reserve ratios, the discount rate, and open market operations. Required reserve ratios are changed infrequently. The discount rate and open market operations are used more frequently. Let's see how these tools work.

How Required Reserve Ratios Work

When the Fed *increases* the required reserve ratio, the banks must hold more reserves. To increase their reserves, the banks must *decrease* their lending, which *decreases* the quantity of money. When the Fed *decreases* the required reserve ratio, the banks may hold less reserves. To decrease their reserves, the banks *increase* their lending, which *increases* the quantity of money.

How the Discount Rate Works

When the Fed *increases* the discount rate, the banks must pay a higher price for any reserves that they borrow from the Fed. Faced with higher cost of reserves, the banks try to get by with smaller reserves. But with a given required reserve ratio, the banks must also *decrease* their lending to decrease their borrowed reserves. So the quantity of money *decreases*. When the Fed *decreases* the discount rate, the banks pay a lower price for any reserves that they borrow from the Fed. Faced with lower cost of reserves, the banks are willing to borrow more reserves and *increase* their lending. So the quantity of money *increases*.

How an Open Market Operation Works

When the Fed *buys* securities in an open market operation, the monetary base *increases*, banks *increase* their lending, and the quantity of money *increases*. When the Fed *sells* securities in an open market operation, the monetary base *decreases*, banks *decrease* their lending, and the quantity of money *decreases*. Open market operations are used more frequently than the other two tools and are the most complex in their operation. So we'll study this tool in greater detail than the other two.

When the Fed conducts an open market operation, the reserves of the banking system (a component of the monetary base) change. To see why, we'll trace the effects of an open market operation when the Fed *buys* securities. (The effects of a sale of securities is the reverse of what we'll see here.)

The Fed Buys Securities Suppose the Fed buys $100 million of U.S. government securities in the open market. There are two cases to consider: when the Fed buys from a commercial bank and when it buys from the public (a person or business that is not a commercial bank). The outcome is essentially the same in either case, but you might need to be convinced of this fact, so we'll study the two cases, starting with the simplest case, in which the Fed buys from a commercial bank.

Buys from Commercial Bank When the Fed buys $100 million of securities from the Manhattan Commercial Bank, two things happen:

1. The Manhattan Commercial Bank has $100 million less securities, and the Fed has $100 million more securities.
2. The Fed pays for the securities by crediting the Manhattan Commercial Bank's deposit account at the Fed with $100 million.

Figure 31.3(a) shows the effects of these actions on the balance sheets of the Fed and the Manhattan Commercial Bank. Ownership of the securities passes from the commercial bank to the Fed, so the bank's assets decrease by $100 million and the Fed's assets increase by $100 million, as shown by the blue arrow running from the Manhattan Commercial Bank to the Fed. The Fed pays for the securities by crediting the Manhattan Commercial Bank's deposit account— its reserves—at the Fed with $100 million, as shown by the green arrow running from the Fed to the Manhattan Commercial Bank. This action increases the monetary base and increases the reserves of the banking system.

The Fed's assets increase by $100 million, and its liabilities also increase by $100 million. The commercial bank's total assets remain constant, but their composition changes. Its holdings of government securities decrease by $100 million, and its deposits at the Fed increase by $100 million. So the bank has additional reserves, which it can use to make loans.

FIGURE 31.3

The Fed Buys Securities in the Open Market

(a) The Fed buys securities from a commercial bank

(b) The Fed buys securities from the public

We've just seen that when the Fed buys government securities from a bank, the bank's reserves increase. But what happens if the Fed buys government securities from the public—say from Goldman Sachs, a financial services company?

Buys from Public When the Fed buys $100 million of securities from Goldman Sachs, three things happen:

1. Goldman Sachs has $100 million less securities, and the Fed has $100 million more securities.

2. The Fed pays for the securities with a check for $100 million drawn on itself, which Goldman Sachs deposits in its account at the Manhattan Commercial Bank.

3. The Manhattan Commercial Bank collects payment of this check from the Fed, and $100 million is deposited in Manhattan's deposit account at the Fed.

Figure 31.3(b) shows the effects of these actions on the balance sheets of the Fed, Goldman Sachs, and the Manhattan Commercial Bank. Ownership of the securities passes from Goldman Sachs to the Fed, so Goldman Sachs's assets decrease by $100 million and the Fed's assets increase by $100 million, as shown by the blue arrow running from Goldman Sachs to the Fed. The Fed pays for the securities with a check payable to Goldman Sachs, which Goldman Sachs deposits in the Manhattan Commercial Bank. This payment increases Manhattan's reserves by $100 million, as shown by green arrow running from the Fed to Manhattan Commercial Bank. It also increases Goldman Sachs's deposit at the Manhattan Commercial Bank by $100 million, as shown by the red arrow running from the Manhattan Commercial Bank to Goldman Sachs. Just as when the Fed buys from a bank, this action increases the monetary base and increases the reserves of the banking system.

Again, the Fed's assets increase by $100 million, and its liabilities also increase by $100 million. Goldman Sachs has the same total assets as before, but their composition has changed. It now has more money and fewer securities. The Manhattan Commercial Bank's total assets increase, and so do its liabilities. Its deposits at the Fed—its reserves—increase by $100 million, and its deposit liability to Goldman Sachs increases by $100 million. Because its reserves have increased by the same amount as its deposits, the bank has excess reserves, which it can use to make loans.

We've studied what happens when the Fed *buys* government securities from either a bank or the public. When the Fed *sells* securities, all the transactions and events you've just studied work in reverse. (Trace the process again but with the Fed selling and the banks or public buying securities.)

The effects of an open market operation on the balance sheets of the Fed and the banks that we've just described are not the end of the story—they are just the beginning. With an increase in their reserves, the banks are able to make more loans, which increases the quantity of money. With a decrease in reserves, the banks must cut back on their loans and the quantity of money decreases.

A change in the monetary base that results from an open market operation has ripple effects through the economy. First, it has a multiplier effect on the quantity of money. Second, it changes interest rates. Third, it changes aggregate expenditure and real GDP. We are going to study these ripple effects in the rest of this chapter. We begin by studying the multiplier effect of an open market operation on the quantity of money. To do so, we build on the link between bank reserves and bank deposits that you studied in Chapter 30. But first we examine a related broader link between the monetary base and the quantity of money.

Monetary Base and Bank Reserves

We've defined the *monetary base* as the sum of Federal Reserve notes, coins, and banks' deposits at the Fed. The monetary base is held either by banks as *reserves* or outside the banks as currency in circulation. When the monetary base increases, both bank reserves and currency in circulation increase. But only the increase in bank reserves can be used by banks to make loans and create additional money. An increase in currency held outside the banks is called a **currency drain**. A currency drain reduces the amount of additional money that can be created from a given increase in the monetary base.

The **money multiplier** is the amount by which a change in the monetary base is multiplied to determine the resulting change in the quantity of money. It is related to, but differs from, the deposit multiplier that we studied in Chapter 30. The *deposit multiplier* is the amount by which a change in bank reserves is multiplied to determine the change in bank deposits.

Let's now look at the money multiplier.

The Multiplier Effect of an Open Market Operation

Figure 31.4 shows the multiplier effect of an open market purchase of securities from the banks. Initially, the banks' reserves increase but the quantity of money does not change. The banks have excess reserves, and the following sequence of events takes place:

- Banks lend excess reserves.
- The money supply increases.
- New deposits are used to make payments.
- Some of the new money is held as currency—a *currency drain*.
- Some of the new money remains on deposit in banks.
- Banks' required reserves increase.
- Excess reserves decrease but remain positive.

The sequence repeats in a series of rounds, but each round begins with a smaller quantity of excess reserves than did the previous one. The process continues until excess reserves have finally been eliminated.

Figure 31.5 keeps track of the increases in reserves, loans, deposits, currency, and money that results from an open market operation of $100,000. In this figure, the *currency drain* is 33.33 percent and the *required reserve ratio* is 10 percent. These numbers are assumed to keep the arithmetic simple.

The Fed buys $100,000 of securities from the banks. The banks' reserves increase by this amount, but deposits do not change. The banks have excess reserves of $100,000, and they lend those reserves. When the banks lend $100,000 of excess reserves, $66,667 remains in the banks as deposits and $33,333 drains off and is held outside the banks as currency. The quantity of money has now increased by $100,000—the increase in deposits plus the increase in currency holdings.

The increased bank deposits of $66,667 generates an increase in required reserves of 10 percent of that amount, which is $6,667. Actual reserves have

---

FIGURE 31.4

A Round in the Multiplier Process Following an Open Market Operation

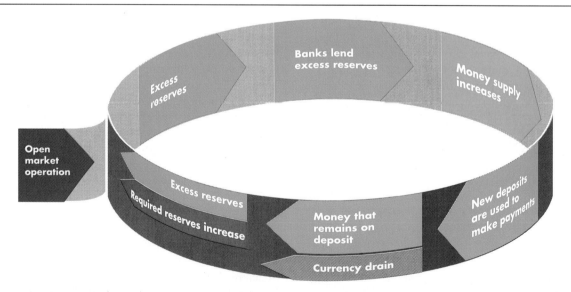

An open market operation increases bank reserves and creates excess reserves. Banks lend the excess reserves, and new loans are used to make payments. Households and firms receiving payments keep some of the receipts in the form of currency—a currency drain—and place the rest on deposit in banks. The increase in bank deposits increases banks' reserves but also increases banks' required reserves. Required reserves increase by less than actual reserves, so the banks still have some excess reserves, though less than before. The process repeats until excess reserves have been eliminated.

FIGURE 31.5

The Multiplier Effect of an Open Market Operation

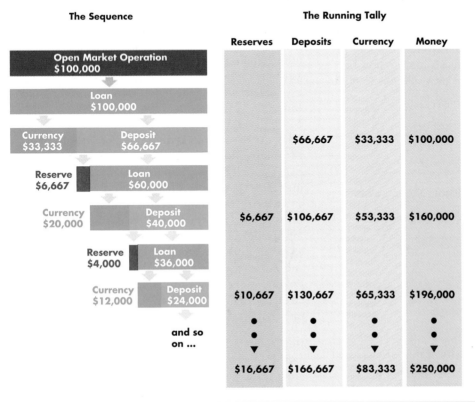

The Sequence

The Running Tally

	Reserves	Deposits	Currency	Money
Open Market Operation $100,000				
Loan $100,000				
Currency $33,333 / Deposit $66,667		$66,667	$33,333	$100,000
Reserve $6,667 / Loan $60,000				
Currency $20,000 / Deposit $40,000	$6,667	$106,667	$53,333	$160,000
Reserve $4,000 / Loan $36,000				
Currency $12,000 / Deposit $24,000	$10,667	$130,667	$65,333	$196,000
and so on ...	● ● ▼	● ● ▼	● ● ▼	● ● ▼
	$16,667	$166,667	$83,333	$250,000

When the Fed provides the banks with $100,000 of additional reserves in an open market operation, the banks lend those reserves. Of the amount lent, $33,333 (33.33 percent) leaves the banks in a currency drain and $66,667 remains on deposit. With additional deposits, required reserves increase by $6,667 (10 percent required reserve ratio) and the banks lend $60,000. Of this amount, $20,000 leaves the banks in a currency drain and $40,000 remains on deposit. The process repeats until the banks have created enough deposits to eliminate their excess reserves. An additional $100,000 of reserves creates $250,000 of money.

---

increased by the same amount as the increase in deposits—$66,667. So the banks now have excess reserves of $60,000. At this stage, we have gone once around the circle shown in Fig. 31.4. The process we've just described repeats but begins with excess reserves of $60,000. Figure 31.5 shows the next two rounds. At the end of the process, the quantity of money has increased by a multiple of the increase in the monetary base. In this case, the increase is $250,000, which is 2.5 times the increase in the monetary base.

An open market *sale* works similarly to an open market purchase, but it *decreases* the quantity of money. (Trace the process again but with the Fed selling and the banks or public buying securities.)

When the Fed undertakes an open market operation, it is trying to influence the course of the economy. But the Fed's influence is indirect. You've now studied the initial effect of the Fed's actions, which is to change the quantity of money.

R E V I E W

◼ When the Fed buys securities in the open market, the monetary base and bank reserves increase and banks have excess reserves. When the Fed sells securities in the open market, the monetary base and bank reserves decrease and banks have a shortage of reserves.

◼ With excess reserves, the banks increase their lending and the quantity of money increases.

◼ With a shortage of reserves, the banks decrease their lending and the quantity of money decreases.

When the Fed changes the quantity of money, it sets off a ripple effect, the next part of which is a change in interest rates. Why do interest rates change when the quantity of money changes? We'll discover the answer by studying the demand for money.

The Demand for Money

THE AMOUNT OF MONEY WE RECEIVE EACH WEEK in payment for our labor is income—a flow. The amount of money that we hold in our wallet or in a deposit account at the bank is an inventory—a stock. There is no limit to how much income we would like to receive each week. But there is a limit to how big an inventory of money each of us would like to hold on to and not spend.

The Influences on Money Holding

The quantity of money that people choose to hold depends on four main factors:

- The price level
- The interest rate
- Real GDP
- Financial innovation

Let's look at each of them.

The Price Level The quantity of money measured in dollars is called the quantity of *nominal money*. The quantity of nominal money demanded is proportional to the price level, other things remaining the same. That is, if the price level (GDP deflator) increases by 10 percent, people will want to hold 10 percent more nominal money than before, other things being equal. What matters is not the number of dollars that you hold but their buying power. If you hold $20 to buy your weekly movies and soda, you will increase your money holding to $22 if the prices of movies and soda—and your wage rate—increase by 10 percent.

The quantity of money measured in constant dollars (for example, in 1992 dollars) is called *real money*. Real money is equal to nominal money divided by the price level. It is the quantity of money measured in terms of what it will buy. In the above example, when the price level rises by 10 percent and you increase your average cash holding by 10 percent, you are keeping your *real* cash holding constant. Your $22 at the new price level buys the same quantity of goods and is the same quantity of *real money* as your $20 at the original price level. The quantity of real money held does not depend on the price level.

The Interest Rate A fundamental principle of economics is that as the opportunity cost of something increases, people try to find substitutes for it. Money is no exception. The higher the opportunity cost of holding money, other things being equal, the lower is the quantity of real money demanded. But what is the opportunity cost of holding money? It is the interest rate that you can earn by holding money minus the interest rate that you must forgo on other assets that you could hold instead of money.

The interest rate that you earn on currency and some checking deposits is zero. So the opportunity cost of holding these items is the interest rate on other assets such as a savings bond or Treasury bill. By holding money instead, you forgo the interest that you otherwise would have received. This forgone interest is the opportunity cost of holding money.

Money loses value because of inflation. So, why isn't the inflation rate part of the cost of holding money? It is: Other things being equal, the higher the expected inflation rate, the higher are interest rates and the higher, therefore, is the opportunity cost of holding money. (The forces that make interest rates change to reflect changes in the expected inflation rate are described in Chapter 32 on pp. 728–729.)

Real GDP The quantity of money that households and firms plan to hold depends on the amount they are spending, and the quantity of money demanded in the economy as a whole depends on aggregate expenditure—real GDP.

Again, suppose that you hold an average of $20 to finance your weekly purchases of movies and soda. Now imagine that the prices of these goods and of all other goods remain constant but that your income increases. As a consequence, you now spend more, and you also keep a larger amount of money on hand to finance your higher volume of expenditure.

Financial Innovation Technological change and the arrival of new financial products change the quantity of money held. The major financial innovations are the widespread use of:

1. Daily interest checking deposits
2. Automatic transfers between checking and savings deposits
3. Automatic teller machines
4. Credit cards

These innovations have occurred because of the development of computing power that has lowered the cost of calculations and record keeping.

We summarize the effects of the influences on money holding by using the demand for money curve.

The Demand for Money Curve

The *demand for money* is the relationship between the quantity of real money demanded and the interest rate, when all other influences on the amount of money that people wish to hold remain the same. Figure 31.6 shows a demand for money curve, MD. When the interest rate rises, everything else remaining the same, the opportunity cost of holding money rises and the quantity of money demanded decreases—there is a movement along the demand for money curve. Similarly, when the interest rate falls, the opportunity cost of holding money falls, and the quantity of money demanded increases—there is a downward movement along the demand for money curve.

Shifts in the Demand Curve for Real Money

A change in real GDP or financial innovation changes the demand for money and shifts the demand curve for real money. Figure 31.7 illustrates the change in the demand for money. A decrease in real GDP decreases the demand for money and shifts the demand curve leftward from MD_0 to MD_1. An increase in real GDP has the opposite effect. It increases the demand for money and shifts the demand curve rightward from MD_0 to MD_2.

The influence of financial innovation on the demand for money curve is more complicated. It might increase the demand for some types of deposits, decrease the demand for others, and decrease the demand for currency. We'll look at the effects of financial innovation by studying the demand for money in the United States.

FIGURE 31.6

The Demand for Money ◆

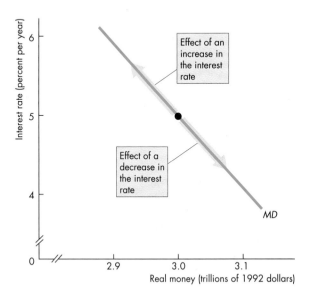

FIGURE 31.7

Changes in the Demand for Money ◆

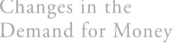
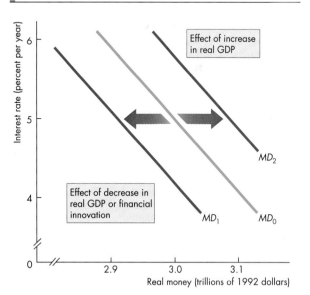

The demand for money curve, MD, shows the relationship between the quantity of money that people plan to hold and the interest rate, other things remaining the same. The interest rate is the opportunity cost of holding money. A change in the interest rate brings a movement along the demand curve.

A decrease in real GDP decreases the demand for money and shifts the demand curve leftward from MD_0 to MD_1. An increase in real GDP increases the demand for money and shifts the demand curve rightward from MD_0 to MD_2. Financial innovation generally decreases the demand for money.

The Demand for Money in the United States

Figure 31.8 shows the relationship between the interest rate and the quantity of real money demanded in the United States between 1970 and 1996. Each dot shows the interest rate and the amount of real money held in a given year. In 1970, the demand for M1 (shown in part a) was MD_{70}. During the early 1970s, the spread of credit cards decreased the demand for M1 (currency and checking deposits) and this financial innovation shifted the demand for M1 curve leftward to MD_{76}. But over the years, real GDP growth increased the demand for M1, and by 1994, the demand for M1 curve had shifted rightward to MD_{94}.

Further financial innovation, probably arising from the further increased use of credit cards, decreased the demand for M1 and shifted the demand curve leftward again.

In 1970, the demand for M2 (shown in part b) was MD_{70}. The spread of credit cards that decreased the demand for M1 during the period did not decrease demand for M2. The reason is that most of the new financial products were M2 deposits. So from 1970 through 1989, the demand for M2 increased and the demand for M2 curve shifted rightward to MD_{89}. But in the period after 1989, the main innovations were in financial products that compete with deposits of all kinds. So the demand for M2 decreased, and the demand for M2 curve shifted leftward to MD_{96}.

FIGURE 31.8

The Demand for Money in the United States

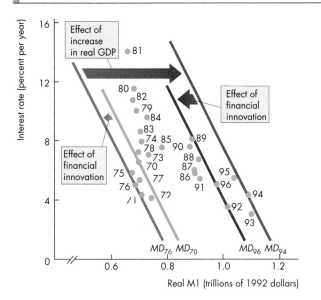

(a) M1 demand

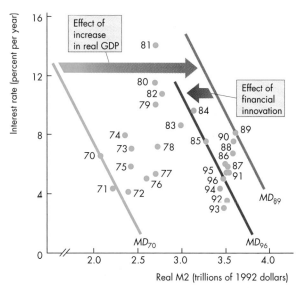

(b) M2 demand

The dots show the quantity of real money and the interest rate in each year between 1970 and 1996. In 1970, the demand for M1 was MD_{70} in part (a). The demand for M1 decreased during the early 1970s because of financial innovation, and the demand curve shifted leftward to MD_{76}. But the demand for M1 has increased because of real GDP growth, and by 1994, the demand curve had shifted rightward to MD_{94}. Further financial

innovation decreased the demand for M1 in 1995 and 1996 and shifted the demand curve leftward again to MD_{96}. In 1970, the demand for M2 curve was MD_{70} in part (b). The growth of real GDP increased the demand for M2, and by 1989, the demand curve had shifted rightward to MD_{89}. During the 1990s, new substitutes for M2 decreased the demand for M2 and the demand curve shifted leftward to MD_{96}.

Source: Economic Report of the President, 1997, and the author's calculations and assumptions.

REVIEW

- The demand for money curve shows the relationship between the quantity of real money demanded and the interest rate with all other influences on money holding unchanged.
- An increase in the interest rate decreases the quantity of money demanded and brings a movement along the demand curve for real money.
- Other influences on the quantity of real money demanded are real GDP and financial innovation.
- An increase in real GDP increases the demand for money and shifts the demand curve rightward.
- Financial innovations have decreased the demand for M1. These innovations initially increased the demand for M2, but later the demand for M2 also decreased.

We now know what determines the demand for money. And we've seen that a key factor is the interest rate—the opportunity cost of holding money. But what determines the interest rate? Let's find out.

Interest Rate Determination

AN INTEREST RATE IS THE PERCENTAGE YIELD on a financial security such as a *bond* or a *stock*. The higher the price of a financial asset, other things remaining the same, the lower is the interest rate. An example will make this relationship clear. Suppose the federal government sells a bond that promises to pay $10 a year. If the price of the bond is $100, the interest rate is 10 percent per year—$10 is 10 percent of $100. If the price of the bond is $50, the interest rate is 20 percent—$10 is 20 percent of $50. And if the price of the bond is $200, the interest rate is 5 percent—$10 is 5 percent of $200.

You've just seen the link between the price of a bond and the interest rate. People divide their wealth between bonds (and other interest-bearing financial assets) and money, and the amount they hold as money depends on the interest rate. We can study the forces that determine the interest rate either in the market for bonds or the market for money. Because the Fed can influence the *supply* of money, we focus on the market for money.

Money Market Equilibrium

The interest rate is determined by the supply of and demand for money. The quantity of money supplied is determined by the actions of the banking system and the Fed. On any given day, the supply of money is a fixed quantity. The *real* quantity of money supplied is equal to the nominal quantity supplied divided by the price level. At a given moment in time, there is a particular price level, and so the quantity of real money supplied is also a fixed amount. The supply curve of real money is shown in Fig. 31.9 as the vertical line labeled *MS*. The quantity of real money supplied is $3.0 trillion.

FIGURE 31.9
Money Market Equilibrium

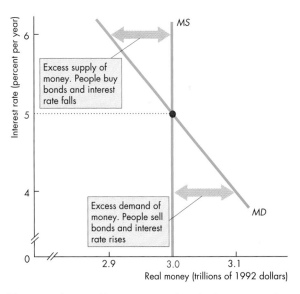

Money market equilibrium occurs when the interest rate has adjusted to make the quantity of money demanded equal to the quantity supplied. Here, equilibrium occurs at an interest rate of 5 percent. At interest rates above 5 percent, the quantity of money demanded is less than the quantity supplied, so people buy bonds, and the interest rate falls. At interest rates below 5 percent, the quantity of real money demanded exceeds the quantity supplied, so people sell bonds and the interest rate rises. Only at 5 percent is the quantity of real money in existence willingly held.

On any given day, all the influences on the demand for money except for the interest rate are constant. But the lower the interest rate, the greater is the quantity of money demanded. Figure 31.9 shows a demand for money curve, *MD*.

Equilibrium When the quantity of money supplied equals the quantity of money demanded, the money market is in equilibrium. Figure 31.9 illustrates equilibrium in the money market. Equilibrium is achieved by changes in the interest rate. If the interest rate is too high, people demand a smaller quantity of money than the quantity supplied. They are holding too much money. In this situation, they try to get rid of money by buying bonds. As they do so, the price of a bond rises and the interest rate falls to the equilibrium rate. Conversely, if the interest rate is too low, people demand a larger quantity of money than the quantity supplied. They are holding too little money. In this situation, they try to get more money by selling bonds. As they do so, the price of a bond falls and the interest rate rises to the equilibrium rate. Only when the interest rate is at the level at which people are holding the quantity of money supplied do they willingly hold the money and take no actions that change the interest rate.

Changing the Interest Rate

Suppose that the economy is overheating and the Fed fears inflation. It decides to take action to decrease aggregate demand and spending. To do so, it wants to raise interest rates and discourage borrowing and expenditure on goods and services. What does the Fed do?

The Fed sells securities in the open market. As it does so, it mops up bank reserves and induces the banks to cut their lending. The banks make a smaller quantity of new loans each day until the stock of loans outstanding has fallen to a level that is consistent with the new lower level of reserves. The money supply decreases.

Suppose that the Fed undertakes open market operations on a sufficiently large scale to decrease the money supply from $3.0 trillion to $2.9 trillion. As a consequence, the supply curve of real money shifts leftward, as shown in Fig. 31.10, from MS_0 to MS_1.

The demand for money is shown by *MD*. With an interest rate of 5 percent and $2.9 trillion of money in the economy, firms and households are now holding less money than they wish to hold. They attempt to increase their money holding by selling financial

Interest Rate Changes

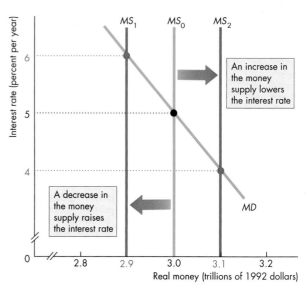

An open market sale of securities shifts the money supply curve leftward to MS_1 and the interest rate rises to 6 percent. An open market purchase of securities shifts the money supply curve rightward to MS_2 and the interest rate falls to 4 percent.

assets. As they do so, the prices of bonds fall and the interest rate rises. When the interest rate has increased to 6 percent, people are willing to hold the smaller $2.9 trillion of money that the Fed and the banks have created.

Conversely, suppose that the Fed fears recession and decides to stimulate spending by increasing the money supply. If the Fed increases the real money supply to $3.1 trillion, the supply of money curve shifts rightward from MS_0 to MS_2. Equilibrium occurs when the interest rate has fallen to 4 percent.

R E V I E W

▪ Short-term interest rates are determined by the demand for and supply of money. When the quantity of money demanded equals the quantity supplied, the interest rate is at its equilibrium level.

▪ To increase the interest rate, the Fed sells securities and decreases the money supply. To decrease the interest rate, the Fed buys securities and increases the money supply.

Monetary Policy

YOU HAVE NOW LEARNED A GREAT DEAL ABOUT the Fed, the monetary policy actions it can take, and the effects of those actions on short-term interest rates. Most of the "secrets of the temple" have been revealed. But you are possibly thinking: All this sounds nice in theory, but does it really happen? Does the Fed actually do the things we've learned about in this chapter? Indeed, it does happen, sometimes with dramatic effect.

To see the Fed in action, we'll do two things. First, we'll look at the fluctuations in short-term interest rates in the United States since 1970 and see how the Fed has influenced those fluctuations. Second, we'll focus on two episodes in the life of the Fed. One is from the turbulent years of the early 1980s when the Fed was struggling to eradicate a stubborn inflation. The other is from the period since a stock market crash of 1987 during which the Fed tried to keep inflation in check without killing economic growth.

The Fed in Action

You've seen that the immediate effect of the Fed's actions is a change in the short-term interest rate. Figure 31.11 shows the course of four short-term interest rates since 1970:

1. The 3-month Treasury bill rate, which is the interest rate paid by the federal government on 3-month loans

2. The 6-month commercial bill rate, which is the interest rate paid by large corporations on 6-month loans

3. The discount rate, which is the interest rate charged to banks by the Fed when the banks borrow reserves

4. The federal funds rate, which is the interest rate that the banks charge each other on overnight loans of reserves

Notice how closely these four interest rates move together. The interest rate that the Fed directly controls is the discount rate, and the rate that it closely

FIGURE 31.11

Short-Term Interest Rates

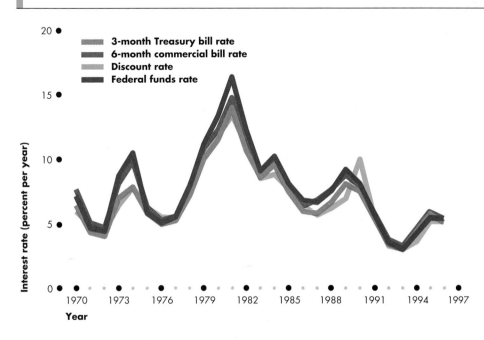

The Fed directly determines the discount rate (the rate at which the Fed lends reserves to banks) and closely monitors the federal funds rate (the rate at which banks lend reserves to each other). All short-term interest rates move up and down together, so the Fed influences all short-term rates such as the 3-month Treasury bill rate (the rate at which the federal government borrows in the short term) and the 6-month commercial bill rate (the rate at which big corporations borrow in the short term).

Source: *Economic Report of the President,* 1997

monitors is the federal funds rate, but because the short-term rates all move up and down together, the Fed is effectively able to influence all these rates.

Do short-term interest rates rise and fall in response to changes in the quantity of money, as the theory we've just studied predicts? Mostly they do, but not quite always. Figure 31.12 illustrates this connection. It shows the federal funds rate and a measure of the quantity of money. This measure of money is M2 expressed as a percentage of GDP. The reason for looking at M2 is that it is this measure of money that the Fed has placed greatest emphasis on. The reason for expressing M2 as a percentage of GDP is that we can see both the supply-side and demand-side effects on interest rates in a single measure. Interest rates rise if the quantity of money decreases. Interest rates also rise if the demand for money increases. But the demand for money increases if GDP increases. So the ratio of M2 to GDP rises either if the supply of money increases (M2 increases) or the demand for money decreases (GDP decreases).

You can see by studying Fig. 31.12 that between 1970 and 1990, the rises and falls in the interest rate were exactly matched by decreases and increases in the ratio of M2 to GDP. An increase in the supply of money relative to the demand for money brought a fall in the interest rate (1970–1972, 1974–1977, and 1981–1986). A decrease in the supply of money relative to the demand for money brought a rise in the interest rate (1972–1974, 1977–1981, and 1986–1989).

You can also see in Fig. 31.12 that after 1990, the relationship between money and interest rates broke down. When the interest rate fell through 1993, the M2 to GDP ratio did not increase. The reason is that the demand for M2 fell because of the availability of some new substitute ways of holding wealth—bond and equity mutual funds. These funds were growing through the 1980s, but they grew more quickly during the 1990s, and their growth disturbed the traditional relationship between M2 and short-term interest rates. Consequently, after 1990, the Fed began to pay less attention to M2.

FIGURE 31.12

Money and Interest Rates

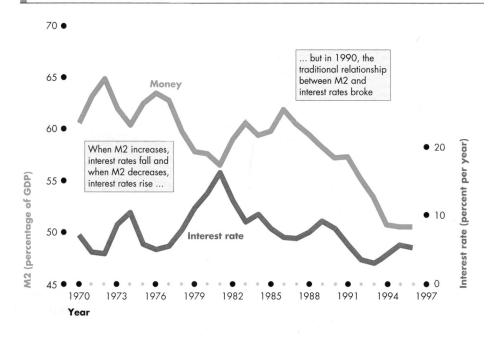

When the ratio of M2 to GDP (measured on the left scale) rises, either the supply of money increases or the demand for money decreases. The result, before 1990, is a fall in the federal funds rate (measured on the right scale). Similarly, when the ratio of M2 to GDP falls, either the supply of money has decreased or the demand for money has increased and (again before 1990) the federal funds rate rises. After 1990, the relationship between M2 and interest rates broke down because new substitutes for M2 decreased the demand for M2.

Source: *Economic Report of the President*, 1997, and the author's calculations.

You've now seen that we can explain short-term interest rate fluctuations as arising from fluctuations in the supply of money relative to the demand for money. But this relationship doesn't tell us whether actions by the Fed or fluctuations in GDP brought the fluctuations in the M2 to GDP ratio. Do the Fed's own actions move interest rates around? Let's look at the Fed in action.

Paul Volcker's Fed   At the start of Paul Volcker's term of office as chairman of the Fed, which began in August 1979, the United States was locked in the grips of double-digit inflation. Volcker ended that inflation. He did so by forcing interest rates sharply upward from 1979 through 1981. This increase in interest rates resulted from the Fed using open market operations and increases in the discount rate to keep the banks short of reserves, which in turn held back the growth in the supply of loans and of money relative to the growth in their demand.

As we saw in Fig. 31.10, to increase interest rates, the Fed has to cut the real money supply. In practice, because the economy is growing and because prices are rising, a *slowdown* in nominal money supply growth is enough to increase interest rates. It is not necessary to actually *cut* the nominal money supply.

When Volcker became chairman of the Fed, the money supply was growing at more than 8 percent a year. Volcker slowed down that money supply growth to 6.5 percent in 1981. As a result, interest rates increased. The Treasury bill rate—the rate at which the government borrows—increased from 10 percent to 14 percent. The rate at which big corporations borrow increased from 9 percent to 14 percent. Mortgage rates—the rates at which homebuyers borrow—increased from 11 percent to 15 percent. The economy went into recession. The money supply growth slowdown and interest rate hike cut back the growth rate of aggregate demand. Real GDP fell, and the inflation rate slowed down.

Alan Greenspan's Fed   Alan Greenspan became chairman of the Fed in August 1987. In the two preceding years, the money supply had grown at a rapid pace, interest rates had tumbled, and the stock market had boomed. Then, suddenly and with no warning, stock prices fell, bringing fears of economic calamity and recession. This was Alan Greenspan's first test as Fed chairman.

The Fed's immediate reaction to the new situation was to emphasize the flexibility and sensitivity of the financial system and to make reserves plentiful to avoid any fear of a banking crisis. But as the months passed, it became increasingly clear that the economy was not heading for any kind of a recession. Unemployment continued to fall, income growth continued to be strong, and the fears that emerged were of inflation, not recession.

Seeking to avoid a serious upturn in inflation, the Fed slowed money growth and, just as Paul Volcker had done eight years earlier, forced interest rates sharply upward. Open market operations were targeted toward creating a shortage of reserves in the banking system to slow the money supply growth rate. As a consequence, during the year from May 1988 to May 1989, the M1 measure of the money supply was virtually constant and the M2 measure grew by only 2.4 percent, both down from growth rates of around 5 percent a year earlier and down from around 10 percent a year before the stock market crash. The slowdown in money supply growth increased interest rates throughout 1988. The interest rate on U.S. government 3-month Treasury bills increased from less than 6 percent a year at the start of 1988 to almost 9 percent a year by early 1989.

As 1989 advanced, concern about inflation remained, but renewed fears of recession returned as an increasing number of signs of a slowing economy emerged. Interest rates were gradually lowered, and the money supply was permitted to grow more quickly. By 1990, recession had become a reality. At first, the Fed's reaction was to adopt a neutral position, waiting for signs of recovery from an increase in investment and consumption expenditure. But as the months passed and recovery seemed elusive, the Fed eventually began to stimulate spending with a series of interest rate cuts. During 1991, interest rates declined by three percentage points as the Fed tried to encourage an increase in borrowing and spending.

By mid-1991, the recovery had begun and real GDP expanded. By 1997, this expansion was still going strong and set to break a record to become the longest peacetime expansion. The Fed played a role in keeping the expansion alive and in holding inflation in check. It did so by trying to anticipate unwanted deviations in either direction. Through 1992 and 1993, the Fed permitted rapid money growth and kept interest rates low. During 1994, the Fed slowed money growth and pushed interest rates upward. It permitted rates to fall again during 1996 and nudged them up slightly in the first quarter of 1997.

Profiting by Predicting the Fed

Every day, the Fed influences interest rates by its open market operations. By buying securities and increasing the money supply, the Fed can lower interest rates; by selling securities and lowering the money supply, the Fed can increase interest rates. Sometimes such actions are taken to offset other influences and keep interest rates steady. At other times, the Fed moves interest rates up or down. The higher the interest rate, the lower is the price of a bond; the lower the interest rate, the higher is the price of a bond. Thus predicting interest rates is the same as predicting bond prices. Predicting that interest rates are going to fall is the same as predicting that bond prices are going to rise—a good time to buy bonds. Predicting that interest rates are going to rise is the same as predicting that bond prices are going to fall—a good time to sell bonds.

Because the Fed is the major player whose actions influence interest rates and bond prices, predicting the Fed is profitable and a good deal of effort goes into that activity. But people who anticipate that the Fed is about to increase the money supply buy bonds right away, pushing their prices upward and pushing interest rates downward *before* the Fed acts. Similarly, people who anticipate that the Fed is about to decrease the money supply sell bonds right away, pushing their prices downward and pushing interest rates upward before the Fed acts. In other words, bond prices and interest rates change as soon as the Fed's actions are foreseen. By the time the Fed actually takes its actions, if those actions are correctly foreseen, they have no effect. The effects occur in anticipation of the Fed's actions. Only changes in the money supply that are not foreseen change the interest rate at the time that those changes occur.

The Ripple Effects of Monetary Policy

You've now seen that the Fed's actions do indeed change interest rates and that the Fed tries to influence the course of the economy. These monetary policy measures work by changing aggregate demand. When the Fed slows money growth and pushes interest rates up, it decreases aggregate demand, which in turn slows both real GDP growth and inflation. When the Fed speeds money growth and lowers interest rates, it increases aggregate demand, which in turn speeds real GDP

growth and inflation. The mechanism through which aggregate demand changes involves several channels. Higher interest rates bring a decrease in consumption expenditure and investment. Tighter bank credit brings fewer loans and reinforces the effects of higher interest rates on consumption expenditure and investment.

Higher interest rates bring an increase in the exchange rate that makes U.S. exports more expensive and makes imports less costly. So net exports decrease. The decreases in consumption, investment, and net exports all combine to decrease aggregate demand, which in turn slows the growth rate of real GDP and the inflation rate. Schematically, the effects of the Fed's actions ripple through the economy in the following way:

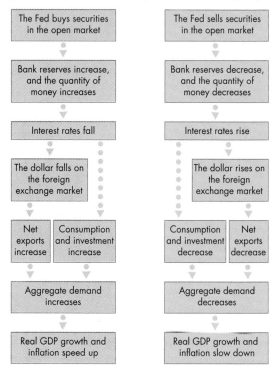

Interest Rates and the Business Cycle

You've seen the connection between the Fed's actions and interest rates in Fig. 31.12. What about the ripple effects that we've just described? Do they really occur? Do changes in interest rates ultimately influence the real GDP growth rate? Yes they do. You can see these effects in Fig. 31.13. The blue line in this figure shows the short-term interest rate minus the long-term interest rate. The short-term interest rate is influenced by the Fed in the way that you studied

FIGURE 31.13
Interest Rates and Real GDP Growth

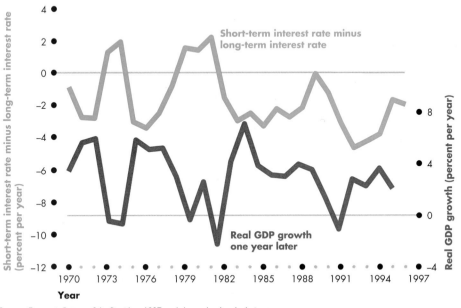

When the Fed increases short-term interest rates, the short-term rate rises above the long-term rate and, later, real GDP growth slows down. Similarly, when the Fed decreases short-term interest rates, the short-term rate falls below the long-term rate and, later, real GDP growth speeds up.

Source: *Economic Report of the President,* 1997, and the author's calculations.

earlier in this chapter. And changes in short-term rates have some influence on the long-term interest rate. But this influence is small, and the long-term interest rate is determined by saving and investment plans (see Chapter 26, pp. 575–577) and by long-term inflation expectations (see Chapter 32, pp. 728–729). The red line in Fig. 31.13 is the real GDP growth rate *one year later.* You can see that when short-term interest rates rise or long-term interest rates fall, the real GDP growth rate slows down in the following year. Long-term interest rates fluctuate less than short-term rates, so when short-term rates rise above long-term rates, it is because the Fed has pushed short-term rates upward. And when short-term rates fall below long-term rates, it is because the Fed has pushed short-term rates downward. So when the Fed stimulates aggregate demand (pushes short-term rates downward), the GDP growth rate speeds up, and when the Fed lowers aggregate demand (pushes short-term rates upward), the real GDP growth rate slows down. The inflation rate also increases and decreases in sympathy with these fluctuations in real GDP growth.

R E V I E W

- The Fed directly controls the discount rate, closely monitors the federal funds rate, and influences all short-term interest rates.
- Fluctuations in short-term interest rates usually mirror fluctuations in the ratio of M2 to GDP.
- When the money supply change is *un*anticipated, interest rates change at the same time as the change in the money supply. When a money supply change is *anticipated*, interest rates change ahead of the change in the money supply.
- When the Fed lowers (raises) interest rates, aggregate demand increases (decreases) and real GDP growth and inflation speed up (slow down).

◆ *Reading Between the Lines* on pages 708–709 looks at the Fed in action during 1996. Now that you know how the Fed determines the quantity of money and interest rates, we're going to explore the influence of money (and other factors) on inflation.

Policy WATCH

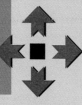 The Fed in Action

Essence of THE STORY

■ At the end of 1996, it was expected that the Fed would not increase interest rates in the immediate future.

■ For the seventh consecutive meeting, the FOMC decided against making any changes to monetary policy.

■ Policy makers agree that inflation has not increased enough to require tighter credit conditions.

THE DENVER POST, DECEMBER 20, 1996

Fed Won't Hike Rates, Experts Say

WASHINGTON—The Federal Reserve will leave the economy on autopilot in 1997, barring any blips on its radar screen that indicate inflation is taking off.

The vast majority of Wall Street economists say the Fed remains more likely to raise interest rates in the new year than lower them. But at present, there is little evidence that price pressures are on an upward trajectory, leaving the Fed with a steady flight path for monetary policy in the months ahead.

"The Fed is absolutely, flatly, and firmly on hold for a while," said John Williams, chief economist at Bankers Trust Co.

Earlier this week, the Federal Open Market Committee left its monetary policy unchanged, signaling it is comfortable with U.S. economic conditions. That marked the seventh consecutive time the FOMC took no action on rates.

That lack of a rate action reflects a consensus among policy makers that inflation hasn't risen enough to necessitate tighter credit conditions, observers said. The Fed's steady policy also suggests policy makers are satisfied with the extent to which growth has moderated since the second quarter of 1996, when gross domestic product expanded at a 4.7 percent annual pace.

Dow Jones News Service. Reprinted with permission.

Economic

A N A L Y S I S

■ Approximately every 6 weeks, the FOMC meets to review the state of the economy and set policy guidelines for open market operations. For most of 1996, the FOMC made no policy changes.

■ Figure 1 shows the economy in 1995 and 1996.

■ In 1995, real GDP was $6.7 trillion and the price level was 108, at the intersection of the aggregate demand curve AD_{95} and the short-run aggregate supply curve SAS_{95}. Also, real GDP was equal to potential GDP—the economy was on long-run aggregate supply curve LAS_{95}.

■ By 1996, real GDP had increased to $6.9 trillion and the price level had increased to 110, at the intersection of the aggregate demand curve AD_{96} and the short-run aggregate supply curve SAS_{96}. Real GDP remained at potential GDP—the economy was on long-run aggregate supply curve LAS_{96}.

■ Looking forward to 1997, the Fed was comfortable with the state of

the U.S. economy. Figure 2 shows the Fed's forecast of aggregate demand for 1997 as AD_{97} and short-run aggregate supply curve SAS_{97}. The Fed expected real GDP to grow to $7.05 trillion and the price level to rise to 113.

■ If aggregate demand increases to AD_0, we will have an inflationary gap. Inflation and real GDP will increase. To counter such an increase, the Fed might tighten money and raise interest rates.

■ If aggregate demand increases to AD_1, we will have a recessionary gap. Inflation and real GDP will decrease. To counter such an increase, the Fed might loosen money and lower interest rates.

■ You can see the dilemma the Fed faces every year. If aggregate demand increases by too much, the Fed must try to dampen the economy. If aggregate demand increases by too little, the Fed must try to stimulate the economy. But to be effective, the Fed must anticipate the change in aggregate demand correctly.

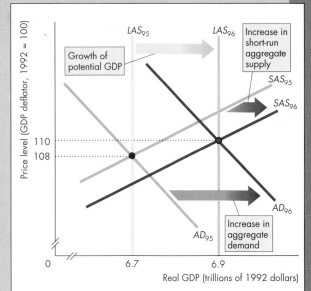

Figure 1 The economy in 1995 and 1996

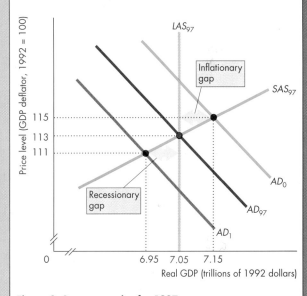

Figure 2 Some scenarios for 1997

You're

THE VOTER

■ Why did the Fed believe that no monetary policy action was needed during 1996?

■ Did the Fed change interest rates in 1997? If so, by how much, in which direction, and why?

■ What should the Fed do if a recession appears to be likely? What should the Fed do if inflation appears to be likely?

SUMMARY

Key Points

The Federal Reserve System (pp. 690–693)

■ The Federal Reserve System is the central bank of the United States.

■ The Fed influences the economy by setting the required reserve ratio for banks, by setting the discount rate—the interest rate at which it is willing to lend reserves to the banking system—and by open market operations.

Controlling the Money Supply (pp. 693–697)

■ By buying government securities in the market (an open market purchase), the Fed is able to increase the monetary base and the reserves available to banks.

■ There follows an expansion of bank lending and the quantity of money increases.

■ By selling government securities, the Fed is able to decrease the monetary base and bank reserves and decrease the quantity of money.

The Demand for Money (pp. 698–701)

■ The quantity of money demanded is the amount of money that people plan to hold.

■ The quantity of real money equals the quantity of nominal money divided by the price level.

■ The quantity of real money demanded depends on the interest rate and real GDP. A higher interest rate induces a smaller quantity of real money demanded.

Interest Rate Determination (pp. 701–702)

■ Changes in interest rates achieve equilibrium in the markets for money and financial assets.

■ Money market equilibrium achieves an interest rate (and an asset price) that makes the quantity of real money available willingly held.

■ If the quantity of real money is increased by the actions of the Fed, the interest rate falls and the prices of financial assets rise.

Monetary Policy (pp. 703–707)

■ The Fed directly controls the discount rate and closely targets the federal funds rate, but all short-term rates fluctuate together and the Fed influences all short-term interest rates.

■ People attempt to profit by predicting the actions of the Fed. To the extent that they can predict the Fed, interest rates and the price of financial assets move in anticipation of the Fed's actions rather than in response to them.

■ Consequently, interest rates change when the Fed changes the money supply only if the Fed catches people by surprise. Anticipated changes in the money supply produce interest rate changes by themselves.

■ When the Fed lowers interest rates, it increases aggregate demand, which speeds real GDP growth and inflation. And when the Fed raises interest rates, it decreases aggregate demand, which slows real GDP growth and inflation.

Key Figures

Key Terms

Central bank, 690
Currency drain, 695
Discount rate, 691
Federal Open Market Committee, 690
Federal Reserve System, 690
Monetary base, 693
Monetary policy, 690
Money multiplier, 695
Open market operation, 691

QUESTIONS

1. What is the Federal Reserve System?

2. What are the three main components in the structure of the Federal Reserve System?

3. What are the three policy tools of the Fed? Which of these is the Fed's most frequently used tool?

4. What is the effect of a change in required reserves?

5. What is the effect of a change in the discount rate?

6. What is the effect of an open market operation?

7. If the Fed wants to decrease the quantity of money, does it buy or sell U.S. government securities in the open market?

8. Trace the events that follow an open market purchase of securities by the Fed from a commercial bank.

9. Trace the events that follow an open market purchase of securities by the Fed from the public.

10. Trace the events that follow an open market sale of securities by the Fed to a commercial bank.

11. Trace the events that follow an open market sale of securities by the Fed to the public.

12. What is the money multiplier?

13. Why does an open market operation have a multiplier effect on the quantity of money?

14. Distinguish between nominal money and real money.

15. What is the opportunity cost of holding money?

16. What do we mean by the demand for money?

17. What determines the demand for money?

18. What happens to the interest rate on a bond if the price of the bond increases?

19. How does equilibrium come about in the money market?

20. What happens to the interest rate if the money supply increases?

21. Trace the ripple effects of the Fed's actions when it increases the interest rate.

22. Explain why it pays people to try to predict the Fed's actions.

PROBLEMS

1. You are given the following information about the economy of Nocoin: The banks have deposits of $300 billion. Their reserves are $15 billion, two thirds of which is in deposits with the central bank. There are $30 billion notes outside the banks. There are no coins in Nocoin!
   a. Calculate the monetary base.
   b. Calculate the currency drain.
   c. Calculate the money supply.
   d. Calculate the money multiplier.

2. Suppose that the Bank of Nocoin, the central bank, undertakes an open market purchase of securities of $0.5 million. What happens to the money supply? Explain why the change in the money supply is not equal to the change in the monetary base.

3. You are given the following information about the economy of Miniland: For each $1 increase in real GDP, the demand for money increases by one quarter of a dollar, other things remaining the same. Also, if the interest rate increases by 1 percentage point (for example, from 4 percent to 5 percent), the quantity of real money demanded falls by $50. If real GDP is $4,000 and the price level is 1,
   a. At what interest rate is no money held?
   b. How much real money is held at an interest rate of 10 percent a year?
   c. Draw a graph of the demand for money.

4. Given the demand for money in Miniland in Problem 3, if the price level is 1, real GDP is $4,000, and the real money supply is $750,
   a. What is the equilibrium interest rate?
   b. What is the equilibrium quantity of real money held?

5. Suppose that in Problem 4, the Bank of Miniland, the central bank, wants to lower the interest rate by 1 percentage point. By how much would it have to change the real money supply to achieve that objective?

6. The figure shows the demand for real money in Upland.

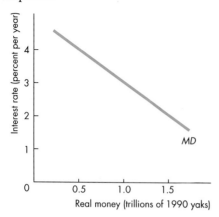

a. In the figure, draw the supply of money curve if the interest rate in Upland is 3 percent a year.

b. Suppose that the Bank of Upland (the central bank) wants to lower the interest rate by 1 percentage point. By how much must it change the real money supply to achieve that objective? Draw the new supply of money curve.

c. Suppose that to change the quantity of money in part (b), the Bank of Upland uses open market operations. Does the Bank of Upland make an open market purchase or an open market sale of securities?

7. Starting from above full-employment equilibrium, briefly explain with the aid of a figure the short-run effect on the price level and real GDP of an open market sale of securities by the Fed. Does such an action help to avoid inflation? Does such an action lower real GDP in the long run?

http://hepg.awl.com/parkin/econ100

CRITICAL THINKING

1. Study *Reading Between the Lines* on pp. 708–709 and then answer the following questions:
   a. Why did the Fed repeatedly *not* increase interest rates during 1996?
   b. What does the Fed look at when it is deciding whether to change interest rates?
   c. What are the risks from the Fed raising interest rates and from not raising interest rates? Which is the more risky in your opinion and why?
   d. When the Fed does raise interest rates, what actions does it take?

2. Could the Volcker Fed have brought inflation under control without creating a deep recession? If you think the answer is "no," do you think it was wise to lower inflation? If you think the answer is "yes," what would the Fed have had to do differently?

3. Visit the World Wide Web site of the Fed at http://www.bog.frb.fed.us/ (or by using the link on the Parkin Web site) and obtain the latest data on M1, M2, and some short-term interest rates. Then answer the following questions.
   a. Is the Fed trying to slow the economy or speed it up? How can you tell which?
   b. What open market operations do you think the Fed has undertaken during the past month?
   c. Skim the latest minutes of the FOMC, which you can find at the Fed's Web site, and see whether you can discover the open market operations planned.
   d. In the light of the Fed's recent actions, what ripple effects do you expect over the coming months?
   e. What do you think the effects of the Fed's recent actions will be on bond prices and stock prices?

4. Visit the World Wide Web site of the Fed at http://www.bog.frb.fed.us/ (or by using the link on the Parkin Web site) and look at the current economic conditions described in the Beige Book. On the basis of current forecasts by the Fed, do you predict that the Fed will raise interest rates, lower interest rates, or hold interest rates steady? Write a brief summary of your predictions and reasons.

32

Inflation

At the end of the third century A.D., Roman Emperor Diocletian struggled to contain an inflation that raised prices by more than 300 percent a year. At the end of the twentieth century, Russian President Boris Yeltsin struggled to contain a severe inflation that raised prices at a rate of close to 1,000 percent a year. But the most rapid recent inflations have been in Brazil, where the inflation rate hit 40 percent *per month* in 1994, and in Zaire, which had an inflation rate of 75 percent *per month*. What causes rapid inflation? ◆ In comparison with the cases just described, the United States has had remarkable price stability. Nevertheless, during the 1970s, the U.S. price level more than doubled—an inflation of more than 100 percent over the decade. Today, along with the other rich industrial countries, the United States has a low inflation rate at about 2.5 percent a year.

From Rome to Russia

Why do some countries have a low inflation rate? And why did a more serious inflation break out in the United States during the 1970s? ◆ Most of life's big economic decisions—whether to buy or rent a home, whether to save more for retirement—turn on what is going to happen to inflation. Will inflation increase so our savings buy less? Will inflation decrease so our debts are harder to repay? To make good decisions, we need good forecasts of inflation, and not for just next year but for many years into the future. How do people try to forecast inflation? And how do expectations of inflation influence the economy? ◆ As the inflation rate rises and falls, the unemployment rate and interest rates also fluctuate. What are the links between inflation and the economy that make unemployment and interest rates fluctuate when inflation fluctuates? ◆ In this chapter, you will learn about the forces that generate inflation, the effects of inflation, and the way in which people try to forecast inflation. You will pull together several of the threads you have been following through your study of macroeconomics. And again, you will use the *AS-AD* model of Chapter 24. But first, let's recall what inflation is and how it is measured.

After studying this chapter, you will be able to:

- **Distinguish between inflation and a one-time rise in the price level**

- **Explain the different ways in which inflation can be generated**

- **Describe how people try to forecast inflation**

- **Explain the short-run and long-run relationships between inflation and unemployment**

- **Explain the short-run and long-run relationships between inflation and interest rates**

Inflation and the Price Level

WE DON'T HAVE MUCH INFLATION TODAY, BUT during the 1970s it was a major problem. **Inflation** is a process in which the *price level is rising* and *money is losing value*.

If the price level rises persistently, then people need more and more money to make transactions. Incomes rise, so firms must pay out more in wages and other payments to resource owners. And prices rise, so consumers must take more money with them when they go shopping. But the value of money gets smaller and smaller.

A change in one price is not inflation. For example, if the price of hot dogs jumps to $25 and all other money prices fall slightly so that the price level remains constant, there is no inflation. Instead, the relative price of hot dogs has increased. If the price of hot dogs and all other prices rise by a similar percentage, there is inflation.

But a one-time jump in the price level is not inflation. Instead, inflation is an ongoing *process*. Figure 32.1 illustrates this distinction. The red line shows the price level rising continuously. That is inflation. The blue line shows a one-time jump in the price level. This economy is not experiencing inflation. Its price level is constant most of the time.

Inflation is a serious problem, and preventing inflation is the main task of monetary policy and the actions of the Fed. We are going to learn how inflation arises and see how we can avoid the situation shown in the cartoon. But first, let's see how we calculate the inflation rate.

To measure the inflation *rate,* we calculate the annual percentage change in the price level. For

"I told you the Fed should have tightened."

Drawing by Mankoff; © 1997 The New Yorker Magazine, Inc.

FIGURE 32.1

Inflation Versus a One-Time Rise in the Price Level

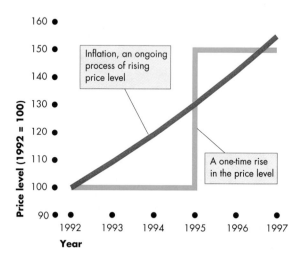

Along the red line, an economy experiences inflation because the price level is rising persistently. Along the blue line, an economy experiences a one-time rise in the price level.

example, if this year's price level is 126 and last year's price level was 120, the inflation rate is 5 percent per year. That is,

$$\text{Inflation rate} = \frac{126 - 120}{120} \times 100$$

$$- \ 5 \text{ percent per year}$$

This equation shows the connection between the *inflation rate* and the *price level.* For a given price level last year, the higher the price level in the current year, the higher is the inflation rate. If the price level is *rising*, the inflation rate is *positive*. If the price level rises at a *faster* rate, the inflation rate *increases*. Also, the higher the new price level, the lower is the value of money, and the higher is the inflation rate.

Inflation can result from either an increase in aggregate demand or a decrease in aggregate supply. These two sources of impulses that can get inflation started are called:

- Demand pull
- Cost push

We'll first study a demand-pull inflation.

Demand-Pull Inflation

AN INFLATION THAT RESULTS FROM AN INITIAL increase in aggregate demand is called **demand-pull inflation**. Such an inflation can arise from any factor that increases aggregate demand such as an:

1. Increase in the money supply
2. Increase in government purchases
3. Increase in exports

Inflation Effect of an Increase in Aggregate Demand

Suppose that last year the price level was 110 and real GDP was $7 trillion. Potential GDP was also $7 trillion. Figure 32.2(a) illustrates this situation. The aggregate demand curve is AD_0, the short-run

aggregate supply curve is SAS_0, and the long-run aggregate supply curve is LAS.

In the current year, aggregate demand increases to AD_1. Such a situation arises if, for example, the Fed loosens its grip on the money supply, or the government increases its purchases of goods and services, or exports increase.

With no change in potential GDP, and with no change in the money wage rate, the long-run aggregate supply curve and the short-run aggregate supply curve remain at LAS and SAS_0.

The price level and real GDP are determined at the point where the aggregate demand curve AD_1 intersects the short-run aggregate supply curve. The price level rises to 113, and real GDP increases above potential GDP to $7.5 trillion. The economy experiences a 2.7 percent rise in the price level (a price level of 113 compared with 110) and a rapid expansion of real GDP. Unemployment falls below the natural rate. The next step in the unfolding story is a rise in wages.

FIGURE 32.2

A Demand-Pull Rise in the Price Level

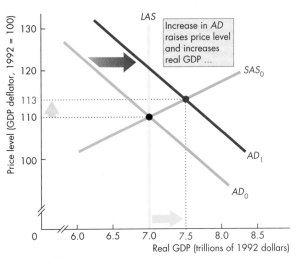

(a) Initial effect

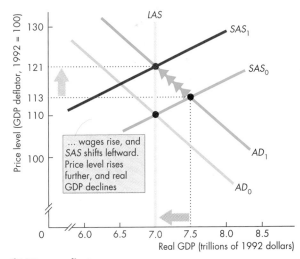

(b) Wages adjust

In part (a), the aggregate demand curve is AD_0, the short-run aggregate supply curve is SAS_0, and the long-run aggregate supply curve is LAS. The price level is 110, and real GDP is $7 trillion, its long-run level. Aggregate demand increases to AD_1 (because, for example, the Fed increases the money supply, or the government increases its purchases of goods and services,

or exports increase). The new equilibrium occurs where AD_1 intersects SAS_0. The price level rises to 113, and real GDP increases to $7.5 trillion. In part (b), starting from above full employment, wages begin to rise and the short-run aggregate supply curve shifts leftward toward SAS_1. The price level rises further, and real GDP returns to its long-run level.

Wage Response

Real GDP cannot remain above potential GDP forever. With unemployment below its natural rate, there is a shortage of labor. In this situation, wages begin to rise. As they do so, short-run aggregate supply decreases and the SAS curve starts to shift leftward. The price level rises further, and real GDP begins to decrease.

With no further change in aggregate demand—the aggregate demand curve remains at AD_1—this process ends when the short-run aggregate supply curve has shifted to SAS_1 in Fig. 32.2(b). At this time, the price level has increased to 121 and real GDP has returned to potential GDP of $7 trillion, the level from which it started.

A Demand-Pull Inflation Process

The process we've just studied eventually ends when, for a given increase in aggregate demand, wages have adjusted enough to restore the real wage rate to its full-employment level. We've studied a one-time rise in the price level like that described in Fig. 32.1(b). For inflation to proceed, aggregate demand must persistently increase.

The only way in which aggregate demand can persistently increase is if the quantity of money persistently increases. Suppose the government has a large budget deficit that it finances by selling bonds to the Fed. When the Fed buys these bonds, it creates more money. In this situation, aggregate demand increases year after year. The aggregate demand curve keeps shifting rightward. This persistent increase in aggregate demand puts continual upward pressure on the price level. The economy now experiences demand-pull inflation.

Figure 32.3 illustrates the process of demand-pull inflation. The starting point is the same as that shown in Fig. 32.2. The aggregate demand curve is AD_0, the short-run aggregate supply curve is SAS_0, and the long-run aggregate supply curve is LAS. Real GDP is $7 trillion, and the price level is 110. Aggregate demand increases, shifting the aggregate demand curve to AD_1. Real GDP increases to $7.5 trillion, and the price level rises to 113. The economy is at an above full-employment equilibrium. There is a shortage of labor, and the wage rate rises, shifting the short-run aggregate supply curve to SAS_1. The price level rises to 121, and real GDP returns to potential GDP.

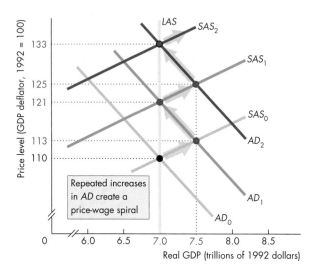

FIGURE 32.3

A Demand-Pull Inflation Spiral

Each time the money supply increases, aggregate demand increases, and the aggregate demand curve shifts rightward from AD_0 to AD_1 to AD_2, and so on. Each time real GDP goes above potential GDP and unemployment goes below the natural rate, the money wage rate rises and the short-run aggregate supply curve shifts leftward from SAS_0 to SAS_1 to SAS_2, and so on. As aggregate demand continues to increase, the price level rises from 110 through 113, 121, 125, to 133, and so on. There is a perpetual demand-pull inflation. Real GDP fluctuates between $7 trillion and $7.5 trillion.

But the money supply increases again, and aggregate demand continues to increase. The aggregate demand curve shifts rightward to AD_2. The price level rises further to 125, and real GDP again exceeds potential GDP at $7.5 trillion. Yet again, the wage rate rises and decreases short-run aggregate supply. The SAS curve shifts to SAS_2, and the price level rises further to 133. As the money supply continues to grow, aggregate demand increases and the price level rises in an ongoing demand-pull inflation process.

The process you have just studied generates inflation—an ongoing process of a rising price level.

Demand-Pull Inflation in Kalamazoo You may better understand the inflation process that we've just described by considering what is going on in an individual part of the economy, such as a Kalamazoo soda-bottling plant. Initially, when aggregate demand increases, the demand for soda increases and the price of soda rises. Faced with a higher price, the soda plant works overtime and increases production. Conditions are good for workers in Kalamazoo, and the soda factory finds it hard to hang onto its best people. To do so, it has to offer higher wages. As wages increase, so do the soda factory's costs.

What happens next depends on what happens to aggregate demand. If aggregate demand remains constant (as in Fig. 32.2b), the firm's costs are increasing but the price of soda is not increasing as quickly as its costs. Production is scaled back. Eventually, wages and costs increase by the same percentage as the price of soda. In real terms, the soda factory is in the same situation as initially—before the increase in aggregate demand. The plant produces the same amount of soda and employs the same amount of labor as before the increase in demand.

But if aggregate demand continues to increase, so does the demand for soda, and the price of soda rises at the same rate as wages. The soda factory continues to operate above full employment, and there is a persistent shortage of labor. Prices and wages chase each other upward in an unending spiral.

Demand-Pull Inflation in the United States   A demand-pull inflation like the one you've just studied occurred in the United States during the 1960s. In 1960, inflation was a moderate 2 percent a year, but its rate increased slowly to 3 percent by 1966. Then, in 1967, a large increase in government purchases on the Vietnam War and an increase in spending on social programs, together with an increase in the growth rate of the money supply, increased aggregate demand more quickly. Consequently, the rightward shift of the aggregate demand curve speeded up and the price level increased more quickly. Real GDP increased above potential GDP, and the unemployment rate fell below the natural rate.

With unemployment below the natural rate, the money wage rate started to rise more quickly and the short-run aggregate supply curve shifted leftward. The Fed responded with a further increase in the money supply growth rate, and a demand-pull inflation spiral unfolded. By 1970, the inflation rate had reached 6 percent a year.

For the next three years, aggregate demand continued to grow quickly and the inflation rate remained around 6 percent a year.

- Demand-pull inflation begins when an increase in aggregate demand increases real GDP and increases the price level.
- At above full employment, the wage rate rises, short-run aggregate supply decreases, real GDP decreases, and the price level rises further.
- If aggregate demand keeps increasing, wages chase prices in an unending inflation spiral.

Next, let's see how shocks to aggregate supply can create cost-push inflation.

Cost-Push Inflation

AN INFLATION THAT RESULTS FROM AN INITIAL increase in costs is called **cost-push inflation**. The two main sources of increases in costs are:

1. An increase in money wage rates
2. An increase in the money prices of raw materials

At a given price level, the higher the cost of production, the smaller is the amount that firms are willing to produce. So if money wage rates rise or if the prices of raw materials (for example, oil) rise, firms decrease their supply of goods and services. Aggregate supply decreases, and the short-run aggregate supply curve shifts leftward.[1] Let's trace the effects of such a decrease in short-run aggregate supply on the price level and real GDP.

Initial Effect of a Decrease in Aggregate Supply

Suppose that last year the price level was 110 and real GDP was $7 trillion. Potential real GDP was also $7 trillion. Figure 32.4 illustrates this situation. The aggregate demand curve was AD_0, the short-run aggregate supply curve was SAS_0, and the long-run aggregate supply curve was LAS. In the current year, the world's oil producers form a price-fixing organization

---

[1] Some cost-push forces, such as an increase in the price of oil accompanied by a decrease in the availability of oil, can also decrease long-run aggregate supply. We'll ignore such effects here and examine cost-push factors that change only short-run aggregate supply.

FIGURE 32.4

A Cost-Push Rise in the Price Level

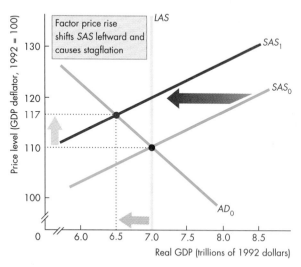

Initially, the aggregate demand curve is AD_0, the short-run aggregate supply curve is SAS_0, and the long-run aggregate supply curve is LAS. A decrease in aggregate supply (for example, resulting from an increase in the world price of oil) shifts the short-run aggregate supply curve to SAS_1. The economy moves to the point where the short-run aggregate supply curve SAS_1 intersects the aggregate demand curve AD_0. The price level rises to 117, and real GDP decreases to $6.5 trillion. The economy experiences inflation and a contraction of real GDP—*stagflation*.

that strengthens their market power and increases the relative price of oil. They raise the nominal price of oil, and this action decreases short-run aggregate supply. The short-run aggregate supply curve shifts leftward to SAS_1. The price level rises to 117, and real GDP decreases to $6.5 trillion. The combination of a rise in the price level and a decrease in real GDP is called **stagflation**.

This event is a one-time rise in the price level like that in Fig. 32.1(b). It is not inflation. In fact, a supply shock on its own cannot cause inflation. Something more must happen to enable a one-time supply shock to be converted into a process of money supply growth and ongoing inflation. The money supply must persistently increase. And it often does increase, as you will now see.

Aggregate Demand Response

When real GDP falls, the unemployment rate rises above the natural rate. In such a situation, there is usually an outcry of concern and a call for action to restore full employment. Suppose that the Fed increases the money supply. Aggregate demand increases. In Fig. 32.5, the aggregate demand curve shifts rightward to AD_1. The increase in aggregate demand has restored full employment. But the price level rises to 121, a 10 percent increase over the initial price level.

A Cost-Push Inflation Process

The oil producers now see the prices of everything that they buy increase by 10 percent. So they increase the price of oil again to restore its new high relative price. Figure 32.6 continues the story.

FIGURE 32.5

Aggregate Demand Response to Cost Push

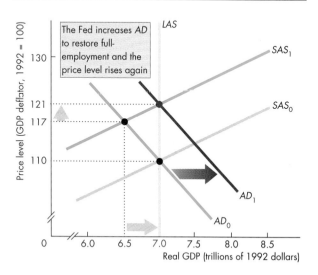

Following a cost-push increase in the price level, real GDP is below potential GDP and unemployment is above the natural rate. If the Fed responds by increasing aggregate demand to restore full employment, the aggregate demand curve shifts rightward to AD_1. The economy returns to full employment, but at the expense of more inflation. The price level rises to 121.

The short-run aggregate supply curve now shifts to SAS_2, and another bout of stagflation ensues. The price level rises further to 129, and real GDP falls to $6.5 trillion. Unemployment increases above its natural rate. If the Fed responds yet again with an increase in the money supply, aggregate demand increases and the aggregate demand curve shifts to AD_2. The price level rises even higher—to 133—and full employment is again restored. A cost-push inflation spiral results. But if the Fed does not respond, the economy remains below full employment.

You can see that the Fed has a dilemma. If it increases the money supply to restore full employment, it invites another oil price hike that will call forth yet a further increase in the money supply.

FIGURE 32.6
A Cost-Push
Inflation Spiral

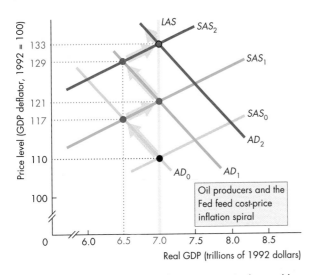

When a cost increase (for example, an increase in the world oil price) decreases short-run aggregate supply from SAS_0 to SAS_1, the price level rises to 117 and real GDP decreases to $6.5 trillion. The Fed responds with an increase in the money supply that shifts the aggregate demand curve from AD_0 to AD_1. The price level rises again to 121, and real GDP returns to $7 trillion. A further cost increase occurs, which shifts the short-run aggregate supply curve again, this time to SAS_2. Stagflation is repeated, and the price level now rises to 129. The Fed responds again, and the cost-price inflation spiral continues.

Inflation will rage along at a rate decided by the oil-exporting nations. If the Fed keeps the lid on money supply growth, real GDP remains below potential GDP.

Cost-Push Inflation in Kalamazoo What is going on in the Kalamazoo soda-bottling plant when the economy is experiencing cost-push inflation? When the oil price increases, so do the costs of bottling soda. These higher costs decrease the supply of soda, increasing its price and decreasing the quantity produced. The soda plant lays off some workers. This situation will persist until either the Fed increases aggregate demand or the price of oil falls. If the Fed increases aggregate demand, as it did in the mid-1970s, the demand for soda increases and so does its price. The higher price of soda brings higher profits, and the bottling plant increases its production. The soda factory rehires the laid-off workers.

Cost-Push Inflation in the United States A cost-push inflation like the one you've just studied occurred in the United States during the 1970s. It began in 1974 when the Organization for Petroleum Exporting Countries (OPEC) raised the price of oil fourfold. The higher oil price decreased aggregate supply, which caused the price level to rise more quickly and real GDP to shrink. The Fed then faced a dilemma. Would it increase the quantity of money and accommodate the cost-push forces or would it keep aggregate demand growth in check by limiting money growth? In 1975, 1976, and 1977, the Fed repeatedly allowed the money supply to grow quickly, and inflation proceeded at a rapid rate. In 1979 and 1980, OPEC was again able to push oil prices higher. On that occasion, the Fed decided not to respond to the oil price hike with an increase in the money supply. The result was a recession but also, eventually, a fall in inflation.

R E V I E W

- Cost-push inflation starts with an increase in the money wage rate or in the money price of a raw material that decreases aggregate supply.
- Real GDP decreases, and the price level rises— *stagflation* occurs.
- If the Fed increases aggregate demand to restore full employment, freewheeling cost-push inflation ensues.

Effects of Inflation

REGARDLESS OF WHETHER INFLATION IS DEMAND-pull or cost-push, the failure to correctly *anticipate* it results in unintended consequences. These unintended consequences impose costs in both labor markets and capital markets. Let's examine these costs.

Unanticipated Inflation in the Labor Market

Unanticipated inflation has two main consequences for the operation of the labor market:

- Redistribution of income
- Departure from full employment

Redistribution of Income   Unanticipated inflation redistributes income between employers and workers. Sometimes employers gain at the expense of workers, and sometimes they lose. If an unexpected increase in aggregate demand increases the inflation rate, then wages will not have been set high enough. Profits will be higher than expected, and wages will buy fewer goods than expected. In this case, employers gain at the expense of workers. But if aggregate demand is expected to increase at a rapid rate and it fails to do so, workers gain at the expense of employers. With a high inflation rate anticipated, wages are set too high and profits are squeezed. Redistribution between employers and workers creates an incentive for both firms and workers to try to forecast inflation correctly.

Departures from Full Employment

Redistribution brings gains to some and losses to others. But departures from full employment impose costs on everyone. To see why, let's return to the soda-bottling plant in Kalamazoo.

If the bottling plant and its workers do not anticipate inflation, but inflation occurs, the money wage rate does not rise to keep up with inflation. The real wage rate falls, and the firm tries to hire more labor and increase production. But because the real wage rate has fallen, the firm has a hard time attracting the labor it wants to employ. It pays overtime rates to its existing work force, and because it runs its plant at a faster pace, it incurs higher plant maintenance and parts replacement costs. But also, because the real wage rate has fallen, workers begin to quit the bottling plant to find jobs that pay a real wage rate that is closer to one that prevailed before the outbreak of inflation. This labor turnover imposes additional costs on the firm. So even though its production increases, the firm incurs additional costs, and its profits do not increase as much as they otherwise would. The workers incur additional costs of job search, and those who remain at the bottling plant wind up feeling cheated. They've worked overtime to produce the extra output, and when they come to spend their wages, they discover that prices have increased, so their wages buy a smaller quantity of goods and services than expected.

If the bottling plant and its workers anticipate a high inflation rate that does not occur, they increase the money wage rate by too much, and the real wage rate rises. At the higher real wage rate, the firm lays off some workers and the unemployment rate increases. Those workers who keep their jobs gain, but those who become unemployed lose. Also, the bottling plant loses because its output and profits fall.

Unanticipated Inflation in the Capital Market

Unanticipated inflation has two consequences for the operation of the capital market. They are:

- Redistribution of income
- Too much or too little lending and borrowing

Redistribution of Income   Unanticipated inflation redistributes income between borrowers and lenders. Sometimes borrowers gain at the expense of lenders, and sometimes they lose. When inflation is unexpected, interest rates are not set high enough to compensate lenders for the falling value of money. In this case, borrowers gain at the expense of lenders. But if inflation is expected and then fails to occur, interest rates are set too high. In this case, lenders gain at the expense of borrowers. Redistributions of income between borrowers and lenders create an incentive for both groups to try to forecast inflation correctly.

Too Much or Too Little Lending and Borrowing

If the inflation rate turns out to be either higher or lower than expected, the interest rate does not incorporate a correct allowance for the falling value of money and the real interest rate is either lower or higher than it otherwise would be. When the real interest rate turns out to be too low, which occurs when inflation is *higher* than expected, borrowers wish they had borrowed more and lenders wish they had lent less. Both groups would have made different lending and borrowing decisions with greater foresight about the inflation rate. When the real interest rate turns out to be too high, which occurs when inflation is *lower* than expected, borrowers wish they had borrowed less and lenders wish they had lent more. Again, both groups would have made different lending and borrowing decisions with greater foresight about the inflation rate.

So unanticipated inflation imposes costs regardless of whether the inflation turns out to be higher or lower than anticipated. The presence of these costs gives everyone an incentive to forecast inflation correctly. Let's see how people go about this task.

Forecasting Inflation

Inflation is difficult to forecast. The reasons are, first, there are several sources of inflation—the demand-pull and cost-push sources you've just studied. Second, the speed with which a change in either aggregate demand or aggregate supply translates into a change in the price level varies. This speed of response also depends, as you will see below, on the extent to which the inflation is anticipated.

Because inflation is costly and difficult to forecast, people devote considerable resources to improving inflation forecasts. Some people specialize in forecasting, and others buy forecasts from specialists. The specialist forecasters are economists who work for public and private macroeconomic forecasting agencies and for banks, insurance companies, labor unions, and large corporations. The returns these specialists make depend on the quality of their forecasts, so they have a strong incentive to forecast as accurately as possible. The most accurate forecast possible is the one that is based on all the relevant information and is called a **rational expectation**.

A rational expectation is not a correct forecast. It is simply the best forecast available. It will often turn out to be wrong, but no other forecast that could have been made with the information available could be predicted to be better.

You've seen the effects of inflation when people fail to anticipate it. And you've seen why it pays to try to anticipate inflation. Let's now see what happens if inflation is correctly anticipated.

Anticipated Inflation

In the demand-pull and cost-push inflations that we studied earlier in this chapter, money wages are sticky. When aggregate demand increases, either to set off a demand-pull inflation or to accommodate cost-push inflation, the money wage does not change immediately. But if people correctly anticipate increases in aggregate demand, they will adjust money wage rates so as to keep up with anticipated inflation.

In this case, inflation proceeds with real GDP equal to potential GDP and unemployment equal to the natural rate. Figure 32.7 explains why. Suppose that last year the price level was 110 and real GDP was $7 trillion, which is also potential GDP. The aggregate demand curve was AD_0, the aggregate supply curve was SAS_0, and the long-run aggregate supply curve was LAS.

Suppose that potential GDP does not change, so the LAS curve does not shift. Also suppose that aggregate demand is expected to increase and that the expected aggregate demand curve for this year is AD_1. In anticipation of this increase in aggregate demand, money wage rates rise and the short-run aggregate supply curve shifts leftward. If the money wage rate rises by the same percentage as the price level rises, the short-run aggregate supply curve for next year is SAS_1.

If aggregate demand turns out to be the same as expected, the aggregate demand curve is AD_1 and with the short-run aggregate supply curve SAS_1 the actual price level is 121. Between last year and this year, the price level increased from 110 to 121 and the economy experienced an inflation rate of 10 percent, the same as the inflation rate that was anticipated. If this anticipated inflation is ongoing, in the following year aggregate demand increases (as anticipated) and the aggregate demand curve shifts to AD_2. The money wage rate rises to reflect the anticipated inflation, and the short-run aggregate supply curve shifts to SAS_2. The price level rises by a further 10 percent to 133.

What has caused this inflation? The immediate answer is that because people expected inflation, wages were increased and prices increased. But the expectation was correct. Aggregate demand was expected to increase, and it did increase. Because aggregate demand was *expected* to increase from AD_0 to AD_1, the short-run aggregate supply curve shifted from SAS_0 to SAS_1. Because aggregate demand actually did increase by the amount that was expected, the actual aggregate demand curve shifted from AD_0

to AD_1. The combination of the anticipated and actual increases in aggregate demand produced an increase in the price level that was anticipated.

Only if aggregate demand growth is correctly forecasted does the economy follow the course described in Fig. 32.7. If the expected growth rate of aggregate demand is different from its actual growth rate, the expected aggregate demand curve shifts by an amount that is different from the actual aggregate demand curve. The inflation rate departs from its expected level, and to some extent, there is unanticipated inflation.

FIGURE 32.7
Anticipated Inflation

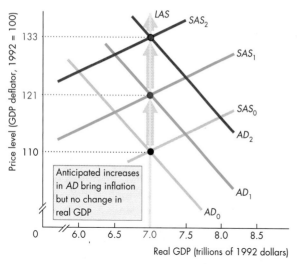

Potential real GDP is $7 trillion. Last year, aggregate demand was AD_0, and the short-run aggregate supply curve was SAS_0. The actual price level was the same as the expected price level—110. This year, aggregate demand is expected to increase to AD_1. The rational expectation of the price level changes from 110 to 121. As a result, wages rise and the short-run aggregate supply curve shifts to SAS_1. If aggregate demand actually increases as expected, the actual aggregate demand curve AD_1 is the same as the expected aggregate demand curve. Equilibrium occurs at a real GDP of $7 trillion and an actual price level of 121. The inflation is correctly anticipated. Next year the process continues with aggregate demand increasing as expected to AD_2 and wages rising to shift the short-run aggregate supply curve to SAS_2. Again, real GDP remains at $7 trillion, and the price level rises, as anticipated, to 133.

Unanticipated Inflation

When aggregate demand increases by *more* than expected, there is some unanticipated inflation that looks just like the demand-pull inflation that you studied earlier. Some inflation is expected, and the money wage rate is set to reflect that expectation. The SAS curve intersects the LAS curve at the expected price level. Aggregate demand then increases, but by more than expected. So the AD curve intersects the SAS curve at a level of real GDP that exceeds potential GDP. With real GDP above potential GDP and unemployment below the natural rate, the money wage rate rises. So the price level rises further. If aggregate demand increases again, a demand-pull inflation spiral unwinds.

When aggregate demand increases by *less* than expected, there is some unanticipated inflation that looks like the cost-push inflation that you studied earlier. Again, some inflation is expected, and the money wage rate is set to reflect that expectation. The SAS curve intersects the LAS curve at the expected price level. Aggregate demand then increases, but by less than expected. So the AD curve intersects the SAS curve at a level of real GDP below potential GDP. Aggregate demand increases to restore full employment. But if aggregate demand is expected to increase by more than it actually does, wages again rise, short-run aggregate supply again decreases, and a cost-push spiral unwinds.

We've seen that only when inflation is unanticipated does real GDP depart from potential GDP. When inflation is anticipated, real GDP remains at potential GDP. Does this mean that an anticipated inflation has no costs?

The Costs of Anticipated Inflation

The costs of an anticipated inflation depend on its rate. At a moderate rate of 2 or 3 percent a year, the cost is probably small. But as the anticipated inflation rate rises, so do its costs, and an anticipated inflation at a rapid rate can be extremely costly.

Anticipated inflation decreases potential GDP and slows economic growth. These adverse consequences arise for three major reasons:

- Transactions costs
- Tax effects
- Increased uncertainty

Transactions Costs The first transactions costs are known as the "boot leather costs." These are costs that arise from an increase in the velocity of circulation of money and an increase in the amount of running around that people do to try to avoid incurring losses from the falling value of money.

When money loses value at a rapid anticipated rate, it does not function well as a store of value and people try to avoid holding money. They spend their incomes as soon as they receive them, and firms pay out incomes—wages and dividends—as soon as they receive revenue from their sales. The velocity of circulation increases. During the 1920s, when inflation in Germany reached *hyperinflation* levels (rates more than 50 percent a month), wages were paid and spent twice in a single day!

The range of estimates of the boot leather costs is large. Some economists put the cost at close to zero. Others estimate it to be as much 2 percent of GDP for a 10 percent inflation. For a rapid inflation, these costs are much more.

The boot leather costs of inflation are just one of several transactions costs that are influenced by the inflation rate. At high anticipated inflation rates, people seek alternatives to money as a means of payment and use tokens and commodities or even barter, all of which are less efficient than money as a means of payment. For example, in Israel during the 1980s, when inflation reached 1,000 percent a year, the U.S. dollar started to replace the increasingly worthless shekel. Consequently, people had to keep track of the exchange rate between the shekel and the dollar hour by hour and had to engage in many additional and costly transactions in the foreign exchange market.

Because anticipated inflation increases transactions costs, it diverts resources from producing goods and services and it decreases potential GDP. The faster the anticipated inflation rate, the greater is the decrease in potential GDP and the further leftward does the *LAS* curve shift.

Tax Effects Anticipated inflation interacts with the tax system and creates serious distortions in incentives. Its major effect is on real interest rates.

Anticipated inflation swells the dollar returns on investments. But dollar returns are taxed, so the effective tax rate rises. This effect becomes serious at even modest inflation rates. Let's consider an example.

Suppose the real interest rate is 4 percent a year and the tax rate is 50 percent. With no inflation, the nominal interest rate is also 4 percent a year and 50 percent of this rate is taxable. The real *after-tax* interest rate is 2 percent a year (50 percent of 4 percent). Now suppose the inflation rate is 4 percent a year, so the nominal interest rate is 8 percent a year. The nominal *after-tax* rate is 4 percent a year (50 percent of 8 percent). Now subtract the 4 percent inflation rate from this amount, and you see that the *real after-tax interest rate* is zero! The true tax rate on interest income is 100 percent.

The higher the inflation rate, the higher is the effective tax rate on income from capital. And the higher the tax rate, the higher is the interest rate paid by borrowers and the lower is the after-tax interest rate received by lenders (see Chapter 29, p. 658).

With a low after-tax real interest rate, the incentive to save is weakened and the saving rate falls. With a high cost of borrowing, the amount of investment decreases. And with a fall in saving and investment, the pace of capital accumulation slows and so does the long-term growth rate of real GDP.

Increased Uncertainty When the inflation rate is high, there is increased uncertainty about the long-term inflation rate. Will inflation remain high for a long time or will price stability be restored? This increased uncertainty makes long-term planning difficult and gives people a shorter-term focus. Investment falls, and so the growth rate slows.

But this increased uncertainty also misallocates resources. Instead of concentrating on the activities at which they have a comparative advantage, people find it more profitable to search for ways of avoiding the losses that inflation inflicts. As a result, inventive talent that might otherwise work on productive innovations works on finding ways of profiting from the inflation instead.

The implications of inflation for economic growth have been estimated to be enormous. Peter Howitt of Ohio State University, building on work by Robert Barro of Harvard University, has estimated that if inflation is lowered from 3 percent a year to zero, the growth rate of real GDP will rise by between 0.06 and 0.09 percentage points a year. These numbers might seem small. But they are growth rates. After 30 years, real GDP would be 2.3 percent higher and the present value of all the future output would be 85 percent of current GDP—almost $6 trillion! In the rapid anticipated inflations of Brazil and Russia, the costs are much greater than the numbers given here.

REVIEW

- Wrong inflation forecasts are costly, and to minimize forecasting errors, people use all the available information and make a *rational expectation*.
- Anticipated changes in aggregate demand and aggregate supply result in anticipated inflation.
- A rapid anticipated inflation diverts resources from producing goods and services and decreases potential GDP.

You've seen that an increase in aggregate demand that is not fully anticipated increases both the price level and real GDP. It also decreases unemployment. Similarly, a decrease in aggregate demand that is not fully anticipated decreases the price level and real GDP. It also increases unemployment. Do these relationships mean that there is a tradeoff between inflation and unemployment? That is, does low unemployment always bring inflation and does low inflation bring high unemployment? We explore these questions next.

Inflation and Unemployment: The Phillips Curve

THE AGGREGATE SUPPLY–AGGREGATE DEMAND model focuses on the price level and real GDP. Knowing how these two variables change, we can work out what happens to the inflation rate and the unemployment rate. But the model does not place inflation and unemployment at the center of the stage.

A more direct way of studying inflation and unemployment uses a relationship called the Phillips curve. The Phillips curve approach uses the same basic ideas as the *AS-AD* model, but it focuses directly on inflation and unemployment. The Phillips curve is so named because New Zealand economist A.W. Phillips popularized it. A **Phillips curve** is a curve that shows a relationship between inflation and unemployment. There are two time frames for Phillips curves:

- The short-run Phillips curve
- The long-run Phillips curve

The Short-Run Phillips Curve

The **short-run Phillips curve** is a curve that shows the tradeoff between inflation and unemployment, holding constant:

1. The expected inflation rate
2. The natural unemployment rate

You've just seen what determines the expected inflation rate. The natural rate of unemployment and the factors that influence it are explained in Chapter 25 on pp. 552, 557–559.

Figure 32.8 shows a short-run Phillips curve, *SRPC*. Suppose that the expected inflation rate is 10 percent a year and the natural unemployment rate is

FIGURE 32.8
A Short-Run Phillips Curve

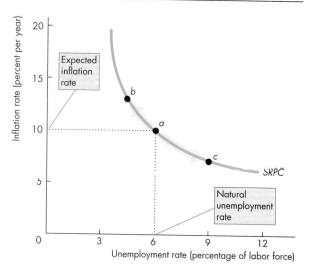

The short-run Phillips curve (*SRPC*) shows the relationship between inflation and unemployment at a given expected inflation rate and given natural unemployment rate. With an expected inflation rate of 10 percent a year and a natural unemployment rate of 6 percent, the short-run Phillips curve passes through point *a*. An unanticipated increase in aggregate demand lowers unemployment and increases inflation—a movement up the short-run Phillips curve. An unanticipated decrease in aggregate demand increases unemployment and lowers inflation—a movement down the short-run Phillips curve.

6 percent, point *a* in the figure. A short-run Phillips curve passes through this point. If inflation rises above its expected rate, unemployment falls below its natural rate. This joint movement in the inflation rate and the unemployment rate is illustrated as a movement up the short-run Phillips curve from point *a* to point *b* in the figure. Similarly, if inflation falls below its expected rate, unemployment rises above the natural rate. In this case there is movement down the short-run Phillips curve from point *a* to point *c*.

This negative relationship between inflation and unemployment along the short-run Phillips curve is explained by the aggregate supply–aggregate demand model. Figure 32.9 shows the connection between the two approaches. Initially, the aggregate demand curve is AD_0, the short-run aggregate supply curve is SAS_0, and the long-run aggregate supply curve is *LAS*. Real GDP is $7 trillion, and the price level is 100. Aggregate demand is expected to increase, and the aggregate demand curve is expected to shift rightward to AD_1. Anticipating this increase in aggregate demand, the money wage rate rises, which shifts the short-run aggregate supply curve to SAS_1. What happens to actual inflation and real GDP depends on the *actual* change in aggregate demand.

First, suppose that aggregate demand actually increases by the amount expected, so the aggregate demand curve shifts to AD_1. The price level rises from 100 to 110, and the inflation rate is an anticipated 10 percent a year. Real GDP remains at potential GDP, and unemployment remains at the natural rate. The economy moves to point *a* in Fig. 32.9, and it can equivalently be described as being at point *a* on the short-run Phillips curve in Fig. 32.8.

Alternatively, suppose that aggregate demand is expected to increase to AD_1 but actually increases by more than expected to AD_2. The price level now rises to 113, a 13 percent inflation rate. Real GDP increases above potential GDP, and unemployment falls below the natural rate. We can now describe the economy as moving to point *b* in Fig. 32.9 or at point *b* on the short-run Phillips curve in Fig. 32.8.

Finally, suppose that aggregate demand is expected to increase to AD_1 but actually remains at AD_0. The price level now rises to 107, a 7 percent inflation rate. Real GDP falls below potential GDP, and unemployment rises above the natural rate. We can now describe the economy as moving to point *c* in Fig. 32.9 or at point *c* on the short-run Phillips curve in Fig. 32.8.

FIGURE 32.9

AS-AD and the Short-Run Phillips Curve

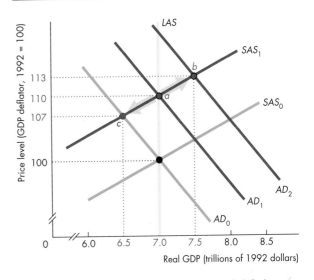

If aggregate demand is expected to increase and shift the aggregate demand curve from AD_0 to AD_1, then the money wage rate rises by an amount that shifts the short-run aggregate supply curve from SAS_0 to SAS_1. The price level rises to 110, a 10 percent rise, and the economy is at point *a* in this figure and at point *a* on the short-run Phillips curve in Fig. 32.8. If, with the same expectations, aggregate demand increases and shifts the aggregate demand curve from AD_0 to AD_2, the price level rises to 113, a 13 percent rise, and the economy is at point *b* in this figure and at point *b* on the short-run Phillips curve in Fig. 32.8. If, with the same expectations, aggregate demand does not change, the price level rises to 107, a 7 percent rise, and the economy is at point *c* in this figure and at point *c* on the short-run Phillips curve in Fig. 32.8.

The short-run Phillips curve is like the short-run aggregate supply curve. A movement along the *SAS* curve that brings a higher price level and an increase in real GDP is equivalent to a movement along the short-run Phillips curve that brings an increase in the inflation rate and a decrease in the unemployment rate. (Similarly, a movement along the *SAS* curve that brings a lower price level and a decrease in real GDP is equivalent to a movement along the short-run Phillips curve that brings a decrease in the inflation rate and an increase in the unemployment rate.)

The Long-Run Phillips Curve

The **long-run Phillips curve** is a curve that shows the relationship between inflation and unemployment when the actual inflation rate equals the expected inflation rate. The long-run Phillips curve is vertical at the natural unemployment rate. It is shown in Fig. 32.10 as the vertical line *LRPC*. The long-run Phillips curve tells us that any anticipated inflation rate is possible at the natural unemployment rate. This proposition is the same as the one you discovered in the *AS-AD* model. When inflation is anticipated, real GDP equals potential GDP. And with real GDP equal to potential GDP, unemployment is at the natural rate.

When the expected inflation rate changes, the short-run Phillips curve shifts. If the expected inflation rate is 10 percent a year, the short-run Phillips curve is $SRPC_0$. If the expected inflation rate falls to

7 percent a year, the short-run Phillips curve shifts downward to $SRPC_1$. The distance by which the short-run Phillips curve shifts downward when the expected inflation rate falls is equal to the change in the expected inflation rate.

To see why the short-run Phillips curve shifts when the expected inflation rate changes, let's do a thought experiment. There is full employment, and a 10 percent a year anticipated inflation is raging. The Fed now begins an attack on inflation by slowing money supply growth. Aggregate demand growth slows, and the inflation rate falls to 7 percent a year. At first, this decrease in inflation is *un*anticipated, so wages continue to rise at their original rate. The short-run aggregate supply curve shifts leftward at the same pace as before. Real GDP falls, and unemployment increases. In Fig. 32.10, the economy moves from point *a* to point *c* on $SRPC_0$.

If the actual inflation rate remains steady at 7 percent a year, this rate eventually comes to be expected. As this happens, wage growth slows and the short-run aggregate supply curve shifts leftward less quickly. Eventually, it shifts leftward at the same pace at which the aggregate demand curve is shifting rightward. The actual inflation rate equals the expected inflation rate, and full employment is restored. Unemployment is back at its natural rate. In Fig. 32.10, the short-run Phillips curve has shifted from $SRPC_0$ to $SRPC_1$ and the economy is at point *d*.

An increase in the expected inflation rate has the opposite effect to that shown in Fig. 32.10. Another important source of shifts in the Phillips curve is a change in the natural rate of unemployment.

Changes in the Natural Unemployment Rate

The natural unemployment rate changes for many reasons (see Chapter 25, pp. 557–558). A change in the natural unemployment rate shifts both the short-run and long-run Phillips curves. Figure 32.11 illustrates such shifts. If the natural unemployment rate increases from 6 percent to 9 percent, the long-run Phillips curve shifts from $LRPC_0$ to $LRPC_1$, and if expected inflation is constant at 10 percent a year, the short-run Phillips curve shifts from $SRPC_0$ to $SRPC_1$. Because the expected inflation rate is constant, the short-run Phillips curve $SRPC_1$ intersects the long-run curve $LRPC_1$ (point *e*) at the same inflation rate at which the short-run Phillips curve $SRPC_0$ intersects the long-run curve $LRPC_0$ (point *a*).

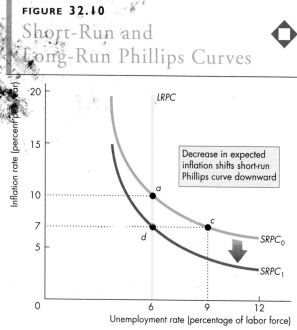

FIGURE 32.10

Short-Run and Long-Run Phillips Curves

Decrease in expected inflation shifts short-run Phillips curve downward

The long-run Phillips curve is *LRPC*, a vertical line at the natural unemployment rate. A fall in expected inflation shifts the short-run Phillips curve downward. For example, when the expected inflation rate falls from 10 percent a year to 7 percent a year, the short-run Phillips curve shifts downward from $SRPC_0$ and $SRPC_1$. The new short-run Phillips curve intersects the long-run Phillips curve at the new expected inflation rate—point *d*. With the original expected inflation rate (of 10 percent), an actual inflation rate of 7 percent a year would occur at an unemployment rate of 9 percent, at point *c*.

The U.S. Phillips Curve

Figure 32.12(a) is a scatter diagram of inflation and unemployment since 1960. The Phillips curve does not jump out of this figure. But we can interpret the data in terms of a shifting short-run Phillips curve as in Fig. 32.12(b). During the 1960s, the natural rate of unemployment was 5 percent and the expected inflation rate was 2 percent a year (point a), so the short-run Phillips curve was $SRPC_0$. During the 1970s and through 1981, the expected inflation rate and the natural unemployment rate increased and the short-run Phillips curve shifted rightward to $SRPC_1$, $SRPC_2$, and $SRPC_3$. During the 1980s and 1990s, the expected inflation rate and the natural unemployment rate decreased and the short-run Phillips curve shifted leftward. By the early 1990s, the curve was back at $SRPC_1$. And by 1996, the natural unemployment rate and the expected inflation rate were back around their 1960s levels, so the short-run Phillips curve was back at $SRPC_0$.

FIGURE 32.12
Phillips Curves in the United States

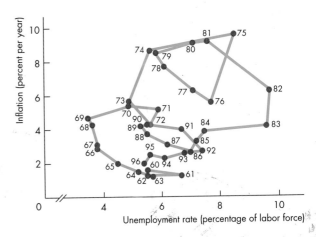

(a) Time sequence

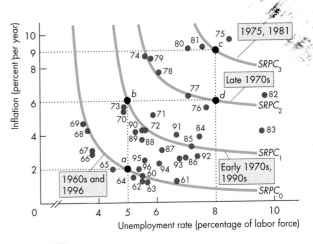

(b) Four Phillips curves

In part (a), each dot represents the combination of inflation and unemployment for a particular year in the United States. There is no clear relationship between the two variables. Part (b) interprets the data with a shifting short-run Phillips curve. The black dots a, b, c, and d show the combination of the natural rate of unemployment and the expected inflation rate in different periods. The short-run Phillips curve was $SRPC_0$ during the 1960s and in 1996. It was $SRPC_1$ during the early 1970s and 1990s, $SRPC_2$ during the late 1970s, and $SRPC_3$ (briefly) in 1975 and 1981.

FIGURE 32.11
A Change in the Natural Unemployment Rate

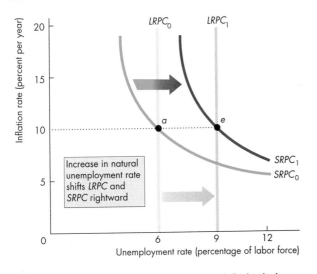

A change in the natural unemployment rate shifts both the short-run and long-run Phillips curves. Here the natural unemployment rate increases from 6 percent to 9 percent, and the two Phillips curves shift right to $SRPC_1$ and $LRPC_1$. The new long-run Phillips curve intersects the new short-run Phillips curve at the expected inflation rate—point e.

R E V I E W

- Unanticipated changes in the inflation rate bring movements along the short-run Phillips curve.
- An unanticipated increase in the inflation rate lowers the unemployment rate, and an unanticipated decrease in the inflation rate raises the unemployment rate.
- A change in the expected inflation rate shifts the short-run Phillips curve (upward for an increase in inflation and downward for a decrease in inflation) by an amount equal to the change in the expected inflation rate.
- A change in the natural unemployment rate shifts both the short-run and long-run Phillips curves (rightward for an increase in the natural rate and leftward for a decrease).
- The relationship between inflation and unemployment in the United States can be interpreted by a short-run Phillips curve that shifts.

So far, we've studied the effects of inflation on real GDP, real wages, employment, and unemployment. But inflation lowers the value of money and changes the real value of the amounts borrowed and repaid. As a result, interest rates are influenced by inflation. Let's see how.

Interest Rates and Inflation

TODAY, BUSINESSES IN THE UNITED STATES CAN borrow at interest rates of around 6 percent a year. Businesses in Russia pay interest rates of 60 percent a year, and those in Turkey pay 75 percent a year. Although U.S. interest rates have never been as high as these two cases, during the 1980s, U.S. businesses faced interest rates of 16 percent or higher. Why do interest rates vary so much both across countries and over time? The answer is because the inflation rate varies. When the inflation rate changes, nominal interest rates change to make borrowers pay the amount that compensates lenders for the fall in the value of money. Let's see how inflation affects borrowers and lenders and how it leads to changes in interest rates.

The Effects of Inflation on Borrowers and Lenders

The *nominal* interest rate is the price paid by a borrower to compensate a lender for two things: the amount loaned and the fall in the value of money that results from inflation. The *real* interest rate is the price paid by a borrower to compensate a lender only for the amount loaned. It is the real cost of a loan to the borrower and the real return on a loan to the lender. The forces of demand and supply determine an equilibrium real interest rate that does not depend on the inflation rate. These same forces also determine an equilibrium nominal interest rate that does depend on the inflation rate and that equals the equilibrium real interest rate plus the expected inflation rate.

To see why these outcomes occur, imagine that there is no inflation and that the nominal interest rate is 4 percent a year. The real interest rate is also 4 percent a year. The amount that businesses and people want to borrow equals the amount that businesses and people want to lend at this real interest rate. Walt Disney Corporation is willing to pay an interest rate of 4 percent a year to get the funds it needs to pay for its global investment in new theme parks. Sue and thousands of people like her are willing to lend Disney the amount it needs for its theme parks if they can get a *real* return of 4 percent a year. (Sue wants to buy a new car, and she plans to save enough to do so.)

Now suppose inflation breaks out at a steady 6 percent a year. All dollar prices and values, including theme park profits and car prices rise by 6 percent a year. If Disney was willing to pay a 4 percent interest rate when there was no inflation, it is now willing to pay 10 percent interest. The reason is that its profits are rising by 6 percent a year, so it is *really* paying only 4 percent. Similarly, if Sue was willing to lend at a 4 percent interest rate when there was no inflation, she is now willing to lend only if she gets 10 percent interest. The price of the car Sue is planning on buying is rising by 6 percent a year, so she is *really* getting only a 4 percent interest rate.

Because borrowers are willing to pay the higher rate and lenders are willing to lend only if they receive the higher rate, when inflation is anticipated, the *nominal interest rate* increases by an amount equal to the expected inflation rate. The *real interest rate* remains constant. The real interest rate might change because the supply of saving or investment demand has changed for some other reason. But a change in the expected inflation rate alone does not change the real interest rate.

Do the effects of inflation on interest rates that we've just described actually occur? Let's look at the U.S. experience.

Inflation and Interest Rates in the United States

Figure 32.13 shows the relationship between inflation and nominal interest rates in the United States between 1960 and 1996. Each point represents a year. The interest rate is that paid by large corporations on 6-month loans. The blue line shows the relationship between the nominal interest rate and the inflation rate if the real interest rate is constant at 2.1 percent a year, which is its actual average value in this period. When the red dot lies above the blue line, the real interest rate exceeds 2.1 percent a year, and when the red dot lies below the blue line, the real interest rate is less than 2.4 percent a year.

FIGURE 32.13

Inflation and the Interest Rate

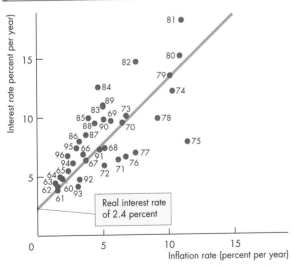

Other things remaining the same, the higher the expected inflation rate, the higher is the nominal interest rate. A graph showing the relationship between nominal interest rates and the actual inflation rate reveals that the influence of inflation on nominal interest rates is a powerful one.

Source: Economic Report of the President, 1997.

There is a positive relationship between the inflation rate and the interest rate, but the real interest rate has not been constant. During the 1960s, inflation and nominal interest rates were low. In the early 1970s, inflation began to increase, but it was not expected to increase much and certainly not to persist. As a result, nominal interest rates did not rise very much at that time. During the late 1970s and early 1980s, inflation of close to 10 percent a year came to be expected as an ongoing and highly persistent phenomenon. As a result, nominal interest rates increased to around 15 percent a year. Then in 1984 and 1985, the inflation rate fell—at first unexpectedly. Interest rates began to fall but not nearly as quickly as the inflation rate. Short-term interest rates fell more quickly than long-term interest rates because, at that time, it was expected that inflation would be lower in the short term but not as low in the longer term.

By the 1990s, inflation and the nominal interest rate had returned to their 1960s levels, and with inflation near its expected rate, the real interest rate was close to its long-term average of 2.1 percent a year.

The relationship between inflation and interest rates is even more dramatically illustrated by international experience. For example, in recent years, Chile has experienced an inflation rate of around 30 percent with nominal interest rates of about 40 percent. Brazil has experienced inflation rates and nominal interest rates of 40 percent a *month*. At the other extreme, countries such as Japan and Belgium have low inflation and low nominal interest rates.

R E V I E W

- The real interest rate is equal to the nominal interest rate minus the inflation rate.
- An increase in the inflation rate brings an increase in the nominal interest rate.

Reading Between the Lines on pages 730–731 looks at the current low inflation in the United States and the Fed's actions to keep it that way.

You have now completed your study of inflation. This material, together with that on economic growth (Chapter 27), gives a good overview of the long-term problems that confront a modern economy such as that of the United States. Our task in the following chapter is to focus more sharply on the problems of short-term fluctuations and the business cycle.

Keeping Inflation Down

THE CINCINNATI ENQUIRER, JANUARY 22, 1997

Greenspan Reports Economy Still Strong

BY LAURA COHN AND MICHAEL MCKEE
BLOOMBERG NEWS

The U.S. economy remains strong with few signs of immediate inflationary pressures even as an era of low wage gains may be ending, Federal Reserve Chairman Alan Greenspan said Tuesday.

"The economy has retained considerable vigor, with few signs of the imbalances and inflationary tensions that have disrupted past expansions," Mr. Greenspan said. "By some important measures of price trends, inflation actually slowed a bit in 1996."

Analysts interpreted Mr. Greenspan's comments to the Senate Budget committee as suggesting the Fed's policy-making Open Market committee won't raise interest rates when it meets Feb. 4-5.

Still, the Fed chairman left the door ajar for action later if inflation accelerates because of rising wage levels. Though it has taken a while, tight labor markets are beginning to put upward pressure on wages.

"The relatively modest wage gains we've seen are a transitional rather than a lasting phenomenon," Mr. Greenspan said. "Indeed, the recent pickup in some measures of wages suggests that the transition may already be running its course."

If that's the case, the Fed chairman suggested the central bank will have to consider raising the federal funds rate on overnight bank loans it controls.

So far, wages have increased only at a modest pace and that has kept prices in check, according to Sung Won Sohn, chief economist at Norwest Corp. Mr. Greenspan "made it clear that we are probably at the end of that good luck period," Mr. Sohn said. "From here on, we should expect somewhat higher rate of wage gains and, therefore, inflation."

Mr. Sohn also said Mr. Greenspan's comments—as well as the overall economic outlook—suggest the Fed will raise the rate on overnight bank loans by about a quarter percent this spring from 5.25 percent. That's "likely to be followed by another couple of tightenings later this year," he said. ...

Bloomberg News. Reprinted with permission.

Essence of THE STORY

■ The U.S. economy continues to expand with few signs of inflation. According to some measures, inflation slowed during 1996.

■ Wage gains were moderate during 1996, but the latest upswing in wage rates could indicate that inflation might accelerate.

■ To combat inflation, the Fed may raise interest rates in the spring and follow this with further increases later.

Economic

A N A L Y S I S

■ Figure I shows the inflation rate and the earnings growth rate from January 1995 to December 1996. Inflation has been on a slight upward trend since late 1995.

■ Figure 2 interprets the changes in inflation and unemployment by using the Phillips curve.

■ In January 1995, the long-run Phillips curve was $LRPC_0$ at the (assumed) natural unemployment rate of 5.7 percent. The short-run Phillips curve was $SRPC_0$, and unemployment was slightly below the natural rate.

■ With unemployment below the natural rate, inflation increased. The expected inflation rate also increased and the short-run Phillips curve shifted upward to $SRPC_1$.

■ In May 1995, the unemployment rate remained below the natural rate.

■ But during the rest of 1995 and the first half of 1996, the natural rate of unemployment decreased to (an assumed) 5.5 percent and the long-run Phillips curve shifted leftward to $LRPC_1$. The short-run Phillips curve also shifted leftward to $SRPC_2$.

■ In February 1996, unemployment was close to the new natural rate.

■ During the second half of 1996, the natural rate of unemployment remained at (an assumed) 5.5 percent but the actual unemployment rate decreased below the natural rate.

■ By September 1996, the inflation rate had increased to 3 percent a year.

■ The long-run Phillips curve remained at $LRPC_1$, but the expected inflation rate increased and by December 1996, the short-run Phillips curve shifted back to $SRPC_0$.

■ Whether inflation is going to continue to increase depends on how rapidly the money supply grows. The Fed is committed to maintaining non-inflationary money growth, and Fig. 3 shows that it is succeeding.

■ From April 1995 to March 1996, M2 growth increased. Through the rest of 1996, M2 growth has been steady at about 4 percent a year.

■ An M2 growth rate of this magnitude is likely to keep inflation low.

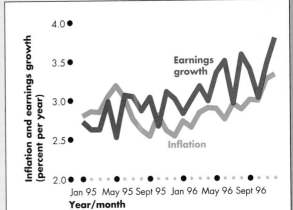

Figure 1 Inflation

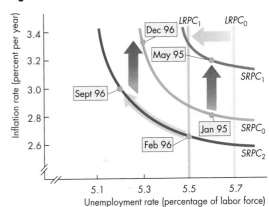

Figure 2 Phillips curves

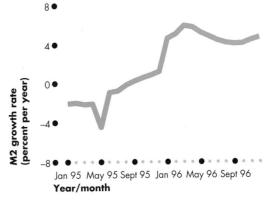

Figure 3 M2 money growth

SUMMARY

Key Points

Inflation and the Price Level (p. 714)

■ Inflation is a process of persistently rising prices and falling value of money.

Demand-Pull Inflation (pp. 715–717)

■ Demand-pull inflation arises from increasing aggregate demand.

■ Its main sources are increases in the money supply or in government purchases.

Cost-Push Inflation (pp. 717–719)

■ Cost-push inflation can result from any factor that decreases aggregate supply.

■ Its main sources are increasing wage rates and increasing prices of key raw materials.

Effects of Inflation (pp. 720–724)

■ Inflation is costly when it is unanticipated because it creates inefficiencies and redistributes income and wealth.

■ People try to anticipate inflation to avoid its costs.

■ Forecasts of inflation based on all the available relevant information are called rational expectations.

■ A moderate anticipated inflation has a small cost. But a rapid anticipated inflation is costly because it decreases potential GDP and slows growth.

Inflation and Unemployment: The Phillips Curve (pp. 724–728)

■ The short-run Phillips curve shows the tradeoff between inflation and unemployment when the expected inflation rate and the natural unemployment rate are constant.

■ The long-run Phillips curve, which is vertical, shows that when the actual inflation rate equals the expected inflation rate, the unemployment rate equals the natural unemployment rate.

■ Unexpected changes in the inflation rate bring movements along the short-run Phillips curve.

■ Changes in expected inflation shift the short-run Phillips curve.

■ Changes in the natural unemployment rate shift both the short-run and long-run Phillips curves.

Interest Rates and Inflation (pp. 728–729)

■ The higher the expected inflation rate, the higher is the nominal interest rate.

■ As the anticipated inflation rate rises, borrowers willingly pay a higher interest rate and lenders successfully demand a higher interest rate.

■ The nominal interest rate adjusts to equal the real interest rate plus the expected inflation rate.

Key Figures

Key Terms

QUESTIONS

1. What is inflation and how is its rate measured?
2. Distinguish between the price level and the inflation rate.
3. Distinguish between a one-time change in the price level and inflation.
4. Distinguish between demand-pull inflation and cost-push inflation.
5. What are the factors that can start a demand-pull inflation?
6. Explain the sequence of events that unfold when a demand-pull inflation spiral occurs.
7. What are the factors that can start a cost-push inflation?
8. Explain the sequence of events that unfold when a cost-push inflation spiral occurs.
9. Why is unanticipated inflation costly?
10. What are the losses that a person suffers in labor markets when inflation is unanticipated?
11. What are the losses that a person suffers in capital markets when inflation is unanticipated?
12. Explain why unanticipated inflation does not only redistribute income but also creates inefficiency.
13. Why do people devote resources to trying to forecast inflation?
14. What is a rational expectation?
15. What causes an anticipated inflation?
16. Describe the sequence of events that unfold during an anticipated inflation.
17. What are the costs of anticipated inflation?
18. What does the short-run Phillips curve show?
19. What is held constant when there is a movement along a short-run Phillips curve?
20. What does the long-run Phillips curve show?
21. What is held constant when there is a movement along a long-run Phillips curve?
22. What have been the main causes of shifts in the U.S. short-run Phillips curve during the 1970s, 1980s, and 1990s?
23. Why do nominal interest rates vary so much both across countries and over time?
24. What is the relationship between inflation and the nominal interest rate in the United States?

PROBLEMS

1. Work out the effects on the price level of the following unexpected events:
   a. An increase in the money supply
   b. An increase in government purchases of goods and services
   c. An increase in income taxes
   d. An increase in investment demand
   e. An increase in the wage rate
   f. An increase in labor productivity
2. Work out the effects on the price level of the events listed in problem 1 when they are correctly anticipated.
3. The figure shows an economy's long-run aggregate supply curve, LAS, three aggregate demand curves, AD_0, AD_1, and AD_2, and three short-run aggregate supply curves, SAS_0, SAS_1, and SAS_2. The economy starts out on the curves AD_0 and SAS_0.

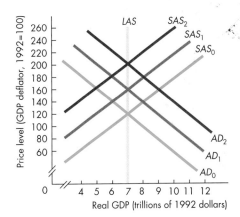

Some events then occur that take the economy to the other aggregate demand curves and short-run aggregate supply curves.
   a. Describe the sequence of events in the figure if there is a demand-pull inflation.
   b. Describe the sequence of events in the figure if there is a cost-push inflation.
   c. Describe the sequence of events in the figure if there is an anticipated inflation.
4. In the economy in problem 3, aggregate demand unexpectedly increases to AD_1.
   a. What is the price level in the short run?
   b. What is real GDP in the short run?
   c. What is the price level in the long run?
   d. What is real GDP in the long run?

5. An economy has a natural unemployment rate of 4 percent when its expected inflation is 6 percent. Its inflation and unemployment history is as follows:

Inflation rate (percent per year)	Unemployment rate (percent)
10	2
8	3
6	4
4	5
2	6

a. Draw a diagram of this economy's short-run and long-run Phillips curves.
b. If the actual inflation rate rises from 6 percent a year to 8 percent a year, what is the change in the unemployment rate? Explain why it occurs.
c. If the natural unemployment rate rises to 5 percent, what is the change in the unemployment rate? Explain why it occurs.
d. Go back to part (b). If the expected inflation rate falls to 4 percent a year, what is the change in the unemployment rate? Explain why it occurs.

CRITICAL THINKING

1. Study *Reading Between the Lines* on pp. 730–731 and then answer the following questions:
   a. What does Alan Greenspan say about the likelihood of inflation increasing?
   b. Is the news article describing a cost-push inflation or a demand-pull inflation or an anticipated inflation? Provide detailed reasons.
   c. If the Fed tightens money and raises interest rates, how do you think that action will influence inflation and unemployment in the short run?
   d. If the Fed tightens money and raises interest rates, how do you think that action will influence inflation and unemployment in the long run?
   e. If the Fed raises interest rates in 1997, does that make it likely that interest rates will be higher or lower than they otherwise would have been in 1998?

2. In light of what you have learned in this chapter, what do you think the Fed should do during 1998 to keep inflation in check?

3. If inflation rates of 10 percent a year (as we had during the 1970s) returned in the United States, who would benefit and who would lose?

4. "The Phillips curve is a menu from which the government must chose how much inflation and how much unemployment to buy." Evaluate this statement. Under what conditions is it true? Under what conditions is it false?

5. If the Fed aimed to use monetary policy to lower the unemployment rate to 3 percent, what do you predict would happen to:
   a. Unemployment in the short run?
   b. Unemployment in the long run?
   c. Inflation in the short run?
   d. Inflation in the long run?
   e. The short-run Phillips curve?
   f. The long-run Phillips curve?
   g. Potential GDP?
   h. The growth rate of potential GDP?

Understanding and Smoothing the Business Cycle

To cure a disease, doctors must first understand how the disease responds to different treatments. It helps to understand the mechanisms that operate to cause the disease, but sometimes, a workable cure can be found even before the full story of the causes has been told. ◆ Curing economic ills is similar to curing our medical ills. We need to understand how the economy responds to the treatments we might prescribe for it. And sometimes, we want to try a cure, even though we don't fully understand the reasons for the problem we're trying to control. ◆ You have already encountered a lot of what is known about macroeconomic performance. You've seen how the pace of capital accumulation and technological change determine the long-term growth trend. You've learned how fluctuations around the long-term trend can be generated by changes in aggregate demand and aggregate supply. And you've learned about the key sources of fluctuations in aggregate demand and aggregate supply. ◆ The two chapters in this part build of everything you've studied in macroeconomics. The central tool they use is the *AS–AD* model. But they use it to explain the big picture or grand vision that different schools of thought hold concerning the way the economy operates and what is important. ◆ In Chapter 33, you will learn about alternative visions of the business cycle. All of these visions can be translated in the *AS–AD* model. And doing so helps us to compare and contrast the competing visions. But one theory of the cycle, the new *real business cycle (RBC)* theory, is more at home with the demand and supply model of microeconomics (Chapter 4) than the *AS–AD* model. Most economists have not embraced the real business cycle approach. It is an extreme view. But the method that real business cycle theory uses is here to stay. This method is to build a (mathematical) model of the entire economy and then see, in a computer simulation, what kind of cycle the model creates. The economy on the computer is then calibrated to the real economy and the cycles are compared. The computer model can be treated with a variety of 'medications' and their effects observed. This new style of business cycle research cannot be explained in detail without using advanced mathematical ideas. But the economics that underlies it can be explained and Chapter 33 shows you the nature of the model that real business cycle theorists have used. ◆ In Chapter 34, we turn to the policy debate. There, you will study the alternative approaches that have been proposed to speed growth, smooth the business cycle, and contain inflation. Again, the *AS–AD* model is the workhorse you will use to compare the effects of alternative policy strategies. ◆ Before we embark on the next two chapters, we're going to meet two economists whose ideas about business cycles and macroeconomic policy have been influential. They are Irving Fisher and Frederic S. Mishkin.

Business Cycles

The Economist:
Irving Fisher

Irving Fisher (1867–1947) is the greatest American-born economist. The son of a Congregational minister who died as Irving was finishing high school, he paid his way through Yale and earned enough money to support his mother and younger brother by tutoring his fellow students.

Irving Fisher came to economics by way of mathematics. He was Yale's first Ph.D. candidate in pure economics, but was a student in the math department!

The contributions that Fisher made to economics cover the entire subject. He is best known for his work on the quantity theory of money (Chapter 30, pp. 679–683) and the relation between interest rates and inflation (Chapter 32, pp. 728–729). But he also wrote on the business cycle. He believed that the Great Depression was caused because the fall in the price level increased the real burden of debts. He wrote from experience: He had borrowed heavily to buy stocks in the rising market of the late 1920s and lost a fortune of perhaps 10 million dollars in the crash of 1929.

> "*...in the great booms and depressions, ... the two big bad actors are debt disturbances and price level disturbances.*"
>
> IRVING FISHER
>
> "*The Debt Deflation Theory of Depressions*"
>
> ECONOMETRICA, 1933

The Issues
and Ideas

Economic activity has fluctuated between boom and bust for as long as we've had records. And understanding the sources of economic fluctuations has turned out to be difficult. One reason is that there are no simple patterns. Every new episode of the business cycle is different from its predecessor in some way. Some cycles are long and some short, some are mild and some severe, some begin in the United States and some abroad. We never know with any certainty when the next turning point (down or up) is coming or what will cause it. A second reason is that the apparent waste of resources during a recession or depression seems to contradict the very foundation of economics: Resources are limited and people have unlimited wants—there is scarcity. A satisfactory theory of the business cycle must explain why scarce resources don't *always* get fully employed.

One theory is that recessions result from insufficient aggregate demand. The solution is to increase government spending, cut taxes, and cut interest rates. But demand stimulation must not be overdone. Countries that stimulate aggregate demand too much, such as Brazil, find their economic growth rates sagging, unemployment rising, and inflation accelerating.

Today's new theory, real

business cycle theory, predicts that fluctuations in aggregate demand have no effect on output and employment and change only the price level and inflation rate. But this theory ignores the real effects of financial collapse of the type that occurred in the 1930s. If banks fail on a large scale and people lose their wealth, other firms also begin to fail and jobs are destroyed. Unemployed people cut their spending, and output falls further. Demand stimulation may not be called for, but action to ensure that sound banks survive certainly is.

While economists are trying to understand the sources of the business cycle, the government and the Fed are doing the best they can to moderate the cycle. In the years since World War II, there appears to have been some success. Although the business cycle has not disappeared, it has become much less severe.

THEN ...

What happens to the economy when people lose confidence in banks? They withdraw their funds. These withdrawals feed on themselves, creating a snowball of withdrawals and, eventually, panic. Short of funds with which to repay depositors, banks call in loans and previously sound businesses are faced with financial distress. They close down and lay off workers. And recession deepens and turns into depression. Bank failures and the resulting decline in the nation's supply of money and credit were a significant factor in deepening and prolonging the Great Depression. But they taught us the importance of stable financial institutions and gave rise to the establishment of federal deposit insurance to prevent future financial collapse.

... AND NOW

How can a building designed as a shop have no better use than to be boarded up and left empty? Not enough aggregate demand, say the Keynesians. Not so, say the real business cycle theorists. Technological change has reduced the building's current productivity as a shop to zero. But its expected future productivity is sufficiently high that it is not efficient to refit the building for some other purpose.

All unemployment, whether of buildings or people, can be explained in a similar way. For example, how can it be that during a recession, a person trained as a shop clerk is without work? Not enough aggregate demand is one answer. Another is that the current productivity of shop clerks is low, but their expected future productivity is sufficiently high that it does not pay an unemployed clerk to retrain for a job that is currently available.

It is now almost 70 years since the Great Depression. Although we've had many recessions since then, none compare with the severity of that event. Some credit for avoiding another major depression must go to the Federal Reserve board. You'll next meet Professor Frederick Mishkin, current VP and director of research at the Fed of New York.

Frederic S. Mishkin is currently an executive vice president and director of research at the Federal Reserve Bank of New York. He is on leave from the Graduate School of Business at Columbia University. Professor Mishkin was born in New York City in 1951. He received his Ph.D. from MIT in 1976 and has taught at the University of Chicago, Northwestern University, Princeton University, and Columbia University.

Professor Mishkin's research focuses on monetary policy and its impact on financial markets and the aggregate economy.

Michael Parkin talked with Professor Mishkin about his work, the role the Fed plays in monetary policy, and the legacy of Irving Fisher.

The views expressed here are those of Professor Mishkin and do not represent those of the Federal Reserve Bank of New York or the Federal Reserve System.

Why are you an economist?

The Great Depression was the most important event in my father's life, and we talked about it continually at the dinner table. We also talked about the stock market. These discussions piqued my interest in economics. When I went to college, I thought of becoming a physicist, but I realized that economics has many of same attributes. Both disciplines demand thinking logically and are consistently based on models. The real-world problems that were implicit in the study of economics proved much more interesting to me then. I realized that economics was my calling, and in fact, it was one of the best choices I've ever made.

What are the most basic principles that you find yourself repeatedly returning to in your professional life, and especially in your life as the director of research at the New York Fed.

A key principle is that incentives are everything. Particularly in today's world, where you need creativity, you cannot motivate people to do good research by just commanding them. You instead need to motivate them by saying, "Do your own work, figure it out yourself, but, on the other hand, I'm going to give you the right incentives." A second principle is the concept of backward induction. If you think about where you want to be and work backwards, you are frequently way ahead of the game. Not only are these two concepts extremely useful in thinking about real-world economic problems, they've been absolutely invaluable to me in managing the Fed's research group of 150 people. We have an annual evaluation process followed by a salary review, and promotions are determined by how well people are doing and how well they respond to incentives.

> *A key principle is that incentives are everything.*

Does the work of Federal Reserve banks directly contribute to the quality of the monetary policy that is developed?

In economics we never really have answers, but we are able to understand things better through research that initiates debate and makes good policy outcomes more likely. Many of the new ideas that are published in the academic journals have helped to guide policy makers. I have stressed the value of basic research here at the Federal Reserve Bank of New York and have emphasized our need to be at the very frontier of ideas. We also have to make decisions from day to day that involves much more nitty-gritty research. For example, we have to forecast the economy and try to understand what's going on in the inflation process.

We are enjoying one of longest uninterrupted recoveries in U.S. economic history, and there's little sign of either serious inflation or a serious recession. To what do you attribute this successful run? What part do you think the Fed can take credit for, and where else would you allocate credit, if anywhere?

There's a fair amount of credit due to the Fed, but I'm going to use an adage that my mother always said to me, "It's better to be lucky than good, but it's even better to be good and lucky." The Fed has been both good and lucky. The "good" part is that the Fed has acted in accordance with the results of economic research that indicates that good monetary policy is forward looking. There are lags from monetary policy to inflation on the order of two to three years. This indicates that monetary policy actions today have little effect on today's inflation but are highly relevant to what will happen to future inflation. We must look to the future if we are to promote a stable economic environment in which we have very low inflation. In February 1994, when the Fed

> *Monetary policy actions today have little effect on today's inflation but are highly relevant to what will happen to future inflation.*

started to raise interest rates, unemployment was close to the 7 percent range and inflation pressures were nonexistent. Yet, looking several years down the road, we realized that if we did not start to raise interest rates and tighten monetary policy, then we would eventually have an overheated economy with inflation out of control. The preemptive policy of raising interest rates was extremely successful because it helped the inflation rate to stay very low, and the economy continued to grow at a sustainable pace. Another benefit of pursuing a preemptive policy is that markets and businesses understand that the central bank will be serious about controlling inflation. That produces a much more stable environment because businesses know they can't solve their problems by just raising prices. Instead,

they have to be efficient and keep costs low. The Fed has also been "lucky." Even if the Fed is doing the right thing during a business cycle expansion, there may be a tendency for the economy to overheat a little bit and a little bit of inflation to occur. This has not happened. The economy is about as good as it can get, and that requires not only good policy but also some luck.

The traditional categories for discussing policy involve terms such as *rules*, *discretion*, and *fixed rules* versus *feedback rules*. Is that language of use in thinking about Fed policy?

I think that there's a problem with the dichotomy between rules and discretion. One part of the literature views rules as being critical to solving problems such as time inconsistency. Trying to do what looks good right now but not worrying about the future may result in a sequence of policies that lead to poor outcomes in the long run. You have to avoid the temptation to do what looks like the right thing today and ignore the long run. That's one of the reasons why people feel that rules are important. On the other hand, the criticism of rules is that they are too rigid, particularly for dealing with unexpected events. Rules can, in that situation, lead to a very bad outcome. An alternative is to pursue a policy that is basically constrained discretion. It's rulelike, but without a rigid rule. For example, inflation-targeting regimes that have been pursued in many countries throughout the world in recent years are neither a rule nor discretion. They are, instead, constrained discretion. My view is that a good monetary policy should always be rulelike; but, on the other hand, the idea of putting in fixed rules is probably not a good idea.

For the past 15 years the real business cycle research agenda has downplayed the role of money. How do you evaluate the recent real business cycle research program?

The real business cycle literature takes the view that monetary policy is not important to the actual short-term business cycle. I think that monetary policy is more important to the business cycle than real business cycle models give credit for. There is evidence that monetary policy has been important. For example, during the early 1980s, the Federal Reserve took very active steps to get inflation under control and the result was a quite severe recession, but eventually the tight monetary policy produced the right outcome, which was low inflation. I would also characterize the Great Depression as a period where monetary policy performed very poorly and contributed to the most severe economic contraction in the U.S. history. I think monetary policy actions were extremely important during that episode and extremely important during the period 1980 to 1982. On the other hand, real business cycle literature points out that the degree of control that monetary policy authorities can exert on the business cycle is indeed limited, and I am quite sympathetic to this view. The idea that the monetary authorities are able to tweak the business cycle at every turn is just not correct because the actual degree of certainty as to what will happen as a result of certain monetary policy actions is by no means clear. The real business cycle literature has made people aware that monetary policy cannot be fully in control of what

happens in the business cycle. On the other hand, I think that it's overstretching to say that monetary policy actions don't have real effects.

How can students help themselves to be more able to address interesting, real problems?

It is critical to get students to apply what they learn in class to their everyday lives. I tell my students that they must be reading newspapers such as *The Wall Street Journal, The Financial Times*, or *The New York Times* for business and financial news. I also tell students that they actually can use economic principles such as adverse selection and moral hazard to solve real-world problems every day. For example, if somebody's a rich person and is thinking about getting married, he or she faces an adverse selection problem: Does the other person love me because I'm wealthy rather than because I'm a lovable person?

In addition to managing the research group, I participate in the management committee of the bank. I've been able to actively contribute to the management of this bank because I can use economic principles to discuss what I think would be sensible solutions to problems. Economics is wonderful training for being able to

solve many problems that hit you every day.

What, for you, is the legacy of Irving Fisher?

Irving Fisher is one of the extraordinary American economists. He's famous for the quantity theory of money, which is extremely useful in thinking about the importance of money to the economy. He was a pioneer whose work on interest rates is still valuable today in thinking about how to conduct monetary policy. He also did path-breaking work for which he was not famous. For example, his paper "The Debt Deflation Theory of the Great Depression" has led to a much better understanding of financial crises in today's world.

What can an undergraduate gain from taking an economics course?

Economics is an important part of a liberal arts education and is essential for law and MBA students. For the first time in my life, I've actually been a manager, and one of the things that is really striking is how useful economic concepts have been to helping me to be effective. I now can go back to my MBA students and show them that many of these concepts are ones that I actually used in practice to make me a better manager.

Economics is not only useful in helping people become professionals, but also extremely useful in terms of making them better educated citizens. Yes, I do want to train people to help them be successful directly in their careers, but I also want to make them more successful, generally, as people. I think economics is a very powerful tool in achieving that.

33

The Business Cycle

The 1920s were years of unprecedented prosperity for Americans. After the horrors of World War I (1914–1918), the economic machine was back at work, producing such technological marvels as cars and airplanes, telephones and vacuum cleaners. Houses and apartments were being built at a frantic pace. Then, almost without warning, in October 1929, came a devastating stock market crash. Overnight, the values of stocks and shares traded on Wall Street fell by 30 percent. During the four succeeding years, there followed the most severe economic contraction in recorded history. By 1933, real GDP had fallen by 30 percent, unemployment had increased to 25 percent of the labor force, and employment was down 20 percent.

Must What Goes Up Always Come Down?

What caused the Great Depression? ◆ By the standard of the Great Depression, recent recessions have been mild. But recessions have not gone away. Our economy has experienced 15 recessions since 1920 and 10 since the end of World War II in 1945. For 16 months, from November 1973 through March 1975, real GDP fell by 5 percent. It fell again in 1980 and yet again in back-to-back recessions in 1981–1982. Most recently, real GDP decreased for 8 months in 1990–1991. Between these recessions, expansions took real GDP and income per person to new heights. Since the 1990–1991 recession, real GDP has grown steadily. By the end of 1996, it was some 15 percent higher than it had been in the 1990–1991 recession. What causes a repeating sequence of recessions and expansions in our economy? Must what goes up always come down? Will we have another recession? When? Before 2000? ◆ We are going to explore the business cycle in this chapter. You will see how all the strands of macroeconomics that you've been following come together and weave a complete picture of the forces and mechanisms that generate economic growth and fluctuations in production, employment and unemployment, and inflation.

After studying this chapter, you will be able to:

- Distinguish among the different theories of the business cycle

- Explain the Keynesian and monetarist theories of the business cycle

- Explain the new classical and new Keynesian theories of the business cycle

- Explain real business cycle theory

- Describe the origins of and the mechanisms at work during two recent recessions and during the Great Depression

Cycle Patterns, Impulses, and Mechanisms

YOU'VE LOOKED AT THE BUSINESS CYCLE AT several points in your study of macroeconomics. You met it first in Chapter 22, which defines the phases of the cycle and describes its history. You learned about a framework for studying the business cycle—the aggregate supply–aggregate demand model—in Chapter 24. In Chapter 25, you saw how unemployment fluctuates over the business cycle. In Chapter 28, you focused on business cycle turning points and the inventory changes and expenditure multiplier effects that operate as the economy swings from expansion to recession and from recession to expansion. In Chapter 29, you studied the ways in which fiscal policy influences and is influenced by the business cycle. Finally, you saw in Chapters 30 through 32 how money influences economic fluctuations and how inflation and the business cycle intertwine.

You've also looked at another type of economic fluctuation: the productivity growth slowdown of the 1970s. This slowdown is not classified as a business cycle event, but it has some similarities. It is part of an overall process of economic growth, the pace of which fluctuates. The processes of growth and of the business cycle are intimately connected. In fact, according to one view, they are all manifestations of the same phenomenon.

This chapter brings all these strands in your previous study of macroeconomics together and gives you an opportunity both to review what you have learned and to put it to work in a focused way in interpreting and making sense of particular episodes in our economic history.

We'll get moving by first returning to the facts about the business cycle and looking at the complex patterns it makes.

Business Cycle Patterns

The business cycle is an irregular and nonrepeating up-and-down movement of business activity that takes place around a generally rising trend and that shows great diversity. Each recession, expansion, and turning point has been dated by the National Bureau of Economic Research (NBER). The NBER has identified 15 recessions and expansions since 1920. On the average, recessions have lasted for just over a year and real GDP has fallen from peak to trough by more than 6 percent. Expansions have lasted for almost 4 years on the average, and real GDP has increased from trough to peak by an average of 22 percent. But these averages hide huge variations from one cycle to another.

Figure 33.1 shows the range of variation across the different recessions and expansions. It shows the total percentage change in real GDP during successive recessions and expansion. You can see that the Great Depression was much more severe than anything that followed it. Over a 43-month period, real GDP shrank by 33 percent. The second most severe recession was also in the 1930s. Another relatively severe recession occurred at the end of World War II in 1945. The only other recession that comes close to these is the OPEC recession of 1974–1975, which lasted for 16 months, during which real GDP fell by 5 percent. The other recessions since 1950, including the most recent 1990–1991 recession, have been much milder than those of the 1930s. The biggest expansion occurred during World War II. But the other two big expansions were in the 1960s and 1980s. There is no correlation between the length of an expansion and the length of the preceding recession.

With this enormous diversity of experience, there is no simple explanation for the business cycle. Also, there is no (currently available) way of forecasting when the next turning point will come. But there is a body of theory about the business cycle that helps us to understand its causes. A good place to begin studying this theory is to distinguish the possible ways in which cycles can be created.

Cycle Impulses and Mechanisms

Cycles are a widespread physical phenomenon. In a tennis match, the ball cycles from one side of the court to the other and back again. Every day, the earth cycles from day to night and back to day. A child on a rocking horse creates a cycle as the horse swings back and forth.

The tennis ball cycle is the simplest. It is caused by the actions of the players. Each time the ball changes direction (at each turning point), the racket (an outside force) is applied. The day-night-day cycle is the most subtle. This cycle is caused by the rotation of the earth. No new force is applied each day to make the sun rise and set. It happens because of

FIGURE 33.1

Some Business Cycle Patterns

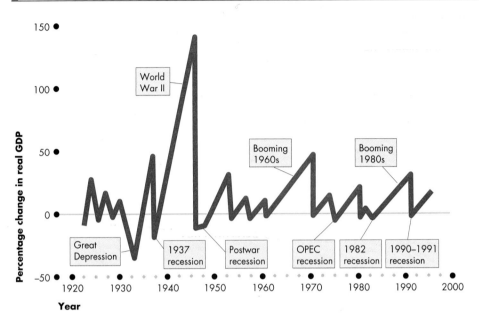

Recessions have lasted from 43 months during the Great Depression, when real GDP fell by 33 percent, to 6 months in 1980, when real GDP fell by 2.5 percent. The mildest recession lasted through most of 1970, when real GDP fell by 1 percent. Recessions have been less severe in the post-World War II period. Expansions have lasted from 6 months in 1980 to more than 100 months during the 1960s. Expansions have become longer and stronger during the post-World War II period.

Source: National Bureau of Economic Research and the author's calculations.

the design of the objects that interact to create the cycle. Nothing happens at a turning point (sunrise and sunset) that is any different from what is happening at other points except that the sun comes into or goes out of view. The child's rocking horse cycle is a combination of these two cases. To start the horse rocking, some outside force must be exerted (as in the tennis ball cycle). But once the horse is rocking, the to-and-fro cycle continues for some time with no further force being applied (as in the day-night-day cycle). The rocking horse cycle eventually dies out unless the horse is pushed again, and each time the horse is pushed, the cycle temporarily becomes more severe.

The economy is a bit like all three of these examples. It can be hit by shocks (like a tennis ball) that send it in one direction or another, it can cycle indefinitely (like the turning of day into night), and it can cycle in swings that get milder until another shock sets off a new burst of bigger swings (like a rocking horse). While none of these analogies is perfect, they all contain some insights into the business cycle.

Different theories of the cycle emphasize different outside forces (different tennis rackets) and different cycle mechanisms (different solar system and rocking horse designs).

Although there are several different theories of the business cycle, they all agree about one aspect of the cycle: the central role played by investment and the accumulation of capital.

The Central Role of Investment and Capital

Whatever the shocks are that hit the economy, they hit one crucial variable: investment. Recessions begin when investment in new capital slows down, and they turn into expansions when investment speeds up. Investment and capital interact like the spinning earth and the sun to create an ongoing cycle.

In an expansion, investment proceeds at a rapid rate and the capital stock grows quickly. But rapid capital growth means that the amount of capital per hour of labor is growing. Equipped with more capital, labor becomes more productive. But the *law of diminishing returns* begins to operate. The law of diminishing returns states that as the quantity of capital increases, with the quantity of labor remaining the same, the gain in productivity from the additional units of capital eventually diminishes. Diminishing returns to capital bring a fall in the profit rate, and with a lower profit rate, the incentive to invest weakens. As a result, investment eventually falls. When it falls by a large amount, recession begins.

In a recession, investment is low and the capital stock grows slowly. In a deep recession, the capital stock might actually fall. Slow capital growth (or even a falling capital stock) means that the amount of capital per hour of labor is falling. With a low amount of capital per hour of labor, businesses begin to see opportunities for profitable investment and the pace of investment eventually picks up. As it does so, recession turns into expansion.

The *AS-AD* Model

Investment and capital are a crucial part of the business cycle mechanism, but they are just one part. To study the broader business cycle mechanism, we need a broader framework. That framework is the *AS-AD* model of Chapter 24. All the theories of the business cycle can be described in terms of the *AS-AD* model. Theories differ both in what they identify as the impulse and in the cycle mechanism. But all theories can be thought of as making assumptions about the factors that make either aggregate supply or aggregate demand fluctuate and assumptions about how they interact with each other to create a business cycle. Business cycle impulses can affect either the supply side or the demand side of the economy or both. But there are no pure supply-side theories. We will classify all theories of the business cycle as either:

■ Aggregate demand theories
■ Real business cycle theory

We'll study the aggregate demand theories first. Then we'll study real business cycle theory, which is a more recent approach that isolates a shock that has both aggregate supply and aggregate demand effects.

Aggregate Demand Theories of the Business Cycle

THREE TYPES OF AGGREGATE DEMAND THEORY OF the business cycle have been proposed. They are:

■ Keynesian theory
■ Monetarist theory
■ Rational expectations theories

Keynesian Theory

The **Keynesian theory of the business cycle** regards volatile expectations as the main source of economic fluctuations. This theory is distilled from Keynes' *General Theory of Employment, Interest, and Money*. We'll explore the Keynesian theory by looking at its main impulse and the mechanism that converts that impulse into a real GDP cycle.

Keynesian Impulse The *impulse* in the Keynesian theory of the business cycle is *expected future sales and profits*. A change in expected future sales and profits changes the demand for new capital and changes the level of investment.

Keynes had a sophisticated theory about *how* expected sales and profits are determined. He reasoned that these expectations would be volatile because most of the events that shape the future are unknown and impossible to forecast. So, he reasoned, news or even rumors about future tax rate changes, interest rate changes, advances in technology, global economic and political events, or any other of the thousands of relevant factors that influence sales and profits change expectations in ways that can't be quantified but that have large effects.

To emphasize the volatility and diversity of sources of changes in expected sales and profits, Keynes described these expectations as *animal spirits*. In using this term, Keynes was not saying that expectations are irrational. Rather, he meant that because future sales and profits are impossible to forecast, it might be rational to take a view about them based on rumors, guesses, intuition, and instinct. Further, it might be rational to *change* one's view of the future, perhaps radically, in the light of scraps of new information.

Keynesian Cycle Mechanism In the Keynesian theory, once a change in animal spirits has changed investment, a cycle mechanism begins to operate that has two key elements. First, the initial change in investment has a multiplier effect. The change in investment changes *aggregate* expenditure, real GDP, and disposable income. The change in disposable income changes consumption expenditure, and aggregate demand changes by a multiple of the initial change in investment. (This mechanism is described in detail in Chapter 28, pp. 626–633.) The aggregate demand curve shifts rightward in an expansion and leftward in a recession.

The second element of the Keynesian cycle mechanism is the response of real GDP to a change in aggregate demand. The short-run aggregate supply curve is horizontal (or nearly so). With a horizontal *SAS* curve, swings in aggregate demand translate into swings in real GDP with no changes in the price level. But the short-run aggregate supply curve depends on the money wage rate. If the money wage rate is fixed (sticky), the *SAS* curve does not move. And if the money wage rate changes, the *SAS* curve shifts. In the Keynesian theory, the response of the money wage rate to changes in aggregate demand are *asymmetric*.

On the downside, when aggregate demand decreases and unemployment rises, the money wage rate does not change. It is completely rigid in the downward direction. With a decrease in aggregate demand and no change in the money wage rate, the economy gets stuck in a below full-employment equilibrium. No natural forces operate to restore full employment. The economy remains in that situation until animal spirits are lifted and investment increases.

On the upside, when aggregate demand increases and unemployment falls below the natural rate, the money wage rate rises quickly. It is flexible in the upward direction. At above full employment, the horizontal *SAS* curve plays no role and only the vertical *LAS* curve is relevant. With an increase in aggregate demand and an accompanying rise in the money wage rate, the price level rises quickly to eliminate the shortages and bring the economy back to full employment. The economy remains in that situation until animal spirits fall and investment and aggregate demand decrease.

Figures 33.2 and 33.3 illustrate the Keynesian theory of the business cycle by using the aggregate supply–aggregate demand model. In Fig. 33.2, the economy is initially at full employment (point *a*) on the long-run aggregate supply curve (*LAS*), the aggregate demand curve (*AD*₀), and the short-run

FIGURE 33.2

A Keynesian Recession

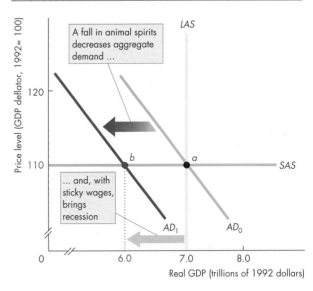

The economy is operating at point *a* at the intersection of the long-run aggregate supply curve (*LAS*), the short-run aggregate supply curve (*SAS*), and the aggregate demand curve (*AD*₀). A Keynesian recession begins when a fall in animal spirits causes investment demand to decrease. Aggregate demand decreases, and the *AD* curve shifts leftward to *AD*₁. With sticky money wages, real GDP decreases to $6 trillion and the price level does not change. The economy moves to point *b*.

aggregate supply curve (*SAS*). A fall in animal spirits decreases investment, and a multiplier process decreases aggregate demand. The aggregate demand curve shifts leftward to *AD*₁. With a fixed money wage rate, real GDP falls to $6 trillion and the economy moves to point *b*. Unemployment has increased and there is a surplus of labor. But the money wage rate does not fall, and the economy remains at point *b* until some force moves it away.

That force is shown in Fig. 33.3. Here, starting out at point *b*, a rise in animal spirits increases investment. The multiplier process kicks in, and aggregate demand increases. The *AD* curve shifts to *AD*₂, and real GDP begins to increase. An expansion is under way. As long as real GDP remains below potential GDP ($7 trillion in this example), the money wage rate and the price level remain constant. But real

FIGURE 33.3
A Keynesian Expansion

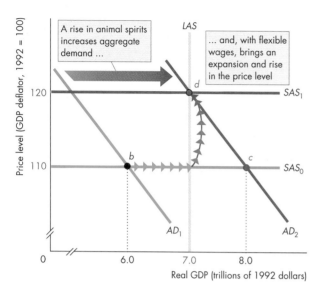

Starting at point b, a Keynesian expansion begins when a rise in animal spirits causes investment demand to increase. Aggregate demand increases, and the AD curve shifts rightward to AD_2. With sticky money wages, real GDP increases to $7 trillion. But the economy does not go all the way to point c. When full employment is reached, the money wage rate rises and the SAS curve shifts upward toward SAS_1. The price level rises as the economy heads toward point d.

GDP never increases to point c, the point of intersection of SAS_0 and AD_2. The reason is that once real GDP exceeds potential GDP and unemployment falls below the natural rate, the money wage rate begins to rise and the SAS curve starts to shift upward toward SAS_1. As the money wage rate rises, the price level also rises and real GDP growth slows. The economy follows a path like the one shown by the arrows connecting point b, the initial equilibrium, with point d, the final equilibrium.

The Keynesian business cycle is mainly like a tennis match. It is caused by outside forces—animal spirits—that change direction and set off a process that ends at an equilibrium that must be hit again by the outside forces to disturb it.

Monetarist Theory

The **monetarist theory of the business cycle** regards fluctuations in the money stock as the main source of economic fluctuations. This theory is distilled from the writings of Milton Friedman and several other economists. We'll explore the monetarist theory as we did the Keynesian theory, by looking first at its main impulse and second at the mechanism that creates a cycle in real GDP.

Monetarist Impulse   The *impulse* in the monetarist theory of the business cycle is the *growth rate of the quantity of money*. A speedup in money growth brings expansion, and a slowdown in money growth brings recession. The source of the change in the growth rate of the quantity of money is the monetary policy actions of the Fed.

Monetarist Cycle Mechanism   In the monetarist theory, once the Fed has changed the money growth rate, a cycle mechanism begins to operate that, like the Keynesian mechanism, first affects aggregate demand. When the money growth rate increases, the quantity of real money in the economy increases. Interest rates fall, and real money balances increase. The foreign exchange rate also falls—the dollar loses value on the foreign exchange market. These initial financial market effects begin to spill over into other markets. Investment demand and exports increase, and consumers spend more on durable goods. These initial changes in expenditure have a multiplier effect, just as investment has in the Keynesian theory. Through these mechanisms, a speedup in money growth shifts the aggregate demand curve rightward and brings an expansion. Similarly, a slowdown in money growth shifts the aggregate demand curve leftward and brings a recession.

The second element of the monetarist cycle mechanism is the response of aggregate supply to a change in aggregate demand. The short-run aggregate supply curve is upward-sloping. With an upward-sloping SAS curve, swings in aggregate demand translate into swings in both real GDP and the price level. But monetarists believe that real GDP deviations from full employment are temporary in both directions.

In monetarist theory, the money wage rate is only *temporarily sticky*. When aggregate demand decreases and unemployment rises, the money wage rate eventually begins to fall. As the money wage rate falls, so does the price level and after a period of adjustment, full employment is restored. When aggregate demand increases and unemployment falls below the natural rate, the money wage rate begins to rise. As the money wage rate rises, so does the price level. And through a period of adjustment, real GDP returns to potential GDP and the unemployment rate returns to the natural rate.

Figure 33.4 illustrates the monetarist theory. In part (a), the economy is initially at full employment (point *a*) on the long-run aggregate supply curve (*LAS*), the aggregate demand curve (*AD₀*), and the short-run aggregate supply curve (*SAS₀*). A slowdown in the money growth rate decreases aggregate

demand and the aggregate demand curve shifts leftward to *AD₁*. Real GDP decreases to $6.5 trillion, and the economy goes into recession (point *b*). Unemployment increases and there is a surplus of labor. The money wage rate begins to fall. As the money wage falls, the short-run aggregate supply curve starts to shift rightward toward *SAS₁*. The price level falls, and real GDP begins to expand as the economy moves to point *c*, its new full-employment equilibrium.

Figure 33.4(b) shows the effects of the opposite initial money shock—a speedup in money growth. Here, starting out at point *c*, a speedup in the money growth rate increases aggregate demand and shifts the *AD* curve to *AD₂*. Both real GDP and the price level

---

FIGURE 33.4
A Monetarist Business Cycle

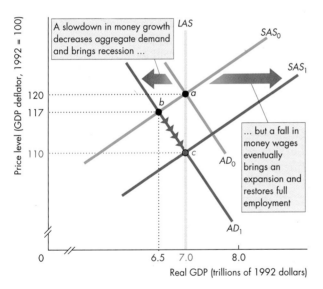

(a) Recession

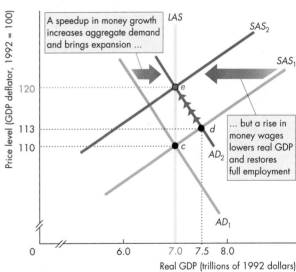

(b) Expansion

A monetarist recession begins when a slowdown in money growth decreases aggregate demand. The *AD* curve shifts leftward from *AD₀* to *AD₁* (in part a). With sticky money wages, real GDP decreases to $6.5 trillion and the price level falls to 117 as the economy moves from point *a* to point *b*. With a surplus of labor, the money wage rate falls and the *SAS* curve shifts rightward to *SAS₁*. The price level falls further and real GDP returns to potential GDP at point *c*.

Starting at point *c* (part b), a monetarist expansion begins when an increase in money growth increases aggregate demand and shifts the *AD* curve rightward to *AD₂*. With sticky money wages, real GDP rises to $7.5 trillion, the price level rises to 113, and the economy moves to point *d*. With a shortage of labor, the money wage rate rises and the *SAS* curve shifts toward *SAS₂*. The price level rises and real GDP decreases to potential GDP as the economy heads toward point *e*.

increase as the economy moves to point *d*, the point of intersection of SAS_1 and AD_2. With real GDP above potential GDP and unemployment below the natural rate, the money wage rate begins to rise and the *SAS* curve starts to shift leftward toward SAS_2. As the money wage rate rises, the price level also rises and real GDP decreases. The economy moves from point *d* to point *e*, its new full-employment equilibrium.

The monetarist business cycle is like a rocking horse. It needs an outside force to get it going, but once going, it rocks back and forth (but just once). It doesn't matter in which direction the force initially hits. If it is a money growth slowdown, the economy cycles with a recession followed by expansion. If it is a money growth speedup, the economy cycles with an expansion followed by recession.

Rational Expectations Theories

A **rational expectation** is a forecast that is based on all the available relevant information (see Chapter 32, p. 721). Rational expectations theories of the business cycle are theories based on the view that money wages are determined by a rational expectation of the price level. Two distinctly different rational expectations theories of the cycle have been proposed. A **new classical theory of the business cycle** regards *unanticipated* fluctuations in aggregate demand as the main source of economic fluctuations. This theory is based on the work of Robert E. Lucas, Jr., (see the part opener on pp. 465–470) and several other economists, including Thomas J. Sargent and Robert J. Barro. A different **new Keynesian theory of the business cycle** also regards *unanticipated* fluctuations in aggregate demand as the main source of economic fluctuations but it leaves room for *anticipated* demand fluctuations to play a role. We'll explore these theories as we did the Keynesian and monetarist theories, by looking first at the main impulse and second at the cycle mechanism.

Rational Expectations Impulse The *impulse* that distinguishes the rational expectations theories from the other aggregate demand theories of the business cycle is the *unanticipated change in aggregate demand*. A larger than anticipated increase in aggregate demand brings an expansion, and a smaller than anticipated increase in aggregate demand brings a recession. Any factor that influences aggregate demand—for exam-

ple, fiscal policy, monetary policy, or developments in the world economy that influence exports—whose change is not anticipated can bring a change in real GDP.

Rational Expectations Cycle Mechanisms To describe the rational expectations cycle mechanisms, we'll deal first with the new classical version. When aggregate demand decreases, if the money wage rate doesn't change, real GDP and the price level both decrease. The fall in the price level increases the *real* wage rate, and employment decreases and unemployment increases. In the new classical theory, these events occur only if the decrease in aggregate demand is not anticipated. If the decrease in aggregate demand *is* anticipated, the price level is expected to fall and both firms and workers will agree to a lower money wage rate. By doing so, they can prevent the real wage from rising and avoid a rise in the unemployment rate.

Similarly, if firms and workers anticipate an increase in aggregate demand, they expect the price level to rise and will agree to a higher money wage rate. By doing so, they can prevent the real wage rate from falling and avoid a fall in the unemployment rate below the natural rate.

Only fluctuations in aggregate demand that are unanticipated and not taken into account in wage agreements bring changes in real GDP. *Anticipated* changes in aggregate demand change the price level, but they leave real GDP and unemployment unchanged and do not create a business cycle.

New Keynesian economists, like new classical economists, believe that money wages are influenced by rational expectations of the price level. But new Keynesians emphasize the long-term nature of most wage contracts. They say that *today's* money wages are influenced by *yesterday's* rational expectations. These expectations, which were formed in the past, are based on old information that might now be known to be incorrect. After they have made a long-term wage agreement, both firms and workers might anticipate a change in aggregate demand, which they expect will change the price level. But because they are locked into their agreement, they are unable to change money wages. So money wages are sticky in the new Keynesian theory, and with sticky money wages, even an *anticipated* change in aggregate demand changes real GDP.

New classical economists believe that long-term contracts are renegotiated when conditions change to make them outdated. So they do not regard long-term contracts as an obstacle to money wage flexibility, provided that both parties to an agreement recognize the changed conditions. If both firms and workers expect the price level to change, they will change the agreed money wage rate to reflect that shared expectation. In this situation, anticipated changes in aggregate demand change the money wage rate and the price level and leave real GDP unchanged.

The distinctive feature of both versions of the rational expectations theory of the business cycle is the role of unanticipated changes in aggregate demand. Figure 33.5 illustrates the effect of unanticipated changes on real GDP and the price level.

Potential GDP is $7 trillion, and the long-run aggregate supply curve is *LAS*. Aggregate demand is expected to be *EAD*. Given potential GDP and *EAD*, the money wage rate is set at the level that is expected to bring full employment. At this money wage rate, the short-run aggregate supply curve is *SAS*. Imagine that initially aggregate demand equals expected aggregate demand, so there is full employment. Real GDP is $7 trillion, and the price level is 110. Then, unexpectedly, aggregate demand turns out to be less than expected and the aggregate demand curve shifts leftward to AD_0 (in Fig. 33.5a). Many different aggregate demand shocks, such as a slowdown in the money growth rate or a collapse of exports, could have caused this shift. A recession

---

FIGURE 33.5

A Rational Expectations Business Cycle

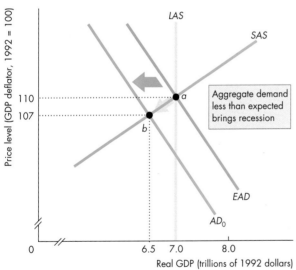

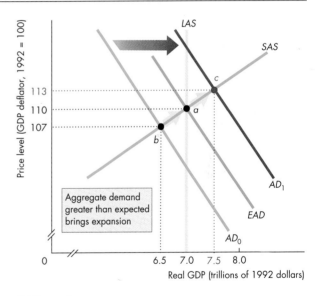

(a) Recession

(b) Expansion

The economy is expected to be at point *a* at the intersection of the long-run aggregate supply curve, *LAS*; the short-run aggregate supply curve, *SAS*; and the *expected* aggregate demand curve, *EAD*. A rational expectations recession begins when an unanticipated fall in aggregate demand shifts the *AD* curve leftward to AD_0. With money wage rates based on the expectation that aggregate demand will be *EAD*, real GDP falls to $6.5 trillion and the price level falls to 107 as the economy moves to point *b*. As long as aggregate demand is *expected* to

be *EAD*, there is no change in the money wage rate.

A rational expectations expansion begins when an unanticipated rise in aggregate demand shifts the *AD* curve rightward from AD_0 to AD_1. With money wage rates based on the expectation that aggregate demand will be *EAD*, real GDP increases to $7.5 trillion and the price level rises to 113 as the economy moves to point *c*. Again, as long as aggregate demand is *expected* to be *EAD*, there is no change in the money wage rate.

begins. Real GDP falls to $6.5 trillion, and the price level falls to 107. The economy moves to point *b*. Unemployment increases, and there is a surplus of labor. But aggregate demand is expected to be at *EAD,* so the money wage rate doesn't change and the short-run aggregate supply curve remains at *SAS.*

The recession ends when aggregate demand increases to its expected level. And a larger increase that takes aggregate demand to a level that exceeds *EAD* brings an expansion. In Fig. 33.5(b), the aggregate demand curve shifts rightward to *AD*₁. Such an increase in aggregate demand might be caused by a speedup in the money growth rate or an export boom. Real GDP now increases to $7.5 trillion, and the price level rises to 113. The economy moves to point *c*. Unemployment is now below the natural rate. But aggregate demand is expected to be at *EAD,* so the money wage rate doesn't change and the short-run aggregate supply curve remains at *SAS.*

Fluctuations in aggregate demand between *AD*₀ and *AD*₁ around expected aggregate demand *EAD* bring fluctuations in real GDP and the price level between points *b* and *c*.

The two versions of the rational expectations theory differ in their predictions about the effects of a change in expected aggregate demand. The new classical theory predicts that as soon as expected aggregate demand changes, the money wage rate also changes, so the *SAS* curve shifts. The new Keynesian theory predicts that the money wage rate changes only gradually when new contracts are made, so the *SAS* curve moves only slowly. This difference between the two theories is crucial for policy. According to the new classical theory, anticipated policy actions change the price level only and have no effect on real GDP and unemployment. The reason is that when policy is expected to change, the money wage rate changes, so the *SAS* curve shifts and offsets the effects of the policy action on real GDP. In contrast, in the new Keynesian theory, because the money wage rate changes only when new contracts are made, even anticipated policy actions change real GDP and can be used in an attempt to stabilize the cycle.

Like the monetarist business cycle, these rational expectations cycles are similar to rocking horses. They need an outside force to get them going, but once going, the economy rocks around its full employment point. The new classical horse rocks faster and comes to rest more quickly than the new Keynesian horse.

AS-AD General Theory

All the theories of the business cycle that we've considered can be viewed as particular cases of the more general *AS-AD* theory. In this more general theory, the impulses of both the Keynesian and monetarist theories can change aggregate demand. A multiplier effect makes aggregate demand change by more than any initial change in one of its components. The money wage rate can be viewed as responding to changes in the expected price level. Even if the money wage is flexible, it will change only to the extent that price level expectations change. As a result, the money wage rate will adjust gradually.

Although in all three types of business cycle theory that we've considered, the cycle is caused by fluctuations in aggregate demand, the possibility that an occasional aggregate supply shock might occur is not ruled out. A recession could occur because aggregate supply falls. For example, a widespread drought that cuts agricultural production could cause a recession in an economy that has a large agricultural sector. But these aggregate demand theories of the cycle regard aggregate supply shocks as rare rather than normal events. Aggregate demand fluctuations are the normal ongoing sources of fluctuations.

REVIEW

- Keynesian theory says that the business cycle is caused by volatile expectations about future sales and profits—*animal spirits*—a multiplier effect, and sticky money wages.
- Monetarist theory says that the business cycle is caused by the Fed speeding up and slowing the growth rate of money, which changes spending plans.
- New classical and new Keynesian theories (rational expectations theories) say that the business cycle is caused by unanticipated fluctuations in aggregate demand.
- In the new classical theory, the money wage rate responds to price level expectations, and in the new Keynesian theory, the money wage rate is set by long-term contracts.

A new theory of the business cycle challenges the mainstream and traditional aggregate demand theories that you've just studied. It is called the real business cycle theory. Let's look at this new cycle theory.

Real Business Cycle Theory

THE NEWEST THEORY OF THE BUSINESS CYCLE, known as **real business cycle theory** (or RBC theory), regards random fluctuations in productivity as the main source of economic fluctuations. These productivity fluctuations are assumed to result mainly from fluctuations in the pace of technological change, but they might also have other sources such as international disturbances, climate fluctuations, or natural disasters. The origins of real business cycle theory can be traced to the rational expectations revolution set off by Robert E. Lucas, Jr., but the first demonstration of the power of this theory was given by Edward Prescott and Finn Kydland and by John Long and Charles Plosser. Today, real business cycle theory is part of a broad research agenda called *dynamic general equilibrium analysis*, and hundreds of young macroeconomists do research on this topic.

Like our study of the aggregate demand theories, we'll explore RBC theory by looking first at its impulse and second at the mechanism that converts that impulse into a cycle in real GDP.

The RBC Impulse

The *impulse* in RBC theory is the *growth rate of productivity* that results from *technological change*. RBC theorists believe this impulse to be generated mainly by the process of research and development that leads to the creation and use of new technologies. Sometimes, technological progress is rapid and productivity grows quickly; at other times, progress is slow and productivity grows moderately. Occasionally, technological change is so far-reaching that it makes a large amount of existing capital, especially human capital, obsolete. It also, initially, destroys jobs and shuts down businesses. These initial effects of far-reaching technological change *decrease* productivity and can trigger a recession. Ultimately, such technological change creates both jobs and businesses and brings massive gains in productivity. Other shocks, such as the world oil embargo of the mid-1970s, can temporarily decrease productivity.

To isolate the RBC theory impulse—the growth rate of productivity that results from technological change—economists use the tool of growth accounting, which is explained in Chapter 27, on pp. 593–595.

FIGURE 33.6
The Real Business Cycle Impulse

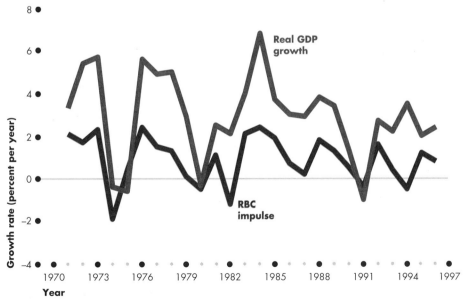

The real business cycle is caused by changes in technology that bring fluctuations in the growth rate of productivity. The fluctuations in productivity growth shown here are calculated by using growth accounting (the one third rule) to remove the contribution of capital accumulation to productivity growth. Productivity fluctuations are correlated with real GDP fluctuations. Economists are not sure what the productivity variable actually measures or what causes it to fluctuate.

Source: *Economic Report of the President,* 1997, and the author's calculations.

Figure 33.6 shows the RBC impulse for the United States from 1970 to 1996. The figure also shows that fluctuations in productivity growth are correlated with real GDP fluctuations. This RBC productivity variable is a catchall, and economists are not sure what it actually measures or what causes it to fluctuate.

The RBC Mechanism

According to RBC theory, two immediate effects follow from a change in productivity that get an expansion or a contraction going:

1. Investment demand changes.
2. The demand for labor changes.

We'll study these effects and their consequences during a recession. In an expansion, they work in the direction opposite to what is described here.

A wave of technological changes makes some existing capital obsolete and temporarily lowers productivity. Firms expect the future profits to fall and see their labor productivity falling. With lower profit expectations, they cut back their purchases of new capital, and with lower labor productivity, they plan to lay off some workers. So the initial effect of a temporary fall in productivity is a decrease in investment demand and a decrease in the demand for labor.

Figure 33.7 illustrates these two initial effects of a decrease in productivity. Part (a) shows investment demand, *ID*, and saving supply, *SS* (both of which are explained in Chapter 26, pp. 569–570 and 572–573). Initially, investment demand is ID_0 and the equilibrium investment and saving arc $1 trillion at a real interest rate of 6 percent a year. A decrease in productivity decreases investment demand and the *ID* curve shifts leftward to ID_1. The real interest rate falls to 4 percent, and investment and saving decrease to $0.7 trillion.

Part (b) shows the demand for labor, *LD*, and the supply of labor, *LS* (which are explained in Chapter 25, p. 554). Initially, the demand for labor is LD_0, and equilibrium employment is 200 billion hours a year at a real wage rate of $15 an hour. The decrease in productivity decreases the demand for labor, and the *LD* curve shifts leftward to LD_1.

Before we can determine the new level of employment and real wage rate, we need to take a ripple effect into account—the key ripple effect in RBC theory.

The Key Decision: When to Work? According to RBC theory, people decide *when* to work by doing a cost-benefit calculation. They compare the return from working in the current period with the *expected* return from working in a later period. You make such a comparison every day in school. Suppose your goal in this course is to get an A. To achieve this goal, you work pretty hard most of the time. But during the few days before the midterm and final exams, you work especially hard. Why? Because you believe that the return from studying close to the exam is greater than the return from studying when the exam is a long time away. So during the term, you take time off for the movies and other leisure pursuits, but at exam time, you work every evening and weekend.

Real business cycle theory says that workers behave like you. They work fewer hours, sometimes zero hours, when the real wage rate is temporarily low, and they work more hours when the real wage rate is temporarily high. But to properly compare the current wage rate with the expected future wage rate, workers must use the real interest rate. If the real interest rate is 6 percent a year, a real wage of $1 an hour earned this week will become $1.06 a year from now. If the real wage rate is expected to be $1.05 an hour next year, today's real wage of $1 looks good. By working longer hours now and shorter hours a year from now, a person can get a 1 percent higher real wage rate. But suppose the real interest rate is 4 percent a year. In this case, $1 earned now is worth $1.04 next year. Working fewer hours now and more next year is the way to get a 1 percent higher real wage rate.

So the when-to-work decision depends on the real interest rate. The lower the real interest rate, other things remaining the same, the smaller is the supply of labor. Many economists believe this *intertemporal substitution* effect to be of negligible size. RBC theorists believe that the effect is large, and it is the key element in the RBC mechanism.

You've seen in Fig. 33.7(a) that the decrease in investment demand lowers the real interest rate. This fall in the real interest rate lowers the return to current work and decreases the supply of labor. In Fig. 33.7(b), the labor supply curve shifts leftward to LS_1. The effect of a productivity shock on the demand for labor is larger than the effect of the fall in the real interest rate on the supply of labor. That is, the *LD* curve shifts farther leftward than does the *LS* curve. As a result, the real wage rate falls to $14.50 an hour and the level of employment falls to 195 billion hours. A recession has begun and is intensifying.

FIGURE 33.7

Capital and Labor Markets in a Real Business Cycle

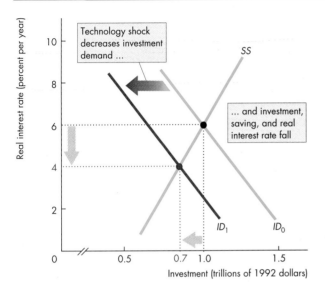

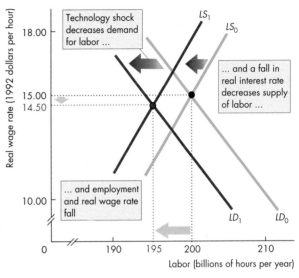

(a) Investment, saving, and interest rate

(b) Labor and wage rate

Saving supply is *SS* (part a), and initially, investment demand is *ID₀*. The real interest rate is 6 percent, and saving and investment are $1 trillion. In the labor market (part b), the demand for labor is *LD₀* and the supply of labor is *LS₀*. The real wage rate is $15 an hour, and employment is 200 billion hours. A technological change temporarily decreases productivity, and both investment demand and the demand for labor decrease.

The two demand curves shift leftward to *ID₁* and *LD₁*. In part (a), the real interest rate falls to 4 percent a year and investment and saving decrease. In part (b), the fall in the real interest rate decreases the supply of labor (the when-to-work decision) and the supply curve shifts leftward to *LS₁*. Employment falls to 195 billion hours, and the real wage rate falls to $14.50 an hour. A recession is under way.

Real GDP and the Price Level The next part of the RBC story traces the consequences of the changes you've just seen for real GDP and the price level. With a decrease in employment, aggregate supply decreases, and with a decrease in investment demand, aggregate demand decreases. Figure 33.8 illustrates these effects, using the *AS-AD* framework. Initially, the long-run aggregate supply curve is *LAS₀*, and the aggregate demand curve is *AD₀*. The price level is 110, and real GDP is $7 trillion. There is no short-run aggregate supply curve in this figure because in RBC theory, the *SAS* curve has no meaning. The labor market moves relentlessly toward its equilibrium, and the money wage rate adjusts freely (either upward or downward) to ensure that the real wage rate keeps the quantity of labor demanded equal to the quantity supplied. In RBC theory, unemploy-

ment is always at the natural rate, and the natural rate fluctuates over the business cycle because the amount of job search fluctuates.

The decrease in employment decreases total production and aggregate supply decreases. The *LAS* curve shifts leftward to *LAS₁*. The decrease in investment demand decreases aggregate demand, and the *AD* curve shifts leftward to *AD₁*. The price level falls to 107, and real GDP decreases to $6.8 trillion. The economy has gone through a recession.

What Happened to Money? The name *real* business cycle theory is no accident. It reflects the central prediction of the theory. Real things, not nominal or monetary things, cause the business cycle. If the quantity of money changes, aggregate demand changes. But if there is no real change—with no

FIGURE 33.8

AS-AD in a Real Business Cycle

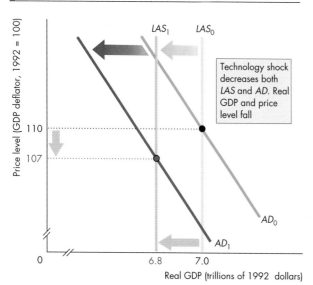

Initially, the long-run aggregate supply curve is LAS_0, and the aggregate demand curve is AD_0. Real GDP is $7 trillion (which equals potential GDP), and the price level is 110. There is no SAS curve in the real business cycle theory because the money wage rate is flexible. The technological change described in Fig. 33.7 temporarily decreases potential GDP, and the LAS curve shifts leftward to LAS_1. The fall in investment demand decreases aggregate demand, and the AD curve shifts leftward to AD_1. Real GDP decreases to $6.8 trillion, and the price level falls to 107. The economy has gone into recession.

change in the use of resources and no change in potential GDP—the change in money changes only the price level. In real business cycle theory, this outcome occurs because the aggregate supply curve is the LAS curve, which pins real GDP down at potential GD. So when AD changes, only the price level changes.

Cycles and Growth The shock that drives the business cycle of RBC theory is the same as the force that generates economic growth: technological change. On the average, as technology advances, productivity grows. But it grows at an uneven pace. You saw this fact when you studied growth accounting in Chapter

27. There, we focused on slow-changing trends in productivity growth. Real business cycle theory uses the same idea but says that there are frequent shocks to productivity that are mostly positive but that are occasionally negative.

Criticisms of Real Business Cycle Theory

RBC theory is controversial, and when economists discuss it, they often generate more heat than light. Its detractors claim that its basic assumptions are just too incredible. Money wages *are* sticky, they claim, so to assume otherwise is at odds with a clear fact. Intertemporal substitution is too weak, they say, to account for large fluctuations in labor supply and employment with small real wage changes.

But what really kills the RBC story, say most economists, is an implausible impulse. Technology shocks are not capable of creating the swings in productivity that growth accounting reveals. These swings in productivity are caused by something, they concede, but they are as likely to be caused by *changes in aggregate demand* as by technology. If the fluctuations in productivity are caused by aggregate demand fluctuations, then the traditional demand theories are needed to explain them. Fluctuations in productivity do not cause the cycle but are caused by it!

Building on this theme, the critics point out that the so-called productivity fluctuations that growth accounting measures are correlated with changes in the growth rate of money and other indicators of changes in aggregate demand.

Defense of Real Business Cycle Theory

The defenders of RBC theory claim that the theory works. It explains the macroeconomic facts about the business cycle and is consistent with the facts about economic growth. In effect, a single theory explains *both growth and cycles*. The growth accounting exercise that explains slowly changing trends also explains the more frequent business cycle swings. Its defenders also claim that RBC theory is consistent with a wide range of *micro*economic evidence about labor supply decisions, labor demand and investment demand decisions, and information on the distribution of income between labor and capital.

RBC theorists acknowledge that money and the business cycle are correlated. That is, rapid money growth and expansion go together, and slow money growth and recession go together. But, they argue, causation does not run from money to real GDP as the traditional aggregate demand theories state. Instead, they view causation as running from real GDP to money—so-called reverse causation. In a recession, the initial fall in investment demand that lowers the interest rate decreases the demand for bank loans and lowers the profitability of banking. So banks increase their reserves and decrease their loans. The quantity of bank deposits and hence the quantity of money decrease. This reverse causation is responsible for the correlation between money growth and real GDP according to real business cycle theory.

Its defenders also argue that the RBC view is significant because it at least raises the possibility that the business cycle is efficient. The business cycle does not signal an economy that is misbehaving; it is business as usual. If this view is correct, it means that policy designed to smooth the cycle is misguided. Only by taking out the peaks can the troughs be smoothed out. But peaks are bursts of investment to take advantage of new technologies in a timely way. So smoothing the cycle means delaying the benefits of new technologies.

R E V I E W

- Real business cycle (RBC) theory says that economic fluctuations are caused by technological change that makes productivity growth fluctuate.
- A fall in productivity decreases both investment demand and the demand for labor and lowers the real interest rate. The lower real interest rate decreases the supply of labor and employment, and the real wage rate falls.
- A fall in productivity decreases both long-run aggregate supply and aggregate demand and decreases both real GDP and the price level.

You've now reviewed the main theories of the business cycle. Your next task is to examine some actual business cycles. In pursuing this task, we will focus on the recession phase of the cycle. We'll do this mainly because it is the recessions that cause the most trouble. We begin by looking at two recent recessions.

Two Recent Recessions

IN THE THEORIES OF THE BUSINESS CYCLE THAT you've studied, recessions can be triggered by a variety of forces, some on the aggregate demand side and some on the aggregate supply side. Let's identify the shocks that triggered two recent recessions: the OPEC recession of 1974–1975 and the 1990–1991 recession.

The OPEC Recession

During the early 1970s, real GDP was on trend and growing at a rate similar to its long-run average growth rate. Unemployment ranged between 5 and 6 percent, and inflation ranged between 3 and 6 percent a year. More and more people were enjoying and sharing in the benefits of sustained economic expansion. But undercurrents were at work that would bring extraordinary change during the mid-1970s.

Toward the end of 1973, the U.S. and world economies were dealt a devastating blow. The Organization of Petroleum Exporting Countries (OPEC), which controlled 68 percent of world oil production (outside the Communist countries), imposed an oil embargo and increased the price of a barrel of oil from $2.60 to $11.65—a 348 percent increase. The price hike had dramatic macroeconomic effects. For the next two years, the U.S. economy went into a severe recession.

Figure 33.9 shows the severity of the OPEC recession and illustrates the forces that caused the recession by using the mainstream AS-AD framework. Before the oil price hike, the aggregate demand and short-run aggregate supply curves were AD_{73} and SAS_{73}, respectively. Real GDP was $3.9 trillion, and the GDP deflator was 35.4. Through the subsequent two years, aggregate demand continued to increase and the aggregate demand curve shifted rightward to AD_{75}. When OPEC increased the price of crude oil, the prices of other fuels as well as the prices of many other raw materials also increased. The index of all commodity prices excluding fuel increased by 63 percent in 1973 and 24 percent in 1974. Labor costs also started to increase more quickly. As a result of these resource price increases, the short-run aggregate supply curve shifted leftward to SAS_{75}. This shift in the short-run aggregate supply curve, triggered by the oil price increase, was the single most significant event producing the OPEC recession. Real GDP fell to $3.87 trillion, and the GDP deflator increased to

FIGURE 33.9

The OPEC Recession

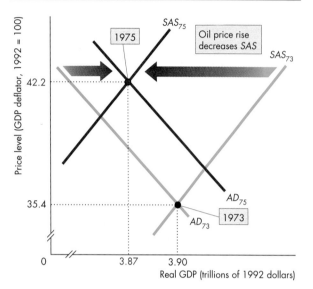

In 1973, the economy was on its aggregate demand curve, AD_{73}, and its short-run aggregate supply curve, SAS_{73}, with real GDP at $3.9 trillion and a GDP deflator of 35.4. Between 1973 and 1975, aggregate demand continued to increase at a moderate pace and the aggregate demand curve shifted to AD_{75}. In 1974, OPEC increased the price of oil by 348 percent. Other input prices and wages increased, and the short-run aggregate supply curve shifted to SAS_{75}. The large shift of the SAS curve combined with the moderate shift of the AD curve led to stagflation—a decrease in real GDP and rising inflation.

42.2—an almost 20 percent increase in the price level over the two years of recession. Thus during the OPEC recession, real GDP decreased and the inflation rate increased. This combination of events gave rise to a new word, *stagflation*, a combination of falling real GDP and rising inflation.

The 1990–1991 Recession

At the beginning of 1990, the economy was at full employment. The unemployment rate was just above 5 percent, and inflation was steady at 4 percent a year. But the events of 1990 disturbed this situation and brought an end to the longest peacetime expansion in U.S. history.

The dominant events of 1990 were the Persian Gulf crisis and the ensuing Gulf War triggered by Saddam Hussein's invasion of Kuwait. The Gulf crisis brought shocks to both aggregate demand and aggregate supply. The aggregate demand shocks went in both directions. First, fiscal policy became less restrained as government purchases increased to cope with the military consequences of the crisis. The Gulf situation also increased uncertainty about expected sales and profits, which brought a fall in investment. With a fall in investment, aggregate demand decreased. Although fiscal policy was working in the direction opposite to this change in investment, it was not strong enough to prevent aggregate demand from decreasing.

FIGURE 33.10

The 1990–1991 Recession

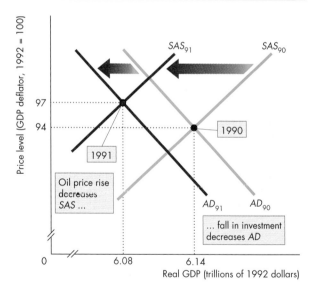

In 1990, the economy was on its aggregate demand curve, AD_{90}, and its short-run aggregate supply curve, SAS_{90}, with real GDP at $6.14 trillion and a GDP deflator of 94. A large increase in oil prices decreased aggregate supply and shifted the short-run aggregate supply curve to SAS_{91}. Uncertainty surrounding the world economy lowered profit expectations, leading to a fall in investment and a decrease in aggregate demand. The aggregate demand curve shifted to AD_{91}. The combination of a decrease in both aggregate supply and aggregate demand puts the economy into recession.

On the supply side, the Gulf crisis put the world energy markets into turmoil yet again. Between April 1990 and October 1990, the price of crude oil more than doubled. This oil price increase operated in a way similar to that of the 1970s. It decreased short-run aggregate supply.

Figure 33.10 shows how the combined effects of these forces started the 1990–1991 recession. In mid-1990, the economy was on aggregate demand curve AD_{90} and short-run aggregate supply curve SAS_{90} with real GDP at $6.14 trillion and the GDP deflator at 94. By mid-1991, the short-run aggregate supply curve had shifted to SAS_{91}, and investment uncertainty had shifted the aggregate demand curve to AD_{91}. Real GDP had decreased to $6.08 trillion. The GDP deflator increased to 97, which slowed the inflation rate slightly to 3.2 percent over the year.

You've seen how aggregate demand and aggregate supply changed in two recent recessions. What happened in the labor market during these recessions?

The Labor Market in the OPEC Recession

During the OPEC recession, the real wage rate fell from $14.64 an hour in 1973 to $14.49 an hour in 1975.[1] Aggregate hours decreased from 157 billion in 1973 to 155 billion in 1975. What caused this decrease in both employment and the real wage rate? We've seen that there are two views about the labor market. The traditional view is that the money wage rate is sticky and changes only gradually. The real business cycle view is that the money wage rate is flexible and adjusts to keep the labor market in equilibrium. Let's see how these two views explain the changes in the real wage rate and employment during the OPEC recession.

Sticky Wage Theory Figure 33.11 illustrates the labor market in 1973 and 1975 according to the sticky wage view. In 1973, the demand for labor was LD_{73} and the supply of labor was LS_{73}. The real wage rate, $14.64 an hour, and the level of employment, 157 billion hours, are determined at the intersection of these two curves. The unemployment rate in 1973

---

[1] The measure of real wage rates used here is aggregate wages, salaries, and benefits divided by aggregate hours—see Fig. 25.5, p. 548.

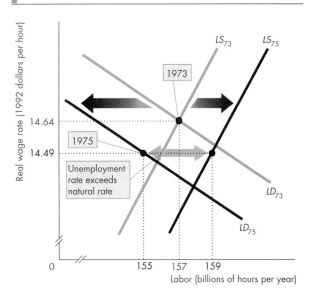

FIGURE 33.11

The Sticky Wage View

In 1973, the demand for labor was LD_{73} and the supply of labor was LS_{73}. If the quantity of labor demanded equaled the quantity supplied in 1973, the real wage rate of $14.64 an hour and employment of 157 billion hours are at the point of intersection of LD_{73} and LS_{73}. The OPEC oil price hike lowered the productivity of labor, so the demand for labor decreased and the demand for labor curve shifted leftward to LD_{75}. An increase in the population increased the supply of labor and shifted the supply curve rightward to LS_{75}. The real wage rate fell, but not by enough to bring about equality between the quantities of labor supplied and demanded. The quantity demanded was 155 billion hours, but the quantity supplied was 159 billion hours. Unemployment increased.

was 4.9 percent, which we will assume was equal to the natural rate, so there was full employment. (This is an assumption, not a fact.)

The OPEC oil price hike lowered labor productivity, which in turn decreased the demand for labor. The labor demand curve shifted leftward to LD_{75}. There were four main reasons for this decrease in labor productivity. First, OPEC restricted the supply of crude oil, which meant that some firms experienced temporary shortages of fuel and so had to slow down production. Second, faced with higher energy prices, firms economized on the use of energy. For example, transportation companies lowered truck speeds and airlines pruned schedules to get better payloads. Again, production per hour of labor fell. Third, labor resources that were previously used in production were redirected to designing and building more fuel-efficient equipment. For example, automakers designed smaller, more fuel-efficient cars. Yet again, production per work-hour fell. Fourth, gas-guzzling planes and road vehicles and energy-hungry furnaces and industrial equipment were scrapped at a more rapid than normal pace, a process that decreased the capital stock and so further cut labor productivity.

In the sticky wage view, the real wage rate is determined in the short run by the gradually changing money wage rate and the price level. Between 1973 and 1975, the money wage rate increased by 18 percent. But the price level increased by 19 percent, so the real wage rate fell by 1 percent, to $14.49. At this real wage rate and with the new demand for labor curve, employment decreased to 155 billion hours in 1975.

Through 1974 and 1975, the population increased, and as a result, the supply of labor increased. If there were no other influences on the supply of labor, the supply curve shifted rightward from LS_{73} to LS_{75}. At the real wage rate of $14.49, the quantity of labor supplied was 159 billion hours. Unemployment increased above the natural rate. The unemployment rate increased from 4.9 percent in 1973 to 8.5 percent in 1975.

What were the forces preventing the real wage rate from falling in 1975? Given that both the money wage rate and the price level had increased by almost 20 percent, it seems hard to believe that the money wage was sticky. The flexible wage theory has an answer.

Flexible Wage Theory The flexible wage theory is that the money wage rate adjusts to maintain equality between the quantity of labor demanded and the quantity supplied. Fluctuations in unemployment are fluctuations in the natural rate of unemployment. Let's examine the OPEC recession again and see how we can interpret it in terms of this alternative theory.

Figure 33.12 illustrates the flexible wage view of the OPEC recession. The 1973 demand and supply curves, LD_{73} and LS_{73}, are identical to those in Fig. 33.11, and they determine the 1973 (assumed) full-employment equilibrium. Following the oil price hike, the demand for labor fell and the demand curve shifted leftward to LD_{75}, just as it did in Fig. 33.11.

So far, the flexible wage and sticky wage stories have been the same. The difference arises on the supply side of the labor market. An increase in the population increased the supply of labor. But a fall in the real interest rate—the when-to-work decision—decreased the supply of labor. The real interest rate, which had been around 1 percent a year in 1973, fell to almost *minus* 1 percent a year in 1975. With a low (negative) real interest rate, 1975 was for many people a good year in which to borrow and look for a better job rather than work. This factor was so strong, according to the flexible wage view, that it more than counteracted the increase in the population. So the supply of labor decreased. The labor supply curve shifted leftward to LS_{75} in Fig. 33.12.

FIGURE 33.12

The Flexible Wage View

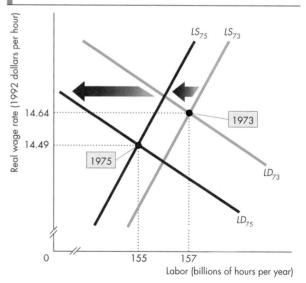

During the OPEC recession, the real wage rate fell from $14.64 an hour to $14.49 an hour and employment fell from 157 billion hours to 155 billion hours. These movements of the real wage rate and employment are consistent with the flexible wage theory. A fall in the real interest rate made 1975 a bad year for working and a good year for searching for a better job, so the supply of labor decreased. The supply of labor curve shifted leftward to LS_{75}, and the 1975 equilibrium is at the intersection of LD_{75} and LS_{75}. According to the flexible wage theory, the increase in unemployment that occurred between 1973 and 1975 is interpreted as a temporary increase in the natural rate of unemployment.

The new supply of labor curve intersected the new demand for labor curve at a real wage rate of $14.49 an hour and an employment level of 155 billion hours. You can't see it in Fig. 33.12, but the natural rate of unemployment increased through 1975, according to the flexible wage view. In deciding not to work, more people searched for new and better jobs, so job search and unemployment increased. People who had previously worked in energy-using jobs looked for higher-paid energy-saving jobs.

We've interpreted the labor market in the OPEC recession in two ways. Can we also interpret the 1990–1991 recession in these same two ways?

The Labor Market in the 1990–1991 Recession

During the 1990–1991 recession, the real wage rate *increased* from $17.32 an hour in 1990 to $17.45 an hour in 1991, and aggregate hours decreased from 203 billion in 1990 to 201 billion in 1992. Why did the real wage rate increase when hours decreased and the economy was in recession?

Sticky Wage Theory A sticky wage story can be told about money wages in the 1990–1991 recession that is based on the rational expectations theories of the business cycle. According to this view, the money wage rate in 1991 was determined by decisions made in 1990 based on the price level then expected for 1991. Prices had increased during 1990 by about 4.5 percent a year. Assuming that this rate would continue through 1991 and allowing for a small expected rise in labor productivity, employers and workers agreed to increase the money wage rate by almost 5 percent.

In reality, the inflation rate slowed in 1991 to less than 4 percent. As a result, the real wage rate increased by 1 percent. With an increase in the real wage rate, the quantity of labor demanded decreased and employment fell.

Can the flexible wage theory interpret the 1990–1991 change in employment and the real wage rate?

Flexible Wage Theory The flexible wage theory has a difficult time accounting for the events we've just described. For the real wage rate to rise and employment to fall, the supply of labor must have decreased and by more than the decrease in the demand for labor. But the influences on the supply

of labor worked in the wrong direction in 1991. The working-age population increased that year by almost 1 percent. More significant, though, the real interest rate *increased*. So the when-to-work decision and the population change both increased the supply of labor.

The failure of a simple flexible wage theory to explain the rise in the real wage rate and the fall in employment does not mean that the entire approach is invalid. Many economists believe that a more detailed microeconomic story about labor reallocation across sectors and changes in wage rates for individual jobs can explain even the 1990–1991 recession in terms of flexible wages.

Determining which of the two wage theories is correct is not just an academic curiosity. It is crucial for the design of antirecessionary policy. If the flexible wage theory is correct, there is only one aggregate supply curve—the vertical long-run aggregate supply curve. This fact means that any attempt to bring the economy out of recession by increasing aggregate demand—for example, by lowering interest rates and increasing the money supply or by fiscal policy measures—is doomed to failure and can result only in a higher price level (more inflation). Conversely, if the sticky wage theory is correct, then the short-run aggregate supply curve slopes upward. An increase in aggregate demand, although increasing the price level somewhat, increases real GDP and will bring the economy out of a recession.

R E V I E W

■ The OPEC recession was triggered by a supply shock—an increase in the price of oil.

■ The 1990–1991 recession was triggered by a supply shock—the Gulf crisis, which increased the price of oil—and a demand shock—increased uncertainty, which lowered investment demand.

■ The labor market can be interpreted by using either the sticky wage theory or the flexible wage theory during the OPEC recession but by using only the sticky wage theory during the 1990–1991 recession.

You've now seen how business cycle theory can be used to interpret two recent recessions. But can we use business cycle theory to explain the greatest of recessions—the Great Depression? Let's find out.

The Great Depression

THE LATE 1920S WERE YEARS OF ECONOMIC
boom. New houses and apartments were built on an
unprecedented scale, new firms were created, and the
capital stock of the nation expanded. At the beginning of 1929, U.S. real GDP exceeded potential
GDP and the unemployment rate was a low 3.2 percent. But as that eventful year unfolded, increasing
signs of economic weakness began to appear. The
most dramatic events occurred in October when the
stock market collapsed, losing more than one third of
its value in two weeks. The four years that followed
were years of monstrous economic depression.

Figure 33.13 shows the dimensions of the Great
Depression. On the eve of the Great Depression in
1929, the economy was on aggregate demand curve
AD_{29} and short-run aggregate supply curve SAS_{29}.
Real GDP was $1,028 billion (1992 dollars), and the
GDP deflator was 15.

In 1930, there was a widespread expectation that
the price level would fall, and the money wage rate fell.
With a lower money wage rate, the short-run aggregate supply curve shifted from SAS_{29} to SAS_{30}. But
increased pessimism and uncertainty decreased investment and the demand for consumer durables, and
aggregate demand decreased to AD_{30}. In 1930, real
GDP decreased to $936 billion (a 9 percent decrease)
and the price level fell to 14.6 (a 3 percent fall).

In a normal recession, the economy might have
remained below full employment for a year or so and
then started to expand. But the recession of 1930 was
not a normal one. In 1930 and the next two years,
the economy was further bombarded with huge negative demand shocks (the sources of which we'll look
at in a moment). The aggregate demand curve shifted
leftward all the way to AD_{33}. With a depressed economy, the price level was expected to fall and wages
fell in line with those expectations. The money wage
fell from 55¢ an hour in 1930 to 44¢ an hour by
1933. As a result of lower wages, the aggregate supply
curve shifted from SAS_{30} to SAS_{33}. But the size of the
shift of the short-run aggregate supply curve was
much less than the decrease in aggregate demand. As
a result, the aggregate demand curve and the short-
run aggregate supply curve intersected in 1933 at a
real GDP of $734 billion (a decrease of 29 percent
from 1929) and a GDP deflator of 11.4 (a decrease
of 24 percent from 1929).

FIGURE 33.13

The Great Depression

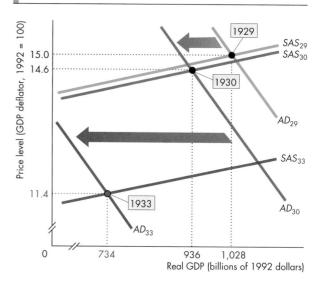

In 1929, real GDP was $1,028 billion and the GDP deflator
was 15—at the intersection of AD_{29} and SAS_{29}. Increased pessimism and uncertainty resulted in a decrease in investment
and aggregate demand decreased to AD_{30}. The money wage
rate decreased, so the short-run aggregate supply curve
shifted to SAS_{30}. Real GDP and the price level fell. In the next
three years, decreases in the money supply and investment
decreased aggregate demand, shifting the aggregate demand
curve to AD_{33}. Again, to some degree, the decrease in aggregate demand was anticipated, so wages fell and the short-run
aggregate supply curve shifted to SAS_{33}. By 1933, real GDP had
fallen to $734 billion (71 percent of its 1929 level) and the
GDP deflator had fallen to 11.4 (76 percent of its 1929 level).

Although the Great Depression brought enormous hardship, the distribution of that hardship was
uneven. Twenty-five percent of the work force had no
jobs at all. Also at that time, there were virtually no
organized social security and unemployment programs in place. So for many families there was virtually no income. But the pocketbooks of those who
kept their jobs barely noticed the Great Depression.
It is true that wages fell from 57¢ an hour in 1929 to
44¢ an hour in 1933. But at the same time, the price
level fell by a larger percentage, so real wages actually
increased. Thus people who had jobs became better
off during the Great Depression.

You can begin to appreciate the magnitude of the Great Depression if you compare it with the two recessions that we studied earlier in this chapter. Between 1973 and 1975, real GDP fell by 1.8 percent. From mid-1990 to mid-1991, it fell by 1.6 percent. A hypothetical 1999 Great Depression would lower real GDP by 30 percent, to less than its 1979 level.

Why the Great Depression Happened

The late 1920s were years of economic boom, but they were also years of increasing uncertainty. The main source of increased uncertainty was international. The world economy was going through tumultuous times. The patterns of world trade were changing as Britain, the traditional economic powerhouse of the world, began its period of relative economic decline and new economic powers such as Japan began to emerge. International currency fluctuations and the introduction of restrictive trade policies by many countries (see Chapter 35) further increased the uncertainty faced by firms. There was also domestic uncertainty arising from the fact that there had been such a strong boom in recent years, especially in the capital goods sector and housing. No one believed that this boom would last forever, but many people thought it had a lot farther to run and there was great uncertainty about how demand would change.

This environment of uncertainty led to a slowdown in consumer spending, especially on new homes and household appliances. By the fall of 1929, the uncertainty had reached a critical level and contributed to the stock market crash. The stock market crash, in turn, heightened people's fears about economic prospects in the foreseeable future. Fear fed fear. Investment collapsed. The building industry almost disappeared. An industry that had been operating flat out just two years earlier was now building virtually no new houses and apartments. It was this drop in investment and a drop in consumer spending on durables that led to the initial leftward shift of the aggregate demand curve from AD_{29} to AD_{30} in Fig. 33.13.

At this stage, what became the Great Depression was no worse than many previous recessions had been. What distinguishes the Great Depression from previous recessions are the events that followed between 1930 and 1933. But economists, even to

this day, have not come to agreement on how to interpret those events. One view, argued by Peter Temin,[2] is that spending continued to fall for a wide variety of reasons—including a continuation of increasing pessimism and uncertainty. According to Temin's view, the continued contraction resulted from a collapse of expenditure that was independent of the decrease in the quantity of money. The investment demand curve shifted leftward. Milton Friedman and Anna J. Schwartz have argued that the continuation of the contraction was almost exclusively the result of the subsequent worsening of financial and monetary conditions.[3] According to Friedman and Schwartz, it was a severe cut in the money supply that lowered aggregate demand, prolonging the contraction and deepening the depression.

Although there is disagreement about the causes of the contraction phase of the Great Depression, the disagreement is not about the elements at work but about the degree of importance attached to each. Everyone agrees that increased pessimism and uncertainty lowered investment demand, and everyone agrees that there was a massive contraction of the real money supply. Temin and his supporters assign primary importance to the fall in autonomous expenditure and secondary importance to the fall in the money supply. Friedman and Schwartz and their supporters assign primary responsibility to the money supply and regard the other factors as being of limited importance.

Let's look at the contraction of aggregate demand a bit more closely. Between 1930 and 1933, the nominal money supply decreased by 20 percent. This decrease in the money supply was not directly induced by the Fed's actions. The *monetary base* (currency in circulation and bank reserves) hardly fell at all. But the bank deposits component of the money supply suffered an enormous collapse. It did so primarily because a large number of banks failed. Before the Great Depression, fueled by increasing stock prices and booming business conditions, bank loans expanded. But after the stock market crash and the downturn, many borrowers found themselves in hard economic times. They could not pay the interest on

---

[2] Peter Temin, *Did Monetary Forces Cause the Great Depression?* (New York: W. W. Norton, 1976).
[3] Milton Friedman and Anna J. Schwartz developed this explanation in *A Monetary History of the United States: 1867–1960* (Princeton, N.J.: Princeton University Press, 1963), Chapter 7.

their loans, and they could not meet the agreed repayment schedules. Banks had deposits that exceeded the realistic value of the loans that they had made. When depositors withdrew funds from the banks, the banks lost reserves. Many of them simply couldn't meet their depositors' demands to be repaid.

Bank failures feed on themselves and create additional failures. Seeing banks fail, people become anxious to protect themselves and so take their money out of the banks. Such were the events of 1930. The quantity of notes and coins in circulation increased, and the volume of bank deposits declined. But the very action of taking money out of the bank to protect one's wealth accentuated the process of banking failure. Banks were increasingly short of cash and unable to meet their obligations.

What role did the stock market crash of 1929 play in producing the Great Depression? It certainly created an atmosphere of fear and panic and probably also contributed to the overall air of uncertainty that dampened investment spending. It also reduced the wealth of stockholders, encouraging them to cut back on their consumption spending. But the direct effect of the stock market crash on consumption, although a contributory factor to the Great Depression, was not the major source of the drop in aggregate demand. It was the collapse in investment arising from increased uncertainty that brought the 1930 decline in aggregate demand.

The stock market crash was a predictor of severe recession. It reflected the expectations of stockholders concerning future profit prospects. As those expectations became pessimistic, people sold their stocks. There were more sellers than buyers and the prices of stocks were bid lower and lower. That is, the behavior of the stock market was a consequence of expectations about future profitability, and those expectations were lowered as a result of increased uncertainty.

Can It Happen Again?

Because we have an incomplete understanding of the causes of the Great Depression, we cannot be sure whether such an event will happen again. The economic turmoil of the 1920s that preceded the Depression certainly can happen again. But there are some significant differences between the economy of the 1990s and that of the 1930s that make a severe depression much less likely today than it was 60 years ago. The most significant features of the economy

that make severe depression less likely today are:

■ Bank deposit insurance
■ The Fed's role as lender of last resort
■ Taxes and government spending
■ Multi-income families

Let's examine these in turn.

Bank Deposit Insurance As a result of the Great Depression, the federal government established, in the 1930s, the Federal Deposit Insurance Corporation (FDIC). The FDIC insures bank deposits for up to $100,000 per deposit, so most depositors need no longer fear bank failure. If a bank fails, the FDIC pays the deposit holders. With federally insured bank deposits, the key event that turned a fairly ordinary recession into the Great Depression is most unlikely to occur. It was the fear of bank failure that caused people to withdraw their deposits from banks. The aggregate consequence of these individually rational acts was to cause the very bank failures that were feared. With deposit insurance, most depositors have nothing to lose if a bank fails and so have no incentive to take actions that are likely to give rise to that failure.

Some recent events reinforce this conclusion. With massive failures of S&Ls in the 1980s and with bank failures in New England in 1990 and 1991, there was no tendency for depositors to panic and withdraw their funds in a self-reinforcing run on similar institutions.

Lender of Last Resort The Fed is the lender of last resort in the U.S. economy. If a single bank is short of reserves, it can borrow reserves from other banks. If the entire banking system is short of reserves, banks can borrow from the Fed. By making reserves available (at a suitable interest rate), the Fed is able to make the quantity of reserves in the banking system respond flexibly to the demand for those reserves. Bank failure can be prevented, or at least contained to cases in which bad management practices are the source of the problem. Widespread failures of the type that occurred in the Great Depression can be prevented.

It is now generally agreed that the Fed made a serious mistake in its handling of monetary policy during the Great Depression. With one eye on the international situation, the Fed *increased* the discount rate sharply from 1.5 percent to 3.5 percent just when the banks needed to borrow more. It was only long after the event, when Friedman and Schwartz examined the contraction years of the Great Depression, that economists came to realize that the Fed would have had to *decrease* the discount rate and *increase* the monetary base to have prevented the intensification of the contraction. Now that this lesson has been learned and there is such widespread agreement about the matter, there is at least some chance that the mistake will not be repeated.

The last time the Fed was confronted by a similar problem, although on a much smaller scale, was in October 1987. At that time, a severe stock market crash triggered fears of a new Great Depression. The Fed Chairman, Alan Greenspan, told the U.S. banking and financial community that the Fed had both the ability and the intent to maintain calm financial conditions and to supply sufficient reserves to ensure that the banking system did not begin to contract.

Taxes and Government Spending   The government sector was a much smaller part of the economy in 1929 than it has become today. On the eve of that earlier recession, government purchases of goods and services were less than 9 percent of GDP. Today, government purchases exceed 20 percent of GDP. Government transfer payments were less than 6 percent of GDP in 1929. Today, they exceed 15 percent of GDP.

A larger level of government purchases of goods and services means that when recession hits, a large component of aggregate demand does not decline. But government transfer payments are the most sensitive economic stabilizer. When the economy goes into recession and depression, more people qualify for unemployment benefits and social security. As a consequence, although disposable income decreases, the extent of the decrease is moderated by the existence of such programs. Consumption expenditure, in turn, does not decline by as much as it would in the absence of such government programs. The limited decline in consumption spending further limits the overall decrease in aggregate expenditure, thereby limiting the magnitude of an economic downturn.

Multi-Income Families   At the time of the Great Depression, families with more than one wage earner were much less common than they are today. The labor force participation rate in 1929 was around 55 percent. Today, it is 67 percent. Thus even if the unemployment rate increased to around 25 percent today, close to 50 percent of the adult population

would actually have jobs. During the Great Depression, less than 40 percent of the adult population had work. Multi-income families have greater security than single-income families do. The chance of both (or all) income earners in a family losing their jobs simultaneously is much lower than the chance of a single earner losing work. With greater family income security, family consumption is likely to be less sensitive to fluctuations in family income that are seen as temporary. Thus when aggregate income falls, it might not induce a cut in consumption. For example, during the OPEC recession, as real GDP fell, personal consumption expenditure actually increased. In 1990–1991, when real GDP fell by $60 billion, consumption expenditure fell by only $26 billion.

For the four reasons we have just reviewed, it appears that the economy has better shock-absorbing characteristics today than it had in the 1920s and 1930s. Even if there is a collapse of confidence, leading to a fall in investment, today's shock absorbers will not translate that initial shock into the large and prolonged fall in real GDP and rise in unemployment that occurred more than 60 years ago.

Because the economy is now more immune to severe recession than it was in the 1930s, even a stock market crash of the magnitude that occurred in 1987 had barely noticeable effects on spending. A crash of a similar magnitude in 1929 resulted in the near collapse of housing investment and consumer durable purchases. In the period following the 1987 stock market crash, investment and spending on durable goods hardly changed.

None of this is to say that there might not be a deep recession or even a Great Depression in the last half of the 1990s (or beyond). But it would take a very severe shock to trigger one.

◆   We have now completed our study of the business cycle. During an expansion, analysts use the theories you have studied to try to forecast the next recession. You can see an example of this activity in *Reading Between the Lines* on pp. 764–765.

We have also completed our study of the science of macroeconomics and learned about the influences on long-term economic growth and inflation as well as the business cycle. We have discovered that these issues pose huge policy challenges. How can we speed up the rate of economic growth while at the same time keeping inflation low and avoiding big swings of the business cycle? Our task in the next chapter is to study these macroeconomic policy challenges.

The 1990s Expansion

THE ARIZONA REPUBLIC, DECEMBER 29, 1996

Can Economic Expansion Keep From Faltering?

BY VIVIAN MARINO
THE ASSOCIATED PRESS

WASHINGTON—Just as the economy helped evict George Bush from the White House four years ago, it renewed Bill Clinton's lease in 1996.

Jobs were plentiful. Incomes rose. The stock market marched further into record territory. ...

How much of the credit does Clinton truly deserve? Will the economic expansion—the third longest in the country's history—continue during his second term, or through 1997, for that matter?

Only two other presidents this century—John F. Kennedy and Lyndon B. Johnson—have avoided recessions while in office. No two-term president has managed to escape one.

Some believe Clinton will rewrite history. Forty-four top economic forecasters surveyed recently by the National Association of Business Economists predicted the expansion that began in March 1991 would continue into the 21st century, with growth averaging 2.5 percent over the next five years.

Others believe the cycle is winding down. ...

Heading into 1997, the economy does appear to be moderating.

Recent data show new home sales plunged nearly 9 percent in October.

Unemployment climbed to a four-month high of 5.4 percent in November, after hovering near 5 percent in August.

The gross domestic product ... rose at a weaker-than-estimated 2 percent annual rate in the third quarter, less than half the nearly 5 percent pace in the April-to-June quarter.

Most economists believe the GDP will average 2.5 percent growth for all of 1996 and ease to between 2 percent and 2.25 percent in 1997. ...

The year ends with relatively low interest rates, around 7.5 percent for a 30-year fixed-rate mortgage, and low inflation, around 3 percent.

Other positive economic signs linger: Consumer confidence is at a seven-year high. The manufacturing sector of the economy remains at a five-month high in terms of growth. And the stock market has continued to break records, with the Dow Jones industrial average rising nearly 500 points in November alone. ...

Clinton takes credit for cutting the federal budget deficit in each year of office. It also was during his tenure that median household income rose for the first time in six years—2.7 percent in 1995. ...

Essence of THE STORY

■ Three presidents this century have escaped recessions while in office: Kennedy, Johnson, and Clinton.

■ During President Clinton's first term, unemployment was low, household incomes increased, and the Dow Jones industrial index expanded.

■ Some economists believe the expansion that began in March 1991 will continue into the twenty-first century. Others believe the expansion is slowing.

■ Some recent data show that unemployment is climbing and GDP growth is slowing.

■ But consumer confidence is high, the manufacturing sector is at a five-month high in terms of growth, and the stock market continues to break records.

■ President Clinton takes credit for cutting the budget deficit during each year in office.

Economic

A N A L Y S I S

■ Presidents Kennedy and Johnson and, to date, President Clinton have all escaped recessions while holding office. But there are some significant differences between the two eras.

■ Figure 1 shows the economy during the Kennedy-Johnson era. When President Kennedy took office in 1960, real GDP was $2.3 trillion. At the end of President Johnson's term, real GDP was $3.3 trillion.

■ During these years, real GDP grew at a rate of 4.9 percent per year and the inflation rate was 2.2 percent per year.

■ In 1960, the economy was in a recessionary gap. Figure 1 shows this gap. The aggregate demand curve AD_{60} intersects the short-run supply curve SAS_{60} to the left of the long-run aggregate supply curve LAS_{60}.

■ In 1968, the economy was in an inflationary gap. Figure 1 shows this gap. The aggregate demand curve AD_{68} intersects the short-run supply curve SAS_{68} to the right of the long-run aggregate supply curve LAS_{68}.

■ In 1993, when President Clinton took office, the economy was in a recessionary gap similar to that inherited by President Kennedy. Figure 2 shows the situation. Real GDP was $6.2 trillion in 1992. In 1996, real GDP was $6.9 trillion, which equaled potential GDP.

■ During President Clinton's first term of office, real GDP growth was 2.8 percent per year and the inflation rate was 2.6 percent per year.

■ These episodes have contrasting policies. The Kennedy-Johnson period was one of expansionary fiscal policy. Government consumption expenditure increased by 4.7 percent per year.

■ In contrast during the first Clinton term, government consumption expenditure increased only 1 percent over the entire four-year period.

■ The Kennedy-Johnson period was also a period of rapid monetary growth. The M2 growth rate was almost 8 percent per year. In contrast, during President Clinton's first term, M2 grew by only 2.6 percent per year.

■ The economic expansion during the 1960s exceeded the expansion of potential GDP and was policy driven. President Johnson bears some of the responsibility for the 1960s expansion being too strong and starting the inflationary 1970s.

■ The economic expansion of the 1990s is an expansion of potential GDP and is not driven by policy. More likely, supply-side factors are at work, for which President Clinton can take limited credit.

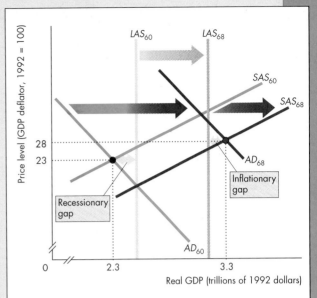

Figure 1 Kennedy-Johnson years

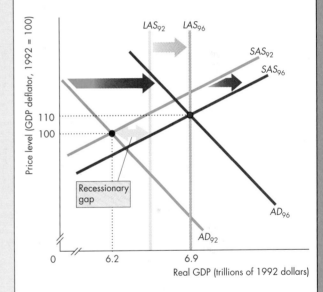

Figure 2 Clinton years

SUMMARY

Key Points

Cycle Patterns, Impulses, and Mechanisms (pp. 742–744)

- Since 1920, there have been fifteen recessions and expansions.
- The Great Depression was the most severe contraction of real GDP, and the postwar recessions have been milder than the prewar recessions.

Aggregate Demand Theories of the Business Cycle (pp. 744–750)

- Keynesian business cycle theory identifies volatile expectations about future sales and profits as the main source of economic fluctuations.
- Monetarist business cycle theory identifies fluctuations in the money stock as the main source of economic fluctuations.
- Rational expectations theory identifies unanticipated fluctuations in aggregate demand as the main source of economic fluctuations.

Real Business Cycle Theory (pp. 751–755)

- In real business cycle (RBC) theory, economic fluctuations are caused by fluctuations in the influence of technological change on productivity growth.
- A temporary slowdown in the pace of technological change decreases investment demand and both the demand for labor and supply of labor decrease.

Two Recent Recessions (pp. 755–759)

- The OPEC recession was triggered by an increase in the price of oil and an oil embargo, which decreased aggregate supply.
- The 1990–1991 recession resulted from the Gulf crisis, which increased the price of oil and decreased aggregate supply, and a decrease in investment, which decreased aggregate demand.

The Great Depression (pp. 760–763)

- The Great Depression started with increased uncertainty, which brought a fall in investment (especially in housing) and spending on consumer durables.
- There then followed a near total collapse of the financial system. Banks failed and the money supply fell, resulting in a continued fall in aggregate demand.
- The Great Depression itself produced a series of reforms that make a repeat of such a depression much less likely.

Key Figures

Key Terms

QUESTIONS

1. Describe an average recession and expansion.

2. Have recessions been getting more severe or less severe?

3. Distinguish between a cycle impulse and a cycle mechanism, and identify the impulse and mechanism in three analogies given in this chapter.

4. What is the Keynesian theory of the business cycle? Carefully distinguish between its impulse and its mechanism.

5. What is the monetarist theory of the business cycle? Carefully distinguish between its impulse and its mechanism.

6. What are the rational expectations theories of the business cycle? Carefully distinguish between their impulses and their mechanisms.

7. What is the key difference between new classical theory and new Keynesian theory of the business cycle?

8. What is the impulse that causes economic fluctuations according to real business cycle theory?

9. In real business cycle theory, what happens to investment demand and the demand for labor if a technological change brings a large increase in productivity?

10. How is the labor supply decision influenced by the real interest rate?

11. Why is there no short-run aggregate supply curve in real business cycle theory?

12. List the main arguments against and in favor of real business cycle theory.

13. When did the Great Depression and the OPEC recession occur?

14. What triggered the OPEC recession and the 1990–1991 recession?

15. Which one of the OPEC recession and the 1990–1991 recession was a period of stagflation?

16. Describe the changes in employment and real wages in the OPEC recession. What is the sticky wage theory of these changes? What is the flexible wage theory of these changes?

PROBLEMS

Use the figure on the next page, which shows the economy of Virtualreality, for all the following problems.

1. When the economy is in a long-run equilibrium, it is at points *b, e,* and *h*. When a recession occurs in Virtualreality, the economy moves away from these points to one of the two other points identified in each of the three parts of the figure.

   a. If the Keynesian theory is the correct explanation for the recession, to which points does the economy move?

   b. If the monetarist theory is the correct explanation for the recession, to which points does the economy move?

   c. If the new classical rational expectations theory is the correct explanation for the recession, to which points does the economy move?

   d. If the new Keynesian rational expectations theory is the correct explanation for the recession, to which points does the economy move?

   e. If real business cycle theory is the correct explanation for the recession, to which points does the economy move?

2. Suppose that when the recession occurs in Virtualreality, the economy moves to *a, f,* and *i*. Which, if any, theory of the business cycle explains this outcome?

3. Suppose that when the recession occurs in Virtualreality, the economy moves to *c, f,* and *i*. Which, if any, theory of the business cycle explains this outcome?

4. Suppose that when the recession occurs in Virtualreality, the economy moves to *a, d,* and *i*. Which, if any, theory of the business cycle explains this outcome?

5. Suppose that when the recession occurs in Virtualreality, the economy moves to *c, d,* and *i*. Which, if any, theory of the business cycle explains this outcome?

6. Suppose that when the recession occurs in Virtualreality, the economy moves to *a, f,* and *g*. Which, if any, theory of the business cycle explains this outcome?

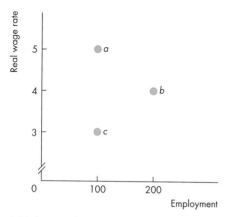

(a) Labor market

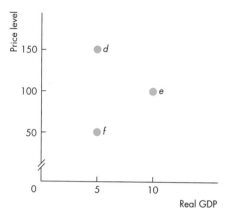

(b) AS-AD

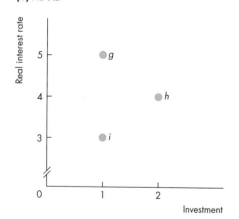

(c) Investment

CRITICAL THINKING

1. Study *Reading Between the Lines* on pp. 764–765 and then answer the following questions:
   a. What are the alternative views about the U.S. economy expressed in the article?
   b. What is the relevance, if any, of the information given in the article about the number of presidents who have avoided recessions?
   c. What does the article regard as positive signs that point to continued expansion?
   d. What does the article regard as negative signs that point to recession?
   e. Can you detect any clues in the news article to tell you whether the author is a Keynesian, monetarist, new classical, new Keynesian, or real business cycle supporter?
   f. What policy actions, if any, do you think the Fed or Congress needs to take in 1997 and 1998 to keep the economy growing and to prevent a new recession?

2. Describe the changes in employment and real wages during the 1990–1991 recession. What is the sticky wage theory of these changes? What is the flexible wage theory of these changes?

3. Describe the changes in real GDP, employment and unemployment, and the price level that occurred during the Great Depression years of 1929–1933.

4. List all of the features of the U.S. economy during the current year that you can think of that are consistent with a pessimistic outlook for the next two years.

5. List all of the features of the U.S. economy during the current year that you can think of that are consistent with an optimistic outlook for the next two years.

6. How do you think the U.S. economy is going to evolve over the next year or two? Explain your predictions, drawing on the pessimistic and optimistic factors that you have listed in the previous two questions and on your knowledge of macroeconomic theory.

34

Macroeconomic Policy Challenges

From 1991 through 1997, the U.S. economy performed well. Real GDP expanded by 2.6 percent a year, unemployment fell to below 5 percent, and the inflation rate remained below 3 percent a year. The United States was not alone in achieving a strong macroeconomic performance. Real GDP expanded in Canada by 2.5 percent a year and in the developing countries of Asia by 8 percent a year. But not all countries and regions shared in this solid growth. Japan's real GDP expanded by a lackluster 1 percent a year, and in Russia, real GDP shrank for five successive years to less than two thirds of its 1990 level. ◆ There were clouds, even in the U.S. economic sky. Interest rates remained relatively high, and the federal budget deficit stubbornly persisted. Also, there were questions about how fast U.S. real GDP could grow over the longer term. Had the potential GDP growth rate increased? Had the natural rate of unemployment decreased? Or was real GDP now above potential GDP? Was the economy overheating again? If it was overheating, was inflation about to increase? And when is the next recession coming? ◆ The variety of macroeconomic performance raises questions about macroeconomic policy. Can policy improve performance? Specifically, can the federal government use its fiscal policy to speed up long-term growth, keep inflation in check, and maintain a low unemployment rate? Can the Fed use its monetary policy to achieve any of these ends? Are some policy goals better achieved by fiscal policy and some by monetary policy? What specific policy actions do the best job? Are some ways of conducting policy better than others? ◆ In this chapter, we're going to study the challenges of achieving the highest sustainable long-term growth rate and low unemployment while avoiding inflation. At the end of the chapter, you will have a deeper understanding of the macroeconomic policy problems facing the United States today.

What Can Policy Do?

After studying this chapter, you will be able to:

- ■ Describe the goals of macroeconomic policy and the main features of fiscal policy and monetary policy since 1960

- ■ Explain how fiscal policy and monetary policy influence long-term economic growth

- ■ Evaluate fixed-rule and feedback-rule policies to stabilize the business cycle

- ■ Explain how fiscal policy influences the natural rate of unemployment

- ■ Explain why lowering inflation usually brings recession

Policy Goals

MACROECONOMIC POLICY GOALS FALL INTO TWO big categories: domestic and international. We study international macroeconomic policy issues in Chapters 35 and 36. Here, we focus on domestic policy. The four main domestic macroeconomic policy goals are to:

- Achieve the highest sustainable rate of potential GDP growth
- Smooth out avoidable business cycle fluctuations
- Maintain low unemployment
- Maintain low inflation

Potential GDP Growth

Rapid sustained real GDP growth can make a profound contribution to economic well being. With a growth rate of 2 percent a year, it takes more than 30 years for production to double. With a growth rate of 5 percent a year, production more than doubles in just 15 years. And with a growth rate of 10 percent a year, as some Asian countries are achieving, production doubles in just 7 years. The limits to *sustainable* growth are determined by the availability of natural resources, by environmental considerations, and by the willingness of people to save and invest in new capital and new technologies rather than consume everything they produce.

How fast can the economy grow over the long term? Between 1988 and 1995, through one complete business cycle, potential GDP grew at a rate of 2 percent a year.[1] But the U.S. population grows at about 1 percent a year, so the growth rate of real GDP per person was 1 percent a year, which means that output per person doubles every 70 years. Most economists believe that the U.S. economy can maintain a long-term growth rate of potential GDP of 2.5 percent a year. This growth rate would double output per person every 48 years. A few economists believe that with the right policies, sustainable growth of 5 percent a year is possible. This growth rate would double output per person every 18 years, increase it more than sixfold over 48 years, and increase it more than twelvefold in 70 years. So increasing the long-term growth rate is of critical importance.

[1] This number and the other numbers in this paragraph are based on the official measure of real GDP. If we take inflation bias into account, the growth rates might be as much as 1 percent per year more than these.

The Business Cycle

Potential GDP probably does not grow at a constant rate. Fluctuations in the pace of technological advance and in the pace of investment in new capital bring fluctuations in potential GDP. So some fluctuations in real GDP represent fluctuations in potential GDP. But when real GDP grows less quickly than potential GDP, output is lost, and when real GDP grows more quickly than potential GDP, bottlenecks arise. Keeping real GDP growth steady and equal to potential GDP growth avoids these problems.

It is not known how smooth real GDP growth can be made. Real business cycle theory regards all the fluctuations in real GDP as fluctuations in potential GDP. The aggregate demand theories regard most of the fluctuations in real GDP as being avoidable deviations from potential GDP.

Unemployment

When real GDP growth slows, unemployment rises above the natural rate of unemployment. The higher the unemployment rate, the longer is the time taken by unemployed people to find jobs. Productive labor is wasted, and there is a slowdown in the accumulation of human capital. If high unemployment persists, serious psychological and social problems arise for the unemployed workers and their families.

When real GDP growth speeds up, unemployment decreases and falls below the natural rate of unemployment. The lower the unemployment rate, the harder it becomes for expanding industries to get the labor they need to keep growing. If extremely low unemployment persists, serious bottlenecks and production dislocations occur.

Keeping unemployment at the natural rate avoids both of these problems. But just what is the natural rate of unemployment? Assessments vary. The actual average unemployment rate over the most recent business cycle—1988 to 1996—was 6 percent. Most economists would put the natural rate at about 5.5 percent. A few economists believe that the natural rate is lower than this, perhaps as low as 5 percent. At the other extreme, real business cycle theorists believe that the natural rate fluctuates and always equals the actual unemployment rate.

If the natural rate of unemployment becomes high, then a goal of policy becomes lowering the natural rate itself. This goal is independent of smoothing the business cycle.

Inflation

When inflation fluctuates unpredictably, money becomes less useful as a measuring rod for conducting transactions. In extreme cases, it becomes useless and is abandoned as the means of payment. Borrowers and lenders and employers and workers must take on extra risks. Keeping the inflation rate steady and predictable avoids these problems.

What is the most desirable inflation rate? Some economists say that the *rate* of inflation doesn't matter much as long as the rate is *predictable*. But most economists believe that price stability, which they translate as an inflation rate between 0 and 3 percent a year, is desirable. The reason why zero is not the target is that some price increases are due to quality improvements—a measurement bias in the price index—so a *measured* inflation rate between 0 and 3 percent a year is equivalent to price stability.

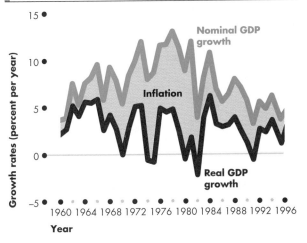

FIGURE 34.1

Macroeconomic Performance: Real GDP and Inflation

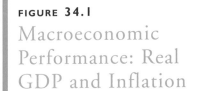

Real GDP growth and inflation fluctuate a great deal, and during the 1970s, inflation mushroomed (the height of the green shaded area) and real GDP growth slowed. This macroeconomic performance falls far short of the goals of a high and stable real GDP growth rate and low and predictable inflation.

Source: The Economic Report of the President, 1997.

The Two Core Policy Indicators: Real GDP Growth and Inflation

Although macroeconomic policy pursues the four goals we've just considered, the goals are not independent ones. Three of these goals—increasing the real GDP growth rate, smoothing the business cycle, and maintaining low unemployment—are linked together. Real GDP growth tells us directly about the long-term goal of high sustainable growth and the business cycle. It also has a strong link to unemployment. If growth becomes too rapid, unemployment falls below the natural rate, and if growth becomes too slow, unemployment rises above the natural rate. So keeping real GDP growing steadily at its maximum sustainable rate is equivalent to avoiding business fluctuations and keeping unemployment at the natural rate.

There are some connections between real GDP growth and inflation, but over the long run, these two variables are largely independent. So two variables, real GDP growth and inflation, are the core policy targets.

Policy performance, judged by the two core policy targets—real GDP growth and inflation—is shown in Fig. 34.1. Here the red line shows real GDP growth. Real GDP growth averaged 4 percent a year during the 1960s, but after 1970, the growth rate fell to less than 2.5 percent a year. Real GDP growth has fluctuated between a high of 6.8 percent in 1984 and a low of –2.1 percent in 1982. The height of the green shaded area shows inflation. The inflation rate was low during the 1960s, exploded during the 1970s, and then fell through the 1980s. During the 1990s, inflation returned to its 1960s level.

REVIEW

- The goals of domestic macroeconomic policy are the highest sustainable rate of potential GDP growth, small business cycle fluctuations, low unemployment, and low inflation.
- Keeping real GDP growing steadily at its highest sustainable rate is equivalent to avoiding business cycle fluctuations and keeping unemployment at the natural rate.

We've examined the policy goals. Let's now look at the policy tools and the way they have been used

Policy Tools and Performance

THE TOOLS THAT ARE USED TO TRY TO ACHIEVE macroeconomic performance objectives are fiscal policy and monetary policy. **Fiscal policy**, which is described in Chapter 29, is the use of the federal budget to achieve macroeconomic objectives. The detailed fiscal policy tools are tax rates, benefit rates, and government purchases of goods and services. These tools work by influencing aggregate supply and aggregate demand in the ways explained in Chapter 24. **Monetary policy**, which is described in Chapter 31, is the adjustment of the quantity of money in circulation and interest rates by the Federal Reserve (the Fed) to achieve macroeconomic objectives. These tools work by changing aggregate demand. How have the tools actually been used in the United States? Let's answer this question by summarizing the main directions of fiscal and monetary policy over the years since 1960.

Fiscal Policy Since 1960

Figure 34.2 gives a broad summary of fiscal policy since 1960. It shows the levels of government revenues and expenditures and the budget balance (each as a percentage of GDP). So that you can see the political context of fiscal policy, the figure also shows the terms of administrations and the names of the incumbent presidents.

Fiscal policy was mildly expansionary during the Kennedy years and strongly expansionary during the later Johnson years when the Vietnam War buildup occurred. During Nixon's presidency, spending growth was kept moderate. But under the pressure of the first OPEC oil shock, spending soared during Ford's presidency. The Carter years began with spending cuts, but then spending climbed to a new high. During the first Reagan term, spending continued to increase at first but it was later held in check, and then during the second Reagan term, spending was cut. During the Bush years, government purchases took an increased percentage of GDP but taxes took a smaller percentage. As the 1991 recession

FIGURE 34.2

The Fiscal Policy Record: A Summary

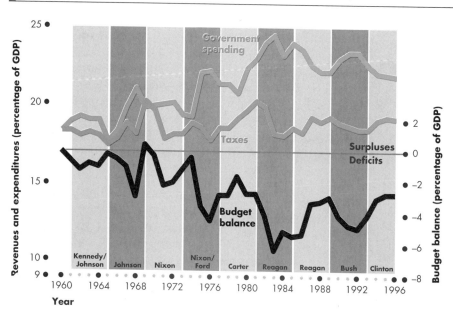

Fiscal policy is summarized here by the performance of government spending, taxes, and the budget balance. Spending has been on an upward trend, and because spending has increased more than taxes, a deficit has emerged. Cycles in spending and taxes have resulted in cycles in the deficit that often have been expansionary in the year before an election and contractionary in the year following an election.

...mic Report of the President, 1997, and the author's calculations.

intensified and the 1992 election drew closer, tax cuts became the rage, especially in Congress, and revenues decreased. But a tax bill in 1993 increased taxes, so revenues increased during the Clinton presidency. At the same time, spending was held in check and decreased as a percentage of GDP.

The budget balance tells an interesting story. During the terms of Johnson, Nixon, and Ford and the first Reagan term, the budget deficit decreased in the immediate postelection year and increased as the next election approached.

Let's now look at monetary policy.

Monetary Policy Since 1960

Figure 34.3 shows three broad measures of monetary policy. They are the growth rate of M2, the federal funds rate, and the real federal funds rate. The M2 growth rate tells us how monetary policy was influencing an important determinant of aggregate demand. The federal funds rate tells us how the Fed was acting to change money growth. And the real federal funds rate tells us how the Fed was acting

on the opportunity cost of short-term funds that influences spending plans.

Figure 34.3 also identifies the election years, the presidents, and the Fed chairs. The Fed has had five chairs during this period. Notice that the term of a Fed chair does not coincide with the term of a president. William McChesney Martin was a long-serving chair whose term began in 1951. He retired in 1969 and was replaced by Arthur Burns, who served until 1977. William Miller had the shortest term and was replaced by Paul Volcker in 1979. The next chair, Alan Greenspan, was appointed by President Reagan in 1987 and has served under three presidents.

First, let's look at some of the monetary policy trends. During the 1960s, the M2 growth rate averaged 7 percent a year and ranged between a low of 4 percent in 1969 and a high of 9 percent in 1967. It then increased to average 10 percent a year between 1970 and 1983 and hit a peak of 14 percent in 1976. M2 growth fell steadily from 12 percent in 1983 to less than 1 percent in 1994 but then increased in 1995. The federal funds rate trended upward from 1960 through 1981 and then trended downward. The real federal funds rate fell through 1975 and

---

FIGURE 34.3
The Monetary Policy Record: A Summary

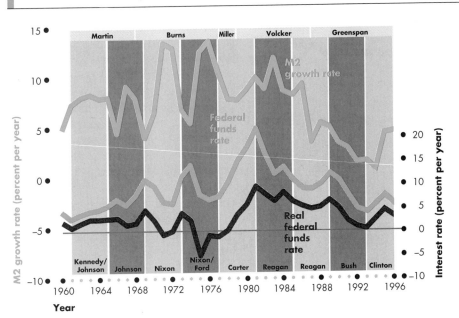

The monetary policy record is summarized here by the growth rate of M2 and the federal funds rate. Fluctuations in M2 growth have coincided with elections, the growth rate usually increasing in the year before an election. Important exceptions are 1979–1980 and 1991–1992, when monetary policy did not become expansionary and the incumbent President lost the election.

Source: The Economic Report of the President, 1997.

then increased and remained high through most of the 1980s. It fell during the early 1990s but then began to rise again through 1995.

The general upward trend in M2 growth brought the 1970s inflation, which brought rising *nominal* interest rates but, at first, falling real interest rates. The subsequent sharp downward trend in M2 growth brought falling inflation and falling nominal interest rates but was accompanied by high real interest rates.

Next, look at the cycles. The peaks and troughs in M2 growth more or less coincide with the opposite turning points in the federal funds rate. When the Fed cuts the federal funds rate, M2 growth speeds up; when the Fed increases the federal funds rate, M2 growth slows down. But notice also a remarkable fact about the monetary policy cycles. There is a tendency for the federal funds rate to rise and the M2 growth rate to decrease immediately following an election and for the federal funds rate to fall and the M2 growth rate to increase as the next election approaches. Usually, the incumbent president or his party's successor has won the election. There are two exceptions. In 1980, M2 growth increased, but not as quickly as the demand for money. Interest rates increased, the economy slowed, and Jimmy Carter lost his reelection bid. In 1992, M2 growth slowed, interest rates rose, and George Bush lost his reelection bids. A coincidence? Perhaps, but presidents take a keen interest in what the Fed is up to.

REVIEW

- The macroeconomic policy tools are fiscal policy and monetary policy.
- Fiscal policy was expansionary during the Kennedy, Johnson, Ford, and first Reagan terms; moderate during the Nixon and Bush terms; and contractionary during the Carter, second Reagan, and Clinton terms.
- Money supply growth increased at the end of the 1960s and remained high through the 1970s. It slowed through the 1980s and 1990s.

You've now studied the goals of policy and seen the broad trends and cycles in fiscal and monetary policy. Let's now study the ways in which policy might be used better to achieve its goals. We'll begin by looking at long-term growth policy.

Long-Term Growth Policy

THE SOURCES OF THE LONG-TERM GROWTH OF potential GDP, which are explained in Chapter 27 (pp. 591–592), are the accumulation of physical and human capital and the advance of technology. Chapter 27 briefly examines the range of policies that might achieve faster growth. Here, we probe more deeply into the problem of boosting the long-term growth rate.

Monetary policy can contribute to long-term growth by keeping the inflation rate low. (Chapter 32, pp. 722–723 explains some connections between inflation on growth.) Fiscal policy and other policies can also contribute to growth by influencing the private decisions on which long-term growth depends in three areas. All growth policies increase:

- National saving
- Investment in human capital
- Investment in new technologies

National Saving

National saving equals private saving plus government saving. Figure 34.4 shows national saving and its private and government components since 1960. From 1960 through 1982, national saving (green line) fluctuated around an average of 20 percent of GDP. There then began a steady slide that saw national saving sink to 14 percent of GDP in 1993 before beginning to rise again. Private saving (blue line) actually increased as a percentage of GDP between 1960 and 1984, when it peaked at 22 percent of GDP. Government saving (the vertical gap between the blue line and the green line) was generally positive before 1975 and became increasingly negative (government dissaving) during the 1980s.

The data you have just examined are for *gross* saving. Each year, national wealth grows by the amount of *net* saving, which equals gross saving minus the value of capital that is scrapped during the year. Figure 34.4 shows U.S. net saving as a percentage of GDP. You can see that net saving (red line) followed a falling trend through 1993. The reason is that capital depreciated at an increasing rate. During the 1960s, depreciation ranged between 10 percent and 14 percent of GDP. This percentage edged upward and was around 12 percent by the mid-1990s. In the 1982 recession, it reached 14 percent of GDP. As a result of the fall in gross saving and the increase in the depreciation rate, net saving in the United States sank to an all-time low of 2.4 percent of GDP in 1993. But since 1993, the net saving rate has been rising.

U.S. investment, one of the engines of growth, is not limited by U.S. saving. The reason is that foreign saving can be harnessed to finance U.S. investment. But boosting the U.S. saving rate can help to bring faster real GDP growth for two reasons. First, the U.S. economy is a significant proportion of the world economy, so an increase in U.S. saving would increase world saving and bring lower real interest rates around the world. With lower real interest rates, investment would be boosted everywhere. The U.S. economy and the world economy could grow faster. Second, with more domestic saving, there might be an increase in

domestic investment in high-risk–high-return new technologies that could boost U.S. growth.

How can national saving be increased? The two points of attack are:

■ Increasing government saving
■ Increasing private saving

Increasing Government Saving   Government saving has been negative since 1975, and its average during the 1990s has been –2.2 percent of GDP. Increasing government saving means reducing or eliminating the federal deficit. But as is explained in Chapter 29, achieving a substantial cut in the deficit will be hard work and will be achieved only by cuts in such sensitive areas as Social Security, Medicaid, and Medicare.

Increasing Private Saving   Private saving has fallen from its peak of the mid-1980s, but even in the low years of 1992 and 1993, private saving was the same percentage of GDP it had been in 1960. The main way in which government actions can boost private saving is by increasing the after-tax rate of return on saving. This is what government policy has sought to do, but on only one type of asset: individual retirement accounts (IRAs). By putting their savings into IRAs, people can avoid income tax on their interest income. But they cannot use their IRAs (without tax penalties) until they reach the age of 59 1/2. Also, there are limits to the amount that can be accumulated tax-free in an IRA. The Clinton administration has proposed expanding IRAs.

Private saving probably could be stimulated more effectively by cutting taxes on interest income and capital gains across the board and replacing the lost government revenue from such a tax cut with a national consumption tax or a national sales tax. Whether such restructuring of taxes is politically feasible or desirable is a question that goes beyond the scope of macroeconomics.

Private Saving and Inflation   Inflation erodes the value of money and other financial assets such as bonds, and uncertainty about future inflation discourages saving. One further policy, therefore, that increases the saving rate is a monetary policy that preserves stable prices and minimizes uncertainty about the future value of money. Chapter 32 (pp. 722–723) spells out the broader connection between inflation and real GDP and explains why low inflation brings greater output and faster growth.

FIGURE 34.4

Saving Rates in the United States: 1960–1996

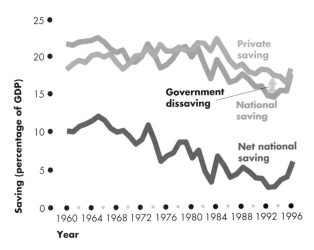

U.S. national saving (green line) peaked in 1979 and has fallen since that year. Both government saving and private saving have contributed to the fall. U.S. net saving (red line) has fallen even faster than national saving and has been on a downward trend since the mid-1960s. It hit an all-time low of 2.4 percent of GDP in 1993. It has increased since then.

Source: The Economic Report of the President, 1997.

Investment in Human Capital

The accumulation of human capital plays a crucial role in economic growth, and two areas are relevant: schooling and on-the-job experience. Economic research shows that both schooling and on-the-job training pay. That is, on the average, the greater the number of years a person remains in school and the greater the number of years of work experience, the higher are that person's earnings. Furthermore, schooling and on-the-job experience yield one of the highest rates of return available.

If education and on-the-job training yield higher earnings, why does the government need a policy toward investment in human capital? Why can't people simply be left to get on with making their own decisions about how much human capital to acquire? The answer is that the *social* returns to human capital probably exceed the *private* returns. The extra productivity that comes from the *interactions* of well-educated and experienced people exceeds what each individual could achieve alone. So, left to ourselves, we would probably accumulate too little human capital. Let's look at some aspects of education and training policies.

Education and Training Policies Governments attempt to increase human capital by subsidizing schooling. They also help to set the standards of achievement for the school system.

The United States has achieved a high standard on some dimensions of schooling but not on all dimensions. For example, in 1996, 63 percent of high school graduates enrolled in postsecondary education (one of the highest percentages in the world) but 13 percent of high school students dropped out and did not graduate.

The Goals 2000: Educate America Act of 1994 and President Clinton's second term education initiative are examples of attempts to improve the quality of schooling. The 1994 Act pays special attention to improving each child's state of preparation for school and performance in school, especially in mathematics and science, two areas in which U.S. schoolchildren are not leading the world. A further feature of Goals 2000 is to improve college access, especially for adults who can benefit from retraining.

The scope for government training programs is limited, but the government can set an example as an employer and it can encourage best-practice training programs for workers.

Investment In New Technologies

Investment in new technologies is the third area in which policy can influence economic growth. As Chapter 27 explains, investment in new technologies is special for two reasons. First, it appears not to run into the problem of diminishing returns that plague the other types of capital and the other factors of production. Second, the benefits of new technologies spill over to influence all parts of the economy, not just the firms undertaking the investment. For these reasons, increasing the rate of investment in new technologies is a promising way of boosting long-term growth. But how can government policy influence the pace of technological change?

Government can fund and provide tax incentives for research and development activities. Through the National Science Foundation, the public universities, and various research establishments, governments fund a large amount of basic research. Also, the federal government encourages business research with a Research and Experiment Tax Credit (R&E credit). This credit is available to firms that spend more on research and development than some threshold amount. The idea is to stimulate more expenditure on these activities than would occur otherwise. The effectiveness of the R&E credit is not certain, but there is some evidence that it is a cost-effective way of boosting research.

R E V I E W

- Long-term growth policies focus on increasing saving and increasing investment in human capital and new technologies.
- The U.S. net saving rate has been on a negative trend since the mid-1970s. To increase the saving rate, government saving and the after-tax return on private saving must be increased and inflation must be kept in check.
- Human capital investment might be increased with improved education and on-the-job training programs.
- Investment in new technologies can be encouraged by government funding and tax incentives.

We've seen how government might use its fiscal and monetary policies to influence long-term growth. How can it influence the business cycle and unemployment? Let's now address this question.

Business Cycle and Unemployment Policy

MANY DIFFERENT FISCAL AND MONETARY POLICIES can be pursued to stabilize the business cycle and cyclical unemployment. But all these polices fall into three broad categories:

- Fixed-rule policies
- Feedback-rule policies
- Discretionary policies

Fixed-Rule Policies

A **fixed-rule policy** specifies an action to be pursued independently of the state of the economy. An everyday life example of a fixed rule is a stop sign. It says, "Stop regardless of the state of the road ahead—even if no other vehicle is trying to use the road." One fixed-rule policy, proposed by Milton Friedman, is to keep the quantity of money growing at a constant rate year in and year out, regardless of the state of the economy, to make the *average* inflation rate zero. Another fixed-rule policy is to balance the federal budget. Fixed rules are rarely followed in practice, but they have some merits in principle, and later in this chapter, we will study how they would work if they were pursued.

Feedback-Rule Policies

A **feedback-rule policy** specifies how policy actions respond to changes in the state of the economy. A yield sign is an everyday feedback rule. It says, "Stop if another vehicle is attempting to use the road ahead, but otherwise, proceed." A macroeconomic feedback-rule policy is one that changes the money supply, interest rates, or even tax rates in response to the state of the economy. Some feedback rules guide the actions of policy makers. For example, the Fed's Federal Open Market Committee used a feedback rule when it kept pushing interest rates ever higher through 1994 in response to persistently falling unemployment and strong real GDP growth. Other feedback-rule policies are automatic. Examples are the automatic increase in tax revenues and decrease in transfer payments during an expansion and the automatic decrease in tax revenues and increase in transfer payments during a recession.

Discretionary Policies

A **discretionary policy** responds to the state of the economy in a possibly unique way that uses all the information available, including perceived lessons from past "mistakes." An everyday discretionary policy occurs at an unmarked intersection. Each driver uses discretion in deciding whether to stop and how slowly to approach the intersection. Most macroeconomic policy actions have an element of discretion because every situation is to some degree unique. For example, through 1994, the Fed increased interest rates several times but by small increments. It might have delayed increasing rates until it was more sure that higher rates were needed and then increased them by a larger increment. The Fed used discretion based on lessons it had learned from earlier expansions. But despite the fact that all policy actions have an element of discretion, they can be regarded as modifications of a basic feedback-rule policy.

We'll study the effects of business cycle policy by comparing the performance of real GDP and the price level under a fixed rule and a feedback rule. Because the business cycle can result from demand shocks or supply shocks, we need to consider these two cases. We'll begin by studying demand shocks.

Stabilizing Aggregate Demand Shocks

We'll study an economy that starts out at full employment and has no inflation. Figure 34.5 illustrates this situation. The economy is on aggregate demand curve AD_0 and short-run aggregate supply curve SAS. These curves intersect at a point on the long-run aggregate supply curve, LAS. The GDP deflator is 110, and real GDP is $7 trillion. Now suppose that there is an unexpected and temporary decrease in aggregate demand. Let's see what happens.

Perhaps investment decreases because of a wave of pessimism about the future, or perhaps exports decrease because of a recession in the rest of the world. Regardless of the origin of the decrease in aggregate demand, the aggregate demand curve shifts leftward, to AD_1 in Fig. 34.5. Aggregate demand curve AD_1 intersects the short-run aggregate supply curve, SAS, at a GDP deflator of 105 and a real GDP of $6.5 trillion. The economy is in a recession. Real GDP is less than potential GDP, and unemployment is above its natural rate.

FIGURE 34.5

A Decrease in Aggregate Demand

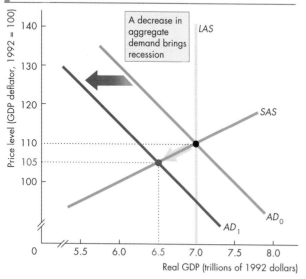

The economy starts out at full employment on aggregate demand curve AD_0 and short-run aggregate supply curve SAS, the two curves intersecting on the long-run aggregate supply curve, LAS. Real GDP is $7 trillion, and the GDP deflator is 110. A fall in aggregate demand (due to pessimism about future profits, for example) unexpectedly shifts the aggregate demand curve to AD_1. Real GDP falls to $6.5 trillion, and the GDP deflator falls to 105. The economy is in a recession.

Suppose that the decrease in aggregate demand from AD_0 to AD_1 is temporary. As confidence in the future improves, firms' investment picks up, or as economic expansion proceeds in the rest of the world, exports gradually increase. As a result, the aggregate demand curve gradually returns to AD_0, but it takes some time to do so.

We are going to work out how the economy responds under two alternative policies during the period in which aggregate demand gradually increases to its original level: a fixed rule and a feedback rule.

Fixed Rule: Monetarism   The fixed rule that we'll study here is one in which government purchases of goods and services, taxes, and the money supply remain constant. Neither fiscal policy nor monetary policy responds to the depressed economy. This is the rule advocated by monetarists. A **monetarist** is

an economist who believes that fluctuations in the money stock are the main source of economic fluctuations—the monetarist theory of the business cycle (see Chapter 33, p. 746).

Figure 34.6(a) illustrates the response of the economy under a fixed rule when the decrease in aggregate demand to AD_1 is *temporary*. Gradually, aggregate demand returns to its original level and the aggregate demand curve shifts rightward to AD_0. As it does so, real GDP and the GDP deflator gradually increase. The GDP deflator gradually returns to 110 and real GDP to $7 trillion, as shown in Fig. 34.6(a). Throughout this process, the economy experiences more rapid growth than usual but beginning from a state in which real GDP is less than potential GDP. Also throughout the adjustment, unemployment remains above the natural rate.

Figure 34.6(b) illustrates the response of the economy under a fixed rule when the decrease in aggregate demand to AD_1 is *permanent*. Gradually, with unemployment above the natural rate, the money wage rate falls and the short-run aggregate supply curve shifts rightward to SAS_1. As it does so, real GDP gradually increases and the GDP deflator falls. Real GDP gradually returns to potential GDP of $7 trillion, and the GDP deflator gradually falls to 95, as shown in Fig. 34.6(b). Again, throughout the adjustment, real GDP is less than potential GDP and unemployment exceeds the natural rate.

Let's contrast the adjustment under a fixed-rule policy with that under a feedback-rule policy.

Feedback Rule: Keynesian Activism   The feedback rule that we'll study is one in which government purchases of goods and services increase, tax rates decrease, and the money supply increases when real GDP falls below potential GDP. In other words, both fiscal policy and monetary policy become expansionary when real GDP is less than potential GDP. When real GDP exceeds potential GDP, both policies operate in reverse, becoming contractionary. This rule is advocated by Keynesian activists. A **Keynesian activist** is an economist who believes that fluctuations in aggregate demand combined with sticky wages (and/or sticky prices) are the main source of economic fluctuations—the Keynesian and new Keynesian theories of the business cycle (see Chapter 33, pp. 744, 748).

Figure 34.6(c) illustrates the response of the economy under this feedback-rule policy. When aggregate demand decreases to AD_1, the expansionary fiscal and

FIGURE 34.6

Two Stabilization Policies: Aggregate Demand Shock

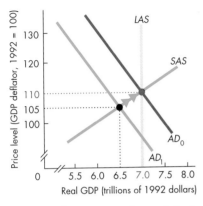

(a) Fixed rule: temporary demand shock

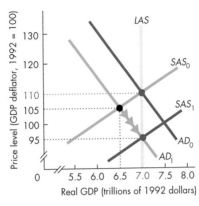

(b) Fixed rule: permanent demand shock

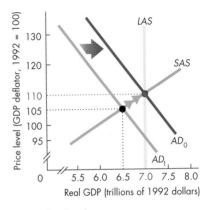

(c) Feedback rule

Aggregate demand has fallen from AD_0 to AD_1, and the economy is in a recession. Real GDP has fallen to $6.5 trillion, and the GDP deflator has fallen to 105. A fixed-rule stabilization policy (parts a and b) leaves aggregate demand at AD_1, so real GDP remains at $6.5 trillion and the GDP deflator remains at 105. If the aggregate demand shock is temporary (part a), aggregate demand subsequently returns to its original level and the aggregate demand curve shifts back to AD_0. As it does, real GDP increases back to $7 trillion and the GDP deflator increases to 110. If the demand shock is permanent (part b),

aggregate demand remains at AD_1. Eventually, because unemployment is above the natural rate, the money wage rate falls and the SAS curve shifts to SAS_1. The price level falls further (to a GDP deflator of 95), and real GDP returns to $7 trillion. Part (c) shows a feedback rule. With the economy in recession, expansionary fiscal and monetary policies increase aggregate demand and shift the aggregate demand curve from AD_1 to AD_0. Real GDP returns to $7 trillion and the GDP deflator returns 110.

monetary policies increase aggregate demand, shifting the aggregate demand curve immediately to AD_0. As other influences begin to increase aggregate demand, fiscal and monetary policies become contractionary and hold the aggregate demand curve steady at AD_0. Real GDP is held steady at $7 trillion, and the GDP deflator remains at 110.

The Two Rules Compared   Under a fixed-rule policy, the economy goes into a recession and stays there for as long as it takes for aggregate demand to increase again under its own steam. Only gradually does the aggregate demand curve return to its original position and the recession come to an end.

Under a feedback-rule policy, the economy is pulled out of its recession by the policy action. Once back at potential GDP, real GDP is held there by a gradual, policy-induced decrease in aggregate demand that exactly offsets the increase in aggregate demand coming from private spending decisions.

The price level and real GDP decrease and increase by exactly the same amounts under the two policies, but real GDP stays below potential GDP for longer with a fixed rule than it does with a feedback rule.

The Fed's Feedback Rule: 1992–1996   The Fed tries to operate a feedback rule like the one you've just studied. At the end of 1992, real GDP was below potential GDP and unemployment was above the natural rate. Through 1992, the Fed gradually lowered interest rates and speeded up money growth. The economy expanded. By 1994, real GDP was close to potential GDP and was growing faster than potential GDP. To prevent an outbreak of inflation, the Fed increased interest rates and slowed money growth. As the economy slowed during 1995, the Fed lowered interest rates and speeded up money growth. Real GDP growth again speeded up in 1996. And again, in early 1997, the Fed applied the monetary brake.

So Feedback Rules Are Better?   Isn't it obvious that a feedback rule is better than a fixed rule? Can't the government and the Fed use feedback rules to keep the economy close to full employment with a stable price level? Of course, unforecasted events—such as a collapse in business confidence—will hit the economy from time to time. But by responding with a change in tax rates, spending, interest rates, and money supply, can't the government and the Fed minimize the damage from such a shock? It appears to be so from our analysis, and the Fed did a pretty good job during 1992–1996.

Despite the apparent superiority of a feedback rule, many economists remain convinced that a fixed rule stabilizes aggregate demand more effectively than a feedback rule does. These economists assert that fixed rules are better than feedback rules because:

- Potential GDP is not known.
- Policy lags are longer than the forecast horizon.
- Feedback-rule policies are less predictable than fixed-rule policies.

Let's look at these assertions.

Knowledge of Potential GDP   To decide whether a feedback policy needs to stimulate or retard aggregate demand, it is necessary to determine whether real GDP is currently above or below potential GDP. But potential GDP is not known with certainty. It depends on a large number of factors, one of which is the level of employment when unemployment is at its natural rate. But uncertainty and disagreement exist about how the labor market works, so we can only estimate the natural rate of unemployment. As a result, there is uncertainty about the *direction* in which a feedback policy should be pushing the level of aggregate demand.

Policy Lags and the Forecast Horizon   The effects of policy actions taken today are spread out over the following two years or even more. But no one is able to forecast accurately that far ahead. The forecast horizon of the policy makers is less than 1 year. Further, it is not possible to predict the precise timing and magnitude of the effects of policy actions. Thus feedback policies that react to today's economy may be inappropriate for the state of the economy at that uncertain future date when the policy's effects are felt.

For example, suppose that today the economy is in recession. The Fed reacts with an increase in the money supply growth rate. When the Fed puts on the monetary accelerator, the first reaction is a fall in interest rates. Some time later, lower interest rates produce an increase in investment and the purchases of consumer durable goods. Some time still later, this increase in expenditure increases income; higher income in turn induces higher consumption expenditure. Later yet, the higher expenditure increases the demand for labor, and eventually, wages and prices rise. The industries and regions in which spending increases occur vary, and so does the impact on employment. It can take from 9 months to 2 years for an initial action by the Fed to cause a change in real GDP, employment, and the inflation rate.

By the time the Fed's actions are having their maximum effect, the economy has moved on to a new situation. Perhaps a world economic slowdown has added a new negative effect on aggregate demand that is offsetting the Fed's expansionary actions. Or perhaps a boost in business confidence has increased aggregate demand yet further, adding to the Fed's own expansionary policy. Whatever the situation, the Fed can take the appropriate actions today only if it can forecast those future shocks to aggregate demand.

Thus to smooth the fluctuations in aggregate demand, the Fed needs to take actions today, based on a forecast of what will be happening over a period stretching 2 or more years into the future. It is no use taking actions a year from today to influence the situation that then prevails. By then it will be too late.

If the Fed is good at economic forecasting and bases its policy actions on its forecasts, then the Fed can deliver the type of aggregate-demand-smoothing performance that we assumed in the model economy that we studied earlier in this chapter. But if the Fed takes policy actions that are based on today's economy rather than on the forecasted economy a year into the future, then those actions will often be inappropriate ones.

When unemployment is high and the Fed puts its foot on the accelerator, it speeds the economy back to full employment. But the Fed might not be able to see far enough ahead to know when to ease off the accelerator and gently tap the brake, holding the economy at its full-employment point. Usually, the Fed keeps its foot on the accelerator for too long, and after the Fed has taken its foot off the accelerator pedal, the economy races through the full-employment point and starts to experience shortages and inflationary pressures. Eventually, when inflation increases and unemployment falls below its natural rate, the Fed steps on the brake, pushing the economy back below full employment.

According to advocates of fixed rules, the Fed's own reactions to the current state of the economy is one of the major sources of fluctuations in aggregate demand and the major factor that people have to forecast to make their own economic choices.

During 1994, the Fed tried hard to avoid the problems just described. It increased interest rates early in the expansion and by small increments. In 1995, after real GDP growth slowed down but before any serious signs of recession were on the horizon, it began to cut interest rates. And in 1997, before inflation turned seriously upward, the Fed squeezed the monetary brake. It is too early to tell whether the Fed now knows enough to avoid some of the mistakes of the past. But its actions during 1992–1996 were gentler and better timed than in previous cycles.

The problems for fiscal policy feedback rules are more severe than those for monetary policy because of the lags in the implementation of fiscal policy. The Fed can take actions relatively quickly. But before a fiscal policy action can be taken, the entire legislative process must be completed. Thus even before a fiscal policy action is implemented, the economy may have moved on to a new situation that calls for a different feedback policy from the one that is in the legislative pipeline.

Predictability of Policies   To make decisions about long-term contracts for employment (wage contracts) and for borrowing and lending, people have to anticipate the future course of prices—the future inflation rate. To forecast the inflation rate, it is necessary to forecast aggregate demand. And to forecast aggregate demand, it is necessary to forecast the policy actions of the government and the Fed.

If the government and the Fed stick to rock-steady, fixed rules for tax rates, spending programs, and money supply growth, then policy itself cannot be a contributor to unexpected fluctuations in aggregate demand.

In contrast, when a feedback rule is being pursued, there is more scope for the policy actions to be unpredictable. The main reason is that feedback rules are not written down for all to see. Rather, they have to be inferred from the behavior of the government and the Fed.

Thus with a feedback policy, it is necessary to predict the variables to which the government and Fed react and the extent to which they react. Consequently, a feedback rule for fiscal and monetary

policies can create more unpredictable fluctuations in aggregate demand than a fixed rule can.

Economists disagree about whether those bigger fluctuations offset the potential stabilizing influence of the predictable changes the Fed makes. No agreed measurements have been made to settle this dispute. Nevertheless, the unpredictability of the Fed in its pursuit of feedback policies is an important fact of economic life. And the Fed does not always go out of its way to make its reactions clear. Even in Congressional testimony, Federal Reserve Board chairmen are reluctant to make the Fed's actions and intentions entirely plain. (It has been suggested that two former chairmen of the Federal Reserve Board, the pipe-puffing Arthur Burns and the cigar-puffing Paul Volcker, carried their own smokescreens around with them, as if to exemplify the Fed's mysteriousness and unpredictability. The nonsmoking Alan Greenspan seems to be running a more open and predictable Fed.)

It is not surprising that the Fed seeks to keep *some* of its actions behind a smokescreen. First, the Fed wants to maintain as much freedom of action as possible and so does not want to state with too great a precision the feedback rules that it will follow in any given circumstances. Second, the Fed is part of a political process and, although legally independent of the federal government, is not immune to subtle influence. For at least these two reasons, the Fed does not specify feedback rules as precisely as the one we've analyzed in this chapter. As a result, the Fed cannot deliver an economic performance that has the stability that we generated in the model economy.

To the extent that the Fed's actions are discretionary and unpredictable, they lead to unpredictable fluctuations in aggregate demand. These fluctuations, in turn, produce fluctuations in real GDP, employment, and unemployment.

If it is difficult for the Fed to pursue a predictable feedback stabilization policy, it is probably impossible for Congress to do so. The stabilization policy of Congress is formulated in terms of spending programs and tax laws. Because these programs and laws are the outcome of a political process that is constrained only by the Constitution, there can be no effective way in which a predictable feedback fiscal policy can be adhered to.

We reviewed three reasons why feedback-rule policies might not be more effective than fixed-rule policies in controlling aggregate demand. But there is a fourth reason why some economists prefer fixed rules: Not all shocks to the economy are on the demand side. Most advocates of feedback rules believe that most fluctuations do come from aggregate demand. Some advocates of fixed rules believe that aggregate supply fluctuations are the dominant ones. Let's now see how aggregate supply fluctuations affect the economy under a fixed rule and a feedback rule. We will also see why the economists who believe that aggregate supply fluctuations are the dominant ones also favor a fixed rule rather than a feedback rule.

Stabilizing Aggregate Supply Shocks

Real business cycle theorists believe that fluctuations in real GDP (and in employment and unemployment) are caused not by fluctuations in aggregate demand but by fluctuations in productivity growth. According to real business cycle theory, there is no useful distinction between long-run aggregate supply and short-run aggregate supply. Because wages are flexible, the labor market is always in equilibrium and unemployment is always at its natural rate. The vertical long-run aggregate supply curve is also the short-run aggregate supply curve. Fluctuations occur because of shifts in the long-run aggregate supply curve. Normally, the long-run aggregate supply curve shifts to the right—the economy expands. But the pace at which the long-run aggregate supply curve shifts to the right varies. Also, on occasion, the long-run aggregate supply curve shifts leftward, bringing a decrease in aggregate supply and a fall in real GDP.

If the real business cycle theory is correct, economic policy that influences the aggregate demand curve has no effect on real GDP. But it does affect the price level. If a feedback-rule policy is used to increase aggregate demand every time real GDP decreases, and if the real business cycle theory is correct, the feedback-rule policy will make price level fluctuations more severe than they otherwise would be. To see why, consider Fig. 34.7.

Imagine that the economy starts out on aggregate demand curve AD_0 and long-run aggregate supply curve LAS_0 at a GDP deflator of 110 and with real GDP equal to $7 trillion. Now suppose that the long-run aggregate supply curve shifts to LAS_1. An actual decrease in long-run aggregate supply can occur as a result of a severe drought or other natural catastrophe or perhaps as the result of a disruption of international trade such as the OPEC embargo of the 1970s.

FIGURE 34.7

Responding to a Productivity Growth Slowdown

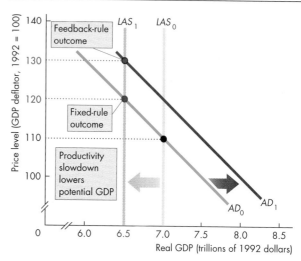

A productivity growth slowdown shifts the long-run aggregate supply curve from LAS_0 to LAS_1. Real GDP decreases to $6.5 trillion, and the GDP deflator rises to 120. With a fixed rule, there is no change in the money supply, taxes, or government spending; aggregate demand stays at AD_0; and that is the end of the matter. With a feedback rule, the Fed increases the money supply and the Congress cuts taxes or increases spending, intending to increase real GDP. Aggregate demand shifts to AD_1, but the result is an increase in the price level—the GDP deflator rises to 130—with no change in real GDP.

Fixed Rule   With a fixed rule, the fall in the long-run aggregate supply has no effect on the policies of the Fed or the government and no effect on aggregate demand. The aggregate demand curve remains AD_0. Real GDP decreases to $6.5 trillion, and the GDP deflator increases to 120.

Feedback Rule   Now suppose that the Fed and the government use feedback rules. In particular, suppose that when real GDP decreases, the Fed increases the money supply and Congress enacts a tax cut to increase aggregate demand. In this example, the money supply and tax cut shift the aggregate demand curve to AD_1. The policy goal is to bring real GDP back to $7 trillion. But the long-run aggregate supply curve has shifted, and so potential GDP has decreased to $6.5 trillion. The increase in aggregate demand cannot bring forth an increase in output if the economy does not have the capacity to produce that output. So real GDP stays at $6.5 trillion, but the price level rises still further—the GDP deflator goes to 130. You can see that in this case, the attempt to stabilize real GDP using a feedback-rule policy has no effect on real GDP but generates a substantial price level increase.

We've now seen some of the shortcomings of using feedback rules for stabilization policy. Some economists believe that these shortcomings are serious and want to constrain Congress and the Fed so that they use fixed rules. Others, regarding the potential advantages of feedback rules as greater than their costs, advocate the continued use of such policies but with an important modification that we'll now look at.

Nominal GDP Targeting

Nominal GDP targeting is an attempt to keep the growth rate of nominal GDP steady. This policy target was first proposed by a leading Keynesian activist, James Tobin of Yale University. It is a policy that recognizes the strengths of a fixed rule but that regards the monetarist fixed rule as inappropriate. Instead, nominal GDP targeting uses feedback rules for fiscal and monetary policy to hit a fixed nominal GDP growth target.

Because nominal GDP growth equals the real GDP growth rate plus the inflation rate, keeping nominal GDP growth steady does not directly target either real GDP growth or inflation. But nominal GDP usually grows quickly because the inflation rate is high. And nominal GDP usually grows slowly because real GDP growth is negative—the economy is in recession. So the idea is that, by keeping nominal GDP growth steady, both excessive inflation and severe recession might be avoided.

Nominal GDP targeting uses feedback rules. Expansionary fiscal and/or monetary actions increase aggregate demand when nominal GDP is below target and contractionary fiscal and/or monetary actions decrease aggregate demand when nominal GDP is above target. The main problem with nominal GDP targeting is that there are long and variable time lags between the identification of a need to change aggregate demand and the effects of the policy actions that are taken.

Natural Rate Policies

The business cycle and unemployment policies we've considered have been directed at smoothing the business cycle and minimizing *cyclical unemployment*. It is also possible to pursue policies aimed at lowering the natural rate of unemployment. But there are no costless ways of lowering the natural rate of unemployment. Let's look at two possible ways.

One policy tool is unemployment insurance. To lower the natural rate of unemployment, the government might reduce the unemployment benefit, or shorten the period for which benefits are paid, or restrict benefits to people who undertake training programs that increase the likelihood of their finding jobs. With reduced benefits, an unemployed person would spend less time looking for a job and would accept a job even if it were not a good match for the person's skills. But such a policy might create hardship and have a cost that exceeds the cost of a high natural rate of unemployment.

The government might lower the minimum real wage rate. It could achieve a cut in the minimum wage either by holding the minimum money wage rate constant and letting inflation cut the minimum real wage rate or by cutting the minimum money wage rate. A lower minimum wage increases the quantity of labor demanded and lowers unemployment. The government faces a tradeoff between real wages and unemployment.

REVIEW

▪ Fixed-rule policies keep fiscal and monetary policy set steady and independent of the state of the economy.

▪ Feedback policies cut taxes, increase spending, and speed up money supply growth when the economy is in recession and reverse these measures when the economy is overheating.

▪ Successful feedback rules require knowledge of the source of shocks (demand side or supply side), an ability to forecast as far ahead as the policy actions have effects, and clarity about the feedback rules being used.

We've studied growth policy and business cycle and unemployment policy. Let's now study inflation policy.

Inflation Policy

THERE ARE TWO INFLATION POLICY PROBLEMS. In times of price level stability, the problem is to prevent inflation from breaking out. In times of inflation, the problem is to reduce its rate and restore price stability. Preventing inflation from breaking out means avoiding both demand-pull and cost-push forces. Avoiding demand-pull inflation is the flip side of avoiding demand-driven recession and is achieved by stabilizing aggregate demand. So the business cycle and unemployment policy we've just studied is also an anti-inflation policy. But avoiding cost-push inflation raises some special issues that we need to consider. So we will look at two issues for inflation policy:

■ Avoiding cost-push inflation
■ Slowing inflation

Avoiding Cost-Push Inflation

Cost-push inflation is inflation that has its origins in cost increases. In 1973–1974 and again in 1979, the world oil price exploded. Cost shocks such as these become inflationary if they are accommodated by an increase in the quantity of money. Such an increase in the quantity of money can occur if a monetary policy feedback rule is used. A fixed-rule policy for the money stock makes cost-push inflation impossible. Let's see why.

Figure 34.8 shows the economy at full employment. Aggregate demand is AD_0, short-run aggregate supply is SAS_0, and long-run aggregate supply is LAS. Real GDP is $7 trillion, and the GDP deflator is 110. Now suppose that OPEC tries to gain a temporary advantage by increasing the price of oil. The short-run aggregate supply curve shifts leftward from SAS_0 to SAS_1.

FIGURE 34.8

Responding to an OPEC Oil Price Increase

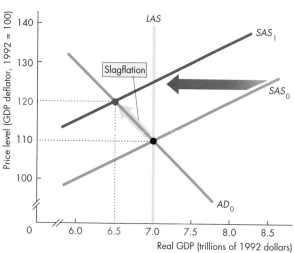

(a) Fixed rule

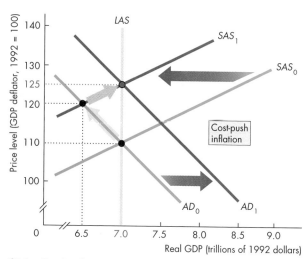

(b) Feedback rule

The economy starts out on AD_0 and SAS_0, with a GDP deflator of 110 and real GDP of $7 trillion. OPEC forces up the price of oil, and the short-run aggregate supply curve shifts to SAS_1. Real GDP decreases to $6.5 trillion, and the GDP deflator increases to 120. With a fixed-rule policy (part a), the Fed makes no change to aggregate demand. The economy stays in

a recession until resource prices fall and the economy returns to its original position. With a feedback-rule policy (part b), the Fed injects additional money and the aggregate demand curve shifts to AD_1. Real GDP returns to $7 trillion (potential GDP), but the GDP deflator increases to 125. The economy is set for another round of cost-push inflation.

Monetarist Fixed Rule   Figure 34.8(a) shows what happens if the Fed follows a fixed rule for monetary policy and the government follows a fixed rule for fiscal policy. Suppose that the fixed rule is for zero money growth and no change in taxes or government purchases of goods and services. With these fixed rules, the Fed and the government pay no attention to the fact that there has been an increase in the price of oil. No policy actions are taken. The short-run aggregate supply curve has shifted to SAS_1, but the aggregate demand curve remains at AD_0. The GDP deflator rises to 120, and real GDP falls to $6.5 trillion. The economy has experienced *stagflation*. With unemployment above the natural rate, the money wage rate will eventually fall. The low level of real GDP and low sales will probably also bring a fall in the price of oil. These events will shift the short-run aggregate supply curve back to SAS_0. The GDP deflator will fall to 110, and real GDP will increase to $7 trillion. But this adjustment might take a long time.

Keynesian Feedback Rule   Figure 34.8(b) shows what happens if the Fed and government operate a feedback rule. The starting point is the same as before—the economy is on SAS_0 and AD_0 with a GDP deflator of 110 and real GDP of $7 trillion. OPEC raises the price of oil, and the short-run aggregate supply curve shifts to SAS_1. Real GDP decreases to $6.5 trillion, and the price level rises to 120.

A feedback rule is followed. With potential GDP perceived to be $7 trillion and with actual real GDP at $6.5 trillion, the Fed pumps money into the economy and the government increases its spending and lowers taxes. Aggregate demand increases, and the aggregate demand curve shifts rightward to AD_1. The price level rises to 125, and real GDP returns to $7 trillion. The economy moves back to full employment but at a higher price level. The economy has experienced *cost-push inflation*.

The Fed responded in the way we've just described to the first wave of OPEC price increases in the mid-1970s. OPEC sees the same advantage in forcing up the price of oil again. A new rise in the price of oil decreases aggregate supply, and the short-run aggregate supply curve shifts leftward once more. The Fed chases it with an increase in aggregate demand, and the economy is in a freewheeling inflation. Realizing this danger, the Fed did *not* respond in the early 1980s to the second wave of OPEC price increases as it had done before. Instead, the Fed held firm and even slowed down the growth of aggregate demand

to further dampen the inflation consequences of OPEC's actions.

Incentives to Push Up Costs   You can see that there are no checks on the incentives to push up *nominal* costs if the Fed accommodates price hikes. If some group sees a temporary gain from pushing up the price at which they are selling their resources and if the Fed always accommodates the increase to prevent unemployment and slack business conditions from emerging, then cost-push elements will have a free rein. But when the Fed pursues a fixed-rule policy, the incentive to attempt to steal a temporary advantage from a price increase is severely weakened. The cost of higher unemployment and lower output is a consequence that each group will have to face and recognize.

Thus a fixed rule can deliver steady inflation, while a feedback rule, in the face of cost-push pressures, leaves inflation free to rise and fall at the whim of whichever group believes a temporary advantage to be available from pushing up its price.

Slowing Inflation

So far, we've concentrated on *avoiding* inflation. But often the problem is not to avoid inflation but to tame it. The United States was in such a situation during the late 1970s and early 1980s. How can inflation, once it has set in, be cured? We'll look at two cases:

- A surprise inflation reduction
- A credible announced inflation reduction

A Surprise Inflation Reduction   We'll use two equivalent approaches to study the problem of lowering inflation: the aggregate supply–aggregate demand model and the Phillips curve. The *AS-AD* model tells us about real GDP and the price level, while the Phillips curve, which is explained in Chapter 32 (pp. 724–728), lets us keep track of inflation and unemployment.

Figure 34.9 illustrates the economy at full employment with inflation raging at 10 percent a year. In part (a), the economy is on aggregate demand curve AD_0 and short-run aggregate supply curve SAS_0. Real GDP is $7 trillion, and the GDP deflator is 110. With real GDP equal to potential GDP on the *LAS* curve, the economy is at full employment. Equivalently, in part (b), the economy is on its long-run Phillips curve, *LRPC*, and short-run Phillips curve, $SRPC_0$. The

FIGURE 34.9

Lowering Inflation

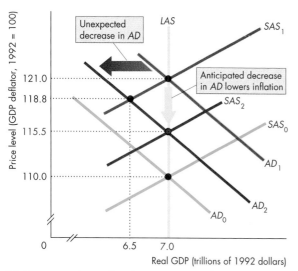

(a) Aggregate demand and aggregate supply

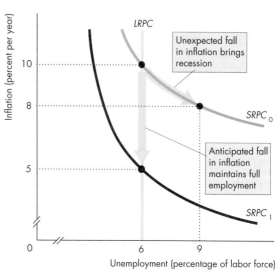

(b) Phillips curves

In part (a), aggregate demand is AD_0, short-run aggregate supply is SAS_0, and real GDP and potential GDP are $7 trillion on the long-run aggregate supply curve LAS. The aggregate demand curve is expected to shift and actually shifts to AD_1. The short-run aggregate supply curve shifts to SAS_1. The GDP deflator rises to 121, but real GDP remains at $7 trillion. Inflation is proceeding at a 10 percent a year, and this inflation rate is anticipated. In part (b), which shows this same situation, the economy on the short-run Phillips curve $SRPC_0$ and on the long-run Phillips curve $LRPC$. Unemployment is at the natural rate of 6 percent, and inflation is 10 percent a year. An unex-

pected slowdown in aggregate demand growth means that the aggregate demand curve shifts from AD_0 to AD_2, real GDP falls to $6.5 trillion, and inflation slows to 8 percent (GDP deflator is 118.8). Unemployment rises to 9 percent as the economy slides down $SRPC_0$. An anticipated, credible, announced slowdown in aggregate demand growth means that when the aggregate demand curve shifts from AD_0 to AD_2, the short-run aggregate supply curve shifts from SAS_0 to SAS_2. The short-run Phillips curve shifts to $SRPC_1$. Inflation slows to 5 percent, real GDP remains at $7 trillion, and unemployment remains at its natural rate of 6 percent.

inflation rate of 10 percent a year is anticipated, so unemployment is at its natural rate, 6 percent of the labor force.

Next year, aggregate demand is *expected* to increase and the aggregate demand curve in Fig. 34.9(a) is expected to shift rightward from AD_0 to AD_1. In expectation of this increase in aggregate demand, wages increase to shift the short-run aggregate supply curve from SAS_0 to SAS_1. If expectations are fulfilled, the GDP deflator rises to 121—a 10 percent inflation—and real GDP remains at potential GDP. In part (b), the economy remains at its original position—unemployment is at the natural rate, and the inflation rate is 10 percent a year.

Now suppose that no one is expecting the Fed to change its policy, but the Fed actually tries to slow

inflation. It raises interest rates and slows money growth. Aggregate demand growth slows, and the aggregate demand curve (in part a) shifts rightward from AD_0 not to AD_1, as people expect, but only to AD_2.

With no change in the expected inflation rate, wage rates rise by the same amount as before and the short-run aggregate supply curve shifts leftward from SAS_0 to SAS_1. Real GDP decreases to $6.5 trillion, and the GDP deflator rises to 118.8—an inflation rate of 8 percent a year. In Fig. 34.9(b), the economy moves along the short-run Phillips curve $SRPC_0$ as unemployment rises to 9 percent and inflation falls to 8 percent a year. The Fed's policy has succeeded in slowing inflation but at the cost of recession. Real GDP is below potential GDP, and unemployment is above its natural rate.

A Credible Announced Inflation Reduction

Suppose that instead of simply slowing down the growth of aggregate demand, the Fed announces its intention ahead of its action and in a credible and convincing way so that its announcement is believed. That is, the Fed's policy is anticipated. Because the lower level of aggregate demand is expected, wages increase at a pace consistent with the lower level of aggregate demand. The short-run aggregate supply curve (in Fig. 34.9a) shifts leftward from SAS_0 but only to SAS_2. Aggregate demand increases by the amount expected, and the aggregate demand curve shifts from AD_0 to AD_2. The GDP deflator rises to 115.5—an inflation rate of 5 percent a year—and real GDP remains at potential GDP.

In Fig. 34.9(b), the lower expected inflation rate shifts the short-run Phillips curve downward to $SRPC_1$, and inflation falls to 5 percent a year, while unemployment remains at its natural rate of 6 percent.

A credible announced inflation reduction lowers inflation but with no accompanying loss of output or increase in unemployment.

Inflation Reduction in Practice

When the Fed in fact slowed inflation in 1981, we paid a high price. The Fed's policy action was unpredicted. It occurred in the face of wages that had been set at too high a level to be consistent with the growth of aggregate demand that the Fed subsequently allowed. The consequence was recession—a decrease in real GDP and a rise in unemployment. Could the Fed have lowered inflation without causing recession by telling people far enough ahead of time that it did indeed plan to lower inflation?

The answer appears to be no. The main reason is that people expect the Fed to behave in line with its record, not with its stated intentions. How many times have you told yourself that it is your firm intention to take off 10 unwanted pounds or to keep within your budget and put a few dollars away for a rainy day, only to discover that, despite your very best intentions, your old habits win out in the end?

To form expectations of the Fed's actions, people look at the Fed's past *actions*, not its stated intentions. On the basis of such observations—called Fed-watching—they try to work out what the Fed's policy is, to forecast its future actions, and to forecast the effects of those actions on aggregate demand and inflation. The Greenspan Fed, like the Volcker Fed

that preceded it, has built a reputation for being anti-inflationary. That reputation is valuable because it helps the Fed to contain inflation and lowers the cost of eliminating inflation if it temporarily returns. The reason is that with a low expected inflation rate, the short-run Phillips curve is in a favorable position (like $SRPC_1$ in Fig. 34.9b). The Fed's action during the 1990s have been designed to keep inflation expectations low and prevent the gains made during the 1980s recession from being eroded.

A Truly Independent Fed

A radical suggestion for strengthening the Fed's reputation as the guardian of price stability is to make the Fed more independent of government and to charge it with the single responsibility of achieving and maintaining price level stability. Some central banks are more independent than the Fed. The German and Swiss central banks are the best examples. Another example is the New Zealand central bank. All these central banks have the responsibility of stabilizing prices but not real GDP and of pursuing their objective without interference from the government. Recent research on central bank performance has strengthened the view that a more independent central bank can deliver a lower average inflation rate without creating either a higher unemployment rate or a lower real GDP growth rate.

R E V I E W

■ A fixed rule gives more effective protection against a cost-push inflation than a feedback rule does.

■ When inflation is tamed, a recession usually results because people form policy expectations based on past policy actions.

■ By establishing a reputation of being an inflation fighter, the Fed has strengthened the expectation that it will maintain low inflation and possibly lowered the cost of fighting inflation.

◆ *Reading Between the Lines* on pp. 788–789 looks at the challenges the Fed faced in 1997 as it sought to keep the economy expanding but avoid renewed inflation.

You've now completed your study of macroeconomics. In the remaining chapters we shift our focus to the international economy.

Policy
WATCH

Steering the Course

THE NEW YORK TIMES, *JANUARY 2, 1997*

Outlook '97: Economy & Industry

By LOUIS UCHITELLE

The current economic recovery is nearly six years old, and the annual inflation rate is a meager 3.2 percent—the lowest level since World War II for an expansion this old. Economists are coming up with all sorts of explanations for the unusual milestone. And gradually many are concluding that inflation has become harder to explain.

The most striking aspect of this milestone is the scramble it is provoking among economists to repair the theory that they use to link unemployment and inflation. The theory, a keystone of economic policy, says that when the unemployment rate falls below a certain flash point, inflation soon accelerates. But the flash point foreseen in theory, 6 percent, was breached months ago, and nothing happened. The unemployment rate went as low as 5.1 percent, and still nothing happened. ...

The theoretical concept, known as the natural rate of unemployment, holds that at a certain level, the unemployment rate is just high enough to avoid labor shortages that would push up wages, prompting companies to raise prices to cover the additional labor costs. This equilibrium level, at which the inflation rate neither rises nor falls, has varied from decade to decade, but when the unemployment rate moves below what the Federal Reserve and the economists consider the natural rate, a series of responses develops that usually end in recession.

The Federal Reserve raises interest rates to discourage business activity. The unemployment rate then rises as people lose jobs, and the inflation rate falls. But instead of stopping at the natural rate, restoring an equilibrium, the unemployment rate often keeps rising as the economy slows. This sequence in the 1960's and the 1980's, the two other periods since World War II when a recovery has lasted as long as the current one, culminated in recessions. But with the natural rate theory so much in doubt today, the odds of a repeat performance are less. ...

Still, many forecasters and economists, particularly on Wall Street, where nervousness about inflation is part of the landscape, insist that the natural rate thesis remains valid and will show itself in 1997 in rising prices. "It is as important as ever," said Albert M. Wojnilower, senior economic adviser for Clipper Asset Management, "but no one is so sure anymore where the natural rate is." ...

Essence of THE STORY

■ The current economic recovery is almost six years old, and the annual inflation rate is 3.2 percent.

■ The theory of the natural rate of unemployment holds that inflation will accelerate if unemployment falls below the natural rate. In the 1990s, the natural rate was believed to be 6 percent.

■ During 1996, the unemployment rate fell below 6 percent but inflation did not accelerate.

■ The 1960s and 1980s expansions ended when unemployment fell below the danger point, inflation broke out, and the Fed raised interest rates

■ Forecasters and economists are divided on the natural rate thesis.

Economic

A N A L Y S I S

■ The Fed faces a constant stabilization policy dilemma: whether to tighten or loosen its grip on money growth by raising or lowering short-term interest rates.

■ During 1996, the economy experienced slow growth and the unemployment rate averaged 5.4 percent. The kept M2 money growth steady at around 4 percent per year.

■ Has the Fed done enough to stabilize the economy and prevent a return of inflation?

■ The theory of inflation predicts that the inflation rate rises if aggregate demand grows more quickly than potential GDP. Equivalently, the inflation rate rises if the unemployment rate falls below the natural rate.

■ The three figures show how the change in the inflation rate and the unemployment rate have been related since 1960.

■ In the 1960s, the natural rate of unemployment was about 5.4 percent (Fig. 1). In the 1970s, it was about 7.5 percent (Fig. 2), and in the late 1980s and 1990s, it fell to less than 6 percent (Fig. 3). (These are estimates of the natural rate.)

■ When the unemployment rate goes into the danger zone below the natural rate, the inflation rate usually increases. When the unemployment rate exceeds the natural rate, the inflation rate usually falls. (There were only two exceptions, in 1975 and 1987.)

■ By studying the shifting relationship between the change in the inflation rate and the unemployment rate, the Fed tries to estimate the natural rate and decide whether to tighten or loosen its monetary policy.

■ No one knows what the natural rate is. The natural rate keeps changing, and although we can estimate what it has been in the past, we cannot know its current and future levels.

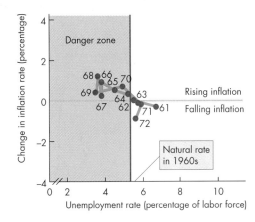

Figure 1 1960 to 1972

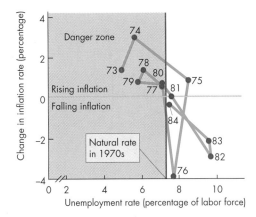

Figure 2 1973 to 1984

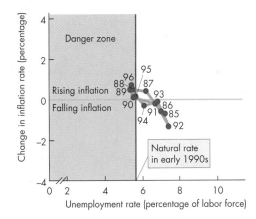

Figure 3 1985 to 1996

You're

THE VOTER

■ Why does the Fed need to estimate the natural rate of unemployment?

■ What are the main pros and cons of the Fed forgetting about the natural rate of unemployment and fixing the growth rate of M2?

■ What are the main pros and cons of the Fed raising interest rates every time the economy moves into the inflation danger zone?

SUMMARY

Key Points

Policy Goals (pp. 770–771)

▨ The goals of macroeconomic policy are to achieve the highest sustainable rate of long-term real GDP growth, smooth unavoidable business cycle fluctuations, maintain low unemployment, and avoid inflation.

Policy Tools and Performance (pp. 772–774)

▨ Fiscal policy was expansionary during the Kennedy years, the late 1960s and early 1970s, and the early Reagan 1980s. It was contractionary during the Carter, later Reagan, and Clinton years.

▨ The M2 growth rate increased during the 1970s, peaked in 1976, and then fell.

Long-Term Growth Policy (pp. 774–776)

▨ Policies to increase the long-term growth rate focus on increasing saving and investment in human capital and new technologies.

▨ To increase the saving rate, government saving must increase or incentives for private saving must be strengthened by increasing after-tax returns.

▨ Human capital investment might be increased with improved education and by improving on-the-job training programs.

▨ Investment in new technologies can be encouraged by tax incentives.

Business Cycle and Unemployment Policy (pp. 777–783)

▨ In the face of an aggregate demand shock, a fixed-rule policy takes no action. Real GDP and the price level fluctuate.

▨ In the face of an aggregate demand shock, a feedback-rule policy takes offsetting fiscal and monetary action. An ideal feedback rule keeps the economy at full employment, with stable prices.

▨ Some economists say that a feedback rule creates fluctuations because it requires greater knowledge of the economy than we have, operates with time lags that extend beyond the forecast horizon, and introduces unpredictability about policy reactions.

▨ In the face of a productivity growth slowdown, both rules have the same effect on output. A feedback rule brings a higher inflation rate than a fixed rule does.

▨ Nominal GDP targeting might avoid the extremes of inflation and recession.

Inflation Policy (pp. 784–787)

▨ A fixed rule minimizes the threat of cost-push inflation. A feedback rule validates cost-push inflation and leaves the price level and inflation rate free to move to wherever they are pushed.

▨ Inflation can be tamed, at little or no cost in terms of lost output or excessive unemployment, by slowing the growth of aggregate demand in a credible and predictable way. But usually, when inflation is slowed down, a recession occurs.

Key Figures

Key Terms

QUESTIONS

1. What are the four goals of macroeconomic policy?
2. What are the two core goals of policy and why are they core?
3. Describe the main features of fiscal policy since 1960. In which periods did fiscal policy increase aggregate demand? In which periods did fiscal policy decrease aggregate demand?
4. Describe the main features of monetary policy since 1960. In which periods was monetary policy inflationary? In which periods did monetary policy fight inflation?
5. What three things can policy do to try to speed potential GDP growth?
6. What is the distinction between a fixed-rule policy, a feedback-rule policy, and discretionary policy? Provide an example of each type of policy both in everyday life and in macroeconomics.
7. What are the effects of a temporary decrease in aggregate demand if the Fed adopts a fixed-rule policy.
8. How do real GDP and the price level respond to a permanent decrease in aggregate demand when the Fed adopts:
   a. A fixed-rule monetary policy?
   b. A feedback-rule policy?
9. Explain the main problems in using fiscal policy for smoothing the business cycle.
10. Why do economists disagree with each other on the appropriateness of fixed-rule and feedback-rule policies?
11. What are the effects of a rise in the price of oil on real GDP and the price level if the Fed employs:
    a. A fixed-rule policy?
    b. A feedback-rule policy?
12. What is nominal GDP targeting and why might it reduce real GDP fluctuations and inflation?
13. How can the Fed avoid cost-push inflation? Does a fixed rule or a feedback rule do the better job?
14. Why is lowering inflation costly?
15. What must the Fed do to minimize the cost of lowering inflation?
16. Why does having a reputation as an inflation fighter help in fighting inflation?

PROBLEMS

1. A productivity growth slowdown has occurred. Explain its possible origins and describe a policy package that is designed to speed up growth again.
2. The economy shown in the figure is initially on aggregate demand curve AD_0 and short-run aggregate supply curve SAS. Then aggregate demand decreases, and the aggregate demand curve shifts leftward to AD_1.

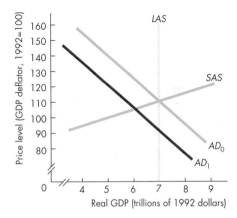

a. What are the initial equilibrium real GDP and price level?
b. If the decrease in aggregate demand is temporary and the government follows a fixed-rule fiscal policy, what happens to real GDP and the price level? Trace the immediate effects and the adjustment as aggregate demand returns to its original level.
c. If the decrease in aggregate demand is temporary and the government follows a feedback-rule fiscal policy, what happens to real GDP and the price level? Trace the immediate effects and the adjustment as aggregate demand returns to its original level.
d. If the decrease in aggregate demand is permanent and the government follows a fixed-rule fiscal policy, what happens to real GDP and the price level?
e. If the decrease in aggregate demand is permanent and the government follows a feedback-rule fiscal policy, what happens to real GDP and the price level?

3. The economy shown in the figure is initially on aggregate demand curve *AD* and short-run aggregate supply curve SAS_0. Then short-run aggregate supply decreases, and the short-run aggregate supply curve shifts leftward to SAS_1.

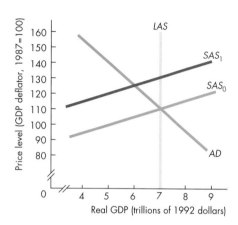

a. What are the initial equilibrium real GDP and price level?
b. What type of event could have caused the decrease in short-run aggregate supply?
c. If the government follows a fixed-rule monetary policy, what happens to real GDP and the price level? Trace the immediate effects and the adjustment as the short-run aggregate supply returns to its original level.
d. If the government follows a feedback-rule monetary policy, what happens to real GDP and the price level? Trace the immediate effects and the adjustment as aggregate demand and short-run aggregate supply respond to the policy action.

4. The economy is experiencing 10 percent inflation and 7 percent unemployment. Set out policies for the Fed and Congress to pursue that will lower both inflation and unemployment. Explain how and why your proposed policies will work.

http://hepg.awl.com/parkin/econ100

CRITICAL THINKING

1. Study *Reading Between the Lines* on pp. 788–789 and then:
   a. Describe the dilemma faced by the Fed and explain why the dilemma was particularly acute during 1997.
   b. What is the short-run relationship between inflation and unemployment?
   c. What signs do you look for to determine whether the economy is in the "danger zone"?
   d. What in your opinion does the Fed's dilemma of 1997 tell us about the relative merits of a fixed-rule monetary policy and a feedback-rule monetary policy?
2. The economy is booming and inflation is beginning to rise, but it is widely agreed that a massive recession is just around the corner. Weigh the advantages and disadvantages of the Congress pursuing a fixed-rule and a feedback-rule *fiscal* policy.
3. The economy is in a recession, and inflation is falling. It is widely agreed that a strong recovery is just around the corner. Weigh the advantages and disadvantages of the Fed pursuing a fixed-rule and a feedback-rule policy.
4. You have been hired to draw up an economic plan that will maximize the chance of the President being reelected.
   a. What are the macroeconomic stabilization policy elements in that plan?
   b. What do you have to make the economy do in an election year?
   c. What policy actions would help the President achieve reelection?
   (In dealing with this problem, be careful to take into account the effects of your proposed policy on expectations and the effects of those expectations on actual economic performance.)
5. Visit the World Wide Web site of the Economic Report of the President at http://www.stat-usa.gov/BEN/erp1/erp.html (or via the link at the Parkin Web site) and review Chapter 2 of the report, "Macroeconomic Policy and Performance." Write a summary and critique of this chapter.

Part 11

The Global Economy

It's a Small World

The scale of international trade, borrowing, and lending, both in absolute dollar terms and as a percentage of total world production expands every year. One country, Singapore, imports and exports goods and services in a volume that exceeds its Gross Domestic Product. The world's largest nation, China, returned to the international economic stage during the 1980s and is now a major producer of manufactured goods. ◆ International economic activity is large because today's economic world is small and because communication is so incredibly fast. But today's world is not a new world. From the beginning of recorded history, people have traded over large and steadily increasing distances. The great Western civilizations of Greece and Rome traded not only around the Mediterranean but also into the Gulf of Arabia. The great Eastern civilizations traded around the Indian Ocean. By the Middle Ages, the East and the West were trading routinely overland on routes pioneered by Venetian traders and explorers such as Marco Polo. When, in 1497, Vasco da Gama opened a sea route between the Atlantic and Indian Oceans around Africa, a new trade between East and West began, which brought tumbling prices of Eastern goods tumbled in Western markets. ◆ The European discovery of America and the subsequent opening up of Atlantic trade continued the process of steady globalization. So, the developments of the 1990s, amazing though many of them are, represent a continuation of an ongoing expansion of human horizons. ◆ The two chapters in this final part study the interaction of nations in today's global economy. ◆ In Chapter 35, you will learn about international trade in goods and services. Here, you will come face to face with one of the biggest policy issues of all ages, free trade versus protection. You will learn how all nations can benefit from free international trade. And you will see how protection from competition brings big benefits to a few and small losses to the many. The total gains from protection are dwarfed by the losses, but because the losses are spread thinly and the gains thickly, protectionism always has its supporters and political backers. ◆ In Chapter 36, you will learn about international borrowing and lending and the exchange rate. You will discover that the size of our international deficit depends not on how efficient we are, but on how much we save relative to how much we invest. Nations with low saving rates, everything else being the same, have international deficits. ◆ You'll also discover why foreign exchange rates fluctuate so much. ◆ But first, we'll spend some time with the economist who first explained the fundamental idea of comparative advantage, David Ricardo. And we'll talk with one of today's leading international economists, Stanley Fischer, formally a professor at MIT and now First Deputy Managing Director of the International Monetary Fund.

Understanding the Gains from International Trade

The Economist: David Ricardo

David Ricardo (1772–1832) was a highly successful 27-year-old stockbroker when he stumbled on a copy of Adam Smith's *The Wealth of Nations* (see p. 2) on a weekend visit to the country. He was immediately hooked and went on to become the most celebrated economist of his age and one of the all-time great economists. One of his many contributions was to develop the principle of comparative advantage, the foundation on which the modern theory of international trade is built. The example he used to illustrate this principle was the trade between England and Portugal in cloth and wine.

The General Agreement on Tariffs and Trade (GATT) was established as a reaction against the devastation wrought by beggar-my-neighbor tariffs imposed during the 1930s. But it is also a triumph for the logic first worked out by Smith and Ricardo.

"Under a system of perfectly free commerce, each country naturally devotes its capital and labor to such employments as are most beneficial to each."

DAVID RICARDO

THE PRINCIPLES OF POLITICAL ECONOMY AND TAXATION,

1817

The Issues and Ideas

Until the mid-eighteenth century, it was generally believed that the purpose of international trade was to keep exports greater than imports and to pile up gold. If gold were accumulated, it was believed, the nation would prosper; and if gold were lost through an international deficit, the nation would be drained of money and impoverished. These beliefs are called *mercantilism*, and the *mercantilists* were pamphleteers who advocated with missionary fervor the pursuit of an international surplus. If exports did not exceed imports, the mercantilists wanted imports restricted.

In the 1740s, David Hume explained that as the quantity of money (gold) changes, so also does the price level, and the nation's *real* wealth is unaffected. In the 1770s, Adam Smith argued that import restrictions would lower the gains from specialization and make a nation poorer, and 30 years later, David Ricardo proved the law of comparative advantage and demonstrated the superiority of free trade. Mercantilism was intellectually bankrupt but remained politically powerful.

Gradually, through the nineteenth century, the mercantilist influence waned and North America and Western Europe prospered in an environment of increasingly free international trade. But despite remarkable advances in economic understanding, mercantilism never quite died. It had a brief and devastating revival in the 1920s and 1930s when tariff hikes brought about the collapse of international trade and accentuated the Great Depression. It subsided again after World War II with the establishment of the General Agreement on Tariffs and Trade (GATT).

But mercantilism lingers on. The often expressed view that the United States should restrict Japanese imports and reduce its deficit with Japan and fears that the NAFTA will bring economic ruin to the United States are modern manifestations of mercantilism. It would be interesting to have David Hume, Adam Smith, and David Ricardo commenting on these views. But we know what they would say—the same things that they said to the eighteenth century mercantilists. And they would still be right today.

THEN ...

In the eighteenth century, when mercantilists and economists were debating the pros and cons of free international exchange, the available transportation technology limited the gains from international trade. Sailing ships with tiny cargo holds took close to a month to cross the Atlantic Ocean. But the potential gains were large, and so was the incentive to cut shipping costs. By the 1850s, the clipper ship had been developed, cutting the journey from Boston to Liverpool to only $12^{1}/_{4}$ days. Half a century later, 10,000-ton steamships were sailing between America and England in just 4 days. As sailing times and costs declined, so the gains from international trade increased and the volume of trade expanded.

... AND NOW

The container ship has revolutionized international trade and contributed to its continued expansion. Today, most goods cross the oceans in containers—metal boxes—packed into and piled on top of ships like the one above.

Container technology has cut the cost of ocean shipping by economizing on handling and by making cargoes harder to steal, lowering insurance costs. It is unlikely that there would be much international trade in goods such as television sets and VCRs without this technology. High-value and perishable cargoes such as flowers and fresh foods, as well as urgent courier packages, travel by air. Every day, dozens of cargo-laden 747s fly between every major U.S city and destinations across the Atlantic and Pacific oceans.

As the world economy has become more integrated, new international institutions have evolved. One of these institutions is the International Monetary Fund, or IMF. Let's talk with Stanley Fischer, one of today's outstanding economists, who now plays a leading role at the IMF.

Talking with

Stanley Fischer has served as the First Deputy Managing Director of the International Monetary Fund since 1994. Born in Zambia in 1943, he received a B.S. and an M.S. from the London School of Economics in 1965 and 1966, respectively, and a Ph.D. from MIT in 1969. Professor Fischer has taught at the University of Chicago and MIT. He served as Vice President of Development Economics and Chief Economist at the World Bank from 1988 to 1992.

Michael Parkin talked with Professor Fischer about his work at the International Monetary Fund and World Bank, the goals of these two institutions, the importance of trade liberalization, and how the thinking of economists such as David Ricardo provide insights to address today's international trade challenges.

Dr. Fischer, how did you get into economics?

I was at high school in Zimbabwe (then Rhodesia) and went through the British educational system, and in the sixth grade I began to specialize in physics, chemistry, and math. Then I heard about economics, and switched one of my science courses to economics—and loved it.

This was the perfect field, one that provided an analytic way of understanding an important part of how societies work, and also one in which I could use my quantitative skills. I went to the London School of Economics for my Bachelor's and Master's degrees and then to MIT for my Ph.D. My first appointment was at the University of Chicago, at a time when Milton Friedman was still the dominant influence there.

As someone who has worked both at the University of Chicago and at MIT, how would you characterize the two approaches to economics?

When I was at Chicago in the early 1970s, MIT was more theoretical and Chicago was low-tech and more policy-oriented. Now they've switched: Chicago's macro is far more theoretical and less policy-oriented than that at MIT.

One of the things I learned at Chicago was to try to figure out whether a particular theoretical point was quantitatively important (though I should have learned that at MIT, from Bob Solow, who is famous for his back-of-the-envelope calculations). I remember Milton Friedman saying in one of the first Money Workshops I went to, "There's no reason to think the real interest rate should vary systematically with inflation." I replied, "Oh, but you know that in the Sidrauski (non-maximizing) model, changes in the inflation rate change capital intensity and so the real interest rate." And he said, "Well now, how does that work?" And then we went through the exercise of calculating the possible size of the various effects involved and concluded that the overall effect would have to be very small. Of course, as later empirical work shows, the real interest rate is negatively affected by inflation, just not mainly through that particular mechanism.

What is the role of the IMF and what are the main problems that it seeks to address?

The IMF has three main functions. The first is *surveillance*, which means that it is an institution in which countries discuss problems of the international economy, as well as each other's economies. Twice a year, the Fund staff presents its survey of the world economy, the *World Economic Outlook.*

In addition, Fund staff presents an annual report—the Article IV report—on the economy of each member country. The Article IV reports are based on the staff's analysis and discussions with the economic policy makers in each country.

The second function of the Fund is to *make loans to countries* that are in economic trouble. These loans typically provide balance of payments support to countries in crisis and countries to which the private capital markets are reluctant to lend. The biggest such loan ever made was to Mexico in 1995, after its December 1994 devaluation, when the private capital markets dried up and the country had to achieve a massive turnaround—8 percent of GDP—in its balance of payments within a year. These loans come with conditions on the country's policies that were designed to deal with the problems that caused the crisis.

The third IMF function is technical assistance and training. We provide technical assistance to

help improve the monetary and fiscal systems, for instance, to explain how to set up a system to undertake open market operations or how to institute a value-added tax. This is hands-on advice. We also provide technical assistance to improve statistical systems. We provided a lot of technical assistance to the transition economies of Eastern Europe and the former Soviet Union. Many of those countries now have well-functioning central banks after only 5 years of transition.

You've also worked at the World Bank. What is the role of the World Bank and what are the main problems that it seeks to address?

The World Bank was established at the end of World War II to lend to countries undergoing reconstruction and also to lend to developing countries. At that time, private capital flows were small and very little went to developing countries. Initially, the Bank lent to finance projects, such as ports or dams, and it still does project lending. Over time, it was realized that lending for projects didn't do a whole lot for development in the face of bad economic policies. In the late 1970s, and particularly the 1980s, the Bank began to undertake *lending for structural adjustment*—providing loans to governments on the condition they change their economic policies, for instance, and most important, by liberalizing trade.

International trade is an important factor in the success of any country. How has trade liberalization featured in the success cases of countries such as Mexico?

Mexico was a closed economy in the 1970s and even in the early 1980s. The World Bank, in collaboration with the Fund, encouraged the authorities to liberalize their

Every one of the successful East Asian countries has succeeded by integrating with the world economy.

trade regime. The World Bank didn't pull its punches on these issues, and it was right. The success of the Mexican reforms is evident from the differences in the response of the economy to its debt crises in 1982 and 1995. In the 1980s, it took Mexico about 8 years to dig out from its crisis. In 1995, it took only 2 years to adjust and to resume growth at 5 percent a year, as well as to repay most of the loans made by the United States and the IMF. That contrast is a result of the reforms Mexico undertook during the 1980s and early 1990s. It is now a much more open, flexible, and private-sector-oriented economy.

What are the gains and losses of the international trade liberalization process of the post–World War II years? Have the industrial countries or the developing countries gained most?

I'm not sure there's a scientific way of making that appraisal. But if you were to look at what has happened in the postwar period to the industrialized countries, which, despite some slowing since the 1960s, have grown faster, more consistently, and with less disruption than in any period of similar length in history, you would have to say that the architecture of the postwar economy has been very successful. And then if you look at the developing countries, you will find that, on the average, they have grown faster yet. In the most populous part of the globe, namely, East Asia and China and, to some extent, India, we have had absolutely unprecedented growth. Every one of the successful East Asian countries has succeeded by integrating with the world economy, by promoting exports and increasing imports, especially of capital and intermediate goods. This process of opening up and using world markets for exports and imports has been absolutely critical. This outcome is what most economists from Adam Smith and David Ricardo on would have predicted.

The one part of the world where progress has, on the average, been most disappointing, is Africa. But there are countries in Africa that have done well and others that have not. The countries that have been serious about trying to trade in the global economy and about implementing market-friendly policies have done better on the whole. There are countries where the per capita income has grown substantially. We have seen significant growth in per capita income in Africa in the last few years. The prospects for South Africa look good, and that could be very important for a large part of the continent. In addition, there are countries such as Mozambique and Uganda, which have begun growing very fast after terrible civil wars, and there is Botswana, which has been one of the fastest-growing economies in the world for the past two decades.

What do you foresee as the challenges facing the world economy?
There are the continuing challenges of making sure that this present period of lower inflation and reasonable growth continues.

Second, to make sure that the global trading system keeps opening up—a task in which the newly created World Trade Organization (WTO) has a vital role to play. Third, to focus on the challenge of opening capital accounts—not one of the original functions of the IMF but becoming an increasingly important part of our activities. That's a challenge. Bringing the transition economies, particularly Russia, into the global system is a huge challenge. Bringing the countries that have been failing, many of them in Africa, into the global system is another major challenge. In addition, there is the challenge of maintaining momentum in a variety of countries where things are changing. For example, India used to be regarded as inherently a 3 percent a year growth country; in fact, it's been growing at 5 to 7 percent a year for the last few years. Maintaining that growth rate would make all the difference. In the Middle East, similarly, we're seeing signs of countries turning around. For the IMF, World Bank, and WTO the challenges facing the world economy are to keep the good things

---

For the IMF, World Bank, and WTO, the challenges facing the world economy are to keep the good things going and take care of the countries that are falling behind.

---

going and take care of the countries that are falling behind.

What kinds of jobs do economics graduates get in international organizations such as the IMF and the World Bank? What should students be doing as undergraduates to prepare themselves to be in such positions?
People who want to work in the Fund and the Bank should take courses in macroeconomics, international trade and finance, development, monetary economics, and public finance. From the viewpoint of the Bank, it would also be useful to study more micro-oriented policy issues. The Fund and the Bank have entry programs designed for people who may be destined for their professional ranks. The World Bank's is called Young Professionals, and the IMF's is called the Economist Program.

The IMF and the World Bank are terrific places to work. You get to use your analytic skills all the time, in the real world. You have to decide what really matters, you have to be sure that what you're recommending will improve the lives of people. And then if you work in the operational parts of the Fund or Bank, you have to persuade the countries with which you're working that you're right. If you are right, and if you succeed, you have the satisfaction of having done something useful.

In the process, you'll have had the benefit of learning some diplomacy. You are also likely to learn some humility—for you will realize that the really hard work of implementing policies is done by the politicians and officials of the countries that undertake them. Your job is to help them do their own jobs better, always bearing in mind that the benefits or costs are borne by their people.

35

Trading with the World

Since ancient times, people have expanded their trading as far as technology allowed. Marco Polo opened up the silk route between Europe and China in the thirteenth century. Today, container ships laden with cars and machines and Boeing 747s stuffed with farm-fresh foods ply sea and air routes, carrying billions of dollars worth of goods. Why do people go to such great lengths to trade with those in other nations? ◆ Low-wage Mexico has entered into a free trade agreement with high-wage Canada and the United States—the North American Free Trade Agreement, or NAFTA. According to Texas billionaire Ross Perot, this agreement will

Silk Routes and Sucking Sounds

cause a "giant sucking sound" as jobs are transferred from Michigan to Mexico. Is Ross Perot right? How can we compete with a country that pays its workers a fraction of U.S. wages? Are there any industries, besides perhaps the Hollywood movie industry, in which we have an advantage? ◆ In 1930, Congress passed the Smoot-Hawley Act, which imposed a 45 percent tariff (rising to 60 percent by 1933) on one third of U.S. imports. This move provoked widespread retaliation and a tariff war among the world's major trading countries. After World War II, a process of trade liberalization brought about a gradual reduction of tariffs. What are the effects of tariffs on international trade? Why don't we have completely unrestricted international trade? ◆ In this chapter, we're going to learn about international trade. We'll discover how all nations can gain by specializing in producing the goods and services in which they have a comparative advantage and trading with other countries. We'll discover that *all* countries can compete, no matter how high their wages. We'll also explain why countries restrict trade.

After studying this chapter, you will be able to:

- Describe the patterns in international trade

- Explain comparative advantage and explain why all countries can gain from international trade

- Explain how economies of scale and diversity of taste lead to gains from trade

- Explain why trade restrictions reduce our imports, exports, and consumption possibilities

- Explain the arguments used to justify trade restrictions and show how they are flawed

- Explain why we have trade restrictions

Patterns and Trends in International Trade

THE GOODS AND SERVICES THAT WE BUY FROM people in other countries are called **imports**. The goods and services that we sell to people in other countries are called **exports**. What are the most important things that we import and export? Most people would probably guess that a rich nation such as the United States imports raw materials and exports manufactured goods. Although that is one feature of U.S. international trade, it is not its most important feature. The vast bulk of our exports *and* imports is manufactured goods. We sell foreigners earth-moving equipment, airplanes, supercomputers, and scientific equipment, and we buy televisions, VCRs, blue jeans, and T-shirts from them. Also, we are a major exporter of agricultural products and raw materials. We also import and export a huge volume of services.

Trade in Goods

Manufactured goods account for 50 percent of our exports and for 60 percent of our imports. Industrial materials (raw materials and semimanufactured items) account for 17 percent of our exports and for 20 percent of our imports, and agricultural products account for only 7 percent of our exports and 3 percent of our imports. Our largest individual export and import items are capital goods and autos.

But goods account for only 74 percent of our exports and 83 percent of our imports. The rest of our international trade is in services.

Trade in Services

You may be wondering how a country can "export" and "import" services. Here are some examples.

If you take a vacation in France and travel there on an Air France flight from New York, you import transportation services from France. The money you spend in France on hotel bills and restaurant meals is also classified as the import of services. Similarly, the vacation taken by a French student in the United States counts as an U.S. export of services to France.

When we import TV sets from South Korea, the owner of the ship that transports them might be Greek and the company that insures them might be British. The payments that we make for the transportation

and insurance are imports of services. Similarly, when an American shipping company transports California wine to Tokyo, the transportation cost is an export of a service to Japan. Our international trade in these types of services is large and growing.

Geographical Patterns

The United States has trading links with every part of the world, but Canada is our biggest single trading partner for both exports and imports. We buy 45 percent of our imports from Japan and other Asian countries such as China, Hong Kong, South Korea, and Taiwan, and we sell a similar percentage of our exports to Asia, Europe, Latin America, and Canada.

Trends in the Volume of Trade

In 1960, we exported less than 5 percent of total output and imported 4 1/2 percent of the goods and services that we consumed ourselves. Over the years since then, these percentages have steadily increased, and today they are more than twice their 1960 levels.

On the export side, capital goods, automobiles, food, and raw materials have remained large items and held a roughly constant share of total exports, but the composition of imports has changed. Food and raw material imports have fallen steadily. Imports of fuel increased dramatically during the 1970s but fell during the 1980s. Imports of machinery have grown and today they approach 50 percent of total imports.

Balance of Trade and International Borrowing

The value of exports minus the value of imports is called the **balance of trade.** In 1996, the U.S. balance of trade was a negative $95 billion. Our imports were $95 billion more than our exports. When we import more than we export, as we did in 1996, we borrow from foreigners or sell some of our assets. When we export more than we import, we make loans to foreigners or buy some of their assets.

We study the *balance* of trade in Chapter 36. In this chapter, our goal is to understand the factors that influence the *volume* and *directions* of international trade rather than its balance. And the keys to this understanding are the concepts of opportunity cost and comparative advantage.

Opportunity Cost and Comparative Advantage

THE FUNDAMENTAL FORCE THAT GENERATES international trade is *comparative advantage*. And the basis of comparative advantage is divergent *opportunity costs*. You met these ideas in Chapter 3, when we learned about the gains from specialization and exchange between Tom and Nancy.

Tom and Nancy each specialize in producing just one good and then trade with each other. Most nations do not go to the extreme of specializing in a single good and importing everything else. Nonetheless, nations can increase the consumption of all goods if they redirect their scarce resources toward the production of those goods and services in which they have a comparative advantage.

To see how this outcome occurs, we'll apply the same basic ideas we learned in the case of Tom and Nancy to trade among nations. We'll begin by recalling how we can use the production possibility frontier to measure opportunity cost. Then we'll see how divergent opportunity costs bring comparative advantage and gains from trade for countries as well as for individuals even though no country completely specializes in the production of just one good.

Opportunity Cost in Farmland

Farmland (a fictitious country) can produce grain and cars at any point inside or along its production possibility frontier, *PPF*, shown in Fig. 35.1. (We're holding constant the output of all the other goods that Farmland produces.) The Farmers (the people of Farmland) are consuming all the grain and cars that they produce, and they are operating at point *a* in the figure. That is, Farmland is producing and consuming 15 billion bushels of grain and 8 million cars each year. What is the opportunity cost of a car in Farmland?

We can answer that question by calculating the slope of the production possibility frontier at point *a*. The magnitude of the slope of the frontier measures the opportunity cost of one good in terms of the other. To measure the slope of the frontier at point *a*, place a straight line tangential to the frontier at point *a* and calculate the slope of that straight line. Recall that the formula for the slope of a line is the change in the value of the variable measured on the *y*-axis divided by the change in the value of the variable measured on the *x*-axis as we move along the line.

Here, the variable measured on the *y*-axis is billions of bushels of grain, and the variable measured on the *x*-axis is millions of cars. So the slope is the change in the number of bushels of grain divided by the change in the number of cars.

As you can see from the red triangle at point *a* in the figure, if the number of cars produced increases by 2 million, grain production decreases by 18 billion bushels. Therefore the magnitude of the slope is 18 billion divided by 2 million, which equals 9,000. To get one more car, the people of Farmland must give up 9,000 bushels of grain. Thus the opportunity cost of 1 car is 9,000 bushels of grain. Equivalently, 9,000 bushels of grain cost 1 car. For the people of Farmland, these opportunity costs are the prices they face. The price of a car is 9,000 bushels of grain, and the price of 9,000 bushels of grain is 1 car.

FIGURE 35.1

Opportunity Cost in Farmland

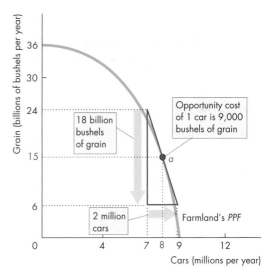

Farmland produces and consumes 15 billion bushels of grain and 8 million cars a year. That is, it produces and consumes at point *a* on its production possibility frontier. Opportunity cost is equal to the magnitude of the slope of the production possibility frontier. The red triangle tells us that at point *a*, 18 billion bushels of grain must be forgone to get 2 million cars. That is, at point *a*, 2 million cars cost 18 billion bushels of grain. Equivalently, 1 car costs 9,000 bushels of grain or 9,000 bushels cost 1 car.

Opportunity Cost in Mobilia

Figure 35.2 shows the production possibility frontier of Mobilia (another fictitious country). Like the Farmers, the Mobilians consume all the grain and cars that they produce. Mobilia consumes 18 billion bushels of grain a year and 4 million cars, at point a'.

Let's calculate the opportunity costs in Mobilia. At point a', the opportunity cost of a car is equal to the magnitude of the slope of the red line tangential to the production possibility frontier, *PPF*. You can see from the red triangle that the magnitude of the slope of Mobilia's production possibility frontier is 6 billion bushels of grain divided by 6 million cars, which equals 1,000 bushels of grain per car. To get one more car, the Mobilians must give up 1,000 bushels of grain. Thus the opportunity cost of 1 car is 1,000 bushels of grain, or, equivalently, the opportunity cost of 1,000 bushels of grain is 1 car. These are the prices faced in Mobilia.

FIGURE 35.2
Opportunity Cost in Mobilia

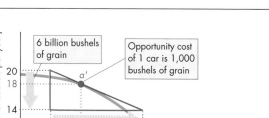

Mobilia produces and consumes 18 billion bushels of grain and 4 million cars a year. That is, it produces and consumes at point a' on its production possibility frontier. Opportunity cost is equal to the magnitude of the slope of the production possibility frontier. The red triangle tells us that at point a', 6 billion bushels of grain must be forgone to get 6 million cars. That is, at point a', the opportunity cost of 6 million cars is 6 billion bushels of grain. Equivalently, 1 car costs 1,000 bushels of grain or 1,000 bushels of grain cost 1 car.

Comparative Advantage

Cars are cheaper in Mobilia than in Farmland. One car costs 9,000 bushels of grain in Farmland but only 1,000 bushels of grain in Mobilia. But grain is cheaper in Farmland than in Mobilia—9,000 bushels of grain costs only 1 car in Farmland, while that same amount of grain costs 9 cars in Mobilia.

Mobilia has a comparative advantage in car production. Farmland has a comparative advantage in grain production. A country has a **comparative advantage** in producing a good if it can produce that good at a lower opportunity cost than any other country.

Let's see how opportunity cost differences and comparative advantage generate gains from international trade.

Gains from Trade

IF MOBILIA BOUGHT GRAIN FOR WHAT IT COSTS Farmland to produce it, then Mobilia could buy 9,000 bushels of grain for 1 car. That is much lower than the cost of growing grain in Mobilia, for there it costs 9 cars to produce 9,000 bushels of grain. If the Mobilians can buy grain at the low Farmland price, they will reap some gains.

If the Farmers can buy cars for what it costs Mobilia to produce them, they will be able to obtain a car for 1,000 bushels of grain. Because it costs 9,000 bushels of grain to produce a car in Farmland, the Farmers would gain from such an opportunity.

In this situation, it makes sense for Mobilians to buy their grain from Farmers and for Farmers to buy their cars from Mobilians. Let's see how such profitable international trade comes about.

Reaping the Gains from Trade

We've seen that the Farmers would like to buy their cars from the Mobilians and that the Mobilians would like to buy their grain from the Farmers. Let's see how the two groups do business with each other, by concentrating our attention on the international market for cars.

Figure 35.3 illustrates such a market. The quantity of cars *traded internationally* is measured on the x-axis. On the y-axis, we measure the price of a car. This price is expressed as the number of bushels of grain that a car costs—the opportunity cost of a car.

FIGURE 35.3
International Trade
in Cars

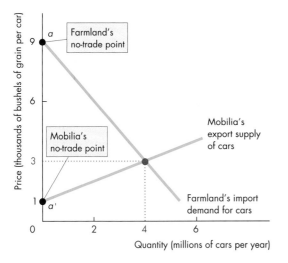

As the price of a car decreases, the quantity of imports demanded by Farmland increases—Farmland's import demand curve for cars is downward sloping. As the price of a car increases, the quantity of cars supplied by Mobilia for export increases—Mobilia's export supply curve of cars is upward sloping. Without international trade, the price of a car is 9,000 bushels of grain in Farmland (point *a*) and 1,000 bushels of grain in Mobilia (point *a'*).

With free international trade, the price of a car is determined where the export supply curve intersects the import demand curve—a price of 3,000 bushels of grain. At that price, 4 million cars a year are imported by Farmland and exported by Mobilia. The value of grain exported by Farmland and imported by Mobilia is 12 billion bushels a year, the quantity required to pay for the cars imported.

If no international trade takes place, the price of a car in Farmland is 9,000 bushels of grain, indicated by point *a* in the figure. Again, if no trade takes place, the price of a car in Mobilia is 1,000 bushels of grain, indicated by point *a'* in the figure. The no-trade points *a* and *a'* in Fig. 35.3 correspond to the points identified by those same letters in Figs. 35.1 and 35.2. The lower the price of a car (in terms of grain), the greater is the quantity of cars that the Farmers are willing to import from the Mobilians. This fact is illustrated by the downward-sloping curve, which shows Farmland's import demand for cars.

The Mobilians respond in the opposite direction. The higher the price of cars (in terms of bushels of grain), the greater is the quantity of cars that Mobilians are willing to export to Farmers. This fact is reflected in Mobilia's export supply of cars—the upward-sloping line in Fig. 35.3.

The international market in cars determines the equilibrium price and quantity traded. This equilibrium occurs where the import demand curve intersects the export supply curve. In this case, the equilibrium price of a car is 3,000 bushels of grain. Four million cars a year are exported by Mobilia and imported by Farmland. Notice that the price at which cars are traded is lower than the initial price in Farmland but higher than the initial price in Mobilia.

Balanced Trade

The number of cars exported by Mobilia—4 million a year—is exactly equal to the number of cars imported by Farmland. How does Farmland pay for its cars? By exporting grain. How much grain does Farmland export? You can find the answer by noticing that for 1 car, Farmland has to pay 3,000 bushels of grain. Hence, for 4 million cars, they have to pay 12 billion bushels of grain. Thus Farmland's exports of grain are 12 billion bushels a year. Mobilia imports this same quantity of grain.

Mobilia is exchanging 4 million cars for 12 billion bushels of grain each year, and Farmland is doing the opposite, exchanging 12 billion bushels of grain for 4 million cars. Trade is balanced between these two countries. The value received from exports equals the value paid out for imports.

Changes in Production and Consumption

We've seen that international trade makes it possible for Farmers to buy cars at a lower price than that at which they can produce them for themselves. Equivalently, Farmers can sell their grain for a higher price. International trade also enables Mobilians to sell their cars for a higher price. Equivalently, Mobilians can buy grain for a lower price. Thus everybody gains. How is it possible for *everyone* to gain? What are the changes in production and consumption that accompany these gains?

An economy that does not trade with other economies has identical production and consumption possibilities. Without trade, the economy can consume only what it produces. But with international trade, an economy can consume different quantities of goods from those that it produces. The production possibility frontier describes the limit of what a country can produce, but it does not describe the limits to what it can consume. Figure 35.4 will help you to see the distinction between production possibilities and consumption possibilities when a country trades with other countries.

First of all, notice that the figure has two parts, part (a) for Farmland and part (b) for Mobilia. The production possibility frontiers that you saw in Figs. 35.1 and 35.2 are reproduced here. The slopes of the two black lines in the figure represent the opportunity costs in the two countries when there is no international trade. Farmland produces and consumes at point *a*, and Mobilia produces and consumes at *a'*. Cars cost 9,000 bushels of grain in Farmland, and 1,000 bushels of grain in Mobilia.

Consumption Possibilities   The red line in each part of Fig. 35.4 shows the country's consumption possibilities with international trade. These two red lines have the same slope, and the magnitude of that slope is the opportunity cost of a car in terms of grain on the world market—3,000 bushels per car. The *slope* of the consumption possibilities line is common to both countries because its magnitude equals the *world* price. But the position of a country's consumption possibilities line depends on the country's production possibilities. A country cannot produce outside its production possibility curve, so its consumption possibility curve touches its production possibility curve. Thus Farmland could choose to consume at point *b* with no international trade or at any point on its red consumption possibilities line with international trade.

Free Trade Equilibrium   With international trade, the producers of cars in Mobilia can get a higher price for their output. As a result, they increase the quantity of car production. At the same time, grain producers in Mobilia get a lower price for their grain, and so they reduce production. Producers in Mobilia adjust their output by moving along their production possibility frontier until the opportunity cost in Mobilia equals the world price (the opportunity cost in the world market). This situation arises when Mobilia is producing at point *b'* in Fig. 35.4(b).

But the Mobilians do not consume at point *b'*. That is, they do not increase their consumption of cars and decrease their consumption of grain. Instead, they sell some of their car production to Farmland in exchange for some of Farmland's grain. They trade internationally. But to see how that works out, we first need to check in with Farmland to see what's happening there.

In Farmland, producers of cars now get a lower price and producers of grain get a higher price. As a consequence, producers in Farmland decrease car production and increase grain production. They adjust their outputs by moving along the production possibility frontier until the opportunity cost of a car in terms of grain equals the world price (the opportunity cost on the world market). They move to point *b* in part (a). But the Farmers do not consume at point *b*. Instead, they trade some of their additional grain production for the now cheaper cars from Mobilia.

The figure shows us the quantities consumed in the two countries. We saw in Fig. 35.3 that Mobilia exports 4 million cars a year and Farmland imports those cars. We also saw that Farmland exports 12 billion bushels of grain a year and Mobilia imports that grain. Thus Farmland's consumption of grain is 12 billion bushels a year less than it produces, and its consumption of cars is 4 million a year more than it produces. Farmland consumes at point *c* in Fig. 35.4(a).

Similarly, we know that Mobilia consumes 12 billion bushels of grain more than it produces and 4 million cars fewer than it produces. Thus Mobilia consumes at *c'* in Fig. 35.4(b).

Calculating the Gains from Trade

You can now literally see the gains from trade in Fig. 35.4. Without trade, Farmers produce and consume at point *a* (part a)—a point on Farmland's production possibility frontier. With international trade, Farmers consume at point *c* in part (a)—a point *outside* the production possibility frontier. At point *c*, Farmers are consuming 3 billion bushels of grain a year and 1 million cars a year more than before. These increases in consumption of both cars and grain, beyond the limits of the production possibility frontier, are the gains from international trade. Mobilians also gain. Without trade, they consume at point *a'* in part (b)—a point on Mobilia's production possibility frontier. With international trade, they consume at point *c'*—a point outside the

FIGURE 35.4

Expanding Consumption Possibilities

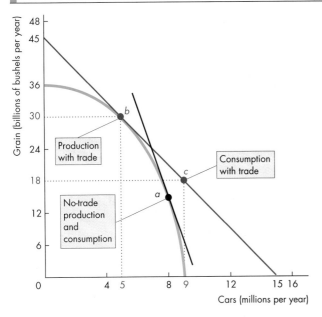

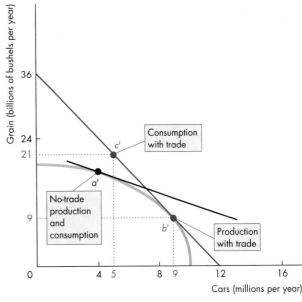

(a) Farmland

With no international trade, the Farmers produce and consume at point *a* and the opportunity cost of a car is 9,000 bushels of grain (the slope of the black line in part a). Also, with no international trade, the Mobilians produce and consume at point *a'* and the opportunity cost of 1,000 bushels of grain is 1 car (the slope of the black line in part b). Goods can be exchanged internationally at a price of 3,000 bushels of grain for 1 car along the red line in each part of the figure. In part (a), Farmland decreases its production of cars and

(b) Mobilia

increases its production of grain, moving from *a* to *b*. It exports grain and imports cars, and it consumes at point *c*. The Farmers have more of both cars and grain than they would if they produced all their own goods—at point *a*. In part (b), Mobilia increases car production and decreases grain production, moving from *a'* to *b'*. Mobilia exports cars and imports grain, and it consumes at point *c'*. The Mobilians have more of both cars and grain than they would if they produced all their own goods—at point *a'*.

production possibility frontier. With international trade, Mobilia consumes 3 billion bushels of grain a year and 1 million cars a year more than without trade. These are the gains from international trade for Mobilia.

Gains for All

Trade between the Farmers and the Mobilians does not create winners and losers. Everyone wins. Sellers add the net demand of foreigners to their domestic demand, and so their market expands. Buyers are faced with domestic supply plus net foreign supply and so have a larger supply available to them.

REVIEW

▥ When countries have divergent opportunity costs, they can gain from international trade.

▥ Each country can buy some goods and services from another country at a lower opportunity cost than that at which it can produce them for itself.

▥ Gains arise when each country increases its production of those goods and services in which it has a comparative advantage.

▥ All countries gain from international trade. There are no losers.

Gains from Trade in Reality

THE GAINS FROM TRADE THAT WE HAVE JUST studied between Farmland and Mobilia in grain and cars occur in a model economy—in a world economy that we have imagined. But these same phenomena occur every day in the real global economy.

Comparative Advantage in the Global Economy

We buy TVs and VCRs from Korea, machinery from Europe, and fashion goods from Hong Kong. In exchange, we sell machinery, grain and lumber, airplanes, computers and financial services. All this international trade is generated by comparative advantage, just like the international trade between Farmland and Mobilia in our model economy. All international trade arises from comparative advantage, even when trade is in similar goods such as tools and machines. At first thought, it seems puzzling that countries exchange manufactured goods. Why doesn't each developed country produce all the manufactured goods its citizens want to buy?

Trade in Similar Goods

Why does the United States produce automobiles for export and at the same time import large quantities of them from Canada, Japan, Korea, and Western Europe? Wouldn't it make more sense to produce all the cars that we buy here in the United States? After all, we have access to the best technology available for producing cars. Autoworkers in the United States are surely as productive as their fellow workers in Canada, Western Europe, and Asian countries. So why does the United States have a comparative advantage in some types of cars and Japan and Europe in others?

Diversity of Taste and Economies of Scale

The first part of the answer is that people have a tremendous diversity of taste. Let's stick with the example of cars. Some people prefer a sports car, some prefer a limousine, some prefer a regular, full-size car, and some prefer a minivan. In addition to size and type of car, there are many other dimensions in which cars vary. Some have low fuel consumption, some have high performance, some are spacious and comfortable, some have a large trunk, some have four-wheel drive, some have front-wheel drive, some have a radiator grill that looks like a Greek temple, and others look like a wedge. People's preferences across these many dimensions vary. The tremendous diversity in tastes for cars means that people value variety and are willing to pay for it in the marketplace.

The second part of the answer to the puzzle is *economies of scale*—the tendency for the average cost to be lower, the larger the scale of production. In such situations, larger and larger production runs lead to ever lower average costs. Many goods, including cars, experience economies of scale. For example, if a car producer makes only a few hundred (or perhaps a few thousand) cars of a particular type and design, the producer must use production techniques that are much more labor-intensive and much less automated than those employed to make hundreds of thousands of cars in a particular model. With short production runs and labor-intensive production techniques, costs are high. With very large production runs and automated assembly lines, production costs are much lower. But to obtain lower costs, the automated assembly lines have to produce a large number of cars.

It is the combination of diversity of taste and economies of scale that determines opportunity cost, produces comparative advantages, and generates such a large amount of international trade in similar commodities. With international trade, each car manufacturer has the whole world market to serve. Each producer can specialize in a limited range of products and then sell its output to the entire world market. This arrangement enables large production runs on the most popular cars and feasible production runs even on the most customized cars demanded by only a handful of people in each country.

The situation in the market for cars is also present in many other industries, especially those producing specialized equipment and parts. For example, the United States exports computer central processor chips but imports memory chips, exports mainframe computers but imports PCs, exports specialized video equipment but imports VCRs. Thus international exchange of similar but slightly differentiated manufactured products is a highly profitable activity.

Let's next see what happens when governments restrict international trade. We'll see that free trade brings the greatest possible benefits. We'll also see why, in spite of the benefits of free trade, governments sometimes restrict trade.

Trade Restrictions

GOVERNMENTS RESTRICT INTERNATIONAL TRADE to protect domestic industries from foreign competition by using two main tools:

1. Tariffs
2. Nontariff barriers

A **tariff** is a tax that is imposed by the importing country when an imported good crosses its international boundary. A **nontariff barrier** is any action other than a tariff that restricts international trade. Examples of nontariff barriers are quantitative restrictions and licensing regulations that limit imports. First, let's look at tariffs.

The History of Tariffs

U.S. tariffs today are modest compared with their historical levels. Figure 35.5 shows the average tariff rate—total tariffs as a percentage of total imports.

You can see in this figure that this average reached a peak of 20 percent in 1933. In that year, three years after the passage of the Smoot-Hawley Act, one third of imports was subject to a tariff, and on those imports, the tariff rate was 60 percent. (The average tariff in Fig. 35.5 for 1933 is 60 percent multiplied by 0.33, which equals 20 percent.) Today, the average tariff rate is only 4 percent.

The reduction in tariffs since World War II followed the signing in 1947 of the **General Agreement on Tariffs and Trade** (GATT). Since its formation, the GATT has organized several rounds of negotiations that have resulted in tariff reductions. One of these, the Kennedy Round which began in the early 1960s, resulted in large tariff cuts starting in 1967. Another, the Tokyo Round, resulted in further tariff cuts in 1979. The most recent, the Uruguay Round, which started in 1986 and was completed in 1994, was the most ambitious and comprehensive of the rounds. The Uruguay Round also led to the creation of a new **World Trade Organization** (WTO). Membership of the WTO brings greater obligations on countries to observe the GATT rules.

FIGURE **35.5**

U.S. Tariffs: 1930–1996

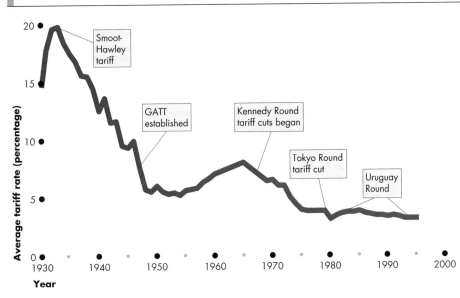

The Smoot-Hawley Act, which was passed in 1930, took U.S. tariffs to a peak average rate of 20 percent in 1933. (One third of imports was subject to a tariff rate of 60 percent.) Since the establishment of GATT in 1947, tariffs have steadily declined in a series of negotiating rounds, the most significant of which are identified in the figure. Tariffs are now as low as they have ever been.

Sources: U.S. Bureau of the Census, *Historical Statistics of the United States, Colonial Times to 1970,* Bicentennial Edition, Part 1 (Washington, D.C., 1975), Series U-212: *Statistical Abstract of the United States: 1986,* 106th edition (Washington, D.C., 1985); and *Statistical Abstract of the United States: 1996,* 116th edition (Washington, D.C., 1996).

In addition to the agreements under the GATT and the WTO, the United States is a party to the **North American Free Trade Agreement** (NAFTA), which became effective on January 1, 1994, and under which barriers to international trade between the United States, Canada, and Mexico will be virtually eliminated after a 15-year phasing-in period.

In other parts of the world, trade barriers have virtually been eliminated among the member countries of the European Union, which has created the largest unified tariff-free market in the world. In 1994, discussions among the Asia-Pacific Economic group (APEC) led to an agreement in principle to work toward a free-trade area that embraces China, all the economies of East Asia and the South Pacific, and the United States and Canada. These countries include the fastest-growing economies and hold the promise of heralding a global free-trade area.

The effort to achieve freer trade underlines the fact that trade in some goods is still subject to extremely high tariffs. The highest tariffs faced by U.S. buyers are those on textiles and footwear. A tariff of more than 10 percent (on the average) is imposed on almost all our imports of textiles and footwear. For example, when you buy a pair of blue jeans for $20, you pay about $5 more than you would if there were no tariffs on textiles. Other goods protected by tariffs are agricultural products, energy and chemicals, minerals, and metals. The meat, cheese, and sugar that you consume cost significantly more because of protection than they would with free international trade.

The temptation on governments to impose tariffs is a strong one. First, tariffs provide revenue to the government. Second, they enable the government to satisfy special interest groups in import-competing industries. But, as we'll see, free international trade brings enormous benefits that are reduced when tariffs are imposed. Let's see how.

How Tariffs Work

To analyze how tariffs work, let's return to the example of trade between Farmland and Mobilia. Figure 35.6 shows the international market for cars in which these two countries are the only traders. The volume of trade and the price of a car are determined at the point of intersection of Mobilia's export supply curve of cars and Farmland's import demand curve for cars.

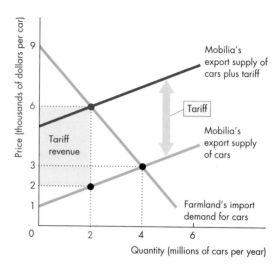

FIGURE 35.6
The Effects of a Tariff

Farmland imposes a tariff on car imports from Mobilia. The tariff increases the price that Farmers have to pay for cars. It shifts the supply curve of cars in Farmland leftward. The vertical distance between the original supply curve and the new one is the amount of the tariff, $4,000 per car. The price of cars in Farmland increases, and the quantity of cars imported decreases. The government of Farmland collects a tariff revenue of $4,000 per car—a total of $8 billion on the 2 million cars imported. Farmland's exports of grain decrease because Mobilia now has a lower income from its exports of cars.

In Fig. 35.6, these two countries trade cars and grain in exactly the same way that we saw in Fig. 35.3. Mobilia exports cars, and Farmland exports grain. The volume of car imports into Farmland is 4 million a year, and the world market price of a car is 3,000 bushels of grain. Fig. 35.6 expresses prices in dollars rather than in units of grain and is based on a money price of grain of $1 a bushel. With grain costing $1 a bushel, the money price of a car is $3,000.

Now suppose that the government of Farmland, perhaps under pressure from car producers, decides to impose a tariff on imported cars. In particular, suppose that a tariff of $4,000 per car is imposed. (This is a huge tariff, but the car producers of Farmland are pretty fed up with competition from Mobilia.) What happens?

- The supply of cars in Farmland decreases.
- The price of a car in Farmland rises.
- The quantity of cars imported by Farmland decreases.
- The government of Farmland collects the tariff revenue.
- Resource use is inefficient.
- The *value* of exports changes by the same amount as the *value* of imports and trade remains balanced.

Change in the Supply of Cars Farmland cannot buy cars at Mobilia's export supply price. It must pay that price plus the $4,000 tariff. So the supply curve in Farmland shifts leftward. The new supply curve is that labeled "Mobilia's export supply of cars plus tariff." The vertical distance between Mobilia's export supply curve and the new supply curve is the tariff of $4,000 a car.

Rise in Price of Cars A new equilibrium occurs where the new supply curve intersects Farmland's import demand curve for cars. That equilibrium is at a price of $6,000 a car, up from $3,000 with free trade.

Fall in Imports Car imports fall from 4 million to 2 million cars a year. At the higher price of $6,000 a car, Farmland's car producers increase their production. Grain production in Farmland decreases as resources are moved into the expanding car industry.

Tariff Revenue Total expenditure on imported cars by the Farmers is $6,000 a car multiplied by the 2 million cars imported ($12 billion). But not all of that money goes to the Mobilians. They receive $2,000 a car, or $4 billion for the 2 million cars. The difference—$4,000 a car, or a total of $8 billion for the 2 million cars—is collected by the government of Farmland as tariff revenue.

Inefficiency The people of Farmland are willing to pay $6,000 for the marginal car imported. But the opportunity cost of that car is $2,000. So there is a gain from trading an extra car. In fact, there are gains—willingness to pay exceeds opportunity cost—all the way up to 4 million cars a year. Only when 4 million cars are being traded is the maximum price that a Farmer is willing to pay equal to the minimum price that is acceptable to a Mobilian. Thus restricting trade reduces the gains from trade.

Trade Remains Balanced With free trade, Farmland was paying $3,000 a car and buying 4 million cars a year from Mobilia. Thus the total amount paid to Mobilia for imports was $12 billion a year. With a tariff, Farmland's imports have been cut to 2 million cars a year and the price paid to Mobilia has also been cut to only $2,000 a car. Thus the total amount paid to Mobilia for imports has been cut to $4 billion a year. Doesn't this fact mean that Farmland now has a balance of trade surplus?

It does not. The price of cars in Mobilia has fallen. But the price of grain remains at $1 a bushel. So the relative price of cars has fallen, and the relative price of grain has increased. With free trade, the Mobilians could buy 3,000 bushels of grain for one car. Now they can buy only 2,000 bushels for a car. With a higher relative price of grain, the quantity demanded by the Mobilians decreases and Mobilia imports less grain. But because Mobilia imports less grain, Farmland exports less grain. In fact, Farmland's grain industry suffers from two sources. First, there is a decrease in the quantity of grain sold to Mobilia. Second, there is increased competition for inputs from the now expanded car industry. Thus the tariff leads to a contraction in the scale of the grain industry in Farmland.

It seems paradoxical at first that a country imposing a tariff on cars hurts its own export industry, decreasing its exports of grain. It may help to think of it this way: Mobilians buy grain with the money they make from exporting cars to Farmland. If they export fewer cars, they cannot afford to buy as much grain. In fact, in the absence of any international borrowing and lending, Mobilia must cut its imports of grain by exactly the same amount as the loss in revenue from its export of cars. Grain imports into Mobilia are cut back to a value of $4 billion, the amount that can be paid for by the new lower revenue from Mobilia's car exports. Thus trade is still balanced. The tariff cuts imports and exports by the same amount. The tariff has no effect on the *balance* of trade, but it reduces the *volume* of trade.

The result that we have just derived is perhaps one of the most misunderstood aspects of international economics. On countless occasions, politicians and others call for tariffs to remove a balance of trade deficit or argue that lowering tariffs would produce a balance of trade deficit. They reach this conclusion by failing to work out all the implications of a tariff.

Let's now turn our attention to the other tool for restricting trade: nontariff barriers.

Nontariff Barriers

The two main forms of nontariff barriers are:

1. Quotas
2. Voluntary export restraints

A **quota** is a quantitative restriction on the import of a particular good, which specifies the maximum amount of the good that can be imported in a given period of time. A **voluntary export restraint** (VER) is an agreement between two governments in which the government of the exporting country agrees to restrain the volume of its own exports.

Quotas are especially prominent in textiles and agriculture. Voluntary export restraints are used to regulate trade between Japan and the United States.

How Quotas and VERs Work

To see how a quota works, suppose that Farmland imposes a quota that restricts its car imports to 2 million cars a year. Figure 35.7 shows the effects of this action. The quota is shown by the vertical red line at 2 million cars a year. Because it is illegal to exceed the quota, car importers buy only that quantity from Mobilia, for which they pay $2,000 a car. But because the import supply of cars is restricted to 2 million cars a year, people in Farmland are willing to pay $6,000 per car. This is the price of a car in Farmland.

The value of imports falls to $4 billion, exactly the same as in the case of the tariff. So with lower incomes from car exports and with a higher relative price of grain, Mobilians cut back on their imports of grain in exactly the same way that they did under a tariff.

The key difference between a quota and a tariff lies in who collects the gap between the import supply price and the domestic price. In the case of a tariff, it is the government of the importing country. In the case of a quota, it goes to the person who has the right to import under the import quota regulations.

A voluntary export restraint is like a quota arrangement in which quotas are allocated to each exporting country. The effects of voluntary export restraints are similar to those of quotas but differ from them in that the gap between the price in the importing country and the export price is captured not by domestic importers but by the foreign exporter. The government of the exporting country has to establish procedures for allocating the restricted volume of exports among its producers.

FIGURE 35.7

The Effects of a Quota

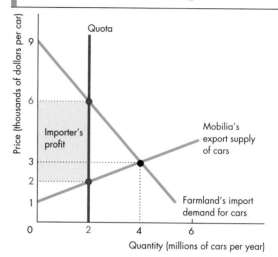

Farmland imposes a quota of 2 million cars a year on car imports from Mobilia. That quantity appears as the vertical line labeled "Quota." Because the quantity of cars supplied by Mobilia is restricted to 2 million, the price at which those cars will be traded increases to $6,000. Importing cars is profitable because Mobilia is willing to supply cars at $2,000 each. There is competition for import quotas.

R E V I E W

- When a country opens itself up to international trade and trades freely at world market prices, it expands its consumption possibilities.
- When trade is restricted, some of the gains from trade are lost.
- A country might be better off with restricted trade than with no trade but not as well off as it could be if it engaged in free trade.
- A tariff reduces the volume of imports, but it also reduces the volume of exports.
- Under both free trade and restricted trade (and without international borrowing and lending), the value of imports equals the value of exports. With restricted trade, both the total value of exports and the total value of imports are less than under free trade, but trade is still balanced.

Let's now look at some commonly heard arguments for restricting international trade.

The Case Against Protection

FOR AS LONG AS NATIONS AND INTERNATIONAL trade have existed, people have debated whether a country is better off with free international trade or with protection from foreign competition. The debate continues, but for most economists, a verdict has been delivered and is the one you have just seen. Free trade promotes prosperity for all: protection is inefficient. We've seen the most powerful case for free trade in the example of how Farmland and Mobilia both benefit from their comparative advantage. But there is a broader range of issues in the free trade versus protection debate. Let's review these issues.

Three arguments for restricting international trade are:

■ The national security argument
■ The infant-industry argument
■ The dumping argument

Let's look at each in turn.

The National Security Argument

The national security argument for protection is that a country must protect industries that produce defense equipment and armaments and those on which the defense industries rely for their raw materials and other intermediate inputs. This argument for protection does not withstand close scrutiny.

First, it is an argument for international isolation, for in a time of war, there is no industry that does not contribute to national defense. Second, if the case is made for boosting the output of a strategic industry, it is more efficient to achieve this outcome with a subsidy to the firms in the industry financed out of taxes. Such a subsidy would keep the industry operating at the scale judged appropriate, and free international trade would keep the prices faced by consumers at their world market levels.

The Infant-Industry Argument

The so-called **infant-industry argument** for protection is that it is necessary to protect a new industry to enable it to grow into a mature industry that can compete in world markets. The argument is based on the idea of *dynamic comparative advantage*, which can arise from *learning-by-doing* (see Chapter 3).

Learning-by-doing is a powerful engine of productivity growth, and comparative advantage evolves and changes because of on-the-job experience. But these facts do not justify protection.

First, the infant-industry argument is valid only if the benefits of learning-by-doing *not only* accrue to the owners and workers of the firms in the infant industry but also *spill over* to other industries and parts of the economy. For example, there are huge productivity gains from learning-by-doing in the manufacture of aircraft. But almost all of these gains benefit the stockholders and workers of Boeing and other aircraft producers. Because the people making the decisions, bearing the risk, and doing the work are the ones who benefit, they take the dynamic gains into account when they decide on the scale of their activities. In this case, almost no benefits spill over to other parts of the economy, so there is no need for government assistance to achieve an efficient outcome.

Second, even if the case is made for protecting an infant industry, it is more efficient to do so by a subsidy to the firms in the industry, with the subsidy financed out of taxes.

The Dumping Argument

Dumping occurs when a foreign firm sells its exports at a lower price than its cost of production. Dumping might be used by a firm that wants to gain a global monopoly. In this case, the foreign firm sells its output at a price below its cost to drive domestic firms out of business. When the domestic firms have gone, the foreign firm takes advantage of its monopoly position and charges a higher price for its product. Dumping is usually regarded as a justification for temporary countervailing tariffs.

But there are powerful reasons to resist the dumping argument for protection. First, it is virtually impossible to detect dumping because it is hard to determine a firm's costs. As a result, the test for dumping is whether a firm's export price is below its domestic price. But this test is a weak one because it can be rational for a firm to charge a low price in markets in which the quantity demanded is highly sensitive to price and a higher price in a market in which demand is less price-sensitive.

Second, it is hard to think of a good that is produced by a natural *global* monopoly. So even if all the domestic firms were driven out of business in some industry, it would always be possible to find several and usually many alternative foreign sources of supply and to buy at prices determined in competitive markets.

Third, if a good or service were a truly global natural monopoly, the best way of dealing with it would be by regulation—just as in the case of domestic monopolies. Such regulation would require international cooperation.

The three arguments for protection that we've just examined have an element of credibility. The counterarguments are in general stronger, so these arguments do not make the case for protection. But they are not the only arguments that you might encounter. The many other arguments that are commonly heard are quite simply wrong. They are fatally flawed. The most common of them are that protection:

■ Saves jobs
■ Allows us to compete with cheap foreign labor
■ Brings diversity and stability
■ Penalizes lax environmental standards
■ Protects national culture
■ Prevents rich countries from exploiting developing countries

Saves Jobs

The argument is: When we buy shoes from Brazil or shirts from Taiwan, U.S. workers lose their jobs. With no earnings and poor prospects, these workers become a drain on welfare and spend less, causing a ripple effect of further job losses. The proposed solution to this problem is to ban imports of cheap foreign goods and protect U.S. jobs. The proposal is flawed for the following reasons.

First, free trade does cost some jobs, but it also creates other jobs. It brings about a global rationalization of labor and allocates labor resources to their highest-value activities. Because of international trade in textiles, tens of thousands of workers in the United States have lost jobs because textile mills and other factories have closed. But tens of thousands of workers in other countries have gotten jobs because textile mills have opened there. And tens of thousands of U.S. workers have gotten better-paying jobs than textile workers because other export industries have expanded and created more jobs than have been destroyed.

Second, imports create jobs. They create jobs for retailers that sell imported goods and firms that service those goods. They also create jobs by creating incomes in the rest of the world, some of which are spent on imports of U.S.-made goods and services.

Although protection does save particular jobs, it does so at inordinate cost. For example, textile jobs are protected in the United States by quotas imposed under an international agreement called the Multifiber Arrangement. It has been estimated by the U.S. International Trade Commission (ITC) that because of quotas, 72,000 jobs exist in textiles that would otherwise disappear and annual clothing expenditure in the United States is $15.9 billion, or $160 per family higher than it would be with free trade. Equivalently, the ITC estimates that each textile job saved costs $221,000 a year.

Allows Us to Compete with Cheap Foreign Labor

With the removal of protective tariffs in U.S. trade with Mexico, Ross Perot said we would hear a "giant sucking sound" of jobs rushing to Mexico (one of which is shown in the cartoon). Let's see what's wrong with this view.

The labor cost of a unit of output equals the wage rate divided by labor productivity. For example, if a U.S. auto worker earns $30 an hour and produces 15

"I don't know what the hell happened—one minute I'm at work in Flint, Michigan, then there's a giant sucking sound and suddenly here I am in Mexico."

Drawing by M. Stevens; © 1993
The New Yorker Magazine, Inc.

units of output an hour, the average labor cost of a unit of output is $2. If a Mexican auto assembly worker earns $3 an hour and produces 1 unit of output an hour, the average labor cost of a unit of output is $3. Other things remaining the same, the higher a worker's productivity, the higher is the worker's wage rate. High-wage workers have high productivity. Low-wage workers have low productivity.

Although high-wage U.S. workers are more productive, on the average, than low-wage Mexican workers, there are differences across industries. U.S. labor is relatively more productive in some activities than in others. For example, the productivity of U.S. workers in producing movies, financial services, and customized computer chips is relatively higher than in the production of metals and some standardized machine parts. The activities in which U.S. workers are relatively more productive than their Mexican counterparts are those in which the United States has a *comparative advantage*. By engaging in free trade, increasing our production and exports of the goods and services in which we have a comparative advantage and decreasing our production and increasing our imports of the goods and services in which our trading partners have a comparative advantage, we can make ourselves and the citizens of other countries better off.

Brings Diversity and Stability

A diversified investment portfolio is less risky than one that has all the eggs in one basket. The same is true for an economy's production. A diversified economy fluctuates less than an economy that produces only one or two goods.

But big, rich, diversified economies like those of the United States, Japan, and Europe do not have this type of stability problem. Even a country like Saudi Arabia that produces almost only one good (oil) can benefit from specializing in the activity at which it has a comparative advantage and then investing in a wide range of other countries to bring greater stability to its income and consumption.

Penalizes Lax Environmental Standards

A new argument for protection is that many poorer countries, such as Mexico, do not have the same environment policies that we have and, because they

are willing to pollute and we are not, we cannot compete with them without tariffs. So if they want free trade with the richer and "greener" countries, they must clean up their environments to our standards.

This argument for trade restrictions is weak. First, not all poorer countries have significantly lower environmental standards than the United States has. Many poor countries and the former Communist countries of Eastern Europe do have bad environment records. But some countries enforce strict laws. Second, a poor country cannot afford to be as concerned about its environment as a rich country can. The best hope for a better environment in Mexico and in other developing countries is rapid income growth through free trade. As their incomes grow, developing countries will have the *means* to match their desires to improve their environment. Third, poor countries have a comparative advantage at doing "dirty" work, which helps rich countries achieve higher environment standards than they otherwise could.

Protects National Culture

The national culture argument for protection is not heard much in the United States, but it is a commonly heard argument in Canada and Europe.

The expressed fear is that free trade in books, magazines, movies, and television programs means U.S. domination and the end of local culture. So, the reasoning continues, it is necessary to protect domestic culture industries from free international trade to ensure the survival of a national cultural identity.

Protection of these industries is common and takes the form of nontariff barriers. For example, local content regulations on radio and television broadcasting and in magazines is often required.

The cultural identity argument for protection has no merit, and it is one more example of rent-seeking (see Chapter 13, pp. 277–278). Writers, publishers, and broadcasters want to limit foreign competition so that they can earn larger economic profits. There is no actual danger to national culture. In fact, many of the creators of so-called American cultural products are not Americans, but the talented citizens of other countries, ensuring the survival of their national cultural identities in Hollywood! Also, if national culture is in danger, there is no surer way of helping it on its way out than by impoverishing the nation whose culture it is. And protection is an effective way of doing just that.

Prevents Rich Countries from Exploiting Developing Countries

Another new argument for protection is that international trade must be restricted to prevent the people of the rich industrial world from exploiting the poorer people of the developing countries, forcing them to work for slave wages.

Wage rates in some developing countries are indeed very low. But by trading with developing countries, we increase the demand for the goods that these countries produce, and, more significantly, we increase the demand for their labor. When the demand for labor in developing countries increases, the wage rate also increases. So, far from exploiting people in developing countries, trade improves their opportunities and increases their incomes.

We have reviewed the arguments that are commonly heard in favor of protection and the counter-arguments against them. There is one counter-argument to protection that is general and quite overwhelming. Protection invites retaliation and can trigger a trade war. The best example of a trade war occurred during the Great Depression of the 1930s when the Smoot-Hawley Tariff was introduced. Country after country retaliated with its own tariff, and in a short period, world trade had almost disappeared. The costs to all countries were large and led to a renewed international resolve to avoid such self-defeating moves in the future. They also led to the creation of GATT and are the impetus behind NAFTA, APEC, and the European Union.

REVIEW

- Trade restrictions aimed at national security goals, stimulating the growth of new industries, and restraining foreign monopoly have little merit.
- Trade restrictions to save jobs, compensate for low foreign wages, make the economy more diversified, compensate for costly environmental policies, protect national culture, and protect developing countries from being exploited are misguided.
- The main arguments against trade restrictions are that subsidies and antitrust policies can achieve domestic goals more efficiently than protection and that protection can trigger a trade war in which all countries lose.

Why Is International Trade Restricted?

WHY, DESPITE ALL THE ARGUMENTS AGAINST protection, is trade restricted? There are two key reasons:

- Tariff revenue
- Rent seeking

Tariff Revenue

Government revenue is costly to collect. In the developed countries such as the United States, a well-organized tax-collection system is in place that can generate billions of dollars of income tax and sales tax revenues. This tax-collecting system is made possible by the fact that most economic transactions are done by firms that must keep properly audited financial records. Without such records, the revenue collection agencies (the Internal Revenue Service in the United States) would be severely hampered in the work. Even with audited financial accounts, some proportion of potential tax revenue is lost. Nonetheless, for the industrialized countries, the income tax and sales taxes are the major sources of revenue and the tariff plays a very small role.

But governments in developing countries have a difficult time collecting taxes from their citizens. Much economic activity takes place in an informal economy with few financial records. So only a small amount of revenue is collected from income taxes and sales taxes in these countries. The one area in which economic transactions are well recorded and audited is in international trade. So this activity is an attractive base for tax collection in these countries and is used much more extensively than in the developed countries.

Rent Seeking

The major reason why international trade is restricted is because of rent seeking. Free trade increases consumption possibilities *on the average* but not everyone shares in the gain and some people even lose. Free trade brings benefits to some and imposes costs on others, with total benefits exceeding total costs. It is the uneven distribution of costs and benefits that is the principal source of impediment to achieving more liberal international trade.

Returning to our example of trade in cars and grain between Farmland and Mobilia, the benefits to Farmland from free trade accrue to all the producers of grain and those producers of cars who would not have to bear the costs of adjusting to a smaller car industry. These costs are transition costs, not permanent costs. The costs of moving to free trade are borne by those car producers and their employees who have to become grain producers. The number of people who gain will, in general, be enormous compared with the number who lose. The gain per person will therefore be rather small. The loss per person to those who bear the loss will be large. Because the loss that falls on those who bear it is large, it will pay those people to incur considerable expense to lobby against free trade. On the other hand, it will not pay those who gain to organize to achieve free trade. The gain from trade for any one individual is too small for that individual to spend much time or money on a political organization to achieve free trade. The loss from free trade will be seen as being so great by those bearing that loss that they *will* find it profitable to join a political organization to prevent free trade. Each group is optimizing—weighing benefits against costs and choosing the best action for themselves. The anti-free-trade group will, however, undertake a larger quantity of political lobbying than the pro-free-trade group.

Compensating Losers

If, in total, the gains from free international trade exceed the losses, why don't those who gain compensate those who lose so that everyone is in favor of free trade? To some degree, such compensation does take place. When Congress approved the NAFTA deal with Canada and Mexico, it set up a $56 million fund to support and retrain workers who lost their jobs because of the new trade agreement. During the first six months of the operation of NAFTA, only 5,000 workers applied for benefits under this scheme.

The losers from freer international trade are also compensated indirectly through the normal unemployment compensation arrangements. But only limited attempts are made to compensate those who lose from free international trade. The main reason why full compensation is not attempted is that the costs of identifying all the losers and estimating the value of their losses would be enormous. Also, it would never

be clear whether a person who has fallen on hard times is suffering because of free trade or for other reasons, perhaps reasons that are largely under the control of the individual. Furthermore, some people who look like losers at one point in time may, in fact, wind up gaining. The young auto worker who loses his job in Michigan and becomes a computer assembly worker in Minneapolis resents the loss of work and the need to move. But a year or two later, looking back on events, he counts himself fortunate. He has made a move that has increased his income and given him greater job security.

It is because we do not, in general, compensate the losers from free international trade that protectionism is such a popular and permanent feature of our national economic and political life.

R E V I E W

- International trade is restricted because tariffs raise revenue for governments and because tariffs create gains (economic rents) for some and losses for others.
- The revenue from tariffs is important for developing countries but not for developed countries such as the United States.
- Gains from trade are spread thinly, and gains from protection accrue to a few people. It pays the few to organize to ensure that their interests are protected.

◆ You've now seen how free international trade enables all nations to gain from specialization and trade. By producing goods in which we have a comparative advantage and trading some of our production for that of others, we expand our consumption possibilities. Placing impediments on that trade restricts the extent to which we can gain from specialization and trade. Opening our country up to free international trade expands the market for the things that we sell and raises their relative price. The market for the things that we buy also expands, and the relative price falls. *Reading Between the Lines* on pp. 816–817 looks at a recent example of the removal and reintroduction of a tariff in the small but politically sensitive market for brooms.

In the final chapter, we're going to examine the balance of international trade and the forces that influence the exchange rate.

Policy
WATCH

NAFTA in Action

THE ORLANDO SENTINEL, July 30, 1996

U.S. Broom Makers Swept Aside by NAFTA

THE ASSOCIATED PRESS

GREENUP, ILL.—In a long room filled with the smell of straw and the clatter of stitching machines, Ed Graves feeds fistfuls of broomcorn under a thin wire.

He works quickly, cutting the extra stalks away with a long knife as the spinning machine turns wood, wire and straw into the familiar shape of a household broom.

It's a good job, the top of the broom-making profession. He can earn up to $100 a day.

But it's a job Graves and fellow employees at the Quinn Broom Works fear could soon be gone, the victim of the North American Free Trade Agreement and cheaper labor at broom factories in Mexico.

The U.S. broom industry is a small one—only about 600 workers scattered in small plants in Illinois, Ohio, California, Texas and the Southeast. But small broom makers such as the Quinn Broom Works could be among the first manufacturers protected from Mexican competition under NAFTA.

On Friday, the U.S. International Trade Commission recommended restoring a 32 percent tariff on Mexican brooms. The ITC ruled that competition from Mexican factories poses a serious threat to the domestic broom industry. ...

Last year, the average Mexican broom cost $1.92, compared with $3 to $3.40 a broom for U.S.-made brooms ... .

"Our sales are down from the first of the year because of NAFTA by about 50 percent," said Alvin Wingler of Warren Manufacturing in Arcola, Ill. "We were closed down for three weeks, and for another few weeks we ran at 25 percent of our production capacity." ...

The Associated Press. Reprinted with permission.

- American broom makers fear that cheap Mexican labor and NAFTA will destroy their jobs.

- One manufacturer says that NAFTA has decreased broom sales by 50 percent.

- Broom makers could be one of the first to be protected from Mexican competition under NAFTA.

- The International Trade Commission is recommending the restoration of a 32 percent tariff on Mexican brooms.

- Mexican brooms sell at an average price of $1.92. American brooms sell in the $3.00 to $3.40 price range.

Economic

A N A L Y S I S

■ On January 1, 1994, the United States, Mexico, and Canada began a process of tariff reduction that by 2009 will have eliminated most restrictions on trade among the three countries.

■ One tariff eliminated was that on brooms. But protests from U.S. broom producers have brought the broom tariff back.

■ Brooms come in many types. The price of the simplest, least durable, and cheapest broom is less than $2. The most elaborate, durable, hand-made brooms cost as much as $50!

■ To study the economics of trade in brooms, we'll consider a standard broom that costs $2 to produce in Mexico.

■ Figure 1 shows the U.S. market for this standard broom, both with and without a tariff. The demand curve is D. The supply curve of Mexican brooms is S_M. The supply curve of U.S. brooms is S_{US}.

■ With no tariff, QC_1 brooms are bought in the United States. Of these, QP_1 are produced in the United States and the rest are imported, as shown by the arrow in Fig. 1.

■ To keep the numbers simple, suppose we put a 50 percent tariff on broom imports. The price of the Mexican broom is now $2 plus the $1 tariff, so the supply curve of brooms from Mexico shifts to become S_M + tariff.

■ With the tariff, QC_0 brooms are bought in the United States. Of these, QP_0 are produced in the United States and the rest are imported. U.S. consumption and imports decrease and U.S. production increases.

■ Figure 2 shows the winners and the losers in the United States.

■ U.S producers gain additional economic profit (the blue area) and the U.S. government collects additional revenue (the purple area).

■ The loser is the U.S. consumer. The consumers' loss equals the producers' gain plus the government's gain plus the deadweight loss, shown by the two gray areas.

■ The sum of the blue, purple, and gray areas is the loss of consumer surplus that results from the tariff.

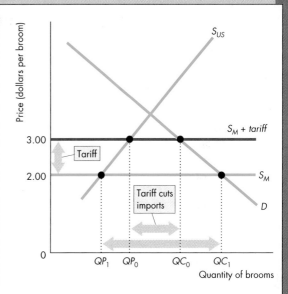

Figure 1 Tariffs and imports

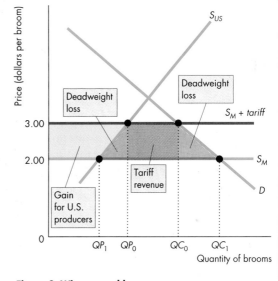

Figure 2 Winners and losers

You're

THE VOTER

■ Are you for or against the tariff on brooms?

■ What do you predict Mexico will do about the broom tariff?

■ Write a report to your Congress member explaining why you favor or oppose the removal of the broom tariff.

SUMMARY

Key Points

Patterns and Trends in International Trade (p. 800)

- Large flows of trade take place between countries, most of which is in manufactured goods exchanged among rich industrialized countries.
- Since 1960, the volume of U.S. trade, as a percentage of total output, has more than doubled.

Opportunity Cost and Comparative Advantage (pp. 801–802)

- When opportunity costs between countries diverge, comparative advantage enables countries to gain from international trade.

Gains from Trade (pp. 802–805)

- By increasing its production of goods in which it has a comparative advantage and then trading some of the increased output, a country can consume at a point outside its production possibility frontier.
- In the absence of international borrowing and lending, trade is balanced as prices adjust to reflect the international supply of and demand for goods.
- The world price balances the production and consumption plans of the trading parties. At the equilibrium price, trade is balanced.

Gains from Trade in Reality (p. 806)

- Comparative advantage explains the international trade that takes place in the world.
- But trade in similar goods arises from economies of scale in the face of diversified tastes.

Trade Restrictions (pp. 807–810)

- Countries restrict international trade by imposing tariffs and quotas.
- Trade restrictions raise the domestic price of imported goods, lower the volume of imports, and reduce the total value of imports.

- Trade restrictions also reduce the total value of exports by the same amount as the reduction in the value of imports.

The Case Against Protection (pp. 811–814)

- Arguments that protection is necessary for national security, to allow infant industries the chance to grow, and to prevent dumping are weak.
- Arguments that protection saves jobs, allows us to compete with cheap foreign labor, makes the economy diversified and stable, protects national culture, and is needed to offset the costs of environmental policies are fatally flawed.

Why is International Trade Restricted? (pp. 814–815)

- Trade is restricted because tariffs raise government revenue and because protection brings a small loss to a large number of people and a large gain per person to a small number of people.

Key Figures

Key Terms

QUESTIONS

1. What are the main exports and imports of the United States?
2. With which countries does the United States do most of its international trade?
3. What is comparative advantage?
4. Why does comparative advantage lead to gains from international trade?
5. Explain what the gains from trade are.
6. Explain why international trade brings gains to all countries.
7. Explain why all countries have a comparative advantage in something.
8. Explain why, when a country begins to trade, the price received for the good exported rises and the price paid for the good imported falls.
9. Explain why we import and export such large quantities of certain similar goods—such as cars.
10. What are the main ways in which we restrict international trade?
11. What are the GATT and the WTO? When was each established and what is its role?
12. What is NAFTA? When did it begin, and what have its effects to date been?
13. What are the effects of a tariff?
14. What are the effects of a quota?
15. What are the effects of a voluntary export restraint?
16. What is an infant industry? Explain why some people argue that an infant industry needs protection from international competition and also explain the main flaws in the argument.
17. What is dumping? Explain why dumping occurs.
18. Describe the main trends in tariffs.
19. What are the main arguments for trade restrictions? Explain the flaw in each argument.
20. Why do countries restrict international trade?
21. What is a voluntary export restraint and who gains from it?
22. Explain the effect of trade with low-wage countries on jobs in the United States.

PROBLEMS

1. Figures 35.1 and 35.2 illustrate Farmland's and Mobilia's production possibilities.
   a. Calculate Farmland's opportunity cost of a car when it produces 2 million cars a year.
   b. Calculate Mobilia's opportunity cost of a car when it produces 8 million cars a year.
   c. With no trade, Farmland produces 2 million cars and Mobilia produces 8 million cars. Which country has a comparative advantage in the production of cars?
   d. If there is no trade between Farmland and Mobilia, how much grain is consumed and how many cars are bought in each country?

2. Suppose that the two countries in problem 1 trade freely.
   a. Which country exports grain?
   b. What is the change in the amount of each good produced by each country?
   c. What is the change in the amount of each good consumed by each country?
   d. What can you say about the price of a car under free trade?

3. Compare the total production of each good produced in problems 1 and 2.

4. Why does Mobilia export cars in the chapter (pp. 797–801) but import them in problem 2?

5. The following figure depicts the international market for soybeans.

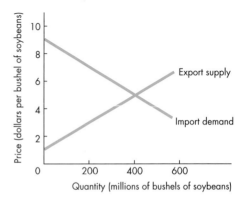

   a. If the two countries did not engage in international trade, what would be the prices of soybeans in the two countries?

b. What is the world price of soybeans if there is free trade between these countries?

c. What quantities of soybeans are traded?

d. What is the balance of trade?

6. If the country in problem 5 that imports soybeans imposes a tariff of $2 per bushel, what is the world price of soybeans and what quantity of soybeans gets traded internationally? What is the price of soybeans in the importing country? Calculate the tariff revenue.

7. The importing country in problem 5(b) imposes a quota of 300 million bushels on imports of soybeans.

   a. What is the price of soybeans in the importing country?

   b. What is the revenue from the quota?

   c. Who gets this revenue?

8. The exporting country in problem 5(b) imposes a VER of 300 million bushels on its exports of soybeans.

   a. What is the world price of soybeans now?

   b. What is the revenue of soybean growers in the exporting country?

   c. Which country gains from the VER?

9. Suppose that the exporting country in problem 5(b) subsidizes production by paying its farmers $1 a bushel for soybeans harvested.

   a. What is the price of soybeans in the importing country?

   b. What action might soybean growers in the importing country take? Why?

10. Countries Atlantis and Magic Kingdom produce only food and balloon rides. The figure shows their production possibility frontiers.

   a. If Atlantis produces at point *a*, what is its opportunity cost of a balloon ride?

   b. What are the consumption possibilities of Atlantis?

   c. If Magic Kingdom produces at point *a'*, what is its opportunity cost of a balloon ride?

   d. What are the consumption possibilities of Magic Kingdom?

   e. Which country has a comparative advantage in producing food?

11. If Atlantis and Magic Kingdom in problem 10 enter into a free trade agreement:

   a. How does the price of a balloon ride in each country change?

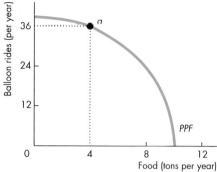

(a) Atlantis

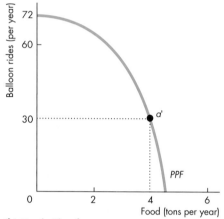

(b) Magic Kingdom

b. How does the price of food in each country change?

c. Which country exports balloon rides?

d. Which country exports food?

e. What are the gains from trade for each country?

f. Are there any losers as a result of the free trade agreement?

CRITICAL THINKING

1. Study *Reading Between the Lines* on pp. 816–817, and then answer the following questions.

   a. Why did NAFTA give U.S broom producers a hard time?

   b. What are the effects of the tariff on brooms?

   c. Who are the winners and who are the losers from the tariff on brooms?

   d. Why do you think the government reinstated the tariff on brooms?

36

The Balance of Payments and the Dollar

In 1988, the United States owned $1.9 trillion in assets abroad and foreigners owned $1.9 trillion of assets in the United States. Before 1988, U.S. residents' ownership of foreign assets exceeded foreigners' ownership of assets in the United States; since 1988, the balance has tipped increasingly the other way. During these years, foreign entrepreneurs such as Australian-born Rupert Murdoch and Sony's Akio Mori roamed the United States with giant shopping carts and loaded them up with such items as Twentieth Century Fox, the Rockefeller Center, and MGM. Why have foreigners been buying more U.S. real estate and businesses than Americans have been buying abroad? ◆ In 1971, one U.S. dollar was enough to buy 360 Japanese yen. By mid-1995, that same dollar bought only 84 yen. But the slide from 360 to 84 yen was not a smooth one. At some times, the dollar held its own or even rose in value against the Japanese currency, as it did, for example, in 1982. But at other times, the dollar's slide was precipitous, as in the period between 1985 and 1988 and again in 1995. But since mid-1995, the dollar has increased against the yen, and by April 1997, it had climbed to more than 120 yen. The dollar has risen in recent years against the German mark, the French franc, the Swiss franc, and the Canadian dollar. But it has fallen slightly against the British pound. What makes our dollar fluctuate in value against other currencies? Why were the fluctuations particularly extreme during the 1980s? Is there anything we can do or should do to stabilize the value of the dollar? ◆ We're going to discover why the U.S. economy has become attractive for foreign investors, why the dollar fluctuates against the values of other currencies, and why interest rates vary from country to country.

A Climbing Debt and a Tumbling Dollar

After studying this chapter, you will be able to:

- Explain how international trade is financed

- Describe a country's balance of payments accounts

- Explain what determines the amount of international borrowing and lending

- Explain why the United States changed from being a lender to being a borrower in the mid-1980s

- Explain how the foreign exchange value of the dollar is determined

- Explain why the foreign exchange value of the dollar fluctuates

Financing International Trade

WHEN A SONY STORE IN THE UNITED STATES imports CD players from Japan, it does not pay for them with U.S. dollars—it uses Japanese yen. And when a French construction company buys an earth mover from Caterpillar, Inc., it uses U.S. dollars. Whenever we buy things from another country, we use the currency of that country to make the transaction. It doesn't make any difference what the item being traded is; it might be a consumption good or a capital good, a building, or even a firm.

We're going to study the markets in which money—different types of currency—is bought and sold. But first we're going to look at the scale of international trading and borrowing and lending and at the way in which we keep our records of these transactions. Such records are called the balance of payments accounts.

Balance of Payments Accounts

A country's **balance of payments accounts** records its international trading, borrowing, and lending. There are in fact three balance of payments accounts:

1. Current account
2. Capital account
3. Official settlements account

The **current account** records payments for imports of goods and services from abroad, receipts from exports of goods and services sold abroad, net interest paid abroad, and net transfers (such as foreign aid payments). The *current account balance* equals exports minus imports, net interest, and net transfers. The **capital account** records foreign investment in the United States minus U.S. investment abroad. The **official settlements account** records the change in official U.S. reserves. **Official U.S. reserves** are the government's holdings of foreign currency. If U.S. official reserves increase, the *official settlements account balance* is negative. The reason is that holding foreign money is like investing abroad. U.S. investment abroad is a minus item in the capital account. By the same reasoning, if official reserves decrease, the *official settlements account balance* is positive.

The sum of the balances on the three accounts always equals zero. That is, to pay for our current account deficit, either we must borrow more from abroad than we lend abroad or use our official reserves to cover the shortfall.

Table 36.1 shows the U.S. balance of payments accounts in 1996. Items in the current account and capital account that provide foreign currency to the United States have a plus sign; items that cost the United States foreign currency have a minus sign. The table shows that in 1996, U.S. imports exceeded U.S. exports and the United States had a current account deficit of $160 billion. How do we pay for our current account deficit? We pay by borrowing from the rest of the world. The capital account tells us by how much. We borrowed $430 billion (foreign investment in the United States) but made loans of $240 billion (U.S. investment abroad). Thus our identified net foreign borrowing was $190 billion. There is a statistical discrepancy of $40 billion between our capital account and current account transactions such as unidentified borrowing from the rest of the world, illegal international trade— for example, the import of illegal drugs—and

---

TABLE 36.1

U.S. Balance of Payments Accounts in 1996

Current account	Billions of dollars
Imports of goods and services	−940
Exports of goods and services	+830
Net interest income	−10
Net transfers	−40
Current account balance	−160
Capital account	
Foreign investment in the United States	+430
U.S. investment abroad	−240
Statistical discrepancy	−40
Capital account balance	+150
Official settlements account	
Decrease in official U.S. reserves	10

Source: *Survey of Current Business* (January 1997), vol. 77. Data for the full year of 1996 were not available when this book went to press. The data here cover January to September 1996 and have been scaled up by the author to an annual rate.

transactions that are not reported in order to illegally evade tariffs or other international trade protection measures.

Our net borrowing from abroad minus our current account deficit is the change in official U.S. reserves. In 1996 those reserves decreased by $10 billion. Net borrowing from foreigners was $150 billion, the current account deficit was $160 billion, and the difference, $10 billion, was the decrease in official U.S. reserves.

The numbers in Table 36.1 give a snapshot of the balance of payments accounts in 1996. Figure 36.1 puts that snapshot into perspective by showing the balance of payments between 1975 and 1996. Because the economy grows and the price level rises, changes in the dollar value of the balance of payments do not convey much information. To remove the influences of growth and inflation, Fig. 36.1 shows the balance of payments as a percentage of nominal GDP.

As you can see, the capital account balance is almost a mirror image of the current account balance. The official settlements balance is very small in comparison with the balances on these other two accounts. A large current account deficit (and capital account surplus) emerged during the 1980s but declined from 1987 to 1991. Since then, it has increased again.

You will perhaps obtain a better understanding of the balance of payments accounts and the way in which they are linked together if you consider the income and expenditure, borrowing and lending, and bank account of an individual.

Individual Analogy   An individual's current account records the income from supplying the services of factors of production and the expenditure on goods and services. Consider, for example, Joanne. She worked in 1995 and earned an income of $25,000. Joanne has $10,000 worth of investments that earned her an interest income of $1,000. Joanne's current account shows an income of $26,000. Joanne spent $18,000 buying goods and services for consumption. She also bought a new house, which cost her $60,000. So Joanne's total expenditure was $78,000. The difference between her expenditure and income is $52,000 ($78,000 minus of $26,000). This amount is Joanne's current account deficit.

FIGURE 36.1

The Balance of Payments: 1975–1996

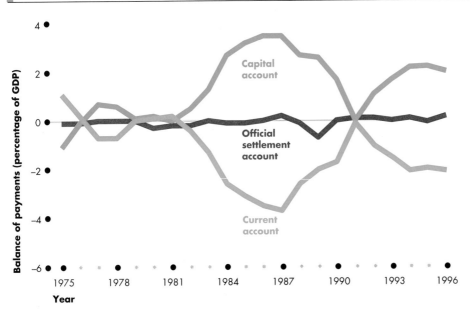

During the 1970s, fluctuations in the balance of payments were small, but during the 1980s, a large current account deficit arose. That deficit decreased in the late 1980s but increased again after 1991. The capital account balance mirrors the current account balance. When the current account balance is negative, the capital account balance is positive—we borrow from the rest of the world. Fluctuations in the official settlements balance are small in comparison with fluctuations in the current account balance and the capital account balance.

Source: *Economic Report of the President*, 1997, and *Survey of Current Business* (January 1997), vol. 77.

To pay for expenditure of $52,000 in excess of her income, Joanne has to use the money that she has in the bank or has to take out a loan. In fact, Joanne took a mortgage of $50,000 to help buy her house. This mortgage was the only borrowing that Joanne did, so her capital account surplus was $50,000. With a current account deficit of $52,000 and a capital account surplus of $50,000, Joanne is still $2,000 short. She got that $2,000 from her own bank account. Her cash holdings decreased by $2,000.

Joanne's income from her work is analogous to a country's income from its exports. Her income from her investments is analogous to a country's interest income from foreigners. Her purchases of goods and services, including her purchase of a house, are analogous to a country's imports. Joanne's mortgage—borrowing from someone else—is analogous to a country's borrowing from the rest of the world. The change in her own bank account is analogous to the change in the country's official reserves.

Borrowers and Lenders, Debtors and Creditors

A country that is borrowing more from the rest of the world than it is lending to it is called a **net borrower**. Similarly, a **net lender** is a country that is lending more to the rest of the world than it is borrowing from it. A net borrower might be going deeper into debt or might simply be reducing its net assets held in the rest of the world. The total stock of foreign investment determines whether a country is a debtor or creditor. A **debtor nation** is a country that during its entire history has borrowed more from the rest of the world than it has lent to it. It has a stock of outstanding debt to the rest of the world that exceeds the stock of its own claims on the rest of the world. The United States became a debtor nation in 1989. A **creditor nation** is a country that has invested more in the rest of the world than other countries have invested in it. The largest creditor nation today is Japan.

At the heart of the distinction between a net borrower/net lender and a debtor/creditor nation is the distinction between flows and stocks, which you have encountered many times in your study of macroeconomics. Borrowing and lending are flows—amounts borrowed or lent per unit of time. Debts are stocks—amounts owed at a point in time. The flow of borrowing and lending changes the stock of debt. But the outstanding stock of debt depends mainly on past flows of borrowing and lending, not on the current period's flows. The current period's flows determine the *change* in the stock of debt outstanding.

When a nation has a string of current account deficits, it eventually becomes a net debtor nation.

The United States is a newcomer to the ranks of net borrower nations. Throughout the 1960s and most of the 1970s, the United States had a surplus on its current account and a deficit on its capital account. Thus the country was a net lender to the rest of the world. It was not until 1983 that the United States became a significant net borrower from the rest of the world. Between 1983 and 1987, its borrowing increased each year. It then decreased and was briefly zero in 1991, after when it started to increase again. The average net foreign borrowing by the United States between 1983 and 1995 was $91 billion a year.

Most countries are net borrowers like the United States. But a small number of countries, including Japan and oil-rich Saudi Arabia, are net lenders.

The United States is not only a net borrower nation. It is also a debtor nation. That is, its total stock of borrowing from the rest of the world exceeds its lending to the rest of the world. The largest debtor nations are the capital-hungry developing countries. The international debt of these countries grew from less than a third to more than a half of their gross domestic product during the 1980s and created what was called the "Third World debt crisis."

Should the United States be concerned about the switch from being a net lender to being a net borrower? The answer to this question depends mainly on what the net borrower is doing with the borrowed money. If borrowing is financing investment that in turn is generating economic growth and higher income, borrowing is not a problem. If the borrowed money is being used to finance consumption, then higher interest payments are being incurred, and as a consequence, consumption will eventually have to be reduced. In this case, the more the borrowing and the longer it goes on, the greater is the reduction in consumption that will eventually be necessary. We'll see below whether the United States is borrowing for investment or for consumption.

Current Account Balance

What determines a country's current account balance and net foreign borrowing? You've seen that net exports (*NX*) is the main item in the current account.

We can define the current account balance (*CAB*) as

$$CAB = NX + \text{Net interest income} + \text{Net transfers.}$$

Fluctuations in net exports are the main source of fluctuations in the current account balance. The other two items are small and have trends but do not fluctuate much. So we can study the current account balance by looking at what determines net exports.

Net Exports

Net exports are determined by the government budget and private saving and investment. To see how net exports are determined, we need to recall some of the things that we learned about the National Income and Product Accounts in Chapter 23. Table 36.2 will refresh your memory and summarize some calculations. Part (a) lists the national income variables that are needed, with their symbols. Part (b) defines three surpluses and deficits.

Net exports is exports of goods and services minus imports of goods and services.

The **government sector surplus or deficit** is equal to net taxes minus government purchases of goods and services. If that number is positive, a government sector surplus is lent to other sectors; if that number is negative, a government deficit must be financed by borrowing. The government sector deficit is the sum of the deficits of the federal, state, and local governments.

The **private sector surplus or deficit** is saving minus investment. If saving exceeds investment, a private sector surplus is lent to other sectors. If investment exceeds saving, a private sector deficit is financed by borrowing from other sectors.

Part (b) also shows the values of these deficits and surpluses for the United States in 1996. As you can see, net exports were –$99 billion, a deficit of $99 billion. The government sector's revenue from net taxes was $1,340 billion, and it purchased $1,407 billion worth of goods and services. The government sector deficit was $67 billion. The private sector saved $1,084 billion and invested $1,116 billion, so it had a deficit of $32 billion.

Part (c) shows the relationship among the three deficits. From the national income accounts, we know that real GDP (*Y*) is the sum of consumption expenditure (*C*), investment, government purchases, and net exports. Real GDP also equals the sum of consumption expenditure, saving, and taxes. Rearranging these equations tells us that net exports is the sum of the government sector deficit and the private

---

TABLE 36.2

Net Exports, the Government Budget, Saving, and Investment

	Symbols and equations	United States in 1996* (billions of dollars)
(a) Variables		
Exports	X	855
Imports	M	954
Government purchases	G	1,407
Net taxes	T	1,340
Investment	I	1,116
Saving	S	1,084
(b) Surpluses and deficits		
Net exports	$X - M$	$855 - 954 = -99$
Government sector	$T - G$	$1,340 - 1,407 = -67$
Private sector	$S - I$	$1,084 - 1,116 = -32$
(c) Relationship among surpluses and deficits		
National accounts	$Y = C + I + G + X - M$	
	$= C + S + T$	
Rearranging	$X - M = S - I + T - G$	
Net exports	$X - M$	–99
equals:		
Government sector	$T - G$	–67
plus		
Private sector	$S - I$	–32

Source: National Income and Product Accounts and *Survey of Current Business*, (January 1997), vol. 77.

*The National Income and Product Accounts measures of exports and imports are different from the Balance of Payments Accounts measures in Table 36.1 on p. 822.

sector deficit. In the United States in 1996, the government sector had a deficit of $67 billion and the private sector had a deficit of $32 billion. The government sector deficit plus the private sector deficit equals net exports of –$99 billion.

The Twin Deficits

You've seen that net exports equal the sum of the government sector deficit and the private sector deficit. But how do these deficits fluctuate over time? Figure 36.2 answers this question. It shows the government sector deficit (the red line) and net exports *two years later* (the blue line).

You can see that there is a strong tendency for net exports to decrease (to become increasingly negative) when the government budget has gone into a deeper deficit (has become increasingly negative). Because of the tendency for the government sector

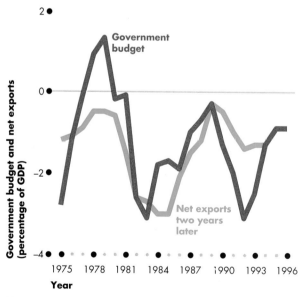

FIGURE 36.2

The Twin Deficits

Net exports and the government budget deficit move in similar ways but with a time lag of two years. If the government sector deficit increases, as it did in 1980–1983 and again in 1990–1992, net exports two years later decrease.

Source: Survey of Current Business, March 1997, Vol. 77.

deficit and the net exports deficit to move in the same direction, they are sometimes called the **twin deficits**.

Why are the two deficits linked? It is because capital is highly mobile in today's world. If the U.S. government increases expenditure or lowers taxes, total spending in the United States rises. But with the economy at or near full employment, the extra goods and services demanded are sucked in from the rest of the world. Imports rise. Capital flows in to pay for those imports. Saving and investment don't change. In reality, these adjustments take time, which is why net exports lag behind the government sector deficit by about two years.

Is U.S. Borrowing for Consumption or Investment?

In 1996, net exports were a negative $99 billion and this amount was borrowed from abroad. Did we borrow for consumption or to finance investment? The answer depends on how much of the government sector deficit arises from investment. The government buys structures such as highways and dams that exceed $200 billion a year. This expenditure adds to the nation's capital and increases productivity. Government also spends on education and health care services, which increase *human capital*. Our international borrowing is financing private and public investment, not consumption.

R E V I E W

- When we buy goods from or invest in the rest of the world, we use foreign currency; and when foreigners buy goods from or invest in the United States, they use U.S. currency.

- We record international transactions in the balance of payments accounts—current account (exports and imports of goods and services), capital account (net foreign borrowing or lending), and official settlements account (change in holdings of a foreign currencies).

- The net exports deficit is equal to the sum of the government sector deficit and the private sector deficit.

- Changes in the government sector deficit can change both the private sector deficit and the net exports deficit.

The Exchange Rate

WHEN WE BUY FOREIGN GOODS OR INVEST IN another country, we have to obtain some of that country's currency to make the transaction. When foreigners buy U.S.-produced goods or invest in the United States, they have to obtain some U.S. dollars. We get foreign currency, and foreigners get U.S. dollars in the foreign exchange market. The **foreign exchange market** is the market in which the currency of one country is exchanged for the currency of another. The foreign exchange market is not a place like a downtown flea market or produce market. The market is made up of thousands of people—importers and exporters, banks, and specialists in the buying and selling of foreign exchange, called foreign exchange brokers. The foreign exchange market opens on Monday morning in Hong Kong, which is still Sunday evening in New York. As the day advances, markets open in Singapore, Tokyo, Bahrain, Frankfurt, London, New York, Chicago, and San Francisco. As the West Coast markets close, Hong Kong is only an hour away from opening for the next day of business. The sun barely sets on the foreign exchange market. Dealers around the world are in continual contact by telephone, and on a typical day in 1996, $1.3 trillion changed hands.

The price at which one currency exchanges for another is called a **foreign exchange rate**. For example, in April 1997, one U.S. dollar bought 123 Japanese yen. The exchange rate was 123 yen per dollar. We've just expressed the exchange rate between the yen and the dollar as a number of yen per dollar.

The actions of the foreign exchange brokers make the foreign exchange market highly efficient. Exchange rates are almost identical around the world. If U.S. dollars were cheap in London and expensive in Tokyo, people would buy in London and sell in Tokyo. The London price would rise and the Tokyo price would fall until the prices were equal.

Figure 36.3 shows the exchange rate of the U.S. dollar in terms of the Japanese yen between 1975 and 1997. From 1975 to 1978 and again from 1982 to 1995, the value of the dollar fell against the yen—the dollar depreciated. **Currency depreciation** is the fall in the value of one currency in terms of another currency. For example, if the dollar falls from 100 yen to 80 yen, the dollar depreciates by 20 percent. From 1978 to 1982 and again during 1996 and 1997, the

FIGURE 36.3

The Exchange Rate

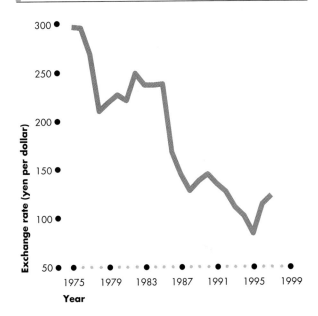

The exchange rate is the price at which two currencies can be traded. The yen-dollar exchange rate, expressed as yen per dollar, shows that the dollar has generally fallen in value—depreciated—against the yen. But since 1995, the dollar has risen against the yen.

Source: Economic Report of the President, 1997.

dollar rose in value against the yen—the dollar appreciated. **Currency appreciation** is the rise in the value of one currency in terms of another currency. For example, if the dollar rises from 100 yen to 120 yen, the dollar appreciates by 20 percent.

Why does the U.S. dollar sometimes depreciate and sometimes appreciate? What happened during 1996 and 1997 to make the dollar appreciate? To answer this question, we need to understand the forces that determine the exchange rate.

The exchange rate is a price—the price of one country's money in terms of another country's money. And like all prices, demand and supply determine the exchange rate. So to understand the forces that determine the exchange rate, we need to study demand and supply in the foreign exchange market. We'll begin by looking at the demand side of the market.

Demand in the Foreign Exchange Market

The quantity of dollars demanded in the foreign exchange market is the amount that traders plan to buy during a given time period at a given exchange rate. This quantity depends on many factors. The main ones are:

- The exchange rate
- Interest rates in the United States and other countries
- The expected future exchange rate

Let's look first at the relationship between the quantity of dollars demanded in the foreign exchange market and the exchange rate.

The Law of Demand for Foreign Exchange

People do not buy dollars because they enjoy them. The demand for dollars is a *derived demand*. People demand dollars so that they can buy U.S.-made goods and services (U.S. exports). They also demand dollars so that they can buy U.S. assets such as bank accounts, bonds, stocks, businesses, and real estate. Nevertheless, the law of demand applies to dollars just as it does to anything else that people value.

Other things remaining the same, the higher the exchange rate, the smaller is the quantity of dollars demanded in the foreign exchange market. For example, if the price of the U.S. dollar rises from 100 yen to 120 yen but nothing else changes, the quantity of U.S. dollars that people plan to buy in the foreign exchange market decreases. Why does the exchange rate influence the quantity of dollars demanded?

There are two separate reasons, and they are related to the two sources of the derived demand for dollars:

- Exports effect
- Expected profit effect

Exports Effect The larger the value of U.S. exports, the larger is the quantity of dollars demanded in the foreign exchange market. But the value of U.S. exports depends on the exchange rate. The lower the exchange rate, with everything else the same, the cheaper are U.S.-produced goods and services and the greater is the value of U.S. exports and the greater is the quantity of U.S. dollars demanded on the foreign exchange market to pay for these exports.

Expected Profit Effect The larger the expected profit from holding dollars, the greater is the quantity of dollars demanded in the foreign exchange market. But expected profit depends on the exchange rate. The lower the exchange rate, other things remaining the same, the larger is the expected profit from buying dollars and the greater is the quantity of dollars demanded on the foreign exchange market.

To understand this effect, suppose you think the dollar will be worth 120 yen by the end of the month. If today, a dollar costs 115 yen, you buy dollars. But a person who thinks that the dollar will be worth 115 yen at the end of the month does not buy dollars. Now suppose the exchange rate falls to 110 yen per dollar. More people think they can profit from buying dollars, so the quantity of dollars demanded increases.

For the two reasons we've just reviewed, other things remaining the same, when the foreign exchange rate rises, the quantity of dollars demanded decreases, and when the foreign exchange rate falls, the quantity of dollars demanded increases. Figure 36.4 shows the demand curve for U.S. dollars in the foreign exchange market. In this figure, when the foreign exchange rate rises, other things remaining the same, there is a decrease in the quantity of dollars demanded and a movement upward along the demand curve as shown by the arrow. When the exchange rate falls, other things remaining the same, there is an increase in the quantity of dollars demanded and a movement downward along the demand curve as shown by the arrow.

Changes in the Demand for Dollars

A change in any other influence on the dollars that people plan to buy in the foreign exchange market brings a change in the demand for dollars and a shift in the demand curve for dollars. Demand either increases or decreases. These other influences are:

- Interest rates in the United States and other countries
- The expected future exchange rate

Interest Rates in the United States and Other Countries People and businesses buy financial assets to make a return. The higher the interest rate that people can make on U.S. assets compared with foreign assets, the more U.S. assets they buy. What matters is not the level of U.S. interest rates, but the U.S. interest rate minus the foreign interest rate, a

FIGURE 36.4

The Demand for Dollars

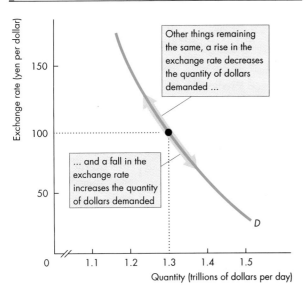

Other things remaining the same, a rise in the exchange rate decreases the quantity of dollars demanded ...

... and a fall in the exchange rate increases the quantity of dollars demanded

The quantity of dollars that people plan to buy depends on the exchange rate. Other things remaining the same, if the exchange rate rises, the quantity of dollars demanded decreases and there is a movement upward along the demand curve for dollars. If the exchange rate falls, the quantity of dollars demanded increases and there is a movement downward along the demand curve for dollars.

gap that is called the **U.S. interest rate differential**. If the U.S. interest rate rises and the foreign interest rate remains constant, the U.S. interest rate differential increases. The larger the U.S. interest rate differential, the greater is the demand for U.S. assets and the greater is the demand for dollars on the foreign exchange market.

The Expected Future Exchange Rate   Other things remaining the same, the higher the expected future exchange rate, the greater is the demand for dollars. To see why, suppose you are Toyota's finance manager. The exchange rate is 100 yen per dollar and you think that by the end of the month, it will be 120 yen per dollar. You spend 100,000 yen today and buy $1,000. At the end of the month, the dollar is 120 yen, as you predicted it would be, and you sell the $1,000. You get 120,000 yen. You've made a profit of 20,000 yen, or almost $167. The higher the

expected future exchange rate, other things remaining the same, the greater is the expected profit and the greater is the demand for dollars today.

Figure 36.5 summarizes the above discussion of the influences on the demand for dollars. A rise in the U.S. interest differential or a rise in the expected future exchange rate increases the demand for dollars and shifts the demand curve rightward from D_0 to D_1. A fall in the U.S. interest differential or a fall in the expected future exchange rate decreases the demand for dollars and shifts the demand curve leftward from D_0 to D_2.

FIGURE 36.5

Changes in the Demand for Dollars

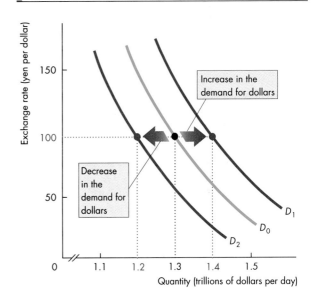

Increase in the demand for dollars

Decrease in the demand for dollars

A change in any influence on the quantity of dollars that people plan to buy, other than the exchange rate, brings a change in the demand for dollars.

The demand for dollars:

Increases if:	Decreases if:
■ The U.S. interest rate differential increases	■ The U.S. interest rate differential decreases
■ The expected future exchange rate rises	■ The expected future exchange rate falls

Supply in the Foreign Exchange Market

The quantity of U.S. dollars supplied in the foreign exchange market is the amount that traders plan to sell during a given time period at a given exchange rate. This quantity depends on many factors. The main ones are:

- The exchange rate
- Interest rates in the United States and other countries
- The expected future exchange rate

Let's look first at the relationship between the quantity of dollars supplied in the foreign exchange market and the exchange rate.

The Law of Supply for Foreign Exchange

People supply dollars in the foreign exchange market when they buy other currencies. And they buy other currencies so that they can buy foreign-made goods and services (U.S. imports). They also supply dollars and buy foreign currencies so that they can buy foreign assets such as bank accounts, bonds, stocks, businesses, and real estate. The law of supply applies to dollars just as it does to anything else that people plan to sell.

Other things remaining the same, the higher the exchange rate, the greater is the quantity of dollars supplied in the foreign exchange market. For example, if the price of the U.S. dollar rises from 100 yen to 120 yen but nothing else changes, the quantity of yen that people plan to buy in the foreign exchange market increases and so the quantity of U.S. dollars supplied increases. Why does the exchange rate influence the quantity of dollars supplied?

There are two reasons and they parallel the two reasons on the demand side of the market:

- Imports effect
- Expected profit effect

Imports Effect   The larger the value of U.S. imports, the larger is the quantity of foreign currency demanded to pay for these imports. And when people buy foreign currency, they supply dollars. So the larger the value of U.S. imports, the greater is the quantity of

dollars supplied in the foreign exchange market. But the value of U.S. imports depends on the exchange rate. The higher the exchange rate, with everything else the same, the cheaper are foreign-produced good and services to Americans, the more the United States imports, and the greater is the quantity of U.S. dollars supplied on the foreign exchange market to pay for these imports.

Expected Profit Effect   The larger the expected profit from holding a foreign currency, the greater is the quantity of that currency demanded and the greater is the quantity of dollars supplied in the foreign exchange market. But the expected profit from holding a foreign currency depends on the exchange rate. The higher the exchange rate, other things remaining the same, the larger is the expected profit from selling dollars and the greater is the quantity of dollars supplied on the foreign exchange market.

FIGURE 36.6
The Supply of Dollars

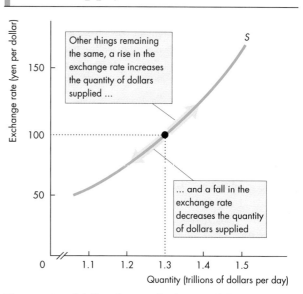

The quantity of dollars that people plan to sell depends on the exchange rate. Other things remaining the same, if the exchange rate rises, the quantity of dollars supplied increases and there is a movement upward along the supply curve for dollars. If the exchange rate falls, the quantity of dollars supplied decreases and there is a movement downward along the supply curve for dollars.

For the two reasons we've just reviewed, other things remaining the same, when the foreign exchange rate rises, the quantity of dollars supplied increases, and when foreign exchange rate falls, the quantity of dollars supplied decreases. Figure 36.6 shows the supply curve for U.S. dollars in the foreign exchange market. In this figure, when the foreign exchange rate rises, other things remaining the same, there is an increase in the quantity of dollars supplied and a movement upward along the supply curve as shown by the arrow. When the exchange rate falls, other things remaining the same, there is a decrease in the quantity of dollars supplied and a movement downward along the supply curve as shown by the arrow.

Changes in the Supply of Dollars

A change in any other influence on the dollars that people plan to sell in the foreign exchange market brings a change in the supply of dollars and a shift in the supply curve for dollars. Supply either increases or decreases. These other influences parallel the other influences on demand but have exactly the opposite effects. These influences are:

- Interest rates in the United States and other countries
- The expected future exchange rate

Interest Rates in the United States and Other Countries   The larger the U.S. interest rate differential, the smaller is the demand for foreign assets and so the smaller is the supply of dollars in the foreign exchange market.

The Expected Future Exchange Rate   Other things remaining the same, the higher the expected future exchange rate, the smaller is the supply of dollars. To see why, suppose the dollar is trading at 100 yen per dollar today and you think that by the end of the month, the dollar will be 120 yen per dollar. You were planning on selling dollars today, but you decide to hold off and wait until the end of the month. If you supply dollars today, you get only 100 yen per dollar. But at the end of the month, if the dollar is 120 yen per dollar as you predict, you'll get 120 yen for each dollar you supply. You'll make a profit of 20 percent. So, the higher the expected

future exchange rate, other things remaining the same, the smaller is the expected profit from selling U.S. dollars today and the smaller is the supply of dollars today.

Figure 36.7 summarizes the above discussion of the influences on the supply of dollars. A rise in the U.S. interest differential or a rise in the expected future exchange rate decreases the supply of dollars and shifts the demand curve leftward from S_0 to S_1. A fall in the U.S. interest differential or a fall in the expected future exchange rate increases the supply of dollars and shifts the supply curve rightward from S_0 to S_2.

FIGURE 36.7
Changes in the Supply of Dollars

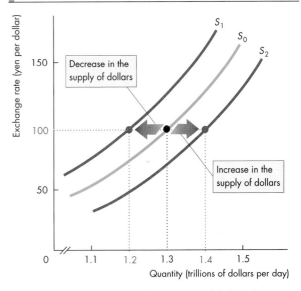

A change in any influence on the quantity of dollars that people plan to sell, other than the exchange rate, brings a change in the supply of dollars.
   The supply of dollars:

Increases if:	Decreases if:
■ The U.S. interest rate differential decreases	■ The U.S. interest rate differential increases
■ The expected future exchange rate falls	■ The expected future exchange rate rises

Market Equilibrium

Figure 36.8 shows how demand and supply in the foreign exchange market determine the exchange rate. The demand curve is *D*, and the supply curve is *S*. Just like all the other markets you've studied, the price (the exchange rate) acts as a regulator.

If the exchange rate is too high, there is a surplus of dollars—the quantity supplied exceeds the quantity demanded. In Fig. 36.8, if the exchange rate is 150 yen per dollar, there is a surplus of dollars. If the exchange rate is too low, there is a shortage of dollars—the quantity supplied is less than the quantity demanded. In Fig. 36.8, if the exchange rate is 50 yen per dollar, there is a shortage of dollars.

At the equilibrium exchange rate, there is neither a shortage nor a surplus. The quantity supplied equals the quantity demanded. In Fig. 36.8, the equilibrium exchange rate is 100 yen per dollar. At this exchange rate, the quantity demanded equals the quantity supplied and $1.3 trillion a day is bought and sold.

The foreign exchange market is constantly pulled to its equilibrium by the forces of supply and demand. Foreign exchange dealers are constantly looking for the best price they can get. If they are selling, they want the highest price available. If they are buying, they want the lowest price available. Information flows from dealer to dealer through the worldwide computer network, and the price adjusts second by second to keep buying plans and selling plans in balance. That is, price adjusts second by second to keep the market at its equilibrium.

Changes in the Exchange Rate

If the demand for dollars increases and the supply of dollars does not change, the exchange rate rises. If the demand for dollars decreases and the supply of dollars does not change, the exchange rate falls. Similarly, if the supply of dollars decreases and the demand for dollars does not change, the exchange rate rises. If the supply of dollars increases and the demand for dollars does not change, the exchange rate falls.

These predictions about the effects of changes in demand and supply are the same as for other markets.

Why the Exchange Rate Is Volatile Sometimes the dollar depreciates and at other times it appreciates, but the quantity of dollars traded each day barely changes. Why? The main reason is that supply and demand are not independent of each other in the foreign exchange market.

When we studied the demand for dollars and the supply of dollars, we saw that unlike other markets, the demand side and the supply side of the market have some common influences. A change in the expected future exchange rate or a change in the U.S. interest rate differential changes both demand and supply—and in opposite directions. These common influences on both demand and supply explain why the exchange rate can be volatile at times, even though the quantity of dollars traded does not change.

Everyone in the foreign exchange market is potentially a demander and a supplier. Each has a price above which he or she will sell and below which he or she will buy. Let's see how these common supply and demand effects work by looking at two episodes: one in which the dollar appreciated and one in which it depreciated.

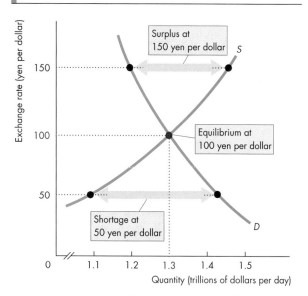

FIGURE 36.8
Equilibrium Exchange Rate

The demand curve for dollars is *D*, and the supply curve is *S*. If the exchange rate is 150 yen per dollar, there is a surplus of dollars and the exchange rate falls. If the exchange rate is 50 yen per dollar, there is a shortage of dollars and the exchange rate rises. If the exchange rate is 100 yen per dollar, there is neither a shortage nor a surplus of dollars and the exchange rate remains constant. The market is in equilibrium.

A Depreciating Dollar: 1994–1995   Between 1994 and the summer of 1995, the dollar fell from 100 yen to a low of 84 yen per dollar. Figure 36.9(a) explains this fall. In 1994, the demand and supply curves were those labeled D_{94} and S_{94}. The exchange rate was 100 yen per dollar. During 1994, traders expected the U.S. dollar to depreciate. They expected a lower exchange rate. As a result, the demand for dollars decreased and the supply of dollars increased. The demand curve shifted leftward to D_{95}, and the supply curve shifted rightward to S_{95}. The exchange rate fell to 84 yen per dollar.

An Appreciating Dollar: 1995–1997   Between 1995 and 1997, the dollar appreciated against the yen. It rose from 84 yen to 123 yen per dollar. Figure 36.9(b) explains why this happened. In 1995, the demand and supply curves were those labeled D_{95} and S_{95}. The exchange rate was 84 yen per dollar— where the supply and demand curves intersect. During the next two years, Japan was in recession

and the U.S. economy was expanding. Interest rates in Japan fell, and the yen was expected to depreciate. The demand for yen decreased. As a result, the demand for dollars increased, and the supply of dollars decreased. The demand curve shifted from D_{95} to D_{97}, and the supply curve shifted from S_{95} to S_{97}. These two shifts reinforced each other, and the exchange rate increased to 123 yen per dollar.

Exchange Rate Expectations

The changes in the exchange rate that we've just examined occurred in part because the exchange rate was *expected to change.* This explanation sounds a bit like a self-fulfilling forecast. But what makes expectations change? The answer is new information about the deeper forces that influence the value of money. Two such forces are:

- Purchasing power parity
- Interest rate parity

FIGURE 36.9

Exchange Rate Fluctuations

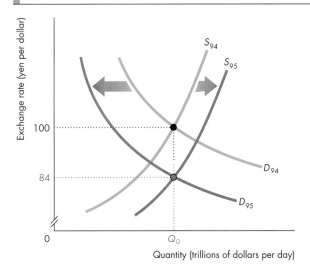

(a) 1994 to 1995

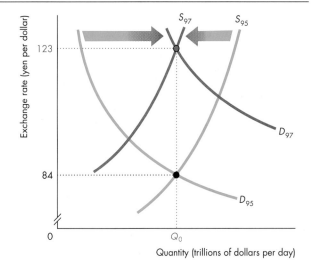

(b) 1995 to 1997

The exchange rate fluctuates because changes in demand and supply are not independent of each other. Everyone in the foreign exchange market is a potential buyer and seller. Between 1994 and 1995 (in part a), the dollar depreciated from 100 to 84 yen per dollar. The exchange rate was expected to depreciate, which decreased the demand for dollars and increased the

supply. Between 1995 and 1997 (part b), the dollar appreciated from 84 to 123 yen per dollar. This appreciation occurred because a weak Japanese economy and low interest rates in Japan generated an expectation of a weak yen and a strong dollar. The supply of dollars decreased, the demand for dollars increased, and the dollar rose in value.

Purchasing Power Parity Money is worth what it will buy. But two kinds of money, U.S. dollars and Canadian dollars for example, might buy different amounts of goods and services. Suppose a Big Mac costs $4 (Canadian) in Toronto and $3 (U.S.) in New York. If the Canadian dollar exchange rate is $1.33 Canadian per U.S. dollar, the two monies have the same value. You can buy a Big Mac in both Toronto and New York for either $4 Canadian or $3 U.S.

The situation we've just described is called **purchasing power parity**, which means *equal value of money*. If purchasing power parity does not prevail, some powerful forces go to work. To understand these forces, let's suppose that the price of a Big Mac in New York rises to $4 U.S., but in Toronto it remains at $4 Canadian. Suppose the exchange rate remains at $1.33 Canadian per U.S. dollar. In this case, a Big Mac in Toronto still costs $4 Canadian or $3 U.S. But in New York, it costs $4 U.S. or $5.33 Canadian. Money buys more in Canada than in the United States. Money is not of equal value in both countries.

If all (or most) prices have increased in the United States and not increased in Canada, then people will generally expect that the value of the U.S. dollar on the foreign exchange market must fall. In this situation, the exchange rate is expected to fall. The demand for U.S. dollars decreases and the supply of U.S. dollars increases. The exchange rate falls, as expected. If the exchange rate falls to $1.00 Canadian and there are no further price changes, purchasing power parity is restored. A Big Mac now costs $4 in either U.S. or Canadian dollars in both New York and Toronto.

If prices increase in Canada and other countries but remain constant in the United States, then people will generally expect that the value of the U.S. dollar on the foreign exchange market is too low and that it is going to rise. In this situation, the exchange rate is expected to rise. The demand for U.S. dollars increases and the supply of U.S. dollars decreases. The exchange rate rises, as expected.

Ultimately, the value of money is determined by the price level, which in turn is determined by aggregate supply and aggregate demand (see Chapter 24, pp. 524–525, and Chapter 32, pp. 715–719.) So the deeper forces that influence the exchange rate have tentacles that spread throughout the economy. If prices in the United States rise faster than those in other countries, the exchange rate falls. And if prices rise more slowly in the United States than in other countries, the exchange rate rises.

Interest Rate Parity Money is worth what it can earn. Again, two kinds of money, Canadian dollars and U.S. dollars for example, might earn different amounts. Suppose a Canadian dollar bank deposit in Toronto earns 5 percent a year and a U.S. dollar bank deposit in New York earns 3 percent a year. In this situation, why does anyone deposit money in New York? Why doesn't all the money flow to Toronto? The answer is: Because of exchange rate expectations. Suppose people expect the Canadian dollar to depreciate by 2 percent a year. This 2 percent depreciation must be subtracted from the 5 percent interest to obtain the net return of 3 percent a year that an American expects to earn by depositing funds in a Toronto bank. The two returns are equal. This situation is one of **interest rate parity**, which means *equal interest rates*.

Adjusted for risk, interest rate parity always prevails. Funds move to get the highest return available. If for a few seconds a higher return is available in New York than in Toronto, the demand for U.S. dollars rises and the exchange rate rises until expected interest rates are equal.

The Fed in the Foreign Exchange Market

Interest rates in the United States are determined by the demand for and supply of money (see Chapter 31, pp. 701–702). But the supply of money is influenced by the Fed, so ultimately, the exchange rate is influenced by monetary policy. When interest rates in the United States rise, relative to those in other countries, the demand for U.S. dollars increases, the supply decreases, and the exchange rate rises. (Similarly, when interest rates in the United States fall, relative to those in other countries, the demand for U.S. dollars decreases, the supply increases, and the exchange rate falls.)

But the Fed can intervene directly in the foreign exchange market. It can buy or sell dollars and try to smooth out fluctuations in the exchange rate. Let's look at the foreign exchange interventions that the Fed can make.

Suppose the Fed wants the exchange rate to be steady at 120 yen per dollar. If the exchange rate rises above 120 yen per dollar, the Fed sells dollars. If the exchange rate falls below 120 yen per dollar, the Fed buys dollars. By these actions, it changes supply or demand and keeps the exchange rate close to its target rate of 120 yen per dollar.

Figure 36.10 shows this Fed intervention in the foreign exchange market. The supply of dollars is S, and initially the demand for dollars is D_0. The equilibrium exchange rate is 120 yen per dollar. This exchange rate is the Fed's target rate, shown by the horizontal red line in the figure.

When the demand for dollars increases and the demand curve shifts rightward to D_1, the Fed sells $0.1 trillion. This action increases the supply of dollars by $0.1 trillion and prevents the exchange rate from rising. When the demand for dollars decreases and the demand curve shifts leftward to D_2, the Fed buys $0.1 trillion. This action decreases the supply of dollars by $0.1 trillion and prevents the exchange rate from falling.

If the demand for dollars fluctuates between D_1 and D_2 and on the average is D_0, the Fed can repeatedly intervene in the way we've just seen. Sometimes

the Fed buys and sometimes it sells, but on the average, it neither buys nor sells.

But suppose the demand for dollars increases permanently from D_0 to D_1. The Fed cannot now maintain the exchange rate at 120 yen per dollar indefinitely. To do so, the Fed would have to sell dollars every day. When the Fed sells dollars in the foreign exchange market, it buys foreign currency. So the Fed would be piling up foreign currency.

Now suppose the demand for dollars decreases permanently from D_0 to D_2. Again the Fed cannot maintain the exchange rate at 120 yen per dollar indefinitely. In this situation, to hold the exchange rate at 120 yen per dollars, the Fed would have to buy dollars every day. When the Fed buys dollars in the foreign exchange market, it uses its holdings of foreign currency. So the Fed would be losing foreign currency. Eventually, it would run out of foreign currency and would then have to abandon its attempt to fix the exchange rate.

FIGURE 36.10
Foreign Exchange Market Intervention

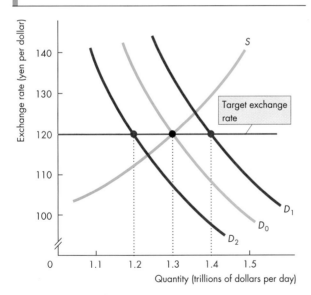

Initially, the demand for dollars is D_0, the supply of dollars is S, and the exchange rate is 120 yen per dollar. The Fed can intervene in the foreign exchange market to keep the exchange rate close to its target rate (120 yen in this example). If demand increases from D_0 to D_1, the Fed sells dollars to increase supply. If demand decreases from D_0 to D_2, the Fed buys dollars to decrease supply. Persistent intervention on one side of the market cannot be sustained.

R E V I E W

- The exchange rate is determined by demand and supply in the foreign exchange market.
- Changes in interest rates and in the expected future exchange rate change both demand and supply and bring changes in the exchange rate.
- Expectations are influenced by purchasing power parity and interest rate parity and by the wider influences on the price level and interest rates.
- The Fed can intervene in the foreign exchange market to try to smooth out fluctuations in the exchange rate but it cannot resist a permanent change in the equilibrium exchange rate.

Reading Between the Lines on pages 836–837 looks at exchange rates in 1997 and the relative purchasing power of different currencies in terms of a Big Mac.

You have now reached the end of your economics course. Go back to the big ideas that define the way of economic thinking (on pp. 6–11) and see how much more they mean to you now than they did when you first read them. I hope that your instructor and I have helped to open your eyes and shown you a new way of seeing the world. If we have, you can now do your own "reading between the lines" every day. Keep your economics text handy. Use it to refresh you memory of the economic principles that help you make sense of your world.

Policy
WATCH

Purchasing Power Parity

THE ECONOMIST, APRIL 12, 1997

Big MacCurrencies

Is the world's exchange-rate system on the brink of collapse? Just like the old gold standard and the fixed rates of the Bretton Woods system, another international currency benchmark could be doomed: the hamburger standard. For more than a decade, *The Economist's* Big Mac index has provided a delectable guide to whether currencies are at their "correct" level. But news in February that McDonald's was about to slash the American price of its Big Mac by 65% sent shivers through financial markets. Would this blatant competitive devaluation reduce the hamburger standard to ashes?

It certainly threatened to leave us in a pickle. The Big Mac index is based on the theory of purchasing-power parity (PPP)—the notion that a dollar should buy the same amount in all countries. In the long run, argue PPP fans, currencies should move towards the rate which equalises the prices of an identical basket of goods in each country. Our "basket" is a McDonald's Big Mac, which is now produced in over 100 countries. The Big Mac PPP is the exchange rate that would leave hamburgers costing the same in America as abroad. Comparing actual exchange rates with PPP provides one indication of whether a currency is under- or over-valued.

The hamburger standard

	Big Mac prices		Local currency under(-)/over(+) valuation,†%
	In local currency	In dollars	
United States‡	$2.42	2.42	—
Argentina	Peso2.50	2.50	+3
Australia	A$2.50	1.94	−20
Austria	Sch34.00	2.82	+17
Belgium	BFr109	3.09	+28
Brazil	Real2.97	2.81	+16
Britain	£ 1.81	2.95	+22
Canada	C$2.88	2.07	−14
Chile	Peso1,200	2.88	+19
China	Yuan9.70	1.16	−52
Czech Republic	CKr53.0	1.81	−25
Denmark	DKr25.75	3.95	+63
France	FFr17.5	3.04	+26
Germany	DM4.90	2.86	+18
Hong Kong	HK$9.90	1.28	−47
Hungary	Forint271	1.52	−37
Israel	Shekel11.5	3.40	+40
Italy	Lire4,600	2.73	+13
Japan	¥294	2.34	−3
Malaysia	M$3.87	1.55	−36
Mexico	Peso14.9	1.89	−22
Netherlands	Fl5.45	2.83	+17
New Zealand	NZ$3.25	2.24	−7
Poland	Zloty4.30	1.39	−43
Russia	Rouble11,000	1.92	−21
Singapore	S$3.00	2.08	−14
South Africa	Rand7.80	1.76	−27
South Korea	Won2,300	2.57	+6
Spain	Pta375	2.60	+7
Sweden	SKr26.0	3.37	+39
Switzerland	SFr5.90	4.02	+66
Taiwan	NT$68.0	2.47	+2
Thailand	Baht46.7	1.79	−26

†Against dollar ‡Average of New York, Chicago, San Francisco and Atlanta

Source: McDonald's

Essence of
THE STORY

■ *The Economist* publishes a Big Mac index of world currencies.

■ The index is based on the price of a McDonald's Big Mac, which is now produced in over 100 countries.

■ The Big Mac purchasing-power parity (PPP) is the exchange rate that makes a Big Mac cost the same in all countries.

■ *The Economist* uses this index to judge whether currencies are at their "correct" PPP level.

■ In April 1997, the Big Mac cost an average of $2.42 (including tax) in the United States. It cost least in China, $1.16, and most in Switzerland, $4.02.

■ *The Economist* concludes that the Chinese yuan is the most undervalued currency (by 52%) and the Swiss franc the most overvalued (by 66%).

Economic

ANALYSIS

■ Although *The Economist* is having a bit of fun with its Big Mac index, it is also doing some misleading and potentially wrong economics.

■ The basic assumption is that a Big Mac is the same good the world over. Because it is the same good, it should have the same price. Any price differences are due to currencies being undervalued or overvalued.

■ The assumption is wrong. When McDonald's sells a Big Mac, it sells a *service*—a fast food service—as well as a good.

■ And the price of the service component of a Big Mac varies from place to place and depends on local demand and supply conditions.

■ The figure shows the range of prices *inside the United States*. The highest price is in New York City, where a Big Mac costs $3.13 with tax. The lowest price is in Jonesboro, Arkansas, where the price is $1.80.

■ Of the 32 countries in *The Economist's* table, 21 have prices that fall inside the range of those in the United States.

■ Four of *The Economist's* countries, Switzerland, Denmark, Israel, and Sweden have prices that exceed that in New York City.

■ Seven of *The Economist's* countries, Thailand, South Africa, Malaysia, Hungary, Poland, Hong Kong, and China, have prices below those in Jonesboro.

■ There are many reasons why the local price of a Big Mac varies—some demand-side and some supply-side.

■ A major supply-side influence is the cost of labor. An hour of labor in Switzerland costs 75 times that of an hour of labor in China!

■ To make PPP comparisons, we must use goods that are easily transported among countries and that have a small or no service component. The price of a floppy disk, a PC, or a computer chip would do a much better job of revealing PPP than the price of a Big Mac.

■ *The Economist* should replace its Big Mac standard with the Intel chip standard.

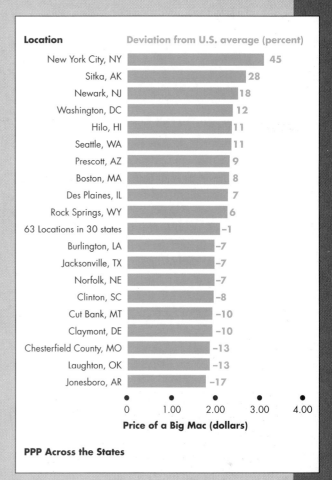

Location	Deviation from U.S. average (percent)
New York City, NY	45
Sitka, AK	28
Newark, NJ	18
Washington, DC	12
Hilo, HI	11
Seattle, WA	11
Prescott, AZ	9
Boston, MA	8
Des Plaines, IL	7
Rock Springs, WY	6
63 Locations in 30 states	−1
Burlington, LA	−7
Jacksonville, TX	−7
Norfolk, NE	−7
Clinton, SC	−8
Cut Bank, MT	−10
Claymont, DE	−10
Chesterfield County, MO	−13
Laughton, OK	−13
Jonesboro, AR	−17

Price of a Big Mac (dollars)

PPP Across the States

You're

THE VOTER

■ Why does it matter if the dollar is undervalued or overvalued?

■ What can the Fed do if it believes the dollar is undervalued or overvalued?

■ Thinking only about your own economic well being, what is better for you, an undervalued or an overvalued dollar?

SUMMARY

Key Points

Financing International Trade (pp. 822–826)

- International trade, borrowing, and lending are financed by using foreign currency.
- A country's international transactions are recorded in its balance of payments accounts.
- Historically, the United States has been a net lender to the rest of the world, but in 1983 that situation changed and the United States became a net borrower. In 1989, the United States became a net debtor.
- The net exports deficit is equal to the government sector deficit plus the private sector deficit.

The Exchange Rate (pp. 827–835)

- Foreign currency is obtained in exchange for domestic currency in the foreign exchange market.
- The exchange rate is determined by demand and supply in the foreign exchange market.
- The lower the exchange rate, the greater is the quantity of dollars demanded. A change in the exchange rate brings a movement along the demand curve for dollars.
- Changes in the U.S. interest rate differential and the expected future exchange rate change the demand for dollars and shift the demand curve.
- The lower the exchange rate, the smaller is the quantity of dollars supplied. A change in the exchange rate brings a movement along the supply curve for dollars.
- Changes in the U.S. interest rate differential and the expected future exchange rate change the supply of dollars and shift the supply curve.
- Fluctuations in the exchange rate occur because fluctuations in the demand for and supply of dollars are not independent.
- The Fed can intervene in the foreign exchange market to smooth fluctuations in the dollar.

Key Figures and Table

Key Terms

QUESTIONS

1 What are the three accounts that make up the balance of payments accounts?

2 What are the transactions that are recorded in the current account and the capital account?

3. What is the relationship between the balance on the current account, the capital account, and the official settlements account?

4. Distinguish between a country that is a net borrower and one that is a debtor nation. Are net borrowers always debtor nations? Are debtor nations always net borrowers?

5. What is the connection between a country's net exports and the government sector deficit and the private sector deficit?

6. Why do fluctuations in the government sector balance lead to fluctuations in net exports?

7. What is a currency appreciation? What is a currency depreciation?

8. Explain why the quantity of dollars demanded in the foreign exchange market depends on the exchange rate.

9. Explain why the quantity of dollars supplied in the foreign exchange market depends on the exchange rate.

10. Review the main influences on the demand for dollars in the foreign exchange market.

11. Review the main influences on the supply of dollars in the foreign exchange market.

12. Why does the foreign exchange value of the dollar fluctuate so much?

13. What is purchasing power parity? Give an example of purchasing power parity.

14. What is interest rate parity? Give an example of interest rate parity.

15. How can the Fed limit the fluctuations in the exchange rate?

PROBLEMS

1. The citizens of Silecon, whose currency is the grain, conduct the following transactions in 1995:

Item	Billions of grains
Imports of goods and services	350
Exports of goods and services	500
Borrowing from the rest of the world	60
Lending to the rest of the world	200
Increase in official reserves	10

a. Set out the three balance of payments accounts for Silecon.

2. The figure at the bottom of the next page shows the flows of income and expenditure in Dream Land in 1996. The amounts are in millions of dollars. GDP in Dream Land is $60 million.
a. Calculate Dream Land's net exports.
b. Calculate saving in Dream Land.
c. Calculate the government sector deficit.
d. Calculate the private sector deficit.
e. Show the relationship between your answers to (a), (c), and (d).

3. You are told the following about Ecflex, whose currency is the band:

Item	Billion bands
GDP	100
Consumption expenditure	60
Government purchases of goods and services	24
Investment	22
Exports of goods and services	20
Government budget deficit	4

Calculate the following for Ecflex:
a. Imports of goods and services
b. Saving
c. Net taxes
d. Private sector deficit

💻 4. The foreign exchange market is shown in the figure. The demand for dollars and the supply of dollars decrease.

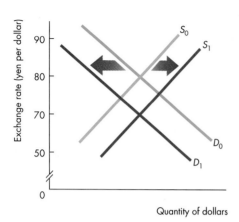

a. Explain the influences on the market that might have decreased the demand for dollars and the supply of dollars.
b. Explain what happens to the exchange rate when the demand for dollars and the supply of dollars decrease.
c. What action would the Fed have to undertake to keep the exchange rate steady?
d. In part (c), describe the effects of the Fed's actions on official U.S. reserves.

🌐 http://hepg.awl.com/parkin/econ100

CRITICAL THINKING

1. Study *Reading Between the Lines* on pp. 836–837 and then answer the following questions.
   a. Which currencies does *The Economist* claim are undervalued and which overvalued?
   b. What is PPP?
   c. What is the key assumption used by *The Economist* to make its PPP calculations?
   d. What is wrong with *The Economist's* assumptions?
   e. Use the Parkin Internet exchange to share information on the prices of floppy disks around the world and do a PPP comparison based on the floppy disk standard.

🌐 2. Visit *FRED*, the Federal Reserve Bank of St. Louis Economic database on the World Wide Web at http://www.stls.frb.org/fred/fred.html (or via the link at the Parkin Web site) and find data on the exchange rate and international trade.
   a. When did the United States last have a current account surplus?
   b. Does the United States have a surplus or a deficit in trade in goods?
   c. Does the United States have a surplus or a deficit in trade in services?
   d. How has foreign investment in the United States changed during the past 10 years?
   e. Do you think the U.S. balance of payments record is a matter for concern? Why or why not?

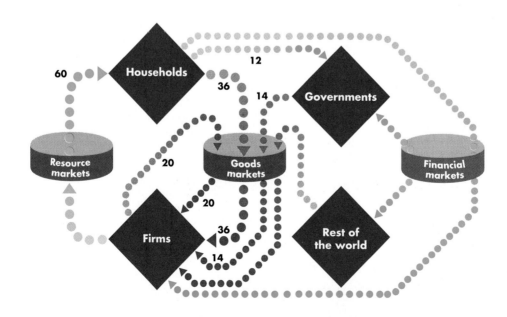

Glossary

Above full-employment equilibrium A macroeconomic equilibrium in which real GDP exceeds potential GDP.

Absolute advantage A person has an absolute advantage in the production of two goods if by using the same quantities of inputs, that person can produce more of both goods than another person; a country has an absolute advantage if its output per unit of inputs of all goods is larger than that of another country.

Adverse selection The tendency for people to enter into agreements in which they can use their private information to their own advantage and to the disadvantage of the less-informed party.

Aggregate demand The relationship between the aggregate quantity of real GDP demanded and the price level.

Aggregate hours The total number of hours worked by all the people employed, both full time and part time, during a year.

Aggregate planned expenditure The expenditure that households, firms, governments, and foreigners plan to undertake in given circumstances. It is the sum of planned consumption expenditure, planned investment, planned government purchases of goods and services, and planned exports minus planned imports.

Aggregate production function The relationship between the quantity of real GDP supplied and the quantities of labor and capital and the state of technology.

Antitrust law A law that regulates and prohibits certain kinds of market behavior, such as monopoly and monopolistic practices.

Automatic fiscal policy A change in fiscal policy that is triggered by the state of the economy.

Automatic stabilizers Mechanisms that stabilize real GDP without explicit action by the government.

Autonomous expenditure The sum of those components of aggregate planned expenditure that are not influenced by real GDP.

Average cost pricing rule A rule that sets price equal to average total cost.

Average fixed cost Total fixed cost per unit of output—total fixed cost divided by output.

Average product The average product of a resource. It equals total product divided by the quantity of the resource employed.

Average revenue Revenue per unit of output sold—total revenue divided by the quantity sold. Average revenue also equals price.

Average tax rate The percentage of income that is paid in tax.

Average total cost Total cost per unit of output.

Average variable cost Total variable cost per unit of output.

Balanced budget A government budget in which tax revenues and expenditures are equal.

Balanced budget amendment A requirement that the federal government's budget be balanced.

Balance of payments accounts A country's record of international trading, borrowing, and lending.

Balance of trade The value of exports minus the value of imports.

Barriers to entry Legal or natural constraints that protect a firm from potential competitors.

Barter The direct exchange of one good or service for other goods and services.

Below full-employment equilibrium A macroeconomic equilibrium in which potential GDP exceeds real GDP.

Big tradeoff The conflict between equity and efficiency.

Bilateral monopoly A situation in which there is a single seller (a monopoly) and a single buyer (a monopsony).

Black market An illegal trading arrangement in which the price exceeds the legally imposed price ceiling.

Bond A legally enforceable debt obligation to pay specified amounts of money at specified future dates.

Bond market A market in which the bonds of corporations and governments are traded.

Budget deficit A government's budget balance that is negative—expenditures exceed tax revenues.

Budget line The limits to a household's consumption choices.

Budget surplus A government's budget balance that is positive—tax revenues exceed expenditures.

Business cycle The periodic but irregular up-and-down movement in production.

Capital The equipment, buildings, tools, and manufactured goods that we use to produce other goods and services.

Capital account A record of foreign investment in a country minus its investment abroad.

Capital accumulation The growth of capital resources.

Capital gain The income received by selling a stock or bond for a higher price than the price paid for it.

Capital stock The total quantity of plant, equipment, buildings, and inventories.

Capture theory A theory of regulation that states that the regulations are supplied to satisfy the demand of producers to maximize producer surplus—to maximize economic profit.

Cartel A group of firms that has entered into a collusive agreement to restrict output and increase prices and profits.

Central bank A bank's bank and a public authority charged with regulating and controlling a country's monetary policy and financial institutions and markets.

Ceteris paribus Other things being equal—all other relevant things remaining the same.

Chain-weighted output index An index that measures the growth rate of real GDP.

Change in demand A change in buyers' plans that occurs when some influence on those plans other than the price of the good changes. It is illustrated by a shift of the demand curve.

Change in supply A change in sellers' plans that occurs when some influence on those plans other than the price of the good changes. It is illustrated by a shift of the supply curve.

Change in the quantity demanded A change in buyers' plans that occurs when the price of a good changes but all other influences on buyers' plans remain unchanged. It is illustrated by a movement along the demand curve.

Change in the quantity supplied A change in sellers' plans that occurs when the price of a good changes but all other influences on sellers' plans remain unchanged. It is illustrated by a movement along the supply curve.

Classical growth theory A theory of economic growth based on the view that real GDP growth is temporary and that when real GDP per person increases above subsistence level, a population explosion brings real GDP back to subsistence level.

Coase theorem The proposition that if property rights exist and transactions costs are low, private transactions are efficient—equivalently, with property rights and low transaction costs, there are no externalities.

Collective bargaining A process of negotiation between representatives of employers and unions.

Collusive agreement An agreement between two (or more) producers to restrict output so as to increase prices and profits.

Command system A system in which some people give orders and other people obey them.

Commercial bank A firm, licensed either by the Comptroller of the Currency (in the U.S. Treasury) or by a state agency to receive deposits and make loans.

Comparative advantage A person or country has a comparative advantage in an activity if that person or country can perform the activity at a lower opportunity cost than anyone else or any other country.

Complement A good that is used in conjunction with another good.

Constant returns to scale Technological conditions under which a given percentage increase in all the firm's inputs results in the firm's output increasing by the same percentage.

Consumer efficiency A situation that occurs when consumers cannot become better off by reallocating their budget.

Consumer equilibrium A situation in which a consumer has allocated his or her income in the way that maximizes his or her utility.

Consumer Price Index An index that measures the average level of prices of the goods and services that a typical urban family buys.

Consumer surplus The value that the consumer gets from each unit of a good minus the price paid for it.

Consumption expenditure The total amount spent on consumption goods and services.

Consumption function The relationship between consumption expenditure and disposable income, other things remaining the same.

Contractionary fiscal policy A decrease in government expenditures or an increase in tax revenues.

Contestable market A market in which one firm (or a small number of firms) operates but in which entry and exit are free, so the firm (or firms) in the industry faces competition from potential entrants.

Convertible paper money A paper claim to a commodity (such as gold) that circulates as a means of payment.

Cooperative equilibrium The outcome of a collusive agreement between players when the players make and share the monopoly profit.

Copyright A government-sanctioned exclusive right granted to the inventor of a good, service, or productive process to produce, use, and sell the invention for a given number of years.

Cost-push inflation An inflation that results from an initial increase in costs.

Council of Economic Advisers The President's council whose main work is to monitor the economy and keep the President and the public well informed about the current state of the economy and the best available forecasts of where it is heading.

Craft union A group of workers who have a similar range of skills but work for many different firms in many different industries and regions.

Credit union A financial intermediary owned by its depositors, who are a social or economic group, that accepts savings deposits and makes mostly consumer loans.

Creditor nation A country that during its entire history has invested more in the rest of the world than other countries have invested in it.

Cross elasticity of demand The responsiveness of the demand for a good to the price of a substitute or complement, other things remaining the same. It is calculated as the percentage change in the quantity demanded of the good divided by the percentage change in the price of the substitute or complement.

Cross-section graph A graph that shows the values of an economic variable for different groups in a population at a point in time.

Crowding-out effect The tendency for a government budget deficit to decrease in investment.

Currency The bills and coins that we use today.

Currency appreciation The rise in the value of one currency in terms of another currency.

Currency depreciation The fall in the value of one currency in terms of another currency.

Currency drain An increase in currency held outside the banks.

Current account A record of receipts from the sale of goods and services to foreigners, the payments for goods and services bought from foreigners, the interest payments paid to and received from the rest of the world, and net transfers paid to foreigners.

Cyclical unemployment The fluctuations in unemployment over the business cycle.

Cyclically adjusted deficit The budget deficit that would occur if the economy were at full employment.

Deadweight loss A measure of inefficiency. It is equal to the loss in total surplus (consumer surplus plus producer surplus) when output is below or above its efficient level.

Debtor nation A country that during its entire history has borrowed more from the rest of the world than it has lent to it.

Decentralized planning An economic system that combines state ownership of capital and land with incentives based on a mixture of market prices and laws and regulations.

Decreasing returns to scale Technological conditions under which a given percentage increase in all the firm's inputs results in the firm's output increasing by a smaller percentage.

Deflation A process in which the price level falls—a negative inflation.

Demand The relationship between the quantity of a good that consumers plan to buy and the price of the good, when all other influences on buyers' plans remain the same. It is described by a demand schedule and illustrated by a demand curve.

Demand curve A curve that shows the relationship between the quantity demanded of a good and its price when all other influences on consumers' planned purchases remain the same.

Demand-pull inflation An inflation that results from an initial increase in aggregate demand.

Deposit multiplier The amount by which an increase in bank reserves is multiplied to calculate the increase in bank deposits.

Depreciation The decrease in the capital stock resulting from wear and tear and the scrapping of existing capital.

Derived demand Demand for a productive resource which is derived from the demand for the goods and services produced by the resource.

Diminishing marginal rate of substitution The general tendency for the marginal rate of substitution of one good for another to diminish as a consumer moves along an indifference curve increasing consumption of the first good.

Diminishing marginal returns The tendency for the marginal product of an additional resource eventually to be less than the marginal product of the previous unit of the resource.

Diminishing marginal utility The marginal utility that a consumer gets from a good decreases as more of the good is consumed.

Direct relationship A relationship between two variables that move in the same direction.

Discounting The conversion of a future amount of money to its present value.

Discount rate The interest rate at which the Fed stands ready to lend reserves to commercial banks.

Discouraged workers People who are available and willing to work but who have given up the effort to find work.

Discretionary fiscal policy A policy action that is initiated by an act of Congress.

Discretionary policy A policy that responds to the state of the economy

in a possibly unique way that uses all the information available, including perceived lessons from past "mistakes."

Disposable income Aggregate income minus taxes plus transfer payments.

Dominant strategy equilibrium The outcome of a game in which there is a single best strategy (a dominant strategy) for each player, regardless of the strategy of the other players.

Dumping The sale of a good or service to a foreign country at a price that is less than the cost of producing the good or service.

Duopoly A market structure in which two producers of a good or service compete.

Dynamic comparative advantage A comparative advantage that a person or country possesses as a result of having specialized in a particular activity and then, as a result of learning-by-doing, having become the producer with the lowest opportunity cost.

Economic depreciation The change in the market price of a piece of capital over a given period.

Economic efficiency A situation that occurs when the cost of producing a given output is as low as possible.

Economic growth The expansion of production possibilities that results from capital accumulation and technological change.

Economic information Data on prices, quantities, and qualities of goods and services and factors of production.

Economic model A description of some aspect of the economic world that includes only those features of the world that are needed for the purpose at hand.

Economic profit A firm's total revenue minus its opportunity cost.

Economic rent The income received by the owner of a resource over and above the amount required to induce that owner to offer the resource for use.

Economic theory A generalization that summarizes what we think we understand about the economic choices that people make and the performance of industries and entire economies.

Economic welfare A comprehensive measure of the general state of economic well-being.

Economics The science that explains the choices we make and how those choices change as we cope with scarcity.

Economies of scope Decreases in average total cost that occur when a firm uses specialized resources to produce a range of goods and services.

Efficiency wage The wage rate that maximizes profit.

Efficient Resource use is efficient when we produce the goods and services that we value most highly.

Efficient market A market in which the actual price embodies all currently available relevant information. Resources are sent to their highest-valued use.

Elastic demand Demand with a price elasticity greater than 1; other things remaining the same, the percentage change in the quantity demanded exceeds the percentage change in price.

Elasticity of supply The responsiveness of the quantity supplied of a good to a change in its price, other things remaining the same.

Employment Act of 1946 A landmark Congressional act that recognized a role for government actions to reduce unemployment, keep the economy expanding, and keep inflation in check.

Employment-to-population ratio The percentage of people of working age who have jobs.

Entitlement spending Spending on government programs that entitle suitably qualified individuals and businesses to receive benefits and that result in transfer payments that depend on the economic state of individual citizens and businesses.

Entrants People who enter the labor force.

Entrepreneurship The resource that organizes the other three factors of production—labor, land, and capital. Entrepreneurs come up with new ideas about what, how, when, and where to produce, make business decisions, and bear the risk that arise from their decisions.

Equation of exchange An equation that states that the quantity of money multiplied by the velocity of circulation equals GDP.

Equilibrium expenditure The level of aggregate expenditure that occurs when aggregate planned expenditure equals real GDP.

Equilibrium price The price at which the quantity demanded equals the quantity supplied.

Equilibrium quantity The quantity bought and sold at the equilibrium price.

Equity In economics, equity has two meanings: economic justice or fairness and the owner's stake in a business.

Exchange efficiency A situation in which a good or service is exchanged at a price that equals both the marginal social benefit and the marginal social cost of the good or service. All the gains from trade have been realized.

Excess reserves A bank's actual reserves minus its required reserves.

Excise tax A tax on the sale of a particular commodity.

Exhaustible natural resources Natural resources that can be used only once and that cannot be replaced once they have been used.

Expansion A business cycle phase in which real GDP increases.

Expansionary fiscal policy An increase in government expenditure or a decrease in tax revenues.

Expected utility The average utility arising from all possible outcomes.

Exports The goods and services that we sell to people in other countries.

External benefits Benefits that accrue to people other than the buyer of the good.

External costs Costs that are not borne by the producer of the good but borne by someone else.

External diseconomies Factors outside the control of a firm that raise the firm's costs as the industry produces a larger output.

External economies Factors beyond the control of a firm that lower the firm's costs as the industry produces a larger output.

Externality A cost or a benefit that arises from an economic transaction and that falls on people who do not participate in the transaction.

Factors of production The economy's productive resources—land, labor, capital, and entrepreneurship. Also called productive resources.

Federal budget A statement of the federal government's financial plan,

itemizing programs and their costs, tax revenues, and the proposed deficit or surplus.

Federal Open Market Committee The main policy-making organ of the Federal Reserve System.

Federal Reserve System The central bank of the United States.

Feedback-rule policy A rule that specifies how policy actions respond to changes in the state of the economy.

Financial innovation The development of new financial products—new ways of borrowing and lending.

Financial intermediary A firm that takes deposits from households and firms and makes loans to other households and firms.

Firm An institution that hires productive resources and that organizes those resources to produce and sell goods and services.

Fiscal policy The government's attempt to influence the economy by setting and changing taxes, its purchases of goods and services, and transfer payments to achieve macroeconomic objectives such as full employment, sustained long-term economic growth, and low inflation.

Fixed-rule policy A rule that specifies an action to be pursued independently of the state of the economy.

Four-firm concentration ratio A measure of market power that is calculated as the percentage of the value of sales accounted for by the four largest firms in an industry.

Flow A quantity per unit of time.

Foreign exchange market The market in which the currency of one country is exchanged for the currency of another.

Foreign exchange rate The price at which one currency exchanges for another.

Free rider A person who consumes a good without paying for it.

Frictional unemployment The unemployment that arises from normal labor turnover—people entering and leaving the labor force and from ongoing creation and destruction of jobs.

Full employment A situation in which the quantity of labor demanded equal the quantity supplied. At full employment, the unemployment rate equals the natural rate of unemploy-

ment and all unemployment is frictional and structural.

Game theory The main tool that economists use to analyze strategic behavior—behavior that takes into account the expected behavior of others and the mutual recognition of independence.

GDP deflator A price index that measures the average level of the prices of all goods and services that are included in GDP.

General Agreement on Tariffs and Trade (GATT) An international agreement designed to reduce tariffs on international trade.

Goods and services All the things that people are willing to pay for.

Government budget deficit The deficit that arises when federal government expenditure exceed the taxes collected.

Government debt The total amount of borrowing that the government has undertaken. It equals the sum of past budget deficits minus budget surpluses.

Government purchases Goods and services bought by the government.

Government purchases multiplier The magnification effect of a change in government purchases of goods and services on equilibrium expenditure and real GDP.

Government sector surplus or deficit An amount equal to net taxes minus government purchases of goods and services.

Great Depression A decade (1929–1939) of high unemployment and stagnant production throughout the world economy.

Gross domestic product (GDP) The value of aggregate production in a country in a year.

Gross investment The total amount spent on adding to the capital stock and on replacing depreciated capital.

Growth accounting A method of calculating how much real GDP growth has resulted from growth of labor and capital and how much is attributable to technological change.

Herfindahl-Hirschman Index A measure of market power, that is calculated as the square of the market share of each firm (as a percentage) summed over the largest 50 firms (or over all firms if there are fewer than 50) in a market.

Human capital The skill and knowledge that people obtain from education and on-the-job training.

Implicit rental rate The rent that a firm pays to itself for the use of its own assets.

Imports The goods and services that we buy from people in other countries.

Incentive An inducement to take a particular action.

Incentive regulation scheme A regulation that gives a firm an incentive to operate efficiently and keep costs under control.

Income effect The change in consumption that results from a change in the consumer's income, other things remaining the same.

Income elasticity of demand The responsiveness of demand to a change in income, other things remaining the same. It is calculated as the percentage change in the quantity demanded divided by the percentage change in income.

Increasing marginal returns The tendency for the marginal product of an additional unit of a resource initially to exceed the marginal product of the previous unit of the resource.

Increasing returns to scale Technological conditions under which a given percentage increase in all the firm's inputs results in the firm's output increasing by a larger percentage.

Indifference curve A line that shows combinations of goods among which a consumer is indifferent.

Induced expenditure The sum of the components of aggregate expenditure that varies with real GDP.

Induced taxes Taxes that vary as real GDP varies.

Industrial union A group of workers who have a variety of skills and job types but work for the same industry.

Inelastic demand A demand with a price elasticity between 0 and 1; the percentage change in the quantity demanded is less than the percentage change in price.

Infant-industry argument The argument that protection is necessary to enable an infant industry to grow into a mature industry that can compete in world markets.

Inferior good A good for which demand decreases as income increases.

Inflation A process in which the price level is rising and money is losing value.

Inflationary gap The amount by which real GDP exceeds potential GDP.

Information cost The opportunity cost of economic information—the cost of acquiring information on prices, quantities, and qualities of goods and services and resources.

Insider-outsider theory A theory of job rationing that says that to be productive, new workers—outsiders—must receive on-the-job training from existing workers—insiders.

Intellectual property rights Property rights for discoveries owned by the creators of knowledge.

Interest rate parity A situation in which the return on assets in different currencies are equal.

Intermediate goods and services Goods and services that firms buy from each other and use as inputs in the goods and services that they eventually sell to final users.

Inverse relationship A relationship between variables that move in opposite directions.

Investment The purchase of new plant, equipment, and buildings and additions to inventories.

Investment demand The relationship between investment and real interest rate, other influences on investment remaining the same.

Job leavers People who voluntarily quit their jobs.

Job losers People who are laid off, either permanently or temporarily, from their jobs.

Job rationing The practice of paying employed people a wage that creates an excess supply of labor and a shortage of jobs and increases the natural rate of unemployment.

Job search The activity of people looking for acceptable vacant jobs.

Keynesian activist An economist who believes that fluctuations in aggregate demand combined with sticky wages (and/or sticky prices) are the main source of economic fluctuations.

Keynesian theory of the business cycle A theory that regards volatile expectations as the main source of economic fluctuations.

Labor The time and effort that people allocate to producing goods and services.

Labor demand curve A curve that shows the quantity of labor that firms plan to hire at each possible real wage rate.

Labor force The sum of the people who are employed and who are unemployed.

Labor force participation rate The percentage of the working-age population who are members of the labor force.

Labor supply curve A curve that shows the quantity of labor that households plan to supply at each possible real wage rate.

Labor union An organized group of workers whose purpose is to increase wages and to influence other job conditions.

Land All the gifts of nature that we use to produce goods and services.

Law of diminishing returns As a firm uses more of a variable input with a given quantity of other inputs (fixed inputs), the marginal product of the variable input eventually diminishes.

Learning-by-doing People become more productive in an activity (learn) just by repeatedly producing a particular good or service (doing).

Legal monopoly A market structure in which there is one firm and entry is restricted by the granting of a public franchise, government license, patent, or copyright.

Limit pricing The practice of charging a price below the monopoly profit-maximizing price and producing a quantity greater than that at which marginal revenue equals marginal cost so as to deter entry.

Linear relationship A relationship between two variables that is illustrated by a straight line.

Liquidity The property of being instantly convertible into a means of payment with little loss in value.

Local public good A public good that is consumed by all the people who live in a particular area.

Long run A period of time in which a firm can vary the quantities of all its inputs.

Long-run aggregate supply curve The relationship between the real GDP supplied and the price level in the long run when real GDP equals potential GDP.

Long-run average cost curve The relationship between the lowest attainable average total cost and output when both capital and labor are varied.

Long-run cost The cost of production when a firm uses the economically efficient quantities of labor and capital.

Long-run industry supply curve A curve that shows how the quantity supplied by an industry varies as the market price varies after all the possible adjustments have been made, including changes in plant size and the number of firms in the industry.

Long-run macroeconomic equilibrium A situation that occurs when real GDP equals potential GDP—the economy is on its long-run aggregate supply curve.

Long-run Phillips curve A curve that shows the relationship between inflation and unemployment when the actual inflation rate equals the expected inflation rate.

Lorenz curve A curve that graphs the cumulative percentage of income or wealth against the cumulative percentage of families or population.

Lump-sum tax multiplier The magnification effect of a change in lump-sum taxes on equilibrium expenditure and real GDP.

Lump-sum taxes Taxes that do not vary with real GDP.

M1 A measure of money that consists of currency and traveler's checks plus checking deposits owned by individuals and businesses.

M2 A measure of money that consists of M1 plus savings deposits and time deposits.

Macroeconomic long run A time frame that is sufficiently long for real GDP to return to potential GDP.

Macroeconomics The study of the national economy and the global economy, the way that economic aggregates grow and fluctuate, and the effects of government actions on them.

Macroeconomic short run A period during real GDP has decreased below or increased above potential GDP.

Marginal benefit The benefit that a person receives from consuming one more unit of a good or service. It is measured as the maximum amount that a person is willing to pay for one more unit of the good or service.

Marginal cost The opportunity cost of producing one more unit of a good or service. It is the best alternative forgone. It is calculated as the increase in total cost divided by the increase in output.

Marginal cost pricing rule A rule that sets the price of a good or service equal to the marginal cost of producing it.

Marginal product The extra output produced as a result of a small increase in the variable input. It is calculated as the increase in total product divided by the increase in the variable input employed, when the quantities of all other factors are constant.

Marginal propensity to consume The fraction of an increase in disposable income that is consumed.

Marginal propensity to import The fraction of an increase in real GDP that is spent on imports.

Marginal propensity to save The fraction of an increase in disposable income that is saved.

Marginal rate of substitution The rate at which a person will give up good y (the good measured on the y-axis) to get more of good x (the good measured on the x-axis) and at the same time remain indifferent (remain on the same indifference curve).

Marginal revenue The change in total revenue received from selling one additional unit of the good or service. It is calculated as the change in total revenue divided by the change in quantity sold.

Marginal revenue product The change in total revenue that results from employing one more unit of a resource while the quantity of all other resources remains the same. It is calculated as the increase in total revenue divided by the increase in the quantity of the resource.

Marginal social benefit The marginal benefit received by the buyer of a good (marginal private benefit) plus the marginal benefit received by others (external benefit).

Marginal social cost The marginal cost incurred by the producer of a good (marginal private cost) plus the marginal cost imposed on other members of society (external cost).

Marginal tax rate The percentage of an additional dollar of income that is paid in tax.

Marginal utility The change in total utility resulting from a one-unit increase in the quantity of a good consumed.

Marginal utility per dollar spent The marginal utility obtained from the last unit of a good consumed divided by the price of the good.

Market Any arrangement that enables buyers and sellers to get information and to do business with each other.

Market demand The relationship between the quantity demanded of a good or service by everyone in the population and its price. It is illustrated by the market demand curve.

Market failure A state in which the market does not use resources efficiently.

Means of payment A method of settling a debt.

Microeconomics The study of the decisions of people and businesses, the interactions of those decisions in markets, and the effects of government regulation and taxes on the prices and quantities of goods and services.

Minimum wage law A regulation that makes the hiring of labor below a specified wage rate illegal.

Monetarist An economist who believes that fluctuations in the money stock are the main source of economic fluctuations.

Monetarist theory of the business cycle A theory that regards fluctuations in the money stock as the main source of economic fluctuations.

Monetary base The sum of the Federal Reserve notes, coins, and banks' deposits at the Fed.

Monetary policy The Federal Reserve's attempt to keep inflation in check, maintain full employment, moderate the business cycle, and contribute towards achieving long-term growth by adjusting the quantity of money in circulation and interest rates.

Money Any commodity or token that is generally acceptable as a means of payment.

Money market mutual fund A financial institution that obtains funds by selling shares and that uses these funds to buy highly liquid assets such as U.S. Treasury bills.

Money multiplier The amount by which a change in the monetary base is multiplied to determine the resulting change in the quantity of money.

Monopolistic competition A market in which a large number of firms compete by making similar but slightly different products.

Monopoly An industry that produces a good or service for which no close substitute exists and in which there is one supplier that is protected from competition by a barrier preventing the entry of new firms.

Monopsony A market in which there is a single buyer.

Moral hazard A situation in which one of the parties to an agreement has an incentive after the agreement is made to act in a manner that brings additional benefits to himself or herself at the expense of the other party.

Multiplier The amount by which a change in autonomous expenditure is magnified or multiplied to determine the change in equilibrium expenditure and real GDP.

Nash equilibrium The outcome of a game that occurs when player A takes the best possible action given the action of player B, and player B takes the best possible action given the action of player A.

Natural monopoly A monopoly that occurs when one firm can supply the entire market at a lower price than two or more firms can.

National saving Saving by households and businesses plus government saving.

Natural rate of unemployment The unemployment rate when the economy is at full employment. There is no cyclical unemployment, all unemployment is frictional and structural.

Negative income tax A redistribution scheme that gives every family a guaranteed minimum annual income and taxes all income above the guaranteed minimum at a fixed marginal tax rate.

Negative relationship A relationship between variables that move in opposite directions.

Neoclassical growth theory A theory of economic growth that proposes that real GDP grows because technological change induces saving and investment.

Net borrower A country that is borrowing more from the rest of the world than it is lending to it.

Net exports The exports of goods and services minus imports of goods and services.

Net investment Net increase in the capital stock—gross investment minus depreciation.

Net lender A country that is lending more to the rest of the world than it is borrowing from it.

Net present value The present value of the future flow of marginal revenue product generated by capital minus the cost of the capital.

Net taxes Taxes paid to governments minus transfer payments received from governments.

New classical theory of the business cycle A rational expectations theory of the business cycle that regards unanticipated fluctuations in aggregate demand as the main source of economic fluctuations.

New growth theory A theory of economic growth based on the idea that real GDP grows because of the choices that people make in the pursuit of ever greater profit and that growth can persist indefinitely.

New Keynesian theory of the business cycle A rational expectations theory of the business cycle that regards unanticipated fluctuations in aggregate demand as the main source of economic fluctuations but leaves room for anticipated demand fluctuations to play a role.

Nominal GDP GDP valued in current prices.

Nominal GDP targeting An attempt to keep the growth rate of nominal GDP steady.

Nonexhaustible natural resources Natural resources that can be used repeatedly without depleting what is available for future use.

Nontariff barrier Any action other than a tariff that restricts international trade.

Normal good A good for which demand increases as income increases.

Normal profit The expected return for supplying entrepreneurial ability.

North American Free Trade Agreement An agreement signed in 1994 between the United States, Canada, and Mexico to virtually eliminate all barriers to international trade between them in 15 years.

Official settlements account A record of the change in a country's official reserves.

Official U.S. reserves The government's holdings of foreign currency.

Oligopoly A market in which a small number of firms compete.

Open market operation The purchase or sale of government securities by the Federal Reserve System in the open market.

Opportunity cost The opportunity cost of an action is the highest-valued alternative forgone.

Patent A government-sanctioned exclusive right granted to the inventor of a good, service, or productive process to produce, use, and sell the invention for a given number of years.

Payoff matrix A table that shows the payoffs for every possible action by each player for every possible action by each other player.

Perfect competition A market in which there are many firms each selling an identical product; there are many buyers; there are no restrictions on entry into the industry; firms in the industry have no advantage over potential new entrants; and firms and buyers are well informed about the price of each firm's product.

Perfectly elastic demand Demand with an infinite price elasticity; the quantity demanded changes by a large percentage in response to a tiny price change.

Perfectly inelastic demand Demand with a price elasticity of zero; the quantity demanded remains constant when the price changes.

Phillips curve A curve that shows a relationship between inflation and unemployment.

Political equilibrium The outcome that results from the choices of voters, politicians, and bureaucrats.

Positive relationship A relationship between two variables that move in the same direction.

Potential GDP The value of production when all the economy's resources (labor, land, capital, and entrepreneurship) are fully employed. Unemployment is at its natural rate and the economy is at full employment.

Poverty A state in which a family's income is too low to be able to buy the quantities of food, shelter, and clothing that are deemed necessary.

Present value The amount of money that, if invested today, will grow to be as large as a given future amount when the interest that it will earn is taken into account.

Price ceiling A regulation that makes it illegal to charge a price higher than a specified level.

Price discrimination The practice of selling different units of a good or service for different prices or of charging one customer different prices for different quantities bought.

Price effect The change in consumption that results from a change in the price of a good or service, other things remaining the same.

Price elasticity of demand A measure of the responsiveness of the quantity demanded of a good to a change in its price, with all other influences on buyers' plans remaining the same.

Price level The average level of prices as measured by a price index.

Price taker A firm that cannot influence the price of the good or service it produces.

Principal-agent problem The problem of devising compensation rules that induce an agent to act in the best interest of a principal.

Principle of minimum differentiation The tendency for competitors to make themselves identical as they try to appeal to the maximum number of clients or voters.

Private information Information that is available to one person but is too costly for anyone else to obtain.

Private sector surplus or deficit An amount equal to saving minus investment.

Producer efficiency A situation in which firms cannot lower the cost of producing a given output by changing the resources they use.

Producer surplus The price a producer gets for a good or service minus the opportunity cost of producing it.

Product differentiation Making a good or service slightly different from that of a competing firm.

Production efficiency A situation in which the economy cannot produce more of one good without producing less of some other good.

Production function The relationship between the maximum output attainable and the quantities of both labor and capital.

Production possibility frontier The boundary between those combinations of goods and services that can be produced and those that cannot.

Productive resources The economy's resources—land, labor, capital, and entrepreneurship. Also called the economy's resources.

Productivity Production per unit of resource used in the production of goods and services.

Productivity function A relationship that shows how real GDP per hour of labor changes as the amount of capital per hour of labor changes with a given state of technology.

Productivity growth slowdown A slowdown in the growth rate of output per person.

Progressive income tax A tax on income at a marginal rate that increases with the level of income.

Property rights Social arrangements that govern the ownership, use, and disposal of resources, goods, and services.

Proportional income tax A tax on income that remains at a constant rate, regardless of the level of income.

Public good A good or service that can be consumed simultaneously by everyone, even if they don't pay for it.

Public interest theory A theory of regulation that states that regulations are supplied to satisfy the demand of consumers and producers to maximize total surplus—that is, to attain efficiency.

Purchasing power parity A situation in which the value of different money (different currencies) is equal.

Quantity demanded The amount of a good or service that consumers plan to buy during a given time period at a particular price.

Quantity supplied The amount of a good or service that producers plan to sell during a given time period at a particular price.

Quantity theory of money The proposition that in the long run, an increase in the quantity of money brings an equal percentage increase in the price level.

Quota A quantitative restriction on the import of a particular good, which specifies the maximum amount that can be imported in a given time period.

Rate of return regulation A regulation that determines a regulated price by setting the price at a level that enables the regulated firm to earn a specified target percent return on its capital.

Rational expectation A forecast based on all available relevant information.

Rational ignorance The decision not to acquire information because the cost of doing so exceeds the expected benefit.

Real business cycle theory A theory that regards random fluctuations in productivity as the main source of economic fluctuations.

Real Gross Domestic Product (real GDP) The value of total production of all the nation's farms, factories, shops, and offices linked back to the prices of a single year. It is calculated as GDP in the base year scaled up by the growth rate of real GDP since the base year.

Real income A household's income expressed not as money but as a quantity of goods that the household can afford to buy.

Real interest rate The nominal interest rate adjusted for inflation; the nominal interest rate minus the inflation rate.

Real wage rate The quantity of goods ands services that an hour's work can buy.

Recession A business cycle phase in which real GDP decreases for at least two successive quarters.

Recessionary gap The amount by which potential GDP exceeds real GDP.

Reentrants People who reenter the labor force.

Regressive income tax A tax on income at a marginal rate that decreases with the level of income.

Relative price The ratio of the price of one good or service to the price of another good or service. A relative price is an opportunity cost.

Rent ceiling A regulation that makes it illegal to charge a rent higher than a specified level.

Rent seeking The activity of trying to obtain a monopoly from which an economic profit can be made.

Required reserve ratio The ratio of reserves to deposits that banks are required, by regulation, to hold.

Reservation price The highest price that a buyer is willing to pay for a good.

Reserve ratio The fraction of a bank's total deposits that are held in reserves.

Reserves Cash in a bank's vault plus the bank's deposits at Federal Reserve banks.

Resources The economy's resources are land, labor, capital, and entrepreneurship. Also called the productive resources or factors of production.

Returns to scale The increase in output that results when a firm increases all its inputs by the same percentage.

Risk A situation in which more than one outcome might occur and the probability of each possible outcome can be estimated.

Saving The amount of income remaining after meeting consumption expenditures.

Saving function The relationship between saving and disposable income, other things remaining the same.

Savings and loan association (S&L) A financial intermediary that receives checking deposits and savings deposits and that makes personal, commercial, and home-purchase loans.

Savings bank A financial intermediary that is owned by its depositors and accepts deposits and makes loans, mostly home-purchase loans.

Saving supply The relationship between saving and the real interest rate, other things remaining the same.

Scarcity The state in which the resources available are insufficient to satisfy people's wants.

Scatter diagram A diagram that plots the value of one economic variable against the value of another.

Search activity The time spent looking for someone with whom to do business.

Short run The short run in microeconomics has two meanings. For the firm, it is the period of time in which the quantity of at least one input is fixed and the quantities of the other inputs can be varied. The fixed input is usually capital—that is, the firm has a given plant size. For the industry, the short run is the period of time in which each firm has a given plant size and the number of firms in the industry is fixed.

Short-run aggregate supply curve A curve that shows the relationship between the quantity of real GDP supplied and the price level in the short run when the money wage rate, other resource prices, and potential GDP remain constant.

Short-run industry supply curve A curve that shows the quantity supplied by the industry at each price varies when the plant size of each firm and the number of firms in the industry remain the same.

Short-run macroeconomic equilibrium A situation that occurs when the quantity of real GDP demanded equals quantity of real GDP supplied—at the point of intersection of the *AD* curve and the *SAS* curve.

Short-run Phillips curve A curve that shows the relationship between inflation and unemployment, when the expected inflation rate and the natural rate of unemployment remain the same.

Shutdown point The output and price at which the firm just covers its total variable cost. In the short run, the firm is indifferent between producing the profit-maximizing output and shutting down temporarily.

Signal An action taken outside a market that conveys information that can be used by that market.

Single-price monopoly A monopoly that sells each unit of its output for a same price.

Slope The change in the value of the variable measured on the *y*-axis divided by the change in the value of the variable measured on the *x*-axis.

Stagflation The combination of a rise in the price level and a decrease in real GDP.

Stock A quantity that exists at a point in time.

Strategies All the possible actions of each player in a game.

Structural deficit A budget that is in deficit when real GDP equals potential GDP; expenditures exceed tax revenues.

Structural unemployment The unemployment that arises when changes in technology or international competition change the skills needed to perform jobs or change the locations of jobs.

Subsidy A payment made by the government to producers that depends the level of output.

Subsistence real wage rate The minimum real wage rate needed to maintain life.

Substitute A good that can be used in place of another good.

Substitution effect The effect of a change in price of one good or service on the quantity bought when the consumer remains indifferent between the original and the new consumption situations—that is, the consumer remains on the same indifference curve.

Sunk cost A cost that has been incurred and that cannot be reversed.

Supply The relationship between the quantity of a good that producers plan to sell and the price of the good when all other influences on sellers' plans remain the same. It is described by a supply schedule and illustrated by a supply curve.

Supply curve A curve that shows the relationship between the quantity supplied and the price of a good when all other influences on producers' planned sales remain the same.

Tariff A tax that is imposed by the importing country when an imported good crosses its international boundary.

Technological efficiency A situation that occurs when it is not possible to increase output without increasing inputs.

Time-series graph A graph that measures time (for example, months or years) on the *x*-axis and the variable or variables in which we are interested on the *y*-axis.

Total cost The cost of all the productive resources that a firm uses.

Total fixed cost The cost of the fixed inputs.

Total product The total output produced by a firm in a given period of time.

Total revenue The value of a firm's sales. It is calculated as the price of the good multiplied by the quantity sold.

Total revenue test A method of estimating the price elasticity of demand by observing the change in total revenue that results from a change in the price, when all other influences on the quantity sold remain the same.

Total utility The total benefit that a person gets from the consumption of goods and services.

Total variable cost The cost of all the variable inputs.

Tradeoff A constraint that involves giving up one thing to get something else.

Transactions costs The costs incurred in searching for someone with whom to do business, in reaching an agreement about the price and other aspects of the exchange, and in ensuring that the terms of the agreement are fulfilled.

Trend The general direction (rising or falling) in which a variable is moving over the long term.

Twin deficits The tendency for the government sector deficit and the net exports deficit to move together.

Uncertainty A situation in which more than one event might occur but it is not known which one.

Unemployed A person who does not have a job but is available for work, is willing to work, and has made some effort to find work within the previous four weeks.

Unemployment Resources that are available but are not being used.

Unemployment rate The percentage of the people in the labor force who are unemployed.

Unit elastic demand Demand with a price elasticity of 1; the percentage change in the quantity demanded equals the percentage change in price.

U.S. interest rate differential The interest rate on a U.S. dollar asset minus the interest rate on a foreign currency asset.

Utility The benefit or satisfaction that a person gets from the consumption of a good or service.

Utility of wealth The amount of utility that a person attaches to a given amount of wealth.

Value The maximum amount that a person is willing to pay for a good. The value of one more unit of the good or service is its marginal benefit.

Value added The value of a firm's output minus the value of the intermediate goods that the firm buys from other firms.

Velocity of circulation The average number of times a dollar of money is used annually to buy the goods and services that make up GDP.

Voluntary export restraint An agreement between two countries in which the government of the exporting country agrees to reduce the volume of its own exports to the other country.

Wealth The value of all the things that people own.

Working-age population The total number of people aged 16 years and over who are not in jail, hospital, or some other form of institutional care.

World Trade Organization An international organization that places obligations on its member countries to observe the GATT rules.

Index

Key concepts and pages on which they are defined appear in **boldface type**.

Four Alternative Sequences for a Macro Principles Course

Early Long-Term Growth	Late Long-Term Growth	Keynesian Perspective	Monetarist Perspective
5 A First Look at Macroeconomics	**5** A First Look at Macroeconomics	**5** A First Look at Macroeconomics	**5** A First Look at Macroeconomics
6 Measuring GDP, Inflation, and Economic Growth	**6** Measuring GDP, Inflation, and Economic Growth	**6** Measuring GDP, Inflation, and Economic Growth	**6** Measuring GDP, Inflation, and Economic Growth
8 Employment and Unemployment	**8** Employment and Unemployment	**8** Employment and Unemployment	**8** Employment and Unemployment
9 Capital, Investment, and Saving	**7** Aggregate Supply and Aggregate Demand	**11** Expenditure Multipliers	**7** Aggregate Supply and Aggregate Demand
10 Economic Growth	**11** Expenditure Multipliers	**7** Aggregate Supply and Aggregate Demand	**13** Money
7 Aggregate Supply and Aggregate Demand	**12** Fiscal Policy	**12** Fiscal Policy	**14** Monetary Policy
11 Expenditure Multipliers	**13** Money	**13** Money	**15** Inflation
12 Fiscal Policy	**14** Monetary Policy	**14** Monetary Policy	**11** Expenditure Multipliers
13 Money	**15** Inflation	**15** Inflation	**12** Fiscal Policy
14 Monetary Policy	**9** Capital, Investment, and Saving	**9** Capital, Investment, and Saving	**9** Capital, Investment, and Saving
15 Inflation	**10** Economic Growth	**10** Economic Growth	**10** Economic Growth
16 The Business Cycle	**16** The Business Cycle	**16** The Business Cycle	**16** The Business Cycle
17 Macroeconomic Policy Challenges	**17** Macroeconomic Policy Challenges	**17** Macroeconomic Policy Challenges	**17** Macroeconomic Policy Challenges
19 The Balance of Payments and the Dollar (optional)	**19** The Balance of Payments and the Dollar (optional)	**19** The Balance of Payments and the Dollar (optional)	**19** The Balance of Payments and the Dollar (optional)

The Addison-Wesley Series in Economics

Abel/Bernanke
Macroeconomics

Allen
Managerial Economics

Berndt
The Practice of Econometrics

Bierman/Fernandez
Game Theory with Economic Applications

Binger/Hoffman
Microeconomics with Calculus

Boyer
Principles of Transportation Economics

Branson
Macroeconomic Theory and Policy

Brown/Hogendorn
International Economics: Theory and Context

Browning/Zupan
Microeconomic Theory and Applications

Bruce
Public Finance and the American Economy

Burgess
The Economics of Regulation and Antitrust

Byrns/Stone
Economics

Canterbery
The Literate Economist: A Brief History of Economics

Carlton/Perloff
Modern Industrial Organization

Caves/Frankel/Jones
World Trade and Payments: An Introduction

Cooter/Ulen
Law and Economics

Eaton/Mishkin
Reader to accompany The Economics of Money, Banking, and Financial Markets

Ehrenberg/Smith
Modern Labor Economics

Ekelund/Tollison
Economics: Private Markets and Public Choice

Filer/Hamermesh/Rees
The Economics of Work and Pay

Fusfeld
The Age of the Economist

Ghiara
Learning Economics: A Practical Workbook

Gibson
International Finance

Gordon
Macroeconomics

Gregory
Essentials of Economics

Gregory/Ruffin
Economics

Gregory/Stuart
Russian and Soviet Economic Structure and Performance

Griffiths/Wall
Intermediate Microeconomics

Gros/Steinherr
Winds of Change: Economic Transition in Central and Eastern Europe

Hartwick/Olewiler
The Economics of Natural Resource Use

Hogendorn
Economic Development

Hoy/Livernois/McKenna/ Rees/Stengos
Mathematics for Economics

Hubbard
Money, the Financial System, and the Economy

Hughes/Cain
American Economic History

Husted/Melvin
International Economics

Invisible Hand Software
Economics in Action

Jehle/Reny
Advanced Microeconomic Theory

Klein
Mathematical Methods for Economics

Krugman/Obstfeld
International Economics: Theory and Policy

Laidler
The Demand for Money: Theories, Evidence, and Problems

Lesser/Dodds/Zerbe
Environmental Economics and Policy

Lipsey/Courant
Economics

McCarty
Dollars and Sense

Melvin
International Money and Finance

Miller
Economics Today

Miller/Benjamin/North
The Economics of Public Issues

Miller/Fishe
Microeconomics: Price Theory in Practice

Miller/VanHoose
Essentials of Money, Banking, and Financial Markets

Mills/Hamilton
Urban Economics

Mishkin
The Economics of Money, Banking, and Financial Markets

Parkin
Economics

Phelps
Health Economics

Riddell/Shackelford/Stamos
Economics: A Tool for Critically Understanding Society

Ritter/Silber/Udell
Principles of Money, Banking, and Financial Markets

Rohlf
Introduction to Economic Reasoning

Ruffin/Gregory
Principles of Economics

Salvatore
Microeconomics

Sargent
Rational Expectations and Inflation

Scherer
Industry Structure, Strategy, and Public Policy

Schotter
Microeconomics

Sherman/Kolk
Business Cycles and Forecasting

Smith
Case Studies in Economic Development

Studenmund
Using Econometrics

Su
Economic Fluctuations and Forecasting

Tietenberg
Environmental and Natural Resource Economics

Tietenberg
Environmental Economics and Policy

Todaro
Economic Development

Waldman/Jensen
Industrial Organization: Theory and Practice

Zerbe/Dively/Lesser
Benefit-Cost Analysis